FIFTH EDITION

MEN'S LIVES

Michael S. Kimmel

Michael A. Messner

Allyn and Bacon

Boston ■ London ■ Toronto ■ Sydney ■ Tokyo ■ Singapore

To our sons,

Zachery Aaron Kimmel,

Miles Hondagneu-Messner, and Sasha Hondagneu-Messner,

and the egalitarian world we hope they will help to build.

Series Editor: Sarah L. Kelbaugh
Editor in Chief, Social Science: Karen Hanson
Editoral Assistant: Lori Flickinger
Composition Buyer: Linda Cox
Manufacturing Buyer: Megan Cochran
Editorial-Production Service: Susan McNally
Production Administrator: Deborah Brown
Cover Administrator: Linda Knowles
Designer: Denise Hoffman, Glenview Studios

Library of Congress Cataloging-in-Publication Data

Men's lives / [compiled by] Michael S. Kimmel, Michael A. Messner. —5th ed.
    p. cm.
   ISBN 0-205-32105-4
   1. Men—United States—Attitudes. 2. Masculinity—United States.
 3. Men—United States—Sexual behavior. I. Kimmel, Michael S.
 II. Messner, Michael A.

HQ1090.3.M465 2000
305.31—dc21   00-030605

Printed in the United States of America

10 9 8 7 6 5 4 3 2 1   05 04 03 02 01 00

CONTENTS

PREFACE

Over the past twelve years, we have been teaching courses on the male experience, or "men's lives." Our courses have reflected both our own education and recent research by feminist scholars and profeminist men in U.S. society. (By profeminist men, we mean active supporters of women's efforts against male violence and claims for equal opportunity, political participation, sexual autonomy, family reform, and equal education.) Gender, scholars have demonstrated, is a central feature of social life—one of the chief organizing principles around which our lives revolve. Gender shapes our identities and the institutions in which we find ourselves. In the university, women's studies programs and courses about women in traditional disciplines have explored the meaning of gender in women's lives. But what does it mean to be a man in contemporary U.S. society?

This anthology is organized around specific themes that define masculinity and the issues men confront over the course of their lives. In addition, a social-constructionist perspective has been included that examines how men actively construct masculinity within a social and historical context. Related to this construction and integrated in our examination are the variations that exist among men in relation to class, race, and sexuality.

We begin Part One with issues and questions that unravel the "masculine mystique" and reveal various dimensions of men's position in society and their relationships with women and with other men. Parts Two through Nine examine the different issues that emerge for men at different times of their lives and the ways in which their lives change over time. We touch on central moments related to boyhood, adolescence, sports, occupations, marriage, and fatherhood, and explore men's emotional and sexual relationships with women and with other men. The final part, "Men, Movements, and the Future," explores some of the ways in which men are changing and some possible directions by which they might continue to change.

Although a major component of the traditional, normative definition of masculinity is independence, we are pleased to acknowledge those colleagues and friends whose criticism and support have been a constant help throughout our work on this project. Karen Hanson and Sarah Kelbaugh, our editors at Allyn and Bacon, inherited this project and have embraced it as their own, facilitating our work at every turn. Chris Cardone and Bruce Nichols, our original editors, were supportive from the start and helped get the project going. Many other scholars who work on issues of masculinity, such as Bob Blauner, Robert Brannon, Harry Brod, Rocco Capraro, Bob Connell, James Harrison, Jeff Hearn, Joe Pleck, Tony Rotundo, Don Sabo, and Peter Stein, have contributed to a supportive intellectual community in which to work.

We also thank the following reviewers for their helpful comments and suggestions: Parvin Abyanch, California State University, Pomona; Alice Abelkemp, University of New Orleans; Ron Matson, Wichita State University; Gul Ozyegin, College of William and Mary; and Mindy Stombler, Texas Technical University. Colleagues at the State University of New York at Stony Brook and the University of Southern California have also been supportive of this project. We are especially grateful to Diane Barthel, Ruth Schwartz Cowan, John Gagnon, Barry Glassner, Norman Goodman, Nilufer Isvan, Carol Jacklin, and Barrie Thorne. A fellowship from the Lilly Foundation supported Kimmel's work on pedagogical issues of teaching about men and masculinity.

This book is the product of the profeminist men's movement as well—a loose network of men who support a feminist critique of traditional masculinity and women's struggles to enlarge the scope of their personal autonomy and public power. These men are engaged in a variety of efforts to transform masculinity in ways that allow men to live fuller, richer, and healthier lives. The editors of *Changing Men* (with whom we worked as Book Review Editor and Sports Editor), the late Mike Biernbaum and Rick Cote, have labored for more than a decade to provide a forum for antisexist men. We acknowledge their efforts with gratitude and respect.

Our families, friends, and colleagues have provided a rare atmosphere that combines intellectual challenge and emotional support. We are grateful to Judith Brisman, Martin Duberman, Eli Zal, Kate Ellis, Frances Goldin, Cathy Greenblat, Pam Hatchfield, Sandi Kimmel, David Levin, Mary Morris and Larry O'Connor, Lillian and Hank Rubin, and Mitchell Tunick. We want especially to acknowledge our fathers and mothers for providing such important models—not of being women or men, but of being adults capable of career competence, emotional warmth, and nurturance (these are not masculine or feminine traits).

Finally, we thank Amy Aronson and Pierette Hondagneu-Sotelo, who have chosen to share our lives, and our sons, to whom we dedicate this edition of the book, who didn't have much of a choice about it. Together they fill our lives with so much joy.

M.S.K.
M.A.M.

This is a book about men. But, unlike other books about men, which line countless library shelves, this is a book about men *as men*. It is a book in which men's experiences are not taken for granted as we explore the "real" and significant accomplishments of men, but a book in which those experiences are treated as significant and important in themselves.

Men as "Gendered Beings"

But what does it mean to examine men "as men"? Most courses in a college curriculum are about men, aren't they? But these courses routinely deal with men only in their public roles, so we come to know and understand men as scientists, politicians, military figures, writers, and philosophers. Rarely, if ever, are men understood through the prism of gender.

But listen to some male voices from some of these "ungendered" courses. Take, for example, composer Charles Ives, debunking "sissy" types of music; he said he used traditional tough guy themes and concerns in his drive to build new sounds and structures out of the popular musical idiom (cf. Wilkinson 1986: 103). Or architect Louis Sullivan, describing his ambition to create "masculine forms": strong, solid, commanding respect. Or novelist Ernest Hemingway, retaliating against literary enemies by portraying them as impotent or homosexual.

Consider also political figures, such as Cardinal Richelieu, the seventeenth-century French First Minister to Louis XIII, who insisted that it was "necessary to have masculine virtue and do everything by reason" (cited in Elliott 1984: 20). Closer to home, recall President Lyndon Baines Johnson's dismissal of a political adversary: "Oh him. He has to squat to piss!" Or his boast that during the Tet offensive in the Vietnam War, he "didn't just screw Ho Chi Minh. I cut his pecker off!"

Democrats have no monopoly on unexamined gender coloring their political rhetoric. Richard Nixon was "afraid of being acted upon, of being inactive, of being soft, or being thought impotent, of being dependent upon anyone else," according to his biographer, Bruce Mazlish. And don't forget Vice-President George Bush's revealing claim that in his television debate with Democratic challenger Geraldine Ferraro he had "kicked ass." (That few political pundits criticized such unapologetic glee concerning violence against women is again indicative of how invisible gender issues are in our culture.) Indeed, recent political campaigns have revolved, in part, around gender issues, as each candidate attempted to demonstrate that he was not a "wimp" but was a "real man." (Of course, the few successful female politicians face the double task of convincing the electorate that they are not the "weak-willed wimps" that their gender implies in the public mind while at the same time demonstrating that they are "real women.")

These are just a few examples of what we might call gendered speech, language that uses gender terms to make its case. And these are just a few of the thousands of examples one could find in every academic discipline of how men's lives are organized around gender issues and how gender remains one of the organizing principles of social life. We come to know ourselves and our world through the prism of gender. Only we act as if we didn't know it.

Fortunately, in recent years, the pioneering work of feminist scholars, both in traditional disciplines and in women's studies, and of feminist women in the political arena has made us aware of the centrality of gender in our lives. Gender, these scholars have demonstrated, is a central feature of social life, one of the central organizing principles around which our lives revolve. In the social sciences, gender has now taken its place alongside class and race as one of the three central mechanisms by which power and resources are distributed in our society and the three central themes out of which we fashion the meanings of our lives.

We certainly understand how this works for women. Through women's studies courses and also in courses about women in traditional disciplines, students have explored the complexity of women's lives, the hidden history of exemplary women, and the daily experiences of women in the routines of their lives. For women, we know how gender works as one of the formative elements out of which social life is organized.

The Invisibility of Gender: A Sociological Explanation

Too often, though, we treat men as if they had no gender, as if only their public personae were of interest to us as students and scholars, as if their interior experience of gender was of no significance. This became evident when one of us was in a graduate seminar on feminist theory several years ago. A discussion between a white woman and a black woman revolved around the question of whether their similarities as women were greater than their racial differences as black and white. The white woman asserted that the fact that they were both women bonded them, in spite of their racial differences. The black woman disagreed.

"When you wake up in the morning and look in the mirror, what do you see?" she asked.

"I see a woman," replied the white woman.

"That's precisely the issue," replied the black woman. "I see a black woman. For me, race is visible every day, because it is how I am not privileged in this culture. Race is invisible to you, which is why our alliance will always seem somewhat false to me."

Witnessing this exchange, Michael Kimmel was startled. When he looked in the mirror in the morning, he saw, as he put it, "a human being: universally generalizable. The generic person."

What had been concealed—that he possessed both race and gender—had become strikingly visible. As a white man, he was able not to think about the ways in which gender and race had affected his experiences.

There is a sociological explanation for this blind spot in our thinking: the mechanisms that afford us privilege are very often invisible to us. What makes us marginal (unempowered, oppressed) are the mechanisms that we understand, because those are the ones that are most painful in daily life. Thus, white people rarely think of themselves as "raced" people, rarely think of race as a central element in their experience. But people of color are marginalized by race, and so the centrality of race both is painfully obvious and needs study urgently. Similarly, middle-class people do not acknowledge the importance of social class as an organizing principle of social life, largely because for them class is an invisible force that makes everyone look pretty much the same. Working-class people, on the other hand, are often painfully aware of the centrality of class in their lives. (Interestingly, upper-class people are often more aware of class dynamics than are middle-class people. In part, this may be the result of the emphasis on status within the upper class, as lineage, breeding, and family honor take center stage. In part, it may also be the result of a peculiar marginalization of the upper class in our society, as in the overwhelming number of television shows and movies that are ostensibly about just plain [i.e., middle-class] folks.)

In this same way, men often think of themselves as genderless, as if gender did not matter in the daily experiences of our lives. Certainly, we can see the biological sex of individuals, but we rarely understand the ways in which *gender*—that complex of social meanings that is attached to biological sex—is enacted in our daily lives. For example, we treat male scientists as if their being men had nothing to do with the organization of their experiments, the logic of scientific inquiry, or the questions posed by science itself. We treat male political figures as if masculinity were not even remotely in their consciousness as they do battle in the political arena.

This book takes a position directly opposed to such genderlessness for men. We believe that men are also "gendered," and that this gendering process, the transformation of biological males into socially interacting men, is a central experience for men. That we are unaware of it only helps to perpetuate the inequalities based on gender in our society.

In this book, we will examine the various ways in which men are gendered. We have gathered together some of the most interesting, engaging, and convincing materials from the past decade that have been written about men. We believe that *Men's Lives* will allow readers to explore the meanings of masculinity in contemporary U.S. culture in a new way.

Earlier Efforts to Study Men

Certainly, researchers have been examining masculinity for a long time. Historically, there have been three general models that have governed social scientific research on men and masculinity. *Biological models* have focused on the ways in which innate biological differences between males and females programmed different social behaviors. *Anthropological models* have examined masculinity cross-culturally, stressing the variations in the behaviors and attributes associated with being a man. And, until recently, *sociological models* have stressed how socialization of boys and girls included accommodation to a "sex role" specific to one's biological sex. Although each of these perspectives helps us to understand the meaning of masculinity and femininity, each is also limited in its ability to explain fully how gender operates in any culture.

Relying on differences in reproductive biology, some scholars have argued that the physiological organization of males and females makes inevitable the differences we observe in psychological temperament and social behaviors. One perspective holds that differences in endocrine functioning are the cause of gender difference, that testosterone predisposes males toward aggression, competition, and violence, whereas estrogen predisposes females toward passivity, tenderness, and exaggerated emotionality. Others insist that these observed behavioral differences derive from the differences between the size or number of sperm and eggs. Since a male can produce 100 million sperm with each ejaculation, whereas a female can produce fewer than 20 eggs capable of producing healthy offspring over the course of her life, these authors suggest that men's "investment" in their offspring is significantly less than women's investment. Other authors arrive at the same conclusion by suggesting that the different size of egg and sperm, and the fact that the egg is the source of the food supply, impels temperamental differences. Reproductive "success" to males means the insemination of as many females as possible; to females, reproductive success means carefully choosing one male to mate with and insisting that he remain present to care for and support their offspring. Still other authors argue that male and female behavior is governed by different halves of the brain; males are ruled by the left hemisphere, which controls rationality and abstract thought, whereas females are governed by the right hemisphere, which controls emotional affect and creativity. (For examples of these works, see Wilson 1976; Trivers 1972; Goldberg 1975; and Goldberg, 1986.)

Observed normative temperamental differences between women and men that are assumed to be of biological origin are easily translated into political prescriptions. In this ideological sleight of hand, what is *normative* (i.e., what is prescribed) is translated into what is *normal*, and the mechanisms of this transformation are the assumed biological imperative. George Gilder, for example, assembles the putative biological differences between women and men into a call for a return to traditional gender roles. Gilder believes that male sexuality is, by nature, wild and lusty, "insistent" and "incessant," careening out of control and threatening anarchic disorder, unless it can be controlled and constrained. This is the task of women. When women refuse to apply the brakes to male sexuality—by asserting their own or by choosing to pursue a life outside the domestic sphere—they abandon their "natural" function for illusory social gains. Sex education, abortion, and birth control are all condemned as facilitating women's escape from biological necessity. Similarly, he argues against women's employment, since the "unemployed man can contribute little to the community and will often disrupt it, but the woman may even do more good without a job than with one" (Gilder 1986: 86).

The biological argument has been challenged by many scholars on several grounds. The implied causation between two observed sets of differences (biological differences and different behaviors) is misleading, since there is no logical reason to assume that one caused the other, or that the line of causation moves only from the biological to the social. The selection of biological evidence is partial, and generalizations from "lower" animal species to human beings are always suspect. One sociologist asks if these differences are "natural," why their enforcement must be coercive, why males and females have to be forced to assume the rules that they are naturally supposed to play (see Epstein, 1986:8). And one primatologist argues that the evidence adduced to support the current status quo might also lead to precisely the opposite conclusions, that biological differences would impel female promiscuity and male fragility (see Hardy 1981). Biological differences between males and females would appear to set some parameters for differences in social behavior, but would not dictate the temperaments of men and women in any one culture. These psychological and social differences would appear to be the result far more of the ways in which cultures interpret, shape, and modify these biological inheritances. We may be born males or females, but we become men and women in a cultural context.

Anthropologists have entered the debate at this point, but with different positions. For example, some anthropologists have suggested that the universality of gender differences comes from specific cultural adaptations to the environment, whereas others describe the cultural variations of gender roles, seeking to demonstrate the fluidity of gender and the primacy of cultural organization. Lionel Tiger and Robin Fox argue that the sexual division of labor is universal because of the different nature of bonding for males and females. "Nature," they argue, "intended mother and child to be together" because she is the source of emotional security and food; thus, cultures have prescribed various behaviors for women that emphasize nurturance and emotional connection (Tiger and Fox, 1984: 304). The bond between men is forged through the necessity of "competitive cooperation" in hunting; men must cooperate with members of their own tribe in the hunt and yet compete for scarce resources with men in other tribes. Such bonds predispose men toward the organization of the modern corporation or governmental bureaucracy.

Such anthropological arguments omit as much as they include, and many scholars have pointed out problems with the model. Why did not intelligence become sex linked, as this model (and the biological model) would imply? Such positions also reveal a marked conservatism: the differences between women and men are the differences that nature or cultural evolution intended, and are therefore not to be tampered with.

Perhaps the best known challenge to this anthropological argument is the work of Margaret Mead. Mead insisted that the variations among cultures in their prescriptions of gender roles required the conclusion that culture was the more decisive cause of these differences. In her classic study, *Sex and Temperament in Three Primitive Societies* (1935), Mead observed such wide variability among gender role prescriptions—and such marked differences from our own—that any universality implied by biological or anthropological models had to be rejected. And although the empirical accuracy of Mead's work has been challenged in its specific arguments, the general theoretical arguments remain convincing.

Psychological theories have also contributed to the discussion of gender roles, as psychologists have specified the specific developmental sequences for both males and females. Earlier theorists observed psychological distancing from the mother as the precondition for independence and autonomy, or suggested a sequence that placed the capacity for abstract reason as the developmental stage beyond relational reasoning. Since it is normative for males to exhibit independence and the capacity for abstract reason, it was argued that males are more successful at negotiating these psychological passages, and implied that women somehow lagged behind men on the ladder of developmental success. (Such arguments may be found in Freud, Erikson, and Kohlberg.)

But these models, too, have been challenged, most recently by sociologist Nancy Chodorow, who argued that women's ability to connect contains a more fundamentally human trait than the male's need to distance, and by psychologist Carol Gilligan, who claimed that women's predisposition toward relational reasoning may contain a more humane strategy of thought than recourse to abstract principles. Regardless of our assessment of these arguments, Chodorow and Gilligan rightly point out that the highly ideological assumptions that make masculinity the normative standard against which the psychological development of *both* males and females was measured would inevitably make femininity problematic and less fully developed. Moreover, Chodorow explicitly insists that these "essential" differences between women and men are socially constructed and thus subject to change.

Finally, sociologists have attempted to synthesize these three perspectives into a systematic explanation of "sex roles." These are the collection of attitudes, attributes, and behaviors that is seen as appropriate for males and appropriate for females. Thus, masculinity is associated with technical mastery, aggression, competitiveness, and cognitive abstraction, whereas femininity is associated with emotional nurturance, connectedness, and passivity. Sex role theory informed a wide variety of prescriptive literature (self-help books) that instructed parents on what to do if

they wanted their child to grow up as a healthy boy or girl.

The strongest challenge to all these perspectives, as we have seen, came from feminist scholars, who have specified the ways in which the assumptions about maturity, development, and health all made masculinity the norm against which both genders were measured. In all the social sciences, these feminist scholars have stripped these early studies of their academic facades to reveal the unexamined ideological assumptions contained within them. By the early 1970s, women's studies programs began to articulate a new paradigm for the study of gender, one that assumed nothing about men or women beforehand, and that made no assumptions about which gender was more highly developed. And by the mid-1970s, the first group of texts about men appeared that had been inspired by these pioneering efforts by feminist scholars.

Thinking About Men: The First Generation

In the mid-1970s, the first group of works on men and masculinity appeared that was directly influenced by these feminist critiques of the traditional explanations for gender differences. Some books underscored the costs to men of traditional gender role prescriptions, exploring how some aspects of men's lives and experiences are constrained and underdeveloped by the relentless pressure to exhibit other behaviors associated with masculinity. Books such as Marc Feigen-Fasteau's *The Male Machine* (1974) and Warren Farrell's *The Liberated Man* (1975) discussed the costs to men's health—both physical and psychological—and the quality of relationships with women, other men, and their children of the traditional male sex role.

Several anthologies explored the meanings of masculinity in the United States by adopting a feminist-inspired prism through which to view men and masculinity. For example, Deborah

David and Robert Brannon's *The Forty-Nine Percent Majority* (1976) and Joseph Pleck and Jack Sawyer's *Men and Masculinity* (1974) presented panoramic views of men's lives, from within a framework that accepted the feminist critique of traditional gender arrangements. Elizabeth Pleck and Joseph Pleck's *The American Man* (1980) suggested a historical evolution of contemporary themes. These works explored both the "costs" and the privileges of being a man in modern U.S. society.

Perhaps the single most important book to criticize the normative organization of the male sex role was Joseph Pleck's *The Myth of Masculinity* (1981). Pleck carefully deconstructed the constituent elements of the male sex role and reviewed the empirical literature for each component part. After demonstrating that the empirical literature did not support these normative features, Pleck argued that the male sex role model was incapable of describing men's experiences. In its place, he posited a male "sex role strain" model that specified the contemporary sex role as problematic, historically specific, and also an unattainable ideal.

Building on Pleck's work, a critique of the sex role model began to emerge. Sex roles had been cast as the static containers of behaviors and attitudes, and biological males and females were required to fit themselves into these containers, regardless of how ill-fitting these clusters of behaviors and attitudes felt. Such a model was ahistorical and suggested a false cultural universalism, and was therefore ill equipped to help us understand the ways in which sex roles change, and the ways in which individuals modify those roles through the enactments of gender expectations. Most telling, however, was the way in which the sex role model ignored the ways in which definitions of masculinity and femininity were based on, and reproduced, relationships of power. Not only do men as a group exert power over women as a group, but the definitions of masculinity and femininity reproduce those power relations. Power dynamics are an essential element in both the definition and the enactments of gender.

This first generation of research on masculinity was extremely valuable, particularly since it challenged the unexamined ideology that made masculinity the gender norm against which both men and women were measured. The old models of sex roles had reproduced the domination of men over women by insisting on the dominance of masculine traits over feminine traits. These new studies argued against both the definitions of either sex and the social institutions in which those differences were embedded. Shapers of the new model looked at "gender relations" and understood how the definition of either masculinity or femininity was relational, that is, how the definition of one gender depended, in part, on the understanding of the definition of the other.

In the early 1980s, the research on women again surged ahead of the research on men and masculinity. This time, however, the focus was not on the ways in which sex roles reproduce the power relations in society, but rather on the ways in which femininity is experienced differently by women in various social groups. Gradually, the notion of a single femininity—which was based on the white middle-class Victorian notion of female passivity, langorous beauty, and emotional responsiveness—was replaced by an examination of the ways in which women differ in their gender role expectations by race, class, age, sexual orientation, ethnicity, region, and nationality.

The research on men and masculinity is now entering a new stage, in which the variations among men are seen as central to the understanding of men's lives. The unexamined assumption in earlier studies had been that one version of masculinity—white, middle-aged, middle-class, heterosexual—was the sex role into which all men were struggling to fit in our society. Thus, working-class men, men of color, gay men, and younger and older men were all observed as departing in significant ways from the traditional definitions of masculinity. Therefore, it was easy to see these men as enacting "problematic" or "deviant" versions of masculinity. Such theoretical assertions, however, reproduce precisely the power relationships that keep these men in subordinate positions in our society. Not only does middle-class, middle-aged, heterosexual white masculinity become the standard against which all men are measured, but this definition, itself, is used against those who do not fit as a way to keep them down. The normative definition of masculinity is not the "right" one, but it is the one that is dominant.

The challenge to the hegemonic definition of masculinity came from men whose masculinity was cast as deviant: men of color, gay men, and ethnic men. We understand now that we cannot speak of "masculinity" as a singular term, but must examine *masculinities*: the ways in which different men construct different versions of masculinity. Such a perspective can be seen in several recent works, such as Harry Brod's *The Making of Masculinities* (1987), Michael Kimmel's *Changing Men: New Directions in Research on Men and Masculinity* (1987), and Tim Carrigan, Bob Connell, and John Lee's "Toward a New Sociology of Masculinity" (1985). Bob Connell's *Gender and Power* (1987) and Jeff Hearn's *The Gender of Oppression* (1987) represent the most sophisticated theoretical statements of this perspective. Connell argues that the oppression of women is a chief mechanism that links the various masculinities, and that the marginalization of certain masculinities is an important component of the reproduction of male power over women. This critique of the hegemonic definition of masculinity as a perspective on men's lives is one of the organizing principles of our book, which is the first college-level text in this second generation of work on men and masculinities.

Now that we have reviewed some of the traditional explanations for gender relations and have situated this book within the research on gender in general, and men in particular, let us briefly outline exactly the theoretical perspective we have employed in the book. Not only does our theoretical framework provide the organizing principle of the book as a whole, it also provided some of the criteria for the selection of the articles that are included.

The Social Construction of Masculinities

Men are not born, growing from infants through boyhood to manhood, to follow a predetermined biological imperative encoded in their physical organization. To be a man is to participate in social life as a man, as a gendered being. Men are not born; they are made. And men make themselves, actively constructing their masculinities within a social and historical context.

This book is about how men are made and how men make themselves in contemporary U.S. society. It is about what masculinity means, about how masculinity is organized, and about the social institutions that sustain and elaborate it. It is a book in which we will trace what it means to be a man over the course of men's lives.

Men's Lives revolves around three important themes that are part of a social scientific perspective. First, we have adopted a *social constructionist* perspective. By this we mean that the important fact of men's lives is not that they are biological males, but that they become men. Our sex may be male, but our identity as men is developed through a complex process of interaction with the culture in which we both learn the gender scripts appropriate to our culture and attempt to modify those scripts to make them more palatable. The second axis around which the book is organized follows from our social constructionist perspective. As we have argued, the experience of masculinity is not uniform and universally generalizable to all men in our society. Masculinity differs dramatically in our society, and we have organized the book to illustrate the *variations* among men in the construction of masculinity. Third, we have adopted a *life course* perspective, to chart the construction of these various masculinities in men's lives and to examine pivotal developmental moments or institutional locations during a man's life in which the meanings of masculinity are articulated. Social constructionism, variations among men, and the life course perspective define the organization of this book and the criteria we have used to select the articles included.

The Social Constructionist Model

The social constructionist perspective argues that the meaning of masculinity is neither transhistorical nor culturally universal, but rather varies from culture to culture and within any one culture over time. Thus, males become men in the United States in the late twentieth century in a way that is very different from men in Southeast Asia, or Kenya, or Sri Lanka. The meaning of masculinity varies from culture to culture.

Men's lives also vary within any one culture over time. The experience of masculinity in the contemporary United States is very different from that experience 150 years ago. Who would argue that what it meant to be a "real man" in seventeenth-century France (at least among the upper classes)—high-heeled patent leather shoes, red velvet jackets covering frilly white lace shirts, lots of rouge and white powder makeup, and a taste for the elegant refinement of ornate furniture—bears much resemblance to the meaning of masculinity among a similar class of French men today?

A perspective that emphasizes the social construction of gender is, therefore, both *historical* and *comparative*. It allows us to explore the ways in which the meanings of gender vary from culture to culture, and how they change within any one culture over historical time.

Variations Among Men

Masculinity also varies *within* any one society according to the various types of cultural groups that compose it. Subcultures are organized around other poles, which are the primary way in which people organize themselves and by which resources are distributed. And men's experiences differ from one another in the ways in which social scientists have identified as the chief structural mechanisms along which power and resources are distributed. We cannot speak of masculinity in the United States as if it were a single, easily identifiable commodity. To do so is to risk positing one version of masculinity as normative and making all other masculinities problematic.

In the contemporary United States, masculinity is constructed differently by class culture, by race and ethnicity, and by age. And each of these axes of masculinity modifies the others. Black masculinity differs from white masculinity, yet each of them is also further modified by class and age. A 30-year-old middle-class black man will have some things in common with a 30-year-old middle-class white man that he might not share with a 60-year-old working-class black man, although he will share with him elements of masculinity that are different from those of the white man of his class and age. The resulting matrix of *masculinities* is complicated by cross-cutting elements; without understanding this, we risk collapsing all masculinities into one hegemonic version.

The challenge to a singular definition of masculinity as the normative definition is the second axis around which the readings in this book revolve.

The Life Course Perspective

The meaning of masculinity is not constant over the course of any man's life, but will change as he grows and matures. The issues confronting a man about proving himself and feeling successful and the social institutions in which he will attempt to enact his definitions of masculinity will change throughout his life. Thus, we have adopted a *life course perspective* to discuss the ways in which different issues will emerge for men at different times of their lives, and the ways in which men's lives, themselves, change over time. The life course perspective we have employed will examine men's lives at various pivotal moments in their development from young boys to adults. Like a slide show, these points will freeze the action for a short while, to afford us the opportunity to examine in more detail the ways in which different men in our culture experience masculinity at any one time.

The book's organization reflects these three concerns. The first part sets the context through which we shall examine men's lives. Parts Two through Nine follow those lives through their full course, examining central moments experienced by men in the United States today. Specifically, Parts Two and Three touch on boyhood and adolescence, discussing some of the institutions organized to embody and reproduce masculinities in the United States, such as fraternities, the Boy Scouts, and sports groups. Part Four, "Men and Work," explores the ways in which masculinities are constructed in relation to men's occupations. Part Five, "Men and Health: Body and Mind," deals with heart attacks, stress, AIDS, and other health problems among men. Part Six, "Men in Relationships," describes men's emotional and sexual relationships. We deal with heterosexuality and homosexuality, mindful of the ways in which variations are based on specific lines (class, race, ethnicity). Part Seven, "Male Sexualities," studies the normative elements of heterosexuality and probes the controversial political implications of pornography as a source of both straight and gay men's sexual information. Part Eight, "Men in Families," concentrates on masculinities within the family and the role of men as husbands, fathers, and senior citizens. Part Nine, "Masculinities in the Media," explores the different ways the media presents modes of masculinity. Part Ten, "Men, Movements, and the Future," examines some of the ways in which men are changing and points to some directions in which men might continue to change.

Our perspective, stressing the social construction of masculinities over the life course, will, we believe, allow a more comprehensive understanding of men's lives in the United States today.

References

Brod, Harry, ed. *The Making of Masculinities.* Boston: Unwin, Hyman, 1987.

Carrigan, Tim, Bob Connell, and John Lee. "Toward a New Sociology of Masculinity" in *Theory and Society,* 1985, *5*(14).

Chodorow, Nancy. *The Reproduction of Mothering.* Berkeley: University of California Press, 1978.

Connell, R. W. *Gender and Power.* Stanford, CA: Stanford University Press, 1987.

David, Deborah, and Robert Brannon, eds. *The Forty-Nine Percent Majority.* Reading, MA: Addison-Wesley, 1976.

Elliott, J. H. *Richelieu and Olivares.* New York: Cambridge University Press, 1984.

Epstein, Cynthia Fuchs. "Inevitability of Prejudice" in *Society,* Sept. /Oct., 1986.

Farrell, Warren. *The Liberated Man.* New York: Random House, 1975.

Feigen-Fasteau, Marc. *The Male Machine.* New York: McGraw-Hill, 1974.

Gilligan, Carol. *In a Different Voice.* Cambridge, MA: Harvard University Press, 1982.

Gilder, George. *Men and Marriage.* Gretna, LA: Pelican Publishers, 1986.

Goldberg, Steven. *The Inevitability of Patriarchy.* New York: William Morrow & Co., 1975.

——— "Reaffirming the Obvious" in *Society,* Sept./Oct., 1986.

Hearn, Jeff. *The Gender of Oppression.* New York: St. Martin's Press, 1987.

Hrdy, Sandra Blaffer. *The Woman That Never Evolved.* Cambridge, MA: Harvard University Press, 1981.

Kimmel, Michael S., ed. *Changing Men: New Directions in Research on Men and Masculinity.* Newbury Park, CA: Sage Publications, 1987.

Mead, Margaret. *Sex and Temperament in Three Primitive Societies.* New York: McGraw-Hill, 1935.

Pleck, Elizabeth, and Joseph Pleck, eds. *The American Man.* Englewood Cliffs, NJ: Prentice-Hall, 1980.

Pleck, Joseph. *The Myth of Masculinity.* Cambridge, MA: M.I.T. Press, 1981.

——— and Jack Sawyer, eds. *Men and Masculinity.* Englewood Cliffs, NJ: Prentice-Hall, 1974.

Tiger, Lionel, and Robin Fox. *The Imperial Animal.* New York: Holt, Rinehart & Winston, 1984.

Trivers, Robert. "Parental Investment and Sexual Selection" in *Sexual Selection and the Descent of Man* (B. Campbell, ed.). Chicago: Aldine Publishers, 1972.

Wilkinson, Rupert. *American Tough: The Tough Guy Tradition and American Character.* New York: Harper & Row, 1986.

Wilson, E. O. *Sociobiology: The New Synthesis.* Cambridge, MA: Harvard University Press, 1976.

PART ONE

Perspectives on Masculinities

A quick glance at any magazine rack or television talk-show is enough to make you aware that these days, men are confused. What does it mean to be a "real man"? How are men supposed to behave? What are men supposed to feel? How are men to express their feelings? Who are we supposed to be like: Tootsie or Rambo? Clint Eastwood or Phil Donahue? Rhett Butler or Ashley Wilkes? Dennis Rodman or Bill Clinton?

We are daily bombarded with images and handy rules to help us negotiate our way through a world in which all the rules seem to have suddenly vanished or changed. Some tell us to reassert traditional masculinity against all contemporary challenges. But a strength built only on the weakness of others hardly feels like strength at all. Others tell us that men are in power, the oppressor. But if men are in power as a group, why do individual men often feel so powerless? Can men change?

These questions will return throughout this book. In this section, several authors begin to examine some of the issues that define the depth of the question about men and masculinity. These

articles begin to unravel the "masculine mystique" and suggest various dimensions of men's position in society, their power, their powerlessness, and their confusion. Michael Kaufman takes men's problematic relationship to violence as a core theme in men's experience in society.

But we cannot speak of "masculinity" as some universal category that is experienced in the same ways by each man. "All men are alike," runs a popular wisdom. But are they really? Are gay men's experiences with work, relationships, love, and politics similar to those of heterosexual men? Do black and Chicano men face the same problems and conflicts in their daily lives that white men face? Do middle-class men have the same political interests as blue-collar men? The answers to these questions, as the articles in this part suggest, are not simple.

Although earlier studies of men and masculinity focused on the apparently universal norms of masculinity, recent work has attempted to demonstrate how different the worlds of various men are. Men are divided along the same lines that divide any other group: race, class, sexual orientation, ethnicity, age, and geographic region. Men's lives vary in crucial ways, and understanding these variations will take us a long way toward understanding men's experiences.

Earlier studies that suggested a single universal norm of masculinity reproduced some of the problems they were trying to solve. To be sure, *all* benefit from the inequality between women and men; for example, think of how rape jokes or male-exclusive sports culture provide contexts for the bonding of men across class, race, and ethnic lines

while denying full participation to women. But the single, seemingly universal masculinity obscured ways in which some men hold and maintain power over other men in our society, hiding the fact that all men do not share equally in the fruits of gender inequality.

Here is how sociologist Erving Goffman put it in his important book *Stigma* (New York: Doubleday, 1963, p. 128):

> In an important sense there is only one complete unblushing male in America: a young, married, white, urban, northern, heterosexual Protestant father of college education, fully employed, of good complexion, weight, and height, and a recent record in sports. Every American male tends to look out upon the world from this perspective, this constituting one sense in which one can speak of a common value system in America. Any male who fails to qualify in any one of these ways is likely to view himself—during moments at least—as unworthy, incomplete, and inferior.

As Goffman suggests, middle-class, white, heterosexual masculinity is used as the marker against which other masculinities are measured, and by which standard they may be found wanting. What is *normative* (prescribed) becomes translated into what is *normal*. In this way, heterosexual men maintain their status by the oppression of gay men;

middle-aged men can maintain their dominance over older and younger men; upper-class men can exploit working-class men; and white men can enjoy privileges at the expense of men of color.

The articles by Manning Marable and Maxine Baca Zinn challenge popularly held negative stereotypes of black and Chicano males as pathologically "macho." Instead, they suggest that an understanding of ethnic minority men must begin with a critical examination of how institutionalized racism, particularly (but not exclusively) in the economy, shapes and constrains the possibilities, choices, and personal lifestyles of black and Latino men. Calls for "changing masculinities," these articles suggest, must involve an emphasis on *institutional* transformation, to which Marable's argument gives a special political urgency.

Yen le Espiritu explores the gendered stereotype of Asian-American men. And Philippe Bourgois provides a fascinating look inside the world of Puerto Rican crack dealers in east Harlem, exploring the ways in which different definitions of masculinity are expressed.

Finally, the article by R. W. Connell suggests that although diverse masculinities are expressed in a variety of places, there are large-scale structural forces—the globalizing economy, political integration—that construct both new hegemonic forms and new local expressions of masculinity. Today's hegemonic definition is seen on CNN International: at home in business hotels in every city in the world, he wears well-tailored business suits, talks on his cell phone, works on a laptop computer, and always flies business class. Our inquiry into men's lives must, therefore, pay attention to both this emerging hegemonic definition and the variety of local and regional expressions.

Michael Kaufman

The Construction of Masculinity and the Triad of Men's Violence

The all too familiar story: a woman raped, a wife battered, a lover abused. With a sense of immediacy and anger, the women's liberation movement has pushed the many forms of men's violence against women—from the most overt to the most subtle in form—into popular consciousness and public debate. These forms of violence are one aspect of our society's domination by men that, in outcome, if not always in design, reinforce that domination. The act of violence is many things at once. At the same instant it is the individual man acting out relations of sexual power; it is the violence of a society—a hierarchical, authoritarian, sexist, class-divided, militarist, racist, impersonal, crazy society—being focused through an individual man onto an individual woman. In the psyche of the individual man it might be his denial of social powerlessness through an act of aggression. In total these acts of violence are like a ritualized acting out of our social relations of power: the dominant and the weaker, the powerful and the powerless, the active and the passive . . . the masculine and the feminine.

For men, listening to the experience of women as the objects of men's violence is to shatter any complacency about the sex-based status quo. The power and anger of women's responses forces us to rethink the things we discovered when we were very young. When I was eleven or twelve years old a friend told me the difference between fucking and raping. It was simple: with rape you tied the woman to a tree. At the time the anatom-

Reprinted from *Beyond Patriarchy: Essays on Pleasure, Power, and Change,* edited by Michael Kaufman. Toronto: Oxford University Press, 1987. Reprinted by permission.

ical details were still a little vague, but in either case it was something "we" supposedly did. This knowledge was just one part of an education, started years before, about the relative power and privileges of men and women. I remember laughing when my friend explained all that to me. Now I shudder. The difference in my responses is partially that, at twelve, it was part of the posturing and pretense that accompanied my passage into adolescence. Now, of course, I have a different vantage point on the issue. It is the vantage point of an adult, but more importantly my view of the world is being reconstructed by the intervention of that majority whose voice has been suppressed: the women.

This relearning of the reality of men's violence against women evokes many deep feelings and memories for men. As memories are recalled and recast, a new connection becomes clear: violence by men against women is only one corner of a triad of men's violence. The other two corners are violence against other men and violence against oneself.

On a psychological level the pervasiveness of violence is the result of what Herbert Marcuse called the "surplus repression" of our sexual and emotional desires.[1] The substitution of violence for desire (more precisely, the transmutation of violence into a form of emotionally gratifying activity) happens unequally in men and women. The construction of masculinity involves the construction of "surplus aggressiveness." The social context of this triad of violence is the institutionalization of violence in the operation of most aspects of social, economic, and political life.

The three corners of the triad reinforce one another. The first corner—violence against women—cannot be confronted successfully without simultaneously challenging the other two corners of the triad. And all this requires a dismantling of the social feeding ground of violence: patriarchal, heterosexist, authoritarian, class societies. These three corners and the societies in which they blossom feed on each other. And together, we surmise, they will fall.

The Social Context

In spite of proclamations from the skewed research of sociobiologists, there is no good evidence that men's violence is the inevitable and natural result of male genes or hormones. To the contrary, anthropology tells us of many early societies with little or no violence against women, against children, or among men. However, given the complexity of the issues concerning the roots of violence, the essential question for us is not whether men are predisposed to violence but what society does with this violence. Why has the linchpin of so many societies been the manifold expression of violence perpetrated disproportionately by men? Why are so many forms of violence sanctioned or even encouraged? Exactly what is the nature of violence? And how are patterns of violence and the quest for domination built up and reinforced?

In other words, the key questions having to do with men's violence are not biological but are related to gender and society—which is why I speak not of "male violence" (a biological category) but rather of "men's violence" (the gender category).

For every apparently individual act of violence there is a social context. This is not to say there are no pathological acts of violence; but even in that case the "language" of the violent act, the way the violence manifests itself, can only be understood within a certain social experience. We are interested here in the manifestations of violence that are accepted as more or less normal, even if reprehensible: fighting, war, rape, assault,

psychological abuse, and so forth. What is the context of men's violence in the prevalent social orders of today?

Violence has long been institutionalized as an acceptable means of solving conflicts. But now the vast apparati of policing and war making maintained by countries the world over pose a threat to the future of life itself.

"Civilized" societies have been built and shaped through the decimation, containment, and exploitation of other peoples: extermination of native populations, colonialism, and slavery. Our relationship with the natural environment has often been described with the metaphor of rape. An attitude of conquering nature, of mastering an environment waiting to be exploited for profit, has great consequences when we possess a technology capable of permanently disrupting an ecological balance shaped over hundreds of millions of years.

The daily work life of industrial, class societies is one of violence. Violence poses as economic rationality as some of us are turned into extensions of machines, while others become brains detached from bodies. Our industrial process becomes the modern-day rack of torture where we are stretched out of shape and ripped limb from limb. It is violence that exposes workers to the danger of chemicals, radiation, machinery, speedup, and muscle strain.

The racism, sexism, and heterosexism that have been institutionalized in our societies are socially regulated acts of violence. Our cities, our social structure, our work life, our relation with nature, our history, are more than a backdrop to the prevalence of violence. They are violence; violence in an institutionalized form encoded into physical structures and socioeconomic relations. Much of the sociological analysis of violence in our societies implies simply that violence is learned by witnessing and experiencing social violence: man kicks boy, boy kicks dog.[2] Such experiences of transmitted violence are a reality, as the analysis of wife battering indicates, for many batterers were themselves abused as children. But more essential is that our personalities and sexuality, our needs and fears, our strengths and weaknesses, our selves are created—not simply learned—through our lived reality. The violence of our social order nurtures a psychology of violence, which in turn reinforces the social, economic and political structures of violence. The ever-increasing demands of civilization and the constant building upon inherited structures of violence suggest that the development of civilization has been inseparable from a continuous increase in violence against humans and our natural environment.

It would be easy, yet ultimately not very useful, to slip into a use of the term "violence" as a metaphor for all our society's antagonisms, contradictions, and ills. For now, let us leave aside the social terrain and begin to unravel the nature of so-called individual violence.

The Triad of Men's Violence

The longevity of the oppression of women must be based on something more than conspiracy, something more complicated than biological handicap and more durable than economic exploitation (although in differing degrees all these may feature).

—Juliet Mitchell[3]

It seems impossible to believe that mere greed could hold men to such a steadfastness of purpose.

—Joseph Conrad[4]

The field in which the triad of men's violence is situated is a society, or societies, grounded in structures of domination and control. Although at times this control is symbolized and embodied in the individual father—patriarchy, by definition—it is more important to emphasize that patriarchal structures of authority, domination, and control are diffused throughout social, economic, political, and ideological activities and in our relations to the natural environment. Perhaps more than in any previous time during the long epoch of patriarchy, authority does *not* rest with the father, at least in much of the advanced

capitalist and noncapitalist world. This has led more than one author to question the applicability of the term patriarchy.[5] But I think it still remains useful as a broad, descriptive category. In this sense Jessica Benjamin speaks of the current reign of patriarchy without the father. "The form of domination peculiar to this epoch expresses itself not directly as authority but indirectly as the transformation of all relationships and activity into objective, instrumental, depersonalized forms."[6]

The structures of domination and control form not simply the background to the triad of violence, but generate, and in turn are nurtured by, this violence. These structures refer both to our social relations and to our interaction with our natural environment. The relation between these two levels is obviously extremely complex. It appears that violence against nature—that is, the impossible and disastrous drive to dominate and conquer the natural world—is integrally connected with domination among humans. Some of these connections are quite obvious. One thinks of the bulldozing of the planet for profit in capitalist societies, societies characterized by the dominance of one class over others. But the link between the domination of nature and structures of domination of humans go beyond this.

The Individual Reproduction of Male Domination

No man is born a butcher.

—Bertolt Brecht[7]

In a male-dominated society men have a number of privileges. Compared to women we are free to walk the streets at night, we have traditionally escaped domestic labor, and on average we have higher wages, better jobs, and more power. But these advantages in themselves cannot explain the individual reproduction of the relations of male domination, that is, why the individual male from a very early age embraces masculinity. The embracing of masculinity is not only a "socialization" into a certain gender role, as if there is a preformed human being who learns a role that he then plays for the rest of his life, rather, through his psychological development he embraces and takes into himself a set of gender-based social relations: the person that is created through the process of maturation becomes the personal embodiment of those relations. By the time the child is five or six years old, the basis for lifelong masculinity has already been established.

The basis for the individual's acquisition of gender is that the prolonged period of human childhood results in powerful attachments to parental figures. (Through a very complex process, by the time a boy is five or six he claims for himself the power and activity society associates with masculinity.) He embraces the project of controlling himself and controlling the world. He comes to personify activity. Masculinity is a reaction against passivity and powerlessness, and with it comes a repression of a vast range of human desires and possibilities: those that are associated with femininity.

Masculinity is unconsciously rooted before the age of six, is reinforced as the child develops, and then positively explodes at adolescence, obtaining its definitive shape for the individual. The masculine norm has its own particular nuances and traits dependent on class, nation, race, religion, and ethnicity. And within each group it has its own personal expression. In adolescence the pain and fear involved in repressing "femininity" and passivity start to become evident. For most of us, the response to this inner pain is to reinforce the bulwarks of masculinity. The emotional pain created by obsessive masculinity is stifled by reinforcing masculinity itself.

The Fragility of Masculinity

Masculinity is power. But masculinity is terrifyingly fragile because it does not really exist in the sense we are led to think it exists; that is, as a biological reality—something real that we have inside ourselves. It exists as ideology; it exists as scripted behavior; it exists within "gendered" relationships. But in the end it is just a social institution with a tenuous relationship to that with which

it is supposed to be synonymous: our maleness, our biological sex. The young child does not know that sex does not equal gender. For him to be male is to be what he perceives as being masculine. The child is father to the man. Therefore, to be unmasculine is to be desexed—"castrated."

The tension between maleness and masculinity is intense because masculinity requires a suppression of a whole range of human needs, aims, feelings, and forms of expression. Masculinity is one-half of the narrow, surplus-repressive shape of the adult human psyche. Even when we are intellectually aware of the difference between biological maleness and masculinity, the masculine ideal is so embedded within ourselves that it is hard to untangle the person we might want to become (more "fully human," less sexist, less surplus-repressed, and so on) from the person we actually are.

But as children and adolescents (and often as adults), we are not aware of the difference between maleness and masculinity. With the exception of a tiny proportion of the population born as hermaphrodites, there can be no biological struggle to be male. The presence of a penis and testicles is all it takes. Yet boys and men harbor great insecurity about their male credentials. This insecurity exists because maleness is equated with masculinity; but the latter is a figment of our collective, patriarchal, surplus-repressive imaginations.

In a patriarchal society being male is highly valued, and men value their masculinity. But everywhere there are ambivalent feelings. That the initial internalization of masculinity is at the father's knee has lasting significance. Andrew Tolson states that "to the boy, masculinity is both mysterious and attractive (in its promise of a world of work and power), and yet, at the same time, threatening (in its strangeness, and emotional distance). . . . It works both ways; attracts and repels in dynamic contradiction. This simultaneous distance and attraction is internalized as a permanent emotional tension that the individual must, in some way, strive to overcome."[8]

Although maleness and masculinity are highly valued, men are everywhere unsure of their own masculinity and maleness, whether consciously or not. When men are encouraged to be open, as in men's support and counseling groups, it becomes apparent that there exists, often under the surface, an internal dialogue of doubt about one's male and masculine credentials.

Men's Violence Against Women

> In spite of the inferior role which men assign to them, women are the privileged objects of their aggression.
>
> —Simone de Beauvoir[9]

Men's violence against women is the most common form of direct, personalized violence in the lives of most adults. From sexual harassment to rape, from incest to wife battering to the sight of violent pornographic images, few women escape some form of men's aggression.

My purpose here is not to list and evaluate the various forms of violence against women, nor to try to assess what can be classed as violence per se.[10] It is to understand this violence as an expression of the fragility of masculinity combined with men's power. I am interested in its place in the perpetuation of masculinity and male domination.

In the first place, men's violence against women is probably the clearest, most straightforward expression of relative male and female power. That the relative social, economic, and political power can be expressed in this manner is, to a large part, because of differences in physical strength and in a lifelong training (or lack of training) in fighting. But it is also expressed this way because of the active/passive split. Activity as aggression is part of the masculine gender definition. That is not to say this definition always includes rape or battering, but it is one of the possibilities within a definition of activity that is ultimately grounded in the body.

Rape is a good example of the acting out of these relations of power and of the outcome of fragile masculinity in a surplus-repressive society. In the testimonies of rapists one hears over and over again expressions of inferiority, powerlessness, anger. But who can these men feel superior

to? Rape is a crime that not only demonstrates physical power, but that does so in the language of male–female sex-gender relations. The testimonies of convicted rapists collected by Douglas Jackson in the late 1970s are chilling and revealing.[11] Hal: "I feel very inferior to others. . . . I felt rotten about myself and by committing rape I took this out on someone I thought was weaker than me, someone I could control." Len: "I feel a lot of what rape is isn't so much sexual desire as a person's feelings about themselves and how that relates to sex. My fear of relating to people turned to sex because . . . it just happens to be the fullest area to let your anger out on, to let your feelings out on."

Sometimes this anger and pain are experienced in relation to women but just as often not. In either case they are addressed to women who, as the Other in a phallocentric society, are objects of mystification to men, the objects to whom men from birth have learned to express and vent their feelings, or simply objects with less social power and weaker muscles. It is the crime against women par excellence because, through it, the full weight of a sexually based differentiation among humans is played out.

Within relationships, forms of men's violence such as rape, battering, and what Meg Luxton calls the "petty tyranny" of male domination in the household[12] must be understood both "in terms of violence directed against women as women and against women as wives."[13] The family provides an arena for the expression of needs and emotions not considered legitimate elsewhere.[14] It is the one of the only places where men feel safe enough to express emotions. As the dams break, the flood pours out on women and children.[15] The family also becomes the place where the violence suffered by individuals in their work lives is discharged. "At work men are powerless, so in their leisure time they want to have a feeling that they control their lives."[16]

While this violence can be discussed in terms of male aggression, it operates within the dualism of activity and passivity, masculinity and femininity. Neither can exist without the other. This is not to blame women for being beaten, nor to excuse men who beat. It is but an indication that the various forms of men's violence against women are a dynamic affirmation of a masculinity that can only exist as distinguished from femininity. It is my argument that masculinity needs constant nurturing and affirmation. This affirmation takes many different forms. The majority of men are not rapists or batterers, although it is probable that the majority of men have used superior physical strength or some sort of physical force or threat of force against a woman at least once as a teenager or an adult. But in those who harbor great personal doubts or strongly negative self-images, or who cannot cope with a daily feeling of powerlessness, violence against women can become a means of trying to affirm their personal power in the language of our sex-gender system. That these forms of violence only reconfirm the negative self-image and the feelings of powerlessness shows the fragility, artificiality, the precariousness of masculinity.

Violence Against Other Men

At a behavioral level, men's violence against other men is visible throughout society. Some forms, such as fighting, the ritualized display of violence of teenagers and some groups of adult men, institutionalized rape in prisons, and attacks on gays or racial minorities, are very direct expressions of this violence. In many sports, violence is incorporated into exercise and entertainment. More subtle forms are the verbal putdown or, combined with economic and other factors, the competition in the business, political, or academic world. In its most frightening form, violence has long been an acceptable and even preferred method of addressing differences and conflicts among different groups and states. In the case of war, as in many other manifestations of violence, violence against other men (and civilian women) combines with autonomous economic, ideological, and political factors.

But men's violence against other men is more than the sum of various activities and types of behavior. In this form of violence a number of things are happening at once, in addition to the autonomous factors involved. Sometimes mutual, sometimes one-sided, there is a discharge of aggression and hostility. But at the same time as discharging aggression, these acts of violence and the ever-present potential for men's violence against other men reinforce the reality that relations between men, whether at the individual or state level, are relations of power.[17]

Most men feel the presence of violence in their lives. Some of us had fathers who were domineering, rough, or even brutal. Some of us had fathers who simply were not there enough; most of us had fathers who either consciously or unconsciously were repelled by our need for touch and affection once we had passed a certain age. All of us had experiences of being beaten up or picked on when we were young. We learned to fight, or we learned to run; we learned to pick on others, or we learned how to talk or joke our way out of a confrontation. But either way these early experiences of violence caused an incredible amount of anxiety and required a huge expenditure of energy to resolve. That anxiety is crystallized in an unspoken fear (particularly among heterosexual men): all other men are my potential humiliators, my enemies, my competitors.

But this mutual hostility is not always expressed. Men have formed elaborate institutions of male bonding and buddying: clubs, gangs, teams, fishing trips, card games, bars, and gyms, not to mention that great fraternity of Man. Certainly, as many feminists have pointed out, straight male clubs are a subculture of male privilege. But they are also havens where men, by common consent, can find safety and security among other men. They are safe houses where our love and affection for other men can be expressed.

Freud suggested that great amounts of passivity are required for the establishment of social relations among men but also that this very passivity arouses a fear of losing one's power. (This fear takes the form, in a phallocentric, male-dominated society, of what Freud called "castration anxiety.") There is a constant tension of activity and passivity. Among their many functions and reasons for existence, male institutions mediate this tension between activity and passivity among men.

My thoughts take me back to grade six and the constant acting out of this drama. There was the challenge to fight and a punch in the stomach that knocked my wind out. There was our customary greeting with a slug in the shoulder. Before school, after school, during class change, at recess, whenever you saw another one of the boys whom you hadn't hit or been with in the past few minutes, you'd punch each other on the shoulder. I remember walking from class to class in terror of meeting Ed Skagle in the hall. Ed, a hefty young football player a grade ahead of me, would leave a big bruise with one of his friendly hellos. And this was the interesting thing about the whole business; most of the time it was friendly and affectionate. Long after the bruises have faded, I remember Ed's smile and the protective way he had of saying hello to me. But we couldn't express this affection without maintaining the active/passive equilibrium. More precisely, within the masculine psychology of surplus aggression, expressions of affection and of the need for other boys had to be balanced by an active assault.

But the traditional definition of masculinity is not only surplus aggression. It is also exclusive heterosexuality, for the maintenance of masculinity requires the repression of homosexuality.[18] Repression of homosexuality is one thing, but how do we explain the intense fear of homosexuality, the homophobia, that pervades so much male interaction? It isn't simply that many men may choose not to have sexual relations with other men; it is rather that they will find this possibility frightening or abhorrent.

Freud showed that the boy's renunciation of the father—and thus men—as an object of sexual love is a renunciation of what are felt to be passive sexual desires. For the boy to deviate from this norm is to experience severe anxiety, for what appears to be at stake is his ability to be active. Erotic attraction to other men is sacrificed because there is no model central to our society of active, erotic love for other males. The emotionally charged physical attachments of childhood with father and friends eventually breed feelings of passivity and danger and are sacrificed. The anxiety caused by the threat of losing power and activity is "the motive power behind the 'normal' boy's social learning of his sex and gender roles." Boys internalize "our culture's definition of 'normal' or 'real' man: the possessor of a penis, therefore loving only females and that actively; the possessor of a penis, therefore 'strong' and 'hard,' not 'soft,' 'weak,' 'yielding,' 'sentimental,' 'effeminate,' 'passive.' To deviate from this definition is not to be a real man. To deviate is to arouse [what Freud called] castration anxiety."[19]

Putting this in different terms, the young boy learns of the sexual hierarchy of society. This learning process is partly conscious and partly unconscious. For a boy, being a girl is a threat because it raises anxiety by representing a loss of power. Until real power is attained, the young boy courts power in the world of the imagination (with superheroes, guns, magic, and pretending to be grown-up). But the continued pull of passive aims, the attraction to girls and to mother, the fascination with the origin of babies ensure that a tension continues to exist. In this world, the only thing that is as bad as being a girl is being a sissy, that is, being like a girl.[20] Although the boy doesn't consciously equate being a girl or sissy with homosexual genital activity, at the time of puberty these feelings, thoughts, and anxieties are transferred onto homosexuality per se.

For the majority of men, the establishment of the masculine norm and the strong social prohibitions against homosexuality are enough to bury the erotic desire for other men. The repression of our bisexuality is not adequate, however, to keep this desire at bay. Some of the energy is transformed into derivative pleasures—muscle building, male comradeship, hero worship, religious rituals, war, sports—where our enjoyment of being with other men or admiring other men can be expressed. These forms of activity are not enough to neutralize our constitutional bisexuality, our organic fusion of passivity and activity, and our love for our fathers and our friends. The great majority of men, in addition to those men whose sexual preference is clearly homosexual, have, at some time in their childhood, adolescence, or adult life, had sexual or quasi-sexual relations with other males, or have fantasized or dreamed about such relationships. Those who don't (or don't recall that they have), invest a lot of energy in repressing and denying these thoughts and feelings. And to make things worse, all those highly charged male activities in the sports field, the meeting room, or the locker room do not dispel eroticized relations with other men. They can only reawaken those feelings. It is, as Freud would have said, the return of the repressed.

Nowhere has this been more stunningly captured than in the wrestling scene in the perhaps mistitled book, *Women in Love*, by D. H. Lawrence. It was late at night. Birkin had just come to Gerald's house after being put off following a marriage proposal. They talked of working, of loving, and fighting, and in the end stripped off their clothes and began to wrestle in front of the burning fire. As they wrestled, "they seemed to drive their white flesh deeper and deeper against each other, as if they would break into a oneness." They entwined, they wrestled, they pressed nearer and nearer. "A tense white knot of flesh [was] gripped in silence." The thin Birkin "seemed to penetrate into Gerald's more solid, more diffuse bulk, to interfuse his body through the body of the other, as if to bring it subtly into subjection, always seizing with some rapid necromantic foreknowledge every motion of the other flesh, converting and counteracting it, playing upon the limbs and trunk of Gerald like some hard wind. . . . Now and again came a sharp gasp of breath, or a sound like a sigh, then the rapid thudding of movement on the thickly-carpeted floor, then the strange sound of flesh escaping under flesh."[21]

The very institutions of male bonding and patriarchal power force men to constantly reexperience their closeness and attraction to other men, that is, the very thing so many men are afraid of. Our very attraction to ourselves, ambivalent

as it may be, can only be generalized as an attraction to men in general.

A phobia is one means by which the ego tries to cope with anxiety. Homophobia is a means of trying to cope, not simply with our unsuccessfully repressed, eroticized attraction to other men, but with our whole anxiety over the unsuccessfully repressed passive sexual aims, whether directed toward males or females. Homophobia is not merely an individual phobia, although the strength of homophobia varies from individual to individual. It is a socially constructed phobia that is essential for the imposition and maintenance of masculinity. A key expression of homophobia is the obsessive denial of homosexual attraction; this denial is expressed as violence against other men. Or to put it differently, men's violence against other men is one of the chief means through which patriarchal society simultaneously expresses and discharges the attraction of men to other men.[22]

The specific ways that homophobia and men's violence toward other men are acted out varies from man to man, society to society, and class to class. The great amount of *directly expressed* violence and violent homophobia among some groups of working class youth would be well worth analyzing to give clues to the relation of class and gender.

This corner of the triad of men's violence interacts with and reinforces violence against women. This corner contains part of the logic of surplus aggression. Here we begin to explain the tendency of many men to use force as a means of simultaneously hiding and expressing their feelings. At the same time the fear of other men, in particular the fear of weakness and passivity in relation to other men, helps create our strong dependence on women for meeting our emotional needs and for emotional discharge. In a surplus-repressive patriarchal and class society, large amounts of anxiety and hostility are built up, ready to be discharged. But the fear of one's emotions and the fear of losing control mean that discharge only takes place in a safe situation. For many men that safety is provided by a relationship with a woman where the commitment of one's friend or lover creates the sense of security. What is more, because it is a relationship with a woman, it unconsciously resonates with that first great passive relation of the boy with his mother. But in this situation and in other acts of men's violence against women, there is also the security of interaction with someone who does not represent a psychic threat, who is less socially powerful, probably less physically powerful, and who is herself operating within a pattern of surplus passivity. And finally, given the fragility of masculine identity and the inner tension of what it means to be masculine, the ultimate acknowledgement of one's masculinity is in our power over women. This power can be expressed in many ways. Violence is one of them.

When I speak of a man's violence against himself I am thinking of the very structure of the masculine ego. The formation of an ego on an edifice of what Herbert Marcuse called surplus repression and surplus aggression is the building of a precarious structure of internalized violence. The continual conscious and unconscious blocking and denial of passivity and all the emotions and feelings men associate with passivity—fear, pain, sadness, embarrassment—is a denial of part of what we are. The constant psychological and behavioral vigilance against passivity and its derivatives is a perpetual act of violence against oneself.

The denial and blocking of a whole range of human emotions and capacities are compounded by the blocking of avenues of discharge. The discharge of fear, hurt, and sadness, for example (through crying or trembling), is necessary because these painful emotions linger on even if they are not consciously felt. Men become pressure cookers. The failure to find safe avenues of emotional expression and discharge means that a whole range of emotions are transformed into anger and hostility. Part of the anger is directed at oneself in the form of guilt, self-hate, and various physiological and psychological symptoms. Part is directed at other men. Part of it is directed at women.

By the end of this process, our distance from ourselves is so great that the very symbol of male-ness is turned into an object, a thing. Men's preoccupation with genital power and pleasure combines with a desensitization of the penis. As best he can, writes Emmanuel Reynaud, a man gives it "the coldness and the hardness of metal." It becomes his tool, his weapon, his thing. "What he loses in enjoyment he hopes to compensate for in power; but if he gains an undeniable power symbol, what pleasure can he really feel with a weapon between his legs?"[23]

Beyond Men's Violence

Throughout Gabriel García Márquez's *Autumn of the Patriarch*, the ageless dictator stalked his palace, his elephantine feet dragging forever on endless corridors that reeked of corruption. There was no escape from the world of terror, misery, and decay that he himself had created. His tragedy was that he was "condemned forever to live breathing the same air which asphyxiated him."[24] As men, are we similarly condemned; or is there a road of escape from the triad of men's violence and the precarious structures of masculinity that we ourselves recreate at our peril and that of women, children, and the world?

Prescribing a set of behavioral or legal changes to combat men's violence against women is obviously not enough. Even as more and more are convinced there is a problem, this realization does not touch the unconscious structures of masculinity. Any man who is sympathetic to feminism is aware of the painful contradiction between his conscious views and his deeper emotions and feelings.

The analysis in this article suggests that men and women must address each corner of the triad of men's violence and the socioeconomic, psychosexual orders on which they stand. Or to put it more strongly, it is impossible to deal successfully with any one corner of this triad in isolation from the others.

The social context that nurtures men's violence and the relation between socioeconomic transformation and the end of patriarchy have been major themes of socialist feminist thought.

This framework, though it is not without controversy and unresolved problems, is one I accept. Patriarchy and systems of authoritarianism and class domination feed on each other. Radical socioeconomic and political change is a requirement for the end of men's violence. But organizing for macrosocial change is not enough to solve the problem of men's violence, not only because the problem is so pressing here and now, but because the continued existence of masculinity and surplus aggressiveness works against the fundamental macrosocial change we desire.

The many manifestations of violence against women have been an important focus of feminists. Women's campaigns and public education against rape, battering, sexual harassment, and more generally for control by women of their bodies are a key to challenging men's violence. Support by men, not only for the struggles waged by women, but in our own workplaces and among our friends is an important part of the struggle. There are many possible avenues for work by men among men. These include: forming counselling groups and support services for battering men (as is now happening in different cities in North America); championing the inclusion of clauses on sexual harassment in collective agreements and in the constitutions or bylaws of our trade unions, associations, schools, and political parties; raising money, campaigning for government funding, and finding other means of support for rape crisis centers and shelters for battered women; speaking out against violent and sexist pornography; building neighborhood campaigns against wife and child abuse; and personally refusing to collude with the sexism of our workmates, colleagues, and friends. The latter is perhaps the most difficult of all and requires patience, humor, and support from other men who are challenging sexism.

But because men's violence against women is inseparable from the other two corners of the triad of men's violence, solutions are very complex and difficult. Ideological changes and an awareness of problems are important but insufficient. While we can envisage changes in our child-rearing arrangements (which in turn would require radical economic changes) lasting solutions have to go far deeper. Only the development of non-surplus-repressive societies (whatever these might look like) will allow for the greater expression of human needs and, along with attacks on patriarchy per se, will reduce the split between active and passive psychological aims.[25]

The process of achieving these long-term goals contains many elements of economic, social, political, and psychological change, each of which requires a fundamental transformation of society. Such a transformation will not be created by an amalgam of changed individuals; but there *is* a relationship between personal change and our ability to construct organizational, political, and economic alternatives that will be able to mount a successful challenge to the status quo.

One avenue of personal struggle that is being engaged in by an increasing number of men has been the formation of men's support groups. Some groups focus on consciousness raising, but most groups stress the importance of men talking about their feelings, their relations with other men and with women, and any number of problems in their lives. At times these groups have been criticized by some antisexist men as yet another place for men to collude against women. The alternatives put forward are groups whose primary focus is either support for struggles led by women or the organization of direct, antisexist campaigns among men. These activities are very important, but so too is the development of new support structures among men. And these structures must go beyond the traditional form of consciousness raising.

Consciousness raising usually focuses on manifestations of the oppression of women and on the oppressive behavior of men. But as we have seen, masculinity is more than the sum total of oppressive forms of behavior. It is deeply and unconsciously embedded in the structure of our egos and superegos; it is what we have become. An awareness of oppressive behavior is important, but too often it only leads to guilt about being a man. Guilt is a profoundly conservative emotion and as such is not particularly useful for bringing about change. From a position of insecurity and guilt, people do not change or inspire others to change. After all, insecurity about one's male credentials played an important part in the individual acquisition of masculinity and men's violence in the first place.

There is a need to promote the personal strength and security necessary to allow men to make more fundamental personal changes and to confront sexism and heterosexism in our society at large. Support groups usually allow men to talk about our feelings, how we too have been hurt growing up in a surplus-repressive society, and how we, in turn, act at times in an oppressive manner. We begin to see the connections between painful and frustrating experiences in our own lives and related forms of oppressive behavior. As Sheila Rowbotham notes, "the exploration of the internal areas of consciousness is a political necessity for us."[26]

Talking among men is a major step, but it is still operating within the acceptable limits of what men like to think of as rational behavior. Deep barriers and fears remain even when we can begin to recognize them. As well as talking, men need to encourage direct expression of emotions—grief, anger, rage, hurt, love—within these groups and the physical closeness that has been blocked by the repression of passive aims, by social prohibition, and by our own superegos and sense of what is right. This discharge of emotions has many functions and outcomes: like all forms of emotional and physical discharge it lowers the tension within the human system and reduces the likelihood of a spontaneous discharge of emotions through outer- or inner-directed violence.

But the expression of emotions is not an end in itself; in this context it is a means to an end. Stifling the emotions connected with feelings of hurt and pain acts as a sort of glue that allows the original repression to remain. Emotional discharge, in a situation of support and encouragement, helps unglue the ego structures that require us to operate in patterned, phobic, oppressive, and surplus-aggressive forms. In a sense it loosens up the repressive structures and allows us fresh in-

sight into ourselves and our past. But if this emotional discharge happens in isolation or against an unwitting victim, it only reinforces the feelings of being powerless, out of control, or a person who must obsessively control others. Only in situations that contradict these feelings—that is, with the support, affection, encouragement, and backing of other men who experience similar feelings—does the basis for change exist.[27]

The encouragement of emotional discharge and open dialogue among men also enhances the safety we begin to feel among each other and in turn helps us to tackle obsessive, even if unconscious, fear of other men. This unconscious fear and lack of safety are the experience of most heterosexual men throughout their lives. The pattern for homosexual men differs, but growing up and living in a heterosexist, patriarchal culture implants similar fears, even if one's adult reality is different.

Receiving emotional support and attention from a group of men is a major contradiction to experiences of distance, caution, fear, and neglect from other men. This contradiction is the mechanism that allows further discharge, emotional change, and more safety. Safety among even a small group of our brothers gives us greater safety and strength among men as a whole. This gives us the confidence and sense of personal power to confront sexism and homophobia in all its various manifestations. In a sense, this allows us each to be a model of a strong, powerful man who does not need to operate in an oppressive and violent fashion in relation to women, to other men, or to himself. And that, I hope, will play some small part in the challenge to the oppressive reality of patriarchal, authoritarian, and class societies. It will be changes in our own lives inseparably intertwined with changes in society as a whole that will sever the links in the triad of men's violence.

Notes

My thanks to those who have given me comments on earlier drafts of this paper, in particular my father, Nathan Kaufman, and to Gad Horowitz. As well, I extend my appreciation to the men I have worked with in various counseling situations who have helped me develop insights into the individual acquisition of violence and masculinity.

1. Herbert Marcuse, *Eros and Civilization* (Boston: Beacon Press, 1975; New York: Vintage, 1962); Gad Horowitz, *Repression* (Toronto: University of Toronto Press, 1977).

2. This is the approach, for example, of Suzanne Steinmetz. She says that macrolevel social and economic conditions (such as poverty, unemployment, inadequate housing, and the glorification and acceptance of violence) lead to high crime rates and a tolerance of violence that in turn leads to family aggression. See her *Cycle of Violence* (New York: Praeger, 1977), 30.

3. Juliet Mitchell, *Psychoanalysis and Feminism* (New York: Vintage, 1975), 362.

4. Joseph Conrad, *Lord Jim* (New York: Bantam Books, 1981), 146; first published 1900.

5. See, for example, Michele Barrett's thought-provoking book *Women's Oppression Today* (London: Verso/New Left Books, 1980), 10–19, 250–1.

6. Jessica Benjamin, "Authority and the Family Revisited: or, A World Without Fathers?" *New German Critique* (Winter 1978), 35.

7. Bertolt Brecht, *Three Penny Novel*, trans. Desmond I. Vesey (Harmondsworth: Penguin, 1965), 282.

8. Andrew Tolson, *The Limits of Masculinity* (London: Tavistock, 1977), 25.

9. Simone de Beauvoir, in the *Nouvel Observateur*, Mar. 1, 1976. Quoted in Diana E. H. Russell and Nicole Van de Ven, eds., *Crimes Against Women* (Millbrae, Calif.: Les Femmes, 1976), xiv.

10. Among the sources on male violence that are useful, even if sometimes problematic, see Leonore E. Walker, *The Battered Woman* (New York: Harper Colophon, 1980); Russell and Van de Ven, *op. cit.*; Judith Lewis Herman, *Father–Daughter Incest* (Cambridge, Mass.: Harvard University Press, 1981); Suzanne K. Steinmetz, *The Cycle of Violence* (New York: Praeger, 1977); Sylvia Levine and Joseph Koenig, *Why Men Rape* (Toronto: Macmillan, 1980); Susan Brownmiller, *op. cit.*; and Connie Guberman and Margie Wolfe, eds., *No Safe Place* (Toronto: Women's Press, 1985).

11. Levine and Koenig, *op. cit.*, pp. 28, 42, 56, 72.

12. Meg Luxton, *More Than a Labour of Love* (Toronto: Women's Press, 1980), 66.

13. Margaret M. Killoran, "The Sound of Silence Breaking: Toward a Metatheory of Wife Abuse" (M.A. thesis, McMaster University, 1981), 148.

14. Barrett and MacIntosh, *op. cit.*, 23.

15. Of course, household violence is not monopolized by men. In the United States roughly the same number of domestic homicides are committed by each sex. In 1975, 8.0% of homicides were committed by husbands against wives and 7.8% by wives against husbands. These figures, however, do not indicate the chain of violence, that is, the fact that most of these women were reacting to battering by their husbands. (See Steinmetz, *op. cit.*, p. 90.) Similarly, verbal and physical abuse of children appears to be committed by men and women equally. Only in the case of incest is there a near monopoly by men. Estimates vary greatly, but between one-fifth and one-third of all girls experience some sort of sexual contact with an adult male, in most cases with a father, stepfather, other relative, or teacher. (See Herman, *op. cit.*, 12 and *passim*.)

16. Luxton, *op. cit.*, p. 65.

17. This was pointed out by I. F. Stone in a 1972 article on the Vietnam war. At a briefing about the U.S. escalation of bombing in the North, the Pentagon official described U.S. strategy as two boys fighting: "If one boy gets the other in an arm lock, he can probably get his adversary to say 'uncle' if he increases the pressure in sharp, painful jolts and gives every indication of willingness to break the boy's arm" ("Machismo in Washington," reprinted in Pleck and Sawyer, *op. cit.*, 131). Although women are also among the victims of war, I include war in the category of violence against men because I am here referring to the causality of war.

18. This is true both of masculinity as an institution and masculinity for the individual. Gay men keep certain parts of the self-oppressive masculine norm intact simply because they have grown up and live in a predominantly heterosexual, male-dominated society.

19. Horowitz, *op. cit.*, 99.

20. This formulation was first suggested to me by Charlie Kreiner at a men's counseling workshop in 1982.

21. D. H. Lawrence, *Women in Love* (Harmondsworth: Penguin, 1960), 304–5; first published 1921.

22. See Robin Wood's analysis of the film *Raging Bull*. M. Kaufman, ed. *Beyond Patriarchy* (Toronto: Oxford University Press, 1987).

23. Emmanuel Reynaud, *Holy Virility*, translated by Ros Schwartz (London: Plato Press, 1983), 41–2.

24. Gabriel García Márquez, *Autumn of the Patriarch*, trans. Gregory Rabassa (Harmondsworth: Penguin, 1972), 111; first published 1967.

25. For a discussion on non-surplus-repressive societies, particularly in the sense of being complementary with Marx's notion of communism, see Horowitz, *op. cit.*, particularly chapter 7, and also Marcuse, *op. cit.*, especially chaps. 7, 10, and 11.

26. Rowbotham, *op. cit.*, 36.

27. As is apparent, although I have adopted a Freudian analysis of the unconscious and the mechanisms of repression, these observations on the therapeutic process—especially the importance of a supportive counseling environment, peer-counseling relations, emotional discharge, and the concept of contradiction—are those developed by forms of co-counseling, in particular, reevaluation counseling. But unlike the latter, I do not suppose that any of us can discharge all of our hurt, grief, and anger and uncover an essential self simply because our "self" is created.

Manning Marable

The Black Male:
Searching Beyond Stereotypes

What is a Black man? Husband and father. Son and brother. Lover and boyfriend. Uncle and grandfather. Construction worker and share-cropper. Minister and ghetto hustler. Doctor and mine-worker. Auto mechanic and presidential candidate.

What is a Black man in an institutionally racist society, in the social system of modern cap-italist America? The essential tragedy of being Black and male is our inability, as men and as people of African descent, to define ourselves without the stereotypes the larger society imposes upon us, and through various institutional means perpetuates and permeates within our entire cul-ture. Our relations with our sisters, our parents and children, and indeed across the entire spec-trum of human relations are imprisoned by im-ages of the past, false distortions that seldom if ever capture the essence of our being. We cannot come to terms with Black women until we un-derstand the half-hidden stereotypes that have crippled our development and social conscious-ness. We cannot challenge racial and sexual in-equality, both within the Black community and across the larger American society, unless we comprehend the critical difference between the myths about ourselves and the harsh reality of being Black men.

Manning Marable, "The Black Male: Searching Beyond Stereotypes," in R. Majors and J. Gordon, eds., *The American Black Male* (Chicago: Nelson-Hall, 1993).

Confrontation with White History

The conflicts between Black and white men in contemporary American culture can be traced di-rectly through history to the earliest days of chat-tel slavery. White males entering the New World were ill adapted to make the difficult transition from Europe to the American frontier. As recent historical research indicates, the development of what was to become the United States was ac-complished largely, if not primarily, by African slaves, men and women alike. Africans were the first to cultivate wheat on the continent; they showed their illiterate masters how to grow indigo, rice, and cotton; their extensive knowledge of herbs and roots provided colonists with medicines and preservatives for food supplies. It was the Black man, wielding his sturdy axe, who cut down most of the virgin forest across the southern colonies. And in times of war, the white man re-luctantly looked to his Black slave to protect him and his property. As early as 1715, during the Yemassee Indian war, Black troops led British regulars in a campaign to exterminate Indian tribes. After another such campaign in 1747, the all-white South Carolina legislature issued a pub-lic vote of gratitude to Black men, who "in times of war, behaved themselves with great faithful-ness and courage, in repelling the attacks of his Majesty's enemies." During the American Revo-lution, over two thousand Black men volunteered to join the beleaguered Continental Army of George Washington, a slaveholder. A generation later, two thousand Blacks from New York joined the state militia's segregated units during the War of 1812, and Blacks fought bravely under Andrew Jackson at the Battle of New Orleans. From Crispus Attucks to the 180,000 Blacks who fought in the Union Army during the Civil War, Black men gave their lives to preserve the liberties of their white male masters.

The response of white men to the many sacrifices of their sable counterparts was, in a word, contemptuous. Their point of view of Black males was conditioned by three basic beliefs. Black men were only a step above the animals—possessing awesome physical power but lacking in intellectual ability. As such, their proper role in white society was as laborers, not as the managers of labor. Second, the Black male represented a potential political threat to the entire system of slavery. And third, but by no means last, the Black male symbolized a lusty sexual potency that threatened white women. This uneven mixture of political fears and sexual anxieties was reinforced by the white males' crimes committed against Black women, the routine rape and sexual abuse that all slave societies permit between the oppressed and the oppressor. Another dilemma, seldom discussed publicly, was the historical fact that some white women of social classes were not reluctant to request the sexual favors of their male slaves. These inherent tensions produced a racial model of conduct and social context that survived the colonial period and continued into the twentieth century. The white male–dominated system dictated that the only acceptable social behavior of any Black male was that of subservience—the loyal slave, the proverbial Uncle Tom, the ever-cheerful and infantile Sambo. It was not enough that Black men must cringe before their white masters; they must express open devotion to the system of slavery itself. Politically, the Black male was unfit to play even a minor role in the development of democracy. Supreme Court Chief Justice Roger B. Tawney spoke for his entire class in 1857: "Negroes [are] beings of an inferior order, and altogether unfit to associate with the white race, either by social or political relations; and so far inferior that they have no rights which the white man was bound to

respect." Finally, Black males disciplined for various crimes against white supremacy—such as escaping from the plantation, or murdering their masters—were often punished in a sexual manner. On this point, the historical record is clear. In the colonial era, castration of Black males was required by the legislatures of North and South Carolina, Virginia, Pennsylvania, and New Jersey. Black men were castrated simply for striking a white man or for attempting to learn to read and write. In the late nineteenth century, hundreds of Black male victims of lynching were first sexually mutilated before being executed. The impulse to castrate Black males was popularized in white literature and folklore, and even today, instances of such crimes are not entirely unknown in the rural South.

The relations between Black males and white women were infinitely more complex. Generally, the vast majority of white females viewed Black men through the eyes of their fathers and husbands. The Black man was simply a beast of burden, a worker who gave his life to create a more comfortable environment for her and her children. And yet, in truth, he was still a man. Instances of interracial marriage were few, and were prohibited by law even as late as the 1960s. But the fear of sexual union did not prohibit many white females, particularly indentured servants and working-class women, from soliciting favors from Black men. In the 1840s, however, a small group of white middle-class women became actively involved in the campaign to abolish slavery. The founders of modern American feminism—Susan B. Anthony, Elizabeth Cady Stanton, and Lucretia Mott—championed the cause of emancipation and defended Blacks' civil rights. In gratitude for their devotion to Black freedom, the leading Black abolitionist of the period, Frederick Douglass, actively promoted the rights of white women against the white male power structure. In 1848, at the Seneca Falls, New York, women's rights convention, Douglass was the only man, Black or white, to support the extension of voting rights to all women. White women looked to Douglass for leadership in the battle against sexual and racial discrimination. Yet curiously, they were frequently hostile to the continued contributions of Black women to the cause of freedom. When the brilliant orator Sojourner Truth, second only to Douglass as a leading figure in the abolitionist movement, rose to lecture before an 1851 women's convention in Akron, Ohio, white women cried out, "Don't let her speak!" For these white liberals, the destruction of slavery was simply a means to expand democratic rights to white women: the goal was defined in racist terms. Black men like Douglass were useful allies only so far as they promoted white middle-class women's political interests.

The moment of truth came immediately following the Civil War, when Congress passed the Fifteenth Amendment, which gave Black males the right to vote. For Douglass and most Black leaders, both men and women, suffrage was absolutely essential to preserve their new freedoms. While the Fifteenth Amendment excluded females from the electoral franchise, it nevertheless represented a great democratic victory for all oppressed groups.

For most white suffragists, however, it symbolized the political advancement of the Black male over white middle-class women. Quickly their liberal rhetoric gave way to racist diatribes. "So long as the Negro was lowest in the scale of being, we were willing to press his claims," wrote Elizabeth Cady Stanton in 1865. "But now, as the celestial gate to civil rights is slowly moving on its hinges, it becomes a serious question whether we had better stand aside and see 'Sambo' walk into the kingdom first." Most white women reformists concluded that "it is better to be the slave of an educated white man than of a degraded, ignorant black one." They warned whites that giving the vote to the Black male would lead to widespread rape and sexual assaults against white women of the upper classes. Susan B. Anthony vowed, "I will cut off this right arm of mine before I will ever work for or demand the ballot for the Negro and not the [white] woman." In contrast, Black women leaders like Sojourner Truth and Frances E. Watkins Harper understood that the enfranchisement of Black men was an essential step for the democratic rights of all people.

The division between white middle-class feminists and the civil rights movement of Blacks, beginning over a century ago, has continued today in debates over affirmative action and job quotas. White liberal feminists frequently use the rhetoric of racial equality but often find it difficult to support public policies that will advance Black males over their own social group. Even in the 1970s, such liberal women writers as Susan Brownmiller continued to resurrect the myth of the "Black male-as-rapist" and sought to define white women in crudely racist terms. The weight of white history, from white women and men alike, has been an endless series of stereotypes used to frustrate the Black man's images of himself and to blunt his constant quest for freedom.

Confronting the Black Woman

Images of our suffering—as slaves, sharecroppers, industrial workers, and standing in unemployment lines—have been intermingled in our relationship with the Black woman. We have seen her straining under the hot southern sun, chopping cotton row upon row, and nursing our children on the side. We have witnessed her come home, tired and weary after working as a nurse, cook, or maid in white men's houses. We have seen her love of her children, her commitment to the church, her beauty and dignity in the face of political and economic exploitation. And yet, so much is left unsaid. All too often the Black male, in his own silent suffering, fails to communicate his love and deep respect for the mother, sister, grandmother, and wife who gave him the courage and commitment to strive for freedom. The veils of oppression, and the illusions of racial stereotypes, limit our ability to speak the inner truths about ourselves and our relationships to Black women.

The Black man's image of the past is, in most respects, a distortion of social reality. All of us can feel the anguish of our great-grandfathers as they witnessed their wives and daughters being raped by their white masters, or as they wept when their families were sold apart. But do we feel the double bondage of the Black woman, trying desperately to keep her family together and yet at times distrusted by her own Black man? Less than a generation ago, most Black male social scientists argued that the Black family was effectively destroyed by slavery; that the Black man was much less than a husband or father; and that the result was a "Black matriarchy" that crippled the economic, social, and political development of the Black community. Back in 1965, Black scholar C. Eric Lincoln declared that the slavery experience had "stripped the Negro male of his masculinity" and "condemned him to a eunuch-like existence in a culture that venerates masculine primacy." The rigid rules of Jim Crow applied more to Black men than to their women, according to Lincoln: "Because she was frequently the white man's mistress, the Negro woman occasionally flaunted the rules of segregation. . . . The Negro [male] did not earn rewards for being manly, courageous, or assertive, but for being accommodating—for fulfilling the stereotype of what he has been forced to be." The social by-product of Black demasculinization, concluded Lincoln, was the rise of Black matriarchs, who psychologically castrated their husbands and sons. "The Negro female has had the responsibility of the Negro family for so many generations that she accepts it, or assumes it, as second nature. Many older women have forgotten why the responsibility developed upon the Negro woman in the first place, or why it later became institutionalized," Lincoln argues. "And young Negro women do not think it absurd to reduce the relationship to a matter of money, since many of them probably grew up in families where the only income was earned by the mothers: the fathers may not have been in evidence at all." Other Black sociologists perpetuated these stereotypes, which only served to turn Black women and men against each other instead of focusing their energies and talents in the struggle for freedom.

Today's social science research on Black female–male relations tells us what our common sense should have indicated long ago—that the essence of Black family and community life has been a positive, constructive, and even heroic experience. Andrew Billingsley's *Black Families in White America* illustrates that the Black "extended family" is part of our African heritage that was never eradicated by slavery or segregation. The Black tradition of racial cooperation, the collectivist rather than individualistic ethos, is an outgrowth of the unique African heritage that we still maintain. It is clear that the Black woman was the primary transmitter and repositor of the cultural heritage of our people and played a central role in the socialization and guidance of Black male and female children. But this fact does not in any way justify the myth of a "Black matriarchy." Black women suffered from the economic exploitation and racism Black males experienced—but they also were trapped by institutional sexism and all of the various means of violence that have been used to oppress all women, such as rape, "wife beating," and sterilization. The majority of the Black poor throughout history have been overwhelmingly female; the lowest paid major group within the labor force in America is black women, not men.

In politics, the sense of the Black man's relations with Black women are again distorted by stereotypes. Most of us can cite the achievement of the great Black men who contributed to the freedom of our people: Frederick Douglass, W. E. B. Du Bois, Marcus Garvey, Martin Luther King, Jr., Malcolm X, Paul Robeson, Medgar Evers, A. Philip Randolph. Why then are we often forgetful of Harriet Tubman, the fearless conductor on the Underground Railroad, who spirited over 350 slaves into the North? What of Ida B. Wells, newspaper editor and antilynching activist; Mary Church Terrell, educator, member of the Washington, D.C., Board of Education from 1895 to 1906, and civil rights leader; Mary McLeod Bethune, college president and director of the Division of Negro Affairs for the National Youth Administration; and Fannie Lou Hamer, courageous desegregation leader in the South during the 1960s? In simple truth, the cause of Black freedom has been pursued by Black women and men equally. In Black literature, the eloquent appeals to racial equality penned by Richard Wright, James Baldwin, and Du Bois are paralleled in the works of Zora Neale Hurston, Alice Walker, and Toni Morrison. Martin Luther King, Jr., may have expressed for all of us our collective vision of equality in his "I Have a Dream" speech at the 1963 March on Washington—but it was the solitary act of defiance by the Black woman, Rosa Parks, that initiated the great Montgomery bus boycott in 1955 and gave birth to the modern civil rights movement. The struggle of our foremothers and forefathers transcends the barrier of gender, as Black women have tried to tell their men for generations. Beyond the stereotypes, we find a common heritage of suffering, and a common will to be free.

The Black Man Confronts Himself

The search for reality begins and ends with an assessment of the actual socioeconomic condition of Black males within the general context of the larger society. Beginning in the economic sphere, one finds that the illusion of Black male achievement in the marketplace is undermined by statistical evidence. Of the thousands of small businesses initiated by Black entrepreneurs each year, over 90 percent go bankrupt within thirty-six months. The Black businessman suffers from redlining policies of banks, which keep capital outside his hands. Only one out of two hundred Black businessmen have more than twenty paid employees, and over 80 percent of all Black men who start their own firms must hold a second job, working sixteen hours and more each day to provide greater opportunities for their families and communities. In terms of actual income, the gap between the Black man and the white man has increased in the past decade. According to the Bureau of Labor Statistics, in 1979 only forty-six thousand Black men earned salaries between $35,000 and $50,000 annually. Fourteen thousand Black men (and only two thousand Black women) earned $50,000 to $75,000 that year. And in the highest income level, $75,000 and above, there

were four thousand Black males compared to five hundred and forty-eight thousand white males. This racial stratification is even sharper at the lower end of the income scale. Using 1978 poverty statistics, only 11.3 percent of all white males under fourteen years old live in poverty, while the figure for young Black males is 42 percent. Between the ages of fourteen and seventeen, 9.6 percent of white males and 38.6 percent of Black males are poor. In the age group eighteen to twenty-one years, 7.5 percent of white males and 26.1 percent of all Black males are poor. In virtually every occupational category, Black men with identical or superior qualifications earn less than their white male counterparts. Black male furniture workers, for example, earn only 69 percent of white males' average wages; in printing and publishing, 68 percent; in all nonunion jobs, 62 percent.

Advances in high-technology leave Black males particularly vulnerable to even higher unemployment rates over the next decades. Millions of Black men are located either in the "old line" industries such as steel, automobiles, rubber, and textiles, or in the public sector—both of which have experienced severe job contractions. In agriculture, to cite one typical instance, the disappearance of Black male workers is striking. As late as forty years ago, two out of every five Black men were either farmers or farm workers. In 1960, roughly 5 percent of all Black men were still employed in agriculture, and another 3 percent owned their own farms. By 1983, however, less than 130,000 Black men worked in agriculture. From 1959 to 1974, the number of Black-operated cotton farms in the South dropped from 87,074 to 1,569. Black tobacco farmers declined in number from 40,670 to barely 7,000 during the same period. About three out of four black men involved in farming today are not self-employed.

From both rural and urban environments, the numbers of jobless Black adult males have soared since the late 1960s. In 1969, for example, only 2.5 percent of all Black married males with families were unemployed. This percentage increased to about 10 percent in the mid-1970s, and with the recession of 1982–1984 exceeded 15 percent. The total percentage of all Black families without a single income earner jumped from 10 percent in 1968 to 18.5 percent in 1977—and continued to climb into the 1990s.

These statistics fail to convey the human dimensions of the economic chaos of Black male joblessness. Thousands of jobless men are driven into petty crime annually, just to feed their families; others find temporary solace in drugs or alcohol. The collapse of thousands of black households and the steady proliferation of female-headed, single-parent households is a social consequence of the systematic economic injustice inflicted upon Black males.

Racism also underscores the plight of Black males within the criminal justice system. Every year in this country there are over 2 million arrests of Black males. About three hundred thousand Black men are currently incarcerated in federal and state prisons or other penal institutions. At least half of the Black prisoners are less than thirty years of age, and over one thousand are not even old enough to vote. Most Black male prisoners were unemployed at the time of their arrests; the others averaged less than $8,000 annual incomes during the year before they were jailed. And about 45 percent of the thirteen hundred men currently awaiting capital punishment on death row are Afro-Americans. As Lennox S. Hinds, former National Director of the National Conference of Black Lawyers has stated, "Someone black and poor tried for stealing a few hundred dollars has a 90 percent likelihood of being convicted of robbery with a sentence averaging between 94 to 138 months. A white business executive who embezzled hundreds of thousands of dollars has only a 20 percent likelihood of conviction with a sentence averaging about 20 to 48 months." Justice is not "color blind" when Black males are the accused.

What does the economic and social destruction of Black males mean for the Black community as a whole? Dr. Robert Staples, associate professor of sociology at the University of California–San Francisco, cites some devastating statistics of the current plight of younger Black males:

> Less than twenty percent of all black college graduates in the early 1980s are males. The vast majority of young black men who enter college drop out within two years.
>
> At least one-fourth of all black male teenagers never complete high school.
>
> Since 1960, black males between the ages of 15 to 20 have committed suicide at rates higher than that of the general white population. Suicide is currently the third leading cause of death, after homicides and accidents, for black males aged 15 to 24.
>
> About half of all black men over age 18 have never been married [or are] separated, divorced, or widowed.
>
> Despite the fact that several million black male youths identify a career in professional athletics as a desirable career, the statistical probability of any black man making it to the pros exceeds 20,000 to one.
>
> One half of all homicides in America today are committed by black men—whose victims are other black men.
>
> The typical black adult male dies almost three years before he can even begin to collect Social Security.

Fred Clark, a staff psychologist for the California Youth Authority, states that the social devastation of an entire generation of Black males has made it extremely difficult for eligible Black women to locate partners. "In Washington, D.C., it is estimated that there is a one to twelve ratio of black [single] males to eligible females," Clark observes. "Some research indicates that the female is better suited for surviving alone than the male. There are more widowed and single black females than males. Males die earlier and more quickly than females when single. Single black welfare mothers seem to live longer than single unemployed black males."

Every socioeconomic and political indicator illustrates that the Black male in America is facing an unprecedented crisis. Despite singular examples of successful males in electoral politics, business, labor unions, and the professions, the overwhelming majority of Black men find it difficult to acquire self-confidence and self-esteem within the chaos of modern economic and social life. The stereotypes imposed by white history and by the lack of knowledge of our own past often convince many younger Black males that their struggle is too overwhelming. Black women have a responsibility to comprehend the forces that destroy the lives of thousands of their brothers, sons, and husbands. But Black men must understand that they, too, must overcome their own inherent and deeply ingrained sexism, recognizing that Black women must be equal partners in the battle to uproot injustice at every level of the society. The strongest ally Black men have in their battle to achieve Black freedom is the Black woman. Together, without illusions and false accusations, without racist and sexist stereotypes, they can achieve far more than they can ever accomplish alone.

References

Billingsley, A. 1968. *Black Families in White America*. Englewood Cliffs, NJ: Prentice-Hall.

Clark, K. 1965. *Dark Ghetto*. New York: Harper and Row.

Davis, A. Y. 1981. *Women, Race and Class*. New York: Random House.

Lincoln, C. E. 1965. "The Absent Father Haunts the Negro Family." *New York Times Magazine*, Nov. 28.

Marable, M. 1983. *How Capitalism Underdeveloped Black America*. Boston: South End Press.

Maxine Baca Zinn

Chicano Men and Masculinity

Only recently have social scientists begun to systematically study the male role. Although men and their behavior had been assiduously studied (Pleck and Brannon, 1978), masculinity as a specific topic had been ignored. The scholar's disregard of male gender in the general population stands in contrast to the preoccupation with masculinity that has long been exhibited in the literature on minority groups. The social science literature on Blacks and Chicanos specifically reveals a long-standing interest in masculinity. A common assumption is that gender roles among Blacks are less dichotomous than among Whites, and more dichotomous among Chicanos. Furthermore, these differences are assumed to be a function of the distinctive historical and cultural heritage of these groups. Gender segregation and stratification, long considered to be a definitive characteristic of Chicanos, is illustrated in Miller's descriptive summary of the literature:

> Sex roles are rigidly dichotomized with the male conforming to the dominant–aggressive archetype, and the female being the polar opposite—subordinate and passive. The father is the unquestioned patriarch—the family provider, protector and judge. His word is law and demands strict obedience. Presumably, he is perpetually obsessed with the need to prove his manhood, oftentimes through excessive drinking, fighting, and/or extramarital conquests (1979:217).

M. Baca Zinn, "Chicano Family Research: Conceptual Distortions and Alternative Directions" appeared in *The Journal of Ethnic Studies* 10:2, pp. 29–44. Reprinted with permission.

The social science image of the Chicano male is rooted in three interrelated propositions: (1) That a distinctive cultural heritage has created a rigid cult of masculinity, (2) That the masculinity cult generates distinctive familial and socialization patterns, and (3) That these distinctive patterns ill-equip Chicanos (both males and females) to adapt successfully to the demands of modern society.

The machismo concept constitutes a primary explanatory variable for both family structure and overall subordination. Mirandé critically outlines the reasoning in this interpretation:

> The macho male demands complete deference, respect and obedience not only from the wife but from the children as well. In fact, social scientists maintain that this rigid male-dominated family structure has negative consequences for the personality development of Mexican American children. It fails to engender achievement, independence, self-reliance or self-worth—values which are highly esteemed in American society. . . . The authoritarian Mexican American family constellation then produces dependence and subordination and reinforces a present time orientation which impedes achievement (1977:749).

In spite of the widely held interpretation associated with male dominance among Chicanos, there is a growing body of literature which refutes past images created by social scientists. My purpose is to examine empirical challenges to machismo, to explore theoretical developments in the general literature on gender, and to apply both of these to alternative directions for studying and understanding Chicano men and masculinity. My central theme is that while ethnic status may be associated with differences in masculinity, those differences can be explained by structural variables rather than by references to common cultural heritage.

Theoretical Challenges to Cultural Interpretations: The Universality of Male Dominance

The generalization that culture is a major determinant of gender is widely accepted in the social sciences. In the common portrayal of Chicanos, exaggerated male behavior is assumed to stem from inadequate masculine identity.

> The social science literature views machismo as a compensation for feelings of inadequacy and worthlessness. This interpretation is rooted in the application of psychoanalytic concepts to explain both Mexican and Chicano gender roles. The widely accepted interpretation is that machismo is the male attempt to compensate for feelings of internalized inferiority by exaggerated masculinity. "At the same time that machismo is an expression of power, its origin is ironically linked to powerlessness and subordination." The common origins of inferiority and machismo are said to lie in the historical conquest of Mexico by Spain involving the exploitation of Indian women by Spanish men thus producing the hybrid Mexican people having an inferiority complex based on the mentality of a conquered people (Baca Zinn, 1980b:20).

The assumption that male dominance among Chicanos is rooted in their history and embedded in their culture needs to be critically assessed against recent discussions concerning the universality of male dominance. Many anthropologists consider all known societies to be male dominant to a degree (Stockard and Johnson 1980:4). It has been argued that in all known societies male activities are more highly valued than female activities, and that this can be explained in terms of the division of labor between domestic and public spheres of society (Rosaldo, 1973). Women's child-bearing abilities limit their participation in public sphere activities and allow men the freedom to participate in and control the public sphere. Thus in the power relations between the sexes, men have been found to be dominant over women and to control economic resources (Spence 1978:4).

While differing explanations of the cause of male dominance have been advanced, recent literature places emphasis on networks of social relations between men and women and the status structures within which their interactions occur. This emphasis is crucial because it alerts us to the importance of structural variables in understanding sex stratification. Furthermore, it casts doubt on interpretations which treat culture (the systems of shared beliefs and orientations unique to groups) as the cause of male dominance. If male dominance is universal, then it cannot be reduced to the culture of a particular category of people.

Challenges to Machismo

Early challenges to machismo emerged in the protest literature of the 1960s and 1970s and have continued unabated. Challenges are theoretical, empirical, and impressionistic. Montiel, in the first critique of machismo, set the stage for later refutations by charging that psychoanalytic constructs resulted in indiscriminate use of machismo, and that this made findings and interpretations highly suspect (1970). Baca Zinn (1975:25) argued that viewing machismo as a compensation for inferiority (whether its ultimate cause is seen as external or internal to the oppressed), in effect blames Chicanos for their own subordination. Sosa Riddell proposed that the machismo myth is exploited by an oppressive society which encourages a defensive stance on the part of Chicano men (1974). Delgado (1974:6), in similar fashion, wrote that stereotyping acts which have nothing to do with machismo and labeling them as such was a form of societal control.

Recent social science literature on Chicanos has witnessed an ongoing series of empirical challenges to the notion that machismo is the norm in marital relationships (Grebler, Moore, and

Guzman, 1970; Hawkes and Taylor, 1975; Ybarra, 1977; Cromwell and Cromwell, 1978; Cromwell and Ruiz, 1979; Baca Zinn, 1980a). The evidence presented in this research suggests that in the realm of marital decision making, egalitarianism is far more prevalent than macho dominance.

Cromwell and Ruiz find that the macho characterization prevalent in the social science literature is "very compatible with the social deficit model of Hispanic life and culture" (1979:355). Their re-analysis of four major studies on marital decision making (Cromwell, Corrales, and Torsellio, 1973; Delchereo, 1969; Hawkes and Taylor, 1975; and Cromwell and Cromwell, 1978) concludes that "the studies suggest that while wives make the fewest unilateral decisions and husbands make more, joint decisions are by far the most common in these samples . . ." (1979:370).

Other studies also confirm the existence of joint decision making in Chicano families and furthermore they provide insights as to factors associated with joint decision making, most importantly that of wives' employment. For example, Ybarra's survey of 100 married Chicano couples in Fresno, California, found a range of conjugal role patterns with the majority of married Chicano couples sharing decision making. Baca Zinn (1980a) examined the effects of wives' employment outside of the home and level of education through interviews and participation in an urban New Mexico setting. The study revealed differences in marital roles and marital power between families with employed wives and nonemployed wives. "In all families where women were not employed, tasks and decision making were typically sex segregated. However, in families with employed wives, tasks and decision making were shared" (1980a:51).

Studies of the father role in Chicano families also called into question the authoritative unfeeling masculinized male figure (Mejia, 1976; Luzod and Arce, 1979). These studies are broadly supportive of the marital role research which points to a more democratic egalitarian approach to family roles. Luzod and Arce conclude:

It is not our contention to say that no sex role differences occur within Chicano families, but rather [that they] demonstrate the level of importance which both the father and mother give to respective duties as parents as well as the common hopes and desires they appear to share [more] equally for their progeny than was commonly thought. It therefore appears erroneous to focus only on maternal influences in the Chicano family since Chicano fathers are seen as being important to the children and moreover may provide significant positive influences on the development of their children (1979:19).

Recent empirical refutations of supermasculinity in Chicano families have provided the basis of discussions of the Chicano male role (Valdez, 1980; Mirandé, 1979, 1981). While these works bring together in clear fashion impressionistic and empirical refutations of machismo, they should be considered critical reviews rather than conceptual refutations. In an important essay entitled, "Machismo: Rucas, Chingasos, y Chingaderas" (1981), Mirandé critically assesses the stereotypic components of machismo, yet he asserts that it also has authentic components having to do with the resistance of oppression. While this is a significant advance, it requires conceptual focus and analysis.

Unanswered Questions, Unresolved Issues, and Unrecognized Problems

The works discussed above provide a refutation of the simplistic, one-dimensional model of Chicano masculinity. As such they constitute important contributions to the literature. My own argument does not contradict the general conclusion that machismo is a stereotype, but attempts to expand it by posing some theoretical considerations.

In their eagerness to dispute machismo and the negative characteristics associated with the trait, critics have tended to neglect the phenomenon of male dominance at societal, institutional, and interpersonal levels. While the cultural stereotype of machismo has been in need of critical analysis, male dominance does exist among Chicanos. Assertions such as the following require careful examination:

> There is sufficient evidence to seriously question the traditional male dominant view (Mirandé, 1979:47).

Although male dominance may not typify marital decision making in Chicano families, it should not be assumed that it is nonexistent either in families or in other realms of interaction and organization.

Research by Ybarra (1977) and Baca Zinn (1980) found both egalitarian and male-dominant patterns of interaction in Chicano families. They found these patterns to be associated with distinct social conditions of families, most notably wives' employment. The finding that male dominance can be present in some families but not in others, depending on specific social characteristics of family members, is common in family research.

The important point is that we need to know far more than we do about which social conditions affecting Chicanos are associated with egalitarianism and male dominance at both micro and macro levels of organization. Placing the question within this framework should provide significant insights by enlarging the inquiry beyond that of the culture stereotype of machismo. It is necessary to guard against measuring and evaluating empirical reality against this stereotype. The dangers of using a negative ideal as a normative guide are raised by Eichler (1980). In a provocative work, she raises the possibility that the literature challenging gender stereotypes, while explicitly attempting to overcome past limitations of the gender roles research may operate to reinforce the stereotype. Thus, it could be argued that energy expended in refuting machismo may devote too much attention to the concept, and overlook whole areas of inquiry. We have tended to assume that ethnic groups vary in the demands imposed on men and women. "Ethnic differences in sex roles have been discussed by large numbers of social scientists" (Romer and Cherry, 1980: 246). However, these discussions have treated differences as cultural or subcultural in nature. Davidson and Gordon are critical of subcultural explanations of differences in gender roles because they "fail to investigate the larger political and economic situations that affect groups and individuals. They also fail to explain how definition of the roles of women and men, as well as those associated with ethnicity, vary over time and from place to place" (1979:124).

1. What specific social conditions are associated with variation in gender roles among Chicanos?
2. If there are ethnic differences in gender roles, to what extent are these a function of shared beliefs and orientations (culture) and to what extent are they a function of men's and women's place in the network of social relationships (structure)?
3. To what extent are gender roles among Chicanos more segregated and male dominated than among other social groups?
4. How does ethnicity contribute to the subjective meaning of masculinity (and femininity)?

Structural Interpretations of Gender Roles

There is a good deal of theoretical support for the contention that masculine roles and masculine identity may be shaped by a wide range of variables having less to do with culture than with common structural position. Chafetz calls into question the cultural stereotype of machismo by proposing that it is a socioeconomic characteristic:

> . . . more than most other Americans, the various Spanish speaking groups in this country (Mexican American, Puerto Rican, Cuban), . . . stress dominance, aggressiveness, physical prowess and other stereotypical masculine traits. Indeed the masculine sex role for this group is generally described by reference to the highly stereotyped notion of machismo. In fact, a strong emphasis on masculine aggressiveness and dominance may be characteristic of most groups in the lower ranges of the socioeconomic ladder (1979:54).

Without discounting the possibility that cultural differences in male roles exist, it makes good conceptual sense to explain these differences in terms of sociostructural factors. Davidson and Gordon suggest that the following social conditions affect the development of gender roles in ethnic groups: (1) the position of the group in the stratification system, (2) the existence of an ethnic community, (3) the degree of self identification with the minority group (1979:120). Romer and Cherry more specifically propose that ethnic or subcultural sex role definitions can be viewed as functions of the specific and multiple role demands made on a given subgroup such as skilled or unskilled workers, consumers, etc., and the cultural prism through which these role expectations are viewed (1980:246). Both of these discussions underscore the importance of the societal placement of ethnics in the shaping of gender roles. This line of reasoning should not be confused with "culture of poverty" models which posit distinctive subcultural traits among the lower class. However, it can be argued that class position affects both normative and behavioral dimensions of masculinity.

The assumption that Chicanos are more strongly sex typed in terms of masculine identity is called into question by a recent study. Senour and Warren conducted research to question whether ethnic identity is related to masculine and feminine sex role orientation among Blacks, Anglos, and Chicanos. While significant sex differences were found in all categories, Senour and Warren concluded that Mexican American males did not emerge as super masculine in comparison to Black and Anglo males (1976:2).

There is some support for this interpretation. In roles dealing with masculinity among Black males, Parker and Kleiner (1977) and Staples (1978) find that role performance must be seen in light of the structurally generated inequality in employment, housing, and general social conditions. Staples writes:

. . . men often define their masculinity in terms of the ability to impregnate women and to re-

produce prolifically children who are extensions of themselves, especially sons. For many lower income black males there is an inseparable link between their self image as men and their ability to have sexual relations with women and the subsequent birth of children from those sexual acts. At the root of this virility cult is the lack of role fulfillment available to men of the underclass. The class factor is most evident here, if we note that middle class black males sire fewer children than any other group in this society (1978:178).

What is most enlightening about Staples' discussion of masculinity is that it treats male behavior and male identity not as a subcultural phenomenon, but as a consequence of social structural factors associated with race and class.

A thoughtful discussion of inequality, race, and gender is provided by Lewis (1977). Her analysis enlarges upon Rosaldo's model of the domestic public split as the source of female subordination and male dominance discussed earlier. It has pertinent structural considerations. Lewis acknowledges the notion of a structural opposition between the domestic and public spheres which offers useful insights in understanding differential participation and evaluation of men and women. Nevertheless, she argues that its applicability to racial minority men and women may be questionable since historically Black men (like Black women) have been excluded from participation in public sphere institutions. Lewis asserts:

What the black experience suggests is that differential participation in the public sphere is a symptom rather than a cause of structural inequality. While inequality is manifested in the exclusion of a group from public life, it is actually generated in the groups' unequal access to power and resources in a hierarchically arranged social order. Relationships of dominance and subordination, therefore, emerge from a basic structural opposition between groups which is reflected in exclusion of the subordinate group from public life (1977:342).

Lewis then argues that among racially oppressed groups, it is important to distinguish between the public life of the dominant and the dominated societies. Using this framework we recognize a range of male participation from token admittance to the public life of the dominant group to its attempts to destroy the public life within a dominated society. She points to the fact that Mexican American men have played strong public roles in their own dominated society, and as Mexican Americans have become more assimilated to the dominating society, sex roles have become less hierarchical. The significant feature of this argument has to do with the way in which attention is brought to shifts in power relationships between the dominant society and racial minorities, and how these shifts effect changes in relationships between the sexes. Lewis' analysis makes it abundantly clear that minority males' exclusion from the public sphere requires further attention.

Chicano Masculinity as a Response to Stratification and Exclusion

There are no works, either theoretical or empirical, specifically devoted to the impact of structural exclusion on male roles and male identity. However, there are suggestions that the emphasis on masculinity might stem from the fact that alternative roles and identity sources are systematically blocked from men in certain social categories. Lillian Rubin, for example, described the marital role egalitarianism of middle-class professional husbands as opposed to the more traditional authoritarian role of working class husbands in the following manner:

> . . . the professional male is more secure, has more status and prestige than the working class man, factors which enable him to assume a less overtly authoritarian role within the family. There are, after all, other places, other situations where his authority and power are tested and accorded legitimacy. At the same time, the demands of his work role for a satellite wife require that he risk the consequences of a more egalitarian family ideology. In contrast, for the working class men, there are few such re-

wards in the world outside the home. The family is usually the only place where he can exercise power, demand obedience to his authority. Since his work role makes no demands for wifely participation, he is under fewer and less immediate external pressures to accept the egalitarian ideology (Rubin, 1976:99).

Of course, Rubin is contrasting behaviors of men in different social classes, but the same line of thinking is paralleled in Ramos' speculation that for some Chicanos what has been called "machismo" may be a "way of feeling capable in a world that makes it difficult for Chicanos to demonstrate their capabilities" (Ramos, 1979:61).

We must understand that while maleness is highly valued in our society, it interacts with other categorical distinctions in both manifestation and meaning. As Stoll (1974:124) presents this idea, our society is structured to reward some categories in preference to others (e.g., men over women) but the system is not perfectly rational. First, the rewards are scarce; second, other categories such as race, ethnicity, and other statuses are included in the formula. Furthermore, the interaction of different categories with masculinity contributes to multiple societal meanings of masculinity, so that "one can never be sure this aspect of one's self will not be called into dispute. One is left having to account for oneself, thus to be on the defensive" (Stoll, 1974:124). It is in light of the societal importance attributed to masculinity that we must assess Stoll's contention that "gender identity is a more profound personal concern for the male in our society than it is for women, because women can take it for granted that they are female" (Stoll, 1974:105). This speculation may have implications for Chicanos as well. Perhaps it will be found that ethnic differences in the salience of gender are not only one of degree but that their relative significance has different meanings. In other words, gender may not be a problematic identifier for women if they can take it for granted, though it may be primary because many still participate in society through their gender roles. On the other hand, men in certain social categories have had more roles and sources of identity open to them. However, this has not been the case for Chicanos or other men of color. Perhaps manhood takes on greater importance for those who do not have access to socially valued roles. Being male is one sure way to acquire status when other roles are systematically denied by the workings of society. This suggests that an emphasis on masculinity is not due to a collective internalized inferiority, rooted in a subcultural orientation. To be "hombre" may be a reflection of both ethnic and gender components and may take on greater significance when other roles and sources of masculine identity are structurally blocked. Chicanos have been excluded from participation in the dominant society's political–economic system. Therefore, they have been denied resources and the accompanying authority accorded men in other social categories. My point that gender may take on a unique and greater significance for men of color is not to justify traditional masculinity, but to point to the need for understanding societal conditions that might contribute to the meaning of gender among different social categories. It may be worthwhile to consider some expressions of masculinity as attempts to gain some measure of control in a society that categorically denies or grants people control over significant realms of their lives.

Turner makes this point about the male posturing of Black men: "Boastful, or meek, these performances are attempts by black men to actualize control in some situation" (Turner, 1977:128). Much the same point is made in discussions of Chicanos. The possibility has been raised that certain aggressive behaviors on the part of Chicano men were "a calculated response to hostility, exclusion, and racial domination," and a "conscious rejection of the dominant society's definition of Mexicans as passive, lazy, and indifferent" (Baca Zinn, 1975:23). Mirandé (1981:35) also treats machismo as an adaptive characteristic, associated with visible and manifest resistance of Chicano men to racial oppression. To view Chicano male behavior in this light is not to disregard possible maladaptive consequences of overcompensatory

masculinity, but rather to recast masculinity in terms of responses to structural conditions.

Differences in normative and behavioral dimensions of masculinity would be well worth exploring. Though numerous recent studies have challenged macho male dominance in the realm of family decision making, there is also evidence that patriarchal *ideology* can be manifested even in Chicano families where decision making is not male dominant. Baca Zinn's findings of *both* male dominant and egalitarian families revealed also that the ideology of patriarchy was expressed in all families studied:

> Patriarchal ideology was expressed in statements referring to the father as the "head" of the family, as the "boss," as the one "in charge." Informants continually expressed their beliefs that it "should be so." Findings confirmed that while male dominance was a cultural ideal, employed wives openly challenged that dominance on a behavioral level (1975:15).

It is possible that such an ideology is somehow associated with family solidarity. This insight is derived from Michel's analysis of family values (cited in Goode, 1963:57). Drawing on cross cultural studies, she reports:

> . . . the concept of the strength or solidarity of the family is viewed as being identical with the father . . . the unity of the family is identified with the prerogatives of the father.

If this is the case, it is reasonable to suggest that the father's authority is strongly upheld because family solidarity is important in a society that excludes and subordinates Chicanos. The tenacity of patriarchy may be more than a holdover from past tradition. It may also represent a contemporary cultural adaptation to the minority condition of structural discrimination.

Conclusion

The assumption that male dominance among Chicanos is exclusively a cultural phenomenon is contradicted by much evidence. While many of the concerns raised in this paper are speculative in nature, they are nevertheless informed by current conceptualization in relevant bodies of literature. They raise the important point that we need further understanding of larger societal conditions in which masculinity is embedded and expressed. This forces us to recognize the disturbing relationship between the stratification axes of race, class, and sex. To the extent that systems of social inequality limit men's access to societally valued resources, they also contribute to sexual stratification. Men in some social categories will continue to draw upon and accentuate their masculinity as a socially valued resource. This in turn poses serious threats to sexual equality. We are compelled to move the study of masculinity beyond narrow confines of subcultural roles, and to make the necessary theoretical and empirical connections between the contingencies of sex and gender and the social order.

References

Baca Zinn, Maxine.

1975 "Political Familism: Toward Sex Role Equality in Chicano Families," *International Journal of Chicano Studies Research*. 6:13–26.

1980a "Employment and Education of Mexican American Women: The Interplay of Modernity and Ethnicity in Eight Families." *Harvard Educational Review*. 50:47–62.

1980b "Gender and Ethnic Identity Among Chicanos." *Frontiers*: V(2)18–24.

Chafetz, Janet Saltzman.

1974 *Masculine/Feminine or Human*. E. E. Itasca. Ill.: Peacock Publishers, Inc.

Cromwell, Vicky L. and Ronald E. Cromwell.

1978 "Perceived Dominance in Decision-Making and Conflict Resolution Among Anglo, Black and Chicano Couples." *Journal of Marriage and the Family*. 40(Nov.):749–759.

Cromwell, Ronald E. and Rene E. Ruiz.

1979 "The Myth of Macho Dominance in Decision Making Within Mexican and Chicano Families." *Hispanic Journal of Behavioral Sciences*. 1:355–373.

Davidson, Laurie and Laura Kramer Gordon.

1979 *The Sociology of Gender*. Rand McNally College Publishing Co.

Delgado, Abelardo.

1974 "Machismo." *La Luz*. (Dec.):6.

Eichler, Margrit.

1980 *The Double Standard: A Feminist Critique of Feminist Social Science*. St. Martin's Press.

Grebler, Leo, Joan W. Moore and Ralph C. Guzman.

1970 *The Mexican American People: The Nation's Second Largest Minority*. New York: The Free Press.

Hawkes, Glenn R. and Minna Taylor.

1975 "Power Structure in Mexican and Mexican-American Farm Labor Families." *Journal of Marriage and the Family*. 37:807–811.

Hyde, Janet Shibley and B. G. Rosenberg.

1976 Half the Human Experience. *The Psychology of Women*. D. C. Heath and Company.

Lewis, Diane K.

1977 "A Response to Inequality: Black Women, Racism, and Sexism." *SIGNS: Journal of Women in Culture and Society*. 3:339–361

Luzod, Jimmy A. and Carlos H. Arce.

1979 "An Exploration of the Father Role in the Chicano Family." Paper presented at the National Symposium on the Mexican American Child. Santa Barbara, California.

Mejia, Daniel P.

1976 Cross-Ethnic Father Role: Perceptions of Middle Class Anglo American Parents, Doctoral Dissertation, University of California, Irvine.

Miller, Michael V.

1975 "Variations in Mexican-American Family Life: A Review Synthesis." Paper presented at Rural Sociological Society, San Francisco, California.

Mirandé, Alfredo.

1977 "The Chicano Family: A Reanalysis of Conflicting Views." *Journal of Marriage and the Family*. 39:747–756.

1979 "A Reinterpretation of Male Dominance in the Chicano Family." *Family Coordinator*. 28(4): 473–497.

1981 "Machismo: Rucas, Chingasos, y Chingaderas." *De Colores*. Forthcoming.

Montiel, Miguel.

1970 "The Social Science Myth of the Mexican American Family." *El Grito*. 3:56–63.

Parker, Seymour and Robert J. Kleiner.

1977 "Social and Psychological Dimensions of the Family Role Performance of the Negro Male." Pp. 102–117 in Doris Y. Wilkinson and Ronald L. Taylor (editors), *The Black Male in America*. Nelson-Hall.

Pleck, Joseph H. and Robert Brannon.

1978 "Male Roles and the Male Experience: Introduction." *Journal of Social Issues.* 34:1–4.

Ramos, Reyes.

1979 "The Mexican American: Am I Who They Say I Am?" Pp. 49–66 in Arnulfo D. Trejo (editor), *The Chicanos as We See Ourselves.* The University of Arizona Press.

Riddell, Adaljisa Sosa.

1974 "Chicanas and El Movimiento." *Aztlan.* 5 (1 and 2):155–165.

Romer, Nancy and Debra Cherry.

1980 "Ethnic and Social Class Differences in Children's Sex-Role Concepts." *Sex Roles.* 6:245–263.

Rosaldo, Michelle and Louise Lamphere.

1974 *Woman, Culture, and Society.* Stanford: Stanford University Press.

Rubin, Lillian.

1976 *Worlds of Pain.* Basic Books.

Senour, Maria Neito and Lynda Warren.

1976 "Sex and Ethnic Differences in Masculinity, Femininity and Anthropology." Paper presented at the meeting of the Western Psychological Association, Los Angeles, California.

Spence, Janet T. and Robert L. Helmreich.

1978 *Masculinity and Femininity: The Psychological Dimensions, Correlates and Antecedents.* University of Austin Press.

Staples, Robert.

1978 "Masculinity and Race: The Dual Dilemma of Black Men." *Journal of Social Issues.* 34:169–183.

Stockard, Jean and Miriam M. Johnson.

1980 *Sex Roles.* Englewood Cliffs, New Jersey: Prentice-Hall

Stoll, Clarice Stasz.

1974 *Male and Female: Socialization, Social Roles, and Social Structure.* William C. Brown Publishers.

Turner, William H.

1977 "Myths and Stereotypes: The African Man in America." Pp. 122–144 in Doris Y. Wilkinson and Ronald L. Taylor (editors), *The Black Male in America.* Nelson-Hall.

Valdez, Ramiro.

1980 "The Mexican American Male: A Brief Review of the Literature." *Newsletter of the Mental Health Research Project*, I.D.R.A. San Antonio: 4–5.

Ybarra-Soriano, Lea.

1977 *Conjugal Role Relationships in the Chicano Family.* Ph.D. diss. University of California at Berkeley.

Yen Le Espiritu

All Men Are *Not* Created Equal: Asian Men in U.S. History

Today, virtually every major metropolitan market across the United States has at least one Asian American female newscaster. In contrast, there is a nearly total absence of Asian American men in anchor positions (Hamamoto, 1994, p. 245; Fong-Torres, 1995). This gender imbalance in television news broadcasting exemplifies the racialization of Asian American manhood: Historically, they have been depicted as either asexual or hypersexual; today, they are constructed to be less successful, assimilated, attractive, and desirable than their female counterparts (Espiritu, 1996, pp. 95–98). The exclusion of Asian men from Eurocentric notions of the masculine reminds us that not all men benefit—or benefit equally—from a patriarchal system designed to maintain the unequal relationship that exists between men and women. The feminist mandate for gender solidarity tends to ignore power differentials among men, among women, and between white women and men of color. This exclusive focus on gender bars traditional feminists from recognizing the oppression of men of color: the fact that there are men, and not only women, who have been "feminized" and the fact that some white middle-class women hold cultural power and class power over certain men of color (Cheung, 1990, pp. 245–246; Wiegman, 1991, p. 311). Presenting race and gender as relationally constructed, King-Kok Cheung (1990) exhorted white scholars to acknowledge that, like female voices, "the voices of many men of color have been historically silenced or dismissed" (p. 246). Along the same line, black feminists have referred to "racial patriarchy"—a

concept that calls attention to the white/patriarch master in U.S. history and his dominance over the black male as well as the black female (Gaines, 1990, p. 202).

Throughout their history in the United States, Asian American men, as immigrants and citizens of color, have faced a variety of economic, political, and ideological racism that have assaulted their manhood. During the pre–World War II period, racialized and gendered immigration policies and labor conditions emasculated Asian men, forcing them into womanless communities and into "feminized" jobs that had gone unfilled due to the absence of women. During World War II, the internment of Japanese Americans stripped Issei (first generation) men of their role as the family breadwinner, transferred some of their power and status to the U.S.-born children, and decreased male dominance over women. In the contemporary period, the patriarchal authority of Asian immigrant men, particularly those of the working class, has also been challenged due to the social and economic losses that they suffered in their transition to life in the United States. As detailed below, these three historically specific cases establish that the material existences of Asian American men have historically contradicted the Eurocentric, middle-class constructions of manhood.

Asian Men in Domestic Service

Feminist scholars have argued accurately that domestic service involves a three-way relationship between privileged white men, privileged white women, and poor women of color (Romero,

1992). But women have not been the only domestic workers. During the pre–World War II period, racialized and gendered immigration policies and labor conditions forced Asian men into "feminized" jobs such as domestic service, laundry work, and food preparation.[1] Due to their non-citizen status, the closed labor market, and the shortage of women, Asian immigrant men, first Chinese and later Japanese, substituted to some extent for female labor in the American West. David Katzman (1978) noted the peculiarities of the domestic labor situation in the West in this period: "In 1880, California and Washington were the only states in which a majority of domestic servants were men" (p. 55).

At the turn of the twentieth century, lacking other job alternatives, many Chinese men entered into domestic service in private homes, hotels, and rooming houses (Daniels, 1988, p. 74). Whites rarely objected to Chinese in domestic service. In fact, through the 1900s, the Chinese houseboy was the symbol of upper-class status in San Francisco (Glenn, 1986, p. 106). As late as 1920, close to 50 percent of the Chinese in the United States were still occupied as domestic servants (Light, 1972, p. 7). Large numbers of Chinese also became laundrymen, not because laundering was a traditional male occupation in China, but because there were very few women of any ethnic origin—and thus few washerwomen—in gold-rush California (Chan, 1991, pp. 33–34). Chinese laundrymen thus provided commercial services that replaced women's unpaid labor in the home. White consumers were prepared to patronize a Chinese laundryman because as such he "occupied a status which was in accordance with the social definition of the place in the economic hierarchy suitable for a member of an 'inferior race'" (cited in Siu, 1987, p. 21). In her autobiographical fiction *China Men*, Maxine Hong Kingston presents her father and his partners as engaged in their laundry business for long periods each day—a business considered so low and debased that, in their songs, they associate it with the washing of menstrual blood (Goellnicht, 1992, p. 198). The existence of the Chinese houseboy and launderer—and their

forced "bachelor" status—further bolstered the stereotype of the feminized and asexual or homosexual Asian man. Their feminization, in turn, confirmed their assignment to the state's labor force which performed "women's work."

Japanese men followed Chinese men into domestic service. By the end of the first decade of the twentieth century, the U.S. Immigration Commission estimated that 12,000 to 15,000 Japanese in the western United States earned a living in domestic service (Chan, 1991, pp. 39–40). Many Japanese men considered housework beneath them because in Japan only lower-class women worked as domestic servants (Ichioka, 1988, p. 24). Studies of Issei occupational histories indicate that a domestic job was the first occupation for many of the new arrivals; but unlike Chinese domestic workers, most Issei eventually moved on to agricultural or city trades (Glenn, 1986, p. 108). Filipino and Korean boys and men likewise relied on domestic service for their livelihood (Chan, 1991, p. 40). In his autobiography *East Goes West*, Korean immigrant writer Younghill Kang (1937) related that he worked as a domestic servant for a white family who treated him "like a cat or a dog" (p. 66).

Filipinos, as stewards in the U.S. Navy, also performed domestic duties for white U.S. naval officers. During the ninety-four years of U.S. military presence in the Philippines, U.S. bases served as recruiting stations for the U.S. armed forces, particularly the navy. Soon after the United States acquired the Philippines from Spain in 1898, its navy began actively recruiting Filipinos—but only as stewards and mess attendants. Barred from admissions to other ratings, Filipino enlistees performed the work of domestics, preparing and serving the officers' meals, and caring for the officers' galley, wardroom, and living spaces. Ashore, their duties ranged from ordinary housework to food services at the U.S. Naval Academy hall. Unofficially, Filipino stewards also have been ordered to perform menial chores such as walking the officers' dogs and acting as personal servants for the officers' wives (Espiritu, 1995, p. 16).

As domestic servants, Asian men became subordinates of not only privileged white men but also privileged white women. The following testimony from a Japanese house servant captures this unequal relationship:

> Immediately the ma'am demanded me to scrub the floor. I took one hour to finish. Then I had to wash windows. That was very difficult job for me. Three windows for another hour! . . . The ma'am taught me how to cook. . . . I was sitting on the kitchen chair and thinking what a change of life it was. The ma'am came into the kitchen and was so furious! It was such a hard work for me to wash up all dishes, pans, glasses, etc., after dinner. When I went into the dining room to put all silvers on sideboard, I saw the reflection of myself on the looking glass. In a white coat and apron! I could not control my feelings. The tears so freely flowed out from my eyes, and I buried my face with my both arms (quoted in Ichioka, 1988, pp. 25–26).

The experiences of Asian male domestic service workers demonstrate that not all men benefit equally from patriarchy. Depending on their race and class, men experience gender differently. While male domination of women may tie all men together, men share unequally in the fruits of this domination. For Asian American male domestic workers, economic and social discriminations locked them into an unequal relationship with not only privileged white men but also privileged white women (Kim, 1990, p. 74).

The racist and classist devaluation of Asian men had gender implications. The available evidence indicates that immigrant men reasserted their lost patriarchal power in racist America by denigrating a weaker group: Asian women. In *China Men*, Kingston's immigrant father, having been forced into "feminine" subject positions, lapses into silence, breaking the silence only to utter curses against women (Goellnicht, 1992, pp. 200–201). Kingston (1980) traces her father's abuse of Chinese women back to his feeling of emasculation in America: "We knew that it was to feed us you had to endure demons and physical labor" (p. 13). On the other hand, some men

brought home the domestic skills they learned on the jobs. Anamaria Labao Cabato relates that her Filipino-born father, who spent twenty-eight years in the navy as a steward, is "one of the best cooks around" (Espiritu, 1995, p. 143). Leo Sicat, a retired U.S. Navy man, similarly reports that "we learned how to cook in the Navy, and we brought it home. The Filipino women are very fortunate because the husband does the cooking. In our household, I do the cooking, and my wife does the washing" (Espiritu, 1995, p. 108). Along the same line, in some instances, the domestic skills which men were forced to learn in their wives' absence were put to use when husbands and wives reunited in the United States. The history of Asian male domestic workers suggests that the denigration of women is only one response to the stripping of male privilege. The other is to institute a revised domestic division of labor and gender relations in the families.

Changing Gender Relations: The Wartime Internment of Japanese Americans

Immediately after the bombing of Pearl Harbor, the incarceration of Japanese Americans began. On the night of 7 December 1941, working on the principle of guilt by association, the Federal Bureau of Investigation (FBI) began taking into custody persons of Japanese ancestry who had connections to the Japanese government. On 19 February 1942, President Franklin Delano Roosevelt signed Executive Order 9066, arbitrarily suspending civil rights of U.S. citizens by authorizing the "evacuation" of 120,000 persons of Japanese ancestry into concentration camps, of whom approximately fifty percent were women and sixty percent were U.S.-born citizens (Matsumoto, 1989, p. 116).

The camp environment—with its lack of privacy, regimented routines, and new power hierarchy—inflicted serious and lasting wounds on Japanese American family life. In the crammed twenty-by-twenty-five-foot "apartment" units, tensions were high as men, women, and children struggled to recreate family life under very trying conditions. The internment also transformed the balance of power in families: husbands lost some of their power over wives, as did parents over children. Until the internment, the Issei man had been the undisputed authority over his wife and children: he was both the breadwinner and the decision maker for the entire family. Now "he had no rights, no home, no control over his own life" (Houston and Houston, 1973, p. 62). Most important, the internment reverted the economic roles—and thus the status and authority—of family members. With their means of livelihood cut off indefinitely, Issei men lost their role as breadwinners. Despondent over the loss of almost everything they had worked so hard to acquire, many Issei men felt useless and frustrated, particularly as their wives and children became less dependent on them. Daisuke Kitagawa (1967) reports that in the Tule Lake relocation center, "the [Issei] men looked as if they had suddenly aged ten years. They lost the capacity to plan for their own futures, let alone those of their sons and daughters" (p. 91).

Issei men responded to this emasculation in various ways. By the end of three years' internment, formerly enterprising, energetic Issei men had become immobilized with feelings of despair, hopelessness, and insecurity. Charles Kikuchi remembers his father—who "used to be a perfect terror and dictator"—spending all day lying on his cot: "He probably realizes that he no longer controls the family group and rarely exerts himself so that there is little family conflict as far as he is concerned" (Modell, 1973, p. 62). But others, like Jeanne Wakatsuki Houston's father, reasserted their patriarchal power by abusing their wives and children. Stripped of his roles as the protector and provider for his family, Houston's father "kept pursuing oblivion through drink, he kept abusing Mama, and there seemed to be no way out of it for anyone. You couldn't even run" (Houston and Houston, 1973, p. 61). The experiences of the Issei men underscore the intersections of racism and sexism—the fact that men of color

live in a society that creates sex-based norms and expectations (i.e., man as breadwinner) which racism operates simultaneously to deny (Crenshaw, 1989, p. 155).

Camp life also widened the distance and deepened the conflict between the Issei and their U.S.-born children. At the root of these tensions were growing cultural rifts between the generations as well as a decline in the power and authority of the Issei fathers. The cultural rifts reflected not only a general process of acculturation, but were accelerated by the degradation of everything Japanese and the simultaneous promotion of Americanization in the camps (Chan, 1991, p. 128; see also Okihiro, 1991, pp. 229–232). The younger Nisei also spent much more time away from their parents' supervision. As a consequence, Issei parents gradually lost their ability to discipline their children, whom they seldom saw during the day. Much to the chagrin of the conservative parents, young men and women began to spend more time with each other unchaperoned—at the sports events, the dances, and other school functions. Freed from some of the parental constraints, the Nisei women socialized more with their peers and also expected to choose their own husbands and to marry for "love"—a departure from the old customs of arranged marriage (Matsumoto, 1989, p. 117). Once this occurred, the prominent role that the father plays in marriage arrangements—and by extension in their children's lives—declined (Okihiro, 1991, p. 231).

Privileging U.S. citizenship and U.S. education, War Relocation Authority (WRA) policies regarding camp life further reverted the power hierarchy between the Japan-born Issei and their U.S.-born children. In the camps, only Nisei were eligible to vote and to hold office in the Community Council; Issei were excluded because of their alien status. Daisuke Kitagawa (1967) records the impact of this policy on parental authority: "In the eyes of young children, their parents were definitely inferior to their grown-up brothers and sisters, who as U.S. citizens could elect and be elected members of the Community

Council. For all these reasons many youngsters lost confidence in, and respect for, their parents" (p. 88). Similarly, the WRA salary scales were based on English-speaking ability and on citizenship status. As a result, the Nisei youths and young adults could earn relatively higher wages than their fathers. This shift in earning abilities eroded the economic basis for parental authority (Matsumoto, 1989, p. 116).

At war's end in August 1945, Japanese Americans had lost much of the economic ground that they had gained in more than a generation. The majority of Issei women and men no longer had their farms, businesses, and financial savings; those who still owned property found their homes dilapidated and vandalized and their personal belongings stolen or destroyed (Broom and Riemer, 1949). The internment also ended Japanese American concentration in agriculture and small businesses. In their absence, other groups had taken over these ethnic niches. This loss further eroded the economic basis of parental authority since Issei men no longer had businesses to hand down to their Nisei sons (Broom and Riemer, 1949, p. 31). Historian Roger Daniels (1988) declared that by the end of World War II, "the generational struggle was over: the day of the Issei had passed" (286). Issei men, now in their sixties, no longer had the vigor to start over from scratch. Forced to find employment quickly after the war, many Issei couples who had owned small businesses before the war returned to the forms of manual labor in which they began a generation ago. Most men found work as janitors, gardeners, kitchen helpers, and handymen; their wives toiled as domestic servants, garment workers, and cannery workers (Yanagisako, 1987, p. 92).

Contemporary Asian America: The Disadvantaged

Relative to earlier historical periods, the economic pattern of contemporary Asian America is considerably more varied, a result of both the postwar restructured economy and the 1965 Immigration Act.[2] The dual goals of the 1965 Immigration Act—to facilitate family reunification and to admit educated workers needed by the U.S. economy—have produced two distinct chains of emigration from Asia: one comprising the relatives of working-class Asians who had immigrated to the United States prior to 1965; the other of highly trained immigrants who entered during the late 1960s and early 1970s (Liu, Ong, and Rosenstein, 1991). Given their dissimilar backgrounds, Asian Americans "can be found throughout the income spectrum of this nation" (Ong, 1994, p. 4). In other words, today's Asian American men both join whites in the well-paid, educated, white collar sector of the workforce *and* join Latino immigrants in lower-paying secondary sector jobs (Ong and Hee, 1994). This economic diversity contradicts the model minority stereotype—the common belief that most Asian American men are college educated and in high-paying professional or technical jobs.

The contemporary Asian American community includes a sizable population with limited education, skills, and English-speaking ability. In 1990, 18 percent of Asian men and 26 percent of Asian women in the United States, age 25 and over, had less than a high school degree. Also, of the 4.1 million Asians 5 years and over, 56 percent did not speak English "very well" and 35 percent were linguistically isolated (U.S. Bureau of the Census, 1993, Table 2). The median income for those with limited English was $20,000 for males and $15,600 for females; for those with less than a high school degree, the figures were $18,000 and $15,000, respectively. Asian American men and women with both limited English-speaking ability and low levels of education fared the worst. For a large portion of this disadvantaged population, even working full-time, full-year brought in less than $10,000 in earnings (Ong and Hee, 1994, p. 45).

The disadvantaged population is largely a product of immigration: Nine tenths are immigrants (Ong and Hee, 1994). The majority enter as relatives of the pre-1956 working-class Asian immigrants. Because immigrants tend to have socioeconomic backgrounds similar to those of their sponsors, most family reunification immigrants represent a continuation of the unskilled and semiskilled Asian labor that emigrated before 1956 (Liu, Ong, and Rosenstein, 1991). Southeast Asian refugees, particularly the second-wave refugees who arrived after 1978, represent another largely disadvantaged group. This is partly so because refugees are less likely to have acquired readily transferable skills and are more likely to have made investments (in training and education) specific to the country of origin (Chiswick, 1979; Montero, 1980). For example, there are significant numbers of Southeast Asian military men with skills for which there is no longer a market in the United States. In 1990, the overall economic status of the Southeast Asian population was characterized by unstable, minimum-wage employment, welfare dependency, and participation in the informal economy (Gold and Kibria, 1993). These economic facts underscore the danger of lumping all Asian Americans together because many Asian men do not share in the relatively favorable socioeconomic outcomes attributed to the "average" Asian American.

Lacking the skills and education to catapult them into the primary sector of the economy, disadvantaged Asian American men and women work in the secondary labor market—the labor-intensive, low-capital service, and small manufacturing sectors. In this labor market, disadvantaged men generally have fewer employment options than women. This is due in part to the decline of male-occupied manufacturing jobs and the concurrent growth of female-intensive industries in the United States, particularly in service, micro-electronics, and apparel manufacturing. The garment industry, microelectronics, and canning industries are top employers of immigrant women (Takaki, 1989, p. 427; Mazumdar, 1989, p. 19; Villones, 1989, p. 176; Hossfeld, 1994, pp. 71–72). In a study of Silicon Valley (California's famed high-tech industrial region), Karen Hossfeld (1994) reported that the employers interviewed preferred to hire immigrant women over immigrant men for entry-level, operative jobs (p. 74).

The employers' "gender logic" was informed by the patriarchal and racist beliefs that women can afford to work for less, do not mind dead-end jobs, and are more suited physiologically to certain kinds of detailed and routine work. As Linda Lim (1983) observes, it is the "*comparative disadvantage* of women in the wage-labor market that gives them a comparative advantage vis-à-vis men in the occupations and industries where they are concentrated—so-called female ghettoes of employment" (p. 78). A white male production manager and hiring supervisor in a California Silicon Valley assembly shop discusses his formula for hiring:

> Just three things I look for in hiring [entry-level, high-tech manufacturing operatives]: small, foreign, and female. You find those three things and you're pretty much automatically guaranteed the right kind of work force. These little foreign gals are grateful to be hired—very, very grateful—no matter what (Hossfeld, 1994, p. 65).

Refugee women have also been found to be more in demand than men in secretarial, clerical, and interpreter jobs in social service work. In a study of Cambodian refugees in Stockton, California, Shiori Ui (1991) found that social service agency executives preferred to hire Cambodian women over men when both had the same qualifications. One executive explained his preference, "It seems that some ethnic populations relate better to women than men. . . . Another thing is that the pay is so bad" (cited in Ui, 1991, p. 169). As a result, in the Cambodian communities in Stockton, it is often women—and not men—who have greater economic opportunities and who are the primary breadwinners in their families (Ui, 1991, p. 171).

Due to the significant decline in the economic contributions of Asian immigrant men, women's earnings comprise an equal or greater share of the family income. Because the wage each earns is low, only by pooling incomes can a husband and wife earn enough to support a family (Glenn, 1983, p. 42). These shifts in resources have challenged the patriarchal authority of Asian men. Men's loss of status and power—not only in the public but also in the domestic arena—places severe pressure on their sense of well-being. Responding to this pressure, some men accepted the new division of labor in the family (Ui, 1991, pp. 170–173); but many others resorted to spousal abuse and divorce (Luu, 1989, p. 68). A Korean immigrant man describes his frustrations over changing gender roles and expectations:

> In Korea [my wife] used to have breakfast ready for me. . . . She didn't do it any more because she said she was too busy getting ready to go to work. If I complained she talked back at me, telling me to fix my own breakfast. . . . I was very frustrated about her, started fighting and hit her (Yim, 1978, quoted in Mazumdar, 1989, p. 18).

Loss of status and power has similarly led to depression and anxieties in Hmong males. In particular, the women's ability—and the men's inability—to earn money for households "has undermined severely male omnipotence" (Irby and Pon, 1988, p. 112). Male unhappiness and helplessness can be detected in the following joke told at a family picnic, "When we get on the plane to go back to Laos, the first thing we will do is beat up the women!" The joke—which generated laughter by both men and women—drew upon a combination of "the men's unemployability, the sudden economic value placed on women's work, and men's fear of losing power in their families" (Donnelly, 1994, pp. 74–75). As such, it highlights the interconnections of race, class, and gender—the fact that in a racist and classist society, working-class men of color have limited access to economic opportunities and thus limited claim to patriarchal authority.

Conclusion

A central task in feminist scholarship is to expose and dismantle the stereotypes that traditionally have provided ideological justifications for women's subordination. But to conceptualize oppression only in terms of male dominance and female subordination is to obscure the centrality of classism, racism, and other forms of inequality in U.S. society (Stacey and Thorne, 1985, p. 311). The multiplicities of Asian men's lives indicate that ideologies of manhood and womanhood have as much to do with class and race as they have to do with sex. The intersections of race, gender, and class mean that there are also hierarchies among women and among men and that some women hold power over certain groups of men. The task for feminist scholars, then, is to develop paradigms that articulate the complicity among these categories of oppression, that strengthen the alliance between gender and ethnic studies, and that reach out not only to women, but also to men, of color.

Notes

1. One of the most noticeable characteristics of pre–World War II Asian America was a pronounced shortage of women. During this period, U.S. immigration policies barred the entry of most Asian women. America's capitalist economy also wanted Asian male workers but not their families. In most instances, families were seen as a threat to the efficiency and exploitability of the workforce and were actively prohibited.

2. The 1965 Immigration Act ended Asian exclusion and equalized immigration rights for all nationalities. No longer constrained by exclusion laws, Asian immigrants began arriving in much larger numbers than ever before. In the 1980s, Asia was the largest source of U.S. legal immigrants, accounting for 40 percent to 47 percent of the total influx (Min, 1995, p. 12).

References

Broom, Leonard and Ruth Riemer. 1949. *Removal and Return: The Socio-Economic Effects of the War on Japanese Americans*. Berkeley: University of California Press.

Chan, Sucheng. 1991. *Asian Americans: An Interpretive History*. Boston: Twayne.

Cheung, King-Kok. 1990. "The Woman Warrior Versus the Chinaman Pacific: Must a Chinese American Critic Choose Between Feminism and Heroism?" Pp. 234–251 in *Conflicts in Feminism*, edited by Marianne Hirsch and Evelyn Fox Keller. New York and London: Routledge.

Chiswick, Barry. 1979. "The Economic Progress of Immigrants: some apparently universal patterns." In W. Fellner (ED.), *Contemporary Economic Problems.* pp. 357–399. Washington, DC: American Enterprise Institute.

Crenshaw, Kimberlee. 1989. "Demarginalizing the Intersection of Race and Sex: A Black Feminist Critique of Antidiscrimination Doctrine, Feminist Theory and Antiracist Politics." In *University of Chicago Legal Forum: Feminism in the Law: Theory, Practice, and Criticism* (pp. 139–167). Chicago: University of Chicago Press.

Daniels, Roger. 1988. *Asian America: Chinese and Japanese in the United States Since 1850.* Seattle: University of Washington Press.

Donnelly, Nancy D. 1994. *Changing Lives of Refugee Hmong Women.* Seattle: Washington University Press.

Espiritu, Yen Le. 1995. *Filipino American Lives.* Philadelphia: Temple University Press.

Espiritu, Yen Le. 1996. *Asian American Women and Men: Labor, Laws, and Love.* Thousand Oaks, CA: Sage.

Fong-Torres, Ben. 1995. "Why Are There No Male Asian Anchor*men* on TV?" Pp. 208–211 in *Men's Lives*, 3rd ed., edited by Michael S. Kimmel and Michael A. Messner. Boston: Allyn and Bacon.

Gaines, Jane. 1990. "White Privilege and Looking Relations: Race and Gender in Feminist Film Theory." Pp. 197–214 in *Issues in Feminist Film Criticism*, edited by Patricia Erens. Bloomington: Indiana University Press.

Glenn, Evelyn Nakano. 1983. "Split Household, Small Producer and Dual Wage Earner: An Analysis of Chinese-American Family Strategies." *Journal of Marriage and the Family*, February: 35–46.

Glenn, Evelyn Nakano. 1986. *Issei, Nisei, War Bride: Three Generations of Japanese American Women at Domestic Service.* Philadelphia: Temple University Press.

Goellnicht, Donald C. 1992. "Tang Ao in America: Male Subject Positions in *China Men.*" Pp. 191–212 in *Reading the Literatures of Asian America*, edited by Shirley Geok-lin-Lim and Amy Ling. Philadelphia: Temple University Press.

Gold, Steve and Nazli Kibria. 1993. "Vietnamese Refugees and Blocked Mobility." *Asian and pacific migration review* 2:27–56.

Hamamoto, Darrell. 1994. *Monitored Peril: Asian Americans and the Politics of Representation.* Minneapolis: University of Minnesota Press.

Hossfeld, Karen J. 1994. "Hiring Immigrant Women: Silicon Valley's 'Simple Formula.' " Pp. 65–93 in *Women of Color in U.S. Society*, edited by Maxine Baca Zinn and Bonnie Thornton Dill. Philadelphia: Temple University Press.

Houston, Jeanne Wakatsuki and James D. Houston. 1973. *Farewell to Manzanar.* San Francisco: Houghton Mifflin.

Ichioka, Yuji. 1988. *The Issei: The World of the First Generation Japanese Immigrants, 1885–1924.* New York: The Free Press.

Irby, Charles and Ernest M. Pon. 1988. "Confronting New Mountains: Mental Health Problems Among Male Hmong and Mien Refugees. *Amerasia Journal* 14: 109–118.

Kang, Younghill. 1937. *East Goes West.* New York: C. Scribner's Sons.

Katzman, David. 1978. "Domestic Service: Women's Work." Pp. 377–391 in *Women Working: Theories and Facts in Perspective*, edited by Ann Stromberg and Shirley Harkess. Palo Alto: Mayfield.

Kim, Elaine. 1990. " 'Such Opposite Creatures': Men and Women in Asian American Literature." *Michigan Quarterly Review*, 68–93.

Kingston, Maxine Hong. 1980. *China Men.* New York: Knopf.

Kitagawa, Daisuke. 1967. *Issei and Nisei: The Internment Years.* New York: Seabury Press.

Kitano, Harry H. L. 1991. "The Effects of the Evacuation on the Japanese Americans." Pp. 151–162 in *Japanese Americans: From Relocation to Redress*, edited by Roger Daniels, Sandra C. Taylor, and Harry Kitano. Seattle: University of Washington Press.

Light, Ivan. 1972. *Ethnic Enterprise in America: Business and Welfare Among Chinese, Japanese, and Blacks.* Berkeley and Los Angeles: University of California Press.

Lim, Linda Y. C. 1983. "Capitalism, Imperialism, and Patriarchy: The Dilemma of Third-World Women Workers in Multinational Factories." Pp. 70–91 in *Women, Men, and the International Division of Labor*, edited by June Nash and Maria Patricia Fernandez-Kelly. Albany: State University of New York.

Liu, John, Paul Ong, and Carolyn Rosenstein. 1991. "Dual Chain Migration: Post-1965 Filipino Immigration to the United States." *International Migration Review* 25 (3): 487–513.

Luu, Van. 1989. "The Hardships of Escape for Vietnamese Women." Pp. 60–72 in *Making Waves: An Anthology of Writings by and about Asian American Women*, edited by Asian Women United of California. Boston: Beacon Press.

Matsumoto, Valerie. 1989. Nisei Women and Resettlement During World War II. Pp. 115–126 in *Making Waves: An Anthology of Writings by and about Asian American Women*, edited by Asian Women United of California. Boston: Beacon Press.

Mazumdar, Sucheta. 1989. "General Introduction: A Woman-Centered Perspective on Asian American History." Pp. 1–22 in *Making Waves: An Anthology by and about Asian American Women*, edited by Asian Women United of California. Boston: Beacon Press.

Min, Pyong Gap. 1995. Korean Americans. Pp. 199–231 in *Asian Americans: Contemporary Trends and Issues*, edited by Pyong Gap Min. Thousand Oaks, CA: Sage.

Modell, John, ed. 1973. *The Kikuchi Diary: Chronicle from an American Concentration Camp*. Urbana: University of Illinois Press.

Montero, Darrell. 1980. *Vietnamese Americans: Patterns of Settlement and Socioeconomic Adaptation in the United States*. Boulder, CO: Westview.

Okihiro, Gary Y. 1991. *Cane Fires: The Anti-Japanese Movement in Hawaii, 1865–1945*. Philadelphia: Temple University Press.

Ong, Paul. 1994. "Asian Pacific Americans and Public Policy." Pp. 1–9 in *The State of Asian Pacific America: Economic Diversity, Issues, & Policies*, edited by Paul Ong. Los Angeles: LEAP Asian Pacific American Public Policy Institute and UCLA Asian American Studies Center.

Ong, Paul and Suzanne Hee. 1994. "Economic Diversity." Pp. 31–56 in *The State of Asian Pacific America: Economic Diversity, Issues, & Policies*, edited by

Paul Ong. Los Angeles: LEAP Asian Pacific American Public Policy Institute and UCLA Asian American Studies Center.

Romero, Mary. 1992. *Maid in the U.S.A.* New York: Routledge.

Siu, Paul. 1987. *The Chinese Laundryman: A Study in Social Isolation*. New York: New York University Press.

Stacey, Judith and Barrie Thorne. 1985. "The Missing Feminist Revolution in Sociology." *Social Problems* 32: 301–316.

Takaki, Ronald. 1989. *Strangers from a Different Shore: A History of Asian Americans*. Boston: Little, Brown.

Ui, Shiori. 1991. " 'Unlikely Heroes': The Evolution of Female Leadership in a Cambodian Ethnic Enclave." Pp. 161–177 in *Ethnography Unbound: Power and Resistance in the Modern Metropolis*, edited by Michael Burawoy et al. Berkeley: University of California Press.

U.S. Bureau of the Census. 1993. *We the American Asians*. Washington, DC: U.S. Government Printing Office.

Villones, Rebecca. 1989. "Women in the Silicon Valley." Pp. 172–176 in *Making Waves: An Anthology of Writings by and about Asian American Women*, edited by Asian Women United of California. Boston: Beacon Press.

Wiegman, Robyn. 1991. "Black Bodies/American Commodities: Gender, Race, and the Bourgeois Ideal in Contemporary Film." Pp. 308–328 in *Unspeakable Images: Ethnicity and the American Cinema*, edited by Lester Friedman. Urbana and Chicago: University of Illinois Press.

Yanagisako, Sylvia Junko. 1987. "Mixed Metaphors: Native and Anthropological Models of Gender and Kinship Domains." Pp. 86–118 in *Gender and Kinship: Essays Toward a Unified Analysis*, edited by Jane Fishburne Collier and Sylvia Junko Yanagisako. Stanford: Stanford University Press.

Philippe Bourgois

In Search of Masculinity:
Violence, Respect, and Sexuality among
Puerto Rican Crack Dealers in East Harlem

For several decades young African-American and Latino men in the inner cities of the United States have been killed at considerably higher rates than soldiers in the line of fire during World War II. More inner-city African-American and Latino men are under supervision by the criminal justice system than are enrolled in higher education (Mauer 1992). Although accurate figures for Puerto Rican males on the U.S. mainland are usually not disaggregated in census statistics, their levels of violence and institutional incarceration probably parallel those of urbanized African-Americans. Policy Advocates and community leaders specifically identify young, inner-city Puerto Rican men—the focus of this article—as being in a state of crisis (Pérez and Cruz 1994).

Public discussion of the problems faced by poor men of color tend to fuel polemical, moralistic debates that blame the psychological deficiencies of pathological individuals or the social pathology of "subcultures" (cf. *New York Times Magazine* 1994). U.S. politicians and the media in the 1990s have largely responded with traditional "family value" crusades. Individualist, blame-the-victim, and ethnocentric analyses of poverty and social marginalization are standard fare in the United States where social theory in the post-World War II decades has been traumatized by a McCarthyist terror of political economy and an "all-American" tendency towards cultural essen-

Philippe Bourgois, "In Search of Masculinity" appeared in *The British Journal of Criminology* 36, pp. 412–427. Reprinted by permission of Oxford University Press.

tialism or even biological determinist/racist interpretations of social inequality (see the critiques by Katz 1986 and the special issue of *Critique of Anthropology* 1993). Building on conservative interpretations of Oscar Lewis's (1966) culture of poverty concept, and Daniel Moynihan's denunciation of the black family (Rainwater and Yancey 1967), analyses of intrapersonal violence tend to be dominated by psychologists and social workers who focus on the inter-generational transmission of abuse within a therapeutic analytic framework. With notable exceptions (Feldman 1991; Sluka 1990), the growing literature by anthropologists on violence neglects the problems of the industrialized world. Instead anthropologists pursue their "predilection for the exotic" by conducting participant-observation studies on the margins of the world economy, leaving little room for dialogue with other disciplines (see bibliographical review by Ferguson 1988).

Progressive, culturally sensitive critiques of the ethnocentrism and class-bias inherent in most discussions of African-American families notwithstanding (Burton 1991; Jarrett 1994; Stack 1975), paternal abandonment and domestic violence among the inner-city poor in the United States are serious problems. To reach any understanding of why such large numbers of poor men are killing one another and are abandoning or abusing their progeny in the United States, one must set the debate in its larger social structural and political ideological contexts. Most obviously, the restructuring of the global economy has decimated the employment opportunities of the entry-level working class. This results directly in an exacerbation of the material crisis in the reproduction of the conjugal and even the extended family in the United States. As a matter of fact, the U.S. Census Bureau's normally dry, impersonal statistical summaries uncharacteristically used the adjective "alarming" in a 1994 report to describe the over 100 percent increase in family poverty rates for young workers during the 1980s and early 1990s (DeParle 1994: A8). Parallel to these economic shifts, public sector services for the working poor have broken down in the context of an explicitly political hostility to the fate of the marginal (Wacquant 1995). Predictably, this has been accompanied by a rise in urban racial segregation and a polarization of cultural hostility across class and ethnic lines (Tonry 1995).

Working-Class Patriarchy in Flux in East Harlem

The escalation of social marginalization in the United States has had grave consequences for how poor men "do masculinity" (Messerschmidt 1993) as they take refuge in the underground economy and increase their levels of domestic and interpersonal violence. Traditional working-class patriarchy has been thrown into a prolonged material and ideological crisis as increasingly large numbers of men are unable to reproduce what some theorists, building on Gramsci (1991), have called "hegemonic masculinity" (Connell 1987; Messerschmidt 1993). Fewer and fewer men are able to find stable, unionized jobs that pay them a family wage with family benefits as factories relocate overseas in search of inexpensive labour. Unable to provide economically for their conjugal unit, they lose the material legitimation for demanding autocratic "respect" and domineering control over their wives and children.

At the same time that working-class patriarchy has been undermined economically by the restructuring of the global economy, women of all social classes have entered the labour force in increasing numbers since World War II. Furthermore, major cultural and political movements have mobilized women across the globe. As feminist women of colour have noted, this women's movement has been dominated by an anglo-centric middle-class bias which defines emancipation in terms of individual rights and upward economic mobility (Acosta-Belén 1993; Mohanty 1984; see also Jaggar 1983). Nevertheless, throughout most sectors of U.S. society, there has been an ideological dislocation in post–World War II forms of patriarchal social organization. Of course, the reorganization of family arrangements, the restructuring of gendered labour markets, and the transformation of ideologies around sexuality has been a highly uneven and political process. Furthermore, the fundamental ideologies that enforce male domination remain in place. Like patriarchal Luddites, resisting change, men often attempt to reassert their declining level of patriarchal control over women and children through violence.

In the Puerto Rican case, the change in power relations has been further polarized since World War II by a massive rural to urban migration set in a hostile cultural context. The Puerto Rican experience is dramatic by world standards because of the island's colonial relationship to the United States (Meléndez and Meléndez 1993; Rivera-Batiz and Santiago 1994). Few peoples in recent history have experienced such rapid economic changes; such a diasporic emigration; or have suffered such intense social marginalization and cultural denigration (Bonilla and Campos 1986; Dietz 1986; Rodríguez 1989). A Puerto Rican case study, consequently, allows for a detailed examination of how major historical changes affect men and women differently. Puerto Ricans in the United States reveal the centrality of gender and sexual category alongside class and ethnicity in the social pressure cooker that historical experiences of domination and resistance always render so dynamic and painful.

Second-generation inner-city Puerto Rican men who participate in the underground economy offer a particularly poignant example of how social suffering is complexly gendered. For these reasons, when I lived with my family in East

Harlem, New York, during the late 1980s through the early 1990s in order to study street-level crack dealers, gender power relations—and specifically the relationship between interpersonal violence and masculine struggles for dignity—emerged as a central research focus (Bourgois 1995a). In these pages I will explore how inner-city Puerto Rican men, who are confined to the margins of a nation that is explicitly hostile to their culture and no longer requires their labour power, reconstruct their notions of masculine dignity around interpersonal violence, economic parasitism, and sexual domination. Increasingly large proportions of frustrated, desperate men have taken refuge in a street culture of resistance that roots its material base and its ideological appeal in the growing drug economy, which offers a concrete alternative to exclusion from the legal economy and its anglo-centric culture. Through my ethnographic dialogues I hope to show that rather than being mere pawns of larger social structural and ideological forces, drug dealers who participate in street culture are active agents seeking dignity—even if violently and self-destructively. What might be "explained" as individual psychopathology or dismissed as some kind of cultural essentialist machismo (see discussions by Paredes 1971 and Ramírez 1993) needs to be contextualized in history and understood as the expression of contradictory struggles for power and meaning.

The Historical Context

In the decades following World War II between one third and one half of Puerto Rico's population migrated to New York City in search of employment in factory sweatshops (Bonilla and Campos 1986; Bose 1986). They arrived at precisely the historical moment when these kinds of manufacturing jobs were leaving the industrialized countries as multinational corporations have increasingly sought out lower labour costs and more pliant governments throughout the Third World (Rodríguez 1989; Bourgois 1995b; Sassen

1991). This sets the stage for the dramatic changes in family structure and male power roles among second- and third-generation East Harlem residents. Coming primarily from the poorest sectors of society, and often arriving directly from sugar plantations, marginal family farms, or decaying coffee haciendas, definitions of masculinity among Puerto Rican immigrants are embedded in interpersonal webs of "respeto [respect]" defined around gender, age, kinship, and community status. Puerto Ricans still often refer to the long-since urbanized descendants of immigrants from the countryside as "jibaros," a term that is loosely definable as "hillbillies" or "country bumpkins." In the classic "traditional" setting of the family farm, the worth of the autocratic pater familias hinged most immediately on the larger community's perception of the respect accorded to him by his wife and her abundant children. Several generations later on the inner-city street, the idealized legacies of the hierarchies and prestiges that were formerly rooted in the rural family and in the personal hierarchies of small farming or plantation communities have been redefined into an explicitly misogynist and sexually violent street culture. The traditional search for respect has been radically transformed into a fear of disrespect. Unemployed or drug dealing/addicted men find themselves flitting homeless from one sexual relationship to another, without the protection of a family or an economically viable community.

Vivid memories of a rural patriarchy repeatedly surface in the idealized childhood reminiscences of the mothers of the crack dealers I befriended:

> Mrs. Ortiz: What I liked best about life in Puerto Rico was that we kept all our traditions. And in my village, everyone was either an Uncle, or an Aunt. And when you walked by someone older, you had to ask for their blessing. It was respect.
>
> In those days children were respectful. There was a lot of respect in those days. My father was very strict. When a visitor came, my father only spoke to us with his eyes, because chil-

dren were not supposed to be in the room. He would just look at us, and that meant we had to disappear; we had to go to our room. We weren't allowed to be in the same room as the older folks.

I tried to teach my children a little of what my father had taught me.

Mrs. Ortiz's son, Primo, the manager of the crackhouse where I spent much of my time, can no longer "speak" to his children "with his eyes" and expect to have his commands immediately obeyed. A man's oppressive power in his home in rural Puerto Rico was predicated upon his being able to work hard and provide materially for his wife and children. He was supposed to co-ordinate the labor power of his wife and children around the agricultural cycles and intermittent wage labour opportunities of the precarious semi-subsistence rural economy. In inner-city New York, the increasingly large cohort of male high school dropouts who are excluded from the new service sector jobs that require a minimal education and which entail public subservience to anglo-dominated professional office culture have lost the material basis for the patriarchal family pre-rogative of rural Puerto Rico. Former modali-ties of male respect can no longer be achieved through a conjugal household or an extended kin-based community. Instead, the unemployed or drug dealing man lashes out at the women and children he can no longer support or control ef-fectively. The memory of his grandfather's for-mer power hangs heavily upon him as he harks back to a patriarchal "jibaro" past he can no longer reproduce.

The Polarization of Domestic Violence

This was the case for Primo's father when he lost his job at a garment factory and became "a nasty alcoholic (*borrachón sucio*)." Primo's earliest mem-ories of his father are of him beating up his mother. Worse yet, all the subsequent men in

Primo's mother's life offered the growing boy a similarly brutal masculine model defined around physically victimizing women.

> Primo: When I was a kid I never liked'ed no-body to be with my mother. I didn't like any of her men, because I didn't like it when they would have fits, and hit her; get wild and beat her down.
>
> There was this one guy when I was still a little kid in the seventies, named Luis, who was dat-ing my mother. He would hurt her, just to hurt her.
>
> One time he got wild on my mom . . . I was sleeping, and woke'd up.
>
> My mother called the cops, and the mother-fucker grabbed a knife. My heart stopped. That was the only time I got up and came through for my mother. I stood in between after he had made a coupla swings.

Primo reproduced this cycle of brutality 15 years later when he too beat up his girlfriend in front of her children. Powerlessly struggling with his inability to hold a steady job and earn respect though economic faithfulness to his household, he had pursued the street male role of gigolo, and was living off a woman named Candy, who was one of the few female sellers in the crack dealing network I befriended. Primo pretended publicly to enjoy "free loading (*cacheteando*)" on Candy's generosity and love for him. In fact, in private retrospective conversations Primo admitted that he was also in love. After several months of the patriarchal role reversal of being economically supported by a woman and forced to satisfy her sexual desires upon demand, however, he attempted to recoup his personal sense of male respect by the only means immediately at his disposal: public physi-cal violence. Years later in crackhouse conversa-tions, he emphasized his outrage over how his sense of masculinity was "dissed" (disrespected) by Candy's violation of domestic roles:

> Primo: That woman "dissed" me. She was making so, fucking, much money. That bitch was making even more than I knew about.

That bitch was no good. It was like the kids were all living without their mother. The kids were taking care of themselves. Her baby, Lillian, was less than a year old. Hell! Junior was the mother. He was changing the diapers.

And sometimes I felt sorry and shit, so I would do it. I was there, changing the diapers and she wasn't around.

Worse yet, Candy inverted patriarchal sexuality:

Primo: Plus, you see, like, when she would come home, she used to get in a mood, or something, and I didn't wanna BOTHER . . . It was fucked up, because she had grabbed a knife (distant gunshots).

Upon leaving Candy's household following a violent break-up, Primo returned to full-time crack dealing. On slow nights he would provide me and the crackhouse lookout, Caesar, with detailed accounts of the final fight that ended his economically and sexually dependent relationship with Candy. The fight began when Primo refused to make love to Candy. This prompted her to accuse him of having outside girlfriends. It was almost as if Primo used the tape-recorded conversations in the crackhouse as therapy to resolve the confusion generated by the gender taboos that he had broken when he lived off Candy. He also needed to bond with his male friends in the crackhouse by celebrating his ability to triumph over a misbehaving woman. His description climaxed with how he managed to disarm Candy, in order to beat her more severely in front of her children:

Primo: As soon as she put the gun down—I don't remember exactly where she put it, but I saw her take out the clip—I went, "Fucking Bitch!" (swinging both fists). And I mushed her. I was pissed man. I shouted, "Come on, Bitch! I'm not playing with you anymore."

Philippe: What about he kids?

Primo: The kids were there in the room all nervous, I guess they were crying . . . Put it this way: the children knew their mother was wrong, but I was hitting their mother, and they wanted to jump on me. When I saw their faces, I knew

that I had to be prepared for them, too. I was ready to like, block their swings.

Vulnerable Males

In contrast to the legitimation that Primo constructs for his violence against Candy, Primo condemns his own father's violence toward his mother and sisters. He explicitly sees his father as a failure; he was never able to respect him as a patriarchally socialized child should:

Primo: My father's a sick man now. He's got diabetes. He's a chronic drinker; and when he gets drunk he gets violent. So its like he's no fucking good, so why be with him? That's why my mother had to say, "Hike!" (grinning abruptly and jerking his thumb over his shoulder like a sports umpire calling an out).

And every time I would see my father, once they were separated—'cause they were never divorced—it was every other week. And he was just like not correct. Always with a beer in his hand. Always drunk and crying. We were kids. We were thinking "Fuck you. I don't care." He used to buy us candy. And we used to be chillin' with our candy. And then he used to come to me, and ask, "Is you mother with anybody?" I don't remember my answers but I probably used to say "yes," or whatever. He was drunk and stupid.

Maybe he regretted the things that he did. And he could have been better off. I don't remember really too hard. And then he collapses, shakes. I used to hate that.

This particular detail of Primo's father collapsing in a shaking fit of jealousy when his son tells him about his estranged wife's new lover refers to a Puerto Rican psychosomatic medical condition known as *ataque de nervios* (Lewis-Fernandez 1992; Guarnaccia *et al.* 1989). These "nervous attacks" usually afflict women, and are associated with jealousy, abuse, and/or failure in love. The fact that Primo's father might engage in such a feminine expression of angry vulnerability in front of his children and close friends illustrates the sense of male impotence he must have felt as a failed labour migrant in the United States. He would respond by beating up the nearest vulnerable female, whose respect he was no longer capable of commanding.

> Primo: Then he used to start off fighting with my sister, the oldest one. Later, she would hit me.

Ultimately Primo recognizes that he too is a failure as a man. He specifically identifies this in biological terms as a "male thing." In Primo's poignant description of how several generations of men in his immediate lineage have all been crushed, one can discern the gender-specific experience of social marginalization in the Puerto Rican diaspora:

> Primo: I tell you Felipe, I gotta check myself out. 'Cause like I was telling my mother, in my family, it goes like this: all the men are bugged . . . My mother's oldest brother is bugged. He stands in the window talking to himself . . . My mother's other brother—another uncle of mine—he just walks along like a zombie, and he don't look at nobody. I'm his nephew and his godson. He writes some script, it look like shorthand, but it is absolutely no fucking shorthand. He writes in his notebook and scribble scrabble on the notebook. But the guy has his job. He keeps his job. He keeps his place, but he is out of his mind . . . If you look at him walking down the street, he look like a bum. He just walks straight, looking down. He's bugged . . . I remember when he wasn't bugged. He and my mother went to Puerto Rico, when he wasn't bugged. You know, I tell my mother I got a feeling that all the people in my family, I mean all the guys, are gonna snap one day in the future. I think about myself in the future and I'm gonna be bugged . . . But for some reason, somehow, my grandfather wasn't bugged. My grandfather passed away, he wasn't bugged, he just died.

Significantly, none of Primo's sisters—he had no brothers—was involved in the underground economy or even participated in street culture's violence. They all either worked full-time at entry-level jobs in the service sector (i.e., managing a McDonald's, attending customers in a clothes boutique, and working as a nurse's aide in East Harlem's municipal hospital) or were married in long-term relationships raising young children. Primo's pride in his sisters' success illustrates, not only how rigidly women's roles are defined, but also, once again, how differently women are affected by the experience of growing up poor in the inner city.

> Primo: You know my mom's good! She raised up three beautiful daughters that didn't fuck up . . . Maybe they got married early and bullshit, but there's nothing about drugs in the streets. They know what's good and wrong. My sisters ain't violent. They not in the street—none a' that.

Conjugal Stability and Legal Employment

In contrast to their often bravado behavior and explicitly misogynist diatribes, most of the two dozen crack dealers who I befriended admitted to aspiring to an ideal-type, middle-class, nuclear family. In fact, many had actually lived in stable households with the mothers of their children for significant periods of time. This usually occurred during their periods of stable, legal employment. The complex interrelationship between joblessness, personal pathology, family instability, and structural vulnerability in the labour market came up frequently in our conversations. The following account of the relationship between employment and drug use in Primo's life illustrates the interaction between personality and social structure in the construction of masculine subjectivities.

> Primo: I was 19 when I had my kid. He was born in '83, on May 20-something. We were teenagers going steady—me and Sandra. I had found a job and stayed steady with her. We got a crib, and I was making good money . . . I was a good nigga', boy. Every penny that I used to get was for my hobby, which was radio CB-ing. She got pregnant. We didn't really want it. But then I told her, "I'm just as responsible as you are, so if you keep it, I'll take the consequences." So she kept it. It's too bad. But that's

all right . . . And I wasn't selling drugs or doing nothing. I was a goodie, goodie. I had money in the bank, I had money in the house. Sandra never suffered. She was big, and pregnant, and fat . . . When Papito was born I was working at U.S. Litho. I was a good nigga'. I had good hours. I was working from 4:00 to 12:00 at nights . . . I was a hard worker, I was into that overtime. Whatever they give me, I gonna work. I want to bring money to the house . . . This is how I stopped sniffing (cocaine): one day, my son wanted to play with me. I was in the rocking chair, and I didn't want to play with him. It was like, "Leave-me-alone" type shit. And I was thinking about it, and I realized it. I noticed my son was growing up. Plus I bled one time . . . I said, "Nah, this can't be." This ain't me, 'cause I'm always lovable with my kids, singing songs, little school songs that I learned when I was a kid in school . . . I used to sit in a rocking chair, reading him his ABCs and numbers, just to keep his mind busy. You got to read to your kids when they're little, like even when they're only months old, so that they always got things in their brain . . . Then at work they changed my hours to 2:00 a.m. to 10:00 a.m. I said, "I can't handle them hours; I have a family." . . . I used to fall asleep on the job; 'cause I had my son. And this girl, Sandra, my son's mother, had found work off the books. And as she was leaving, I was coming in, and my son was on top of me. He wanted to play. He already slept, you know, so I couldn't sleep . . . And that's when I started fucking up. That's when I started smoking "woolies" (marijuana cigarettes laced with crack), and I was drinking a little. I was staying up all day, and then I didn't want to go to work . . . Man, it's like, oh, God! I used to come from work; I didn't know whether to go to sleep, or hang out and sleep later. And my son, was there, wide awake; he was two, and wanted to play with me. So they fired me because I was falling asleep on the job. They said, "We have to let you go because you have a family, and I know you want to be with your family, because you have these hours, and we can't switch you back to the daylight hours. We need somebody for these hours, where you don't seem to fit in." . . . They were firing everybody; just looking for

reasons. It was like business was bad . . . After that I went AWOL smoking crack.

Primo acutely felt his failure as a father—and as a man:

> You know, Felipe? Now my son is 6 years old. It gets me sad when I think about shit like that . . . It's like, I'm not there for 'im. Just like my father was never there for me . . . And my son loved being with me. Sometimes I was always fixing something in the apartment. So this kid, he used to grab tools, and just start hammering things, like, look at me, and start trying to do the same thing. I love that shit . . . That's why I used to cry a lot when I first left my son. It was only a couple of months after they fired me at U.S. Litho . . . I used to go to the bathroom and cry like a bitch. 'Cause I knew I was leaving soon and that meant: no more kid . . . But you know what, man! I believe in . . . I believe that when you're with someone, and you have a child, you should make the fucking best of it, whether you're doing good or not. You gotta make a commitment; like a family thing, like old-fashioned.
>
> Philippe: What the hell are you talking about?!
>
> Primo: It always seems like I'm full of shit when I say things like that, 'cause I don't support my kid, but that's because, I . . . right now, I'm not supporting my son, but . . . Matter of fact, you know last weekend, when we were talking one time about the last time we had cried, that's the last time I teared, was last weekend. I was thinking about my little nigga'. I was supposed to keep him for the weekend, but I called too late. I fucked up. It was a hassle. (Perking up again) Matter of fact, I remember my father once saying to my mother that he used to cry, because he misses me, because I'm his only son. Now I feel bad, 'cause a few days away from today, it's Papito's birthday, and I'm not gonna give him anything. I don't got the money.
>
> Philippe: You wouldn't rather have those 25 dollars you just paid for the dope (heroin) and the perico (cocaine), to spend on your son's birthday present instead?
>
> Primo (sniffing from a packet of heroin): Well . . . I'll definitely get him a present. I love that nigga'.

Stable legal employment for both spouses is crucial for enabling young men to begin defining masculinity around sharing in the material and emotional reproduction of children. The problem is that most of the legal jobs available to high school drop-outs in New York City are not only poorly remunerated but are also considered to be feminizing. This is because the service sector, specifically office support services in the finance, real estate, and insurance (FIRE) industries, have been the fastest growing employers since the 1970s. Most of the supervisors at the lowest levels of the service sector are women, and street culture castigates males who are publicly subordinated across gender lines. Typically, in their angrier memories of disrespect at work, many of the male crack dealers refer to their female bosses in explicitly sexist language, often insulting their body parts, and dismissing them with street slang and sexualized curses. They often describe their female supervisors as having male sexual organs and they describe themselves and the other men around them at work as being effeminate.

> Caesar: I lasted in the mail room for like eight months at this advertising agency that works with pharmaceutical shit. They used to trust me . . . But I had a prejudiced boss. She was a fucking ho' (prostitute). She was white. I had to take a lot of shit from that fat, ugly bitch, and be a wimp . . . I didn't like it but I kept on working, because "Fuck it!," you don't want to fuck up the relationship. So you just be a punk . . . Oh my God! I hated that head supervisor. That bitch was REALLY nasty. She got her rocks off on firing people, man. You can see that on her face, boy. She made this one fucking guy that worked with me cry—and beg for his job back . . .

The changing high-tech, office service jobs of the post-industrial, globally-linked economy offer few opportunities for young men from the inner city who have dropped out of high school. Not only do young men have difficulty politely taking orders from women, but they often consider it to be downright emasculating to have to run and fetch coffee for their work-place supervisors

and, worse yet, to have to deliver their services with a cheerful smile. Consequently, even when they endure in their positions as messengers, copy machine operators, or mail room clerks they tend to develop reputations for having "bad attitudes"; this further limits their opportunities for upward mobility in office place hierarchies.

Primo never bought Papito, his 7-year-old son, a birthday present. In fact, he did not even go to visit him that week. Coincidentally, during these same days my preteenage neighbours, Manny and Angel, forced me to witness on my tenement stoop the flip side of the father/son generation gap. Eyes sparkling, Angel told me proudly, "I'm going to see my father this weekend." His little brother Manny immediately responded with his eyes dull and sad, "I'm not gonna see my father; he's in jail." As if by script, just moments later we saw another little boy, my neighbour's 3-year-old son nicknamed Papo, shrieking with delight. A 20-year-old man swaggered up almost embarrassedly to hug the little boy, mumbling affectionately *"ay mi hijo* (Oh my son) God bless you!" The mother watched, revealing no emotion. Papo's father had just been allowed out of prison for the afternoon on a drug/rehabilitation/work-release arrangement. An hour or so later, little Papo was screeching again, but this time in anguish. His father had to leave in a hurry to report back to prison before dusk. The superintendent of our tenement later explained to me that Papo's father was the person who had burglarized Papo's mother's apartment two-and-a-half years ago when Papo was only 6 months old. Papo's father had known the apartment was empty because he was supposed to be meeting his infant son in the park at the time. His new girlfriend served as look-out while he stole the VCR and television from out of his son's apartment.

Investing in Promiscuity

Sexual conquest and promiscuity represent another important forum for redefining masculine dignity in street culture that is related to the imperative to glorify one's economic parasitism on the mothers, lovers, wives, and children one can no longer support (Anderson 1989; De la Cancela 1986). Primo's look-out, Caesar, was most adamant in celebrating sexually his inability to maintain a family. Unable to reproduce the patriarchal aspirations of his grandfather's generation within the context of a nuclear family and an extended kin-based community, he concentrated his male energies into macho one-upmanship and sexual belt-notching. He worked hard at exaggerating his sexual promiscuity and hard heartedness:

> Caesar: We's just like those green sea turtles that be in the Galapagos. Those turtles get out of the shell, and they run to the sea, and they never know who their parents was . . . They go through their whole life. Then they bone somebody or they get bone't. They have kids and they never see them . . . I don't feel guilty about the kids I got thrown around out there, because I have no heart Felipe. I'll fuck anybody, anytime. Besides these bitches is crazy nowadays.

Primo also sexualized his notion of male power. One late night after finishing his shift at the crackhouse, I accompanied Primo to visit a social club to drink bootleg liquor. Swigging from his drink and giggling, Primo waved at three women who were playing pool together. Feigning an old-fashioned Puerto Rican rural accent, he said in Spanish, "Look how well my women get along with each other (*Mira como mis mujeres se llevan bien*)."

At the time Primo was under pressure from his probation officer to find a job. A New York City Narcotics Circuit judge had given him a two-to-four-year suspended sentence for selling crack to an undercover agent. One of the conditions for his supervised freedom was that he find legal employment. As he plotted which one of "his women" he was going to spend the night with, I purposefully reminded him that he had to call the employment office early the next morning if he did not want to be sent to prison. Primo simply changed the unpleasant subject and took refuge in his sexual promiscuity.

Primo (sombrely): Oh shit, Felipe, you're right! But you know what? (chuckling) Out of all these bitches hanging around, I take that one (pointing to Maria) . . . (sombrely again) This has happened to me before. One day in front of the Game Room, I saw a legion of girls on the corner (chuckling again). Like a herd of girls talking to each other. And when I looked, I said, "God damn! I had all of them." It was my ex-wife Sandra, Candy, Maria, Jaycee, and I think some other girl that I don't remember.

Philippe: How'd that make you feel—good?

Primo: No. It felt'ed weird. (Noticing Caesar eavesdropping eagerly through the blasting music) No, it felt'ed good, then weird . . . I'm telling you Felipe, I got a golden dick. All my cousins be that way (slapping Caesar five). We all got golden dicks.

Gang Rape

Toward the end of my residence in East Harlem several of the crack dealers with whom I had developed my closest relationships admitted to having been gang rapists in their adolescence. The gang literature in the United States, written primarily by criminologists and sociologists, only occasionally mentions rape (Campbell 1991; Huff 1990). It is usually presented as an initiation ritual and it is sometimes noted that this violent act serves to bond the boys homoerotically and misogynistically (Bourgois 1995a: ch. 5). Participating in gang rape is one of the ways youths achieve their manhood.

All these ritualized dimensions—coming of age, mutual bonding, and ritual initiation—apply to the accounts of adolescent gang rape provided by the crack dealers. Primo, for example, had difficulties becoming sexually aroused when his companions would begin to rape one of the girls in their network. He felt humiliated and excluded when they sent him home for being "too little" to join in their sexual violence.

> Primo: Back in those days I was younger. My dick wouldn't stand up. It was like nasty to me; I wasn't down with it. I can't handle that. So

they be goin' upstairs with a girl, and of course they already knew that I'm not going to be down with it, so they ask me (in a hostile voice), "What'cha gonna do man? Go home or what?" . . . So fuck it, the best thing I could do is break out. "See you guys tomorrow;" or else, I just wait downstairs in the bar, or something.

Primo gained acceptance from the older boys that he admired by becoming an active accomplice in their gang rapes.

Primo: I wasn't really with it, but I used to act wild too, because the bitch is gonna have to pass through the wild thing. And sometimes, it could be me acting stupid with a bat or something, so that she has got to stay in the room with whoever is there . . . Sometimes the older guys, they would play the nice role for awhile with the girl, but once they get that piece of pussy, she gets dished. It's like psshhht, pssht (making slapping motions). She gets beat down: "I own you now, bitch." That was back in the days. Nobody is with that shit no more. Pussy is too easy to get nowadays.

In addition to emphasizing the ritual dimension to adolescent gang rape and its particular frequency in the youth gang context, it is important to understand public rape within the same context that I have presented domestic violence. Gang rape is an extension into the public domain of males trying to reassert the anachronistic patriarchal power relations of previous generations that have been undermined by shifts in gender power relations. As girls increasingly carve out more autonomous roles in public male-dominated settings, boys lash out violently. They legitimatize their sexual violence against young teenage girls, claiming that they are "teaching them a lesson." As a matter of fact, the street expression for gang rape is "to run a train on a bitch." Sometimes the expression is modified into "training a bitch," as if the assaulted person were a dog being taught a lesson, or a new trick. Primo, who was aware of my horror and anger over his accounts of gang rape, often argued with me to try to make me—and any future reader of these tape recorded dialogues—understand the street's dichotomy between worthy and unworthy rape victims:

Primo: Put it this way, Felipe, these bitches were young, dumb, and full-a-cum. If they are hanging out too much, and they start seeing that we are wild, and if they are still hanging out, then we know that we can take them.

Philippe: That is some sick shit you're saying. You motherfuckers were nothin' but a bunch of perverts.

Primo (frustrated): I mean look at their attitude; if they hang out too long, believe me, then they know what's happening. If the girl is gonna hang then she's gonna get dicked. I mean these bitches, they would just keep hanging out, and hanging out. They be coming back to the bar everyday, so then we know that they really want a dick . . . They would take the bitch aside, because we had her *confianza* (trust). By then it was easy to force her into doing it with all of us . . . Besides the bitch get smacked, or something, if she don't.

Philippe: That's rape, man. Don't you understand?

Primo: I mean the way I remember it (speaking directly into my tape-recorder), I was so fucking young. It looked at it like, most likely, whoever never came back to hang out at the club passed through some trauma, and it's gonna be hidden within in their life, for the rest of their life, and they're never goin' a hang again. Instead they go home, and chill the fuck out, and keep a dark secret for the rest of their life. (Looking at me defensively) I used to feel sorry, sometimes too, for them . . . But some bitches was more suitable, and used to just come back and hang. 'Cause I guess it was like they was on the streets, and they passed through their first shit, and now fuck it: *"Voy a hangear"* (I'm going to hang out).

Philippe (interrupting): Come on, man, get real! Nobody likes going through that shit.

Primo (speaking slowly): Well . . . It was their decision, Felipe. I mean, the first time, maybe they weren't into it. Sometimes there be tears in their eyes. They didn't want to be forced.

Caesar (laughing at Primo's confusion and my anger, grabbing the taperecorder from me):

But they were forced; but they liked'ed it; and they come back for more; 'cause they're with it. They just get used to the fact: "We own you now bitch!"

Philippe: You motherfuckers are sick! (Loud gunshots in the nearby background followed by the sound of someone running.)

Primo (running to peek through the door at the noises outside): No! You gotta understand Felipe, even when they say no, they're loving it.

Despite their rationalization of their violence against women as patriarchal justice, they ultimately considered the women they abused to be a reflection of their own sense of internalized worthlessness.

Primo: We used to talk between each other, that these women are living fucked up, because they want to hang out with us . . . And what the fuck we got to offer? Nothing! We used to wonder.

Caesar: We don't be doing nothing! Bitch be stupid to go with a nigga' like us.

Individual Responsibility and Social Structural Victimization

It is impossible to present ethnographic dialogues on experiences of oppression and social marginalization without conjuring negative images that risk re-enforcing racial- and class-based stereotypes. An open, uncensored discussion of masculinity in street culture risks creating a forum for the public humiliation of the poor and powerless. Chicano cultural critics have long since noted how anglo perceptions of latino machismo reflect deep-seated historical prejudices (Paredes 1971). This is exacerbated by the fact that ethnocentric assumptions are so unconsciously ingrained in the public "common sense" that descriptions of extreme social misery and brutality such as those presented in these pages are interpreted as a cultural reflection of a particular ethnic community— in this case Puerto Rican immigrants in the United States. Obviously, such an "airing-of-dirty-laundry" interpretation runs counter to the theoretical and political arguments of this article, which are opposed to cultural essentialist explanations for human action. The same applies to any interpretation that claims women on the street and in the household have provoked male violence against themselves because of their demands for greater rights. That kind of blame-the-victim perspective not only glorifies the stability of previous patriarchal status quos, but also overly individualizes the long-term macro-structural transformations in gender relations that are occurring across the globe. As has been the case historically for all major power shifts between antagonistic groups, the complicated process whereby women are carving out a new public space for themselves is rife with contradictory outcomes and human pain. As I noted in the opening pages, this is exacerbated by the fact that the fundamental status quo that enforces male domination has not been altered. As many feminist theorists have long since noted, many of the struggles and achievements of women in the past decades have been framed in terms of individual rights that ultimately largely mirror or invert patriarchal models of "empowerment" (Butler and Scott 1992; Jaggar 1983). On another theoretical plane part of the problem with understanding experiences of oppression and resistance—whether masculine or not—is that, as Jefferson (1994) notes, the relationship between personality and society is poorly understood. Agency/structure relationships are usually presented in dualistic terms—if addressed at all (see theoretical critique by Giddens 1991). Sexuality, family organization, gender-power relationships, and the cultural construction of intimacy are crucial issues affecting the minute details of our daily quality of life. In many respects they remain taboo subjects for ethnographers who are under an unconscious mandate to present positive images of the people whom with they study and live. Quantitative survey researchers have never had any direct access to these complex dimensions of daily life since most people conceal their intimate experiences of violence, sexuality, substance abuse, etc. from even their closest friends—let alone outside interviewers or survey researchers.

There is no definitive solution to the complex problems inherent in the politics of representation of intimate ethnographic conversations across racial and class-based lines. The men in these pages often behave in cruel and violent ways, not only against the women and children in their lives but also against themselves. Despite the risks of writing this difficult material for outsiders to read, however, I feel that if I failed to confront it—especially the most painful dimensions of misogyny and sexual violence in street culture and in individual action—I would be colluding in the sexist status quo. While all of the crack dealers are victims from a social structural perspective, they are also agents of destruction in their daily lives. They wreak havoc on their loved ones and on their larger community. Of course, from an analytical perspective the particularly brutal form that masculinity has assumed on the streets of inner city USA—where crime rates, murder rates, and incarceration rates are the highest in the entire industrialized world—is ultimately a reflection, not just on the political economic model of the United States but rather of the fundamental lack of basic human rights among the socially marginal in the United States—most notably the lack of individual freedom, access to health care, shelter, education, and public safety by inner-city residents. The polarization of formerly rural-based patriarchal masculine subjectivities toward greater public violence, widespread sexual abuse, and overt economic parasitism on inner-city streets are merely symptomatic expressions of these basic political and cultural inequities. Behind the most gruesome of the crackhouse conversations evoked in these pages lies the massive public and private sector breakdown that has occurred since World War II in most U.S. inner cities, and the de facto apartheid ideology that legitimates a public "common sense" tolerating rising levels of immiseration among the working-poor.

References

Acosta-Belén, E. (1993), "Defining a Common Ground: The Theoretical Meeting of Women's, Ethnic, and Area Studies," in E. and C. E. Bose, eds., *Researching Women in Latin America and the Caribbean*, 175–86. Boulder, CO: Westview Press.

Anderson, E. (1989), "Sex Codes and Family Life Among Poor Inner-City Youths," *The Annals of the American Academy of Political and Social Science*, 501: 59–78.

Baca Zinn, M. (1989), "Family, Race, and Poverty in the Eighties," *Signs: Journal of Women in Culture and Society*, 14: 856–74.

Bonilla, F., and Campos, R. (1986), *Industry and Idleness*, New York: Centro de Estudios Puertorriqueños, Hunter College.

Bose, C. E. (1986), "Puerto Rican Women in the United States: An Overview," in E. Acosta-Belén, ed., *The Puerto Rican Woman: Perspectives on Culture, History, and Society*, 2nd edn, 147–69. New York: Praeger.

Bourgois, P. (1995a), *In Search of Respect: Selling Crack in El Barrio*. New York: Cambridge University Press.

—— (1995b), "The Political Economy of Resistance and Self-Destruction in the Crack Economy: An Ethnographic Perspective," *Annals of the New York Academy of Sciences*, 719: 97–118. Special Issue, "The Anthropology of Lower Income Urban Enclaves: The Case of East Harlem," ed. J. Freidenberg.

Burton, L. (1991), "Caring for Children," *The American Enterprise*, 2/3: 34–7.

Butler, J., and Scott, J., eds. (1992), *Feminists Theorize the Political*. New York: Routledge.

Campbell, A. (1991), *The Girls in the Gang*, 2nd edn. Cambridge, MA: Basil Blackwell.

Connell, R. W. (1987), *Gender and Power*. Stanford, CA: Stanford University Press.

Cook-Lynn, E. (1989), "The Broken Cord," review, *Wicazo Sa*, 5/2: 42–5.

Critique of Anthropology (1993), Special issue on US inner-city poverty and the "underclass debate," 13/3.

De la Cancela, V. (1986), "A Critical Analysis of Puerto Rican Machismo: Implications for Clinical Practice," *Psychotherapy*, 23/2: 291–96.

DeParle, J. (1994), "Sharp Increase Along the Borders of Poverty," *New York Times*, 31 March, A8.

Dietz, J. L. (1986), *Economic History of Puerto Rico: Institutional Change and Capitalist Development*. Princeton: Princeton University Press.

Dorris, M. (1989), *The Broken Cord: A Family's Ongoing Struggle with Fetal Alcohol Syndrome*. New York: Harper and Rowe.

Feldman, A. (1991), *Formations of Violence: The Narrative of the Body and Political Terror in Northern Ireland*. Chicago: University of Chicago Press.

Ferguson, B., with Farragher, L. (1988), *The Anthropology of War: A Bibliography*. New York: H. F. Guggenheim Foundation.

Giddens, A. (1991), *Modernity and Self-Identity: Self and Society in the Late Modern Age*. Cambridge: Polity Press.

Gramsci, A. (1971), *Selections from the Prison Notebooks*. London: Lawrence and Wishart.

Guarnaccia, P. J., De la Cancela, V., and Carrillo, E. (1989), "The Multiple Meaning of Ataques de Nervios in the Latino Community." *Medical Anthropology*, 11: 47–62.

Huff, C. R., ed. (1990), *Gangs in America*. Newbury Park, CA: Sage.

Hunt, R. C. (1971) "Components of Relationships in the Family: A Mexican Village," in F. L. K. Hsu, ed., *Kinship and Culture*, 106–43. Chicago: Aldine.

Jaggar, A. (1983), *Feminist Politics and Human Nature*. Sussex: The Harvester Press.

Jarret, R. L. (1994), "Living Poor: Family Life Among Single Parent African-American Women," *Social Problems*, 41/1: 30–49.

Jefferson, T. (1994), "Theorizing Masculine Subjectivity," in T. Newburn and E. Stanko, eds., *Just Boys Doing Business? Men, Masculinities, and Crime*, 10–31. London: Routledge.

Katz, M. (1986), *In the Shadow of the Poorhouse: A Social History of Welfare in America*. New York: Basic Books.

Lewis, O. (1966), *La Vida: A Puerto Rican Family in the Culture of Poverty—San Juan and New York*. New York: Random House.

Lewis-Fernández, R. (1992). "Ataques de Nervios or Panic Attacks: An Embodied Contestation of Puerto Rican Ethnicity," paper prepared for AAA session on "Healing, Bodily Practices, and Caribbean Ethnicity," San Francisco, 2 December.

Malveaux, J. (1987), "The Political Economy of Black Women," in M. Davis, M. Marable, F. Pfeil, and M. Sprinker, eds., *The Year Left 2: An American Socialist Yearbook*, 52–73. London: Verso.

Mauer, M. (1992), "Americans Behind Bars: One Year Later," The Sentencing Project, Washington, DC.

Meléndez, E., and Meléndez, E., eds. (1993), *Colonial Dilemma: Critical Perspectives on Contemporary Puerto Rico*. Boston: South End Press.

Messerschmidt, J. W. (1993), *Masculinities and Crime: Critique and Reconceptualization of Theory*. Lanham, MD: Rowman and Littlefield, Inc.

Mohanty, C. T. (1984), "Under Western Eyes: Feminist Scholarship and Colonial Discourses," *Boundary 2*, XII/3, XIII/1: 333–58.

New York Times Magazine (1994), "Who Will Help the Black Man? A Symposium Moderated by Bob Herbert," 4 December, 72–7, 90, 92–3, 109–10.

Paredes, A. (1971), "The United States, Mexico, and Machismo," *Journal of the Folklore Institute*, 8/1: 17–37.

Pérez, S., and Cruz, S. (1994), *Speaking out Loud: Conversations with Young Puerto Rican Men*. National Council of La Raza: Washington, DC.

Pollitt, K. (1990), "A New Assault on Feminism," *The Nation*, March 408–17.

Rainwater, L., and Yancey, W., eds. (1967), *The Moynihan Report and the Politics of Controversy*. Boston: MIT Press.

Ramírez, R. (1993), *Dime Capitán: Reflexiones sobre la Masculinidad*. San Juán: Huracán Ediciones.

Rapp, R. (1987), "Urban Kinship in Contemporary America: Families, Classes and Ideology," in Leith Mullings, ed., *Cities of the United States: Studies in Urban Anthropology*, 219–43. New York: Columbia University Press.

Rivera-Batiz, F. L. and Santiago, C. (1994), "The Labour Market and Socioeconomic Performance of the Puerto Rican Population in the United States 1980–1990," monograph prepared for The National Puerto Rican Coalition, Washington, DC.

Rodríguez, C. E. (1989), *Puerto Ricans: Born in the USA*. Winchester, MA: Unwin Hyman.

Sassen, S. (1991), *The Global City*. Princeton: Princeton University Press.

Singer, M., Valentin, F., Baer, H., and Jia, Z. (1992), "Why Does Juán Garcia Have a Drinking Problem? The Perspective of Critical Medical Anthropology," *Medical Anthropology*, 14: 77–108.

Sluka, J. A. (1990), "Participant Observation in Violent Social Contexts," *Human Organization*, 49/2: 111–26.

Stack, C. (1975), *All Our Kin: Strategies for Survival in a Black Community* New York: Harper.

Tonry, M. (1995), *Malign Neglect—Race, Crime, and Punishment in America*. New York: Oxford University Press.

Wacquant, L. (1995), "The New Urban Colour Line: The State and Fate of the Ghetto in Postfordist America," in C. J. Calhoun, ed., *Social Theory and the Politics of Identity*. New York: Basil Blackwell.

R. W. Connell

Masculinities and Globalization

The Ethnographic Moment in Studies of Masculinity

The current wave of research and debate on masculinity stems from the impact of the women's liberation movement on men, but it has taken time for this impact to produce a new intellectual agenda. Most discussions of men's gender in the 1970s and early 1980s centered on an established concept, the male sex role, and an established problem: how men and boys were socialized into this role. There was not much new empirical research. What there was tended to use the more abstracted methods of social psychology (e.g., paper-and-pencil masculinity/femininity scales) to measure generalized attitudes and expectations in ill-defined populations. The largest body of empirical research was the continuing stream of quantitative studies of sex differences—which continued to be disappointingly slight (Carrigan, Connell, and Lee 1985).

The concept of a unitary male sex role, however, came under increasing criticism for its multiple oversimplifications and its incapacity to handle issues about power (Kimmel 1987; Connell 1987). New conceptual frameworks were proposed that linked feminism work on institutionalized patriarchy, gay theoretical work on homophobia, and psychoanalytic ideas about the person (Carrigan, Connell, and Lee 1985; Hearn 1987). Increasing attention was given to certain studies that located issues about masculinity in a fully described local context, whether a British

printing shop (Cockburn 1983) or a Pauan mountain community (Herdt 1981). By the late 1980s, a genre of empirical research based on these ideas was developing, most clearly in sociology but also in anthropology, history, organization studies, and cultural studies. This has borne fruit in the 1990s in what is now widely recognized as a new generation of social research on masculinity and men in gender relations (Connell 1995; *Widersprueche* 1995; Segal 1997).

Although the recent research has been diverse in subject matter and social location, its characteristic focus is the construction of masculinity in a particular milieu or moment—a clergyman's family (Tosh 1991), a professional sports career (Messner 1992), a small group of gay men (Connell 1992), a bodybuilding gym (Klein 1993), a group of colonial schools (Morrell 1994), an urban police force (McElhinny 1994), drinking groups in bars (Tomsen 1997), a corporate office on the verge of a decision (Messerschmidt 1997). Accordingly, we might think of this as the "ethnographic moment" in masculinity research, in which the specific and the local are in focus. (This is not to deny that this work *deploys* broader structural concepts, simply to note the characteristic focus of the empirical work and its analysis.)

The ethnographic moment brought a much-needed gust of realism to debates on men and masculinity, a corrective to the simplifications of role theory. It also provided a corrective to the trend in popular culture where vague discussions of men's sex roles were giving way to the mysti-

Author's Note: *This article is revised from an address, "Men in the World: Masculinities and Globalization," given at the Colloquium on "Masculinities in Southern Africa," University of Natal–Durban, July 1997.*

cal generalities of the mythopoetic movement and the extreme simplifications of religious revivalism.

Although the rich detail of the historical and field studies defies easy summary, certain conclusions emerge from this body of research as a whole. In short form, they are the following.

Plural Masculinities   A theme of theoretical work in the late 1980s, the multiplicity of masculinities has now been very fully documented by descriptive research. Different cultures and different periods of history construct gender differently. Striking differences exist, for instance, in the relationship of homosexual practice to dominant forms of masculinity (Herdt 1984). In multicultural societies, there are varying definitions and enactments of masculinity, for instance, between Anglo and Latino communities in the United States (Hondagneu-Sotelo and Messner 1994). Equally important, more than one kind of masculinity can be found within a given cultural setting or institution. This is particularly well documented in school studies (Foley 1990) but can also be observed in workplaces (Messerschmidt 1997) and the military (Barrett 1996).

Hierarchy and Hegemony   These plural masculinities exist in definite social relations, often relations of hierarchy and exclusion. This was recognized early, in gay theorists' discussions of homophobia; it has become clear that the implications are far-reaching. There is generally a hegemonic form of masculinity, the most honored or desired in a particular context. For Western popular culture, this is extensively documented in research on media representations of masculinity (McKay and Huber 1992). The hegemonic form need not be the most common form of masculinity. Many men live in a state of some tension with, or distance from, hegemonic masculinity; others (such as sporting heroes) are taken as exemplars of hegemonic masculinity and are required to live up to it strenuously (Connell 1990a). The dominance of hegemonic masculinity over other forms may be quiet and implicit, but it may also be ve-

hement and violent, as in the important case of homophobic violence.

Collective Masculinities   Masculinities, as patterns of gender practice, are sustained and enacted not only by individuals but also by groups and institutions. This fact was visible in Cockburn's (1983) pioneering research on informal workplace culture, and it has been confirmed over and over: in workplaces (Donaldson 1991), in organized sport (Whitson 1990; Messner 1992), in schools (Connell 1996), and so on. This point must be taken with the previous two: institutions may construct multiple masculinities and define relationships between them. Barrett's (1996) illuminating study of hegemonic masculinity in the U.S. Navy shows how this takes different forms in the different subbranches of the one military organization.

Bodies as Arenas   Men's bodies do not determine the patterns of masculinity, but they are still of great importance in masculinity. Men's bodies are addressed, defined and disciplined (as in sport; see Theberge 1991), and given outlets and pleasures by the gender order of society. But men's bodies are not blank slates. The enactment of masculinity reaches certain limits, for instance, in the destruction of the industrial worker's body (Donaldson 1991). Masculine conduct with a female body is felt to be anomalous or transgressive, like feminine conduct with a male body; research on gender crossing (Bolin 1988) shows the work that must be done to sustain an anomalous gender.

Active Construction   Masculinities do not exist prior to social interaction, but come into existence as people act. They are actively produced, using the resources and strategies available in a given milieu. Thus the exemplary masculinities of sports professionals are not a product of passive disciplining, but as Messner (1992) shows, results from a sustained, active engagement with the demands of the institutional setting, even to the point of serious bodily damage from "playing hurt" and accumulated stress. With boys learning masculinities, much of what was previously taken as socialization appears, in close-focus studies of schools (Walker 1988; Thorne 1993), as the outcome of intricate and intense maneuvering in peer groups, classes, and adult-child relationships.

Contradiction Masculinities are not homogeneous, simple states of being. Close-focus research on masculinities commonly identifies contradictory desires and conduct; for instance, in Klein's (1993) study of bodybuilders, the contradiction between the heterosexual definition of hegemonic masculinity and the homosexual practice by which some of the bodybuilders finance the making of an exemplary body. Psychoanalysis provides the classic evidence of conflicts within personality, and recent psychoanalytic writing (Chodorow 1994; Lewes 1988) has laid some emphasis on the conflicts and emotional compromises within both hegemonic and subordinated forms of masculinity. Life-history research influenced by existential psychoanalysis (Connell 1995) has similarly traced contradictory projects and commitments within particular forms of masculinity.

Dynamics Masculinities created in specific historical circumstances are liable to reconstruction and any pattern of hegemony is subject to contestation, in which a dominant masculinity may be displaced. Heward (1988) shows the changing gender regime of a boys' school responding to the changed strategies of the families in its clientele. Roper (1991) shows the displacement of a production-oriented masculinity among engineering managers by new financially oriented generic managers. Since the 1970s, the reconstruction of masculinities has been pursued as a conscious politics. Schwalbe's (1996) close examination of one mythopoetic group shows the complexity of the practice and the limits of the reconstruction.

If we compare this picture of masculinity with earlier understandings of the male sex role, it is clear that the ethnographic moment in research has already had important intellectual fruits.

Nevertheless, it has always been recognized that some issues go beyond the local. For instance, mythopoetic movements such as the highly visible Promise Keepers are part of a spectrum of masculinity politics; Messner (1997) shows for the United States that this spectrum involves at least eight conflicting agendas for the remaking of masculinity. Historical studies such as Phillips (1987) on New Zealand and Kimmel (1996) on the United States have traced the changing public constructions of masculinity for whole countries over long periods; ultimately, such historical reconstructions are essential for understanding the meaning of ethnographic details.

I consider that this logic must now be taken a step further, and in taking this step, we will move toward a new agenda for the whole field. What happens in localities is affected by the history of whole countries, but what happens in countries is affected by the history of the world. Locally situated lives are now (indeed, have long been) powerfully influenced by geopolitical struggles, global markets, multinational corporations, labor migration, transnational media. It is time for this fundamental fact to be built into our analysis of men and masculinities.

To understand local masculinities, we must think in global terms. But how? That is the problem pursued in this article. I will offer a framework for thinking about masculinities as a feature of world society and for thinking about men's gender practices in terms of the global structure and dynamics of gender. This is by no means to reject the ethnographic moment in masculinity research. It is, rather, to think how we can use its findings more adequately.

The World Gender Order

Masculinities do not first exist and then come into contact with femininities; they are produced together, in the process that constitutes a gender order. Accordingly, to understand the masculinities on a world scale, we must first have a concept of the globalization of gender.

This is one of the most difficult points in current gender analysis because the very conception is counterintuitive. We are so accustomed to thinking of gender as the attribute of an individual, even as an unusually intimate attribute, that it requires a considerable wrench to think of gender on the vast scale of global society. Most relevant discussions, such as the literature on women and development, fudge the issue. They treat the entities that extend internationally (markets, corporations, intergovernmental programs, etc.) as ungendered in principle—but affecting unequally gendered recipients of aid in practice, because of bad policies. Such conceptions reproduce the familiar liberal-feminist view of the state as in principle gender-neutral, though empirically dominated by men.

But if we recognize that very large scale institutions such as the state are themselves gendered, in quite precise and specifiable ways (Connell 1990b), and if we recognize that international relations, international trade, and global markets are inherently an arena of gender formation and gender politics (Enloe 1990), then we can recognize the existence of a world gender order. The term can be defined as the structure of relationships that interconnect the gender regimes of institutions, and the gender orders of local society, on a world scale. That is, however, only a definition. The substantive questions remain: what is the shape of that structure, how tightly are its elements linked, how has it arisen historically, what is its trajectory into the future?

Current business and media talk about globalization pictures a homogenizing process sweeping across the world, driven by new technologies, producing vast unfettered global markets in which all participate on equal terms. This is a misleading image. As Hirst and Thompson (1996) show, the global economy is highly unequal and the current degree of homogenization is often overestimated. Multinational corporations based in the three major economic powers (the United States, European Union, and Japan) are the major economic actors worldwide.

The structure bears the mark of its history. Modern global society was historically produced, as Wallerstein (1974) argued, by the economic and political expansion of European states from the fifteenth century on and by the creation of colonial empires. It is in this process that we find the roots of the modern world gender order. Imperialism was, from the start, a gendered process. Its first phase, colonial conquest and settlement, was carried out by gender-segregated forces, and it resulted in massive disruption of indigenous gender orders. In its second phase, the stabilization of colonial societies, new gender divisions of labor were produced in plantation economies and colonial cities, while gender ideologies were linked with racial hierarchies and the cultural defense of empire. The third phase, marked by political decolonization, economic neocolonialism, and the current growth of world markets and structures of financial control, has seen gender divisions of labor remade on a massive scale in the "global factory" (Fuentes and Ehrenreich 1983), as well as the spread of gendered violence alongside Western military technology.

The result of this history is a partially integrated, highly unequal, and turbulent world society, in which gender relations are partly but unevenly linked on a global scale. The unevenness becomes clear when different substructures of gender (Connell 1987; Walby 1990) are examined separately.

The Division of Labor A characteristic feature of colonial and neocolonial economies was the restructuring of local production systems to produce a male wage worker–female domestic worker couple (Mies 1986). This need not produce a "housewife" in the Western suburban sense, for instance, where the wage work involved migration to plantations or mines (Moodie 1994). But it has generally produced the identification of masculinity with the public realm and the money economy and of femininity with domesticity, which is a core feature of the modern European gender system (Holter 1997).

Power Relations The colonial and postcolonial world has tended to break down purdah systems of patriarchy in the name of modernization, if not of women's emancipation (Kandiyoti 1994). At the same time, the creation of a westernized public realm has seen the growth of large-scale organizations in the form of the state and corporations, which in the great majority of cases are culturally masculinized and controlled by men. In *comprador* capitalism, however, the power of local elites depends on their relations with the metropolitan powers, so the hegemonic masculinities of neocolonial societies are uneasily poised between local and global cultures.

Emotional Relations Both religious and cultural missionary activity has corroded indigenous homosexual and cross-gender practice, such as the native American *berdache* and the Chinese "passion of the cut sleeve" (Hinsch 1990). Recently developed Western models of romantic heterosexual love as the basis for marriage and of gay identity as the main alternative have now circulated globally—though as Altman (1996) observes, they do not simply displace indigenous models, but interact with them in extremely complex ways.

Symbolization Mass media, especially electronic media, in most parts of the world follow North American and European models and relay a great deal of metropolitan content; gender imagery is an important part of what is circulated. A striking example is the reproduction of a North American imagery of femininity by Xuxa, the blonde television superstar in Brazil (Simpson 1993). In counterpoint, exotic gender imagery has been used in the marketing strategies of newly industrializing countries (e.g., airline advertising from Southeast Asia)—a tactic based on the longstanding combination of the exotic and the erotic in the colonial imagination (Jolly 1997).

Clearly, the world gender order is not simply an extension of a traditional European-American gender order. That gender order was changed by colonization, and elements from other cultures now circulate globally. Yet in no sense do they mix on equal terms, to produce a United Colours of Benetton gender order. The culture and institutions of the North Atlantic countries are hegemonic within the emergent world system. This is crucial for understanding the kinds of masculinities produced within it.

The Repositioning of Men and the Reconstruction of Masculinities

The positioning of men and the constitution of masculinities may be analyzed at any of the levels at which gender practice is configured: in relation to the body, in personal life, and in collective social practice. At each level, we need to consider how the processes of globalization influence configurations of gender.

Men's bodies are positioned in the gender order, and enter the gender process, through body-reflexive practices in which bodies are both objects and agents (Connell 1995)—including sexuality, violence, and labor. The conditions of such practice include where one is and who is available for interaction. So it is a fact of considerable importance for gender relations that the global social order distributes and redistributes bodies, through migration, and through political controls over movement and interaction.

The creation of empire was the original "elite migration," though in certain cases mass migration followed. Through settler colonialism, something close to the gender order of Western Europe was reassembled in North America and in Australasia. Labor migration within the colonial systems was a means by which gender practices were spread, but also a means by which they were reconstructed, since labor migration was itself a gendered process—as we have seen in relation to the gender division of labor. Migration from the colonized world to the metropole became (except for Japan) a mass process in the decades after World War II. There is also migration within the periphery, such as the creation of a very large immigrant labor force mostly from other Muslim countries, in the oil-producing Gulf states.

These relocations of bodies create the possibility of hybridization in gender imagery, sexuality, and other forms of practice. The movement is not always toward synthesis, however, as the race/ethnic hierarchies of colonialism have been recreated in new contexts, including the politics of the metropole. Ethnic and racial conflict has been growing in importance in recent years, and as Klein (1997) and Tillner (1997) argue, this is a fruitful context for the production of masculinities oriented toward domination and violence. Even without the context of violence, there can be an intimate interweaving of the formation of masculinity with the formation of ethnic identity, as seen in the study by Poynting, Noble, and Tabar (1997) of Lebanese youths in the Anglo-dominant culture of Australia.

At the level of personal life as well as in relation to bodies, the making of masculinities is shaped by global forces. In some cases, the link is indirect, such as the working-class Australian men caught in a situation of structural unemployment (Connell 1995), which arises from Australia's changing position in the global economy. In other cases, the link is obvious, such as the executives of multinational corporations and the financial sector servicing international trade. The requirements of a career in international business set up strong pressures on domestic life: almost all multinational executives are men, and the assumption in business magazines and advertising directed toward them is that they will have dependent wives running their homes and bringing up their children.

At the level of collective practice, masculinities are reconstituted by the remaking of gender meanings and the reshaping of the institutional contexts of practice. Let us consider each in turn.

The growth of global mass media, especially electronic media, is an obvious "vector" for the globalization of gender. Popular entertainment circulates stereotyped gender images, deliberately made attractive for marketing purposes. The example of Xuxa in Brazil has already been mentioned. International news media are also controlled or strongly influenced from the metropole and circulate Western definitions of authoritative masculinity, criminality, desirable femininity, and so on. But there are limits to the power of global mass communications. Some local centers of mass entertainment differ from the Hollywood model, such as the Indian popular film industry centered in Bombay. Further, media research emphasizes that audiences are highly selective in their reception of media messages, and we must allow for popular recognition of the fantasy in mass entertainment. Just as economic globalization can be exaggerated, the creation of a global culture is a more turbulent and uneven process than is often assumed (Featherstone 1995).

More important, I would argue, is a process that began long before electronic media existed, the export of institutions. Gendered institutions not only circulate definitions of masculinity (and femininity), as sex role theory notes. The functioning of gendered institutions, creating specific conditions for social practice, calls into existence specific patterns of practice. Thus, certain patterns of collective violence are embedded in the organization and culture of a Western-style army, which are different from the patterns of precolonial violence. Certain patterns of calculative egocentrism are embedded in the working of a stock market; certain patterns of rule following and domination are embedded in a bureaucracy.

Now, the colonial and postcolonial world saw the installation in the periphery, on a very large scale, of a range of institutions on the North Atlantic model: armies, states, bureaucracies, corporations, capital markets, labor markets, schools, law courts, transport systems. These are gendered institutions and their functioning has directly reconstituted masculinities in the periphery. This has not necessarily meant photocopies of European masculinities. Rather, pressures for change are set up that are inherent in the institutional form.

To the extent that particular institutions become dominant in world society, the patterns of masculinity embedded in them may become global standards. Masculine dress is an interesting indicator: almost every political leader in the world now wears the uniform of the Western business executive. The more common pattern, however, is not the complete displacement of local patterns but the articulation of the local gender order with the gender regime of global-model institutions. Case studies such as Hollway's (1994) account of bureaucracy in Tanzania illustrate the point; there, domestic patriarchy articulated with masculine authority in the state in ways that subverted the government's formal commitment to equal opportunity for women.

We should not expect the overall structure of gender relations on a world scale simply to mirror patterns known on the smaller scale. In the most vital of respects, there is continuity. The world gender order is unquestionably patriarchal, in the sense that it privileges men over women. There is a patriarchal dividend for men arising from unequal wages, unequal labor force participation, and a highly unequal structure of ownership, as well as cultural and sexual privileging. This has been extensively documented by feminist work on women's situation globally (e.g., Taylor 1985), though its implications for masculinity have mostly been ignored. The conditions thus exist for the production of a hegemonic masculinity on a world scale, that is to say, a dominant form of masculinity that embodies, organizes, and legitimates men's domination in the gender order as a whole.

The conditions of globalization, which involve the interaction of many local gender orders, certainly multiply the forms of masculinity in the global gender order. At the same time, the specific shape of globalization, concentrating economic and cultural power on an unprecedented scale, provides new resources for dominance by particular groups of men. This dominance may become institutionalized in a pattern of masculinity that becomes, to some degree, standardized across localities. I will call such patterns *globalizing masculinities,* and it is among them, rather than narrowly within the metropole, that we are likely

to find candidates for hegemony in the world gender order.

Globalizing Masculinities

In this section, I will offer a sketch of major forms of globalizing masculinity in the three historical phases identified above in the discussion of globalization.

Masculinities of Conquest and Settlement

The creation of the imperial social order involved peculiar conditions for the gender practices of men. Colonial conquest itself was mainly carried out by segregated groups of men—soldiers, sailors, traders, administrators, and a good many who were all these by turn (such as the Rum Corps in early New South Wales, Australia). They were drawn from the more segregated occupations and milieu in the metropole, and it is likely that the men drawn into colonization tended to be more rootless. Certainly the process of conquest could produce frontier masculinities that combined the occupational culture of these groups with an unusual level of violence and egocentric individualism. The vehement contemporary debate about the genocidal violence of the Spanish conquistadors—who in fifty years completely exterminated the population of Hispaniola—points to this pattern (Bitterli 1989).

The political history of empire is full of evidence of the tenuous control over the frontier exercised by the state—the Spanish monarchs unable to rein in the conquistadors, the governors in Sydney unable to hold back the squatters and in Capetown unable to hold back the Boers, gold rushes breaking boundaries everywhere, even, an independent republic set up by escaped slaves in Brazil. The point probably applies to other forms of social control too, such as customary controls on men's sexuality. Extensive sexual exploitation of indigenous women was a common feature of conquest. In certain circumstances, frontier masculinities might be reproduced as a local cultural tradition long after the frontier had passed, such as the gauchos of southern Southern America, the cowboys of the western United States.

In other circumstances, however, the frontier of conquest and exploitation was replaced by a frontier of settlement. Sex ratios in the colonizing population changed, as women arrived and locally born generations succeeded. A shift back toward the family patterns of the metropole was likely. As Cain and Hopkins (1993) have shown for the British empire, the ruling group in the colonial world as a whole was an extension of the dominant class in the metropole, the landed gentry, and tended to reproduce its social customs and ideology. The creation of a settler masculinity might be the goal of state policy, as it seems to have been in late-nineteenth-century New Zealand, as part of a general process of pacification and the creation of an agricultural social order (Phillips 1987). Or it might be undertaken through institutions created by settler groups, such as the elite schools in Natal studies by Morrell (1994).

The impact of colonialism on the construction of masculinity among the colonized is much less documented, but there is every reason to think it was severe. Conquest and settlement disrupted all the structures of indigenous society, whether or not this was intended by the colonizing powers (Bitterli 1989). Indigenous gender orders were no exception. Their disruption could result from the pulverization of indigenous communities (as in the seizure of land in eastern North America and southeastern Australia), through gendered labor migration (as in gold mining with Black labor in South Africa; see Moodie 1994), to ideological attacks on local gender arrangements (as in the missionary assault on the *berdache* tradition in North America; see Williams 1986). The varied course of resistance to colonization is also likely to have affected the making of masculinities. This is clear in the region of Natal in South Africa, where sustained resistance to colonization by the Zulu kingdom was a key to the mobilization of ethnic-national masculine identities in the twentieth century (Morrell 1996).

Masculinities of Empire

The imperial social order created a hierarchy of masculinities, as it created a hierarchy of communities and races. The colonizers distinguished "more manly" from "less manly" groups among their subjects. In British India, for instance, Bengali men were supposed effeminate while Pathans and Sikhs were regarded as strong and warlike. Similar distinctions were made in South Africa between Hottentots and Zulus, in North America between Iroquois, Sioux, and Cheyenne on one side, and southern and southwestern tribes on the other.

At the same time, the emerging imagery of gender difference in European culture provided general symbols of superiority and inferiority. Within the imperial "poetics of war" (MacDonald 1994), the conqueror was virile, while the colonized were dirty, sexualized, and effeminate or childlike. In many colonial situations, indigenous men were called "boys" by the colonizers (e.g., in Zimbabwe; see Shire 1994). Sinha's (1995) interesting study of the language of political controversy in India in the 1880s and 1890s shows how the images of "manly Englishman" and "effeminate Bengali" were deployed to uphold colonial privilege and contain movements for change. In the late nineteenth century, racial barriers in colonial societies were hardening rather than weakening, and gender ideology tended to fuse with racism in forms that the twentieth century has never untangled.

The power relations of empire meant that indigenous gender orders were generally under pressure from the colonizers, rather than the other way around. But the colonizers too might change. The barriers of late colonial racism were not only to prevent pollution from below but also to forestall "going native," a well-recognized possibility—the starting point, for instance, of Kipling's famous novel *Kim* ([1901] 1987). The pressures, opportunities, and profits of empire might also work changes in gender arrangements among the colonizers, for instance, the division of labor in households with a large supply of indigenous workers as domestic servants (Bulbeck 1992). Empire might also affect the gender order of the metropole itself by changing gender ideologies, divisions of labor, and the nature of the metropolitan state. For instance, empire figured prominently as a source of masculine imagery in Britain, in the Boy Scouts, and in the cult of Lawrence of Arabia (Dawson 1991). Here we see examples of an important principle: the interplay of gender dynamics between different parts of the world order.

The world of empire created two very different settings for the modernization of masculinities. In the periphery, the forcible restructuring of economies and workforces tended to individualize, on one hand, and rationalize, on the other. A widespread result was masculinities in which the rational calculation of self-interest was the key to action, emphasizing the European gender contrast of rational man/irrational woman. The specific form might be local—for instance, the Japanese "salaryman," a type first recognized in the 1910s, was specific to the Japanese context of large, stable industrial conglomerates (Kinmonth 1981). But the result generally was masculinities defined around economic action, with both workers and entrepreneurs increasingly adapted to emerging market economies.

In the metropole, the accumulation of wealth made possible a specialization of leadership in the dominant classes, and struggles for hegemony in which masculinities organized around domination or violence were split from masculinities organized around expertise. The class compromises that allowed the development of the welfare state in Europe and North America were paralleled by gender compromises—gender reform movements (most notably the women's suffrage movement) contesting the legal privileges of men and forcing concessions from the state. In this context, agendas of reform in masculinity emerged: the temperance movement, companionate marriage, homosexual rights movements, leading eventually to the pursuit of androgyny in "men's liberation" in the 1970s (Kimmel and Mosmiller 1992).

Not all reconstructions of masculinity, however, emphasized tolerance or moved toward androgyny. The vehement masculinity politics of fascism, for instance, emphasized dominance and difference and glorified violence, a pattern still found in contemporary racist movements (Tillner 1997).

Masculinities of Postcolonization and Neoliberalism

The process of decolonization disrupted the gender hierarchies of the colonial order and, where armed struggle was involved, might have involved a deliberate cultivation of masculine hardness and violence (as in South Africa; see Xaba 1997). Some activists and theorists of liberation struggles celebrated this, as a necessary response to colonial violence and emasculation; women in liberation struggles were perhaps less impressed. However one evaluates the process, one of the consequences of decolonization was another round of disruptions of community-based gender orders and another step in the reorientation of masculinities toward national and international contexts.

Nearly half a century after the main wave of decolonization, the old hierarchies persist in new shapes. With the collapse of Soviet communism, the decline of postcolonial socialism, and the ascendancy of the new right in Europe and North America, world politics is more and more organized around the needs of transnational capital and the creation of global markets.

The neoliberal agenda has little to say, explicitly, about gender: it speaks a gender-neutral language of "markets," "individuals," and "choice." But the world in which neoliberalism is ascendant is still a gendered world, and neoliberalism has an implicit gender politics. The "individual" of neoliberal theory has in general the attributes and interests of a male entrepreneur, the attack on the welfare state generally weakens the position of women, while the increasingly unregulated power of transnational corporations places strategic power in the hands of particular groups of men. It is not surprising, then, that the installation of capitalism in Eastern Europe and the former Soviet Union has been accompanied by a reassertion of dominating masculinities and, in some situations, a sharp worsening in the social position of women.

We might propose, then, that the hegemonic form of masculinity in the current world gender order is the masculinity associated with those who control its dominant institutions: the business executives who operate in global markets, and the political executives who interact (and in many contexts, merge) with them. I will call this *transnational business masculinity*. This is not readily available for ethnographic study, but we can get some clues to its character from its reflections in management literature, business journalism, and corporate self-promotion, and from studies of local business elites (e.g., Donaldson 1997).

As a first approximation, I would suggest this is a masculinity marked by increasing egocentrism, very conditional loyalties (even to the corporation), and a declining sense of responsibility for others (except for purposes of image making). Gee, Hull, and Lankshear (1996), studying recent management textbooks, note the peculiar construction of the executive in "fast capitalism" as a person with no permanent commitments, except (in effect) to the idea of accumulation itself. Transnational business masculinity is characterized by a limited technical rationality (management theory), which is increasingly separate from science.

Transnational business masculinity differs from traditional bourgeois masculinity by its increasingly libertarian sexuality, with a growing tendency to commodify relations with women. Hotels catering to businessmen in most parts of the world now routinely offer pornographic videos, and in some parts of the world, there is a well-developed prostitution industry catering for international businessmen. Transnational business masculinity does not require bodily force, since the patriarchal dividend on which it rests is accumulated by impersonal, institutional means. But corporations increasingly use the exemplary bodies of elite sportsmen as a marketing tool (note the phenomenal growth of corporate "sponsorship" of sport in the last generation) and indirectly

as a means of legitimation for the whole gender order.

Masculinity Politics on a World Scale

Recognizing global society as an arena of masculinity formation allows us to pose new questions about masculinity politics. What social dynamics in the global arena give rise to masculinity politics, and what shape does global masculinity politics take?

The gradual creation of a world gender order has meant many local instabilities of gender. Gender instability is a familiar theme of poststructuralist theory, but this school of thought takes as a universal condition a situation that is historically specific. Instabilities range from the disruption of men's local cultural dominance as women move into the public realm and higher education, through the disruption of sexual identities that produced "queer" politics in the metropole, to the shifts in the urban intelligentsia that produced "the new sensitive man" and other images of gender change.

One response to such instabilities, on the part of groups whose power is challenged but still dominant, is to reaffirm *local* gender orthodoxies and hierarchies. A masculine fundamentalism is, accordingly, a common response in gender politics at present. A soft version, searching for an essential masculinity among myths and symbols, is offered by the mythopoetic men's movement in the United States and by the religious revivalists of the Promise Keepers (Messner 1997). A much harder version is found, in that country, in the right-wing militia movement brought to world attention by the Oklahoma City bombing (Gibson 1994), and in contemporary Afghanistan, if we can trust Western media reports, in the militant misogyny of the Talibaan. It is no coincidence that in the two latter cases, hardline masculine fundamentalism goes together with a marked anti-internationalism. The world system—rightly enough—is seen as the source of pollution and disruption.

Not that the emerging global order is a hotbed of gender progressivism. Indeed, the neoliberal agenda for the reform of national and international economies involves closing down historic possibilities for gender reform. I have noted how it subverts the gender compromise represented by the metropolitan welfare state. It has also undermined the progressive-liberal agendas of sex role reform represented by affirmative action programs, antidiscrimination provisions, child care services, and the like. Right-wing parties and governments have been persistently cutting such programs, in the name of either individual liberties or global competitiveness. Through these means, the patriarchal dividend to men is defended or restored, without an *explicit* masculinity politics in the form of a mobilization of men.

Within the arenas of international relations, the international state, multinational corporations, and global markets, there is nevertheless a deployment of masculinities and a reasonably clear hegemony. The transnational business masculinity described above has had only one major competitor for hegemony in recent decades, the rigid, control-oriented masculinity of the military, and the military-style bureaucratic dictatorships of Stalinism. With the collapse of Stalinism and the end of the cold war, Big Brother (Orwell's famous parody of this form of masculinity) is a fading threat, and the more flexible, calculative, egocentric masculinity of the fast capitalist entrepreneur holds the world stage.

We must, however, recall two important conclusions of the ethnographic moment in masculinity research: that different forms of masculinity exist together and the hegemony is constantly subject to challenge. These are possibilities in the global arena too. Transnational business masculinity is not completely homogenous; variations of it are embedded in different parts of the world system, which may not be completely compatible. We may distinguish a Confucian variant, based in East Asia, with a stronger commitment to hierarchy and social consensus, from a secularized Christian variant, based in North America, with more hedonism and individualism and

greater tolerance for social conflict. In certain arenas, there is already conflict between the business and political leaderships embodying these forms of masculinity: initially over human rights versus Asian values, and more recently over the extent of trade and investment liberalization.

If there are contenders for hegemony, there is also the possibility of opposition to hegemony. The global circulation of "gay" identity (Altman 1996) is an important indication that nonhegemonic masculinities may operate in global arenas, and may even find a certain political articulation, in this case around human rights and AIDS prevention.

Critiques of dominant forms of masculinity have been circulating for some time among heterosexual men, or among groups that are predominantly heterosexual. English-language readers will be most familiar with three Anglophone examples: the antisexist or profeminist men's groups in the United States, with their umbrella group NOMAS (National Organization for Men Against Sexism), which has been running since the early 1980s (Cohen 1991); the British new left men's groups, which produced the remarkable magazine *Achilles Heel* (Seidler 1991); and the Canadian White Ribbon campaign, the most successful mass mobilization of men opposing men's violence against women (Kaufman 1997).

There are parallel developments in other language communities. In Germany, for instance, feminists launched a discussion of the gender of men in the 1980s (Metz-Goeckel and Mueller 1986; Hagemann-White and Rerrich 1988), which has been followed by an educational (Kindler 1993), a popular-psychology (Hollstein 1992), and a critical (*Widersprueche* 1995; BauSteineMaenner 1996) debate among men about masculinities and how to change them. In Scandinavia, gender reform and debates about men (Oftung 1994) have led to the "father's quota" of paternal leave in Norway (Gender Equality Ombudsman 1997) and to a particularly active network of masculinity researchers. In Japan, a media debate about men's liberation and some pioneering books about changing masculinities (Ito 1993; Nakamura

1994) have been followed by the foundation of a men's center and diversifying debates on change.

These developments at national or regional levels have very recently begun to link internationally. An International Association for Studies of Men has begun to link men involved in critical studies of masculinity. Certain international agencies, including the United Nations Educational, Scientific and Cultural Organization (UNESCO) (1997), have sponsored conferences to discuss the policy implications of new perspectives on masculinity.

Compared with the concentration of institutional power in multinational businesses, these initiatives remain small scale and dispersed. They are, nevertheless, important in potential. I have argued that the global gender order contains, necessarily, greater plurality of gender forms than any local gender order. This must reinforce the consciousness that masculinity is not one fixed form. The plurality of masculinities at least symbolically prefigures the unconstrained creativity of a demographic gender order.

Concluding Note on Research

If the perspective set out in this article holds well, it suggests a significant refocusing of the research agenda on masculinities. There is already a move beyond strictly local studies in the direction of comparative studies from different parts of the world (Cornwall and Lindisfarne 1994; UNESCO 1997). My argument suggests moving beyond this again, to study of the global arena itself, both as a venue for the social construction of masculinities and as a powerful force in local gender dynamics. Such a move will require a reconsideration of research methods, since the life-history and ethnographic methods that have been central to recent work on masculinities give limited grasp on the very large scale institutions, markets, and mass communications that are in play on the world scale. Finally, the typical researcher of recent years—the individual scholar with a personal research project—will need to be supplemented by international teams, able to work together for significant periods, to investigate issues of the scale and complexity we must now address.

References

Altman, Dennis. 1996. Rupture or continuity? The internationalization of gay identities. *Social Text* 48 (3): 77–94.

Barrett, Frank J. 1996. The organizational construction of hegemonic masculinity: The case of the U.S. Navy. *Gender, Work and Organization* 3 (3): 129–42.

BauSteineMaenner, ed. 1996. *Kritische Maenerforschung* [Critical research on men]. Berlin: Argument.

Bitterli, Urs. 1989. *Cultures in conflict: Encounters between European and non-European cultures, 1492–1800.* Stanford, CA: Stanford University Press.

Bolin, Anne. 1988. *In Search of Eve: Transsexual rites of passage.* Westport, CT: Bergin & Garvey.

Bulbeck, Chilla. 1992. *Australian women in Papua New Guinea: Colonial passages 1920–1960.* Cambridge, U.K.: Cambridge University Press.

Cain, P. J., and A. G. Hopkins. 1993. *British imperialism: Innovation and expansion, 1688–1914.* New York: Longman.

Carrigan, Tim, Bob Connell, and John Lee. 1985. Toward a new sociology of masculinity. *Theory and Society* 14 (5): 551–604.

Chodorow, Nancy. 1994. *Femininities, masculinities, sexualities: Freud and beyond.* Lexington: University Press of Kentucky.

Cockburn, Cynthia. 1983. *Brothers: Male dominance and technological change.* London: Pluto.

Cohen, Jon. 1991. NOMAS: Challenging male supremacy. *Changing Men* (Winter/Spring): 45–46.

Connell, R. W. 1987. *Gender and power.* Cambridge, MA: Polity.

———. 1990a. An iron man: The body and some contradictions of hegemonic masculinity. In *Sport, men and the gender order: Critical feminist perspectives*, edited by Michael A. Messner and Donald F. Sabo, 83–95. Champaign, IL: Human Kinetics Books.

———. 1990b. The state, gender and sexual politics: Theory and appraisal. *Theory and Society* 19:507–44.

———. 1992. A very straight gay: Masculinity, homosexual experience, and the dynamics of gender. *American Sociological Review* 57 (6): 735–51.

———. 1995. *Masculinities.* Cambridge, MA: Polity.

————. 1996. Teaching the boys: New research on masculinity, and gender strategies for schools. *Teachers College Record* 98 (2): 206–35.

Cornwall, Andrea, and Nancy Lindisfarne, eds. 1994. *Dislocating masculinity: Comparative ethnographies.* London: Routledge.

Dawson, Graham. 1991. The blond Bedouin: Lawrence of Arabia, imperial adventure and the imagining of English-British masculinity. In *Manful assertions: Masculinities in Britain since 1800*, edited by Michael Roper and John Tosh, 113–44. London: Routledge.

Donaldson, Mike. 1991. *Time of our lives: Labour and love in the working class.* Sydney: Allen & Unwin.

————. 1997. Growing up very rich: The masculinity of the hegemonic. Paper presented at the conference Masculinities: Renegotiating Genders, June, University of Wollongong, Australia.

Enloe, Cynthia. 1990. *Bananas, beaches and bases: Making feminist sense of international politics.* Berkeley: University of California Press.

Featherstone, Mike. 1995. *Undoing culture: Globalization, postmodernism and identity.* London: Sage.

Foley, Douglas E. 1990. *Learning capitalist culture: Deep in the heart of Tejas.* Philadelphia: University of Pennsylvania Press.

Fuentes, Annette, and Barbara Ehrenreich. 1983. *Women in the global factory.* Boston: South End.

Gee, James Paul, Glynda Hull, and Colin Lankshear. 1996. *The new work order: Behind the language of new capitalism.* Sydney: Allen & Unwin.

Gender Equality Ombudsman. 1997. *The father's quota.* Information sheet on paternal leave entitlements, Oslo.

Gibson, J. William. 1994. *Warrior dreams: Paramilitary culture in post-Vietnam America.* New York: Hill and Wang.

Hagemann-White, Carol, and Maria S. Rerrich, eds. 1988. *FrauenMaennerBilder* (Women, Imaging, Men). Bielefeld: AJZ-Verlag.

Hearn, Jeff. 1987. *The gender of oppression: Men, masculinity and the critique of Marxism.* Brighton, U.K.: Wheatsheaf.

Herdt, Gilbert H. 1981. *Guardians of the flutes: Idioms of masculinity.* New York: McGraw-Hill.

————, ed. 1984. *Ritualized homosexuality in Melanesia.* Berkeley: University of California Press.

Heward, Christine. 1988. *Making a man of him: Parents and their sons' education at an English public school 1929–1950.* London: Routledge.

Hinsch, Bret. 1990. *Passions of the cut sleeve: The male homosexual tradition in China.* Berkeley: University of California Press.

Hirst, Paul, and Grahame Thompson. 1996. *Globalization in question: The international economy and the possibilities of governance.* Cambridge, MA: Polity.

Hollstein, Walter. 1992. *Machen Sie Platz, mein Herr! Teilen statt Herrschen* [Sharing instead of dominating]. Hamburg: Rowohlt.

Hollway, Wendy. 1994. Separation, integration and difference: Contradictions in a gender regime. In *Power/gender: Social relations in theory and practice*, edited by H. Lorraine Radtke and Henderikus Stam, 247–69. London: Sage.

Holter, Oystein Gullvag. 1997. Gender, patriarchy and capitalism: A social forms analysis. Ph.D. diss., University of Oslo, Faculty of Social Science.

Hondagneu-Sotelo, Pierrette, and Michael A. Messner. 1994. Gender displays and men's power: The "new man" and the Mexican immigrant man. In *Theorizing masculinities*, edited by Harry Brod and Michael Kaufman, 200–218. Thousand Oaks, CA: Sage.

Ito Kimio. 1993. *Otokorashisa-no-yukue* [Directions for masculinities]. Tokyo: Shinyo-sha.

Jolly, Margaret. 1997. From point Venus to Bali Ha'i: Eroticism and exoticism in representations of the Pacific. In *Sites of desire, economies of pleasure: Sexualities in Asia and the Pacific*, edited by Lenore Manderson and Margaret Jolly, 99–122. Chicago: University of Chicago Press.

Kandiyoti, Deniz. 1994. The paradoxes of masculinity: Some thoughts on segregated societies. In *Dislocating masculinity: Comparative ethnographies*, edited by Andrea Cornwall and Nancy Lindisfarne, 197–213. London: Routledge.

Kaufman, Michael. 1997. Working with men and boys to challenge sexism and end men's violence. Paper presented at UNESCO expert group meeting on Male Roles and Masculinities in the Perspective of a Culture of Peace, September, Oslo.

Kimmel, Michael S. 1987. Rethinking "masculinity": New directions in research. In *Changing men: New directions in research on men and masculinity*, edited by Michael S. Kimmel, 9–24. Newbury Park, CA: Sage.

————. 1996. *Manhood in America: A cultural history.* New York: Free Press.

Kimmel, Michael S., and Thomas E. Mosmiller, eds. 1992. *Against the tide: Pro-feminist men in the United*

States, 1776–1990, a documentary history. Boston: Beacon.

Kindler, Heinz. 1993. *Maske(r)ade: Jungen- und Maennerarbeit fuer die Praxis* [Work with youth and men]. Neuling: Schwaebisch Gmuend und Tuebingen.

Kinmonth, Earl H. 1981. *The self-made man in Meiji Japanese thought: From Samurai to salary man*. Berkeley: University of California Press.

Kipling, Rudyard. [1901] 1987. *Kim*. London: Penguin.

Klein, Alan M. 1993. *Little big men: Bodybuilding subculture and gender construction*. Albany: State University of New York Press.

Klein, Uta. 1997. Our best boys: The making of masculinity in Israeli society. Paper presented at UNESCO expert group meeting on Male Roles and Masculinities in the Perspectives of a Culture of Peace, September, Oslo.

Lewes, Kenneth. 1988. *The psychoanalytic theory of male homosexuality*. New York: Simon & Schuster.

MacDonald, Robert H. 1994. *The language of empire: Myths and metaphors of popular imperialism, 1880–1918*. Manchester, U.K.: Manchester University Press.

McElhinny, Bonnie. 1994. An economy of affect: Objectivity, masculinity and the gendering of police work. In *Dislocating masculinity: Comparative ethnographies*, edited by Andrea Cornwall and Nancy Lindisfarne, 159–71. London: Routledge.

McKay, Jim, and Debbie Huber. 1992. Anchoring media images of technology and sport. *Women's Studies International Forum* 15 (2): 205–18.

Messerschmidt, James W. 1997. *Crime as structured action: Gender, race, class, and crime in the making*. Thousand Oaks, CA: Sage.

Messner, Michael A. 1992. *Power at play: Sports and the problem of masculinity*. Boston: Beacon.

———. 1997. *The politics of masculinities: Men in movements*. Thousand Oaks, CA: Sage.

Metz-Goeckel, Sigrid, and Ursula Mueller. 1986. *Der Mann: Die Brigitte-Studie* [The male]. Beltz: Weinheim & Basel.

Mies, Maria. 1986. *Patriarchy and accumulation on a world scale: Women in the international division of labour*. London: Zed.

Moodie, T. Dunbar. 1994. *Going for gold: Men, mines, and migration*. Johannesburg: Witwatersrand University Press.

Morrell, Robert. 1994. Boys, gangs, and the making of masculinity in the White secondary schools of Natal, 1880–1930. *Masculinities* 2 (2): 56–82.

———, ed. 1996. *Political economy and identities in KwaZulu-Natal: Historical and social perspectives*. Durban, Natal: Indicator Press.

Nakamura Akira. 1994. *Watashi-no Danseigaku* [My men's studies]. Tokyo: Kindaibugei-sha.

Oftung, Knut, ed. 1994. *Menns bilder og bilder av menn* [Images of men]. Oslo: Likestillingsradet.

Phillips, Jock. 1987. *A man's country? The image of the Pakeha male, a history*. Auckland: Penguin.

Poynting, S., G. Noble, and P. Tabar. 1997. "Intersections" of masculinity and ethnicity: A study of male Lebanese immigrant youth in Western Sydney. Paper presented at the conference Masculinities: Renegotiating Genders, June, University of Wollongong, Australia.

Roper, Michael. 1991. Yesterday's model: Product fetishism and the British company man, 1945–85. In *Manful assertions: Masculinities in Britain since 1800*, edited by Michael Roper and John Tosh, 190–211. London: Routledge.

Schwalbe, Michael. 1996. *Unlocking the iron cage: The men's movement, gender politics, and the American culture*. New York: Oxford University Press.

Segal, Lynne. 1997. *Slow motion: Changing masculinities, changing men*. 2d ed. London: Virago.

Seidler, Victor J. 1991. *Achilles heel reader: Men, sexual politics and socialism*. London: Routledge.

Shire, Chenjerai. 1994. Men don't go to the moon: Language, space and masculinities in Zimbabwe. In *Dislocating masculinity: Comparative ethnographies*, edited by Andrea Cornwall and Nancy Lindisfarne, 147–58. London: Routledge.

Simpson, Amelia. 1993. *Xuxa: The mega-marketing of gender, race and modernity*. Philadelphia: Temple University Press.

Sinha, Mrinalini. 1995. *Colonial masculinity: The manly Englishman and the effeminate Bengali in the late nineteenth century*. Manchester: U.K.: Manchester University Press.

Taylor, Debbie. 1985. Women: An analysis: In *Women: A world report*, 1–98. London: Methuen.

Theberge, Nancy. 1991. Reflections on the body in the sociology of sport. *Quest* 43:123–34.

Thorne, Barrie. 1993. *Gender play: Girls and boys in school*. New Brunswick, NJ: Rutgers University Press.

Tillner, Georg. 1997. Masculinity and xenophobia. Paper presented at UNESCO meeting on Male Roles and Masculinities in the Perspective of a Culture of Peace, September, Oslo.

Tomsen, Stephen. 1997. A top night: Social protest, masculinity and the culture of drinking violence. *British Journal of Criminology* 37 (1): 90–103.

Tosh, John. 1991. Domesticity and manliness in the Victorian middle class: The family of Edward White Benson. In *Manful assertions: Masculinities in Britain since 1800*, edited by Michael Roper and John Tosh, 44–73. London: Routledge.

United Nations Educational, Scientific and Cultural Organization (UNESCO). 1997. *Male roles and masculinities in the perspective of a culture of peace: Report of expert group meeting, Oslo, 24–28 September 1997*. Paris: Women and a Culture of Peace Programme, Culture of Peace Unit, UNESCO.

Walby, Sylvia. 1990. *Theorizing patriarchy*. Oxford, U.K.: Blackwell.

Walker, James C. 1988. *Louts and legends: Male youth culture in an inner-city school*. Sydney: Allen & Unwin.

Wallerstein, Immanuel. 1974. *The modern world-system: Capitalist agriculture and the origins of the European world-economy in the sixteenth century*. New York: Academic Press.

Whitson, David. 1990. Sport in the social construction of masculinity. In *Sport, men, and the gender order: Critical feminist perspectives*, edited by Michael A. Messner and Donald F. Sabo, 19–29. Champaign, IL: Human Kinetics Books.

Widersprueche. 1995. Special issue: Maennlichkeiten. Vol. 56/57.

Williams, Walter L. 1986. *The spirit and the flesh: Sexual diversity in American Indian culture*. Boston: Beacon.

Xaba, Thokozani. 1997. Masculinity in a transitional society: The rise and fall of the "young lions." Paper presented at the conference Masculinities in Southern Africa, June, University of Natal-Durban, Durban.

PART TWO

Boyhood

"**O**ne is not born, but rather becomes, a woman," wrote the French feminist thinker Simone de Beauvoir in her ground-breaking book *The Second Sex* (NY: Vintage, 1958). The same is true for men. And the social processes by which boys become men are complex and important. How does early childhood socialization differ for boys and girls? What specific traits are emphasized for boys that mark their socialization as different? What types of institutional arrangements reinforce those traits? How do the various institutions in which boys find themselves—school, family, and circles of friends—influence their development? What of the special institutions that promote "boy's life" or an adolescent male subculture?

During childhood and adolescence, masculinity becomes a central theme in a boy's life. *New York Times* editor A. M. Rosenthal put the dilemma this way: "So there I was, 13 years old, the smallest boy in my freshman class at DeWitt Clinton High School,

smoking a White Owl cigar. I was not only little, but I did not have longies—long trousers—and was still in knickerbockers. Obviously, I had to do something to project my fierce sense of manhood" (*New York Times*, 26 April 1987). That the assertion of manhood is part of a boy's natural development is suggested by Roger Brown, in his textbook *Social Psychology* (NY: Free Press, 1965, p. 161):

> In the United States, a *real* boy climbs trees, disdains girls, dirties his knees, plays with soldiers, and takes blue for his favorite color. When they go to school, real boys prefer manual training, gym, and arithmetic. In college the boys smoke pipes, drink beer, and major in engineering or physics. The real boy matures into a "man's man" who plays poker, goes hunting, drinks brandy, and dies in the war.

The articles in this section address the question of boys' development, focusing on the institutions that shape boys' lives. C. Shawn McGuffey and B. Lindsay Rich, as well as Pat Mahony, and Ellen Jordan and Angela Cowan describe the gender socialization of schooling, both inside the classroom and on the playground. Mike Messner, Geoffrey Canada, and Martin Espada examine the extracurricular socialization that occurs in organized sports, on the streets, and in the Latino community. And Ritch C. Savin-Williams recounts the consequences of early childhood sexual feelings for gay and bisexual boys.

For every boy aged 5 - 12 in the U.S.,
2 G.I. Joe products are sold yearly.

DEMILITARIZE THE PLAYGROUND

C. Shawn McGuffey
B. Lindsay Rich

Playing in the Gender Transgression Zone

Race, Class, and Hegemonic Masculinity in Middle Childhood

By now, R. W. Connell's concept of "hegemonic masculinity" has wide currency among students of gender.[1] The concept implies that there is a predominant way of doing gender relations (typically by men and boys, but not necessarily limited to men and boys) that enforces the gender order status quo: It elevates the general social status of masculine over feminine qualities and privileges some masculine qualities over others. The notion that "masculinities" and "femininities" exist and can be interrogated as negotiated realities allows us to further our understanding about the larger gender order in which they are embedded.

We want to caution, however, against the temptation to overgeneralize the concept of hegemonic masculinity. To do so runs the risk of glossing the modalities, both historical and social-spatial (in terms of class, ethnoracial, sexual, and age variations), in which hegemonic masculinity emerges. We believe that hegemonic masculinity, while having general qualities as a form of social power, may take on many valences and nuances, depending on the social setting and the social actors involved. Connell (1987, 1995, 36–37) is himself careful to make sorts of qualifications we make here while similarly claiming the general analytic utility of the concept. We agree with advocates of the concept that it indeed gives us great theoretical leverage and explanatory power toward clarifying and refining how and why men's dominance works at higher levels of social organization, perhaps even at the global level (Connell 1995; Hawkesworth 1997). In this article, we provide evidence of how hegemonic masculinity is manifest in middle childhood play and used to re-create a gender order among children wherein the larger social relations of men's dominance are learned, employed, reinforced, and potentially changed. Specifically, we present and discuss the results of a preliminary participant observation study of microlevel processes of gender boundary negotiation in middle childhood (ages 5–12).

Providing empirical evidence about the ways in which boys and girls negotiate gender relations within specific social contexts can further understanding about why gender relations take the forms they do in childhood. Using the concept of hegemonic masculinity as a heuristic tool, we decided to focus on how gender relations—specifically, the enactment of masculine hegemony within these relations—were "done" (West and Zimmerman 1987). We eschew the notion that men and women (or boys and girls) merely enact "sex roles" as handed-down scripts. Rather, while acknowledging structural gender socialization implied by the concept of role, we focus on the ways in which the relations between girls and

Author's Note: We would like to thank the anonymous reviewers of *Gender & Society*, Beth Schneider, Neil Quisenberry, and Naomi Gerstel for helpful comments and suggestions on an earlier draft of this article.

boys are negotiated (Connell 1987, 1995; Messner 1998).

There are at least two important reasons for this focus when studying children. First, even when "gender roles" are "visible" to and internalized by kids, the meanings attached to them are partly context specific and negotiable. Second, the relative status of gender-typed behaviors implied by conceptualizing multiple, contested forms of masculinity or femininity is a dynamic, historical process that must be continually created or re-created; it happens most palpably at the micro-level, in face-to-face social interactions of individuals and small groups. Connell (1995, 65), borrowing from Kosik (1976), used the term *onto-formative* to capture the emergent process through which social agents actually create or re-create gender dynamics in, during, and through social interaction. Thus, we want to emphasize the context-bound nature of hegemonic masculinity as a style of gender domination that emerges in this specific middle-childhood context.

A substantial amount of research has been dedicated to studying how boys and girls both segregate and organize themselves within the same gender groupings. Barrie Thorne (1994), for instance, has documented numerous examples of boys organizing themselves in larger, hierarchical groups and occupying more space than their female counterparts. While Thorne asserts that children in middle childhood "use the frame of play as a guise for often serious, gender-related messages" (p. 5), few have explored the power of dynamics of gender boundary negotiations as they are "played out" in childhood.

We analyze the process of gender boundary negotiation by focusing on the intersection of gender-segregated activities. Since boys and girls tend to organize themselves into gender-homogenous groups, they are generally aware that their sphere of "gender-appropriate" activities has boundaries. When they transgress these bounds, they enter a contested area that we refer to as the "gender transgression zone" (GTZ). Since gender identity is a "continual process whereby meanings are attributed by and to individuals through social interaction" (Bird 1996, 122), this contentious area is extremely consequential to the development of children. In the GTZ, gender boundaries are constantly being negotiated. Therefore, it is in the GTZ that we should expect to find continuities, as well as changes, in the construction of "gendered" activities and thus the definition of what is hegemonically masculine and what is "other," typically defined as "effeminate." Related research has demonstrated that an important, if not the central, criterion for defining one's masculinity is to distance oneself from anything feminine (e.g., Bird 1996; McCreary 1994).[2]

Considering the importance of the GTZ as the social location where hegemonic notions of gender are challenged and defended, who ultimately decides the rules of negotiation in the GTZ and how? The evidence from this study suggests that high-status boys control the rules of the game in the GTZ. By learning and enforcing hegemonic masculinity (in this setting, the dominant boys' style stresses emotional detachment, competition and rivalry, public attention-getting for victories, and the sexual objectification of females), high-status boys control gender boundaries within the GTZ.

After describing the setting, sample, and method of data collection, our argument develops by first analyzing the principle of homosocial organization among the boys in a status hierarchy and the homosocial organizational strategies of girls in nonhierarchical small cliques. Using the notion of "gender patrolling," we discuss how heterosocial "playing" occurs in the GTZ and show how the dominant high-status boys exercise hegemony through patrolling. Finally, we examine how the GTZ is (re)produced and how it is changed.

Setting, Sample, and Method

The results reported here are the product of discussions we had during and after the first author observed and participated an average of seven hours daily in these processes as a camp counselor at a children's summer camp in a mid-sized southeastern city. This participant observation was carried out over a period of nine weeks in the summer of 1996, involving a total of approximately 315 hours. The camp itself serves a fairly broad range of families, both in terms of class standing and ethnoracial characteristics. Camp registration forms indicated the household income and racial identification of each child participating in the program. Most children came from middle- to lower-middle-class families, with some poor children attending who were aided by a limited number of scholarships to help pay camp fees. The ethnoracial composition of the sample was as follows: 67 percent white, 25 percent African American, 5 percent Asian or Asian American, and the remaining 3 percent comprising various multiethnic, Arabic, and Latino peoples. These percentages are precise approximations because although there was some turnover in children over the weeks (about 20 percent each two-week session), it had very little impact on the ethnoracial composition. The camp averaged 77 participants per week—ages 5 to 12—with approximately 80 percent of those enrolled returning each week. The gender composition of the children held quite steady throughout the nine weeks at 54 percent girls, 46 percent boys.

The routine of this summer camp was heavily marked by a lot of "playing." Although each day differed depending on the daily field trip, campers arrived at approximately 8:00 a.m. and had free time—unorganized play in which they could participate in a variety of activities from board games to basketball—until 8:30. At this time, the children were organized into four age groups (5–6, 7–8, 9–10, 11–12) in which counselors informed the campers of the day's activities. The camp had three large areas of play that sponsored assorted games and activities (e.g., prison ball, field hockey, and kick ball) and an arts and crafts facility. The four groups participated in each of the four activities on a rotating basis. Around noon, the participants had lunch and soon after loaded the buses for the daily field trip.

Field trips included outings to the local pool, planetarium, parks, and numerous other places. Depending on when the children returned to the campsite, the camp resumed its age-ranked rotation or played large games that included the participation of all campers. Five-thirty until close was always the designated free time. During free time, lunch, snack, and field trips, children were free to interact with children from other age groups. In sum, this summer camp typically involved the children in plenty of play activity, most of which was not organized on a gender-segregated basis.

As a counselor, the first author supervised the children's activities and assisted in the daily functioning of the site. He kept a log of findings, based on notes taken throughout the day and detailed recollections of gender play and interactions, with many verbatim quotes. Those logs were systematized and typed up every evening after work. Once a week, we had extensive discussions based on these accumulating logs, relating the concrete activities and events of the camp to our evolving formations and theoretical understandings. Early on in this process, we decided that particular attention should be placed on how and where gender boundaries were created and how they were transgressed. We made the methodological decision to be vigilant to both homosocial transgression (i.e., children engaging in gender-appropriate activities among members of the same gender) and to heterosocial transgression (i.e., boys or girls engaging in gender-appropriate activities among members of the other gender). We believe that this aided tremendously in allowing us to narrow the observational target and increase the quality of the data collected. In addition to participant observation, the first author interviewed 22 of the children and 6 parents near the end of the summer to gain insight into the ways children and parents constructed meanings around the observed gendering processes. Finally, when we refer to specific children in this study, we designate ethnoracial, gender, and age distinctions as follows: W = White, B = Black, A = Asian, B = Boy, G =

Girl, and a number representing the age of the child. For example, an African American girl who is seven years old will be represented as (BG7). If a child is of a racial category other than white, Black, or Asian, his or her specific classification will be marked accordingly.

Organization of Homosocial Status Systems

When examined as two separate social groups, boys and girls organize themselves differently based on distinct systems of valuing. We must reiterate that masculinity and femininity are not bipolar or opposites but are rather "separate and relatively independent dimensions" (Absi-Semaan, Crombie, and Freeman 1993, 188). Gender is a social construction that is constantly being modified as individuals mature. What may be gender appropriate at one stage in life may be gender inappropriate at a later stage. Boys, for example, are free to touch each other affectionately in early middle childhood, but this is subsequently stigmatized, with a few exceptions (such as victory celebrations). As "independent dimensions," one can develop a clearer view of masculinity and femininity by studying how they differ in context to intragender (homosocial) relations and then how they interact in intergender (heterosocial) relations. Homosocial relationships—nonsexual attractions held by members of the same sex—define how heterosocial relationships are maintained. Thus, it is essential to understand how boys and girls organize themselves within each homosocial group to understand how they negotiate boundaries between the two (Bird 1996).[3]

Structural Formation of Boys in Middle Childhood

Boys in middle childhood organize themselves in a definite hierarchical structure in which the high-status boys decide what is acceptable and valued— that which is hegemonically masculine—and what is not. A boy's rank in the hierarchy is chiefly determined by his athletic ability. Researchers have identified sports as a central focus in boys' development (Fine 1992; Messner 1992, 1994). Boys in this context were observed using words such as *captain, leader,* and various other ranking references, even when they were not playing sports. Messner (1994, 209) explains the attraction of sports in hegemonic masculinity as a result of young males finding the "rulebound structure of games and sports to be a psychologically 'safe' place in which [they] can get (non-intimate) connection with others within a context that maintains clear boundaries, distance, and separation from others." Sharon Bird (1996) identifies three characteristics in maintaining hegemonic masculinity: emotional detachment, competitiveness, and the sexual objectification of women, in which masculinity is thought of as different from and better than femininity. As another essential feature of hegemonic masculinity, we want to add to these characteristics the ability to draw attention to one's self. Because hegemony is sustained publicly, being able to attract positive attention to one's self is vital. The recognition a boy receives from his public performance of masculinity allows him to maintain his high status and/or increase his rank in the hierarchy.

Conflicts and disagreements in the boys' hierarchy are resolved by name-calling and teasing, physical aggression, and exclusion from the group. These forms of aggression structure and maintain the hierarchy by subordinating alternate propositions and identities that threaten hegemonic masculinity. Although direct and physical aggression are the most physically damaging, the fear of being exiled from the group is the most devastating since the hierarchy confirms masculinity and self-worth for many young boys. According to Kaufman (1995, 16), the basis for a hegemonic masculinity is "unconsciously rooted before the age of six" and "is reinforced as the child develops." Lower-status boys adhere to the hegemonic rules as established by the top boys even if they do not receive any direct benefits from the hierarchy within the homosocial context. The overwhelming majority of boys support hegemonic masculinity in relation to subordinated masculinities and femininities because it not only gives boys power over an entire sex (i.e., girls), but it also gives them the opportunity to acquire power over members of their own sex. This helps maintain the hierarchical frame by always giving boys—even low-status boys—status and power over others. Connell (1987, 183) states that hegemonic masculinity "is always constructed in relation to various subordinated masculinities as well as in relation to women." Connell (1995, 79) describes this pan-masculine privilege over girls and women as the "patriarchal dividend." Hegemonic masculinity is publicly used to sustain the power of high-status boys over subordinate boys and boys over girls.

Emotional detachment, competitiveness, and attention arousal could be witnessed in any game of basketball. High-status boys in our study generally performed the best and always distinguished themselves after scoring points. Three high-status boys demonstrate this particularly well. After scoring, Adam[4] (WB11) usually jumped in the air, fist in hand, and shouted either, "In your face!" or "You can't handle this!" Brian's (BB11) style consisted of a little dance followed by, "It's all good and it's all me!" Darrel (BB11) also had a shuffle he performed and ended his routine with, "You can't handle my flow!" or "Pay attention and take notes on how a real 'G' [man] does it." These three are also the most aggressive, oftentimes running over their own teammates. By constantly displaying their athletic superiority, these high-status boys are validating their position and maintaining separation from lower-status boys. Most boys usually did some "attention getting" as well when they scored.

The sexual objectification of women can easily be seen in boys' homosocial interactions. Sexually degrading remarks by boys about women and girls at the pool were common; harassment by young boys occasionally occurred. In one instance at a nearby swimming pool, an adolescent girl, approximately 16 years old, was on her stomach sunbathing with the top portion of her bikini unfastened. Adam (WB11)—the highest-ranked boy—walked over to the young lady and asked if he could put some tanning lotion on her back. After she refused his offer, Adam—with a group of boys urging him on—poured cold water on her back, causing her to instinctively raise up and reveal her breasts. While he was being disciplined, the other boys cheered him on, and Adam smiled with pride. In "The Dirty Play of Little Boys," Gary Fine (1992, 137) argues that "given the reality that many talkers have not reached puberty, we can assume that their sexual interests are more social than physiological. Boys wish to convince their peers that they are sexually mature, active, and knowledgeable" and, we might add, definitely heterosexual.

Despite the fact that there were definite racial and class differences in the boys' hierarchy, these factors had surprisingly little consequence for rankings in the power structure. Black and/or economically disadvantaged boys were just as likely to hold high positions of authority as their white and/or middle-class counterparts. Though a white middle-class boy (Adam) was the highest-ranked youth in the boys' hierarchy, two poor Black youths (Brian and Darrel) held the second and third positions in the hierarchy. Furthermore, when Adam went on a two-week vacation with his family, Darrel surpassed Brian and assumed the alpha position in the boys' social order. Nonetheless, upon his return, Adam reasserted his dominance in the group.

Structural Formation of Girls in Middle Childhood

Girls' homosocial organizational forms are distinct from boys. The tendency toward a single hierarchy, for example, is quite rare. Social aggression (e.g., isolating a member of the group) is used to mark boundaries of femininity. These boundaries do not seem to involve a singular notion of hegemonic femininity with which to subordinate other forms or to heighten public notice of a higher-status femininity. Girls' boundaries are less defined than boys'. The girls in our study generally organized themselves in small groups ranging from two to four individuals. These groups, nonetheless, usually had one girl who was of higher status than the other girls in the clique. The highest-status girl was generally the one considered the most sociable and the most admired by others in the immediate clique as well as others in the camp. Much as Luria and Thorne (1994, 52) observed, the girls were connected by shifting alliances. Girls deal with personal conflicts by way of exclusion from the group and social manipulation. Social manipulation includes gossiping, friendship bartering, and indirectly turning the group against an individual. Contrary to the findings of many sociologists and anthropologists who only characterize aggression in physical aspects, we—like Kaj Bjorkqvist (1994) in "Sex Differences in Physical, Verbal, and Indirect Aggression"—found that girls display just as much aggression as boys but in different ways. When Elaine (WG8), for example, would not share her candy with her best friends Brandi (WG8) and Darlene (WG7), Brandi and Darlene proclaimed that Elaine could no longer be their friend. Elaine then joined another group of girls. This is quite representative of what happens when one girl is excluded from a clique. To get back at Brandi and Darlene, Elaine told her new "best friends" that Brandi liked Kevin (biracial B11) and that Darlene urinated on herself earlier that day. This soon spread throughout the camp, and Darlene and Brandi were teased for the rest of the day, causing them to cry. As Bjorkqvist (1994, 180) suggests, there is no reason to believe that girls are any less aggressive than boys. In fact, social manipulation may be more damaging than physical aggression because though physical wounds heal, gossip and group exclusion can persist eternally (or at least until the end of summer).

Unlike the boys who perform or comply with a predominant form of masculinity, no such form of hegemonic femininity was observed. Connell (1987) explains the lack of a hegemonic form of femininity as the result of the collective subordination of women to the men's homosocial hierarchy. According to Connell, since power rests in the men's (boys') sphere, there is no reason to form power relations over other women (girls). Hence, "no pressure is set up to negate or subordinate other forms of femininity in the way hegemonic masculinity must negate other masculinities" (Connell 1987, 187). Girls were inclined to gather in different groups, or cliques, reflective of various ways to define femininity; they gathered with those who defined their girlhood on the same terms. Just as Ann Beutel and Margaret Marini (1995, 436) discovered in their work, "Gender and Values," girls in our study also formed girl cliques "characterized by greater emotional intimacy, self-disclosure, and supportiveness." Intimacy helps ensure faithfulness to the group. All the girl groups—regardless of racial makeup, socioeconomic background, or age differences—had an idea of being "nice," which enhanced clique solidarity. Various girls were asked to give a definition of what it meant to be nice: "Nice just means, you know, helping each other out" (BG12); "Nice just means doing the right thing" (BG7); "Nice means . . . getting along" (WG11). Despite this notion of being nice, however, being nice in one group may be seen as being mean in another. In some groups, for example, it was considered nice for one girl to ask another if the former could have some of the other's chips at lunch. In others, though, this was considered rude; the nice, or proper, conduct was to wait until one was offered some chips. Nice was relative to the particular group. Being nice among the girls observed in this study generally entailed sharing, the aversion of physical and direct aggression, and the avoidance of selfish acts.

The organization of African American girls was somewhat unique. As mentioned, campers were divided into four age groups. In each age group, there were no more than four or five Black girls. Within these age groups, African American girls had the same structural patterns as Caucasians—small cliques of two to four in which a person may drift from clique to clique at a given time. There were no problems with the Black girls mixing with the white girls in age groups or organized activities.

During times when the campers were not restricted to specific groups (e.g., snack time, most field trips, at the pool, group games, and free time), however, the preponderance of African American girls gravitated to each other, despite age differences. This differs from previous research that notes that children in middle childhood associate with near-aged members (Absi-Semaan, Crombie, and Freeman 1993; Andersen 1993; Beutel and Marini 1995; Block 1984; Curran and Renzetti 1992; Luria and Thorne 1994). The first author also visited another camp with similar demographics and observed a similar lack of age segregation among African American girls. African American girls formed larger groups and occupied more space than white girls.

In general, Black girls were more assertive and therefore less likely to be bothered by boys. A loose hierarchy formed in which the older girls made most of the decisions for the younger ones in the group. This hierarchy was by no means hegemonic as in the boys' hierarchy. Rather, this hierarchy used a communal approach to decision making, with the older girls working to facilitate activities for the group. This process was illustrated every day as this group of girls decided which activity they would participate in at free time. The oldest girls—Brittany (BG11), Alexia (BG12), and Melanie (BG11)—would give options such as arts and crafts, checkers, basketball, and jump roping for the group to choose from. After considering all the options—taking into account what they had played the day before, the time left to participate in the activity, and the consensus of the group—the older girls indirectly shifted the focus to a particular activity that seldom received objection from the younger girls in the clique.

To make sense of our findings regarding the African American girl clique, we compared our field notes to Marjorie Harness Goodwin's (1994) "Social Differentiation and Alliance Formation in an African-American Children's Peer Group," a study that observed Black girls organizing larger coalitions than the relatively small associations typical of white girls. Goodwin's study, nonetheless, revealed age segregation. We believe cross-age interaction was prominent with the African American girls in our study because they were in

the minority, whereas Black girls were a majority in Goodwin's sample. This minority ethnoracial/ gender status may have contributed to undercutting the typical age divisions among the Black girls. Since Black and white boys did not exhibit social racial segregation in the boys' hierarchy, we do not believe ethnoracial differences directly account for the separation of Black and white girls. Because the Black girls tended to be more assertive as a whole, they gravitated toward one another, despite age differences. In addition, the racial connection allowed this girl peer group to foster and reinforce its own assertive, yet nurturing, characteristics in an environment where these attributes might otherwise be eclipsed. In other words, by pulling together, they created a clique that supports their culture of femininity.

Moreover, whereas the boys displayed little class segregation, the girls were clearly marked by class affiliations. Girls usually formed groups with other girls from their neighborhood. Most of the girls in a clique knew each other as neighbors or schoolmates. Even when girls switched groups or bartered for friendship, they often did so along class lines. This was especially evident in the unstructured activities in which children could freely choose to associate with whomever they wanted (e.g., snack time and free time). The data here suggest that class and racial distinctions are more salient for girls than boys in middle childhood.

The Gender Transgression Zone

How do boys and girls negotiate boundaries in the GTZ? This area of activity—where boys and girls conduct heterosocial relations in hopes of either expanding or maintaining current gender boundaries in child culture—is where gender transgression takes place. A boy playing hand-clapping games (e.g., patty cake) or a girl completing an obstacle course that is designed to determine one's "manliness" are instances of transgression that occur in this zone. Figure 1 illustrates the areas of discussion for the rest of the article.

■ FIGURE 1

The Gender Transgression Zone and Its Boundaries

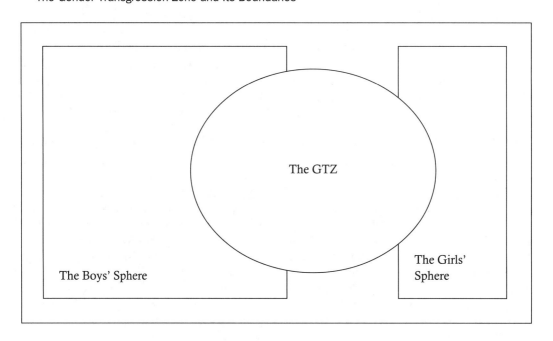

The left rectangle represents the boys' sphere of gender-appropriate activity, the right rectangle represents the girls' sphere, and the central oval represents the GTZ. The right rectangle, the bounds of femininity, is purposely drawn smaller; although girls have a wider range of possible normative femininities than the narrower hegemonic form of masculinity predominant among boys, girls control fewer resources and retain less power. The GTZ extends farther into the masculine realm because girls cross over more than boys and receive fewer sanctions for gender deviations. This figure, nonetheless, is not static. Since gender is continually (re)structured and (re)shaped, these boundaries are constantly shifting and challenged.

Hegemonic Masculinity in the Gender Transgression Zone

Boys spend the majority of their time trying to maintain current gender boundaries. It is through the enforcement of gender boundaries that boys construct their social status. High-status boys are especially concerned with gender maintenance because they have the most to lose. By maintaining gender boundaries, top boys secure resources for themselves—such as playing area, social prestige/status, and power. The social prestige procured by high-status boys causes lower-status boys and girls to grant deference to high-ranked boys. If a high-ranked boy insults a lower-status boy or interrupts girls' activities, he is much less likely to be socially sanctioned by boys or girls. The position of lower-status boys in the hierarchy prevents them from challenging the higher-ranked boy's authority, while the collective subordination of girls to boys inhibits much dissension from girls. Connell (1987, 187) would likely suggest that girls' deference to high-status boys in an adaptive strategy to "the global dominance of heterosexual men."

To young children, "masculinity is power" (Kaufman 1995, 16). As a social construction, then, masculinity is maintained through a hegemonic process that excludes femininity and alternate masculinities. Hence, in the GTZ, boys seldom accept deviant boys or girls. Just as boys actively participate in the maintenance of the hegemonic hierarchy by using name-calling, physical aggression, and exclusion to handle personal conflicts, these same tactics are used to handle gender transgressors. The GTZ, then, is where hegemonic masculinity flexes its social muscle.

Boys Patrolling Boys in the GTZ

High-status boys maximize the influence of hegemonic masculinity and minimize gender transgressors by identifying social deviants and labeling them as outcasts. A continuous process occurs of homosocial patrolling and stigmatizing anomalies. Boys who deviate are routinely chastised for their aberrant behavior. Two examples of this process are particularly obvious. Joseph (WB7) is a seven-year-old who is recognized as a "cry baby." He is not very coordinated and gets along better with girls than boys. Because Joseph is so young, he is not directly affected by the full scrutiny of the solidified form of hegemonic masculinity. His age still allows him the luxury of displaying certain behaviors (e.g., crying) that are discredited in subsequent stages of middle childhood. Although the first author did not observe any kids in Joseph's own age group calling Joseph names, many older boys figure that he will "probably be gay when he grows up," as stated by Daniel (WB10). Fewer of the older boys associate with Joseph during free time, and he is not allowed around the older boys as are some of the other more "hegemonically correct" younger boys.

Phillip (WB10) was rejected by all the boys, which, in turn, aided in the maintenance of hegemonic masculinity. Phillip acted rather feminine and looked feminine as well. He lacked coordination, was small in stature, and had shoulder-length hair. Phillip often played with girls and preferred stereotypically feminine activities (e.g., jump rope). It was not uncommon to hear him being referred to as a faggot, fag, or gay. He was the ultimate pariah in the boys' sphere. He was constantly rejected from all circles of boys but got along quite fine with girls. His untouchable status was exemplified clearly in two instances. First, during a game of trains and tunnels—which requires partners linking arms—all players voluntarily paired up with same-sex companions except Phillip. As parents came to pick up their children, however, cross-gendered pairs began to form. This caused little disruption. However, there came a point when a hegemonically masculine boy, Sean (WB9), should have paired up with Phillip. Upon finding out who his new partner would be, Sean violently rejected Phillip. Sean was told that if he did not accept Phillip as his partner, he would have to sit out the rest of the game. Sean screamed, "I don't care if I have to sit out the whole summer 'cause I'm not going to let that faggot touch me!" In another situation during an arts and crafts activity, Phillip finished early. When kids finished early, the staff usually asked them to help an individual who was having problems. Usually everyone accepted help. However, when Phillip attempted to assist Markus (WB9), Markus rejected him harshly. Nonetheless, Markus did accept help from Karen (WG10). Phillip threatened a boy's masculinity because Phillip had been labeled homosexual; receiving help from a girl in this particular area is non-threatening. If Joseph's behavior continues, we expect that he will experience the same harsh rejections that Phillip received. By stigmatizing Joseph and rejecting Phillip, homophobia emerges as a cautionary tale in the GTZ that deters other boys from deviating from the norm out of fear of rejection.

The boys in our case study used Joseph and Phillip to represent what would happen to other boys who transgressed the bound of hegemonic masculinity. If a boy started slipping from gender-appropriate activities, then other boys would simply associate him with one of the two pariahs, Joseph or Phillip, or call him a fag to get him back in the hegemonic group. The boys devalue homosexuality; the threat of being labeled gay is used as a control mechanism to keep boys conforming to the norms of hegemonic masculinity. George Lehne (1992, 389) says that the fear of being labeled gay "is a threat used by societies and individuals to enforce social conformity in the male role, and maintain social control . . . used in many ways to encourage certain types of male behavior and to define the limits of 'acceptable' masculinity." Talk of faggots and gays is also used to help define a boy's own masculinity.[5] By negatively talking about gays and excluding members who are presumed homosexual, individual boys are defining their own heterosexuality, while collectively they are endorsing hegemonic masculinity. Because most of these boys are not sexually mature or knowledgeable, many do not have an accurate conception of homosexuality (or, for that matter, heterosexuality) at this age. Gay bashing is another way boys can separate themselves from gender-deviant behavior.

Boys Patrolling Girls in the GTZ

Just as it is important for boys to patrol their own sex, it is equally important for boys to monitor the activities of girls and to keep them out of the boys' domain. If girls entered the boys' sphere in substantial numbers, the hegemonic hierarchy would be jeopardized. Girls who enter the boys' realm, therefore, are made to feel inadequate by the boys. The few girls who do succeed in the boys' sphere, nevertheless, are either marginalized or adopted into boys' middle-childhood culture (masculinized). Marginalization or masculinization depends on the girls' overall athletic prowess and emotional detachment while in the boys' sphere. This is illustrated by the following incident.

During one of the camp field trips, campers went to a university athletic training center. During the tennis rotation, Adrianne (WG10) was put with three boys. Adrianne, who took tennis lessons, was ignored by the boys. While the boys were arguing over the proper way to hit a backhand, Adrianne sat quietly on the sideline. When one boy finally asked her if she knew how to hit a backhand, she shook her head no. The first author knew this was incorrect because Adrianne had explained to him the proper way to hit a backhand earlier that day. Therefore, the first author asked Adrianne why she responded no. She replied, "When you're with boys, sometimes it's better to pretend like you don't know stuff because they're going to ignore you or tell you you're wrong."

Marginalization also occurs when girls meet some, but not all, of the requirements of hegemonic masculinity. The group of African American girls, for example, was marginalized. Many were just as assertive, and two were more athletic than some boys of high status. Yet, these girls remained marginal, retaining too many feminine characteristics, such as expressive acts of emotion when comforting teammates when they performed poorly in an activity. When a group of boys was asked why they did not associate with these girls who were more athletic than many of the boys in the hierarchy, Adam replied, "They're just different. I don't know about them. That whole group of them are just different. They're all weird."

Girl masculinization occurs when boys dissociate a girl from her feminine gender. The best example of a girl being adopted into a hegemonic masculine identity is Patricia (WG11). She is very athletic and can outplay many boys in basketball, the game that seemed to most signify one's masculinity at this site.[6] She also remained emotionally detached while interacting with boys. One time at the playground, Adam (WB11) created an obstacle course that he contended proved whether or not one was a "man." Some of the "manhood" tests were very dangerous—such as balancing on the rails of a high overhang—and had to be stopped. Each boy who completed a task successfully received applause and high fives. Those who did not complete successfully were laughed at because, according to the other boys, they were not "men." There was one catch to this test of masculinity—Patricia. She completed the numerous tasks faster and better than many of the boys. She did not get the screams of jubilation and high fives as did the other boys at first. As she proved her "manhood," however, she began to be accepted by the boys. By the end of the tests, Patricia was proclaimed a "man." About eight weeks later, when the first author asked a group of boys why Patricia was accepted as a member of their group, Adam, the apparent spokesman for the hierarchy, said, "Well, Patricia is not really a girl. Technically she is, but not really. I mean, come on, she acts like a boy most of the time. She even passed the 'manhood' test, remember?" Though this reveals Patricia's acceptance into the boys' hierarchy, she had to forfeit her feminine gender. As Thorne (1994) recognizes, girls who successfully transgress into the boys' activities under boys' terms do not challenge stereotypical gender norms. Hence, Patricia's participation in boys' activities "does little to challenge existing arrangements" (Thorne 1994, 133).

Hegemonic masculinity in middle childhood maintains itself in regards to girls in the GTZ. Girls are not welcome into the boys' sphere, which occupies more space. If girls partially meet standards, they are marginalized and thought of as "weird." In a way, they are almost degendered. Girls who fit all hegemonic requirements (tomboys) are conceptualized as masculine, or a boy/man. This reasoning is especially disturbing because masculinity is not only maintaining and defining itself, but it is also defining femininity.

Femininity in the Gender Transgression Zone

As previously stated, girls find various forms of femininity acceptable, despite how different the form may be from their own. With this in mind, one can understand that while some girls do not challenge gender boundaries, those who do are not stigmatized by other girls. To test this observation, a group of girls (who were stereotypically "gender appropriate") were asked during lunch one day their views about the behavior of various girls who transgressed into the boys' sphere. Speaking of Patricia (WG11)—the girl who was

proclaimed a "man"—Melissa (WG11) said, "She's pretty nice," and Lucia (WG9) added, "Yeah, she's pretty cool. . . . She just likes to do different stuff. There's nothing wrong with that." They were then asked about the various members of the Black girl clique, and Melissa responded, "They're nice to [us]." When the girls were specifically asked if there was anything wrong with the way these gender transgressors behaved, Melissa and Lucia simply said no. Even Robin (WG10), who was not completely comfortable with the actions of these transgressors, replied, "I guess not. They just have their own way of acting. I just don't think it's very lady-like acting." As one can see, gender transgression is virtually accepted among even gender-traditional girls. Nevertheless, girls deal with clique deviants—those who are not "nice" relative to the clique's definition—just as they handle personal conflicts: exclusion from a particular group and social manipulation.

Girls Patrolling Girls in the GTZ

As girls get older, they recognize the higher value that society puts on masculine traits as well as the resources accumulated in the boys' sphere. Girls also see masculinity as power (Connell 1987). With increasing encouragement from the larger society (parents, teachers, and other pro-feminist role models), many girls attempt to access these resources as they mature. It should be noted, however, that high-status girls in these small groups also have social power in their cliques. The highest-ranked girl largely dictated who was gossiped about and who would be banished from the group. Yet, girls' resources were limited in comparison to their masculine-gendered playmates because their resources did not extend much further than their small clique. Interestingly, girls who dare to participate in the boys' realm not only avoid stigmatization from most girls but are often praised by other girls if they succeed in the boy's sphere. For the most part, girls only receive restrictions from the prime agents of hegemonic masculinity at play—boys. Though girl's relations generally consist of small, intimate groupings when dealing with each other, large group affiliation and support seem to be the gender strategy when girls transgress onto traditional boys' turf. This was observed frequently throughout the summer.

Whenever a girl beat a boy in an athletic event, girls, as a collectivity, cheered them on despite age differences. During a Connect Four contest, Travis (WB9), the champion, was bragging about winning—especially when he beat girls. He would say, "It only takes me two minutes to beat girls," and "Girls aren't a challenge." This changed, however, when Corisa (BG6) started to play. Corisa beat Travis four times in a row. Girls of all ages rallied behind Corisa. For the duration of the day, girls praised Corisa, and some even introduced their parents to Corisa in admiration. One introduction went as follows: "Mommy, this is Corisa. She beat boys in Connect Four." Thorne (1994) also observed similar reactions in her work when a girl beat up a boy. Thorne writes, "[A] ripple of excitement moved among the girls, including me; I think it gave us a sense that one of our kind could resist and even herself exert . . . dominance over boys" (p. 133).

The best example of group solidarity in resistance to boys' dominance was provided one day when leaving the swimming pool. Molly (WG9)—whose eyes were irritated by chlorine and was basically walking to the locker room with her eyes closed—accidentally entered the boys locker room while the campers were changing. Many of the boys laughed at her and ridiculed Molly for her mistake. Brian (BB11) said, "She just wanted to look at our private stuff," and Thomas (WB12) called her a "slut." Molly started to cry. Girls, however, came to Molly's rescue. While Molly's immediate clique comforted her, the other girls scared off boys who attempted to harass Molly for the rest of the day. Crysta (BG9) and Brittany (BG11) were the most effective protectors. This was surprising because even though Molly and Crysta were in the same age group, they did not get along, and Brittany—who is in the oldest group—to the best of our knowledge, had never even talked to Molly. As a gen-

der strategy, girls—regardless of age, class, or racial differences—united together to combat the dominance of boys.

Girls Patrolling Boys in the GTZ

Without a uniform or constant form of femininity, girls were more lenient to both girls and boys when either ventured into the GTZ. Girls accepted Joseph and Phillip, both gender-deviant boys, into all their activities without a problem. These boys, nevertheless, had to adhere to the same principles of "niceness" as did the girls. If the boys did not, they were punished in the same manner as girls—exclusion and social manipulation. When Joseph (WB7) did not share his "Now and Later" candy during lunch one day with the group of girls he was eating with, he soon found himself eating alone and the subject of much gossip in the girls' sphere.

"Alphas Rule! Others Drool!" Or How High-Status Boys Direct Change in the GTZ

The top-ranked boys in the hierarchy direct the actions of all the boys who aspire to hegemonic masculinity (or are, at least, complicit with it). High-status boys are primarily concerned with maintaining gender boundaries to retain status and all the luxuries that are a result of being hegemonically masculine. Dominant boys make decisions for the group and can manipulate the other boys to sustain high-status and its privileges. Examples of status privileges include being picked first for teams, getting first dibs on other people's lunches, being allowed to cut in line, and being freed by other males during prison ball—a game similar to dodge ball—with no reciprocal obligation to free low- or middle-status boys.

High-status boys have the unique power of negotiating gender boundaries by accepting, denying, or altering gender codes. The power of high-status boys to alter gender boundaries was strikingly borne out of a series of events that, for weeks, redefined a feminine gender-stereotyped activity, hand-clapping games, into a hegemonically masculine one. This example of the de-feminization (and thus, from the hegemonic standpoint, destigmatization of girls' behavior) illustrates the ruling dynamic of gender relations in the GTZ. In this camp, boys who even entertained the notion of playing hand-clapping games were confronted, ridiculed, and/or excluded by proponents of hegemonic masculinity.

Here is how the defeminization occurred. One day, right before the closing of the camp, Adam—the highest-ranked boy—was the only boy left waiting for his mother to pick him up. Four girls remained as well and were performing the *Rockin' Robin* hand-clapping routine. When one of the girls left, one of the three remaining girls asked Adam if he would like to learn the routine. He angrily replied, "No, that's girly stuff." Having been a camp counselor for three years, the first author knows every clapping routine from *Bo Bo See Aut In Totin* to *Miss Susie's Steamboat*. He, therefore, volunteered. The girls were amazed that he knew so many of what they referred to as "their" games. After a while, only two girls remained and *Rockin' Robin* requires four participants. Surprisingly, Adam asked to learn. Before he left, Adam had learned the sequence and was having a good time.

We believe that Adam transgressed for three reasons. One, all the other boys were gone, so there were no relevant or important (to him) witnesses to his transgression. Thorne (1994, 54) repeatedly states that witnesses hinder gender deviance: "Teasing makes cross-gender interaction risky, increases social distance between girls and boys, and has the effect of making and policing gender boundaries." Second, Adam saw the first author participate freely in an activity that was previously reserved for girls. Third, as the highest-ranking boy, Adam has a certain degree of freedom that allows him to transgress with little stigmatization. Thorne asserts that the highest-status boy in a hierarchy has "extensive social leeway" (p. 123) since his masculinity is rarely questioned. The next day, Adam was seen perfecting the routine he learned the day before. Many of the boys looked curiously and questioned

why Adam was partaking in such an activity. Soon after, other boys started playing, and boys and girls were interacting heterosocially in what was formerly defined as a "girls-only" activity. Cross-gendered hand-clapping games continued for the rest of the summer and remained an area in which both girls and boys could come together. Defeminization occurred because Adam—the highest-status boy—set the standard and affirmed this type of entertainment as acceptable for boys. This incident supports our view that high-status boys control gender negotiations by showing that gender boundaries can be modified if someone of high status changes the standard of hegemonic masculinity.

To make hand-clapping more masculine, nonetheless, the first author documented boys changing the verses of the most popular hand-clapping game, *Rockin' Robin*, to further defeminize the activity. One of the original verses is "All the little birdies on J-Bird Street like to hear the robin go tweet, tweet, tweet." The boys changed this to "All the little birdies on J-bird Street like to hear the robin say eat my meat!" About a month later, the first author discovered another altered verse from the boys. They changed "Brother's in jail waiting for bail" to "Brother's in jail raising hell!" Since these verses were not condoned at the camp—though we are sure the children used them out of the hearing distance of counselors—girls cleverly modified one of the profane verses by singing, "Brother's in jail raising H-E- double hockey sticks!' This, too, the boys picked up and started applying as their own. Hand-clapping games moved from the girls' sphere to the GTZ. Defeminization of hand clapping exposes the constant fluctuation and restructuring of gender norms in childhood play.

Boys in middle childhood organize themselves in a definite hierarchy that is run by high-status boys in accordance with the hegemonic form of masculinity that they embody and police in the GTZ. Boys are not accepting of deviant boys or girls. Gender deviants are handled by teasing and name-calling, marginalization and exclusion from the group, and physical aggression.

High-status boys, though, have the unique power to negotiate gender boundaries by either accepting, denying, or altering gender codes. Girls who enter the boys' realm are made to feel inadequate by the boys. Those girls who do succeed in the boys' sphere, nevertheless, are either marginalized from or masculinized into boys' middle-childhood culture. They are forced to leave their femininity behind if they want to cross the border fully. Therefore, no feminization of hegemonic masculinity is allowed. As can be seen in the hand-clapping phenomenon, the redefinition entails defeminization.

Conclusion

The findings of this preliminary research suggest that hegemonic masculinity in middle childhood not only regulates boys' homosocial boundaries but also controls the rules of gender negotiation and transgression for both boys and girls. The foundation of the boys' hierarchy is based on an idea of supremacy. The top boys rule the hierarchy and manipulate it so that it preserves their position and thus their higher status. Hegemonic masculinity is public and is used to sustain the power of high-status boys over subordinate boys and over girls. The overwhelming majority of boys support hegemonic masculinity because it gives power over the other sex. It also gives them the opportunity to acquire power over members of their own sex. We argue that our data support the claim that even though most boys do not directly enjoy the benefits of hegemonic masculinity as do higher-status boys (because that status is restricted to a few), they express complicity with the hegemonic regime because the gender order ensures them social status over girls.

On the other side of the gender divide, girls, realizing the power that is retained in the boys' sphere, have an incentive to transgress into boys' territory with few sanctions from their own homosocial sphere. Thus, those who successfully transgress boys' boundaries receive communal support from other girls, even when they are not in the same intimate association or clique. To combat the invasion of gender transgressors, high-status boys handle gender deviants by name-calling, exclusion from the group, and physical aggression. High-status boys lead their army of lower-status, complicit boys—using the social construction of hegemonic masculinity to unite them—against intruders. High-status boys use aggressive, athletic, and boastful behavior to display and sustain their position. By keeping the lower strata of the hierarchy intact—by way of internal struggles for ascendancy in the boys' hierarchy and the constant subordination of gender deviants—high-status boys continue their reign by continually defining what is masculine, what is feminine, and reserving the authority to sanction all gender transgressions in hopes of sustaining valued resources and social prestige.

This study reveals that race and class intersect with gender in complicated ways for boys and girls. Boys revealed little to no racial or class segregation in the hegemonic hierarchy. Boys of various racial and class designations held positions of high authority in the power structure. This is likely attributable to the unstructured nature of the day camp. Free of the institutionally discriminatory practices of the larger social world, a boy had considerable opportunities for upward mobility in the hierarchy since social achievement was chiefly based on athletic ability. Conversely, girls often separated on racial and class divisions. Since white girls formed smaller associations based on precamp friendships from their neighborhoods and school, class and race had visible consequences for girls' cliques. Similar to Goodwin's (1994) research, African American girls formed a larger group during non-age-specific activities and occupied more space than their white counterparts. In addition, a girl's status largely depended on her relationships with others (or other children's perceptions of her). Consequently, boys tended to have more chances to improve their social status relative to girls due to boys' connection to hegemonic masculinity. The actions of hegemonically masculine boys and the collective insurgence of gender-transgressive girls and their supporters are potentially important sources of change in the gender order of childhood. Further research might look for variations in the types of behaviors manifest in the GTZ and in the characteristics of hegemonic masculinity within other domains of childhood.

Notes

1. To the best of our knowledge, this concept was first set out in his book *Gender and Power* (Connell 1987, 183–88).

2. The pre-Oedipal psychodynamics of this process are detailed in Chodorow (1978).

3. Bird (1996) explains how homosocial interactions maintain gender boundaries among adult men. Beutel and Marini (1995) discuss the contrasting value systems of males and females.

4. The names of children in this study are pseudonyms.

5. This may be part and parcel of what McCreary (1994) refers to as the universal avoidance of femininity: Homophobia may be a rejection of the "abnormality" of being attracted to boys (i.e., being "girlish").

6. At the other site that the first author visited, football was the most masculinizing athletic activity.

References

Absi-Semaan, N., G. Crombie, and C. Freeman. 1993. Masculinity and femininity in middle childhood: Developmental and factor analyses. *Sex Roles* 28 (3/4): 187–206.

Andersen, Margaret L. 1993. *Thinking about women.* New York: Macmillan.

Beutel, Ann M., and Margaret M. Marini. 1995. Gender and values. *American Sociological Review* 60 (3): 436–38.

Bird, Sharon R. 1996. Welcome to the men's club: Homosociality and the maintenance of hegemonic masculinity. *Gender & Society* 10 (2): 120–32.

Bjorkqvist, Kaj. 1994. Sex differences in physical, verbal, and indirect aggression: A review of recent research. *Sex Roles* 30 (3/4): 177–88.

Block, Jeanne H. 1984. *Sex role identity and ego development.* San Francisco: Jossey-Bass.

Chodorow, Nancy. 1978. *The reproduction of mothering: Psychoanalysis and the sociology of gender.* Berkeley: University of California Press.

Connell, R. W. 1987. *Gender & power.* Stanford, CA: Stanford University Press.

———. 1995. *Masculinities.* Berkeley: University of California Press.

Curran, Daniel J., and Claire M. Renzetti. 1992. *Women, men, and society.* 2d ed. Needham Heights, MA: Allyn & Bacon.

Fine, Gary Alan. 1992. The dirty play of little boys. In *Men's lives,* edited by Michael S. Kimmel and Michael A. Messner. New York: Macmillan.

Goodwin, Marjorie Harness. 1994. Social differentiation and alliance formation in an African-American children's peer group. In *Gender roles through the life span,* edited by Michael R. Stevenson. Muncie, IN: Ball State University.

Hawkesworth, Mary. 1997. Confounding gender. *Signs: Journal of Women in Culture and Society* 22 (3): 649–86.

Kaufman, Michael. 1995. The construction of masculinity and the triad of men's violence. In *Men's lives,* edited by Michael Kimmel and Michael Messner. New York: Macmillan.

Kosik, Karel. 1976. *Dialectics of the concrete: A study on problems of man and the world.* Dordrecht, the Netherlands: D. Reidel.

Lehne, Gregory K. 1992. Homophobia among men: Supporting and defining the male role. In *Men's lives,* edited by Michael S. Kimmel and Michael Messner. New York: Macmillan.

Luria, Zella, and Barrie Thorne. 1994. Sexuality and gender in children's daily worlds. In *Sociology: Windows on society,* edited by John W. Heereen and Marylee Mason. Los Angeles: Roxbury.

McCreary, Donald R. 1994. The male role and avoiding femininity. *Sex Roles* 31 (9): 517–32.

Messner, Michael A. 1992. *Power at play: Sports and the problem of masculinity.* Boston: Beacon.

———. 1994. The meaning of success: The athletic experience and the development of male identity. In *Sociology: Windows on society,* edited by John W. Hareen and Marylee Mason. Los Angeles: Roxbury.

———. 1998. The limits of "the male sex role": An analysis of the men's liberation and men's rights movements discourse. *Gender & Society* 12 (3): 255–76.

Thorne, Barrie. 1994. *Gender play: Girls and boys in school.* New Brunswick, NJ: Rutgers University Press.

West, Candace, and Don H. Zimmerman. 1987. Doing gender. *Gender & Society* 1 (2): 125–51.

Michael A. Messner

Boyhood, Organized Sports, and the Construction of Masculinities

The rapid expansion of feminist scholarship in the past two decades has led to fundamental reconceptualizations of the historical and contemporary meanings of organized sport. In the nineteenth and twentieth centuries, modernization and women's continued movement into public life created widespread "fears of social feminization," especially among middle-class men (Hantover 1978; Kimmel 1987). One result of these fears was the creation of organized sport as a homosocial sphere in which competition and (often violent) physicality was valued, while "the feminine" was devalued. As a result, organized sport has served to bolster a sagging ideology of male superiority, and has helped to reconstitute masculine hegemony (Bryson 1987; Hall 1988; Messner 1988; Theberge 1981).

The feminist critique has spawned a number of studies of the ways that women's sport has been marginalized and trivialized in the past (Greendorfer 1977; Oglesby 1978; Twin 1978), in addition to illuminating the continued existence of structural and ideological barriers to gender equality within sport (Birrell 1987). Only recently, however, have scholars begun to use feminist insights to examine men's experiences in sport (Kidd 1987; Messner 1987; Sabo 1985). This article explores the relationship between the construction of masculine identity and boyhood participation in organized sports.

I view gender identity not as a "thing" that people "have," but rather as a *process of construc-*

Michael A. Messner, *Journal of Contemporary Ethnography*, Vol. 18, No. 4, January 1990, 416–444, copyright © 1990 by Sage Publications, Inc. Reprinted by permission of Sage Publications, Inc.

tion that develops, comes into crisis, and changes as a person interacts with the social world. Through this perspective, it becomes possible to speak of "gendering" identities rather than "masculinity" or "femininity" as relatively fixed identities or statuses.

There is an agency in this construction; people are not passively shaped by their social environment. As recent feminist analyses of the construction of feminine gender identity have pointed out, girls and women are implicated in the construction of their own identities and personalities, both in terms of the ways that they participate in their own subordination and the ways that they resist subordination (Benjamin 1988; Haug 1987). Yet this self-construction is not a fully conscious process. There are also deeply woven, unconscious motivations, fears, and anxieties at work here. So, too, in the construction of masculinity. Levinson (1978) has argued that masculine identity is neither fully "formed" by the social context, nor is it "caused" by some internal dynamic put into place during infancy. Instead, it is shaped and constructed through the interaction between the internal and the social. The internal gendering identity may set developmental "tasks," may create thresholds of anxiety and ambivalence, yet it is only through a concrete examination of people's interactions with others within social institutions that we can begin to understand both the similarities and differences in the construction of gender identities.

In this study I explore and interpret the meanings that males themselves attribute to their boyhood participation in organized sport. In what ways do males construct masculine identities within the institution of organized sports? In what ways do class and racial differences mediate this relationship and perhaps lead to the construction of different meanings, and perhaps different masculinities? And what are some of the problems and contradictions within these constructions of masculinity?

Description of Research

Between 1983 and 1985, I conducted interviews with 30 male former athletes. Most of the men I interviewed had played the (U.S.) "major sports"—football, basketball, baseball, track. At the time of the interview, each had been retired from playing organized sports for at least five years. Their ages ranged from 21 to 48, with the median, 33; 14 were black, 14 were white, and two were Hispanic; 15 of the 16 black and Hispanic men had come from poor or working-class families, while the majority (9 of 14) of the white men had come from middle-class or professional families. All had at some time in their lives based their identities largely on their roles as athletes and could therefore be said to have had "athletic careers." Twelve had played organized sports through high school, 11 through college, and seven had been professional athletes. Though the sample was not randomly selected, an effort was made to see that the sample had a range of difference in terms of race and social class backgrounds, and that there was some variety in terms of age, types of sports played, and levels of success in athletic careers. Without exception, each man contacted agreed to be interviewed.

The tape-recorded interviews were semi-structured and took from one and one-half to six hours, with most taking about three hours. I asked each man to talk about four broad eras in his life: (1) his earliest experiences with sports in boyhood, (2) his athletic career, (3) retirement or disengagement from the athletic career, and (4) life after the athletic career. In each era, I focused the interview on the meanings of "success and failure," and on the boy's/man's relationships with family, with other males, with women, and with his own body.

In collecting what amounted to life histories of these men, my overarching purpose was to use feminist theories of masculine gender identity to explore how masculinity develops and changes as boys and men interact within the socially constructed world of organized sports. In addition to using the data to move toward some generalizations about the relationship between "masculinity and sport," I was also concerned with sorting out some of the variations among boys, based on class and racial inequalities, that led them to relate differently to athletic careers. I divided my sample into two comparison groups. The first group was made up of 10 men from higher-status backgrounds, primarily white, middle-class, and professional families. The second group was made up of 20 men from lower-status backgrounds, primarily minority, poor, and working-class families.

Boyhood and the Promise of Sports

Zane Grey once said, "All boys love baseball. If they don't they're not real boys" (as cited in Kimmel 1990). This is, of course, an ideological statement; in fact, some boys do *not* love baseball, or any other sports, for that matter. There are millions of males who at an early age are rejected by, become alienated from, or lose interest in organized sports. Yet all boys are, to a greater or lesser extent, judged according to their ability, or lack of ability, in competitive sports (Eitzen, 1975; Sabo, 1985). In this study I focus on those males who did become athletes—males who eventually poured thousands of hours into the development of specific physical skills. It is in boyhood that we can discover the roots of their commitment to athletic careers.

How did organized sports come to play such a central role in these boy's lives? When asked to recall how and why they initially got into playing sports, many of the men interviewed for this study seemed a bit puzzled: after all, playing sports was "just the thing to do." A 42-year-old black man who had played college basketball put it this way:

It was just what you did. It's kind of like, you went to school, you played athletics, and if you didn't, there was something wrong with you. It was just like brushing your teeth: it's just what you did. It's part of your existence.

Spending one's time playing sports with other boys seemed as natural as the cycle of the seasons: baseball in the spring and summer, football in the fall, basketball in the winter—and then it was time to get out the old baseball glove and begin again. As a black 35-year-old former professional football star said:

> I'd say when I wasn't in school, 95% of the time was spent in the park playing. It was the only thing to do. It just came as natural.

And a black, 34-year-old professional basketball player explained his early experiences in sports:

> My principal and teacher said, "Now if you work at this you might be pretty damned good." So it was more or less a community thing—everybody in the community said, "Boy, if you work hard and keep your nose clean, you gonna be good." Cause it was natural instinct.

"It was natural instinct." "I was a natural." Several athletes used words such as these to explain their early attraction to sports. But certainly there is nothing "natural" about throwing a ball through a hoop, hitting a ball with a bat, or jumping over hurdles. A boy, for instance, may have amazingly dexterous inborn hand–eye coordination, but this does not predispose him to a career of hitting baseballs any more than it predisposes him to a life as a brain surgeon. When one listens closely to what these men said about their early experiences in sports, it becomes clear that their adoption of the self-definition of "natural athlete" was the result of what Connell (1990) has called "a collective practice" that constructs masculinities. The boyhood development of masculine identity and status—truly problematic in a society that offers no official rite of passage into adulthood—results from a process of interaction with people and social institutions. Thus, in discussing early motivations in sports, men commonly talk of the importance of relationships with family members, peers, and the broader community.

Family Influences

Though most of the men in this study spoke of their mothers with love, respect, even reverence, their descriptions of their earliest experiences in sports are stories of an exclusively male world. The existence of older brothers or uncles who served as teachers and athletic role models—as well as sources of competition for attention and status within the family—was very common. An older brother, uncle, or even close friend of the family who was a successful athlete appears to have acted as a sort of standard of achievement against whom to measure oneself. A 34-year-old black man who had been a three-sport star in high school said:

> My uncles—my Uncle Harold went to the Detroit Tigers, played pro ball—all of 'em, everybody played sports, so I wanted to be better than anybody else. I knew that everybody in this town knew them—their names were something. I wanted my name to be just like theirs.

Similarly, a black 41-year-old former professional football player recalled:

> I was the younger of three brothers and everybody played sports, so consequently I was more or less forced into it. 'Cause one brother was always better than the next brother and then I came along and had to show them that I was just as good as them. My oldest brother was an all-city ballplayer, then my other brother comes along he's all-city and all-state, and then I have to come along.

For some, attempting to emulate or surpass the athletic accomplishments of older male family members created pressures that were difficult to deal with. A 33-year-old white man explained that he was a good athlete during boyhood, but the constant awareness that his two older brothers had been better made it difficult for him to feel good about himself, or to have fun in sports:

> I had this sort of reputation that I followed from the playgrounds through grade school, and through high school. I followed these guys who were all-conference and all-state.

Most of these men, however, saw their relationships with their athletic older brothers and uncles in a positive light; it was within these relationships that they gained experience and developed motivations that gave them a competitive "edge" within their same-aged peer group. As a 33-year-old black man describes his earliest athletic experiences:

My brothers were role models. I wanted to prove—especially to my brothers—that I had heart, you know, that I was a man.

When asked, "What did it mean to you to be 'a man' at that age?" he replied:

Well, it meant that I didn't want to be a so-called scaredy-cat. You want to hit a guy even though he's bigger than you to show that, you know, you've got this macho image. I remember that at that young an age, that feeling was exciting to me. And that carried over, and as I got older, I got better and I began to look around me and see, well hey! I'm competitive with these guys, even though I'm younger, you know? And then of course all the compliments come— and I began to notice a change, even in my parents—especially in my father—he was proud of that, and that was very important to me. He was extremely important . . . he showed me more affection, now that I think of it.

As this man's words suggest, if men talk of their older brothers and uncles mostly as role models, teachers, and "names" to emulate, their talk of their relationships with their fathers is more deeply layered and complex. Athletic skills and competition for status may often be learned from older brothers, but it is in boys' relationships with fathers that we find many of the keys to the emotional salience of sports in the development of masculine identity.

Relationships with Fathers

The fact that boys' introductions to organized sports are often made by fathers who might otherwise be absent or emotionally distant adds a powerful emotional charge to these early experiences (Osherson 1986). Although playing organized sports eventually came to feel "natural" for all of the men interviewed in this study, many needed to be "exposed" to sports, or even gently "pushed" by their fathers to become involved in activities like Little League baseball. A white, 33-year-old man explained:

I still remember it like it was yesterday—Dad and I driving up in his truck, and I had my glove and my hat and all that—and I said, "Dad, I don't want to do it." He says, "What?" I says, "I don't want to do it." I was nervous. That I might fail. And he says, "Don't be silly. Lookit: There's Joey and Petey and all your friends out there." And so Dad says, "You're gonna do it, come on." And in my memory he's never said that about anything else; he just knew I needed a little kick in the pants and I'd do it. And once you're out there and you see all the other kids making errors and stuff, and you know you're better than those guys, you know: Maybe I *do* belong here. As it turned out, Little League was a good experience.

Some who were similarly "pushed" by their fathers were not so successful as the aforementioned man had been in Little League baseball, and thus the experience was not altogether a joyous affair. One 34-year-old white man, for instance, said he "inherited" his interest in sports from his father, who started playing catch with him at the age of four. Once he got into Little League, he felt pressured by his father, one of the coaches, who expected him to be the star of the team:

I'd go 0-for-four sometimes, strike out three times in a Little League game, and I'd dread the ride home. I'd come home and he'd say, "Go in the bathroom and swing the bat in the mirror for an hour," to get my swing level . . . It didn't help much, though, I'd go out and strike out three or four times again the next game too [laughs ironically].

When asked if he had been concerned with having his father's approval, he responded:

Failure in his eyes? Yeah, I always thought that he wanted me to get some kind of [athletic] scholarship. I guess I was afraid of him when I was a kid. He didn't hit that much, but he had a rage about him—he'd rage, and that voice would just rattle you.

Similarly, a 24-year-old black man described his awe of his father's physical power and presence, and his sense of inadequacy in attempting to emulate him:

> My father had a voice that sounded like rolling thunder. Whether it was intentional on his part or not, I don't know, but my father gave me a sense, an image of him being the most powerful being on earth, and that no matter what I ever did I would never come close to him . . . There were definite feelings of physical inadequacy that I couldn't work around.

It is interesting to note how these feelings of physical inadequacy relative to the father lived on as part of this young man's permanent internalized image. He eventually became a "feared" high school football player and broke school records in weight-lifting, yet,

> As I grew older, my mother and friends told me that I had actually grown to be a larger man than my father. Even though in time I required larger clothes than he, which should have been a very concrete indication, neither my brother nor I could ever bring ourselves to say that I was bigger. We simply couldn't conceive of it.

Using sports activities as a means of identifying with and "living up to" the power and status of one's father was not always such a painful and difficult task for the men I interviewed. Most did not describe fathers who "pushed" them to become sports stars. The relationship between their athletic strivings and their identification with their fathers was more subtle. A 48-year-old black man, for instance, explained that he was not pushed into sports by his father, but was aware from an early age of the community status his father had gained through sports. He saw his own athletic accomplishments as a way to connect with and emulate his father:

> I wanted to play baseball because my father had been quite a good baseball player in the Negro leagues before baseball was integrated, and so

he was kind of a model for me. I remember, quite young, going to a baseball game he was in—this was before the war and all—I remember being in the stands with my mother and seeing him on first base, and being aware of the crowd . . . I was aware of people's confidence in him as a serious baseball player. I don't think my father ever said anything to me like "play sports" . . . [But] I knew he would like it if I did well. His admiration was important . . . he mattered.

Similarly, a 24-year-old white man described his father as a somewhat distant "role model" whose approval mattered:

> My father was more of an example . . . he definitely was very much in touch with and still had very fond memories of being an athlete and talked about it, bragged about it. . . . But he really didn't do that much to teach me skills, and he didn't always go to every game I played like some parents. But he approved and that was important, you know. That was important to get his approval. I always knew that playing sports was important to him, so I knew implicitly that it was good and there was definitely a value on it.

First experiences in sports might often come through relationships with brothers or older male relatives, and the early emotional salience of sports was often directly related to a boy's relationship with his father. The sense of commitment that these young boys eventually made to the development of athletic careers is best explained as a process of development of masculine gender identity and status in relation to same-sex peers.

Masculine Identity and Early Commitment to Sports

When many of the men in this study said that during childhood they played sports because "it's just what everybody did," they of course meant that it was just what *boys* did. They were introduced to organized sports by older brothers and fathers, and once involved, found themselves playing within an exclusively male world. Though the separate (and unequal) gendered worlds of boys and girls came to appear as "natural," they were in fact socially constructed. Thorne's observations of children's activities in schools indicated that rather than "naturally" constituting "separate gendered cultures," there is considerable interaction between boys and girls in classrooms and on playgrounds. When adults set up legitimate contact between boys and girls, Thorne observed, this usually results in "relaxed interactions." But when activities in the classroom or on the playground are presented to children as sex-segregated activities and gender is marked by teachers and other adults ("boys line up here, girls over there"), "gender boundaries are heightened, and mixed-sex interaction becomes an explicit arena of risk" (Thorne 1986; 70). Thus sex-segregated activities such as organized sports as structured by adults, provide the context in which gendered identities and separate "gendered cultures" develop and come to appear natural. For the boys in this study, it became "natural" to equate masculinity with competition, physical strength, and skills. Girls simply did not (could not, it was believed) participate in these activities.

Yet it is not simply the separation of children, by adults, into separate activities that explains why many boys came to feel such a strong connection with sports activities, while so few girls did. As I listened to men recall their earliest experiences in organized sports, I heard them talk of insecurity, loneliness, and especially a need to connect with other people as a primary motivation in their early sports strivings. As a 42-year-old white man stated, "The most important thing was just being out there with the rest of the guys—being friends." Another 32-year-old interviewee was born in Mexico and moved to the United States at a fairly young age. He never knew his father, and his mother died when he was only nine years old. Suddenly he felt rootless, and threw himself into sports. His initial motivations, however, do not appear to be based on a need to compete and win:

Actually, what I think sports did for me is it brought me into kind of an instant family. By being on a Little League team, or even just playing with all kinds of different kids in the neighborhood, it brought what I really wanted, which was some kind of closeness. It was just being there, and being friends.

Clearly, what these boys needed and craved was that which was most problematic for them: connection and unity with other people. But why do these young males find *organized sports* such an attractive context in which to establish "a kind of closeness" with others? Comparative observations of young boys' and girls' game-playing behaviors yield important insights into this question. Piaget (1965) and Lever (1976) both observed that girls tend to have more "pragmatic" and "flexible" orientations to the rules of games; they are more prone to make exceptions and innovations in the middle of a game in order to make the game more "fair." Boys, on the other hand, tend to have a more firm, even inflexible orientation to the rules of a game; to them, the rules are what protects any fairness. This difference, according to Gilligan (1982), is based on the fact that early developmental experiences have yielded deeply rooted differences between males' and females' developmental tasks, needs, and moral reasoning. Girls, who tend to define themselves primarily through connection with others, experience highly competitive situations (whether in organized sports or in other hierarchical institutions) as threats to relationships, and thus to their identities. For boys, the development of gender identity involves the construction of positional identities, where a sense of self is solidified through separation from others (Chodorow 1978). Yet feminist psychoanalytic theory has tended to oversimplify the internal lives of men (Lichterman 1986). Males do appear to develop positional identities, yet despite their fears of intimacy, they also retain a human need for closeness and unity with others. This ambivalence toward intimate relationships is a major thread running through masculine development throughout the life course. Here we can conceptualize what Craib (1987) calls the "elective affinity" between personality and social structure: For the boy who both seeks and fears attachment with others, the rule-bound structure of organized sports can promise to be a safe place in which to seek nonintimate attachment with others within a context that maintains clear boundaries, distance, and separation.

Competitive Structures and Conditional Self-Worth

Young boys may initially find that sports gives them the opportunity to experience "some kind of closeness" with others, but the structure of sports and athletic careers often undermines the possibility of boys learning to transcend their fears of intimacy, thus becoming able to develop truly close and intimate relationships with others (Kidd 1990; Messner 1987). The sports world is extremely hierarchical, and an incredible amount of importance is placed on winning, on "being number one." For instance, a few years ago I observed a basketball camp put on for boys by a professional basketball coach and his staff. The youngest boys, about eight years old (who could barely reach the basket with their shots) played a brief scrimmage. Afterwards, the coaches lined them up in a row in front of the older boys who were sitting in the grandstands. One by one, the coach would stand behind each boy, put his hand on the boy's head (much in the manner of a priestly benediction), and the older boys in the stands would applaud and cheer, louder or softer, depending on how well or poorly the young boy was judged to have performed. The two or three boys who were clearly the exceptional players looked confident that they would receive the praise they were due. Most of the boys, though, had expressions ranging from puzzlement to thinly disguised terror on their faces as they awaited the judgments of the older boys.

This kind of experience teaches boys that it is not "just being out there with the guys—being friends," that ensures the kind of attention and connection that they crave; it is being *better* than the other guys—*beating* them—that is the key to

acceptance. Most of the boys in this study did have some early successes in sports, and thus their ambivalent need for connection with others was met, at least for a time. But the institution of sport tends to encourage the development of what Schafer (1975) has called "conditional self-worth" in boys. As boys become aware that acceptance by others is contingent upon being good—a "winner"—narrow definitions of success, based upon performance and winning become increasingly important to them. A 33-year-old black man said that by the time he was in his early teens:

> It was expected of me to do well in all my contests—I mean by my coaches, my peers, and my family. So I in turn expected to do well, and if I didn't do well, then I'd be very disappointed.

The man from Mexico, discussed above, who said that he had sought "some kind of closeness" in his early sports experiences began to notice in his early teens that if he played well, was a *winner*, he would get attention from others:

> It got to the point where I started realizing, noticing that people were always there for me, backing me all the time—sports got to be really fun because I always had some people there backing me. Finally my oldest brother started going to all my games, even though I had never really seen who he was [laughs]—after the game, you know, we never really saw each other, but he was at all my baseball games, and it seemed like we shared a kind of closeness there, but only in those situations. Off the field, when I wasn't in uniform, he was never around.

By high school, he said, he felt "up against the wall." Sports hadn't delivered what he had hoped it would, but he thought if he just tried harder, won one more championship trophy, he would get the attention he truly craved. Despite his efforts, this attention was not forthcoming. And, sadly, the pressures he had put on himself to excel in sports had taken most of the fun out of playing.

For many of the men in this study, throughout boyhood and into adolescence, this conscious striving for successful achievement became the primary means through which they sought connection with other people (Messner 1987). But it is important to recognize that young males' internalized ambivalences about intimacy do not fully determine the contours and directions of their lives. Masculinity continues to develop through interaction with the social world—and because boys from different backgrounds are interacting with substantially different familial, educational, and other institutions, these differences will lead them to make different choices and define situations in different ways. Next, I examine the differences in the ways that boys from higher- and lower-status families and communities related to organized sports.

Status Differences and Commitments to Sports

In discussing early attractions to sports, the experiences of boys from higher- and lower-status backgrounds are quite similar. Both groups indicate the importance of fathers and older brothers in introducing them to sports. Both groups speak of the joys of receiving attention and acceptance among family and peers for early successes in sports. Note the similarities, for instance, in the following descriptions of boyhood athletic experiences of two men. First, a man born in a white, middle-class family:

> I loved playing sports so much from a very early age because of early exposure. A lot of the sports came easy at an early age, and because they did, and because you were successful at something, I think that you're inclined to strive for that gratification. It's like, if you're good, you like it, because it's instant gratification. I'm doing something that I'm good at and I'm gonna keep doing it.

Second, a black man from a poor family:

> Fortunately I had some athletic ability, and, quite naturally, once you start doing good in whatever it is—I don't care if it's jacks—you show off what you do. That's your ability,

that's your blessing, so you show it off as much as you can.

For boys from both groups, early exposure to sports, the discovery that they had some "ability," shortly followed by some sort of family, peer, and community recognition, all eventually led to the commitment of hundreds and thousands of hours of playing, practicing, and dreaming of future stardom. Despite these similarities, there are also some identifiable differences that begin to explain the tendency of males from lower-status backgrounds to develop higher levels of commitment to sports careers. The most clear-cut difference was that while men from higher-status backgrounds are likely to describe their earliest athletic experiences and motivations almost exclusively in terms of immediate family, men from lower-status backgrounds more commonly describe the importance of a broader community context. For instance, a 46-year-old man who grew up in a "poor working class" black family in a small town in Arkansas explained:

> In that community, at the age of third or fourth grade, if you're a male, they expect you to show some kind of inclination, some kind of skill in football or basketball. It was an expected thing, you know? My mom and my dad, they didn't push at all. It was the general environment.

A 48-year-old man describes sports activities as a survival strategy in his poor black community:

> Sports protected me from having to compete in gang stuff, or having to be good with my fists. If you were an athlete and got into the fist world, that was your business, and that was okay—but you didn't have to if you didn't want to. People would generally defer to you, give you your space away from trouble.

A 35-year-old man who grew up in "a poor black ghetto" described his boyhood relationship to sports similarly:

> Where I came from, either you were one of two things: you were in sports or you were out on the streets being a drug addict, or breaking into places. The guys who were in sports, we had it

a little easier, because we were accepted by both groups. . . . So it worked out to my advantage, cause I didn't get into a lot of trouble—some trouble, but not a lot.

The fact that boys in lower-status communities faced these kinds of realities gave salience to their developing athletic identities. In contrast, sports were important to boys from higher-status backgrounds, yet the middle-class environment seemed more secure, less threatening, and offered far more options. By the time most of these boys got into junior high or high school, many had made conscious decisions to shift their attentions away from athletic careers to educational and (nonathletic) career goals. A 32-year-old white college athletic director told me that he had seen his chance to pursue a pro baseball career as "pissing in the wind," and instead, focused on education. Similarly, a 33-year-old white dentist who was a three-sport star in high school, decided not to play sports in college, so he could focus on getting into dental school. As he put it,

> I think I kind of downgraded the stardom thing. I thought it was small potatoes. And sure, that's nice in high school and all that, but on a broad scale, I didn't think it amounted to all that much.

This statement offers an important key to understanding the construction of masculine identity within a middle-class context. The status that this boy got through sports had been *very* important to him, yet he could see that "on a broad scale," this sort of status was "small potatoes." This sort of early recognition is more than a result of the oft-noted middle-class tendency to raise "future-oriented" children (Rubin 1976; Sennett and Cobb 1973). Perhaps more important, it is that the *kinds* of future orientations developed by boys from higher-status backgrounds are consistent with the middle-class context. These men's descriptions of their boyhoods reveal that they grew up immersed in a wide range of institutional frameworks, of which organized sports was just one. And—importantly—they could see that the

status of adult males around them was clearly linked to their positions within various professions, public institutions, and bureaucratic organizations. It was clear that access to this sort of institutional status came through educational achievement, not athletic prowess. A 32-year-old black man who grew up in a professional-class family recalled that he had idolized Wilt Chamberlain and dreamed of being a pro basketball player, yet his father discouraged his athletic strivings:

> He knew I liked the game. I *loved* the game. But basketball was not recommended; my dad would say, "That's a stereotyped image for black youth. . . . When your basketball is gone and finished, what are you gonna do? One day, you might get injured. What are you gonna look forward to?" He stressed education.

Similarly, a 32-year-old man who was raised in a white, middle-class family, had found in sports a key means of gaining acceptance and connection in his peer group. Yet he was simultaneously developing an image of himself as a "smart student," and becoming aware of a wide range of nonsports life options:

> My mother was constantly telling me how smart I was, how good I was, what a nice person I was, and giving me all sorts of positive strokes, and those positive strokes became a self-motivating kind of thing. I had this image of myself as smart, and I lived up to that image.

It is not that parents of boys in lower-status families did not also encourage their boys to work hard in school. Several reported that their parents "stressed books first, sports second." It's just that the broader social context—education, economy, and community—was more likely to *narrow* lower-status boys' perceptions of real-life options, while boys from higher-status backgrounds faced an expanding world of options. For instance, with a different socioeconomic background, one 35-year-old black man might have become a great musician instead of a star professional football running back. But he did not. When he was a child, he said, he was most interested in music:

> I wanted to be a drummer. But we couldn't afford drums. My dad couldn't go out and buy me a drum set or a guitar even—it was just one of those things; he was just trying to make ends meet.

But he *could* afford, as could so many in his socioeconomic condition, to spend countless hours at the local park, where he was told by the park supervisor

> that I was a natural—not only in gymnastics or baseball—whatever I did, I was a natural. He told me I shouldn't waste this talent, and so I immediately started watching the big guys then.

In retrospect, this man had potential to be a musician or any number of things, but his environment limited his options to sports, and he made the best of it. Even within sports, he, like most boys in the ghetto, was limited:

> We didn't have any tennis courts in the ghetto—we used to have a lot of tennis balls, but no racquets. I wonder today how good I might be in tennis if I had gotten a racquet in my hands at an early age.

It is within this limited structure of opportunity that many lower-status young boys found sports to be *the* place, rather than *a* place, within which to construct masculine identity, status, the relationships. A 36-year-old white man explained that his father left the family when he was very young and his mother faced a very difficult struggle to make ends meet. As his words suggest, the more limited a boy's options, and the more insecure his family situation, the more likely he is to make an early commitment to an athletic career:

> I used to ride my bicycle to Little League practice—if I'd waited for someone to pick me up and take me to the ball park I'd have never played. I'd get to the ball park and all the other kids would have their dad bring them to practice or games. But I'd park my bike to the side and when it was over I'd get on it and go home.

Sports was the way for me to move everything to the side—family problems, just all the embarrassments—and think about one thing, and that was sports . . . In the third grade, when the teacher went around the classroom and asked everybody, "What do you want to be when you grow up?," I said, "I want to be a major league baseball player," and everybody laughed their heads off.

This man eventually did enjoy a major league baseball career. Most boys from lower-status backgrounds who make similar early commitments to athletic careers are not so successful. As stated earlier, the career structure of organized sports is highly competitive and hierarchical. In fact, the chances of attaining professional status in sports are approximately 4:100,000 for a white man, 2:100,000 for a black man, and 3:1 million for a Hispanic man in the United States (Leonard and Reyman 1988). Nevertheless, the immediate rewards (fun, status, attention), along with the constricted (nonsports) structure of opportunity, attract disproportionately large numbers of boys from lower-status backgrounds to athletic careers as their major means of constructing a masculine identity. These are the boys who later, as young men, had to struggle with "conditional self-worth," and, more often than not, occupational dead ends. Boys from higher-status backgrounds, on the other hand, bolstered their boyhood, adolescent, and early adult status through their athletic accomplishments. Their wider range of experiences and life chances led to an early shift away from sports careers as the major basis of identity (Messner 1989).

Conclusion

The conception of the masculinity–sports relationship developed here begins to illustrate the idea of an "elective affinity" between social structure and personality. Organized sports is a "gendered institution"—an institution constructed by gender relations. As such, its structure and values (rules, formal organization, sex composition, etc.), reflect dominant conceptions of masculinity and femininity. Organized sports is also a "gendering institution"—an institution that helps to construct the current gender order. Part of this construction of gender is accomplished through the "masculinizing" of male bodies and minds.

Yet boys do not come to their first experiences in organized sports as "blank slates," but arrive with already "gendering" identities due to early developmental experiences and previous socialization. I have suggested here that an important thread running through the development of masculine identity is males' ambivalence toward intimate unity with others. Those boys who experience early athletic successes find in the structure of organized sport an affinity with this masculine ambivalence toward intimacy: The rule-bound, competitive, hierarchical world of sport offers boys an attractive means of establishing an emotionally distant (and thus "safe") connection with others. Yet as boys begin to define themselves as "athletes," they learn that in order to be accepted (to have connection) through sports, they must be winners. And in order to be winners, they must construct relationships with others (and with themselves) that are consistent with the competitive and hierarchical values and structure of the sports world. As a result, they often develop a "conditional self-worth" that leads them to construct more instrumental relationships with themselves and others. This ultimately exacerbates their difficulties in constructing intimate relationships with others. In effect, the interaction between the young male's preexisting internalized ambivalence toward intimacy with the competitive hierarchical institution of sport has resulted in the construction of a masculine personality that is characterized by instrumental rationality, goal-orientation, and difficulties with intimate connection and expression (Messner 1987).

This theoretical line of inquiry invites us not simply to examine how social institutions "socialize" boys, but also to explore the ways that boys' already-gendering identities interact with social institutions (which, like organized sport, are themselves the product of gender relations).

This study has also suggested that it is not some singular "masculinity" that is being constructed through athletic careers. It may be correct, from a psychoanalytic perspective, to suggest that all males bring ambivalences toward intimacy to their interactions with the world, but "the world" is a very different place for males from different racial and socioeconomic backgrounds. Because males have substantially different interactions with the world, based on class, race, and other differences and inequalities, we might expect the construction of masculinity to take on different meanings for boys and men from differing backgrounds (Messner 1989). Indeed, this study has suggested that boys from higher-status backgrounds face a much broader range of options than do their lower-status counterparts. As a result, athletic careers take on different meanings for these boys. Lower-status boys are likely to see athletic careers as *the* institutional context for the construction of their masculine status and identities, while higher-status males make an early shift away from athletic careers toward other institutions (usually education and nonsports careers). A key line of inquiry for future studies might begin by exploring this irony of sports careers: Despite the fact that "the athlete" is currently an example of an exemplary form of masculinity in public ideology, the vast majority of boys who become most committed to athletic careers are never well-rewarded for their efforts. The fact that class and racial dynamics lead boys from higher-status backgrounds, unlike their lower-status counterparts, to move into nonsports careers illustrates how the construction of different kinds of masculinities is a key component of the overall construction of the gender order.

References

Birrell, S. (1987) "The woman athlete's college experience: knowns and unknowns." *J. of Sport and Social Issues* 11: 82–96.

Benjamin, J. (1988) *The Bonds of Love: Psychoanalysis, Feminism, and the Problem of Domination.* New York: Pantheon.

Bryson, L. (1987) "Sport and the maintenance of masculine hegemony." Women's Studies International *Forum* 10: 349–360.

Chodorow, N. (1978) *The Reproduction of Mothering.* Berkeley: Univ. of California Press.

Connell, R. W. (1987) *Gender and Power.* Stanford, CA: Stanford Univ. Press.

Connell, R. W. (1990) "An iron man: the body and some contradictions of hegemonic masculinity." In M. A. Messner and D. F. Sabo (eds.) *Sport, Men and the Gender Order: Critical Feminist Perspectives.* Champaign, IL: Human Kinetics.

Craib, I. (1987) "Masculinity and male dominance." *Soc. Rev.* 38: 721–743.

Eitzen, D. S. (1975) "Athletics in the status system of male adolescents: a replication of Coleman's *The Adolescent Society.*" *Adolescence* 10: 268–276.

Gilligan, C. (1982) *In a Different Voice: Psychological Theory and Women's Development.* Cambridge, MA: Harvard Univ. Press.

Greendorfer, S. L. (1977) "The role of socializing agents in female sport involvement." *Research Q.* 48: 304–310.

Hall, M. A. (1988) "The discourse on gender and sport: from femininity to feminism." *Sociology of Sport J.* 5: 330–340.

Hantover, J. (1978) "The boy scouts and the validation of masculinity." *J. of Social Issues* 34: 184–195.

Haug, F. (1987) *Female Sexualization.* London: Verso.

Kidd, B. (1987) "Sports and masculinity," pp. 250–265 in M. Kaufman (ed.) *Beyond Patriarchy: Essays by Men on Pleasure, Power, and Change.* Toronto: Oxford Univ. Press.

Kidd, B. (1990) "The men's cultural centre: sports and the dynamic of women's oppression/men's repression," In M. A. Messner and D. F. Sabo (eds.) *Sport, Men and the Gender Order: Critical Feminist Perspectives.* Champaign, IL: Human Kinetics.

Kimmel, M. S. (1987) "Men's responses to feminism at the turn of the century." *Gender and Society* 1: 261–283.

Kimmel, M. S. (1990) "Baseball and the reconstitution of American masculinity: 1880–1920." In M. A. Messner and D. F. Sabo (eds.) *Sport, Men and the Gender Order: Critical Feminist Perspectives.* Champaign, IL: Human Kinetics.

Leonard, W. M. II and J. M. Reyman (1988) "The odds of attaining professional athlete status: refining the computations." *Sociology of Sport J.* 5: 162–169.

Lever, J. (1976) "Sex differences in the games children play." *Social Problems* 23: 478–487.

Levinson, D. J. et al. (1978) *The Seasons of a Man's Life.* New York: Ballantine.

Lichterman, P. (1986) "Chodorow's psychoanalytic sociology: a project half-completed." *California Sociologist* 9: 147–166.

Messner, M. (1987) "The meaning of success: the athletic experience and the development of male identity," pp. 193–210 in H. Brod (ed.) *The Making of Masculinities: The New Men's Studies.* Boston: Allen and Unwin.

Messner, M. (1988) "Sports and male domination: the female athlete as contested ideological terrain." *Sociology of Sport J.* 5: 197–211.

Messner, M. (1989) "Masculinities and athletic careers." *Gender and Society* 3: 71–88.

Oglesby, C. A. (Ed.) (1978) *Women and Sport: From Myth to Reality.* Philadelphia: Lea & Febiger.

Osherson, S. (1986) *Finding Our Fathers: How a Man's Life Is Shaped by His Relationship with His Father.* New York: Fawcett Columbine.

Piaget, J. H. (1965) *The Moral Judgment of the Child.* New York: Free Press.

Rubin, L. B. (1976) *Worlds of Pain: Life in the Working Class Family.* New York: Basic Books.

Sabo, D. (1985) "Sport, patriarchy and male identity: new questions about men and sport." *Arena Rev.* 9: 2.

Schafer, W. E. (1975) "Sport and male sex role socialization." *Sport Sociology Bull.* 4: 47–54.

Sennett, R. and J. Cobb (1973) *The Hidden Injuries of Class.* New York: Random House.

Theberge, N. (1981) "A critique of critiques: radical and feminist writings on sport." *Social Forces* 60: 2.

Thorne, B. (1986) "Girls and boys together . . . but mostly apart: gender arrangements in elementary schools," pp. 167–184 in W. W. Hartup and Z. Rubin (eds.) *Relationships and Development.* Hillsdale, NJ: Lawrence Erlbaum.

Twin, S. L. [ed.] (1978) *Out of the Bleachers: Writings on Women and Sport.* Old Westbury, NY: Feminist Press.

Geoffrey Canada

Learning to Fight

On Union Avenue, failure to fight would mean that you would be set upon over and over again. Sometimes for years. Later I would see what the older boys did to Butchie.

Butchie was a "manchild," very big for his age. At thirteen he was the size of a fully grown man. Butchie was a gentle giant. He loved to play with the younger boys and was not particularly athletic. Butchie had one flaw: he would not fight. Everyone picked on him. The older teenagers (fifteen and sixteen) were really hard on him. He was forever being punched in the midsection and chest by the older boys for no reason. (It was against the rules to punch in the face unless it was a "fair fight.")

I don't know what set the older boys off, or why they picked that Saturday morning, but it was decided that Butchie had to be taught a lesson. The older boys felt that Butchie was giving the block a bad reputation. Everyone had to be taught that we didn't tolerate cowards. Suddenly two of them grabbed Butchie. Knowing that something was wrong, that this was not the rough and tumble play we sometimes engaged in, Butchie broke away. Six of the older boys took off after him. Butchie zigzagged between the parked cars, trying desperately to make it to his building and the safety of his apartment. One of the boys cut him off and, kicking and yelling, Butchie was snagged.

By the time the other five boys caught up, Butchie was screaming for his mother. We knew that his mother often drank heavily on the week-

From *Fist Stick Knife Gun* by Geoffrey Canada. Copyright © 1995 by Geoffrey Canada. Adapted by permission of Beacon Press, Boston.

ends and were not surprised when her window did not open and no one came to his aid. One of the rules of the block was that you were not allowed to cry for your mother. Whatever happened you had to "take it like a man." A vicious punch to the stomach and a snarled command, "Shut the fuck up," and Butchie became quiet and stopped struggling. The boys marched him up the block, away from his apartment. Butchie, head bowed, hands held behind his back, looked like a captured prisoner.

There are about twelve of us younger boys out that morning playing football in the street. When the action started we stopped playing and prepared to escape to our individual apartment buildings. We didn't know if the older boys were after us, too—they were sometimes unpredictable—and we nervously kept one eye on them and one on a clear avenue of escape. As they marched Butchie down the block it became apparent that we were meant to learn from what was going to happen to Butchie, that they were really doing this for us.

The older boys took Butchie and "stretched" him. This was accomplished by four boys grabbing Butchie, one on each arm, one on each leg. Then they placed him on the trunk of a car (in the early 1960s the cars were all large) and pulled with all their might until Butchie was stretched out over the back of the car. When Butchie was completely, helplessly exposed, two of the boys began to punch him in his stomach and chest. The beating was savage. Butchie's cries for help seemed only to infuriate them more. I couldn't believe that a human body could take that amount of punishment. When they finished with him, Butchie just collapsed in the fetal position and cried. The older boys walked away talking, as if nothing had happened.

To those of us who watched, the lesson was brutal and unmistakable. No matter who you fought, he could never beat you *that* bad. So it was better to fight even if you couldn't win than to end up being "stretched" for being a coward. We all fought, some with more skill and determination than others, but we all fought.

The day my bother John went out to play on the block and had to fight Paul Henry there was plenty of wild swinging and a couple of blows landed, but they did no real damage. When no one got the better of the other after six or seven minutes, the fight was broken up. John and Paul Henry were made to shake hands and became best of friends in no time.

John was free. He could go outside without fear. I was still trapped. I needed help figuring out what would happen when I went outside. John was not much help to me about how the block worked. He was proud that he could go out and play while we were still stuck in the house. I mentioned something about going downstairs and having Ma come down to watch over me and John laughed at me, called me a baby. He had changed, he had accepted the rules—no getting mothers to fight your battles. His only instructions to me were to fight back, don't let the boys your age hit you without hitting back. Within a week I decided I just couldn't take it, and I went downstairs.

The moment I went outside I began to learn about the structure of the block and its codes of conduct. Each excursion taught me more. The first thing I learned was that John, even though he was just a year older than me, was in a different category than I was. John's peers had some status on the block; my peers were considered too young to have any.

At the top of the pecking order were the young adults in their late teens (seventeen, eighteen, and nineteen). They owned the block; they were the strongest and the toughest. Many of them belonged to a gang called the Disciples. Quite a few had been arrested as part of a police crack-

down on gangs in the late fifties and early sixties. Several came out of jail during my first few years on Union Avenue. They often spent large amounts of time in other areas of the Bronx, so they were really absentee rulers.

At this time there were some girls involved in gang activities as well; many of the larger male gangs had female counterparts whose members fought and intimidated other girls. On Union Avenue there was a group of older girls who demanded respect, and received it, from even the toughest boys on the block. Some of these girls were skilled fighters, and boys would say "she can fight like a boy" to indicate that a girl had mastered the more sophisticated techniques of fist-fighting. Girls on Union Avenue sometimes found themselves facing the same kind of violence as did boys, but this happened less often. All in all there was less pressure on girls to fight for status, although some did; for girls to fight there usually had to be a major triggering incident.

But status was a major issue for boys on the block. The next category in the pecking order was the one we all referred to as the "older boys," fifteen and sixteen years old. They belonged to a group we sometimes called the Young Disciples, and they were the real rulers of Union Avenue. This was the group that set the rules of conduct on the block and enforced law and order. They were the ones who had stretched Butchie.

Next were boys nine, ten, and eleven, just learning the rules. While they were allowed to go into the street and play, most of them were not allowed off the block without their mother's permission. My brother John belonged to this group.

The lowest group was those children who could not leave the sidewalk, children too young to have any status at all. I belonged to this group and I hated it. The sidewalk, while it provided plenty of opportunity to play with other children, seemed to me to be the sidelines. The real action happened in the street.

There were few expectations placed on us in terms of fighting, but we were not exempt. There was very little natural animosity among us. We played punchball, tag, and "red light, green light, one-two-three." It was the older boys who caused the problems. Invariably, when the older boys were sitting on the stoop and one of them had a brother, or cousin amongst us, it would be he who began the prelude to violence.

I'd been outside for more than a week and thought that I had escaped having to fight anyone because all the boys were my friends. But sure enough, Billy started in on me.

"David, can you beat Geoff?"

David looked at me, then back at Billy. "I don't know."

"What! You can't beat Geoff? I thought you was tough. You scared? I know you ain't scared. You betta not be scared."

I didn't like where this conversation was heading. David was my friend and I didn't know Billy, he was just an older boy who lived in my building. David looked at me again and this time his face changed, he looked threatening, he seemed angry.

"I ain't scared of him."

I was lost. Just ten minutes before David and I were playing, having a good time. Now he looked like I was his worst enemy. I became scared, scared of David, scared of Billy, scared of Union Avenue. I looked for help to the other boys sitting casually on the stoop. Their faces scared me more. Most of them barely noticed what was going on, the rest were looking half interested. I was most disheartened by the reaction of my brother John. Almost in a state of panic, I looked to him for help. He looked me directly in the eye, shook his head no, then barely perceptibly pointed his chin toward David as if to say, Quit stalling, you know what you have to do. Then he looked away as if this didn't concern him at all.

The other sidewalk boys were the only ones totally caught up in the drama. They knew that their day would also come, and they were trying to learn what they could about me in case they had to fight me tomorrow, or next week, or whenever.

During the time I was sizing up my situation I made a serious error. I showed on my face what was going on in my head. My fear and my con-

fusion were obvious to anyone paying attention. This, I would later learn, was a rookie mistake and could have deadly consequences on the streets.

Billy saw my panic and called to alert the others. "Look at Geoff, he's scared. He's scared of you, David. Go kick his ass."

It was not lost on me that the questioning part of this drama was over. Billy had given David a direct command. I thought I was saved, however, because Billy had cursed. My rationale was that no big boy could use curses at a little boy. My brother would surely step in now and say, "C'mon, Billy, you can't curse at my little brother. After all, he's only seven." Then he would take me upstairs and tell Ma.

When I looked at John again I saw only that his eyes urged me to act, implored me to act. There would be no rescue coming from him. What was worse, the other older boys had become interested when Billy yelled, "Kick his ass," and were now looking toward David and me. In their eyes this was just a little sport, not a real fight, but a momentary distraction that could prove to be slightly more interesting than talking about the Yankees, or the Giants, or their girlfriends. They smiled at my terror. Their smiles seemed to say, "I remember when I was like that. You'll see, it's not so bad."

Thinking on your feet is critical in the ghetto. There was so much to learn and so much of it was so important. It was my brother's reaction that clued me in. I knew John. He was a vicious tease at times, but he loved me. He would never allow me to be harmed and not help or at least go for help. He was telling me I had to go through this alone. I knew I could run upstairs, but what about tomorrow? Was I willing to become a prisoner in my apartment again? And what about how everyone was smiling at me? How was I ever going to play in the street with them if they thought I was such a baby? So I made the decision not to run but to fight.

I decided to maximize the benefits the situation afforded. I said, not quite with the conviction that I'd hoped for, "I'm not afraid of David. He can't beat me. C'mon. David, you wanna fight?"

There was only one problem—I didn't know how to fight. I hadn't seen Dan taking back John's coat, or John's fight with Paul Henry. But a funny thing happened after I challenged David. When I looked back at him, he didn't look quite so confident. He didn't look like he wanted to fight anymore. This gave me courage.

Billy taunted David, "You gonna let him talk to you like that? Go on, kick his ass."

Then Paul Henry chimed in, "Don't be scared, little Geoff. Go git him."

I was surprised. I didn't expect anyone to support me, especially not Paul Henry. But as I would learn later, most of these fights were viewed as sport by the bystanders. You rooted for the favorite or the underdog. Almost everyone had someone to root for them when they fought.

David put up his balled-up fists and said, "Come on." I didn't know how to fight, but I knew how to pretend fight. So I "put up my dukes" and stood like a boxer. We circled one another.

"Come on."

"No, *you* come on."

Luckily for me, David didn't know how to fight either. The older boys called out encouragement to us, but we didn't really know how to throw a punch. At one point we came close enough to one another for me to grab David, and we began to wrestle. I was good at this, having spent many an hour wrestling with my three brothers.

Wrestling wasn't allowed in a "real" fight, but they let us go at it a few moments before they broke us up. The older boys pronounced the fight a tie and made us shake hands and "be friends." They rubbed our heads and said, "You're all right," and then gave us some pointers on how to really fight. We both basked in the glory of their attention. The other sidewalk boys looked at us with envy. We had passed the first test. We were on our way to becoming respected members of Union Avenue.

David and I became good friends. Since we'd had a tie we didn't have to worry about any other older boys making us fight again. The rule was that if you fought an opponent, and could prove it by having witnesses, you didn't have to fight that person again at the command of the older boys. This was important, because everyone, and I mean everyone, had to prove he could beat other boys his age. Union Avenue, like most other inner-city neighborhoods, had a clear pecking order within the groups as well as between them when it came to violence. The order changed some as boys won or lost fights, but by and large the same boys remained at the top. New boys who came on the block had to be placed in the pecking order. If they had no credentials, no one to vouch for their ability, they had to fight different people on the block until it could be ascertained exactly where they fit in. If you refused to fight, you moved to the bottom of the order. If you fought and lost, your status still remained unclear until you'd won a fight. Then you'd be placed somewhere between the person you lost to and the person you beat.

The pecking order was important because it was used to resolve disputes that arose over games, or girls, or money, and also to maintain order and discipline on the block. Although we were not a gang, there were clear rules of conduct, and if you broke those rules there were clear consequences. The ranking system also prevented violence because it gave a way for boys to back down; if everybody knew you couldn't beat someone and you backed down, it was no big deal most of the time.

My "fight" with David placed me on top of the pecking order for boys on the sidewalk. I managed to get through the rest of the summer without having to fight anyone else. I had learned so much about how Union Avenue functioned that I figured I would soon know all I needed about how to survive on the block.

Ellen Jordan

Angela Cowan

Warrior Narratives in the Kindergarten Classroom: Renegotiating the Social Contract?

The "social contract" becomes part of the lived experience of little boys when they discover that the school forbids the warrior narratives through which they initially define masculinity and imposes a different, public sphere: masculinity of rationality and responsibility. They learn that these narratives are not to be lived but only experienced symbolically through fantasy and sport in the private sphere of desire. Little girls, whose gender-defining fantasies are not repressed by the school, have less lived awareness of the social contract.

Since the beginning of second wave feminism, the separation between the public (masculine) world of politics and the economy and the private (feminine) world of the family and personal life has been seen as highly significant in establishing gender difference and inequality (Eisenstein 1984). Twenty years of feminist research and speculation have refined our understanding of this divide and how it has been developed and reproduced. One particularly striking and influential account is that given by Carole Pateman in her book *The Sexual Contract* (1988).

Pateman's broad argument is that in the modern world, the world since the Enlightenment, a "civil society" has been established. In this civil

Author's Note: The research on which this article is based was funded by the Research Management Committee of the University of Newcastle. The observation was conducted at East Maitland Public School and the authors would like to thank the principal, teachers, and children involved for making our observer so welcome.

Ellen Jordan and Angela Cowan, *Gender & Society*, Vol. 9 No. 6, pp. 727–743, copyright © 1995 by Sage Publications. Reprinted by permission of Sage Publicatons, Inc.

society, patriarchy has been replaced by a fratriarchy, which is equally male and oppressive of women. Men now rule not as fathers but as brothers, able to compete with one another, but presenting a united front against those outside the group. It is the brothers who control the public world of the state, politics, and the economy. Women have been given token access to this world because the discourses of liberty and universalism made this difficult to refuse, but to take part they must conform to the rules established to suit the brothers.

This public world in which the brothers operate together is conceptualized as separate from the personal and emotional. One is a realm where there is little physicality—everything is done rationally, bureaucratically, according to contracts that the brothers accept as legitimate. Violence in this realm is severely controlled by agents of the state, except that the brothers are sometimes called upon for the supreme sacrifice of dying to preserve freedom. The social contract redefines the brawling and feuding long seen as essential characteristics of masculinity as deviant, even criminal, while the rest of physicality—sexuality, reproduction of the body, daily and intergenerationally—is left in the private sphere. Pateman quotes Robert Unger, "The dichotomy of the public and private life is still another corollary of the separation of understanding and desire. . . . When reasoning, [men] belong to a public world. . . . When desiring, however, men are private beings" (Pateman 1989, 48).

This is now widely accepted as the way men understand and experience their world. On the other hand, almost no attempt has been made to look at how it is that they take these views on board, or why the public/private divide is so much more deeply entrenched in their lived experience than in women's. This article looks at one strand in the complex web of experiences through which this is achieved. A major site where this occurs is the school, one of the institutions particularly characteristic of the civil society that emerged with the Enlightenment (Foucault 1980, 55–7). The school does not deliberately condition boys and not girls into this dichotomy, but it is, we believe, a site where what Giddens (1984, 10–3) has called a cycle of practice introduces little boys to the public/private division.

The article is based on weekly observations in a kindergarten classroom. We examine what happens in the early days of school when the children encounter the expectations of the school with their already established conceptions of gender. The early months of school are a period when a great deal of negotiating between the children's personal agendas and the teacher's expectations has to take place, where a great deal of what Genovese (1972) has described as accommodation and resistance must be involved.

In this article, we focus on a particular contest, which, although never specifically stated, is central to the children's accommodation to school: little boys' determination to explore certain narratives of masculinity with which they are already familiar—guns, fighting, fast cars— and the teacher's attempts to outlaw their importation into the classroom setting. We argue that what occurs is a contest between two definitions of masculinity: what we have chosen to call "warrior narratives" and the discourses of civil society—rationality, responsibility, and decorum— that are the basis of school discipline.

By "warrior narratives," we mean narratives that assume that violence is legitimate and justified when it occurs within a struggle between good and evil. There is a tradition of such narratives, stretching from Hercules and Beowulf to Superman and Dirty Harry, where the male is depicted as the warrior, the knight-errant, the superhero, the good guy (usually called a "goody" by Australian children), often supported by brothers in arms, and always opposed to some evil figure, such as a monster, a giant, a villain, a criminal, or, very simply, in Australian parlance, a "baddy." There is also a connection, it is now often suggested, between these narratives and the activity that has come to epitomize the physical expression of masculinity in the modern era: sport (Crosset 1990; Duthie 1980, 91–4; Messner 1992, 15). It is as sport that the physicality and desire usually lived out in the private sphere are permitted a ritualized public presence. Even though the violence once characteristic of the warrior has, in civil society and as part of the social contract, become the prerogative of the state, it can still be re-enacted symbolically in countless sporting encounters. The mantle of the warrior is inherited by the sportsman.

The school discipline that seeks to outlaw these narratives is, we would suggest, very much a product of modernity. Bowles and Gintis have argued that "the structure of social relations in education not only inures the student to the discipline of the work place, but develops the types of personal demeanor, modes of self-presentation, self-image, and social-class identifications which are the crucial ingredients of job adequacy" (1976, 131). The school is seeking to introduce the children to the behavior appropriate to the civil society of the modern world.

An accommodation does eventually take place, this article argues, through a recognition of the split between the public and the private. Most boys learn to accept that the way to power and respectability is through acceptance of the conventions of civil society. They also learn that warrior narratives are not a part of this world; they can only be experienced symbolically as fantasy or sport. The outcome, we will suggest, is that little boys learn that these narratives must be left behind in the private world of desire when they participate in the public world of reason.

The Study

The school where this study was conducted serves an old-established suburb in a country town in New South Wales, Australia. The children are predominantly Australian born and English speaking, but come from socioeconomic backgrounds ranging from professional to welfare recipient. We carried out this research in a classroom run by a teacher who is widely acknowledged as one of the finest and most successful kindergarten teachers in our region. She is an admired practitioner of free play, process writing, and creativity. There was no gender definition of games in her classroom. Groups composed of both girls and boys had turns at playing in the Doll Corner, in the Construction Area, and on the Car Mat.

The research method used was nonparticipant observation, the classic mode for the sociological study of children in schools (Burgess 1984; Goodenough 1987; Thorne 1986). The group of children described came to school for the first time in February 1993. The observation sessions began within a fortnight of the children entering school and were conducted during "free activity" time, a period lasting for about an hour. At first we observed twice a week, but then settled to a weekly visit, although there were some weeks when it was inconvenient for the teacher to accommodate an observer.

The observation was noninteractive. The observer stationed herself as unobtrusively as possible, usually seated on a kindergarten-sized chair, near one of the play stations. She made pencil notes of events, with particular attention to accurately recording the words spoken by the children,

and wrote up detailed narratives from the notes, supplemented by memory, on reaching home. She discouraged attention from the children by rising and leaving the area if she was drawn by them into any interaction.

This project thus employed a methodology that was ethnographic and open-ended. It was nevertheless guided by certain theories, drawn from the work on gender of Jean Anyon, Barrie Thorne, and R. W. Connell, of the nature of social interaction and its part in creating personal identity and in reproducing the structures of a society.

Anyon has adapted the conceptions of accommodation and resistance developed by Genovese (1972) to understanding how women live with gender. Genovese argued that slaves in the American South accommodated to their contradictory situation by using certain of its aspects, for example, exposure to the Christian religion, to validate a sense of self-worth and dignity. Christian beliefs then allowed them to take a critical view of slavery, which in turn legitimated certain forms of resistance (Anyon 1983, 21). Anyon lists a variety of ways in which women accommodate to and resist prescriptions of appropriate feminine behavior, arguing for a significant level of choice and agency (Anyon 1983, 23–6).

Thorne argues that the processes of social life, the form and nature of the interactions, as well as the choices of the actors, should be the object of analysis. She writes, "In this book I begin not with individuals, although they certainly appear in the account, but with *group life*—with social relations, the organization and meanings of social situations, the collective practices through which children and adults create and recreate gender in their daily interactions" (1993, 4).

These daily interactions, Connell (1987, 139–41) has suggested, mesh to form what Giddens (1984, 10–3) has called "cyclical practices." Daily interactions are neither random nor specific to particular locations. They are repeated and recreated in similar settings throughout a society. Similar needs recur, similar discourses are available, and so similar solutions to problems are adopted; thus, actions performed and discourses adopted to achieve particular ends in particular situations have the unintended consequence of producing uniformities of gendered behavior in individuals.

In looking at the patterns of accommodation and resistance that emerge when the warrior narratives that little boys have adapted from television encounter the discipline of the classroom, we believe we have uncovered one of the cyclical practices of modernity that reveal the social contract to these boys.

Warrior Narratives in the Doll Corner

In the first weeks of the children's school experience, the Doll Corner was the area where the most elaborate acting out of warrior narratives was observed. The Doll Corner in this classroom was a small room with a door with a glass panel opening off the main area. Its furnishings—stove, sink, dolls' cots, and so on—were an attempt at a literal re-creation of a domestic setting, revealing the school's definition of children's play as a preparation for adult life. It was an area where the acting out of "pretend" games was acceptable.

Much of the boys' play in the area was domestic:

> Jimmy and Tyler were jointly ironing a tablecloth. "Look at the sheet is burnt, I've burnt it," declared Tyler, waving the toy iron above his head. "I'm telling Mrs. Sandison," said Jimmy worriedly. "No, I tricked you. It's not really burnt. See," explained Tyler, showing Jimmy the black pattern on the cloth. (February 23, 1993)

> "Where is the baby, the baby boy?" Justin asked, as he helped Harvey and Malcolm settle some restless teddy babies. "Give them some potion." Justin pretended to force feed a teddy, asking "Do you want to drink this potion?" (March 4, 1993)

On the other hand, there were attempts from the beginning by some of the boys and one of the girls to use this area for nondomestic games and, in the case of the boys, for games based on warrior narratives, involving fighting, destruction, goodies, and baddies.

> The play started off quietly, Winston cuddled a teddy bear, then settled it in a bed. Just as Winston tucked in his bear, Mac snatched the teddy out of bed and swung it around his head in circles. "Don't hurt him, give him back," pleaded Winston, trying vainly to retrieve the teddy. The two boys were circling the small table in the center of the room. As he ran, Mac started to karate chop the teddy on the arm, and then threw it on the floor and jumped on it. He then snatched up a plastic knife, "This is a sword. Ted is dead. They all are." He sliced the knife across the teddy's tummy, repeating the action on the bodies of two stuffed dogs. Winston grabbed the two dogs, and with a dog in each hand, staged a dog fight. "They are alive again." (February 10, 1993)

> Three boys were busily stuffing teddies into the cupboard through the sink opening. "They're in jail. They can't escape," said Malcolm. "Let's pour water over them." "Don't do that. It'll hurt them," shouted Winston, rushing into the Doll Corner. "Go away, Winston. You're not in our group," said Malcolm. (February 12, 1993)

The boys even imported goodies and baddies into a classic ghost scenario initiated by one of the girls:

> "I'm the father," Tyler declared. "I'm the mother," said Alanna. "Let's pretend it's a stormy night and I'm afraid. Let's pretend a ghost has come to steal the dog." Tyler nodded and placed the sheet over his head. Tyler moaned, "ooooOOOOOOOAHHHH!!!" and moved his outstretched arms toward Alanna. Jamie joined the game and grabbed a sheet from the doll's cradle, "I'm the goody ghost." "So am I," said Tyler. They giggled and wrestled each other to the floor. "No! you're the baddy ghost," said Jamie. Meanwhile, Alanna was making ghostly noises and moving around the boys. "Did you like the game? Let's play it again," she suggested. (February 23, 1993)

In the first two incidents, there was some conflict between the narratives being invoked by Winston and those used by the other boys. For

Winston, the stuffed toys were the weak whom he must protect knight-errant style. For the other boys, they could be set up as the baddies whom it was legitimate for the hero to attack. Both were versions of a warrior narrative.

The gender difference in the use of these narratives has been noted by a number of observers (Clark 1989, 250–2; Paley 1984; Thorne 1993, 98–9). Whereas even the most timid, least physically aggressive boys—Winston in this study is typical—are drawn to identifying with the heroes of these narratives, girls show almost no interest in them at this early age. The strong-willed and assertive girls in our study, as in others (Clark 1990, 83–4; Walkerdine 1990, 10–2), sought power by commandeering the role of mother, teacher, or shopkeeper, while even the highly imaginative Alanna, although she enlivened the more mundane fantasies of the other children with ghosts, old widow women, and magical mirrors, seems not to have been attracted by warrior heroes.[1]

Warrior narratives, it would seem, have a powerful attraction for little boys, which they lack for little girls. Why and how this occurs remains unexplored in early childhood research, perhaps because data for such an explanation are not available to those doing research in institutional settings. Those undertaking ethnographic research in preschools find the warrior narratives already in possession in these sites (Davies 1989, 91–2; Paley 1984, 70–3, 116). In this research, gender difference in the appeal of warrior narratives has to be taken as a given—the data gathered are not suitable for constructing theories of origins; thus, the task of determining an explanation would seem to lie within the province of those investigating and theorizing gender differentiation during infancy, and perhaps, specifically, of those working in the tradition of feminist psychoanalysis pioneered by Dinnerstein (1977) and Chodorow (1978). Nevertheless, even though the cause may remain obscure, there can be little argument that in the English-speaking world for at least the last hundred years—think of Tom Sawyer playing Robin Hood and the pirates and Indians in J. M.

Barrie's *Peter Pan*—boys have built these narratives into their conceptions of the masculine.

Accommodation Through *Bricolage*

The school classroom, even one as committed to freedom and self-actualization as this, makes little provision for the enactment of these narratives. The classroom equipment invites children to play house, farm, and shop, to construct cities and roads, and to journey through them with toy cars, but there is no overt invitation to explore warrior narratives.

In the first few weeks of school, the little boys un-self-consciously set about redressing this omission. The method they used was what is known as *bricolage*—the transformation of objects from one use to another for symbolic purposes (Hebdige 1979, 103). The first site was the Doll Corner. Our records for the early weeks contain a number of examples of boys rejecting the usages ascribed to the various Doll Corner objects by the teacher and by the makers of equipment and assigning a different meaning to them. This became evident very early with their use of the toy baby carriages (called "prams" in Australia). For the girls, the baby carriages were just that, but for many of the boys they very quickly became surrogate cars:

> Mac threw a doll into the largest pram in the Doll Corner. He walked the pram out past a group of his friends who were playing "crashes" on the Car Mat. Three of the five boys turned and watched him wheeling the pram toward the classroom door. Mac performed a sharp three-point turn; raced his pram past the Car Mat group, striking one boy on the head with the pram wheel. (February 10, 1993)
>
> "Brrrrmmmmmm, brrrrrmmmmmm," Tyler's revving engine noises grew louder as he rocked the pram back and forth with sharp jerking movements. The engine noise grew quieter as he left the Doll Corner and wheeled the pram around the classroom. He started to run with the pram when the teacher could not observe him. (March 23, 1993)

The boys transformed other objects into masculine appurtenances: knives and tongs became weapons, the dolls' beds became boats, and so on.

Mac tried to engage Winston in a sword fight using Doll Corner plastic knives. Winston backed away, but Mac persisted. Winston took a knife but continued to back away from Mac. He then put down the knife, and ran away half-screaming (semi-seriously, unsure of the situation) for his teacher. (February 10, 1993)

In the literature on youth subcultures, bricolage is seen as a characteristic of modes of resistance. Hebdige writes:

It is through the distinctive rituals of consumption, through style, that the subculture at once reveals its "secret" identity and communicates its forbidden meanings. It is predominantly the way commodities are *used* in subculture which mark the subculture off from more orthodox cultural formations. . . . The concept of *bricolage* can be used to explain how subcultural styles are constructed. (1979, 103)

In these early weeks, however, the boys did not appear to be aware that they were doing anything more than establishing an accommodation between their needs and the classroom environment.

This mode of accommodation was rejected by the teacher, however, who practiced a gentle, but steady, discouragement of such bricolage. Even though the objects in this space are not really irons, beds, and cooking pots, she made strong efforts to assert their cultural meaning, instructing the children in the "proper" use of the equipment and attempting to control their behavior by questions like "Would you do that with a tea towel in your house?" "Cats never climb up on the benches in *my* house." It was thus impressed upon the children that warrior narratives were inappropriate in this space.

The children, our observations suggest, accepted her guidance, and we found no importation of warrior narratives into the Doll Corner after the first few weeks. There were a number of elaborate and exciting narratives devised, but they

were all to some degree related to the domestic environment. For example, on April 20, Justin and Nigel used one of the baby carriages as a four-wheel drive, packed it with equipment and went off for a camping trip, setting out a picnic with Doll Corner tablecloths, knives, forks, and plates when they arrived. On May 18, Matthew, Malcolm, Nigel, and Jonathan were dogs being fed in the Doll Corner. They then complained of the flies, and Jonathan picked up the toy telephone and said, "Flycatcher! Flycatcher! Come and catch some flies. They are everywhere." On June 1, the following was recorded:

"We don't want our nappies [diapers] changed," Aaron informed Celia, the mum in the game. "I'm pooing all over your clothes mum," Mac declared, as he grunted and positioned himself over the dress-up box. Celia cast a despairing glance in Mac's direction, and went on dressing a doll. "I am too; poohing all over your clothes mum," said Aaron. "Now mum will have to clean it all up and change my nappy," he informed Mac, giggling. He turned to the dad [Nigel], and said in a baby voice, "Goo-goo; give him [Mac] the feather duster." "No! give him the feather duster; he did the longest one all over the clothes," Mac said to Nigel. (June 1, 1993)

Although exciting and imaginative games continued, the bricolage virtually disappeared from the Doll Corner. The intention of the designer of the Doll Corner equipment was increasingly respected. Food for the camping trip was bought from the shop the teacher had set up and consumed using the Doll Corner equipment. The space invaded by flies was a domestic space, and appropriate means, calling in expert help by telephone, were used to deal with the problem. Chairs and tables were chairs and tables, clothes were clothes and could be fouled by appropriate inhabitants of a domestic space, babies. Only the baby carriages continued to have an ambiguous status, to maintain the ability to be transformed into vehicles of other kinds.

The warrior narratives—sword play, baddies in jail, pirates, and so on—did not vanish from the boys' imaginative world, but, as the later observations show, the site gradually moved from the Doll Corner to the Construction Area and the Car Mat. By the third week in March (that is, after about six weeks at school), the observer noticed the boys consistently using the construction toys to develop these narratives. The bricolage was now restricted to the more amorphously defined construction materials.

> Tyler was busy constructing an object out of five pieces of plastic straw (clever sticks). "This is a water pistol. Everyone's gonna get wet," he cried as he moved into the Doll Corner pretending to wet people. The game shifted to guns and bullets between Tyler and two other boys. "I've got a bigger gun," Roger said, showing off his square block object. "Mine's more longer. Ehehehehehehehe, got you," Winston yelled to Roger, brandishing a plastic straw gun. "I'll kill your gun," Mac said, pushing Winston's gun away. "No Mac. You broke it. No," cried Winston. (March 23, 1993)
>
> Two of the boys picked up swords made out of blue- and red-colored plastic squares they had displayed on the cupboard. "This is my sword," Jamie explained to Tyler. "My jumper [sweater] holds it in. Whichever color is at the bottom, well that's the color it shoots out. Whoever is bad, we shoot with power out of it." "Come on Tyler," he went on. "Get your sword. Let's go get some baddies." (March 30, 1993)

The toy cars on the Car Mat were also pressed into the service of warrior narratives:

> Justin, Brendan, and Jonathan were busy on the Car Mat. The game involved police cars that were chasing baddies who had drunk "too much beers." Justin explained to Jonathan why his car had the word "DOG" written on the front. "These are different police cars, for catching robbers taking money." (March 4, 1993)
>
> Three boys, Harvey, Maurice, and Marshall, were on the Car Mat. "Here comes the baddies," Harvey shouted, spinning a toy car around the mat. "Crasssshhhhh everywhere." He crashed his car into the other boys' cars and they responded with laughter. "I killed a bad-

die everyone," said Maurice, crashing his cars into another group of cars. (May 24, 1993)

A new accommodation was being proposed by the boys, a new adaptation of classroom materials to the needs of their warrior narratives.

Classroom Rules and Resistance

Once again the teacher would not accept the accommodation proposed. Warrior narratives provoked what she considered inappropriate public behavior in the miniature civil society of her classroom. Her aim was to create a "free" environment where children could work independently, learn at their own pace, and explore their own interests, but creating such an environment involved its own form of social contract, its own version of the state's appropriation of violence. From the very first day, she began to establish a series of classroom rules that imposed constraints on violent or disruptive activity.

The belief underlying her practice was that firmly established classroom rules make genuine free play possible, rather than restricting the range of play opportunities. Her emphasis on "proper" use of equipment was intended to stop it being damaged and consequently withdrawn from use. She had rules of "no running" and "no shouting" that allowed children to work and play safely on the floor of the classroom, even though other children were using equipment or toys that demanded movement, and ensured that the noise level was low enough for children to talk at length to one another as part of their games.

One of the outcomes of these rules was the virtual outlawing of a whole series of games that groups of children usually want to initiate when they are playing together, games of speed and body contact, of gross motor self-expression and skill. This prohibition affected both girls and boys and was justified by setting up a version of public and private spaces: The classroom was not the proper place for such activities, they "belong" in the playground.[2] The combined experience of many teachers has shown that it is almost impossible for children to play games involving car crashes and guns without violating these rules; therefore, in this classroom, as in many others (Paley 1984, 71, 116), these games were in effect banned.

These rules were then policed by the children themselves, as the following interchange shows:

> "Eeeeeheeeeeeheeeeh!" Tyler leapt about the room. A couple of girls were saying, "Stop it Tyler" but he persisted. Jane warned, "You're not allowed to have guns." Tyler responded saying, "It's not a gun. It's a water pistol, and that's not a gun." "Not allowed to have water pistol guns," Tony reiterated to Tyler. "Yes, it's a water pistol," shouted Tyler. Jane informed the teacher, who responded stating, "NO GUNS, even if they are water pistols." Tyler made a spear out of Clever Sticks, straight after the banning of gun play. (March 23, 1993)

The boys, however, were not prepared to abandon their warrior narratives. Unlike gross motor activities such as wrestling and football, they were not prepared to see them relegated to the playground, but the limitations on their expression and the teacher disapproval they evoked led the boys to explore them surreptitiously; they found ways of introducing them that did not violate rules about running and shouting.

As time passed, the games became less visible. The warrior narratives were not so much acted out as talked through, using the toy cars and the construction materials as a prompt and a basis:

> Tyler was showing his plastic straw construction to Luke. "This is a Samurai Man and this is his hat. A Samurai Man fights in Japan and they fight with the Ninja. The bad guys who use cannons and guns. My Samurai is captain of the Samurai and he is going to kill the sergeant of the bad guys. He is going to sneak up on him with a knife and kill him." (June 1, 1993)

> Malcolm and Aaron had built boats with Lego blocks and were explaining the various components to Roger. "This ship can go faster," Malcolm explained. "He [a plastic man] is the boss

of the ship. Mine is a goody boat. They are not baddies." "Mine's a steam shovel boat. It has wheels," said Aaron. "There it goes in the river and it has to go to a big shed where all the steam shovels are stopping." (June 11, 1993)

It also became apparent that there was something covert about this play. The cars were crashed quietly. The guns were being transformed into water pistols. Swords were concealed under jumpers and only used when the teacher's back was turned. When the constructed objects were displayed to the class, their potential as players in a fighting game was concealed under a more mundane description. For example:

> Prior to the free play, the children were taking turns to explain the Clever Stick and Lego Block constructions they had made the previous afternoon. I listened to Tyler describe his Lego robot to the class: "This is a transformer robot. It can do things and turn into everything." During free play, Tyler played with the same robot explaining its capacities to Winston: "This is a terminator ship. It can kill. It can turn into a robot and the top pops off." (March 23, 1993)

Children even protested to one another that they were not making weapons, "This isn't a gun, it's a lookout." "This isn't a place for bullets, it's for petrol."

The warrior narratives, it would seem, went underground and became part of a "deviant" masculine subculture with the characteristic "secret" identity and hidden meanings (Hebdige 1979, 103). The boys were no longer seeking accommodation but practicing hidden resistance. The classroom, they were learning, was not a place where it was acceptable to explore their gender identity through fantasy.

This, however, was a message that only the boys were receiving. The girls' gender-specific fantasies (Davies 1989, 118–22; Paley 1984, 106–8) of nurturing and self-display—mothers, nurses, brides, princesses—were accommodated easily within the classroom. They could be played

out without contravening the rules of the miniature civil society. Although certain delightful
activities—eating, running, hugging, and kissing
(Best 1983, 110)—might be excluded from this
public sphere, they were not ones by means of
which their femininity, and thus their subjectivity, their conception of the self, was defined.

Masculinity, the School Regime, and the Social Contract

We suggest that this conflict between warrior narratives and school rules is likely to form part of
the experience of most boys growing up in the industrialized world. The commitment to such narratives was not only nearly 100 percent among the
boys we observed, but similar commitment is, as
was argued above, common in other sites. On the
other hand, the pressure to preserve a decorous
classroom is strong in all teachers (with the possible exception of those teaching in "alternative"
schools) and has been since the beginnings of
compulsory education. Indeed, it is only in classrooms where there is the balance of freedom and
constraint we observed that such narratives are
likely to surface at all. In more formal situations,
they would be defined as deviant and forced underground from the boys' first entry into school.

If this is a widely recurring pattern, the question then arises: Is it of little significance or is it
what Giddens (1984, 10–3) would call one of the
"cyclical practices" that reproduce the structures
of our society? The answer really depends on
how little boys "read" the outlawing of their warrior narratives. If they see it as simply one of the
broad constraints of school against which they
are continually negotiating, then perhaps it has
no significance. If, on the other hand, it has in
their minds a crucial connection to the definition
of gender, to the creation of their own masculine
identity, to where they position particular sites
and practices on a masculine to feminine continuum, then the ostracism of warrior narratives may
mean that they define the school environment as
feminine.

There is considerable evidence that some primary school children do in fact make this cate-
gorization (Best 1983, 14–5; Brophy 1985, 118;
Clark 1990, 36), and we suggest here that the out-
lawry of the masculine narrative contributes to
this. Research by Willis (1977) and Walker (1988)
in high schools has revealed a culture of resistance
based on definitions of masculinity as *antagonistic*
to the demands of the school, which are construed
as feminine by the resisters. It might therefore
seem plausible to see the underground perpetuation of the warrior narrative as an early expression of this resistance and one that gives some
legitimacy to the resisters' claims that the school
is feminine.

Is the school regime that outlaws the warrior
narratives really feminine? We would argue,
rather, that the regime being imposed is based on
a male ideal, an outcome of the Enlightenment
and compulsory schooling. Michel Foucault has
pointed out that the development of this particular regime in schools coincided with the emergence of the prison, the hospital, the army
barracks, and the factory (Foucault 1980, 55–7).
Although teachers in the first years of school are
predominantly female, the regime they impose is
perpetuated by male teachers (Brophy 1985, 121),
and this preference is endorsed by powerful and
influential males in the society at large. The kind
of demeanor and self-management that teachers
are trying to inculcate in the early school years is
the behavior expected in male-dominated public
arenas like boardrooms, courtrooms, and union
mass meetings.[3]

Connell (1989, 291) and Willis (1977, 76, 84)
provide evidence that by adolescence, boys from
all classes, particularly if they are ambitious, come
to regard acquiescence in the school's demands
as compatible with constructing a masculine identity. Connell writes:

> Some working class boys embrace a project of
> mobility in which they construct a masculinity
> organized around themes of rationality and re-
> sponsibility. This is closely connected with the
> "certification" function of the upper levels of

the education system and to a key form of masculinity among professionals. (1989, 291)

Rationality and responsibility are, as Weber argued long ago, the primary characteristics of the modern society theorized by the Enlightenment thinkers as based on a social contract. This prized rationality has been converted in practice into a bureaucratized legal system where "responsible" acceptance by the population of the rules of civil society obviates the need for individuals to use physical violence in gaining their ends or protecting their rights, and where, if such violence is necessary, it is exercised by the state (Weber 1978, 341–54). In civil society, the warrior is obsolete, his activities redefined bureaucratically and performed by the police and the military.

The teacher in whose classroom our observation was conducted demonstrated a strong commitment to rationality and responsibility. For example, she devoted a great deal of time to showing that there was a cause and effect link between the behavior forbidden by her classroom rules and classroom accidents. Each time an accident occurred, she asked the children to determine the cause of the accident, its result, and how it could have been prevented. The implication throughout was that children must take responsibility for the outcomes of their actions.

> Mac accidentally struck a boy, who was lying on the floor, in the head with a pram wheel. He was screaming around with a pram, the victim was playing on the Car Mat and lying down to obtain a bird's eye view of a car crash. Mac rushed past the group and collected Justin on the side of the head. Tears and confusion ensued. The teacher's reaction was to see to Justin, then stop all play and gain children's attention, speaking first to Mac and Justin plus Justin's group:
>
> T. How did Justin get hurt? M. [No answer] T. Mac, what happened?
>
> M. I was wheeling the pram and Justin was in the way.
>
> T. Were you running? M. I was wheeling the pram.

The teacher now addresses the whole class:

> T. Stop working everyone, eyes to me and listen. Someone has just been hurt because someone didn't remember the classroom rules. What are they Harvey?
>
> (Harvey was listening intently and she wanted someone who could answer the question at this point).
>
> H. No running in the classroom. T. Why?
>
> Other children offer an answer.
>
> Chn. Because someone will get hurt.
>
> T. Yes, and that is what happened. Mac was going too quickly with the pram and Justin was injured. Now how can we stop this happening next time?
>
> Chn. No running in the classroom, only walk. (February 10, 1993)
>
> Malcolm, walking, bumped Winston on the head with a construction toy. The teacher intervened.
>
> T. [To Malcolm and Winston] What happened?
>
> W. Malcolm hit me on the head.
>
> M. But it was an accident. I didn't mean it. I didn't really hurt him.
>
> T. How did it happen? M. It was an accident. W. He [Malcolm] hit me.
>
> T. Malcolm, I know you didn't mean to hurt Winston, so how did it happen?
>
> M. I didn't mean it.
>
> T. I know you didn't mean it, Malcolm, but why did Winston get hurt?
>
> Chn. Malcolm was running.
>
> M. No I wasn't.
>
> T. See where everyone was sitting? There is hardly enough room for children to walk. Children working on the floor must remember to leave a walking path so that other children can move safely around the room. Otherwise someone will be hurt, and that's what has happened today. (February 23, 1993)

This public-sphere masculinity of rationality and responsibility, of civil society, of the social contract is not the masculinity that the boys are bringing into the classroom through their warrior narratives. They are using a different, much older version—not the male as responsible citizen, the producer and consumer who keeps the capitalist system going, the breadwinner, and caring father of a family. Their earliest vision of masculinity is the male as warrior, the bonded male who goes out with his mates and meets the dangers of the world, the male who attacks and defeats other males characterized as baddies, the male who turns the natural products of the earth into weapons to carry out these purposes.

We would argue, nevertheless, that those boys who aspire to become one of the brothers who wield power in the public world of civil society ultimately realize that conformity to rationality and responsibility, to the demands of the school, is the price they must pay. They realize that although the girls can expect one day to become the brides and mothers of their pretend games, the boys will never, except perhaps in time of war, be allowed to act out the part of warrior hero in reality.

On the other hand, the school softens the transition for them by endorsing and encouraging the classic modern transformation and domestication of the warrior narrative, sport (Connell 1987, 177; Messner 1992, 10–2). In the school where this observation was conducted, large playground areas are set aside for lunchtime cricket, soccer, and basketball; by the age of seven, most boys are joining in these games. The message is conveyed to them that if they behave like citizens in the classroom, they can become warriors on the sports oval.

Gradually, we would suggest, little boys get the message that resistance is not the only way to live out warrior masculinity. If they accept a public/private division of life, it can be accommodated within the private sphere; thus, it becomes possible for those boys who aspire to respectability, figuring in civil society as one of the brothers, to accept that the school regime and its expectations are masculine and to reject the attempts of the "resisters" to define it (and them) as feminine. They adopt the masculinity of rationality and responsibility as that appropriate to the public sphere, while the earlier, deeply appealing

masculinity of the warrior narratives can still be experienced through symbolic reenactment on the sports field.

Conclusion

We are not, of course, suggesting that this is the only way in which the public/private division becomes part of the lived awareness of little boys. We do, however, believe that we have teased out one strand of the manner in which they encounter it. We have suggested that the classroom is a major site where little boys are introduced to the masculinity of rationality and responsibility characteristic of the brothers in civil society; we have been looking at a "cycle of practice" where, in classroom after classroom, generation after generation, the mode of masculinity typified in the warrior narratives is first driven underground and then transferred to the sports field. We are, we would suggest, seeing renegotiated for each generation and in each boy's own life the conception of the "social contract" that is characteristic of the era of modernity, of the Enlightenment, of democracy, and of capitalism. We are watching reenacted the transformation of violence and power as exercised by body over body, to control through surveillance and rules (Foucault 1977, 9; 1984, 66–7), the move from domination by individual superiors to acquiescence in a public sphere of decorum and rationality (Pateman 1988).

Yet, this is a social *contract*, and there is another side to the bargain. Although they learn that they must give up their warrior narratives of masculinity in the public sphere, where rationality and responsibility hold sway, they also learn that in return they may preserve them in the private realm of desire as fantasy, as bricolage, as a symbolic survival that is appropriate to the spaces of leisure and self-indulgence, the playground, the backyard, the television set, the sports field. Although this is too large an issue to be explored in detail here, there may even be a reenactment in the school setting of what Pateman (1988, 99–115) has defined as the sexual contract, the male right to dominate women in return for accepting the constraints of civil society. Is this, perhaps, established for both boys and girls by means of the endemic misogyny—invasion of girls' space (Thorne 1986, 172; 1993, 63–88), overt expressions of aversion and disgust (D'Arcy 1990, 81; Goodenough 1987, 422), disparaging sexual innuendo (Best 1983, 129; Clark 1990, 38–46; Goodenough, 1987, 433)—noted by so many observers in the classrooms and playgrounds of modernity? Are girls being contained by the boys' actions within a more restricted, ultimately a private, sphere because, in the boys' eyes, they have not earned access to the public sphere by sharing their ordeal of repression, resistance, and ultimate symbolic accommodation of their gender-defining fantasies?

Notes

1. Some ethnographic studies describe a "tomboy" who wants to join in the boys' games (Best 1983, 95–7; Davies 1989, 93, 123; Thorne 1993, 127–9), although in our experience, such girls are rare, rarer even than the boys who play by choice with girls. The girls' rejection of the warrior narratives does not appear to be simply the result of the fact that the characters are usually men. Bronwyn Davies, when she read the role-reversal story *Rita the Rescuer* to preschoolers, found that many boys identified strongly with Rita ("they flex their muscles to show how strong they are and fall to wrestling each other on the floor to display their strength"), whereas for most girls, Rita remained "other" (Davies 1989, 57–8).

2. This would seem to reverse the usual parallel of outdoor/indoor with public/private. This further suggests that the everyday equation of "public" with "visible" may not be appropriate for the specialized use of the term in sociological discussions of the public/private division. Behavior in the street may be more visible than what goes on in a courtroom, but it is nevertheless acceptable for the street behavior to be, to a greater degree, personal, private, and driven by "desire."

3. There are some groups of men who continue to reject these modes of modernity throughout their lives. Andrew Metcalfe, in his study of an Australian mining community, has identified two broad categories of miner, the "respectable," and the "larrikin" (an Australian slang expression carrying implications of non-conformism, irreverence, and impudence). The first are committed to the procedural decorums of union meetings, sporting and hobby clubs, welfare groups, and so on; the others relate more strongly to the less disciplined masculinity of the pub, the brawl, and the racetrack (Metcalfe, 1988, 73–125). This distinction is very similar to that noted by Paul Willis in England between the "ear'oles" and the "lads" in a working-class secondary school (Willis, 1977). It needs to be noted that this is not a *class* difference and that demographically the groups are identical. What distinguishes them is, as Metcalfe points out, their relative commitment to the respectable modes of accommodation and resistance characteristic of civil society of larrikin modes with a much longer history, perhaps even their acceptance or rejection of the social contract.

References

Anyon, Jean. 1983. Intersections of gender and class: Accommodation and resistance by working-class and affluent females to contradictory sex-role ideologies. In *Gender, class and education*, edited by Stephen Walker and Len Barton. Barcombe, Sussex: Falmer.

Best, Raphaela. 1983. *We've all got scars: What girls and boys learn in elementary school.* Bloomington: Indiana University Press.

Bowles, Samuel, and Herbert Gintis. 1976. *Schooling in capitalist America: Educational reform and the contradictions of economic life.* London: Routledge and Kegan Paul.

Brophy, Jere E. 1985. Interactions of male and female students with male and female teachers. In *Gender influences in classroom interaction*, edited by L. C. Wilkinson and C. B. Marrett. New York: Academic Press.

Burgess, R. G., ed. 1984. *The research process in educational settings: Ten case studies.* Lewes: Falmer.

Chodorow, Nancy. 1978. *The reproduction of mothering: Psychoanalysis and the sociology of gender.* Berkeley: University of California Press.

Clark, Margaret. 1989. Anastasia is a normal developer because she is unique. *Oxford Review of Education* 15:243–55.

———. 1990. *The great divide: Gender in the primary school.* Melbourne: Curriculum Corporation.

Connell, R. W. 1987. *Gender and power: Society, the person and sexual politics.* Sydney: Allen and Unwin.

————. 1989. Cool guys, swots and wimps: The interplay of masculinity and education. *Oxford Review of Education* 15:291–303.

Crosset, Todd. 1990. Masculinity, sexuality, and the development of early modern sport. In *Sport, men and the gender order*, edited by Michael E. Messner and Donald F. Sabo. Champaign, IL: Human Kinetics Books.

D'Arcy, Sue. 1990. Towards a non-sexist primary classroom. In *Dolls and dungarees: Gender issues in the primary school curriculum*, edited by Eva Tutchell. Milton Keynes: Open University Press.

Davies, Bronwyn. 1989. *Frogs and snails and feminist tales: Preschool children and gender*. Sydney: Allen and Unwin.

Dinnerstein, Myra. 1977. *The mermaid and the minotaur: Sexual arrangements and human malaise*. New York: Harper and Row.

Duthie, J. H. 1980. Athletics: The ritual of a technological society? In *Play and culture*, edited by Helen B. Schwartzman. West Point, NY: Leisure.

Eisenstein, Hester. 1984. *Contemporary feminist thought*. London: Unwin Paperbacks.

Foucault, Michel. 1977. *Discipline and punish: The birth of the prison*. Translated by Alan Sheridan. New York: Pantheon.

————. 1980. Body/power. In *power/knowledge: Selected interviews and other writings 1972–1977*, edited by Colin Gordon. Brighton: Harvester

————. 1984. Truth and power. In *The Foucault reader*, edited by P. Rabinow. New York: Pantheon.

Genovese, Eugene E. 1972. *Roll, Jordan, roll: The world the slaves made*. New York: Pantheon.

Giddens, Anthony. 1984. *The constitution of society: Outline of the theory of structuration*. Berkeley: University of California Press.

Goodenough, Ruth Gallagher. 1987. Small group culture and the emergence of sexist behaviour: A comparative study of four children's groups. In *Interpretive ethnography of education*, edited by G. Spindler and L. Spindler. Hillsdale, NJ: Lawrence Erlbaum.

Hebdige, Dick. 1979. *Subculture: The meaning of style*. London: Methuen.

Messner, Michael E. 1992. *Power at play: Sports and the problem of masculinity*. Boston: Beacon.

Metcalfe, Andrew. 1988. *For freedom and dignity: Historical agency and class structure in the coalfields of NSW*. Sydney: Allen and Unwin.

Paley, Vivian Gussin. 1984. *Boys and girls: Superheroes in the doll corner*. Chicago: University of Chicago Press.

Pateman, Carole. 1988. *The sexual contract*. Oxford: Polity.

————. 1989. The fraternal social contract. In *The disorder of women*. Cambridge: Polity.

Thorne, Barrie. 1986. Girls and boys together . . . but mostly apart: Gender arrangements in elementary schools. In *Relationships and development*, edited by W. W. Hartup and Z. Rubin. Hillsdale, NJ: Lawrence Erlbaum.

————. 1993. *Gender play: Girls and boys in school*. New Brunswick, NJ: Rutgers University Press.

Walker, J. C. 1988. *Louts and legends: Male youth culture in an inner-city school*. Sydney: Allen and Unwin.

Walkerdine, Valerie. 1990. *Schoolgirl fictions*. London: Verso.

Weber, Max. 1978. *Selections in translation*. Edited by W. G. Runciman and translated by Eric Matthews. Cambridge: Cambridge University Press.

Willis, Paul. 1977. *Learning to labour: How working class kids get working class jobs*. Farnborough: Saxon House.

Ritch C. Savin-Williams

Memories of Same-Sex Attractions

Recalling their childhood, gay/bisexual youths often report the pervasiveness of distinct, early memories of same-sex attractions. They remember particular feelings or incidents from as young as four or five years of age that, in retrospect, reflect the first manifestations of sexual orientation. These memories often comprise some of the youths' earliest recollections of their lives, present in some rudimentary form for many years before the ability to label sexual feelings and attractions emerges, usually after pubertal onset.[1]

Indeed, over 80 percent of the interviewed youths reported same-sex attractions prior to the physical manifestations of puberty. By the completion of puberty, all youths recalled attractions that they later labeled as "homosexual." Nearly half noted that their feelings for other males were some of their very first memories, present prior to beginning elementary school. Revelation for one youth came through his kindergarten naps: "Dreams of naked men and curious about them. Really wanting to look at them." Another youth was acting on his sexually charged feelings at age four: "I particularly remember an incident with a cousin in the bathroom and we both having hardons and feeling a tingling sensation when we rubbed against each other. I wanted to repeat it, and did!"

The origins of these feelings and their meanings are difficult to discern because prepubertal children are seldom asked if they have sexual attractions for other boys or girls. Thus, clinicians, educators, researchers, and other interested pro-

fessionals must rely on retrospective data from adolescents and young adults. Although these later recollections may be distorted by an awareness of current sexual identity, they provide an invaluable source of information.

Gay/bisexual youths often recall a vague but distinct sense of *being different* from other boys. Indeed, characterizing most developmental models of sexual identity is an introductory stage in which an individual has an unequivocal cognitive and/or emotional realization that he or she is "different" from others. An individual may feel alienated from others with very little awareness that homosexuality is the relevant issue.[2] For example, sociologist and sex educator Richard Troiden proposes a coming-out model that begins with an initial sense that one is marginalized in conjunction with perceptions of being different from peers.[3] This undeniable feeling may be the first internal, emotional revelation of sexual orientation, although it is not likely to be perceived initially as sexual but rather as a strongly experienced sense of not fitting in or of not having the same interests as other boys/girls.

The existence of these early feelings implies that youths have both an awareness of a normative standard of how boys are supposed to act, feel, and behave and a belief that they violate this ideal. Troiden describes this conflation of feeling different and gender inappropriate:

> It is not surprising that "prehomosexuals" used gender metaphors, rather than sexual metaphors, to interpret and explain childhood feelings of difference. . . . Children do not appear to define their sexual experimentation in heterosexual or homosexual terms. The socially created categories of homosexual, heterosexual,

and bisexual hold little or no significance for them. (p. 52)

Retrospectively, the gay/bisexual youths interviewed for this book reported three somewhat overlapping sources as a basis for their initial awareness of differentness:

- a pervasive and emotional captivation with other boys that felt passionate, exotic, consuming, and mysterious;
- a strongly felt desire to engage in play activities and to possess traits usually characteristic of girls;
- disinterest or, in more extreme cases, a revulsion in typical boys' activities, especially team sports and rough-and-tumble physical play.[4]

These three sources are not mutually exclusive—many youths recalled instances of all three during their childhood. For example, one youth who felt apart and isolated during his childhood was obsessed with wanting to be around adult men, frequently developed crushes on male teachers, and spent considerable time with neighborhood girls, particularly enjoying their games of hopscotch and jump rope. He was called "sissy" and "girly" by other boys, and he detested team sports and all things athletic, especially locker rooms.

The prevalence of these three is difficult to determine because few researchers have systematically asked boys the relevant questions that probe these issues. It also bears noting that not all gay or bisexual individuals recall this sense of being different during childhood and adolescence and that these feelings and attractions are not solely the domain of sexual-minority youths. Heterosexual boys may also feel different, have same-sex attractions or desires, enjoy feminine activities, and avoid aggressive pursuits.

Youths interviewed for this book easily and at times graphically remembered these same-sex attractions that emanated from their earliest childhood memories. Despite the dramatic significance that these early homoerotic attractions would have, at the time they felt natural, om-nipresent. Many recalled these attractions to other males by identifying concrete, distinct memories prior to first grade. Without great fanfare, with no clashing of cymbals, and with no abiding shock, later homoerotic attractions were felt to be contiguous with these early feelings.

Captivation with Masculinity

Of the three sources for feeling different, the vast majority of the gay/bisexual youths interviewed for this book attributed to themselves an early sense that in some fundamental way they differed from other boys. This difference was an obsession of always wanting to be near other males. Most boys did not at the time believe that these attractions were sexually motivated; they were just overwhelmed with an all-consuming desire to be with other males. Some became flushed or excited when they made contact, especially physical, with other boys or men; some arranged their lives so as to increase time spent with males, while others avoided males because they were frightened by the male aura. Above all else, their obsession with males was mysterious and pervasive. It was also present from an early age, from first memories.

One youth's childhood was one massive memory of men. He decided that the death of his father ten years earlier was the reason that he would always need guys in his life.

> I can remember wanting the men who visited us to hug me when I was real little, maybe three or four. I've always wanted to touch and be touched by guys, and I was a lot. Guys loved to manhandle me. They would throw me up in the air and I'd touch the ceiling and I'd scream and would love it and would do anything to make it happen more and more. It never was enough and I'd tire them out or I'd go to someone else who would toss me. Sometimes I would be teased for the "little points" [erections] in my pants, but no one, including myself, made much of it.
>
> I think I spent my childhood fantasizing about men, not sexually of course, but just being close to them and having them hold me or hug me. I'd feel safe and warm. My dad gave me this

and my older brother Mitchell gave me this but all of this was never enough. With the other men I'd feel flushed, almost hot. Maybe those were hot flashes like what women get! Those were good days.

Although he may have been an extreme case, other youths also recalled distinct attractions to men that a decade or more later were still vivid, emotional, and construed as significant. This obsession with males remained at the time nameless for the following three youths.

> I was seven at the time and Will, who was working for us doing yard work, was twenty-one and a college student/athlete. One night when my parents went to a hotel for their anniversary dinner and whatever, they asked Will to stay the night to watch over me. He was in a sleeping bag on the floor and I knew he was nude and he was next to my bed and I kept wondering what was in the sleeping bag. I just knew that I wanted to get in with him but I didn't know why or that I could because I didn't want to bother him. I didn't sleep the whole night.

> Maybe it was third grade and there was an ad in the paper about an all-male cast for a movie. This confused me but fascinated—intrigued—me so I asked the librarian and she looked all flustered, even mortified, and mumbled that I ought to ask my parents.

> It was very clear to me around six years of age. There was a TV beer commercial which featured several soccer players without shirts on. I mentioned to my brother how much I liked this TV show because the guys didn't have shirts on. I remember this but I'm sure I had thoughts before this.

Those who monopolized their attention were occasionally same-age boys, but were more often older teenagers and adults—male teachers, coaches, cousins, or friends of the family. Public male figures were also sources of fantasies—Superman, Scott Baio, Duran Duran, John Ritter, Bobby Ewing, and Hulk Hogan. Others turned pages in magazines and catalogs to find male models in various stages of undress; especially popular were underwear advertisements. The

captivation with men had a familiar tone—a drive for male contact or the male image from an early age with little understanding of what it meant—and a common emotional quality—excitement, euphoria, mystery.

These same-sex attractions were not limited to gay boys. Bisexual youths recalled similar early homoerotic captivation with men.

> Technically it could be either male or female, no matter. I just was into naked bodies. I had access and took, without him knowing it, dad's *Penthouse* magazines. Such a big fuss, but actually in them and whatever else I could find, turned on by both the girls and the men. The men I recall most vividly. It was the hairless, feminine guys with big penises and made-up faces. I loved make-up on my guys, the eyelashes and the eyes, blue shadow, but mostly it was the look. Tight jeans, lean bodies.

Homoerotic desires were often interpreted as natural and hence characteristic of all boys. Many youths articulated that their desire for the "male touch" was deeply embodied in their natural self. By this they implied that their attractions to boys were not a matter of choice or free will but were of early and perhaps, they speculated, genetic origins. For example, one youth never felt that he had a choice regarding his intense attractions to adult males.

> My infatuation with my day camp counselor I didn't choose. Why him and not his girlfriend? I never chose my love objects but I was always attracted to guys. In all of my early dreams and fantasies I always centered on guys whether they were sexual or not. What I wanted to do was to get close to them and I knew that innately, perhaps even by the age of six or seven. I felt it was okay because God said it was okay.

Similarly, many other youths noted that their homoerotic desires were never a matter of choice but "just were." Most believed that they were gay or bisexual in large part because of genetic factors or the "way the cards were dealt—luck of the draw, like something in the neuro-structure or hormonal."

I'd dream of my uncle and wake up all euphoric and sweaty and eroticized. Another dream that I had at six was of my [boy] classmates playing around in their underwear with these big cocks sticking out. It just happened. How could I choose these things to dream about, to check out the cocks in my mom's *Playgirl*, and to cut out pictures of guys from movie magazines? I was very intrigued by all of this and knew somehow it related to me.

Maybe my child sex play taught me how to be gay but then maybe it only reinforced what already was. I know that I've been gay for a long time, probably I was born with it. I assumed when I was young that all people had a pee pee. It doesn't have to be genetic but then it could happen during the first year of life. I think I was born being gay, leaning toward homosexuality, and development just sort of pushed it further.

My brother is gay, my uncle is gay, my father acts like he is gay sometimes, and my mother is hanging out with feminist support groups and really butch-looking women. Did I really have a choice?!

I can't stand the smell of women. Who really cares? I could have gone straight but it would have been torture. I am what I am, from birth.

Some youths simply assumed, based on the egocentric principle that their thoughts and feelings were shared by others, that all boys must feel as they do but were simply not talking about their desires. With age, however, they came to realize that perhaps they were more "into it."

I guess I was pretty touchable—and I still am based on what guys I know or am with tell me. I didn't understand why because I thought all kids liked it. Others have told me that they liked it too but somehow I think I liked it more. I craved and adored it and my day would not be a good one unless I had this contact. Only later did I find out why I liked being touched by guys.

Another youth decided that he would simply "outgrow" his obsession with males. He was not, however, going to let this future keep him from enjoying this wonderful pleasure at the moment.

As a child I knew I was attracted to males. I was caught by my mother looking at nude photographs of men in her magazines and I heard my father say to her that, "He'll grow out of it," and so I thought and hoped I would. But until then I just settled back and enjoyed my keen curiosity to see male bodies.

You see, it did not feel threatening because (a) it felt great, and (b) father said I would grow out of it, and he was always right. So why not enjoy it until it went away?

Other youths, however, recognized that these undeniably homoerotic attractions were not typical of other boys. They knew they were extreme cases but they "could not help it."

Even at eight I could tell that my interest in guys was way beyond normal. Like this time that we were out with my friend Chad's big brother catching fireflies and he took off his shirt and I forgot about the fireflies and just stared at his chest. Chad got really irritated and called out, "Hey homo give me the jar!" I'm sure I blushed.

When we played truth-or-dare I always wanted to be dared to kiss one of the guys. No one ever dared me to do that, probably because they knew that I'd like it. And I would have! I knew it was strange of me and that they didn't want to kiss boys. They all knew that too but I really didn't care.

Eventually, most youths understood that these undeniable attractions were the wrong ones to have. Despite the belief that they had no choice in matters of their attractions, most inevitably came to appreciate that they should hide their attractions. Snide remarks made by peers, prohibitions taught by parents, and the silence imposed by religion and by teachers all contributed to this realization. Thus, although early obsessions with males were experienced as instinctive, most of the gay/bisexual youths acknowledged from an early age that their impulses were somehow "wrong" but not necessarily "bad."

Despite the presence of an older gay brother, one youth was vulnerable to society's negative messages about homosexuality. His concern centered on being "strike two" for his mother.

Well, I knew enough to hide Sean's *Jock* after I looked at it. It was not guilt—it was too much fun!—but fear that I felt. I was afraid if mother found out that she would feel bad that she had two failures and that Sean would kill me for getting into his stockpile.

Very few youths made the connection during their childhood that these attractions that felt so natural and significant placed them in the stigmatized category of "homosexual." Although most had a passing acquaintance with the concept and had seen "homosexuals" displayed in the media, relatively few would have situated themselves in this category at this point in their lives. One youth believed that "it" was something to be outgrown: "I thought maybe that it was just a stage that I was going through. But if it wasn't a stage then it was probably no problem for me to worry about now." Other youths, however, were worried.

> Something was different about me. I knew that. I was afraid of what it meant, and I prayed to God that whatever it was that He would take it away. It was a burden but I liked it, and so I felt guilty about liking it.

It was not until many years later, with the onset of sexual maturations that these attractions would be fully linked with sexuality and perhaps a sexual identity. Homosensuality for these youths was not foreign but natural, a lifelong intrigue with men's bodies. However, as the societal wrongness of their intuitive obsession with masculinity became increasingly apparent, many youths hoped that their attractions were a phase to be outgrown or that their feelings would make sense in some distant future.

The feared repercussions from family members and peers if they were known to have gay traits served as a powerful reason for the boys to feel that their same-sex desires and acts were improper and should not be shared with others. Acting on them was thought to be wrong because if caught, punishment would likely ensue. Balancing desire and fear became a significant dilemma. Eventually, many of the youths recognized that others rarely shared or understood their same-sex desires. This pact of secrecy with themselves was a major theme for many of the youths. It did not, however, always inhibit their sexual behavior; a significant number of the boys acted on their sexual desires during childhood, as is apparent in Chapter Four.

Acting Like a Girl

A second source of feeling different, not explicitly linked with same-sex attractions, involved cultural definitions of gender—how a boy should *not* act, think, and feel. Characteristics deemed not appropriate for boys included observable behaviors such as play with girl-typed toys, especially dolls; involvement in female activities and games; cross-dressing; sex-role motor behavior including limp wrists, high-pitched voices, and dramatic gestures; and stated interests such as wishing to be a girl, imagining self as dancer or model, and preferring female friends and being around older women. These boys did not wonder, "Why am I gay?" but "Why do I act like a girl?[5] For example, one youth recalled his childhood in the following way:

> I knew that a boy wasn't supposed to kiss other boys, although I did. I knew it was wrong, so this must be some indication that I knew. I also knew that I wasn't supposed to cross my legs at he knees, but I wouldn't like quickly uncross my legs whenever that was the case. So this is certainly at a young age that I noticed this. I think I knew that it was sort of a female thing, sort of an odd thing, and I knew that boys weren't supposed to do that.

Many boys who fit the category of gender bending were at once erotically drawn to boys and men (the first source) but were repelled by their behavior, their standard of dress and cleanliness, and their barbarian nature. They felt ambivalent regarding their attractions to males; intrigued by male bodies and the masculinity mystique, these youths saw men as enigmatic and unapproachable.

Psychotherapist Richard Isay characterizes this sense of gender atypicality in some pregay boys: "They saw themselves as more sensitive than other boys; they cried more easily, had their feelings more readily hurt, had more aesthetic interests, enjoyed nature, art, and music, and were drawn to other 'sensitive' boys, girls, and adults" (p. 23).[6] Indeed, research amply demonstrates that gender nonconformity is one of the best childhood predictors of adult homosexuality in me.[7] Findings from prospective studies are fairly straightforward: The proportion of *extremely* feminine boys who eventually profess a same-sex sexual orientation approaches 100 percent. However, the fraction of these gender-nonconforming boys in the total population remains considerably below that of gay men. Thus, while the vast majority of extremely feminine boys eventually adopt a gay or bisexual identity in adulthood, so do an unknown number of boys who are not particularly feminine.

Feeling more similar to girls than to boys, one youth described his experience "as if I was from a different planet than other boys." He was not alone; a substantial proportion of the gay/bisexual youths recalled that this "girl-like syndrome" was the basis of how they differed from their male peers. Of all boys interviewed, over one-third described their self-image as being more similar to that of girls than boys, and nearly all of these boys reported that this sense of themselves permeated areas of their lives.

One consequence of having more culturally defined feminine than masculine interests was that many boys with gender-atypical characteristics felt most comfortable in the company of girls and women or preferred spending time alone. Two youths described their gender nonconformity during their childhood years.

> I had mostly friends who were girls and I can remember playing jump rope, dolls, and hop-scotch with them, and I can remember being very interested in hairstyling and practicing on dolls. I got into sewing and knitting. I played make-believe, read spy and adventure stories, house with my sisters. I had a purse and dolls that they gave me. We did everything together.

> I was never close with my brother and we never did anything together. I was always accepted by girls and few other boys were.

> Thinking back I did play with girls in the neighborhood a lot. I loved actually to kiss girls and I was always wanting to kiss girls and I thought this might be a little strange or weird because I liked girls so much at such a young age. I just felt very comfortable with them. I felt more self-conscious around boys because I always wondered what they were thinking about.

The extent to which such behavior could produce a gender-bender who is accepted by girls as one of them is illustrated by a third youth.

> I was even invited to slumber parties and I always went. They were so much fun! Just the five of us in our gowns, with lace and bows that my mom had made for my sister and I "borrowed," laughing, sneaking cigarettes, and gossiping about other girls.

Thus, almost without exception boys who displayed early gender-atypical behavior strongly preferred hanging out with girls rather than with boys. Girls were far less likely to reject the "feminine" boys, a reaction that has been confirmed by research studies.[8] If such youths had male friends it was usually one best friend, perhaps a neighbor who also disliked masculine activities.

> I have always been gay although I did not know what that meant at the time. But I knew that I always felt queer, out of place in my hometown. . . . Mostly I spent my time alone in the house or with girls at school. We ate lunch together and talked in between classes. I always felt that girls received the short end of the stick. I really did not have many friends because I lived in a rural area. I felt rejected and I feared being rejected.

> I have usually had one best male friend, who might change every other year or so but who always was like me in hating sports. Like Tim who was one of my best friends because he lived across the street and was handy, someone so I would not be alone. We spent time together but I am not sure what else we ever did. Otherwise I hung with girls.

Not uncommonly, boys who displayed interest in gender-atypical pursuits fervently expressed strong preferences for solo activities such as reading and make-believe games, or for artistic endeavors.

But my major activity during childhood was drawing and I was sort of known as "The Artist," even as early as third and fourth grades. Today I can see some very gay themes in my drawings! Whenever anyone in the class wanted anything drawn then they asked me. No matter how much they had ridiculed me I agreed to do it.

A second youth made up plays for the neighborhood, role-played TV characters, and cartooned.

I took part in dance, ballet, singing, and had good manners. I liked Broadway musicals, Barbra, Bette, Joan, Liz, Judy, and Greta . . . I did drama, lots and lots of drama! Anything pretend. I did lots of skits for the Mickey Mouse Club, play writing, and office decorating.

Unclear from these accounts is whether the decision to spend time alone was one freely chosen by the gay/bisexual youths or was a consequence of exclusion dictated by others. That is, were they loners by choice or by circumstance? Although most evidence supports the banishment hypothesis, time alone may have been desired and pursued for creative reasons; time alone may have enhanced their creative efforts. One youth found that he spent a lot of time "doing nothing, just being alone, playing the violin, planting flowers, and arranging flowers." Another youth loved "building and creating things like castles and bridges and rivers in the backyard. Maybe it was because I was an only child but I was into any kind of art and I also composed on the piano." When asked about his childhood activities, a third youth was merely succinct: "Shopped. Homework. Masturbated. Read."

Most difficult for many gender-atypical gay/bisexual boys was the almost universal harassment they received from their peers. As a consequence

of associating with girls and not boys, spending considerable time alone, and appreciating female activities, they faced almost daily harassment from peers, usually boys but sometimes girls, teachers, parents, and siblings. Perhaps most insufferable to their male peers was the gay/bisexual boys' feminine gross and fine motor behavior. Their hand gestures, standing and sitting posture, leg and hip movement, voice pitch and cadence, and head tilt conveyed to others that these boys were girllike and hence weak and deplorable. The reactions they received from peers went beyond mere teasing, which most youths receive during childhood and adolescence as a mechanism for social bonding, to outright verbal abuse that was harassing and sometimes extremely destructive to a sense of self. The abuse was occasionally physically expressed and always had emotional and self-image consequences.

Below is a list of names that boys with gender-atypical characteristics reported that they were called by age mates. Not all youths recalled or wanted to remember the exact names.

• sissy	• clumsy	• bitchy	• fag
• queer	• little girl	• cry baby	• fem
• gayson	• faggot	• super fem	• queer bait
• fruitcake	• wimpy	• fruit	• gay
• schoolboy	• pansy	• gaylord	• Janus
• fairy	• softy	• girl	• fag boy
• girly	• homo	• cocksucker	• lisp
• wimp	• gay guy	• Avon Lady	• Safety Girl
• Tinkerbell	• flamer	• mommy's boy	

One youth reported that in grammar school he was voted "The Person Most Likely to Own a Gay Bar."

The specific provocation that elicited these names during school, on the bus, and in the neighborhood varied, but several patterns are discernible. The abuse usually occurred because a boy was perceived as a misfit, as acting too much "like a girl." Three youths provided testimonies from their lives:

Because I was somewhat effeminate in my behavior and because I wore "girly" shoes. Some said that I was a little girl because I couldn't play baseball. I played the clarinet in school and this was defined as a female instrument so I got some teasing for that. I thought I could control my behavior but it got so bad that my family decided to pull me out of the public school to go to a private Catholic school where the teasing receded.

Because I was weak and a cry baby. I was not in the "in" crowd. Also because of the way I dressed and that I got good grades. I was very thin and got every disease that came around. I had all sorts of allergies and was always using all sorts of drugs. I was told I looked like a girl. I played with Barbies and taught her how to sit up and later how to fly. I just wasn't masculine enough I guess.

People thought that perhaps I might be gay because they thought I was just way too nice and also because I was flamboyant. They really didn't think I was like homosexually gay. It was just a term they used for me because it seemed to fit my personality. People said I'm gay because of my mannerisms, also because I slur my s's and I'm so flamboyant. I think it's the way that I walked, the way I talked, the way I carried myself. I had a soft voice. Lots of boys blew me kisses. My voice is just not masculine. Also I tended to be very giggly and flighty and flaky and silly at times.

One youth believed that "most kids were just looking for a laugh" and that he was the easiest target, because of his femininity, they could find. He was their "amusement for the day."

In no story were girls the only ones who verbally abused a youth for being gender nonconforming. On many occasions, however, boys acted alone. Perhaps the most usual pattern was for boys, or a subset of boys, to be the persistent ridiculers with a few girls chiming in when present.

Some of the jocks really bothered me but mostly it was these three guys every day making my life miserable. Always done by males who really had this pecking order. Real bullies!

This was mostly males—this one guy seemed to have it out for me. But some of the girls who hung out with him also did it. The girls thought I was bitchy and called me "fag" and "homo."

Although reactions to being victimized by peer ridicule were diverse, the most common responses, illustrated by three youths, were to ignore, withdraw, or cry.

I took it without saying anything back. I'd pretend that I didn't hear them or hide my feelings. I hated it but didn't say anything back. Guess I was benign to it. Just sat there and took it. I did that for protection. I was so much of a misfit that bullies did it to me. I offended them in some way. Just a horrible, wrenching experience.

I became more withdrawn and thus more of an outcast. I'd cower and keep my distance, keeping it inside myself. I did nothing or remained silent or said "leave me alone." Once I fought back and lost, which made me withdraw even more.

I was very, very sensitive and would cry very easily. I had very little emotional control at the time. Cry, yell at them, cry some more. I would tell my mother and cry and she'd try to comfort me or she'd just dismiss it all. I would tell the guys that I had told my mother and they would make more fun of me.

Not all boys reacted so passively to the verbal assault. Several developed innovative, self-enhancing ways to cope with peer harassment. For example, one youth noted an unusual situation:

All my boyfriends, the jock types, always protected me and punished those who teased me. I would just turn away as if I never gave notice because I knew that I would be protected by all the guys, the jocks, that I was having sex with. I never did try to get back at them [the harassers]. Once they realized this then they kept quiet.

Another used his intelligence and experience as strategies for coping with peer harassment.

I think it was because I was so flamboyant and I was not so sports-oriented. If they said it to my face then I would say "get out of my face!" Or I would point out their stupidity. I considered them to be rather stupid, so immature. I'd been around the world and I knew I could say things that would damage them because I was smarter than them and because I had so many female friends. I tried to ignore it because I knew that I was better than them. I sort of got respect for not fighting back or sometimes I would say, "I like girls! What's *your* problem?"

It is difficult to ascertain the true impact on a youth of this constant bombardment of negative peer review. Few of the boys thought it was anything but negative. Most felt that the most significant effect of the verbal harassment was what it did to their personality: They became increasingly withdrawn from social interactions, despondent, and self-absorbed. The aftermath for the four youths below was a decrease in their self-image and self-worth.

I felt very conscious about my voice and somewhat shameful that I wasn't masculine enough. I actually just sort of retreated more and became more introverted. I felt rejected and it hurt my self-esteem. I took the ridicule to heart and I blamed myself.

Because I knew that indeed I had the attractions to guys I knew that they were right and that I was a disgusting human being. I just spent a lot more time alone to avoid the pain. I just sort of blocked it all internally because it hurt so much. I just sort of erased all my memories of my childhood so I can't give you much detail.

A real nightmare! I really felt like I had no friends. It really did lower my self-esteem and it made me focus on sort of my outer appearance and ignore the inner. It devastated me because I felt everything they said was true. I was quiet and kept it inside.

Heightened my sense of being different. Caused me to withdraw and not feel good about myself. Cut off from people and became shy. Became introverted, guilty. I hated that time. Childhood was supposed to be happy times but it was not. Later, I dropped out of school, thought about suicide, and ran away from home.

Although none of the boys felt that the labeling made him gay, many believed that the name-calling contributed to their negative image of

homosexuality. Hence, the ridicule became a central factor in who they are. The abuse also kept them in the closet for a considerably longer period of time. These effects are apparent in the two narratives below:

It just sort of reinforced that men are scum. I viewed being a fag as so negative that it hurt my self-image for them to call me that. I didn't like myself, so being gay is bad and what they're saying I knew it to be true because I am bad and being gay is bad and I'm gay. It's made me think of males only as sex objects because I wanted to be hated by men because I didn't like myself. I started back in elementary school to believe it was true.

I had such a hostile view towards homosexuality, so it was hard to come out as a result of this stigma because I had really low self-esteem. It affected me by not having a positive attitude about homosexuality in general. I needed at least a positive or even neutral point of view and that would have made my gay life so much easier. I continue to suppress things.

It was the rare youth for whom anything positive emerged from the verbal ridicule. One youth noted that "teasing sort of helped me to deal with my gay identity at a very early age because everyone was calling my attention to it." He was proud to be effeminate; he reported that the teasing made him stronger and was thus beneficial.

I wore stylish clothes and was my own individual self. My teachers appreciated this but not the slobs. Because of this a lot of them said that I was gay and so I thought I must be, although I did not know what this meant except that it meant I would not be shoveling cow shit!

Unfortunately, few youths could recall such positive aspects to their gender atypicality. More often, the consequences of being true to their nature were that other boys viewed them as undesirable playmates and as "weird." Labeled sissy or effeminate, they were rejected by boys, and, equally important, they had little desire to fraternize with their male peers. Because other boys did not constitute an enjoyable or safe context for play or socializing, the youths often turned to girls for activities and consolation. They preferred to dance rather than shovel shit, to sing rather than yell "hike," and to draw rather than bash heads. Thus, childhood was usually experienced as a traumatizing time by youths who did not conform to cultural sex roles. The fortunate ones sought and found girls for solace and support. Girls became their saviors, offering sources of emotional sustenance as the male world of childhood became increasingly distasteful. It was to these girls that many gay/bisexual males subsequently disclosed their sexual affiliations during middle or late adolescence (see Chapter Seven).

Not Acting Like a Boy

A third source of feeling different among the interviewed youths originated from a disinterest or abhorrence of typical masculine activities, which may or may not have occurred in the presence of a captivation with masculinity (first source) or of high levels of femininity (second source). Thus, a lack of masculinity did not necessarily imply that such youths were fond of female activities or were drawn to or hung out with girls. Many reported never playing house, dressing up as a girl, or having a passing acquaintance with Barbie. In the absence of typical expressions of femininity, boys without masculine interests were usually loners or spent time with one or several best male friends.

Compared with what is known about gender-atypical boys, considerably less is known concerning those who during childhood do not fit cultural images of how a boy should act, think, and feel. Characteristics labeled as unmasculine or as failure to conform to gender expectations include observable behaviors such as avoidance of rough-and-tumble play, typical boys' games, and athletic activities; no imagining of oneself as a sports figure; and no desire to grow up to be like one's father. These boys did not wonder, "Why am I gay?" but "Why don't I act like a boy?"[9]

Childhood activities that constitute "unmasculine" all share the characteristic of being gender

neutral by North American standards, suitable for both boys and girls. Within this gender non-partisanship, active and passive patterns were evident in the interviews. Some boys were as active as masculine-inclined peers but in nonmasculine, nonathletic—at least in a team sports sense—activities.

> My friend and me made roads and gardens. I liked to sort of build cities and bridges outside and in the garden. Played in the woods, hiked in the woods, camped out, and hide and seek. Ted and I were almost inseparable for a couple of years. I also biked, swam a lot, jumped on the trampoline. Biking was my way of dealing with stress. I was into matchbox cars.

> I enjoyed playing office, playing grow-up, walking around the city basically looking at other people. Mind games and chess with my brothers. Creative imaginative play. Discovering and enjoying spending a lot of time on bike trips, going to new places. Getting out of the house and being outside, just wandering off by myself.

More common were boys who spent considerable time alone pursuing passive activities. This passivity should not be equated, however, with having a bad time or having a bad childhood. Many recalled an enjoyable if unconventional life during childhood.

> At school I hung out with myself but on weekends it was primarily guys in the neighborhood and we would like watch TV and videos. They were like my best friends and we were not really into moving sports. We were more into passive activities like music and cards. I've always been in the band. Hanging out at the mall. A couple of us guys would do this.

> Very quiet pursuits, stamps, cooking, which my mother liked. Guess I played verbal games, board games with the family, Risk and Candy-land, and crossword puzzles. Did a lot with my family, like family vacations, visiting historical things. I read, played with Lincoln Logs, fantasizing, spending time by myself, drawing, and swinging. I loved the freedom of the swing and I'd do it for hours. Oh yes, I loved croquet!

> I read a lot—like the encyclopedia, the phone book, science fiction, science, mystery, and

gothic novels. I had a comic book collection and Star Wars cards. I spent most of my other time drawing maps. I was really into getting any information anywhere I could, even from the atlas or an almanac. I can remember actually setting out to read the dictionary, although I don't think I got very far. Almost every book in the public library later on.

Most explicitly, unmasculine youths felt particularly ill at ease with archetypal male sports, especially loathing team sports such as baseball, basketball, and football. If they became involved in competitive, aggressive sports it was in response to family or peer pressure. Perhaps forced by a father or coach to participate in sports as a right fielder, a defensive back, or a bench warmer, they deeply resented such coercion and their inevitable failure. Severely repulsed by many typical masculine pursuits, this source of trauma was to be avoided at all costs, even at the price of disappointing parents. Unmasculine youths often shared with the following very gender-atypical youth his rejection of masculine activities and hence of masculinity.

> I did not play basketball or wrestle and I was not a farmer nor a slob nor did I shovel cow shit like my classmates. Girl, they would come in smelling like they looked and you can be sure it was not a number Chanel ever heard of! There was no way that I was going to let this be a part of what I wanted for my life.

> Well they [parents] wanted me to try at least one sport but I was always sort of the last chosen. I knew I was effeminate and clumsy and my father ridiculed me for it. So I avoided sports and I did this by going home for lunch and visiting my female friends rather than playing sports with the other guys during recess.

For one youth, the appeal or even logic of sports baffled and befuddled him.

> I really did not care about most sports and I still do not. I liked more intellectual than physical things. I enjoyed more talking philosophy, writing poetry, and drawing than spending time throwing stupid balls away, then running after the stupid balls, trying to find the stupid balls, and then throwing the stupid balls back to the same person so that he could throw it away again and have somebody run after it, find it, and throw it back to him again. Sounds real intelligent does it not?! Doing these stupid ball tricks made Bill [twin brother] real popular and me really unpopular. Where is the fairness in that?

> I only played sports during recess when I had to. I hated little boy games such as basketball, kickball, football, baseball, or anything that had a ball or a peck order. It was very aggressive and used all of the wrong parts of my anatomy and my personality.

The most aversive aspect of sports was its aggressive, dominant, physical nature. One youth remarked that in sports someone always has to lose—"and it was usually me!" This reflected not only his own personal experience of losing but also an antipathy to his life philosophy of peace, harmony, cooperation. Another youth astutely recognized another reason not to become involved in sports—his true nature might emerge and become figuratively and physically visible.

> I was not on any team sport because I was so self-conscious about being around other males. I was afraid of how I might be looked upon by them and what I might do or say or look at if I was around them a lot. What would I do in the locker room? What would happen to "George," who has a mind of his own? Maybe my feelings might come out and then where would I be?

Other youths reported that they wanted to participate in sports but could not because of physical problems. One noted, "I could never much be a sports person because I had a coordination problem because of my vision that caused me to be physically awkward." Another compensated by reading about sports: "Well, I read the sports pages and sports books! I hated gym because I was overweight. I could not do sports because I felt so evil watching men strip naked in the locker room and I couldn't take it." A third youth was on the swim team before getting pneumonia, forcing him to quit. His restitution was to remain active: "I hung out at the beach (yes, looking at the guys!), played Atari, skateboarded, and played Pogo."

Those who became involved in sports almost preferred individual to team sports. These "jocks" included the two youths below.

Some track, cross-country, swimming. I never liked the team sports. I had to do soccer in fourth grade because my best friends were into it but I disliked it immensely. Guess I was mid-level in ability and lower than that in interest but it gave me something to do and kept me around guys. I lived in a very sex-segregated rural area. I gave all of these up in junior high, except swimming in the Scout pool.

I was really into sports. Let's see. Gymnastics in fourth to sixth grades; bowling in third; darts in third; ping pong whenever; dodge the ball in second to fourth; volleyball in sixth.

Perhaps because of their paltry athleticism and low levels of masculine interests, these boys were not immune to peer ridicule and teasing. They were not, however, ridiculed nearly to the degree that gender-noncomforming boys were. They were often teased for non-gender-related characteristics or for individualized perceived deficits in physical features ("fatty"), in normative masculine behavior ("wimp"), or in desirable kinds of intelligence ("nerd"). Some were also called names more typical of effeminate youths ("fag") without, they almost universally acknowledged, the connotation of sexuality. One youth defended himself by asserting, "Being called a fag really was not a sexual thing. It was more that it reflected on my low self-esteem and that I was so wimpy."

The most common name callers were same-age, same-sex peers, although occasionally girls also participated. One youth had an unusual experience. Called "nerd" by three girls who were making his life miserable, "several boys seemed to go out of their way to protect me and shield me from this kind of teasing. Of course I was giving them answers on their exams!" Otherwise he simply withdrew. Because ridicule was seemingly random and seldom daily, it was sometimes difficult for unmasculine youths to understand what provoked the name calling.

One youth reported that he enjoyed his life as a loner and that others seemed more upset than he was that he was spending so much time alone. With his involvement in computers, the complaints lessened, perhaps, he guessed, because others envied his knowledge and saw it as a means to earn a good living. He was subject, however, to the taunts of male peers. Occasionally he was ridiculed by several boys on the school bus and during recess for reasons that were beyond his control.

At first I didn't understand why they were on my case, but since I didn't fit in in a lot of ways, they had their way. It was just the usual thing. Probably because I wasn't good at sports but I can't remember what I was called. In gym classes primarily by macho males. Nothing I didn't want to remember. I really can't remember too much of it or certainly not the names. It just seemed like I was teased about as much as anyone else was. Not every day, maybe once a month, and I just sort of reacted passively. Never really a major thing or very threatening, just sort of stupid kids' stuff. Just sort of let it go away.

I didn't fit in because I was against the intellectualism of the smart kids and I wasn't a jock. Hence I was not respected. I have no real memories of the exact names but I think they weren't happy ones because I was thin and, oh yes, my ears stuck out so I was called "monkey face."

The name-calling message might be that the boy was too feminine or not masculine enough, but more commonly it was because he was simply different or had undesirable characteristics. Very few felt that being gay was a cause of the verbal abuse. The following youths recounted the reasons they believed they suffered at the hands of their peers.

I was awkward and wore glasses. I had a speech impediment and a birthmark. I was ostracized, sort of left out because I wasn't conforming and I was very shy. I was sort of known as an only child and thus a spoiled brat with very little social skills. I was never teased about being gay. For being fat and overweight. Maybe I was teased more than average. It did hurt. I reacted by just crying because I really couldn't ignore it. It was a weight issue and not a sexual identity issue.

Because I was quiet, shy, and geekish. For being physically awkward, being different, bookish. As a kid I was teased for having cow eyes because my eyes were large. For not going to church. Very low-class assholes, mostly males. Then I went to a school for gifted children and it stopped.

I was ridiculed about being a softy and brain box because I was so intellectual or consumed in the books. They said I got good grades because I was kissing teachers' asses. I think I was just different from all of them and the teachers liked me because I liked learning. Perhaps it happened because I went to an all-male Catholic school.

I was shy and I got called Spock a lot because of my eyes which were real dark. They thought I was wearing eye shadow.

The most common response of the youths was to remain silent. One youth felt scared and frightened but "later it just got to be an annoyance. My response was to remain rather stoic." Another hated gym because he was not "graceful" and because of a particular nemesis.

A classic case of one guy on my case which I usually ignored. But one day he threw me to the gym floor but a guy came to my rescue. He was bigger than me so my reaction was basically to brave it, to try to show that it did not affect me by just walking away. I would usually not talk back and I would not cry.

A second common response was to simply avoid situations where one might be ridiculed. This was not always an easy task.

Being not good at sports, I tried to avoid all sporting situations if at all possible. I just felt like I was left out of everything. I sort of internalized it but I can't really remember how I reacted. I dreaded going to the gym. I was afraid

and felt that I was bullied. I was not verbally equipped to deal with this kind of teasing. I really didn't fight back until high school.

A third response, somewhat less prevalent, was to feel extremely hurt and cry, either publicly or in private. One youth grew to hate and fear school. "It was very painful and I was upset by it and I cried. In fact, so much so I didn't want to go to school." Another cried in private.

I was teased for being very heavy and for being slow. I reacted by being very hurt; I couldn't accept it. I cried a lot, not in front of them but in the bathroom or my room. My out was always, "Well, I'm smart."

Finally, several youths reported that they surprised their tormentors by behaving in a very masculine way, fighting back against the name-calling.

I rode the bus. I felt singled out and ridiculed. Initially what I did was simply relax and ignore it but then at one point I actually fought back, physically and verbally attacking sort of the main person who was ridiculing me the most. If I did fight back, which was the case occasionally, I would usually win. Because it was a small school, the word got out and after that I had no problems. I gained in popularity and the teasing tapered off to almost nothing.

There were rumors about me being gay. I got teasing when my friend told others that we had slept together. I confronted these people but it didn't help. I ended up going back at others or attacking them. I confronted them, "Why are you so interested in my sexuality?" After awhile they left me alone. I denied being gay but I knew I was. I wasn't ashamed but I wanted the ridiculing to stop. I was very wicked to others.

The immediate effects of the ridicule are difficult to determine. However, based on their reports, consequences appear far less severe than they were for youths who enacted femininity, perhaps because the ridicule was not as frequent and did not focus on a central aspect of their sexuality. For example, one youth noted that the name-calling had no repercussion on his sexuality because he did not interpret the ridicule as emanating from his unconventional sexuality. He did not feel that the abuse made him gay or caused him to delay self-identifying as gay. He felt, however, that the ridicule contributed to this tendency to withdraw from social settings, causing him to be more introverted and self-effacing.

> It had no real implications for my sexual identification. Everybody in my school was teased; everyone was called faggot, so I really didn't feel like I was singled out. But it made me trust people less. Hurt my self-esteem. I still need to be liked by others and if not, it upsets me. Maybe why I spent so much time alone. People hurt you. On the good side, I developed good sarcastic skills and a dry wit.

Including those who had many feminine characteristics during childhood, as many as three-quarters of the gay/bisexual youths interviewed had few interests or characteristics usually attributed to men in North American culture. Being *neither* particularly masculine *nor* feminine resulted in youths occupying the middle rung of the peer-group status hierarchy. When not alone, they were usually with a best buddy or a small group of male friends with whom they spend considerable time. Although they were seldom as frequently ridiculed by peers as were youths who were gender atypical in their lifestyle, such youths still faced verbal abuse, usually from same-age boys. The personal characteristics that became targets of abuse were notably analogous to those that heterosexual boys also receive teasing about if they are "unconventional": physical features, personality characteristics, and intelligence. Similar to other gay/bisexual youths, however, most recalled early, intense, natural attractions to other boys and men.

Acting Like a Boy

Not all of the gay/bisexual boys felt different from peers, acted in gender-atypical ways, expressed effeminate gestures and postures, or disliked team sports during their childhood. One in ten was masculine in appearance, behavior, and interests—

nearly indistinguishable from their childhood masculine heterosexual peers. Although these relatively rare boys recalled, in retrospect, that they might have had "nonsexual" attractions to males during early childhood, they had few memories of *sexual* attractions to girls, boys, or anything else. Now, however, they believe that their same-sex attractions have always been a natural part of who they are.

Many of these youths reminisced that as children they chased girls, but this was more of a game that they joined with other boys than a statement about their sexuality or their true sexual interests. As adolescents they were simply disinterested in sexual relations with girls, in being emotionally intimate with girls, or in developing romantic relationships with girls. Most never fantasized about girls. The gay youths with masculine characteristics often had difficulty articulating precisely what it was about sexuality that excited them. Many failed to recall any prepubertal sexual or erotic attractions; thus, in some respects, they appeared to be asexual, especially during the years preceding adolescence. One youth reported "a vague sense that although I did not desire intimate relations with girls, I was not sure what I wanted." Unsure of how they "became gay," the youths characterized their life before puberty as "sexless" and as deeply invested in masculine activities, especially sports.

One youth, who would later run track and play high-school baseball and football, remembered his childhood as his "glory years." Girls were not an integral part of his life.

> As a child I used to run a lot, just everywhere I could, and play tag, swimming, kickball, and softball. Loved making forts. Building blocks, Legos, war games. Just like my best buddy, which changed from time to time, well at least every year I would develop a best buddy, and it was always the best looking guy in my class who was my best friend—always an athlete. I hung around totally guys.
>
> Maybe I just did not have time but I was not into sex. I would have to say that I was sexless because I cannot remember any sexual thoughts. I

was not interested in girls even though I had several girlfriends. In general I felt left out of what my teammates said they were going through.

When asked during the interview to elaborate *any* aspect of his childhood sexuality, he drew a blank. He had many stories of athletic exploits but no sexual ones. Years after pubertal onset he discovered his sexuality and expressed wonderment regarding the location of his sexual desires during childhood.

Similar to this youth, others appeared in most respects to be the traditional, heterosexual boy next door. This was especially evident in their play activities and partners. They enjoyed their popularity with other boys, and they often developed a best friendship with another boy, usually a teammate on a sports team. One swimmer noted that the time he spent "with Jared and the other guys on the swim team was the happiest time of my life."

The sports acumen of these youths was equal or superior to many of their heterosexual peers. However, a distinct bias existed in terms of liking and participating in individual rather than team sports. While many played competitive team sports, their participation appeared more obligatory as an important aspect of male culture than a real choice. Their true love was more apparent in individual sports, especially swimming, track, tennis, and wrestling. Similar to other gay/bisexual youths, many disliked the aggressive, competitive nature of team sports.

> For Dad I did baseball—and it wasn't that I was bad, because I made the team and started— but I just couldn't get into it. Like I refused to slide because I was afraid I'd hurt the other guy, and I was just not going to go crashing into fences to catch a ball! I didn't like being challenged at sports because I was afraid I wasn't good enough so I went into individual sports like tennis, track, and swimming. Dad and I reached a compromise with my track, especially when I won the state 1000M.

> As a child I really liked horseplay, tag, and wrestling. I have to admit that I hated the Little League but as a kid I played Little League for

five years, usually at second base. Later tennis, two years of which were on varsity and I lettered. Also track and lifted weights. I was accepted by everyone, but the baseball guys who were so cutthroat; every game was the end of the universe for them!

As a result of their peer status, few of these boys were teased by others. When they were, it was usually within the context of normative male bonding—teasing in good humor. Although relatively few heard references to being gay, they nonetheless dreaded such accusations. One youth feared that his friends would notice his head turning when a good-looking guy passed by.

In contrast to the gay/bisexual youths previously discussed, masculine youths by disposition looked and acted like other boys their age, participated in typical masculine pursuits, and "fooled" peers into believing that they were heterosexual. They claimed no memories of homoerotic or even sexual attractions during childhood, perhaps, one might speculate, because the realization that the true objects of their sexual desires were boys would have caused them considerable grief and confusion. They were often perceived to be social butterflies and they actively engaged in male-male competitive sports, although their preference was individual sports. Their male friendships were critical to maintain; they wanted and needed to be members of the "male crowd." From all appearances they succeeded in creating a facade of heterosexuality, in being accepted as "one of the guys."

Reflections on the Childhood of Gay/Bisexual Youths

From an early age, the vast majority of the gay/bisexual youths believed that they were different from other boys their age and that regardless of the source of this feeling, it was a natural, instinctual, and omnipresent aspect of themselves. The pattern that most characterized the youths' awareness, interpretation, and affective responses to childhood attractions consisted of an overwhelming desire to be in the company of men. They wanted to touch, smell, see, and hear masculinity. This awareness originated from earliest childhood memories; in this sense, they "always felt gay."

Most ultimately recognized, however, that these feelings were not typical of other boys and that it would be wrong or unwise to express them because of family and peer prohibitions. Others simply assumed that all boys felt as they did and could not understand why their friends were not as preoccupied as they were with homoerotic desires. Although these attractions may have felt natural, the youths were told by parents, friends, religious leaders, teachers, and dogma that such desires were evil and sinful. Many knew that their homosensuality was ill-advised, but they did not thus conclude that it made them sick or immoral.

Beyond this common pattern, two other sources of "feeling different" characterized the vast majority of the gay/bisexual youths. Many were dominated by an overwhelming sense that their difference was attributed to their feminine appearance, behavior, and interests. In many respects these characteristics typify the stereotype that many, gay and nongay alike, have of gay males. Youths so feminized felt natural and true to self, despite the fact that their gender noncomformity was frequently and severely punished with ostracism. Most of these youths detested cultural definitions of masculinity and felt at odds with other boys because they did not share their peers' interest in team sports, competition, and aggressive pursuits. Being an outcast in the world of male peers was usually felt to be unfair and unnecessary, but also inevitable. To avoid becoming expatriated, these boys developed friendships with girls, perhaps because of common interests such as attractions to boys and appreciation of the arts, creativity, clothing, and manners. They felt more comfortable and had greater comraderie with girls than with boys. Few wanted to change either their genitalia or their behavior; they did not view themselves as women in disguise—they were simply repulsed by the "grossness" of masculinity and attracted to the sensitivities of femininity.

Other youths failed to duplicate standard masculine characteristics without necessarily as-

suming feminine traits. In this they may well have resembled heterosexual peers who were also neither particularly masculine nor feminine in behavior. They differed, however, in the direction of their sexual attractions. Being disinterested in team sports and other typical aggressive and competitive pursuits caused them to feel unmasculine, but they did not thus necessarily construe themselves as feminine. Relatively few spent time with girls or participated in girl games. Rather, their activities can be characterized as "appropriate" for either girls or boys.

Many of these youths felt that they simply faded into the background when with peers. Most were loners for a considerable period during their childhood; when they socialized with peers they were usually with one or two male friends. Although they were spared the vicious, pervasive verbal abuse that their effeminate counterparts received during childhood, they were not immune from harassment. Boys still ridiculed them for their physical features, lack of ability in athletic pursuits, and unconventional behavior or intelligence.

In contrast to these gay/bisexual youths was a much smaller group of youths who were nearly indistinguishable from masculine heterosexual boys their age. Constituting at least one of every ten youths interviewed, their participation in typical masculine pursuits, especially individual and team sports, blended them into the fabric of male culture. Many were socially active and one might speculate that their male friendships were an enjoyable sublimation of homoerotic attractions that they only later, often during adolescence or young childhood, recognized. Their failure to recognize any sexual feelings during childhood could be attributed to the direction their sexual attractions might take if they were allowed into consciousness. In this respect, their psychic investment was to conceal this secret from themselves and others.

Unknown is the etiology of these patterns and their long-term effects on other aspects of development, including participation in sexual activities, self-recognition of a sexual identity, disclosure of that identity to others, romantic relationships with other males, and developing a positive sense of self.

Although several of the interviewed youths experienced same-sex attractions as arising abruptly and unexpectedly, for the vast majority these feelings emerged as gradual, inevitable, and not particularly surprising. In this sense, these findings are at odds with the theme of this book—diversity in developmental patterns. Few if any youths believed that they could control the direction of their sexual feelings and no youth believed that he ultimately chose his sexual orientation or sexual attractions. The incorporation of the various masculine and feminine behavioral patterns was felt by youths to be less a matter of choice than an experienced naturalness that was derived from their biological heritage and, less commonly, from early socialization processes beyond their control. On his emerging sexuality, one youth reflected, "It was like being visited by an old friend." This awareness may have emerged early or late, surfaced gradually or arrived instantaneously, felt normal or wrong, motivated sexual activity or abstinence—but it was one aspect of the self that was present without invitation. Future development, discussed in the following chapters, was simply an unfolding of that which was already present, with puberty playing a crucial turning point for many youths in clarifying for them that their homosensuality had a sexual component. From this awareness often loomed first sexual encounters, which occurred during the earliest years of childhood or waited until young adulthood. They too were interpreted by the youths in diverse ways, thus having a differential impact on the eventual incorporation of a gay or bisexual identity.

Notes

1. See early account in A. P. Bell, M. S. Weinberg, and S. K. Hammersmith (1981), *Sexual Preference: Its Development in Men and Women* (Bloomington, IN: Indiana University Press). For data on gay youths see G. Herdt and A. Boxer (1993), *Children of Horizons: How Gay and Lesbian Teens Are Leading a New Way Out*

of the Closet (Boston: Beacon) and R. C. Savin-Williams (1990), *Gay and Lesbian Youth: Expressions of Identity* (New York: Hemisphere).

2 J. Sophie presents a synthesis of coming-out models in her 1985/1986 article, "A Critical Examination of Stage Theories of Lesbian Identity Development," *Journal of Homosexuality*, 12, 39–51.

3 Revised in his 1989 article, R. R. Troiden, "The Formation of Homosexual Identities," *Journal of Homosexuality, 17,* 43–73. Additional empirical evidence is available in references in endnote 1 and B. S. Newman and P. G. Muzzonigro (1993), "The Effects of Traditional Family Values on the Coming Out Process of Gay Male Adolescents," *Adolescence, 28,* 213–226, and S. K. Tellijohann and J. P. Price (1993), "A Qualitative Examination of Adolescent Homosexuals' Life Experiences: Ramifications for Secondary School Personnel," *Journal of Homosexuality, 26,* 41–56.

4. For a comprehensive review of this literature see J. M. Bailey and K. J. Zucker (1995), "Childhood Sex-Typed Behavior and Sexual Orientation: A Conceptual Analysis and Quantitative Review," *Developmental Psychology, 31,* 43–55.

5. For a review of studies using these measures, see endnote 4 and J. M. Bailey (1996), "Gender Identity," in R. C. Savin-Williams and K. M. Cohen (Eds.), *The Lives of Lesbians, Gays, and Bisexuals: Children to Adults*, pp. 71–93 (Fort Worth, TX: Harcourt Brace); R. Green (1987), *The "Sissy Boy Syndrome" and the Development of Homosexuality* (New Haven, CT: Yale University Press); G. Phillips and R. Over (1992), "Adult Sexual Orientation in Relation to Memories of Childhood Gender Conforming and Gender Nonconforming Behaviors," *Archives of Sexual Behavior, 21,* 543–558; and B. Zuger (1984), "Early Effeminate Behavior in Boys: Outcome and Significance for Homosexuality," *Journal of Nervous and Mental Disease, 172,* 90–97.

6. From R. A. Isay (1989), *Being Homosexual: Gay Men and Their Development* (New York: Farrar Straus Grove).

7. See sources in endnotes 1 and 4.

8. Experimental evidence is supplied In K. J. Zucker, D. N. Wilson-Smith, J. A. Kurita, and A. Stern (1995), "Children's Appraisals for Sex-Typed Behavior in their Peers," *Sex Roles, 33,* 703–725.

9. See references in endnotes 4 and 5.

Martin Espada

The Puerto Rican Dummy and the Merciful Son

I have a four-year-old son named Clemente. He is not named for Roberto Clemente, the baseball player, as many people are quick to guess, but rather for a Puerto Rican poet. His name, in translation, means "merciful." Like the cheetah, he can reach speeds of up to sixty miles an hour. He is also, demographically speaking, a Latino male, a "macho" for the twenty-first century.

Two years ago, we were watching television together when a ventriloquist appeared with his dummy. The ventriloquist was Anglo; the dummy was a Latino male, Puerto Rican, in fact, like me, like my son. Complete with pencil mustache, greased hair, and jawbreaking Spanish accent, the dummy acted out an Anglo fantasy for an Anglo crowd that roared its approval. My son was transfixed; he did not recognize the character onscreen because he knows no one who fits that description, but he sensed my discomfort. Too late, I changed the channel. The next morning, my son watched Luis and María on *Sesame Street*, but this was inadequate compensation. *Sesame Street* is the only barrio on television, the only neighborhood on television where Latino families live and work, but the comedians are everywhere, with that frat-boy sneer, and so are the crowds.

However, I cannot simply switch off the comedians, or explain them (how do you explain to a preschooler that a crowd of strangers is angrily laughing at the idea of *him*?). We live in western Massachusetts, not far from Springfield and Holyoke, hardscrabble small cities that, in

the last generation, have witnessed a huge influx of Puerto Ricans, now constituting some of the poorest Puerto Rican communities in the country. The evening news from Springfield features what I call "the Puerto Rican minute." This is the one minute of the newscast where we see the faces of Puerto Rican men, the mug shot or the arraignment in court or witnesses pointing to the bloodstained sidewalk, while the newscaster solemnly intones the mantra of gangs, drugs, jail. The notion of spending the Puerto Rican minute on a teacher or a health care worker or an artist in the community never occurs to the television journalists who produce this programming.

The Latino male is the bogeyman of the Pioneer Valley, which includes the area where we live. Recently, there was a rumor circulating in the atmosphere that Latino gangs would be prowling the streets on Halloween, shooting anyone in costume. My wife, Katherine, reports that one Anglo gentlemen at the local swimming pool took responsibility for warning everyone, a veritable Paul Revere in swim trunks wailing that "The Latinos are going to kill kids on Halloween!" Note how 1) Latino gangs became "Latinos" and 2) Latinos and "kids" became mutually exclusive categories. My wife wondered if this warning contemplated the Latino males in her life, if this racially paranoid imagination included visions of her professor husband and his toddling offspring as gunslingers in full macho swagger, hunting for "gringos" in Halloween costumes. The rumor, needless to say was unfounded.

Then there is the national political climate. In 1995, we saw the spectacle of a politician, California Governor Pete Wilson, being seriously considered for the presidency on the strength of his support for Proposition 187, the most blatantly anti-Latino initiative in recent memory. There is no guarantee, as my son grows older, that this political pendulum will swing back to the left; if anything, the pendulum may well swing farther to the right. That means more fear and fury and bitter laughter.

Into this world enters Clemente, which raises certain questions: How do I think of my son as a Latino male? How do I teach him to disappoint and disorient the bigots everywhere around him, all of whom have bought tickets to see the macho pantomime? At the same time, how do I teach him to inoculate himself against the very real diseases of violence and sexism and homophobia infecting our community? How do I teach Clemente to be Clemente?

My son's identity as a Puerto Rican male has already been reinforced by a number of experiences I did not have at so early an age. At age four, he has already spent time in Puerto Rico, whereas I did not visit the island until I was ten years old. From the time he was a few months old, he has witnessed his Puerto Rican father engaged in the decidedly nonstereotypical business of giving poetry readings. We savor new Spanish words together the same way we devour mangoes together, knowing the same tartness and succulence.

And yet, that same identity will be shaped by negative as well as positive experiences. The ventriloquist and his Puerto Rican dummy offered Clemente a glimpse of his inevitable future: Not only bigotry, but his growing awareness of that bigotry, his realization that some people have contempt for him because he is Puerto Rican. Here his sense of maleness will come into play, because he must learn to deal with his own rage, his inability to extinguish the source of his torment.

My father has good reason for rage. A brown-skinned man, he learned rage when he was arrested in Biloxi, Mississippi, in 1950, and spent a week in jail for refusing to go to the back of the bus. He learned rage when he was denied a college education and instead struggled for years working for an electrical contractor, hating his

work and yearning for so much more. He learned rage as the political triumphs of the 1960s he helped to achieve were attacked from without and betrayed from within. My father externalized his rage. He raged at his enemies and he raged at us. A tremendous ethical and cultural influence for us nonetheless, he must have considered himself a failure by the male career-obsessed standards of the decade into which I was born: the 1950s.

By adolescence, I had learned to internalize my rage. I learned to do this, not so much in response to my father, but more in response to my own growing awareness of bigotry. Having left my Brooklyn birthplace for the town of Valley Stream, Long Island, I was dubbed a spic in an endless torrent of taunting, bullying, and brawling. To defend myself against a few people would have been feasible; to defend myself against dozens and dozens of people deeply in love with their own racism was a practical impossibility. So I told no one, no parent or counselor or teacher or friend, about the constant racial hostility. Instead, I punched a lamp, not once but twice, and watched the blood ooze between my knuckles as if somehow I could leech the poison from my body. My evolving manhood was defined by how well I could take punishment, and paradoxically I punished myself for not being man enough to end my own humiliation. Later in life, I would emulate my father and rage openly. Rarely, however, was the real enemy within earshot, or even visible.

Someday, my son will be called a spic for the first time; this is as much a part of the Puerto Rican experience as the music he gleefully dances to. I hope he will tell me. I hope that I can help him handle the glowing toxic waste of his rage. I hope that I can explain clearly why there are those waiting for him to explode, to confirm their stereotypes of the hot-blooded, bad-tempered Latino male who has, without provocation, injured the Anglo innocents. His anger—and that anger must come—has to be controlled, directed, creatively channeled, articulated—but not all-consuming, neither destructive nor self-destructive. I keep it between the covers of the book I write.

The anger will continue to manifest itself as he matures and discovers the utter resourcefulness of bigotry, the ability of racism to change shape and survive all attempts to snuff it out. "Spic" is a crude expression of certain sentiments that become subtle and sophisticated and insidious at other levels. Speaking of crudity, I am reminded of a group organized by white ethnics in New York during the 1960s under the acronym of SPONGE: The Society for the Prevention of the Niggers Getting Everything. When affirmative action is criticized today by Anglo politicians and pundits with exquisite diction and erudite vocabulary, that is still SPONGE. When and if my son is admitted to school or obtains a job by way of affirmative action, and is resented for it by his colleagues, that will be SPONGE, too.

Violence is the first cousin to rage. If learning to confront rage is an important element of developing Latino manhood, then the question of violence must be addressed with equal urgency. Violence is terribly seductive; all of us, especially males, are trained to gaze upon violence until it becomes beautiful. Beautiful violence is not only the way to victory for armies and football teams; this becomes the solution to everyday problems as well. For many characters on the movie or television screen, problems are solved by *shooting* them. This is certainly the most emphatic way to win an argument.

Katherine and I try to minimize the seductiveness of violence for Clemente. No guns, no soldiers, and so on. But his dinosaurs still eat each other with great relish. His trains still crash, to their delight. He is experimenting with power and control, with action and reaction, which brings him to an imitation of violence. Needless to say, there is a vast difference between stegosaurus and Desert Storm.

Again, all I can do is call upon my own experience as an example. I not only found violence seductive; at some point, I found myself enjoying it. I remember one brawl in Valley Stream when I snatched a chain away from an assailant, knocked him down, and needlessly lashed the chain across his knees as he lay sobbing in the street. That I was now the assailant with the chain did not occur to me.

I also remember the day I stopped enjoying the act of fistfighting. I was working as a bouncer in a bar, and found myself struggling with a man who was so drunk that he appeared numb to the blows bouncing off his cranium. Suddenly, I heard my first echo: *thok.* I was sickened by the sound. Later, I learned that I had broken my right ring finger with that punch, but all I could recall was the headache I must have caused him. I never had a fistfight again. Parenthetically, that job ended another romance: the one with alcohol. Too much of my job consisted of ministering to people who had passed out at the bar, finding their hats and coats, calling a cab, dragging them in their stupor down the stairs. Years later, I channeled those instincts cultivated as a bouncer into my work as a legal services lawyer, representing Latino tenants, finding landlords who forgot to heat buildings in winter or exterminate rats to be more deserving targets of my wrath. Eventually, I even left the law.

Will I urge my son to be a pacifist, thereby gutting one of the foundations of traditional manhood, the pleasure taken in violence and the power derived from it? That is an ideal state. I hope that he lives a life that permits him pacifism. I hope that the world around him evolves in such a way that pacifism is a viable choice. Still, I would not deny him the option of physical self-defense. I would not deny him, on philosophical grounds, the right to resistance in any form that resistance must take to be effective. Nor would I have him deny the right to others, with the luxury of distance. Too many people in this world still need a revolution.

When he is old enough, Clemente and I will talk about matters of justification, which must be carefully and narrowly defined. He must understand that abstractions like "respect" and "honor" are not reasons to fight in the street, and abstractions like "patriotism" and "country" are not reasons to fight on the battlefield. He must understand that violence against women is not acceptable, a message which will have to be somehow repeated every time another movie trailer blazes the art of misogyny across his subconscious mind. Rather than sloganizing, however, the best way I can communicate that message is by the way I treat his mother. How else will he know that jealousy is not love, that a lover is not property?

Knowing Katherine introduced me to a new awareness of many things: compassion and intimacy, domestic violence and recovery. Her history of savage physical abuse as a child—in a Connecticut farming community—compelled me to consider what it means to heal another human being, or to help that human being heal herself. What small gestures begin to restore humanity?

When the Leather Is a Whip

At night,
with my wife
sitting on the bed,
I turn from her
to unbuckle
my belt
so she won't see
her father
unbuckling
his belt

Clemente was born on December 28, 1991. This was a difficult birth. Katherine's coccyx, or tailbone, broken in childhood, would break again during delivery. Yet only with the birth could we move from gesture to fulfillment, from generous moments to real giving. The extraordinary healing that took place was not only physical but emotional and spiritual as well. After years of constant pain, her coccyx bone set properly, as if a living metaphor for the new opportunity represented by the birth of this child.

White Birch

Two decades ago rye whiskey
scalded your father's throat,
stinking from the mouth
as he stamped his shoe
in the groove between your hips,
dizzy flailing cartwheel down the stairs.

The tail of your spine split,
became a scraping hook.
For twenty years a fire raced
across the boughs of your bones,
his drunken mouth a movie
flashing with every stabbed gesture.

Now the white room of birth is throbbing:
the numbers of palpitating red on the
    screen of machinery
tentacled to your arm; the oxygen mask
    wedged
in a wheeze on your face; the numbing
    medication
injected through the spine.
The boy was snagged on that spiraling bone.

Medical fingers prodded your raw pink
    center
while you stared at a horizon of water
no one else could see, creatures leaping
    silver
with tails that slashed the air
like your agonized tongue.

You were born in the river valley,
hard green checkerboard of farms,
a town of white birches
and a churchyard from the workhorse time,
weathered headstones naming women
drained of blood with infants coiled inside
the caging hips, hymns swaying
as if lanterns over the mounded earth.

Then the white birch of your bones,
resilient and yielding, yielded again,
root snapped as the boy spilled out of you
into hands burst open by beckoning
and voices pouring praise like water,
two beings tangled in exhaustion,
blood-painted, but full of breath.
After a generation of burning
the hook unfurled in your body,
the crack in the bone dissolved:
One day you stood, expected again
the branch of nerves
fanning across your back to flame,
and felt only the grace of birches.

Obviously, my wife and son had changed me, had even changed my poetry. This might be the first Puerto Rican poem swaying with white birch trees instead of coconut palms. On the other hand, Katherine and I immediately set about making this a Puerto Rican baby. I danced him to sleep with blaring salsa. Katherine painted *coquis*—tiny Puerto Rican frogs—on his pajamas. We spoon-fed him rice and beans. He met his great-grand-mother in Puerto Rico.

The behavior we collectively refer to as "macho" has deep historical roots, but the trigger is often a profound insecurity, a sense of being threatened. Clemente will be as secure as possible, and that security will stem in large part from self-knowledge. He will know the meaning of his name.

Clemente Soto Vélez was a great Puerto Rican poet, a fighter for the independence of Puerto Rico who spent years in prison as a result. He was also our good friend. The two Clementes met once, when the elder Clemente was eighty-seven years old and the younger Clemente was nine months. Fittingly, it was Columbus Day, 1992, the five-hundredth anniversary of the con-quest. We passed the day with a man who devoted his life and his art to battling the very colonialism personified by Columbus. The two Clementes traced the topography of one another's faces. Even from his sickbed, the elder Clemente was gentle and generous. We took photographs, signed books. Clemente Soto Vélez died the following spring, and eventually my family and I visited the grave in the mountains of Puerto Rico. We found the grave unmarked but for a stick with number and letter, so we bought a gravestone and gave the poet his name back. My son still asks to see the framed photograph of the two Clementes, still asks about the man with the long white hair who gave him *his* name. This will be family legend, family ritual, the origins of the name explained in greater and greater detail as the years pass, a source of knowledge and power as meaningful as the Book of Genesis.

Thankfully, Clemente also has a literal mean-ing: "merciful." Every time my son asks about his name, an opportunity presents itself to teach the power of mercy, the power of compassion. When Clemente, in later years, consciously acts out these qualities, he does so knowing that he is doing what his very name expects of him. His name gives him the beginnings of a moral code, a goal to which he can aspire. "Merciful": Not the first word scrawled on the mental blackboard next to the phrase "Puerto Rican male." Yet how appro-priate, given that, for Katherine and me, the act of mercy has become an expression of gratitude for Clemente's existence.

Because Clemente Means Merciful

—*for Clemente Gilbert-Espada*
February 1992

At three AM, we watched
the emergency room doctor
press a thumb against your cheekbone
to bleach your eye with light.
The spinal fluid was clear, drained
from the hole in your back,
but the X ray film
grew a stain on the lung,
explained the seizing cough,
the wailing heat of fever:
pneumonia at the age
of six weeks, a bedside vigil.
Your mother slept beside you,
the stitches of birth still burning.
When I asked, "Will he be OK?"
no one would answer: "Yes."
I closed my eyes and dreamed
my father dead, naked on a steel table
as I turned away. In the dream,
when I looked again,
my father had become my son.

So the hospital kept us: the oxygen mask,
a frayed wire taped to your toe
for reading the blood,
the medication forgotten from shift to
    shift,
a doctor bickering with radiology over the
    film,
the bald girl with a cancerous rib removed,

the pediatrician who never called, the
    yawning intern,
the hospital roommate's father
from Guatemala, ignored by the doctors
as if he had picked their morning coffee,
the checkmarks and initials of five AM,
the pages of forms flipping like a deck of
    cards,
recordkeeping for the records office,
the lawyers and the morgue.

One day, while the laundry
in the basement hissed white sheets,
and sheets of paper documented dwindling
    breath,
you spat mucus, gulped air, and lived.
We listened to the bassoon of your lungs,
the cadenza of the next century, resonate.
The Guatemalan father
did not need a stethoscope to hear
the breathing, and he grinned.
I grinned too, and because Clemente
means merciful, stood beside the
    Guatemalteco,
repeating in Spanish everything
that was not said to him.

I know someday you'll stand beside
the Guatemalan fathers,
speak in the tongue
of all the shunned faces,
breathe in a music
we have never heard, and live
by the meaning of your name.

Inevitably, we try to envision the next century. Will there by a mens' movement in twenty years, when my son is an adult? Will it someday alienate and exclude Clemente, the way it has alienated and excluded me? The counterculture can be as exclusive and elitist as the mainstream; to be kept out of both is a supreme frustration. I sincerely do not expect the mens' movement to address its own racism. The self-congratulatory tone of that movement drowns out any significant self-criticism. I only wish that the mens' movement wouldn't be so *proud* of its own ignorance.

The blatant expropriation of Native American symbols and rituals by certain factions of the movement leaves me with a twitch in my face. What should Puerto Rican men do in response to this colonizing definition of maleness, particularly considering the presence of our indigenous Taíno blood?

I remember watching one such mens' movement ritual, on public television, I believe, and becoming infuriated because the drummer couldn't keep a beat. I imagined myself cloistered in a tent with some Anglo accountant from the suburbs of New Jersey, stripped to the waist and whacking a drum with no regard for rhythm, the difference being that I could hear Mongo Santamaría in my head, and he couldn't. I am torn between hoping that the mens' movement reforms itself by the time by son reaches adulthood, or that it disappears altogether, its language going the way of Esperanto.

Another habit of language that I hope is extinct by the time Clemente reaches adulthood is the Anglo use of the term "macho." Before this term came into use to define sexism and violence, no particular ethnic or racial group was implicated by language itself. "Macho," as employed by Anglos, is a Spanish word that particularly seems to identify Latino male behavior as the very standard of sexism and violence. This connection, made by Anglos both intuitively and explicitly, then justifies a host of repressive measures against Latino males, as our presence on the honor roll of many a jail and prison will attest. In nearby Holyoke, police officers routinely round up Puerto Rican men drinking beer on the stoop, ostensibly for violating that city's "open container" ordinance, but also as a means of controlling the perceived threat of macho volatility on the street. Sometimes, of course, that perception turns deadly. I remember at age fifteen, hearing about a friend of my father's, Martín "Tito" Pérez, who was "suicided" in a New York City jail cell. A grand jury determined that it is possible for a man to hang himself with his hands cuffed behind him.

While Latino male behavior is, indeed, all too often sexist and violent, Latino males in this country are in fact no worse in that regard than their Anglo counterparts. Arguably, European and European-American males have set the world standard for violence in the twentieth century, from the Holocaust to Hiroshima to Vietnam.

Yet, any assertiveness on the part of Latino males, especially any form of resistance to Anglo authority, is labeled macho and instantly discredited. I can recall one occasion, working for an "alternative" radio station in Wisconsin, when I became involved in a protest over the station's refusal to air a Spanish-language program for the local Chicano community. When a meeting was held to debate the issue, the protesters, myself included, became frustrated and staged a walkout. The meeting went on without us, and we later learned that we were *defended*, ironically enough, by someone who saw us as acting macho. "It's their culture," this person explained apologetically to the gathered liberal intelligentsia. We got the program on the air.

I return, ultimately, to that ventriloquist and his Puerto Rican dummy, and I return, too, to the simple fact that my example as a father will have much to do with whether Clemente frustrates the worshippers of stereotype. To begin with, my very *presence*—as an attentive father and husband—contradicts the stereotype. However, too many times in my life, I have been that Puerto Rican dummy, with someone else's voice coming out of my mouth, someone else's hand in my back making me flail my arms. I have read aloud a script of cruelty or rage, and swung wildly at imagined or distant enemies. I have satisfied audiences who expected the macho brute, who were thrilled when my shouting verified all their anthropological theories about my species. I served the purposes of those who would see the Puerto Rican species self-destruct, become as rare as the parrots of our own rain forest.

But, in recent years, I have betrayed my puppeteers and disappointed the crowd. When my new sister-in-law met me, she pouted that I did not look Puerto Rican. I was not as "scary" as she expected me to be; I did not roar and flail. When a teacher at a suburban school invited me to read there, and openly expressed the usual unspoken expectations, the following incident occurred, proving that sometimes a belly laugh is infinitely more revolutionary than the howl of outrage that would have left me pegged, yet again, as a snarling, stubborn macho.

My Native Costume

When you come to visit,
said a teacher
from the suburban school,

don't forget to wear
your native costume.

But I'm a lawyer,
I said.
My native costume
is a pinstriped suit.

You know, the teacher said,
a Puerto Rican costume.

Like a guayabera?
The shirt? I said.
But it's February.

The children want to see
a native costume,
the teacher said.

So I went
to the suburban school,
embroidered guayabera
short sleeved shirt
over a turtleneck,
and said, Look kids,
cultural adaptation.

The Puerto Rican dummy brought his own poems to read today. *Claro que sí.* His son is always watching.

Pat Mahony

Girls Will Be Girls and Boys Will Be First

In this chapter I explore some of the underlying themes and negative consequences of the ways that the "underachievement of boys" are currently being expressed. My argument is not that the education of boys is unimportant but that the assumptions and purposes underpinning the current obsession with their academic performance are misconceived. As a consequence, key questions concerning the role of schools in the social construction of masculinities are omitted; the practices and consequences of different masculinities in relation to women become invisible; and the effects on different groups of boys of the internal orderings of masculinities are obscured. In relation to the last and sensitized by recent work on women and social class (Mahony and Zmroczek 1997), there is, for example, a great deal of work to be done in identifying how boys from working-class backgrounds are subordinated by the practices, values, and conceits of white, middle-class modes of masculinity. This chapter is critical of the way that the debates about boys are currently being expressed while welcoming the fact that after generations of breaking their bodies by providing fodder for coal mines, factories, and battlefields, serious questions are being forced on us about the education of working-class boys.

At the present time, a number of interdependent issues and themes tumble over each other, coalesce around and find expression in current concerns about boys. The "problem" emerges differently in different countries depending on how issues inherent in the restructurings of patriarchal

Reprinted from *Failing Boys?*, D. Epstein, J. Elwood, V. Hey, & J. Maw (eds.), pp. 37–55, Open University Press 1998.

capitalism are being perceived, experienced, and responded to. In order to trace such themes, I look first at the different and sometimes contradictory claims made in relation to the "evidence" on the underachievement of boys. Next, I place the concern with academic achievement within the wider context of the changing global economy which is framing the education and social policies of national governments. In this I consider the effects of the restructuring of capitalism and some patriarchal investments in and anxieties about these. I move on to explore some of the negative consequences of the English response to these wider changes before moving on to draw out some of the dilemmas involved both in current policy and in proposals for change.

Noisy Data

First, it is important to note that Michèle Cohen's work (1996: 8–9) demonstrates that the preoccupation with masculinity is not new:

> The question then, is not why there was an anxiety about masculinity at a specific time, say the eighteenth century, but how the anxiety about masculinity is articulated at any particular historical moment—or geographical space.

Second, it is interesting to note that the current preoccupation with the "what about the boys" debate is not confined to the United Kingdom. Heard from an international perspective, there is a din of anxiety but with enough variations on a theme to alert us to the possibility that a number of concerns are gathering round this one issue. Only in some countries is the examination performance of boys being played in a major key and even here, there are conflicting claims about which groups of boys are underachieving, in which curriculum areas, at which level of qualification, according to which definitions of underachievement and according to what evidence.

In Australia, Martin Mills and Bob Lingard (1997: 278) describe the debate as developing in response to the claim that girls were outperforming boys in the public exam held at the end of secondary schooling. They suggest that closer analysis of the data revealed that:

> a small group of mainly middle class girls are now performing as well as, and thus challenging, the dominance of middle class boys in the high status, "masculinist" subjects such as Maths, Chemistry and to a lesser extent Physics.

In another article they alert us to the existence of "a particular version of masculinity politics" which is "a recuperative, reactionary politics which seeks to reassert male dominance and traditional sex roles and in some manifestations is explicitly anti-feminist, even misogynist" (Lingard and Mills 1997: 4).

In England, the problem has been defined by the Chief Inspector of Schools as "the failure of boys and in particular white working class boys" (Pyke 1996: 2). In this case the evidence does not support the claim that boys *per se* are underachieving once we move beyond the public examinations at 16 plus. In relation to A level, for example, Patricia Murphy and Jannette Elwood (1998: 19) point out that, "whilst males continue to outperform females in mathematics, males now outperfom females in English." In fact, as Arnot, David and Weiner (1996) demonstrate, male students continue to achieve higher performances in relation to their entry than female students in nearly all subjects.

Odette Parry's discussion of Caribbean examination results add a further dimension to the debate. She cites evidence from the World Bank claiming that "females do better than males at both primary and secondary levels of schooling" (Parry 1996: 2–3). She goes on to note that "subject choices follow the traditional pattern with girls highly visible in arts and boys in science." When she compares English grade results with physics we find that "81.4% of the grade one (English) results were taken by females and 60.7% of the grade one physics went to males." These figures bear a striking resemblance to patterns of gender-segregated achievement identified in the United Kingdom in the 1980s (Mahony 1985). However, at the time, such data was taken as signifying the "underachievement of girls." Seen in its historical context, similar evidence is being used across time and place to signify opposite conclusions. This raises a separate but related issue.

When the focus was on the alleged underachievement of girls, it took a good deal of persuasion by (mainly) feminists before policy makers would look beyond the innate capacities of girls themselves for explanations of "failure" in maths and science. Such responses have not figured highly in relation to the "underachievement of boys" though, inflamed by racist accounts of intelligence, they may lurk behind some teachers' explanations of the achievement gap "between the Black and white boys in this school" (MA student's statement in class). By and large what was once evidence of the problem *of* girls has now become, not even the problem *of* boys but the problem *for* boys. The first casualty is that many of the gains made for girls, such as sensitivity to the messages contained in course materials, are increasingly being eroded as the belief takes hold that "girls have had it too good for too long" (Barber 1994: 2). Some educationists argued in the 1980s that these messages matter, not because of any causal relationship between girls' achievement and images in textbooks (if this had been the case girls would never have succeeded in anything), but because the images were degrading and distorting in portraying boys as adventurous and active while girls dripped around waiting for the first opportunity to serve them (Moys 1980). I will return to this point later but for the moment we need only to note that "achievement" and "underachievement" like other relational concepts, drifts into finer and finer specificity the more data becomes available. We could commit the rest of our lives in trying to find out which boys are underachieving, in relation to whom, in what areas, when, in which countries and why. Or we could ask another question. Why is there such a concern, even an obsession with academic achievement in the first place? I shall now go on to locate this obsession within the rise of the "competition state." This in turn has generated a whole variety of education policy reforms within which the "underachievement of boys" can be partly (but not entirely) understood.

Education and the Global Community

The "underachievement of boys" has to be seen in part within a broader context of change.

> As the world is characterised by increasing interpenetration and the crystallisation of transnational markets and structures, the state itself is having to act more and more like a market player, that shapes its policies to promote, control, and maximise returns from market forces in an international setting. (Cerny 1990: 230)

In the United Kingdom (as elsewhere) the preoccupation with increasing the competitiveness of the nation state plc in the global economy is pervasive and although the precise contribution of schooling to such competitiveness is controversial, the belief that national prosperity depends on high levels of knowledge and skill (one of the principles of microeconomic reform) is clearly presumed in the major educational policy documents of governments as far apart as Australia or New Zealand and the United Kingdom (Grace 1991; Knight *et al.* 1994).

In England it is a belief which is evident in the education policies of the Labour government (albeit set alongside a new concern with inequality):

> The Government's policy decisions, and the framework within which the DfEE [Department for Education and Employment] operates, will be shaped by powerful economic, social and technological forces. We believe the most important are:
> - globalisation—new opportunities and risks in an increasingly global economy where goods, services, capital and information are highly mobile and success depends more and more on the skills of the workforce. (DfEE 1997a)

Within this and in the words of David Blunkett, the Secretary of State for Education:

> We are talking about investing in human capital in the age of knowledge. To compete in the global economy, to live in a civilised society and to develop the talents of each and every one of us, we will have to unlock the potential of every young person. (DfEE 1997b: 3)

In this respect there has been little change in government policy from the former Conservative government in which competition in the global economy clearly underpinned the school effectiveness movement and defined the priorities of schooling. As the Chief Executive of the Teacher Training Agency (the body responsible for teacher training in England) put it:

> everyone is now agreed that the top priority in education is the need to raise pupils' standards of learning. . . . And there is a widespread awareness that, in a competitive world, constant progress is necessary just to maintain parity with other nations. (Millett 1996)

Finally, as has been argued elsewhere (Hextall and Mahony 1998), it has provided a dominant theme within the Teacher Training Agency's (TTA) reconstruction of what it means to teach and of what constitutes career progression in teaching.[1]

At the time of writing, it is too early to identify the continuities and discontinuities in the recently elected Labour government's policies but the former Conservative government's strategy for levering up standards of achievement in school is well known. In pursuit of global competitiveness, the drive to school effectiveness was directly tied to the National Curriculum and judged in accordance with criteria derived from it, mediated through performance indicators of published league tables of examination results and inspection reports. In a context of competition between schools for students, academic achievement becomes highly visible and even heightened through such mechanisms as parental choice and "measures" of individual teacher effectivity while explanations of, and solutions to, underachievement proliferate. Individual students or groups of students (such as boys) thus become crucial in determining the overall academic performance of schools, geared to the demands of the competition state. Since the demands of the global economy have become one of the major new plausibilities in Britain, it is worth noting (Mahony and Moos 1997: 12) that the Danish Minister for Education, Ole Vig Jensen has been very direct in rejecting a model of education based on the economic rationalism underpinning so much of recent education policy in the United Kingdom: "Our educational system shall not be a product of a global educational race without thinking of the goals and ideals we want in Denmark." But the "global race" is not the end of the story.

Lean, Mean, and Flexible

If one driving force in policy reform has been the need to increase "effectiveness" then the other two of the "virtuous three Es of economy, efficiency, and effectiveness" (Pollitt 1993: 59) have involved the need to reduce public expenditure. To this end new public management (NPM) or New Managerialism has been introduced across all parts of the UK public sector, in most OECD countries (Shand 1996) and may even be having an impact further afield in countries such as Pakistan and Kenya (Davies 1994). There is increasing evidence that different countries and sectors have introduced NPM in different ways according to their diverse historical and cultural traditions (Ferlie et al. 1996). For example, changes in the United Kingdom have been marked in particular ways by the influence of the New Right and their nostalgia for a fictitious age when "traditional values" were beyond question and by a particularly hard version of market liberalism. Broadly conceived, NPM in the United Kingdom is viewed as a way of dispersing the management, reporting and accounting approaches of the public sector and modeling them by different degrees along the lines of "best," i.e. "efficient," commercial practice.

The imperative to reduce public expenditure marks a change of view in which public spending,

for example, on unemployment benefit, is no longer seen as an entitlement of citizens or as a social investment but as an unproductive cost. Such expenditure becomes identified as a drain on the public purse along with those who "consume" it. Here the call for a highly skilled labour force connects with the demonization of the "work shy" in the need for an increased inculcation of the work ethic. The slide from "unemployment" to an assumption of "unemployability" easily passes unnoticed giving rise to the assumption that the conditions creating both are the same. Today's underachieving boy stands at the brink of tomorrow's unemployed youth in the form of public burden number one. I shall return later to say more about the labour market, but for the moment I want to pick up another strand of the argument.

Me Tarzan, You Jane

One of the issues in the movement towards various forms of NPM is how the values and motivations of particular powerful groups of white, male elites (Hutton 1995) have connected with the "efficiency fetish" (Lingard 1995). Such men are powerful within the transnational organizations such as the World Bank as well as influencing policy in or behind national governments and their departments.

Within a restructuring of capitalism the patriarchal cage seems to have been rattled by a belief that men are losing economic ground to women. There is indeed an issue emerging in some areas of the labour market which, as I shall suggest later, forms a significant element in the concerns about "underachieving" boys. But for white male elites the "natural order" is not about to be overturned and any panic in that direction is unfortunately unwarranted with women constituting fewer than 5 percent of senior management in the United Kingdom and United States (2 per cent in Australia), 5 percent of UK Institute of Directors and less than 1 per cent of chief executives (Collinson and Hearn 1996).

Weiner et al. (1997: 13) note that when it was newly formed in 1995, appointments to the Department for Education and Employment were "overwhelmingly male at all senior levels despite the fact that the Secretary of State was a woman." In an age of the calculative frameworks of managerialism, it would be pertinent to know whether these DfEE officials mirror the new generation of economics graduates described in Pusey's study of government restructuring in Canberra (1991), for as Prue Hyman (1994: 33–4) argues:

> free rider behaviour (selfish unwillingness to pay for public goods) was more prevalent in economics graduates . . . selfish behaviour in an experimental game was more common both among economics majors than others and among men than women.

It would also be interesting to know how far they reject offensive modes of management-speak "full of lurid gender terminology: thrusting entrepreneurs, opening up virgin territory, aggressive lending, etc." (Connell 1993: 614) and how far the sexualized discourse of management has connected for male managers in education with the "pre-pubescent boy's fantasy of being 'big,' one's potency being judged according to the size of one's budget" (Hoggett 1996: 15).

Collinson and Hearn (1996: 3–4) suggest that the 1990s has brought an increased evaluation of managers and their performance, one criterion being "the masculinist concern with personal power and the ability to control others and self." They too argue that conventional managerial discourse has become redolent with highly (hetero) sexualized talk of "penetrating markets" and "getting into bed with suppliers/customers/ competitors."

Given the restructuring of the public sector in line with "best commercial practice," it is not surprising to find similar versions of masculinism in evidence. According to Clarke and Newman (1997: 70):

> many public sector organisations have taken on images of competitive behaviour as requiring hard, macho or "cowboy" styles of working. It is as if the unlocking of the shackles of bureaucratic constraints has at last allowed public

sector managers to become "real men," released from the second-class status of public functionaries by their exposure to the "real world" of the market place.

There are other indications that while capitalism has fiddled, patriarchy has burned, even without the help of the efficiency fetish or its first cousin, the achievement fetish. This provides further evidence that the economic argument is not the only or indeed a sufficient explanatory framework for understanding the current concern about boys. In Denmark anxieties have been expressed about the demise of the "Real Man":

> The newest tendencies in Denmark support the statement that: "Real men are a scarce commodity," and that boys ought to be allowed to be more "macho" . . . Projects aimed at and for boys are being initiated in kindergartens at a rate unheard of up to now, because the predominantly women staff have been exposed to a good deal of male criticism. This criticism has made the women preschool teachers battle with their own insecurity and many of them now allow "boys' anxiety-based aggression" to run free by buying weapons and war toys and encouraging boys to let loose their wild ideas. Furthermore there is a call for more men teachers. In Viborg the head of a preschool teachers training college in the media has advertised not only for men or for qualified men, but for "Real Men" . . . (Kruse 1996: 438–9)

Kruse goes on to decide the arguments of a number of prominent men among whom is former teacher and author Bertill Nordahl:

> school is a terrible place for boys. In school they are trapped by "The Matriarchy" and are dominated by women who cannot accept boys as they are. The women teachers mainly wish to control and to suppress boys. According to him, men teachers are not a lot better off, over-run as they are by women and female values, which undermine their masculinity and self-esteem. In order to survive in the workplace dominated by women, they submit themselves to female values—thereby becoming *vatpikke* (cotton wool pricks). (Kruse 1996: 439)

As I have suggested, what is interesting about this version of the "what about the boys?" movement is its independence from any statistics on achievement.

I now move on to discuss some of the negative effects of NPM on schools. I have written elsewhere about the negative effects of NPM on feminist work in teacher education (Mahony 1997) so I shall limit my comments to the school context.

The Problem with Basics

The blinkered preoccupation with achievement, defined narrowly as subject knowledge, literacy, and numeracy has been the subject of some criticism both within the United Kingdom and elsewhere. Commenting on issues which arose from a school effectiveness research project McGraw et al. (1992: 174) concluded that:

> School effectiveness is about a great deal more than maximizing academic achievement. Learning and the love of learning; personal development and self-esteem; life skills, problem solving and learning how to learn; the development of independent thinkers and well rounded confident individuals; all rank as highly or more highly as the outcomes of effective schooling as success in a narrow range of academic disciplines.

Even within the school effectiveness "movement," a major figure in the United Kingdom has argued that:

> In Britain and internationally, there is a sense in which the entire enterprise of school effectiveness appears in a "time warp." The studies that have been conducted are all aging rapidly and are of less and less use in the educational world of the 1990's. This world has new needs at the level of pupil outcomes from schools— the skills to access information and to work collaboratively in groups, and the social outcomes of being able to cope in a highly complex world are just three new educational goals which are never used as outcomes in the school effectiveness literature. (Reynolds 1994: 23)

The effects of current UK plc definitions of what it means to "become educated" are highlighted when one works with teachers in other countries, many of whom cite UK research and development from the 1980s (derided by our own Government) as inspiring their current initiatives. Much of that work was undertaken by classroom teachers, yet such is the degree of centralization of educational policy in this country that teachers' voices have increasingly been removed from policy-making circles, their professionalism undermined and their creativity stifled (Mahony and Hextall 1997a).

In addition, teacher "efficiency" is in the process of being reconstructed through a revised appraisal system, performance-related pay, inspection reports on individual teachers, development of teaching standards, and the restructuring of the profession into four stages.

None of this is likely to foster a climate in which teachers will find it easy to be creative about developing different ways of working with different groups of young people. Nor will they be thoroughly prepared or motivated to engage in the kind of progressive work which I suggest later is necessary if we are seriously asking "What about the boys?" Such work which may well "rock the boat" will require a fresh look at gender relations in a context where over the last few years, we have witnessed a full frontal *attack* on such work in schools. Many new teachers in the United Kingdom have never known a time when the purposes of schooling went beyond the pursuit of higher academic standards. They do not remember that in the run-up to the 1987 general election "equal opportunities" were derided as the invention of the "loony Left" and our alleged intention to deprive children of a good education. They probably do not remember that one book in one teachers' centre in one London borough which told the story of a girl visiting her father and his male lover, became a *cause célèbre*; that lies abounded in the tabloid press which told of gay sex being taught to 5-year-olds and of traditional children's stories being rewritten by teachers obsessed with sex equality (Cooper 1989). They may believe along with a first-year undergraduate student teacher that "being OK about gays in school is against the law" or that "teachers in the old days" (defined as the 1980s!) "were too political." Thus when John Major (Chitty and Simon 1993) dismissed the politics of "gender, race and class" as diverting schools from their "true purposes," his words probably fell on uncritical ears. It will take time and considerable political will to put issues of social justice back on the agenda for schools and there is no guarantee that our first-year student will ever come to understand the following quotation as located precisely within the politics of gender (and class).

> In 1995 the proportion of men receiving 1st class honours degrees in History at Cambridge was three times that of women . . . men fare better because they adopt a punchy, aggressive and adversarial approach in their essays. (Targett 1996: 3)

There are further problems with our obsession with narrow definitions of academic achievement. It leads to a "sex war" mentality in which our ever increasing preoccupation with who is doing better than whom leads each year to a media panic expressed in such headlines in the *Times Educational Supplement* as "Male brain rattled by curriculum oestrogen" (15 March 1996), "Perils of ignoring our lost boys" (28 June 1996) and in the *Guardian* "Girls on top of the learning curve" (19 October 1996). It is a short step from this kind of headline to the conclusion expressed by our Chief Inspector for Schools in *The Times* and repeated in the *Times Educational Supplement* that "the failure of boys and in particular white working class boys is one of the most disturbing problems we face within the whole education system." It fuels the claim made the year before that "girls have had their way for long enough, now it's time for the boys" and the call for "reverse discrimination" (Smith 1995). And it heightens the pressure to pour resources into researching the causes of the "underachievement of boys," and to change classroom practice in ways which benefit boys (Klein 1995).

Furthermore, it is not clear where the contexts exist in which different value positions about the purposes of schooling or the different needs of young people, positioned differently by class, "race," gender, sexuality or ability, could even be debated.

We have seen so far that the concern about boys fits into a wider set of issues about the relationship of the nation state to the global economy and into a range of anxieties concerned with reasserting patriarchal dominance. Having outlined some of the negative responses in the United Kingdom, I now move on to a consideration of the terrain between schools and the global economy constituted by the world of paid work. This forms the immediate context into which young people move and to which the achievement effort is partly directed. Here again we see an interweaving of the issues I have raised so far as we reflect on what it means to be prepared for, and positioned within, a changing labour market.

The World of McWork

> A quiet revolution is going on which is transforming the lives of millions of workers in Britain. The world of full-time pensionable employment is retreating before their eyes; and in its stead is emerging an insecure world of contract work, part-time jobs and casualised labour. (Hutton 1995: 20)

This "quiet revolution" has had dramatic effects on economic inequality in the United Kingdom. Lean and Ball (1996: 1) note that according to the Human Development Report published by the UN Development Programme:

> Britain is now the most unequal country in the Western world . . . The report shows that the poorest 40 per cent of Britons share a lower proportion of the national wealth—14.6 per cent— than any other Western country. The richest fifth of Britons enjoy on average, incomes 10 times as high as the poorest fifth.

The gendered effects of poverty within these statistics are not mentioned nor, conversely, have the effects on children's educational potential featured highly within the school-effectiveness movement. The displacement of the "masculine" manufacturing base by the "feminine" service sector has meant that an increasing proportion of casualized work is being carried out by white and black working class women (EOC 1997). It would seem that since 1977 when Paul Willis wrote *Learning to Labour: How Working Class Kids Get Working Class Jobs*, it is the world which has changed, not the boys and there is no longer a fit between large areas of it and many of the boys. This raises the spectre of the "traditional" heterosexual nuclear family being made unstable by the "underachievement of boys."

If such employment as is available for groups for young working-class people exists largely in the service industries, then it has to be recognized that these require high levels of expertise in the expressive aspects of customer service. Qualities such as "warmth, empathy, sensitivity to unspoken needs and high levels of interpersonal skills to build an effective relationship with customers" (Devereux 1996: 13) would seem to be at odds with masculinities encouraged in, and adopted by, some adolescent boys. The latter poses a really difficult challenge for the demands of the labour market, the problem for some boys seems to be that they are not more like girls. It would follow that some masculinities need to change. On the other hand any attempt to critique or transform such masculinities strikes at the heart of the gender regime from which men earn the "patriarchal dividend" (Connell 1995: 41). How far there really is a need for everyone to achieve high levels of academic knowledge in order to ensure UK plc's competitiveness in the global economy and how far the real problem lies in the threat to the "natural order" of the working class male breadwinner would be a question worthy of further pursuit.

Evidence from one region in the south-east of England indicates that the reconstruction of masculinities will be hard to achieve. In a project undertaken with 130 14-years-olds, about their attitudes to school subjects and their ambitions for the future (Mahony and Frith 1995), it emerged that for many boys, biological accounts of gender were alive and kicking. Being good at (or bad at) different subjects was a matter beyond their control—"It's in yer brain" as one boy said and there was nothing to be done for some boys from whom it was not "in yer brain" but to "f— about." Girls on the other hand tended to think that if "you work harder maybe you get to like it and get better at it."

Students of both sexes thought that some subjects were easier for girls or boys though their reasons differed; boys again tended to blame the gendered nature of "natural ability" whereas girls cited "what you're used to since you were little."

Whether the boys really did believe in "nature" rather than "nurture" is a moot point. In one report: "Staff felt that boys appeared more concerned with preserving an image of reluctant involvement or disengagement; for many boys, it is not acceptable for them to be seen to be interested or stimulated by academic work" (Hofkins 1995: 5). Two points need to be interjected here about the ways in which biological determinism rolls on and off the explanatory stage. First, biological determinism is not the quaint prerogative of 14-year-old boys in south-east England but pervasive across other sites. One recent example occurred during my recent period of jury service on a case involving violent assault, when a barrister said, "You may think there is a little too much testosterone in this case, but unfortunately that is natural." It remains unclear what would have been the point of punishing the accused, if found guilty, but then perhaps it is a mistake to seek logical argument in the legitimating discourses of male violence.

In an opposite tendency, anecdoctal evidence from teachers suggests that girls are increasingly acting in ways conventionally associated with particular forms of masculinity (for example, in their increased tendency to resort to physical violence). Here, femininities and masculinities are not regarded as biologically fixed but as fluid and (in the case of the girls) as both amenable to, and in need of, reconstruction. That such a strategy (to eliminate masculinist behaviour) should not have occurred to our money conscious policy makers as a way of cutting the cost of policing, prosecuting and imprisoning men (and a few women) is perhaps no surprise. It would after all undercut one of the major props in the maintenance of patriarchal power.

To return to the study, it was predominantly the male students who wanted to get a job at 16 rather than continuing into further education and mostly the boys who were unclear about the future. They also tended to be less informed than the girls about relevant pathways to different occupations, despite the fact that all the students had spent a considerable amount of time studying "careers." For example, one student who wanted to be a PE teacher said he would either go to college to study English, media, and art or get a job.

Where they had them, the ambitions of the white working-class boys clustered simultaneously round two poles of the male labour market. On the one hand they aspired to enter the middle-class professions even though 40 percent of them could not accurately spell their chosen "career." Given what is known about the widening social class divisions in access to higher education and the social class backgrounds and exclusionary networking practices of members of the legal and medical professions, it is highly unlikely that the opportunity will really exist for these boys to become a "barraster," "solister," "docter," or "arcatec." Perhaps knowing this, they nearly always proposed alternatives to their preferred futures such as "getting a practical job," "a physical job," "a job using my body," "being a courier," or "driving a big lorry." Not one of them wanted to work in the service industries, a common aspiration for the girls and none predicted that he would find employment there. This raises a further set of complexities. Does the future lie in the reskilling (and "feminization"?) of working-class boys so that they can displace working-class women at the edge of the labour market or does it reside in encouraging them into modes of perceived middle-class masculinity so that they can enter the more stable ranks of the managerial classes? These dilemmas are further cross-cut by the recognition that masculinities are neither fixed nor framed solely by social class but by sexuality, region, age, ability, and by ethnicity as well as by the availability and nature of work, being shaped in part by economic policies geared to the needs of multinational companies, operating across national borders. In any event, there are real problems in the 1990s around the claim that some masculinities need to be reconstructed. Let us briefly explore these.

From Pen to Practice

First, a perspective favouring the reconstruction of particular masculinities will not be easy to introduce, even if the grounds on which it is advanced were reframed in terms of the employability of boys. The attack on the equity work of the 1980s at least in the United Kingdom has probably left too much detritus in the popular imagination for the arguments to be taken seriously and the anti-feminist backlash inherent in some forms of masculinity politics seem set to exploit this (Connell 1997). Second, though recent literature has stressed the transformational potential of "variety, difference and plurality, both between men and men and within individual boys and men" (Jackson and Salisbury 1996: 109) and though these particular authors make a rare and much welcome foray into suggesting practical strategies for working with boys (Salisbury and Jackson 1996), it is not clear how the cracks and fissures in the constructions of masculinities could be systematically exploited in school to produce new gender regimes. How would this much needed work stand alongside the competition to achieve higher academic results, defined within "Blairjorism" as the true purposes of schooling? How could the attempt to soften the hard competitive edges of some forms of masculinity sit comfortably within a context where *increased* competitiveness (in the global economy) has all but become the national anthem for the millennium? Within the increasingly managerialist restructuring of schools (Mahony and Hextall

1997b), it may even be that masculinist values are on the increase:

> Organisations clearly reproduce themselves. People in power (who are mostly men) mentor, encourage, and advance people who are most like themselves . . . a number of studies have shown that as women move up the organizational hierarchy, their identification with the masculine model of managerial success becomes so important that they end up rejecting even the few valued feminine managerial traits they may have endorsed. (Kanter 1993: 72)

The second problem in the United Kingdom is that few are now qualified to do such work. Nor is it clear how teachers could become qualified in the current climate. The priorities for continuing professional development for teachers are being centrally defined around the need to increase teachers' subject knowledge and their "leadership" skills and the spaces for thinking about the wider purposes of schooling are not evident within the framework of national standards for teaching currently being developed by the TTA.

The increasing gap between research and practice in the education of teachers does not help matters. As teachers work longer and harder to ensure that theirs is an "effective school" so, in parallel, researchers are striving to meet the demands of the academy for the publication of yet more academically orientated texts. Theory and practice become progressively estranged, to the detriment of both.

Within the academy there is a further problem. Just as it is easy for researchers to get lost in the detailed data on underachievement, so the temptation is to be drawn into the increasingly detailed exploration of masculinities, femininities, ethnicities, sexualities, or class identities. This is an attractive option, to be sure, easier than trying to change the world and allowing a sensitive subject to be avoided. This is that masculinities, for all their variety and internal jockeying, coalesce around a main axis of power relations with women. This awareness and its implications for action are low on both the research and practice agenda, not helped in either case by the way that

the "underachievement of boys" debate has been framed. Responsibility for this cannot be laid at the door of the pressing demands of the global economy. Other countries inhabit the same globe without feeling the need to deny that expressions of male power in the form of sexual violence are issues which have to be dealt with in school.

The European Dimension

A European workshop on in-school "prevention" of sexual violence against girls and boys was recently held in Germany. The workshop grew out of the joint local government/European Union financed PETZE project, set up in Schleswig Holstein to develop a teachers' INSET programme on sexual violence against girls and boys (Schmidt and Peter 1996). Sixty men and women (of whom I was one) from thirteen countries participated in the workshop including doctors, government officials, academics, and youth workers. In preparation, a survey was conducted on the activities of the fifteen member states in relation to "prevention work" in school, how questions of sexual violence were discussed and how teachers were supported in this work. The questionnaire from the United Kingdom was not filled in though a note was attached explaining that it was "impossible to fill it in because such work is the responsibility of the LEAs [local education authorities]" (Kavemann 1996). *The Leeds Inter-Agency School Project* (1996: 1), however, suggests that "LMS has made it difficult to promote and resource such work across the LEA." Delegates from various countries reported that "we are very worried that we will go the same way as the English— obsessed with exams" and the question "How have you in your country let this happen?" was one I could not answer, even in my own language.

Astounding was the similarity of the evidence of sexual violence quoted from many of the countries. As definitions of sexual violence vary and research methods change, so the findings of prevalence studies vary. However, bearing this difficulty in mind, much of the evidence presented at the workshop confirmed the findings of Kelly et al.

(1991) that if unwanted sexual events or interactions are included then one in two women and one in four men will have experienced at least one event before the age of 18. If "abuse attempts successfully resisted" and "less serious" forms of abuse are excluded then one in five women and one in fourteen men experienced at least one event before the age of 18.

The outcome of the workshop was that agreement on a five-page resolution was reached and sent off "to Europe." Read out of the context in which it was produced and from a perspective which theorizes the continuum of sexual violence as functioning to maintain patriarchal domination, the first paragraph of the resolution is less than perfect:

> The most far-reaching aim of prevention is to change social structures of power and violence between the sexes and the generations which produce sexual abuse of children, particularly of girls, to abolish the myths around sexual violence and the denial of its devastating consequences. (European workshop 1996: 81)

On the other hand, as the culmination of the participants' work over 3 days, in which the predominant theme had been men's sexual violence and its functioning in the social control of women, it provided evidence that perhaps we need to look outside England for examples of broader and more equitable views of the "true purposes of schooling" and of what it means to take a wider view of gender relations. Masculinities form only part of this wider perspective and the "underachievement of boys" an even smaller part.

Conclusion

I have argued that the "underachievement of boys" debate is part of a much bigger bundle of anxieties around "What about the boys?" and that these cannot be understood outside various forms of patriarchal capitalist restructurings occurring within different sites. There is an untidy heap of issues around what it means to engage with the problem which range from the diversionary through to the radical. Even from a radical

perspective which explores the potential for transforming masculinities, the danger is that the wider spectrum of gender relations and the positionings of women within it, will be overlooked. In particular, sexual violence, its devastating effects on individuals and its functioning in the social control of women are not high on the agenda in some of the theorizing around masculinities and the difficulties of educating women and men teachers to undertake transformational work in this country should not be underestimated within the purposes of schooling as defined by Blairjorism.

As a way forward we might explore the potential for exploiting at a national level the contradictions between education policy in the United Kingdom and what is currently being recommended as best practice by transnational organizations such as the OECD (Townshend 1996). We might also consider the possibilities afforded by forging alliances with other groups expressing dissatisfaction with current definitions of the purposes of schooling (Gardiner 1997). Finally, we need to question whether there are spaces in which it might be possible to overcome some of the difficulties I have highlighted in order to engage in radical work at the level of the "local." Some of the work currently being conducted under the banner of "underachieving boys" would be an obvious starting point notwithstanding the fact that teachers willing and able to do it will need time, acknowledgement, and support.

Evidence which gives cause for optimism at the level of the local suggests that parents' views of the purposes of schooling are rather wider than those pursued over recent years (Mahony and Moos 1997). There are also practical examples where such views are being accessed and developed to legitimate a broader view of the purposes of the individual school (MacBeath et al. 1996).

Even though these local spaces may provide opportunities for radical work, such possibilities mark the beginning, not the end of current debates. They raise but do not resolve wide-ranging concerns evident throughout the whole area of public-sector reorganization over patterns of centralization/decentralization and questions of accountability and representation (Mahony and Hextall 1997a). We are led ultimately to questions about forms of social participation and control, the nature of society itself in the late 1990s and the representation of different voices and value positions within it. As is often the case, issues of gender lead ultimately to questions concerned with what kind of society we want, who the "we" is who wants it and the nature of our powers to achieve it.

Note

1. The data on the Teacher Training Agency was gathered during an ESRC funded project "The Policy Context and Impact of the Teacher Training Agency" undertaken with Ian Hextall from September 1995 to November 1996.

References

Arnot, M., David, M. and Weiner, G. (1996) *Educational Reforms and Gender Equality in Schools.* Manchester: Equal Opportunities Commission.

Barber, M. (1994) Report into school students' attitudes, *Guardian,* 23 August.

Cerny, P. (1990) *The Changing Architecture of Politics: Structure, Agency and the Future of the State.* London: Sage Publications.

Chitty, C. and Simon, B. (eds) (1993) Extract from John Major's speech to the 1992 Conservative Party conference, in *Education Answers Back: Critical Responses to Government Policy.* London: Wishart.

Clarke, J. and Newman, J. (1997) *The Managerial State.* London: Sage Publications.

Cohen, M. (1996) *Fashioning Masculinity: National Identity and Language in the Eighteenth Century.* London: Routledge.

Collinson, D. and Hearn J. (eds) (1996) *Men as Managers, Managers as Men.* London: Sage Publications.

Connell, R. W. (1993) The big picture: masculinities in recent world history. *Theory and Society,* 22: 597–624.

Connell, R. W. (1995) *Masculinities.* Sydney: Allen and Unwin.

Connell, R. W. (1997) Men, masculinities and feminism. *Social Alternatives,* 16: 7–10.

Cooper, D. (1989) Positive images in Haringey: a struggle for identity, in C. Jones and P. Mahony (eds) *Learning our Lines: Sexuality and Social Control in Education.* London: The Women's Press.

Davies, L. (1994) *Beyond Authoritarian School Management: The Challenge of Transparency.* Derbyshire: Education Now Publishing Cooperative.

Department for Education and Employment (DfEE) (1997a) *Learning and Working Together for the Future.* London: HMSO.

Department for Education and Employment (DfEE) (1997b) *Excellence in Schools.* London: HMSO.

Devereux, C. (1996) *Cross Cultural Standards of Competence in Customer Service.* Cheam: W. A. Consultants.

Equal Opportunities Commission [EOC] (1997) 'Briefings on Women and Men in Britain: The Labour Market', Manchester: Equal Opportunities Commission.

European Workshop (1996) Prevention of sexual violence against girls and boys in school. Documentation. Ministry of Education, Science, Research and Cultural Affairs of the Land of Schlewig-Holstein, Germany.

Ferlie, E., Pettigrew, A., Ashburner, L. and Fitgerald, L. (1996) *The New Public Management in Action.* Oxford: Oxford University Press.

Gardiner, J. (1997) Editors back new progressivism, *Times Educational Supplement, 24 January.*

Grace, G. (1991) Welfare Labourism versus the New Right: the struggle in New Zealand's educational policy. *International Studies in the Sociology of Education,* 1: 25–41.

Hextall, I. and Mahony, P. (1998) Effective teachers for effective schools, in R. Slee, S. Tomlinson and G. Weiner (eds) *Effective for Whom?* London: Falmer Press.

Hofkins, D. (1995) Why teenage boys think success is sad, *Times Educational Supplement,* 18 August.

Hoggett, P. (1996) New modes of control in the public service. *Public Administration,* 74: 9–31.

Hutton, W. (1995) *The State We're In.* London: Jonathan Cape.

Hyman, P. (1994) *Women and Economics: A New Zealand Feminist Perspective.* Wellington, New Zealand: Bridget Williams Book Ltd.

Jackson, D. and Salisbury J. (1996) Why should secondary schools take working with boys seriously? *Gender and Education*, 8: 103–15.

Kanter, R. M. (1993) *Men and Women of the Corporation*, 2nd edn. New York: Basic Books.

Kavemann, B. (1996) Verbal comment made during presentation of *Evaluation of a Survey of the European Union Member States Concerning Prevention of Sexual Violence against Girls and Boys*. Schleswig-Holstein: Ministry of Education, Science, Research and Culture.

Kelly, L., Regan, L. and Burton, S. (1991) *An Exploratory Study of the Prevalence of Sexual Abuse in a Sample of 16–21 Year Olds*. London: Child Abuse Studies Unit, University of North London.

Klein, R. (1995) Tails of snips and snails, *Times Educational Supplement*, 9 June.

Knight, J., Lingard, B. and Barlett, L. (1994) Reforming teacher education policy under Labor Governments in Australia 1983–93. *British Journal of Sociology of Education*, 15: 451–66.

Kruse, A.-M. (1996) Approaches to teaching girls and boys: current debates, practices and perspectives in Denmark, in P. Mahony (ed.) *Changing Schools: Some International Feminist Perspectives on Working with Girls and Boys*. Special Issue, *Women's Studies International Forum,* 19: 429–45.

Lean, G. and Ball, G. (1996) UK most unequal Country in the West, *Independent on Sunday*, 21 July.

Leeds Inter-Agency School Project (1996) *Summary, Key Issues and Recommendations*. Leeds: Leeds City Council.

Lingard, B. (1995) Re-articulating relevant voices in reconstructing teacher education. The Annual Harry Penny Lecture, University of South Australia.

Lingard, B. and Mills, M. (1997) Masculinity politics: an introduction. *Social Alternatives*, 16: 4–6.

MacBeath, J., Boyd, J., Rand, B. and Bell, S. (1996) *Schools Speak for Themselves: Towards a Framework for Self-Evaluation*. Strathclyde Quality in Education Centre, University of Strathclyde.

McGraw, B., Piper, K., Banks, D. and Evans, B. (1992) *Making Schools More Effective*. Victoria: Australian Council for Educational Research (ACER).

Mahony, P. (1985) *Schools for the Boys?* London: Hutchinson.

Mahony, P. (1997) Talking heads: feminist perspectives on public sector reform in teacher education. *Discourse*, 18: 87–102.

Mahony, P. and Frith, R. (1995) *Factors Influencing Girls' and Boys' Option Choices in Year 9*. Report to Essex Careers and Business Partnership. London: Roehampton Institute.

Mahony, P. and Hextall, I. (1997a) Problems of accountability in reinvented government: a case study of the Teacher Training Agency. *Journal of Education Policy*, 12: 267–78.

Mahony, P. and Hextall, I. (1997b) Sounds of silence: the social justice agency of the Teacher Training Agency. *International Studies in Sociology of Education*, 7: 137–56.

Mahony, P. and Moos, L. (1997) Facts and fictions of school leadership. Paper presented at European Conference on Educational Research, Frankfurt, Germany, 24–26 September.

Mahony, P. and Zmroczek, C. (1997) *Class Matters: "Working Class" Women's Perspectives on Social Class*. London: Taylor and Francis.

Millett, A. (1996) *Chief Executive's Annual Lecture*. London: Teacher Training Agency.

Mills, M. and Lingard, B. (1997) Masculinity politics, myths and boys' schooling. *British Journal of Educational Studies*, 45: 276–92.

Moys, A. (1980) *Modern Languages Examinations at 16+*. London: Centre for Information on Language Teaching Research.

Murphy, P. and Elwood, J. (1998) Gendered experiences, choices and achievement: exploring the links, in D. Epstein, J. Maw, J. Elwood and V. Hey (eds) *International Journal of Inclusive Education: Special Issue on Boys' "Underachievement,"* 2(2): 95–118.

Parry, O. (1996) Cultural contexts and school failure: underachievement of Caribbean males in Jamaica, Barbados and St. Vincent and the Grenadines. Paper presented to ESRC seminar series "Gender and Schooling: Are Boys Now Underachieving?," University of London Institute of Education.

Pollitt, C. (1993) *Managerialism and the Public Services*, 2nd edn. Oxford: Blackwell Publishers.

Pusey, M. (1991) *Economic Rationalism in Canberra: A Nation-Building State Changes its Mind*. New York: Cambridge University Press.

Pyke, N. (1996) Boys "read less than girls," *Times Educational Supplement*, 15 March.

Reynolds, D. (1994) School effectiveness and quality in education, in P. Ribnew and E. Burridge (eds) *Improving Education: Promoting Quality in Schools.* London: Cassell.

Salisbury, J. and Jackson, D. (1996) *Challenging Macho Values: Practical Ways of Working with Adolescent Boys.* London: Falmer Press.

Schmidt, B. and Peter, A. (1996) The Petze Project: working with teachers on the prevention of sexual violence against girls and boys in Germany, in P. Mahony (ed.) *Changing Schools: Some International Feminist Perspectives on Working with Girls and Boys.* Special issue *Women's Studies International Forum*, 19: 395–407.

Shand, D. (1996) The new public management: an international perspective. Paper presented to Public Services Management 2000 Conference, University of Glamorgan, 11 October.

Smith, M. J. (1995) Silence of the lads, *Times Educational Supplement*, 24 March.

Targett, S. (1996) Women told to take risks to get a first, *Times Higher Educational Supplement*, 1 November.

Townshend, J. (1996) An overview of OECD work on teachers, their pay and conditions, teaching quality and the continuing professional development of teachers. Paper presented at UNESCO International Conference on Education, Geneva, October.

Weiner, G., Arnot, M. and David, M. (1997) Is the future female? Female success, male disadvantage and changing gender patterns in education, in A. H. Halsey, P. Brown, H. Lauder and A. Stuart-Wells (eds) *Education: Culture, Economy and Society.* Oxford: Oxford University Press.

Willis, P. (1977) *Learning to Labour: How Working Class Kids Get Working Class Jobs.* Aldershot: Saxon House.

PART THREE

THREE

Collegiate Masculinities: Privilege and Peril

The old social science orthodoxy about sex role socialization, from the 1950s until today, held that three institutions—family, church, and school—formed the primary sites of socialization, and the impact of education, family values, and religious training was decisive in shaping people's lives. This view tended to emphasize the centrality of adults in boys' lives. Because adults themselves were constructing the models of socialization, this conclusion seems understandable. But as social scientists began to ask boys and girls about the forces that influenced them, they heard about the increasing importance of peer groups and the media—two arenas where adults had far less reach. In recent years, researchers have begun to explore how homosocial peer groups affect men's lives.

The articles in Part Three focus on masculinities in college, a place where the all-male peer group is especially salient. How does collegiate life organize and reproduce the definitions of masculinity that we learn as young boys? How do specific all-male subcultures develop within these institutions, and what roles do they play? Part Three explores male bonding within collegiate organizations, such as fraternities and athletic teams, and within the traditions of an all-male military institution. In recent years these institutions have been increasingly scrutinized and criticized, and some group members have felt besieged and unfairly picked on. Who's right?

Two of the articles in this section focus specifically on fraternities and the role of fraternity culture on campus life. The articles by Peter Lyman and by A. Ayres Boswell and Joan Spade ask: How is hegemonic masculinity reproduced in fraternity life? Why are fraternity men more likely to be accused of sexual assault? Todd Crosset, Jeffrey Benedict, and Mark McDonald report the results of a survey about campus sexual assault and participation in NCAA athletics. Timothy Jon Curry explores the fusion of the two, observing how fraternal bonding takes place in the locker room. Finally, John Stoltenberg suggests an alternative collegiate masculinity, one increasingly focused on supporting women's equality as an expression of what it means to be a man.

Tank McNamara © 1989 Millar/Hinds. Distributed by Universal Press Syndicate. Reprinted with permission. All rights reserved.

Peter Lyman

The Fraternal Bond as a Joking Relationship: A Case Study of the Role of Sexist Jokes in Male Group Bonding

One evening during dinner, 45 fraternity men suddenly broke into the dining room of a nearby campus sorority, surrounded the 30 women residents, and forced them to watch while one pledge gave a speech on Freud's theory of penis envy as another demonstrated various techniques of masturbation with a rubber penis. The women sat silently, staring downward at their plates, and listened for about 10 minutes, until a woman law student who was the graduate resident in charge of the house walked in, surveyed the scene and demanded, "Please leave immediately!" As she later described that moment, "There was a mocking roar from the men, 'It's tradition.' I said, 'That's no reason to do something like this, please leave!' And they left. I was surprised. Then the women in the house started to get angry. And the guy who made the penis-envy speech came back and said to us, 'That was funny to me. If that's not funny to you I don't know what kind of sense of humor you have, but I'm sorry.' "

That night the women sat around the stairwell of their house discussing the event, some angry and others simply wanting to forget the whole thing. They finally decided to ask the university to require that the men return to discuss the event. When university officials threatened to take action, the men agreed to the meeting. I had served as a faculty resident in student housing for two years and had given several talks in the dorm

From *Changing Men*, edited by Michael Kimmel. Newbury Park, CA: Sage Publications, 1987. Reprinted by permission.

about humor and gender, and was asked by both the men and the women involved to attend the discussion as a facilitator, and was given permission to take notes and interview the participants later, provided I concealed their identities.

The penis-envy ritual had been considered a successful joke in previous years by both "the guys and the girls," but this year it failed, causing great tension between two groups that historically had enjoyed a friendly joking relationship. In the women's view, the joke had not failed because of its subject; they considered sexual jokes to be a normal part of the erotic joking relationship between men and women. They thought it had failed because of its emotional structure, the mixture of sexuality with aggression and the atmosphere of physical intimidation in the room that signified that the women were the object of a joking relationship between the men. A few women argued that the failed joke exposed the latent domination in men's relation to women, but this view was labeled "feminist" because it endangered the possibility of reconstituting the erotic joking relationship with the men. Although many of the men individually regretted the damage to their relationship with women friends in the group, they argued that the special male bond created by sexist humor is a unique form of intimacy that justified the inconvenience caused the women. In reinterpreting these stories as social constructions of gender, I will focus upon the way the joke form and joking relationships reveal the emotional currents underlying gender in this situation.

The Sociology of Jokes

Although we conventionally think of jokes as a meaningless part of the dramaturgy of everyday life, this convention is part of the way that the social function of jokes is concealed and is necessary if jokes are to "work." It is when jokes fail that the social conflicts that the joke was to reconstruct or "negotiate" are uncovered, and the tensions and emotions that underlie the conventional order of everyday social relations are revealed.

Joking is a special kind of social relationship that suspends the rules of everyday life in order to preserve them. Jokes indirectly express the emotions and tensions that may disrupt everyday life by "negotiating" them (Emerson 1969, 1970), reconstituting group solidarity by shared aggression and cathartic laughter. The ordinary consequences of forbidden words are suspended by meta-linguistic gestures (tones of voice, facial expressions, catch phrases) that send the message "this is a joke," and emotions that would ordinarily endanger a social relationship can be spoken safely within the micro-world created by the "the joke form" (Bateson 1955).

Yet jokes are not just stories, they are a theater of domination in everyday life, and the success or failure of a joke marks the boundary within which power and aggression may be used in a relationship. Nearly all jokes have an aggressive content, indeed shared aggression toward an outsider is one of the primary ways by which a group may overcome internal tension and assert its solidarity (Freud 1960, p. 102). Jokes both require and renew social bonds; thus Radcliffe-Brown pointed out that "joking relationships" between mothers-in-law and their sons-in-law provide a release for tension for people structurally bound to each other but at the same time feeling structural conflict with each other (Radcliffe-Brown 1959). Joking relationships in medicine, for example, are a medium for the indirect expression of latent emotions or taboo topics that if directly expressed would challenge the physician's authority or disrupt the need to treat life and death situations as ordinary work (see Coser 1959; Emerson 1969, 1970).

In each of the studies cited above, the primary focus of the analysis was upon the social function of the joke, not gender, yet in each case the joke either functioned through a joking relationship between men and women, such as in Freud's or Radcliffe-Brown's analysis of mother-in-law jokes, or through the joking relationship between men and women. For example, Coser describes the role of nurses as a safe target of jokes: as a surrogate for the male doctor in patient jokes challenging medical authority; or as a surrogate for the patient in the jokes with which doctors expressed anxiety. Sexist jokes, therefore, should be analyzed not only in general terms of the function of jokes as a means of defending social order, but in specific terms as the mechanism by which the order of gender domination is sustained in everyday life. From this perspective, jokes reveal the way social organizations are gendered, namely, built around the emotional rules of male bonding. In this case study, gender is not only the primary content of men's jokes, but the emotional structures of the male bond is built upon a joking relationship that "negotiates" the tension men feel about their relationship with each other, and with women.

Male bonding in everyday life frequently takes the form of a group joking relationship by which men create a serial kind of intimacy to "negotiate" the latent tension and aggression they feel toward each other. The humor of male bonding relationships generally is sexual and aggressive, and frequently consists of sexist or racist jokes. As Freud (1960, p. 99) observed, the jokes that individual men direct toward women are generally erotic, tend to clever forms (like the double entendre), and have a seductive purpose. The jokes that men tell about women in the presence of other men are sexual and aggressive rather than erotic and use hostile rather than clever verbal forms; and, this paper will argue, have the creation of male group bonding as their purpose. While Freud analyzed jokes in order to reveal the unconscious, in this article, relationships will be analyzed to uncover the emotional dynamics of male friendships.

The failed penis-envy joke reveals two kinds of joking relationships between college men and women. First, the attempted joke was part of an ongoing joking relationship between "the guys and the girls," as they called each other. The guys used the joking relationship to negotiate the tension they felt between sexual interest in the girls and fear of commitment to them. The guys contrasted their sense of independence and play in male friendships to the sense of dependence they felt in their relationships with women, and used hostile joking to negotiate their fear of the "loss of control" implied by intimacy. Second, the failure of the joke uncovered the use of sexist jokes in creating bonds between men; through their own joking relationships (which they called friendship), the guys negotiated the tension between their need for intimacy with other men and their fear of losing their autonomy as men to the authority of the work world.

The Girls' Story

The women frequently had been the target of fraternity initiation rites in the past, and generally enjoyed this joking relationship with the men, if with a certain ambivalence. "There was a naked Christmas Carol event, they were singing 'We wish you a Merry Christmas,' and 'Bring on the hasty pudding' was the big line they liked to yell out. And we had five or six pledges who had to strip in front of the house and do naked jumping jacks on the lawn, after all the women in the house were lined up on the steps to watch." The women did not think these events were hostile because they had been invited to watch, and the men stood with them watching, suggesting that the pledges, not the women, were the targets of the joke. This made the joke sexual, not sexist, and part of the normal erotic joking relationship between the guys and girls. Still, these jokes were ritual events, not real social relationships; one woman said, "We

were just supposed to watch, and the guys were watching us watch. The men set up the stage and the women are brought along to observe. They were the controlling force, then they jump into the car and take off."

At the meeting with the men, two of the women spoke for the group while 11 others sat silently in the center, surrounded by about 30 men. Each tried to explain to the men why the joke had not been funny. The first began, "I'm a feminist, but I'm not going to blame anyone for anything. I just want to talk about my feelings." When she said, "these guys pile in, I mean these huge guys," the men exploded in loud cathartic laughter, and the women joined in, releasing some of the tension of the meeting. She continued, "Your humor was pretty funny as long as it was sexual, but when it went beyond sexual to sexist, then it became painful. You were saying 'I'm better than you.' When you started using sex as a way of proving your superiority it hurt me and made me angry."

The second woman speaker criticized the imposition of the joke form itself, saying that the men's raid had the tone of a symbolic rape. "I admit we knew you were coming over, and we were whispering about it. But it went too far, and I felt afraid to say anything. Why do men always think about women in terms of violating them, in sexual imagery? You have to understand that the combination of a sexual topic with the physical threat of all of you standing around terrified me. I couldn't move. You have to realize that when men combine sexuality and force it's terrifying to women." This woman alluded to having been sexually assaulted in the past, but spoke in a nonthreatening tone that made the men listen silently.

The women spoke about feeling angry about the invasion of their space, about the coercion of being forced to listen to the speeches, and about being used as the object of a joke. But they reported their anger as a psychological fact, a statement about a past feeling, not an accusation. Many began by saying, "I'm not a feminist, but . . . ," to reassure the men that although they felt angry, they were not challenging traditional gender relations. The women were caught in a double-bind; if they spoke angrily to the men they would violate the taboo against the expression of anger by women (Miller 1976, p. 102). If they said nothing, they would internalize their anger, and traditional feminine culture would encourage them to feel guilty about feeling angry at all (Bernardez 1978; Lerner 1980). In part they resolved the issue by accepting the men's construction of the event as a joke, although a failed joke; accepting the joke form absolved the men of responsibility, and transformed a debate about gender into a debate about good and bad jokes.

To be accepted as a joke, a cue must be sent to establish a "frame" [for] the latent hostility of the joke content in a safe context; the men sent such a cue when they stood next to the women during the naked jumping jacks. If the cue "this is a joke" is ambiguous, or is not accepted, the aggressive content of the joke is revealed and generally is responded to with anger or aggression, endangering the relationship. In part the women were pointing out to the men that the cue "this is a joke" had not been given in this case, and the aggressive content of the joke hurt them. If the cue is given properly and accepted, the everyday rules of social order are suspended and the rule "this is fun" is imposed on the expression of hostility.

Verbal aggression mediated by the joke form generally will be [accepted] without later consequences in the everyday world, and will be judged in terms of the formal intention of jokes, shared play marked by laughter in the interest of social order. By complaining to the university, the women had suspended the rules of joke culture, and attempted to renegotiate them by bringing in an observer; even this turned out to be too aggressive, and the women retreated to traditional gender relationships. The men had formally accepted this shift of rules in order to avoid punishment from the university, however their defense of the joke form was tacitly a defense of traditional gender rules that would define male sexist jokes toward women as erotic, not hostile.

In accepting the construction of the event as "just a joke" the women absolved the men of responsibility for their actions by calling them "little boys." One woman said, "It's not wrong, they're just boys playing a prank. They're little boys, they don't know what they're doing. It was unpleasant, but we shouldn't make a big deal out of it." In appealing to the rules of the joke form the men were willing to sacrifice their relationship to the women to protect the rules. In calling the men "little boys" the women were bending the rules trying to preserve the relationship through a patient nurturing role (see Gilligan 1982, p. 44).

In calling the guys "little boys," the girls had also created a kind of linguistic symmetry between "the boys and the girls." With the exception of the law student, who called the girls "women," the students called the men "guys" and the women "girls." Earlier in the year the law student had started a discussion about this naming practice. The term "women" had sexual connotations that made "the girls" feel vulnerable, and "gals," the parallel to "guys," connoted "older women" to them. While the term "girls" refers to children, it was adopted because it avoided sexual connotations. Thus the women had no term like "the guys," which is a bonding term that refers to a group of friends as equals; the women often used the term "the guys" to refer to themselves in a group. As the men's speeches were to make clear, the term "guys" refers to a bond that is exclusively male, which is founded upon the emotional structure of the joke form, and which justifies it.

The Guys' Story

Aside from the roar of laughter when a woman referred to their intimidating size, the men interrupted the women only once. When a woman began to say that the men obviously intended to intimidate them, the men loudly protested that the women couldn't possibly judge their intentions, that they intended the whole event only as a joke, and the intention of a joke is, by definition, just fun.

At this point the two black men in the fraternity intervened to explain the rules of male joke culture to the women. The black men said that in a sense they understood what the women meant, it is painful being the object of aggressive jokes. In fact, they said, the collective talk of the fraternity at meals and group events was made up of nothing but jokes, including many racist jokes. One said, "I know what you mean. I've had to listen to things in the house that I'd have hit someone for saying if I'd heard them outside." There was again cathartic laughter among the guys, for the male group bond consisted almost entirely of aggressive words that were barely contained by the responsibility absolving rule of the joke form. A woman responded, "Maybe people should be hit for saying those things, maybe that's the right thing to do." But the black speaker was trying to explain the rules of male joke culture to the women, "if you'd just ignored us, it wouldn't have been any fun." To ignore a joke, even though it makes you feel hurt or angry, is to show strength or coolness, the two primary masculine ideals of the group.

Another man tried to explain the failure of the joke in terms of the difference between the degree of "crudeness" appropriate among the guys and between "guys and girls." He said, "As I was listening at the edge of the room, near the door, and when I looked at the guys I was laughing but when I looked at the girls I was embarrassed. I could see both sides at the same time. It was too crude for your sense of propriety. We have a sense of crudeness you don't have. That's a cultural aspect of the difference between girls and guys."

The other men laughed as he mentioned "how crude we are at the house," and one of the black men added, "you wouldn't believe how crude it gets." Many of the men said privately that while they individually found the jokes about women vulgar, the jokes were justified because they were necessary for the formation of the fraternal bond. These men thought the mistake had been to reveal their crudeness to the women, this was "in bad taste."

In its content, the fraternal bond was almost entirely a joking relationship. In part, the joking was a kind of "signifying" or "dozens," a ritual exchange of insults that functioned to create group solidarity. "If there's one theme that goes on, it's the emphasis on being able to take a lot of ridicule, of shit, and not getting upset about it. Most of the interaction we have is verbally abusing each other, making disgusting references to your mother's sexuality, or the women you were seen with, or your sex organ, the size of your sex organ. And you aren't cool unless you can take it without trying to get back." Being cool is an important male value in other settings as well, such as sports or work; the joke form is a kind of male pedagogy in that, in one guy's words, it teaches "how to keep in control of your emotions."

But the guys themselves would not have described their group as a joking relationship or even as a male bond; they called it friendship. One man said he had found perhaps a dozen guys in the house who were special friends, "guys I could cry in front of." Yet in interviews, no one could recall any of the guys actually crying in front of each other. One said, "I think the guys are very close, they would do nearly anything for each other, drive each other places, give each other money. I think when they have problems about school, their car, or something like that, they can talk to each other. I'm not sure they can talk to each other about problems with women though." The image of crying in front of the other guys was a moving symbol of intimacy to the guys, but in fact crying would be an admission of vulnerability, which would violate the ideals of "strength" and "being cool."

Although the fraternal bond was idealized as a unique kind of intimacy upon which genuine friendship was built, the content of the joking relationship was focused upon women, including much "signifying" talk about mothers. The women interpreted the sexist jokes as a sign of vulnerability. "The thing that struck me the most about our meeting together," one said, "was when the men said they were afraid of trusting women, afraid of being seen as jerks." According to her, this had been the women's main reaction to the meeting by the other women, "How do you tell men that they don't have to be afraid, and what do you do with women who abuse that kind of trust?" One of the men on the boundary of the group remarked that the most hostile misogynist jokes came from the men with the fewest intimate relationships with women. "I think down deep all these guys would love to have satisfying relationships with women. I think they're scared of failing, of having to break away from the group they've become comfortable with. I think being in a fraternity, having close friendships with men is a replacement for having close relationships with women. It'd be painful for them because they'd probably fail."

Joking mobilized the commitment of the men to the group by policing the individual men's commitments to women and minimized the possibility of dyadic withdrawal from the group (see Slater 1963). "One of the guys just acquired a girlfriend a few weeks ago. He's someone I don't think has had a woman to be friends with, maybe ever, at least in a long time. Everybody has been ribbing him intensely the last few weeks. It's good natured in tone. Sitting at dinner they've invented a little song they sing to him. People yell questions about his girlfriend, the size of her vagina, does she have big breasts."

Since both the jokes and the descriptions of the parties have strong homoerotic overtones, including the exchange of women as sexual partners, jokes were also targeted at homosexuality, to draw an emotional line between the homosocial male bond and homosexual relationships. Being called "queer," however, did not require a sexual relationship with another man, but only visible signs of vulnerability or nurturing behavior.

Male Bonding as a Joking Relationship

Fraternal bonding is an intimate kind of male group friendship that suspends the ordinary rules and responsibilities of everyday life through joking relationships. To the guys, dyadic friendship with a woman implied "loss of control," namely, responsibility for work and family. In dealing with women, the group separated intimacy from sex, defining the male bond as intimate but not sexual (homosocial), and relationships with women as sexual but not intimate (heterosexual). The intimacy of group friendship was built upon shared spontaneous action, "having fun," rather than the self-disclosure that marks women's friendships (see Rubin 1983, p. 13). One of the men had been inexpressive as he listened to the discussion, but spoke about fun in a voice filled with emotion, "The penis-envy speech was a hilarious idea, great college fun. That's what I joined the fraternity for, a good time. College is a stage in my life to do crazy and humorous things. In 10 years when I'm in the business world I won't be able to carry on like this [again cathartic laughter from the men]. The initiation was intended to be humorous. We didn't think through how sensitive you women were going to be."

This speech gives the fraternal bond a specific place in the life cycle. The joking relationship is a ritual bond that creates a male group bond in the transition between boyhood and manhood, after the separation from the family, where the authority of mothers limits fun, but before becoming subject to the authority of work. One man later commented on the transitional nature of the male bond, "I think a lot of us are really scared of losing total control over our own lives. Having to sacrifice our individuality. I think we're scared of work in the same way we're scared of women." In this sense individuality is associated with what the guys called "strength," both the emotional strength suggested by being cool, and the physical strength suggested by facing the risks of sports and the paramilitary games they liked to play.

The emotional structure of the joking relationship is built upon the guys' latent anger about the discipline that middle-class male roles imposed upon them, both marriage rules and work rules. The general relationship between organization of men's work and men's domination of women was noted by Max Weber (1958, pp.

345–346), who described "the vocational specialist" as a man mastered by the rules of organization that create an impersonal kind of dependence, and who therefore seeks to create a feeling of independence through the sexual conquest of women. In each of the epochs of Western history, Weber argues, the subordination of men at work has given rise to a male concept of freedom based upon the violation of women. Although Weber tied dependence upon rules to men's need for sexual conquest through seduction, this may also be a clue to the meaning of sexist jokes and joking relationships among men at work. Sexist jokes may not be simply a matter of recreation or a means of negotiating role stress, they may be a reflection of the emotional foundations of organizational life for men. In everyday work life, sexist jokes may function as a ritual suspension of the rules of responsibility for men, a withdrawal into a microworld in which their anger about dependence upon work and women may be safely expressed.

In analyzing the contradictions and vulnerabilities the guys felt about relationships with women and the responsibilities of work, I will focus upon three dimensions of the joking relationship: (1) the emotional content of the jokes; (2) the erotics of rule breaking created by the rules of the joke form; and (3) the image of strength and "being cool" they pitted against the dependence represented by both women and work.

The Emotional Dynamic of Sexist Jokes

When confronted by the women, the men defended the joke by asserting the formal rule that the purpose of jokes is play, then by justifying the jokes as necessary in order to create a special male bond. The defense that jokes are play defines aggressive behavior as play. This defense was far more persuasive to the men than to the women, since many forms of male bonding play are rule-governed aggression, as in sports and games. The second defense, asserting the relation between sexist jokes and male bonds, points out the social function of sexist jokes among the guys, to control the threat that individual men might form intimate

emotional bonds with women and withdraw from the group. Each defense poses a puzzle about the emotional dynamics of male group friendship, for in each case male group friendship seems more like a defense against vulnerability than a positive ideal.

In each defense, intimacy is split from sexuality in order to eroticize the male bond, thereby creating an instrumental sexuality directed at women. The separation of intimacy from sexuality transforms women into "sexual objects," which both justifies aggression at women by suspending their relationships to the men and devalues sexuality itself, creating a disgust at women as the sexual "object" unworthy of intimate attention. What is the origin of this conjunction between the devaluation of sexuality and the appropriation of intimacy for the male bond?

Chodorow (1978, p. 182) argues that the sense of masculine identity is constructed by an early repression of the son's erotic bond with his mother; with this repression the son's capacity for intimacy and commitment is devalued as feminine behavior. Henceforth men feel ambivalent about intimate relationships with women, seeking to replicate the fusion of intimacy and sexuality that they had experienced in their primal relationships to their mothers, but at the same time fearing engulfment by women in heterosexual relationships, like the engulfment of their infant selves by their mothers (Chodorow 1976). Certainly the content of the group's joke suggests this repression of the attachment to the mother, as well as hostility to her authority in the family. One man reported, "There's an awful lot of jokes about people's mothers. If any topic of conversation dominates the conversation it's 'heard your mother was with Ray [one of the guys] last night.' The guys will say incredibly vulgar things about their mothers, or they'll talk about the anatomy of a guy's girlfriends, or women they'd like to sleep with." While the guys' signifying mother jokes suggest the repression Chodorow describes, the men realized that their view of women made it unlikely that marriage would be a positive experience. One said, "I think a lot of us expect to marry someone pretty enough that other men will think we got a good catch, someone who is at least marginally interesting to chat with, but not someone we'd view as a friend. But at the same time, a woman who will make sufficient demands that we won't be able to have any friends. So we'll be stuck for the rest of our lives without friends."

While the emotional dynamic of men's "heterosexual knots" may well begin in this primordial separation of infant sons from mothers, its structure is replicated in the guys' ambivalence about their fathers, and their anger about the dependence upon rules in the work world. Yet the guys themselves described the fraternal bond as a way of creating "strength" and overcoming dependence, which suggests a positive ideal of male identity. In order to explore the guys' sense of the value of the male bond, their conception of strength and its consequences for the way they related to each other and to women has to be taken seriously.

Strength

Ultimately the guys justified the penis-envy joke because it created a special kind of male intimacy, but while the male group is able to appropriate its members' needs for intimacy and commitment, it is not clear that it is able to satisfy those needs, because strength has been defined as the opposite of intimacy. "Strength" is a value that represents solidarity rather than intimacy, the solidarity of a shared risk in rule-governed aggressive competition; its value is suggested by the cathartic laughter when the first woman speaker said, "These guys poured in, these huge guys."

The eros detached from sexuality is attached to rules, not to male friends; the male bond consists of an erotic toward rules, and yet the penis-envy joke expresses most of all the guys' ambivalence about rules. Like "the lads," the male gangs who roam the English countryside, "getting in trouble" by enforcing social mores in unsocial ways (Peters 1972), "the guys" break the rules in rule-governed ways. The joke form itself suggests this ambivalence about rules and

acts as a kind of pedagogy about the relationship between rules and aggression in male work culture. The joke form expresses emotions and tensions that might endanger the order of the organization, but that must be spoken lest they damage social order. Jokes can create group solidarity only if they allow dangerous things to be said; allow a physical catharsis of tension through laughter; or create the solidarity of an "in group" through shared aggression against an "out group." In each case there is an erotic in joke forms: an erotic of shared aggression, of shared sexual feeling, or an erotic of rule breaking itself.

It has been suggested that male groups experience a high level of excitement and sexual arousal in public acts of rule breaking (Thorne & Luria 1986). The penis-envy speech is precisely such an act, a breaking of conventional moral rules in the interest of group arousal. In each of the versions of the joking relationship in this group there is such an erotic quality: in the sexual content of the jokes, in the need for women to witness dirty talk or naked pledges, in the eros of aggression of the raid and jokes themselves. The penis-envy speech, a required event for all members of the group, is such a collective violation of the rules, and so is the content of their talk, a collective dirty talking that violates moral rules. The cathartic laughter that greeted the words, "You wouldn't believe what we say at the house," testifies to the emotional charge invested in dirty talk.

Because the intimacy of the guys' bond is built around an erotic of rule breaking, it has the serial structure of shared risk rather than the social structure of shared intimacy. In writing about the shared experience of suffering and danger of men at war, J. Glenn Gray (1959, pp. 89–90) distinguishes two kinds of male bonding, comradeship and friendship. Comradeship is based upon an erotic of shared danger, but is based upon the loss of an individual sense of self to a group identity, while friendship is based upon an individual's intellectual and emotional affinity to another individual. In the eros of friendship one's sense of self is heightened; in the eros of comradeship a sense of self is replaced by a sense of group membership. In this sense the guys were seeking comradeship, not friendship, hence the group constructed its bond through an erotic of shared activities with an element of risk, shared danger, or rule breaking: in sports, in paramilitary games, in wild parties, in joking relations. The guys called the performance of these activities "strength," being willing to take risks as a group and remaining cool.

Thus the behavior that the women defined as aggressive was seen by the men as a contest of strength governed by the rules of the joke form, to which the proper response would have been to remain "cool." To the guys, the masculine virtue of "strength" has a positive side, to discover oneself and to discover a sense of the other person through a contest of strength that is governed by rules. To the guys, "strength" is not the same as power or aggression because it is governed by rules, not anger; it is anger that is "uncool."

"Being Cool"

It is striking that the breaking of rules was not spontaneous, but controlled by the rules of the joke form: that aggressive talk replaces action; that talk is framed by a social form that requires the consent of others; that talk should not be taken seriously. This was the lesson that the black men tried to teach the women in the group session: In the male world, aggression is not defined as violent if it is rule governed rather than anger governed. The fraternal bond was built upon this emotional structure, for the life of the group centered upon the mobilization of aggressive energies in rule-governed activities (in sports, games, jokes, parties), in each arena aggression was highly valued (strength) only when it was rule governed (cool). Getting angry was called "losing control" and the guys thought they were most likely to lose control when they experienced themselves as personally dependent, as in relationships with women and at work.

Rule-governed aggression is a conduct that is very useful to organizations, in that it mobilizes aggressive energies but binds them to order by rules (see Benjamin 1980, p. 154). The male sense of order is procedural rather than substantive because the male bond is formal (rule governed), rather than personal (based upon intimacy and commitment). Male groups in this sense are shame cultures, not guilt cultures, because the male bond is a group identity that subordinates the individual to the rules, and because social control is imposed through collective judgments about self-control, such as "strength" and "cool." The sense of order within such male groups is based upon the belief that all members are equally dependent upon the rules and that no personal dependence is created within the group. This is not true of the family or of relations with women, both of which are intimate, and, from the guys' point of view, are "out of control" because they are governed by emotion.

The guys face contradictory demands from work culture about the use of aggressive behavior. Aggressive conduct is highly valued in a competitive society when it serves the interests of the organization, but men also face a strong taboo against the expression of anger at work when it is not rule governed. "Competition" imposes certain rules upon aggressive group processes: Aggression must be calculated, not angry; it must be consistent with the power hierarchy of the organization, serving authority and not challenging it; if expressed, it must be indirect, as in jokes; it must serve the needs of group solidarity, not of individual autonomy. Masculine culture separates anger from aggression when it combines the value "strength" with the value "being cool." While masculine cultures often define the expression of anger as "violent" or "loss of control," anger, properly defined, is speech, not action; angry speech is the way we can defend our sense of integrity and assert our sense of justice. Thus it is anger that challenges the authority of the rules, not aggressive behavior in itself, because anger defends the self, not the organization.

The guys' joking relationship taught them a pedagogy for the controlled use of aggression in the work world, to be able to compete aggressively without feeling angry. The guys recognized the relationship between their male bond and the work world by claiming that "high officials of the university know about the way we act and they understand what we are doing." While this might be taken as evidence that the guys were internalizing their fathers' norms and thus inheriting the mantle of patriarchy, the guys described their fathers as slaves to work and women, not as patriarchs. The guys also asserted themselves against the authority of their fathers by acting out against the authority of rules in the performance of "strength."

The guys clearly benefited from the male authority that gave them the power to impose the penis-envy joke upon the women with essentially no consequences. Men are allowed to direct anger and aggression toward women because social norms governing the expression of anger or humor generally replicate the power order of the group. It is striking, however, that the guys would not accept the notion that men have more power than women do; to them it is not men who rule, but rules that govern men. These men had so internalized the governing of male emotions by rules that their anger itself could emerge only indirectly through rule-governed forms, such as jokes and joking relationships. In these forms their anger could serve only order, not their sense of self or justice.

References

Bateson, G. (1972). A theory of play and fantasy. In *Steps toward an ecology of mind* (pp. 177–193). New York: Ballantine.

Benjamin, J. (1978). Authority and the family revisited, or, A world without fathers. *New German Critique, 4*(3), 13, 35–57.

Benjamin, J. (1980). The bonds of love: Rational violence and erotic domination. *Feminist Studies, 6*(1), 144–174.

Berndardez, T. (1978). Women and anger. *Journal of the American Medical Women's Association, 33*(5), 215–219.

Bly, R. (1982). What men really want: An interview with Keith Thompson. *New Age*, pp. 30–37, 50–51.

Chodorow, N. (1976). Oedipal asymmetries, heterosexual knots. *Social Problems, 23*, 454–468.

Chodorow, N. (1978). *The reproduction of mothering*. Berkeley: University of California Press.

Coser, R. (1959). Some social functions of laughter: A study of humor in a hospital setting. *Human Relations, 12*, 171–182.

Emerson, J. (1969). Negotiating the serious import of humor. *Sociometry, 32*, 169–181.

Emerson, J. (1970). Behavior in private places. In H. P. Dreitzel (Ed.), *Recent sociology: Vol. 2. Patterns in communicative behavior*. New York: Macmillan.

Freud, S. (1960). *Jokes and their relation to the unconscious*. New York: Norton.

Gilligan, C. (1982). *In a different voice*. Cambridge, MA: Harvard University Press.

Gray, G. J. (1959). *The warriors: Reflections on men in battle*. New York: Harper & Row.

Lerner, H. E. (1980). Internal prohibitions against female anger. *American Journal of Psychoanalysis, 40*, 137–148.

Miller, J. B. (1976). *Toward a new psychology of women*. Boston: Beacon.

Peters, E. L. (1972). Aspects of the control of moral ambiguities. In M. Gluckman (Ed.), *The allocation of responsibility* (pp. 109–162). Manchester: Manchester University Press.

Radcliffe-Brown, A. (1959). *Structure and function in primitive society*. Glencoe, IL: Free Press.

Rubin, L. (1983). *Intimate strangers*. New York: Harper & Row.

Slater, P. (1963). On social regression. *American Sociological Review, 28*, 339–364.

Thorne, B., & Luria, Z. (1986). Sexuality and gender in children's daily worlds. *Social Problems*.

Weber, M. (1958). Religions of the world and their directions. In H. Gerth & C. W. Mills (Eds.), *From Max Weber*. New York: Oxford University Press.

ARTICLE 15

A. Ayres Boswell
Joan Z. Spade

Fraternities and Collegiate Rape Culture: Why Are Some Fraternities More Dangerous Places for Women?

Date rape and acquaintance rape on college campuses are topics of concern to both researchers and college administrators. Some estimate that 60 to 80 percent of rapes are date or acquaintance rape (Koss, Dinero, Seibel, and Cox 1988). Further, 1 out of 4 college women say they were raped or experienced an attempted rape, and 1 out of 12 college men say they forced a woman to have sexual intercourse against her will (Koss, Gidycz, and Wisniewski 1985).

Although considerable attention focuses on the incidence of rape, we know relatively little about the context or the *rape culture* surrounding date and acquaintance rape. Rape culture is a set of values and beliefs that provide an environment conducive to rape (Buchwald, Fletcher, & Roth 1993; Herman 1984). The term applies to a generic culture surrounding and promoting rape, not the specific settings in which rape is likely to occur. We believe that the specific settings also are im-

Author's Note: An earlier version of this article was presented at the annual meeting of the American Sociological Association, August 1993. Special thanks go to Barbara Frankel, Karen Hicks, and Jennifer Vochko for their input into the process and final version and to Judith Gerson, Sue Curry Jansen, Judith Lasker, Patricia Yancey Martin, and Ronnie Steinberg for their careful readings of draft of this article for many helpful comments.

portant in defining relationships between men and women.

Some have argued that fraternities are places where rape is likely to occur on college campuses (Martin and Hummer 1989; O'Sullivan 1993; Sanday 1990) and that the students most likely to accept rape myths and be more sexually aggressive are more likely to live in fraternities and sororities, consume higher doses of alcohol and drugs, and place a higher value on social life at college (Gwartney-Gibbs and Stockard 1989; Kalof and Cargill 1991). Others suggest that sexual aggression is learned in settings such as fraternities and is not part of predispositions or preexisting attitudes (Boeringer, Shehan, and Akers 1991). To prevent further incidences of rape on college campuses, we need to understand what it is about fraternities in particular and college life in general that may contribute to the maintenance of a rape culture on college campuses.

Our approach is to identify the social contexts that link fraternities to campus rape and promote a rape culture. Instead of assuming that all fraternities provide an environment conducive to rape, we compare the interactions of men and women at fraternities identified on campus as being especially *dangerous* places for women, where the likelihood of rape is high, to those seen as *safer* places, where the perceived probability of rape occurring is lower. Prior to collecting data for our study, we found that most women students identified some fraternities as having more sexually aggressive members and a higher probability of rape. These women also considered other fraternities as relatively safe houses, where a women could go and get drunk if she wanted to and feel secure that the fraternity men would not take advantage of her. We compared parties at houses identified as high-risk and low-risk houses as well as at two local bars frequented by college students. Our analysis provides an opportunity to examine situations and contexts that hinder or facilitate positive social relations between undergraduate men and women.

The abusive attitudes toward women that some fraternities perpetuate exist within a general culture where rape is intertwined in traditional gender scripts. Men are viewed as initiators of sex and women as either passive partners or active resisters, preventing men from touching their bodies (LaPlante, McCormick, and Brannigan 1980). Rape culture is based on the assumptions that men are aggressive and dominant whereas women are passive and acquiescent (Buchwald et al. 1993; Herman 1984). What occurs on college campuses is an extension of the portrayal of domination and aggression of men over women that exemplifies the double standard of sexual behavior in U.S. society (Barthel 1988; Kimmel 1993).

Sexually active men are positively reinforced by being referred to as "studs," whereas women who are sexually active or report enjoying sex are derogatorily labeled as "sluts" (Herman 1984; O'Sullivan 1993). These gender scripts are embodied in rape myths and stereotypes such as "She really wanted it; she just said no because she didn't want me to think she was a bad girl" (Burke, Stets, and Pirog-Good 1989; Jenkins and Dambrot 1987; Lisak and Roth 1988; Malamuth 1986; Muehlenhard and Linton 1987; Peterson and Franzese 1987). Because men's sexuality is seen as more natural, acceptable, and uncontrollable than women's sexuality, many men and women excuse acquaintance rape by affirming that men cannot control their natural urges (Miller and Marshall 1987).

Whereas some researchers explain these attitudes toward sexuality and rape using an individual or a psychological interpretation, we argue that rape has a social basis, one in which both men and women create and recreate masculine and feminine identities and relations. Based on the assumption that rape is part of the social construction of gender, we examine how men and women "do gender" on a college campus (West and Zimmerman 1987). We focus on fraternities because they have been identified as settings that encourage rape (Sanday 1990). By comparing fraternities that are viewed by women as places where there is a high risk of rape to those where women believe there is a low risk of rape as well as two local commercial bars, we seek to identify characteristics that make some social settings more likely places for the occurrence of rape.

Method

We observed social interactions between men and women at a private coeducational school in which a high percentage (49.4 percent) of students affiliate with Greek organizations. The university has an undergraduate population of approximately 4,500 students, just more than one third of whom are women; the students are primarily from upper-middle-class families. The school, which admitted only men until 1971, is highly competitive academically.

We used a variety of data collection approaches: observations of interactions between men and women at fraternity parties and bars, formal interviews, and informal conversations. The first author, a former undergraduate at this school and a graduate student at the time of the study, collected the data. She knew about the social life at the school and had established rapport and trust between herself and undergraduate students as a teaching assistant in a human sexuality course.

The process of identifying high- and low-risk fraternity houses followed Hunter's (1953) reputational approach. In our study, 40 women students identified fraternities that they considered to be high risk, or to have more sexually aggressive members and higher incidence of rape, as well as fraternities that they considered to be safe houses. The women represented all four years of undergraduate college and different living groups (sororities, residence halls, and off-campus housing). Observations focused on the four fraternities named most often by these women as high-risk houses and the four identified as low-risk houses.

Throughout the spring semester, the first author observed at two fraternity parties each weekend at two different houses (fraternities could have parties only on weekends at this campus). She also observed students' interactions in two popular university bars on weeknights to provide a comparison of students' behavior in non-Greek settings. The first local bar at which she observed was popular with seniors and older students; the second bar was popular with first-, second-, and third-year undergraduates because the management did not strictly enforce drinking age laws in this bar.

The observer focused on the social context as well as interaction among participants at each setting. In terms of social context, she observed the following: ratio of men to women, physical setting such as the party decor and theme, use and control of alcohol and level of intoxication, and explicit and implicit norms. She noted interactions between men and women (i.e., physical contact, conversational style, use of jokes) and the relations among men (i.e., their treatment of pledges and other men at fraternity parties). Other than the observer, no one knew the identity of the high- or low-risk fraternities. Although this may have introduced bias into the data collection, students on this campus who read this article before it was submitted for publication commented on how accurately the social scene is described.

In addition, 50 individuals were interviewed including men from the selected fraternities, women who attended those parties, men not affiliated with fraternities, and self-identified rape victims known to the first author. The first author approached men and women by telephone or on campus and asked them to participate in interviews. The interviews included open-ended questions about gender relations on campus, attitudes about date rape, and their own experiences on campus.

To assess whether self-selection was a factor in determining the classification of the fraternity, we compared high-risk houses to low-risk houses on several characteristics. In terms of status on campus, the high- and low-risk houses we studied attracted about the same number of pledges; however, many of the high-risk houses had more members. There was no difference in grade point averages for the two types of houses. In fact, the highest and lowest grade point averages were found in the high-risk category. Although both high- and low-risk fraternities participated in sports, brothers in the low-risk houses tended to play intramural sports whereas brothers in the high-risk houses were more likely to be varsity athletes. The high-risk houses may be more aggressive, as they had a slightly larger number of disciplinary incidents and their reports were more severe, often with physical harm to others and damage to property. Further, in year-end reports, there was more property damage in the high-risk houses. Last, more of the low-risk houses participated in a campus rape-prevention program. In summary, both high- and low-risk fraternities seem to be equally attractive to freshmen men on this campus, and differences between the eight fraternities we studied were not great; however, the high-risk houses had a slightly larger number of reports of aggression and physical destruction in the houses and the low-risk houses were more likely to participate in a rape prevention program.

Results

The Settings

Fraternity Parties We observed several differences in the quality of the interaction of men and women at parties at high-risk fraternities compared to those at low-risk houses. A typical party at a low-risk house included an equal number of women and men. The social atmosphere was friendly, with considerable interaction between women and men. Men and women danced in groups and in couples, with many of the couples kissing and displaying affection toward each other. Brothers explained that, because many of the men in these houses had girlfriends, it was normal to see couples kissing on the dance floor. Coed groups engaged in conversations at many of these houses, with women and men engaging in friendly exchanges, giving the impression that they knew each other well. Almost no cursing and yelling was observed at parties in low-risk houses; when pushing occurred, the participants apologized. Respect for women extended to the women's bathrooms, which were clean and well supplied.

At high-risk houses, parties typically had skewed gender ratios, sometimes involving more men and other times involving more women. Gender segregation also was evident at these parties, with the men on one side of a room or in the bar drinking while women gathered in another area. Men treated women differently in the high-risk houses. The women's bathrooms in the high-risk houses were filthy, including clogged toilets and vomit in the sinks. When a brother was told of the mess in the bathroom at a high-risk house, he replied, "Good, maybe some of these beer wenches will leave so there will be more beer for us."

Men attending parties at high-risk houses treated women less respectfully, engaging in jokes, conversations, and behaviors that degraded women. Men made a display of assessing women's bodies and rated them with thumbs up or thumbs down for the other men in the sight of the women. One man attending a party at a high-risk fraternity said to another, "Did you know that this week is Women's Awareness Week? I guess that means we get to abuse them more this week." Men behaved more crudely at parties at high-risk houses. At one party, a brother dropped his pants, including his underwear, while dancing in front of several women. Another brother slid across the dance floor completely naked.

The atmosphere at parties in high-risk fraternities was less friendly overall. With the exception of greetings, men and women rarely smiled or laughed and spoke to each other less often than

was the case at parties in low-risk houses. The few one-on-one conversations between women and men appeared to be strictly flirtatious (lots of eye contact, touching, and very close talking). It was rare to see a group of men and women together talking. Men were openly hostile, which made the high-risk parties seem almost threatening at times. For example, there was a lot of touching, pushing, profanity, and name calling, some done by women.

Students at parties at the high-risk houses seemed self-conscious and aware of the presence of members of the opposite sex, an awareness that was sexually charged. Dancing early in the evening was usually between women. Close to midnight, the sex ratio began to balance out with the arrival of more men or more women. Couples began to dance together but in a sexual way (close dancing with lots of pelvic thrusts). Men tried to pick up women using lines such as "Want to see my fish tank?" and "Let's go upstairs so that we can talk; I can't hear what you're saying in here."

Although many of the same people who attended high-risk parties also attended low-risk parties, their behavior changed as they moved from setting to setting. Group norms differed across contexts as well. At a party that was held jointly at a low-risk house with a high-risk fraternity, the ambience was that of a party at a high-risk fraternity with heavier drinking, less dancing, and fewer conversations between women and men. The men from both high- and low-risk fraternities were very aggressive; a fight broke out, and there was pushing and shoving on the dance floor and in general.

As others have found, fraternity brothers at high-risk houses on this campus told about routinely discussing their sexual exploits at breakfast the morning after parties and sometimes at house meetings (cf. Martin and Hummer 1989; O'Sullivan 1993; Sanday 1990). During these sessions, the brothers we interviewed said that men bragged about what they did the night before with stories of sexual conquests often told by the same men, usually sophomores. The women involved in these exploits were women they did not know or knew but did not respect, or *faceless victims*. Men usually treated girlfriends with respect and did not talk about them in these storytelling sessions. Men from low-risk houses, however, did not describe similar sessions in their houses.

The Bar Scene The bar atmosphere and social context differed from those of fraternity parties. The music was not as loud, and both bars had places to sit and have conversations. At all fraternity parties, it was difficult to maintain conversations with loud music playing and no place to sit. The volume of music at parties at high-risk fraternities was even louder than it was at low-risk houses, making it virtually impossible to have conversations. In general, students in the local bars behaved in the same way that students did at parties in low-risk houses with conversations typical, most occurring between men and women.

The first bar, frequented by older students, had live entertainment every night of the week. Some nights were more crowded than others, and the atmosphere was friendly, relaxed, and conducive to conversation. People laughed and smiled and behaved politely toward each other. The ratio of men to women was fairly equal, with students congregating in mostly coed groups. Conversation flowed freely and people listened to each other.

Although the women and men at the first bar also were at parties at low- and high-risk fraternities, their behavior at the bar included none of the blatant sexual or intoxicated behaviors observed at some of these parties. As the evenings wore on, the number of one-on-one conversations between men and women increased and conversations shifted from small talk to topics such as war and AIDS. Conversations did not revolve around picking up another person, and most people left the bar with same-sex friends or in coed groups.

The second bar was less popular with older students. Younger students, often under the legal drinking age, went there to drink, sometimes after leaving campus parties. This bar was much smaller and usually not as crowded as the first

bar. The atmosphere was more mellow and relaxed than it was at the fraternity parties. People went there to hang out and talk to each other.

On a couple of occasions, however, the atmosphere at the second bar became similar to that of a party at a high-risk fraternity. As the number of people in the bar increased, they removed chairs and tables, leaving no place to sit and talk. The music also was turned up louder, drowning out conversation. With no place to dance or sit, most people stood around but could not maintain conversations because of the noise and crowds. Interactions between women and men consisted mostly of flirting. Alcohol consumption also was greater than it was on the less crowded nights, and the number of visibly drunk people increased. The more people drank, the more conversation and socializing broke down. The only differences between this setting and that of a party at a high-risk house were that brothers no longer controlled the territory and bedrooms were not available upstairs.

Gender Relations

Relations between women and men are shaped by the contexts in which they meet and interact. As is the case on other college campuses, *hooking up* has replaced dating on this campus, and fraternities are places where many students hook up. Hooking up is a loosely applied term on college campuses that had different meanings for men and women on this campus.

Most men defined hooking up similarly. One man said it was something that happens

> when you are really drunk and meet up with a woman you sort of know, or possibly don't know at all and don't care about. You go home with her with the intention of getting as much sexual, physical pleasure as she'll give you, which can range anywhere from kissing to intercourse, without any strings attached.

The exception to this rule is when men hook up with women they admire. Men said they are less likely to press for sexual activity with someone they know and like because they want the relationship to continue and be based on respect.

Women's version of hooking up differed. Women said they hook up only with men they cared about and described hooking up as kissing and petting but not sexual intercourse. Many women said that hooking up was disappointing because they wanted longer-term relationships. First-year women students realized quickly that hook-ups were usually one-night stands with no strings attached, but many continued to hook up because they had few opportunities to develop relationships with men on campus. One first-year woman said that "70 percent of hook-ups never talk again and try to avoid one another; 26 percent may actually hear from them or talk to them again, and 4 percent may actually go on a date, which can lead to a relationship." Another first-year woman said, "It was fun in the beginning. You get a lot of attention and kiss a lot of boys and think this is what college is about, but it gets tiresome fast."

Whereas first-year women get tired of the hook-up scene early on, many men do not become bored with it until their junior or senior year. As one upperclassman said, "The whole game of hooking up became really meaningless and tiresome for me during my second semester of my sophomore year, but most of my friends didn't get bored with it until the following year."

In contrast to hooking up, students also described monogamous relationships with steady partners. Some type of commitment was expected, but most people did not anticipate marriage. The term *seeing each other* was applied when people were sexually involved but free to date other people. This type of relationship involved less commitment than did one of boyfriend/girlfriend but was not considered to be a hook-up.

The general consensus of women and men interviewed on this campus was that the Greek system, called "the hill," set the scene for gender relations. The predominance of Greek membership and subsequent living arrangements segregated men and women. During the week, little interaction occurred between women and men after their first year in college because students in fraternities or sororities live and dine in separate

quarters. In addition, many non-Greek upper-class students move off campus into apartments. Therefore, students see each other in classes or in the library, but there is no place where students can just hang out together.

Both men and women said that fraternities dominate campus social life, a situation that everyone felt limited opportunities for meaningful interactions. One senior Greek man said,

> This environment is horrible and so unhealthy for good male and female relationships and interactions to occur. It is so segregated and male dominated. . . . It is our party, with our rules and our beer. We are allowing these women and other men to come to our party. Men can feel superior in their domain.

Comments from a senior woman reinforced his views: "Men are dominant; they are the kings of the campus. It is their environment that they allow us to enter; therefore, we have to abide by their rules." A junior women described fraternity parties as

> good for meeting acquaintances but almost impossible to really get to know anyone. The environment is so superficial, probably because there are so many social cliques due to the Greek system. Also, the music is too loud and the people are too drunk to attempt to have a real conversation, anyway.

Some students claim that fraternities even control the dating relationships of their members. One senior woman said, "Guys dictate how dating occurs on this campus, whether it's cool, who it's with, how much time can be spent with the girlfriend and with the brothers." Couples either left campus for an evening or hung out separately with their own same-gender friends at fraternity parties, finally getting together with each other at about 2 A.M. Couples rarely went together to fraternity parties. Some men felt that a girlfriend was just a replacement for a hook-up. According to one junior man, "Basically a girlfriend is someone you go to at 2 A.M. after you've hung out with the guys. She is the sexual outlet that the guys can't provide you with."

Some fraternity brothers pressure each other to limit their time with and commitment to their girlfriends. One senior man said, "The hill [fraternities] and girlfriends don't mix." A brother described a constant battle between girlfriends and brothers over who the guy is going out with for the night, with the brothers usually winning. Brothers teased men with girlfriends with remarks such as "whipped" or "where's the ball and chain?" A brother from a high-risk house said that few brothers at his house had girlfriends; some did, but it was uncommon. One man said that from the minute he was a pledge he knew he would probably never have a girlfriend on this campus because "it was just not the norm in my house. No one has girlfriends; the guys have too much fun with [each other]."

The pressure on men to limit their commitment to girlfriends, however, was not true of all fraternities or of all men on campus. Couples attended low-risk fraternity parties together, and men in the low-risk houses went out on dates more often. A man in one low-risk house said that about 70 percent of the members of his house were involved in relationships with women, including the pledges (who were sophomores).

Treatment of Women

Not all men held negative attitudes toward women that are typical of a rape culture, and not all social contexts promoted the negative treatment of women. When men were asked whether they treated the women on campus with respect, the most common response was "On an individual basis, yes, but when you have a group of men together, no." Men said that, when together in groups with other men, they sensed a pressure to be disrespectful toward women. A first-year man's perception of the treatment of women was that "they are treated with more respect to their faces, but behind closed doors, with a group of men present, respect for women is not an issue." One senior man stated, "In general, college-aged men don't treat women their age with respect because 90 percent of them think of women as merely a means to sex." Women reinforced this perception.

A first-year women stated, "Men here are more interested in hooking up and drinking beer than they are in getting to know women as real people." Another woman said, "Men here use and abuse women."

Characteristic of rape culture, a double standard of sexual behavior for men versus women was prevalent on this campus. As one Greek senior man stated, "Women who sleep around as sluts and get bad reputations; men who do are champions and get a pat on the back from their brothers." Women also supported a double standard for sexual behavior by criticizing sexually active women. A first-year woman spoke out against women who are sexually active: "I think some girls here make it difficult for the men to respect women as a whole."

One concrete example of demeaning sexually active women on this campus is the "walk of shame." Fraternity brothers come out on the porches of their houses the night after parties and heckle women walking by. It is assumed that these women spent the night at fraternity houses and that the men they were with did not care enough about them to drive them home. Although sororities now reside in former fraternity houses, this practice continues and sometimes the victims of hecklings are sorority women on their way to study in the library.

A junior man in a high-risk fraternity described another ritual of disrespect toward women called "chatter." When an unknown woman sleeps over at the house, the brothers yell degrading remarks out the window at her as she leaves the next morning such as "Fuck that bitch" and "Who is that slut?" He said that sometimes brothers harass the brothers whose girlfriends stay over instead of heckling those women.

Fraternity men most often mistreated women they did not know personally. Men and women alike reported incidents in which brothers observed other brothers having sex with unknown women or women they knew only casually. A sophomore woman's experience exemplifies this anonymous state: "I don't mind if 10 guys were watching or it was videotaped. That's expected on this campus. It's the fact that he didn't apologize or even offer to drive me home that really upset me." Descriptions of sexual encounters involved the satisfaction of men by nameless women. A brother in a high-risk fraternity described a similar occurrence:

> A brother of mine was hooking up upstairs with an unattractive woman who had been pursuing him all night. He told some brothers to go outside the window and watch. Well, one thing led to another and they were almost completely naked when the woman noticed the brothers outside. She was then unwilling to go any further, so the brother went outside and yelled at the other brothers and then closed the shades. I don't know if he scored or not, because the woman was pretty upset. But he did win the award for hooking up with the ugliest chick that weekend.

Attitudes Toward Rape

The sexually charged environment of college campuses raises many questions about cultures that facilitate the rape of women. How women and men define their sexual behavior is important legally as well as interpersonally. We asked students how they defined rape and had them compare it to the following legal definition: the perpetration of an act of sexual intercourse with a female against her will and consent, whether her will is overcome by force or fear resulting from the threat of force, or by drugs or intoxicants; or when, because of mental deficiency, she is incapable of exercising rational judgment. (Brownmiller 1975, 368)

When presented with this legal definition, most women interviewed recognized it as well as the complexities involved in applying it. A first-year woman said, "If a girl is drunk and the guy knows it and the girl says, 'Yes, I want to have sex,' and they do, that is still rape because the girl can't make a conscious, rational decision under the influence of alcohol." Some women disagreed. Another first-year woman stated, "I don't think it is fair that the guy gets blamed when both people involved are drunk."

The typical definition men gave for rape was "when a guy jumps out of the bushes and forces himself sexually onto a girl." When asked what date rape was, the most common answer was "when one person has sex with another person who did not consent." Many men said, however, that "date rape is when a woman wakes up the next morning and regrets having sex." Some men said that date rape was too gray an area to define. "Consent is a fine line," said a Greek senior man student. For the most part, the men we spoke with argued that rape did not occur on this campus. One Greek sophomore man said, "I think it is ridiculous that someone here would rape someone." A first-year man stated, "I have a problem with the word rape. It sounds so criminal, and we are not criminals; we are sane people."

Whether aware of the legal definitions of rape, most men resisted the idea that a woman who is intoxicated is unable to consent to sex. A Greek junior man said, "Men should not be responsible for women's drunkenness." One first-year man said, "If that is the legal definition of rape, then it happens all the time on this campus." A senior man said, "I don't care whether alcohol is involved or not; that is not rape. Rapists are people that have something seriously wrong with them." A first-year man even claimed that when women get drunk, they invite sex. He said, "Girls get so drunk here and then come to us. What are we supposed to do? We are only human."

Discussion and Conclusion

These findings describe the physical and normative aspects of one college campus as they relate to attitudes about and relations between men and women. Our findings suggest that an explanation emphasizing rape culture also must focus on those characteristics of the social setting that play a role in defining heterosexual relationships on college campuses (Kalof and Cargill 1991). The degradation of women as portrayed in rape culture was not found in all fraternities on this campus. Both group norms and individual behavior changed as students went from one place to another. Although individual men are the ones who rape, we found that some settings are more likely places for rape than are others. Our findings suggest that rape cannot be seen only as an isolated act and blamed on individual behavior and proclivities, whether it be alcohol consumption or attitudes. We also must consider characteristics of the settings that promote the behaviors that reinforce a rape culture.

Relations between women and men at parties in low-risk fraternities varied considerably from those in high-risk houses. Peer pressure and situational norms influenced women as well as men. Although many men in high- and low-risk houses shared similar views and attitudes about the Greek system, women on this campus, and date rape, their behaviors at fraternity parties were quite different.

Women who are at highest risk of rape are women whom fraternity brothers did not know. These women are faceless victims, nameless acquaintances—not friends. Men said their responsibility to such persons and the level of guilt they feel later if the hook-ups end in sexual intercourse are much lower if they hook up with women they do not know. In high-risk houses, brothers treated women as subordinates and kept them at a distance. Men in high-risk houses actively discouraged ongoing heterosexual relationships, routinely degraded women, and participated more fully in the hook-up scene; thus, the probability that women would become faceless victims was higher in these houses. The flirtatious nature of the parties indicated that women go to these parties looking for available men, but finding boyfriends or relationships was difficult at parties in high-risk houses. However, in the low-risk houses, where more men had long-term relationships, the women were not strangers and were less likely to become faceless victims.

The social scene on this campus, and on most others, offers women and men few other options to socialize. Although there may be no such thing as a completely safe fraternity party for women, parties at low-risk houses and commercial bars encouraged men and women to get to know each

other better and decreased the probability that women would become faceless victims. Although both men and women found the social scene on this campus demeaning, neither demanded different settings for socializing, and attendance at fraternity parties is a common form of entertainment.

These findings suggest that a more conducive environment for conversation can promote more positive interactions between men and women. Simple changes would provide the opportunity for men and women to interact in meaningful ways such as adding places to sit and lowering the volume of music at fraternity parties or having parties in neutral locations, where men are not in control. The typical party room in fraternity houses includes a place to dance but not to sit and talk. The music often is loud, making it difficult, if not impossible, to carry on conversations; however, there were more conversations at the low-risk parties, where there also was more respect shown toward women. Although the number of brothers who had steady girlfriends in the low-risk houses as compared to those in the high-risk houses may explain the differences, we found that commercial bars also provided a context for interaction between men and women. At the bars, students sat and talked and conversations between men and women flowed freely, resulting in deep discussions and fewer hook-ups.

Alcohol consumption was a major focus of social events here and intensified attitudes and orientations of a rape culture. Although pressure to drink was evident at all fraternity parties and at both bars, drinking dominated high-risk fraternity parties, at which nonalcoholic beverages usually were not available and people chugged beers and became visibly drunk. A rape culture is strengthened by rules that permit alcohol only at fraternity parties. Under this system, men control the parties and dominate the men as well as the women who attend. As college administrators crack down on fraternities and alcohol on campus, however, the same behaviors and norms may transfer to other places such as parties in apartments or private homes where administrators have much less control. At commercial bars, interaction and socialization with others were as important as drinking, with the exception of the nights when the bar frequented by under-class students became crowded. Although one solution is to offer nonalcoholic social activities, such events receive little support on this campus. Either these alternative events lacked the prestige of the fraternity parties or the alcohol was seen as necessary to unwind, or both.

In many ways, the fraternities on this campus determined the settings in which men and women interacted. As others before us have found, pressures for conformity to the norms and values exist at both high-risk and low-risk houses (Kalof and Cargill 1991; Martin and Hummer 1989; Sanday 1990). The desire to be accepted is not unique to this campus or the Greek system (Holland and Eisenhart 1990; Horowitz 1988; Moffat 1989). The degree of conformity required by Greeks may be greater than that required in most social groups, with considerable pressure to adopt and maintain the image of their houses. The fraternity system intensifies the "groupthink syndrome" (Janis 1972) by solidifying the identity of the in-group and creating an us/them atmosphere. Within the fraternity culture, brothers are highly regarded and women are viewed as outsiders. For men in high-risk fraternities, women threatened their brotherhood; therefore, brothers discouraged relationships and harassed those who treated women as equals or with respect. The pressure to be one of the guys and hang out with the guys strengthens a rape culture on college campus by demeaning women and encouraging the segregation of men and women.

Students on this campus were aware of the contexts in which they operated and the choices available to them. They recognized that, in their interactions, they created differences between men and women that are not natural, essential, or biological (West and Zimmerman 1987). Not all men and women accepted the demeaning treatment of women, but they continued to participate in behaviors that supported aspects of a rape culture. Many women participated in the hook-up scene even after they had been humiliated and hurt because they had few other means of initiating contact with men on campus. Men and women alike played out this scene, recognizing its injustices in many cases but being unable to change the course of their behaviors.

Although this research provides some clues to gender relations on college campuses, it raises many questions. Why do men and women participate in activities that support a rape culture when they see its injustices? What would happen if alcohol were not controlled by groups of men who admit that they disrespect women when they get together? What can be done to give men and women on college campuses more opportunities to interact responsibly and get to know each other better? These questions should be studied on other campuses with a focus on the social settings in which the incidence of rape and the attitudes that support a rape culture exist. Fraternities are social contexts that may or may not foster a rape culture.

Our findings indicate that a rape culture exists in some fraternities, especially those we identified as high-risk houses. College administrators are responding to this situation by providing counseling and educational programs that increase awareness of date rape including campaigns such as "No means no." These strategies are important in changing attitudes, values, and behaviors; however, changing individuals is not enough. The structure of campus life and the impact of that structure on gender relations on campus are highly determinative. To eliminate campus rape culture, student leaders and administrators must examine the situations in which women and men meet and restructure these settings to provide opportunities for respectful interaction. Change may not require abolishing fraternities; rather, it may require promoting settings that facilitate positive gender relations.

References

Barthel, D. 1988. *Putting on appearances: Gender and advertising*. Philadelphia: Temple University Press.

Boeringer, S. B., C. L. Shehan, and R. L. Akers, 1991. Social contexts and social learning in sexual coercion and aggression: Assessing the contribution of fraternity membership. *Family Relations* 40:58–64.

Brownmiller, S. 1975. *Against our will: Men, women and rape.* New York: Simon & Schuster.

Buchwald, E., P. R. Fletcher, and M. Roth, eds. 1993. *Transforming a rape culture.* Minneapolis, MN: Milkweed Editions.

Burke, P., J. E. Stets, and M. A. Pirog-Good. 1989. Gender identity, self-esteem, physical abuse and sexual abuse in dating relationships. In *Violence in dating relationships: Emerging social issues*, edited by M. A. Pirog-Good and J. E. Stets. New York: Praeger.

Gwartney-Gibbs, P., and J. Stockard. 1989. Courtship aggression and mixed-sex peer groups. In *Violence in dating relationships: Emerging social issues*, edited by M. A. Pirog-Good and J. E. Stets. New York: Praeger.

Herman, D. 1984. The rape culture. In *Women: A feminist perspective*, edited by J. Freeman. Mountain View, CA: Mayfield.

Holland, D. C., and M. A. Eisenhart. 1990. *Educated in romance: Women, achievement, and college culture.* Chicago: University of Chicago Press.

Horowitz, H. L. 1988. *Campus life: Undergraduate cultures from the end of the 18th century to the present.* Chicago: University of Chicago Press.

Hunter, F. 1953. *Community power structure.* Chapel Hill: University of North Carolina Press.

Jenkins, M. J., and F. H. Dambrot. 1987. The attribution of date rape: Observer's attitudes and sexual experiences and the dating situation. *Journal of Applied Social Psychology* 17:875–95.

Janis, I. L. 1972. *Victims of groupthink.* Boston: Houghton Mifflin.

Kalof, L., and T. Cargill. 1991. Fraternity and sorority membership and gender dominance attitudes. *Sex Roles* 25:417–23.

Kimmel, M. S. 1993. Clarence, William, Iron Mike, Tailhook, Senator Packwood, Spur Posse, Magic . . . and us. In *Transforming a rape culture*, edited by E. Buchwald, P. R. Fletcher, and M. Roth. Minneapolis, MN: Milkweed Editions.

Koss, M. P., T. E. Dinero, C. A. Seibel, and S. L. Cox. 1988. Stranger and acquaintance rape: Are there differences in the victim's experience? *Psychology of Women Quarterly* 12:1–24.

Koss, M. P., C. A. Gidycz, and N. Wisniewski. 1985. The scope of rape: Incidence and prevalence of sexual aggression and victimization in a national sample of higher education students. *Journal of Consulting and Clinical Psychology* 55:162–70.

LaPlante, M. N., N. McCormick, and G. G. Brannigan. 1980. Living the sexual script: College students' views of influence in sexual encounters. *Journal of Sex Research* 16:338–55.

Lisak, D., and S. Roth. 1988. Motivational factors in nonincarcerated sexually aggressive men. *Journal of Personality and Social Psychology* 55:795–802.

Malamuth, N. 1986. Predictors of naturalistic sexual aggression. *Journal of Personality and Social Psychology* 50:953–62.

Martin, P. Y., and R. Hummer. 1989. Fraternities and rape on campus. *Gender & Society* 3:457–73.

Miller, B., and J. C. Marshall. 1987. Coercive sex on the university campus. *Journal of College Student Personnel* 28:38–47.

Moffat, M. 1989. *Coming of age in New Jersey: College life in American culture.* New Brunswick, NJ: Rutgers University Press.

Muehlenhard, C. L., and M. A. Linton. 1987. Date rape and sexual aggression in dating situations: Incidence and risk factors. *Journal of Counseling Psychology* 34:186–96.

O'Sullivan, C. 1993. Fraternities and the rape culture. In *Transforming a rape culture*, edited by E. Buchwald, P. R. Fletcher, and M. Roth. Minneapolis, MN: Milkweed Editions.

Peterson, S. A., and B. Franzese. 1987. Correlates of college men's sexual abuse of women. *Journal of College Student Personnel* 28:223–28.

Sanday, P. R. 1990. *Fraternity gang rape: Sex, brotherhood, and privilege on campus.* New York: New York University Press.

West, C., and D. Zimmerman. 1987. Doing gender. *Gender & Society* 1:125–51.

Todd W. Crosset
Jeffrey R. Benedict
Mark A. McDonald

Male Student–Athletes Reported for Sexual Assault: A Survey of Campus Police Departments and Judicial Affairs Offices

In recent years, an ongoing public debate has developed regarding the propensity of athletes to commit sexual assault. A succession of publicized rape cases during the 1980s involving high-profile athletes led to increased coverage of sexual assault by sports reporters. During the first half of the 1990s, the unabated number of allegations involving athletes in rape cases (for a summary, see Nelson 1994) has fed the debate. Some members of the media have suggested that athletes are more prone to commit acts of sexual aggression (Eskanazi 1990; Hofmann 1986; Kirshenbaum 1989; Larimer 1991; Toufexis 1990). This claim is disputed by those who believe that athletes are scrutinized more intensely because of their notoriety (Dershowitz 1994). They contend that thousands of rape cases go unmentioned in news reports each year, yet seldom does a case involving an athlete or any other celebrity go unpublicized. This practice, they argue, creates a distorted perception regarding the proportion of athletes who commit sexual assault and fails to account for the large number of athletes who do not commit sexually aggressive acts.

Social scientists have offered little to inform this debate. The purpose of this study is to re-

Todd W. Crosset, Jeffrey R. Benedict, & Mark A. McDonald, *Journal of Sport & Social Issues*, vol. 19, pp. 126–140. Reprinted by permission of Sage Publications, Inc.

search the association between reported incidents of sexual assault and athletic affiliation in a rigorous fashion.

Introduction

Social Milieu and Sexual Aggression

A number of researchers concerned with sexually aggressive behavior adopt what Malamuth, Sockloskie, Koss, and Tanaka (1991) call an "ecological approach." This approach starts with the recognition that sexually aggressive behavior is a form of violence and not a form of sexuality. It argues that aggression against women results from a complex combination of social and psychological factors, with primary emphasis on sociological factors. Employing multiple regression analysis, Malamuth et al. note that proximate social factors such as peer group environment and masculine hostility toward women have far more influence as predictors of sexual aggression than do distal factors such as violence experienced as a child. Malamuth et al. conclude that future research should focus on the following social factors: (a) factors that contribute to the practice and acceptance of coercion and hostility, (b) factors that promote aggression against targets perceived as weaker or as out groups (e.g., sex segregation), and (c) factors that promote sexism and violence against women (e.g., eroticism of domination).

This approach is supported by the work of anthropologist Peggy Sanday (1981), who found that the frequency of rape varied substantially from one tribal society to another. Cultures that displayed a high level of tolerance for violence, male dominance, and sex segregation had the highest frequency of rape (both individual and gang). These societal characteristics are the basis of what Sanday (1990) calls "rape cultures," which lack the social constraints that discourage sexual aggression or contain social arrangements that encourage sexual aggression. Sanday's findings support the contention that sexual assault is not simply the result of an individual's biological makeup or psychological disposition; rather, it is a behavior that is socially encouraged (Brownmiller 1975; Russell 1975; Sanday 1981, 1990).

Athletes and Sexual Assault

Beginning in the late 1970s, academics and social critics began discussing connections between the culture of sport and violence against women (Sabo & Runfola 1980). In many regards, men's sport resembles a "rape culture." Athletics is highly sex segregated. By design, dominant forms of sport promote hostile attitudes toward rivals and gaining at the expense of another team or person (Kidd 1990; Messner 1992; Messner & Sabo 1994). Male athletic teams often garner high status for physically dominating others (Sabo 1980). Further, organized competitive sports for men have been described as supporting male dominance and sexist practices (Bryson 1987; Kidd 1990; MacKinnon 1987; Messner 1992; Whitson 1990). Curry (1991), in his study of conversation fragments from a male locker room, found statements that were consistent with what might be found in a "rape culture."

Social scientists have been conducting empirical research on the relationship between athletic participation and sexual assault for a relatively short period of time (Koss & Gaines 1993). Prior to the early 1990s, there were few attempts to document the connection between athletes and sexual assault.

To date, most academic references to athletes as sexual aggressors involve gang rapes (Ehrhart & Sandler 1985, as cited by Koss & Gaines 1993; O'Sullivan 1991). This literature identifies members of fraternities, followed by members of athletic teams, as the "most likely to engage in group sexual assault" (O'Sullivan 1991, p. 144).[1] O'Sullivan argues that cohesiveness gained through team membership, sex-segregated housing, and prestige can be factors in facilitating illicit activities. The group dynamics outlined by O'Sullivan confirm those identified by Sanday (1990), who has conducted extensive research on gang rape in college fraternities. Sanday concludes that the group environment binds men emotionally to one another and contributes to their seeing sex relations from a position of power and status.

There is little doubt that men in sex-segregated groups (sports teams, fraternities, military, etc.) are more likely to commit acts of group sexual assault (Ehrhart & Sandler 1992; O'Sullivan 1991; Sanday 1981, 1990). However, there is a lack of scholarly research on athletes as individual perpetrators of simple rape or aggravated rape.

Using multiple regression analysis of data collected through self-reports, Koss and Gaines (1993) attempted to ascertain the influence of athletic affiliation on sexual aggression. They compared the influence of alcohol use, nicotine use, fraternity membership, and athletic affiliation on sexual aggressive behavior on a Division I college campus. Whereas alcohol and nicotine use were strongly associated with the incidence of sexual assault, varsity athletic participation in "revenue-producing sports" was weakly associated with sexually aggressive behavior by men against women at the university.

The study by Koss and Gaines (1993) has limitations. Because they examined only one campus, Koss and Gaines are reluctant to make generalizations applicable to other universities. Further, their comparison population was taken from introductory courses consisting predominantly of first- and second-year students whose average age was 18.9 years. The athletic population was over-sampled and selected from all years. The result is a comparison of the group-affiliated student–athlete against "newer" students less likely to have developed strong campus affiliations. In addition, the study used only self-reported data, which carries inherent limitations on validity (Koss & Gaines 1993). Finally, Koss and Gaines do not distinguish between individual rape and gang rape. Despite these limitations, the research of Koss and Gaines is a groundbreaking step in understanding sexual aggression and college athletes. It is the first rigorous empirical research that identifies athletic affiliation as a predictor (albeit slight) of sexual aggression.

The nature of sexual assault makes it difficult to study. Clinical research in this area is both impractical and unethical. Correlational data can be collected from self-reports or official reports, but both types of data have limitations. Further, we cannot draw conclusions about causality from correlational research. Muehlenhard and Linton (1987) recommend that data from different types of studies converge to provide insight into the problem of sexual assault. Therefore, the design and methodology of this study is to address some of the limitations of the work of Koss and Gaines (1993) and Curry (1991) and determine whether the findings based on official reports of sexual assault are consistent with the findings of previous studies.

The objective of the present study is to examine the relationship between membership on men's varsity sports teams in NCAA Division I universities and officially reported sexual assaults. The study compares the rates of reported sexual assaults for varsity athletes with the rest of the male student population. The data were obtained from records at 30 Division I American universities; 107 cases of sexual assault were examined. The study uses statistical analyses to test the purported relationship between membership on a varsity sports team and officially reported sexual assaults.

Method

In general, there are three locations on a college campus where a victim can officially report sexual assault: campus police, judicial affairs,[2] or a rape crisis/counseling center. Of these, only the first two keep records on the perpetrator. However, at nearly all institutions, neither campus police nor judicial affairs offices indicate whether an alleged perpetrator is a student–athlete. Institutions participating in our study were asked to provide the total number of male students enrolled, student–athletes enrolled, sexual assaults reported, and sexual assaults reported that involved a student–athlete by cross-referencing the names of accused perpetrators with the names on official athletic rosters. The figures were calculated at each institution to protect privacy rights.

We purposely selected Division I institutions and, whenever possible, selected schools with highly ranked popular sports. We assumed that these institutions were most likely to support insulated athletic subworlds and systems of affiliation among athletes that, according to the literature (Curry 1991; Messner 1992; Messner & Sabo 1994; Sabo 1980), might lead to problematic behavior.

Two Data Sets

We speculated that the initial response to and subsequent adjudication of incidents of sexual assault differed considerably between campus police and judicial affairs officials. Further, we thought that these differences are understood on some level by victims. Campus police officers operate under the same guidelines as do civil police officers. In most cases, a victim would file an official report with campus police only if she desired to file criminal charges and pursue justice through the state court system. By contrast, administrators in judicial affairs are empowered to independently determine the facts in an alleged assault without being subjected to the strict laws of evidence required in a court of law. Although unable to mete out punishment in the same manner as the criminal justice system, institutions are able to provide more immediate recourse to a victim while maintaining her privacy. Through either a student court or a private hearing conducted by a judicial officer or dean, a school can stipulate disciplinary action that ranges from probation to expulsion. A victim who is seeking a timely response, an immediate separation from the perpetrator with respect to housing or class schedules, or adjudication without a criminal trial may be more inclined to report the incident to judicial affairs.

In other words, although both judicial affairs and campus police process official reports of sexual assault, their functions are not identical. Therefore, we have approached the data as two distinct sample sets. Data were collected from 20 campus police departments and 10 judicial affairs offices.

Campus Police Data Set   With regard to campus police departments, our survey group includes institutions from all geographic regions of the United States. We targeted schools with perennial Top 20 basketball or football teams. Schools that landed teams in the men's Top 20 poll for either basketball or football in at least 2 of the 3 years between 1991 and 1993 were mailed surveys. Of the 49 schools targeted, 20 responded—a response rate of 41%. All the reports were usable. The high rate of usability was enhanced by the Campus Security Act (1987), which requires campus police departments to allow public access to information regarding all crime on campus.

Judicial Affairs Data Set   Because judicial affairs offices are not required by the Campus Security Act to reveal information regarding violations of the student codes of conduct, data were much more difficult to obtain than they were from campus police departments. To facilitate a high response rate, we conducted telephone interviews with a judicial affairs representative from institutions in the original sample. Many institutions with Top 20 basketball and football teams were reluctant to participate in this study. Therefore, in addition to 8 Division I institutions with Top 20

athletic programs, we petitioned 8 Division I institutions that did not have perennial Top 20 basketball or football teams. Of these 16 schools that initially agreed to be part of the survey, 12 were able to complete the project (75% response rate) and 10 provided usable data. Judicial affairs offices were asked to provide 3 years of data, covering the academic years from 1991 through 1993. Among the respondents, 2 schools did not have records for 1991 and 1 school did not have data from 1993. Of the 10 schools supplying usable data, 5 were perennial Top 20 football or basketball schools according to our operational definition.

Problems and Solutions

Asking for information regarding sexual assaults on campuses poses a number of problems for the researcher. First, this information is extremely sensitive and potentially damaging to the reputation of an institution. Initially, we assured confidentiality to all potential participants. To overcome further hesitancy on the part of institutions, we garnered the support of two influential people—Jim Ferrier, a member of the International Association of Campus Law Enforcement Administrators, and Carol Bohmer, a legal scholar who has trained judicial affairs officers at institutions around the country. We included their names in the cover letter of our survey. As a result, we were able to gain the cooperation of both police departments and judicial affairs offices at a significant number of schools.

Second, each institution has an obligation to protect the privacy of both the victim and the accused. In keeping with privacy protection laws, the names of individuals accused of sexual assault were neither requested nor revealed. Instead, each participating institution was asked to internally review the names of those students accused of sexual offenses and determine whether they appeared on a varsity team roster at the time of the assault. This required a considerable amount of effort on the part of participating institutions.

Finally, the institutions we surveyed do not adhere to universal definitions for student codes of conduct violations. Rather than asking participating schools to conform to a researcher-created definition of sexual assault, we allowed each institution to maintain its own definition of sexual assault. This procedure ensures that we are reporting data based on codes of conduct violations as described at each institution. The overlap between institutional definitions of sexual assault ensures that all perpetrators reported in this study are accused of either rape, attempted rape, unwanted touching of intimate parts of another person, or the use of threats or intimidation to gain an advantage in nonconsensual sexual contact.

Findings

A summary of the data collected from the two sample sets is listed in Table 16.1.[3]

Male student–athletes comprised 3.8% of the total male student population yet represented 5.5% of the reported sexual assaults to campus police ($n = 38$). For the combined 3 years of the 10 judicial affairs offices, male student–athletes comprised 3.3% of the total male population, yet represented 19% of the perpetrators reported ($n = 69$). A two-tailed t test was conducted on these data to compare the sexual assault perpetrator rate of male student–athletes with that of the rest of the male student population. This test was chosen because we did not hypothesize from the outset the direction of the difference between the student–athletes and the rest of the male student population. We tested for significance to the .05 level, or a confidence level of higher than 95%.

Because the judicial affairs data come from different years at the same campuses, we needed to test the appropriateness of combining the 3 years of judicial affairs data. First, the annual data were tested for significance. Then a regression analysis was conducted to determine the appropriateness of combining the 3 years of data for further analysis.[4] Because we found no significant difference between the years, we were able to combine the 3 years to create a larger sample for analysis.

Table 16.2 shows the results of the t test for the campus police questionnaire, each year of the judicial affairs questionnaire, and the combined data from judicial affairs.

Campus Police Questionnaire Results

The t test reveals that, in the reported sexual assaults to campus police, there is no significant difference between male student–athletes and other male students, $t = -0.70$, $p = .490$. That is, given the current data sample, we cannot state with

■ **TABLE 16.1**
Summary of Data Collected from Two Sample Sources

	Campus Police Questionnaire[a]	Judicial Affairs Questionnaire (1991–1993)[b]
Men not on intercollegiate sport teams		
Student population	182,091	252,630
Perpetrators	36	56
Men on intercollegiate sport teams		
Athlete population	6,975	8,739
Perpetrators	2	13

a. Institutions reporting = 20.
b. Institutions reporting = 10; annual reports = 27 (1991 = 8, 1992 = 10, 1993 = 9).

■ **TABLE 16.2**

Results of *t* Test for Campus Police Questionnaire (CPQ) and Judicial Affairs
Questionnaire (JAQ)

Survey	Number of Male Nonvarsity Athlete Perpetrators	Men/1,000 Incident Rate	Number of Male Student–Athlete Perpetrators	Men/1,000 Incident Rate	*t* Statistics
CPQ (1992)	36	0.19	2	0.33	–0.70
JAQ (1991)	16	0.20	5	2.21	–2.45*
JAQ (1992)	19	0.21	6	1.72	–1.29
JAQ (1993)	23	0.25	2	0.67	–0.57
JAQ (1991–1993)	56	0.22	13	1.49	–2.47*

*$p < .05$.

confidence that collegiate athletes are reported to campus police at a higher rate than are other male students.

Judicial Affairs Questionnaire Results

For the annual data collected from the judicial affairs offices, only in the 1991 academic year are there statistically significant differences between male student–athletes and other male students, $t = -2.45$, $p < .05$, with regard to the rate of being reported for sexual assault. In this year, male student–athletes comprised 2.8% of the total male student population and represented 24% of the perpetrators reported to judicial affairs for sexual assault ($n = 21$).

By contrast, there were no significant differences in sexual assault incident rates between these two groups based on the 1992 data, $t = -1.29$, $p = .229$, or on the 1993 data, $t = -0.57$, $p = .582$. In 1992, student–athletes comprised 3.7% of the total male student population and represented 24% of the perpetrators reported to judicial affairs for sexual assault ($n = 25$). In 1993, student–athletes comprised 3.4% of the population and represented 8.7% of the perpetrators reported to judicial affairs for sexual assault ($n = 25$).

The *t* test performed on the combined judicial affairs data (1991–1993) reveals statistically significant differences between male student–athletes

and other male students, $t = -2.47$, $p < .05$. For the combined 3 years, male student–athletes comprised 3.3% of the total male population yet represented 19% of the reported perpetrators ($n = 69$). This result indicates an association between collegiate athletic membership and reports of sexual assault to judicial affairs offices.

Finally, we conducted a comparison of student–athletes involved in the revenue-producing contact sports of football and basketball to all other students–athletes. This comparison was made with the combined judicial affairs data (1991–1993). A two-tailed *t* test indicated that the difference in incident rates between these groups approached significance but was not quite statistically significant, $t = 1.41$, $p = .17$. However, it should be noted that, in this sample, male football and basketball players comprised 30% of the student-athlete population, yet are responsible for 67% of the reported sexual assaults.

Limitations

Our data included only those sexual assaults officially reported to either campus police or judicial affairs. Some estimates suggest that 84% of all rapes go unreported (National Victim's Center, 1992). Although the conditions under which women will report sexual assault are not fully understood, we can assume that reports are not random. Any sample based on official reports, therefore, is not a representative sample of sexual assaults that take place on college campuses. The benefit of working with officially reported sexual assaults is the general high reliability of the claims.[5] Further, the small sample size prevents us from using highly sophisticated statistical tests in our data analysis. Therefore, our study does not include an analysis of all the factors associated with men's sexual aggression toward women; we have no information on the circumstances in which actual cases of sexual aggression occurred. We know only whether the reported perpetrator was a member of an intercollegiate sport team. Given the limitations of the data, we can report only on the statistical relationship between membership on men's intercollegiate sport teams in Division I universities and the incidence of reported sexual assaults at those universities.

Conclusion

Given the nature and scope of this research, conclusions based on the data are necessarily limited. For example, to draw conclusions as to the frequency of sexual assault committed by athletes would be a misapplication of these findings. Further, it needs to be reiterated that it is not clear whether the association between athletic affiliation and sexual assault is causal or the result of behavior only indirectly related to sport.

Nonetheless, this research indicates that male college student–athletes, compared with the rest of the male student population, are responsible for a significantly higher percentage of the sexual assaults reported to judicial affairs offices on the campuses of Division I institutions. Although reports of sexual assault by student–athletes to campus police are not statistically different from those by other male students, athletes are nonetheless slightly overrepresented. When the two data sets are viewed concurrently, athletes appear to be disproportionately involved in incidents of sexual assault on college campuses. Further, these

findings lend support to other research that links athletic participation and sexual aggression (Curry 1991; Koss & Gaines 1993).

This research makes three significant contributions to this area of study. First, because it relies on official reports, it can be used to counter those who would dismiss the findings based on data from self-reports (Koss & Gaines 1993). The findings of this study do not contradict those of Koss and Gaines, enhancing the validity of their findings. We can state with increasing confidence that there is some connection between the dynamics of being involved on a men's intercollegiate sports team, particularly in the contact sports of football and basketball in Division I universities, and reported cases of sexual assault at those institutions.

Second, we investigated 30 Division I institutions across the United States, 25 of which support top-ranked teams in either football or basketball. Previous researchers have been reluctant to make broad conclusions on the basis of research drawn from single institutions (Curry 1991; Koss & Gaines 1993). Because we sampled a number of institutions, we can assume that our conclusions are generally representative of other large Division I campuses with strong athletic programs.

Finally, this study contributes to a small body of empirical research on an issue that is much discussed yet rarely studied. Popular sports journalism and scholarship alike have attributed one in three sexual assaults committed on college campuses to athletes (Bohmer & Parrot 1993; Deford 1993; Eskanazi 1990; Kane & Disch 1993; Kirshenbaum 1989; Melnick 1992; Nelson 1991, 1994; Toufexis 1990). However, after extensive review of the literature, there does not appear to be any empirical evidence to substantiate this claim, which appears consistently in both academic and sport journalism publications.

Claims that one in three campus sexual assaults is committed by a student–athlete have two primary sources: Richard Hofmann (1986) of the *Philadelphia Daily News* and Gerald Eskanazi (1990) of the *New York Times*. In 1986, Hofmann wrote a four-part series on athletes and sexual assault. Hofmann does not contend that his investigation is scientific. He acknowledges that the figures used in his articles were based on an informal poll of university officials. The findings from this poll were then compared to FBI Uniform Crime Reports. Despite the obvious flaws in this type of comparison, both scholars and journalists have relied on the Hofmann piece to assert that athletes are much more likely to commit sexual assaults.

Askanazi (1990) misrepresented the work of a leading researcher in the area of sexual assault on campus, Mary Koss. He cites a 3-year National Institute of Mental Health study by Koss claiming that, of the cases studied, athletes were involved about a third of the time. Koss did not control for athletic affiliation in this study and disputes the findings Eskanazi attributes to her.[6]

Implications

Clearly, caution must be employed when discussing the implications of our findings. The popular press has overstated the problem in the past, in part by misrepresenting scientific research. At the same time, the findings of this research clearly indicate the existence of a problem. To suggest that all of these cases are simply a result of athletes being targeted because of their high profile status denies reality. The best interest of institutions cannot be served until those working within the institution admit that a problem exists. Athletic departments and coaches have an obvious interest in learning about and addressing the factors that are contributing to athletes being reported for individual acts of sexual assault (and gang rapes) at a higher rate than that of other male students. Reducing the number of sexual attacks committed by athletes on campus will require a significant effort from athletic departments, coaches, and other educational personnel.

Further Research

The lack of rigorous research in this area points to one obvious avenue of study: replication. In addition to replication, we see three broad research needs: exploration of variables associated with sexually aggressive behavior, factors influencing reporting rates, and efficacy of intervention programs.

From the current research, we are unable to explain the association between varsity athletic membership and sexual assault. It is possible that the association we found has little to do with athletic participation but rather is associated with some other behavior only indirectly related to athletics. Despite the association between intercollegiate athletic membership and reported sexual assaults, far stronger associations have been found between sexual assault and alcohol use, nicotine use, and hostile attitudes toward women (Koss & Gaines 1993). Those who attempt replication, then, will want to test more variables.

Further, there is a need for more studies so that we can learn more about patterns within and between universities and develop explanations for those patterns. For example, although the sample size was small, the data hinted that sexual assault was not endemic to all sports. Contact sports such as football and basketball were overrepresented, raising the possibility that athletes trained to use physical domination on the field are more likely to carry these lessons into their relationships. Even here, reports were not uniform from school to school, suggesting that the social environment of programs may vary significantly and have a substantial impact on the rate of sexual assault.

Conversations between members of the research team and university officials indicated that the prevalence of reported sexual assaults by athletes was dramatic in some instances following changes in coaching staffs. This suggests that coaches may have a significant impact on the team's social milieu and thus on athletes' behavior outside of sport. A qualitative approach to this topic might prove most beneficial.

There is also a need to explore factors influencing rates of reporting. The disparity between the data sets (police and judicial affairs) not only confirms our speculation about the differences between these two reporting sites but also reinforces our earlier cautions about official reports not producing representative samples. This disparity also suggests a new avenue of research: Under what conditions do women report sexual assaults committed by athletes? One possible explanation for the disparity is that women believe that the university will provide swifter recourse while significantly reducing the amount of public humiliation that accompanies a criminal trial. In addition, victims may anticipate an extremely negative response from the broader community if they were to press criminal charges against a Division I athlete. Conversely, women may perceive more severe retribution from other male groups (e.g., fraternity members) with whom they socialize on a regular basis (Martin & Hummer 1989) than they do from athletes, who are less likely to be a part of their daily lives. Clearly, more research is needed in this area.

Finally, if sexual aggression is a form of behavior that is influenced by social and group cultural factors, subject to control and change, intervention and education may reduce the frequency of sexually aggressive behavior among men, including athletes. Recently, educators have developed sexual assault prevention programs specifically designed to reach athletes (Parrot 1994). Social researchers must go beyond describing the problem; they must document the relative success of these programs and make recommendations for more effective interventions.

Notes

1. Of the 24 campus gang rapes analyzed by O'Sullivan (1991), 54% were committed by fraternities, 38% by athletes, and 8% by other groups.

2. In general, the term *judicial affairs* refers to a department with jurisdiction over university and college code of conduct violations. Every institution has a method of disciplining students who violate university rules. Although there is not a universal protocol for establishing a judicial affairs office, schools typically have either a dean or judicial affairs director who is responsible for overseeing any alleged violations of the student code of conduct. Most institutions have either a student court or a body of administrators that hears complaints and determines appropriate sanctions.

3. It should be noted that the original data set included two gang rapes, one of which was committed by a group of student–athletes. Due to the focus of our research, we excluded this data from our sample.

4. The dependent variable for this analysis was the difference between the incident rates for student–athletes and those for other male students. Two dummy variables, coded for year (1991, 1992, 1993), were the independent variables. The regression results showed that neither of the coefficients for the independent variables was statistically significant, $t = 1.44$, $p = .16$; $t = .49$, $p = .63$. Thus the differences between the incident rates were not statistically related to the year of data collection. Therefore, it was determined that combining the 3 years of judicial affairs data for analysis purposes would be appropriate.

5. Although a more representative sample might have been gathered through self-reports, the reliability of this form of data has been the subject of considerable attack in the popular press. Admittedly, there are some limitations inherent with research based on self-reported data. They are nowhere near as pronounced as they appear in the press (see, e.g., Rophie 1993). The most public attacks have been authored by academics and students who do not have training in statistical research. The willingness of the media to publish these attacks speaks to the level of hostility gender researchers face in these rather reactionary times (Faludi 1991).

6. Based on a personal conversation with Mary Koss.

References

Bohmer, C., & Parrot, A. (1993). *Sexual assault on campus: The problem and the solution.* Lexington, MA: Lexington.

Brownmiller, S. (1975). *Against our will.* New York: Simon & Schuster.

Bryson, L. (1987). Sport and maintenance of masculine hegemony. *Women's Studies International Forum, 10,* 349–360.

Curry, T. (1991). Fraternal bonding in the locker room: A profeminist analysis of talk about competition and women. *Sociology of Sport Journal, 8,* 119–135.

Deford, F. (1993, March 24). Does team sports culture encourage prospect of rape? *National Public Radio* (Washington, DC).

Dershowitz, A. (1994, August 6). When women cry rape—falsely. *Boston Herald*, p. 13.

Ehrhart, J., & Sandler, D. (1992). *Campus gang rape: Party games?* Washington, DC: Center for Women Policy Studies.

Eskanazi, G. (1990, June 3). The male athlete and sexual assault. *New York Times*, sec. 8, pp. 1, 4.

Faludi, S. (1991). *Backlash: The undeclared war against American women*. New York: Crown.

Hofmann, R. (1986, March 17). Rape and the college athlete. *Philadelphia Daily News*, sec. 9, p. 102.

Kane, M. J., & Disch, L. (1993). Sexual violence and the reproduction of male power in the locker room: The "Lisa Olson incident." *Sociology of Sport Journal, 10*, 4.

Kidd, B. (1990). The men's cultural center: Sports and the dynamic of women's oppression/men's repression. In M. Messner & D. Sabo (Eds.), *Sport, men and the gender order: Critical feminist perspectives*. Champaign, IL: Human Kinetics.

Kirshenbaum, J. (1989, February 27). An American disgrace: A violent and unprecedented lawlessness has arisen among college athletes in all parts of the country. *Sports Illustrated*, p. 16.

Koss, M., & Gaines, J. (1993). The prediction of sexual aggression by alcohol use, athletic participation and fraternity affiliation. *Journal of Interpersonal Violence, 8*, 94–108.

Larimer, T. (1991, December 16). Under pressure to produce winners, some college coaches turn to risky recruits. *The Sporting News*, p. 8.

Malamuth, N., Sockloskie, R., Koss, P., & Tanaka, T. (1991). Characteristics of aggressors against women: Testing a model using a national sample of college students. *Journal of Consulting and Clinical Psychology, 50*, 670–681.

MacKinnon, C. (1987). *Feminism unmodified: Discourses on life and law*. Cambridge, MA: Harvard University Press.

Martin, P., & Hummer, R. (1989). Fraternities and rape on campus. *Gender & Society, 3*, 457–473.

Melnick, M. (1992). Male athletes and sexual assault. *Journal of Physical Education, Recreation, and Dance, 63*(5); pp. 32–35.

Messner, M. (1992). *Power at play: Sports and the problems of masculinity*. Boston: Beacon.

Messner, M., & Sabo, D. (1994). *Sex, violence, and power in sports: Rethinking masculinity*. Freedom, CA: Crossing.

Muehlenhard, C., & Linton, M., (1987). Date rape and sexual aggression in dating situations: Incidence and risk factors. *Journal of Counseling Psychology, 34*, 186–196.

National Victim's Center. (1992, April 23). *Rape in America: Report to the nation*. Arlington, VA: Author.

Nelson, M. B. (1991). *Are we winning yet? How women are changing sports and sports are changing women*. New York: Random House.

Nelson, M. B. (1994). *The stronger women get, the more men love football: Sexism and the American culture of sports*. New York: Harcourt Brace.

O'Sullivan, C. (1991). Acquaintance gang rape on campus. In A. Parrot & L. Bechhofer (Eds.), *Acquaintance rape: The hidden crime* (pp. 120–156). New York: Wiley.

Parrot, A. (1994, January). A rape awareness and prevention model for male athletes. *Journal of American College Health, 42*, 179–184.

Parrot, A., & Bechhofer, L. (1991). *Acquaintance rape: The hidden crime*. New York: Wiley.

Rophie, K. (1993, June 13). Date rape's other victim. *New York Times Magazine*, p. 26.

Russell, D. (1975). *The politics of rape: The victim's perspective*. New York: Stein & Day.

Sabo, D. (1980). Best years of my life? In D. Sabo & R. Runfola (Eds.), *Jock: Sports and male identity* (pp. 74–78). Englewood Cliffs, NJ: Prentice-Hall.

Sabo, D., & Runfola, R. (1980). *Jock: Sports and male identity*. Englewood Cliffs, NJ: Prentice-Hall.

Sanday, P. (1981). The socio-cultural context of rape: A cross-cultural study. *Journal of Social Issues, 37*(4), 5–27.

Sanday, P. (1990). *Fraternity gang rapes: Sex, brotherhood, and privilege on campus*. New York: New York University Press.

Toufexis, A. (1990, August 6). Sex in the sporting life: Do athletic teams unwittingly promote assaults and rapes? *Time*, p. 76.

Whitson, D. (1990). Sport and the social construction of masculinity. In M. Messner & D. Sabo (Eds.), *Sport, men and the gender order: Critical feminist perspectives* (pp. 19–30). Champaign, IL: Human Kinetics.

A R T I C L E   1 7

Timothy Jon Curry

Fraternal Bonding in the Locker Room: A Profeminist Analysis of Talk About Competition and Women

The men's locker room is enshrined in sports mythology as a bastion of privilege and a center of fraternal bonding. The stereotyped view of the locker room is that it is a retreat from the outside world where athletes quietly prepare themselves for competition, noisily celebrate an important victory, or silently suffer a defeat. Given the symbolic importance of this sports shrine, it is surprising that there have been so few actual studies of the dynamics of male bonding in locker rooms. The purpose of this study was to explore a new approach to this aspect of fraternal bonding, by collecting locker room talk fragments and interpreting them from a profeminist perspective. Profeminism in this context meant adapting a feminist perspective to men's experience in sport, giving special attention to sexist and homophobic remarks that reveal important assumptions about masculinity, male dominance, and fraternal bonding.

Although seldom defined explicitly, the fraternal bond is usually considered to be a force, link, or affectionate tie that unites men. It is characterized in the literature by low levels of disclosure and intimacy. Sherrod (1987), for example, suggests that men associate different meanings with friendships than women do, and that men tend to derive friendships from doing things together while women are able to maintain friend-

Reprinted by permission from T. J. Curry, 1991, "Fraternal Bonding in the Locker Room: A Profeminist Analysis of Talk about Competition and Women," *Sociology of Sport Journal* 8(2): 119–135.

ships through disclosures. This view implies that men need a reason to become close to one another and are uncomfortable about sharing their feelings.

Some of the activities around which men bond are negative toward women and others who are perceived as outsiders to the fraternal group. For example, Lyman (1987) describes how members of a fraternity bond through sexist joking relationships, and Fine (1987) notes the development of sexist, racist, and homophobic attitudes and jokes even among preadolescent Little Leaguers. Sanday (1990) examines gang rape as a by-product of male bonding in fraternities, and she argues that the homophobic and homosocial environments of such all-male groups make for a conducive environment for aggression toward women.

Sport is an arena well suited for the enactment and perpetuation of the male bond (Messner 1987). It affords separation and identity building as individual athletes seek status through making the team and winning games (Dunning 1986), and it also provides group activity essential for male bonding (Sherrod 1987) while not requiring much in the way of intimate disclosures (Sabo & Panepinto 1990). Feminist scholars have pointed out that the status enhancement available to men through sports is not as available to women, and thus sport serves to legitimate men's domination of women and their control of public life (Bryson 1987; Farr 1988). In addition, since most sports are rule bound either by tradition or by explicit formal codes, involvement in sports is part of the typical rights-and-rules orientation of boys' socialization in the United States (Gilligan 1982).

For young men, sport is also an ideal place to "do gender"—display masculinity in a socially approved fashion (West & Zimmerman 1987). In fact the male bond is apparently strengthened by an effective display of traditional masculinity and threatened by what is not considered part of standard hegemonic masculinity. For example, as Messner (1989 p. 192) relates, a gay football player who was aggressive and hostile on the field felt "compelled to go along with a lot of locker room garbage because I wanted that image [of attachment to more traditional male traits]—and I know a lot of others who did too . . . I know a lot of football players who very quietly and secretly like to paint, or play piano. And they do it quietly, because this to them is threatening if it's known by others." Since men's bonding is based on shared activity rather than on self-disclosures (Sherrod 1987), it is unlikely that teammates will probe deeply beneath these surface presentations.

Deconstructing such performances, however, is one way of understanding "the interactional scaffolding of social structure and the social control process that sustains it" in displays of masculinity central to fraternal bonding (West & Zimmerman 1987 p. 147). Pronger (1990, pp. 192–213) has provided one such deconstruction of doing gender in the locker room from the perspective of a homosexual. He notes the irony involved in maintaining the public façade of heterosexuality while privately experiencing a different reality.

Two other studies of locker rooms emphasized the cohesive side of male bonding through sports, but neither of these studies was concerned specifically with gender displays or with what male athletes say about women (Snyder 1972; Zurcher 1982). The uproar over the sexual harassment of a woman reporter in the locker room of the NFL's New England Patriots, described by Heymann (1990), suggests that this work is a timely and important undertaking.

Procedures

This study of locker room talk follows Snyder (1972), who collected samples of written messages and slogans affixed to locker room walls. However, since the messages gathered by Snyder were originally selected by coaches and were meant to serve as normative prescriptions that would contribute to winning games, they mostly revealed an idealistic, public side of locker room culture. From reading these slogans one would get the impression that men's sports teams are characterized by harmony, consensus, and "esoteric in-group traditions" (Snyder 1972, p. 99).

The approach taken here focuses on the spoken aspects of locker room culture—the jokes and put-downs typically involved in fraternal bonding (Fine 1987; Lyman 1987). Although this side of locker room culture is ephemeral, situational, and generally not meant for display outside of the all-male peer groups, it is important in understanding how sport contributes to male bonding, status attainment, and hegemonic displays of masculinity.

The Talk Fragments

The talk fragments were gathered in locker rooms from athletes on two teams participating in contact sports at a large midwestern university with a "big time" sports program. The first team was approached at the beginning of its season for permission to do a field study. Permission was granted and assurances were made that anonymity would be maintained for athletes and coaches. I observed the team as a nonparticipant sport sociologist, both at practices and during competition, for well over a month before the first talk fragments were collected. The talk fragments were gathered over a 2-month period and the locker room was visited frequently to gather field notes. Note gathering in the locker room was terminated upon saturation; however, the team's progress was followed and field observations continued until the end of the season.

Intensive interviews were conducted with some of the athletes and coaches during all 9 months of the research. These interviews concerned not only locker room interaction but also the sport background and life histories of the respondents. Additionally, after the talk fragments were gathered, five of the athletes enrolled in my class on sport sociology and wrote term papers on their experiences in sport. These written documents, along with the interviews and observations made outside the locker room, provided a rich variety of materials for the contextual analysis and interpretation of the conversations held inside the locker room. They also lent insight into how the athletes themselves defined locker room talk.

The talk fragments were collected in plain view of the athletes, who had become accustomed to the presence of a researcher taking notes. Fragments of talk were written down as they occurred and were reconstructed later. Such obvious note taking may have influenced what was said, or more likely what was not said. To minimize the obtrusiveness of the research, eye contact was avoided while taking notes. A comparison between the types of conversations that occurred during note taking versus when note taking was not done yielded few differences. Even so, more talk fragments were gathered from a second locker room as a way of both increasing the validity of the study and protecting the anonymity of the athletes and coaches from the first locker room.

The Second Locker Room

Field notes concerning talk from a second locker room were gathered by a senior who had enjoyed a successful career as a letterman. His presence in the locker room as a participant observer was not obtrusive, and the other student-athletes reacted to him as a peer. He gathered talk fragments over a 3-month period while his team was undergoing conditioning and selection procedures similar in intensity to that of the original team. He met with me every week and described his perceptions of interaction in the locker room. His collection of talk fragments was included as part of a written autobiographical account of his experience in sport while at college. These research procedures were modeled after Zurcher's (1983) study of

hashers in a sorority house and Shaw's (1972) autobiographical account of his experience in sport.

One additional point needs to be stressed here: Unlike anecdotal accounts of locker room behavior or studies based on the recollections of former athletes, these conversations were systematically gathered live and in context over a relatively brief period of time. Consequently the stories and jokes may not be as extreme as those remembered by athletes who reflect upon their entire career in sport (e.g., Messner 1987; Pronger 1990), or as dramatic as the episode of sexual harassment that took place in the locker room of the New England Patriots (Heymann 1990).

The strength of this study lies in situating the conversations within the context of the competitive environment of elite collegiate sport rather than capturing the drama of a single moment or the recollections of particularly memorable occasions. In other words, no one study, including this one, can hope to cover the entire gambit of locker room culture and various distinctive idiocultures of different teams (Fine 1987). A variety of studies that use different methods and incorporate different perspectives are needed for that endeavor.

Profeminist Perspective

Messner (1990) has recently argued that a profeminist perspective is needed to overcome male bias in research in the sociology of sport. For decades, Messner claims, male researchers have been prone to writing about sport from a masculine standpoint and have neglected gender issues. He further states that since men have exclusive access to much of the social world of sport, they also have the primary responsibility of providing a more balanced interpretation of that world by paying special attention to gender oppression. He maintains that such balance is best achieved at this point by adopting a value-centered feminist perspective rather than a supposedly value-free but androcentric perspective.

Adopting a feminist standpoint requires assuming that "feminist visions of an egalitarian society are desirable" (Messner 1990, p. 149). Ultimately, research guided by such an assumption will contribute to a deeper understanding of the costs and the privileges of masculinity and may help build a more just and egalitarian world. Messner does not offer explicit guidelines as to how an androcentric researcher might begin to undertake such a shift in perspectives, however, although he does refer to a number of exemplary studies.

As a method of consciously adopting a profeminist perspective in this research, a review of feminist literature on sports and socialization was undertaken, feminist colleagues were consulted on early drafts of the manuscript, and a research assistant trained in feminist theory was employed to help with the interpretation of talk fragments. She shared her ideas and observations regarding the talk fragments, written documents, and field notes with me and suggested some additional references and sources that proved useful.

The talk fragments were selected and arranged to provide a sense of the different themes, ideas, and attitudes encountered. In focusing on the talk fragments themselves, two categories emerged (through a grounded theory approach) as especially important for situating and interpreting locker room behavior from a profeminist perspective: (a) the dynamics of competition, status attainment, and bonding among male athletes, and (b) the dynamics of defending one's masculinity through homophobic talk and talk about women as objects. A numbering system for each talk fragment (Athlete 1, 2, Sam, etc.) is used below to keep track of the different speakers. Names have been changed and the numbering system starts over for each talk fragment.

Competition, Status Attainment, and Bonding

Locker room talk is mostly about the common interests that derive from the shared identities of male student-athlete. Underlying these interactions is an ever present sense of competition, both for status and position on the team itself and between the team and its opponents. While sport provides an activity to bond around, one's position

on the team is never totally secure. An injury or poor performance may raise doubts about one's ability and lead to one's replacement. Such basic insecurities do not promote positive social relationships in the locker room, and they help explain some of the harshness of the talk that the athletes directed toward each other and toward women.

For example, competition can have a subtle influence on the relationships athletes have with others on the team and cause them to be quite tentative, as illustrated by the following statements obtained from two interviews:

> One of the smaller guys on the team was my best friend . . . maybe I just like having a little power over [him] . . . It doesn't matter if the guy is your best friend, you've got to beat him, or else you are sitting there watching. Nobody wants to watch.

> That's one of my favorite things about the sport, I enjoy the camaraderie. [Who are your friends?] Usually it's just the starters . . . you unite behind each other a lot. The other guys don't share the competition with you like the starters do.

The competition can extend beyond sport itself into other domains. It is not unusual for athletes to have as their closest friends men who are not on the team, which helps them maintain some defensive ego boundaries between themselves and the team. It also provides a relief from the constant competition, as one athlete indicates:

> [My] better friends aren't on the team. Probably because we are not always competing. With my [athlete] friends, we are always competing . . . like who gets the best girls, who gets the best grades . . . Seems like [we] are competitive about everything, and it's nice to have some friends that don't care . . . you can just relax.

Competition, Emotional Control, and Bonding

A variety of studies have indicated that male athletes are likely to incorporate competitive motivation as part of their sport identity (e.g., Curry & Weiss 1989). As competition and status attainment become important for the male athlete in establishing his identity, noninstrumental emotion becomes less useful, perhaps even harmful to his presentation of a conventionally gendered self (Sherrod 1987). In addition, by defining themselves in terms of what is not feminine, men may come to view emotional displays with disdain or even fear (Herek 1987). However, control over emotions in sport is made difficult by the passions created by an intense desire to win. One athlete described his feelings of being consumed by competition while in high school and his need to control the emotions:

> My junior year, I had become so obsessed with winning the district . . . I was so overcome that I lost control a week before the tournament. I was kicking and screaming and crying on the sofa . . . since then I have never been the same. True, now I work harder than that year but now when I start to get consumed [with something] I get fearful and reevaluate its importance.

As part of learning to control emotions, the athletes have learned to avoid public expressions of emotional caring or concern for one another even as they bond, because such remarks are defined as weak or feminine. For example, the remarks of the following athlete illustrate how this type of socialization can occur through sport. This athlete's father was very determined that his son would do well in sports, so much so that he forced the boy to practice daily and became very angry with the boy's mistakes. To understand his father's behavior, the boy went to his mother:

> I would come up from the cellar and be upset with myself, and I would talk to my mother and say, "Why does he yell so much?" and she would say, "He only does it because he loves you."

While the father emphasized adherence to rules and discipline, the boy had to depend on his mother to connect him to his father's love. Distancing from each other emotionally is of course dysfunctional for the relationships among male athletes and leads to an impoverishment of relationships (Messner 1987).

Maintaining a "safe" distance from one another also influences what is said and what is not said in front of others about topics of mutual concern, such as grades and women. Failure to address such common problems openly means that they must be dealt with indirectly or by denial. For example, the deriding of academic work by male athletes has been noted by other investigators (Adler & Adler 1991) and is not typical of female athletes (Meyer 1990). The reason may be that when athletes make comments that might be construed as asking for help or encouragement, their behavior is considered nonmasculine. They are thus subject to ridicule, as illustrated in the following two talk fragments:

Fragment 1

Athlete 1: [Spoken to the athlete who has a locker near him, but loud enough to be heard by others] What did you get on your test?

Athlete 2: 13 [pause], that's two D+'s this week. That's a student-athlete for you. [sighs, then laughs quietly]

Athlete 1: That's nothing to laugh about.

Athlete 2: [contritely] I mean an athlete-student, but things are looking up for me. I'm going to do better this week. How did you do on that test?

Athlete 1: Got a 92.

Athlete 3: Yeah, who did you cheat off of? [group laughter]

Fragment 2

Athlete 1: [To coach, shouted across room] I'm doing real bad in class.

Coach: Congratulations!

Athlete 1: [serious tone, but joking] Will you call the professor up and tell him to give me an A?

Coach: [Obviously sarcastically] Sure thing, would tonight at 9 be all right?

Competition and a Sense of Self

Considering the time-consuming nature of big-time college sports, it is not surprising that they become the central focus of athletes' lives. Approximately 30 hours a week were spent in practice, and often the athletes were too tired after a hard practice to do much else than sleep.

Fragment 3

Athlete 1: [collapses on bench] Shit, I'm going to bed right now, and maybe I'll make my 9 o'clock class tomorrow.

Athlete 2: 40 minutes straight! I thought he'd never stop the drills.

Athlete 1: Left you gasping for air at the end, didn't it?

Athlete 2: You mean gasping for energy.

Sports and competition become the greater part of the athlete's world. Through his strivings to excel, to be a part of the team and yet stand out on his own, he develops a conception of how he is. Thus the athlete's sense of self can be seen as being grounded in competition, with few alternative sources of self-gratification (Adler & Adler 1991). The rewards for such diligence are a heightened sense of self-esteem. When one athlete was asked what he would miss most if he were to leave sports, he declared, "the competition . . . the attitude I feel about being [on the team]. It makes me feel special. You're doing something that a lot of people can't do, and wish they could do." In other words, his knowledge of his "self" includes status enhancing presumptions about character building through sport.

This attitude is not atypical. For example, another man claimed, "I can always tell a [refers to athletes in same sport he plays]. They give off cues—good attitude, they are sure of themselves, bold, not insecure." This sense of specialness and status presumption cements the male bond and may temporarily cut across social class and racial differences. Later in life the experiences and good memories associated with fellowship obtained through sport may further sociability and dominance bonding (Farr 1988). For the elite college athlete, however, this heightened self-esteem is obtained at some costs to other activities. Often academic studies and social or romantic involvements get defined as peripheral to the self and are referred to with contempt in the locker room, as illustrated in the next fragment:

Most everyone has vacated the locker room for the showers. Sam and a few of his friends are left behind. Sam is red shirting (saving a year's eligibility by not participating on the team except for practices) and will not be traveling with the team. What he is going to do instead is the subject of several jokes once all the coaches have left the locker room:

Fragment 4

Athlete 1: What are you going to do, Sam, go to the game?

Sam: I can't, I sold my ticket. [laughs] I'm going to the library so I can study. [cynically] Maybe I'll take my radio so I can listen to the game. [pause] I hate my classes.

Athlete 1: Oh, come on, that's not the right attitude.

Sam: And I hope to get laid a few times too.

Athlete 1: Hey come on, that's not a nice way to talk.

Sam: How else are you supposed to talk in a locker room?

Sam's comment also leads us directly to the question of peer group influence on presentation of a gendered self. A general rule of male peer groups is that you can say and do some things with your peers that would be inappropriate almost anywhere else. For male athletes this rule translates into an injunction to be insulting and antisocial on occasion (Fine 1987; Lyman 1987). You are almost expected to speak sarcastically and offensively in the locker room, as Sam indicates above. Thus, hostile talk about women is blended with jokes and put-downs about classes and each other. In short, while sport leads to self-enhancement, the peer culture of male athletes also fosters antisocial talk, much of which is directed toward the athletes themselves.

Rigidities of the Bond

Competition in sports, then, links men together in a status enhancing activity in which aggression is valued (Dunning 1986). The bond between male athletes is usually felt to be a strong one, yet it is set aside rather easily. The reason for this is that the bond is rigid, with sharply defined boundaries. For example, when speaking about what it is that bonds athletes to their sport and other athletes, a coach remarks,

> They know they are staying in shape, they are part of something. Some of them stay with it because they don't want to be known as quitters. There's no in-between. You're a [team member or not a team member]. The worst guy on the team is still well thought of if he's out there every day going through it. There's no sympathy in that room. No sympathy if you quit. You might die but you're not going to quit.

This rigid definition of who is or is not a team member reflects Gilligan's (1982) concept of a rights/rules moral system for males, which emphasizes individuality, instrumental relations, achievement, and control. In short the male athlete is either on the team or not. There is no grey area: It is clearly a black or white situation. If one follows the "rules," then he has the "right" to participate in bonding. If one does not follow the rules (i.e., quits), he ceases to exist in a bonding capacity. However, as Coakley (1990) has observed, following the rules to their extremes can lead to "positive" deviance, including a refusal to quit in spite of injury. Athlete 1 below endured a number of small and severe injuries, but throughout his ordeal refused to consider leaving the team.

Fragment 5

Athlete 1: My shin still hurts, can't get it to stop.

Athlete 2: Well, that's it then—time to quit.

Athlete 1: Not me, I'm not a quitter.

Athlete 2: Oh, come on, I can see through that. You'll quit if you have to.

Athlete 1: No way.

Even though injured, an athlete is still a member of the team if he attends practice, even if only to watch the others work out. However, his bond with the others suffers if he cannot participate fully in the sport. Sympathy is felt for such athletes, in that their fate is recognized and understood. As one athlete empathized during an interview, "I feel for the guys who are hurt who are usually

starters . . . [They] feel lonely about it, feel like they want to be back out there, feel like they want to prove something."

Perhaps what these athletes need to prove is that they are still a part of the activity around which the bonds are centered. As Sherrod (1987) suggests, the meanings associated with friendship for men are grounded in activities, giving them a reason to bond. Past success or status as a team member is not enough to fully sustain the bond; bonding requires constant maintenance. With boundaries so rigid, the athletes must constantly establish and reestablish their status as members involved in the bond by the only way they know how: through competition.

Rigid definitions of performance requirements in sport combine to form an either/or situation for the athlete and his ability to bond with teammates. If he stays within these boundaries, he is accepted and the bond remains intact. If he fails, he is rejected and the bond is severed. One athlete sums up this position with the following comments: "You lose a lot of respect for guys like that. Seems like anybody who's quit, they just get pushed aside. Like [name deleted], when he used to be [on the team] he hung around with us, and now that he's not, he ain't around anymore." Thus an athlete may find his relations severed with someone he has known for half his life, through participation in sport in junior high and high school, simply because the other person has left the team.

Talk About Women

Competitive pressures and insecurities surrounding the male bond influence talk about women. As discussed above, competition provides an activity bond to other men that is rewarding, even though the atmosphere of competition surrounding big-time sports generates anxiety and other strong emotions that the athletes seek to control or channel. Competition for positions or status on the team also curtails or conditions friendships, and peer group culture is compatible with antisocial talk and behavior, some of which is directed at the athletes themselves.

The fraternal bond is threatened by inadequate role performance, quitting the team, or not living up to the demands of masculinity. Consequently, fear of weakening the fraternal bond greatly affects how athletes "do gender" in the locker room and influences the comments they make about women. In this regard, locker room talk may again be characterized both by what is said and what is not said. Conversations that affirm a traditional masculine identity dominate, and these include talk about women as objects, homophobic talk and talk that is very aggressive and hostile toward women—essentially talk that promotes rape culture.

Woman as Person, Woman as Object

Two additional distinctions now need to be made in categorizing locker room talk about women. One category concerns women as real people, persons with whom the athletes have ongoing social relationships. This category of locker room talk is seldom about sexual acquisition; most often it is about personal concerns athletes might wish to share with their best friend on the team. Because the athletes do not want their comments to be overheard by others who might react with ridicule, this type of talk usually occurs in hushed tones, as described in the following fragment. Talk about women as objects, on the other hand, often refers to sexual conquests. This type of talk is not hushed. Its purpose seems mainly to enhance the athletes' image of themselves to others as practicing heterosexuals.

Fragment 6

Athlete 1 to 2: I've got to talk to you about [whispers name]. They go over to an empty corner of the locker room and whisper. They continue to whisper until the coaches arrive. The athletes at the other end of the locker room make comments:

Athlete 3: Yeah, tell us what she's got.

Athlete 4: Boy, you're in trouble now.

Assistant coach: You'll have to leave our part of the room. This is where the real men are.

The peer culture of the locker room generally does not support much talk about women as persons. Norms of masculinity discourage talking seriously about social relations, so these types of conversations are infrequent (Fine 1987; Sabo & Panepinto 1990). Inevitably, personal revelations will quickly be followed by male athletic posturing, jokes, and put-downs, as in the talk fragment above. While the jokes may be amusing, they do little to enhance personal growth and instead make a real sharing of intimacies quite difficult. The ridicule that follows these interactions also serves to establish the boundaries of gender appropriate behavior. This ridicule tells the athlete that he is getting too close to femaleness, because he is taking relatedness seriously. "Real men" do not do that. Perhaps just taking the view of women as persons is enough to evoke suspicion in the locker room.

To avoid this suspicion, the athlete may choose to present his attitude toward women in a different way, one that enhances his identity as a "real man." The resulting women-as-objects stories are told with braggadocio or in a teasing manner; they are stage performances usually requiring an audience of more than one, and may be told to no one in particular:

Fragment 7

I was taking a shower with my girlfriend when her parents came home. I never got dressed so fast in my life.

These types of stories elicit knowing smiles or guffaws from the audience, and it is difficult to tell whether or not they are true. In any event the actual truth of such a story is probably less important than the function it serves in buttressing the athlete's claim as a practicing heterosexual.

Fragment 8

Athlete 1: How was your Thanksgiving?

Athlete 2: Fine, went home.

Athlete 1: I bet you spent the time hitting high schools!

Athlete 2: Naw, only had to go back to [one place] to find out who was available.

Women's identities as people are of no consequence in these displays. The fact that women are viewed as objects is also evident in the tendency of men to dissect woman's bodies into parts, which are then discussed separately from the whole person. Athlete 1 in Fragment 9 below is describing a part of a woman's body as if it existed separately from the woman, as if it was in the training room and the woman was not:

Fragment 9

Athlete 1: I just saw the biggest set of Ta-Tas in the training room!

Athlete 2: How big were they?

Athlete 1: Bigger than my mouth.

This perspective toward women highlights the fact that the use of women's bodies is more important than knowing them as people. Perhaps this attitude is also based in the athlete's focus on maintaining control, whether physically through athletic performance or mentally through strict adherence to rules and discipline. Since the male athlete's ideas about control center around physical strength and mental discipline, they stand in sharp contrast to ideas about females, who are generally thought of as physically weak and emotional. Following the implications of these ideas a bit further, women as persons are emotional and cannot be easily controlled; women as objects, however, have no volition and can be more easily controlled.

Doing Gender through Homophobic Talk

From Herek's (1987) notion that through socialization boys learn to be masculine by avoiding that which is feminine or homosexual, it follows that in the locker room an athlete may be singled out if his demeanor is identified as unmasculine in any way. The reasoning may be seen as follows: (a) "real men" are defined by what they are *not*

(women and homosexuals); (b) it is useful to maintain a separation from femaleness or gayness so as not to be identified as such; (c) expression of dislike for femaleness or homosexuality demonstrates to oneself and others that one is separate from it and therefore must be masculine. For example, when an athlete's purple designer underwear is discovered, a teammate asks, "and did you get earrings for Christmas?" When he protests, this replay, directed to all of the athletes in the room is offered: "Guess I hit a . . . nerve. I won't begin on the footsies today, maybe tomorrow."

This example illustrates that every aspect of the athlete's appearance runs the risk of gender assessment. That which is under suspicion of being at odds with traditional definitions of masculinity threatens the bond and will be questioned. Connell (1990, pp. 88–89) provides further graphic example of gender assessment among athletes. He describes the life of a determinedly heterosexual Australian Iron-Man competitor, whose first coital experience at 17 was both arranged and witnessed by his surf-club friends, and who felt he had to "put on a good show for the boys." Presumably, his performance allowed him and his friends to reaffirm to themselves and others that their sexual preferences remained within the boundaries of the bond.

Not only is being homosexual forbidden, but tolerance of homosexuality is theoretically off limits as well. The sanctions associated with this type of boundary maintenance manifest themselves in jokes and story telling about homosexuals.

Fragment 10

Athlete 1: When I was at [high school] we all lined up to watch the other guys come in. Fred pretended to be interested in one of them and said, "I like that one" [he gestures with a limp wrist] . . . . We were all so fucking embarrassed, nobody would give him a ride home. It was the funniest thing!

Athlete 2: Yeah, once we all stopped in at [a local bar] and Tom got up to dance with one of the fags, actually took his hand and started to dance! Boy was the fag surprised. [group laughter]

Making fun of homosexuals by mimicking stereotyped gay gender displays brings laughter in the locker room partly because it helps distance the athletes from being categorized as gay themselves. Such hegemonic gender displays also take more aggressive forms. Perhaps male athletes are especially defensive because of the physical closeness and nudity in the locker room and the contact between males in sport itself. This latter idea is evident in the following remarks of a coach:

> We do so much touching that some people think we're queer. In 37 years I've never for sure met a queer [athlete]. At [a certain college] we had a [teammate] that some of the fellows thought was queer. I said "pound on him, beat on him, see what happens." He quit after 3 days. He never approached anyone anyway.

Locker Room Talk Promotes Rape Culture

Maintaining the appearance of a conventional heterosexual male identity then, is of the utmost importance to the athlete who wants to remain bonded to his teammates. Also, as discussed previously, the perception of women as objects instead of persons encourages expressions of disdain or even hatred toward them on the part of the male athletes. Thus, the striving to do gender appropriately within the constraints of the fraternal bond involves talk that manages to put down women while also ridiculing or teasing each other, as the following fragments indicate:

Fragment 11

Assistant Coach 1: [announcement] Shame to miss the big [football] game, but you have to travel this week to keep you out of trouble. Keep you from getting laid too many times this weekend. Here are the itineraries for the trip. They include a picture of Frank's girlfriend. [Picture is of an obese woman surrounded by children. Frank is one of the best athletes on the team.]

Assistant Coach 2: Yeah, when she sits around the house, she really sits around the house.

Assistant Coach 3: She's so ugly that her mother took her everywhere so she wouldn't have to kiss her good-bye. [group laughter]

Jibes and put-downs about one's girlfriend or lack of sexual success are typified by this exchange. Part of the idealized heterosexual male identity consists of "success" with women, and to challenge that success by poking fun at the athlete's girlfriend is an obvious way to insult him. These jibes were directed at one of the best athletes on the team whose girlfriend was not in town. It is important to note that these insults were delivered by the assistant coaches, who are making use of their masculine identity as a common bond they share with the student-athletes. By ridiculing one of the better athletes, they are not threatening any of the more vulnerable team members and at the same time they are removing some of the social distance between themselves and the students. After receiving such an insult, the athlete has to think of a comeback to top it or lose this round of insulting. Fine (1987) also noted such escalation of insults in his study of the Little League. This attitude is recognized and understood by other athletes:

Fragment 12

You guys harass around here real good. If you knew my mother's name, you would bring her into it too.

Thus a negative view of women prevails in the locker room and serves to facilitate the bond between athletes and their coaches. At times the competition involved with these exchanges does not involve insults directed at one another. The athletes compete instead to see who can express the most negative attitudes toward women, as illustrated by the final comments from a discussion of different types of women:

Fragment 13

Let me tell you about those [names an ethnic minority] women. They look good until they are 20, then they start pushing out the pups. By the time they're 40, they weigh 400 pounds.

This negative orientation is fed by other related attitudes about women, such as those that concern women's sports, as indicated by the following remarks made by a coach: "[Our sport] has been taking a beating in lots of colleges. It's because of the emphasis on women's sports. Too bad, because [our sport] is cheaper. Could make money . . ." (he continues with comments about women's sports not paying their way).

At their extreme, these attitudes promote aggression toward women and create an environment supportive for rape culture (Beneke 1982; Sanday 1990). A fairly mild form of this aggression is suggested in the following talk fragment, in which two athletes are talking about Jerry, an athlete who is a frequent butt of their jokes. Jerry has just left the locker room and this conversation occurs when he is out of hearing distance:

Fragment 14

Athlete 1: Hey Pete, did you know Jerry is a sexual dynamo?

Pete: Why do you say that?

Athlete 1: He said he was with two different girls in the same day and both girls were begging, and I emphasize begging, for him to stop. He said he banged each of them so hard that they begged for him to stop.

Pete: I think he's becoming retarded.

Athlete 1: Do you believe he said this to me?

Pete: Well, what did you do?

Athlete 1: I laughed in his face.

Pete: What did he do?

Athlete 1: Nothing, he just kept telling me about this; it was hilarious.

The preceding fragment can be seen as describing rape in that the women involved with the athlete "begged for him to stop," and in this case the athletes choose to use the story to put down Jerry and thus negate his claim to sexual dynamism. The rape reference is more obvious in the following fragment. To set the scene, the team was visited by high school athletes and their parents; the athletes were being recruited by the coaches. The mother of one recruit drew attention from a group of athletes because she was extremely attractive. This conversation occurs in the locker room after she left with her son:

Fragment 15

Athlete 1: She's too young to be his mother!

Athlete 2: Man, I'd hurt her if I got ahold of her.

Athlete 3: I'd tear her up.

Athlete 4: I'd break her hips. [all laugh]

Athlete 3: Yeah, she was hot!

Thus locker room talk about women, though serving a function for the bonding of men, also promotes harmful attitudes and creates an environment supportive of sexual assault and rape. Competition among teammates, the emphasis upon women as objects, sexual conquest as enviable achievement, peer group encouragement of antisocial comments and behavior, and anxiety about proving one's heterosexuality—all of these ideas are combined in the preceding fragment to promote a selfish, hostile, and aggressive approach to sexual encounters with women.

Conclusions

Sex and aggression are familiar themes in men's talk, and it is no surprise to find them of paramount importance in the locker room. Fine's (1987) work with preadolescent Little League baseball players indicated that the conversations of 9- to 12-year-old boys reflected similar concerns. What comes through less clearly in the conversations is the fulfillment that men find in such talk. It is an affirmation of one's masculine identity to be able to hold one's own in conversations about women, to top someone else's joke, or to share a story that one's peers find interesting. In this way the athlete's identity as a man worthy of bonding with is maintained.

College athletes often speak of the rewards of team membership as being an important reason for participating in a sport, and one of the rewards is the give and take of the peer culture in the locker room. The combination of revelation and braggadocio requires a shifting interpretation between fantasy and reality, and the ready willingness to insult means that a false interpretation may subject one to ridicule.

There are no definitive studies that document the effects of participating in locker room culture. On the one hand, behavior in locker rooms is both ephemeral and situational and probably does not reflect the actual values of all the participants. From this perspective, the locker room is just a place to change clothing and to shower, and one should not make too much of what goes on there. In discussing locker room interaction with some of the athletes involved, I found that most distanced themselves from it and denied its importance to them, particularly with respect to devaluing academic work. In some cases locker room talk even served as a negative reference for athletes, who quietly went about their business and avoided involvement. However, it is important to note that no one ever publicly challenged the dominant sexism and homophobia of the locker room. Whatever oppositional thoughts there may have been were muttered quietly or remained private.

On the other hand, there is evidence that years of participating in such a culture desensitizes athletes to women's and gay rights and supports male supremacy rather than egalitarian relationships with women. For instance, Connell's (1990) life history of an Iron-Man indicated that this incredibly fit young man was unable to tolerate a "girl" who stood up for her own interests, and so had a series of girlfriends who were compliant with his needs and schedule. Moreover, Connell observes that this attitude is typical among the other male supremacists who constitute the Australian surfing subculture.

Another illustration is provided by the harassment of Lisa Olson in the locker room of the New England Patriots. This episode also supports the idea that locker room talk promotes aggressive antifemale behavior. The details of this case involved grown men parading nude around the seated reporter as she was conducting an interview. Some of the men "modeled themselves" before her, and one "adjusted" his genitals and

shook his hips in an exaggerated fashion, and one naked player stood arm's length from her and said "Here's what you want. Do you want to take a bite out of this?"—all to the accompaniment of bantering and derisive laughter (Heymann 1990, p. 9A). No one tried to stop the humiliating activity, nor did management intervene or sincerely apologize until forced to by the NFL Commissioner. In fact, the initial reaction of the team's owner was to support the players. The owner, Victor ("I liked it so much, I bought the company"—Remington) Kiam, was heard to say, "What a classic bitch. No wonder none of the players like her." However, his concern for the sales of his women's shaving products resulted in the following damage control campaign:

> He took out full-page ads in three major U.S. newspapers to protest his innocence, offered testimonials from three people who denied he said anything derogatory about Olson, and blamed the Patriots front office personnel for not telling him of the Olson locker room incident sooner. (Norris 1991, p. 23)

Finally, Sanday (1990, p. 193) concludes her study of gang rape by fraternity members by indicating that "Sexism is an unavoidable by-product of a cultural fascination with the virile, sexually powerful hero who dominates everyone, male and female alike." If this is true, then sexism in locker rooms is best understood as part of a larger cultural pattern that supports male supremacy.

It is my view that sexist locker room talk is likely to have a cumulative negative effect on young men because it reinforces the notions of masculine privilege and hegemony, making that world view seem normal and typical. Moreover, it does so in a particularly pernicious fashion. By linking ideas about masculinity with negative attitudes toward women, locker room culture creates a no-win situation for the athlete who wishes to be masculine and who wants to have successful, loving, nurturing relationships with women: "real men" are not nurturant. Similarly, locker room talk provides no encouragement for the "real man" who seeks egalitarian relationships.

As Pronger (1990) notes, the myth of masculinity prevalent in the locker room cannot be maintained in the face of equitable relations between men and women or in the acceptance of homosexuality.

Finally, by linking ideas about status attainment with male bonding and masculinity, locker room culture makes it more difficult for young men to realize that women also desire success and status attainment through hard work and self-discipline. In other words, through participating in sport young men are taught that discipline and effort are needed for success and that one's acceptance depends on successful performance. But since these lessons are usually learned in all-male groups, they do not generalize easily to women and may create barriers to men's acceptance of women in the workplace.

References

Adler, P. A., & Adler, P. (1991). *Backboards & blackboards: College athletes and role engulfment.* New York: Columbia University Press.

Beneke, T. (1982). *Men on rape.* New York: St. Martin's Press.

Bryson, L. (1987). Sport and the maintenance of masculine hegemony. *Women's Studies International Forum,* 10, 349–360.

Coakley, J. J. (1990). *Sport in society: Issues and controversies.* St. Louis: Mosby.

Connell, R. W. (1990). An Iron Man: The body and some contradictions of hegemonic masculinity. In M. A. Messner & D. F. Sabo (Eds.), *Sport, men, and the gender order* (pp. 83–95). Champaign, IL: Human Kinetics.

Curry, T. J., & Weiss, O. (1989). Sport identity and motivation for sport participation: A comparison between American college athletes and Austrian student sport club members. *Sociology of Sport Journal,* 6, 257–268.

Dunning, E. (1986). Social bonding and violence in sport. In N. Elias & E. Dunning (Eds.), *Quest for excitement: Sport and leisure in the civilizing process* (pp. 224–244). Oxford: Basil Blackwell.

Farr, K. A. (1988). Dominance bonding through the good old boys sociability group. *Sex Roles,* 18, 259–277.

Fine, G. A. (1987). *With the boys: Little League baseball and preadolescent culture.* Chicago: University of Chicago Press.

Gilligan, C. (1982). *In a different voice: Psychological theory and woman's development.* Cambridge, MA: Harvard University Press.

Herek, G. M. (1987). On heterosexual masculinity: Some physical consequences of the social construction of gender and sexuality. In M. S. Kimmel (Ed.), *Changing men: New directions in research on men and masculinity* (pp. 68–82). Beverly Hills: Sage.

Heymann, P. B. (1990, Nov. 28). Report describes what happened in locker room. *USA Today,* pp. 9A, 7C.

Lyman, P. (1987). The fraternal bond as a joking relationship: A case study of the role of sexist jokes in male group bonding. In M. S. Kimmel (Ed.), *Changing men: New directions in research on men and masculinity* (pp. 148–163). Beverly Hills: Sage.

Messner, M. A. (1987). The meaning of success: The athletic experience and the development of male identity. In H. Brod (Ed.), *The making of masculinities: The new men's studies* (pp. 193–209). Boston: Allen and Unwin.

Messner, M. A. (1989). Gay athletes and the gay games: An interview with Tom Waddell. In M. S. Kimmel and M. A. Messner (Eds.), *Men's lives* (pp. 190–193). New York: Macmillian.

Messner, M. A. (1990). Men studying masculinity: Some epistemological issues in sport sociology. *Sociology of Sport Journal,* 7, 136–153.

Meyer, B. B. (1990). From idealism to actualization: The academic performance of female college athletes. *Sociology of Sport Journal,* 7, 44–57.

Norris, M. (1991, Feb. 2). Mr. nice guy. *T.V. Guide,* pp. 22–29.

Pronger, B. (1990). *The arena of masculinity: Sport, homosexuality, and the meaning of sex.* New York: St. Martin's Press.

Sabo, D. F., & Panepinto, J. (1990). Football ritual and the social reproduction of masculinity. In M. A. Messner & D. F. Sabo (Eds.), *Sport, men, and the gender order* (pp. 115–126). Champaign, IL: Human Kinetics.

Sanday, P. R. (1990). *Fraternity gang rapes: Sex, brotherhood, and privilege on campus.* New York: New York University Press.

Shaw, G. (1972). *Meat on the hoof.* New York: St. Martin's Press.

Sherrod, D. (1987). The bonds of men: Problems and possibilities in close male relationships. In H. Brod (Ed.), *The making of masculinities: The new men's studies* (pp. 213–239). Boston: Allen and Unwin.

Snyder, E. E. (1972). Athletic dressing room slogans as folklore: A means of socialization. *International Review of Sport Sociology,* 7, 89–100.

West, C., & Zimmerman, D. H. (1987). Doing gender. *Gender & Society,* 1, 125–149.

Zurcher, L. A. (1983). Dealing with an unacceptable role: Hashers in a sorority house. In L. A. Zurcher (Ed.), *Social roles: Conformity, conflict, and creativity* (pp. 77–89). Beverly Hills: Sage.

Zurcher, L. A. (1982). The staging of emotion: A dramaturgical analysis. *Symbolic Interaction,* 5, 1–19.

John Stoltenberg

"I Am Not a Rapist!"

Why College Guys Are Confronting Sexual Violence

What follows is an emotionally charged conversation among members of a Duke University student organization called Men Acting for Change (MAC), one of many new men's groups at colleges and universities across the United States and Canada. Besides meeting regularly to talk personally, MAC members present programs about gender and sexuality, focusing on sexual violence and homophobia, to fraternities and other campus groups.

MAC came to national prominence in the United States when members appeared in a segment about pornography on the ABC newsmagazine program *20/20*. On January 28, 1993, millions of viewers heard these college-age males speak graphically about the negative effects of pornography, including *Playboy*, on their sex lives and their relationships with women.

A year earlier, Kate Wenner, an ABC producer, asked to pick my brains about how to do a pornography story that hadn't been done before. Over an amiable lunch at a café near Lincoln Center, I suggested she report how pornography has become a primary form of sex education for young men. She liked the idea and tracked down MAC. The resulting broadcast included footage of frank conversations among both female and male Duke students and was perhaps the most astute coverage of pornography's interpersonal effects yet to appear on network television.

After that *20/20* segment aired, MAC members were invited to appear on *Oprah, Donahue, Jerry Springer, Maury Povich,* and *Montel Williams,* but they declined to have their stories sensationalized. Meanwhile *Playboy* went ballistic and, in an apparent attempt at damage control, ridiculed them in print as "the pointy-headed, wet-behind the scrotum boys at Duke."

In January 1994, curious to know what makes MAC tick, I traveled to Durham, North Carolina, to attend the third annual Student Conference on Campus Sexual Violence, to be held at Duke. The brochure promised "focus on student activism and involvement in the anti-rape movement" and quoted Jason Schultz, a conference organizer and *20/20* participant: "Through our work against rape, we take control of our future and generate the skills and perspectives that we need to help make it a better, safer place for both women and men." The afternoon before the conference opened, Jason arranged a private conversation in his home among five MAC members. They understood that I would sit in, ask questions, and try to get an edited transcript of their conversation published where it could contribute to more accurate understanding of the student movement against sexual violence.

As I listened, I realized that these young men had taken the meaning of sexual violence to heart in some intensely personal and generationally specific new ways. Everyone in the group knew friends who had been sexually assaulted. At one point I asked them to estimate how many. One said that one in five of his friends had told him this. Another said fifty. Another said that among his twenty to twenty-five friends who had been

From *Feminism and Men: Towards a Relational Feminism*, edited by Steven Schacht and Doris Ewing, New York: New York University Press.

sexually assaulted, he also knew the perpetrator in half the cases.

At another point one told something he had never before shared with his fellow MAC members: he himself had been sexually molested in his youth. That dramatic moment was generationally specific too, I realized. Such a disclosure would never have occurred among college-age males even a decade before. The vocabulary and sense of social safety would simply not have existed.

I came to understand that what these college-age males had to say is historically unprecedented: they had each become aware, through personal experience, of their own stake in confronting sexual violence.

There is a newsworthy story here, I thought to myself, a trend to be watched. An extraordinary new student-based social-change movement has begun; yet no major news-gathering medium has thought to listen in to the generationally specific experience represented by these five members of MAC.[1] Although they spoke as individuals and from particular viewpoints—the group was a mix of straight, bi, and gay; white and black—they also seemed at times to speak on behalf of many more male agemates than themselves. Quite matter-of-factly, without any prompting, they each described an experience now so common that it may define their generation more profoundly than any war ever has: how it feels to be perceived by female peers as a potential rapist.

Ever since the women's movement began to bring sexual violence to light in the early 1970s, the extent of rape and the extent of women's fears of it have been trivialized, refuted, and ridiculed by mainstream media. Today the aspirations of campus activists to radical gender egalitarianism and eroticized equality are similarly distorted in the popular press. For example, in the early 1990s students at Antioch College developed a comprehensive, nine-page policy spelling out the meaning of consent in sexual contact and conduct; defining and prohibiting a list of offenses that included rape, sexual assault, "sexual imposition," and nondisclosure of a known HIV-positive status; and detailing fair hearing procedures and reme-

dies in case of violation. This path-breaking, gender-neutral, ethically acute initiative was widely sneered at by media commentators who had never read it, never talked to the students who drafted and implemented it. During the 1960s and early 1970s, many "with it" magazine and book editors reveled in the ribald romance of covering the radical student antiwar movement in depth and at length. By contrast, today's middle-age male media decision makers act as if their journalistic radar screens got stuck in time along with the anachronistic sexual politics of their youth. Nostalgic for the 1960s "sexual revolution" days before feminism made "no" even an option for women—when, in the hustle of the time, "Girls say yes to [sex with] boys who say no [to the military]"—today's middle-age male media decision makers package smug blather about "date-rape hysteria" (a *New York* magazine cover story) or "sexual correctedness" (a *Newsweek* cover story) or "do-me feminism" (an *Esquire* cover story) and sign up execrably researched diatribes about "morning-after misgivings" (Katie Roiphe) or "the new Victorianism" (Rene Denfield). Today's middle-age male media decision makers just don't get it.

What this conversation reveals, however, is that a significant subset of young males have started to get it. Typical of a brand-new kind of self-selected peer group, they voice values that do not much resemble the sexual politics of most men their fathers' age. Within their transient, education-centered communities, the social and relational meaning of sexual violence to young women has become apparent to them as an everyday, lived reality. Never before have so many young males struggled to take this reality on board in their moral map of the world, and never before have so many known that others are doing so also.

In the student antiwar movement of the 1960s, many young women of conscience organized politically on behalf of young men whose bodies were then regarded as most at risk—deployable as cannon folder in an immoral military operation. Today, more and more young men of conscience have begun to understand their vital role in the student movement against sexual violence, and this time it is they who have put their lives on the line on behalf of the women whose bodies are most at risk.

For older menfolk—especially those who hold jobs in academia and are therefore in a position to offer material support and substantive resources—this movement presents a classic challenge for teachers: to listen to and learn from students.

When student antiwar activists of the 1960s brought new ideals and values into their subsequent work, family, and civic lives, the cultural and political impact of that movement was felt throughout the larger society for decades. As I write, the president of the United States is a man who in his student days protested the Vietnam War. Who would have guessed back then that the fledgling youth counterculture, vibrantly antimilitarist, would not only help halt a war but one day inform this nation's governance at the highest level?

Today, too, it is easy not to reckon the profound cultural and political shift portended by the values and ideals of young people in the burgeoning campus antirape movement. But who knows? One day this country could elect a president who in her or his student days protested, and helped end, men's war against women.

Q: Why did you get involved in Men Acting for Change?

Warren Hedges (30, Ph.D. candidate in English)²: I got involved because of women I was close to and things they had survived. When I walk on campus at night and a woman in front of me sees I'm a man walking behind her, her shoulders tense up and she starts walking more quickly. Her keys come out of her pocket in case she needs them to defend herself from me. It wouldn't do any good to try and convince her I'm a nice guy or "enlightened." I'm perceived as something that doesn't fit with what I want to be, and the only way to change that is by changing the broader social structure—laws and economic relations and things like that.

In our culture having a penis is supposed to be a package deal: You're supposed to have specific desires (for women) and pursue them in specific ways (aggressively, competitively), identify with men instead of women, have specific—and usually boring—sexual practices. There's this broad cultural discourse saying, "This is who you should be if you happen to have this particular organ." I can't create a space where I can express myself and be more upfront about my desires and my identifications and my practices and so forth without trying to change the larger social structures.

Andy Moose (21, pre-law English major): My reason for doing this came through a slow process, especially with MAC meetings, of having the space to really reflect about how I felt about a lot of emotional and personal issues that I hadn't spent much time as a man thinking about before. I'm in a fraternity and have seen a lot of abuses that go on within that system. I want to stay in there and work to improve the situation so that my fraternity brothers get to that process as well. I've felt it could help them, and also stop a lot of the abuses that were going on to other friends. It's personal for me, rather than seeing a great deal of violence and wanting to work towards stopping that. That's a major concern, but the bigger driving force for me is the personal gains that I see possible for people in working with these issues.

Carlton Leftwich (25, premed): I'm twenty-five years old and I have come to the realization that I've never had a healthy relationship with a woman. There's a lot of issues here that make me reflect on my opinion of women and how I treat them, how I deal with them, and how I could develop a healthy relationship with one. Healthy to me is looking at them and not saying, "Oh, that's a *woman's* point of view"—making everything that she says or feels inferior. I'd like to get on an even keel when discussing something with a woman and not just look at her and say, "She's a totally different kind of thing."

Erick Fink (22, psych major and women's studies minor): I took this intro to women's studies class and it hit me that this feminist stuff made a lot of sense. Like, even though you've never raped anyone or even thought about it, other men are doing that in your name and they're hurting people that you love in your name. All the pressure that men feel to act a certain way and do a certain thing and fit a certain mold—maybe it *used* to work, but it's not working now. And now I'm here, and I'm going to try to do something about it. I feel like I and people with penises have something to gain from the women's movement, a lot to gain: being able to be exactly who you are without having to be "a man" in the traditional sense.

I've felt very limited by patriarchy. My sense of masculinity mostly came from where everybody else's does, TV—"If you do this, chicks will dig you." That was what was masculine for me—how to attract the opposite sex. But I didn't want to be this macho guy. It's not that I didn't want to be; I just wasn't.

Carlton: I never could identify with what straight was—this rugby-playing kind of rough-and-tumble guy, always having to prove that I was macho—so I just automatically thought that I had to be gay, because I was very sensitive and I loved classical music. I was not a quote unquote normal young man, because I never liked football. And I always heard, "Well, all guys like football—if you don't play football you're a sissy."

Jason Schultz (22, public policy major and women's studies minor): In high school I was one of the top ten in my class academically. The other nine were all girls. They were brilliant and they taught me—about math, physics, English. Learning from female peers really had a big influence. The culture tells you women are bimbos, don't know anything, and are ditzes, sex objects; but my reality was different. I had good relationships with women who were intellectual and spoke their mind and wouldn't let me get away with shit—in a very loving way. Not "Get the fuck out" but "You better change or *I'm* going to get the fuck out." When I got to college, the intelligent, assertive, self-confident women started calling themselves feminists, and these were the people I loved to hang out with—"Oh, sure I'll go to your meeting. Oh, that sounds like an interesting class"—and I started to get involved. But for me there was a

piece missing. I went through fraternity rush, didn't find any men that I really liked to hang out with, and felt really stupid. Women in women's studies classes were focusing on women's experience, women's perspective—which made a lot of sense, because it's left out of traditional academia—but nothing was speaking to me on a first-person level. At that time there were a couple other men on campus who wanted the same thing, and it was framed as men interested in confronting sexual violence. It was this group that I felt could look at the other component, the part that I needed to match—not to feel isolated as much as I was sometimes, not to feel like I had to speak for men.

Q: How have you personally been affected by sexual violence?

Jason: My first year in college, a good friend of mine, a female friend, was avoiding me. We weren't communicating; we didn't have the intimacy I enjoyed so much. And I'm like, "What's up with you? what's bugging you? did you flunk some test or something?" I knew that she had gone out with this guy, and I knew who he was, and she told me the story in brief detail: She was raped. And she was like, "That's why I don't feel comfortable around you—it's because I don't know who to trust anymore." I didn't blame her at all. I was pissed at him. I was *really* pissed at him. It made me angry that this guy had ruined a friendship of mine with somebody I cared about. Then when I saw this men-concerned-with-sexual-violence thing, it came together.

As a man doing this kind of work you get stories and stories—it's just exponential. I probably know fifty survivors personally—most of them through campus.

Warren: The first person who told me she had survived a rape—here on campus by another Duke student on Valentine's Day—was during my first year in graduate school. For me it was a real hard lesson learning that just me being sensitive is not enough. This sort of thing was happening to women and it was going to change the way they reacted to all or most men, especially initially. And that prompted me to get involved with this program in Durham with men who batter their wives.

Once it became known on campus that I was concerned about these issues, and once I had a chance to speak at a Take Back the Night march, the number of stories I heard from women just seemed to multiply. One reason MAC had been so important to me is that I feel I've got an emotional support network now—not just feeling utterly overwhelmed by the number of stories that seemed to come flooding in. Probably one in five friends told me—attempted rapes and assaults, but usually rape.

Carlton: When I was growing up I was abused sexually. I just internalized everything and left it there. It was through MAC I could come in contact with people who had a rape encounter and see how they handled it, how they were surviving it, without actually having to admit that I was someone who had been raped also. That was really difficult for me. But to see women have the courage to pick up their lives and keep on going—it's really empowering. I can feel for women a lot more now that I know that it was something that I had no control over and that it wasn't my fault. I can understand that helplessness and that dirty feeling, the pain and sorrow.

Most guys are like, "Well, how do you rape a male?" There are a lot of ways to rape a male. And I would say to any other male survivor, "Don't be ashamed." Even if it happened ten, fifteen, twenty years ago, it still happened, and you're going to have to deal with it. You're going to have to address those feelings. It's not going to be easy, but try and hook up with a group of guys that can really feel for you and care about you. And by caring for women—I guess I took that assumption, that these guys care about women—then they're obviously going to care about my plight and respect me.

Erick: For the women I know that have been sexually assaulted or raped—I'd say twenty to twenty-five percent—it sticks with them; it changes their lives.

Carlton: Your sense of security is gone, and once you lose your sense of security you're never going to get it back.

Erick: There's an awful lot of fear out there—like if there's a woman sitting in a room with me alone, and we're sitting there talking, there's the chance that she is fearful of me.

Carlton: Sometimes I just want to shout, "I'm not going to hurt you!"

Jason: Holding up a sign: "not a rapist"?

Carlton: Yeah.

Andy: My first experience of sexual violence was from the other side, knowing the male who was being accused. During freshman year at Duke, I was faced with a rape case that was going to the Judi [Judicial] Board. This was a huge shock for me—becoming aware of the size of the problem and the frequency with which these acts were going on. It was something I was completely unaware of in high school. Having a very dear personal friend share with me that they were assaulted, coupled with knowing someone accused of the rape—those two things at the same time forced me to try to understand how this could happen. I couldn't just say, "Well, it's obvious these people are incredibly violent," because I wasn't seeing that. How could this happen around me every day and these people don't show me any signs of violent tendencies? How could this be happening with such frequency?

As you begin to get involved, a lot more people, a shocking number, tell you things. It takes you aback, the numbers—between twenty and twenty-five good friends, very close. Mostly women, ninety-some percent. I had one male friend share like that. And there were a number of stories where the male was someone I knew, probably a fourth of them. Actually more than that—probably half.

Talking with other people in MAC and doing programs on sexual violence helped me, because I felt I could do something. In a very basic way that feels good, to fight a situation that before you felt really helpless in. I have a little bit more understanding of how the event could happen—so it's not so much burning hatred towards that individual. I'm not so quick just to discard that person and say, "OK, he raped this woman so now I'm just going to not communicate with him any longer." I don't want to do that. There's definitely resentment and anger, a great deal of anger, and I try to suppress that as much as I can, because when you have these sorts of numbers around you, it's vital that you don't hate and cut that person off just because—. I mean, you become very lonely, obviously.

Q: How do you reach other men?

Jason: Standing up to them never seems to work. It seems to push them farther away, make them reactive. It's a balance of making them feel like I care what they say and being willing to sit down and listen to them for a long time, but then be willing to challenge them. Not saying, "Oh, you're a sexist pig—get the fuck outta here," but when the opportunity is there to say, "What you're saying really bothers me" or "I'd really like to talk to you about this because I'm learning where this is coming from."

Carlton: Don't make men feel like a minority. There are a lot of men out there who really want to understand themselves and their feelings a lot more, and you can really turn somebody off with that raw anger that seems to be associated with feminists. That's intimidating to men. I know it is to me.

Andy: A lot of the successes that I've been a part of talking with fraternity men came from catching them off guard. The minute some discussion on sexual violence comes up they become defensive. When they've gotten in these discussions with women or with non-Greek men, oftentimes it's led to an argument, they didn't feel very good about it, they don't want to talk about it, and so they don't deal with it. If there's something being discussed about a Greek function, they immediately assume that the fraternity men are going to be blamed, and they're going to defend themselves as not being a rapist or whatever. So a lot of the successes have come from surprise, when they realize there's a real conversation that's going to happen and it's not going to become some heated argument—because a lot of men haven't really thought about it much at all, and people really enjoy having an opportunity to reflect about their opinions, to recognize, "Wow, you know, I've thought about this and it really helped."

Erick: I was talking to a good friend and he said, "You know what I think date rape is? I think this woman has sex with this guy and the next morning she decides she shouldn't have done it, so she just screams rape." And I'm like, "Well, you know, I remember not long ago I felt the same way. But if you really think about it, things like that can happen. On a date maybe with somebody that you might know very well or have been seeing for a long time, you could get violent with that person, couldn't you?" And he said, "Uh, I don't know." And I'm like, "Well, have you ever gotten so angry or so frustrated with your girlfriend that you could just—" And he's like, "Sure, I guess so." And there was a relation there, where I could see how he was feeling, and he could see how I was feeling too. I think if he had said that to a woman, she would be very offended—and rightfully so.

Andy: You have to have discussions for the potential rapist, but also focus on how people contribute to an environment or make it easier for a rape to happen. A lot of times they don't recognize how they in a much more subtle way contribute or make these sorts of things easier to happen, by a comment or a particular action in a situation.

Warren: Or by no action.

Andy: Right, exactly, because so quickly they say, "Well, *I'm* not a rapist." They don't think about what environment you're establishing when you're having a party or you're making some joke or you don't say anything in a particular situation. It's better to have dialogue about those issues.

Jason: A lot of men don't hear what feminists are actually saying when it's coming from women. Their words are so devalued, and we value men's words more. My experience has been that it takes some patience, because if somebody said something sexist like "Oh, she deserved to be raped, look at how she's dressed," there's an instinct to want to confront that. But what seems to be more beneficial is to ask questions, maybe let the story weave itself a little more, find a deeper belief system, and figure out what about that issue to confront. I think with some men you can definitely do that.

Warren: My formative experience thinking about male violence was working with men who beat their wives. They were ordered by the courts to attend. The men couldn't leave the program angry because they might go home and beat their partner. That was a real constraint on my need to be vindictive and self-righteous. There was a counselor who put it very well when he said, "Dealing with abusive men is like judo; you gotta grab ahold of their energy and move them someplace they don't expect to end up."

Notes

1. I tried for two years to get this conversation into print. Among the publications that passed on it are *Cosmopolitan, Details, Elle, Glamour, Mademoiselle, Ms., On the Issues, Rolling Stone,* and the *Village Voice.*

2. Ages and academic concentrations are given as of the date of this conversation.

PART FOUR

Men and Work

In what ways is work tied to male identity? Do men gain a sense of fulfillment from their work, or do they view it as necessary drudgery? How might the organization of workplaces play on, reinforce, or sometimes threaten the types of masculinity that males have already learned as youngsters? How does the experience of work (or of not having work) differ for men of different social classes, ethnicities, and sexual preference groups? And how do recent structural changes in society impact upon the masculinity–work relationship? The articles in this section address these issues and more.

The rise of urban industrial capitalism saw the creation of separate "public" and "domestic" spheres of social life. As women were increasingly relegated to working in the home, men were in-

creasingly absent from the home, and the male "breadwinner role" was born. The sexual division of labor, this gendered split between home and workplace, has led to a variety of problems and conflicts for women and for men. Women's continued movement into the paid labor force, higher levels of unemployment, and the rise of a more service-oriented economy have led to dramatic shifts in the quality and the quantity of men's experiences in their work.

Articles by Christine L. Williams and Jennifer Pierce explore the experience of work for men—the former by examining the ways in which men who do "women's work" also "do" gender restoration, the latter by exploring the gender confirmation of the work of corporate lawyers. Timothy Nonn and Lois Weis, Amira Proweller and Craig Centrie explore the gendered meanings of work at the other side of the economic pyramid, among the homeless and among white working-class men.

The work world has also become an arena of the battle of the sexes, as the continuing struggles over sexual harassment make clear. The article by Patti Giuffre and Christine Williams examines the ways in which sexual harassment concerns raise important issues in male-female interactions in all work sites.

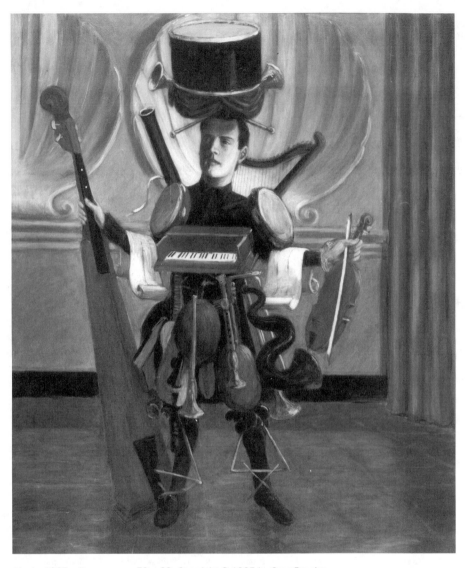

Music, 1985, oil on canvas, 70 × 60. Copyright © 1985 by Greg Drasler.

A R T I C L E   1 9

Christine L. Williams

The Glass Escalator: Hidden Advantages for Men in the "Female" Professions

The sex segregation of the U.S. labor force is one of the most perplexing and tenacious problems in our society. Even though the proportion of men and women in the labor force is approaching parity (particularly for younger cohorts of workers) (U.S. Department of Labor 1991:18), men and women are still generally confined to predominantly single-sex occupations. Forty percent of men or women would have to change major occupational categories to achieve equal representation of men and women in all jobs (Reskin and Roos 1990:6), but even this figure underestimates the true degree of sex segregation. It is extremely rare to find specific jobs where equal numbers of men and women are engaged in the same activities in the same industries (Bielby and Baron 1984).

Most studies of sex segregation in the work force have focused on women's experiences in male-dominated occupations. Both researchers and advocates for social change have focused on the barriers faced by women who try to integrate predominantly male fields. Few have looked at the "flip-side" of occupational sex segregation: the exclusion of men from predominantly female occupations (exceptions include Schreiber 1979;

This research was funded in part by a faculty grant from the University of Texas at Austin. I also acknowledge the support of the sociology departments of the University of California, Berkeley; Harvard University; and Arizona State University. I would like to thank Judy Auerbach, Martin Button, Robert Nye, Teresa Sullivan, Debra Umberson, Mary Waters, and the reviewers at *Social Problems* for their comments on earlier versions of this paper. Copyright © 1992 by the Society for the Study of Social Problems. Reprinted from *Social Problems*, Vol. 39, No.3, August 1992, pp. 253–267 by permission.

Williams 1989; Zimmer 1988). But the fact is that men are less likely to enter female sex-typed occupations than women are to enter male-dominated jobs (Jacobs 1989). Reskin and Roos, for example, were able to identify 33 occupations in which female representation increased by more than nine percentage points between 1970 and 1980, but only three occupations in which the proportion of men increased as radically (1990:20–21).

In this paper, I examine men's underrepresentation in four predominantly female occupations—nursing, librarianship, elementary school teaching, and social work. Throughout the twentieth century, these occupations have been identified with "women's work"—even though prior to the Civil War, men were more likely to be employed in these areas. These four occupations, often called the female "semi-professions" (Hodson and Sullivan 1990), today range from 5.5 percent male (in nursing) to 32 percent male (in social work). (See Table 19.1.) These percentages have not changed substantially in decades. In fact, as Table 19.1 indicates, two of these professions— librarianship and social work—have experienced declines in the proportions of men since 1975. Nursing is the only one of the four experiencing noticeable changes in sex composition, with the proportion of men increasing 80 percent between 1975 and 1990. Even so, men continue to be a tiny minority of all nurses.

Although there are many possible reasons for the continuing preponderance of women in these fields, the focus of this paper is discrimination. Researchers examining the integration of women into "male fields" have identified discrimination as a major barrier to women (Jacobs 1989; Reskin

■ **TABLE 19.1**
Percent Male in Selected Occupations,
Selected Years

Profession	1990	1980	1975
Nurses	5.5	3.5	3.0
Elementary teachers	14.8	16.3	14.6
Librarians	16.7	14.8	18.9
Social workers	31.8	35.0	39.2

Source: U.S. Department of Labor. Bureau of Labor
Statistics. *Employment and Earnings* 38:1 (January 1991),
Table 22 (Employed civilians by detailed occupation),
185; 28:1 (January 1981), Table 23 (Employed persons by
detailed occupation), 180; 22:7 (January 1976), Table 2
(Employed persons by detailed occupation), 11.

1988; Reskin and Hartmann 1986). This discrimination has taken the form of laws or institutionalized rules prohibiting the hiring or promotion
of women into certain job specialties. Discrimination can also be "informal," as when women
encounter sexual harassment, sabotage, or other
forms of hostility from their male co-workers resulting in a poisoned work environment (Reskin
and Hartmann 1986). Women in nontraditional
occupations also report feeling stigmatized by
clients when their work puts them in contact with
the public. In particular, women in engineering
and blue-collar occupations encounter gender-
based stereotypes about their competence which
undermine their work performance (Epstein
1988; Martin 1980). Each of these forms of
discrimination—legal, informal, and cultural—
contributes to women's underrepresentation in
predominantly male occupations.

The assumption in much of this literature is
that any member of a token group in a work setting will probably experience similar discriminatory treatment. Kanter (1977), who is best known
for articulating this perspective in her theory of
tokenism, argues that when any group represents
less than 15 percent of an organization, its members will be subject to predictable forms of discrimination. Likewise, Jacobs argues that "in
some ways, men in female-dominated occupa-

tions experience the same difficulties that women
in male-dominated occupations face" (1989:167),
and Reskin contends that any dominant group in
an occupation will use their power to maintain a
privileged position (1988:62).

However, the few studies that have considered men's experience in gender atypical occupations suggest that men may not face
discrimination or prejudice when they integrate
predominantly female occupations. Zimmer
(1988) and Martin (1988) both contend that the
effects of sexism can outweigh the effects of tokenism when men enter nontraditional occupations. This study is the first to systematically
explore this question using data from four occupations. I examine the barriers to men's entry
into these professions; the support men receive
from their supervisors, colleagues, and clients; and
the reactions they encounter from the public (those
outside their professions).

Methods

I conducted in-depth interviews with 76 men
and 23 women in four occupations from 1985–
1991. Interviews were conducted in four metropolitan areas: San Francisco/Oakland, California; Austin, Texas; Boston, Massachusetts; and
Phoenix, Arizona. These four areas were selected
because they show considerable variation in the
proportions of men in the four professions. For
example, Austin has one of the highest percentages of men in nursing (7.7 percent), whereas
Phoenix's percentage is one of the lowest (2.7
percent) (U.S. Bureau of the Census 1980). The
sample was generated using "snowballing" techniques. Women were included in the sample to
gauge their feelings and responses to men who
enter "their" professions.

Like the people employed in these professions generally, those in my sample were predominantly white (90 percent).[1] Their ages ranged
from 20 to 66 and the average age was 38. The interview questionnaire consisted of several open-
ended questions on four broad topics: motivation
to enter the profession; experiences in training;

career progression; and general views about men's status and prospects within these occupations. I conducted all the interviews, which generally lasted between one and two hours. Interviews took place in restaurants, my home or office, or the respondent's home or office. Interviews were tape-recorded and transcribed for the analysis.

Data analysis followed the coding techniques described by Strauss (1987). Each transcript was read several times and analyzed into emergent conceptual categories. Likewise, Strauss' principle of theoretical sampling was used. Individual respondents were purposely selected to capture the array of men's experiences in these occupations. Thus, I interviewed practitioners in every specialty, oversampling those employed in the *most* gender atypical areas (e.g., male kindergarten teachers). I also selected respondents from throughout their occupational hierarchies—from students to administrators to retirees. Although the data do not permit within-group comparisons, I am reasonably certain that the sample does capture a wide range of experiences common to men in these female-dominated professions. However, like all findings based on qualitative data, it is uncertain whether the findings generalize to the larger population of men in nontraditional occupations.

In this paper, I review individuals' responses to questions about discrimination in hiring practices, on-the-job rapport with supervisors and coworkers, and prejudice from clients and others outside their profession.

Discrimination in Hiring

Contrary to the experience of many women in the male-dominated professions, many of the men and women I spoke to indicated that there is a *preference* for hiring men in these four occupations. A Texas librarian at a junior high school said that his school district "would hire a male over a female."

> **I:** Why do you think that is?
>
> **R:** Because there are so few, and the . . . ones that they do have, the library directors

seem to really . . . think they're doing great jobs. I don't know, maybe they just feel they're being progressive or something, [but] I have had a real sense that they really appreciate having a male, particularly at the junior high. . . . As I said, when seven of us lost our jobs from the high schools and were redistributed, there were only four positions at the junior high, and I got one of them. Three of the librarians, some who had been here longer than I had with the school district, were put down in elementary school as librarians. And I definitely think that being male made a difference in my being moved to the junior high rather than an elementary school.

Many of the men perceived their token status as males in predominantly female occupations as an *advantage* in hiring and promotions. I asked an Arizona teacher whether his specialty (elementary special education) was an unusual area for men compared to other areas within education. He said,

> Much more so. I am extremely marketable in special education. That's not why I got into the field. But I am extremely marketable because I am a man.

In several cases, the more female-dominated the specialty, the greater the apparent preference for men. For example, when asked if he encountered any problem getting a job in pediatrics, a Massachusetts nurse said,

> No, no, none. . . . I've heard this from managers and supervisory-type people with men in pediatrics: "It's nice to have a man because it's such a female-dominated profession."

However, there were some exceptions to this preference for men in the most female-dominated specialties. In some cases, formal policies actually barred men from certain jobs. This was the case in some rural Texas school districts, which refused to hire men in the youngest grades (K–3). Some nurses also reported being excluded from positions in obstetrics and gynecology wards, a policy encountered more frequently in private Catholic hospitals.

But often the pressures keeping men out of certain specialties were more subtle than this. Some men described being "tracked" into practice areas within their professions which were considered more legitimate for men. For example, one Texas man described how he was pushed into administration and planning in social work, even though "I'm not interested in writing policy; I'm much more interested in research and clinical stuff." A nurse who is interested in pursuing graduate study in family and child health in Boston said he was dissuaded from entering the program specialty in favor of a concentration in "adult nursing." A kindergarten teacher described the difficulty of finding a job in his specialty after graduation: "I was recruited immediately to start getting into a track to become an administrator. And it was men who recruited me. It was men that ran the system at that time, especially in Los Angeles."

This tracking may bar men from the most female-identified specialties within these professions. But men are effectively being "kicked upstairs" in the process. Those specialties considered more legitimate practice areas for men also tend to be the most prestigious, better paying ones. A distinguished kindergarten teacher, who had been voted city-wide "Teacher of the Year," told me that even though people were pleased to see him in the classroom, "there's been some encouragement to think about administration, and there's been some encouragement to think about teaching at the university level or something like that, or supervisory-type position." That is, despite his aptitude and interest in staying in the classroom, he felt pushed in the direction of administration.

The effect of this "tracking" is the opposite of that experienced by women in male-dominated occupations. Researchers have reported that many women encounter a "glass ceiling" in their efforts to scale organizational and professional hierarchies. That is, they are constrained by invisible barriers to promotion in their careers, caused mainly by sexist attitudes of men in the highest positions (Freeman 1990).[2] In contrast to the "glass ceiling," many of the men I interviewed seem to encounter a "glass escalator." Often, despite their intentions, they face invisible pressures to move up in their professions. As if on a moving escalator, they must work to stay in place.

A public librarian specializing in children's collections (a heavily female-dominated concentration) described an encounter with this "escalator" in his very first job out of library school. In his first six-months' evaluation, his supervisors commended him for his good work in storytelling and related activities, but they criticized him for "not shooting high enough."

> Seriously. That's literally what they were telling me. They assumed that because I was a male—and they told me this—and that I was being hired right out of graduate school, that somehow I wasn't doing the kind of management-oriented work that they thought I should be doing. And as a result, really they had a lot of bad marks, as it were, against me on my evaluation. And I said I couldn't believe this!

Throughout his ten-year career, he has had to struggle to remain in children's collections.

The glass escalator does not operate at all levels. In particular, men in academia reported some gender-based discrimination in the highest positions due to their universities' commitment to affirmative action. Two nursing professors reported that they felt their own chances of promotion to deanships were nil because their universities viewed the position of nursing dean as a guaranteed female appointment in an otherwise heavily male-dominated administration. One California social work professor reported his university canceled its search for a dean because no minority male or female candidates had been placed on their short list. It was rumored that other schools on campus were permitted to go forward with their searches—even though they also failed to put forward names of minority candidates—because the higher administration perceived it to be "easier" to fulfill affirmative action goals in the social work school. The interviews provide greater evidence of the "glass escalator" at work in the lower levels of these professions.

Of course, men's motivations also play a role in their advancement to higher professional positions. I do not mean to suggest that the men I talked to all resented the informal tracking they experienced. For many men, leaving the most female-identified areas of their professions helped them resolve internal conflicts involving their masculinity. One man left his job as a school social worker to work in a methadone drug treatment program not because he was encouraged to leave by his colleagues, but because "I think there was some macho shit there, to tell you the truth, because I remember feeling a little uncomfortable there . . . ; it didn't feel right to me." Another social worker, employed in the mental health services department of a large urban area in California, reflected on his move into administration:

> The more I think about it, through our discussion, I'm sure that's a large part of why I wound up in administration. It's okay for a man to do the administration. In fact, I don't know if I fully answered a question that you asked a little while ago about how did being male contribute to my advancing in the field. I was saying it wasn't because I got any special favoritism as a man, but . . . I think . . . because I'm a man, I felt a need to get into this kind of position. I may have worked harder toward it, may have competed harder for it, than most women would do, even women who think about doing administrative work.

Elsewhere I have speculated on the origins of men's tendency to define masculinity through single-sex work environments (Williams 1989). Clearly, personal ambition does play a role in accounting for men's movement into more "male-defined" arenas within these professions. But these occupations also structure opportunities for males independent of their individual desires or motives.

The interviews suggest that men's underrepresentation in these professions cannot be attributed to discrimination in hiring or promotions. Many of the men indicated that they received preferential treatment because they were men. Although men mentioned gender discrimination in the hiring process, for the most part they were channelled into the more "masculine" specialties within these professions, which ironically meant being "tracked" into better paying and more prestigious specialties.

Supervisors and Colleagues: The Working Environment

Researchers claim that subtle forms of workplace discrimination push women out of male-dominated occupations (Jacobs 1989; Reskin and Hartmann 1986). In particular, women report feeling excluded from informal leadership and decision-making networks, and they sense hostility from their male co-workers, which makes them feel uncomfortable and unwanted (Carothers and Crull 1984). Respondents in this study were asked about their relationships with supervisors and female colleagues to ascertain whether men also experienced "poisoned" work environments when entering gender atypical occupations.

A major difference in the experience of men and women in nontraditional occupations is that men in these situations are far more likely to be supervised by a member of their own sex. In each of the four professions I studied, men are overrepresented in administrative and managerial capacities, or, as in the case of nursing, their positions in the organizational hierarchy are governed by men (Grimm and Sterm 1974; Phenix 1987; Schmuck 1987; Williams 1989; York, Henley, and Gamble 1987). Thus, unlike women who enter "male fields," the men in these professions often work under the direct supervision of other men.

Many of the men interviewed reported that they had good rapport with their male supervisors. Even in professional school, some men reported extremely close relationships with their male professors. For example, a Texas librarian described an unusually intimate association with two male professors in graduate school:

I can remember a lot of times in the classroom there would be discussions about a particular topic or issue, and the conversation would spill over into their office hours, after the class was over. And even though there were . . . a couple of the other women that had been in on the discussion, they weren't there. And I don't know if that was preferential or not . . . it certainly carried over into personal life as well. Not just at the school and that sort of thing. I mean, we would get together for dinner . . .

These professors explicitly encouraged him because he was male:

I: Did they ever offer you explicit words of encouragement about being in the profession by virtue of the fact that you were male? . . .

R: Definitely. On several occasions. Yeah. Both of these guys, for sure, including the Dean who was male also. And it's an interesting point that you bring up because it was, oftentimes, kind of in a sign, you know. It wasn't in the classroom, and it wasn't in front of the group, or if we were in the student lounge or something like that. It was . . . if it was just myself or maybe another one of the guys, you know, and just talking in the office. It's like . . . you know, kind of an opening-up and saying, "You know, you are really lucky that you're in the profession because you'll really go to the top real quick, and you'll be able to make real definite improvements and changes. And you'll have a real influence," and all this sort of thing. I mean, really, I can remember several times.

Other men reported similar closeness with their professors. A Texas psychotherapist recalled his relationships with his male professors in social work school:

I made it a point to make a golfing buddy with one of the guys that was in administration. He and I played golf a lot. He was the guy who kind of ran the research training, the research part of the master's program. Then there was a sociologist who ran the other part of the research program. He and I developed a good friendship.

This close mentoring by male professors contrasts with the reported experience of women in nontraditional occupations. Others have noted a lack of solidarity among women in nontraditional occupations. Writing about military academies, for example, Yoder describes the failure of token women to mentor succeeding generations of female cadets. She argues that women attempt to play down their gender difference from men because it is the source of scorn and derision.

Because women felt unaccepted by their male colleagues, one of the last things they wanted to do was to emphasize their gender. Some women thought that, if they kept company with other women, this would highlight their gender and would further isolate them from male cadets. These women desperately wanted to be accepted as cadets, not as *women* cadets. Therefore, they did everything from not wearing skirts as an option with their uniforms to avoiding being a part of a group of women. (Yoder 1989:532)

Men in nontraditional occupations face a different scenario—their gender is construed as a *positive* difference. Therefore, they have an incentive to bond together and emphasize their distinctiveness from the female majority.

Close, personal ties with male supervisors were also described by men once they were established in their professional careers. It was not uncommon in education, for example, for the male principal to informally socialize with the male staff, as a Texas special education teacher describes:

Occasionally I've had a principal who would regard me as "the other man on the campus" and "it's us against them," you know? I mean, nothing really that extreme, except that some male principals feel like there's nobody there to talk to except the other man. So I've been in that position.

These personal ties can have important consequences for men's careers. For example, one California nurse, whose performance was judged marginal by his nursing supervisors, was transferred to the emergency room staff (a prestigious promotion) due to his personal friendship with the physician in charge. A Massachusetts teacher acknowledged that his principal's personal interest in him landed him his current job.

I: You had mentioned that your principal had sort of spotted you at your previous job and had wanted to bring you here [to this school]. Do you think that has anything to do with the fact that you're a man, aside from your skills as a teacher?

R: Yes, I would say in that particular case, that was part of it. . . . We have certain things in common, certain interests that really lined up.

I: Vis-à-vis teaching?

R: Well, more extraneous things—running specifically, and music. And we just seemed to get along real well right off the bat. It is just kind of a guy thing; we just liked each other . . .

Interviewees did not report many instances of male supervisors discriminating against them, or refusing to accept them because they were male. Indeed, these men were much more likely to report that their male bosses discriminated against the *females* in their professions. When asked if he thought physicians treated male and female nurses differently, a Texas nurse said:

I think yeah, some of them do. I think the women seem like they have a lot more trouble with the physicians treating them in a derogatory manner. Or, if not derogatory, then in a very paternalistic way than the men [are treated]. Usually if a physician is mad at a male nurse, he just kind of yells at him. Kind of like an employee. And if they're mad at a female nurse, rather than treat them on an equal basis, in terms of just letting their anger out at them as an employee, they're more paternalistic or there's some sexual harassment component to it.

A Texas teacher perceived a similar situation where he worked:

I've never felt unjustly treated by a principal because I'm a male. The principals that I've seen that I felt are doing things that are kind of arbitrary or not well thought out are doing it to everybody. In fact, they're probably doing it to the females worse than they are to me.

Openly gay men may encounter less favorable treatment at the hands of their supervisors. For example, a nurse in Texas stated that one of the physicians he worked with preferred to staff the operating room with male nurses exclusively—as long as they weren't gay. Stigma associated with homosexuality leads some men to enhance, or even exaggerate their "masculine" qualities, and may be another factor pushing men into more "acceptable" specialties for men.

Not all men who work in these occupations are supervised by men. Many of the men interviewed who had female bosses also reported high levels of acceptance—although levels of intimacy with women seemed lower than with other men. In some cases, however, men reported feeling shut-out from decision making when the higher administration was constituted entirely by women. I asked an Arizona librarian whether men in the library profession were discriminated against in hiring because of their sex:

Professionally speaking, people go to considerable lengths to keep that kind of thing out of their [hiring] deliberations. Personally, is another matter. It's pretty common around here to talk about the "old girl network." This is one of the few libraries that I've had any intimate knowledge of which is actually controlled by women. . . . Most of the department heads and upper level administrators are women. And there's an "old girl network" that works just like the "old boy network," except that the important conferences take place in the women's room rather than on the golf course. But the political mechanism is the same, the exclusion of the other sex from decision making is the same. The reasons are the same. It's somewhat discouraging . . .

Although I did not interview many supervisors, I did include 23 women in my sample to ascertain their perspectives about the presence of men in their professions. All of the women I interviewed claimed to be supportive of their male colleagues, but some conveyed ambivalence. For example, a social work professor said she would like to see more men enter the social work profession, particularly in the clinical specialty (where they are underrepresented). Indeed, she favored affirmative action hiring guidelines for men in the profession. Yet, she resented the fact that her department hired "another white male" during a recent search. I questioned her about this ambivalence:

> **I:** I find it very interesting that, on the one hand, you sort of perceive this preference and perhaps even sexism with regard to how men are evaluated and how they achieve higher positions within the profession, yet, on the other hand, you would be encouraging of more men to enter the field. Is that contradictory to you, or . . . ?
>
> **R:** Yeah, it's contradictory.

It appears that women are generally eager to see men enter "their" occupations. Indeed, several men noted that their female colleagues had facilitated their careers in various ways (including mentorship in college). However, at the same time, women often resent the apparent ease with which men advance within these professions, sensing that men at the higher levels receive preferential treatment which closes off advancement opportunities for women.

But this ambivalence does not seem to translate into the "poisoned" work environment described by many women who work in male-dominated occupations. Among the male interviewees, there were no accounts of sexual harassment. However, women do treat their male colleagues differently on occasion. It is not uncommon in nursing, for example, for men to be called upon to help catheterize male patients, or to lift especially heavy patients. Some librarians also said that women asked them to lift and move heavy boxes of books because they were men. Teachers sometimes confront differential treatment as well, as described by this Texas teacher:

As a man, you're teaching with all women, and that can be hard sometimes. Just because of the stereotypes, you know. I'm real into computers . . . and all the time people are calling me to fix their computer. Or if somebody gets a flat tire, they come and get me. I mean, there are just a lot of stereotypes. Not that I mind doing any of those things, but it's . . . you know, it just kind of bugs me that it is a stereotype, "A man should do that." Or if their kids have a lot of discipline problems, that kiddo's in your room. Or if there are kids that don't have a father in their home, that kid's in your room. Hell, nowadays that'd be half the school in my room (laughs). But you know, all the time I hear from the principal or from other teachers, "Well, this child really needs a man . . . a male role model" (laughs). So there are a lot of stereotypes that . . . men kind of get stuck with.

This special treatment bothered some respondents. Getting assigned all the "discipline problems" can make for difficult working conditions, for example. But many men claimed this differential treatment did not cause distress. In fact, several said they liked being appreciated for the special traits and abilities (such as strength) they could contribute to their professions.

Furthermore, women's special treatment sometimes enhanced—rather than poisoned—the men's work environments. One Texas librarian said he felt "more comfortable working with women than men" because "I think it has something to do with control. Maybe it's that women will let me take control more than men will." Several men reported that their female colleagues often cast them into leadership roles. Although not all savored this distinction, it did enhance their authority and control in the workplace. In subtle (and not-too-subtle) ways, then, differential treatment contributes to the "glass escalator" men experience in nontraditional professions.

Even outside work, most of the men interviewed said they felt fully accepted by their female colleagues. They were usually included in informal socializing occasions with the women—even though this frequently meant attending baby showers or Tupperware parties. Many said that they declined offers to attend these events because they were not interested in "women's things," although several others claimed to attend everything: The minority men I interviewed seemed to feel the least comfortable in these informal contexts. One social worker in Arizona was asked about socializing with his female colleagues:

> **I:** So in general, for example, if all the employees were going to get together to have a party, or celebrate a bridal shower or whatever, would you be invited along with the rest of the group?
>
> **R:** They would invite me, I would say, somewhat reluctantly. Being a black male, working with all white females, it did cause some outside problems. So I didn't go to a lot of functions with them . . .
>
> **I:** You felt that there was some tension there on the level of your acceptance . . . ?
>
> **R:** Yeah. It was OK working, but on the outside, personally, there was some tension there. It never came out, that they said, "Because of who you are we can't invite you" (laughs), and I wouldn't have done anything anyway. I would have probably respected them more for saying what was on their minds. But I never felt completely in with the group.

Some single men also said they felt uncomfortable socializing with married female colleagues because it gave the "wrong impression." But in general, the men said that they felt very comfortable around their colleagues and described their workplaces as very congenial for men. It appears unlikely, therefore, that men's underrepresentation in these professions is due to hostility towards men on the part of supervisors or women workers.

Discrimination from "Outsiders"

The most compelling evidence of discrimination against men in these professions is related to their dealings with the public. Men often encounter negative stereotypes when they come into contact with clients or "outsiders"—people they meet outside of work. For instance, it is popularly assumed that male nurses are gay. Librarians encounter images of themselves as "wimpy" and asexual. Male social workers describe being type-cast as "feminine" and "passive." Elementary school teachers are often confronted by suspicions that they are pedophiles. One kindergarten teacher described an experience that occurred early in his career which was related to him years afterwards by his principal:

> He indicated to me that parents had come to him and indicated to him that they had a problem with the fact that I was a male. . . . I recall almost exactly what he said. There were three specific concerns that the parents had: One parent said, "How can he love my child; he's a man." The second thing that I recall, he said the parent said, "He has a beard." And the third thing was, "Aren't you concerned about homosexuality?"

Such suspicions often cause men in all four professions to alter their work behavior to guard against sexual abuse charges, particularly in those specialties requiring intimate contact with women and children.

Men are very distressed by these negative stereotypes, which tend to undermine their self-esteem and to cause them to second-guess their motivations for entering these fields. A California teacher said,

> If I tell men that I don't know, that I'm meeting for the first time, that that's what I do, . . . sometimes there's a look on their faces that, you know, "Oh, couldn't get a real job?"

When asked if his wife, who is also an elementary school teacher, encounters the same kind of prejudice, he said,

> No, it's accepted because she's a woman. . . . I think people would see that as a . . . step up, you know. "Oh, you're not a housewife, you've got a career. That's great . . . that you're out there working. And you have a daughter, but

you're still out there working. You decided not to stay home, and you went out there and got a job." Whereas for me, it's more like I'm supposed to be out working anyway, even though I'd rather be home with [my daughter].

Unlike women who enter traditionally male professions, men's movement into these jobs is perceived by the "outside world" as a step down in status. This particular form of discrimination may be most significant in explaining why men are underrepresented in these professions. Men who otherwise might show interest in and aptitudes for such careers are probably discouraged from pursuing them because of the negative popular stereotypes associated with the men who work in them. This is a crucial difference from the experience of women in nontraditional professions: "My daughter, the physician," resonates far more favorably in most people's ears than "My son, the nurse."

Many of the men in my sample identified the stigma of working in a female-identified occupation as the major barrier to more men entering their professions. However, for the most part, they claimed that these negative stereotypes were not a factor in their own decisions to join these occupations. Most respondents didn't consider entering these fields until well into adulthood, after working in some related occupation. Several social workers and librarians even claimed they were not aware that men were a minority in their chosen professions. Either they had no well-defined image or stereotype, or their contacts and mentors were predominantly men. For example, prior to entering library school, many librarians held part-time jobs in university libraries, where there are proportionally more men than in the profession generally. Nurses and elementary school teachers were more aware that mostly women worked in these jobs, and this was often a matter of some concern to them. However, their choices were ultimately legitimized by mentors, or by encouraging friends or family members who implicitly reassured them that entering these occupations would not typecast them as feminine. In some cases, men were told by recruiters there were spe-

cial advancement opportunities for men in these fields, and they entered them expecting rapid promotion to administrative positions.

I: Did it ever concern you when you were making the decision to enter nursing school, the fact that it is a female-dominated profession?

R: Not really. I never saw myself working on the floor. I saw myself pretty much going into administration, just getting the background and then getting a job someplace as a supervisor and then working, getting up into administration.

Because of the unique circumstances of their recruitment, many of the respondents did not view their occupational choices as inconsistent with a male gender role, and they generally avoided the negative stereotypes directed against men in these fields.

Indeed, many of the men I interviewed claimed that they did not encounter negative professional stereotypes until they had worked in these fields for several years. Popular prejudices can be damaging to self-esteem and probably push some men out of these professions altogether. Yet, ironically, they sometimes contribute to the "glass escalator" effect I have been describing. Men seem to encounter the most vituperative criticism from the public when they are in the most female-identified specialties. Public concerns sometimes result in their being shunted into more "legitimate" positions for men. A librarian formerly in charge of a branch library's children's collection, who now works in the reference department of the city's main library, describes his experience:

R: Some of the people [who frequented the branch library] complained that they didn't want to have a man doing the storytelling scenario. And I got transferred here to the central library in an equivalent job . . . I thought that I did a good job. And I had been told by my supervisor that I was doing a good job.

I: Have you ever considered filing some sort of lawsuit to get that other job back?

R: Well, actually, the job I've gotten now . . . well, it's a reference librarian; it's what I wanted in the first place. I've got a whole lot more authority here. I'm also in charge of the circulation desk. And I've recently been promoted because of my new stature, so . . . no, I'm not considering trying to get that other job back.

The negative stereotypes about men who do "women's work" can push men out of specific jobs. However, to the extent that they channel men into more "legitimate" practice areas, their effects can actually be positive. Instead of being a source of discrimination, these prejudices can add to the "glass escalator effect" by pressuring men to move *out* of the most female-identified areas, and *up* to those regarded more legitimate and prestigious for men.

Conclusion: Discrimination Against Men

Both men and women who work in nontraditional occupations encounter discrimination, but the forms and consequences of this discrimination are very different. The interviews suggest that unlike "nontraditional" women workers, most of the discrimination and prejudice facing men in the "female professions" emanates from outside those professions. The men and women interviewed for the most part believed that men are given fair—if not preferential—treatment in hiring and promotion decisions, are accepted by supervisors and colleagues, and are well-integrated into the workplace subculture. Indeed, subtle mechanisms seem to enhance men's position in these professions—a phenomenon I refer to as the "glass escalator effect."

The data lend strong support for Zimmer's (1988) critique of "gender neutral theory" (such as Kanter's [1977] theory of tokenism) in the study of occupational segregation. Zimmer argues that women's occupational inequality is more a con-

sequence of sexist beliefs and practices embedded in the labor force than the effect of numerical underrepresentation per se. This study suggests that token status itself does not diminish men's occupational success. Men take their gender privilege with them when they enter predominantly female occupations: this translates into an advantage in spite of their numerical rarity.

This study indicates that the experience of tokenism is very different for men and women. Future research should examine how the experience of tokenism varies for members of different races and classes as well. For example, it is likely that informal workplace mechanisms similar to the ones identified here promote the careers of token whites in predominantly black occupations. The crucial factor is the social status of the token's group—not their numerical rarity—that determines whether the token encounters a "glass ceiling" or a "glass escalator."

However, this study also found that many men encounter negative stereotypes from persons not directly involved in their professions. Men who enter these professions are often considered "failures," or sexual deviants. These stereotypes may be a major impediment to men who otherwise might consider careers in these occupations. Indeed, they are likely to be important factors whenever a member of a relatively high status group crosses over into a lower status occupation. However, to the extent that these stereotypes contribute to the "glass escalator effect" by channeling men into more "legitimate" (and higher paying) occupations, they are not discriminatory.

Women entering traditionally "male" professions also face negative stereotypes suggesting they are not "real women" (Epstein 1981; Lorber 1984; Spencer and Podmore 1987). However, these stereotypes do not seem to deter women to the same degree that they deter men from pursuing nontraditional professions. There is ample historical evidence that women flock to male-identified occupations once opportunities are available (Cohn 1985; Epstein 1988). Not so with men. Examples of occupations changing from predominantly female to predominantly male are very rare in our history. The few existing cases—such as medicine—suggest that redefinition of the occupations as appropriately "masculine" is necessary before men will consider joining them (Ehrenreich and English 1978).

Because different mechanisms maintain segregation in male- and female-dominated occupations, different approaches are needed to promote their integration. Policies intended to alter the sex composition of male-dominated occupations—such as affirmative action—make little sense when applied to the "female professions." For men, the major barriers to integration have little to do with their treatment once they decide to enter these fields. Rather, we need to address the social and cultural sanctions applied to men who do "women's work" which keep men from even considering these occupations.

One area where these cultural barriers are clearly evident is in the media's representation of men's occupations. Women working in traditionally male professions have achieved an unprecedented acceptance on popular television shows. Women are portrayed as doctors ("St. Elsewhere"), lawyers ("The Cosby Show," "L.A. Law"), architects ("Family Ties"), and police officers ("Cagney and Lacey"). But where are the male nurses, teachers, and secretaries? Television rarely portrays men in nontraditional work roles, and when it does, that anomaly is made the central focus—and joke—of the program. A comedy series (1991–92) about a male elementary school teacher ("Drexell's Class") stars a lead character who *hates children!* Yet even this negative portrayal is exceptional. When a prime time hospital drama series ("St. Elsewhere") depicted a male orderly striving for upward mobility, the show's writers made him a "physician's assistant," not a nurse or nurse practitioner—the much more likely "real life" possibilities.

Presenting positive images of men in nontraditional careers can produce limited effects. A few social workers, for example, were first inspired to pursue their careers by George C. Scott, who played a social worker in the television drama

series, "Eastside/Westside." But as a policy strategy to break down occupational segregation, changing media images of men is no panacea. The stereotypes that differentiate masculinity and femininity, and degrade that which is defined as feminine, are deeply entrenched in culture, social structure, and personality (Williams 1989). Nothing short of a revolution in cultural definitions of masculinity will effect the broad scale social transformation needed to achieve the complete occupational integration of men and women.

Of course, there are additional factors besides societal prejudice contributing to men's underrepresentation in female-dominated professions. Most notably, those men I interviewed mentioned as a deterrent the fact that these professions are all underpaid relative to comparable "male" occupations, and several suggested that instituting a "comparable worth" policy might attract more men. However, I am not convinced that improved salaries will substantially alter the sex composition of these professions unless the cultural stigma faced by men in these occupations diminishes. Occupational sex segregation is remarkably resilient, even in the face of devastating economic hardship. During the Great Depression of the 1930s, for example, "women's jobs" failed to attract sizable numbers of men (Blum 1991:154). In her study of American Telephone and Telegraph (AT&T) workers, Epstein (1989) found that some men would rather suffer unemployment than accept relatively high paying "women's jobs" because of the damage to their identities this would cause. She quotes one unemployed man who refused to apply for a female-identified telephone operator job:

> I think if they offered me $1000 a week tax free, I wouldn't take that job. When I . . . see those guys sitting in there [in the telephone operating room], I wonder what's wrong with them. Are they pansies or what? (Epstein 1989: 577)

This is not to say that raising salaries would not affect the sex composition of these jobs. Rather, I am suggesting that wages are not the only—or perhaps even the major—impediment to men's entry into these jobs. Further research is needed to explore the ideological significance of the "woman's wage" for maintaining occupational stratification.[3]

At any rate, integrating men and women in the labor force requires more than dismantling barriers to women in male-dominated fields. Sex segregation is a two-way street. We must also confront and dismantle the barriers men face in predominantly female occupations. Men's experiences in these nontraditional occupations reveal just how culturally embedded the barriers are, and how far we have to travel before men and women attain true occupational and economic equality.

Notes

1. According to the U.S. Census, black men and women comprise 7 percent of all nurses and librarians, 11 percent of all elementary school teachers, and 19 percent of all social workers (calculated from U.S. Census 1980: Table 278, 1–197). The proportion of blacks in social work may be exaggerated by these statistics. The occupational definition of "social worker" used by the Census Bureau includes welfare workers and pardon and parole officers, who are not considered "professional" social workers by the National Association of Social Workers. A study of degreed professionals found that 89 percent of practitioners were white (Hardcastle 1987).

2. In April 1991, the Labor Department created a "Glass Ceiling Commission" to "conduct a thorough study of the underrepresentation of women and minorities in executive, management, and senior decision-making positions in business" (U.S. House of Representatives 1991:20).

3. Alice Kessler-Harris argues that the lower pay of traditionally female occupations is symbolic of a patriarchal order that assumes female dependence on a male breadwinner. She writes that pay equity is fundamentally threatening to the "male worker's sense of self, pride, and masculinity" because it upsets his individual standing in the hierarchical ordering of the sexes (1990:125). Thus, men's reluctance to enter these

occupations may have less to do with the actual dollar amount recorded in their paychecks, and more to do with the damage that earning "a woman's wage" would wreak on their self-esteem in a society that privileges men. This conclusion is supported by the interview data.

References

Bielby, William T., and James N. Baron
1984 "A woman's place is with other women: Sex segregation within organizations." In *Sex Segregation in the Workplace: Trends, Explanations, Remedies*, ed. Barbara Reskin, 27–55. Washington, D.C.: National Academy Press.

Blum, Linda M.
1991 *Between Feminism and Labor: The Significance of the Comparable Worth Movement*. Berkeley and Los Angeles: University of California Press.

Carothers, Suzanne C., and Peggy Crull
1984 "Contrasting sexual harassment in female-dominated and male-dominated occupations." In *My Troubles Are Going to Have Trouble with Me: Everyday Trials and Triumphs of Women Workers*, ed. Karen B. Sacks and Dorothy Remy, 220–227. New Brunswick, N.J.: Rutgers University Press.

Cohn, Samuel
1985 *The Process of Occupational Sex-Typing*. Philadelphia: Temple University Press.

Ehrenreich, Barbara, and Deirdre English
1978 *For Her Own Good: 100 Years of Expert Advice to Women*. Garden City, N.Y.: Anchor Press.

Epstein, Cynthia Fuchs
1981 *Women in Law*. New York: Basic Books.
1988 *Deceptive Distinctions: Sex, Gender and the Social Order*. New Haven, Conn.: Yale University Press.
1989 "Workplace boundaries: Conceptions and creations." *Social Research* 56: 571–590.

Freeman, Sue J. M.
1990 *Managing Lives: Corporate Women and Social Change*. Amherst, Mass.: University of Massachusetts Press.

Grimm, James W., and Robert N. Stern
1974 "Sex roles and internal labor market structures: The female semi-professions." *Social Problems* 21: 690–705.

Hardcastle, D. A.
1987 "The social work labor force." Austin, Tex.: School of Social Work, University of Texas.

Hodson, Randy, and Teresa Sullivan
1990 *The Social Organization of Work.* Belmont, Calif.: Wadsworth Publishing Co.

Jacobs, Jerry
1989 *Revolving Doors: Sex Segregation and Women's Careers.* Stanford, Calif.: Stanford University Press.

Kanter, Rosabeth Moss
1977 *Men and Women of the Corporation.* New York: Basic Books.

Kessler-Harris, Alice
1990 *A Woman's Wage: Historical Meanings and Social Consequences.* Lexington, Ky.: Kentucky University Press.

Lorber, Judith
1984 *Women Physicians: Careers, Status, and Power.* New York: Tavistock.

Martin, Susan E.
1980 *Breaking and Entering: Police Women on Patrol.* Berkeley, Calif.: University of California Press.

1988 "Think like a man, work like a dog, and act like a lady: Occupational dilemmas of policewomen." In *The Worth of Women's Work: A Qualitative Synthesis*, ed. Anne Statham, Eleanor M. Miller, and Hans O. Mauksch, 205–223. Albany, N.Y.: State University of New York Press.

Phenix, Katharine
1987 "The status of women librarians." *Frontiers* 9: 36–40.

Reskin, Barbara
1988 "Bringing the men back in: Sex differentiation and the devaluation of women's work." *Gender & Society* 2: 58–81.

Reskin, Barbara, and Heidi Hartmann
1986 *Women's Work, Men's Work: Sex Segregation on the Job.* Washington, D.C.: National Academy Press.

Reskin, Barbara, and Patricia Roos
1990 *Job Queues, Gender Queues: Explaining Women's Inroads into Male Occupations.* Philadelphia: Temple University Press.

Schmuck, Patricia A.
1987 "Women school employees in the United States." In *Women Educators: Employees of Schools in Western Countries*, ed. Patricia A. Schmuck, 75–97. Albany, N.Y.: State University of New York Press.

Schreiber, Carol
1979 *Men and Women in Transitional Occupations.* Cambridge, Mass.: MIT Press.

Spencer, Anne, and David Podmore
1987 *In a Man's World: Essays on Women in Male-Dominated Professions.* London: Tavistock.

Strauss, Anselm L.
1987 *Qualitative Analysis for Social Scientists.* Cambridge, England: Cambridge University Press.

U.S. Bureau of the Census
1980 *Detailed Population Characteristics*, Vol. 1, Ch. D. Washington, D.C.: Government Printing Office.

U.S. Congress. House
1991 *Civil Rights and Women's Equity in Employment Act of 1991.* Report. (Report 102-40, Part I.) Washington, D.C.: Government Printing Office.

U.S. Department of Labor. Bureau of Labor Statistics
1991 *Employment and Earnings.* January. Washington, D.C.: Government Printing Office.

Williams, Christine L.
1989 *Gender Differences at Work: Women and Men in Nontraditional Occupations.* Berkeley, Calif.: University of California Press.

Yoder, Janice D.
1989 "Women at West Point: Lessons for token women in male-dominated occupations." In *Women: A Feminist Perspective*, ed. Jo Freeman, 523–537. Mountain View, Calif.: Mayfield Publishing Company.

York, Reginald O., H. Carl Henley, and Dorothy N. Gamble
1987 "Sexual discrimination in social work: Is it salary or advancement?" *Social Work* 32: 336–340.

Zimmer, Lynn
1988 "Tokenism and women in the workplace." *Social Problems* 35: 64–77.

A R T I C L E   2 0

Jennifer Pierce

Rambo Litigators: Emotional Labor in a Male-Dominated Occupation

Litigation is war. The lawyer is a gladiator and the object is to wipe out the other side.

—Cleveland lawyer quoted in the *New York Times*

A recent spate of articles in the *New York Times* and a number of legal dailies characterized some of America's more flamboyant and aggressive trial lawyers as "Rambo litigators."[1] This hyper-masculine, aggressive image is certainly not a new one. In popular culture and everyday life, jokes and stories abound that characterize lawyers as overly aggressive, manipulative, unreliable, and unethical individuals.[2] What jokes, as well as the popular press, fail to consider is that such behavior is not simply the result of individual failings but is actually required and reinforced by the legal profession itself.

Legal scholar Carrie Menkel-Meadow (1985) suggests that the adversarial model with its emphasis on "zealous advocacy" and "winning" encourages a "macho ethic" in the courtroom (pp. 51–54). Lawyers and teachers of trial lawyers argue that the success of litigators depends on their ability to manipulate people's emotions (Brazil 1978; Turow 1987). Trial lawyers must persuade judges and juries, as well as intimidate witnesses and opposing counsel in the courtroom, in deposition, and in negotiations. The National Institute of Trial Advocacy, for example, devotes a 3-week training seminar to teaching lawyers to

Jennifer Pierce, "Rambo Litigators: Emotional Labor in a Male-Dominated Occupation," in Cheng, ed., *Masculinities in Organizations*, pp. 1–27, Sage Publications, 1993.

hone such emotional skills, thereby improving their success in the courtroom (Rice 1989). This chapter makes this aspect of lawyering explicit by examining the emotional dimension of legal work in a particular specialty of law—litigation. Sociological studies of the legal profession have yet to seriously examine the emotional dimension of lawyering.[3] Although a few studies make reference to the emotional dimension of work, it is not the central focus of their research.[4] For example, Nelson (1988) reduces lawyering to three roles— "finders, minders and grinders," meaning "lawyers who seem to bring in substantial clients . . . lawyers who take care of the clients who are already here and there are the grinders who do the work" (senior partner quoted in Nelson 1988, p. 69). Nelson's reduction of these roles to their instrumental and intellectual dimensions neglects the extent to which instrumental tasks may also contain emotional elements.

The sparse attention other sociological studies have given to this dimension of lawyering is contradicted by my 15 months of field research (from 1988 to 1989) at two large law firms in San Francisco—6 months at a private firm (Lyman, Lyman, and Portia) and 9 months in the legal department of a large corporation (Bonhomie Corporation).[5] Litigators make use of their emotions to persuade juries, judges, and witnesses in the courtroom and in depositions, in communications with opposing counsel, and with clients. However, in contrast to the popular image, intimidation and aggression constitute only one component of the emotional labor required by this profession. Lawyers also make use of strategic friendliness, that is, the use of charm or flattery to manipulate others. Despite the apparent differences in these two types of emotional labor, both use the manipulation of others for a specific end—winning a case. Although other jobs require the use of manipulation to achieve specific ends, such labor may serve different purposes and be embedded in a different set of relationships. Flight attendants, for example, are friendly and reassuring to passengers so as to alleviate their anxiety about flying (Hochschild 1983). However, flight attendants' friendliness takes the form of deference: Their relationship to passengers is supportive and subordinate. By contrast, in litigation, the goal of strategic friendliness is to *win over* or dominate another. As professionals who have a monopoly over specialized knowledge, attorneys hold a superordinate position with respect to clients, witnesses, and jurors and a competitive one with other lawyers. If trial lawyers want to win their cases, they must be able to successfully manipulate and ultimately dominate others for their professional ends.

By doing whatever it takes within the letter of the law to win a case, lawyers effectively fulfill the goal of zealous advocacy: persuading a third party that the client's interests should prevail. In this way, intimidation and strategic friendliness serve to reproduce and maintain the adversarial model. At the same time, by exercising dominance and control over others, trial lawyers also reproduce gender relations. The majority of litigators who *do dominance* are men (88% of litigators are male) and those who defer are either female secretaries and paralegals,[6] other women, or men who become feminized in the process of losing. In addition to creating and maintaining a gendered hierarchy, the form such emotional labor takes is gendered. It is a masculinized form of emotional labor, not only because men do it but because dominance is associated with masculinity

in our culture. West and Zimmerman (1987) argue, for example, that displays of dominance are ways for men to "do gender."[7] Similarly, psychoanalytic feminists equate masculinity with men's need to dominate women (Benjamin 1988; Chodorow 1978). In the case of trial lawyers, the requirements of the profession deem it appropriate to dominate women as well as other men. Such *conquests* or achievements at once serve the goals of effective advocacy and become the means for the trial lawyer to demonstrate a class-specific form of masculinity.

Gamesmanship and the Adversarial Model

Popular wisdom and lawyer folklore portray lawyering as a game, and the ability to play as gamesmanship (Spence 1988). As one of the trial attorneys I interviewed said,

> The logic of gamesmanship is very interesting to me. I like how you make someone appear to be a liar. You know, you take them down the merry path and before they know it, they've said something pretty stupid. The challenge is getting them to say it without violating the letter of the law.

Lawyering is based on gamesmanship—legal strategy, skill, and expertise. But trial lawyers are much more than chess players. Their strategies are not simply cerebral, rational, and calculating moves but highly emotional, dramatic, flamboyant, and shocking presentations that invoke sympathy, distrust, or outrage. In my redefinition of the term, *gamesmanship* involves the utilization of legal strategy through a presentation of an emotional self designed specifically to influence the feelings and judgment of a particular legal audience—the judge, the jury, the witness, or opposing counsel. Furthermore, in my definition, the choices litigators make about selecting a particular strategy are not simply individual, they are institutionally constrained by the structure of the legal profession, formal and informal professional norms such as the American Bar Association's

(1982) *Model Code of Professional Responsibility* and training in trial advocacy through programs sponsored by the National Institute of Trial Advocacy.

The rules governing gamesmanship derive from the adversarial model that underlies the basic structure of our legal system. This model is a method of adjudication that involves two advocates (e.g., the attorneys) presenting their case to an impartial third party (i.e., the judge and the jury) who listens to evidence and argument and declares one party the winner (Luban 1988; Menkel-Meadow 1985). As Menkel-Meadow (1985) observes, the basic assumptions that underlie this set of arrangements are "advocacy, persuasion, hierarchy, competition and binary results (win or lose)." She writes, "The conduct of litigation is relatively similar . . . to a sporting event— there are rules, a referee, an object to the game, and a winner is declared after play is over" (p. 51).

Within this system, the attorney's main objective is to persuade the impartial third party that his client's interests should prevail (American Bar Association 1982, p. 34). However, clients do not always have airtight, defensible cases. How, then, does the *zealous advocate* protect his clients interests and achieve the desired result? When persuasion by appeal to reason breaks down, an appeal to emotions becomes tantamount (Cheatham 1955, pp. 282–283). As legal scholar John Buchan (1939) writes, "The root of the talent is simply the *power to persuade*" [italics added] (pp. 211–213). By appealing to emotions, the lawyer becomes a "con man."[8] He acts "as if" he has a defensible case, he puffs himself up, he bolsters his case. Thus, the successful advocate must not only be smart, but as famous turn-of-the-century trial lawyer Francis Wellman (1903/1986, p. 13) observes, he must also be a "good actor." In his book, *The Art of Cross-Examination*, first published in 1903 and reprinted to the present, Wellman describes how carefully the litigator must present himself to the judge and jury:

> The most cautious cross-examiner will often elicit a damaging answer. Now is the time for the greatest self-control. If you show by your face how the answer hurt, you may lose by that

one point alone. How often one sees a cross-examiner fairly staggered by such an answer. He pauses, blushes . . . [but seldom regains] control of the witness. With the really experienced trial lawyer, such answers, instead of appearing to surprise or disconcert him, will seem to come as a matter of course, and will fall perfectly flat. He will proceed with the next question as if nothing happened, or else perhaps give the witness an incredulous smile, as if to say, "Who do you suppose would believe that for a minute?" (pp. 13–14).

More recently, teacher and lawyer David Berg (1987) advises lawyers to think of themselves as actors, and the jury, an audience. He writes,

> Decorum can make a difference, too. . . . *Stride to the podium* and *exude confidence*, even if there is a chance that the high school dropout on the stand is going to make you look like an idiot. *Take command* of the courtroom. Once you begin, do not grope for questions, shuffle through papers, or take breaks to confer with co-counsel. Let the jury know that you are prepared, that you do not need anyone's advice, and that *you care* about the case . . . because if *you don't care, the jurors won't care*. (1987, p. 28, italics added)

Wellman (1903/1986) and Berg (1987) make a similar point: Trials are the enactment of a drama in the courtroom, and attorneys are the leading actors. Appearance and demeanor are of utmost importance. The lawyer's manner, his tone of voice, his facial expressions are all means to persuade the jury that his client is right. Outrageous behavior is acceptable, as long as it remains within the letter of the law. Not only are trial lawyers expected to act but with a specific purpose in mind: to favorably influence feelings of the jurors. As Berg points out, "if you don't show you care, the jurors won't care."

This emphasis on acting is also evident in the courses taught by the National Institute for Trial Advocacy (NITA) where neophyte litigators learn the basics in presenting a case for trial. NITA's emphasis is on "learning by doing" (Kilpatrick, quoted in Rice 1989). Attorneys do not simply read about cases but practice presenting them in a simulated courtroom with a judge, a jury, and witnesses. In this case, doing means acting. As one of the teacher–lawyers said on the first day of class, "Being a good trial lawyer means being a good actor. . . . Trial attorneys love to perform." Acting, in sociological terms, translates into emotional labor, that is, inducing or suppressing feelings in order to produce an outward countenance that influences the emotions of others. Teacher–lawyers discuss style, delivery, presentation of self, attitude, and professionalism. Participants, in turn, compare notes about the best way to "handle" judges, jurors, witnesses, clients, and opposing counsel. The efforts of these two groups constitute the teaching and observance of "feeling rules" or professional norms that govern appropriate lawyerlike conduct in the courtroom.

The 3-week course I attended[9] took students through various phases of a hypothetical trial—jury selection, opening and closing statements, and direct and cross-examination. Each stage of the trial has a slightly different purpose. For example, the objective of jury selection is to uncover the biases and prejudices of the jurors and to develop rapport with them. On the other hand, an opening statement sets the theme for the case, whereas a direct examination lays the foundation of evidence for the case. Cross-examination is intended to undermine the credibility of the witness, whereas closing represents the final argument. Despite the differing goals that each of these phases has, the means to achieve them is similar in each case, that is, the attempt to persuade a legal audience favorably to one's client through a particular emotional presentation of self.

In their sessions on direct and cross-examination, students were given primarily stylistic, as opposed to substantive, responses on their presentations. They were given finer legal points on the technicalities of their objections—the strength or weakness of their arguments. But in the content analysis of my field notes, I found that 50% to 80% of comments were directed to-ward the attorney's particular style. These comments fell into five categories: (a) personal appearance, (b) presentation of self (nice, aggressive, or sincere manner), (c) tone and level of voice, (d) eye contact, and (e) rapport with others in the courtroom.

For example, in one of the sessions, Tom, a young student–lawyer in the class, did a direct examination of a witness to a liquor store robbery. He solemnly questioned the witness about his work, his special training in enforcing liquor laws, and how he determined whether someone was intoxicated. At one point when the witness provided a detail that Tom had not expected, rather than expressing surprise, Tom appeared nonchalant and continued with his line of questions. At the end of his direct, the teacher–lawyer provided the following feedback:

> Good background development of a witness. Your voice level was appropriate but try modulating it a bit more for emphasis. You also use too many thank you's to the judge. You should ingratiate yourself with the judge but not overly so. You also made a good recovery when the witness said something unexpected.

When Patricia, a young woman attorney, proceeded nervously through the same direct examination, opposing counsel objected repeatedly to some of her questions, which flustered her. The teacher–lawyer told her,

> You talk too fast. And you didn't make enough eye contact with the judge. Plus, you got bogged down in the objections and harassment from opposing counsel. You're recovery was too slow. You've got to be more forceful.

In both these examples, as in most of the sessions that I observed, the focus of the comments was not on the questions asked but on *how* the questions were asked. Tom was told to modulate his voice; Patricia was told not to talk so fast. In addition, the teacher–lawyer directed their attention to rapport with others in the courtroom. Tom was encouraged not to be overly ingratiating with the judge, whereas Patricia was told to pay more attention to the judge. Moreover, the teacher commended Tom for his "recovery," that is, regaining self-composure and control of the witness. He criticized Patricia, on the other hand, for not recovering well from an aggressive objection made by opposing counsel.[10]

In my fieldwork at NITA and in the two law offices, I found two main types of emotional labor: intimidation and strategic friendliness. Intimidation entails the use of anger and aggression, whereas strategic friendliness uses politeness, friendliness, or playing dumb. Both forms are related to gamesmanship. Each involves an emotional presentation of self that is intended to favorably influence the feelings of a particular legal audience toward one's client. Many jobs appear to require strategic friendliness and intimidation. Domestic workers, for example, sometimes "play dumb" so as not to alienate their white female employers (Rollins 1985). For domestic workers, however, this strategy is a means for someone in a subordinate position to survive a degrading job. By contrast, for litigators, strategic friendliness, like intimidation, is a means for an individual with professional status to control and dominate others in an effort to win one's case. Although both the litigator and the domestic worker may play dumb, in each job, the behavior serves different goals that are indicative of their divergent positions in relationship to others.

Intimidation and strategic friendliness not only serve the goals of the adversarial model, but they exemplify a masculine style of emotional labor. They become construed as masculine for several reasons. First, emotional labor in the male-dominated professional strata of the gendered law firm is interpreted as masculine, simply because men do it. Ruth Milkman (1987), for example, suggests that "idioms of sex-typing can be applied to whatever women and men happen to be doing" (p. 50). Male trial attorneys participate in shaping this idiom by describing their battles in the courtroom and with opposing counsel as "macho," "something men get into," and "a male thing." In addition, by treating women lawyers as outsiders

and excluding them from professional networks, they further define their job as exclusively male.

In addition, the underlying purpose of gamesmanship itself, that is, the control and domination of others through manipulation, reflects a particular cultural conception of masculinity. Connell (1987), for example, describes a hegemonic form of masculinity that emphasizes the domination of a certain class of men—middle- to upper-middle class—over other men and over women. Connell's cultural conception of masculinity dovetails neatly with feminist psychoanalytic accounts that interpret domination as a means of asserting one's masculinity (Benjamin 1988; Chodorow 1978). The lawyers I studied also employed a ritual of degradation and humiliation against other men and women who were witnesses or opposing counsel. The remainder of this chapter describes the two main components of emotional labor—intimidation and strategic friendliness—the purpose of each, and shows how these forms become construed as masculine. These forms of emotional labor are explored in practices, such as cross-examination, depositions, jury selection, and in opening and closing statements.

Intimidation

The first and most common form of emotional labor associated with lawyers is intimidation. In popular culture, the tough, hard-hitting, and aggressive trial lawyer is portrayed in television shows, such as *L.A. Law* and *Perry Mason* and in movies, such as *The Firm*, *A Few Good Men*, and *Presumed Innocent*. The news media's focus on famous trial attorneys such as Arthur Liman, the prosecutor of Oliver North in the Iran-Contra trial, also reinforces this image. Law professor Wayne Brazil (1978) refers to this style of lawyering as the *professional combatant*. Others have used terms such as *Rambo litigator, legal terrorists*, and *barbarians of the bar* (Margolick 1988; Miner 1988; Sayler 1988). Trial attorneys themselves call litigators from large law firms "hired guns" (Spangler 1986). The central figure that appears again and again in these images is not only intimidating but strongly masculine. In the old West, hired guns were sharpshooters, men who were hired to kill other men. The strong, silent movie character Rambo is emblematic of a highly stylized, super masculinity. Finally, most of the actors who play tough, hard-hitting lawyers in the television shows and movies mentioned above are men. Thus, intimidation is not simply a form of emotional labor associated with trial lawyers, it is a masculinized form of labor.

Intimidation is tied to cultural conceptions of masculinity in yet another way. In a review of the literature on occupations, Connell (1987) observes that the cult of masculinity in working-class jobs centers on physical prowess and sexual contempt for men in managerial or office positions (p. 180). Like the men on the shop floor in Michael Burawoy's (1979) study who brag about how much they can lift or produce, lawyers in this study boast about "destroying witnesses," "playing hardball," "taking no prisoners," and about the size and amount of their "win." In a middle-class job such as the legal profession, however, intimidation depends not on physical ability but on mental quickness and a highly developed set of social skills. Thus, masculinizing practices, such as aggression and humiliation, take on an emotional and intellectual tone specific to middle-class occupations and professions.

This stance is tied to the adversarial model's conception of the "zealous advocate" (American Bar Association 1982). The underlying purpose of this strategy is to intimidate, scare, or emotionally bully the witness of opposing counsel into submission. A destructive cross-examination is the best example.[11] Trial attorneys are taught to intimidate the witness in cross-examination, "to control the witness by never asking a question to which he does not already know the answer and to regard the impeachment of the witness as a highly confrontational act" (Menkel-Meadow 1985, p. 54). Wellman (1903/1986) describes cross-examination in this way:

It requires the greatest ingenuity; a habit of logical thought; clearness of perception; infinite patience and self-control; the power to read men's minds intuitively, to judge of their characters by their faces, to appreciate their motives; ability to act with force and precision; a masterful knowledge of the subject matter itself; an extreme caution; and, above all *the instinct to discover the weak point in the witness under examination . . .* It is a *mental duel* between counsel and witness. (p. 8, italics added)

Berg (1987) echoes Wellman's words when he begins his lecture on cross-examination by saying, "The common denominator for effective cross-examination is not genius, however. It's a combination of preparation and an instinct for the jugular" (p. 27). Again, cross-examination involves not only acting mean but creating a specific impression on the witness.

In the sections on cross-examination at NITA, teachers trained lawyers how to *act mean.* The demonstration by the teachers on cross-examination best exemplified this point. Two male instructors reenacted an aggressive cross-examination in a burglary case. The prosecutor relentlessly hammered away, until the witness couldn't remember any specific details about what the burglar looked like. At its conclusion, the audience clapped vigorously. Three male students who had been asked to comment on the section responded unanimously and enthusiastically that the prosecutor's approach has been excellent. One student commentator said, "He kept complete control of the witness." Another remarked, "He blasted the witness's testimony." And the third added, "He destroyed the witness's credibility." The fact that a destructive cross-examination served as the demonstration for the entire class underlines the desirability of aggressive behavior as a model for appropriate lawyerlike conduct in this situation. Furthermore, the students' praise for the attorney's tactics collectively reinforce the norm for such behavior.

Teachers emphasized the importance of using aggression on an individual level as well. Before a presentation on cross-examination, Tom, one of the students, stood in the hallway with one of the instructors trying to "psyche himself up to get mad." He repeated over and over to himself, "I hate it when witnesses lie to me, it makes me so mad!" The teacher coached him to concentrate on that thought, until Tom could actually evoke the feeling of anger. He said to me later in an interview, "I really felt mad at the witness when I walked into the courtroom." In the actual cross-examination, each time the witness made an inconsistent statement, Tom became more and more angry: "First, you told us you could see the burglar, now you say your vision was obstructed! So, which is it, Mr. Jones?" The more irate he became, the more intimidated and confused the witness became, until he completely backed down and said, "I don't know," in response to every question. The teacher characterized Tom's performance as "the best in the class," because it was the "the most forceful" and "the most intimidating." Students remarked that he deserved to "win the case."

NITA's teachers also used mistakes to train students in the rigors of cross-examination. For example, when Laura cross-examined the same witness in the liquor store case, a teacher commented on her performance:

> Too many words. You're asking the witness for information. Don't do that in cross-examination. You tell them what the information is. You want to be destructive in cross-examination. When the other side objects to an answer, *you were too nice. Don't be so nice!* [italics added]. Next time, ask to talk to the judge, tell him, "This is crucial to my case." You also asked for information when you didn't know the answer. Bad news. You lost control of the witness.

By being nice and losing control of the witness, Laura violated two norms underlying the classic confrontational cross-examination. A destructive cross-examination is meant to impeach the witness's credibility, thereby demonstrating to the jury the weakness in opposing counsel's case.

In situations that call for such an aggressive cross-examination, being nice implies that the lawyer likes the witness and agrees with his or her testimony. By not being aggressive, Laura created the wrong impression for the jury. Second, Laura lost control of the witness. Rather than guiding the witness through the cross with leading questions[12] that were damaging to opposing counsel's case, she allowed the witness to make his own points. As we will see in the next section of the chapter, being nice can also be used as a strategy for controlling a witness; however, such a strategy is not effective in a destructive cross-examination.

Laura's violation of these norms also serves to highlight the implicitly masculine practices used in cross-examination. The repeated phrase, "keeping complete control of the witness," clearly signals the importance of dominating other women and men. Furthermore, the language used to describe obtaining submission—"blasting the witness," "destroying his credibility," or pushing him to "back down"—is quite violent. In addition, the successful control of the witness often takes on the character of a sexual conquest. One brutal phrase used repeatedly in this way is "raping the witness." Within this discursive field, men who "control," "destroy," or "rape" the witness are seen as "manly," whereas those who lose control are feminized as "sissies" and "wimps" or, in Laura's case, as "too nice."

The combative aspect of emotional labor carries over from the courtroom to other lawyering tasks, such as depositions. Attorneys not only "shred" witnesses in the courtroom but in depositions as well. When I worked at this private firm, Daniel, one of the partners, employed what he called his "cat and mouse game" with one of the key witnesses, Jim, in a deposition that I attended. During the deposition, Daniel aggressively cross-examined Jim. "When did you do this?" "You were lying, weren't you?" Jim lost his temper in response to Daniel's hostile form of interrogation—"You hassle me, man! You make me mad!" Daniel smiled and said, "I'm only trying to get to the truth of the situation." Then, he became aggressive again and said, "You lied to the IRS about how much profit you made, didn't you, Jim!" Jim lost his temper again and started calling Daniel a liar. A heated interchange between Daniel and opposing counsel followed, in which opposing counsel objected to Daniel's "badgering the witness." The attorneys decided to take a brief recess.

When the deposition resumed, Daniel began by accusing John, the other attorney, of withholding crucial documents to the case, while pointing his index finger at him. Opposing counsel stood up and started yelling in a high-pitched voice, "Don't you ever point your finger at me! Don't you ever do that to me! This deposition is over . . . I'm leaving." With that he stood up and began to cram papers into his briefcase in preparation to leave. Daniel immediately backed down, apologized, and said, "Sit down, John, I promise I won't point my finger again." He went on to smooth the situation over and proceeded to tell John in a very calm and controlled voice what his objections were. John made some protesting noises, but he didn't leave. The deposition continued.

In this instance, the deposition, rather than the courtroom, became the *stage* and Daniel took the leading role. His cross-examination was confrontational and his behavior with the witness and opposing counsel was meant to intimidate. After the deposition, Daniel boasted to me and several associates about how mad he had made the witness and how he had "destroyed his credibility." He then proceeded to reenact the final confrontation by imitating John standing up and yelling at him in a falsetto voice. In the discussion that followed, Daniel and his associates gave the effects of his behavior on the "audience" utmost consideration. Hadn't Daniel done a good job forcing the witness to lose control? Hadn't he controlled the situation well? Didn't he make opposing counsel look like a "simpering fool"?

The reenactment and ensuing discussion reveal several underlying purposes of the deposition.

First, it suggests that the deposition was not only a fact-finding mission for the attorney but a show designed to influence a particular audience—the witness. Daniel effectively flustered and intimidated the witness. Second, Daniel's imitation of John with a falsetto voice, "as if" he were a woman, serves as a sort of "degradation ceremony" (Garfinkel 1956). By reenacting the drama, he ridicules the man on the other side before an audience of peers, further denigrating him by inviting collective criticism and laughter from colleagues. Third, the discussion of the strategy builds up and elevates Daniel's status as an attorney for his aggressive, yet rational control of the witness and the situation. Thus, the discussion creates a space for collectively reinforcing Daniel's intimidation strategy.

In addition to highlighting the use of intimidation in depositions, this example also illustrates the way aggression as legal strategy or rule-governed aggression (Benjamin 1988; Lyman 1987) and masculinity become conflated, whereas aggression, which is not rule governed, is ridiculed as feminine. John shows his anger, but it is deemed inappropriate, because he loses control of the situation. Such a display of hostility does not serve the interests of the legal profession, because it does not achieve the desired result—a win for the case. As a result, Daniel and his associate regard John's behavior—his lack of control, his seeming hysteria and high voice, with contempt. This contempt takes on a specific sexual character. Just as the working class "lads" in Paul Willis's (1977) book, *Learning to Labor*, denigrate the "earholes" or sissies for their feminine attributes, Daniel and his colleagues ridicule John for his femalelike behavior. Aggression as legal strategy or maleness is celebrated; contempt is reserved for aggression (or behavior) that is not rule governed and behavior that is also associated with the opposite sex.

Attorneys also used the confrontational approach in depositions at Bonhomie Corporation. In a deposition I sat in on, Mack, a litigator, used an aggressive cross-examination of the key witness.

Q: What were the names of the people that have migrated from one of the violators, as you call it, to Bonhomie Corporation?

A: I don't remember as of now.

Q: Do you have their names written down?

A: No.

Q: Well, if you don't remember their names and they're not written down, how can you follow their migration from one company to another?

A: You can consider it in the process of discovery that I will make some inquiring phone calls.

Q: Did you call anyone to follow their migration?

A: Well, I was unsuccessful as of yet to reach other people.

Q: Who have you attempted to call?

A: I can't tell you at this time. I have a list of processes in my mind to follow.

Q: Do you recall who you called and were not able to reach?

A: No.

Q: What's the list of processes in your mind to follow?

A: It's hard to describe.

Q: In other words, you don't have a list?

A: [quietly] Not really.

Q: Mr. Jensen, instead of wasting everyone's time and money, answer the question yes or no!

Opposing Counsel: Don't badger the witness.

Q: Answer the question, Mr. Jensen, yes or no!

Opposing Counsel: I said, don't badger the witness.

Q: Mr. Jensen, you are still required to answer the question!

A: [quietly] No.

In this case, Mack persisted in badgering the witness, who provided incoherent and vague an-

swers. In response to the question, "Well, if you don't remember their names and they're not written down, how can you follow their migration from one company to another?" the witness gave the vague reply: "You can consider it in the process of discovery that I will make some inquiring phone calls." As the witness became more evasive, the attorney became more confrontational, "Answer the question, Mr. Jensen, yes or no!" By using this approach, the lawyer succeeded in making the witness appear even more uncooperative than he actually was and eventually pushed him to admit that he didn't have a list.

Later, in the same deposition, the attorney's confrontational tactics extended to opposing counsel.

Q: Let's change the subject. Mr. Jensen, can you tell me what representations were made to you about the reliability of the Bonhomie Corporation's spider system?

A: Nancy, the saleslady, said they use it widely in the United States, and could not be but very reliable. And, as we allege, fraudulent, and as somebody referred to it, was the, they wanted to give us the embrace of death to provide us more dependency, and then to go on and control our operation totally [sic].

Q: Who said that?

A: My attorney.

Q: When was that?

Opposing Counsel: Well, I . . .

Mack: I think he's already waived it. All I want to know is when it was supposedly said.

A: Well . . .

Opposing Counsel: I do use some great metaphors.

Mack: Yes, I know, I have read your complaint.

Opposing Counsel: Sorry?

Mack: I have read your complaint. That will be all for today, Mr. Jensen.

Here, the attorney did not stop with badgering the witness. When the witness made the statement about the "embrace of death," Mack was quick to find out who said it. And when opposing counsel bragged about his "great metaphors," Mack parried back with a sarcastic retort, "Yes, I know, I have read your complaint." Having had the final word, he abruptly ended the deposition. Like the other deposition, this one was not only an arena for intimidating the witness but for ridiculing the attorney on the other side. In this way, intimidation was used to control the witness and sarcasm to dominate opposing counsel. In doing so, Mack had achieved the desired result—the witness's submission to his line of questioning and a victory over the other side. Furthermore, in his replay of the deposition to his colleagues, he characterized his victory as a "macho blast against the other side," thereby underscoring the masculine character of his intimidation tactics.

Strategic Friendliness

> Mr. Choate's appeal to the jury began long before final argument. . . . His manner to the jury was that of a *friend* [italics added], a friend solicitous to help them through their tedious investigation; never an expert combatant, intent on victory, and looking upon them as only instruments for its attainment. (Wellman 1903/1986, pp. 16–17)

The lesson implicit in Wellman's anecdote about famous 19th-century lawyer Rufus Choate's trial tactics is that friendliness is another important strategy the litigator must learn and use to be successful in the courtroom. Like the use of aggression, the strategic use of friendliness is another feature of gamesmanship and, hence, another component of emotional labor. As Richard, one of the attorney–teachers at NITA stated, "Lawyers have to be able to vary their styles, they have to be able to have multiple speeds, personalities and style." In his view, intimidation did not always work and he proposed an alternative strategy, what he called "the toe-in-the-sand, aw shucks routine." Rather than adopting an intimidating stance vis-à-vis the witness, he advocated "play-

ing dumb and innocent." "Say to the witness, 'Gee, I don't know what you mean. Can you explain it again?' until you catch the witness in a mistake or an inconsistent statement." Other litigators, such as Leonard Right (1987), call this the "low-key approach." As an illustration of this style, Ring describes how opposing counsel delicately handled the cross-examination of a child witness.

> The lawyer for the defendant . . . stood to cross-examine. Did he attack the details of her story to show inconsistencies? Did he set her up for impeachment by attempting to reveal mistakes, uncertainties and confusion? I sat there praying that he would. But no, he did none of the things a competent defense lawyer is supposed to do. He was old enough to be the girl's grandfather . . . the image came through. He asked her very softly and politely: "Honey, could you tell us again what you saw?" She told it exactly as she had on my direct. I felt relieved. He still wasn't satisfied. "Honey, would you mind telling us again what you saw?" She did again exactly as she had before. He still wasn't satisfied. "Would you do it once more?" She did. She repeated, again, the same story—the same way, in the same words. By that time I got the message. The child had been rehearsed by her mother the same way she had been taught "Mary Had a Little Lamb." I won the case, but it was a very small verdict. (pp. 35–36)

Ring concludes that a low-key approach is necessary in some situations and advises against adhering rigidly to the prototypical combative style.

Similarly, Scott Turow (1987), lawyer and novelist, advises trying a variety of approaches when cross-examining the star witness. He cautions against adopting a "guerrilla warfare mentality" in cross-examination and suggests that the attorney may want to create another impression with the jury:

> Behaving courteously can keep you from getting hurt and, in the process, smooth the path for a win. [In one case I worked on] the cross examination was conducted with a politesse appropriate to a drawing room. I smiled to show

that I was not mean-spirited. The chief executive officer smiled to show that he was not beaten. The commissioners smiled to show their gratitude that everybody was being so nice. And my client won big. (pp. 40–42)

Being nice, polite, welcoming, playing dumb, or behaving courteously are all ways that a trial lawyer can manipulate the witness to create a particular impression for the jury. I term this form of gamesmanship *strategic friendliness*. Rather than bully or scare the witness into submission, this tactic employs the opposite—friendliness, politeness, and tact. Despite this seeming difference, it shares with the former an emphasis on the emotional manipulation of another person for a strategic end—winning one's case. For instance, the attorney in Ring's account is gentle and considerate of the child witness for two strategic reasons. First, by making the child feel comfortable, he brings to light the fact that her testimony has been rehearsed. Second, by playing the polite, gentle grandfatherly role, he has created a favorable impression of himself with the jury. Thus, he simultaneously demonstrates to the jury that the witness has been rehearsed and that he, as opposing counsel, is a nice guy. In this way, he improves his chances for winning. And, in fact, he did. Although he didn't win the case, the verdict for the other side was "small."

Although strategic friendliness may appear to be a softer approach than intimidation, it carries with it a strongly instrumental element. Consider the reasoning behind this particular approach. Ring's attorney is nice to the child witness not because he's altruistically concerned for her welfare. He utilizes gentility as a strategy to achieve the desired result—a big win in the courtroom. It is simply a means to an end. Although this approach may be less aggressive than intimidation, it is no less manipulative. Like the goal of intimidation, the central goal of this component of gamesmanship is to dominate and control others for a specific end. This end is best summed up by litigator Mark Dombroff (1989) who writes, "So long as you don't violate the law, including the rules of procedure and evidence or do violence to the

canons of ethics, winning is the only thing that matters" (p. 13).

This emphasis on winning is tied to hegemonic conceptions of masculinity and competition. Sociologist Mike Messner (1989) argues that achievement in sporting competitions, such as football, baseball, and basketball, serve as a measure of men's self-worth and their masculinity. This can also be carried over into the workplace. For example, in her research on men in sales, Leidner (1993) finds that defining the jobs as competition becomes a means for construing the work as masculine.

For litigators, comparing the number of wins in the courtroom and the dollar amount of damages or settlement awards allows them to interpret their work as manly. At Bonhomie Corporation and at Lyman, Lyman, and Portia, the first question lawyers often asked others after a trial or settlement conference was "Who won the case?" or "How big were the damages?" Note that both Ring and Turow also conclude their pieces with descriptions of their win—"I won the case, but the verdict was small" and "I won big." Trial attorneys who did not "win big" were described as "having no balls," "geeks," or "wimps." The fact that losing is associated with being less than a man suggests that the constant focus on competition and winning is an arena for proving one's masculinity.

One important area that calls for strategic friendliness and focuses on winning is jury selection or *voir dire*. The main purpose of *voir dire* is to obtain personal information about prospective jurors to determine whether they will be fair, "favorably disposed to you, your client, and your case, and will ultimately return a favorable verdict" (Mauet 1980, p. 31). Once an attorney has made that assessment, biased jurors can be eliminated through challenges for cause and peremptory challenges. In an article on jury selection, attorney Peter Perlman (1988) maintains that the best way to uncover the prejudices of the jury "is to conduct *voir dire* in an atmosphere that makes prospective jurors comfortable about disclosing their true feelings" (p. 5). He provides a checklist of strategies for lawyers to use that enable jurors to feel more comfortable. Some of these include the following:

- Given the initial intimidation that jurors feel, try to make them feel as comfortable as possible; approach them in a *natural, unpretentious, and clear manner.*
- Because jurors don't relate to "litigants" or "litigation," humanize the client and the dispute.
- *Demonstrate the sincere* desire to learn of the jurors's feelings. (pp. 5–9, italics added)

Perlman's account reveals that the underlying goal of jury selection is to encourage the jury to open up so that the lawyer can eliminate the jurors he doesn't want and develop a positive rapport with the ones who appear favorable to his case. This goal is supported not only by other writings on jury selection (Blinder 1978; Cartwright 1977; Mauet 1980; Ring 1983) but also through the training offered by NITA. As a teacher–judge said after the class demonstration on jury selection, "Sell your personality to the jury. Try to get liked by the jury. You're not working for a fair jury but one favorable to your side."

At NITA, teachers emphasized this point on the individual level. In their sessions on *voir dire*, students had to select a jury for a case that involved an employee who fell down the steps at work and severely injured herself. (Jurors in the class were other students, in addition to myself.) Mike, one of the students, proceeded with his presentation. He explained that he was representing the wife's employer. He then went on to tell the jury a little bit about himself. "I grew up in a small town in Indiana." Then, he began to ask each of the jurors where they were from, whether they knew the witness or the experts, whether they played sports, had back problems, suffered any physical injuries, and ever had physical therapy. The instructor gave him the following comments:

> The personal comments about yourself seem forced. Good folksy approach, but you went overboard with it. You threw stuff out and let

the jury nibble and you got a lot of information. But the main problem is that you didn't find out how people *feel* about the case or about their relatives and friends.

Another set of comments:

> Nice folksy approach but a bit overdone. Listen to what jurors say, don't draw conclusions. Don't get so close to them, it makes them feel uncomfortable. Use body language to give people a good feeling about you. Good personality, but don't cross certain lines. Never ask someone about their ancestry. It's too loaded a question to ask. Good sense of humor, but don't call one of your prospective jurors a "money man." And don't tell the jury jokes! You don't *win them over* [italics added] that way.

The sporting element to *voir dire* becomes "winning over the jury." This theme also became evident in discussions student lawyers had before and after jury selection. They discussed at length how best "to handle the jurors," "how to get personal information out of them," "how to please them," "how to make them like you," and "how to seduce them to your side." The element of sexual seduction is no more apparent than in the often used phrase, "getting in bed with the jury." The direct reference to sexual seduction and conquest suggests, as it did with the intimidation strategy used in cross-examination, that "winning over the jury" is also a way to prove one's masculinity. Moreover, the desired result in both strategic friendliness and intimidation is similar: obtaining the juror's submission and winning.

Strategic friendliness is used not only in jury selection but in the cross-examination of sympathetic witnesses. In one of NITA's hypothetical cases, a husband's spouse dies of an illness related to her employment. He sues his deceased wife's former employer for her medical bills, her lost wages, and "lost companionship." One of the damaging facts in the case that could hurt his claim for lost companionship was the fact that he had a girlfriend long before his wife died. In typical combative adversarial style, some of the student lawyers tried to bring this fact out in cross-examination to discredit his relationship with his wife. The teacher–judge told one lawyer who presented such an aggressive cross-examination,

> It's too risky to go after him. Don't be so confrontational. And don't ask the judge to reprimand him for not answering the question. This witness is too sensitive. Go easy on him.

The same teacher gave the following comment to another student who had "come on too strong":

> Too stern. Hasn't this guy been through enough already! Handle him with kid gloves. And don't cut him off. It generates sympathy for him from the jury when you do that. It's difficult to control a sympathetic witness. It's best to use another witness's testimony to impeach him.

And to yet another student:

> Slow down! This is a dramatic witness. Don't lead so much. He's a sympathetic witness—the widower—let him do the talking. Otherwise you look like an insensitive jerk to the jury.

In the cross-examination of a sympathetic witness, teachers advised students not to be aggressive but to adopt a gentler approach. Their concern, however, is not for the witness's feelings but how their treatment of the witness appears to the jury. The jury already thinks the witness is sympathetic, because he is a widower. As a result, the lawyers were advised not to do anything that would make the witness appear more sympathetic and them less so. The one student who did well on this presentation demonstrated great concern for the witness. She gently asked him about his job, his marriage, his wife's job, and her illness. Continuing with this gentle approach, she softly asked him whether anyone had been able to provide him comfort during this difficult time. By doing so, she was able to elicit the testimony about the girlfriend in a sensitive manner. By extracting the testimony about the girlfriend, she decreased the jury's level of sympathy for the bereaved widower. How much companionship did he lose, if he was having an affair? At the same time, because she did so in a gentle manner, she

increased the jury's regard for her. She presented herself as a nice person. Her approach is similar to Laura's in using "niceness" as a strategy. However, in Laura's case, being nice was not appropriate to a destructive cross-examination. In the case of cross-examining a sympathetic witness, such an approach is necessary.

Opening statements also provide an opportunity for using the nonconfrontational approach. NITA provided a hypothetical case called *BMI v. Minicom*, involving a large corporation that sues a small business for its failure to pay a contract. Minicom signed a contract for a $20,000 order of computer parts from BMI. BMI shipped the computer parts through UPS to Minicom, but they never arrived. According to the law in the case, the buyer bears the loss, typically through insurance, when the equipment is lost in mail. Mark gave an opening statement that portrayed Minicom as a small business started by ambitious, hard-working college friends "on their way to the big league in business." He played up the difficulties that small businesses face in trying to compete with giant corporations. And at a dramatic moment in the opening, he asked the jury to "imagine a world where cruel giants didn't squeeze out small companies like Minicom." The teacher provided the following comments:

> Good use of evocative imagery. BMI as cruel giant. Minicom squeezing in between the cracks. Great highlighting of the injustice of the situation.

The lawyer for Minicom attempted to gain sympathy from the jury by playing up the underdog role of his client—the small company that gets squeezed between the cracks of the cruel, dominating giant.

In his attempt to counter this image, Robert, the lawyer for BMI, used a courteous opening statement. He attempted to present himself as a nice guy. He took off his jacket, loosened his tie, smiled at the jury, and said, in a friendly conversational tone, "This case is about a broken contract. BMI fulfilled their side of the contract. Mr. Blakey, my client, worked round the clock to get the shipment ready for Minicom. He made phone call after phone call to inventory to make sure the parts got out on time. He checked and rechecked the package before he sent it to Minicom." He paused for dramatic emphasis and, looking sincere and concerned, said, "It's too bad UPS lost the shipment, but that's not BMI's fault. And now, BMI is out $20,000." He received the following comments from the teacher:

> Great use of gestures and eye contact. Good use of voice. You made the case sound simple but important. You humanized yourself and the people at BMI. Good building of sequence.

Here, the attorney for BMI tried to play down his client's impersonal, corporate image by presenting himself as a nice guy. Before he began his opening statement, he took off his jacket and loosened his tie to suggest a more casual and ostensibly less corporate image. He smiled at the jury to let them know that he was friendly—not the cruel giant depicted by opposing counsel. He used a friendly conversational tone to begin his opening statement. And he even admitted that it was not fair that the other side didn't get their computer parts. As the teacher's comments suggest, this strategy was most effective for this particular kind of case.

This approach can also be used in closing statements. In a hypothetical case, during which an insurance company alleged that the claimant set fire to his own business, the lawyer for the store owner tried to defuse the insurance company's strategy with a highly dramatic closing statement:

> Visualize Elmwood Street in 1952. The day Tony Rubino came home from the Navy. His father took him outside to show him a new sign he had made for the family business. It read "Rubino & Son." Standing under the sign "Rubino & Son" with his father was the happiest day of his life. [Pause] The insurance company wants you to believe, ladies and gentlemen of the jury, that Tony set fire to this family jewel. "I'll carry on," he told his father, and he did. . . . [With tears in her eyes, the lawyer concludes] You don't set fire to your father's dream.

The teacher's comments for Janine's closing statement were effusive:

> Great! Well thought out, sounded natural. Good use of details and organization. I especially liked "I don't know what it's like to have a son, but I know what it's like to have a father." And you had tears in your eyes! Gave me the closing-argument goose bumps. Pitched emotion felt real, not phony.

Janine's use of sentimental and nostalgic imagery, the son returning home from the Navy, the beginning of a father and son business, the business as the "family jewel" is reminiscent of a Norman Rockwell painting. It also serves to counter the insurance company's allegation that Tony Rubino set fire to his own store. With the portrait the lawyer paints and the concluding line, "You don't set fire to your father's dream," she rallies the jury's sympathy for Tony Rubino and their antipathy for the insurance company's malicious claim against them. Moreover, her emotional presentation of the story is so effective that the instructor thought it "sounded natural" and "felt real, not phony." The great irony here is that this is not a real case—it is a hypothetical case with hypothetical characters. There is no Tony Rubino, no family store, and no fire. Yet Janine's "deep acting" was so convincing that the teachers believed it was true—it gave him "the closing-argument goose bumps."

Strategic friendliness carries over from the courtroom to depositions. Before deposing a particularly sensitive or sympathetic witness, Joe, one of the attorneys in the private firm, asked me whether "there is anything personal to start the interview with—a sort of warm up question to start things off on a personal note?" I had previously interviewed the woman over the phone, so I knew something about her background. I told him that she was a young mother who had recently had a very difficult delivery of her first child. I added that she was worried about the baby's health, because he had been born prematurely. At the beginning of the deposition later that afternoon, Joe said in a concerned voice that he understood the witness had recently had a baby and was concerned about its health. She appeared slightly embarrassed by the question, but with a slow smile and lots of encouragement from him, she began to tell him all about the baby and its health problems. By the time Joe began the formal part of the deposition, the witness had warmed up and gave her complete cooperation. Later, the attorney bragged to me and one of the associates that he had the witness "eating out of his hand."

After recording these events in my field notes, I wrote the following impressions:

> On the surface, it looks like social etiquette to ask the witness these questions, because it puts her at ease. It lets her know he takes her seriously. But the "personal touch" is completely artificial. He doesn't give a shit about the witness as a person. Or, I should say, only insofar as she's *useful* to him.

Thus, something as innocuous as a personal remark becomes another way to create the desired impression with a witness and thereby manipulate him or her. Perhaps what is most ironic about strategic friendliness is that it requires a peculiar combination of sensitivity to other people and, at the same time, ruthlessness. The lawyer wants to appear kind and understanding, but that is merely a cover for the ulterior motive—winning. Although the outward presentation of self for this form of emotional labor differs from intimidation, the underlying goal is the same: the emotional manipulation of the witness for a favorable result.

Conclusion

In this chapter, I have redefined gamesmanship as the utilization of legal strategy through a presentation of emotional self designed specifically to influence the feelings and judgments of a particular legal audience, such as the judge, the jury, opposing counsel, or the witness. Gamesmanship as emotional labor constitutes two main components—intimidation and strategic friendliness. Despite their apparent differences, both share an emphasis on the manipulation of others toward a strategic end, that is, winning a case. Whereas, the object of intimidation is to "wipe out the other side," playing dumb and being polite represent strategically friendly methods for controlling legal audiences and bringing about the desired "win." Furthermore, I have shown that the attempt to dominate and control judges, juries, and opposing counsel not only serves the goals of the adversarial model but also becomes a means for trial lawyers to assert a hegemonic form of masculinity. Lawyers who gain the other side's submission characterize their efforts as a "macho blast," "a male thing," or "something men get into," whereas those who do not are regarded as "sissies" and "wimps." Thus, it is through their very efforts to be successful litigators that emotional labor in this male-dominated profession is masculinized.

This chapter also suggests many questions for future research on the role of masculinity and emotions in organizations. Masculinity is often a taken-for-granted feature of organizational life. Yet the masculinization of occupations and professions has profound consequences for workers located within them. Not only do male litigators find themselves compelled to act in ways they may find morally reprehensible, but women working in these jobs[13] are increasingly marginalized—facing sex discrimination and sexual harassment (Rhode 1988; Rosenberg, Perlstadt, & Phillips 1993). At the same time, because of its informal and seemingly invisible nature, emotional labor too is often unexamined and unquestioned (Fineman 1993). Given that organizations often intrude on emotional life means that the line between the individual and the job becomes a murky one. The litigator who refuses to play Rambo may not only be unsuccessful, he may find himself without a job. Thus, many questions still require our attention. Is emotional labor gendered in other jobs? Under what conditions? When does emotional labor take on racialized or classed dimensions? When is it exploitative and when is it not? And finally, what role, if any, should emotions play in the workplace?

Notes

1. For examples, see Goldberg (1987), Margolick (1988), Miner (1988), and Sayler (1988).

2. For example, see the *National Law Journal*'s (1986) article, "What America Really Thinks About Lawyers."

3. Classic studies on the legal profession have typically focused on the tension between professionalism and bureaucracy. For examples, see Smigel (1969), Carlin (1962), Spangler (1986), and Nelson (1988).

4. For example, in their classic book, *Lawyers and Their Work*, Johnstone and Hopson (1967) describe 19 tasks associated with the lawyering role. In only 2 of these 19 tasks do Johnstone and Hopson allude to the emotional dimension of lawyering—"emotional support to client" and "acting as a scapegoat" (pp. 119–120).

5. In addition to my field research, I also conducted 60 interviews with lawyers, paralegals, and secretaries, as well as 8 interviews with personnel directors from some of San Francisco's largest law firms. Field work and interviews were also conducted at the National Institute of Trial Advocacy where I spent 3 weeks with litigators during a special training course on trial preparation. These methodological decisions are fully discussed in the introductory chapter to my book, *Gender Trials* (Pierce 1995). Please note, names of organizations and individuals have been changed throughout to protect confidentiality.

6. See Chapter 4, "Mothering Paralegals: Emotional Labor in a Feminized Occupation," in *Gender Trials* (Pierce 1995).

7. West and Zimmerman (1987) conceptualize gender as "a routine accomplishment embedded in everyday interaction" (p. 1).

8. Blumberg (1967) describes lawyers as practicing a "confidence game." In his account, it is the client who is the "mark" and the attorney and other people in the court who collude in "taking him out." In my usage, litigators "con" not only their clients but juries, judges, and opposing counsel as well.

9. Special thanks to Laurence Rose, Lou Natali, and the National Institute of Trial Advocacy for allowing me to attend and observe NITA's special 3-week training seminar on trial advocacy. All interpretations of NITA and its practices are my own and are *not* intended to reflect the goals or objectives of that organization.

10. Women were much more likely to be criticized for being "too nice." The significance of women being singled out for these kinds of "mistakes" is examined in Chapter 5. "Women and Men as Litigators," in *Gender Trials* (Pierce 1995).

11. Mauet describes two approaches to cross-examination. In the first, the purpose is to elicit favorable testimony by getting the witness to agree with the facts that support one's case. On the other hand, a destructive cross-examination "involves asking questions which will discredit the witness or his testimony" (1980, p. 240).

12. The proper form of leading questions is allowed in cross-examination but *not* in direct examination. Mauet (1980) defines a leading question as "one which suggests the answer" and provides examples, such as "Mr. Doe, on December 13, 1977, you owned a car, didn't you?" (p. 247). In his view, control comes by asking "precisely phrased leading questions that never give the witness an opening to hurt you" (p. 243).

13. Women trial lawyers negotiate the masculinized norms of the legal profession in a variety of ways. See Chapter 5, "Women and Men as Litigators," in *Gender Trials* (Pierce 1995).

References

American Bar Association (1982). *Model code of professional responsibility and code of judicial conduct*. Chicago: National Center for Professional Responsibility and ABA.

Benjamin, J. (1988). *The bonds of love: Psychoanalysis, feminism and the problem of domination*. New York: Pantheon.

Berg, D. (1987). Cross-examination. *Litigation: Journal of the Section of Litigation, American Bar Association, 14*(1), 25–30.

Blinder, M. (1978). Picking juries. *Trial Diplomacy, 1*(1), 8–13.

Blumberg, A. (1967). The practice of law as confidence game: Organizational co-optation of a profession. *Law and Society Review, 1*(2), 15–39.

Brazil, W. (1978). The attorney as victim: Toward more candor about the psychological price tag of litigation practice. *Journal of the Legal Profession, 3*, 107–117.

Buchan, J. (1939). The judicial temperament. In J. Buchan, *Homilies and recreations* (3rd ed.). London: Hodder & Stoughton.

Burawoy, M. (1979). *Manufacturing consent*. Chicago: University of Chicago Press.

Carlin, J. (1962). *Lawyers on their own*. New Brunswick, NJ: Rutgers University Press.

Cartwright, R. (1977, June). Jury selection. *Trial, 28*, 13.

Cheatham, E. (1955). *Cases and materials on the legal profession* (2nd ed.). Brooklyn, NY: Foundation.

Chodorow, N. (1978). *The reproduction of mothering: Psychoanalysis and the sociology of gender*. Berkeley & Los Angeles: University of California Press.

Connell, R. W. (1987). *Gender and power: Society, the person and sexual politics*. Stanford, CA: Stanford University Press.

Dombroff, M. (1989, September 25). Winning is everything! *National Law Journal*, p. 13, col. 1.

Fineman, S. (Ed.). (1993). *Emotions in organizations*. Newbury Park, CA: Sage.

Garfinkel, H. (1956). Conditions of successful degradation ceremonies. *American Journal of Sociology, 61*(11), 420–424.

Goldberg, D. (1987, July 1). Playing hardball. *American Bar Association Journal*, p. 48.

Hochschild, A. (1983). *The managed heart: Commercialization of human feeling*. Berkeley & Los Angeles: University of California Press.

Johnstone, Q., & Hopson, D., Jr. (1967). *Lawyers and their work*. Indianapolis, IN: Bobbs-Merrill.

Leidner, R. (1993). *Fast food, fast talk: Service work and the routinization of everyday life*. Berkeley: University of California Press.

Luban, D. (1988). *Lawyers and justice: An ethical study*. Princeton, NJ: Princeton University Press.

Lyman, P. (1987). The fraternal bond as a joking relationship: A case study of sexist jokes in male group bonding. In M. Kimmel (Ed.), *Changing men: New directions in research on men and masculinity* (pp. 148–163). Newbury Park, CA: Sage.

Margolick, D. (1988, August 5). At the bar: Rambos invade the courtroom. *New York Times*, p. B5.

Mauet, T. (1980). *Fundamentals of trial techniques*. Boston: Little, Brown.

Menkel-Meadow, C. (1985, Fall). Portia in a different voice: Speculations on a women's lawyering process. *Berkeley Women's Law Review*, pp. 39–63.

Messner, M. (1989). Masculinities and athletic careers. *Gender & Society, 3*(1), 71–88.

Milkman, R. (1987). *Gender at work*. Bloomington: University of Indiana Press.

Miner, R. (1988, December 19). Lawyers owe one another. *National Law Journal*, pp. 13–14.

Nelson, R. (1988). *Partners with power*. Berkeley & Los Angeles: University of California Press.

Perlman, P. (1988). Jury selection. *The Docket: Newsletter of the National Institute for Trial Advocacy, 12*(2), 1.

Pierce, J. L. (1995). *Gender trials: Emotional lives in contemporary law firms*. Berkeley & Los Angeles: University of California Press.

Rhode, D. (1988). Perspectives on professional women. *Stanford Law Review, 40*, 1163–1207.

Rice, S. (1989, May 24). Two organizations provide training, in-house or out. *San Francisco Banner*, p. 6.

Ring, L. (1983, July). *Voir dire:* Some thoughtful notes on the selection process. *Trial, 19*, 72–75.

Ring, L. (1987). Cross-examining the sympathetic witness. *Litigation: Journal of the Section of Litigation, American Bar Association, 14*(1), 35–39.

Rollins, J. (1985). *Between women: Domestics and their employers*. Philadelphia: Temple University Press.

Rosenberg, J., Perlstadt, H., & Phillips, W. (1993). Now that we are here: Discrimination, disparagement and harassment at work and the experience of women lawyers. *Gender & Society, 7*(3), 415–433.

Sayler, R. (1988, March 1). Rambo litigation: Why hardball tactics don't work. *American Bar Association Journal*, p. 79.

Smigel, E. (1969). *The Wall Street lawyer: Professional or organizational man?* (2nd ed.). New York: Free Press.

Spangler, E. (1986). *Lawyers for hire: Salaried professionals at work*. New Haven, CT: Yale University Press.

Spence, G. (1988). *With justice for none*. New York: Times Books.

Turow, S. (1987). Crossing the star. *Litigation: Journal of the Section of Litigation, American Bar Association, 14*(1), 40–42.

Wellman, F. (1986). *The art of cross-examination: With the cross-examinations of important witnesses in some celebrated cases* (4th ed.). New York: Collier. (Original work published 1903).

West, C., & Zimmerman, D. (1987). Doing gender. *Gender & Society, 1*(2), 125–151.

What America really thinks about lawyers. (1986, October). *National Law Journal*, p. 1.

Willis, P. (1977). *Learning to labor*. Farnborough, UK: Saxon House.

Timothy Nonn

Hitting Bottom: Homelessness, Poverty, and Masculinity

In the dangerous and impoverished Tenderloin district of San Francisco live the men we consider failures. Urban deterioration and public neglect has created a "dumping-ground for unwanted individuals" (North of Market Planning Coalition 1992: 4). Low rents attract immigrants, welfare recipients, and low-income workers. The population is about 40 percent white, one-third Asian American, and one-tenth black and Latino, respectively. There are severe problems with homelessness, AIDS, violence, substance abuse, and unemployment.

In studies of men, poor men are rarely the object of research.[1] This article examines the coping mechanisms poor men develop to resolve their status as "failed men": First, to overcome stigmatization and regain self-worth, Tenderloin men develop "counter-masculinities" within distinct groups; second, some men develop new values in response to a multiplicity of masculinities that allow them to transcend separate groups and identify with the Tenderloin community.

Using a snowball sample, twenty men were interviewed during a six-month period, including twelve whites, six blacks, and two Latinos; twelve were heterosexual, and eight were homosexual. Their ages ranged from twenty-nine to fifty-four; the majority had a high-school education. Many had been homeless, but most were now living in single-room occupancy hotels. Twelve were single, seven were divorced or separated, and one was married. Several have left children behind. Their interactions with women at the time of the interview were very limited. Few had contact with

families or had long-term relationships with women.

Each interview lasted about two hours and included a questionnaire that examined attitudes about gender, race, and sexuality. In the study, I examined how Tenderloin men, as groups, interacted with other men.

Failed Men

A discussion of failure among men must begin with hegemonic masculinity. R. W. Connell writes:

> Hegemonic masculinity is constructed in relation to women and to subordinated masculinities. These other masculinities need not be as clearly defined—indeed, achieving hegemony may consist precisely in preventing alternatives gaining cultural definition and recognition as alternatives, confining them to ghettos, to privacy, to unconsciousness. (Connell 1987: 186)

Connell defines hegemonic masculinity as men's dominance over women. While individuals may change, men's collective power remains embedded in social and cultural institutions. Michael Messner interprets change among white, middle-class men as a matter of personal life-style rather than a restructuring of power and politics (Messner 1993).

Hegemonic masculinity is the standard by which Tenderloin men are judged. The media refers to them as "thugs and bums."[2] Forced to live amidst poverty, drugs, and violence, they are stripped of or denied access to a masculine identity constructed around the role of "the good provider" (see Bernard in this book). As white heterosexuals, they are stripped of an identity associated with privilege and power. As gays or men of color, they are denied access to a masculine ideal associated with heterosexual whites. George, a divorced black Vietnam veteran, says:

> Now, we're talking about that segment of the male population that have been taught some of the same things that all men are taught. So they were straight-up abject failures.[3]

Tenderloin men sometimes refer to each other as "invisible." George describes a homeless man's life:

> I call it the "invisible-man syndrome." That's what you become. Most homeless, but not all, self-medicate. It's that thing that you can turn to when you're suffering. You feel disenfranchised from society. You feel less than human. It tells him—in between those periods where he has some lucidity, in between drug or alcohol bouts—that he is a total failure.

Allan, a forty-six-year-old heterosexual white man, recounts the experience of trying to cash a small check:

> [I went] into the bank to cash a two-dollar check and had to deal with people's feedback. I just want to be invisible. I'm real embarrassed about that. About my economic status. . . . When I was stripped of all those material things that I was taught were the measure of success, and everybody rejected me—even though as a person I hadn't changed—I saw the sort of shallowness. It was very painful and very hard.[4]

Tenderloin men face a lonely end. Before death—having been stripped of everything that qualifies a man for full participation in society—there is the shame of surviving as less than a man. Tenderloin men belong to a "shamed group" (Goffman 1963: 23). David, a heterosexual black homeless man, describes their daily struggle:

> The thing that really hurts and holds people down is when they give completely up. When you give completely up that means you take your energy and give it to drugs or alcohol. . . .

Some homeless men have lost their self-esteem. They have been down for so long. And the system has played this game of chess with them for so long. They've just said, "Oh, forget it." They say, "We'll sell drugs. So if I go to jail, I still have a home." So it don't make any difference. They feel rejected.[5]

Tenderloin men feel trapped in the role of failure.[6] Many hang out day and night on streets "drinking and drugging," talking and begging. The ubiquitous drug trade, routine violence, and crushing poverty combine to form an atmosphere of continual dread and hopelessness within the neighborhood. The men wait in line for hours at churches to receive food, clothing, and lodging. Because it is equally painful to be seen as to be invisible, they are silent and avoid eye contact. They spend a lot of time waiting. The wait transforms them. They dress in a similar ragged way. They walk and talk in a dispirited way. Their faces have the same blank stare or menacing hardness. Some turn into predators in search of victims.[7] Others turn into victims in search of sympathy. George says:

> Your antenna is up for people feeling sorry for you. Part of you becomes a predator. The predator part wants to take advantage. So you can get resources to continue your downward spiral to total destruction. The other part of you feels ashamed because you have violated every man-code that you were ever taught. So you're stuck on stupid. You get to a point where you don't know what to do. You don't give a shit no more about how you're perceived. You can walk down the street smelling like a billy goat. Stuff hanging all over you. You haven't had access to basic hygiene in days and sometimes weeks. You don't care. And the looks don't bother you anymore because you ain't nobody. The productive citizens have that way of not looking at you anyway because you're the invisible man.

The invisibility of Tenderloin men is part of "a pervasive two-role social process" in which failure and success are interrelated (Goffman 1963: 138). They are stigmatized merely by living in an area decimated by poverty, sex and drug markets, and high levels of crime and violence. William Julius Wilson calls them "the permanent underclass" (Wilson 1987: 7). Samuel, a forty-year-old homosexual black man, describes their plight more poignantly: "You're always going to need a place where the lonely souls can go."[8]

Trapped at the bottom of society and stigmatized as failures, Tenderloin men have limited opportunities to claim an identity that fosters self-worth. Charles, a fifty-year-old white gay man, says: "Once you go in there, it's like being an untouchable. You're stigmatized as being this type of sleazy person that does dope and needles, and the whole thing."[9] After a man is stripped of or denied access to symbols of masculinity that confer power and privilege—job, car, home, and family—life becomes a series of challenges to his existence. Some escape the Tenderloin by getting clean, finding work, and moving out. Others descend further into self-destructive behavior and die. Those who remain must adapt to the Tenderloin.

Counter-Masculinities

Counter-masculinities—developed in response to hegemonic masculinity—are coping mechanisms that provide Tenderloin men with a sense of self-worth.[10] A typology of counter-masculinities was found among three groups of Tenderloin men: heterosexual whites, heterosexual blacks and Latinos, and homosexual blacks and whites.

Heterosexual White Men: Urban Hermits

Heterosexual whites are the only men that do not identify with their own group. In the introduction to this book, Michael Kimmel writes that white men see themselves as "the generic person" because "the mechanisms that afford us privilege are very often invisible to us." To escape from the stigma of failure, the "urban hermit" structures identify around the value of self-sufficiency. Power is interpreted as individual achievement. Oscar, a fifty-year-old divorced heterosexual white man, describes a sense of failure:

It's a difficult struggle. But you can't blame anybody but yourself. Because it is you yourself. Like with me. It's me myself that has the illness. Not the people of the government. Not the people of the different businesses. And things like that. It's me.[11]

Although receiving disability benefits, Oscar views himself as self-sufficient and criticizes blacks on welfare for lacking motivation. Men of color similarly criticize whites. Ned, a forty-year-old single heterosexual black man, says:

I feel that most of them have given up. They don't really care or try. I try to respect all men. But it's difficult to understand why a white man would give up on himself given a society that is made for them.[12]

Virtually all heterosexual white men interpret their present hardship as the result of personal failure. Richard Sennett and Jonathan Cobb argue that the "code of respect" in American society demands that "a man should feel responsibility for his own social position—even if, in a class society, he believes men in general are deprived of the freedom to control their lives." Failure is defined according to cultural values in which a man is expected to have the desire and opportunity to work (Sennett and Cobb 1972: 36).

Urban hermits spend most of their time alone in hotel rooms. Many frequent bars and restaurants where they complain that criminals have "taken over" the area and demand that police "clean up the streets."[13] Unable to reconcile belief in white male superiority and life among the disenfranchised, most believe society is falling apart. Frank, a single heterosexual white man, describes whites:

Their spirits are broken. They're outcasts of their families from all over the country. They're in disarray. They're drifting. Some of them never came back from Vietnam. Some of them are screwed up on drugs. It seems to me that America isn't like it used to be. When I grew up it was changing . . . it was breaking apart. My family broke apart, anyway. It was hard on me. They're outcasts from all over the country, and they gravitate here.[14]

Heterosexual white men experience a high level of cultural shock in moving to the Tenderloin.[15] A walk to the store is a challenge to their self-esteem. They confront black and Latino men who threaten their sense of racial superiority and gays who threaten their sexual identity. Oscar believes gays challenge divine law. He says:

> God decided he wanted a man to look like a man and a woman to look like a woman. It's not his fault if some men act like women and women act like men. It's the fault of the people themselves. The people can go without acting that way if they don't want to and they can act that way if they want to. It's up to them.[16]

Heterosexual whites are confused and angry because others appear to violate social norms. Most retreat into isolation. A few imitate other men's behavior. Brad, a twenty-nine-year-old single, heterosexual white man, admires the "sense of family" among Latinos.[17] Many appreciate the nurturing qualities of gays. But other men criticize whites for not knowing themselves. Miguel, a divorced fifty-year-old heterosexual Latino man, says:

> The white man tries too hard to make friends. . . . If you're going to come in here and start trying to be black, they see that already. You're not! But here's a guy and he's trying to talk like us and be cool. It's a front. We know that. Hey, come on. I mean I've studied white folks before, and I know that's not the way white people are supposed to be.[18]

Wanting to belong, and forced to confront their prejudices, heterosexual whites discover that genuineness is vital. But it is difficult for them to adapt. Quinn, a fifty-four-year-old gay white man, says whites are aloof because: "White is right. White isn't going to be criticized. White isn't going to be stopped by police."[19]

The counter-masculinity of the urban hermit discloses an inability to cope with diversity of race, culture, and sexual orientation. As a coping mechanism, it resists the stigma of failure but undermines identity by organizing social relations around poles of independence and dependence.

In the Tenderloin, interdependence is both a reality and a necessity. What heterosexual whites view as self-sufficiency, others view as arrogance. Because the urban hermit is seen as an outcast among outcasts, failure and alienation are not overcome through self-sufficiency.

Heterosexual Black and Latino Men: Cool Pose

Heterosexual blacks and Latinos dominate street life and display what Majors and Billson (1992) call "cool pose." Cool pose is a counter-masculinity that structures identity around the value of respect. Power is interpreted as group solidarity in a racist society. Blacks and Latinos establish social position by displaying aggressiveness or showing deference (Almaguer 1991: 80). Miguel claims the system of respect maintains harmony: "You don't have to trust someone. You just respect them." George uses a hypermasculine facade to obtain respect and to fend off predators. He says:

> One of the techniques you use—and this is a prison technique—is getting big. You work out hard. You carry yourself in an intimidating manner. Your body language says, "I'll kill you if you even think about approaching my space."

The mask of hypermasculinity establishes a man's position in his group.[20] Miguel describes putting on his mask:

> Whenever I walk, I look mean. I make my face look like I got an attitude. Like I just got ripped off. I don't look at the person. I look through them. I'm cutting him. And this guy's thinking, "Hmmm. Let me move out of the way." You could get busted. "Oh, you ain't that tough." But out there you gotta act that way.

"Getting busted" means that someone is able to see through a man's mask. Whites have difficulty distinguishing between actual threats and posturing by blacks and Latinos, and often feel threatened. But Jack, a heterosexual black man, explains that cool pose conceals a sense of failure among men of color living in a white-dominated society:

The one thing I hear from white guys is, "You guys act like you're so proud." They don't realize why we're doing it. It's to survive amongst our own peers. We feel just as bad as he does. The white guy resents that; "How in the hell can he act like that and I'm white? I come from the superior race and I can't act like that. I feel dead." They come from two different worlds.[21]

Ned interprets cool pose in relation to a definition of masculinity that excludes black men in American society:

A black man has to be tough out there on the street. The reason they have to be that way is that they don't have any other outlet for their manhood. They can't show their manhood by being a success economically because society simply will not give them a chance. I mean a black man is even lucky to have a full-time—or even a part-time—job. So he has to show his manhood by acting physically tough. Because mentally tough won't get him anywhere. But there has been no reason that white men have had to be physically tough because they've been able to show their manhood through their nine-to-five. Going to work every day. And making a living.

Cool pose is depicted as "a creative strategy devised by African-American males to counter the negative forces in their lives" (Majors and Billson 1992: 105). Yet, the counter-masculinity of cool pose does not allow heterosexual black and Latino men to escape from failure by structuring identity around the value of respect. While the coping mechanism of cool pose weakens the stigma of failure, it undermines identity by organizing social relations around poles of dominance and submission. What heterosexual men of color view as respect, others view as hostility. By adopting an identity based upon fear and violence, men of color in the Tenderloin in part contribute to their own alienation from other groups and society at large. They are further marginalized in an environment where different social groups demand to live in equality with one another.

Homosexual Black and White Men: Perfect Copy

Gays in the Tenderloin blur gender and sexual boundaries by constructing identity around performance of a series of roles. "Perfect copy" of hypermasculinity redefines and subverts masculinity (Butler 1990: 31). Klaus, a thirty-four-year-old gay white man, interprets his experience with heterosexual men in the Tenderloin:

They feel like their manhood or sexuality has been threatened because I'm more butch than they are. I am more of a man than a straight man can be around here. They're threatened. Not only to me but to themselves.[22]

Gays structure identity around the value of acceptance. Power is interpreted as inclusion of persons who challenge gender and sexual categories. Because identity is in flux, and gender and sexual identity are rendered uncertain, "homosexuality undermines masculinity" (Edwards 1990: 114). Larry, a thirty-three-year-old gay white man, says heterosexuals are simultaneously confused and intrigued by gays:

I think [they] are very jealous of gay men because we're so open and free with our feelings. We speak what we have to say. We don't hide our feelings. We cry at sad movies. Heterosexual men think that men don't cry. But if you go drinking with them, get them drunk or high, they're the first ones that throw their legs in the air or whip out their cocks in front of you and say, "Here. Suck this."[23]

Another gay man believes single heterosexuals are in a predicament because they normally rely on women to provide them with gender identity. Charles says:

Most men depend on women to define that role for them. So a man is what a woman defines him to be. So if you don't have a woman in your life to define you as a man, then you have to depend on all these macho apparatuses. Then you have to prove to other men that you are a man.

Transgenders pose a new challenge by further blurring gender and sexual boundaries. Thomas, a twenty-nine-year-old gay black man, says some men respond favorably:

> It seems to be a turn-on. Especially if everything is in order—the appearance is almost perfect. Woman have a lot to do just getting dressed in the morning. Hair, makeup, clothing, shoes. Everything has to be just right. It's not like men. We can just put on a pair of jeans and a T-shirt. And out the door. I've noticed this especially with straight men. They seem to be really impressed.[24]

Identity is a series of roles that gays perfect in daily encounters. Transgenders further complicate identity when "some transgendered persons consider themselves heterosexual, while others consider themselves homosexual" (Koenig 1993: 10). The counter-masculinity of perfect copy challenges hegemonic masculinity through a multitude of replicated masculinities that blur sexual and gender boundaries. Performance of a series of roles creates security in a homophobic society by destabilizing and redefining social relations. But perfect copy of hypermasculine (or hyperfeminine) roles implies a reliance upon hegemonic masculine ideals. While the coping mechanism of perfect copy resists the stigma of failure, it undermines identity by organizing social relations around poles of performance and observation. Perfect copy contributes to further alienation of gays, because what they view as acceptance, others view as licentiousness.

Counter-masculinities are coping mechanisms that aid Tenderloin men in regaining a sense of self-worth while preventing them from overcoming alienation from other groups of men. For Tenderloin men, masculine identity develops around specific value systems in response to the social system of hegemonic masculinity and an immediately hostile environment (Tong 1971: 8). Paradoxically, counter-masculinities offer resistance to hegemonic masculinity while deepening social divisions. Since the contradictions of counter-masculinities stem from inequitable relations of power, what unites men as a group separates them as a community. The urban hermit devalues interdependence in favor of self-sufficiency; cool pose devalues equality in favor of dominance; and perfect copy devalues mutuality in favor of performance. A new value system constructed around shared power is required to unite Tenderloin men into a community.

Versatile Masculinity

Versatile masculinity is a unique masculine identity that emerges from everyday encounters of Tenderloin men as they collectively resolve the contradictions of counter-masculinities. Versatile masculinity allows men to identify with a transcendent set of values without destroying their group identity or value systems. This new set of values—while not distinctively masculine—is the basis of a masculine identity that binds Tenderloin men together in genuine community.

Versatile masculinity is not a fixed identity but a growing capacity for relating to difference.[25] As a fluid construction that sorts and combines practices, values, and attitudes in a strategic movement, it enables men to flourish in a diverse and dynamic environment. Most important, it is not a way of being but a way of becoming in relationships. David calls it being "flexible":

> So many people [were] raised a certain way, and it stays with them. That's the only way they know. Instead of looking over the whole situation and see this and that. That's the way you have to live. Especially if you're living homeless on the streets. You have to be able to be flexible. Maybe this guy does things a different way. Maybe I can help him do this and he can help me do that. That's where you have to come in and learn it. That's what certain people call "streetwise." Streetwise people are just movable. They're just flexible.

Versatile masculinity does not undermine the different values of Tenderloin men but relates them to a transcendent set of values: honesty, caring, interdependence, and respect. H. Richard

Niebuhr writes that ultimate value is not identifiable with a particular mode of being but "is present whenever being confronts being, wherever there is becoming in the midst of plural, interdependent, and interacting existences. It is not a function of being as such but of being in relation to being" (Niebuhr 1970: 106–7).

Similarly, versatile masculinity creates unity from diversity. Jack believes that acceptance of difference is essential to survival:

> All people are equal. All things are relative. If you exterminate Jews, you exterminate me and you. . . . They're all of our cultures, are relative to keep us together. If I'm not afraid to learn about your culture then I got something to learn. Something that is relative. If everybody was alike, we'd be in trouble. We'd be in real trouble.

As marginalized persons, Tenderloin men are innovative survivors who manifest "creative strategies for survival that then open up new possibilities for everyone" (Duberman 1993: 24). But their experience reveals that only after a man has reached bottom—after he is stripped of or denied access to a masculine identity that provides him with a sense of innate superiority—will he change. Quinn says:

> You bottom out. And you go through the bottom of the barrel and you come up again. You learn a different type of survival skills. . . . But going from the bottom and coming through you run into criminals, junkies, crazies, and everything else. . . . It doesn't make you less of a person. Actually, it can make you a stronger person. And more sensitive.

Versatile masculinity includes three conditions: (1) A man must be stripped of or denied access to a hegemonic masculine identity; (2) a man must adopt a counter-masculinity to reconstruct his identity and resist hegemonic masculine values that stigmatize him as a failure; and (3) a man must experience a multiplicity of masculinities that compel him to develop an identity based on acceptance of difference. When these conditions exist, versatile masculinity drives men to over-come their differences and create a community based on the following values.

Honesty

For Tenderloin men, honesty means genuineness. It is a process of "coming to critical consciousness" (Hooks 1990: 191). Tenderloin men sometimes discard illusions that contribute to lack of self-esteem. Hank, a thirty-six-year-old divorced, heterosexual white man, says:

> I realized that the only way I was going to get clean and sober, and really become a disciple of Christ, was to clean up my act. To become truly honest. Beginning with admitting to myself that I was full of shit. That I was living a lie. Just a lie.[26]

Brad says:

> I feel like if you're genuine with people there's some recognition within them. Or they see something. I know it's happened to me when I just met somebody who is for real and I've been acting like a fool or not being true to myself. It kind of makes me go, "Oh!" and "Yeah!"

In the Tenderloin, because men use every imaginable act to hide from themselves and society, they can easily recognize genuineness. Quinn says: "An honest person is going to recognize another honest person and see a phony."

Caring

Many Tenderloin men have HIV/AIDS. Samuel, who is beginning to display symptoms, has given himself a final task before he dies. He says:

> I'm having a big struggle with a transvestite named Carol who rips me off every second she has a chance to. I keep going back to her. And I tell her, "You got me, girl. But you didn't really have to do that. If you wanted it, just ask me for it. I'll give it to you. And if not, then you can rip me off." She's turned out to be one of my best friends. It's all she's ever known in her life. She's always lived in the ghetto. This is my personal struggle. My personal fight is to just take that one person and make her realize that she doesn't have to keep two steps ahead of me

in order to get what's mine. Because it's all materialistic. If what I have you need, you can have. All you have to do is just ask for it.

Poverty, ostracism, and illness have brought men together to provide and receive care from one another. Allan describes his life at one of the worst slum hotels in the Tenderloin:

> At the Victoria, people will come in who are very different from one another, and sit down and talk and joke with one another. I don't think you could say that those interactions are insincere, or [occur] simply because they're close together. They like each other. They've discovered that we're all human beings with the same needs and very interesting differences. It's an acknowledgment that they're worthwhile. The kinds of sharing of people who don't have a lot to give is striking.

The work of caring is rare among men in our society, because compassion is a value identified with women. For Tenderloin men, caring for one another is tremendously empowering.

Interdependence

Men forced to live at the bottom of society feel insignificant and powerless. A common phrase heard on the streets is "the small people." Masculinity is redefined as an identity based on interdependence. Thomas says:

> Here you kind of like take care of your own. You kind of have to take care of each other here just so everybody survives. If one person doesn't survive, there's a big effect on everybody.

Respect

The most important lesson that Tenderloin men learn is respect for the intrinsic worth of each person. Masculinity includes an identification with humanity rather than only with one's group. This process (especially for heterosexual whites) begins with a period of cultural shock. Eduardo, a thirty-three-year-old single, heterosexual Latino man, says new residents overcome fear when they "start standing in the soup lines and staying in hotels. You realize that the homeless are not un-

like you or I. They're human. You become part of the community."[27] Larry—who once worked as a male prostitute in the Tenderloin—believes faith overcomes barriers between people. He says:

> Mary Magdalene was a prostitute. There are many women and men in this city that are prostitutes. There's nothing wrong with that. They're human beings first. Their titles come afterward. We weren't born what we are today. We were born human beings first. Then we were educated and trained to become who we are. But before we are what we are, we're humans first. A lot of people have lost that track. Lost that faith. To see what the hell we were or where we came from.

George says we all are faced with a choice:

> Basically, they are human beings. The one thing that we have been given is the ability to make choices. That's what separates us from other animals. Outside forces may have an effect, and usually do have an effect, on the choices we have to make. But the fact is, we get to make those choices. So make those choices as a winner—not so much as a winner—but as a human being.

Summary

Tenderloin men construct new masculine identities to resist a sense of failure and to create a sense of belonging. Versatile masculinity develops from their need to safely coexist in a hostile environment, but it also provides a basis for shared power and love in relationships. The Tenderloin men who transform themselves from "failed men" into human beings display a capacity not merely to survive, but also to flourish in a context of adversity and diversity. This is aptly demonstrated by the tenants of a Tenderloin residential hotel—many of whom were once homeless and substance abusers—who have built a beautiful rooftop garden. A resident says it's "a little bit of magic in the Tenderloin." Another is happy to see "a new spirit in this neighborhood" (Maitland 1993). In the Tenderloin, a small space has gradually emerged where men are free to change.

Notes

1. There are several noteworthy works that examine the lives of poor and working-class men. See Eugene V. Debs, *Walls and Bars* (Chicago: Charles H. Kerr and Company, 1973); George Orwell, *Down and Out in Paris and London* (New York: Berkeley Medallion, 1959); James Agee and Walker Evans, *Let Us Now Praise Famous Men* (Boston: Houghton Mifflin Company, 1939); Studs Terkel, *Hard Times: An Oral History of the Great Depression* (New York: Washington Square Press, 1970); Elliot Liebow, *Tally's Corner* (Boston: Little, Brown and Company, 1967); William Julius Wilson, *The Truly Disadvantaged: The Inner City, the Underclass, and Public Policy* (Chicago: University of Chicago Press, 1987); Lillian Rubin, *Worlds of Pain: Life in the Working-Class Family* (New York: Basic Books, 1976); Richard Sennet and Jonathan Cobb, *The Hidden Injuries of Class* (New York: Vintage Books, 1972).

2. Local newspapers regularly describe Tenderloin residents in derogatory terms. See "Cheap wine ban sought in Tenderloin," *San Francisco Chronicle*, 5 April 1989; "Group wants Tenderloin as family neighborhood," *San Francisco Chronicle*, 21 July 1992; "Community policing," *San Francisco Chronicle*, 20 November 1992.

3. Interview with George on 30 April 1993. All names are fictitious.

4. Interview with Allan on 22 June 1993.

5. Interview with David on 1 May 1993.

6. Interview with Peter, a recently married, forty-eight-year-old heterosexual white man, on 27 July 1993.

7. The term "predator" is commonly used to refer to persons (often drug users) who prey on the more vulnerable sectors of the Tenderloin neighborhood, such as the elderly, children, and tourists.

8. Interview with Samuel on 26 August 1993.

9. Interview with Charles on 28 July 1993.

10. Thomas J. Gershick and Adam S. Miller (1993: 5) similarly interpret masculinities of disabled men as coping mechanisms that rely upon, reformulate, or reject the standard of hegemonic masculinity.

11. Interview with Oscar on 19 June 1993.

12. Interview with Ned on 26 July 1993.

13. Interviews with Oscar on 24 April and 19 June 1993.

14. Interview with Frank on 13 August 1993.

15. Bruno Bettelheim (1960: 120) reports that of Jews sent to Nazi concentration camps, middle-class German men experienced the greatest level of initial shock and were the least adaptable prisoners.

16. Interview with Oscar on 19 June 1993.

17. Interview with Brad on 28 July 1993.

18. Interview with Miguel on 23 July 1993.

19. Interview with Quinn on 29 July 1993.

20. Pleck (1987: 31) defines "hypermasculinity" as exaggerated, extreme masculine behavior.

21. Interview with Jack on 23 April 1993.

22. Interview with Klaus on 13 March 1993.

23. Interview with Larry on 16 July 1993.

24. Interview with Thomas on 28 August 1993.

25. Versatility is defined as "the faculty or character of turning or being able to turn readily to a new subject or occupation," or "many-sidedness." In *The Compact Edition of the Oxford English Dictionary* 1971, Oxford University Press.

26. Interview with Hank on 31 July 1993.

27. Interview with Eduardo on 14 May 1993.

References

Almaguer, Tomas. 1991. "Chicano Men: A Cartography of Homosexual Identity and Behavior." *Differences* 3(2).

Bernard, Jessie. 1995. "The Good-Provider Role." In Michael S. Kimmel and Michael A. Messner, eds., *Men's Lives*. New York: Macmillan.

Bettelheim, Bruno. 1960. *The Informed Heart: Autonomy in a Mass Age*. New York: The Free Press.

Butler, Judith. 1990. *Gender Trouble: Feminism and the Subversion of Identity*. New York: Routledge & Kegan Paul.

Connell, R. W. 1987. *Gender and Power*. Stanford, CA: Stanford University Press.

Duberman, Martin. 1993. "A Matter of Difference." *Nation*, 5 July.

Edwards, Tim. 1990. "Beyond Sex and Gender: Masculinity, Homosexuality and Social Theory." In Jeff Hearn and David Morgan, eds., *Men, Masculinities, and Social Theory*. London: Unwin Hyman.

Gershick, Thomas J., and Adam S. Miller. 1994. "Coming to Terms: Masculinity and Physical Disability." In M. Kimmel and M. Messner, eds., *Men's Lives*, 3rd edition. Boston: Allyn & Bacon.

Goffman, Erving. 1963. *Stigma: Notes on the Management of Spoiled Identity*. New York: Touchstone.

hooks, bell. 1990. "Feminism: A Transformational Politic." In Deborah L. Rhode, ed., *Theoretical Perspectives on Sexual Difference*. New Haven: Yale University Press.

Koenig, Karen. 1993. "Transgenders Unite to Fight for Justice and Recognition." *Tenderloin Times*, August.

Maitland, Zane. 1993. "Tenderloin Hotel Has a Rooftop Garden." *San Francisco Chronicle*, 23 July.

Majors, Richard, and Janet Mancini Billson. 1992. *Cool Pose: The Dilemmas of Black Manhood in America*. New York: Lexington Books.

Messner, Michael A. 1993. " 'Changing Men' and Feminist Politics in the United States." *Theory and Society*, August/September.

Niebuhr, H. Richard. 1970. *Radical Monotheism and Western Culture*. New York: Harper Torchbooks.

North of Market Planning Coalition (NOPC). 1992. *Final Report: Tenderloin 2000 Survey and Plan*. San Francisco: NOPC.

Pleck, Joseph H. 1987. "The Theory of Male Sex-Role Identity: Its Rise and Fall, 1936 to the Present." In Harry Brod, ed., *The Making of Masculinities: The New Men's Studies*. New York: Routledge & Kegan Paul.

Sennett, Richard, and Jonathan Cobb. 1972. *The Hidden Injuries of Class*. New York: Vintage Books.

Tong, Ben. 1971. "The Ghetto of the Mind: Notes on the Historical Psychology of Chinese America." *Amerasia Journal*, 1(3). November.

Wilson, William Julius. 1987. *The Truly Disadvantaged: The Inner City, the Underclass, and Public Policy*. Chicago: University of Chicago Press.

A R T I C L E   2 2

Patti A. Giuffre
Christine L. Williams

Boundary Lines: Labeling Sexual Harassment in Restaurants

Sexual harassment occurs when submission to or rejection of sexual advances is a term of employment, is used as a basis for making employment decisions, or if the advances create a hostile or offensive work environment (Konrad and Gutek 1986). Sexual harassment can cover a range of behaviors, from leering to rape (Ellis, Barak, and Pinto 1991; Pryor 1987; Reilly et al. 1992; Schneider 1982). Researchers estimate that as many as 70 percent of employed women have experienced behaviors that may legally constitute sexual harassment (MacKinnon 1979; Powell 1986); however, a far lower percentage of women claim to have experienced sexual harassment. Paludi and Barickman write that "the great majority of women who are abused by behavior that fits legal definitions of sexual harassment—and who are traumatized by the experience—do not label what has happened to them 'sexual harassment' " (1992, 68).

Why do most women fail to label their experiences as sexual harassment? Part of the problem is that many still do not recognize that sexual harassment is an actionable offense. Sexual harassment was first described in 1976 (MacKinnon 1979), but it was not until 1986 that the U.S. Supreme Court included sexual harassment in the category of gender discrimination, thereby making it illegal (Paludi and Barickman 1991);

Patti A. Giuffre and Christine L. Williams, *Gender & Society*, Vol 8, pp. 378–401, copyright © 1994. Reprinted with permission of Sage Publications, Inc.

consequently, women may not yet identify their experiences as sexual harassment because a substantial degree of awareness about its illegality has yet to be developed.

Many victims of sexual harassment may also be reluctant to come forward with complaints, fearing that they will not be believed, or that their charges will not be taken seriously (Jensen and Gutek (1982). As the Anita Hill–Clarence Thomas hearings demonstrated, women who are victims of sexual harassment often become the accused when they bring charges against their assailant.

There is another issue at stake in explaining the gap between experiencing and labeling behaviors "sexual harassment": many men and women experience some sexual behaviors in the workplace as pleasurable. Research on sexual harassment suggests that men are more likely than women to enjoy sexual interactions at work (Gutek 1985; Konrad and Gutek 1986; Reilly et al. 1992), but even some women experience sexual overtures at work as pleasurable (Pringle 1988). This attitude may be especially strong in organizations that use and exploit the bodies and sexuality of the workers (Cockburn 1991). Workers in many jobs are hired on the basis of their attractiveness and solicitousness—including not only sex industry workers, but also service sector workers such as receptionists, airline attendants, and servers in trendy restaurants. According to Cockburn (1991), this sexual exploitation is not completely forced: many people find this dimension of their jobs appealing and reinforcing to their own sense of identity and pleasure; consequently, some men and women resist efforts to expunge all sexuality from their places of work.

This is not to claim that all sexual behavior in the workplace is acceptable, even to some people. The point is that it is difficult to label behavior as sexual harassment because it forces people to draw a line between illicit and "legitimate" forms of sexuality at work—a process fraught with ambiguity. Whether a particular interaction is identified as harassment will depend on the intention of the harasser and the interpretation of the interchange by the victim, and both of these perspectives will be highly influenced by workplace culture and the social context of the specific event.

This article examines how one group of employees—restaurant workers—distinguishes between sexual harassment and other forms of sexual interaction in the workplace. We conducted an in-depth interview study of waitpeople and found that complex double standards are often used in labeling behavior as sexual harassment: identical behaviors are labeled sexual harassment in some contexts and not others. Many respondents claimed that they *enjoyed* sexual interactions involving co-workers of the same race/ethnicity, sexual orientation, and class/status backgrounds. Those who were offended by such interactions nevertheless dismissed them as natural or inevitable parts of restaurant culture.[1] When the same behavior occurred in contexts that upset these hegemonic heterosexual norms—in particular, when the episode involved interactions between gay and heterosexual men, or men and women of different racial/ethnic backgrounds—people seemed willing to apply the label sexual harassment.

We argue that identifying behaviors that occur only in counterhegemonic contexts as sexual harassment can potentially obscure and legitimate more insidious forms of domination and exploitation. As Pringle points out, "Men control women through direct use of power, but also through definitions of pleasure—which is less likely to provoke resistance" (1988, 95). Most

women, she writes, actively seek out what Rich (1980) termed "compulsory heterosexuality" and find pleasure in it. The fact that men and women may enjoy certain sexual interactions in the workplace does not mean they take place outside of oppressive social relationships, nor does it imply that these routine interactions have no negative consequences for women. We argue that the practice of labeling as "sexual harassment" only those behaviors that challenge the dominant definition of acceptable sexual activity maintains and supports men's institutionalized right of sexual access and power over women.

Methods

The occupation of waiting tables was selected to study the social definition of sexual harassment because many restaurants have a blatantly sexualized workplace culture (Cobble 1991; Paules 1991). According to a report published in a magazine that caters to restaurant owners, "Restaurants . . . are about as informal a workplace as there is, so much so as to actually encourage—or at the very least tolerate—sexual banter" (Anders 1993, 48). Unremitting sexual banter and innuendo, as well as physical jostling, create an environment of "compulsory jocularity" in many restaurants (Pringle 1988, 93). Sexual attractiveness and flirtation are often institutionalized parts of a waitperson's job description; consequently, individual employees are often forced to draw the line for themselves to distinguish legitimate and illegitimate expressions of sexuality, making this occupation an excellent context for examining how people determine what constitutes sexual harassment. In contrast, many more sexual behaviors may be labeled sexual harassment in less highly sexualized work environments.[2]

Eighteen in-depth interviews were conducted with male and female wait staff who work in restaurants in Austin, Texas. Respondents were selected from restaurants that employ equal proportions of men and women on their wait staffs. Overall, restaurant work is highly sex segregated:

women make up about 82 percent of all waitpeople (U.S. Department of Labor 1989), and it is common for restaurants to be staffed only by either waitresses or waiters, with men predominating in the higher-priced restaurants (Cobble 1991; Hall 1993; Paules 1991). We decided to focus only on waitpeople who work in mixed-sex groups for two reasons. First, focusing on waitpeople working on integrated staffs enables us to examine sexual harassment between co-workers who occupy the same position in an organizational hierarchy. Co-worker sexual harassment is perhaps the most common form of sexual harassment (Pryor 1987; Schneider 1982); yet most case studies of sexual harassment have examined either unequal hierarchical relationships (e.g., boss–secretary harassment) or harassment in highly skewed gender groupings (e.g., women who work in nontraditional occupations) (Benson and Thomson 1982; Carothers and Crull 1984; Gruber and Bjorn 1982). This study is designed to investigate sexual harassment in unequal hierarchical relationships, as well as harassment between organizationally equal co-workers.

Second, equal proportions of men and women in an occupation implies a high degree of male–female interaction (Gutek 1985). Waitpeople are in constant contact with each other, help each other when the restaurant is busy, and informally socialize during slack periods. In contrast, men and women have much more limited interactions in highly sex-segregated restaurants and indeed, in most work environments. The high degree of interaction among the wait staff provides ample opportunity for sexual harassment between men and women to occur and, concomitantly, less opportunity for same-sex sexual harassment to occur.

The sample was generated using "snowball" techniques and by going to area restaurants and asking waitpeople to volunteer for the study. The sample includes eight men and ten women. Four respondents are Latina/o, two African American, and twelve white. Four respondents are gay or lesbian; one is bisexual; thirteen are heterosexual. (The gay men and lesbians in the sample are

all "out" at their respective restaurants.) Fourteen respondents are single; three are married; one is divorced. Respondents' ages range from 22 to 37.

Interviews lasted approximately one hour, and they were tape-recorded and transcribed for this analysis. All interviews were conducted by the first author, who has over eight years' experience waiting tables. Respondents were asked about their experiences working in restaurants; relationships with managers, customers, and other co-workers; and their personal experiences of sexual harassment. Because interviews were conducted in the fall of 1991, when the issue was prominent in the media because of the Hill–Thomas hearings, most respondents had thought a lot about this topic.

Findings

Respondents agreed that sexual banter is very common in the restaurant: staff members talk and joke about sex constantly. With only one exception, respondents described their restaurants as highly sexualized. This means that 17 of the 18 respondents said that sexual joking, touching, and fondling were common, everyday occurrences in their restaurants. For example, when asked if he or other waitpeople ever joke about sex, one waiter replied, "about 90 percent of [the jokes] are about sex." According to a waitress, "at work . . . [we're] used to patting and touching and hugging." Another waiter said, "I do not go through a shift without someone . . . pinching my nipples or poking me in the butt or grabbing my crotch. . . . It's just what we do at work."

These informal behaviors are tantamount to "doing heterosexuality," a process analogous to "doing gender" (West and Zimmerman 1987).[3] By engaging in these public flirtations and open discussions of sex, men and women reproduce the dominant cultural norms of heterosexuality and lend an air of legitimacy—if not inevitability—to heterosexual relationships. In other words, heterosexuality is normalized and naturalized through its ritualistic public display. Indeed, although most respondents described their workplace as highly sexualized, several dismissed the constant sexual innuendo and behaviors as "just joking," and nothing to get upset about. Several respondents claimed that this is simply "the way it is in the restaurant business," or "just the way men are."

With only one exception, the men and women interviewed maintained that they enjoyed this aspect of their work. Heterosexuality may be normative, and in these contexts, even compulsory, yet many men and women find pleasure in its expression. Many women—as well as men— actively reproduce hegemonic sexuality and apparently enjoy its ritual expression; however, in a few instances, sexual conduct was labeled as sexual harassment. Seven women and three men said they had experienced sexual harassment in restaurant work. Of these, two women and one man described two different experiences of sexual harassment, and two women described three experiences. Table 22.1 describes the characteristics of each of the respondents and their experiences of sexual harassment.

We analyzed these 17 accounts of sexual harassment to find out what, if anything, these experiences shared in common. With the exception of two episodes (discussed later), the experiences that were labeled "sexual harassment" were not distinguished by any specific words or behaviors, nor were they distinguished by their degree of severity. Identical behaviors were considered acceptable if they were perpetrated by some people, but considered offensive if perpetrated by others. In other words, sexual behavior in the workplace was interpreted differently depending on the context of the interaction. In general, respondents labeled their experiences sexual harassment only if the offending behavior occurred in one of three social contexts: (1) if perpetrated by someone in a more powerful position, such as a manager; (2) if perpetrated by someone of a different race/ethnicity; or (3) if perpetrated by someone of a different sexual orientation.

Our findings do not imply that sexual harassment did not occur outside of these three contexts. Instead, they simply indicate that our respondents *labeled* behavior as "sexual harassment" when it occurred in these particular social contexts. We will discuss each of these contexts and speculate on the reasons why they were singled out by our respondents.

Powerful Position

In the restaurant, managers and owners are the highest in the hierarchy of workers. Generally, they are the only ones who can hire or fire waitpeople. Three of the women and one of the men interviewed said they had been sexually harassed by their restaurants' managers or owners. In addition, several others who did not personally experience harassment said they had witnessed managers or owners sexually harassing other waitpeople. This finding is consistent with other research indicating people are more likely to think that sexual harassment has occurred when the perpetrator is in a more powerful position (e.g., Ellis et al. 1991).

Carla describes being sexually harassed by her manager:

> One evening, [my manager] grabbed my body, not in a private place, just grabbed my body, period. He gave me like a bear hug from behind a total of four times in one night. By the end of the night I was livid. I was trying to avoid him. Then when he'd do it, I'd just ignore the conversation or the joke or whatever and walk away.

She claimed that her co-workers often give each other massages and joke about sex, but she did not label any of their behaviors sexual harassment. In fact, all four individuals who experienced sexual harassment from their managers described very similar types of behavior from their co-workers, which they did not define as sexual harassment. For example, Cathy said that she and the other waitpeople talk and joke about sex constantly: "Everybody stands around and talks about sex a lot. . . . Isn't that weird? You know, it's something about working in restaurants and, yeah, so we'll all sit around and talk about sex." She said that talking with her co-worker about sex does not constitute sexual harassment because

■ **TABLE 22.1**

Description of Respondents and Their Reported Experiences
of Sexual Harassment at Work

Pseudonym	Age	Race[a]	SO[b]	MS[c]	Years in Restaurant[d]	Sexualized Environment[e]	Sexually Harassed[f]
Kate	23	W	H	S	1	yes	yes (1)
Beth	26	W	H	S	5	yes	yes (1)
Ann	29	W	H	S	1*	yes	yes (2)
Cathy	29	W	H	S	8 mos.*	yes	yes (3)
Carla	22	W	H	M	5 mos.*	yes	yes (3)
Diana	32	L	H	M	6	no	no
Maxine	30	L	H	M	4	yes	no
Laura	27	W	B	S	2*	yes	yes (1)
Brenda	23	W	L	S	3	yes	yes (2)
Lynn	37	B	L	D	5*	yes	no
Jake	22	W	H	S	1	yes	yes (1)
Al	23	W	H	S	3	yes	no
Frank	29	W	H	S	8	yes	yes (1)
John	31	W	H	S	2	yes	no
Trent	23	W	G	S	1*	yes	no
Rick	24	B	H	S	1.5	yes	yes (2)
David	25	L	H	S	5	yes	no
Don	24	L	G	S	1*	yes	no

a. Race: B = Black, L = Latina/o, W = White.

b. SO = sexual orientation: B = bisexual, G = gay, H = heterosexual, L = lesbian.

c. MS = marital status: D = divorced, M = married, S = single.

d. Years in restaurant refers to length of time employed in current restaurant. An asterisk indicates that respondent has worked in other restaurants.

e. Whether or not the respondent claimed sexual banter and touching were common occurrences in their restaurant.

f. Responded yes or no to the question: "Have you ever been sexually harassed in the restaurant?" Number in parentheses refers to number of incidents described in the interview.

it is "only joking." She does, however, view her male manager as a sexual harasser:

> My employer is very sexist. I would call that sexual harassment. Very much of a male chauvinist pig. He kind of started [saying] stuff like, "You can't really wear those shorts because they're not flattering to your figure. . . . But I like the way you wear those jeans. They look real good. They're tight." It's like, you know [I want to say to him], "You're the owner, you're in power. That's evident. You know, you need to find a better way to tell me these things." We've gotten to a point now where we'll joke around now, but it's never ever sexual, ever. I won't allow that with him.

Cathy acknowledges that her manager may legitimately dictate her appearance at work, but only if he does so in professional—and not personal—

terms. She wants him "to find a better way to tell me these things," implying that he is not completely out of line in suggesting that she wear tight pants. He "crosses the line" when he personalizes his directive, by saying to Cathy "*I like* the way you wear those jeans." This is offensive to Cathy because it is framed as the manager's personal prerogative, not the institutional requirements of the job.

Ann described a similar experience of sexual harassment from a restaurant owner:

> Yeah, there's been a couple of times when a manager has made me feel real uncomfortable and I just removed myself from the situation. . . . Like if there's something I really want him to hear or something I think is really important there's no touching. Like, "Don't touch me while I'm talking to you." You know, because I take that as very patronizing. I actually blew up at one of the owners once because I was having a rough day and he came up behind me and he was rubbing my back, like up and down my back and saying, you know, "Oh, is Ann having a bad day?" or something like that and I shook him off of me and I said, "You do not need to touch me to talk to me."

Ann distinguishes between legitimate and illegitimate touching: If the issue being discussed is "really important"—that is, involving her job status—she insists there be no touching. In these specific situations, a back rub is interpreted as patronizing and offensive because the manager is using his powerful position for his *personal* sexual enjoyment.

One of the men in the sample, Frank, also experienced sexual harassment from a manager.

> I was in the bathroom and [the manager] came up next to me and my tennis shoes were spray-painted silver so he knew it was me in there and he said something about, "Oh, what do you have in your hand there?" I was on the other side of a wall and he said, "Mind if I hold it for a while?" or something like that, you know. I just pretended like I didn't hear it.

Frank also described various sexual behaviors among the wait staff, including fondling, "joking about bodily functions," and "making bikinis out of tortillas." He said, "I mean, it's like, what we do at work. . . . There's no holds barred. I don't find it offensive. I'm used to it by now. I'm guilty of it myself." Evidently, he defines sexual behaviors as "sexual harassment" only when perpetrated by someone in a position of power over him.[4]

Two of the women in the sample also described sexual harassment from customers. We place these experiences in the category of "powerful position" because customers do have limited economic power over the waitperson insofar as they control the tip (Crull 1987). Cathy said that male customers often ask her to "sit on my lap" and provide them with other sexual favors. Brenda, a lesbian, described a similar experience of sexual harassment from women customers:

> One time I had this table of lesbians and they were being real vulgar towards me. Real sexual. This woman kind of tripped me as I was walking by and said, "Hurry back." I mean, gay people can tell when other people are gay. I felt harassed.

In these examples of harassment by customers, the line is drawn using a similar logic as in the examples of harassment by managers. These customers acted as though the waitresses were providing table service to satisfy the customers' private desires, instead of working to fulfill their job descriptions. In other words, the customers' demands were couched in personal—and not professional—terms, making the waitresses feel sexually harassed.

It is not difficult to understand why waitpeople singled out sexual behaviors from managers, owners, and customers as sexual harassment. Subjection to sexual advances by someone with economic power comes closest to the quid pro quo form of sexual harassment, wherein employees are given the option to either "put out or get out." Studies have found that this type of sexual harassment is viewed as the most threatening and unambiguous sort (Ellis et al. 1991; Fitzgerald 1990; Gruber and Bjorn 1982).

But even in this context, lines are drawn between legitimate and illegitimate sexual behavior in the workplace. As Cathy's comments make clear, some people accept the employers' prerogative to exploit the workers' sexuality, by dictating appropriate "sexy" dress, for example. Like airline attendants, waitresses are expected to be friendly, helpful, and sexually available to the male customers (Cobble 1991). Because this expectation is embedded in restaurant culture, it becomes difficult for workers to separate sexual harassment from the more or less accepted forms of sexual exploitation that are routine features of their jobs. Consequently, some women are reluctant to label blatantly offensive behaviors as sexual harassment. For example, Maxine, who claims that she has never experienced sexual harassment, said that customers often "talk dirty" to her:

> I remember one day, about four or five years ago when I was working as a cocktail waitress, this guy asked me for a "Slow Comfortable Screw" [the name of a drink]. I didn't know what it was. I didn't know if he was making a move or something. I just looked at him. He said, "You know what it is, right?" I said, "I bet the bartender knows!" (laughs). . . . There's another one, "Sex on the Beach." And there's another one called a "Screaming Orgasm." Do you believe that?

Maxine is subject to a sexualized work environment that she finds offensive; hence her experience could fit the legal definition of sexual harassment. But because sexy drink names are an institutionalized part of restaurant culture, Maxine neither complains about it nor labels it sexual harassment: Once it becomes clear that a "Slow Comfortable Screw" is a legitimate and recognized restaurant demand, she accepts it (albeit reluctantly) as part of her job description. In other words, the fact that the offensive behavior is institutionalized seems to make it beyond reproach in her eyes. This finding is consistent with others' findings that those who work in highly sexualized environments may be less likely to label offensive

behavior "sexual harassment" (Gutek 1985; Konrad and Gutek 1986).

Only in specific contexts do workers appear to define offensive words and acts of a sexual nature as sexual harassment—even when initiated by someone in a more powerful position. The interviews suggest that workers use this label to describe their experiences only when their bosses or their customers couch their requests for sexual attentions in explicitly personal terms. This way of defining sexual harassment may obscure and legitimize more institutionalized—and hence more insidious—forms of sexual exploitation at work.

Race/Ethnicity

The restaurants in our sample, like most restaurants in the United States, have racially segregated staffs (Howe 1977). In the restaurants where our respondents are employed, men of color are concentrated in two positions: the kitchen cooks and bus personnel (formerly called busboys). Five of the white women in the sample reported experiencing sexual harassment from Latino men who worked in these positions. For example, when asked if she had ever experienced sexual harassment, Beth said:

> Yes, but it was not with the people . . . it was not, you know, the people that I work with in the front of the house. It was with the kitchen. There are boundaries or lines that I draw with the people I work with. In the kitchen, the lines are quite different. Plus, it's a Mexican staff. It's a very different attitude. They tend to want to touch you more and, at times, I can put up with a little bit of it but . . . because I will give them a hard time too but I won't touch them. I won't touch their butt or anything like that.
>
> [Interviewer: So sometimes they cross the line?]
>
> It's only happened to me a couple of times. One guy, like, patted me on the butt and I went off. I lost my shit. I went off on him. I said, "No. Bad. Wrong. I can't speak Spanish to you but, you know, this is it." I told the kitchen manager who is a guy and he's not . . . the head kitchen manager is not Hispanic. . . . I've had to do that over the years only a couple of times with those guys.

Beth reported that the waitpeople joke about sex and touch each other constantly, but she does not consider their behavior sexual harassment. Like many of the other men and women in the sample, Beth said she feels comfortable engaging in this sexual banter and play with the other waitpeople (who were predominantly white), but not with the Mexican men in the kitchen.

Part of the reason for singling out the behaviors of the cooks as sexual harassment may involve status differences between waitpeople and cooks. Studies have suggested that people may label behaviors as sexual harassment when they are perpetrated by people in lower status organizational positions (Grauerholz 1989; McKinney 1990); however, it is difficult to generalize about the relative status of cooks and waitpeople because of the varied and often complex organizational hierarchies of restaurants (Paules 1991, 107–10). If the cook is a chef, as in higher-priced restaurants, he or she may actually have more status than waitpeople, and indeed may have the formal power to hire and fire the waitstaff. In the restaurants where our respondents worked, the kitchen cooks did not wield this sort of formal control, but they could exert some informal power over the wait staff by slowing down food orders or making the orders look and/or taste bad. Because bad food can decrease the waitperson's tip, the cooks can thereby control the waitperson's income; hence servers are forced to negotiate and to some extent placate the wishes and desires of cooks to perform their jobs. The willingness of several respondents to label the cooks' behavior as sexual harassment may reflect their perception that the cooks' informal demands had become unreasonable. In such cases, subjection to the offensive behaviors is a term of employment, which is quid pro quo sexual harassment. As mentioned previously, this type of sexual harassment is the most likely to be so labeled and identified.

Because each recounted case of sexual harassment occurring between individuals of different occupational statuses involved a minority man sexually harassing a white woman, the racial context seems equally important. For example, Ann also said that she and the other waiters and waitresses joke about sex and touch each other "on the butt" all the time, and when asked if she had ever experienced sexual harassment, she said,

> I had some problems at [a previous restaurant] but it was a communication problem. A lot of the guys in the kitchen did not speak English. They would see the waiters hugging on us, kissing us and pinching our rears and stuff. They would try to do it and I couldn't tell them, "No. You don't understand this. It's like we do it because we have a mutual understanding but I'm not comfortable with you doing it." So that was really hard and a lot of times what I'd have to do is just sucker punch them in the chest and just use a lot of cuss words and they knew that I was serious. And there again, I felt real weird about that because they're just doing what they see go on everyday.

Kate, Carla, and Brenda described very similar racial double standards. Kate complained about a Mexican busser who constantly touched her:

> This is not somebody that I talk to on a friendly basis. We don't sit there and laugh and joke and stuff. So, when he touches me, all I know is he is just touching me and there is no context about it. With other people, if they said something or they touched me, it would be funny or . . . we have a relationship. This person and I and all the other people do not. So that is sexual harassment.

And according to Brenda:

> The kitchen can be kind of sexist. They really make me angry. They're not as bad as they used to be because they got warned. They're mostly Mexican, not even Mexican-American. Most of them, they're just starting to learn English.
> [Interviewer: What do they do to you?]
> Well, I speak Spanish, so I know. They're not as sexual to me because I think they know I don't like it. Some of the other girls will come through and they will touch them like here [points to the lower part of her waist]. . . . I've had some pretty bad arguments with the kitchen.

[Interviewer: Would you call that sexual harassment?]

Yes. I think some of the girls just don't know better to say something. I think it happens a lot with the kitchen guys. Like sometimes, they will take a relleno in their hands like it's a penis. Sick!

Each of these women identified the sexual advances of the minority men in their restaurants as sexual harassment, but not the identical behaviors of their white male co-workers; moreover, they all recognize that they draw boundary lines differently for Anglo men and Mexican men: each of them willingly participates in "doing heterosexuality" only in racially homogamous contexts. These women called the behavior of the Mexican cooks "sexual harassment" in part because they did not "have a relationship" with these men, nor was it conceivable to them that they *could* have a relationship with them, given cultural and language barriers—and, probably, racist attitudes as well. The white men, on the other hand, can "hug, kiss, and pinch rears" of the white women because they have a "mutual understanding"—implying reciprocity and the possibility of intimacy.

The importance of this perception of relationship potential in the assessment of sexual harassment is especially clear in the cases of the two married women in the sample, Diana and Maxine. Both of these women said that they had never experienced sexual harassment. Diana, who works in a family-owned and -operated restaurant, claimed that her restaurant is not a sexualized work environment. Although people occasionally make double entendre jokes relating to sex, according to Diana, "there's no contact whatsoever like someone pinching your butt or something." She said that she has never experienced sexual harassment:

Everybody here knows I'm married so they're not going to get fresh with me because they know that it's not going to go anywhere, you know so . . . and vice versa. You know, we know the guys' wives. They come in here to eat. It's respect all the way. I don't think they could

handle it if they saw us going around hugging them. You know what I mean? It's not right.

Similarly, Maxine, who is Colombian, said she avoids the problem of sexual harassment in her workplace because she is married:

The cooks don't offend me because they know I speak Spanish and they know how to talk with me because I set my boundaries and they know that. . . . I just don't joke with them more than I should. They all know that I'm married, first of all, so that's a no-no for all of them. My brother used to be a manager in that restaurant so he probably took care of everything. I never had any problems anyway in any other jobs because, like I said, I set my boundaries. I don't let them get too close to me.

[Interviewer: You mean physically?]

Not physically only. Just talking. If they want to talk about, "Do you go dancing? Where do you go dancing?" Like I just change the subject because it's none of their business and I don't really care to talk about that with them . . . not because I consider them to be on the lower levels than me or something but just because if you start talking with them that way then you are just giving them hope or something. I think that's true for most of the guys here, not just talking about the cooks. . . . I do get offended and they know that so sometimes they apologize.

Both Maxine and Diana said that they are protected from sexual harassment because they are married. In effect, they use their marital status to negotiate their interactions with their co-workers and to ward off unwanted sexual advances. Furthermore, because they do not view their co-workers as potential relationship "interests," they conscientiously refuse to participate in any sexual banter in the restaurant.

The fact that both women speak Spanish fluently may mean that they can communicate their boundaries unambiguously to those who only speak Spanish (unlike the female respondents in the sample who only speak English). For these two women, sexual harassment from co-workers is not an issue. Diana, who is Latina, talks about "respect all around" in her restaurant; Maxine claims the cooks (who are Mexican) aren't the ones who offend her. Their comments seem to reflect more mutual respect and humanity toward their Latino co-workers than the comments of the white waitresses. On the other hand, at least from Maxine's vantage point, racial harassment is a bigger problem in her workplace than is sexual harassment. When asked if she ever felt excluded from any groups at work, she said:

> Yeah, sometimes. How can I explain this? Sometimes, I mean, I don't know if they do it on purpose or they don't but they joke around you about being Spanish. . . . Sometimes it hurts. Like they say, "What are you doing here? Why don't you go back home?"

Racial harassment—like sexual harassment—is a means used by a dominant group to maintain its dominance over a subordinated group. Maxine feels that, because she is married, she is protected from sexual harassment (although, as we have seen, she is subject to a sexualized workplace that is offensive to her); however, she does experience racial harassment where she works, and she feels vulnerable to this because she is one of very few nonwhites working at her restaurant.

One of the waiters in the sample claimed that he had experienced sexual harassment from female co-workers, and race may have also been a factor in this situation. When Rick (who is African American) was asked if he had ever been sexually harassed, he recounted his experiences with some white waitresses:

> Yes. There are a couple of girls there, waitpeople, who will pinch my rear.
>
> [Interviewer: Do you find it offensive?]
>
> No (laughs) because I'm male. . . . But it is a form of sexual harassment.
>
> [Interviewer: Do you ever tell them to stop?]
>
> If I'm really busy, if I'm in the weeds, and they want to touch me, I'll get mad. I'll tell them to stop. There's a certain time and place for everything.

Rick is reluctant about labeling this interaction "sexual harassment" because "it doesn't bother me unless I'm, like, busy or something like that." In those cases where he is busy, he feels that his female co-workers are subverting his work by pinching him. Because of the race difference, he may experience their behaviors as an expression of racial dominance, which probably influences his willingness to label the behavior as sexual harassment.

In sum, the interviews suggest that the perception and labeling of interactions as "sexual harassment" may be influenced by the racial context of the interaction. If the victim perceives the harasser as expressing a potentially reciprocal relationship interest, they may be less likely to label their experience sexual harassment. In cases where the harasser and victim have a different race/ethnicity and class background, the possibility of a relationship may be precluded because of racism, making these cases more likely to be labeled "sexual harassment."

This finding suggests that the practices associated with "doing heterosexuality" are profoundly racist. The white women in the sample showed a great reluctance to label unwanted sexual behavior sexual harassment when it was perpetrated by a potential (or real) relationship interest—that is, a white male co-worker. In contrast, minority men are socially constructed as potential harassers of white women: any expression of sexual interest may be more readily perceived as nonreciprocal and unwanted. The assumption of racial homogamy in heterosexual relationships thus may protect white men from charges of sexual harassment of white women. This would help to explain why so many white women in the sample labeled behaviors perpetrated by Mexican men as sexual harassment, but not the identical behaviors perpetrated by white men.

Sexual Orientation

There has been very little research on sexual harassment that addresses the sexual orientation of the harasser and victim (exceptions include Reilly et al. 1992; Schneider 1982, 1984). Surveys of sexual harassment typically include questions about marital status but not about sexual orientation (e.g., Fain and Anderton 1987; Gruber and Bjorn 1982; Powell 1986). In this study, sexual orientation was an important part of heterosexual men's perceptions of sexual harassment. Of the four episodes of sexual harassment reported by the men in the study, three involved openly gay men sexually harassing straight men. One case involved a male manager harassing a male waiter (Frank's experience, described earlier). The other two cases involved co-workers. Jake said that he had been sexually harassed by a waiter:

> Someone has come on to me that I didn't want to come on to me. . . . He was another waiter [male]. It was laughs and jokes the whole way until things got a little too much and it was like, "Hey, this is how it is. Back off. Keep your hands off my ass." . . . Once it reached the point where I felt kind of threatened and bothered by it.

Rick described being sexually harassed by a gay baker in his restaurant:

> There was a baker that we had who was really, really gay. . . . He was very straightforward and blunt. He would tell you, in detail, his sexual experiences and tell you that he wanted to do them with you. . . . I knew he was kidding but he was serious. I mean, if he had a chance he would do these things.

In each of these cases, the men expressed some confusion about the intentions of their harassers— "I knew he was kidding but he was serious." Their inability to read the intentions of the gay men provoked them to label these episodes sexual harassment. Each man did not perceive the sexual interchange as reciprocal, nor did he view the harasser as a potential relationship interest. Interestingly, however, all three of the men who described harassment from gay men claimed that sexual banter and play with other *straight* men did not trouble them. Jake, for example, said that "when men get together, they talk sex," regardless of whether there are women around. He acceded, "people find me offensive, as a matter of fact," because he gets "pretty raunchy" talking and

joking about sex. Only when this talk was initiated by a gay man did Jake label it as sexual harassment.

Johnson (1988) argues that talking and joking about sex is a common means of establishing intimacy among heterosexual men and maintaining a masculine identity. Homosexuality is perceived as a direct challenge and threat to the achievement of masculinity and consequently, "the male homosexual is derided by other males because he is not a real man, and in male logic if one is not a real man, one is a woman" (p. 124). In Johnson's view, this dynamic not only sustains masculine identity, it also shores up male dominance over women; thus, for some straight men, talking about sex with other straight men is a form of reasserting masculinity and male dominance, whereas talking about sex with gay men threatens the very basis for their masculine privilege. For this reason they may interpret the sex talk and conduct of gay men as a form of sexual harassment.

In certain restaurants, gay men may in fact intentionally hassle straight men as an explicit strategy to undermine their privileged position in society. For example, Trent (who is openly gay) realizes that heterosexual men are uncomfortable with his sexuality, and he intentionally draws attention to his sexuality in order to bother them:

> [Interviewer: Homosexuality gets on whose nerves?]
>
> The straight people's nerves. . . . I know also that we consciously push it just because, we know, "Okay. We know this is hard for you to get used to but tough luck. I've had my whole life trying to live in this straight world and if you don't like this, tough shit." I don't mean like we're shitty to them on purpose but it's like, "I've had to worry about being accepted by straight people all my life. The shoe's on the other foot now. If you don't like it, sorry."
>
> [Interviewer: Do you get along well with most of the waitpeople?]
>
> I think I get along with straight women. I get along with gay men. I get along with gay women usually. If there's ever going to be a

problem between me and somebody it will be between me and a straight man.

Trent's efforts to "push" his sexuality could easily be experienced as sexual harassment by straight men who have limited experience negotiating unwanted sexual advances. The three men who reported being sexually harassed by gay men seemed genuinely confused about the intentions of their harassers, and threatened by the possibility that they would actually be subjected to and harmed by unwanted sexual advances. But it is important to point out that Trent works in a restaurant owned by lesbians, which empowers him to confront his straight male co-workers. Not all restaurants provide the sort of atmosphere that makes this type of engagement possible; indeed, some restaurants have policies explicitly banning the hiring of gays and lesbians. Clearly, not all gay men would be able to push their sexuality without suffering severe retaliation (e.g., loss of job, physical attacks).

In contrast to the reports of the straight men in this study, none of the women interviewed reported sexual harassment from their gay or lesbian co-workers. Although Maxine was worried when she found out that one of her co-workers was lesbian, she claims that this fact no longer troubles her:

Six months ago I found out that there was a lesbian girl working there. It kind of freaked me out for a while. I was kind of aware of everything that she did towards me. I was conscious if she walked by me and accidently brushed up against me. She's cool. She doesn't bother me. She never touches my butt or anything like that. The gay guys do that to the [straight] guys but they know they're just kidding around. The [straight] guys do that to the [straight] girls, but they don't care. They know that they're not supposed to do that with me. If they do it, I stop and look at them and they apologize and they don't do it anymore. So they stay out of my way because I'm a meanie (laughs).

Some heterosexual women claimed they feel *more* comfortable working with gay men and lesbians. For example, Kate prefers working with

gay men rather than heterosexual men or women. She claims that she often jokes about sex with her gay co-workers, yet she does not view them as potential harassers. Instead, she feels that her working conditions are more comfortable and more fun because she works with gay men. Similarly, Cathy prefers working with gay men over straight men because "gay men are a lot like women in that they're very sensitive to other people's space." Cathy also works with lesbians, and she claims that she has never felt sexually harassed by them.

The gays and lesbians in the study did not report any sexual harassment from their gay and lesbian co-workers. Laura, who is bisexual, said she preferred to work with gays and lesbians instead of heterosexuals because they are "more relaxed" about sex. Brenda said she feels comfortable working around all of her male and female colleagues—regardless of their sexual orientation:

The guys I work with [don't threaten me]. We always run by each other and pat each other on the butt. It's no big deal. Like with my girlfriend [who works at the same restaurant], all the cocktailers and hostesses love us. They don't care that we're gay. We're not a threat. We all kind of flirt but it's not sexual. A lesbian is not going to sexually harass another woman unless they're pretty gross anyway. It has nothing to do with their sexuality; it has to do with the person. You can't generalize and say that gays and lesbians are the best to work with or anything because it depends on the person.

Brenda enjoys flirtatious interactions with both men and women at her restaurant, but distinguishes these behaviors from sexual harassment. Likewise, Lynn, who is a lesbian, enjoys the relaxed sexual atmosphere at her workplace. When asked if she ever joked about sex in her workplace, she said:

Yes! (laughs) All the time! All the time—everybody has something that they want to talk about on sex and it's got to be funny. We have gays. We have lesbians. We have straights. We have people who are real Christian-oriented. But we all jump in there and we all talk about it. It gets real funny at times. . . . I've patted a few butts . . . and I've been patted back by men, and by the women, too! (laughs).

Don and Trent, who are both gay, also said that they had never been sexually harassed in their restaurants, even though both described their restaurants as highly sexualized.

In sum, our interviews suggest that sexual orientation is an important factor in understanding each individual's experience of sexual harassment and his or her willingness to label interactions as sexual harassment. In particular, straight men may perceive gay men as potential harassers. Three of our straight male respondents claimed to enjoy the sexual banter that commonly occurs among straight men, and between heterosexual men and women, but singled out the sexual advances of gay men as sexual harassment. Their contacts with gay men may be the only context where they feel vulnerable to unwanted sexual encounters. Their sense of not being in control of the situation may make them more willing to label these episodes sexual harassment.

Our findings about sexual orientation are less suggestive regarding women. None of the women (straight, lesbian, or bisexual) reported sexual harassment from other female co-workers or from gay men. In fact, all but one of the women's reported cases of sexual harassment involved a heterosexual man. One of the two lesbians in the sample (Brenda) did experience sexual harassment from a group of lesbian customers (described earlier), but she claimed that sexual orientation is *not* key to her defining the situation as harassment. Other studies have shown that lesbian and bisexual women are routinely subjected to sexual harassment in the workplace (Schneider 1982, 1984); however, more research is needed to elaborate the social contexts and the specific definitions of harassment among lesbians.

The Exceptions

Two cases of sexual harassment were related by respondents that do not fit in the categories we have thus far described. These were the only incidents of sexual harassment reported between co-workers of the same race: in both cases, the sexual harasser is a white man, and the victim, a white woman. Laura—who is bisexual—was sexually harassed at a previous restaurant by a cook:

This guy was just constantly badgering me about going out with him. He like grabbed me and took me in the walk-in one time. It was a real big deal. He got fired over it too. . . . I was in the back doing something and he said, "I need to talk to you," and I said, "We have nothing to talk about." He like took me and threw me against the wall in the back. . . . I ran out and told the manager, "Oh my God. He just hit me," and he saw the expression on my face. The manager went back there . . . and then he got fired.

This episode of sexual harassment involved violence, unlike the other reported cases. The threat of violence was also present in the other exception, a case described by Carla. When asked if she had ever been sexually harassed, she said,

I experienced two men, in wait jobs, that were vulgar or offensive and one was a cook and I think he was a rapist. He had the kind of attitude where he would rape a woman. I mean, that's the kind of attitude he had. He would say totally, totally inappropriate [sexual] things.

These were the only two recounted episodes of sexual harassment between "equal" co-workers that involved white men and women, and both involved violence or the threat of violence.[5]

Schneider (1982, 1991) found the greatest degree of consensus about labeling behavior sexual harassment when that behavior involves violence. A victim of sexual harassment may be more likely to be believed when there is evidence of assault (a situation that is analogous to acquaintance rape). The assumption of reciprocity among homogamous couples may protect assailants with similar characteristics to their victims (e.g., class background, sexual orientation, race/ethnicity, age)—*unless* there is clear evidence of physical abuse. Defining only those incidents that involve violence as sexual harassment obscures—and perhaps even legitimatizes—the more common occurrences that do not involve violence, making it all the more difficult to eradicate sexual harassment from the workplace.

Discussion and Conclusion

We have argued that sexual harassment is hard to identify, and thus difficult to eradicate from the workplace, in part because our hegemonic definition of sexuality defines certain contexts of sexual interaction as legitimate. The interviews with waitpeople in Austin, Texas, indicate that how people currently identify sexual harassment singles out only a narrow range of interactions, thus disguising and ignoring a good deal of sexual domination and exploitation that take place at work.

Most of the respondents in this study work in highly sexualized atmospheres where sexual banter and touching frequently occur. There are institutionalized policies and practices in the workplace that encourage—or at the very least tolerate—a continual display and performance of heterosexuality. Many people apparently accept this ritual display as being a normal or natural feature of their work; some even enjoy this behavior. In the in-depth interviews, respondents labeled such experiences as sexual harassment in only three contexts: when perpetrated by someone who took advantage of their powerful position for personal sexual gain; when the perpetrator was of a different race/ethnicity than the victim—typically a minority man harassing a white woman; and when the perpetrator was of a different sexual orientation than the victim—typically a gay man harassing a straight man. In only two cases did respondents label experiences involving co-workers of the same race and sexual orientation as sexual harassment—and both episodes involved violence or the threat of violence.

These findings are based on a very small sample in a unique working environment, and hence it is not clear whether they are generalizable to other work settings. In less sexualized working environments, individuals may be more likely to label all offensive sexual advances as sexual harassment, whereas in more highly sexualized environments (such as topless clubs or striptease bars), fewer sexual advances may be labeled sexual harassment. Our findings do suggest that researchers should pay closer attention to the interaction context of sexual harassment, taking into account not only gender but also the race, occupational status, and sexual orientation of the assailant and the victim.

Of course, it should not matter who is perpetrating the sexually harassing behavior: sexual harassment should not be tolerated under any circumstances. But if members of oppressed groups (racial/ethnic minority men and gay men) are selectively charged with sexual harassment, whereas members of the most privileged groups are exonerated and excused (except in cases where institutionalized power or violence are used), then the patriarchal order is left intact. This is very similar to the problem of rape prosecution: minority men are the most likely assailants to be arrested and prosecuted, particularly when they attack white women (LaFree 1989). Straight white men who sexually assault women (in the context of marriage, dating, or even work) may escape prosecution because of hegemonic definitions of "acceptable" or "legitimate" sexual expression. Likewise, as we have witnessed in current debate on gays in the military, straight men's fears of sexual harassment justify the exclusion of gay men and lesbians, whereas sexual harassment perpetrated by straight men against both straight and lesbian women is tolerated and even endorsed by the military establishment, as in the Tailhook investigation. By singling out these contexts for the label "sexual harassment," only marginalized men will be prosecuted, and the existing power structure that guarantees privileged men's sexual access to women will remain intact.

Sexual interactions involving men and women of the same race and sexual orientation have a hegemonic status in our society, making sexual harassment difficult to identify and eradicate. Our interviews suggest that many men and women are active participants in the sexualized culture of the workplace, even though ample evidence indicates that women who work in these environments suffer negative repercussions to their careers because of it (Jaschik and Fretz 1991; Paludi and Barickman 1991; Reilly et al. 1992; Schneider 1982). This is how cultural hegemony works—by getting under our skins and defining what is and is not pleasurable to us, despite our material or emotional interests.

Our findings raise difficult issues about women's complicity with oppressive sexual relationships. Some women obviously experience pleasure and enjoyment from public forms of sexual engagement with men; clearly, many would resist any attempt to eradicate all sexuality from work—an impossible goal at any rate. Yet, it is also clear that the sexual "pleasure" many women seek out and enjoy at work is structured by patriarchal, racist, and heterosexist norms. Heterosexual, racially homogamous relationships are privileged in our society: they are institutionalized in organizational policies and job descriptions, embedded in ritualistic workplace practices, and accepted as legitimate, normal, or inevitable elements of workplace culture. This study suggests that only those sexual interactions that violate these policies, practices, and beliefs are resisted and condemned with the label "sexual harassment."

We have argued that this dominant social construction of pleasure protects the most privileged groups in society from charges of sexual harassment and may be used to oppress and exclude the least powerful groups. Currently, people seem to consider the gender, race, status, and sexual orientation of the assailant when deciding to label behaviors as sexual harassment. Unless we acknowledge the complex double standards people use in "drawing the line," then sexual domination and exploitation will undoubtedly remain the normative experience of women in the work force.

Notes

1. It could be the case that those who find this behavior extremely offensive are likely to leave restaurant work. In other words, the sample is clearly biased in that it includes only those who are currently employed in a restaurant and presumably feel more comfortable with the level of sexualized behavior than those who have left restaurant work.

2. It is difficult, if not impossible, to specify which occupations are less highly sexualized than waiting tables. Most occupations probably are sexualized in one way or another; however, specific workplaces may be more or less sexualized in terms of institutionalized job descriptions and employee tolerance of sexual banter. For example, Pringle (1988) describes some offices as coolly professional—with minimal sexual joking and play—whereas others are characterized by "compulsory jocularity." Likewise, some restaurants may deemphasize sexual flirtation between waitpeople and customers, and restrain informal interactions among the staff (one respondent in our sample worked at such a restaurant).

3. We thank Margaret Andersen for drawing our attention to this fruitful analogy.

4. It is also probably significant that this episode of harassment involved a gay man and a heterosexual man. This context of sexual harassment is discussed later in this article.

5. It is true that both cases involved cooks sexually harassing waitresses. We could have placed these cases in the "powerful position" category, but did not because in these particular instances, the cooks did not possess institutionalized power over the waitpeople. In other words, in these particular cases, the cook and waitress had equal organizational status in the restaurant.

References

Anders, K. T. 1993. Bad sex: Who's harassing whom in restaurants? *Restaurant Business*, 20 January, pp. 46–54.

Benson, Donna J., and Gregg E. Thomson. 1982. Sexual harassment on a university campus: The confluence of authority relations, sexual interest and gender stratification. *Social Problems* 29:236–51.

Carothers, Suzanne C., and Peggy Crull. 1984. Contrasting sexual harassment in female- and male-dominated occupations. In *My troubles are going to have trouble with me: Everyday trials and triumphs of women workers*, edited by K. B. Sacks and D. Remy. New Brunswick, NJ: Rutgers University Press.

Cobble, Dorothy Sue. 1991. *Dishing it out: Waitresses and their unions in the twentieth century*. Urbana: University of Illinois Press.

Cockburn, Cynthia. 1991. *In the way of women*. Ithaca, NY: I.L.R. Press.

Crull, Peggy. 1987. Searching for the causes of sexual harassment: An examination of two prototypes. In *Hidden aspects of women's work*, edited by Christine Bose, Roslyn Feldberg, and Natalie Sokoloff. New York: Praeger.

Ellis, Shmuel, Azy Barak, and Adaya Pinto. 1991. Moderating effects of personal cognitions on experienced and perceived sexual harassment of women at the workplace. *Journal of Applied Social Psychology* 21:1320–37.

Fain, Terri C., and Douglas L. Anderton. 1987. Sexual harassment: Organizational context and diffuse status. *Sex Roles* 17:291–311.

Fitzgerald, Louise F. 1990. Sexual harassment: The definition and measurement of a construct. In *Ivory power: Sexual harassment on campus*, edited by Michele M. Paludi. Albany: State University of New York Press.

Grauerholz, Elizabeth. 1989. Sexual harassment of women professors by students: Exploring the dynamics of power, authority, and gender in a university setting. *Sex Roles* 21:789–801.

Gruber, James E., and Lars Bjorn. 1982. Blue-collar blues: The sexual harassment of women auto workers. *Work and Occupations* 9:271–98.

Gutek, Barbara A. 1985. *Sex and the workplace*. San Francisco: Jossey-Bass.

Hall, Elaine J. 1993. Waitering/waitressing: Engendering the work of table servers. *Gender & Society* 7:329–46.

Howe, Louise Kapp. 1977. *Pink collar workers: Inside the world of women's work*. New York: Avon.

Jaschik, Mollie L., and Bruce R. Fretz. 1991. Women's perceptions and labeling of sexual harassment. *Sex Roles* 25:19–23.

Jensen, Inger W., and Barbara A. Gutek. 1982. Attributions and assignment of responsibility in sexual harassment. *Journal of Social Issues* 38:122–36.

Johnson, Miriam. 1988. *Strong mothers, weak wives*. Berkeley: University of California Press.

Konrad, Alison M., and Barbara A. Gutek. 1986. Impact of work experiences on attitudes toward sexual harassment. *Administrative Science Quarterly* 31:422–38.

LaFree, Gary D. 1989. *Rape and criminal justice: The social construction of sexual assault*. Belmont, CA: Wadsworth.

MacKinnon, Catherine A. 1979. *Sexual harassment of working women: A case of sex discrimination*. New Haven, CT: Yale University Press.

McKinney, Kathleen. 1990. Sexual harassment of university faculty by colleagues and students. *Sex Roles* 23:421–38.

Paludi, Michele, and Richard B. Barickman. 1991. *Academic and workplace sexual harassment*. Albany: State University of New York Press.

Paules, Greta Foff. 1991. *Dishing it out: Power and resistance among waitresses in a New Jersey restaurant*. Philadelphia: Temple University Press.

Powell, Gary N. 1986. Effects of sex role identity and sex on definitions of sexual harassment. *Sex Roles* 14:9–19.

Pringle, Rosemary. 1988. *Secretaries talk: Sexuality, power and work*. London: Verso.

Pryor, John B. 1987. Sexual harassment proclivities in men. *Sex Roles* 17:269–90.

Reilly, Mary Ellen, Bernice Lott, Donna Caldwell, and Luisa DeLuca. 1992. Tolerance for sexual harassment related to self-reported sexual victimization. *Gender & Society* 6:122–38.

Rich, Adrienne. 1980. Compulsory heterosexuality and lesbian existence. *Signs* 5:631–60.

Schneider, Beth E. 1982. Consciousness about sexual harassment among heterosexual and lesbian women workers. *Journal of Social Issues* 38:75–98.

———. 1984. The office affair: Myth and reality for heterosexual and lesbian women workers. *Sociological Perspectives* 27:443–64.

———. 1991. Put up and shut up: Workplace sexual assaults. *Gender & Society* 5:533–48.

U.S. Department of Labor, Bureau of Labor Statistics. 1989, January. *Employment and earnings*. Washington, DC: Government Printing Office.

West, Candace, and Don H. Zimmerman. 1987. Doing gender. *Gender & Society* 1:125–51.

Lois Weis, Amira Proweller, and Craig Centrie

Re-examining "A Moment in History": Loss of Privilege Inside White Working-Class Masculinity in the 1990s

In the past ten years, we have come a long way toward unraveling the identity production processes of various groups within American society. Feminist work, in particular, has helped us understand the ways in which girls and women fashion their own identities in relation to what Dorothy Smith calls textually mediated discourses. Drawing from Foucault, Smith argues that

> social forms of consciousness, "femininity" included, can be examined as actual practices, actual activities, taking place in real time, in real places, using definite material means and under definite material conditions. Among other matters, this means that we do not neglect the "textual" dimensions of social consciousness. By texts, I mean the more or less permanent and above all replaceable forms of meaning, of writing, painting, television, film, etc. The production, distribution and uses of texts are a pervasive and highly significant dimension of contemporary social organization. "Femininity," I'm going to argue, is a distinctively textual phenomenon. But texts must not be isolated from the practices in which they are embedded and which they organize. (1988: 39)

Smith's observations are helpful as we work toward understanding the production of femininity, and work by Leslie Roman, Linda Valli, Nancy Lesko, Claire Wallace, Amira Proweller, and others enhances our knowledge of the pro-

duction of women's identities. Here we want to shift our gaze to the production of masculinity, and particularly the production of white masculinity. While feminists have undertaken work on the production of femininity and theorized it as such, scholars who have focused on the production of boys' and men's identities have rarely theorized their work specifically along gender lines. Well-known work by Paul Willis, for example, although wholly centered on the production of male culture, does not theorize it as such. Rather he employs a class-based paradigm through which he understands the lads' culture as working class, and develops an analysis through class-based terms. He fails, however, to employ theoretical work on gender to begin to decode these processes as specifically gender-based practices. Where Willis does focus on gender, he employs a classic Marxist notion of gender (and race) that speaks to the divide-and-rule tactics associated with the capitalist class. We want here to place the production of masculinity and, in particular, the production of white masculinity, at the center of our analysis, naming our focus as the culture of working-class men. Along these lines, we will highlight the production of white masculinity in this particular class fraction as it takes shape at the intersectionalities of social class, race, and gender. Theoretically this represents a departure from previous work and relies on Kimberle Crenshaw's important discussion of intersectionality as being key in the production of identity across variegated sites of meaning-making.

On Being White

Theorists and researchers including Dorothy Smith, Carol Cohn, Peggy McIntosh, Leslie Roman, Stanley Aronowitz, Joel Kovel, Judith Rollins, bell hooks, Toni Morrison, and others have argued for the study of privileged standpoints, for "studying up." Few, however, have taken up this challenge. White standpoints, privileged standpoints, are generally taken as an unstated norm, rather than offering a site for theoretical excavation. Certainly the work of Peggy Sanday in her analysis of fraternity men at an elite university stands out as an exception (1990). Dorothy Smith's analysis of corporate workplaces excavates privileged standpoint as does Judith Rollins's (1985) study of domestic workers and their white employers. Roslyn Arlin Michelson, Melvin Oliver, and Stephen Smith similarly focus on privilege when they study the ways in which universities, in spite of affirmative action policies, work to exclude the voices of people of color.

In this discussion, we take up this challenge as we begin to unravel white male identity inside working-class culture in a time of economic restructuring and deindustrialization. Gone are the jobs in heavy industry that sustained white men's fathers and grandfathers, that allowed them to earn the "family wage" which bought them the privilege of dominating their wives and children in the home. Most of the truly "masculine" jobs, those that demand hard physical labor, are gone, replaced by jobs in the service sector, jobs that not only pay less but do not offer the "hard" real confrontation with physicality that was embedded in jobs of former years, jobs that encouraged the production of a certain type of masculinity (Connell 1995). We wonder, then, not only how white males in the 1980s and 1990s, in the midst of feminism, affirmative action, and gay/lesbian rights manage to sustain a sense of self, individually and collectively, but also how they sustain a belief in a system that has, at least for working-class and middle-class white males, begun to crumble, eroding their once-certain advantage over white women and women and men of color (Newman 1993).[1] As scholars begin to recognize that "white is a color" (Roman 1993; Wong 1994), we write in order to make visible the borders, strategies, and fragilities of white, working-class male culture in insecure times, at, in Dorothy Smith's words, "a moment in history."[2]

This renders the study of privilege more complex than standpoint theorists generally recognize. While white working-class men are privileged via their color, they are relatively less privileged than their economically advantaged white male counterparts. Too, they are currently losing the edge they had in the economy over men of color. White working-class men represent a position of privilege at the same time they represent the loss of such privilege. It is this simultaneous moment of privilege and loss that we excavate when we turn our attention to the production of white masculinity. It is their whiteness and maleness which privileges them. But it is also in this space of historical privilege that they begin to confront the realities of loss.

Through an analysis of data collected with poor and working-class white, Latino, and African American men and women, ages 23–35, as to their concrete experiences in family, job, community, religion, political activism, and schooling, we unearth the territory mapped by white men inside in-depth interviews. Interviews were normally done in two segments, each approximately 1–1.5 hours in length, and were conducted with low-income people in Jersey City and Buffalo. Respondents were drawn from meaningful urban communities, to use William Julius Wilson's term, such as schools, Headstart, literacy centers, churches, and social agencies directly involved with local ethnic and racial communities.

We argue that white working-class men feel themselves to be under siege—in their jobs, in their neighborhoods, in their homes, and in their schools. Whether true or not in material terms, they feel themselves to be decentered, to no longer hold the position of privilege that they sense is rightfully theirs. This is, of course, stated in much more coded language, and no individual alleges that whites deserve more in the society simply by virtue of their skin color. That, unfortunately, may be one of the real outcomes of the civil rights struggle—that whites have to justify privilege in ways other than simply skin color. The expectation of privilege due to whiteness and maleness must be coded differently so that the demand for privilege does not rest on skin color alone, or skin color as related to intelligence. (We do, however, see a resurgence of this latter argument as well currently; see Herrnstein, *The Bell Curve.*) Rather, these men are involved in the production of elaborate justifications of privilege, justifications which serve, in their minds, to recenter what they argue is the decentered white male. Much of their identity production swirls around the creation and maintenance of the dark "other" against which their own whiteness and goodness is necessarily understood. The social construction of this goodness, then, provides moral justification for privileged standpoints. We do not mean to argue here that this type of discursive work has not been done historically. Clearly that is not the case, as Toni Morrison and David Roediger make clear. However, what is important in the late twentieth century is that these productions co-exist with a dismantled apartheid legal system. Discursive productions swirling around race therefore undermine ostensible equality under the law. These discursive productions are, as Dorothy Smith reminds us, textually mediated. They do not arise out of the thin air of class culture, "on the ground," so to speak, but are dialectically linked to the media, popular culture, and other forms of consumerist culture that directly articulate with economic arrangements structuring daily experience.

On Whiteness

Recent work by Ruth Frankenburg (1993) is extremely provocative. As she argues, "to speak of the social construction of whiteness" reveals locations, discourses, and material relations to which the term "whiteness" applies. She further asserts that "whiteness refers to a set of locations that are historically, socially, politically, and culturally produced and moreover are intrinsically linked to unfolding relations of domination. Naming 'whiteness' displaces it from the unmarked, unnamed status that is itself an effect of its dominance. Among the effects on white people both of race privilege and of the dominance of whiteness are their seeming normativity, their structured invisibility" (p. 6). As Frankenberg asserts, to analyze whiteness is to focus squarely on a site of constructed dominance.

In the United States, the hierarchies of race, gender, and class are embodied in the contemporary "struggle" of white maleness. As you will hear, these men work to sustain both an identity within dominance and the very hierarchies which assure their ongoing domination. Among the varied demographic categories that spill out of this race/gender hierarchy, white males are the only ones who have a vested interest in maintaining both their position and their web of power. The irony here, of course, is that white working-class males, themselves, are not the biggest beneficiaries of privilege itself. In sustaining the hierarchy, they are reproducing the very conditions that render them relatively expendable in the current economy. The assertion of dominance in one arena (race) implies the lack of such dominance in another (class). To accomplish the myth of race privilege, white males have had to sustain the notion of egalitarianism or at least the potential for equality. White male power necessitates a commitment on the part of white working-class males to engage the struggle for cultural dominance. Yet the location of struggle is far removed from the actual center of power and privilege residing inside the elite community. Lower income and working-class white males form a necessary buffer that, if eliminated or realigned along class rather than race lines, could destabilize elite domination.

Scholars of colonial discourse have highlighted the ways in which discourse about nonwestern "others" are produced simultaneously with the production of discourse about the western white "self," and this work becomes relevant to our analyses of race/gender domination. Scholarship on West European expansion documents the cultural disruptions that took place alongside economic appropriation, as well as the importance of the production of knowledge about groups of people that rendered colonization successful. As Frankenberg states, "The notion of 'epistemic violence' captures the idea that associated with West European colonial expansion is the production of codes of knowing that enabled and rationalized colonial domination from the standpoint of the West, and produced ways of conceiving other societies and cultures whose legacies endure into the present" (p. 16). As she argues:

> Colonial discourse (like racist discourse) is in many ways heterogeneous rather than univocal, not surprising given the extent and geographical dispersion of European colonizing projects. However, if a common thread runs through the whole range of instances of colonial discourse, it is the construction of alterity along social and/or cultural lines—the construction of others conceived as fundamentally different from, and inferior to, white, European metropolitan selves (Said 1979). It must also be noted—and this is a point perhaps more difficult to grasp upon first encounter with it—that it is precisely by means of the construction of a range of others that the self or dominant center constitutes itself. White/European self-constitution is, in other words, fundamentally tied to the process of discursive production of others, rather than preexisting that process (p. 63).

It is precisely this point that gives rise to the voices inside Afrocentric scholarship, particularly the work of Asante (1990, 1991), which assert that the colonial European has no identity other than that which has been constructed vis-a-vis "others." In the United States, Mohanty (1988) and Roediger (1992) talk carefully about the production of white racial identity and the ways in which this identity is intimately tied to the production of black identity. What is important here is that the legacy of colonialism, more specifically the legacy of colonial discourse, rendered the category "white," a simultaneously *empty* but *normative*

space—in other words, "white" could easily be defined in relation to the constructed other. It is by these very processes of othering that "white" becomes the norm against which all other communities (of color) are judged (usually to a deviant). Colonialism and neocolonialism have sanctioned the normativity and structured invisibility of the West, partially through the production of knowledge but mainly by positioning an "other" as knowledge consumer. This has served to bolster the inscrutability of whiteness through naming and labeling the "other." Internal colonialization in the United states has achieved this same dynamic through the marginalization of people of color and the resulting normativity of whiteness. It is, therefore, possible to name cultures precisely because they are excluded from the normative, thus enabling the dominant "white" to engage in a process of establishing what Trin Min-ha (1989) calls boundedness. Thus much of white identity formation, stemming from colonial times to the present, involves drawing boundaries, engaging in boundedness, configuring rings around the substantively empty category "white," while at the same time discursively constructing "others." The dominant white self can, therefore, only be understood in relation to the constructed other. Without it, the white self pales into nonexistence.[3]

Central, then, to the colonial discourse and the construction of whiteness in America is the idea of the "other" being wholly and hierarchically different from the "white" self. Discursively inventing the colonial "other," for example, whites were parasitically producing an apparently stable Western, white self out of a previously nonexistent self. As Gayatri Chakravorty Spivak (1985) argues: "Europe . . . consolidated itself as sovereign subject by defining its colonies as 'others,' even as it constituted them for purposes of administration and the expansion of markets" (as cited in Frankenberg, p. 17). Thus the Western (read white) self and the colonial "other" are products of this discursive construction.

One continuing effect of colonial discourse is the production of an unnamed, unmarked, white, Western self against which all others can be named and judged. It is the unnamed, unmarked, white self which must be deconstructed, named, and marked. This paper takes up this challenge. As we will argue, white male identity is indeed parasitically coproduced as white men name and mark others, thereby naming and marking themselves. At a moment of economic crisis when white working-class males are being squeezed, the construction of others proliferates.[4]

Centered inside these constructions is the white male self—the male "under siege" in the economy, the community, and the family. We now turn to each of these sectors at their complex intersections as we explore the assault on historical privilege as white working-class men forge lives that increasingly appear to hang in the balance.

Under Siege in the Economy

While it is indeed the case that massive restructuring has taken place in the American economy and white working-class male jobs have been substantially reduced and/or pay less than they did before, the changes in the economy are due almost entirely to the concrete decisions made by elites in order to compete more profitably in the global market economy. It is the case that there has been some preferential hiring of people of color and that this accounts for some loss of white male jobs, but the loss of jobs associated with affirmative action policies pales in comparison with job loss associated with massive restructuring and deindustrialization (Perry, Bluestone, and Harrison; Harrison and Bluestone 1988). It is most interesting, therefore, that not one of the white men we interviewed held elites accountable for the relocation of industry, closing of industries, and so forth. Rather the finger was always pointed at affirmative action policies which allegedly accorded preferential treatment to minorities, positioned differently as undeserving. This is why, according to white males, they are not working, or not working in jobs for which they feel entitled.

Because of the economy, many working-class white males have had, at times, to seek and obtain welfare benefits. What they do discursively with welfare is very important here. Welfare becomes a site wherein people of color are defined as lazy and undeserving, while at the same time, white men define themselves as hard working and only going on welfare when absolutely necessary. This set of discursive constructions serves to draw their own boundaries of what constitutes acceptable conditions for "not working," welfare receipts, and government-sponsored programs, thus establishing a state of "boundedness." Having created an "other" who holds a set of unpleasant personal characteristics, white men can, then, at the same time, deny their own participation in the welfare state, their own experiences with unemployment, their own moments on the dole. Race affords them the opportunity to project and deny, defining themselves as the men who know how to take care of the family, and not "live off the government." The subordination of women in these families is absolutely essential to the propping up of white men vis-à-vis men of color. This set of discursively drawn distinctions, however, keeps white men from looking carefully at the real source of their difficulties—elites. It encourages them to trade on their whiteness, offers them a way of being white, and therefore dominant, at the expense of seriously analyzing the system and what it has, in fact, done to working-class white men. The white male critique is grounded fundamentally in the notion that people of color do not want to work.

LW: Are there tensions?

Larry: Probably not so much between them [blacks and Hispanics], but like for us, they think, I mean, it gets me angry sometimes. I don't say I'm better than anybody else. But I work for the things that I have, and they [blacks and Hispanics] figure just because you're ahead, or you know more and you do more, [that it's] because you're white. And that's not really it. We're all equal, and I feel that what I've done, I've worked for myself to get to where I'm at. . . . If they would just really try instead of just kind of hanging out on the street corners. That's something that really aggravates me, to see while I'm rushing to get to work, and everybody is just kind of milling around doing nothing.

At the heart of the white male critique is the notion that people of color, blacks, in particular, simply do not wish to work, that they are lazy. We can hear the victory of psychology over economics in this explanation. Personal, moral attributions of blame thrive despite rampant evidence of private-sector and public-sector abandonment. This is juxtaposed to notions of self which assert that although white men may be out of a job, they always want to work. From this flows an overt racial critique of affirmative action programs, as well as a somewhat more racially coded critique of welfare abusers and cheats. We, actually they, take up the issue of affirmative action first.

> **Pete:** For the most part, it hasn't been bad. It's just that right now with these minority quotas, I think more or less, the white male has become the new minority. And that's not to point a finger at the blacks, Hispanics or the women. It's just that with all these quotas, instead of hiring the best for the job, you have to hire according to your quota system, which is still wrong.
>
> **LW:** Do you have any sense of social movements? Like the Civil Rights Movement?
>
> **Pete:** Civil rights, as far as I'm concerned, is being way out of proportion.
>
> **LW:** Talk to me more about that.
>
> **Pete:** Well, um, granted, um, the Afro-Americans were slaves over two hundred years ago. They were given their freedom. We as a country, I guess you could say, have tried to, well I can't say all of us, but most of us, have tried to, like, make things a little more equal. Try to smooth over some of the rough spots. You have some of these other, you have some of these militants who are now claiming that after all these years, we still owe them. I think the owing time is over for everybody. Because if we go into that, then the Poles are still owed [he is Polish].

The Germans are still owed. Jesus—the Jews are definitely still owed. I mean, you're, you're getting cremated, everybody wants to owe somebody. I think it's time to wipe that slate clean.

The critique of affirmative action (often referred to as "quotas") is that it is not "fair," that it privileges blacks, Hispanics, and at times white women above the white male, and that this contradicts notions of equal opportunity and a flat playing field. It is noteworthy that nowhere in these narratives is there any recognition of the fact that white men as a group have been historically privileged, irrespective of individual merit.

Where men give credence to affirmative action, it takes highly essentialist forms. John, for example, feels that affirmative action programs "have their place," that they "shouldn't be completely out of the question." For example, he feels that "women can speak with women or children a lot better than men can"; and that, "in the areas of crime, you have to have blacks and Hispanics working in community programs, so you have to have certain jobs and responsibilities where they can deal with people, like say, with people of their own race or background." In other words, women should be privileged for *certain* jobs dealing with women and children, and blacks and Hispanics should be privileged in jobs dealing with crime. That is where, he suggests, affirmative action is useful. In general, though, white men concur with Tom when he states, "as soon as they [blacks] don't get a job, they yell discrimination. . . . But the ones who are really lazy, don't want it [to become educated and work one's way up], they start yelling discrimination so they can just get the job and they're not even qualified for it. And they might take it away from, whether it's a, you know, a woman or a guy [white]."

The assertions about affirmative action offer white men a way of "othering" African Americans, in particular. "We," whites, even though we might be unemployed, want to work. "They," blacks, just want a free ride—they just want to get the job without having to really work for it. This encourages the discursive coconstruction of blacks as lazy, as wanting a handout, unlike hard-working whites. This theme is further elaborated in discussions of welfare abusers and cheats.

AP: Have you ever applied for welfare?

Ron: No.

AP: Or, have you ever had to?

Ron: Never had to. I, probably very early in our marriage, um, when the first company I worked for, and they closed up, and um, we, we went through a period where we probably could have, had we applied, I think we would have been eligible. I mean, our income was really low enough that we probably should have.

AP: But you didn't. How come?

Ron: I guess both of us pretty much feel the same way. You know, we look at welfare as being something, um, less than admirable.

AP: And that's what it would have amounted to for you? Sort of less than admirable?

Ron: Yeah, I think, had we been any lower, as far as income and gotten to the point where we absolutely couldn't even afford to eat, um, I mean, I'm not opposed to doing what I have to do. . . . But, um, to me, it should be strictly a last resort. I think the welfare system is very much abused.

AP: Can you talk to me a little about that?

Ron: Well, um, . . . I think for the most part, I think most people get out of life what they put into it. You know, because some people have more obstacles than others, there's no doubt about it. But I think a lot of people just expect things to come to them, and when it doesn't, you know, they've got the government to fall back on. . . . You know, I think it [falling back on the government] is more common for black people. . . . I mean social services, in general, I think, is certainly necessary, and Sheila [wife] and I have taken advantage of them. We've got food stamps several times. . . . But, you know, as soon as

I was able to get off it, I did. And not for any noble reasons, but just, you know, I think I'd rather be able to support myself than have things handed to me.

* * *

CC: What do you think of welfare?

Tom: I think it's good for people who deserve it. And I think there's a lot of people that don't deserve it. The system stinks. If you're on welfare, I think if you're willing to work, I think the . . . you know, I think the State should, I mean look out here, there's a lot of things that need to be cleaned up. Let 'em clean the streets; let 'em do something. Just don't let 'em sit at home and just collect their check. There's some that can't [work]. There's some who deserve it and they have to . . . for the most part, yeah. I mean, if you deserved it, fine. But if you don't, don't play the system.

Katherine Newman's (1993) insights are particularly helpful here. She suggests that:

> American culture is allergic to the idea that impersonal forces control individual destiny. Rather we prefer to think of our lives as products of our own efforts. Through hard work, innate ability and competition, the good prosper and the weak drop by the wayside. Accordingly, the end results in peoples' lives—their occupations, material possessions, and the recognition accorded by friends and associates—are proof of the underlying stuff of which they are made. Of course, when the fairy tale comes true, the flip side of the meritocratic individualism emerges with full force. Those who prosper—the morally superior—deserve every bit of their material comfort. (p. 89)

White men, then, script poor blacks as deserving of their plight and unwilling to work, while they [white men] "sincerely" strive for the American Dream. They, that is, white men are coconstructed as highly deserving, willing to work, and eager to participate in the American economy.

Although there are some exceptions to this, the primary function of discussions about welfare abusers is to draw the boundaries of acceptable welfare receipt *at themselves*—the hard-working white man who is trying to support his family. Pete, for example, states, "There's definitely some people who abuse the system, I can see that. But then there are people who, when you need it, you know, it's like they have something to fall back on. And they're [the case workers] basically shoving everybody into one category. They're [all welfare recipients] all users. But these [the case workers] are the same people that if the county closes them off, they won't have a job, and they're going to be there next too." Since most of the case workers are white, Pete is discursively aligning himself with the hard-working people who have just fallen on hard times, unlike the abusers, largely black, who exploit the system. His criticism of the case workers is that they treat all welfare recipients as cheats, as like African Americans, thus denying differential positionality vis-à-vis welfare.

The discussions of affirmative action and welfare abuse enable white men to draw distinctions between themselves and a largely black "other," whom they discursively construct as lazy, unwilling to do what is necessary to get a job, and more than happy to take advantage of government handouts, including affirmative action programs, which they script as a "handout," as going to those undeserving. In discursively constructing a black "other," white men simultaneously construct themselves as hard working and only going on welfare and accepting government help when absolutely necessary.

This splitting of Self and Other is reminiscent of Weis's working-class white high school boys. Boys in Freeway High constructed the black "other" as highly sexualized and drug prone. This construction at one and the same time served to authorize white boys as clean, respectful of women, and definitely heterosexual. Beyond high school, into young adulthood, these discursive constructions layer on top of one another, so that black men, in particular, are now discursively constructed as lazy, unwilling to work, and so forth. This weaves through the high school con-

structions revolving around drugs and sexuality, ultimately leaving young white men highly resentful of blacks in general, whom they see as drug prone, oversexualized, and lazy, but also of affirmative action programs, in particular, which they feel privilege inferior human beings. This, then, is social critique to white men. Interestingly enough, it leaves totally unexamined and even unrecognized the role of whites who self-consciously closed industries and/or enabled legislation which moved capital across state and international borders, thus interrupting far more white male jobs than affirmative action ever could (or has). (Perry 1987; Bluestone and Harrison 1982).

Under Siege in the Neighborhood

A felt assault invades the perceptions of many white men in talk about their neighborhoods as they begin to express a sense of no longer belonging, or that their neighborhood is "deteriorating," further evidence that it is no longer a space that belongs to them in both physical and psychological terms. Most often this encroaching instability is attributed to an influx of blacks or Hispanics who they clearly position as the Other. As Larry says;

> I really feel—I'm not going to say out of place. I do. I've grown up in the neighborhood [the Italian west side], but I don't really feel as though I belong here anymore. I don't know, not strictly because I'm a white male, and there's not many of us. I mean, there's not really that many in my neighborhood that I can say, "Well, I have a neighbor, the guy who lives next door to me or the somebody across the street." There is, I'm kind of like the minority. I'm, I don't really, there's not a lot of people I associate with. There's some people I'll say hello to, or, you know, you talk with your neighbors to associate.

A focus group discussion with three men in a west-side church uncovers similar sentiments:

> **CC:** What was it like when you guys were little?

Ron: I think it was different—ten times different.

Craig: What did happen? What did you see happen?

Ron: I just seen more kids on the streets, more of them starting to dress up like the rappers on TV, white kids, black kids, Hispanic, it didn't matter. I just seen, you know, more hanging out.

Pete: The west side has always been like a low income type of area, and it's always been a tough neighborhood. But what I think is, more or less, it's getting more violent. We both went to Grover [high school], so we know what it's like to grow up in kind of like a tough atmosphere, but nothing like it is now. There's a lot of drug dealing, a lot of guns.

Ron: The thing is, they're getting younger.

Pete: Thirteen, fourteen-year-old kids are carrying guns. It's really not that out in the open, but you hear about it. You hear about the shootings. . . . There was a rape at School 18 [elementary school], maybe about a month ago. I heard it on the news.

Ron: . . . I did see a drug bust. As a matter of fact, right on my street. The cop more or less blocked me in my driveway, because they just pull up, and they park unmarked cars, and they just rushed into a couple of houses down.

Ron, in an individual interview, elaborates as follows:

A: Just look at the school. It's just . . . you know . . . and you hear the loud music all over the place now. I mean, it's not as bad as I might be making it sound . . . but . . . my car got broken into, stuff like that . . . that never happened back then.

Q: It didn't?

A: Uh uh. I'd say up to four-five years ago, it didn't happen.

Q: Interesting. What proportion of the people are still Italian?

A: There's a lot of older ones still there. Um, oh, my God, I'd say 30 to 40 percent.

Q: Still? Well that's quite high then.

A: . . . See, you have the lower west side and the upper west side, say . . . you know what I'm talking about . . . that's predominantly Puerto Rican. The upper west side still has got a lot of Italians through there.

Q: But you said a lot of the Puerto Ricans and blacks are moving into the upper west side?

A: Oh yeah, they're coming. I mean, which is . . . which is fine. I have no problem with that. A lot of Italians are moving to the North side, so that's starting to be Italian Heaven over there. But there's been a definite change, no doubt about it.

Ron is interesting since he, himself, is a border crosser in the sense that his girlfriend (who he later became engaged to) is Puerto Rican. However this presents no conceptual difficulty for him since she is among those Puerto Rican families that have been there for a while and who also object to the new Puerto Ricans and blacks moving in. As he notes, "Yeh, she'll talk to me. Coming from her mouth herself, she would say the same thing I did. It's really sad I can't walk through my old neighborhood, you know, it's really sick. It's ignorant, you know. They, her family, feels the same way. Her mother, because her mother doesn't have a car, so she has to walk a lot of places, and she knows what's going on."

Dave, who during the course of our interview let us know that he was Native American, said the following:

A: It was a real friendly neighborhood. I lived on Connecticut and Normal Avenue, and at the time, it was a predominantly Italian neighborhood. It was very close knit. I mean, you could leave your doors open and bikes unchained, and all that kind of stuff, and now it's not like that anymore.

Q: How is it different?

A: Well, now it's a Hispanic and black neighborhood, and you practically have to . . . you know . . . chain things up, nail them down, put bolts on them, and it's something that shouldn't be . . . we should all be able to live together and respect each other's personal artifacts, whatever they are.

Many of the white men interviewed hope to exit the areas they define as "under siege" as soon as they can. In Larry's case, he has bought some land in a suburb where his two brothers live, because he can't imagine raising children where he currently resides. Several others plan to move to the suburbs, or to North Buffalo, when they are married, and especially when they have children. This will not necessarily be easy to accomplish, since many are living in properties owned by their parents, properties bought with monies that white privilege was able to amass in the parental generation, when white men were easily able to secure full-time work in industry. Those that foresee staying in the city are working to establish block clubs, neighborhood watches, and small-scale organizations designed to patrol the borders of their communities. Tom, for example, is very active in the block club in his community.

Q: What is the purpose of the block club?

A: To watch the neighborhood. You know, if you see trouble happening, to call 911. Or if one of the neighbors is having a problem, you know, it's better to come out in groups, you know, don't cause any violence. . . . And you know, if we see somebody else, like the lady across the street is an older elderly lady. And we watch for her. You know, we see somebody strange up that driveway or at her house, you know, we'll confront them. We'll ask them [who they are]. And I think that shows too. I think people see that.

While he narrates this as very supportive, and indeed it is in many ways, the borders they are patrolling are those basically encasing the white community against encroaching "others." It is

whiteness that people are attempting to protect in these neighborhoods. This does not deny the fact that some blacks live in white neighborhoods as well, but rather points out that in these white neighborhoods bordered by the "other," it is the other against whom white communities are attempting to protect themselves. This is also not to ignore the fact that several families of color live in these white neighborhoods, but rather to note that these families are considered settled—as "just like us" in the case of the "Spanish" family who lived in the Italian neighborhood. It is the racial "other"—the "other" constructed as lazy, violent, dangerous, as not working, as hanging around, that is at issue here. And it is this group to whom block clubs are formed in response. As Tom says, "If I move, it's going to be because I want to move, not because the kids are going to force me out. You know, I'm not afraid of the kids. I'm not afraid of, you know, people moving in. You know, I'm not afraid of the colored coming in. They don't bother me. If I'm going to move, it will be because [I want to]." In the meantime, he is organizing with other white men and white women to patrol the borders of his neighborhood, a relatively "safe space," from the onslaught of the "other."

Some, like Bill below, recognize that the block clubs can engage in seemingly racist practices:

Q: Do you belong to any groups of any kind?

A: No, none.

Q: Um, any groups that, like anything that tries to change the community? Like, do you belong to a block club?

A: Um, the block club I won't join . . . I totally hate their views. I mean, they're like, "Get them out, kick their ass," just . . .

Q: Who is saying "Get them out, kick their ass"?

A: Oh, people who live a few doors from me. And they're very prejudiced.

Q: So, they're whites?

A: Yeah.

Q: Whites want to kick out the blacks.

A: Exactly. It doesn't matter to them if they're good or bad. You know if they're renters or owners. They just want them out. And talking to them, I mean their views on good white people is ridiculous, because there's a few streets over, um, off William, and he, well, the guy who, whose main view, he loves that area because it's mostly white.

Q: Is that a place called Kaisertown?

A: No. It's off of William by the Dolsky Center. About half way to the Dolsky Center. And, um, I mean, it's equivalency, it's the equivalency of black people, black kids running around in their underwear, where, here's white kids running around in their underwear. It's like, he thinks it's a much better area. Why, because you can buy your crack there? Which, um, he does.

White men then take up a protectionist stance in an effort to secure their "turf" from assault in a time of increasing racial diversification and with that, the fracturing of working-class neighborhoods. Block clubs emerge as freely organized and co-opted spaces for group meeting and exchange designed to bolster the community, but they also exist as a site for the deployment of tactical strategies meant to arm the neighborhood against the other. A "good" community initiative in the interests of engagement across difference thus doubles as a legitimate form of border patrolling. Initiatives on the part of white working-class men need, then, to be seen as counter-strategies for reclaiming lost power and privilege in their communities which they perceive as being under immediate threat of dislocation.

Under Siege in the Home: Contesting Gender Roles

White working-class men express strong sentiment about the family and, specifically, about male roles and responsibilities within the family. The family is idealized and even valorized, at least in theory, if not altogether in practice. For men, who have lost real material space inside shopfloor culture, they turn to the family and attempt to assert or re-assert dominance in that realm. While this may have always been the case, as Lillian Rubin (1976) and others have argued about the working-class family, the move to sustain dominance in the white working-class home is particularly key at this moment in time where there are genuine material losses in other spheres of working-class life. Men no longer have a clear-cut material sphere in which they can assert live power. Working-class men are forced, in a sense, into a symbolic realm, the realm of family, which is not their material space, in order to assert a form of symbolic dominance. Turning to the family as the symbolic domain of male power, they insist or re-insist on reclaiming gender privilege. Much of the patrolling of the borders of the community must be seen in these terms as well. The borders of the community as patrolled by white men are drawn in the name of the family—men are protecting their wives and children (all of whom are constructed as absolutely less than men) from what they construct as an encroaching assault. Thus they envelop the family sphere within their own symbolic dominance, a dominance which they substitute, although not wholly consciously or completely, for their former authority in the material realm.

The next set of conversations was conducted in a focus group in an Italian church located in one of the borderlands of Buffalo. The family is absolutely essential to the construction of manhood in these narratives and, indeed, to the propping up of the discourse of masculinity inside working-class culture:

CC: What do you think the role of the family is right now?

Pete: I think there is definitely a fall in the American family right now.

Ron: That's the major contributor to any of the problem, I think.

Pete: What I see it is, is it used to be a man could work, make a paycheck, and the woman could stay home and be a housewife, but now you need either two incomes or a man cannot support the family, he cannot get a job to support the family, so he bolts, he leaves, and goes on his own, and that's what I see. . . . He takes the easy way out. All the other pressures of the world. . . .

CC: What other pressures?

Pete: The age itself. Men are tempted away from their wives; wives are tempted away from their husbands because of sex.

CC: Is that new, though?

Ron: No. It's not new, but it's more frequent now because of everything—it's just thrown at you no matter what. You could watch TV and you could just turn it—I mean even regular cable—and you could see some gross stuff, even for kids, you know. It's the temptation of bad. It's the temptation of money and it's just, you know, it's the temptation of well, I've got to please myself first.

CC: What do you think is going to happen to the family in the future? Is it going to get better or worse?

Ron: I hate to say it, I don't think it's going to get better.

Pete and Ron attribute what they see as the fall in the American family to a variety of factors. In fact, we hear them searching for explanations as they scan Reagonomics, popular culture (cable TV), commodified sex, and the lack of jobs. However, it is clear in these narratives that the lynchpin of the family is the man as breadwinner and protector of wife and children. The economy and popular culture have made that difficult since two people now need to work, and sex tempts both men and women away from family commitments. Thus there is a moral component to the breakdown of the American family as well. But the male as provider must, they argue, be restored if the family is to regain its strength. There is a clear valorization of traditional gender-based roles, without which the family is undermined.

CC: Do you think that the roles of men and women are now changing to some extent be-

cause of the changes in the family and the changes in society?

Pete: Definitely. There is more of a leadership role for women.

Ron: There is nothing wrong—I mean I agree with women being able to be independent and stuff like that, but the women's lib, when that started, it really threw things into a little bit of chaos too because, like you said, the family. For one thing, it took the mother out of the family.

Pete: Right. The role of the woman has definitely changed because the woman has to work now.

Ron: Now there are babysitters or the baby is at day care all day long.

Pete: I think for one thing, the roles have changed because again, of the single parent households. There is a lot of that, and the mother has to be the father and the mother at the same time.

Ron: Yeah that's true.

Pete: And it's very hard for a mother to discipline a teenage boy.

Ron: You need two parents.

CC: Given everything that you just said right now, what is the meaning of maleness?

Pete: First of all, I think the meaning of maleness is more than, you know, helping to produce a child. I still think that the meaning of maleness is to go out, earn a living, support a family, I still feel that should be the meaning of maleness. I don't know if it is, I really don't think it is.

Ron: . . . Just like pretty much what he said. Just to keep—a real man will keep what he believes in and not stray from it to please everybody. He'll get a wife. He'll love her unconditionally and she, in return, will respect him and want to do things for him, and vice versa, and just to follow the example of maybe the church or of Christ. That's pretty much it. Just an unselfish provider willing to sacrifice for his family, or sacrifice for whoever, and not take everyone else's values, to please the other person.

Pete: . . . I think they should be responsible. The male should be more responsible for the family.

Ron: Right, exactly. That's what he is in society. Like it was back in the days—like the *Leave It to Beaver* times, when the man went out, and the woman stayed home.

Pete: I think that's when there were really no problems in America. I don't know, I wasn't there, but from what I see, it seemed like everything was better.

Men reclaim their waning dominance in the material sector by centering the family in their collective memory of the past as youth coming of age, from which point they move toward its valorization as the main resource for financial, but, even more to the point, emotional support. These same men continue to draw on their memories and present experiences as they pin their hopes for the future on family as well, projecting their own marriages, their own families, and building lives in neighborhoods and communities in proximity to family and kin.

Conversation that captures the importance of the intact family sets the stage for discussion of the central role played by men in the household as they argue their significance to the home space despite the fact that they understand themselves as only symbolically dominant therein. In other words, these men are left to reclaim the waning privileges of male dominance through a traditional vocabulary of gender roles and relationships.

Q: What's the most important thing in terms of life?

Pete: Family.

Q: Why?

Pete: Because that's your flesh and blood. That's who you grew up with. That's who loves you the most. That's your most trusted, prized possession, your family. That is the most important thing in my life.

Q: Anything else?

Pete: Belief in God and sticking together as a family, and that's basically it.

The centrality of family to the provision of emotional support inside working-class culture is best captured in Pete's admission of family as "your most trusted, prize possession." Attaching material value to the family unit allows white working-class men to position the family as the fulcrum point on which masculine domination hinges. This line of argument is sustained inside Tom's attention to the family and the provisor of emotional support whose example makes the future possible.

Q: Could you have predicted that your family would have been so important to you? Do you come from a family where your family is . . .

Tom: Yes, Yes. Even though my sisters—like I said, the one sister—I mean, we . . . I'm still close. I mean, if she calls me to do something, I'll still do it for her. Ahm, my parents were close . . .

Q: So you're not surprised to see this in yourself?

Tom: No. Ahm, my father's brothers and sisters, my mother, on her side, the cousins and that, we're just close. . . . I mean, it just goes from brother to sister, from wife and kids to brother and the whole family.

Establishing the foundational aspects of the family unit, these white working-class men are able to build an argument that validates male authority, albeit symbolic, inside the home. Normalization of working-class cultural forms mandates a vocabulary that subscribes to the traditional sexual division of labor inside the home. Out of these terms, white working-class men position themselves as bordered by white women who they see as not being in their correct place. Men are trying hard to re-assert male dominance in the home, attempting to make certain that they maintain dominance in this symbolic realm. In other words, although the space materially belongs, in large measure, to women, and the men wish it to stay that way, they want to make it absolutely clear that they are dominant symbolically. They are the head of the household even though they do not materially inhabit and/or take care of this household in ways they expect of their women. While this has always gone on, the depth to which this is being asserted, we would argue, is due to the erosion of dominance in their own material space, shop floors, and so forth in the wage labor sector.

Notes

This study is supported through generous funds from the Spencer Foundation. Michelle Fine and Lois Weis are co-investigators on the grant.

1. A similar erosion of privilege existed for white males in the Southern United States after the Civil War. This era found white men "retaliating" for their felt loss of privilege through the organization of hate groups like the Ku Klux Klan.

2. The now classic works of Franz Fanon, *Black Skin, White Masks* and *The Wretched of the Earth* and Albert Memmi's *The Colonizer and the Colonized* have undertaken the delicate task of providing a psychological analysis of the colonial identity complex of both the colonizer and the colonized. These authors have laid the foundation for African American and white scholars to examine the complex nature of racial identity as it intersects with class and gender in the current discourse on the loss of privilege inside the culture of white working-class males.

3. The European construction of the colonized identity has given voice to scholars of color who earlier in the twentieth century began to question its validity. Authors of negritude, among them Aime Cesaire, Leopold Senghor, and Jean Price-Mars, have asked the question—are we French or are we Black—in protest of the French Metropolitan practice of linguistic and cultural imperialism. This movement has given rise to an impressive body of work which deconstructs the identity construction of Caribbean as well as North and West Africans under French colonial or neocolonial domination, legislating French colonialist identification as the "superior white."

4. One might speculate as to the extent to which these proliferations are linked to social change. One might speculate, for example, that the intensification of such coproductions is strongly linked historically to economic crisis and/or colonial expansion. One could empirically examine this claim.

References

Aronowitz, Stanley. 1992. *The Politics of Identity*. New York: Routledge.

Asante, Molefi K., and Mark T. Mattson. 1991. *Historical and Cultural Atlas of Africans*. New York: Maxwell Macmillan International.

Asante, Molefi K. 1990. *Afrocentricity and Knowledge*. Trenton, New Jersey: Africa World Press.

Bluestone, Barry, and Bennett Harison. 1982. *The Deindustrialization of America: Plant Closing, Community Abandonment, and the Dismantling of Basic Industry*. New York: Basic Books.

Cesaire, Aime. 1969. *Return to My Native Land*. Baltimore: Penguin Books.

———. 1955, 1962. *Discourse sur colonialisme*. Paris: Presence Africaine.

———. 1947. *Cahier d'un retour au pays natal*. New York: Brentano's.

Connell, R. W. 1995. *Masculinities*. Cambridge: Polity Press.

Fanon, Franz. 1967. *Black Skin, White Masks*. New York: Grove Weidenfeld.

———. 1967. *Pour la revolution*. New York: Africaine Monthly Review Press.

———. 1963. *The Wretched of the Earth*. New York: Grove Press.

Fine, Michelle. 1993. "Sexuality, Schooling, and Adolescent Females: The Missing Discourse of Desire." In Weis, Lois, and Michelle Fine (eds.), *Beyond Silenced Voices: Class, Race, and Gender in United States Schools*. Albany: State University of New York Press.

Foucault, Michel. 1980. *The History of Sexuality*, Vol. 1. New York: Vintage Press.

Frankenberg, Ruth. 1993. *White Women, Race Matters: The Social Construction of Whiteness*. Minneapolis: University of Minnesota Press.

Harrison, Bennett, and Barry Bluestone. 1988. *The Great U-Turn: Corporate Restructuring and Polarizing of America*. New York: Basic Books.

Herrnstein, Richard J. and Charles M. Murray. 1994. *The Bell Curve: Intelligence and Class Structure in American Life*. New York: Free Press.

hooks, bell. 1989. *Talking Back, Thinking Feminist, Thinking Black*. Boston: South End Press.

Lesko, Nancy. 1988. *Symbolizing Society: Stories, Rites and Structure in a Catholic High School.* New York: Falmer.

Memmi, Albert. 1965. *The Colonizer and the Colonized.* Boston: Beacon Press.

Michelson, Roslyn Arlin, Stephen Samuel Smith, and Melvin L. Oliver. 1993. "Breaking through the Barriers: African American Job Candidates and the Academic Hiring Process." In Lois Weis and Michelle Fine (eds.), *Beyond Silenced Voices.* Albany: State University of New York Press.

Mohanty, C. T. 1988. "Under Western Eyes: Feminist Scholarship and Colonial Discourses." *Feminist Review* 30, 61–88.

Morrison, Toni. 1992. *Playing in the Dark: Whiteness and the Literary Imagination.* Cambridge, Massachusetts: Harvard University Press.

Newman, Katherine S. 1993. *Declining Fortunes: The Withering of American Dream.* New York: Basic Books.

Perry, David. 1987. "The Politics of Dependency in Deindustrializing America: The Case of Buffalo, New York." In Michael Smith and Joe Feagin (eds.), *The Capitalist City: Global Restructuring and Community Politics.* Oxford (Oxfordshire) and New York: Basil Blackwell.

Price-Marce, Jean. 1928. *Ainsi parla l'oncle.* Port Au Prince: Imprinerie du Comparegne.

Proweller, Amira. 1995. "Inside Absence: An Ethnography of Female Identity Construction in an Upper Middle Class Youth Culture." Unpublished Ph.D. dissertation, SUNY Buffalo.

Roediger, David R. 1991. *The Wages of Whiteness: Race and the Making of the American Working Class.* New York: Verso.

Rollins, Judith. 1985. *Between Women: Domestics and Their Employers.* Philadelphia: Temple University Press.

Roman, Leslie G. 1993. "White Is a Color! White Defensiveness, Postmodernism, and Anti-Racist Pedagogy." In Cameron McCarthy and Warren Crichlow (eds.) *Race, Identity, and Representation in Education.* New York: Routledge.

Roman, Leslie, and Linda K. Christian-Smith (eds.). 1988. *Becoming Feminine: The Politics of Popular Culture.* Philadelphia: Falmer Press.

Rubin, Lillian. 1976. *Worlds of Pain.* New York: Basic Books.

Sanday, Peggy. 1990. *Fraternity Gang Rape: Sex, Brotherhood, and Privilege on Campus.* New York: New York University Press.

Senghor, Leopold. 1961. *Nation et voi Africaine du Socialisme.* Paris: Presence Africaine.

Smith, Dorothy E. 1988. "Femininity as Discourse." In Leslie G. Roman and Linda K. Christian-Smith (eds.), *Becoming Feminine: The Politics of Popular Culture.* Philadelphia: Falmer Press.

Spivak, Gayatri Chakravorty. 1990. "Can the Subaltern Speak?" In S. Harasym (ed.), *The Post-Colonial Critic: Issues, Strategies, Dialogues.* New York: Routledge, pp. 271–313.

Trinh, Min-ha. 1989. *Woman, Native, Other.* Bloomington: The University of Indiana Press.

Valli, Linda. 1986. *Becoming Clerical Workers.* Boston: Routledge and Kegan Paul.

Wallace Claire. 1987. *For Richer, for Poorer: Growing Up In and Out of Work.* London, New York: Tavistock.

Whatley, Marianne. 1985, 1987. "Raging Hormones and Powerful Cars: The Construction of Men's Sexuality in School Sex Education and Popular Adolescent Films." In Henry Giroux, *Postmodernism, Feminism, and Cultural Politics: Redrawing Educational Boundaries.* Albany: State University of New York Press, 1991.

Willis, Paul. 1977. *Learning to Labour: How Working Class Kids Get Working Class Jobs.* Farnborough, England: Saxon House.

Wilson, William J. 1980. *The Declining Significance of Race: Blacks and Changing American Institutions.* Chicago: University of Chicago Press.

Wong, Mun. 1994. "Di(s)-secting and di(s)-closing Whiteness, 'Two Tales From Psychology.'" *Feminism and Psychology* 4, 133–153.

PART FIVE

Men and Health: Body and Mind

Why did the gap between male and female life expectancy increase from two years in 1900 to nearly eight years today? Why do men suffer heart attacks and ulcers at such a consistently higher rate than women do? Why are auto insurance rates so much higher for young males than for females of the same age? Are mentally and emotionally "healthy" males those who conform more closely to the dominant cultural prescriptions for masculinity, or is it the other way around?

The articles in this section examine the "embodiment" of masculinity, the ways in which men's mental and physical health express and reproduce the definitions of masculinity we have ingested in our society. Don Sabo offers a compassionate account of how men will invariably confront traditional stereotypes as they look for more nurturing roles. Ann Fausto-Sterling and Gloria Steinem poke holes in the traditional definitions of masculinity, and especially the putative biological basis for gender expression. Susan Bordo's somewhat tongue-in-cheek meditation on Viagra underscores the fears men have about their bodies not performing as power tools.

Alongside these dominant cultural conceptions of masculinity, there have always been masculinities that have been marginalized and subordinated. These can often provide models for resistance to the dominant model, as the articles by Robin Kelley, Rafael Diaz, and Thomas Gerschick and Adam Miller suggest.

You construct intricate rituals which allow you to touch the skin of other men.

Photo courtesy of Barbara Kruger.

Don Sabo

Masculinities and Men's Health: Moving Toward Post-Superman Era Prevention

My grandfather used to smile and say, "Find out where you're going to die and stay the hell away from there." Grandpa had never studied epidemiology (the study of variations in health and illness in society), but he understood that certain behaviors, attitudes, and cultural practices can put individuals at risk for accidents, illness, or death. This chapter presents an overview of men's health that proceeds from the basic assumption that aspects of traditional masculinity can be dangerous to men's health (Sabo & Gordon 1995; Harrison, Chin, & Ficarrotto 1992). First, I identify some gender differences in relation to morbidity (sickness) and mortality (death). Next, I examine how the risk for illness varies from one male group to another. I then discuss an array of men's health issues and a preventive strategy for enhancing men's health.

Gender Differences in Health and Illness

When British sociologist Ashley Montagu put forth the thesis in 1953 that women were biologically superior to men, he shook up the prevailing chauvinistic beliefs that men were stronger, smarter, and better than women. His argument was partly based on epidemiological data that show males are more vulnerable to mortality than females from before birth and throughout the life span.

Reprinted from *Nursing Care in the Community*, 2e, edited by J. Cookfair, St. Louis: Mosby-Year Book.

Mortality

From the time of conception, men are more likely to succumb to prenatal and neonatal death than females. Men's chances of dying during the prenatal stage of development are about 12% greater than those of females and, during the neonatal (newborn) stage, 130% greater than those of females. A number of neonatal disorders are common to males but not females, such as bacterial infections, respiratory illness, digestive diseases, and some circulatory disorders of the aorta and pulmonary artery. Table 24.1 compares male and female infant mortality rates across historical time. Though the infant mortality rate decreases over time, the persistence of the higher rates for males than females suggests that biological factors may be operating. Data also show that males have higher mortality rates than females in every age category, from "under one year" through "over 85" (National Center for Health Statistics 1992). In fact, men are more likely to die in 9 out of the 10 leading causes of death in the United States. (See Table 24.2.)

Females have greater life expectancy than males in the United States, Canada, and postindustrial societies (Verbrugge and Wingard 1987; Waldron 1986). This fact suggests a female biological advantage, but a closer analysis of changing trends in the gap between women's and men's life expectancy indicates that social and cultural factors related to lifestyle, gender identity, and behavior are operating well. Life expectancy among American females is about 78.3 years but 71.3 years for males (National Center for Health

■ **TABLE 24.1**
Infant Mortality Rate

Year	Both Sexes	Males	Females
1940	47.0	52.5	41.3
1950	29.2	32.8	25.5
1960	26.0	29.3	22.6
1970	20.0	22.4	17.5
1980	12.6	13.9	11.2
1989	9.8	10.8	8.8

Note: Rates are for infant (under 1 year) deaths per 1,000 live births for all races.

Source: Adapted from *Monthly Vital Statistics Report*, Vol. 40, No. 8, Supplement 2, January 7, 1992, p. 41.

Statistics 1990). As Waldron's (1995) analysis of shifting mortality patterns between the sexes during the 20th century shows, however, women's relative advantage in life expectancy over men was rather small at the beginning of the 20th century. During the mid-20th century, female mortality declined more rapidly than male mortality, thereby increasing the gender gap in life expectancy. Whereas women benefited from decreased maternal mortality, the midcentury trend toward a lowering of men's life expectancy was slowed by increasing mortality from coronary heart disease and lung cancer that were, in turn, mainly due to higher rates of cigarette smoking among males.

The most recent trends show that differences between women's and men's mortality decreased during the 1980s; that is, female life expectancy was 7.9 years greater than that of males in 1979 and 6.9 years in 1989 (National Center for Health Statistics 1992). Waldron explains that some changes in behavioral patterns between the sexes, such as increased smoking among women, have narrowed the gap between men's formerly higher mortality rates from lung cancer, chronic obstructive pulmonary disease, and ischemic heart disease. In summary, it appears that both biological and sociocultural factors are involved with shaping patterns of men's and women's mortality. In fact, Waldron (1976) suggests that gender-related behaviors rather than strictly biogenic factors account for about three-quarters of the variation in men's early mortality.

Morbidity

Whereas females generally outlive males, females report higher morbidity rates, even after controlling for maternity. National health surveys show

■ **TABLE 24.2**
Death Rates by Sex and 10 Leading Causes: 1989

Cause of Death	Age-Adjusted Death Rate per 100,000 Population			
	Total	Male	Female	Sex Differential
Diseases of the heart	155.9	210.2	112.3	1.87
Malignant neoplasms	133.0	163.4	111.7	1.45
Accidents and adverse effects	33.8	49.5	18.9	2.62
Cerebrovascular disease	28.0	30.4	26.2	1.16
Chronic liver disease, cirrhosis	8.9	12.8	5.5	2.33
Diabetes	11.5	2.0	11.0	1.09
Suicide	11.3	18.6	4.5	4.13
Homicide and legal intervention	9.4	14.7	4.1	3.59

Source: Adapted from the *U.S. Bureau of the Census: Statistical Abstracts of the United States: 1992* (112th ed., p. 84), Washington, DC.

that females experience acute illnesses such as respiratory conditions, infective and parasitic conditions, and digestive system disorders at higher rates than males do; however, males sustain more injuries (Givens 1979; Cypress 1981; Dawson & Adams 1987). Men's higher injury rates are partly owed to gender differences in socialization and lifestyle, such as learning to prove manhood through recklessness, involvement in contact sports, and working in risky blue-collar occupations.

Females are generally more likely than males to experience chronic conditions such as anemia, chronic enteritis and colitis, migraine headaches, arthritis, diabetes, and thyroid disease. However, males are more prone to develop chronic illnesses such as coronary heart disease, emphysema, and gout. Although chronic conditions do not ordinarily cause death, they often limit activity or cause disability.

After noting gender differences in morbidity, Cockerham (1995) asks whether women really do experience more illness than men—or could it be that women are more sensitive to bodily sensations than men, or that men are not as prone as women to report symptoms and seek medical care? He concludes, "The best evidence indicates that the overall differences in morbidity are real" and, further, that they are due to a mixture of biological, psychological, and social influences (p. 42).

Masculinities and Men's Health

There is no such thing as masculinity; there are only masculinities (Sabo & Gordon 1995). A limitation of early gender theory was its treatment of "all men" as a single, large category in relation to "all women" (Connell 1987). The fact is, however, that all men are not alike, nor do all male groups share the same stakes in the gender order. At any given historical moment, there are competing masculinities—some dominant, some marginalized, and some stigmatized—each with its respective structural, psychosocial, and cultural moorings. There are substantial differences between the health options of homeless men, working-class men, lower-class men, gay men, men with AIDS, prison inmates, men of color, and their comparatively advantaged middle- and upper-class, white, professional male counterparts. Similarly, a wide range of individual differences exists between the ways that men and women act out "femininity" and "masculinity" in their everyday lives. A health profile of several male groups is discussed below.

Adolescent Males

Pleck, Sonenstein, and Ku (1992) applied critical feminist perspectives to their research on problem behaviors and health among adolescent males. A national sampling of adolescent, never-married males aged 15–19 were interviewed in 1980 and 1988. Hypothesis tests were geared to assessing whether "masculine ideology" (which measured the presence of traditional male role attitudes) put boys at risk for an array of problem behaviors. The researchers found a significant, independent association with seven of ten problem behaviors. Specifically, traditionally masculine attitudes were associated with being suspended from school, drinking and use of street drugs, frequency of being picked up by the police, being sexually active, the number of heterosexual partners in the last year, and tricking or forcing someone to have sex. These kinds of behaviors, which are in part expressions of the pursuit of traditional masculinity, elevate boys' risk for sexually transmitted diseases, HIV transmission, and early death by accident or homicide. At the same time, however, these same behaviors can also encourage victimization of women through men's violence, sexual assault, unwanted teenage pregnancy, and sexually transmitted diseases.

Adolescence is a phase of accelerated physiological development, and good nutrition during this period is important to future health. Obesity puts adults at risk for a variety of diseases such as coronary heart disease, diabetes mellitus, joint disease, and certain cancers. Obese adolescents are also apt to become obese adults, thus elevating long-term risk for illness. National Health and

Nutrition Examination Surveys show that obesity among adolescents increased by 6% during 1976–80 and 1988–91. During 1988–91, 22% of females of 12–18 years were overweight, and 20% of males in this age group were as well (*Morbidity and Mortality Weekly Report* 1994a).

Males form a majority of the estimated 1.3 million teenagers who run away from home each year in the United States. For both boys and girls, living on the streets raises the risk of poor nutrition, homicide, alcoholism, drug abuse, and AIDS. Young adults in their 20s comprise about 20% of new AIDS cases and, when you calculate the lengthy latency period, it is evident that they are being infected in their teenage years. Runaways are also more likely to be victims of crime and sexual exploitation (Hull 1994).

Clearly, adolescent males face a spectrum of potential health problems—some that threaten their present well-being, and others that could take their toll in the future.

Men of Color

Patterns of health and illness among men of color can be partly understood against the historical and social context of economic inequality. Generally, because African Americans, Hispanics, and Native Americans are disproportionately poor, they are more apt to work in low-paying and dangerous occupations, reside in polluted environments, be exposed to toxic substances, experience the threat and reality of crime, and worry about meeting basic needs. Cultural barriers can also complicate their access to available health care. Poverty is correlated with lower educational attainment, which, in turn, mitigates against adoption of preventive health behaviors.

The neglect of public health in the United States is particularly pronounced in relation to African Americans (Polych & Sabo 1996). For example, in Harlem, where 96% of the inhabitants are African American and 41% live below the poverty line, the survival curve beyond the age of 40 for men is lower than that of men living in Bangladesh (McCord & Freeman 1990). Even though African American men have higher rates

of alcoholism, infectious diseases, and drug-related conditions, for example, they are less apt to receive health care, and when they do, they are more apt to receive inferior care (Bullard 1992; Staples 1995). Statistics like the following led Gibbs (1988) to describe young African American males as an "endangered species":

- The number of young African American male homicide victims in 1977 (5,734) was higher than the number killed in the Vietnam War during 1963–72 (5,640) (Gibbs 1988:258).
- Homicide is the leading cause of death among young African American males. The probability of a black male dying from homicide is about the same as that of a white male dying from an accident (Reed 1991).
- More than 36% of urban African American males are drug and alcohol abusers (Staples 1995).
- In 1993 the rate of contracting AIDS for African American males aged 13 and older was almost 5 times higher than the rate for white males (*Morbidity and Mortality Weekly Report* 1994b).

The health profile of Native Americans and Native Canadians is also poor. For example, alcohol is the number-one killer of Native Americans between the ages of 14 and 44 (May 1986), and 42% of Native American male adolescents are problem drinkers, compared to 34% of same-age white males (Lamarine 1988). Native Americans (10–18 years of age) comprise 34% of in-patient admissions to adolescent detoxification programs (Moore 1988). Compared to the "all race" population, Native American youth exhibit more serious problems in the areas of depression, suicide, anxiety, substance use, and general health status (Blum et al. 1992). The rates of morbidity, mortality from injury, and contracting AIDS are also higher (Sugarman et al. 1993; Metler, et al. 1991).

Like those of many other racial and ethnic groups, the health problems facing American and Canadian natives correlate with the effects of poverty and social marginalization, such as dropping out of school, a sense of hopelessness, the experience of prejudice, poor nutrition, and lack of regular health care. Those who care about men's health, therefore, need to be attuned to the potential interplay between gender, race/ethnicity, cultural differences, and economic conditions when working with racial and ethnic minorities.

Gay and Bisexual Men

Gay and bisexual men are estimated to constitute 5% to 10% of the male population. In the past, gay men have been viewed as evil, sinful, sick, emotionally immature, and socially undesirable. Many health professionals and the wider public have harbored mixed feelings and homophobic attitudes toward gay and bisexual men. Gay men's identity, their lifestyles, and the social responses to homosexuality can impact the health of gay and bisexual men. Stigmatization and marginalization, for example, may lead to emotional confusion and suicide among gay male adolescents. For gay and bisexual men who are "in the closet," anxiety and stress can tax emotional and physical health. When seeking medical services, gay and bisexual men must often cope with the homophobia of health care workers or deal with the threat of losing health care insurance if their sexual orientation is made known.

Whether they are straight or gay, men tend to have more sexual contacts than women do, which heightens men's risk for contracting sexually transmitted diseases (STDs). Men's sexual attitudes and behaviors are closely tied to the way masculinity has been socially constructed. For example, real men are taught to suppress their emotions, which can lead to a separation of sex from feeling. Traditionally, men are also encouraged to be daring, which can lead to risky sexual decisions. In addition, contrary to common myths about gay male effeminacy, masculinity also plays a powerful role in shaping gay and bisexual men's identity and behavior. To the extent that traditional masculinity informs sexual activity of men, masculinity can be a barrier to safer

sexual behavior among men. This insight leads Kimmel and Levine (1989) to assert that "to educate men about safe sex, then, means to confront the issues of masculinity" (p. 352). In addition to practicing abstinence and safer sex as preventive strategies, therefore, they argue that traditional beliefs about masculinity be challenged as a form of risk reduction.

Men who have sex with men remain the largest risk group for HIV transmission. For gay and bisexual men who are infected by the HIV virus, the personal burden of living with an AIDS diagnosis is made heavier by the stigma associated with homosexuality. The cultural meanings associated with AIDS can also filter into gender and sexual identities. Tewksbury's (1995) interviews with 45 HIV positive gay men showed how masculinity, sexuality, stigmatization, and interpersonal commitment mesh in decision making related to risky sexual behavior. Most of the men practiced celibacy in order to prevent others from contracting the disease; others practiced safe sex, and a few went on having unprotected sex.

Prison Inmates

There are 1.3 million men imprisoned in American jails and prisons (Nadelmann & Wenner 1994). The United States has the highest rate of incarceration of any nation in the world, 426 prisoners for every 100,000 people (American College of Physicians 1992), followed by South Africa and the former Soviet Union (Mauer 1992). Racial and ethnic minorities are overrepresented among those behind bars. Black and Hispanic males, for example, comprise 85% of prisoners in the New York State prison system (Green 1991).

The prison system acts as a pocket of risk, within which men already at high risk of having a preexisting AIDS infection are exposed to conditions that further heighten the risk of contracting HIV (Toepell 1992) or other infections such as tuberculosis (Bellin, Fletcher & Safyer 1993) or hepatitis. The corrections system is part of an institutional chain that facilitates transmission of HIV and other infections in certain North

American populations, particularly among poor, inner-city, minority males. Prisoners are burdened not only by social disadvantage but also by high rates of physical illness, mental disorder, and substance abuse that jeopardize their health (Editor, *Lancet* 1991).

AIDS prevalence is markedly higher among state and federal inmates than in the general U.S. population, with a known aggregate rate in 1992 of 202 per 100,000 population (Brewer & Derrickson 1992) compared to a total population prevalence of 14.65 in 100,000 (American College of Physicians 1992). The cumulative total of American prisoners with AIDS in 1989 was estimated to be 5,411, a 72% increase over the previous year (Belbot & del Carmen 1991). The total number of AIDS cases reported in U.S. corrections as of 1993 was 11,565 (a minimum estimate of the true cumulative incidence among U.S. inmates) (Hammett; cited in Expert Committee on AIDS and Prisons 1994). In New York State, at least 10,000 of the state's 55,000 prisoners are believed to be infected (Prisoners with AIDS/HIV Support Action Network 1992). In Canadian federal penitentiaries, it is believed that 1 in 20 inmates is HIV infected (Hankins; cited in Expert Committee on AIDS and Prison 1994).

The HIV virus is primarily transmitted between adults by unprotected penetrative sex or by needle sharing, without bleaching, with an infected partner. Sexual contacts between prisoners occur mainly through consensual unions and secondarily through sexual assault and rape (Vaid; cited in Expert Committee on AIDS and Prisons 1994). The amount of IV drug use behind prison walls is unknown, although it is known to be prevalent and the scarcity of needles often leads to sharing of needles and sharps (Prisoners with AIDS/HIV Support Action Network 1992).

The failure to provide comprehensive health education and treatment interventions in prisons not only puts more inmates at risk for HIV infection, but also threatens the public at large. Prisons are not hermetically sealed enclaves set apart from the community, but an integral part of society (Editor, *Lancet* 1991). Prisoners regularly move in and out of the prison system. In 1989, prisons in the United States admitted 467,227 persons and discharged 386,228 (American College of Physicians 1992). The average age of inmates admitted to prison in 1989 was 29.6, with 75% between 18 and 34 years; 94.3% were male. These former inmates return to their communities after having served an average of 18 months inside (Dubler & Sidel 1989). Within three years, 62.5% will be re-arrested and jailed. Recidivism is highest among poor black and Hispanic men. The extent to which the drug-related social practices and sexual activities of released or paroled inmates who are HIV positive are putting others at risk upon return to their communities is unresearched and unknown.

Male Athletes

Injury is everywhere in sport. It is evident in the lives and bodies of athletes who regularly experience bruises, torn ligaments, broken bones, aches, lacerations, muscle tears, and so forth. For example, about 300,000 football-related injuries per year require treatment in hospital emergency rooms (Miedzian 1991). Critics of violent contact sports claim that athletes are paying too high a physical price for their participation. George D. Lundberg (1994), editor of the *Journal of the American Medical Association,* has called for a ban on boxing in the Olympics and in the U.S. military. His editorial entreaty, though based on clinical evidence for neurological harm from boxing, is also couched in a wider critique of the exploitative economics of the sport.

Injuries are basically unavoidable in sports, but, in traditional men's sports, there has been a tendency to glorify pain and injury, to inflict injury on others, and to sacrifice one's body in order to "win at all costs." The "no pain, no gain" philosophy, which is rooted in traditional cultural equations between masculinity and sports, can jeopardize the health of athletes who conform to its ethos (Sabo 1994).

The connections between sport, masculinity, and health are evidence in Klein's (1993) study of how bodybuilders use anabolic steroids, overtrain, and engage in extreme dietary practices. He spent years as an ethnographic researcher in the muscled world of the bodybuilding subculture, where masculinity is equated to maximum muscularity and men's striving for bigness and physical strength hides emotional insecurity and low self-esteem.

A nationwide survey of American male high school seniors found that 6.6% used or had used anabolic steroids. About two-thirds of this group were athletes (Buckley et al. 1988). Anabolic steroid use has been linked to health risks such as liver disease, kidney problems, atrophy of the testicles, elevated risk of injury, and premature skeletal maturation.

Klein lays bare a tragic irony in American culture—the powerful male athlete, a symbol of strength and health, has often sacrificed his health in pursuit of ideal masculinity (Messner & Sabo 1994).

Men's Health Issues

Advocates of men's health have identified a variety of issues that impact directly on men's lives. Some of these issues may concern you or men you care about.

Testicular Cancer

The epidemiological data on testicular cancer are sobering. Though relatively rare in the general population, it is the fourth most common cause of death among males of 15–35 years accounting for 14% of all cancer deaths for this age group. It is the most common form of cancer affecting males of 20–34 years. The incidence of testicular cancer is increasing, and about 6,100 new U.S. cases were diagnosed in 1991 (American Cancer Society 1991). If detected early, the cure rate is high, whereas delayed diagnosis is life threatening. Regular testicular self-examination (TSE), therefore, is a potentially effective means for ensuring early detection and successful treatment. Regrettably, however, most physicians do not teach TSE techniques (Rudolf & Quinn 1988).

Denial may influence men's perceptions of testicular cancer and TSE (Blesch 1986). Studies show that most males are not aware of testicular cancer, and even among those who are aware, many are reluctant to examine their testicles as a preventive measure. Even when symptoms are recognized, men sometimes postpone seeking treatment. Moreover, men who are taught TSE are often initially receptive, but their practice of TSE decreases over time. Men's resistance to TSE has been linked to awkwardness about touching themselves, associating touching genitals with homosexuality or masturbation, or the idea that TSE is not a manly behavior. And finally, men's individual reluctance to discuss testicular cancer partly derives from the widespread cultural silence that envelops it. The penis is a cultural symbol of male power, authority, and sexual domination. Its symbolic efficacy in traditional, male-dominated gender relations, therefore, would be eroded or neutralized by the realities of testicular cancer.

Diseases of the Prostate

Middle-aged and elderly men are likely to develop medical problems with the prostate gland. Some men may experience benign prostatic hyperplasia, an enlargement of the prostate gland that is associated with symptoms such as dribbling after urination, frequent urination, or incontinence. Others may develop infections (prostatitis) or malignant prostatic hyperplasia (prostate cancer). Prostate cancer is the third leading cause of death from cancer in men, accounting for 15.7 deaths per 100,000 population in 1989. Prostate cancer is now more common than lung cancer (Martin 1990). One in 10 men will develop this cancer by age 85, with African American males showing a higher prevalence rate than whites (Greco & Blank 1993).

Treatments for prostate problems depend on the specific diagnosis and may range from medication to radiation and surgery. As is the case with testicular cancer, survival from prostate cancer is enhanced by early detection. Raising men's awareness about the health risks associated with the prostate gland, therefore, may prevent unnecessary morbidity and mortality. Unfortunately, the more invasive surgical treatments for prostate cancer can produce incontinence and impotence, and there has been no systematic research on men's psychosocial reactions and adjustment to sexual dysfunction associated with treatments for prostate cancer.

Alcohol Abuse

Although social and medical problems stemming from alcohol abuse involve both sexes, males comprise the largest segment of alcohol abusers. Some researchers have begun exploring the connections between the influence of the traditional male role on alcohol abuse. Isenhart and Silversmith (1994) show how, in a variety of occupational contexts, expectations surrounding masculinity encourage heavy drinking while working or socializing during after-work or off-duty hours. Some predominantly male occupational groups, such as longshoremen (Hitz 1973), salesmen (Cosper 1979), and members of the military (Pursch 1976), are known to engage in high rates of alcohol consumption. Mass media play a role in sensationalizing links between booze and male bravado. Postman, Nystrom, Strate, and Weingartner (1987) studied the thematic content of 40 beer commercials and identified a variety of stereotypical portrayals of the male role that were used to promote beer drinking: reward for a job well done; manly activities that feature strength, risk, and daring; male friendship and esprit de corps; romantic success with women. The researchers estimate that, between the ages of 2 and 18, children view about 100,000 beer commercials.

Findings from a Harvard School of Public Health (1994) survey of 17,600 students at 140 colleges found that 44% engaged in "binge drinking," defined as drinking five drinks in rapid succession for males and four drinks for females. Males were more apt to report binge drinking during the past two weeks than females; 50% and 39% respectively. Sixty percent of the males who binge three or more times in the past two weeks reported driving after drinking, compared to 49%

of their female counterparts, thus increasing the risk for accident, injury, and death. Compared to non–binge drinkers, binge drinkers were seven times more likely to engage in unprotected sex, thus elevating the risk for unwanted pregnancy and sexually transmitted disease. Alcohol-related automobile accidents are the top cause of death among 16- to 24-year-olds, especially among males (Henderson & Anderson 1989). For all males, the age-adjusted death rate from automobile accidents in 1991 was 26.2 per 100,000 for African American males and 24.2 per 100,000 for white males, 2.5 and 3.0 times higher than for white and African American females respectively (*Morbidity and Mortality Weekly Report* 1994d). The number of automobile fatalities among male adolescents that results from a mixture of alcohol abuse and masculine daring is unknown.

Men and AIDS

Human immunodeficiency virus (HIV) infection became a leading cause of death among males in the 1980s. Among men aged 25–44 in 1990, HIV infection was the second leading cause of death, compared to the sixth leading cause of death among same-age women (*Morbidity and Mortality Weekly Report* 1993a). Among reported cases of acquired immunodeficiency syndrome (AIDS) for adolescent and adult men in 1992, 60% were men who had sex with other men, 21% were intravenous drug users, 4% were exposed through heterosexual sexual contact, 6% were men who had sex with men and injected drugs, and 1% were transfusion recipients. Among the cases of AIDS among adolescent and adult women in 1992, 45% were intravenous drug users, 39% were infected through heterosexual sexual contact, and 4% were transfusion recipients (*Morbidity and Mortality Weekly Report* 1993a).

Because most AIDS cases have been among men who have sex with other men, perceptions of the epidemic and its victims have been tinctured by sexual attitudes. In North American cultures, the stigma associated with AIDS is fused with the stigma linked to homosexuality. Feelings about men with AIDS can be mixed and complicated by homophobia.

Thoughts and feelings about men with AIDS are also influenced by attitudes toward race, ethnicity, drug abuse, and social marginality. Centers for Disease Control data show, for example, that men of color aged 13 and older constituted 51% (45,039) of the 89,165 AIDS cases reported in 1993. Women of color made up 71% of the cases reported among females aged 13 and older (*Morbidity and Mortality Weekly Report* 1994b). The high rate of AIDS among racial and ethnic minorities has kindled racial prejudices in some minds, and AIDS is sometimes seen as a "minority disease." Although African American or Hispanic males may be at greater risk of contracting HIV/AIDS, just as yellow fingers do not cause lung disease, it is not race or ethnicity that confers risk, but the behaviors they engage in and the social circumstances of their lives.

Perceptions of HIV/AIDS can also be influenced by attitudes toward poverty and poor people. HIV infection is linked to economic problems that include community disintegration, unemployment, homelessness, eroding urban tax bases, mental illness, substance abuse, and criminalization (Wallace 1991). For example, males comprise the majority of homeless persons. Poverty and homelessness overlap with drug addiction, which, in turn, is linked to HIV infection. Of persons hospitalized with HIV in New York City, 9–18% have been found to be homeless (Torres et al. 1990). Of homeless men tested for HIV at a New York City shelter, 62% of those who took the test were seropositive (Ron & Rogers 1989). Among runaway or homeless youth in New York City, 7% tested positive, and this rate rose to 15% among the 19- and 20-year-olds. Of homeless men in Baltimore, 85% admitted to substance use problems (Weinreb & Bassuk 1990).

Suicide

The suicide rates for both African American and white males increased between 1970 and 1989, whereas female rates decreased. Indeed, males are more likely than females to commit suicide from middle childhood until old age (Stillion 1985, 1995). Compared to females, males typically deploy more violent means of attempting suicide (e.g., guns or hanging rather than pills) and are more likely to complete the act. Men's selection of more violent methods to kill themselves is consistent with traditionally masculine behavior (Stillion, White, McDowell, & Edwards 1989).

Canetto (1995) interviewed male survivors of suicide attempts in order to better understand sex differences in suicidal behavior. Although she recognizes that men's psychosocial reactions and adjustments to nonfatal suicide vary by race/ethnicity, socioeconomic status, and age, she also finds that gender identity is an important factor in men's experiences. Suicide data show that men attempt suicide less often than women but are more likely to die than women. Canetto indicates that men's comparative "success" rate points toward a tragic irony in that, consistent with gender stereotypes, men's failure even at suicide undercuts the cultural mandate that men are supposed to succeed at everything. A lack of embroilment in traditionally masculine expectations, she suggests, may actually increase the likelihood of surviving a suicide attempt for some men.

Elderly males in North America commit suicide significantly more often than elderly females. Whereas white women's lethal suicide rate peaks at age 50, white men age 60 and older have the highest rate of lethal suicide, even surpassing the rate for young males (Manton et al. 1987). Canetto (1992) argues that elderly men's higher suicide mortality is chiefly owed to gender differences in coping. She writes,

> older women may have more flexible and diverse ways of coping than older men. Compared to older men, older women may be more willing and capable of adopting different coping strategies—"passive" or "active," "connected" or "independent"—depending on the situation (p. 92).

She attributes men's limited coping abilities to gender socialization and development.

Erectile Disorders

Men often joke about their penises or tease one another about penis size and erectile potency ("not getting it up"). In contrast, they rarely discuss their concerns about impotence in a serious way. Men's silences in this regard are regrettable in that many men, both young and old, experience recurrent or periodic difficulties getting or maintaining an erection. Estimates of the number of American men with erectile disorders range from 10 million to 30 million (Krane, Goldstein, & Saenz de Tejada 1989; National Institutes of Health 1993). The Massachusetts Male Aging Study of the general population of noninstitutionalized, healthy American men between ages 40 and 70 years found that 52% reported minimal, moderate, or complete impotence (Feldman et al. 1994). The prevalence of erectile disorders increased with age, and 9.6% of the men were afflicted by complete impotence.

During the 1960s and 1970s, erectile disorders were largely thought to stem from psychological problems such as depression, financial worries, or work-related stress. Masculine stereotypes about male sexual prowess, phallic power, or being in charge of lovemaking were also said to put too much pressure to perform on some males (Zilbergeld 1993). In contrast, physiological explanations of erectile disorders and medical treatments have been increasingly emphasized since the 1980s. Today diagnosis and treatment of erectile disorders should combine psychological and medical assessment (Ackerman & Carey 1995).

Men's Violence

Men's violence is a major public health problem. The traditional masculine stereotype calls on males to be aggressive and tough. Anger is a byproduct of aggression and toughness and, ultimately, part of the inner terrain of traditional masculinity (Sabo 1993). Images of angry young men are compelling vehicles used by some males to separate themselves from women and to measure their status in respect to other males. Men's anger and violence derive, in part, from sex inequality. Men use the threat or application of violence to maintain their political and economic advantage over women and lower-status men. Male socialization reflects and reinforces these larger patterns of domination.

Homicide is the second leading cause of death among 15- to 19-year-old males. Males aged 15–34 years made up almost half (49%, or 13,122) of homicide victims in the United States in 1991. The homicide rate for this age group increased by 50% from 1985 to 1991 (*Morbidity and Morality Weekly Report* 1994c).

Women are especially victimized by men's anger and violence in the form of rape, date rape, wife beating, assault, sexual harassment on the job, and verbal harassment (Thorne-Finch 1992). That the reality and potential of men's violence impact women's mental and physical health can be surely assumed. However, men's violence also exacts a toll on men themselves in the forms of fighting, gang clashes, hazing, gay-bashing, intentional infliction of injury, homicide, suicide, and organized warfare.

Summary

It is ironic that two of the best-known actors who portrayed Superman have met with disaster. George Reeves, who starred in the original black-and-white television show, committed suicide, and Christopher Reeve, who portrayed the "man of steel" in recent film versions, was paralyzed by an accident during a high-risk equestrian event. Perhaps one lesson to be learned here is that, behind the cultural facade of mythic masculinity, men are vulnerable. Indeed, as we have seen in this chapter, some of the cultural messages sewn into the cloak of masculinity can put men at risk for illness and early death. A sensible preventive health strategy for the 1990s calls upon men to critically evaluate the Superman legacy, that is, to challenge the negative aspects of traditional masculinity that endanger their health, while hanging on to the positive aspects of masculinity and men's lifestyles that heighten men's physical vitality.

The promotion of men's health also requires a sharper recognition that the sources of men's risks for many diseases do not strictly reside in men's psyches, gender identities, or the roles that they enact in daily life. Men's roles, routines, and relations with others are fixed in the historical and structural relations that constitute the larger gender order. As we have seen, not all men or male groups share the same access to social resources, educational attainment, and opportunity that, in turn, can influence their health options. Yes, men need to pursue personal change in order to enhance their health, but without changing the political, economic, and ideological structures of the gender order, the subjective gains and insights forged within individuals can easily erode and fade away. If men are going to pursue self-healing, therefore, they need to create an overall preventive strategy that at once seeks to change potentially harmful aspects of traditional masculinity and meets the health needs of lower-status men.

References

Ackerman, M. D., & Carey, P. C. (1995). *Journal of Counseling & Clinical Psychology, 63*(6), 862–876.

American Cancer Society (1991). Cancer Facts and Figures—1991. Atlanta, GA: American Cancer Society.

American College of Physicians. (1992). The crisis in correctional health care: The impact of the national drug control strategy on correctional health services. *Annals of Internal Medicine, 117*(1), 71–77.

Belbot, B. A., & del Carmen, R. B. (1991). AIDS in prison: Legal issues. *Crime and Delinquency, 31*(1), 135–153.

Bellin, E. Y., Fletcher, D. D., & Safyer, S. M. (1993). Association of tuberculosis infection with increased time in or admission to the New York City jail system. *Journal of the American Medical Association, 269*(17), 2228–2231.

Blesch, K. (1986). Health beliefs about testicular cancer and self-examination among professional men. *Oncology Nursing Forum, 13*(1), 29–33.

Blum, R., Harman, B., Harris, L., Bergeissen, L., & Restrick, M. (1992). American Indian–Alaska native youth health. *Journal of American Medical Association, 267*(12), 1637–1644.

Brewer, T. F., & Derrickson, J. (1992). AIDS in prison: A review of epidemiology and preventive policy. *AIDS, 6*(7), 623–628.

Buckley, W. E., Yesalis, C. E., Friedl, K. E., Anderson, W. A., Streit, A. L., & Wright, J. E. (1988). Estimated prevalence of anabolic steroid use among male high school seniors. *Journal of the American Medical Association, 260*(23), 3441–3446.

Bullard, R. D. (1992). Urban infrastructure: Social, environmental, and health risks to African-Americans. In B. J. Tidwell (Ed.), *The State of Black America* (pp. 183–196). New York: National Urban League.

Canetto, S. S. (1995). Men who survive a suicidal act: Successful coping or failed masculinity? In D. Sabo & D. Gordon (Eds.), *Men's health and illness* (pp. 292–304). Newbury Park, CA: Sage.

Canetto, S. S. (1992). Gender and suicide in the elderly. *Suicide and Life-Threatening Behavior, 22*(1), 80–97.

Cockerham, W. C. (1995). *Medical sociology.* Englewood Cliffs, NJ: Prentice-Hall.

Connell, R. W. (1987). *Gender and power.* Stanford: Stanford University Press.

Cosper, R. (1979). Drinking as conformity: A critique of sociological literature on occupational differences in drinking. *Journal of Studies on Alcoholism, 40,* 868–891.

Cypress, B. (1981). Patients' reasons for visiting physicians: National ambulatory medical care survey, U.S. 1977–78. DHHS Publication No. (PHS) 82-1717, Series 13, No. 56. Hyattsville, MD: National Center for Health Statistics, December, 1981a.

Dawson, D. A., & Adams, P. F. (1987). Current estimates from the national health interview survey: U.S. 1986. Vital Health Statistics Series, Series 10, No. 164. DHHS Publication No. (PHS) 87-1592, Public Health Service. Washington, D.C: U.S. Government Printing Office.

Dubler, N. N., & Sidel, V. W. (1989). On research on HIV infection and AIDS in correctional institutions. *The Milbank Quarterly, 67*(1–2), 81–94.

Editor, (1991, March 16). Health care for prisoners: Implications of "Kalk's refusal." *Lancet, 337,* 647–648.

Expert Committee on AIDS and Prison. (1994). *HIV/AIDS in prisons: Summary report and recommendations to the Expert Committee on AIDS and Prisons* (Ministry of Supply and Services Canada

Catalogue No. JS82-68/2-1994). Ottawa, Ontario, Canada: Correctional Service of Canada.

Feldman, H. A., Goldstein, I., Hatzichristou, D. G., Krane, R. J., & McKinlay, J. B. (1994). Impotence and its medical and psychosocial correlates: Results of the Massachusetts Male Aging Study. *Journal of Urology, 151,* 54–61.

Gibbs, J. T. (Ed.) (1988). *Young, black, and male in America: An endangered species.* Dover, MA: Auburn House.

Givens, J. (1979). Current estimates from the health interview survey: U.S. 1978. DHHS Publication No. (PHS) 80-1551, Series 10, No. 130. Hyattsville, MD: Office of Health Research Statistics, November 1979.

Greco, K. E. & Blank, B. (1993). Prostate-specific antigen: The new early detection test for prostate cancer. *Nurse Practitioner, 18*(5), 30–38.

Green, A. P. (1991). Blacks unheard. *Update* (Winter), New York State Coalition for Criminal Justice, 6–7.

Harrison, J., Chin, J., & Ficarrotto, T. (1992). Warning: Masculinity may be dangerous to your health. In M. S. Kimmel & M. A. Messner (Eds.), *Men's lives* (pp. 271–285). New York: Macmillan.

Harvard School of Public Health. Study reported by Wechler, H., Davenport, A., Dowdall, G., Moeykens, B., & Castillo, S. (1994). Health and behavioral consequences of binge drinking in college: A national survey of students at 140 campuses. *Journal of the American Medical Association, 272*(21), 1672–1677.

Henderson, D. C., & Anderson, S. C. (1989). Adolescents and chemical dependency. *Social Work in Health Care, 14*(1), 87–105.

Hitz, D. (1973). Drunken sailors and others: Drinking problems in specific occupations. *Quarterly Journal of Studies on Alcohol, 34,* 496-505.

Hull, J. D. (1994, November 21). Running scared. *Time, 144*(2), 93–99.

Isenhart, C. E., & Silversmith, D. J. (1994). The influence of the traditional male role on alcohol abuse and the therapeutic process. *Journal of Men's Studies, 3*(2), 127–135.

Kimmel, M. S., and Levine, M. P. (1989). Men and AIDS. In M. S. Kimmel & M. A. Messner (Eds.), *Men's lives* (pp. 344–354) New York: Macmillan.

Klein, A. (1993). *Little big men: Bodybuilding subculture and gender construction.* Albany, NY: SUNY Press.

Krane, R. J., Goldstein, I., & Saentz de Tejjada, I. (1989). Impotence. *New England Journal of Medicine, 321,* 1648–1659.

Lamarine, R. (1988). Alcohol abuse among Native Americans. *Journal of Community Health, 13*(3), 143–153.

Lundberg, G. D. (1994, June 8). Let's stop boxing in the Olympics and the United States military. *Journal of the American Medical Association, 271*(22), 1990.

Manton, K. G., Blazer, D. G., & Woodbury, M. A. (1987). Suicide in middle age and later life: Sex and race specific life table and cohort analyses. *Journal of Gerontology, 42,* 219–227.

Martin, J. (1990). Male cancer awareness: Impact of an employee education program. *Oncology Nursing Forum, 17*(1), 59–64.

Mauer, M. (1992). Men in American prisons: Trends, causes, and issues. *Men's Studies Review, 9*(1), 10–12. A special issue on men in prison, edited by Don Sabo and Willie London.

May, P. (1986). Alcohol and drug misuse prevention programs for American Indians: Needs and opportunities. *Journal of Studies of Alcohol, 47*(3), 187–195.

McCord, C., & Freeman, H. P. (1990). Excess mortality in Harlem. *New England Journal of Medicine, 322*(22), 1606–1607.

Messner, M. A., and Sabo, D. (1994). *Sex, violence, and power in sports: Rethinking masculinity.* Freedom, CA: Crossing Press.

Metler, R., Conway, G., & Stehr-Green, J. (1991). AIDS surveillance among American Indians and Alaskan natives. *American Journal of Public Health, 81*(11), 1469–1471.

Miedzian, M. (1991). *Boys will be boys: Breaking the link between masculinity and violence.* New York: Doubleday.

Montagu, A. (1953). *The natural superiority of women.* New York: Macmillan.

Moore, D. (1988). Reducing alcohol and other drug use among Native American youth. *Alcohol Drug Abuse and Mental Health, 15*(6), 2–3.

Morbidity and Mortality Weekly Report. (1993a). Update: Mortality attributable to HIV infection/AIDS among persons aged 25–44 years—United States, 1990–91. *42*(25), 481–486.

Morbidity and Mortality Weekly Report. (1993b). Summary of notifiable diseases United States, 1992. *41*(55).

Morbidity and Mortality Weekly Report. (1994a). Prevalence of overweight among adolescents—United States, 1988–91. *43*(44), 818–819.

Morbidity and Mortality Weekly Report. (1994b). AIDS among racial/ethnic minorities—United States, 1993. *43*(35), 644–651.

Morbidity and Mortality Weekly Report. (1994c). Homicides among 15–19-year-old males—United States. *43*(40), 725–728.

Morbidity and Mortality Weekly Report. (1994d). Deaths resulting from firearm- and motor-vehicle-related injuries—United States, 1968–1991. *43*(3), 37–42.

Nadelmann, P. & Wenner, L. (1994, May 5). Toward a sane national drug policy [Editorial]. *Rolling Stone,* 24–26.

National Center for Health Statistics. (1990). *Health, United States, 1989.* Hyattsville, MD: Public Health Service.

National Center for Health Statistics. (1992). Advance report of final mortality statistics, 1989. *Monthly Vital Statistics Report, 40* (Suppl. 2) (DHHS Publication No. [PHS] 92-1120).

National Institutes of Health. (1993). Consensus development panel on impotence. *Journal of the American Medical Association, 270,* 83–90.

Pleck, J., Sonenstein, F. L., & Ku, L. C. (1992). In R. Ketterlinus, & M. E. Lamb (Eds.), *Adolescent problem behaviors.* Hillsdale, NJ: Lawrence Erlbaum Associates.

Polych, C., & Sabo, D. (1996). Gender politics, pain, and illness: The AIDS epidemic in North American prisons. In D. Sabo & D. Gordon (Eds.), *Men's health and illness.* Newbury Park, CA: Sage, pp. 139–157.

Postman, N., Nystrom, C., Strate, L., & Weingartner, C. (1987). *Myths, men and beer: An analysis of beer commercials on broadcast television, 1987.* Falls Church, VA: Foundation for Traffic Safety.

Prisoners with AIDS/HIV Support Action Network. (1992). *HIV/AIDS in prison systems: A comprehensive strategy* (Brief to the Minister of Correctional Services and the Minister of Health). Toronto: Prisoners with AIDS/HIV Support Action Network.

Pursch, J. A. (1976). From quonset hut to naval hospital: The story of an alcoholism rehabilitation service. *Journal of Studies on Alcohol, 37,* 1655–1666.

Reed, W. L. (1991). Trends in homicide among African Americans. *Trotter Institute Review, 5,* 11–16.

Ron, A., & Rogers, D. E. (1989). AIDS in New York City: The role of intravenous drug users. *Bulletin of the New York Academy of Medicine, 65*(7), 787–800.

Rudolf, V., & Quinn, K. (1988). The practice of TSE among college men: Effectiveness of an educational program. *Oncology Nursing Forum, 15*(1), 45–48.

Sabo, D., & Gordon, D. (1995). *Men's health and illness: Gender, power, and the body.* Newbury Park, CA: Sage.

Sabo, D. (1994). The body politics of sports injury: Culture, power, and the pain principle. A paper presented at the annual meeting of the National Athletic Trainers Association, Dallas, TX, June 6, 1994.

Sabo, D. (1993). Understanding men. In Kimball, G. (Ed.) *Everything You Need to Know to Succeed after College.* Chico, CA: Equality Press, 71–93.

Staples, R. (1995). Health and illness among African-American Males. In D. Sabo and D. Gordon (Eds.), *Men's health and illness.* Newbury Park, CA: Sage, p. 121–138.

Stillion, J. (1985). *Death and the sexes: An examination of differential longevity, attitudes, behaviors, and coping skills.* New York: Hemisphere.

———. (1995). Premature death among males: Rethinking links between masculinity and health. In D. Sabo & D. Gordon (Eds.), *Men's health and illness.* Newbury Park, CA: Sage, pp. 46–67.

Stillion, J., White, H., McDowell, E. E., & Edwards, P. (1989). Ageism and sexism in suicide attitudes. *Death Studies, 13,* 247–261.

Sugarman, J., Soderberg, R., Gordon, J., & Rivera, F. (1993). Racial misclassification of American Indians: Its effects on injury rates in Oregon, 1989–1990. *American Journal of Public Health, 83*(5), 681–684.

Tewksbury, (1995). Sexual adaptation among gay men with HIV. In D. Sabo & D. Gordon (Eds.), *Men's Health and Illness* (pp. 222–245). Newbury Park, CA: Sage.

Thorne-Finch, R. (1992). *Ending the silence: The origins and treatment of male violence against women.* Toronto: University of Toronto Press.

Toepell, A. R. (1992). *Prisoners and AIDS: AIDS education needs assessment.* Toronto: John Howard Society of Metropolitan Toronto.

Torres, R. A., Mani, S., Altholz, J., & Brickner, P. W. (1990). HIV infection among homeless men in a

New York City shelter. *Archives of Internal Medicine, 150,* 2030–2036.

Verbrugge, L. M., & Wingard, D. L. (1987). Sex differentials in health and mortality. *Women's Health, 12,* 103–145.

Waldron, I. (1995). Contributions of changing gender differences in behavior and social roles to changing gender differences in mortality. In D. Sabo & D. Gordon (Eds.), *Men's health and illness,* Newbury Park, CA: Sage, pp. 22–45.

———. (1986). What do we know about sex differences in mortality? *Population Bulletin of the U.N., No. 18-1985,* 59–76.

———. (1976). Why do women live longer than men? *Journal of Human Stress, 2,* 1–13.

Wallace, R., (1991). Traveling waves of HIV infection on a low dimensional "sociogeographic" network. *Social Science Medicine, 32*(7), 847–852.

Weinreb, L. F., & Bassuk, E. L. (1990). Substance abuse: A growing problem among homeless families. *Family and Community Health, 13*(1), 55–64.

Zilbergeld, B. (1993). *The New Male Sexuality.* New York: Bantam.

Robin D. G. Kelley

Confessions of a Nice Negro, or Why I Shaved My Head

It happened just the other day—two days into the new year, to be exact. I had dashed into the deserted lobby of an Ann Arbor movie theater, pulling the door behind me to escape the freezing winter winds Michigan residents have come to know so well. Behind the counter knelt a young white teenager filling the popcorn bin with bags of that awful pre-popped stuff. Hardly the enthusiastic employee; from a distance it looked like she was lost in deep thought. The generous display of body piercing suggested an X-generation flower-child—perhaps an anthropology major into acid jazz and environmentalism, I thought. Sporting a black New York Yankees baseball cap and a black-and-beige scarf over my nose and mouth, I must have looked like I had stepped out of a John Singleton film. And because I was already late, I rushed madly toward the ticket counter.

The flower child was startled: "I don't have anything in the cash register," she blurted as she pulled the bag of popcorn in front of her for protection.

"Huh? I just want one ticket for *Little Women,* please—the two-fifteen show. My wife and daughter should already be in there." I slowly gestured to the theater door and gave her one of those innocent childlike glances I used to give my mom when I wanted to sit on her lap.

"Oh god . . . I'm so sorry. A reflex. Just one ticket? You only missed the first twenty minutes. Enjoy the show."

Enjoy the show? Barely 1995 and here we go again. Another bout with racism in a so-called liberal college town; another racial drama in which I play the prime suspect. And yet I have to confess the situation was pretty funny. Just two hours earlier I couldn't persuade Elleza, my four-year-old daughter, to put her toys away; time-out did nothing, yelling had no effect, and the evil stare made no impact whatsoever. Thoroughly frustrated, I had only one option left: "Okay, I'm gonna tell Mommy!" Of course it worked.

So those five seconds as a media-made black man felt kind of good. I know it's a product of racism. I know that the myth of black male violence has resulted in the deaths of many innocent boys and men of darker hue. I know that the power to scare is not real power. I know all that—after all, I study this stuff for a living! For the moment, though, it felt good. (Besides, the ability to scare with your body can come in handy, especially when you're trying to get a good seat in a theater or avoid long lines.)

I shouldn't admit this, but I take particular pleasure in putting fear into people on the lookout for black male criminality mainly because those moments are so rare for me. Indeed, my *inability* to employ black-maleness as a weapon is the story of my life. Why I don't possess it, or rather possess so little of it, escapes me. I grew up poor in Harlem and Afrodena (the Negro West Side of Pasadena/Altadena, California). My mom was single during my formative preadolescent years, and for a brief moment she even received a welfare check. A hard life makes a hard nigga, so I've been told.

Never an egghead or a dork, as a teenager I was pretty cool. I did the house-party circuit on Friday and Saturday nights and used to stroll down the block toting the serious Radio Raheem boombox. Why, I even invaded movie theaters in the company of ten or fifteen hooded and high-topped black bodies, colonizing the balconies and occupying two seats per person. Armed with popcorn and Raisinettes as our missiles of choice, we dared any usher to ask us to leave. Those of us who had cars (we called them hoopties or rides back in that day) spent our lunch hours and precious class time hanging out in the school parking lot, running down our Die Hards to pump up Cameo, Funkadelic, Grandmaster Flash from our car stereos. I sported dickies and Levis, picked up that gangsta stroll, and when the shag came in style I was with it—always armed with a silk scarf to ensure that my hair was laid. Granted, I vomited after drinking malt liquor for the first time and my only hit of a joint ended abruptly in an asthma attack. But I was cool.

Sure, I was cool, but nobody feared me. That I'm relatively short with dimples and curly hair, speak softly in a rather medium to high-pitched voice, and having a "girl's name" doesn't help matters. And everyone knows that light skin is less threatening to white people than blue–black or midnight brown. Besides, growing up with a soft-spoken, uncharacteristically passive West Indian mother deep into East Indian religions, a mother who sometimes walked barefoot in the streets of Harlem, a mother who insisted on proper diction and never, ever, ever used a swear word, screwed me up royally. I could never curse right. My mouth had trouble forming the words— "fuck" always came out as "fock" and "goddamn" always sounded like it's spelled, not "gotdayum," the way my Pasadena homies pronounced it in their Calabama twang. I don't ever recall saying the word "bitch" unless I was quoting somebody or some authorless vernacular rhyme. For some unknown reason, that word scared me.

Mom dressed me up in the coolest mod outfits—short pants with matching hats, Nehru jackets, those sixties British-looking turtlenecks. Sure, she got some of that stuff from John's Bargain Store or Goodwill, but I always looked "cute." More stylish than roguish. Kinda like W. E. B. Du Bois as a toddler, or those turn-of-the-century photos of middle-class West Indian boys who grow up to become prime ministers or poets. Ghetto ethnographers back in the late sixties and early seventies would not have found me or my family very "authentic," especially if they had discovered that one of my middle names is Gibran, after the Lebanese poet Kahlil Gibran.

Everybody seemed to like me. Teachers liked me, kids liked me; I even fell in with some notorious teenage criminals at Pasadena High School because *they* liked me. I remember one memorable night in the ninth grade when I went down to the Pasadena Boys' Club to take photos of some of my partners on the basketball team. On my way home some big kids, eleventh-graders to be exact, tried to take my camera. The ringleader pulled out a knife and gently poked it against my chest. I told them it was my stepfather's camera and if I came home without it he'd kick my ass for a week. Miraculously, this launched a whole conversation about stepfathers and how messed up they are, which must have made them feel sorry for me. Within minutes we were cool; they let me go unmolested and I had made another friend.

In affairs of the heart, however, "being liked" had the opposite effect. I can only recall having had four fights in my entire life, all of which were with girls who supposedly liked me but thoroughly beat my behind. Sadly, my record in the boxing ring of puppy love is still 0–4. By the time I graduated to serious dating, being a nice guy seemed like the root of all my romantic problems. I resisted jealousy, tried to be understanding, brought flowers and balloons, opened doors, wrote poems and songs, and seemed to always be on my knees for one reason or another. If you've ever watched "Love Connection" or read *Cosmopolitan,* you know the rest of the story: I practically never had sex and most of the women I dated left me in the cold for roughnecks. My last girlfriend in high school, the woman I took to my prom, the woman I once thought I'd die for, tried to show me the light: "Why do you always ask me what I want? Why don't you just *tell* me what you want me to do? Why don't you take charge and *be a man?* If you want to be a real man you can't be nice all the time!"

I always thought she was wrong; being nice has nothing to do with being a man. While I still think she's wrong, it's an established fact that our culture links manhood to terror and power, and that black men are frequently imaged as the ultimate in hypermasculinity. But the black man as the prototype of violent hypermasculinity is as much a fiction as the happy Sambo. No matter what critics and stand-up comics might say, I know from experience that not all black men— and here I'm only speaking of well-lighted or daytime situations—generate fear. Who scares and who doesn't has a lot to do with the body in question; it is dependent on factors such as age, skin color, size, clothes, hairstyle, and even the sound of one's voice. The cops who beat Rodney King and the jury who acquitted King's assailants openly admitted that the size, shape, and color of his body automatically made him a threat to the officers' safety.

On the other hand, the threatening black male body can take the most incongruous forms. Some of the hardest brothas on my block in West Pasadena kept their perms in pink rollers and hairnets. It was not unusual to see young black men in public with curlers, tank-top undershirts, sweatpants, black mid-calf dress socks, and Stacey Adams shoes, hanging out on the corner or on the basketball court. And we all knew that these brothas were not to be messed with. (The rest of the world probably knows it by now, too, since black males in curlers are occasionally featured on "Cops" and "America's Most Wanted" as notorious drug dealers or heartless pimps.)

Whatever the source of this ineffable terror, my body simply lacked it. Indeed, the older I got, the more ensconced I became in the world of academia, the less threatening I seemed. Marrying and having a child also reduced the threat factor. By the time I hit my late twenties, my wife, Diedra, and I found ourselves in the awkward position of being everyone's favorite Negroes. I don't know how many times we've attended dinner parties where we were the only African Americans in the room. Occasionally there were others, but we seemed to have a monopoly on the dinner party invitations. This not only happened in Ann Arbor, where there is a small but substantial black population to choose from, but in the Negro mecca of Atlanta, Georgia. Our hosts always felt comfortable asking us "sensitive" questions about race that they would not dare ask other black colleagues and friends: What do African Americans think about Farrakhan? Ben Chavis? Nelson Mandela? Most of my black students are very conservative and career-oriented— why is that? How can we mend the relations between blacks and Jews? Do you celebrate Kwanzaa? Do you put anything in your hair to make it that way? What are the starting salaries for young black faculty nowadays?

Of course, these sorts of exchanges appear regularly in most black autobiographies. As soon as they're comfortable, it is not uncommon for white people to take the opportunity to find out everything they've always wanted to know about "us" (which also applies to other people of color, I'm sure) but were afraid to ask. That they feel perfectly at ease asking dumb or unanswerable questions is not simply a case of (mis)perceived racelessness. Being a "nice Negro" has a lot to do with gender, and my peculiar form of "left–feminist–funny-guy" masculinity—a little Kevin Hooks, some Bobby McFerrin, a dash of Woody Allen—is regarded as less threatening than that of most other black men.

Not that I mind the soft-sensitive masculine persona—after all, it is the genuine me, a product of my mother's heroic and revolutionary child-rearing style. But there are moments when I wish I could invoke the intimidation factor of black-maleness on demand. If I only had that look— that Malcolm X/Mike Tyson/Ice Cube/Larry Fishburne/Bigger Thomas/Fruit of Islam look— I could keep the stupid questions at bay, make college administrators tremble, and scare editors into submission. Subconsciously, I decided that I had to do something about my image. Then, as if by magic, my wish was fulfilled.

Actually, it began as an accident involving a pair of electric clippers and sleep deprivation—a bad auto-cut gone awry. With my lowtop fade on the verge of a Sly Stone afro, I was in desperate need of a trim. Diedra didn't have the time to do it, and as it was February (Black History Month), I was on the chitlin' lecture circuit and couldn't spare forty-five minutes at a barber shop, so I elected to do it myself. Standing in a well-lighted bathroom, armed with two mirrors, I started trimming. Despite a steady hand and what I've always believed was a good eye, my hair turned out lopsided. I kept trimming and trimming to correct my error, but as my flattop sank lower, a yellow patch of scalp began to rise above the surrounding hair, like one of those big granite mounds dotting the grassy knolls of Central Park. A nice yarmulke could have covered it, but that would have been more difficult to explain than a bald spot. So, bearing in mind role models like Michael Jordan, Charles Barkley, Stanley Crouch, and Onyx (then the hip-hop group of the hour), I decided to take it all off.

I didn't think much of it at first, but the new style accomplished what years of evil stares and carefully crafted sartorial statements could not: I began to scare people. The effect was immediate and dramatic. Passing strangers avoided me and smiled less frequently. Those who did smile or make eye contact seemed to be deliberately trying to disarm me—a common strategy taught in campus rape-prevention centers. Scaring people was fun for a while, but I especially enjoyed standing in line at the supermarket with my bald head, baggy pants, high-top Reeboks, and long black hooded down coat, humming old standards like "Darn That Dream," "A Foggy Day," and "I Could Write a Book." Now *that* brought some stares. I must have been convincing, since I adore those songs and have been humming them ever since I can remember. No simple case of cultural hybridity here, just your average menace to society with a deep appreciation for Gershwin,

Rodgers and Hart, Van Heusen, Cole Porter, and Jerome Kern.

Among my colleagues, my bald head became the lead subject of every conversation. "You look older, more mature." "With that new cut you come across as much more serious than usual." "You really look quite rugged and masculine with a bald head." My close friends dispensed with the euphemisms and went straight to the point: "Damn. You look scary!" The most painful comment was that I looked like a "B-Boy wannabe" and was "too old for that shit." I had to remind my friend that I'm an OBB (Original B-Boy), that I was in the eleventh grade in 1979 when the Sugar Hill Gang dropped "Rapper's Delight," and that *his* tired behind was in graduate school at the time. Besides, B-Boy was not the intent.

In the end, however, I got more questions than comments. Was I in crisis? Did I want to talk? What was I trying to say by shaving my head? What was the political point of my actions? Once the novelty passed, I began getting those "speak for the race" questions that irritated the hell out of me when I had hair. Why have *black men* begun to shave their heads in greater numbers? Why have so many black athletes decided to shave their heads? Does this new trend have some kind of phallic meaning? Against my better judgment, I found myself coming up with answers to these questions—call it an academician's reflex. I don't remember exactly what I said, but it usually began with black prizefighter Jack Johnson, America's real life "baaad nigger" of the early twentieth century, whose head was always shaved and greased, and ended with the hip-hop community's embrace of an outlaw status. Whatever it was, it made sense at the time.

The publicity photo for my recent book, *Race Rebels,* clearly generated the most controversy among my colleagues. It diverged dramatically from the photo on my first book, where I look particularly innocent, almost angelic. In that first photo I smiled just enough to make my dimples visible; my eyes gazed away from the camera in sort of a dreamy, contemplative pose; my haircut was nondescript and the natural sunlight had a kind of halo effect. The Izod shirt was the icing on the cake. By contrast, the photograph for *Race Rebels* (which Diedra set up and shot, by the way) has me looking directly into the camera, arms folded, bald head glistening from baby oil and rear window light, with a grimace that could give Snoop Doggy Dogg a run for his money. The lens made my arms appear much larger than they really are, creating a kind of Popeye effect. Soon after the book came out, I received several e-mail messages about the photo. A particularly memorable one came from a friend and fellow historian in Australia. In the course of explaining to me how he had corrected one of his students who had read an essay of mine and presumed I was a woman, he wrote: "Mind you, the photo in your book should make things clear—the angle and foreshortening of the arms, and the hairstyle make it one of the more masculine author photos I've seen recently????!!!!!!"

My publisher really milked this photo, which actually fit well with the book's title. For the American Studies Association meeting in Nashville, Tennessee, which took place the week the book came out, my publisher bought a full-page ad on the back cover of an ASA handout, with my mug staring dead at you. Everywhere I turned—in hotel elevators, hallways, lobbies, meeting rooms—I saw myself, and it was not exactly a pretty sight. The quality of the reproduction (essentially a high-contrast xerox) made me appear harder, meaner, and crazier than the original photograph.

The situation became even stranger since I had decided to abandon the skinhead look and grow my hair back. In fact, by the time of the ASA meeting I was on the road (since abandoned) toward a big Black Power Afro—a retro style that at the time seemed to be making a comeback. Worse still, I had come to participate in a roundtable discussion on black hair! My paper, titled "Nap Time: Historicizing the Afro," explored the political implications of competing narratives of the Afro's origins and meaning. Overall, it was a

terrific session; the room was packed and the discussion was stimulating. But inevitably the question came up: "Although this isn't directly related to his paper, I'd like to find out from Professor Kelley why he shaved his head. Professor Kelley, given the panel's topic and in light of the current ads floating about with your picture on them, can you shed some light on what is attractive to black men about baldness?" The question was posed by a very distinguished and widely read African-American literary scholar. Hardly the naif, he knew the answers as well as I did, but wanted to generate a public discussion. And he succeeded. For ten minutes the audience ran the gamut of issues revolving around race, gender, sexuality, and the politics of style. Even the issue of bald heads as phallic symbols came up. "It's probably true," I said, "but when I was cutting my hair at three o'clock in the morning I wasn't thinking 'penis.'" Eventually the discussion drifted from black masculinity to the tremendous workloads of minority scholars, which, in all honesty, was the source of my baldness in the first place. Unlike the golden old days, when doing hair was highly ritualized and completely integrated into daily life, we're so busy mentoring and publishing and speaking and fighting that we have very little time to attend to our heads.

Beyond the session itself, that ad continued to haunt me during the entire conference. Every ten minutes, or so it seemed, someone came up to me and offered unsolicited commentary on the photo. One person slyly suggested that in order to make the picture complete I should have posed with an Uzi. When I approached a very good friend of mine, a historian who is partly my Jewish mother and partly my confidante and *always* looking out for my best interests, the first words out of her mouth were, "Robin, I hate that picture! It's the worst picture of you I've ever seen. It doesn't do you justice. Why did you let them use it?"

"It's not that bad," I replied. "Diedra likes it—she took the picture. You just don't like my bald head."

"No, that's not it. I like the bald look on some men, and you have a very nice head. The problem is the photo and the fact that I know what kind of person you are. None of your gentleness and lovability comes out in that picture. Now, don't get a swelled head when I say this, but you have a delightful face and expression that makes people feel good, even when you're talking about serious stuff. The way you smile, there's something unbelievably safe about you."

It was a painful compliment. And yet I knew deep down that she was telling the truth. I've always been unbelievably safe, not just because of my look but because of my actions. Not that I consciously try to put people at ease, to erase conflict and difference, to remain silent on sensitive issues. I can't quite put my finger on it. Perhaps it's my mother's politeness drills? Perhaps it's a manifestation of my continuing bout with shyness? Maybe it has something to do with the sense of joy I get from stimulating conversations? Or maybe it's linked to the fact that my mom refused to raise me in a manner boys are accustomed to? Most likely it is a product of cultural capital—the fact that I *can* speak the language, (re)cite the texts, exhibit the manners and mannerisms that are inherent to bourgeois academic culture. My colleagues identify with me because I can talk intelligently about their scholarship on their terms, which invariably has the effect of creating an illusion of brilliance. As Frantz Fanon said in *Black Skin, White Masks,* the mere fact that he was an articulate *black* man who read a lot rendered him a stunning specimen of erudition in the eyes of his fellow intellectuals in Paris.

Whatever the source of my ineffable lovability, I've learned that it's not entirely a bad thing. In fact, if the rest of the world could look a little deeper, beyond the hardcore exterior—the wide bodies, the carefully constructed grimaces, the performance of terror—they would find many, many brothas much nicer and smarter than myself. The problem lies in a racist culture, a highly gendered racist culture, that is so deeply enmeshed in the fabric of daily life that it's practically invisible. The very existence of the "nice Negro," like the model-minority myth pinned on Asian Americans, renders the war on those "other," hardcore niggas justifiable and even palatable. In a little-known essay on the public image of world champion boxer Joe Louis, the radical Trinidadian writer C. L. R. James put it best: "This attempt to hold up Louis as a model Negro has strong overtones of condescension and race prejudice. It implies: 'See! When a Negro knows how to conduct himself, he gets on very well and we all love him.' From there the next step is: 'If only all Negroes behaved like Joe, the race problem would be solved.'"[1]

Of course we all know this is a bunch of fiction. Behaving "like Joe" was merely a code for deference and patience, which is all the more remarkable given his vocation. Unlike his predecessor Jack Johnson—the bald-headed prize fighter who transgressed racial boundaries by sleeping with and even marrying white women, who refused to apologize for his "outrageous" behavior, who boasted of his prowess in every facet of life (he even wrapped gauze around his penis to make it appear bigger under his boxing shorts)—Joe Louis was America's hero. As James put it, he was a credit to his race, "I mean the human race."[2] (Re)presented as a humble Alabama boy, God-fearing and devoid of hatred, Louis was constructed in the press as a raceless man whose masculinity was put to good, patriotic use. To many of his white fans, he was a man in the ring and a boy—a good boy—outside of it. To many black folks, he was a hero because he had the license to kick white men's butts and yet maintain the admiration and respect of a nation. Thus, despite similarities in race, class, and vocation, and their common iconization, Louis and Johnson exhibited public behavior that reflected radically different masculinities.

Here, then, is a lesson we cannot ignore. There is some truth in the implication that race (or gender) conflict is partly linked to behavior and how certain behavior is perceived. If our society, for example, could dispense with rigid, archaic notions of appropriate masculine and feminine behavior, perhaps we might create a world that nurtures, encourages, and even rewards nice guys. If violence were not so central to American culture—to the way manhood is defined, to the way in which the state keeps African-American men in check, to the way men interact with women, to the way oppressed peoples interact with one another—perhaps we might see the withering away of white fears of black men. Perhaps young black men wouldn't feel the need to adopt hardened, threatening postures merely to survive in a Doggy-Dogg world. Not that black men ought to become colored equivalents of Alan Alda. Rather, black men ought to be whomever or whatever they want to be, without unwarranted criticism or societal pressures to conform to a particular definition of manhood. They could finally dress down without suspicion, talk loudly without surveillance, and love each other without sanction. Fortunately, such a transformation would also mean the long-awaited death of the "nice Negro."

Not in my lifetime. Any fool can look around and see that the situation for race and gender relations in general, and for black males in particular, has taken a turn for the worse—and relief is nowhere in sight. In the meantime, I will make the most of my "nice Negro" status. When it's all said and done, there is nothing romantic or interesting about playing Bigger Thomas. Maybe I can't persuade a well-dressed white couple to give up their box seats, but at least they'll listen to me. For now. . . .

Notes

1. C. L. R. James, "Joe Louis and Jack Johnson," *Labor Action,* 1 July 1946.

2. Ibid.

Anne Fausto-Sterling

How to Build a Man

How does one become a man? Although poets, novelists, and playwrights long past answered with discussions of morality and honor, these days scholars deliberate the same question using a metaphor—that of social construction. In the current intellectual fashion, men are made, not born. We construct masculinity through social discourse, that array of happenings that covers everything from music videos, poetry, and rap lyrics to sports, beer commercials, and psychotherapy. But underlying all of this clever carpentry is the sneaking suspicion that one must start with a blueprint—or, to stretch the metaphor yet a bit more, that buildings must have foundations. Within the soul of even the most die-hard constructionist lurks a doubt. It is called the body.

In contrast, biological and medical scientists feel quite certain about their world. For them, the body tells the truth. (Never mind that postmodern scholarship has questioned the very meaning of the word "truth.") My task in this essay is to consider the truths that biologists extract from bodies, human and otherwise, to examine scientific accounts—some might even say constructions—of masculinity. To do this, I will treat the scientific/medical literature as yet another set of texts open to scholarly analysis and interpretation.

What are little boys made of? While the nursery rhyme suggests "snips and snails, and puppy-dogs tails," during the past seventy years, medical scientists have built a rather more concrete and certainly less fanciful account. Perhaps the single most influential voice during this pe-

riod has been that of psychologist John Money. Since at least the 1920s, embryologists have understood that during fetal development a single embryonic primordium—the indifferent fetal gonad—can give rise to either an ovary or a testis. In a similar fashion, both male and female external genitalia arise from a single set of structures. Only the internal sex organs—uteri, fallopian tubes, prostates, sperm transport ducts—arise during embryonic development from separate sets of structures. In the 1950s, Money extended these embryological understandings into the realm of psychological development. As he saw it, all humans start on the same road, but the path rapidly begins to fork. Potential males take a series of turns in one direction, potential females in another. In real time, the road begins at fertilization and ends during late adolescence. If all goes as it should, then there are two, and only two, possible destinations—male and female.

But, of course, all does not always go as it should. Money identified the various forks in the road by studying individuals who took one or more wrong turns. From them, he derived a map of the normal. This is, in fact, one of the very interesting things about biological investigators. They use the infrequent to illuminate the common. The former they call abnormal, the latter normal. Often, as is the case for Money and others in the medical world, the abnormal requires management. In the examples I will discuss, management means conversion to the normal. Thus, we have a profound irony. Biologists and physicians use natural biological variation to define normality. Armed with this description, they set out to eliminate the natural variation that gave them their definitions in the first place.

How does all this apply to the construction of masculinity? Money lists ten road signs directing a person along the path to male or female. In most cases these indicators are clear, but, as in any large city these days, sometimes graffiti makes them hard to read and the traveler ends up taking a wrong turn. The first sign is *chromosomal sex*, the presence of an X or a Y chromosome. The second is *gonadal sex*: when there is no graffiti, the Y or the X instructs the fetal gonad to develop into a testis or an ovary. *Fetal hormonal sex* marks the third fork: the embryonic testis must make hormones which influence events to come— particularly the fourth (*internal morphologic sex*), fifth (*external morphologic sex*), and sixth (*brain sex*) branches in the road. All of these, but especially the external morphologic sex at birth, illuminate the road sign for step number seven, *sex of assignment and rearing*. Finally, to become either a true male or a true female in John Money's world, one must produce the right hormones at puberty (*pubertal hormonal sex*), acquire and express a consistent *gender identity and role*, and, to complete the picture, be able to reproduce in the appropriate fashion (*procreative sex*).[1]

Many medical texts reproduce this neat little scheme, and suggest that it is a literal account of the scientific truth, but they neglect to point out how, at each step, scientists have woven into the fabric their own deeply social understandings of what it means to be male or female. Let me illustrate this for several of the branches in the road. Why is it that usually XX babies grow up to be female while XYs become male? Geneticists say that it is because of a specific Y chromosome gene, often abbreviated SDY (for "Sex-Determining Gene" on the Y). Biologists also refer to the SDY as the Master Sex-Determining Gene and say that in its *presence* a male is formed. Females, on the other hand, are said to be the default sex. In the *absence* of the master gene, they just naturally happen. The story of the SDY begins an account of maleness that continues throughout development. A male embryo must activate its master gene and seize its developmental pathway from the underlying female ground plan.

When the SDY gene starts working, it turns the indifferent gonad into a functional testis. One of the first things the testis does is to induce hormone synthesis. It is these molecules that take control of subsequent developmental steps. The first hormone to hit the decks (MIS, or Mullerian Inhibiting Substance) suppresses the development of the internal female organs, which lie in wait ready to unveil their feminine presence. The next, fetal testosterone, manfully pushes over embryonic primordia to develop both the internal and external trappings of physical masculinity. Again, medical texts offer the presence/absence hypothesis. Maleness requires the presence of special hormones; in their absence, femaleness just happens.[2]

Up to this point, two themes emerge. First, masculinity is an active presence which forces itself onto a feminine foundation. Money sometimes calls this "The Adam Principle—adding something to make a male." Second, the male is in constant danger. At any point male development can be derailed: a failure to activate SDY, and the gonad becomes an ovary; a failure to make MIS, and the fetus can end up with fallopian tubes and a uterus superimposed on an otherwise male body; a failure to make fetal testosterone, and, despite the presence of a testis, the embryo develops the external trappings of a baby girl. One fascinating contradiction in the scientific literature illustrates my point. Most texts write that femaleness results from the absence of male hormones, yet at the same time scientists worry about how male fetuses protect themselves from being feminized by the sea of maternal (female) hormones in which they grow.[3] This fear suggests, of course, that female hormones play an active role, after all; but most scientists do not pick up on that bit of logic. Instead, they hunt for special proteins the male embryo makes in order to protect itself from maternally induced feminization. (It seems that mother is to blame even before birth.)

Consider now the birth of a boy-child. He is perfect: Y chromosomes, testes descended into their sweet little scrotal sacs, a beautifully formed penis. He is perfect—except that the penis is very tiny. What happens next? Some medical texts refer to a situation such as this as a social emergency, others see it as a surgical one. The parents want to tell everyone about the birth of their baby boy; the physicians fear he cannot continue developing along the road to masculinity. They decide that creating a female is best. Females are imperfect by nature, and if this child cannot be a perfect or near-perfect male, then being an imperfect female is the best choice. What do the criteria physicians use to make such choices tell us about the construction of masculinity?

Medical managers use the following rule of thumb:

> Genetic females should always be raised as females, preserving reproductive potential, regardless of how severely the patients are virilized. In the genetic male, however, the gender of assignment is based on the infant's anatomy, predominantly the size of the phallus.[4]

Only a few reports on penile size at birth exist in the scientific literature, and it seems that birth size in and of itself is not a particularly good indicator of size and function at puberty. The average phallus at birth measures 3.5 cm (1 to 1.5 inches) long. A baby boy born with a penis measuring only 0.9 inches raises some eyebrows, but medical practitioners do not permit one born with a penis less than 0.6 inches long to remain as a male.[5] Despite the fact that the intact organ promises to provide orgasmic pleasure to the future adult it is surgically removed (along with the testes) and replaced by a much smaller clitoris which may or may not retain orgasmic function. When surgeons turn "Sammy" into "Samantha," they also build her a vagina. Her primary sexual activity is to be the recipient of a penis during heterosexual intercourse. As one surgeon recently commented, "It's easier to poke a hole than build a pole."

All this surgical activity goes on to ensure a congruous and certain sex of assignment and sex of rearing. During childhood, the medical literature insists, boys must have a phallus large enough to permit them to pee standing up, thus allowing them to "feel normal" when they play in little boys' peeing contests. In adulthood, the penis must become large enough for vaginal penetration during sexual intercourse. By and large, physicians use the standard of reproductive potential for making females and phallus size for making males, although Suzanne J. Kessler reports one case of a physician choosing to reassign as male a potentially reproductive genetic female infant rather than remove a well-formed penis.[6]

At birth, then, masculinity becomes a social phenomenon. For proper masculine socialization to occur, the little boy must have a sufficiently large penis. There must be no doubt in the boy's mind, in the minds of his parents and other adult relatives, or in the minds of his male peers about the legitimacy of his male identification. In childhood, all that is required is that he be able to pee in a standing position. In adulthood, he must engage in vaginal heterosexual intercourse. The discourse of sexual pleasure, even for males, is totally absent from this medical literature. In fact, male infants who receive extensive penile surgery often end up with badly scarred and thus physically insensitive members. While no surgeon finds this outcome desirable, in assigning sex to an intersexual infant, sexual pleasure clearly takes a backseat to ensuring heterosexual conventions. Penetration in the absence of pleasure takes precedence over pleasure in the absence of penetration.

In the world of John Money and other managers of intersexuality, men are made not born. Proper socialization becomes more important than genetics. Hence, Money and his followers have a simple solution to accidents as terrible as penile amputation following infant circumcision: raise the boy as a girl. If both the parents and the child remain confident of his newfound female identity, all will be well. But what counts as good mental health for boys and girls? Here, Money and his coworkers focus primarily on female development, which becomes the mirror from which we can reflect the truth about males. Money has published extensively on XX infants born with masculinized genitalia. Usually such children are raised as girls, receiving surgery and hormonal treatments to femininize their genitalia and to ensure a feminine puberty. He notes that frequently such children have a harder time than usual achieving clarity about their femininity. Some signs of trouble are these: in the toddler years, engaging in rough-and-tumble play, and hitting more than other little girls do; in the adolescent years, thinking more about having a career and fantasizing less about marriage than other little girls do; and, as an adolescent and young adult, having lesbian relationships.

The homologue to these developmental variations can be found in Richard Green's description of the "Sissy Boy Syndrome." Green studied little boys who develop "feminine" interests—playing with dolls, wanting to dress in girls' clothing, not engaging in enough rough-and-tumble play. These boys, he argued, are at high risk for becoming homosexuals. Money's and Green's ideas work together to present a picture of normality. And, surprise, surprise, there is no room in the scheme for a normal homosexual. Money makes a remarkable claim. Genetics and even hormones count less in making a man or a woman than does socialization. In sustaining that claim, his strongest evidence, his trump card, is that the child born a male but raised a female becomes a heterosexual female. In their accounts of the power of socialization, Money and his coworkers define heterosexual in terms of the sex of rearing. Thus, a child raised as a female (even if biologically male) who prefers male lovers is psychologically heterosexual, although genetically she is not.

Again, we can parse out the construction of masculinity. To begin with, normally developing little boys must be active and willing to push one another around; maleness and aggression go together. Eventually, little boys become socialized into appropriate adult behavior, which includes heterosexual fantasy and activity. Adolescent boys do not dream of marriage, but of careers and a professional future. A healthy adolescent girl, in contrast, must fantasize about falling in love, mar-

rying, and raising children. Only a masculinized girl dreams of a professional future. Of course, we know already that for men the true mark of heterosexuality involves vaginal penetration with the penis. Other activities, even if they are with a woman, do not really count.

This might be the end of the story, except for one thing. Accounts of normal development drawn from the study of intersexuals contain internal inconsistencies. How *does* Money explain the higher percentage than normal of lesbianism, or the more frequent aggressive behavior among masculinized children raised as girls? One could imagine elaborating on the socialization theme: parents aware of the uncertain sex of their children subconsciously socialize them in some intermediary fashion. Shockingly for a psychologist, however, Money denies the possibility of subconsciously driven behavior. Instead, he and the many others who interpret the development of intersexual children resort to hormonal explanations. If an XX girl, born with a penis, surgically "corrected" shortly after birth, and raised as a girl, subsequently becomes a lesbian, Money and others do not look to faulty socialization. Instead, they explain this failure to become heterosexual by appealing to hormones present in the fetal environment. Excess fetal testosterone caused the masculinization of the genitalia; similarly, fetal testosterone must have altered the developing brain, readying it to view females as appropriate sexual objects. Here, then, we have the last bit of the picture painted by biologists. By implication, normal males become sexually attracted to females because testosterone affects their brain during embryonic development. Socialization reinforces this inclination.

Biologists, then, write texts about human development. These documents, which take the form of research papers, textbooks, review articles, and popular books, grow from interpretations of scientific data. Often written in neutral, abstract language, the texts have the ring of authority. Because they represent scientific findings, one might imagine that they contain no preconceptions, no culturally instigated belief systems. But this turns out not to be the case. Although based in evidence, scientific writing can be seen as a particular kind of cultural interpretation—the enculturated scientist interprets nature. In the process, he or she also uses that interpretation to reinforce old or build new sets of social beliefs. Thus, scientific work contributes to the construction of masculinity, and masculine constructs are among the building blocks for particular kinds of scientific knowledge. One of the jobs of the science critic is to illuminate this interaction. Once this is done, it becomes possible to discuss change.

Notes

1. For a popular account of this picture, see John Money and Patricia Tucker, *Sexual Signatures: On Being a Man or a Woman* (Boston: Little, Brown and Co., 1975).

2. The data do not actually match the presence/absence model, but this does not seem to bother most people. For a discussion of this point, see Anne Fausto-Sterling, "Life in the XY Corral," *Women's Studies International Forum* 12 (1989): 319–31; Anne Fausto-Sterling, "Society Writes Biology/Biology Constructs Gender," *Daedalus* 116 (1987): 61–76; and Anne Fausto-Sterling, *Myths of Gender: Biological Theories about Women and Men* (New York: Basic Books, 1992).

3. I use the phrase "male hormone" and "female hormone" as shorthand. There are, in fact, no such categories. Males and females have the same hormones, albeit in different quantities and sometimes with different tissue distributions.

4. Patricia Donahue, David M. Powell, and Mary M. Lee, "Clinical Management of Intersex Abnormalities," *Current Problems in Surgery* 8 (1991): 527.

5. Robert H. Danish, Peter A. Lee, Thomas Mazur, James A. Amrhein, and Claude J. Migeon, "Micropenis II: Hypogonadotropic Hypogonadism," *Johns Hopkins Medical Journal* 146 (1980): 177–84.

6. Suzanne J. Kessler, "The Medical Construction of Gender: Case Management of Intersexed Infants," *Signs* 16 (1990).

Gloria Steinem

If Men Could Menstruate

A white minority of the world has spent centuries conning us into thinking that a white skin makes people superior—even though the only thing it really does is make them more subject to ultraviolet rays and to wrinkles. Male human beings have built whole cultures around the idea that penis-envy is "natural" to women—though having such an unprotected organ might be said to make men vulnerable, and the power to give birth makes womb-envy at least as logical.

In short, the characteristics of the powerful, whatever they may be, are thought to be better than the characteristics of the powerless—and logic has nothing to do with it.

What would happen, for instance, if suddenly, magically, men could menstruate and women could not?

The answer is clear—menstruation would become an enviable, boastworthy, masculine event:

Men would brag about how long and how much.

Boys would mark the onset of menses, that longed-for proof of manhood, with religious rituals and stag parties.

Congress would fund a National Institute of Dysmenorrhea to help stamp out monthly discomforts.

Sanitary supplies would be federally funded and free. (Of course, some men would still pay for the prestige of commercial brands such as John Wayne Tampons, Muhammad Ali's Rope-a-dope Pads, Joe Namath Jock Shields— "For Those Light Bachelor Days," and Robert "Baretta" Blake Maxi-Pads.)

Military men, right-wing politicians, and religious fundamentalists would cite menstruation ("*men*-struation") as proof that only men could serve in the Army ("you have to give blood to take blood"), occupy political office ("can women be aggressive without that steadfast cycle governed by the planet Mars?"), be priests and ministers ("how could a woman give her blood for our sins?"), or rabbis ("without the monthly loss of impurities, women remain unclean").

Male radicals, left-wing politicians, and mystics, however, would insist that women are equal, just different; and that any woman could enter their ranks if only she were willing to self-inflict a major wound every month ("you *must* give blood for the revolution"), recognize the preeminence of menstrual issues, or subordinate her selfness to all men in their Cycle of Enlightenment.

Street guys would brag ("I'm a three-pad man") or answer praise from a buddy ("Man, you lookin' *good!*") by giving fives and saying, "Yeah, man, I'm on the rag!"

TV shows would treat the subject at length. ("Happy Days": Richie and Potsie try to convince Fonzie that he is still "The Fonz," though he has missed two periods in a row.) So would newspapers. (SHARK SCARE THREATENS MENSTRUATING MEN. JUDGE CITES MONTHLY STRESS IN PARDONING RAPIST.) And movies. (Newman and Redford in "Blood Brothers"!)

Men would convince women that intercourse was *more* pleasurable at "that time of the month." Lesbians would be said to fear blood and therefore life itself—though probably only because they needed a good menstruating man.

Of course, male intellectuals would offer the most moral and logical arguments. How could a woman master any discipline that demanded a sense of time, space, mathematics, or measurement, for instance, without that in-built gift for measuring the cycles of the moon and planets—and thus for measuring anything at all? In the rarefied fields of philosophy and religion, could women compensate for missing the rhythm of the universe? Or for their lack of symbolic death-and-resurrection every month?

Liberal males in every field would try to be kind: the fact that "these people" have no gift for measuring life or connecting to the universe, the liberals would explain, should be punishment enough.

And how would women be trained to react? One can imagine traditional women agreeing to all these arguments with a staunch and smiling masochism. ("The ERA would force house-wives to wound themselves every month": Phyllis Schlafly. "Your husband's blood is as sacred as that of Jesus—and so sexy, too!": Marabel Morgan.) Reformers and Queen Bees would try to imitate men, and *pretend* to have a monthly cycle. All feminists would explain endlessly that men, too, needed to be liberated from the false idea of Martian aggressiveness, just as women needed to escape the bonds of menses-envy. Radical feminists would add that the oppression of the nonmenstrual was the pattern for all other oppressions. ("Vampires were our first freedom fighters!") Cultural feminists would develop a bloodless imagery in art and literature. Socialist feminists would insist that only under capitalism would men be able to monopolize menstrual blood. . . .

In fact, if men could menstruate, the power justifications could probably go on forever.

If we let them.

A R T I C L E   2 8

Thomas J. Gerschick
Adam Stephen Miller

Coming to Terms: Masculinity and Physical Disability

Men with physical disabilities are marginalized and stigmatized in American society. The image and reality of men with disabilities undermine cultural beliefs about men's bodies and physicality. The body is a central foundation of how men define themselves and how they are defined by others. Bodies are vehicles for determining value, which in turn translates into status and prestige. Men's bodies allow them to demonstrate the socially valuable characteristics of toughness, competitiveness, and ability (Messner 1992). Thus, one's body and relationship to it provide a way to apprehend the world and one's place in it. The bodies of men with disabilities serve as a continual reminder that they are at odds with the expectations of the dominant culture. As anthropologist Robert Murphy (1990: 94) writes of his own experiences with disability:

> Paralytic disability constitutes emasculation of a more direct and total nature. For the male, the weakening and atrophy of the body threaten

Reprinted from *masculinities*, 2(1) 1994.

We would like to thank our informants for sharing their time, experiences, and insights. Additionally, we would like to thank the following people for their comments on earlier drafts of this work: Sandra Cole, Harlan Hahn, Michael Kimmel, Michael Messner, Don Sabo, and Margaret Weigers. We, of course, remain responsible for its content. Finally, we are indebted to Kimberly Browne and Erika Gottfried for background research and interview transcriptions. This research was supported by a grant from the Undergraduate Research Opportunity Program at the University of Michigan.

all the cultural values of masculinity: strength, activeness, speed, virility, stamina, and fortitude.

This article seeks to sharpen our understanding of the creation, maintenance, and re-creation of gender identities by men who, by birth, accident, or illness, find themselves dealing with a physical disability. We examine two sets of social dynamics that converge and clash in the lives of men with physical disabilities. On the one side, these men must deal with the presence and pressures of hegemonic masculinity, which demands strength. On the other side, societal members perceive people with disabilities to be weak.

For the present study, we conducted in-depth interviews with ten men with physical disabilities in order to gain insights into the psychosocial aspects of men's ability to come to terms with their physical and social condition. We wanted to know how men with physical disabilities respond to the demands of hegemonic masculinity and their marginalization. For instance, if men with disabilities need others to legitimize their gender identity during encounters, what happens when others deny them the opportunity? How do they reconcile the conflicting expectations associated with masculinity and disability? How do they define masculinity for themselves, and what are the sources of these definitions? To what degree do their responses contest and/or perpetuate the current gender order? That is, what are the political implications of different gender identities and practices? In addressing these questions, we contribute to the growing body of literature on marginalized and alternative gender identities.

We will first discuss the general relationship between physical disability and hegemonic masculinity. Second, we will summarize the methods used in this study. Next, we will present and discuss our central findings. Finally, we discuss how the gender identities and life practices of men with disabilities contribute to the politics of the gender order.

Hegemonic Masculinity and Physical Disability

Recently, the literature has shifted toward understanding gender as an interactive process. Thus, it is presumed to be not only an aspect of what one *is*, but more fundamentally it is something that one *does* in interaction with others (West and Zimmerman 1987). Whereas previously, gender was thought to be strictly an individual phenomenon, this new understanding directs our attention to the interpersonal and institutional levels as well. The lives of men with disabilities provide an instructive arena in which to study the interactional nature of gender and its effect on individual gender identities.

In *The Body Silent*, Murphy (1990) observes that men with physical disabilities experience "embattled identities" because of the conflicting expectations placed on them as men and as people with disabilities. On the one side, contemporary masculinity privileges men who are strong, courageous, aggressive, independent, and self-reliant (Connell 1987). On the other side, people with disabilities are perceived to be, and treated as, weak, pitiful, passive, and dependent (Murphy 1990). Thus, for men with physical disabilities, masculine gender identity and practice are created and maintained at the crossroads of the demands of contemporary masculinity and the stigmatization associated with disability. As such, for men with physical disabilities, being recognized as masculine by others is especially difficult, if not impossible, to accomplish. Yet not being recognized as masculine is untenable because, in our culture,

everyone is expected to display an appropriate gender identity (West and Zimmerman 1987).

Methods

This research was based on in-depth interviews with ten men. Despite the acknowledged problem of identity management in interviews, we used this method because we were most interested in the subjective perceptions and experiences of our informants. To mitigate this dynamic, we relied on probing questions and reinterviews. Informants were located through a snowball sample, utilizing friends and connections within the community of people with disabilities. All of our informants were given pseudonyms, and we further protected their identity by deleting nonessential personal details. The age range of respondents varied from sixteen to seventy-two. Eight of our respondents were white, and two were African American. Geographically, they came from both coasts and the Midwest. All were "mobility impaired," and most were para- or quadriplegics. Given the small sample size and the modicum of diversity within it, this work must necessarily be understood as exploratory.

We interviewed men with physical disabilities for three primary reasons. First, given the diversity of disabilities and our modest resources, we had to bind the sample. Second, mobility impairments tend to be more apparent than other disabilities, such as blindness or hearing loss, and people respond to these men using visual clues. Third, although the literature in this area is scant, much of it focuses on men with physical disabilities.

Due to issues of shared identities, Adam did all the interviews. Interviews were semi-structured and tape-recorded. Initial interviews averaged approximately an hour in length. Additionally, we contacted all of our informants at least once with clarifying questions and, in some cases, to test ideas that we had. These follow-ups lasted approximately thirty minutes. Each informant received a copy of his interview transcript to ensure that we had captured his perspective accurately. We also shared draft copies of this chapter with them and incorporated their insights into the current version.

There were two primary reasons for the thorough follow-up. First, from a methodological standpoint, it was important for us to capture the experience of our informants as fully as possible. Second, we felt that we had an obligation to allow them to control, to a large extent, the representation of their experience.

Interviews were analyzed using an analytic induction approach (Denzin 1989; Emerson 1988; Katz 1988). In determining major and minor patterns of masculine practice, we used the responses to a series of questions including, What is the most important aspect of masculinity to you? What would you say makes you feel most manly or masculine? Do you think your conception of masculinity is different from that of able-bodied men as a result of your disability? If so, how and why? If not, why not? Additionally, we presented our informants with a list of characteristics associated with prevailing masculinity based on the work of R. W. Connell (1987, 1990a, 1990b, 1991) and asked them to rate their importance to their conception of self. Both positive and negative responses to this portion of our questionnaire guided our insight into how each man viewed his masculinity. To further support our discussion, we turned to the limited academic literature in this area. Much more helpful were the wide range of biographical and autobiographical accounts of men who have physical disabilities (see, for instance, Murphy 1990; Callahan 1989; Kriegel 1991; Hahn 1989; and Zola 1982).

Finally, in analyzing the data we were sensitive to making judgments about our informants when grouping them into categories. People with disabilities are shoehorned into categories too much as it is. We sought to discover what was common among their responses and to highlight what we perceived to be the essence of their views. In doing so, we endeavored to provide a conceptual framework for understanding the responses

of men with physical disabilities while trying to be sensitive to their personal struggles.

Disability, Masculinity, and Coming to Terms

While no two men constructed their sense of masculinity in exactly the same way, there appeared to be three dominant frameworks our informants used to cope with their situations. These patterns can be conceived of in relation to the standards inherent in dominant masculinity. We call them the three Rs: *reformulation*, which entailed men's redefinition of hegemonic characteristics on their own terms; *reliance*, reflected by sensitive or hypersensitive adoptions of particular predominant attributes; and *rejection*, characterized by the renunciation of these standards and either the creation of one's own principles and practices or the denial of masculinity's importance in one's life. However, one should note that none of our interviewees *entirely* followed any one of these frameworks in defining his sense of self. Rather, for heuristic reasons, it is best to speak of the major and minor ways each man used these three patterns. For example, some of our informants relied on dominant standards in their view of sexuality and occupation but also reformulated the prevailing ideal of independence.

Therefore, we discuss the *primary* way in which these men with disabilities related to hegemonic masculinity's standards, while recognizing that their coping mechanisms reflected a more complex combination of strategies. In doing so, we avoid "labeling" men and assigning them to arbitrary categories.

Reformulation

Some of our informants responded to idealized masculinity by reformulating it, shaping it along the lines of their own abilities, perceptions, and strengths, and defining their manhood along these new lines. These men tended not to contest these standards overtly, but—either consciously or unconsciously—they recognized in their own condition an inability to meet these ideals as they were culturally conceived.

An example of this came from Damon, a seventy-two-year-old quadriplegic who survived a spinal-cord injury in an automobile accident ten years ago. Damon said he always desired, and had, control of his life. While Damon required round-the-clock personal care assistants (PCAs), he asserted that he was still a very independent person:

> I direct all of my activities around my home where people have to help me to maintain my apartment, my transportation, which I own, and direction in where I go. I direct people how to get there, and I tell them what my needs will be when I am going and coming, and when to get where I am going.

Damon said that his sense of control was more than mere illusion; it was a reality others knew of as well. This reputation seemed important to him:

> People know from Jump Street that I have my own thing, and I direct my own thing. And if they can't comply with my desire, they won't be around. . . . I don't see any reason why people with me can't take instructions and get my life on just as I was having it before, only thing I'm not doing it myself. I direct somebody else to do it. So, therefore, I don't miss out on very much.

Hegemonic masculinity's definition of independence privileges self-reliance and autonomy. Damon required substantial assistance: indeed, some might term him "dependent." However, Damon's reformulation of the independence ideal, accomplished in part through a cognitive shift, allowed him to think otherwise.

Harold, a forty-six-year-old polio survivor, described a belief and practice akin to Damon's. Also a quadriplegic, Harold similarly required PCAs to help him handle daily necessities: Harold termed his reliance on and control of PCAs "acting through others":

> When I say independence can be achieved by acting through other people, I actually mean get-

ting through life, liberty, and the pursuit of happiness while utilizing high-quality and dependable attendant-care services.

As with Damon, Harold achieved his perceived sense of independence by controlling others. Harold stressed that he did not count on family or friends to do favors for him, but *employed* his PCAs in a "business relationship" he controlled. Alternatives to family and friends are used whenever possible because most people with disabilities do not want to burden or be dependent on their families any more than necessary (Murphy 1990).

Social class plays an important role here. Damon and Harold had the economic means to afford round-the-clock assistance. While none of our informants experienced economic hardship, many people with disabilities depend on the welfare system for their care, and the amount and quality of assistance they receive make it much more difficult to conceive of themselves as independent.

A third man who reformulated predominant demands was Brent, a forty-five-year-old administrator. He told us that his paraplegic status, one that he had lived with since he was five years old, had often cast him as an "outsider" to society. This status was particularly painful in his late adolescence, a time when the "sexual revolution" was sweeping America's youth:

> A very important measure of somebody's personhood—manhood—was their sexual ability. . . . What bothers me more than anything else is the stereotypes, and even more so, in terms of sexual desirability. Because I had a disability, I was less desirable than able-bodied people. And that I found very frustrating.

His experiences led him to recast the hegemonic notion that man's relations with a partner should be predominantly physical. As a result, he stressed the importance of emotional relations and trust. This appeared to be key to Brent's definition of his manhood:

> For me, that is my measure of who I am as an individual and who I am as a man—my ability

to be able to be honest with my wife. Be able to be close with her, to be able to ask for help, provide help. To have a commitment, to follow through, and to do all those things that I think are important.

As Connell (1990a) notes, this requires a capacity to not only be expressive, but also to have feelings worth expressing. This clearly demonstrates a different form of masculine practice.

The final case of reformulation came from Robert, a thirty-year-old survivor of a motorcycle accident. Able-bodied for much of his life, Robert's accident occurred when he was twenty-four, leaving him paraplegic. Through five years of intensive physical therapy, he regained 95 percent of his original function, though certain effects linger to this day.

Before his accident, Robert had internalized many of the standards of dominant masculinity exemplified by frequenting bars, leading an active sex life, and riding a motorcycle. But, if our research and the body of autobiographical works from men with physical disabilities has shown anything, it is that coming to terms with a disability eventually changes a man. It appeared to have transformed Robert. He remarked that, despite being generally "recovered," he had maintained his disability-influenced value system:

> I judge people on more of a personal and character level than I do on any physical, or I guess I did; but, you know, important things are guys that have integrity, guys that are honest about what they are doing, that have some direction in their life and know . . . peace of mind and what they stand for.

One of the areas that Robert said took the longest to recover was his sexuality—specifically, his confidence in his sexual ability. While Robert said sexual relations were still important to him, like Brent he reformulated his previous, largely hegemonic notion of male sexuality into a more emotionally and physically egalitarian model:

> I've found a whole different side to having sex with a partner and looking at satisfying the partner rather than satisfying myself; and that has

taken the focus off of satisfying myself, being the big manly stud, and concentrating more on my partner. And that has become just as satisfying.

However, reformulation did not yield complete severance from prevailing masculinity's standards as they were culturally conceived. For instance, despite his reformulative inclinations, Robert's self-described "macho" attitude continued in some realms during his recovery. He, and all others we interviewed, represented the complexity of gender identities and practices; no man's masculinity fell neatly into any one of the three patterns.

For instance, although told by most doctors that his physical condition was probably permanent, Robert's resolve was unyielding. "I put my blinders on to all negative insight into it and just totally focused on getting better," he said. "And I think that was, you know, a major factor on why I'm where I'm at today." This typified the second pattern we identified—reliance on hegemonic masculinity's standards. It was ironic, then, that Robert's tenacity, his never-ending work ethic, and his focused drive to succeed were largely responsible for his almost-complete recovery. While Robert reformulated much of his earlier sense of masculinity, he still relied on this drive.

Perhaps the area in which men who reformulate most closely paralleled dominant masculinity was the emphasis they placed on their occupation. Our sample was atypical in that most of our informants were professionally employed on a full-time basis and could, therefore, draw on class-based resources, whereas unemployment among people with disabilities is very high. Just as societal members privilege men who are accomplished in their occupation, Harold said he finds both "purpose," and success, in his career:

> No one is going to go through life without some kind of purpose. Everyone decides. I wanted to be a writer. So I became a writer and an observer, a trained observer.

Brent said that he drew much of his sense of self, his sense of self-esteem, and his sense of manhood from his occupational accomplishments. Initially, Brent denied the importance of the prevailing ideal that a man's occupational worth was derived from his breadwinner status:

> It is not so important to be the breadwinner as it is to be competent in the world. You know, to have a career, to have my name on the door. That is what is most important. It is that recognition that is very important to me.

However, he later admitted that being the breadwinner still was important to him, although he denied a link between his desires and the "stereotypical" conception of breadwinner status. He maintained that "it's still important to me, because I've always been able to make money." Independence, both economic and physical, were important to all of our informants.

Rejection of hegemonic ideals also occurred among men who primarily depended on a reformulative framework. Harold's view of relationships with a partner dismissed the sexually powerful ideal: "The fact of the matter is that I'm not all that upset by the fact that I'm disabled and I'm a male. I mean, I know what I can do." We will have more to say about the rejection of dominant conceptions of sexuality later.

In brief summary, the subset of our informants whose primary coping pattern involved reformulation of dominant standards recognized their inability to meet these ideals as they are culturally conceived. Confident in their own abilities and values, and drawing from previous experience, they confronted standards of masculinity on their own terms. In doing so, they distanced themselves from masculine ideals.

Reliance

However, not all of the men with physical disabilities we interviewed depended on a reformulative approach. We found that many of our informants *were* concerned with others' views of their masculinity and with meeting the demands of hegemonic masculinity. They primarily used the second pattern, reliance, which involves the internalization of many more of the ideals of predominant masculinity, including physical strength, athleticism, independence, and sexual prowess. Just as some men depended on reformulation for much of their masculine definition, others, despite their inability to meet many of these ideals, relied on them heavily. As such, these men did not seem to be as comfortable with their sense of manhood; indeed, their inability to meet society's standards bothered them very much.

This subset of our informants found themselves in a double bind that left them conflicted. They embraced dominant conceptions of masculinity as a way to gain acceptance from themselves and from others. Yet, they were continuously reminded in their interactions with others that they were "incomplete." As a result, the identity behind the facade suffered; there were, then, major costs associated with this strategy.

The tension between societal expectations and the reality of men with physical disabilities was most clearly demonstrated by Jerry, a sixteen-year-old who had juvenile rheumatoid arthritis. While Jerry was physically able to walk for limited distances, this required great effort on his part; consequently, he usually used a wheelchair. He was concerned with the appearance of his awkward walking. "I feel like I look a little, I don't know, more strange when I walk," he said.

The significance of appearance and external perception of manliness is symptomatic of the difficulty men with physical disabilities have in developing an identity and masculinity free of others' perceptions and expectations. Jerry said:

> I think [others' conception of what defines a man] is very important, because if they don't think of you as one, it is hard to think of yourself as one; or, it doesn't really matter if you think of yourself as one if no one else does.

Jerry said that, particularly among his peers, he was not perceived as attractive as the able-bodied teenagers; thus, he had difficulty in male–female relations beyond landing an occasional date. "[The girls believe] I might be a 'really nice person,' but not like a guy per se," he said. "I think to some extent that you're sort of genderless to them." This clearly represents the emasculation and depersonalization inherent in social definitions of disability.

However, Jerry said that he faced a more persistent threat to his autonomy—his independence and his sense of control—from others being "uncomfortable" around him and persisting in offering him assistance he often did not need. This made him "angry," though he usually did not refuse the help out of politeness. Thus, with members of his social group, he participated in a "bargain": they would socialize with him as long as he remained in a dependent position where they could "help" him.

This forced, situational passivity led Jerry to emphasize his autonomy in other areas. For instance, Jerry avoided asking for help in nearly all situations. This was directly tied to reinforcing his embattled manhood by displaying outward strength and independence:

> If I ever have to ask someone for help, it really makes me like feel like less of a man. I don't like asking for help at all. You know, like even if I could use some, I'll usually not ask just because I can't, I just hate asking. . . . [A man is] fairly self-sufficient in that you can sort of handle just about any situation, in that you can help other people, and that you don't need a lot of help.

Jerry internalized the prevailing masculine ideal that a man should be independent; he relied on that ideal for his definition of manhood. His inability to meet this ideal—partly through his physical condition, and partly from how others treated him—threatened his identity and his sense of manhood, which had to be reinforced even at the expense of self-alienation.

One should not label Jerry a "relier" simply because of these struggles. Being only sixteen years of age—and the youngest participant in our study—Jerry was still developing his sense of masculinity; and, as with many teenagers both able-bodied and disabled, he was trying to fit into his peer group. Furthermore, Jerry will continue to mature and develop his self-image and sense of

masculinity. A follow-up interview in five years might show a degree of resolution to his struggles.

Such a resolution could be seen in Michael, a thirty-three-year-old manager we interviewed, who also internalized many of the standards of hegemonic masculinity. A paraplegic from an auto accident in 1977, Michael struggled for many years after his accident to come to terms with his condition.

His struggles had several sources, all tied into his view of masculinity's importance. The first was that, before his accident, he accepted much of the dominant conception of masculinity. A high-school student, farm hand, and football and track star at the time, Michael said that independence, relations with the women he dated, and physical strength were central to his conception of self.

After his accident, Michael's doctors told him there was a 50–50 chance that he would regain the ability to walk, and he clung to the hope. "I guess I didn't understand it, and had hope that I would walk again," he said. However, he was "depressed" about his situation, "but not so much about my disability, I guess. Because that wasn't real yet."

But coming home three months after his accident didn't alleviate the depression. Instead, it heightened his anxiety and added a new component—vulnerability. In a span of three months, Michael had, in essence, his sense of masculinity and his security in himself completely stripped away. He was in an unfamiliar situation; and far from feeling strong, independent, and powerful, he felt vulnerable and afraid: "No one," he remarked, "can be prepared for a permanent disability."

His reliance on dominant masculinity, then, started with his predisability past and continued during his recovery as a coping mechanism to deal with his fears. The hegemonic standard Michael strove most to achieve was that of independence. It was central to his sense of masculinity before and at the time of our interview. Indeed, it was so important that it frustrated him greatly when he needed assistance. Much like Jerry, he refused to ask for it:

I feel that I should be able to do everything for myself and I don't like it. . . . I don't mind asking for things that I absolutely can't do, like hanging pictures, or moving furniture, or having my oil changed in my car; but there are things that I'm capable of doing in my chair, like jumping up one step. That I feel like I should be able to do, and I find it frustrating when I can't do that sometimes. . . . I don't like asking for [help I don't think I need]. It kind of makes me mad.

When asked if needing assistance was "unmanly," Michael replied, "There's probably some of that in there." For both Michael and Jerry, the independence ideal often led to risk-taking behavior in order to prove to themselves that they were more than their social definition.

Yet, much like Robert, Michael had reformulated his view of sexuality. He said that his physical sexuality made him "feel the most masculine"—apparently another reliant response with a stereotypical emphasis on sexual performance. However, it was more complicated. Michael said that he no longer concentrated on pleasing himself, as he did when able-bodied, but that he now had a more partner-oriented view of sexuality. "I think that my compensation for my feeling of vulnerability is I've overcompensated by trying to please my partner and leave little room to allow my partner to please me. . . . Some of my greatest pleasure is exhausting my partner while having sex." Ironically, while he focused more on his partner's pleasure than ever before, he did so at his own expense; a sense of balancing the needs of both partners was missing.

Thus, sex served multiple purposes for Michael—it gave him and his partner pleasure; it reassured him in his fears and his feelings of vulnerability; and it reconfirmed his masculinity. His sexuality, then, reflected both reliance and reformulation.

While independence and sexuality were both extremely important to Scott, a thirty-four-year-old rehabilitation engineer, he emphasized a third area for his sense of manhood—athletics. Scott served in the Peace Corps during his twenties,

working in Central America. He described his life-style as "rigorous" and "into the whole sports thing," and used a mountain bike as his primary means of transportation and recreation. He was also an avid hockey player in his youth and spent his summers in softball leagues.

Scott acquired a polio-like virus when he was twenty-five years old that left him permanently paraplegic, a situation that he did not initially accept. In an aggressive attempt to regain his physical ability, and similar to Robert, Scott obsessively attacked his rehabilitation

. . . thinking, that's always what I've done with all the sports. If I wasn't good enough, I worked a little harder and I got better. So, I kept thinking my walking isn't very good now. If I push it, it will get better.

But Scott's athletic drive led not to miraculous recovery, but overexertion. When ordered by his doctors to scale back his efforts, he realized he could not recover strictly through tenacity. At the time of our interview, he was ambivalent about his limitations. He clearly did not feel like a failure: "I think that if I wouldn't have made the effort, I always would have wondered, could I have made a difference?" Following the athlete's code of conduct, "always give 110 percent," Scott attacked his recovery. But when his efforts were not enough—when he did not "emerge victorious"—he accepted it as an athlete would. Yet, his limitations also frustrated him at times, and in different areas.

For example, though his physical capacity was not what it was, Scott maintained a need for athletic competition. He played wheelchair basketball and was the only wheelchair-participant in a city softball league. However, he did not return to hockey, the sport he loved as a youngster; in fact, he refused to even try the sled-based equivalent.

Here was Scott's frustration. His spirit of athleticism was still alive, but he lamented the fact that he could not compete exactly as before:

[I miss] the things that I had. I played hockey; that was my primary sport for so many years.

Pretty much, I did all the sports. But, like, I never played basketball; never liked basketball before. Which is why I think I can play now. See, it would be like the equivalent to wheelchair hockey. Some friends of mine have talked to me about it, [but] I'm not really interested in that. Because it wouldn't be real hockey. And it would make me feel worse, rather that better.

In this respect, Scott had not completely come to terms with his limitations. He still wanted to be a "real" athlete, competing in the same sports, in the same ways, with the same rules, with others who shared his desire for competition. Wheelchair hockey, which he derogatorily referred to as "gimp hockey," represented the antithesis of this for him.

Scott's other responses added to this emphasis. What he most disliked about having a disability was "that I can't do the things that I want to be able to do," meaning he could not ride his bike or motorcycle, he could not play "real" hockey, and he was unable to live a freewheeling, spontaneous life-style. Rather, he had to plan ahead of time where he went and how he got there. The frustration caused by having to plan nearly every move was apparent in almost all of our interviews.

However, on the subject of independence, Scott said "I think I'm mostly independent," but complained that there were some situations where he could not meet his expectations and had to depend on his wife. Usually this was not a "major issue," but "there's still times when, yeah, I feel bad about it; or, you know it's the days where she doesn't feel like it, but she kind of has to. That's what bothers me the most, I guess." Thus, he reflected the general desire among men with disabilities not to be a burden of any kind on family members.

Much of the time, Scott accepted being "mostly independent." His reliance on the ideals of athleticism and independence played a significant part in his conception of masculinity and self. However, Scott learned, though to a limited degree, to let go of some of his previous ideals and to accept a different, reformulated notion of independence and competition. Yet, he could not

entirely do so. His emphasis on athletics and independence was still strong, and there were many times when athletics and acceptance conflicted.

However, one should stop short of a blanket assessment of men with disabilities who rely on hegemonic masculinity standards. "Always" is a dangerous word, and stating that "men who rely on hegemonic standards are *always* troubled" is a dangerous assumption. An apparent exceptional case among men who follow a reliant pattern came from Aaron, a forty-one-year-old paraplegic. Rather than experiencing inner turmoil and conflict, Aaron was one of the most upbeat individuals we interviewed. Aaron said that, before his 1976 accident, he was "on top of the world," with a successful business, a commitment to athletics that included basketball shoot-arounds with NBA prospects, and a wedding engagement. Indeed, from the time of his youth, Aaron relied on such hegemonic standards as sexuality, independence, athleticism, and occupational accomplishment.

For example, when asked what masculinity meant to him before his accident, Aaron said that it originally meant sexual conquest. As a teen, he viewed frequent sexual activity as a "rite of passage" into manhood.

Aaron said he had also enjoyed occupational success, and that this success was central to his definition of self, including being masculine. Working a variety of jobs ranging from assembly-line worker to white-collar professional, Aaron said, "I had been very fortunate to have good jobs, which were an important part of who I was and how I defined myself."

According to Aaron, much of his independence ideal came from his father. When his parents divorced, Aaron's father explained to him that, though he was only five, he would have to be "the man of the house." Aaron took this lesson to heart, and strived to fulfill this role both in terms of independence and providing for the family. "My image of manhood was that of a provider," he said, "one who was able to make a contribution to the financial stability of the family in addition to dealing with the problems and concerns that would come up."

His accident, a gunshot wound injuring his spinal cord, left him completely dependent. Predictably, Aaron could not immediately cope with this. "My whole self-image itself was real integrally tied up with the things I used to do," he said. "I found my desire for simple pleasures to be the greatest part of the pain I had to bear."

His pain increased when he left the hospital. His fiancee had left him, and within two years he lost "everything that was important to me"—his house, his business, his savings, most of his friends, and even, for a while, his hope.

However, much as with Robert, Aaron's resiliency eventually turned his life around. Just as he hit bottom, he began telling himself that "if you hold on long enough, if you don't quit, you'll get through it." Additionally, he attacked his therapy with the vengeance he had always devoted to athletics. "I'd never been confronted with a situation in my entire life before that I was not able to overcome by the efforts of my own merit," he said. "I took the same attitude toward this."

Further, he reasserted his sexuality. Though he then wore a colostomy bag, he resumed frequent sexual intercourse, taking the attitude that "this is who I was, and a woman was either going to have to accept me as I was, or she's got to leave me f——— alone."

However, he realized after those five years that his hard work would not be rewarded nor would he be miraculously healed. Figuring that "there's a whole lot of life that I need to live, and this wasn't the most efficient way to live it," he bought a new sport wheelchair, found a job, and became involved in wheelchair athletics. In this sense, a complex combination of all three patterns emerged in Aaron as reliance was mixed with reformulation and rejection.

Furthermore, his soul-searching led him to develop a sense of purpose in his life, and a reason for going on:

> [During my recovery] I felt that I was left here to enrich the lives of as many people as I could before I left this earth, and it gave me a new purpose, a new vision, a new mission, new dreams.

Tenacity, the quest for independence, athletics, and sexual activity carried Aaron through his recovery. Many of these ideals, which had their source in his father's teachings, remained with him as he continued to be active in athletics (everything from basketball to softball to scuba diving), to assert his sexuality, and to aim for complete autonomy. To Aaron, independence, both physical and financial, was more than just a personal ideal; it was one that should be shared by all people with disabilities. As such, he aspired to be a role model for others:

> The work that I am involved in is to help people gain control over their lives, and I think it's vitally important that I walk my talk. If . . . we hold ourselves out to be an organization that helps people gain control over their lives, I think it's vitally important for me as the CEO of that organization to live my life in a way that embodies everything that we say we're about.

Clearly, Aaron was not the same man he was before his disability. He said that his maturity and his experience with disability "made me stronger," and that manhood no longer simply meant independence and sexual conquest. Manhood also meant

> . . . being responsible for one's actions; being considerate of another's feelings; being sensitive to individuals who are more vulnerable than yourself, to what their needs would be; standing up on behalf and fighting for those who cannot speak out for themselves, fight for themselves. It means being willing to take a position and be committed to a position, even when it's inconvenient or costly to take that point of view, and you do it only because of the principle involved.

This dovetailed significantly with his occupation, which was of great importance to him. But as alluded to above, Aaron's emphasis on occupation cannot be seen as mere reliance on the hegemonic conception of occupational achievement. It was more a reformulation of that ideal from self-achievement to facilitating the empowerment of others.

Nevertheless, Aaron's struggle to gain his current status, like the struggle of others who rely on hegemonic masculinity's standards, was immense. Constructing hegemonic masculinity from a subordinated position is almost always a Sisyphean task. One's ability to do so is undermined continuously by physical, social, and cultural weakness. "Understandably, in an effort to cope with this stress (balancing the demands for strength and the societal perception of weakness)," writes political scientist Harlan Hahn, "many disabled men have tended to identify personally and politically with the supposed strength of prevalent concepts of masculinity rather than with their disability" (1989: 3). To relinquish masculinity under these circumstances is to court gender annihilation, which is untenable to some men. Consequently, relying on hegemonic masculinity becomes more understandable (Connell 1990a: 471).

Rejection

Despite the difficulties it presents, hegemony, including that related to gender, is never complete (Janeway 1980, Scott 1985). For some of our informants, resistance took the form of creating alternative masculine identities and subcultures that provided them with a supportive environment. These men were reflected in the final pattern: rejection. Informants who followed this pattern did not so much share a common ideology or set of practices; rather, they believed that the dominant conception of masculinity was wrong, either in its individual emphases or as a practice. One of these men developed new standards of masculinity in place of the ones he had rejected. Another seemingly chose to deny masculinity's importance, although he was neither effeminate nor androgynous. Instead, they both emphasized their status as "persons," under the motto of "people first." This philosophy reflected a key tenet of the Disability Rights Movement.

Alex, a twenty-three-year-old, first-year law student, survived an accident that left him an incomplete quadriplegic when he was fourteen. Before that time, he felt he was an outsider at his private school because he eschewed the superficial, athletically oriented, and materialistic atmosphere. Further, he said the timing of the accident, when many of his peers were defining their social roles, added to this outsider perspective, in that it made him unable to participate in the highly social, role-forming process. "I didn't learn about the traditional roles of sexuality, and whatever the rules are for such behavior in our society, until later," he said. "Because of my physical characteristics, I had to learn a different set of rules."

Alex described himself as a "nonconformist." This simple moniker seemed central to his conception of selfhood and masculinity. Alex, unlike men who primarily reformulate these tenets, rejected the attitudinal and behavioral prescriptions of hegemonic masculinity. He maintained that his standards were his own—not society's—and he scoffed at commonly held views of masculinity.

For example, Alex blamed the media for the idea that men must be strong and attractive, stating "The traditional conception is that everyone has to be Arnold Schwartzenegger . . . [which] probably lead[s] to some violence, unhappiness, and things like that if they [men] don't meet the standards."

As for the importance of virility and sexual prowess, Alex said, "There is a part of me that, you know, has been conditioned and acculturated and knows those [dominant] values"; but he sarcastically laughed at the notion of a man's sexual prowess being reflected in "making her pass out," and summed up his feelings on the subject by adding, "You have to be willing to do things in a nontraditional way."

Alex's most profound rejection of a dominant ideal involved the importance of fathering, in its strictest sense of the man as impregnator:

> There's no reason why we (his fiancee and himself) couldn't use artificial insemination or adoption. Parenting doesn't necessarily involve being the male sire. It involves being a good parent. . . . Parenting doesn't mean that it's your physical child. It involves responsibility and an emotional role as well. I don't think the link

between parenthood is the primary link with sexuality. Maybe in terms of evolutionary purposes, but not in terms of a relationship.

Thus, Alex rejected the procreation imperative encouraged in hegemonic masculinity. However, while Alex took pride at overtly rejecting prevailing masculinity as superficial and silly, even he relied on it at times. Alex said he needed to support himself financially and would not ever want to be an emotional or economic "burden" in a relationship. On one level, this is a common concern for most people, disabled or not. But on another level, Alex admitted that it tied in to his sense of masculinity:

> If I was in a relationship and I wasn't working, and my spouse was, what could be the possible reasons for my not working? I could have just been fired. I could be laid off. Who knows what happened? I guess . . . that's definitely an element of masculinity, and I guess I am just as influenced by that as, oh, as I guess as other people, or as within my definition of masculinity. What do you know? I have been caught.

A different form of rejection was reflected in Leo, a fifty-eight-year-old polio survivor. Leo, who had striven for occupational achievement since his youth, seemed to value many hegemonic traits: independence, money-making ability, and recognition by peers. But he steadfastly denied masculinity's role in shaping his outlook.

Leo said the most important trait to him was his mental capacity and intelligence, since that allowed him to achieve his occupational goals. Yet he claimed this was not related to the prevailing standard. Rather, it tied into his ambitions from before his disability and his willingness to do most anything to achieve his goals.

Before we label him "a rejector," however, note that Leo was a believer in adaptive technology and personal assistance, and he did not see a contradiction between using personal-care assistants and being independent. This seemed to be a reformulation, just as with Damon and Harold, but when we asked Leo about this relation to masculinity, he flatly denied any connection.

Leo explained his renunciation of masculinity by saying "It doesn't mean a great deal . . . it's not how I think [of things]." He said that many of the qualities on our list of hegemonic characteristics were important to him on an individual level but did not matter to his sense of manhood. Leo maintained that there were "external" and "internal" reasons for this.

The external factors Leo identified were the Women's and Disability Rights Movements. Both provided support and alternatives that allow a person with a disability the freedom to be a person, and not (to use Leo's words) a "strange bird." Indeed, Leo echoed the call of the Disability Rights Movement when he described himself as a "person first." In this way, his humanity took precedence and his gender and his disability became less significant.

Also, Leo identified his background as a contributing factor to his outlook. Since childhood, he held a group of friends that valued intellectual achievement over physical performance. In his youth, Leo said he was a member of a group "on the college route." He remained in academia.

Internally, his view of masculinity came from maturity. He had dealt with masculinity and related issues for almost sixty years and reached a point at which he was comfortable with his gender. According to him, his gender conceptions ranged across all three patterns. This was particularly evident in his sexuality. When younger, he relied on a culturally valued, genital sexuality and was concerned with his potency. He wanted to "be on top," despite the physical difficulties this presented him. At the time of our interview, he had a reformulated sexuality. The Women's Movement allowed him to remain sexually active without worrying about "being on top." He even rejected the idea (but not necessarily the physical condition) of potency, noting that it was "even a funny word—potent—that's power."

Further, his age allowed Leo to let go of many of the expectations he had for himself when younger. For instance, he used to overcompensate with great physical activity to prove his manhood and to be "a good daddy." But, he said, he gradually learned that such overcompensation was not necessary.

The practice of "letting go," as Leo and many of our other informants had done, was much like that described by essayist Leonard Kriegel (1991) who, in a series of autobiographical essays, discussed the metaphor of "falling into life" as a way of coping with a disability and masculinity. Kriegel described a common reaction to coping with disability; that is, attempting to "overcome" the results of polio, in his case, by building his upper-body strength through endless hours of exercise. In the end, he experienced premature arthritis in his shoulders and arms. The metaphor of giving up or letting go of behavioral expectations and gender practices as a way to gain greater strength and control over one's life was prevalent among the men who primarily rejected dominant masculinity. As Hahn notes, this requires a cognitive shift and a change in reference group as well as a source of social support:

> I think, ironically, that men with disabilities can acquire strength by acknowledging weakness. Instead of attempting to construct a fragile and ultimately phony identity only as males, they might have more to gain, and little to lose, both individually and collectively, by forging a self-concept about the concept of disability. Certainly this approach requires the exposure of a vulnerability that has been a primary reason for the elaborate defense mechanisms that disabled men have commonly employed to protect themselves (1989:3).

Thus, men with disabilities who rejected or renounced masculinity did so as a process of deviance disavowal. They realized that it was societal conceptions of masculinity, rather than themselves, that were problematic. In doing so, they were able to create alternative gender practices.

Summary and Conclusion

The experiences of men with physical disabilities are important, because they illuminate both the insidious power and limitations of contemporary masculinity. These men have insider knowledge of what the subordinated know about both the gender and social order (Janeway 1980). Additionally, the gender practices of some of these men exemplify alternative visions of masculinity that are obscured but available to men in our culture. Finally, they allow us to elucidate a process of paramount importance: How men with physical disabilities find happiness, fulfillment, and a sense of self-worth in a culture that has, in essence, denied them the right to their own identity, including their own masculinity.

Based on our interviews, then, we believe that men with physical disabilities depend on at least three patterns in their adjustment to the double bind associated with the demands of hegemonic masculinity and the stigmatization of being disabled. While each of our informants used one pattern more than the others, none of them depended entirely on any one of the three.

To judge the patterns and practices associated with any form of masculinity, it is necessary to explore the implications for both the personal life of the individual and the effect on the reproduction of the societal gender order (Connell 1990a). Different patterns will challenge, comply, or actively support gendered arrangements.

The reliance pattern is reflected by an emphasis on control, independence, strength, and concern for appearances. Men who rely on dominant conceptions of masculinity are much more likely to internalize their feelings of inadequacy and seek to compensate or overcompensate for them. Because the problem is perceived to be located within oneself rather than within the social structure, this model does not challenge, but rather perpetuates, the current gender order.

A certain distancing from dominant ideals occurs in the reformulation pattern. But reformulation tends to be an independent project, and class-based resources play an important role. As such, it doesn't present a formidable challenge to the gender order. Connell (1990a: 474) argues that this response may even modernize patriarchy.

The rejection model, the least well represented in this article, offers the most hope for change. Linked closely to a sociopolitical approach that defines disability as a product of interactions between individuals and their environment, disability (and masculinity) is understood as socially constructed.

Members of the Disability Rights Movement, as a result, seek to reconstruct masculinity through a three-prong strategy. First, they focus on changing the frame of reference regarding who defines disability and masculinity, thereby changing the social-construction dynamics of both. Second, they endeavor to help people with disabilities be more self-referent when defining their identities. To do that, a third component must be implemented: support structures, such as alternative subcultures, must exist. If the Disability Rights Movement is successful in elevating this struggle to the level of collective practice, it will challenge the legitimacy of the institutional arrangements of the current gender order.

In closing, there is much fruitful work to be done in the area of masculinity and disability. For instance, we should expect men with disabilities to respond differently to the demands associated with disability and masculinity due to sexual orientation, social class, age of onset of one's disability, race, and ethnicity. However, *how* and *why* gender identity varies for men with disabilities merits further study. We hope that this work serves as an impetus for others to take up these issues.

References

Callahan, John. 1989. *Don't Worry, He Won't Get Far on Foot*. New York: Vintage Books.

Connell, R. W. 1991. "Live Fast and Die Young: The Construction of Masculinity among Young Working-Class Men on the Margin of the Labor Market." *The Australian and New Zealand Journal of Sociology*, Volume 27, Number 2, August, pp. 141–171.

————. 1990a. "A Whole New World: Remaking Masculinity in the Context of the Environmental Movement." *Gender & Society*, Volume 4, Number 4, December, pp. 452–478.

————. 1990b. "An Iron Man: The Body and Some Contradictions of Hegemonic Masculinity," In *Sport, Men, and the Gender Order*, Michael Messner and Donald Sabo, eds. Champaign, IL: Human Kinetics Publishers, Inc., pp. 83–96.

————. 1987. *Gender and Power: Society, the Person, and Sexual Politics*. Stanford, CA: Stanford University Press.

Denzin, Norman. 1989. *The Research Act: A Theoretical Introduction to Sociological Methods*. Englewood Cliffs, NJ: Prentice-Hall.

Emerson, Robert. 1988. "Introduction." In *Contemporary Field Research: A Collection of Readings*, Robert Emerson, ed. Prospect Heights, IL: Waveland Press, pp. 93–107.

Hahn, Harlan. 1989. "Masculinity and Disability." *Disability Studies Quarterly*, Volume 9, Number 3, pp. 1–3.

Janeway, Elizabeth. 1980. *Powers of the Weak*. New York: Alfred A. Knopf.

Katz, Jack. 1988. "A Theory of Qualitative Methodology: The Social System of Analytic Fieldwork." In *Contemporary Field Research: A Collection of Readings*, Robert Emerson, ed. Prospect Heights, IL: Waveland Press, pp. 127–148.

Kriegel, Leonard. 1991. *Falling into Life*. San Francisco: North Point Press.

Messner, Michael A. 1992. *Power at Play: Sports and the Problem of Masculinity*. Boston: Beacon Press.

Murphy, Robert F. 1990. *The Body Silent*. New York: W. W. Norton.

Scott, James C. 1985. *Weapons of the Weak: Everyday Forms of Peasant Resistance*. New Haven: Yale University Press.

West, Candace, and Don H. Zimmerman. 1987. "Doing Gender." *Gender and Society*, Volume 1, Number 2, June, pp. 125–151.

Zola, Irving Kenneth. 1982. *Missing Pieces: A Chronicle of Living with a Disability*. Philadelphia: Temple University Press.

Rafael M. Díaz

Trips to Fantasy Island: Contexts of Risky Sex for San Francisco Gay Men

Promiscuity is famously defined as any amount of sex greater than what you are having. Admittedly, it's an unhelpful word. And yet, "promiscuous" is how many gay men describe at least a part of their life. Some of them mean a kind of innocent, adolescent freedom, but what others really mean is compulsive sex—sex that cannot be credibly taken as political liberation or personal ecstasy because it does not bring joy, cannot be controlled, and is used, exactly like alcohol or drugs, to assuage a non-sexual need. (Jesse Green, "Flirting with Suicide," New York Times Magazine, 15 September 1996).

In the presence of substantial knowledge about how HIV can be transmitted and prevented—and quite often with strong personal intentions to practice safer sex—a substantial number of gay men in San Francisco engage in unprotected anal intercourse in situations that could potentially result in HIV transmission. As a consequence, the number of new HIV infections in the city, particularly among young gay men and gay men of ethnic minority groups, remains unacceptably high (Lemp et al. 1994; Osmond et al. 1994). Even with promising therapeutic regimens in sight, every new infection represents a costly tragedy—personal, interpersonal, societal, and financial. Understanding the nature and context of unprotected sexual practices in situations where HIV could be transmitted (labeled "risky sex"), especially those that occur in the presence of knowledge and skills to avert further infection, is of utmost importance to the work of HIV prevention (Kelly et al. 1991).

Based on psychosocial models of behavior change, behavioral scientists have uncovered important correlates and predictors of risky sex, such as perceived self-efficacy and peer norms for safer sex (Coates et al. 1988). Consequently, prevention programs aimed at promoting self-efficacy and reinforcing social norms for safer sex have been effective in promoting condom use, at least modestly, among vulnerable populations (Bandura 1994). Research on predictors of sexual risk behavior to date, however, has been limited by two serious shortcomings. First, models of behavior change have typically focused on personal (mostly cognitive) variables that predict intentions to practice safer sex, rather than contextual variables that compete against the enactment of safer sex intentions (see critique of behavior change models in Díaz 1998: Chapter 3). By focusing on cognitive predictors of personally formulated intentions, research has missed the situational factors that weaken or break down personal intentionality in sexual practices.

Second, research findings on correlates and predictors of sexual risk have been based mostly on comparisons between men who remain consistently safe (typically labeled the "low-risk" group) and men who, within a given period of time, report at least one instance of unprotected intercourse (typically labeled the "high-risk" group). Such between-group analyses, though useful and somewhat valid, ignore the intra-individual circumstances that might explain episodes of unprotected sex in risky situations for men who otherwise possess all the necessary knowledge, motivation, and skills to practice safer sex. New research is needed on the contexts, situations, and circumstances that undermine men's actual attempts, motivation, and ability to protect themselves against HIV infection.

Overview

We report the results of a qualitative analysis of intra-individual variability in the practice of safer sex. The analysis is based not on comparisons between individuals or groups, but rather on comparisons between sexual episodes—risky and safe, protected and unprotected—within individuals' sexual lives. Thirty interviews, conducted in the context of the San Francisco AIDS Foundation Qualitative Interview Study (QIS; described in the following Methodology section), were included in the analysis. Ten individual interviews were selected from each of the three ethnic groups sampled in QIS: 10 African-American, 10 Latino, and 10 non-Latino White/Caucasian men. All 30 men had reported at least one instance of unprotected anal sex in the last 12 months prior to the study screening interview; the majority of them reported episodes of both protected and unprotected anal intercourse.

Analyses of individual interviews yielded a number of reasons why many gay men in San Francisco engage from time to time in the practice of unprotected anal intercourse, quite often with full awareness of the risks involved. Explicit reasons ranged from an "I just didn't care anymore" attitude stemming from exhaustion about the epidemic, to well-reasoned assessment of acceptable risks (e.g., "He told me he was negative, I'm also negative, and I was the top"). Implicit

reasons ranged from misguided assumptions of partners' HIV serostatus, to blatant distortions of biomedical fact ("my HIV doesn't infect others").

Rather than a "grocery list" of stated and/or implied reasons for risky sex, however, I want to propose a more integrated conceptual framework for understanding unprotected sexual behavior in this vulnerable group of men. Specifically, and based on systematic comparisons of individuals' narratives for their protected and unprotected sexual episodes reported in QIS, I would like to propose, and document with data from interview transcripts, that risky sexual behavior is likely to occur and re-occur in person–situation contexts that have the following six person–situation characteristics:

1. A painful and powerful emotional need-state prior to the sexual encounter, such as extreme feelings of restlessness, loneliness, or despair.

2. The objectification and even "de-humanization" of a sexual partner in fantasy-like fashion, where the partner is seen mostly in terms of satisfying sexual and/or non-sexual personal needs.

3. Sexual activity that seems disconnected or split from the rest of the personal self, that is, sexual behavior that is not well integrated to the cognitive and affective domains of the individual. The sexual split can be extreme, as in the case where the individual's sexual behavior is observed as occurring independently, "on its own," or occurring to someone who the self is detachedly observing.

4. The use and abuse of drugs and/or alcohol to facilitate, maintain, and justify sexual activity that is ultimately experienced as frightening, undesirable, and/or dissonant with personal values and beliefs. In these situations, and mostly through the attributions regarding their effects on the particular individual, the use of substances facilitates the split of sexual behavior.

5. Perceptions of low sexual control or low sense of responsibility throughout the sexual

episode. Control and responsibility for events in the sexual encounter are attributed to substances, circumstances, or the other partner.

6. Negative emotional states—such as guilt and regret—after the sexual encounter, especially those self-deprecatory ruminations that stem from pathologizing world views that prevent individuals from instructive self-observation.

My major claim is that this conceptual framework—labeled Trips to Fantasy Island—is useful to understand the intra-individual variability in safer sex behavior for the majority of the interviews in the study. My major cautionary note is that this framework should *not* be used to further pathologize individuals who engage in unprotected intercourse, whether risky or not. More often than not, reasons for unprotected intercourse are embedded within an ecology of personal, interpersonal and social circumstances that create contexts or situations that increase the probability of HIV transmission (Rotello 1997). It follows that "risky" behavior cannot be understood as a property of individuals or as a product of individual deviance and/or pathology, but it is rather the outcome of structural, cultural, personal, and situational factors that meaningfully (and at times oppressively) interact, and shape sexual encounters between men. Moreover, when these contextual factors or ecology are taken into account, what appears to an outsider as "risky" sexual behavior appears to the individual as a subjectively powerful and meaningful experience. As evident in the remainder of the article and explicitly discussed in the conclusion, the powerful emotions that initiate the "trips" are closely connected to elements of the culture that shape perceptions of self and give meaning to sexual encounters. Also, it must be kept in mind that the narratives gathered for this analysis were provided by individuals who in other contexts and situations were perfectly capable of practicing safer sex.

The label "Trips to Fantasy Island" underscores the fact that, for many of the risky episodes

I studied, men were engaging in sexual activity in an attempt to fulfill or solve, in fantasy-like fashion, what is basically a non-sexual perceived need, whether it is intimacy, masculinity, or self-worth. Thus, at a very basic level, the Fantasy Island framework formalizes a familiar observation, namely that many individuals come to sexual encounters in search of experiences other than simply sex, such as interpersonal connectedness, social acceptance, or personal affirmation. In fact, sexuality can be said to be socially and culturally constructed, to the extent that for a given group or society sex becomes a place, for example, to restore feelings of masculinity–femininity, or assert power, or feel attractive, or experience social connectedness. Psychologically, in those cases where the need for connectedness, affirmation, or self-worth is so great and deeply felt, such needs seem to overpower the concern for safety or health. By the same token, it is not surprising that such needs are really pressing in cultures that worship physical attractiveness, or that demand that masculinity be proven, or where rampant prejudice and discrimination promote social alienation and isolation.

Even though the framework is indeed psychological and developed by someone trained in psychology, I think of it as "contextualized," because it refers to person–situation contexts rather than to cognitive or behavioral constructs that are independent of actual situations. In the Fantasy Island framework, all psychological constructs—emotions, perceptions, and behaviors—become meaningful and integrated only when considered in their whole person–situation context; otherwise, with what we all know about HIV, the sexual episodes would seem totally absurd and crazy.

Not all instances of unprotected intercourse can be explained or understood within this conceptual framework. The framework is offered as only one—yet, in my view, useful—window or perspective to understand the re-occurrence of unprotected risky sexual behavior in the presence of substantial knowledge, motivation, and skills to practice safer sex.

Methodology

Eliciting Sexual Narratives

Men in the study were recruited to participate in an in-depth interview study (QIS) sponsored by the San Francisco AIDS Foundation (SFAF), a well-known non-profit private organization that provides a wide range of HIV/AIDS-related services in the city. Interviews were conducted at the Center for AIDS Prevention Studies (CAPS), a research group affiliated with the University of California San Francisco. Trained interviewers asked men about a diverse set of topics such as family history, participation in gay community, social support networks, and patterns of sexual activity, among others. Somewhere around the second third of the in-depth interview, individual participants were asked to report the frequency of anal intercourse in the past 12 months, and the number of those episodes that were unprotected, with no use of condoms. Study participants were also asked about the number of incidents where condoms might have failed or broken. Questions about the frequency of anal intercourse, though at times shifting abruptly the content of the interviews, served as a good introduction to elicit participants' narratives of selected sexual episodes.

Participants were asked first to describe a sexual episode that involved the use of condoms (i.e. protected sex) and, immediately after, they were asked to describe a sexual episode that involved no condoms at all (i.e. unprotected sex). Narratives about the sexual episodes—including details about setting, location, partners, substance use, emotions, and actual behaviors—were elicited in the following fashion, as in these two examples, taken from two different interviews:

> I would like for you to describe the most recent sexual encounter with another man when you engaged in anal intercourse with a condom that did not break. Try to remember as much about what happened before, during, and after the event. Keeping in mind that I'm interested in your thoughts and feelings. Just tell me about that day, what you were doing and feeling be-

fore you had sex, who it was with, what you talked about, things like that. (Case 13)

> If you would could you talk about the last time that you had anal sex with a condom. The last time you fucked with a condom, what was that like? With whom? Where were you? How'd you feel? What was the day like? How did you lead up to having sex with this person? Where'd you meet up? Things like that. (Case 05)

Similar questions were then asked for the unprotected-sex episodes and, in a few cases, about the episode that involved condom break.

Coding the Interview Transcripts

The narratives of sexual episodes were transcribed (varying in length from one to about fifteen single-spaced pages) and coded under the following categories:

1. Setting/situation
2. Partner characteristics
3. Stated emotions prior, during, and after the episode
4. Actual sexual behavior
5. Associated cognitions
6. Substance use: type and amount, reported effects, and attributions of influence
7. Perceptions and assessments of HIV risk
8. Communication: verbal and non-verbal
9. Disclosure of HIV status
10. Gender attributions
11. Decision-making/intentionality
12. Strategies to reduce risk
13. Attitudes towards condoms
14. Perceptions of responsibility/control

For each of the 30 selected interviews, text from both protected and unprotected episodes was categorized under the same categories. Our goal—one that we easily achieved—was to categorize exhaustively the majority of text given for the sexual episodes.

The Contexts of Risky Sex

In the following sections, and based on the voices and subjective experiences of study participants,

I offer some empirical support for the six hypothesized dimensions, factors, or characteristics of unprotected sexual encounters. Most of these factors are present, in different degrees and combinations, in the narratives of many of the unprotected sexual episodes examined. These six factors constitute the major areas of difference between protected and unprotected events within individuals' sexual lives. I propose that, taken together, the six factors create a particular context of sexual risk, labeled Trips to Fantasy Island, which can explain or give meaning to a large proportion of risky sex reported in the study. All names given to the respondents are fictitious, and are used only for the purpose of ease of presentation; Appendix 1 contains a list of cases cited, listed with their respective fictitious names and information regarding age, ethnicity, and HIV serostatus.

(1) *Negative emotions prior to the sexual encounter*
One of the most striking differences between the protected and unprotected sexual episodes was the emotional state of participants immediately prior to the risky sexual encounter. In contrast to the protected episodes, risky episodes contained a certain emotional heaviness or "thickness" that was not present in the descriptions of protected encounters. The emotional heaviness typically referred to a need-state, a sense of personal isolation, or insecurity that somehow would be relieved by the sexual encounter. Even though at times men expressed this emotional state as "I was very horny" or "I had to have it [sex] that night," further inquiry revealed a set of negative emotions connected to non-sexual needs prior to the sexual encounter.

In the context of the unprotected episodes, men talked about feeling lonely, frustrated, anxious, unattractive, disappointed, drained by multiple losses and, some of them, even highly ambivalent about having sex at all or about entering situations they perceived as potentially dangerous and emotionally unsafe. Consider, for example, the contrasting descriptions of Larry, a 40-year-old Caucasian, HIV-positive gay man.

For the protected episode:

Larry: Things at the time were really good. I was feeling really upbeat.

Int.: How had you been feeling during the day while you were getting ready?

Larry: Excited.

Int.: And your mood was . . .

Larry: Real upbeat, real, a bit anxious, you know.

Int.: Did you have anything particularly stressful at that time in your life?

Larry: No, thankfully I had just gotten rid of that stressful, yucky roommate, so no.

For the unprotected episode, Larry reported the following emotions:

Int.: What had your mood been like during the day as you were getting ready for this date?

Larry: Actually to be real honest with you, I was very anxious about it in a bad way because I always feel terribly afraid to take my clothes off the better looking a man is. And I almost, I really had been thinking of ways to lie out of it. So I wouldn't have to go. 'Cause he was so terribly attractive to me, I didn't want him to see me naked. So I had been feeling real anxious.

While Larry confessed being a bit anxious prior to his protected encounter, his "real anxious" and "terribly afraid" state accompanied his unprotected event. The fear, anxiety, and ultimate ambivalence about meeting his sexual partner manifested both his desire and fear of having sex with someone he considered extremely attractive. Sex with this partner, described by Larry as "tragically handsome" (see next section), involved a test of his personal attractiveness. In the context of a very poor body self-image, Larry ventured to have sex with this handsome "looker," as if sex with this man would validate his own sense of personal attractiveness. In fact, later on in the interview, Larry confessed that he fantasized about this partner telling other people how good and exciting he had been in bed.

Quite often, negative emotional states prior to the unprotected events were connected to feelings of social isolation, loneliness, disappointed love, and accompanying feelings of longing and craving for flesh-to-flesh contact. Michael, a 30-year-old HIV-negative Latino gay man who was pretty upset about the general disconnection between sex and intimacy in his life, and his inability to find a romantic partner, described it in the following way:

Michael: It was during a period when there was this guy who I really had grown to like a lot and I told him that I wanted to be in a relationship with him and he didn't feel the same way, and I was very disappointed. That was on a Saturday. And on Sunday night—Sundays tend to be like, I don't know why, but Sunday afternoon and evening feel depressing to me, and lonely. And so that evening I went out to the bar to see a show and have a couple of drinks . . . I went there for a couple hours and didn't run into any of my friends, didn't get any attention from anyone, and left after a couple of hours feeling pretty low, I think. I was down about 'J' and I was feeling lonely. And from there I decided to go home but instead I ended up going out cruising out to a park.

Int.: What would you say were the things that led you to not use a condom that night?

Michael: Um, more than anything else was that sense that I get when I'm in the midst of being sexually predatory of like just being very single-minded and wanting to find that person and to seduce them and to have sex with them. Um, and I think it's sort of a single-minded strange thing I feel that was happening in the left part of the brain, somehow it's not accessible to use it at that point. That was part of it. I don't know how much my down mental state had to do with it but I do know my mental state has a lot do with when

I pursue sex because pursuing sex is often what I do to fill up loneliness and I know in general pursuing sex like that is about loneliness. I don't know how much not using a condom was about that . . .

With a decreased sense of personal control, and driven by his longing for social connection, Michael found himself in the cruising park having unprotected sex with someone he didn't feel attracted to. In a state he described as "trance-like," and somewhat desperately, Michael attempted to assuage his feelings of loneliness and isolation in the context of an anonymous and unsafe sexual encounter. While quite connected with and articulate about his own emotional states in retrospect, at the time of the encounter Michael felt outside himself: "I just felt like I was just being kind of swept along on the events and that I was not in control of myself."

In what is perhaps an extreme illustration of the point under discussion, Rick, a 38-year-old HIV-positive Caucasian gay man, spoke of his need to find in sex the physical pain that would match his emotional pain. Rick was able to find this physical pain in an anonymous encounter, being penetrated (without condoms) by a man with a larger than normal penis ("donkey-like," "biggest cock I've ever seen") in a cruising park setting. In his own words:

Int.: How had you been feeling that day? What had that day been like for you, beforehand?

Rick: Well, it really, it was a messed up day. I had my house burglarized, my brand new stereo system taken, my TV taken, my VCR taken, my books taken, my rifles taken, kept my clothes and all my paperwork. But all my material stuff was taken, my telephone taken . . . I was wanting something that size [referring to his partner's penis], maybe smaller, I needed somebody to inflict pain on me. That's going back to my adolescence, at least half my life, whenever, whenever, whenever I hurt on the inside, I want to hurt on the outside, too. So that's when I basically, I go out for anal sex. Because it doesn't really hurt, it feels good. It's twisted, but it's a fact.

(2) *Fantasy partner* More often than not, and in sharp contrast to partners for protected sexual events, partners of risky sexual encounters were described in fantasy-like fashion. Fantasies ranged from Hollywood star-like handsome men, to butcher-type, straight-looking men. Interestingly, and in most cases, fantasies were meaningfully connected to the emotional need-state described as preceding the sexual event. For example, a Latino man who is usually on top in anal intercourse, under the influence of drugs becomes an "eager bottom," and thus longs to be penetrated by a "straight-looking" man. In another example, terribly down on account of his varicose veins and plain physical looks, a gay man searches for an encounter with a "tragically handsome man," an exotic-looking "Harry Belafonte with a beard." Another man goes to the Castro (gentrified gay neighborhood) "to get away from it all" and sees his potential sexual partner as a prince-like charmer who helps him forget the ghetto-like horrors of the Tenderloin (poor section of town) and who, in his view, "probably doesn't have HIV" because he looks so clean, decent, smart, and well-educated. In all cases, the partner is unrealistically polarized, in fantasy-like fashion, to exaggerate the quality most needed to satisfy the individual's unmet need—be it physical attractiveness, masculinity, or escaping the devastating consequences of poverty. Let us consider in more detail the nature of fantasy-like sexual partners, by contrasting Larry's sexual partners for both the protected and unprotected sexual episodes he reported in the interview.

For the protected episode, Larry described his partner as follows:

> **Larry:** . . . I really liked him. I liked being with him and so I was pretty excited and he was enough of what I liked, like sensitive and passionate and erotic and kissing and touching . . . we met at the Aliveness project which was an HIV/AIDS/Wellness community dining resource center in Minneapolis. . . . He looked older than me, but he was like 34. . . . White guy.

> **Int.:** Is that a typical type for you?

> **Larry:** Yeah, white, dark hair, bearded, yeah.

On the other hand, for the unprotected event, Larry describes his sexual partner, not at all according to his "type" described above, but rather according to a fantasy that involves god-like physical beauty in a man of color. Not unlike many other examples in the study, Larry has mixed feelings about his fantasy partner and acknowledges feeling used and abused. However, he is powerfully drawn to this exotic, dark, mysterious, and good-looking partner to whom he totally surrenders control:

> I do, like, one black guy every five years, is my average. This guy was so tragically handsome, black guy, bearded black guy. Right, but he's just a macho pig. I'm sure "here's a little honky-boy hole to poke," you know. That's the way I felt. I had a picture of him in my brain because, I mean he's a looker . . . he looks like somebody really famous he looks like. I can't think. Kind of on the order of Harry Belafonte with a beard, yeah. He's not a love-maker, he's just a "sexer." . . . I really, I really have to say that a lot of it is, maybe it's even kind of like, you know, um, worshipping him because he's so hot, you know, so gorgeous, I have to please him, you know, I have to do what he wants me to do. I have to make him say, you know, when he gossips about me to other people about what he did with me, well he was good in bed. You know there's a lot of that stuff going on in my head at that time. Make him wanna see me again, you know.

Eduardo, a 31-year-old, HIV-positive Latino gay man, gave the following account of his unprotected sexual partner:

> He was an Italian guy in North Beach, you know he's very "macho" and straight and, you

know, has a girlfriend, and no one would ever know that he was doing something like this but he felt like doing it tonight. Because he had been partying too. He had been doing coke the night before with his friends. . . . He was very attractive, very, I would never thought if I saw him on the street, you know, that he would do something like this . . . having sex with a guy. He looked like very, like he coulda been a butcher or a cook in like an Italian restaurant. Sort of burly, hairy, short, stocky, muscular, I could see him with like a wife and kids.

Paradoxically, early in the interview, Eduardo had complained about all those "Latino macho men" who pretend they are straight and say, "Oh, you're just sucking my dick or I'm gonna fuck you and I have a wife and kid so it doesn't mean that I'm gay." . . . Eduardo had also confessed his attraction to Latino straight men who, however, could be dangerous ("beat you up or they pull a knife, a gun") if approached for sex. Like many other Latino gay men, Eduardo struggles with the masculine "macho" ideal, the pressures of needing to prove masculinity especially in sexual intercourse, and the imposition of a cultural gender-definition of homosexuality where homosexuals are seen as less than or "failed" men (Díaz 1998). His fantasy partner thus involved a type of man to whom he felt very attracted but who also represented many of the "macho" qualities he so indignantly scorned about his Latino upbringing. The butcher-looking guy, coupled with the ingestion of multiple drugs, allowed Eduardo to lower his anxiety and act out the straight man fantasy in a physically safer context, though definitely unsafe with respect to HIV transmission. Not surprisingly, the power of the masculinity fantasy overpowered the health concern, much to his dismay after the whole thing was over.

For some men in the Tenderloin, struggling with the multiple and devastating effects of poverty, racism, and HIV, the fantasy partner became a travel companion to a cleaner, safer, healthier space, an oasis away from a troubled urban desert. In the fantasy, of course, HIV could not be part of that oasis which the men so badly

needed for rejuvenation and rest. Therefore, in those fantasy-like situations, the partner was assumed HIV-negative or there was simply no talk of HIV, or of condoms, which have come to represent HIV.

Vincent, a 29-year-old, HIV-negative, African-American man from the Tenderloin, told us about going to the Castro "just to get away" and hang out at "The Pendulum," a gay bar where guys "are trying to have something better." The fantasy partner involved in his unprotected episode was described, as Vincent sorted out his reasons for not using condoms:

Vincent: Yeah. And the other person too, I think, at least somebody that, you know, they look pretty clean and decent. You know what I mean it's kinda easy to like not use a condom too.

Int.: What can you, what's that mean? Because I probably have a different idea, you know, what . . . ?

Vincent: Well, when you meet a handsome guy and then they don't show any signs of sickness. I mean, you know. More or less that.

Int.: And that's sort of a way of keeping a little note in your mind that, so, being handsome is one of those things that makes a person seem more likely as not being someone at risk.

Vincent: [?] Smarter,

Int.: So what about things like, you were talking about earlier, people have certain kind of values that you really appreciate to bettering yourself and things like that. Does that also figure into what you think about a person's HIV status and whether you're more likely to . . . ?

Vincent: Yeah.

Int.: So what kind of person is that? Because it comes out in conversation, right?

Vincent: Yeah, it comes out.

Int.: Can you tell from other things like the way they carry themselves, wear their hair?

Vincent: Their hygiene is a lot.

Int.: So if you get near them and they don't smell so great.

Vincent: No way.

Int.: So how 'bout things like if people are professionals.

Vincent: Yeah, man. That would play a good part.

(3) *Non-integrated sex* When study participants described their sexual behavior in protected and unprotected episodes, important differences emerged other than condom use. During the unprotected sex episodes, for lack of better words, sex seemed more disconnected and less integrated to the cognitive and affective domains of the person. In the context of risky episodes, sex was often described as purely physical, just sex, isolated from caresses, kisses, or other signs of interpersonal intimacy—in the words of one participant, "wham-bam, thank you, Sir." In contrast to more playful and affectionate adventures—many of them casual or anonymous—encountered in safer sex episodes, for the unprotected sex encounters, men described feeling like "hunks of meat" or "a robot" or a "sex machine."

Larry's encounter with his bearded Harry Belafonte lookalike did not sound like fun at all:

> He didn't really want to kiss me much or suck my cock, you know, and then I didn't like it because when I'd suck his, he'd shove it at me and I'm like, "Let go of my ears, I know what I'm doing," you know. And, um, and then I just let him throw my legs up like I was some hunk of meat and fuck me violently. And I hated it. I could hardly wait to go after it was over.

In the context of his risky episode, and in more extreme form, Michael spoke about his sexuality as split-off from the rest of his self—he felt as if his sexuality was coming from a very different and isolated part of his brain. In contrast to his playful and affectionate safe encounter at a public cruising beach, Michael described himself as a sexual predator who dehumanized his partner in the risky episode:

Int.: Was there anything about him or the specific circumstances, that setting?

Michael: He was very dehumanized to me. I was definitely only seeing him as someone who might be able to get me off and he was not a full human being to me. That was different from the earlier incident [the protected sexual encounter] that I was telling you about. Part of it has to do with it being nighttime and not being able to see their face but also part of it is I think that it's easier to dehumanize someone for me when I don't feel like I'm really attracted to them. When I feel like I could walk away from that encounter and it wouldn't be a big loss for me, or it wouldn't be difficult, I think it was a lot easier for me to dehumanize someone. When someone is attractive in whatever way you have curiosity about them, you kind of wonder with them but if you knew that you're just with them to have sex and you're not even attracted to them I think they become less than human.

Int.: Like there won't be a romantic fantasy or desire?

Michael: Yeah. There won't be a romantic fantasy or desire and I don't feel obliged to take them in any way around being safe, I feel a lot less obliged to be wanting to take care of them like when I do when I'm with someone I know or like or am attracted to.

It is very important to note that, in the context of this paper, "integrated" sex does not mean sex within boyfriend relationships and, conversely, "non-integrated sex" does not automatically refer to casual or anonymous encounters. That would be a misunderstanding of the point I am trying to convey. In fact, I witnessed descriptions of non-integrated sex in the context of lover relationships and, conversely, a lot of integrated sex in the context of anonymous casual encounters. The central point I am trying to make is that, more often than not, in the context of risky episodes—which happened either with boyfriends or with casual partners—sexuality was described in terms that stressed its "physicality" in a somewhat isolated fashion from other aspects or possible characteristics of a sexual encounter. Also, non-integrated sex in risky situations, while often occurring in contexts that were emotionally charged, could not be described as playful and/or affectionate, involving the whole person.

To stress my point, here is the description of a sexual encounter within a complex lover relationship that, in my view, typifies what I mean by non-integrated sex. Joseph, a 31-year-old HIV-negative Latino gay man, originally from Los Angeles, recounted the following episode that happened prior to a break-up with his troubled lover. His description emerged as he attempted to compare both his protected and unprotected episodes, at the interviewer's request. The sexual split that characterizes this risky episode, in Joseph's point of view, was prompted by the use of speed; other parts of the narrative, however, suggest that relationship issues, other than heavy substance use, might also have played a part in promoting the sexual split. And so the interview goes:

Int.: In the two sorts of sexual events that you've described [protected and unprotected], what's a—how are they alike? Could you compare them and how were they different for you?

Joseph: Well, whereas the experiences with speed [the risky encounter], you know, there was that sexual feeling of—that overwhelming sexual feeling. You know, it's a very kind of, you know, tactile, very sensory feeling. And although I loved him, you know, although when I was on speed, you know, that really kind of didn't mean a lot. You know, at the time it was not something that I thought about. And now, it's more like a, more spiritual, more bonding, more—you know, kind of back and forth and more of an emotional as well as sensory experience now, where there it was just kind of like this sexual frenzy, where it might have—could not

have even been him, it could have been just anyone.

Similar feelings of being overpowered by split-off physical sensations were reported by David, a 29-year-old, HIV-negative Latino gay man, when explaining the context and circumstances that led to his risky episode. His encounter, while not involving the use of drugs, includes many of the hypothesized elements of a risk, such as experiences of loneliness and longing prior to the encounter and an overwhelming set of physical sensations that clouded his judgment and undermined his perceptions of sexual control:

David: That particular day I can't remember exactly, but I know when I go up there [a cruising park], you know, I'm really longing for, you know, contact and really longing to have a connection . . . I mean I'll go over there and substitute, you know, sex, for, you know, being touched or something that's non-sexual just because sex is easier to find than intimacy . . . I said okay, just for a moment. You know, just for, you know, a few minutes because it felt pretty intense. And still sort of that intensity of the connection, no barrier. Not a lot of lubrication. I mean he was—you know, it was just mainly spit, and, you know, so there was a bit more friction and so it was just like sort of overcome with those sensations . . . I was like, Shit! this guy wants to get fucked and you don't have a condom . . . I mean at the time I was overcome with the feelings and the intensity of it . . . Just the intensity of the sensation, it being different than with a condom and a lot of lube. You know, just spit.

This closer look at the voices and subjective experiences of study participants begins to clarify some defining characteristics of what I have called "non-integrated sex":

1. An extreme or exclusive focus on the physicality or physical sensations of a sexual encounter.

2. The relative absence of interpersonal expressions of nurturance, warmth, and other manifestations of intimacy and, at times, sex that can be characterized as forceful or coercive.
3. An objectification of the partner as a purely physical object of pleasure, to the point that men might feel like "hunks of meat" or ignore important aspects of the individual partner, that is, "it could have been just anyone."
4. Reduced levels of verbal communication during the sexual encounter, especially about HIV, in favor of keeping the given fantasy alive and unchallenged.

(4) *Substance use*   A detailed examination of QIS transcripts reveals that more often than not, unprotected sex was accompanied by the use or abuse of substances, mostly drugs, and more specifically, potent stimulants of the central nervous system, such as cocaine or crystal meth (speed). It is important, however, to realize that there is not a direct relationship between substance use and risky sex. In fact, the interview transcripts do contain plenty of evidence regarding unprotected sex without substance use, as well as safer sex in the presence of heavy use of substances.

The task ahead of us is to understand those specific contexts, situations, and circumstances where drugs become important predictors of unprotected sex. My working hypothesis is that drugs will facilitate risky behavior in the context of trips to Fantasy Island, especially when men attribute to the drug powerful effects that are congruent with the purpose of such trips. I propose that drugs become predictors of risky sex, for example, when men believe that drugs make them more courageous to meet partners they ambivalently both want and fear, or when drugs are believed to alleviate anxiety or numb judgment in emotionally loaded situations, allowing them to do what they would not do otherwise for reasons of principle, personal commitment, or safety. In other words, I believe that the use of drugs predicts risky behavior when attributions of drug effects on the particular individuals are consonant with Fantasy island goals, such as "it makes me an eager bottom," "it makes me have compulsive sex—I was like a robot," "it just breaks this thing about anal sex," or "I was just too stoned to care."

Let us examine with more detail the use of alcohol and drugs in the context of specific unprotected sexual episodes. Consider, for example, John's attributions of the effects of speed on his personality and sexual activity. John, a 35-year-old, HIV-positive Caucasian gay man, confesses that he goes on five-day-long speed runs that end up in risky sexual encounters.

> **John:** When I'm on crystal I'm up for five days at a time. It's usually the last two days that I'm on crystal, like let's say I was up, you know, first day I'm like coming up, the next day I usually go dancing, you know, and then like the third, fourth, or fifth day would be when I'd have sex . . .
>
> . . [I] go out, get high, go dancing, come home, get on the sex line, that would be a typical night for me.

Sex for John, however, means multiple anonymous encounters with "two to fifteen people in twenty-four hours . . . with people I've never met before, with people I'll never see again." While he talks openly and frankly about his sex life, John is also very harsh and judgmental about his sexual behavior, reporting that he is disgusted by it all:

> **John:** . . . I feel pretty disgusting when I come down completely from it.
> **Int.:** And disgusting about what?
> **John:** Just what I've done and myself. And I mean it's pretty harsh to have sex with, you know, two to fifteen people in twenty-four hours.
> **Int.:** Um hm. Harsh on the physical self?
> **John:** Mentally. That's just disgusting. You know, I, people I've never met before, people I'll never see again. Whatever.

Int.: So when you're coming down that's when you get that sort of sense of the feeling of disgusting, so to speak.

John: When I've completely come down. Yes.

Setting aside the specific reasons that lead John to pursue what he considers unsatisfying and compulsive sexual encounters, it is important to examine how drug use—and specifically crystal use—facilitates and allows him to do it. How does the drug allow John to do what he considers harsh and disgusting when he is sober? John's attributions of crystal's effects on him contain some important clues to answer this question. First of all, John believes that, under the influence of crystal, he becomes "a different person than what I am right now." As such, the drug facilitates a split between sexual behavior and his affect and cognitions; a split from the more reflective self—cognitively and affectively—that he presents in the interview. If nothing else, the drug may in fact facilitate a silencing of his harsh self-judgments. Second, in John's attribution, crystal has the special ability to make "ugly" things look glamorous, as if possessing an alchemic power of transformation very conducive to the production of Fantasy Island contexts:

John: The way I feel makes me, on crystal, makes me a totally different person than what I am right now. I mean like I'm, I usually hang around with my, some girlfriends of mine that were on crystal and I haven't done it for a long, long time. And I could just see the way I used to be in them just how your whole thinking process changes and . . .

Int.: How did they look to you?

John: Well, they look glamorous but they're just, just, what they're talking about and how "spacey" they were and it's just kind of ugly to me, really an ugly thing.

Drugs, and in particular speed, facilitate many of the hypothesized elements involved in the construct trips to Fantasy Island. In John's case, speed facilitated the split of sexual behavior and moral reasoning—under the influence of speed he could do what he labels "ugly" and "disgusting" things. As a matter of fact, with speed, John goes on the ultimate cognitive–sexual split, on "auto-pilot":

John: Having sex when I'm on crystal is like masturbating, I can do it again, and again, and again and it doesn't give me any great satisfaction it's just like, you know, I get the eternal hard-on and, you know? So, anyways.

Int.: So is that—?

John: It's auto-pilot-sex type thing.

For others, speed facilitates the numbing of the emotional pain that brought about in the first place the whole fantasy encounter; speed may also facilitate the focus on physicality, isolating sexual sensations away from other interpersonal, affective concerns. By promoting the intensification of physical sensations during a sexual encounter, speed helps men shift and refocus their attention away from emotion or health concerns to the point of "I just don't care anymore."

I want to illustrate further and provide empirical support for these claims through the words of Harvey, a 34-year-old, HIV-positive African-American bisexual man, as he speaks of the circumstances leading to his unprotected sexual episode. Like many other men on trips to Fantasy Island, Harvey started his own trip with feelings of emotional pain, hurt, and loneliness brought about by the cruel sexual manipulations of one of his African-American friends:

Int.: How had you been feeling? What was your mood like during the day?

Harvey: Uh, stress. I needed to get out. At least do something. I just needed to get out and do something, I was stressed out.

Int.: You said you were feeling horny?

Harvey: Yeah. Stressed out, horny.

Int.: And you're feeling anxious?

Harvey: Yeah.

Int.: Did you have anything particularly stressful happen yesterday that caused this feeling?

Harvey: Um, one of my friends still calls me. He was talking dirty with me and then said, "Oh, I was just playin' wit ya," and hung the phone up! Uh, we sittin' there talkin' dirty for like about forty-five minutes on the phone, I'm going like, "OK." He said, "Are you ready? I'm comin' over there." "OK." Then he say, "Oh, I'm just joking with you." I said, "You're joking!" I said, "OK. I'll talk to you later." "The jokes I was playin' wit you." I had to go find somebody, I was already aroused, ready to go. I just wanted to go do something.

When Harvey goes out on his expedition, he finds a willing fantasy partner, a "White leather-stud" that offers him an oasis of relief from the interpersonal hurt he had just experienced with his African-American buddy. The partner, in Harvey's words: "He's a stud. He's into leather, he's a stud here. Anything but Black, I think I can't deal with." The "stud" partner, purposefully chosen as White, already stoned with 90cc of injected speed, gives Harvey the drugs—both speed and cocaine—to facilitate the split, the numbing of pain, the focus on physicality needed for his Fantasy Island adventure:

Harvey: That speed helped me to [laughs]. It helped me have my face sorta pale, I mean sorta hot. My cheeks was hot and I had to like run to the bathroom like three times. I never done speed. I went to the bathroom three times and I got an erection! I went to the bathroom and I got erection! I'm going like, I ain't gonna haggle with this. I say, "It's on!" It was on!

Int.: Did you feel you needed the drugs to have sex last night?

Harvey: Yeah. To take away the pain. Yes. But I was just horny I just didn't know what I really wanted; man or woman I's gonna get

it good as I can get. Gonna go out there and get it. And I was out on Folsom, just "on."

Int.: Were you comfortable with how you handled that and how he did?

Harvey: Actually at the time I was so high I didn't care. I'm just being honest with you.

Int.: So you'd say you were higher than you were the other time [the protected event] we talked?

Harvey: Yeah.

Int.: Did being higher make a difference for you in not bothering to talk about condoms or to use one?

Harvey: Yeah. It did cuz I was in the heat of passion of both drugs mixing and so you don't really think, the only thing you thinkin' about is just doin' it. Getting' off! . . . I was too stoned in my mind, I didn't give a care. I mean I didn't care.

This split of sexuality and self, as a result of drug use, even though subjectively experienced in many different ways, was quite prevalent in the risky episodes of QIS. For some men, like Larry and Eduardo, drugs are seen as the only way to break down their psychological barriers and fears about anal sex. For others, drugs allow them to focus narrowly on the sexual satisfaction, isolating or even protecting their sexual desire from other intrusive, potentially disturbing, thoughts or feelings. "When I smoke, nothing else is on my mind but what I want [meaning sex]"—said Mike, a 28-year-old, African-American HIV-negative gay man.

The split can be quite dramatic for some men, like in the case of Bob, a 35-year-old, Caucasian HIV-positive bisexual man, who describes himself as a robot when high on cocaine:

Cocaine is the kind of drug that makes me compulsive to have sex. I really can't have sex unless I got a buzz on. I mean if I'm still thinking kind of clearly, you know what I mean? If I know what I'm doing it's, like, it doesn't feel right. I was, like, I was a robot.

Finally, for some men, encountering and facing their demons (such as issues of physical attractiveness) in the sexual context of Fantasy Island means a feat of courage. As an Iron John, on his way to fight the proverbial dragon, Larry finds a little help in alcohol:

> I was at home alone and I started drinking that beer so I would finally get on that bus to go over there. You know, it seemed better to bolster my confidence with a little alcohol than to bail out and lie.

(5) *Perceptions of low sexual control*   A common denominator for many of the unprotected sexual episodes I studied—whether attributed to substances, difficult circumstances, or coercive partners—was a decreased sense of personal control over the whole situation, including one's own sexual behavior. Some men felt that they could not think clearly, or that they were not totally there, or that events seemed to just happen on their own.

I want to let the QIS men speak for themselves:

Larry

Int.: Did you feel like you even had a choice?

Larry: Um, not really, I felt that I had to give him that because that was what he was expecting and that's what he wanted, you know and that it would be awkward if I refused.

Int.: Did, uh, you feel that he made the decision about not using the condom?

Larry: Oh, definitely, one hundred percent, could care less.

Eduardo

I'm very in control, but I don't think I am when I've been doing crystal. Had I been a little more clearer thinking, I think I probably wouldn't have gone over there.

Joe

But in that kind of sexual frenzy where everything's moving really fast, it didn't happen. I mean we hadn't planned it . . . I was kind of angry, you know, that, you know, where it was uncomfortable and then he was not listening to me, he was not—we were not communicating well. I was telling him to stop and he wouldn't . . . It just happened, you know.

Michael

It [sex] was very strange, I felt like kind of almost disembodied and again it was kind of the sexual trance that I will sometimes go into. Uh, I just felt like I was just kind of being swept along on the events and that I was not in control of myself.

Mike

I was so high I didn't care. I was in the heat of passion of both drugs mixing and so you don't really think, the only thing you thinking about it's just doin' it. Getting off!

David

Just, like, the body takes over. The mind and reason just goes out the window and it's just like oh my God this feels good. I can't stop, it's just at least for me it's been that way. You know.

(6) *Negative emotions following the sexual encounter*   Lastly, I found a substantial amount of unprotected sex to be followed by feelings of depression, guilt, self-hatred, and disgust. With a few notable exceptions, where the unprotected episodes were seen as turning points in their lives, I found many men engaged in painful, self-deprecatory, and regretful rumination about their risky encounters rather than a critical self-reflection about the situations and circumstances that put them at risk or as lessons to be learned for future encounters.

Jesse Greene's comments about "sex that doesn't bring joy," quoted at the beginning of this article, became poignantly clear when listening to men's feelings about "the morning after." Some of the painful feelings were associated with fears about HIV infection following a risky encounter, as evidenced by Michael's interview transcript:

Int.: Um, tell me more about not using the condom?

Michael: I was uh, very shocked immediately afterwards. And I was particularly like frightened that he had, after I had been fucking him, turned around and gone down on me again. I kept thinking about that and I was obsessing about him being HIV-positive and like almost as if he wanted to turn around and clean me up of that somehow, that he felt a sudden remorse or something, so I started obsessing about that.

Int.: And you said that you had some anxiety about his HIV status, afterward?

Michael: Oh! Yeah! A lot!

Int.: How did you feel afterward?

Michael: I felt horrible. It was really horrible. I would say that it was like a big turning point for me around a lot of stuff about my sex and what kind of sex I have and what kind of sex I need. I felt really guilty that after like eight years of taking care of myself around condoms during fucking that I'd slipped that way so I was definitely beating myself up for a while afterwards . . . the effect of not using a condom was a tremendous one, I think for months I was a wreck around that incident.

Painful after-feelings, however, were typically associated with men's puzzlement about doing something they would not do if they had been in their "right mind." In some cases, men felt used, dirty and/or cheap, and had to go home to wash up or literally flush their fantasy partners out of their bodies. In Eduardo's words:

> just thought, "Wow! I should not have done that [unsafe sex], but I did." So I pretty much felt hideous . . . I felt gross. I thought people must be looking at me thinking, Oh, my God, look at this guy, he's been up for two days and he looks like, used, or something.
>
> . . . I just felt really gross.
>
> . . . I mean inside too, I felt like, "What are you doing? Why are you doing this? Why are you continuing to do this?"

In contrast to a description of his protected event as "afterglow city," this is how Larry felt after his troubling risky episode:

> Thank god it didn't hurt. He wasn't too big and I don't know, it was just the right time for me. It didn't hurt physically, but I felt real disgusted as I was walking to the bus, you know. It was a very empty act for me, you know and I felt real, I felt dirty and cheap [. . .] Yeah, yeah, I felt like, why the fuck did I do that? You know, and I couldn't wait to get to the bathroom, you know and just get him out of me.

In John's case, as he comes down from his crystal runs, the feelings of disgust—about his out-of-control sex with so many strangers in one night—are so intense that he must alleviate his anxiety with additional drugs:

> **Int.:** So when you're coming down that's when you get that sort of sense of the feeling of disgusting, so to speak.
>
> **John:** When I've completely come down. Yes.
>
> **Int.:** Um hm. And then was the feeling afterwards of, you called it disgusting?
>
> **John:** See that comes down after I've had a nap or something like, you know, when I first sleep. So, and usually I'd take some pain-killers or, like valiums and alcohol on the way down, you know.

In Conclusion: Individual Pathology or Oppressive Culture?

The risk of sexual transmission of HIV is not randomly distributed in the population; rather, the epidemic is increasingly shaped by the boundaries of poverty, racism, and homophobia. In the perspective of the larger social context, the virus spreads not at random, but within pockets of powerlessness and alienation created by social injustice, inequality, and oppression. Similarly, the risk for HIV is not randomly distributed within individual lives. There are times when, for reasons discussed here, individuals are more vulnerable to act in ways that overpower principles and personal standards of safer sex behavior. There are indeed pockets of powerlessness within individual lives, created by powerful emotional states, different types of partners, and volatile interpersonal situations. More often than not, these are congruent with the social forces that shape, regulate, and give meaning to gay men's sexuality.

It would be very simplistic to attribute the sexual contexts and events described as "Trips to Fantasy Island" to individual pathology or psychological dysfunction. In fact, I want to argue that the non-sexual needs experienced so deeply by the men interviewed, are social and cultural in origin. The non-sexual needs described in connection to the sexual episodes clustered around four specific themes: (1) the need to validate one's sense of physical attractiveness; (2) the need to restore a wounded sense of masculinity; (3) the need to alleviate painful experiences of loneliness and social isolation; and (4) the need to get away, find relief or escape, at least temporarily, from difficult situations brought about by poverty, racism, interpersonal rejection, and AIDS. These "needs" can be traced to sociocultural factors, such as a certain obsession with masculinity and physical beauty found in gay culture, or the perceived lack of models and support to integrate love and sex, intimacy and sexual passion, in long-term gay relationships. The split of sexuality from the cognitive and social domains is perhaps one of the most devastating sequelae of societal homophobia, where closeted sexual lives had to be constructed as the domain of the secret, shameful, and forbidden—what you do with strangers in strange places at strange hours (Díaz 1998). Such negative construction of sexuality in the face of pervasive homophobia does not simply disappear after coming out or moving into the gay neighborhood.

The Fantasy Island analysis leads to the conclusion that the origins of (so-called) risky sexual behavior can be found in elements of our culture, rather than in individuals' pathological impulsiveness or defiant risk-taking. The cultural elements that provide and promote the described contexts

of risk, even though experienced subjectively as psychological states, motivations, and feelings, are more truly a reflection of oppressors in our lives such as homophobia, machismo, sexual silence, poverty, and racism. Those forces converge in a deeply felt sense that something is terribly wrong with us, and many of us go to sexual encounters to find a sense of relief.

Acknowledgements

The research for this article was commissioned and financed by the San Francisco AIDS Foundation, based on data collected in the Qualitative Interview Study (QIS), between January and June 1996. I thank members of the QIS team, in particular, René Durazzo, Ron Stall, Andy Williams, Michael Crosby, and George Ayala for their insightful comments and suggestions, as well as for their collegial support in the writing of this manuscript. I also thank Miguel Casuso for coding all the interview transcripts included in this analysis.

References

Bandura, Albert (1994). "Social Cognitive Theory and Exercise of Control over HIV Infection," in R. DiClemente and J. Peterson (eds) *Preventing AIDS: Theories and Methods of Behavioral Interventions*, pp. 25–59. New York: Plenum Press.

Coates, Tom; Stall, Ron; Catania, Joseph and Kegeles, Susan (1988). "Behavioral Factors in HIV Infection," *AIDS* 2 (Suppl. 1): S239–46.

Díaz, Rafael (1998). *Latino Gay Men and HIV: Culture, Sexuality & Risk Behavior*. New York: Routledge.

Kelly, Jeffrey; Kalichman, Seth; Kauth, Michael; Kilgore, Hilda; Hood, Harold; Campos, Peter; Rao, Stephin; Brasfield, Ted and St Lawrence, Janet (1991). "Situational Factors Associated with AIDS Risk Behavior, Lapses and Coping Strategies Used by Gay Men Who Successfully Avoid Lapses," *American Journal of Public Health* 81(10): 1335–8.

Lemp, George; Hirozawa, Ane; Givertz, Daniel; Nicri, Giuliano; Anderson, Laura; Lindergren, Mary Lou; Janssen, Robert and Katz, Mitchell (1994). "Seroprevalence of HIV and Risk Behaviors among Young Homosexual and Bisexual

Men: The San Francisco/Berkeley Young Men's Survey," *Journal of the American Medical Association* 272: 449–54.

Osmond, Dennis; Page, Kimberly; Wiley, James; Garrett, Karen; Sheppard, Haynes; Moss, Andrew; Schrager, Lewis and Winkelstein, Warren (1994). "HIV Infection in Homosexual and Bisexual Men 18–29 Years of Age: The San Francisco Young Men's Health Study," *American Journal of Public Health* 84: 1933–7.

Rotello, Gabriel (1997). *Sexual Ecology: AIDS and the Destiny of Gay Men.* New York: Dutton.

Bob: 35-year-old, Caucasian, HIV positive.
David: 29-year-old, Latino, HIV positive.
Eduardo: 31-year-old, Latino, HIV positive.
Harvey: 34-year-old, African American, HIV positive.
Joseph: 31-year-old, Latino, HIV negative.
John: 35-year-old, Caucasian, HIV positive.
Larry: 40-year-old, Caucasian, HIV positive.
Michael: 30-year-old, Latino, HIV negative.
Mike: 28-year-old, African American, HIV negative.
Rick: 38-year-old, Caucasian, HIV positive.
Vincent: 29-year-old, African American, HIV negative.

Appendix 1

Study Participants Quoted in the Text
(All names, arranged in alphabetical order, are fictitious)

Susan Bordo

Pills and Power Tools

Viagra. When it went on sale in April of 1998, it broke all records for "fastest takeoff of a new drug" that the Rite Aid drugstore chain had ever seen. It was all over the media. Users were jubilant, claiming effects that lasted through the night, youth restored, better-"quality" erections.

Some even viewed Viagra as a potential cure for social ills. Bob Guccione, publisher of *Penthouse*, hails the drug as "freeing the American male libido" from the emasculating clutches of feminism. This diagnosis doesn't sit very comfortably with current medical wisdom, which has declared impotence to be a physiological problem. I, like Guccione, am skeptical of that declaration—but would suggest a deeper meditation on what's put the squeeze on male libido.

Think, to begin with, of the term: *Impotence.* It rings with disgrace, humiliation—and it's not feminists who invented it. Writer Philip Lopate, in an essay on this body, says that merely to say the word out loud makes him nervous.

Unlike other disorders, impotence implicates the whole man, not merely the body-part. *He is impotent.* Would we ever say about a person with a headache, *"He is a headache"*? Yet this is just what we do with impotence, as Warren Farrell notes. "We make no attempt to separate impotence from the total personality," writes Farrell. "Then, we expect the personality to perform like a machine." "Potency" means power. So I guess it's correct to say that the machine we expect men to perform like is a power tool.

That expectation of men is embedded throughout our culture. To begin with, we encourage men to think of their sexuality as residing in their penises, and give them little encouragement to explore the rest of their bodies. The beauty of the male body has finally been brought out of the cultural closet by Calvin Klein, Versace, and other designers. But notice how many of those new underwear ads aggressively direct our attention to the (often extraordinary) endowments of the models. Many of them stare coldly, challengingly at the viewer, defying the viewer's "gaze" to define them in any way other than how they have chosen to present themselves: powerful, armored, emotionally impenetrable. "I am a rock," their bodies seem to proclaim. Commercial advertisements depict women stroking their necks, their faces, their legs, lost in sensual reverie, taking pleasure in touching themselves—all over. Similar poses with men are very rare. Touching oneself languidly, lost in the sensual pleasure of the body, is too feminine, too "soft," for a real man. Crotch grabbing, thrusting, putting it "in your face"—that's another matter.

There's a fascinating irony in the fact that although it is women whose bodies are most sexually "objectified" by this culture, women's bodies are permitted much greater sexual expression in our cultural representations than men's. In sex scenes, the moaning and writhing of the female partner have become the conventional cinematic code for heterosexual ecstasy and climax. The male's participation largely gets represented via caressing hands, humping buttocks, and—on rare occasions—a facial expression of intense concentration. She's transported to another world; he's the pilot of the ship that takes her there. When men are shown being transported themselves, it's usually been played for comedy (as in Al Pacino's shrieks in *Frankie and Johnny,* Eddie Murphy's moaning in *Boomerang,* Kevin Kline's contortions in *A Fish Called Wanda*), or it's coded to suggest that something is not quite normal with the man—he's sexually enslaved, for example (as with Jeremy Irons in *Damage*). Men's bodies in the movies are action-hero toys—wind them up and watch them perform.

Think of our slang-terms, so many of which encase the penis, like a cyborg, in various sorts of metal or steel armor. Big rig. Blow torch. Bolt. Cockpit. Crank. Crowbar. Destroyer. Dipstick. Drill. Engine. Hammer. Hand tool. Hardware. Hose. Power tool. Rod. Torpedo. Rocket. Spear. Such slang—common among teen-age boys—is violent in what it suggests the machine penis can do to another, "softer" body. But the terms are also metaphorical protection against the failure of potency. A human organ of flesh and blood is subject to anxiety, ambivalence, uncertainty. A torpedo or rocket, on the other hand, would never let one down.

Contemporary urologists have taken the metaphor of man the machine even further. Erectile functioning is "all hydraulics," says Irwin Goldstein of the Boston University Medical Center, scorning a previous generation of researchers who stressed psychological issues. Goldstein was quoted in a November 1997 *Newsweek* cover story called "The New Science of IMPOTENCE," announcing the dawn of the age of Viagra. At the time, the trade name meant little to the casual reader. What caught my eye were the contradictory messages. On the one hand, that ugly shame-inducing word *IMPOTENCE* was emblazoned throughout the piece. On the other hand, we were told in equally bold letters that science was "REBUILDING THE MALE MACHINE." If it's all a matter of fluid dynamics, I thought, why keep the term *impotent,* whose definitions (according to *Webster's Unabridged*) are: "want of power," "weakness," "lack of effectiveness, helplessness" and (only lastly) "lack of ability to engage in sexual intercourse"? In keeping the term *impotence,* I

figured, the drug companies would get to have it both ways: reduce a complex human condition to a matter of chemistry, while keeping the old shame-machine working, helping to assure the flow of men to their doors.

It's remarkable, really, when you think about it, that *impotence* remained a common nomenclature among medical researchers (instead of the more forgiving, if medicalized, *erectile dysfunction*) for so long. *Frigidity*—with its suggestion that the woman is "cold," like some barren tundra—went by the board a long while ago. But *impotence,* no less loaded with ugly gender implications, remained the term of choice—not only for journalists but also for doctors—throughout all of the early reportage on Viagra. "THE POTENCY PILL," *Time* magazine called it, in its May 4th, 1998, issue, three weeks after Viagra went on sale. At the same time, inside the magazine, fancy charts with colored arrows, zigzags, triangles, circles, and boxes show us "How Viagra Works," a cartoonlike hot dog the only suggestion that a penis is involved in any of this.

The drug companies eventually realized that *impotence* was as politically incorrect as *frigidity.* They also, apparently, began to worry about the reputation that Viagra was getting as a magic bullet that could produce rampant erections out of thin air. Pfizer's current ad for Viagra announces "A pill that helps men with erectile dysfunction respond again." *Respond.* The word attempts to create a counter-image not only to the early magic-bullet hype, but also to the curious absence of partners in men's descriptions of the effects of the drug. It's "Stronger." It's "Harder." "Longer-lasting." "Better quality." It's "Firmer." The characters in the drama of Viagra were three: a man, his blessed power pill, and his restored power tool.

The way Viagra is supposed to work—as the Pfizer ad goes on to say—is by helping you "achieve erections the natural way—in response to sexual stimulation." *Natural. Response.* It illustrates its themes with a middle-aged man in a suit dipping his gray-haired partner, smiling ecstatically. *Partners. Happy partners.* A playful, joyous, moment. "Let the dance begin," announces Pfizer

at the very bottom of the ad, as though it were or-
chestrating a timeless, ritual coupling. The way
men *had* been talking about the effects of Viagra,
that dance was entirely between them and their
members.

It wasn't a playful rumba though. More like
a march performed to the finale of the "1812
Overture," accompanied with cannon-blasts.
"This little pill is like a package of dynamite,"
says one user. "Turned into a monster" (says another, with pleasure). "You just keep going all
night. The performance is unbelievable," said
one. I'm not making fun of these responses; I find
them depressing. The men's explosive pride, to
me, is indicative of how small and snail-like these
men had felt before, and of the extravagant relief
now felt at becoming a "real man," imagined in
these comments as some kind of monster Ener-
gizer Bunny (pardon me, *Rabbit.*)

Something else is revealed, too, by the absence of partners in these descriptions of the effects of Viagra. The first "sex life" of most men in
our culture—and a powerful relationship that
often continues throughout their lives—involves
a male, his member, and a magazine (or some
other set of images seemingly designed with male
libido in mind). Given the fast-trigger nature of
adolescent sexuality, it doesn't take much; indeed,
it sometimes seems to the teen-age boy as though
everything female has been put on the face of the
earth just to get men hot. Philip Roth's descriptions of Alex Portnoy masturbating at the sight of
his sister's bra, capable of getting a hard-on even
at the sound of the *word* "panties," are hilarious—
and true to life. Despite myths to the contrary, it's
sometimes not so different for adolescent girls,
either. But when we grow up, those "hard-on"
moments (if, to make a point, I may use that
metaphor in a unisexual way) aren't transformed
into launch-off preparations for a sexual "performance."

It's often been noted that women's sexual
readiness can be subtle to read. We are not
required to cross a dramatic dividing line in order
to engage in intercourse. And we aren't

expected—as men are expected, as men seem to
expect of themselves—to retain that hair-trigger
sexuality of adolescence. Quite the opposite, in
fact; the mythology about women is that we're
"slow-cookers" when it comes to sex. Men, in
contrast, get hit with a double whammy: they feel
that they have to perform and they expect themselves to do so at the mere sight of a fancy
brassiere! It's one reason, I think, why so many
men "trade up" for younger wives as they get
older; they're looking for that quick sexual fix of
adolescence. It's their paradigm of sexual response, their criterion (ironically, since it represents the behavior of a fifteen-year-old) of
manliness.

It comes as no surprise then, to learn that as
sexual "performers," many men seem to expect
no tactile help from the audience except—
hopefully—applause at the end. Gail Sheehy
(who, by the way, has cleaned up her own terminology; in an article from the early nineties, her
term for "male menopause" was *viropause,* now
she calls it *manopause*) reports that Lenore Tiefer's
interviews with hundreds of cops, firemen, sani-
tation workers, and blue-color workers at Mon-
tefiore Medical Center in the Bronx revealed that
most of these men expect, even in their fifties, to
be able to get an erection just from paging through
Playboy. Sheehy goes on: "When the sexologist
suggests that at this age a man often needs physical stimulation they balk: 'C'mon, Doc, it's not
masculine for a woman to have to get it up for
me.' Their wives often echo that rigid code: '*He*
should get it up.'"

Some dance, huh?

Most studies of Viagra's "effectiveness" leave
partners out of the picture, too. When you put
them in, you get a somewhat different picture of
the "success" of the drug. In England, they used
something called a "RigiScan" to measure the
penis's "resistance" against a cloth-covered ring
while Viagra-treated men watched porn movies.
In the United States, the 69 percent "success rate"
that Pfizer submitted to the F.D.A. was based on
questionnaires filled out by patients. "Real soft

data, no pun intended," William Steers, Chief of Urology at the University of Virginia was quoted as saying in the July 6, 1998, *New Yorker*. He went on to note that Pfizer's study included no spousal questionnaires. Steers, cheers to him, *did* ask spouses. It turns out that when you ask women about sex with their "Viagra-enhanced" husbands, their estimation of the success of the drug is always lower than men—is about 48 percent for the women, no matter what measure of "success" you use.

Steers does not provide detail as to what those different measures were. Perhaps "monsters" were not what partners were looking for in bed. Perhaps they didn't appreciate the next-day chafing that usually accompanies "going all night." (I once knew a man who could stay erect all night; it had its upside—so to speak—but I couldn't escape the feeling that a bit of sadism, at the very least a control complex, was fueling his unbending passion.) Perhaps partners didn't want *just* a proud member, but the kind of romantic attention that goes along with the proud member in the romance novels. "We're a very meat-and-potatoes culture," says Karen Martin, a sex therapist in upstate New York. "In other cultures, they toss in a few mushrooms." Maybe the wives of Viagrans wanted a few mushrooms tossed in with the beef.

They are less apt to be served them, however, if the couple has had sexual problems. Such couples may have grown distant from each other, may no longer know how to communicate intimately with each other, physically or verbally. Since the initial wave of enthusiasm about Viagra, therapists have begun to worry that Viagra is providing couples with a way to sidestep dealing not only with relationship problems that may have *contributed* to their sexual difficulties ("just because there is a physiological problem doesn't mean there is no psychological cause," reminds Eileen Palace, director of the Center for Sexual Health at Tulane) but also patterns of alienation, resentment, and anger that may develop *because of* those difficulties. A number of studies have found that when men begin to have erectile difficulties, a common

response is to turn away from *all* romantic and affectionate gestures—kissing, caressing, hugging—so as not to (as one said) "stir things up." Many don't offer manual or oral stimulation in place of intercourse, because that would be to admit to themselves that they can't "perform" the "way a man should." They're often uncomfortable talking about the situation with their wives (and even their doctors, who report that most of the men who are asking for prescriptions for Viagra never mentioned their dysfunction before.) "I would tend to kind of brush the problem under the rug," says one man. "It isn't an easy topic to deal with. It goes to the heart of your masculinity."

Into the middle of all this distance, confusion, anxiety, and strain walks Viagra, and with it the news that the problem is only a malfunctioning hydraulic system—which, like any broken machinery, can be fixed. And "let the dance begin!" Many couples, unsurprisingly, don't know the steps, stumble, and step all over each other's toes.

Let me make it clear that I have no desire to withhold Viagra from the many men who have been deprived of the ability to get an erection by accidents, diabetes, cancer, and other misfortunes to which the flesh—or psyche—is heir. I would, however, like CNN and *Time* to spend a fraction of the time they devote to describing "how Viagra cures" to thinking about that gentleman's astute comment—"It goes to the heart of your masculinity"—and perhaps devoting a few features to exploring the functioning of *that* body part as well.

Such an exploration is, thankfully, occurring in other cultural arenas. Paul Thomas Anderson's *Boogie Nights* told the story of the rise and fall (so to speak) of a mythically endowed young porn star, Dirk Diggler, who does fine so long as he's the most celebrated stallion in the stable but loses his grip in the face of competition. On the surface, the film is about a world far removed from the lives of most men, a commercial underground where men pray for "wood" and lose their jobs unless they can achieve erection on command. On a deeper level, however, the world of the porn actor is simply the most literalized embodiment—and a perfect metaphor—for a masculinity that demands constant performance from men.

Even before he takes up a career that depends on it, Diggler's sense of self is constellated around his penis; he pumps up his ego by looking in the mirror and—like a coach mesmerizing his team before a game—intoning mantras about his superior gifts. That works well, so long as he believes it. But unlike a real power tool, the motor of male self-worth can't simply be switched on and off. In the very final shot of the movie, we see Diggler's fabled organ itself. It's a prosthesis, actually (a fact that annoyed several men I know until I pointed out that it was no more a cheat than implanted breasts passing for the real thing). But prosthesis or not and despite its dimensions, it's no masterful tool. It points downward, weighted with expectation, with shame, looking tired and used. What's ground-breaking about *Boogie Nights* is not that it displays a nude penis, but that it so unflinchingly exposes the job that the mythology of unwavering potency does on the male body. As long as the fortress holds, the sense of power may be intoxicating; but when it cracks—as it's bound to at some point—the whole structure falls to pieces. Those of whom such constancy is expected (or who require it of themselves) are set up for defeat and humiliation.

Unless, of course, he pops his little pill whenever "failure" threatens.

Some of what we now call "impotence" may indeed be physiological in origin. Some may be grounded in deep fears and anxieties. But whatever the cause of a man's sexual problems, the "heart of masculinity" isn't a mechanical pump, and in imagining the penis as such, Viagran science actually administers more of the poison it claims to counteract. Dysfunction is no longer defined as "inability to get an erection" but inability to get an erection that is adequate for "satisfactory sexual performance." *Performance.* Not pleasure. Not feeling. *Performance.* Eighty-five-year-old men are having Viagra heart attacks trying to keep those power tools running.

Sometimes, perhaps, a man's "impotence" may simply be his penis instructing him that his *feelings* are not in synch with the job he's supposed to do—or with the very fact that it's a "job." So, I like Philip Lopate's epistemological metaphor for the penis much better than the machine images. Over the years, he has come to appreciate, he writes, that his penis has its "own specialized form of intelligence." The penis knows that it is not a torpedo, no matter what a culture expects of it or what drugs are relayed to its blood vessels. If we accepted that, the notion that a man requires understanding and "tolerance" when he doesn't "perform" would go by the wayside. ("It's O.K. It happens" still assumes that there is something to be excused.) So, too, would the idea that there ought to be one model for understanding nonarousal. Sometimes, the penis's "specialized intelligence" should be listened to rather than cured.

Viagra, unfortunately, seems to be encouraging rather than deconstructing the expectation that men perform like power tools with only one switch—on or off. Until this expectation is replaced by a conception of manhood that permits men *and* their penises a full range of human feeling, we won't yet have the kind of "cure" we really need.

References

Broder, David. (1998). "Side Effect of Viagra May Be End of a Great Stupidity," *Lexington-Herald Leader,* July 27.

Cameron, Deborah. (1992). "Naming of Parts: Gender, Culture, and Terms for the Penis Among American College Students," *American Speech,* Vol. 67, No. 4, pp. 367–382.

Cowley, Geoffrey. (1998). "Is Sex a Necessity?" *Newsweek,* May 11, pp. 62–63.

Farrell, Warren. (1986). *Why Men Are the Way They Are.* New York: Berkley Books.

Goldstein, Irwin. (1997). "The New Science of IMPOTENCE," *Newsweek,* November, pp. XXX.

Handy, Bruce. (1998). "The Viagra Craze," *Time,* May 4, pp. 50–57.

Hendren, John. (1998). "Pfizer presses Insurers on Viagra," *Washington Post,* July 7, p. E3.

Hitchens, Christopher. (1998). "Viagra Falls," *The Nation,* May 25, p. 8.

Leland, John. (1997). "A Pill for Impotence?" *Newsweek,* November 17, pp. 62–68.

Lopate, Phillip. (1993). "Portrait of My Body," *Michigan Quarterly Review,* Volume XXXII, Number 4, Fall, pp. 656–665.

Martin, Douglas. (1998). "Thanks a Bunch, Viagra," *New York Times,* May 3, p. XXX.

Risher, Michael T. (1998). "Controlling Viagra-Mania," *New York Times,* July 20, p. A19.

Safire, William. (1998). "Is There a Right to Sex?" *New York Times,* July 13, p. A21.

Sharpe, Rochelle. (1998). "FDA Received Data on Adverse Effects from Using Viagra," *Wall Street Journal,* June 29, p. B5.

Steinhauer, Jennifer. (1998). "Viagra's Other Side Effect: Upsets in Many a Marriage," *New York Times,* June 23, pp. B9, B11.

Tiefer, Lenore. (1994). "The Medicalization of Impotence," *Gender and Society,* Vol. 8, No. 3, September, pp. 363–377.

Time, May 4, 1998.

PART SIX

Men in Relationships

Why do many men have problems establishing and maintaining intimate relationships with women? What different forms do male–female relational problems take within different socioeconomic groups? How do men's problems with intimacy and emotional expressivity relate to power inequities between the sexes? Are rape and domestic violence best conceptualized as isolated deviant acts by "sick" individuals, or are they the illogical consequences of male socialization? This complex web of male–female relationships, intimacy, and power is the topic of this section.

And what is the nature of men's relationships with other men? Do men have close friendships with men, or do they simply "bond" around shared activities and interests? How do competition, homophobia, and violence enter into men's relationships with each other? For example, a student recently commented that when he goes to the movies with another male friend, they always leave a seat between them, where they put their coats, because they don't want anyone to think they are there "together."

But what are the costs of this emotional and physical distance? And what are the costs of maintaining emotionally impoverished relationships with other men? How is this emotional distance connected to men's intimate relationships with women? Is it related to Billy Crystal's line in *When Harry Met Sally* that women and men can never be friends because "the sex thing always gets in the way"?

Lillian Rubin begins this section with a psychoanalytic interpretation of male–female relational problems. Early development differences, rooted in the social organization of the nuclear family (especially the fact that it is women who care for infants) have set up the fundamental emotional and sexual differences between women and men that create problems for heterosexual couples. In examining conflicts between black males and females, the late Clyde W. Franklin II focused more on how the larger socioeconomic structure of society places strains on black family life, especially on black males' work and family roles. Articles by Karen Walker and Peter Nardi suggest the different ways men—both straight and gay—develop and sustain their friendships with each other.

The problems in male–female relationships—that such relationships can be distorted by insecurity, anger, the need for control, the need to assert and demonstrate manliness—can take an ugly turn, as described by Tim Beneke in his powerful essay and interview, which invite men to think about rape. Jason Schultz's essay, however, gives us room for hope that the next generation of men, now in their 20s, may struggle with these issues in new and different ways, and develop very different ideas about male–female relationships.

"We've been wandering in the desert for forty years. But he's a man—would he ever ask directions?"

Lillian B. Rubin

The Approach–Avoidance Dance: Men, Women, and Intimacy

For one human being to love another, that is perhaps the most difficult of all our tasks, the ultimate, the last test and proof, the work for which all other work is but preparation.

—Rainer Maria Rilke

Intimacy. We hunger for it, but we also fear it. We come close to a loved one, then we back off. A teacher I had once described this as the "go away a little closer" message. I call it the approach–avoidance dance.

The conventional wisdom says that women want intimacy, men resist it. And I have plenty of material that would *seem* to support that view. Whether in my research interviews, in my clinical hours, or in the ordinary course of my life, I hear the same story told repeatedly. "He doesn't talk to me," says a woman. "I don't know what she wants me to talk about," says a man. "I want to know what he's feeling," she tells me. "I'm not feeling anything," he insists. "Who can feel nothing?" she cries. "I can," he shouts. As the heat rises, so does the wall between them. Defensive and angry, they retreat—stalemated by their inability to understand each other.

Women complain to each other all the time about not being able to talk to their men about the things that matter most to them—about what they themselves are thinking and feeling, about what goes on in the hearts and minds of the men they're relating to. And men, less able to expose themselves and their conflicts—those within themselves or those with the women in their lives—either turn silent or take cover by holding women up to derision. It's one of the norms of male camaraderie to poke fun at women, to complain laughingly about the mystery of their minds, wonderingly about their ways. Even Freud did it when, in exasperation, he asked mockingly, "What do women want? Dear God, what do they want?"

But it's not a joke—not for the women, not for the men who like to pretend it is.

> The whole goddamn business of what you're calling intimacy bugs the hell out of me. I never know what you women mean when you talk about it. Karen complains that I don't talk to her, but it's not talk she wants, it's some other damn thing, only I don't know what the hell it is. Feelings, she keeps asking for. So what am I supposed to do if I don't have any to give her or to talk about just because she decides it's time to talk about feelings? Tell me, will you: maybe we can get some peace around here.

The expression of such conflicts would seem to validate the common understandings that suggest that women want and need intimacy more than men do—that the issue belongs to women alone; that, if left to themselves, men would not suffer it. But things are not always what they seem.

353

And I wonder: "If men would renounce intimacy, what is their stake in relationships with women?"

Some would say that men need women to tend to their daily needs—to prepare their meals, clean their houses, wash their clothes, rear their children—so that they can be free to attend to life's larger problems. And, given the traditional structure of roles in the family, it has certainly worked that way most of the time. But, if that were all men seek, why is it that, even when they're not relating to women, so much of their lives is spent in search of a relationship with another, so much agony experienced when it's not available?

These are difficult issues to talk about—even to think about—because the subject of intimacy isn't just complicated, it's slippery as well. Ask yourself: What is intimacy? What words come to mind, what thoughts?

It's an idea that excites our imagination, a word that seems larger than life to most of us. It lures us, beckoning us with a power we're unable to resist. And, just because it's so seductive, it frightens us as well—seeming sometimes to be some mysterious force from outside ourselves that, if we let it, could sweep us away.

But what is it we fear?

Asked what intimacy is, most of us—men and women—struggle to say something sensible, something that we can connect with the real experience of our lives. "Intimacy is knowing there's someone who cares about the children as much as you do." "Intimacy is a history of shared experience. It's sitting there having a cup of coffee together and watching the eleven o'clock news." "It's knowing you care about the same things." "It's knowing she'll always understand." "It's him sitting in the hospital for hours at a time when I was sick." "It's knowing he cares when I'm hurting." "It's standing by me when I was out of work." "It's seeing each other at our worst." "It's sitting across the breakfast table." "It's talking when you're in the bathroom." "It's knowing we'll begin and end each day together."

These seem the obvious things—the things we expect when we commit our lives to one another in a marriage, when we decide to have children together. And they're not to be dismissed as inconsequential. They make up the daily experience of our lives together, setting the tone for a relationship in important and powerful ways. It's sharing such commonplace, everyday events that determines the temper and the texture of life, that keeps us living together even when other aspects of the relationship seem less than perfect. Knowing someone is there, is constant, and can be counted on in just the ways these thoughts express provides the background of emotional security and stability we look for when we enter a marriage. Certainly a marriage and the people in it will be tested and judged quite differently in an unusual situation or in a crisis. But how often does life present us with circumstances and events that are so out of the range of ordinary experience?

These ways in which a relationship feels intimate on a daily basis are only one part of what we mean by intimacy, however—the part that's most obvious, the part that doesn't awaken our fears. At a lecture where I spoke of these issues recently, one man commented also, "Intimacy is putting aside the masks we wear in the rest of our lives." A murmur of assent ran through the audience of a hundred or so. Intuitively we say, "yes." Yet this is the very issue that also complicates our intimate relationships.

On the one hand, it's reassuring to be able to put away the public persona—to believe we can be loved for who we *really* are, that we can show our shadow side without fear, that our vulnerabilities will not be counted against us. "The most important thing is to feel I'm accepted just the way I am," people will say.

But there's another side. For, when we show ourselves thus without the masks, we also become anxious and fearful. "Is it possible that someone could love the *real* me?" we're likely to ask. Not the most promising question for the further development of intimacy, since it suggests that, whatever else another might do or feel, it's we who have trouble loving ourselves. Unfortunately, such misgivings are not usually experienced consciously. We're aware only that our discomfort has risen, that we feel a need to get away. For the person who has seen the "real me" is also the one who reflects back to us an image that's usually not wholly to our liking. We get angry at that, first at ourselves for not living up to our own expectations, then at the other, who becomes for us the mirror of our self-doubts—a displacement of hostility that serves intimacy poorly.

There's yet another level—one that's further below the surface of consciousness, therefore, one that's much more difficult for us to grasp, let alone to talk about. I'm referring to the differences in the ways in which women and men deal with their inner emotional lives—differences that create barriers between us that can be high indeed. It's here that we see how those early childhood experiences of separation and individuation—the psychological tasks that were required of us in order to separate from mother, to distinguish ourselves as autonomous persons, to internalize a firm sense of gender identity—take their toll on our intimate relationships.

Stop a woman in mid-sentence with the question, "What are you feeling right now?" and you might have to wait a bit while she reruns the mental tape to capture the moment just passed. But, more than likely, she'll be able to do it successfully. More than likely, she'll think for a while and come up with an answer.

The same is not true of a man. For him, a similar question usually will bring a sense of wonderment that one would even ask it, followed quickly by an uncomprehending and puzzled response. "What do you mean?" he'll ask. "I was just talking," he'll say.

I've seen it most clearly in the clinical setting where the task is to get to the feeling level—or, as one of my male patients said when he came into therapy, to "hook up the head and the gut." Repeatedly when therapy begins, I find myself having to teach a man how to monitor his internal states—how to attend to his thoughts and feelings, how to bring them into consciousness. In the early stages of our work, it's a common experience to say to a man, "How does that feel?" and to see a blank look come over his face. Over and over, I find myself listening as a man speaks with

calm reason about a situation which I know must be fraught with pain. "How do you feel about that?" I'll ask. "I've just been telling you," he's likely to reply. "No," I'll say, "you've told me what happened, not how you *feel* about it." Frustrated, he might well respond, "You sound just like my wife."

It would be easy to write off such dialogues as the problems of men in therapy, of those who happen to be having some particular emotional difficulties. But it's not so, as any woman who has lived with a man will attest. Time and again women complain: "I can't get him to verbalize his feelings." "He talks, but it's always intellectualizing." "He's so closed off from what he's feeling, I don't know how he lives that way." "If there's one thing that will eventually ruin this marriage, it's the fact that he can't talk about what's going on inside him." "I have to work like hell to get anything out of him that resembles a feeling that's something besides anger. That I get plenty of—me and the kids, we all get his anger. Anything else is damn hard to come by with him." One woman talked eloquently about her husband's anguish over his inability to get problems in his work life resolved. When I asked how she knew about his pain, she answered:

> I pull for it, I pull hard, and sometimes I can get something from him. But it'll be late at night in the dark—you know, when we're in bed and I can't look at him while he's talking and he doesn't have to look at me. Otherwise, he's just defensive and puts on what I call his bear act, where he makes his warning, go-away faces, and he can't be reached or penetrated at all.

To a woman, the world men live in seems a lonely one—a world in which their fears of exposing their sadness and pain, their anxiety about allowing their vulnerability to show, even to a woman they love, is so deeply rooted inside them that, most often, they can only allow it to happen "late at night in the dark."

Yet, if we listen to what men say, we will hear their insistence that they *do* speak of what's inside them, *do* share their thoughts and feelings with the women they love. "I tell her, but she's never satisfied," they complain. "No matter how much I say, it's never enough," they grumble.

From both sides, the complaints have merit. The problem lies not in what men don't say, however, but in what's not there—in what, quite simply, happens so far out of consciousness that it's not within their reach. For men have integrated all too well the lessons of their childhood—the experiences that taught them to repress and deny their inner thoughts, wishes, needs, and fears; indeed, not even to notice them. It's real, therefore, that the kind of inner thoughts and feelings that are readily accessible to a woman generally are unavailable to a man. When he says, "I don't know what I'm feeling," he isn't necessarily being intransigent and withholding. More than likely, he speaks the truth.

Partly that's a result of the ways in which boys are trained to camouflage their feelings under cover of an exterior of calm, strength, and rationality. Fears are not manly. Fantasies are not rational. Emotions, above all, are not for the strong, the sane, the adult. Women suffer them, not men—women, who are more like children with what seems like their never-ending preoccupation with their emotional life. But the training takes so well because of their early childhood experience when, as very young boys, they had to shift their identification from mother to father and sever themselves from their earliest emotional connection. Put the two together and it does seem like suffering to men to have to experience that emotional side of themselves, to have to give it voice.

This is the single most dispiriting dilemma of relations between women and men. He complains, "She's so emotional, there's no point in talking to her." She protests, "It's him you can't talk to, he's always so darned rational." He says, "Even when I tell her nothing's the matter, she won't quit." She says, "How can I believe him when I can see with my own eyes that something's wrong?" He says, "Okay, so something's wrong! What good will it do to tell her?" She cries, "What

are we married for? What do you need me for, just to wash your socks?"

These differences in the psychology of women and men are born of a complex interaction between society and the individual. At the broadest social level is the rending of thought and feeling that is such a fundamental part of Western thought. Thought, defined as the ultimate good, has been assigned to men; feeling, considered at best a problem, has fallen to women.

So firmly fixed have these ideas been that, until recently, few thought to question them. For they were built into the structure of psychological thought as if they spoke to an eternal, natural, and scientific truth. Thus, even such a great and innovative thinker as Carl Jung wrote, "The woman is increasingly aware that love alone can give her her full stature, just as the man begins to discern that spirit alone can endow his life with its highest meaning. Fundamentally, therefore, both seek a psychic relation one to the other, because love needs the spirit, and the spirit love, for their fulfillment."[1]

For a woman, "love"; for a man, "spirit"— each expected to complete the other by bringing to the relationship the missing half. In German, the word that is translated here as spirit is *Geist*. But *The New Cassell's German Dictionary* shows that another primary meaning of *Geist* is "mind, intellect, intelligence, wit, imagination, sense of reason." And, given the context of these words, it seems reasonable that *Geist* for Jung referred to a man's highest essence—his mind. There's no ambiguity about a woman's calling, however. It's love.

Intuitively, women try to heal the split that these definitions of male and female have foisted upon us.

> I can't stand that he's so damned unemotional and expects me to be the same. He lives in his head all the time, and he acts like anything that's emotional isn't worth dealing with.

Cognitively, even women often share the belief that the rational side, which seems to come so naturally to men, is the more mature, the more desirable.

> I know I'm too emotional, and it causes problems between us. He can't stand it when I get emotional like that. It turns him right off.

Her husband agrees that she's "too emotional" and complains:

> Sometimes she's like a child who's out to test her parents. I have to be careful when she's like that not to let her rile me up because otherwise all hell would break loose. You just can't reason with her when she gets like that.

It's the rational-man–hysterical-woman script, played out again and again by two people whose emotional repertoire is so limited that they have few real options. As the interaction between them continues, she reaches for the strongest tools she has, the mode she's most comfortable and familiar with: She becomes progressively more emotional and expressive. He falls back on his best weapons: He becomes more rational, more determinedly reasonable. She cries for him to attend to her feelings, whatever they may be. He tells her coolly, with a kind of clenched-teeth reasonableness, that it's silly for her to feel that way, that she's just being emotional. And of course she is. But that dismissive word "just" is the last straw. She gets so upset that she does, in fact, seem hysterical. He gets so bewildered by the whole interaction that his only recourse is to build the wall of reason even higher. All of which makes things measurably worse for both of them.

> The more I try to be cool and calm her the worse it gets. I swear, I can't figure her out. I'll keep trying to tell her not to get so excited, but there's nothing I can do. Anything I say just makes it worse. So then I try to keep quiet, but . . . wow, the explosion is like crazy, just nuts.

And by then it *is* a wild exchange that any outsider would agree was "just nuts." But it's not just her response that's off, it's his as well—their conflict resting in the fact that we equate the emotional with the nonrational.

This notion, shared by both women and men, is a product of the fact that they were born and reared in this culture. But there's also a difference between them in their capacity to apprehend the *logic* of emotions—a difference born in their early childhood experiences in the family, when boys had to repress so much of their emotional side and girls could permit theirs to flower. . . . It should be understood: Commitment itself is not a problem for a man; he's good at that. He can spend a lifetime living in the same family, working at the same job—even one he hates. And he's not without an inner emotional life. But when a relationship requires the sustained verbal expression of that inner life and the full range of feelings that accompany it, then it becomes burdensome for him. He can act out anger and frustration inside the family, it's true. But ask him to express his sadness, his fear, his dependency—all those feelings that would expose his vulnerability to himself or to another—and he's likely to close down as if under some compulsion to protect himself.

All requests for such intimacy are difficult for a man, but they become especially complex and troublesome in relations with women. It's another of those paradoxes. For, to the degree that it's possible for him to be emotionally open with anyone, it is with a woman—a tribute to the power of the childhood experience with mother. Yet it's that same early experience and his need to repress it that raises his ambivalence and generates his resistance.

He moves close, wanting to share some part of himself with her, trying to do so, perhaps even yearning to experience again the bliss of the infant's connection with a woman. She responds, woman style—wanting to touch him just a little more deeply, to know what he's thinking, feeling, fearing, wanting. And the fear closes in—the fear of finding himself again in the grip of a powerful woman, of allowing her admittance only to be betrayed and abandoned once again, of being overwhelmed by denied desires.

So he withdraws.

It's not in consciousness that all this goes on. He knows, of course, that he's distinctly uncomfortable when pressed by a woman for more intimacy in the relationship, but he doesn't know why. And, very often, his behavior doesn't please him any more than it pleases her. But he can't seem to help it.

Notes

1. Carl Gustav Jung, *Contributions to Analytical Psychology* (New York: Harcourt, Brace & Co., 1928), p. 185.

A R T I C L E   3 2

Clyde W. Franklin II

Black Male–Black Female Conflict: Individually Caused and Culturally Nurtured

Who is to blame? Currently, there is no dearth of attention directed to Black male–Black female relationships. Books, magazine articles, academic journal articles, public forums, radio programs, television shows, and everyday conversations have been devoted to Black male–Black female relationships for several years. Despite the fact that the topic has been discussed over the past several decades by some authors (e.g., Frazier 1939; Drake and Cayton 1945; Grier and Cobb 1968), Wallace's *Black Macho and the Myth of the Superwoman* has been the point of departure for many contemporary discussions of the topic since its publication in 1979.

Actually, Wallace's analysis was not so different in content from other analyses of Black male–Black female relationships (e.g., Drake and Cayton's analysis of "lower-class life" in *Black Metropolis*). But Wallace's analysis was "timely." Coming so soon on the heels of the Black movement in the late 1960s and early 1970s, and, at a time when many Black male-inspired gains for Blacks were disappearing rapidly, the book was explosive. Its theme, too, was provocative. Instead of repeating the rhetoric of the late 1960s and early 1970s that blamed conflictual relationships between Black men and Black women on White society, Wallace implied that the blame lay with Black males. In other words, the blame lay with those Black warriors who only recently had been perceived as the "saviors" of Black people in America. Wallace's lamenting theme is captured

in a quote from her book: "While she stood by silently as he became a man, she assumed that he would finally glorify and dignify Black womanhood just as the White man has done for White women." Wallace goes on to say that this has not happened for Black women.

Wallace updates her attack on Black men in a later article entitled "A Black Feminist's Search for Sisterhood" (1982:9). Her theme, as before, is that Black men are just as oppressive of Black women as White men. She states:

> Whenever I raised the question of a Black woman's humanity in conversations with a Black man, I got a similar reaction. Black men, at least the ones I knew, seemed totally confounded when it came to treating Black women like people. . . . I discovered my voice and when brothers talked to me, I talked back. This had its hazards. Almost got my eye blackened several times. My social life was like guerilla warfare. Here was the logic behind our grandmother's old saying, "A nigga man ain't shit."

Wallace, however, is not alone in placing the blame on Black men for deteriorating relations between Black men and Black women. Allen (1983:62), in a recent edition of *Essence* magazine, states:

> Black women have a tendency to be male-defined, subjugating their own needs for the good of that fragile male ego. . . . The major contradiction is that we Black women, in our hearts, have a tendency to believe Black men need more support and understanding than we do. We bought the Black Revolutionary line that a woman's place was three paces behind the man.

From *Journal of Black Studies* 15 (2 December 1984): 139–154. Reprinted by permission.

We didn't stomp Stokeley when he made the statement that the only position for a woman in the movement was prone.

Such attacks on Black men have been met with equally ferocious counterattacks by some Black authors (both Black men and Black women). A few months following the publication of Wallace's book, an entire issue of the *Black Scholar* was devoted to Black male–Black female relationships. Of the responses to Wallace by such scholars as Jones (1979), Karenga (1979), Staples (1979), and numerous others, Karenga's response is perhaps the most controversial and maybe the most volatile. Karenga launches a personal attack on Wallace suggesting that she is misguided and perhaps responding from personal hurt. Recognizing the complexity of Black male–Black female relationships, Karenga contends that much of it is due not to Black men but to the White power structure. Along similar lines, Moore (1980) has exhorted Black women to stop criticizing Black men and blame themselves for disintegrating bonds between Black men and Black women.

Staples, in his response to Wallace and others who would place the blame on Black men for disruptive relationships between Black men and Black women, points out that while sexism within the Black culture may be an emerging problem, most Black men do not have the institutionalized power to oppress Black women. He believes that the Black male's "condition" in society is what bothers Black males. Staples devotes much attention to the institutional decimation of Black men and suggests that this is the reason for Black male–Black female conflict. Noting the high mortality and suicide rates of Black men, the fact that a half a million Black men are in prison, one-third of urban Black men are saddled with drug problems, and that 25% to 30% do not have steady employment, Staples implied that Black male–Black female conflict may be related to *choice.* This means that a shortage of Black men may limit the choices that Black women have in selecting partners. As Braithwaite (1981) puts it, the insufficient supply of Black men places Black women at a disadvantage by giving Black men the upper hand. In a specific relationship, for example, if a Black woman fails to comply with the Black man's wishes, the Black man has numerous other options, including not only other Black women but also women of other races.

In a more recent discussion of Black male–Black female relationships, Alvin Poussaint (1982:40) suggests that Black women "adopt a patient and creative approach in exploring and creating new dimensions of the Black male–Black female bond." Others, like Ronald Braithwaite, imply in their analyses of relationships between Black men and Black women that Black women's aggressiveness, thought to be a carryover from slavery, may be partly responsible for Black male–Black female conflict.

Succinctly, by and large, most Black male and Black female authors writing on the subject seem to agree that many Black male–Black female relationships today are destructive and potentially explosive. What they do not agree on, however, are the causes of the problems existing between Black men and Black women. As we have seen, some believe that Black men are the cause. Others contend that Black women contribute disproportionately to Black male–Black female conflict. Still others blame White racism solely, using basic assumptions that may be logically inadequate (see Franklin 1980). Many specific reasons for the conflict often postulated include the notions that Black men are abusive toward Black women, that Black men are irresistibly attracted to White women (despite the fact that only approximately 120,000 Black men were married to White women in 1980), that too many Black men are homosexual, that Black women are too aggressive, that Black women don't support Black men—the list goes on. Few of these reasons, however, really explore the underlying cause of the conflict. Instead, they are descriptions of the conflict-behaviors that are indicators of the tension between Black men and Black women. But what is the cause of the behavior—the cause of the tension that so often disrupts harmony in Black male–Black female relationships?

Given the various approaches many Black authors have taken in analyzing Black male–Black female relationships, it is submitted that two major sources of Black male–Black female conflict can be identified: (1) the noncomplementarity of sex-role definitions internalized by Black males and Black females; and (2) structural barriers in the environments of Black males and Black females. Each source is explored separately below.

Sources of Conflict Between Black Men and Black Women

Sex-Role Noncomplementarity Among Black Males and Black Females

Much Black male–Black female conflict stems directly from incompatible role enactments by Black males and Black females. Incompatible role enactments by Black men and Black women occur because they internalize sex-role definitions that are noncomplementary. For example, a Black woman in a particular conflictual relationship with a Black male may feel that her Black man is supposed to assume a dominant role, but she also may be inclined to exhibit behaviors that are opposed to his dominance and her subordinance. In the same relationship, the Black man may pay lip service to assuming a dominant role but may behave "passively" with respect to some aspects of masculinity and in a dominant manner with respect to other aspects.

One reason for role conflict between Black men and Black women is that many contemporary Black women internalize two conflicting definitions of femininity, whereas many contemporary Black men internalize only a portion of the traditional definition of masculinity. Put simply, numerous Black women hold attitudes that are both highly masculine and highly feminine. On the other hand, their male counterparts develop traits that are highly consistent with certain aspects of society's definition of masculinity, but that are basically unrelated to other aspects of the definition. Thus, in a given relationship, one may find a Black woman who feels and behaves in ways that are both assertive and passive, dominant and subordi-

nant, decisive and indecisive, and so on. Within that same relationship, a Black man may exhibit highly masculine behaviors, such as physical aggressiveness, sexual dominance, and even violence, but behave indifferently with respect to the masculine work ethic—assuming responsibility for family-related activities external to the home, being aggressive in the workplace and the like.

The reason these incongruent attitudes and behaviors exist among Black men and Black women is that they have received contradictory messages during early socialization. It is common for Black women to have received two messages. One message states, "Because you will be a Black woman, it is imperative that you learn to take care of yourself because it is hard to find a Black man who will take care of you." A second message frequently received by young Black females that conflicts with the first message is "your ultimate achievement will occur when you have snared a Black man who will take care of you." In discussing early socialization experiences with countless young Black women in recent years, I have found that most of them agree that these two messages were given them by socialization agents and agencies such as child caretakers, relatives, peer group members, the Black church, and the media.

When internalized, these two messages often produce a Black woman who seems to reject aspects of the traditional female sex role in America such as passivity, emotional and economic dependence, and female subordinance while accepting other aspects of the role such as expressiveness, warmth, and nurturance. This is precisely why Black women seem to be more androgynous than White women. Black women's androgyny, though, may be more a function of necessity than anything else. It may be related to the scarcity of Black men who assume traditional masculine roles in male–female relationships.

Whatever the reason for Black women's androgynous orientations, because of such orientations Black women often find themselves in conflictual relationships with Black men or in no stable relationships at all. The scenario generally can be described as follows. Many Black women in early adulthood usually begin a search for a Black Prince Charming. However, because of the dearth of Black men who can be or are willing to be Prince Charmings for Black women, Black women frequently soon give up the search for such a Black man. They give up the search, settle for less, and "like" what they settle for even less. This statement is important because many Black women's eventual choices are destined to become constant reminders that the "female independence" message received during the early socialization process is the correct message. But, because Black women also have to deal with the second socialization message, many come to feel that they have failed in their roles as women. In an effort to correct their mistakes, Black women often choose to enact the aspect of their androgynous role that is decidedly aggressive and/or independent. They may decide either to "go it alone" or to prod their Black men into becoming Prince Charmings. The first alternative for Black women often results in self-doubt, lowered self-esteem, and, generally, unhappiness and dissatisfaction. After all, society nurtures the "find a man" message far beyond early socialization. The second message, unfortunately, produces little more than the first message because Black women in such situations usually end up in conflictual relationships with Black men, who also have undergone a rather complicated socialization process. Let us explore briefly the conflicting messages numerous Black men receive during early socialization.

One can find generally that Black men, too, have received two conflicting messages during early socialization. One message received by young Black males is "to become a man means that you must become dominant, aggressive, decisive, responsible, and in some instances, violent in social encounters with others." A second message received by young Black males that conflicts with the first is, "You are Black and you must not be too aggressive, too dominant, and so on, because the *man* will cut you down." Internalization of these two messages by some Black men (a sub-

stantial number) produces Black men who enact a portion of the traditional definition of masculinity but remain inactive with respect to other parts of traditional masculinity. Usually those aspects of traditional masculinity that can be enacted within the Black culture are the ones exhibited by these Black men. Other aspects of the sex role that require enactment external to the Black culture (e.g., aggressiveness in the workplace) may be related to impassively by Black men. Unfortunately, these are aspects of the male sex role that must be enacted if a male is to be "productive" in American society.

Too many Black men fail to enact the more "productive" aspects of the male sex role. Instead, "being a man," for many Black males who internalize the mixed messages, becomes simply enacting sexual aggression, violence, sexism, and the like—all of which promote Black male–Black female conflict. In addition, contributing to the low visibility and low salience of "productive" masculine traits among Black men is the second socialization message, which provides a rationale for nonenactment of the role traits. Moreover, the "man will get you" message serves to attenuate Black men's motivations to enact more "positive" aspects of the traditional male sex role. We must keep in mind, however, that not all of the sources of Black male–Black female conflict are social–psychological. Some of the sources are structural, and in the next section these sources are discussed.

Structural Barriers Contributing to Black Male–Black Female Conflict

It is easy to place the blame for Black male–Black female conflict on "White society." Several Black authors have used this explanatory approach in recent years (e.g., Anderson and Mealy 1979). They have suggested that Black male–Black female conflict is a function of America's capitalistic orientation and White society's long-time subjugation of Black people. Certainly historical conditions are important to understand when discussing the status of Black people today. Often, however, too much emphasis is placed on the historical subjugation of Black people as the source of Black male–Black female conflict today. Implicit in such an emphasis is the notion that independent variables existing at some point in the distant past cause a multiplicity of negative behaviors between Black males and Black females that can be capsulized as Black male–Black female conflict. A careful analysis of the contemporary environments of Black men and women today will show, instead, that factors responsible, in part, for Black male–Black female conflict are inextricably interwoven in those environments. In other words, an approach to the analysis of conflict between Black men and Black women today must be ahistorical. Past conditions influence Black male–Black female relationships only in the sense that vestiges of these conditions exist currently and are identifiable.

Our society today undoubtedly remains structured in such a manner that the vast majority of Black men encounter insurmountable barriers to the attainment of a "masculine" status as defined by most Americans (Black and White Americans). Black men still largely are locked within the Black culture (which has relatively limited resources), unable to compete successfully for societal rewards—the attainment of which defines American males as "men." Unquestionably, Black men's powerlessness in society's basic institutions such as the government and the economy contributes greatly to the pathological states of many Black men. The high mortality and suicide rates of young Black men, the high incarceration rates of Black men, the high incidence of drug addiction among Black men, and the high unemployment rate of Black men are all functions of societal barriers to Black male upward mobility. These barriers render millions of Black males socially impotent and/or socially dysfunctional. Moreover, as Staples has pointed out, such barriers also result in a scarcity of functional Black men, thereby limiting Black women's alternatives for mates.

While some may be tempted to argue for a psychological explanation of Black male social impotence, it is suggested here that any such argument is misguided unless accompanied by a recognition of the role of cultural nurturance factors. Cultural nurturance factors such as the rigid castelike social stratum of Blacks in America foster and maintain Black men's social impotence. The result is powerless Black men primed for conflictual relationships with Black women. If Black men in our society were not "American," perhaps cultural nurturance of Black people's status in our society could not be translated into cultural nurturance of Black male–Black female conflict. That Black men are Americanized, however, is seen in the outcome of the Black movement of the last decade.

The Black movement of the late 1960s and early 1970s produced little structural change in America. To be sure, a few Black men (and even fewer Black women) achieved a measure of upward mobility; however, the vast majority did not reap gains from the Black movement. What did happen, though, was that Black people did get a glimpse of the rewards that can be achieved in America through violence and/or aggression. White society did bend when confronted by the Black movement, but it did not break. In addition, the few upward mobility doors that were ajar during the height of the movement were quickly slammed shut when the movement began to wane in the middle and late 1970s. Black men today find themselves in a position similar to the one Black men were in prior to the movement. The only difference this time around is that Black men are equipped with the psychological armor of aggression and violence as well as with a distorted perception of a target—Black women, the ones who "stood silently by."

Wallace's statement that Black women "stood silently by" must not be taken lightly. Black women did this; in addition, they further internalized American definitions of masculinity and femininity. Previously, Black women held modified definitions of masculinity and femininity because the society's definition did not fit their everyday experiences. During the Black movement they were exhorted by Black men to assume a sex role that was more in line with the traditional "feminine" role White women assumed in male–female relationships. Although this may have been a noble (verbal) effort on the part of Black men to place Black women on pedestals, it was shortsighted and doomed to fail. Failure was imminent because even during the peak of the Black movement, societal resistance to structural changes that would benefit Black people was strong. The strength of this resistance dictated that change in Black people's status in America could come about only through the united efforts of both Black men and Black women.

Unfortunately, the seeds of division between Black men and Black women were sown during the Black movement. Black men bought the Moynihan report (1965) that indirectly blamed Black women for Black people's underclass status in America. In doing so, Black men convinced themselves that they could be "men" only if they adopted the White male's sex role. An examination of this role reveals that it is characterized by numerous contradictions. The traditional White masculine role requires men to assume protective, condescending, and generally patriarchal stances with respect to women. It also requires, ironically, that men display dominant, aggressive, and often violent behaviors toward women. Just as important, though, is that White masculine role enactment can occur only when there is full participation in masculinist American culture. Because Black men continue to face barriers to full participation in American society, the latter requirement for White male sex-role assumption continues to be met by only a few Black men. The result has been that many Black men have adopted only a part of the culture's definition of masculinity because they are thwarted in their efforts to participate fully in society. Structural barriers to Black male sex-role adoption, then, have produced a Black male who is primed for a conflictual relationship with Black women. In the next section, an exploration is presented of some possible solutions to Black male–Black female conflict that arise from the interactive relationship between the noncomplementary of sex-role internalization by Black men and Black women and structural barriers to Black men's advancement in American society.

Toward Solving Black Male–Black Female Conflict

Given that societal conditions are extremely resistant to rapid changes, the key to attenuating conflict between Black men and Black women lies in altering three social psychological phenomena: (1) Black male and Black female socialization experiences; (2) Black male and Black female role-playing strategies; and (3) Black male and Black female personal communication mechanisms. I first propose some alterations in Black male and Black female socialization experiences. . . .

Black female socialization must undergo change if Black men and Black women are to enjoy harmonious relationships. Those agents and agencies responsible for socializing young Black females must return to emphasizing a monolithic message in young Black female socialization. This message can stress warmth, caring, and nurturance, but it must stress simultaneously self-sufficiency, assertiveness, and responsibility. The latter portion of this message requires that young Black females must be cautioned against sexual freedom at relatively early ages—not necessarily for moral reasons, but because sexual freedom for Black women seems to operate against Black women's self-sufficiency, assertiveness, and responsibility. It is important to point out here, however, that this type of socialization message must be imparted without the accompanying castigation of Black men. To say "a nigger man ain't shit" informs any young Black female that at least one-half of herself "ain't shit." Without a doubt this strategy teaches self-hate and sets the stage for future Black male–Black female conflict.

Young Black males, on the other hand, must be instructed in self-sufficiency, assertiveness, and responsibility without the accompanying warning opposed to these traits in Black males. Such warnings serve only to provide rationales for future failures. To be sure, Black men do (and will) encounter barriers to upward mobility because they are Black. But, as many Black men have shown, such barriers do not have to be insurmountable. Of course it is recognized that innumerable Black men have been victims of American racist policies, but some, too, have been victims because they perceived only that external factors hindered their upward mobility and did not focus on some internal barriers that may have thwarted their mobility. The former factors are emphasized much too often in the contradictory socialization messages received by most young Black males.

Along with the above messages, young Black males must learn that the strong bonds that they establish with their mothers can be extended to their relationships with other Black women. If Black men perceive their mothers to be symbols of strength and perseverance, they must also be taught that most other Black women acquire these same qualities and have done so for generations. It must become just as "cool," in places like urban Black barbershops, to speak of Black women's strength and dignity as it is now to hear of Black women's thighs, breasts, and hips.

On an issue closely related to the above, few persons reading this article can deny that Black men's attempts to enact the White male sex role in America are laughable. Black men are relatively powerless in this country, and their attempts at domination, aggression, and the like, while sacrificing humanity, are ludicrous. This becomes apparent when it is understood that usually the only people being dominated and aggressed against by Black men are Black women (and other Black men). Moreover, unlike White males, Black males receive no societal rewards for their efforts; instead, the result is Black male–Black female disharmony. Black men must avoid the tendency to emulate the nauseatingly traditional male sex role because their experiences clearly show that such a role is counterproductive for Black people. Because the Black man's experiences are different, his role-playing strategies must be different and made to be more complementary with Black

females' altered role-playing strategies. The Black females' role-playing strategies, as we have seen, are androgynous, emphasizing neither the inferiority nor the superiority of male or female sex roles.

On a final note, it is important for Black people in our society to alter their personal communication mechanisms. Black men and Black women interact with each other in diverse ways and in diverse situations, ranging from intimate to impersonal. Perhaps the most important element of this diverse communication pattern is empathy. For Black people in recent years, this is precisely the element that has undergone unnecessary transformation. As Blacks in America have accepted increasingly White society's definition of male–female relationships, Black men and Black women have begun to interact with each other less in terms of empathy. While Black women have retained empathy in their male–female relationships to a greater degree than Black men have, Black men have become increasingly nonexpressive and nonempathic in their male–female relationships. Nearly 60% of Black women (approximately 25,000) in a recent *Essence* survey cited nonexpressiveness as a problem in male–female relationships; 56% also pointed out that Black male nonempathy was a problem (Edwards 1982). It seems, then, that as Black males have attempted to become "men" in America they have shed some of the important qualities of humanity. Some Black women, too, who have embraced the feminist perspective also have discarded altruism. The result of both phenomena, for Black people as a whole, has been to divide Black men and Black women further. Further movement away from empathic understanding in Black male–Black female relationships by both Black men and Black women undoubtedly will be disastrous for Black people in America.

References

Allen B. 1983 "The Price for Giving It Up." *Essence* (February): 60–62, 118.

Anderson, S. E., and R. Mealy. 1979 "Who Origi-
nated the Crisis: A Historical Perspective." *Black Scholar* (May/June): 40–44.

Braithwaite, R. L. 1981 "Interpersonal Relations be-
tween Black Males and Black Females." In *Black Men*, L. E. Gary, ed., pp. 83–97. Beverly Hills, Calif.: Sage.

Drake, S. C., and H. R. Cayton. 1945 *Black Metropolis*. New York: Harcourt.

Edwards, A. 1982 "Survey Results: How You're Feeling." *Essence* (December): 73–76.

Franklin, C. W., II. 1980 "White Racism As a Cause
of Black Male–Black Female Conflict: A Critique." *Western Journal of Black Studies* 4 (1): 42–49.

Frazier, E. F. 1939 *The Negro Family in the United
States*. Chicago: University of Chicago Press.

Grier, W. II., and P. M. Cobb. 1968 *Black Rage*. New
York: Basic Books.

Jones, T. 1979 "The Need to Go beyond Stereotypes." *Black Scholar* (May/June): 48–49.

Karenga, M. R. 1979 "On Wallace's Myth: Wading
through Troubled Waters." *Black Scholar* (May/
June): 36–39.

Moore, W. F. 1980 "Black Women, Stop Criticizing
Black Men—Blame Yourselves." *Ebony* (December): 128–130.

Moynihan, D. P. 1965 *The Negro Family: The Case for
National Action*. Washington, D.C.: U.S. Department of Labor, Office of Planning and Research.

Poussaint, A. F. 1982 "What Every Black Woman
Should Know about Black Men." *Ebony* (August): 36–40.

Staples, R. 1979 "The Myth of Black Macho: A Response to Angry Black Feminists." *Black Scholar*
(March/April): 24–32.

Wallace, M. 1979 *Black Macho and the Myth of the
Superwoman*. New York: Dial.

———. 1982 "A Black Feminist's Search for Sisterhood." In *All the Blacks Are Men, All the Women
Are White, but Some of Us Are Brave*, G. T. Hull et
al., eds. pp. 5–8. Old Westbury, N.Y.: Feminist
Press.

ARTICLE 33

Karen Walker

"I'm Not Friends the Way She's Friends": Ideological and Behavioral Constructions of Masculinity in Men's Friendships

Contemporary ideologies about men's friendships suggest that men's capacity for intimacy is sharply restricted. In this view, men have trouble expressing their feelings with friends. Whether due to the development of the masculine psyche or cultural prescriptions, men are viewed as highly competitive with friends. Because of their competition, they are unlikely to talk about intimate matters such as feelings and relationships. The literature on gender differences in friendship suggests that the ideologies reflect actual behavior. Researchers have found that men limit verbal self-disclosure with friends, especially when compared to women (Aukett, Ritchie, & Mill 1988; Caldwell & Peplau 1982; Reid & Fine 1992; Rubin 1985; Sherrod 1987; Swain 1989). Men share activities with friends (Rubin 1985; Swain 1987). On the other hand, there are also suggestions that the degree of self-disclosure among men may be underestimated (Hacker 1981; Rawlins 1992; Wright 1982), particularly among men from particular groups (Franklin 1992). My research on friendship shows that men and women share the stereotypes about gender differences in friendship, but in specific friendships, men discuss their relationships and report relying on men friends for emotional support and intimacy (Walker 1994). In addition, many activities of friendship—seeing friends for dinner, sharing rit-

ual events, and visiting—are things both men and women do. Barry Wellman (1992) argues that there has been a widespread "domestication" of male friendship, with men seeing friends in their home in much the same way women do.

In much of the literature on gender differences in friendship, ideology has been mistaken for behavior. In part, researchers seem to have made this mistake because they have asked general, instead of specific, questions about friendship.[1] As a result, they have elicited good representations of what respondents *believe* their behavior is—beliefs that are shaped by the respondents' own ideologies. What they have sometimes failed to elicit is information about specific friendships in which variations from the ideologies may be substantial. Because researchers report what respondents tell them, it is easy to understand why researchers make this mistake. What becomes more difficult to understand is how the confusion between the ideology of friendship and friendship behavior comes to be constructed in everyday life. Why do men maintain their belief that men are less open than women in the face of considerable evidence that they do discuss their feelings with their friends? This is even more crucial because the stereotype of intimate friendship that men believe characterizes women's friendship is currently highly valued. Feminist scholars and writers have successfully revalued women's intimate relationships to the detriment of earlier ideals that privileged male bonding. While not all respondents in this study positively evaluated the stereotype of women's openness with friends, many did, as evidenced by one professional man who said,

> I mean, we [men] talk about sports and politics sometimes, any kind of safe [topic], if you will. Not that any [every] kind of interaction needs to be intimate or this and that, but it's much different when you talk to women. Women catch on. I remember once seeing Robert Bly, and he said something that is really so in my experience, that women get to the heart of things and that they get there so quickly that it makes you, uh, it can put men into a rage because women are able to articulate these kinds of things that men can't.

Given the belief that being intimate and "getting to the heart of things" is good, and given the evidence that men are more intimate in practice than the ideology suggests, *why don't men challenge the ideology?*

There seem to be several answers to this question. First, when men do not conform to the masculine ideals about how they should act with their friends, they are occasionally censured. In the practice of masculine friendship, the positive evaluation of feminine intimacy disappears. Because of their friends' reactions, men come to see their behavior as anomalous and bad, and they do not reevaluate the extent to which the ideology of masculine friendship accurately reflects behavior.

Second, social class influences men's capacities for conforming to gender ideologies. Professional men are somewhat more likely than working-class men to conform to gendered norms with respect to intimate behavior (Franklin 1992; Walker 1994). Also, professional men's social class makes them—with other middle-class men—the primary groups on which cultural stereotypes are based. Literature written specifically about men's friendships often relies on research of middle-class men, particularly college-aged men (Caldwell and Peplau 1982; Rawlins 1992; Reid and Fine 1992; Rubin 1985; Swain 1989). Very recently, some researchers have noted that men who are other than middle-class or white may have different types of friendships from the ideology (Franklin, 1992; Hansen, 1992), but the knowledge of the existence of other forms of masculine friendship among working-class African American and white men has not influenced the ideology of friendship.

Third, there *are* gender differences in behavior, and these differences reinforce stereotypes about gendered forms of friendship, even if the differences differ substantively from the substance of the ideology. For instance, male respondents in this study used the telephone somewhat differently from the ways women used it. Through their use of the telephone men constructed their masculinity, and in so doing they reinforced their notions that men are not open. As I will show, men claimed they called their friends for explicitly instrumental reasons—to make plans, get specific information, and so on—but not to find out how friends were, which they connected to women's telephone use. These practices generally supported the idea that women were better at maintaining friendships and talking to friends about feelings even though men's telephone conversations often included talk about personal matters. But a desire to talk to friends about personal matters was rarely the motive for phone calls.

In this article I examine the ways gender ideology about friendships is maintained through four behaviors and men's interpretations of those behaviors: telephone use, jokes, the use of public space, and how men talk about women. It is only when we understand how men behaviorally construct gender within friendship that we can begin to understand how men use these behavioral constructions to support ideological constructions of masculine friendship practices.

Method of Study

This paper relies on research from a study of men's and women's same-gender and cross-gender friendships. I interviewed 9 working-class and 10 professional men (as well 18 working-class and 15 middle-class women). Within each class I individually interviewed some men who were friends with other respondents in the study. Interviewing friends allowed me to gather information on group interaction that would have been unavailable had I interviewed isolated individuals. In addition, I was able to explore issues that were most salient to groups of friends. Finally, by interviewing friends I could examine the extent to which friends agree on what their interactions were like. This was particularly important when there was a discrepancy between behavior and ideology: Some men did not report on behavior that contradicted the masculine ideology of friendship either because they were unwilling to disclose that their behavior did not match the cultural ideal or because such behavior was somewhat meaningless to them, and they forgot it.

Respondents ranged in age from 27 to 48. Class location was determined by both life style and individuals' work. Thus, working-class respondents tended to have high school educations or less, although one self-employed carpenter had a 4-year degree in accounting. Working-class men were in construction and some service occupations. Most working-class men lived in densely populated urban neighborhoods in row houses or twins in Philadelphia. Professional respondents had graduate degrees, and they worked as academics, administrators, lawyers, and therapists. Professionals lived in the suburbs of Philadelphia or in urban apartments.

Interviews were semistructured, and respondents answered both global questions about their friendship patterns as well as questions about activities and topics of conversations in which they engaged with each friend they named. The use of in-depth interviews that included both global and specific questions allowed me to gather data indicating the frequent discrepancies between cultural ideologies of masculine friendships and actual behaviors. In addition, in-depth interviews allowed me to compare working-class and professional respondents' experiences.

Recently, Christine Williams and Joel Heikes (1993) have observed that male nurses shaped responses to interview questions in ways that took into account the gender of the interviewer. In this study, my status as a woman interviewer appeared to have both positive and negative implications for data collection. On the one hand, being a woman made it more likely that men admitted behavior that contradicted gender ideology. Sociologists studying gender and friendship have consistently argued that men do not engage in self-disclosure with other men (Caldwell & Peplau 1982; Reid & Fine 1992). Other research shows that men are likely to be more self-disclosing with women than with men (O'Meara 1989; Rubin 1985). While my research shows that men engaged in self-disclosure more frequently with friends than the literature suggests, they did so with men they considered close friends. Frequently close friends were people they knew for a long time or people with whom they spent much time. Wright (1982) notes that long-time men friends engage in self-disclosure. I suspected that certain kinds of disclosures that men made during the interviews might have been more difficult to make to an unknown man instead of to me, an unknown woman.

On the other hand, respondents suggested that they more heavily edited their responses to questions about how they discussed women with their men friends than they did other questions. They frequently sprinkled their responses with comments recognizing my gender, "You don't have a gun in there, do you? (laugh)" or "I don't mean to be sexist here." I suspected that responses were much more benign than they would have been if I were a man. Thus, when I discuss men's talk about women below I believe that my data underestimate the extent to which men's talk about women constructs gender tensions.

Behavioral Construction of Masculinity

In recent years sociologists of gender have come to emphasize the active construction of gender. Gender is seen as an ongoing activity fundamental to all aspects of social life rather than a static category in which we place men or women (Connell 1987; Leidner 1991; West & Zimmerman 1987). One advantage of a social constructionist perspective is that it allows researchers to explore both the ideological as well as the behavioral construction of gender. Gender is constructed *ideologically* when men and women believe that certain qualities, such as intimacy, characterize one gender rather than another. The way men and women interpret life and its meaning for them is deeply influenced by their ideological beliefs. Gender is constructed *behaviorally* in the activities men and women do and the way they do them.

Sometimes ideology and behavior match—such as when men talk about gender differences in telephone use and report behavior that differs from women's behavior. Sometimes ideology and behavior do not match. When there is a mismatch, the interesting problem of how ideology is sustained when behavior contradicts it emerges. I argue that, in the specific case of friendship, specific behaviors supported men's gendered ideologies. Men discounted or ignored altogether evidence that discredited a distinctly masculine model of friendship. This occurred because gender is a category culturally defined by multiple qualities. When men included themselves in the masculine gender category based on some behavior, they tended unreflectively to accept as given the cultural boundaries of the entire category *even if other of their behaviors contradicted those boundaries*.

Among respondents there were several ways masculinity was constructed in the activities of friendship. First, where men met, particularly working-class men, became a mark of masculinity. Second, the way men used the telephone distinguished masculine from feminine behavior. Third, men used jokes in particular ways to establish masculinity and also to manage tensions between actual behavior and gender ideologies. Finally, men friends talked about women in ways that emphasized the differences and tensions between men and women.

There are class differences in the behaviors that form particular patterns of masculinity. Differential financial constraints, the social expectations of particular kinds of work, and lifestyle differences played roles in shaping particular forms of masculinity. The use of jokes was somewhat more elaborated among working-class men than among professional men, but reports of jokes and joking behavior emerged in both groups. Professional men talked about wives and the strains of work and family differently from working-class men; as I will discuss, this resulted from different work experiences.

Besides class differences, which I will address throughout the article, there were individual differences. All men did not engage in all the behaviors that I argue contribute to the construction of masculinity. One professional man said that while he talked "about what specific women are like," he did not talk about women in general and men who talked about what women are generally like "would not be my friends." Other men did not report the use of jokes and joking behavior in their friendships. Sociology frequently avoids discussion about individuals who do not participate in the behaviors that the sociologist argues shows the existence of meaningful social patterns. Unfortunately, doing so often reifies behavioral differences. This is a particular problem in the discussion of gender because there is currently (and happily for the existence of a lively, informed debate) a very close link between the results of social research on gender and broad social and political debates about men's and women's differences.

I wish, therefore, to give the reader a general indication of the individual variability in the gendered behaviors in which men engaged. In all the behaviors discussed below at least half, and frequently more, of the men participated in the behaviors whereas few women did. There were, however, individual exceptions to these behaviors, and those exceptions point to a flexibility in gendered behavior that, while not as expansive as many would wish, is broader than we frequently recognize. Current social theory about gender emphasizes the agentic nature of the construction of gender. It is a practice in which men and women have a considerable range of actions from which to choose. At given historical points, certain actions may be dictated more than others, and therefore individual men and women may frequently act in ways that conform to current ideology. But even when cultural ideology demands close adherence to particular practices, the practical nature of gender means that some individuals will not conform. Further, the multiplicity of practices that create gender enables individuals to maintain their positions within gender categories without much difficulty.

Men's Use of Public Space

The use of public space for informal and apparently unplanned socializing is much more common among men than among women, and it marks the gender boundaries between men and women. The frequent use of public space by working-class men for informal socializing emerges in ethnographies of men's groups (Anderson 1976; Kornblum 1974; Liebow 1967; Whyte 1981). Working-class men in this study met in public spaces such as local bars and playgrounds. There they talked about work and family, and they made informal connections with other men. Sometimes they picked up side work, sometimes they hung out. At the time of our interview, one working-class man said that he spent some of his time at a local bar selling advertisements in a book to raise money for a large retirement dinner for a long-time coach of a community football team. He also spent time there drinking and talking to friends.

Working-class men also met in semipublic spaces such as gyms or clubs. While membership in these spaces was frequently restricted, the spaces themselves functioned in similar ways to public spaces. Men met regularly and informally in public and semipublic spaces one or more times a week. Unlike women who made definite plans to meet friends occasionally in bars, the men assumed because of past practice that on particular nights of the week they would meet friends.

Wellman (1992) suggests that the use of public space for male socializing is diminishing, and men's friendships are becoming domesticated as their friendships move into the home and hence more like women's. This phenomenon of domestication was evident among professional respondents, most of whom reported socializing infrequently in public spaces. But it was not evident among the working-class respondents in this study. All but one of the working-class respondents had been brought up in the same communities in which they lived when I interviewed them. Among these men there were long-time, continuous patterns of public socializing. While Wellman's point is important, the domestication of male friendship seems to be influenced by circumstances in men's lives and is probably occurring unevenly. Further, barring significant structural changes in working-class men's formal and informal work lives, the domestication of male friendships is unlikely to be complete.

Men's Telephone Use

Discussions of men's telephone use as a construction of gender make the most sense when contrasted with women's telephone use. Many men noted that their wives used the telephone very differently from them. A few, primarily working-class men, stated that they disliked talking on the telephone, and they used it only for instrumental reasons (e.g., to make appointments or get specific information). Other men, both professional and working class, said their wives called friends just to see how they were doing and then talked for a long time, whereas men did not do so. Thus men ideologically constructed gender through their understandings of telephone practices. In addition, both men and women constructed gender behaviorally through using the telephone in different ways.

Telephone use differed slightly by class and work experiences, but even accounting for the effects of class and work, there were substantial gender differences. Men frequently reported that the purpose of their most recent telephone calls with friends was instrumental: lawyers discussed cases, men discussed upcoming social plans, and some working-class men made plans to do side work together. Because of this instrumental motive for telephone calls to friends, many professional men reported that their frequent telephone contact was from their offices during working hours. Men rarely reported that they called friends just to say "hi" and find out how they were. One professional man, Mike,[2] reported differences between his wife and himself in being friends,

> I'm not friends the way she's friends. *How are you friends differently?* I don't work on them. I don't pick the phone up and call people and say, "How are you?"

While Mike reported that, in fact, he did call one friend to find out how he was doing at least once a year, most telephone contact was initiated when friends made plans to visit from out of town or he had business matters to discuss with friends. One result of this behavior was tremendous attrition in his friendship network over time. Mike was a gregarious man who reported many past and current friends, but he tended to lose touch with past friends once business reasons for keeping in touching with them diminished, even those who continued to live in Philadelphia. He only reported talking to two friends six or more times a year on the telephone. One of those friends was a man with whom he had professional ties, and they called one another when they did business. The other friend, Gene, was one of the few men who called friends for social conversations. The fairly frequent calls between Gene and Mike may have been initiated by Gene.

Gil, a working-class man, usually spoke to friends on the phone to arrange meetings. Although he kept in touch with two friends largely through telephone use (he worked two jobs during the week and one of his friends worked on weekends—theirs was a telephone friendship), he said,

> I don't talk to them a long time because I'm not a phone person. I'd rather see them in person because I don't like holding the phone and talking because you really can't think of things to say too often on the phone, but when you're in person you can think of more things, cause I like prefer sitting and talking to a person face-to-face . . . I'll talk to people 10, 15 minutes sometimes, but I prefer not to if I can. But some

you just can't get off the phone, no matter what you do. And you're like, "Uh, great, well, I'll talk to you a little bit later." And they go into another story. You know [my friend] Cindy will do that, Cindy is great for that. Now Joanne [my wife] can talk on the phone for two to three hours . . . And then the person she's with is not too far away so she could just walk over and talk, you know.

Peter, a young working-class man, reported that he "avoided the phone as much as possible." He did not call friends to chat, and he only used the telephone for social chats with one friend, a woman:

> I'm not a phone person, but yeah, I do [talk to a specific friend] because she talks on the phone, she likes the phone so . . . She'll talk and I'll yes and no (laughs).

Peter did not do side jobs with other men, thus his reasons for using the telephone were sharply limited. Peter and Gil both reported that their telephone preferences were different from those of women they knew. Their general comment "I'm not a phone person" was a representation of their identity, and it was substantiated by their behavior that differs from women's behavior. Typically, working-class men spoke on the telephone once or twice a week to those with whom they did side jobs. One man who ran a bookmaking business with a friend reported that they spoke several times a day about business. Men spoke much less frequently than that to friends for other reasons.

Although most men reported calling friends for instrumental reasons, many men reported that their telephone conversations were not limited to the reason for the call. During telephone calls men discussed their families or their work after they finished with their business. During telephone calls made to discuss social plans several men discussed infertility problems with their wives. Another complained to a friend about his marital problems during a phone call initiated to plan side work. One man called a friend to make plans for a birthday dinner for the caller's wife. During the conversation he told his friend how many feelings the interview I had with him had stirred up (the friend had referred me to him). These conversations, then, had several functions for men's friendships. The telephone was primarily considered a tool for business or to make social plans, but it was also used as means of communicating important personal information. Most men, however, deemphasized the telephone's function in the communication of personal information.

About one fourth of the men reported that they did call friends simply to find out how they were. Most of the time these men reported calling out-of-town friends with whom they lacked other regular means of contact, and most of the time their calls were infrequent—one to three times a year. In one exception, a professional man regularly called friends to see how they were (and sometimes became irritated and upset when the friends did not reciprocate by initiating some percentage of the telephone calls). He talked with one local friend once a week for no other reason than to keep in touch, but this pattern was unique. The friend he called had limited mobility, and the men rarely saw one another. The telephone was a primary vehicle for their friendship. In this instance, the two men's calls differed little from some women's calls.

There was tremendous variation in telephone use among men, but the variation does not erase the differences across genders. While only one quarter of the men in this study reported that they ever called friends to visit over the telephone and three quarters called for instrumental reasons, over four-fifths of the women reported that they called friends to visit. Also, men's reported frequency of telephoning friends was consistently lower than women's. Whereas two-thirds of all women reported that they spoke with at least one friend three or more times a week, less than one quarter of the men did so.

The finding that men use the telephone less than women and that women use it for social visiting has been noted by others (Fischer 1992; Rakow 1991). Fischer (1992) argues,

research shows that, discounting their fewer opportunities for social contact, women are more socially adept and intimate than men, for whatever reasons—psychological constitution, social structure, childhood experiences or cultural norms. The telephone therefore fits the typical female style of personal interaction more closely than it does the typical male style (p. 235).

Fischer's comments may hold a clue about how ideologies of gender are maintained despite the evidence of intimate behaviors among men. Men and women both see the telephone as something women use more than men, and they see it as a way women are intimate. Men's telephone practices provided evidence to respondents that men are incapable of intimacy whereas women are very intimate with friends. Although women used the telephone more often for intimate conversation than men, men used opportunities at work and in public hangouts to talk intimately (one respondent reported that when they got together in the bar "we're worse than a bunch of girls when it comes to that [talking about their spouses]!"). Although telephone patterns are a poor measure of intimacy in friendship, men used them as such. Several men commented on hearing their wives call friends and talk about personal information. Doing so substantiated their impressions of women's friendships. Also, because the men focused on the reasons for their calls rather than on the contents of telephone calls, telephone use acted to provide confirmation that stereotypes about friendship are true.

Men's Jokes

Men's use of jokes is another way in which men construct their masculinity. In his ethnography, *America's Working Man*, David Halle (1984) points to several functions jokes serve among men: they reaffirm values of friendship and generosity, they ritually affirm heterosexuality among men whose social circumstances create a level of physical and emotional intimacy culturally regarded as unmasculine, and they mediate disputes. These functions were evident in the way working-class men talked about jokes and humor in their friendships. They were less evident among the professional men, for reasons suggested by Halle.

Men friends, particularly working-class men, used harsh teasing as a form of social control to reinforce certain behaviors. One working-class man said that he and his friends were the worst "ball breakers" in the world. If a man did not show up at the bar or at some social event then my respondent said they heard about it from all their friends. Among these men the friendship group was highly valued, but also, like many contemporary friendships, somewhat fragile. Work and family responsibilities that kept men away from the friendship group might put a friend at risk of being teased.

Other men said that the failure to reciprocate favors, such as help with household projects, might be a basis for teasing friends. This was a particularly important way of defusing tension as well as reaffirming values of friendship for working-class men. They frequently depended on friends to help them attain higher standards of living: friends provided craft services whose prices are high in the formal market and thus many working-class people's material lives were somewhat improved through the help of friends. Failure to reciprocate had implications not only for friendship but also for family income. Jokes about a friend's failure to reciprocate became a public statement about his failure to conform to recognized norms, and they were a way for someone to handle his anger at his friend.

Another way jokes constructed masculinity was to highlight an activity that was outside the purview of men's activities that they nonetheless did. For instance, Greg and Chris were friends from law school who saw each other seven or eight times a year. One of those times was a yearly shopping trip to buy Christmas presents. Men generally claimed they did not shop—those who did usually said they went to hardware stores when they were doing a project with a friend. The shopping trip Greg and Chris went on was a traditional joke between them both. It began in law school when Greg asked Chris to go with him to

buy a negligee for Greg's girlfriend. When they got to the store Chris ran away and Greg was left feeling terribly embarrassed. Ever since, they went shopping once a year, but both men downplayed the shopping aspect of the trips and highlighted the socializing. They said they did not accomplish very much on their trips. They also said they used the time to buy gag gifts for people instead of serious gifts. Turning the shopping spree into a joke subverted the meaning of shopping as something women do, and the trip became a ritual reaffirmation of masculinity.

Jokes were sometimes used as pseudoinstrumental reasons to call friends on the phone when men lacked instrumental reasons; they thus maintained the masculinity of men's telephone practices. Men called each other and told one another jokes and then moved into more personal topics. Gene, for instance, befriended Al's lover, Ken, before Al died of AIDS. During Al's illness Gene was an important source of support for both men, and he continued to keep in touch with Ken after Al's death. They talked regularly on the telephone, but most of the conversations initiated by Ken began with jokes. After Ken and Gene had exchanged jokes the two men moved on to other topics, including their feelings for Al.

Finally, men used jokes to exaggerate gender differences and denigrate women. Gene considered himself sympathetic to women's issues. He said that he and his friends

> will tell in a joking way, tell jokes that are hostile towards feminism or hostile towards women. It's like there's two levels of it. One is, we think the joke is funny in and of itself or we think the joke is funny because it's so outrageously different from what's politically correct. You know, so we kind of laugh about it, and then we'll laugh that we even had the gall to tell it.

Not all men mentioned the importance of humor to friendship, the existence of jokes among friends, or the tendency to tease friends, but about half the respondents indicated that jokes and teasing were part of their friendship. Also, jokes and joking behavior were not limited solely to men. A few women also told jokes and engaged in joking behavior with their friends, but men emphasized the behavior as part of their friendships, whereas women did not. Also, women reported using jokes in a much more restricted way than men. For men, jokes are an elaborated code with multiple meanings and functions.

Men Talk About Women

Finally, men constructed masculinity through their behavior with men friends through their talk about what women are like. While not every man reported that he engaged in discussions about women with his friends, most men did. Comments about women emphasized men's and women's differences. Men, for instance, discussed how their wives had higher housekeeping standards than they, their wives' greater control over child rearing, and their greater propensity to spend money impulsively; they also discussed women's needs for relationships. These comments helped men interpret their relationships with their wives and served to reassure men that their experiences were not unusual.

> We would talk about like how long it would take them to get dressed . . . my wife took exceptionally long to get dressed, four or five hours in the bathroom. Um, but I mean, I don't think I talk a whole lot about women, when I did I guess I generalized and that kind of stuff, like how a wife expects a husband to kind of do everything for her. (Working-class man)

> What we talked about was the differences, differences we have with our wives in terms of raising kids. . . . And how sometimes we feel, rightly or wrongly, we both agreed that we didn't have quite as much control over the situation or say in the situation as we might have liked . . . That's something that a lot of my friends who have younger kids, I've had that discussion with. I've talked to them about it in terms of something that I think mothers, in particular, have a different input into their child's lives than do fathers. (Professional man)

Through these sorts of discussions with men friends—some brief and jocular, some more sus-

tained and serious—men defined who women are, and who they were, in contrast, as men. These discussions with friends frequently reinforced stereotypes about women and men.

Women were spendthrifts:

> One individual may call me up and say, "Geez, my wife just went out and bought these rugs. I need that like a hole in the head. You know, this is great, I have these oriental rugs now, you know, I'm only going to spill coffee on it." (Professional man)

Women attempted to control men's free time:

> [We might talk about] how much we're getting yelled at or in trouble or whatever, you know what I mean, for not doin' stuff around the house, or workin' over somebody else's house too much or staying out at the bars too late. (Working-class man)

Women were manipulative:

> Sometimes they seem, they don't know what they want, or what they want is something different than what they tell you they want. You know, tough to figure out, [we say] that they can be manipulative . . . Conniving. (Professional man)

Men evaluated women's behaviors and desires through such talk. They reported that such talk was a way of getting feedback on their marital experiences. Talking with friends frequently relieved the tensions men felt in their cross-gender relationships, and it did so without requiring men to change their behaviors vis-à-vis women. Men rarely reported that they accommodated themselves to their wives because their friends suggested that they should: in an unusual case, one working-class man said his friend told him that women needed to be told, "I love you," all the time, and he thought his friend had been helpful in mitigating some strains in his marriage through their talk.

More frequently, men's jokes and comments about women—about their demands for more housekeeping help, their ways with money, and their desires to have men home more often—

served to delegitimize women's demands. Men talked about women as unreasonable; as one man above said, "everybody needs time away." This tendency to delegitimize wives' demands was more apparent among working-class men than among the professional men. Professionals reported that their jobs, not unreasonable wives, prevented them from greater involvement in child care, and they sometimes talked with friends about this as an inevitable part of professional life. The effect, however, was similar because talk among both professional and working-class men friends supported the status quo. Instead of becoming a problem to be solved, professional men and their friends determined that professional life unfortunately, but inevitably, caused men to limit their family involvement. (One man who consistently seemed to play with the boundaries of masculinity had tried to solve the problem through scheduling his work flexibly along the lines that a friend had suggested. He reported that he still did not have enough time for his family.)

These four behaviors: using public spaces for friendship socializing, men's telephone practices, joking, and talking about women in particular ways are some ways that men construct masculinity in their friendships. There are many others. Discussions of sports, for instance, are one obvious other way men construct their masculinity, and such discussions were common among respondents. Like women's telephone use and ease with intimacy, men's talk about sports has become part of our cultural ideology about gendered friendships. Not all respondents, however, participated in such talk, and of those who did, some did not enjoy such talk but engaged in it because it was expected.

Cultural Ideology of Men and Friendship

When I began this article I asked not only how men construct masculinity through their behaviors but also why there was a discrepancy between the cultural ideology of men's friendship's, which maintains that men do not share intimate thoughts

and feelings with one another, and reports of specific behaviors that show that they do. It is in part by recognizing that the construction of gender is an ongoing activity that incorporates many disparate behaviors that this question becomes answerable. While one behavior in an interaction may violate the norms of gender ideology, other behaviors are simultaneously conforming to other ideologies of masculinity. When men reflect back on their behavior they emphasize those aspects of their behavior that give truth to their self-images as men. The other behavior may be reported, but, in this study, it did not discredit men's gender ideologies.

Second, as I noted earlier, masculinity is frequently reified, and behavior that does not conform does not affect the overall picture of masculinity. Men belong in the gender category to which they were assigned at birth, and their past in that category reassures them that they belong there. Occasionally respondents recognized that men do things that contradict gender ideology. One man told me about a friend of his who "does thoughtful things for other men." When I asked what he did, and he said:

> Uh, remembers their birthdays. Will buy them gifts. Uh, and does it in a way that's real, I think, really, uh, I don't know, it's not uh, it's not uh, feminine in the sense of, feminine, maybe in the perjorative sense . . . I mean, I remember that John, uh, John's nurturing I saw, not that I was a recipient of it so much although I was in his company a lot and got to see him. Uh, I thought, boy, this guy's a, this guy's a real man, this guy. This guy's all right, you know.

Though my respondent identified his friend's behavior as different, almost feminine, he made sure to tell me that the man is a "real man." This seemed problematic for him, his language became particularly awkward, full of partial sentences. But in the end, the fact that his friend was a man and that my respondent liked and respected him enabled him to conclude, "this guy's a real man."

At other times, recognition that behavior contradicts gender ideology elicits censure instead of acceptance. When men censure one another for such behavior, they reinforce the idea that such behavior is anomalous and should not be expressed. For instance, Gene, who consciously worked at intimacy with his friends, told me about sitting and drinking with a friend of his one night when Gene was depressed. His friend asked him how things were going and Gene told him he was depressed because he was feeling financial pressures. Gene felt "house poor" and upset with himself for buying a house that would cause him to feel such pressures when he had determined that he would not do such a thing. His friend's response was, "Oh, that's the last time I ask you how you're feeling." On an earlier occasion Gene called his gay friend in California on the telephone crying because he had just broken off with a woman he had been dating. His friend comforted him at the time, but later he said, "I didn't know you had it in you [to express yourself like that]." Gene believed that men had greater difficulties with self-disclosure than women, and these events acted as support for his beliefs instead of counterexamples. In both cases friends had let him know his self-disclosing behavior was either intolerable or unusual. His gay friend seemed to admire Gene's ability to call him up in tears by giving him a back-handed compliment, but this was a man who had rejected many norms of heterosexuality, and who saw Gene as participating in hegemonic masculinity (Connell 1987) and teased him for it. Gene's interpretation of these events coincided with his friends: he was behaving in ways men normally did not.

In another case, Anna, a woman respondent, told me about her husband Tom's experience with his best friend. Anna had been diagnosed with a serious chronic illness that had profound consequences for her lifestyle, and Tom was depressed about it. One night he went out with two friends, Jim, Tom's best friend, and another man who was unhappy about his recent divorce. According to Anna, Jim commented that he wished he did not know either Tom or the other man at the time because they were both so depressed. From this, Anna said she and Tom concluded that men did not express their feelings and were not as intimate with one another as women were.

These sorts of events reinforce men's notions that men are emotionally distant. Self-disclosure and attempts to express one's feelings are seen as anomalous, even if desirable—desirable because the contemporary evaluation on friendship as defined primarily by feminists is that women have better friendships than men. Women, by the way, also reported occasions when their friends were unsympathetic to their expressions of distress. The conclusions women and men drew about their unsympathetic friendship differed, however. Women concluded that particular friends lacked sympathy. Unlike men, they did not think their expressive behavior was inappropriate or unusual.

Conclusion

I have conceptualized gender as an ongoing social creation rather than a role individuals learn or a personality type they develop that causes differences in behavior. Individuals construct gender on an ideological and a behavioral level. On a behavioral level, many social acts contribute to the overall construction of masculinity. Men do not talk on the phone unless they have something specific they wish to find out or arrange. Men friends joke around together. Men hang out in bars. Men also talk about women and their wives in ways that distinguish women from men and define gender tensions and men's solutions to them. Some of these behaviors have become part of the cultural ideology of men's friendships. Respondents, for instance, talked generally about differences between men's and women's telephone use. Some also said that women stayed home with their friends whereas men went out. But the relationship between behavior and ideology is not so direct and simple that behaviors in which most men participate become part of the cultural ideology. To the extent that talking about women, for instance, is perceived as sharing personal information, then talking about women is something men do not recognize as characteristic of their friendships.

Because so many actions construct masculinity and gender is a practice over which individuals have some control, the failure to conform to the cultural ideology of masculine friendship does not necessarily threaten either the cultural ideology or the individual's position in the masculine gender category. This becomes particularly important in understanding why the many men who share personal information with friends continue to believe that men are inexpressive and find intimacy difficult. I have found that the exchange of intimate information is something most respondents, men and women, engaged in, but most people also did it with selected friends. Furthermore, talking about personal matters or sharing feelings frequently constituted a small portion of all friendship interactions. Thus, for men whose identities included a notion that they, as men, were not open with friends, the times when they were open were insignificant. There were many other activities of friendship that men preferred to emphasize.

It is useful to expand the debate over gender differences in friendship to include behaviors other than intimacy that has dominated the recent literature on gender and friendship (Allan 1989; Miller 1983; Rawlins 1992; Rubin 1985; Sherrod 1987; Swain 1987). The narrowness of the debate has limited our understandings of why men's friendships have been meaningful and important to them. Working-class men's reliance on friends for services and material support becomes invisible. The importance of joking behavior as a communicative style and its functions in maintaining stable relationships for both working-class and professional men disappear. Finally, the narrow debate over intimacy obscures some implications of how men talk to one another about women for gender relations and inequality.

A version of this article was presented at the 1993 annual meetings of the American Sociological Association in Miami. The author gratefully acknowledges the comments of Robin Leidner and Vicki Smith.

Notes

1. Some researchers have made this mistake as part of a more general positive evaluation of women. Some of this literature is explicitly feminist and draws on literature which emphasizes and dichotomizes gender differences.

2. All names of the respondents have been changed.

References

Allan, G. (1989). *Friendship: Developing a sociological perspective*. Boulder, CO: Westview.

Anderson, E. (1976). *A place on the corner*. Chicago: University of Chicago Press.

Aukett, R., Ritchie, J., & Mill, K. (1988). Gender differences in friendship patterns. *Sex Roles, 19*, 57–66.

Caldwell, M. A., & Peplau, L. A. (1982). Sex differences in same-sex friendships. *Sex Roles, 8*, 721–732.

Connell, R. W. (1987). *Gender and power*. Stanford, CA: Stanford University Press.

Fischer, C. (1992). *America calling: A social history of the telephone to 1940*. Berkeley: University of California Press.

Franklin, C. W. II (1992). Friendship among Black men. In P. Nardi (Ed.), *Men's friendships* (pp. 201–214). Newbury Park, CA: Sage.

Hacker, H. M. (1981). Blabbermouths and clams: Sex differences in self-disclosure in same-sex and cross-sex friendship dyads. *Psychology of Women Quarterly, 5*, 385–401.

Halle, D. (1984). *America's working man: Work, home, and politics among blue-collar property owners*. Chicago: University of Chicago Press.

Hansen, K. V. (1992). Our eyes behold each other: masculinity and intimate friendship in antebellum New England. In P. Nardi (Ed.), *Men's friendships* (pp. 35–58). Newbury Park, CA: Sage.

Kornblum, W. (1974). *Blue collar community*. Chicago: University of Chicago Press.

Leidner, R. (1991). Serving hamburgers and selling insurance: Gender, work, and identity in interactive service jobs. *Gender & Society, 5*, 154–177.

Liebow, E. (1967). *Tally's corner: A study of Negro street-corner men*. Boston: Little, Brown.

Miller, M. (1983). *Men and friendship*. Boston: Houghton Mifflin.

O'Meara, J. D. (1989). Cross-sex friendship: Four basic challenges of an ignored relationship. *Sex Roles, 21*, 525–543.

Rakow, L. F. (1991). *Gender on the line: Women, the telephone, and community life.* Urbana, IL: University of Illinois Press.

Rawlins, W. (1992). *Friendship matters: Communication, dialectics, and the life course.* New York: Aldine de Gruyter.

Reid, H. M., & Fine, G. A. (1992). Self-disclosure in men's friendships. In P. Nardi (Ed.), *Men's friendships* (pp. 132–152). Newbury Park, CA: Sage.

Rubin, L. (1985). *Just friends: The role of friendship in our lives.* New York: Harper & Row.

Sherrod, D. (1987). The bonds of men: Problems and possibilities in close male relationships. In H. Brod (Ed.), *The making of masculinities* (pp. 213–239). Boston: Allen and Unwin.

Swain, S. (1989). Covert intimacy: Closeness in men's friendships. In B. Risman & P. Schwartz (Eds.), *Gender and intimate relationships,* (pp. 71–86). Belmont, CA: Wadsworth.

Walker, K. (1994). Men, women and friendship: what they say; what they do. *Gender & Society, 8,* 246–265.

Wellman, B. (1992). Men in networks: Private communities, domestic friendships. In P. Nardi (Ed.), *Men's friendships* (pp. 74–114). Newbury Park, CA: Sage.

West, C., & Zimmerman, D. (1987). Doing gender. *Gender & Society, 1,* 125–151.

Whyte, W. F. (1981). *Street corner society: The social structure of an Italian slum* (3rd ed.). Chicago: The University of Chicago Press.

Williams, C. L., & Heikes, E. J. (1993). The importance of researcher's gender in the in-depth interview: Evidence from two case studies of male nurses. *Gender & Society, 7,* 280–291.

Wright, P. (1982). Men's friendships, women's friendships and the alleged inferiority of the latter. *Sex Roles, 8,* 1–20.

Peter M. Nardi

The Politics of Gay Men's Friendships

Towards the end of Wendy Wasserstein's Pulitzer Prize–winning play, *The Heidi Chronicles*, a gay character, Peter Patrone, explains to Heidi why he has been so upset over all the funerals he has attended recently: "A person has so many close friends. And in our lives, our friends are our families" (Wasserstein 1990: 238). In his collection of stories, *Buddies*, Ethan Mordden (1986: 175) observes: "What unites us, all of us, surely, is brotherhood, a sense that our friendships are historic, designed to hold Stonewall together.... It is friendship that sustained us, supported out survival." These statements succinctly summarize an important dimension about gay men's friendships: Not only are friends a form of family for gay men and lesbians, but gay friendships are also a powerful political force.

Mordden's notion of "friends is survival" has a political dimension that becomes all the more salient in contemporary society where the political, legal, religious, economic, and health concerns of gay people are routinely threatened by the social order. In part, gay friendship can be seen as a political statement, since at the core of the concept of friendship is the idea of "being oneself" in a cultural context that may not approve of that self. For many people, the need to belong with others in dissent and out of the mainstream is central to the maintenance of self and identity (Rubin 1986). The friendships formed by a shared marginal identity, thus, take on powerful political dimensions as they organize around a stigmatized status to confront the dominant culture in solidarity. Jerome (1984: 698) believes that friendships have such economic and political implications,

Reprinted by permission of the author.

since friendship is best defined as "the cement which binds together people with interests to conserve."

Suttles (1970: 116) argues that

> The very basic assumption friends must make about one another is that each is going beyond a mere presentation of self in compliance with "social dictates." Inevitably, this makes friendship a somewhat deviant relationship because the surest test of personal disclosure is a violation of the rules of public propriety.

Friendship, according to Suttles (1970), has its own internal order, albeit maintained by the cultural images and situational elements that structure the definitions of friendship. In friendship, people can depart from the routine and display a portion of the self not affected by social control. That is, friendships allow people to go beyond the basic structures of their cultural institutions into an involuntary and uncontrollable exposure of self—to deviate from public propriety (Suttles 1970).

Little (1989) similarly argues that friendship is an escape from the rules and pieties of social life. It's about identity: who one is rather than one's roles and statuses. And the idealism of friendship "lies in its detachment from these [roles and statuses], its creative and spiritual transcendence, its fundamental skepticism as a platform from which to survey the givens of society and culture" (Little 1989: 145). For gay men, these descriptions illustrate the political meaning friendship can have in their lives and their society.

The political dimension of friendship is summed up best by Little (1989; 154–155):

the larger formations of social life—kinship, the law, the economy—must be different where there is, in addition to solidarity and dutiful role-performance, a willingness and capacity for friendship's surprising one-to-one relations, and this difference may be enough to transform social and political life. . . . Perhaps, finally, it is true that progress in democracy depends on a new generation that will increasingly locate itself in identity-shaping, social, yet personally liberating, friendships.

The traditional, nuclear family has been the dominant model for political relations and has structured much of the legal and social norms of our culture. People have often been judged by their family ties and history. But as the family becomes transformed into other arrangements, so do the political and social institutions of society. For example, the emerging concept of "domestic partnerships" has affected a variety of organizations, including insurance companies, city governments, private industry, and religious institutions (Task Force on Family Diversity Final Report 1988).

For many gay people, the "friends as family" model is a political statement, going beyond the practicality of developing a surrogate family in times of needed social support. It is also a way of refocusing the economic and political agenda to include nontraditional family structures composed of both romantic and nonromantic nonkin relationships.

In part, this has happened by framing the discussions in terms of gender roles. The women's movement and the emerging men's movement have highlighted the negative political implications of defining gender roles according to traditional cultural norms or limiting them to biological realities. The gay movement, in turn, has often been one source for redefining traditional gender roles and sexuality. So, for example, when gay men exhibit more disclosing and emotional interactions with other men, it demonstrates the limitations of male gender roles typically enacted among many heterosexual male friends. By calling attention to the impact of homophobia on heterosexual men's lives, gay men's friendships illustrate the potentiality for expressive intimacy among all men.

Thus, the assumptions that biology and/or socialization have inevitably constrained men from having the kinds of relationships and intimacies women often typically have can be called into question. This questioning of the dominant construction of gender roles is in itself a sociopolitical act with major implications on the legal, religious, and economic order.

White (1983:16) also sees how gay people's lives can lead to new modes of behavior in the society at large:

In the case of gays, our childlessness, our minimal responsibilities, the fact that our unions are not consecrated, even our very retreat into gay ghettos for protection and freedom: all of these objective conditions have fostered a style in which we may be exploring, even in spite of our conscious intentions, things as they will someday be for the heterosexual majority. In that world (as in the gay world already), love will be built on esteem rather than passion or convention, sex will be more playful or fantastic or artistic than marital—and friendship will be elevated into the supreme consolation for this continuing tragedy, human existence.

If, as White and others have argued, gay culture in the post-Stonewall, sexual liberation years of the 1970s was characterized by a continuous fluidity between what constituted a friend, a sexual partner, and a lover, then we need to acknowledge the AIDS decade of the 1980s as a source for restructuring of gay culture and the reorganization of sexuality and friendship. If indeed gay people (and men in particular) have focused attention on developing monogamous sexual partnerships, what then becomes the role of sexuality in the initiation and development of casual or close friendships? Clearly, gay culture is not a static phenomenon, unaffected by the larger social order. Certainly, as the moral order in the AIDS years encourages the re-establishment of more traditional relationships, the implications for the ways sexuality and friendships are organized similarly change.

Friends become more important as primary sources of social and emotional support when illness strikes; friendship becomes institutionally organized as "brunch buddies" dating services or "AIDS buddies" assistance groups; and self-help groups emerge centering on how to make and keep new friends without having "compulsive sex." While AIDS may have transformed some of the meanings and role of friendships in gay men's lives from the politicalization of sexuality and friendship during the post-Stonewall 1970s, the newer meanings of gay friendships, in turn, may be having some effect on the culture's definitions of friendships.

Interestingly, the mythical images of friendships were historically more male-dominated: bravery, loyalty, duty, and heroism (see Sapadin 1988). This explained why women were typically assumed incapable of having true friendships. But today, the images of true friendship are often expressed in terms of women's traits: intimacy, trust, caring, and nurturing, thereby excluding the more traditional men from true friendship. However, gay men appear to be at the forefront of establishing the possibility of men overcoming their male socialization stereotypes and restructuring their friendships in terms of the more contemporary (i.e., "female") attributes of emotional intimacy.

To do this at a wider cultural level involves major sociopolitical shifts in how men's roles are structured and organized. Friendships between men in terms of intimacy and emotional support inevitably introduce questions about homosexuality. As Rubin (1985: 103) found in her interviews with men: "The association of friendship with homosexuality is so common among men." For women, there is a much longer history of close connections with other women, so that the separation of the emotional from the erotic is more easily made.

Lehne (1989) has argued that homophobia has limited the discussion of loving male relationships and has led to the denial by men of the real importance of their friendships with other men. In addition, "the open expression of emotion and affection by men is limited by homophobia. . . . The expression of more tender emotions among men is thought to be characteristic only of homosexuals" (Lehne 1989: 426). So men are raised in a culture with a mixed message: strive for healthy, emotionally intimate friendships, but if you appear too intimate with another man you might be negatively labelled homosexual.

This certainly wasn't always the case. As a good illustration of the social construction of masculinity, friendship, and sexuality, one need only look to the changing definitions and concepts surrounding same-sex friendship during the nineteenth century (see Rotundo 1989; Smith-Rosenberg 1975). Romantic friendships could be erotic but not sexual, since sex was linked to reproduction. Because reproduction was not possible between two women or two men, the close relationship was not interpreted as being a sexual one:

> Until the 1880s, most romantic friendships were thought to be devoid of sexual content. Thus a woman or man could write of affectionate desire for a loved one of the same gender without causing an eyebrow to be raised (D'Emilio and Freedman 1988: 121).

However, as same-sex relationships became medicalized and stigmatized in the late 19th century, "the labels 'congenital inversion' and 'perversion' were applied not only to male sexual acts, but to sexual or romantic unions between women, as well as those between men" (D'Emilio and Freedman, 1988: 122). Thus, the twentieth century is an anomaly in its promotion of female equality, the encouragement of male–female friendships, and its suspicion of intense emotional friendships between men (Richards 1987). Yet, in ancient Greece and the medieval days of chivalry, comradeship, virtue, patriotism, and heroism were all associated with close male friendship. Manly love, as it was often called, was a central part of the definition of manliness (Richards 1987).

It is through the contemporary gay, women's, and men's movements that these twentieth century constructions of gender are being questioned. And at the core is the association of close male friendships with negative images of homosexuality. Thus, how gay men structure their emotional lives and friendships can affect the social and emotional lives of all men and women. This is the political power and potential of gay friendships.

References

D'Emilio, John and Freedman, Estelle. (1988). *Intimate Matters: A History of Sexuality in America*. New York: Harper & Row.

Jerome, Dorothy. (1984). Good company: The sociological implications of friendship. *Sociological Review*, 32(4), 696–718.

Lehne, Gregory K. (1989 [1980]). Homophobia among men: Supporting and defining the male role. In M. Kimmel and M. Messner (Eds.), *Men's Lives* (pp. 416–429). New York: Macmillan.

Little, Graham. (1989). Freud, friendship, and politics. In R. Porter and S. Tomaselli (Eds.), *The Dialectics of Friendship* (pp. 143–158). London: Routledge.

Mordden, Ethan. (1986). *Buddies*. New York: St. Martin's Press.

Richards, Jeffrey. (1987). "Passing the love of women": Manly love and Victorian society. In J. A. Mangan and J. Walvin (Eds.), *Manliness and Morality: Middle-Class Masculinity in Britain and America (1800–1940)* (pp. 92–122). Manchester, England: Manchester University Press.

Rotundo, Anthony. (1989). Romantic friendships: Male intimacy and middle-class youth in the northern United States, 1800–1900. *Journal of Social History*, 23(1), 1–25.

Rubin, Lillian. (1985). *Just Friends: The Role of Friendship in Our Lives*. New York: Harper & Row.

Sapadin, Linda. (1988). Friendship and gender: Perspectives of professional men and women. *Journal of Social and Personal Relationships*, 5(4), 387–403.

Smith-Rosenberg, Carroll. (1975). The female world of love and ritual: Relations between women in nineteenth-century America. *Signs*, 1(1): 1–29.

Suttles, Gerald. (1970). Friendship as a social institution. In G. McCall, M. McCall, N. Denzin, G. Suttles, and S. Kurth, *Social Relationships* (pp. 95–135). Chicago: Aldine.

Task Force on Family Diversity. (1988). *Strengthening Families: A Model for Community Action*. City of Los Angeles.

Wasserstein, Wendy. (1990). *The Heidi Chronicles*. San Diego: Harcourt, Brace, Jovanovich.

White, Edmund. (1983). Paradise found: Gay men have discovered that there is friendship after sex. *Mother Jones*, June, 10–16.

Tim Beneke

Men on Rape

Rape may be America's fastest growing violent crime; no one can be certain because it is not clear whether more rapes are being committed or reported. It *is* clear that violence against women is widespread and fundamentally alters the meaning of life for women; that sexual violence is encouraged in a variety of ways in American culture; and that women are often blamed for rape.

Consider some statistics:

- In a random sample of 930 women, sociologist Diana Russell found that 44 percent had survived either rape or attempted rape. Rape was defined as sexual intercourse physically forced upon the woman, or coerced by threat of bodily harm, or forced upon the woman when she was helpless (asleep, for example). The survey included rape and attempted rape in marriage in its calculations. (Personal communication)
- In a September 1980 survey conducted by *Cosmopolitan* magazine to which over 106,000 women anonymously responded, 24 percent had been raped at least once. Of these, 51 percent had been raped by friends, 37 percent by strangers, 18 percent by relatives, and 3 percent by husbands. 10 percent of the women in the survey had been victims of incest. 75 percent of the women had been "bullied into making love." Writer Linda Wolfe, who reported on the survey, wrote in reference to such bullying: "Though such harassment stops short of rape, readers reported that it was nearly as distressing."

- An estimated 2–3 percent of all men who rape outside of marriage go to prison for their crimes.[1]
- The F.B.I. estimates that if current trends continue, one woman in four will be sexually assaulted in her lifetime.[2]
- An estimated 1.8 million women are battered by their spouses each year.[3] In extensive interviews with 430 battered women, clinical psychologist Lenore Walker, author of *The Battered Woman*, found that 59.9 percent had also been raped (defined as above) by their spouses. Given the difficulties many women had in admitting they had been raped, Walker estimates the figure may well be as high as 80 or 85 percent (Personal communication). If 59.9 percent of the 1.8 million women battered each year are also raped, then a million women may be raped in marriage each year. And a significant number are raped in marriage without being battered.
- Between one in two and one in ten of all rapes are reported to the police.[4]
- Between 300,000 and 500,000 women are raped each year outside of marriage.[5]

What is often missed when people contemplate statistics on rape is the effect of the *threat* of sexual violence on women. I have asked women repeatedly, "How would your life be different if rape were suddenly to end?" (Men may learn a lot by asking this question of women to whom they are close.) The threat of rape is an assault upon the meaning of the world; it alters the feel of the human condition. Surely any attempt to comprehend the lives of women that fails to take issues of violence against women into account is misguided.

Through talking to women, I learned: *The threat of rape alters the meaning and feel of the night.* Observe how your body feels, how the night feels, when you're in fear. The constriction in your chest, the vigilance in your eyes, the rubber in your legs. What do the stars look like? How does the moon present itself? What is the difference between walking late at night in the dangerous part of a city and walking late at night in the country, or safe suburbs? When I try to imagine what the threat of rape must do to the night, I think of the stalked, adrenalated feeling I get walking late at night in parts of certain American cities. Only, I remind myself, it is a fear different from any I have known, a fear of being raped.

It is night half the time. If the threat of rape alters the meaning of the night, it must alter the meaning and pace of the day, one's relation to the passing and organization of time itself. For some women, the threat of rape at night turns their cars into armored tanks, their solitude into isolation. And what must the space inside a car or an apartment feel like if the space outside is menacing?

I was running late one night with a close woman friend through a path in the woods on the outskirts of a small university town. We had run several miles and were feeling a warm, energized serenity.

"How would you feel if you were alone?" I asked.

"Terrified!" she said instantly.

"Terrified that there might be a man out there?" I asked, pointing to the surrounding moonlit forest, which had suddenly been transformed into a source of terror.

"Yes."

Another woman said, "I know what I can't do and I've completely internalized what I can't do. I've built a viable life that basically involves never leaving my apartment at night unless I'm directly going some place to meet somebody. It's unconsciously built into what it occurs to women to do." When one is raised without freedom, one may not recognize its absence.

The threat of rape alters the meaning and feel of nature. Everyone has felt the psychic nurturance of nature. Many women are being deprived of that nurturance, especially in wooded areas near cities. They are deprived either because they cannot experience nature in solitude because of threat, or because, when they do choose solitude in nature, they must cope with a certain subtle but nettlesome fear.

Women need more money because of rape and the threat of rape makes it harder for women to earn money. It's simple: if you don't feel safe walking at night, or riding public transportation, you need a car. And it is less practicable to live in cheaper, less secure, and thus more dangerous neighborhoods if the ordinary threat of violence that men experience, being mugged, say, is compounded by the threat of rape. By limiting mobility at night, the threat of rape limits where and when one is able to work, thus making it more difficult to earn money. An obvious bind: women need more money because of rape, and have fewer job opportunities because of it.

The threat of rape makes women more dependent on men (or other women). One woman said: "If there were no rape I wouldn't have to play games with men for their protection." The threat of rape falsifies, mystifies, and confuses relations between men and women. If there were no rape, women would simply not need men as much, wouldn't need them to go places with at night, to feel safe in their homes, for protection in nature.

The threat of rape makes solitude less possible for women. Solitude, drawing strength from being alone, is difficult if being alone means being afraid. To be afraid is to be in need, to experience a lack; the threat of rape creates a lack. Solitude requires relaxation; if you're afraid, you can't relax.

The threat of rape inhibits a woman's expressiveness. "If there were no rape," said one woman, "I could dress the way I wanted and walk the way I wanted and not feel self-conscious about the responses of men. I could be friendly to people. I wouldn't have to wish I was ugly. I wouldn't have to make myself small when I got on the bus. I wouldn't have to respond to verbal abuse from men by remaining silent. I could respond in kind."

If a woman's basic expressiveness is inhibited, her sexuality, creativity, and delight in life must surely be diminished.

The threat of rape inhibits the freedom of the eye. I know a married couple who live in Manhattan. They are both artists, both acutely sensitive and responsive to the visual world. When they walk separately in the city, he has more freedom to look than she does. She must control her eye movements lest they inadvertently meet the glare of some importunate man. What, who, and how she sees are restricted by the threat of rape.

The following exercise is recommended for men.

> Walk down a city street. Pay a lot of attention to your clothing; make sure your pants are zipped, shirt tucked in, buttons done. Look straight ahead. Every time a man walks past you, avert your eyes and make your face expressionless. Most women learn to go through this act each time we leave our houses. It's a way to avoid at least some of the encounters we've all had with strange men who decided we looked available.[6]

To relate aesthetically to the visual world involves a certain playfulness, spirit of spontaneous exploration. The tense vigilance that accompanies fear inhibits that spontaneity. The world is no longer yours to look at when you're afraid.

I am aware that all culture is, in part, restriction, that there are places in America where hardly anyone is safe (though men are safer than women virtually everywhere), that there are many ways to enjoy life, that some women may not be so restricted, that there exist havens, whether psychic, geographical, economic, or class. But they are *havens*, and as such, defined by threat.

Above all, I trust my experience: no woman could have lived the life I've lived the last few years. If suddenly I were restricted by the threat of rape, I would feel a deep, inexorable depression. And it's not just rape; it's harassment, battery, Peeping Toms, anonymous phone calls, exhibitionism, intrusive stares, fondlings—all contributing to an atmosphere of intimidation in women's lives. And I have only scratched the surface; it would take many carefully crafted short stories to begin to express what I have only hinted at in the last few pages. I have not even touched upon what it might mean for a woman to be sexually assaulted. Only women can speak to that. Nor have I suggested how the threat of rape affects marriage.

Rape and the threat of rape pervade the lives of women, as reflected in some popular images of our culture.

"She Asked for It"— Blaming the Victim[7]

Many things may be happening when a man blames a woman for rape.

First, in all cases where a woman is said to have asked for it, her appearance and behavior are taken as a form of speech. "Actions speak louder than words" is a widely held belief; the woman's actions—her appearance may be taken as action—are given greater emphasis than her words; an interpretation alien to the woman's intentions is given to her actions. A logical extension of "she asked for it" is the idea that she wanted what happened to happen; if she wanted it to happen, she *deserved* for it to happen. Therefore, the man is not to be blamed. "She asked for it" can mean either that she was consenting to have sex and was not really raped, or that she was in fact raped but somehow she really deserved it. "If you ask for it, you deserve it," is a widely held notion. If I ask you to beat me up and you beat me up, I still don't deserve to be beaten up. So even if the notion that women asked to be raped had some basis in reality, which it doesn't, on its own terms it makes no sense.

Second, a mentality exists that says: a woman who assumes freedoms normally restricted to a man (like going out alone at night) and is raped is doing the same thing as a woman who goes out in the rain without an umbrella and catches a cold. Both are considered responsible for what happens to them. That men will rape is taken to be a legitimized given, part of nature, like rain or snow. The view reflects a massive abdication of responsibility for rape on the part of men. It is so much easier to think of rape as natural than to acknowledge one's part in it. So long as rape is regarded as natural, women will be blamed for rape.

A third point. The view that it is natural for men to rape is closely connected to the view of women as commodities. If a woman's body is regarded as a valued commodity by men, then of course, if you leave a valued commodity where it can be taken, it's just human nature for men to take it. If you left your stereo out on the sidewalk, you'd be asking for it to get stolen. Someone will just take it. (And how often men speak of rape as "going out and *taking* it.") If a woman walks the streets at night, she's leaving a valued commodity, her body, where it can be taken. So long as women are regarded as commodities, they will be blamed for rape.

Which brings us to a fourth point. "She asked for it" is inseparable from a more general "psychology of the dupe." If I use bad judgment and fail to read the small print in a contract and later get taken advantage of, "screwed" (or "fucked over") then I deserve what I get; bad judgment makes me liable. Analogously, if a woman trusts a man and goes to his apartment, or accepts a ride hitchhiking, or goes out on a date and is raped, she's a dupe and deserves what she gets. "He didn't *really* rape her" goes the mentality—"he merely took advantage of her." And in America it's okay for people to take advantage of each other, even expected and praised. In fact, you're considered dumb and foolish if you don't take advantage of other people's bad judgment. And so, again, by treating them as dupes, rape will be blamed on women.

Fifth, if a woman who is raped is judged attractive by men, and particularly if she dresses to look attractive, then the mentality exists that she attacked him with her weapon so, of course, he counter-attacked with his. The preview to a popular movies states: "She was the victim of her own *provocative beauty*." Provocation: "There is a line which, if crossed, will *set me off* and I will lose

control and no longer be responsible for my behavior. If you punch me in the nose then, of course, I will not be responsible for what happens: you will have provoked a fight. If you dress, talk, move, or act a certain way, you will have provoked me to rape. If your appearance *stuns* me, *strikes* me, *ravishes* me, *knocks me out*, etc., then I will not be held responsible for what happens; you will have asked for it." The notion that sexual feeling makes one helpless is part of a cultural abdication of responsibility for sexuality. So long as a woman's appearance is viewed as a weapon and sexual feeling is believed to make one helpless, women will be blamed for rape.

Sixth, I have suggested that men sometimes become obsessed with images of women, that images become a substitute for sexual feeling, that sexual feeling becomes externalized and out of control and is given an undifferentiated identity in the appearance of women's bodies. It is a process of projection in which one blurs one's own desire with her imagined, projected desire. If a woman's attractiveness is taken to signify one's own lust and a woman's lust, then when an "attractive" woman is raped, some men may think she wanted sex. Since they perceive their own lust in part projected onto the woman, they disbelieve women who've been raped. So long as men project their own sexual desires onto women, they will blame women for rape.

And seventh, what are we to make of the contention that women in dating situations say "no" initially to sexual overtures from men as a kind of pose, only to give in later, thus revealing their true intentions? And that men are thus confused and incredulous when women are raped because in their sexual experience women can't be believed? I doubt that this has much to do with men's perceptions of rape. I don't know to what extent women actually "say no and mean yes"; certainly it is a common theme in male folklore. I have spoken to a couple of women who went through periods when they wanted to be sexual but were afraid to be, and often rebuffed initial sexual advances only to give in later. One point is clear: the ambivalence women may feel about having sex is closely tied to the inability of men to fully accept them as sexual beings. Women have been traditionally punished for being openly and freely sexual; men are praised for it. And if many men think of sex as achievement of possession of a valued commodity, or aggressive degradation, then women have every reason to feel and act ambivalent.

These themes are illustrated in an interview I conducted with a 23-year-old man who grew up in Pittsburgh and works as a file clerk in the financial district of San Francisco. Here's what he said:

"Where I work it's probably no different from any other major city in the U.S. The women dress up in high heels, and they wear a lot of makeup, and they just look really *hot* and really sexy, and how can somebody who has a healthy sex drive not feel lust for them when you see them? I feel lust for them, but I don't think I could find it in me to overpower someone and rape them. But I definitely get the feeling that I'd like to rape a girl. I don't know if the actual act of rape would be satisfying, but the *feeling* is satisfying.

"These women look so good, and they kiss ass of the men in the three-piece suits who are *big* in the corporation, and most of them relate to me like 'Who are *you*? Who are *you* to even *look* at?' They're snobby and they condescend to me, and I resent it. It would take me a lot longer to get to first base than it would somebody with a three-piece suit who had money. And to me a lot of the men they go out with are superficial assholes who have no real feelings or substance, and are just trying to get ahead and make a lot of money. Another thing that makes me resent these women is thinking, 'How could she want to hang out with somebody like that? What does that make her?'

"I'm a file clerk, which makes me feel like a nebbish, a nurd, like I'm not making it, I'm a failure. But I don't really believe I'm a failure because I know it's just a phase, and I'm just doing it for the money, just to make it through this phase. I catch myself feeling like a failure, but I realize that's ridiculous."

What Exactly Do You Go Through When You See These Sexy, Unavailable Women?

"Let's say I see a woman and she looks really pretty and really clean and sexy, and she's giving off very feminine, sexy vibes. I think, 'Wow, I would love to make love to her,' but I know she's not really interested. It's a tease. A lot of times a woman knows that she's looking really good and she'll use that and flaunt it, and it makes me feel like she's laughing at me and I feel *degraded*.

"I also feel dehumanized, because when I'm being teased I just turn off, I cease to be human. Because if I go with my human emotions I'm going to want to put my arms around her and kiss her, and to do that would be unacceptable. I don't like the feeling that I'm supposed to stand there and take it, and not be able to hug her or kiss her; so I just turn off my emotions. It's a feeling of humiliation, because the woman has forced me to turn off my feelings and react in a way that I really don't want to.

"If I were actually desperate enough to rape somebody, it would be from wanting the person, but it would be a very spiteful thing, just being able to say, 'I have power over you and I can do anything I want with you,' because really I feel that *they* have power over *me* just by their presence. Just the fact that they can come up to me and just melt me and make me feel like a dummy makes me want revenge. They have power over me so I want power over them. . . .

"Society says that you have to have a lot of sex with a lot of different women to be a real man. Well, what happens if you don't? Then what are you? Are you half a man? Are you still a boy? It's ridiculous. You see a whiskey ad with a guy and two women on his arm. The implication is that real men don't have any trouble getting women."

How Does It Make You Feel Toward Women to See All These Sexy Women in Media and Advertising Using Their Looks to Try to Get You to Buy Something?

"It makes me hate them. As a man you're taught that men are more powerful than women, and that men always have the upper hand, and that it's a man's society; but then you see all these women and it makes you think, 'Jesus Christ, if we have all the power how come all the beautiful women are telling us what to buy?' And to be honest, it just makes me hate beautiful women because they're using their power over me. I realize they're being used themselves, and they're doing it for money. In *Playboy* you see all these beautiful women who look so sexy and they'll be giving you all these looks like they want to have sex so bad; but then in reality you know that except for a few nymphomaniacs, they're doing it for the money; so I hate them for being used and for using their bodies in that way.

"In this society, if you ever sit down and realize how manipulated you really are it makes you pissed off—it makes you want to take control. And you've been manipulated by women, and they're a very easy target because they're out walking along the streets, so you can just grab one and say, 'Listen, you're going to do what I want you to do,' and it's an act of revenge against the way you've been manipulated.

"I know a girl who was walking down the street by her house, when this guy jumped her and beat her up and raped her, and she was black and blue and had to go to the hospital. That's beyond me. I can't understand how somebody could do that. If I were going to rape a girl, I wouldn't hurt her. I might *restrain* her, but I wouldn't *hurt* her. . . .

"The whole dating game between men and women also makes me feel degraded. I hate being put in the position of having to initiate a relationship. I've been taught that if you're not aggressive with a woman, then you've blown it. She's not going to jump on *you*, so *you've* got to jump on *her*. I've heard all kinds of stories where the woman says, 'No! No! No!' and they end up making great love. I get confused as hell if a woman pushes me away. Does it mean she's trying to be a nice girl and wants to put up a good appearance, or does it mean she doesn't want anything to do with you? You don't know. Probably a lot of men think that women don't feel like real women unless a man tries to force himself on her, unless she brings out the 'real man,' so to speak, and probably too much of it goes on. It goes on in my head that you're complimenting a woman by actually staring at her or by trying to get into her pants. Lately, I'm realizing that when I stare at women lustfully, they often feel more threatened than flattered."

Notes

1. Such estimates recur in the rape literature. See *Sexual Assault* by Nancy Gager and Cathleen Schurr, Grosset & Dunlap, 1976, or *The Price of Coercive Sexuality* by Clark and Lewis, The Women's Press, 1977.

2. *Uniform Crime Reports*, 1980.

3. See *Behind Closed Doors* by Murray J. Strauss and Richard Gelles, Doubleday, 1979.

4. See Gager and Schurr (above) or virtually any book on the subject.

5. Again, see Gager and Schurr, or Carol V. Horos, *Rape*, Banbury Books, 1981.

6. From "Willamette Bridge" in *Body Politics* by Nancy Henley, Prentice-Hall, 1977, p. 144.

7. I would like to thank George Lakoff for this insight.

Jason Schultz

Getting Off on Feminism

When it comes to smashing a paradigm, pleasure is not the most important thing. It is the only *thing.*

—Gary Wolf, *Wired* Magazine

Minutes after my best friend told me he was getting married, I casually offered to throw a bachelor party in his honor. Even though such parties are notorious for their degradation of women, I didn't think this part would be much of a problem. Both the bride and groom considered themselves feminists, and I figured that most of the men attending would agree that sexism had no place in the celebration of this union. In fact, I thought the bachelor party would be a great opportunity to get a group of men together for a social event that didn't degenerate into the typical anti-women, homophobic male-bonding thing. Still, ending one of the most sexist traditions in history—even for one night—was a lot tougher than I envisioned.

I have to admit that I'm not a *complete* iconoclast: I wanted to make the party a success by including at least some of the usual elements, such as good food and drink, great music, and cool things to do. At the same time, I was determined not to fall prey to traditional sexist party gimmicks such as prostitutes, strippers jumping out of cakes, or straight porn. But after nixing all the traditional lore, even *I* thought it sounded boring. What were we going to do except sit around and think about women?

"What about a belly dancer?" one of the ushers suggested when I confided my concerns to him. "That's not as bad as a stripper." I sighed. This was supposed to be an occasion for the groom and his male friends to get together, celebrate the upcoming marriage, and affirm their friendship and connection with each other as men. "What the fuck does hiring a female sex worker have to do with any of that?" I shouted into the phone. I quickly regained my calm, but his suggestion still stung. We had to find some other way.

I wanted my party to be as "sexy" as the rest of them, but I had no idea how to do that in the absence of female sex workers. There was no powerful alternative image in our culture from which I could draw. I thought about renting some gay porn, or making it a cross-dressing party, but many of the guests were conservative, and I didn't want to scare anyone off. Besides, what would it say about a bunch of straight men if all we could do to be sexy was act queer for a night?

Over coffee on a Sunday morning, I asked some of the other guys what they thought was so "sexy" about having a stripper at a bachelor party.

"Well," David said, "it's just a gag. It's something kinda funny and sexy at the same time."

"Yeah," A.J. agreed. "It's not all that serious, but it's something special to do that makes the party cool."

"But *why* is it sexy and funny?" I asked. "Why can't we, as a bunch of guys, be sexy and funny ourselves?"

" 'Cause it's easier to be a guy with other guys when there's a chick around. It gives you all something in common to relate to."

"Hmm. I think I know what you mean," I said. "When I see a stripper, I get turned on, but not in the same way I would if I was with a lover. It's more like going to a show or watching a flick together. It's enjoyable, stimulating, but it's not overwhelming or intimate in the same way that sex is. Having the stripper provides a common emotional context for us to feel turned on. But we don't have to do anything about it like we would if we were with a girlfriend, right?"

"Well, my girlfriend would kill me if she saw me checking out this stripper," Greg replied. "But because it's kind of a male-bonding thing, it's not as threatening to our relationship. It's not because it's the stripper over her, it's because it's just us guys hanging out. It doesn't go past that."

Others agreed. "Yeah. You get turned on, but not in a serious way. It makes you feel sexy and sexual, and you can enjoy feeling that way with your friends. Otherwise, a lot of times, just hanging out with the guys is pretty boring. Especially at a bachelor party. I mean, that's the whole point, isn't it—to celebrate the fact that we're bachelors, and he"—referring to Robert, the groom—"isn't!"

Through these conversations, I realized that having a female sex worker at the party would give the men permission to connect with one another without becoming vulnerable. When men discuss sex in terms of actions—who they "did," and how and where they did it—they can gain recognition and validation of their sexuality from other men without having to expose their *feelings* about sex.

"What other kinds of things make you feel sexy like the stripper does?" I asked several of the guys.

"Watching porn sometimes, or a sexy movie."

A.J. said, "Just getting a look from a girl at a club. I mean, she doesn't even have to talk to you, but you still feel sexy and you can still hang out with your friends."

Greg added, "Sometimes just knowing that my girlfriend thinks I'm sexy, and then talking about her with friends, makes me feel like I'm the man. Or I'll hear some other guy talk about his girlfriend in a way that reminds me of mine, and I'll still get that same feeling. But that doesn't happen very often, and usually only when talking with one other guy.

This gave me an idea. "I've noticed that same thing, both here and at school with my other close guy friends. Why doesn't it happen with a bunch of guys, say at a party?"

"I don't know. It's hard to share a lot of personal stuff with guys," said Adam, "especially about someone you're seeing, if you don't feel comfortable. Well, not comfortable, because I know most of the guys who'll be at the party, but it's more like I don't want them to hassle me, or I might say something that freaks them out."

"Or you're just used to guys talking shit about girls," someone else added. "Like at a party or hanging out together. They rag on them, or pick out who's the cutest or who wants to do who. That's not the same thing as really talking about what makes you feel sexy."

"Hmm," I said. "So it's kind of like if I were to say that I liked to be tied down to the bed, no one would take me seriously. You guys would probably crack up laughing, make a joke or two, but I'd never expect you to actually join in and talk about being tied up in a serious way. It certainly wouldn't feel 'sexy,' would it? At least not as much as the stripper."

"Exactly. You talking about being tied down here is fine, 'cause we're into the subject of sex on a serious kick and all. But at a party, people are bullshitting each other and gabbing, and horsing around. The last thing most of us want is to trip over someone's personal taste or start thinking someone's a little queer."

"You mean queer as in homosexual?" I asked.

"Well, not really, 'cause I think everyone here is straight. But more of queer in the sense of perverted or different. I mean, you grow up in high school thinking that all guys are basically the same. You all want the same thing from girls in the same way. And when someone like you says you like to be tied down, it's kinda weird—almost like a challenge. It makes me have to respond in a way that either shows me agreeing that I also like to be tied down or not. And if someone's a typical guy and he says that, it makes you think he's different—not the same guy you knew in high school. And if he's not the same guy, then it challenges you to relate to him on a different level."

"Yeah, I guess in some ways it's like relating to someone who's gay," Greg said. "He can be cool and all, and you can get along totally great. But there's this barrier that's hard to cross over. It kinda keeps you apart. And that's not what you want to feel toward your friends, especially at a party like this one, where you're all coming together to chill."

As the bachelor party approached, I found myself wondering whether my friends and I could "come together to chill"—and affirm our status as sexual straight men—without buying into homophobic or sexist expressions. At the same time, I was doing a lot of soul-searching on how we could challenge the dominant culture's vision of male heterosexuality, not only by deciding against having a stripper at our party, but also by examining and redefining our own relationships with women.

Sex and the Sensitive Man

According to the prevailing cultural view, "desirable" hetero men are inherently dominant, aggressive, and, in many subtle and overt ways, abusive to women. To be sexy and powerful, straight men are expected to control and contrive a sexuality that reinforces their authority. Opposing these notions of power subjects a straight guy to being branded "sensitive," submissive, or passive—banished to the nether regions of excitement and pleasure, the unmasculine, asexual, "vanilla" purgatory of antieroticism. Just as hetero women are often forced to choose between the images of the virgin and the whore, modern straight men are caught in a cultural tug-of-war between the Marlboro Man and the Wimp.

So where does that leave straight men who want to reexamine what a man is and change it? Can a good man be sexy? Can a sexy man be good? What is good sex, egalitarian sex? More fundamentally, can feminist women and men coexist comfortably, even happily, within the same theoretical framework—or the same bedroom?

Relationships with men remain one of the most controversial topics among feminists today. Having sex, negotiating emotional dependency, and/or raising children force many hetero couples to balance their desire to be together with the oppressive dynamics of sexism. In few other movements are the oppressor group and the oppressed group so intimately linked.

But what about men who support feminism? Shouldn't it be okay for straight feminist women to have sex with them? Straight men aren't always oppressive in their sexuality, are they?

You may laugh at these questions, but they hold serious implications for straight feminist sex. I've seen many relationships between opposite-sex activists self-destruct because critical assumptions about power dynamics and desires were made in the mind, but not in the bed. I've even been told that straight male feminists can't get laid without A) feeling guilty; B) reinforcing patriarchy; or C) maintaining complete passivity during sexual activity. Each of these three options represents common assumptions about the sexuality of straight men who support feminism. Choice A, "feeling guilty," reflects the belief that straight male desire inherently contradicts the goals of feminism and fails to contribute to the empowerment of women. It holds that any man who enjoys sex with a woman must be benefiting from sexist male privilege, not fighting against it. In other words, hetero sex becomes a zero-sum game where if men gain, feminism loses.

Choice B represents the assumption that hetero male sex is inherently patriarchal. Beyond merely being of no help, as in Choice A, straight male sexuality is seen as part of the problem. Within this theory, one often hears statements such as "all heterosexual sex is rape." Even though these statements are usually taken out of context, the ideas behind them are problematic. In essence, they say that you can never have a male/female interaction that isn't caught up in oppressive dynamics. Men and women can never be together, especially in such a vulnerable exchange as sexuality, without being subject to the misdistribution of power in society.

The third choice, "maintaining complete passivity," attempts a logical answer to the above predicament. In order to come even close to achieving equality in heterosexuality (and still get laid), men must "give up" all their power through inactivity. A truly feminist man should take no aggressive or dominant position. He should, in fact, not act at all; he should merely lie back and allow the woman to subvert male supremacy through her complete control of the situation. In other words, for a man and a woman to share sexuality on a "level playing field," the man must remove all symptoms of his power through passivity, even though the causes of that inequality (including his penis!) still exist.

I know of one feminist man whose girlfriend *insisted* that she always be on top when they had intercourse. Her reasoning was simple: a man in a dominant sexual position represents sexist oppression incarnate. Therefore, the only possible way to achieve female empowerment was to subvert this power through her dominance. She even went so far as to stop intercourse before he reached orgasm, as a protest against male sexual entitlement.

The above story represents the *assumption* that sexism functions within male sexuality in a uniform, unvarying way, and that straight women must adapt and strategize within their personal relationships accordingly.

Does it have to be this way? Must male heterosexuality always pose a threat to feminism?

What about the sensitive guy? Wasn't that the male cry (whimper) of the nineties? Sorry, but all the media hype about sensitivity never added up to significant changes in behavior. Straight male sexuality still remains one of the most underchallenged areas of masculinity in America. Some men *did* propose a different kind of sexuality for straight men in the 1970s, one that emphasizes feelings and sensitivity and emotional connection. But these efforts failed to affect our ideas in any kind of revolutionary way. Now, instead of a "sexy" sensitive guy, men's magazines are calling for the emergence of the "Post-Sensitive Man," while scientific studies tell us that women prefer Clint Eastwood over Michael Bolton.

Why did sensitivity fail? Were straight women, even feminists, lying to men about what they wanted? The answer is "yes" and "no." I don't think sensitivity was the culprit. I think the problem was men's passivity, or more specifically, men's lack of assertiveness and power.

In much of our understanding, power is equated with oppression: images of white supremacists dominating people of color, men dominating women, and the rich dominating the poor underline the histories of many cultures and societies. But power need not always oppress others. One can, I believe, be powerful in a nonoppressive way.

In order to find this sort of alternative, we need to examine men's experience with power and sexuality further. Fortunately, queer men and women have given us a leg up on the process by reenergizing the debate about what is good sex and what is fair sex. Gay male culture has a long history of exploring nontraditional aspects of male sexuality, such as cross-dressing, bondage and dominance, and role playing. These dynamics force gay men to break out of a singular experience of male sexual desire and to examine the diversity within male sexuality in the absence of gender oppression. Though gay men's culture still struggles with issues such as the fetishizing of men of color and body fascism, it does invite greater exploration of diversity than straight male culture. Gay culture has broader and more inclusive attitudes about what is sexy and a conception of desire that accommodates many types of sex for many types of gay men. For straight men in our culture, there is such a rigid definition of "sexy" that it leaves us few options besides being oppressive, overbearing, or violent.

Part of the success that gay male culture enjoys in breaking out of monolithic notions of male sexuality lies in the acceptance it receives from its partners and peers. Camp, butch, leather, drag-queer culture is constantly affirming the powerful presence of alternative sexualities. Straight male culture, on the other hand, experiences a lack—a void of acceptance—whenever it tries to assert some image other than the sexist hetero male. Both publicly and in many cases privately, alternative straight male sexualities fail to compete for attention and acceptance among hetero men and women.

Hot, Heavy, and Heterosexual

Without role models and cultural messages to affirm them, new forms of desire fail to stick around in our heads and our hearts. Therefore, straight men and women need to get hot and heavy for an alternative male heterosexuality. Often, women who desire nontraditional types of straight men fail to assert their desires publicly. If and when they find these men, they do so through friendships, long-term relationships, or by accident. They rarely seek them out in bars, one-night stands, or house parties. Sexual desire that results from a friendship or long-term relationship can be wonderful, but it fails to hold the popular "sexy" status that active dating, flirtation, or seduction does. If we truly hope to change straight male sexuality, we must move beyond private one-on-one affirmations and change public and cultural ones.

Unfortunately, it's easier said than done. Whenever I've tried to assert a nonoppressive sexuality with women, I've sunk into a cultural quagmire. I get caught riding that fine line between being a Sensitive New Age Guy and an ass-

hole. Many straight women (both feminist and not) still find an aggressive, dominant man sexy. Many straight women still desire a man to take charge when it comes to romance or intimacy, especially when initiating intercourse. Yet many of the same straight feminist women constantly highlight the abuse and discrimination that many of these men inflict. They often complain about a man who is misogynist while affirming his desirability. This dichotomy of desire is confusing and frustrating.

Admittedly, much of my frustration relates to my own experience. I've always found fierce, independent women attractive—women who say they want a man to support them emotionally, listen to them, and not fight them every step of the way. Yet in reality, these women often lost respect for me and for other men who tried to change our sexuality to meet these needs.

I'd try to play the game, moving in as the aggressive man and then showing a more sensitive side after I'd caught the person's attention. But more often than not, the result was frustrating. I didn't catch a clue until one night when I had an enlightening conversation with one of these women who called herself a feminist. I asked her why guys who tried to accommodate the political desires of straight feminists always seemed to lose out in the end. She said she thought it was because a lot of young straight women who confront gender issues through feminism are constantly trying to redefine themselves in relation to culture and other people in their lives. Therefore, if they pursue relationships with men, many consciously seek out a *traditional* man—not only because it is the kind of man they have been taught to desire, but because he is familiar to them. He is strong, stable, predictable, and powerful. As the woman's identity shifts and changes, she can use the man she is dating as a reference point and source of strength and stability.

If she chooses to become involved with a feminist man who feels the same need to examine assumptions about gender (including his own masculinity) on a political and personal level, both partners are in a state of flux and instability. Both are searching for an understanding of their relationship, but each questions how that relationship is defined, even down to assumptions about men, women, sex, and commitment. Within this shifting matrix, straight feminist men who explore alternative ways of being sexual are often perceived as passive, weak, and in many cases, undesirable. In the end, it seems much easier to choose the traditional male.

Out of the Breeding Box

We need to assert a new feminist sexuality for men, one that competes with the traditional paradigm but offers a more inviting notion of how hetero men can be sexual while tearing apart the oppressive and problematic ways in which so many of us have experienced sexuality in the past. We need to find new, strong values and ideas of male heterosexuality instead of passive identities that try to distance us from sexist men. We need to stop trying to avoid powerful straight sexuality and work to redefine what our power means and does. We need to find strength and desire outside of macho, antiwomen ways of being masculine.

Take the notion of "breeding." Many cultures still assume that the male desire to breed and procreate is the primary purpose of sexuality. This idea, based on outdated notions of Darwinism and evolutionary prophecy, forces us to think of heterosexual men as having a single sexual purpose—ejaculating inside a fertile woman. Be hard, be strong, and cum into any woman's vagina you can find. It's all about sowing seed and proving heterosexuality through the conquest of women. Through this mechanism, reproductive sex is seen as "natural" and most desirable; all other forms of sexual interaction are seen as warm-ups or "foreplay." Breeding prioritizes heterosexuality, and within straight sex, limits its goal to the act of vaginal intercourse.

Yet in a pro–birth control, increasingly queer-friendly world, breeding has become a minuscule aspect of sexuality. Few heterosexual men and women have sex strictly to breed, and gay men and women almost never do. Within this new context, notions of what is "sexy" and what straight men desire have much more to do with how we fuck or how we feel than with what we produce.

Even among young people who have no intention of creating children, breeder assumptions continue to define male heterosexuality. For instance, many of my friends, especially queer ones, will harass me after I've been dating a woman for a while and give me flack for being a "breeder." They assume that the reason I'm with her—the goal of my relationship—is to make sure I cum inside her. Even if I don't want a child, even if I hate intercourse, the assumption about my male heterosexuality is that I will at least act like I'm trying to procreate when I'm having sex. Any possibility of a hetero nonbreeder sexuality doesn't exist. I'm forced into the breeding box, no questions permitted.

I've tried to confront these assumptions actively, but it's difficult. Usually I respond with something crass, such as, "Funny, I don't feel like breeding, just fucking." Or by talking about how *I* prefer to be penetrated sometimes. This may seem extreme, but that's how challenging it feels to try to present a different idea of straight male sexuality—one that isn't predicated on notions of being vanilla or being a breeder.

My critique of breeding is not an attempt to discredit fatherhood. Parenting is as much a part of the revolution as any other personal act. My point is that if we want hetero men to change, we have to give them viable choices. There has to be a difference between acting straight and acting like a breeder. And breeding is just *one* of the many assumptions that our culture applies to male heterosexuality.

It's up to straight men to change these assumptions. Gay men and lesbians have engaged in a cultural dialogue around sexuality over the last twenty-five years; straight women are becoming more and more vocal. But straight men have been almost completely silent. This silence, I think, stems in large part from fear: our cultures tell us that being a "real" man means not being feminine, not being gay, and not being weak. They warn us that anyone who dares to stand up to these ideas becomes a sitting target to have his manhood shot down in flames.

Breaking the Silence

Not becoming a sitting target to have *my* manhood shot down was high on my mind when the evening of my best friend's bachelor party finally arrived. But I was determined not to be silent about how I felt about the party and about new visions for straight men within our society.

We decided to throw the party two nights before the wedding. We all gathered at my house, each of us bringing a present to add to the night's activities. After all the men had arrived, we began cooking dinner, breaking open beer and champagne, and catching up on where we had left off since we last saw each other.

During the evening, we continued to talk off and on about why we didn't have a stripper or prostitute for the party. After several rounds of margaritas and a few hands of poker, tension started to build around the direction I was pushing the conversation.

"So what don't you like about strippers?" David asked me.

This was an interesting question. I was surprised not only by the guts of David to ask it, but also by my own mixed feelings in coming up with an answer. "It's not that I don't like being excited, or turned on, per se," I responded. "In fact, to be honest, watching a female stripper is an exciting and erotic experience for me. But at the same time, it's a very uncomfortable one. I get a sense when I watch her that I'm participating in a misuse of pleasure, if that makes sense."

I looked around at my friends. I couldn't tell whether the confused looks on their faces were due to the alcohol, the poker game, or my answer, so I continued. "Ideally, I would love to sit back and enjoy watching someone express herself sexually through dance, seduction, flirtation—all

the positive elements I associate with stripping," I said. "But at the same time, because so many strippers are poor and forced to perform in order to survive economically, I feel like the turn-on I get is false. I feel like I get off easy, sitting back as the man, paying for the show. No one ever expects me to get up on stage.

"And in that way, it's selling myself short sexually. It's not only saying very little about the sexual worth of the woman on stage, but the sexual worth of me as the viewer as well. By *only* being viewer—just getting off as a member of the audience—the striptease becomes a very limiting thing, an imbalanced dynamic. If the purpose is for me to feel sexy and excited, but not to act on those feelings, I'd rather find a more honest and direct way to do it. So personally, while I would enjoy watching a stripper on one level, the real issues of economics, the treatment of women, and the limitation of my own sexual personae push me to reject the whole stripper thing in favor of something else."

"But what else do you do to feel sexy?" A.J. asked.

"That's a tough question," I said. "Feeling sexy often depends on the way other people act toward you. For me, right now, you guys are a huge way for me to feel sexy. [Some of the men cringe.] I'm not saying that we have to challenge our sexual identities, although that's one way. But we can cut through a lot of this locker-room macho crap and start talking with each other about how we feel sexually, what we think, what we like, etc. Watching the stripper makes us feel sexy because we get turned on through the dynamic between her performance and our voyeurism. We can find that same erotic connection with each other by re-creating that context between us. In such a case, we're still heterosexual—we're no more having sex with each other than we are with the stripper. But we're not relying on the imbalanced dynamic of sex work to feel pleasure as straight men."

I took a deep breath. All right, I thought. Here we go. "What makes me feel sexy? I'll tell you. I feel sexy when I say how much I love licking chocolate off a partner's back. Not just that I like to do it, or talking about how often I do it, but that it feels amazing to taste her sweat and her skin mixed in with the sweetness of the chocolate. I feel sexy when I think about running my fingers through her hair in the shower, or watching her put a condom on me with her tongue. I feel sexy remembering how my muscles stretch and strain after being tied down to the bed, or the difference between leather, lace, and silk rubbing up and down my body. That's some of what makes me feel sexy."

The guys were silent for a few seconds, but soon afterwards, the ice seemed to break. While most of the guys weren't completely satisfied with or prepared for my answer, they seemed to feel that it was a step in the right direction. They agreed that, as heterosexual men, we should be able to share with each other what we find exciting and shouldn't *need* a female stripper to feel sexy. In some ways it may have been the desire to define their own sexuality that changed their minds; in others it may have been a traditionally masculine desire to reject any dependency on women. In any case, other men began to speak of their own experiences with pleasure and desire, and we continued to talk throughout the night, exploring the joys of hot sex, one-night stands, and even our preferences for certain brands of condoms. We discussed the ups and downs of monogamy versus "open" dating and the pains of long-distance relationships.

Some men continued to talk openly about their desire for straight pornography or women who fit the traditional stereotype of femininity. But others contradicted this, expressing their wish to move beyond that image of women in their lives. The wedding, which started out as the circumstance for our gathering, soon fell into the background of our thoughts as we focused away from institutional ideas of breeder sexuality and began to find common ground through our real-life experiences and feelings as straight men. In the end, we all toasted the groom, sharing stories,

jokes, and parts of our lives that many of us had never told. Most importantly, we were able to express ourselves sexually without hiding who we were from each other.

Thinking back on the party, I realized that the hard part was figuring out what we all wanted and how to construct a different way of finding that experience. The other men there wanted it just as much as I did. The problem was that we had no ideas of what a different kind of bachelor party might look like. Merely eliminating the old ways of relating (i.e., the female sex workers) left a gap, an empty space which in many ways *felt* worse than the sexist connection that existed there before; we felt passive and powerless. Yet we found a new way of interacting—one that embraced new ideas and shared the risk of experiencing them.

Was the party sexy? Did we challenge the dominance of oppressive male sexuality? Not completely, but it was a start. I doubt anyone found my party as "sexy" as traditional ones might be, but the dialogue has to start somewhere. It's going to take a while to generate the language and collective tension to balance the cultural image of heterosexual male sexuality with true sexual diversity. Still, one of my friends from high school—who's generally on the conservative end of most issues—told me as he was leaving that of all the bachelor parties he had been to, this was by far the best one. "I had a great time," he said. "Even without the stripper."

Public Pleasure and the Pursuit of Political Change

We need to affirm one another, support one another, help, enable, equip, and empower one another to deal with the present crisis, but it can't be uncritical, because if it's uncritical, then we are again refusing to acknowledge other people's humanity. If we are serious about acknowledging other people's humanity, then we are committed to trusting and believing that they are forever in the process. Growth, development, maturation happens in stages. People grow, develop, and mature along the lines in which they are taught. Disenabling critique and contemptuous feedback hinders.

—Cornel West

The bachelor party was but a small example of the dialogue straight men need to—and can—create. Some of the most amazing conversations I have had have been with other straight and bisexual men about the *pleasure* of sex with women. These conversations have been far from passive, boring, or placid. They have ranged from the many uses of cock rings to issues of consent with S/M and B&D acts to methods of achieving multiple male orgasms. The difference between these conversations and typical sexist male dialogue is that our discourse strives to bypass the mythological nature of straight male bravado and pornographic fantasy and to emphasize straight men asserting themselves as strong voices for equality *and* pleasure in cultural discourses on sexuality.

These public dialogues have been immensely helpful in dispelling overemphasized issues like impotence and premature ejaculation; such conversations have also allowed us to move past the degrading and pornographic lingo used in high school locker rooms to describe sex with women and have pushed us to focus our energy on honest questions, feelings, and *desires*. These are the kinds of voices straight men must claim publicly.

When it comes to sex, feminist straight men must become participants in the discourse about our own sexuality. We have to fight the oppressive images of men as biological breeders and leering animals. We must find ways in which to understand our diverse backgrounds, articulate desires that are not oppressive, and acknowledge the power we hold. We must take center stage when it comes to articulating our views in a powerful voice. I'm not trying to prescribe any particular form of sexuality or specify what straight men should want. But until we begin to generate our own demands and desires in an honest and equitable way for feminist straight women to hear, I don't think we can expect to be both good *and* sexy any time soon.

PART SEVEN

Male Sexualities

How do many men learn to desire women? What are men thinking about when they are sexual with women? Are gay men more sexually promiscuous than straight men? Are gay men more obsessed with demonstrating their masculinity than straight men, or are they likely to be more "effeminate"? Recent research indicates that there are no simple answers to these questions. It is increasingly clear, however, that men's sexuality, whether homosexual, bisexual, or heterosexual, is perceived as an experience of their gender.

Since there is no anticipatory socialization for homosexuality and bisexuality, future straight and gay men receive the same socialization as boys. As a result, sexuality as a gender enactment is often a similar internal experience for all men. Early socialization teaches us—through masturbation, locker-room conversations, sex-ed classes and conversations with parents, and the tidbits that boys will pick up from various media—that sex is private, pleasurable, guilt provoking, exciting, and phallocentric, and that orgasm is the goal toward which sexual experience is oriented.

The articles in this section explore how male sexualities express the issues of masculinity. Michael Messner describes how he "became" 100 percent straight, and M. Rochlin's questionnaire humorously challenges us to question the normative elements of heterosexuality. Stevi Jackson investigates the sexual scandals that rocked the Clinton presidency and led to his impeachment. Robert Staples, Tomas Almaguer, and Susan Cochran and Vickie Mays examine elements of black male and gay male sexuality, exploring the intersection among sexuality, race and ethnicity, and gender.

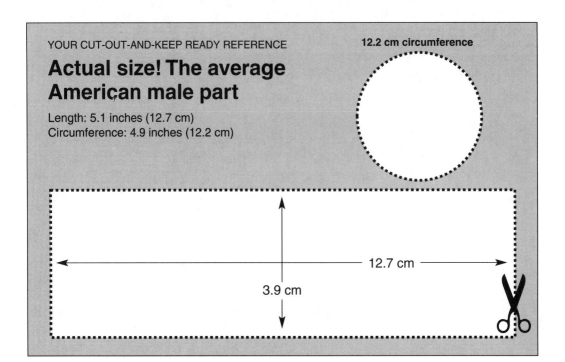

YOUR CUT-OUT-AND-KEEP READY REFERENCE

12.2 cm circumference

Actual size! The average American male part

Length: 5.1 inches (12.7 cm)
Circumference: 4.9 inches (12.2 cm)

12.7 cm

3.9 cm

A R T I C L E   3 7

Michael A. Messner

Becoming 100 Percent Straight

In 1995, as part of my job as the President of the North American Society for the Sociology of Sport, I needed to prepare an hour-long presidential address for the annual meeting of some 200 people. This presented a challenge to me: how might I say something to my colleagues that was interesting, at least somewhat original, and above all, not boring. Students may think that their professors are especially dull in the classroom but, believe me, we are usually much worse at professional meetings. For some reason, many of us who are able to speak to our classroom students in a relaxed manner, using relatively jargon-free language, seem to become robots, dryly reading our papers—packed with impressively unclear jargon—to our yawning colleagues.

Since I desperately wanted to avoid putting 200 sport studies scholars to sleep, I decided to deliver a talk which I entitled "Studying up on sex." The title, which certainly did get my colleagues' attention, was intended as a play on words, a double entendre. "Studying up" has one generally recognizable colloquial meaning, but in sociology it has another. It refers to studying "up" in the power structure. Sociologists have perhaps most often studied "down"—studying the poor, the blue- or pink-collar workers, the "nuts, sluts and perverts," the incarcerated. The idea of "studying up" rarely occurs to sociologists unless and until we live in a time when those who are "down" have organized movements that challenge the institutional privileges of elites. For example, in the wake of labor movements, some sociologists

like C. Wright Mills studied up on corporate elites. Recently, in the wake of racial and ethnic civil rights movements, some scholars like Ruth Frankenberg have begun to study the social meanings of "whiteness." Much of my research, inspired by feminism, has involved a studying up on the social construction of masculinity in sport. Studying up, in these cases, has raised some fascinating new and important questions about the workings of power in society.

However, I realized that when it comes to understanding the social and interpersonal dynamics of sexual orientation in sport we have barely begun to scratch the surface of a very complex issue. Although sport studies have benefited from the work of scholars such as Helen Lenskyj (1986, 1997), Brian Pronger (1990) and others who have delineated the experiences of lesbians and gay men in sports, there has been very little extension of their insights into a consideration of the social construction of heterosexuality in sport. In sport, just as in the larger society, we seem obsessed with asking "how do people become gay?" Imbedded in this question is the assumption that people who identify as heterosexual, or "straight," require no explanation, since they are simply acting out the "natural" or "normal" sexual orientation. We seem to be saying that the "sexual deviants" require explanation, while the experience of heterosexuals, because we are considered normal, seems to require no critical examination or discussion. But I knew that a closer look at the development of sexual orientation or sexual identity reveals an extremely complex process. I decided to challenge myself and my colleagues by arguing that although we have begun to "study up" on corporate elites in sport, on whiteness, on masculinity, it is now time to extend that by studying up on heterosexuality.

But in the absence of systematic research on this topic, where could I start? How could I explore, raise questions about, and begin to illuminate the social construction of heterosexuality for my colleagues? Fortunately, for the previous two years I had been working with a group of five men (three of whom identified as heterosexual, two as gay) mutually to explore our own biographies in terms of the earlier bodily experiences that helped to shape our gender and sexual identities. We modeled our project after that of a German group of feminist women, led by Frigga Haug, who created a research method which they call "memory work." In short, the women would mutually choose a body part, such as "hair," and each would then write a short story based on a particularly salient childhood memory that related to their hair (for example, being forced by parents to cut one's hair, deciding to straighten one's curly hair in order to look more like other girls, etc.). Then the group would read all of the stories and discuss them one by one in the hope of gaining a more general understanding of, and raising new questions about, the social construction of "femininity." What resulted from this project was a fascinating book called *Female Sexualization* (Haug 1987), which my men's group used as the inspiration for our project.

As a research method, memory work is anything but conventional. Many sociologists would argue that this is not really a "research method" at all. The information that emerges from the project cannot be used very confidently as a generalizable "truth," and in this sort of project the researcher is simultaneously part of what is being studied. How, my more scientifically oriented colleagues might ask, is the researcher to maintain his or her objectivity? My answer is that in this kind of project objectivity is not the point. In fact, the strength of this sort of research is the depth of understanding that might be gained through a systematic group analysis of one's experience, one's subjective orientation to social processes. A clear understanding of the subjective aspect of social life—one's bodily feelings, emotions, and reactions to others—is an invaluable window that allows us to see and ask new sociological questions about group interaction and social structure. In

short, group memory work can provide an important, productive, and fascinating insight on social reality, though not a complete (or completely reliable) picture.

As I pondered the lack of existing research on the social construction of heterosexuality in sport, I decided to draw on one of my own stories from my memory work in the men's group. Some of my most salient memories of embodiment are sports memories. I grew up as the son of a high school coach, and I eventually played point guard on my dad's team. In what follows, I juxtapose my story with that of a gay former Olympic athlete, Tom Waddell, whom I had interviewed several years earlier for a book on the lives of male athletes (Messner and Sabo 1994).

Many years ago I read some psychological studies that argued that even for self-identified heterosexuals it is a natural part of their development to have gone through "bisexual" or even "homosexual" stages of life. When I read this, it seemed theoretically reasonable, but did not ring true in my experience. I have always been, I told myself, 100 percent heterosexual! The group process of analyzing my own autobiographical stories challenged the concept I had developed of myself, and also shed light on the way in which the institutional context of sport provided a context for the development of my definition of myself as "100 percent straight." Here is one of the stories.

> When I was in the 9th grade, I played on a "D" basketball team, set up especially for the smallest of high school boys. Indeed, though I was pudgy with baby fat, I was a short 5'2", still pre-pubescent with no facial hair and a high voice that I artificially tried to lower. The first day of practice, I was immediately attracted to a boy I'll call Timmy, because he looked like the boy who played in the *Lassie* TV show. Timmy was short, with a high voice, like me. And like me, he had no facial hair yet. Unlike me, he was very skinny. I liked Timmy right away, and soon we were together a lot. I noticed things about him that I didn't notice about other boys: he said some words a certain way, and it gave me pleasure to try to talk like him.

I remember liking the way the light hit his boyish, nearly hairless body. I thought about him when we weren't together. He was in the school band, and at the football games, I'd squint to see where he was in the mass of uniforms. In short, though I wasn't conscious of it at the time, I was infatuated with Timmy—I had a crush on him. Later that basketball season, I decided—for no reason that I could really articulate then—that I hated Timmy. I aggressively rejected him, began to make fun of him around other boys. He was, we all agreed, a geek. He was a faggot.

Three years later, Timmy and I were both on the varsity basketball team, but had hardly spoken a word to each other since we were freshman. Both of us now had lower voices, had grown to around 6 feet tall, and we both shaved, at least a bit. But Timmy was a skinny, somewhat stigmatized reserve on the team, while I was the team captain and starting point guard. But I wasn't so happy or secure about this. I'd always dreamed of dominating games, of being the hero. Halfway through my senior season, however, it became clear that I was not a star, and I figured I knew why. I was not aggressive enough.

I had always liked the beauty of the fast break, the perfectly executed pick and roll play between two players, and especially the long twenty-foot shot that touched nothing but the bottom of the net. But I hated and feared the sometimes brutal contact under the basket. In fact, I stayed away from the rough fights for rebounds and was mostly a perimeter player, relying on my long shots or my passes to more aggressive teammates under the basket. But now it became apparent to me that time was running out in my quest for greatness: I needed to change my game, and fast. I decided one day before practice that I was gonna get aggressive. While practicing one of our standard plays, I passed the ball to a teammate, and then ran to the spot at which I was to set a pick on a defender. I knew that one could sometimes get away with setting a face-up screen on a player, and then as he makes contact with you, roll your back to him and plant your elbow hard in his stomach. The beauty of this move is that

your own body "roll" makes the elbow look like an accident. So I decided to try this move. I approached the defensive player, Timmy, rolled, and planted my elbow deeply into his solar plexus. Air exploded audibly from Timmy's mouth, and he crumbled to the floor momentarily.

Play went on as though nothing has happened, but I felt bad about it. Rather than making me feel better, it made me feel guilty and weak. I had to admit to myself why I'd chosen Timmy as the target against whom to test out my new aggression. He was the skinniest and weakest player on the team.

At the time, I hardly thought about these incidents, other than to try to brush them off as incidents that made me feel extremely uncomfortable. Years later, I can now interrogate this as a sexual story, and as a gender story unfolding within the context of the heterosexualized and masculinized institution of sport. Examining my story in light of research conducted by Alfred Kinsey a half-century ago, I can recognize in myself what Kinsey saw as a very common fluidity and changeability of sexual desire over the life-course. Put simply, Kinsey found that large numbers of adult, "heterosexual" men had previously, as adolescents and young adults, experienced sexual desire for males. A surprisingly large number of these men had experienced sexual contact to the point of orgasm with other males during adolescence or early adulthood. Similarly, my story invited me to consider what is commonly called the "Freudian theory of bisexuality." Sigmund Freud shocked the post-Victorian world by suggesting that all people go through a stage, early in life, when they are attracted to people of the same sex.[1] Adult experiences, Freud argued, eventually led most people to shift their sexual desire to what he called an appropriate "love object"—a person of the opposite sex. I also considered my experience in light of what lesbian feminist author Adrienne Rich called the institution of compulsory heterosexuality. Perhaps the extremely high levels of homophobia that are often endemic in boys' and men's organized sports led me to deny and repress my own homoerotic desire through a direct and overt rejection of Timmy, through homophobic banter with male peers, and the resultant stigmatization of the feminized Timmy. Eventually I considered my experience in the light of what radical theorist Herbert Marcuse called the sublimation of homoerotic desire into an aggressive, violent act as serving to construct a clear line of demarcation between self and other. Sublimation, according to Marcuse, involved the driving underground, into the unconscious, of sexual desires that might appear dangerous due to their socially stigmatized status. But sublimation involves more than simple repression into the unconscious. It involves a transformation of sexual desire into something else—often into aggressive and violent acting out toward others. These acts clarify the boundaries between oneself and others and therefore lessen any anxieties that might be attached to the repressed homoerotic desire.

Importantly, in our analysis of my story, the memory group went beyond simply discussing the events in psychological terms. The story did perhaps suggest some deep psychological processes at work, but it also revealed the importance of social context—in this case, the context of the athletic team. In short, my rejection of Timmy and the joining with teammates to stigmatize him in ninth grade stands as an example of what sociologist R. W. Connell calls a moment of engagement with hegemonic masculinity, where I actively took up the male group's task of constructing heterosexual/masculine identities in the context of sport. The elbow in Timmy's gut three years later can be seen as a punctuation mark that occurred precisely because of my fears that I might be failing in this goal.

It is helpful, I think, to compare my story with gay and lesbian "coming out" stories in sport. Though we have a few lesbian and bisexual coming out stories among women athletes, there are very few from gay males. Tom Waddell, who as a closeted gay man finished sixth in the decathlon in the 1968 Olympics, later came out and started the Gay Games, an athletic and cultural festival that draws tens of thousands of people every four years. When I interviewed Tom Waddell over a decade ago about his sexual identity and athletic career, he made it quite clear that for many years sports was his closet:

> When I was a kid, I was tall for my age, and was very thin and very strong. And I was usually faster than most other people. But I discovered rather early that I liked gymnastics and I liked dance. I was very interested in being a ballet dancer . . . [but] something became obvious to me right away—that male ballet dancers were effeminate, that they were what most people would call faggots. And I thought I just couldn't handle that . . . I was totally closeted and very concerned about being male. This was the fifties, a terrible time to live, and everything was stacked against me. Anyway, I realized that I had to do something to protect my image of myself as a male—because at that time homosexuals were thought of primarily as men who wanted to be women. And so I threw myself into athletics—I played football, gymnastics, track and field . . . I was a jock—that's how I was viewed, and I was comfortable with that.

Tom Waddell was fully conscious of entering sports and constructing a masculine/heterosexual athletic identity precisely because he feared being revealed as gay. It was clear to him, in the context of the 1950s, that being known as gay would undercut his claims to the status of manhood. Thus, though he described the athletic closet as "hot and stifling," he remained there until several years after his athletic retirement. He even knowingly played along with locker room discussions about sex and women as part of his "cover."

> I wanted to be viewed as male, otherwise I would be a dancer today. I wanted the male, macho image of an athlete. So I was protected by a very hard shell. I was clearly aware of what I was doing . . . I often felt compelled to go along with a lot of locker room garbage because I wanted that image—and I know a lot of others who did too.

Like my story, Waddell's points to the importance of the athletic institution as a context in which peers mutually construct and reconstruct narrow definitions of masculinity. Heterosexuality is considered to be a rock-solid foundation of this concept of masculinity. But unlike my story, Waddell's may invoke a dramaturgical analysis.[2] He seemed to be consciously "acting" to control and regulate others' perceptions of him by constructing a public "front stage" persona that differed radically from what he believed to be his "true" inner self. My story, in contrast, suggests a deeper, less consciously strategic repression of my homoerotic attraction. Most likely, I was aware on some level of the dangers of such feelings, and was escaping the risks, disgrace, and rejection that would likely result from being different. For Waddell, the decision to construct his identity largely within sport was to step into a fiercely heterosexual/masculine closet that would hide what he saw as his "true" identity. In contrast, I was not so much stepping into a "closet" that would hide my identity; rather, I was stepping out into an entire world of heterosexual privilege. My story also suggests how a threat to the promised privileges of hegemonic masculinity—my failure as an athlete—might trigger a momentary sexual panic that can lay bare the constructedness, indeed, the instability of the heterosexual/masculine identity.

In either case, Waddell's or mine, we can see how, as young male athletes, heterosexuality and masculinity was not something we "were," but something we were doing. It is significant, I think, that although each of us was "doing heterosexuality," neither of us was actually "having sex" with women (though one of us desperately wanted to). This underscores a point made by some recent theorists that heterosexuality should not be thought of simply as sexual acts between women and men. Rather, heterosexuality is a constructed identity, a performance, and an institution that is not necessarily linked to sexual acts. Though for one of us it was more conscious than for the other, we were both "doing heterosexual-

ity" as an ongoing practice through which we sought to do two things:

- avoid stigma, embarrassment, ostracism, or perhaps worse if we were even suspected of being gay;
- link ourselves into systems of power, status, and privilege that appear to be the birthright of "real men" (i.e., males who are able to compete successfully with other males in sport, work, and sexual relations with women).

In other words, each of us actively scripted our own sexual and gender performances, but these scripts were constructed within the constraints of a socially organized (institutionalized) system of power and pleasure.

Questions for Future Research

As I prepared to tell this sexual story publicly to my colleagues at the sport studies conference, I felt extremely nervous. Part of the nervousness was due to the fact that I knew some of them would object to my claim that telling personal stories can be a source of sociological insights. But a larger part of the reason for my nervousness was due to the fact that I was revealing something very personal about my sexuality in such a public way. Most of us are not accustomed to doing this, especially in the context of a professional conference. But I had learned long ago, especially from feminist women scholars, and from gay and lesbian scholars, that biography is linked to history. Part of "normal" academic discourse has been to hide "the personal" (including the fact that the researchers are themselves people with values, feelings, and yes, biases) behind a carefully constructed facade of "objectivity." Rather than trying to hide or be ashamed of one's subjective experience of the world, I was challenging myself to draw on my experience of the world as a resource. Not that I should trust my experience as the final word on "reality." White, heterosexual males like me have made the mistake for centuries of calling their own experience "objectivity," and then punishing anyone who does not share their worldview by casting them as "deviant." Instead, I hope to use my experience as an example of how those of us who are in dominant sexual/racial/gender/class categories can get a new perspective on the "constructedness" of our identities by juxtaposing our subjective experiences against the recently emerging worldviews of gay men and lesbians, women, and people of color.

Finally, I want to stress that in juxtaposition neither my own nor Tom Waddell's story sheds much light on the question of why some individuals "become gay" while others "become" heterosexual or bisexual. Instead, I should like to suggest that this is a dead-end question, and that there are far more important and interesting questions to be asked:

- How has heterosexuality, as an institution and as an enforced group practice, constrained and limited all of us—gay, straight, and bi?
- How has the institution of sport been an especially salient institution for the social construction of heterosexual masculinity?
- Why is it that when men play sports they are almost always automatically granted masculine status, and thus assumed to be heterosexual, while when women play sports, questions are raised about their "femininity" and sexual orientation?

These kinds of questions aim us toward an analysis of the working of power within institutions—including the ways that these workings of power shape and constrain our identities and relationships—and point us toward imagining alternative social arrangements that are less constraining for everyone.

Notes

1. The fluidity and changeability of sexual desire over the life course is now more obvious in evidence from prison and military populations, and single-sex boarding schools. The theory of bisexuality is evident, for example, in childhood crushes on same-sex primary schoolteachers.

2. Dramaturgical analysis, associated with Erving Goffman, uses the theater and performance to develop an analogy with everyday life.

References

Haug, Frigga (1987) *Female Sexualization: A Collective Work of Memory*, London: Verso.

Lenskyj, Helen (1986) *Out of Bounds: Women, Sport and Sexuality*, Toronto: Women's Press.

—— (1997) "No fear? Lesbians in sport and physical education," *Women in Sport and Physical Activity Journal* 6(2): 7–22.

Messner, Michael A. (1992) *Power at Play: Sports and the Problem of Masculinity*, Boston: Beacon Press.

—— (1994) "Gay athletes and the Gay Games: in interview with Tom Waddell," in M. A. Messner and D. F. Sabo (eds) *Sex, Violence and Power in Sports: Rethinking Masculinity*, Freedom, CA: The Crossing Press, pp. 113–19.

Pronger, Brian (1990) *The Arena of Masculinity: Sports, Homosexuality, and the Meaning of Sex*, New York: St. Martin's Press.

M. Rochlin

The Heterosexual Questionnaire

1. What do you think caused your heterosexuality?

2. When and how did you decide you were a heterosexual?

3. Is it possible that your heterosexuality is just a phase you may grow out of?

4. Is it possible that your heterosexuality stems from a neurotic fear of others of the same sex?

5. If you have never slept with a person of the same sex, is it possible that all you need is a good Gay lover?

6. Do your parents know that you are straight? Do your friends and/or roommate(s) know? How did they react?

7. Why do you insist on flaunting your heterosexuality? Can't you just be who you are and keep it quiet?

8. Why do heterosexuals place so much emphasis on sex?

9. Why do heterosexuals feel compelled to seduce others into their lifestyle?

10. A disproportionate majority of child molesters are heterosexual. Do you consider it safe to expose children to heterosexual teachers?

11. Just what do men and women *do* in bed together? How can they truly know how to please each other, being so anatomically different?

12. With all the societal support marriage receives, the divorce rate is spiraling. Why are there so few stable relationships among heterosexuals?

13. Statistics show that lesbians have the lowest incidence of sexually transmitted diseases. Is it really safe for a woman to maintain a heterosexual lifestyle and run the risk of disease and pregnancy?

14. How can you become a whole person if you limit yourself to compulsive, exclusive heterosexuality?

15. Considering the menace of overpopulation, how could the human race survive if everyone were heterosexual?

16. Could you trust a heterosexual therapist to be objective? Don't you feel s/he might be inclined to influence you in the direction of her/his own leanings?

17. There seem to be very few happy heterosexuals. Techniques have been developed that might enable you to change if you really want to. Have you considered trying aversion therapy?

18. Would you want your child to be heterosexual, knowing the problems that s/he would face?

Stevi Jackson

A Conventional Affair

One of the more surprising aspects of the Clinton–Lewinsky saga is the lack of critical feminist commentary. With the notable exception of Andrea Dworkin, those feminists willing to commit their thoughts to print have taken the liberal line that it is all a lot of fuss about nothing. Of course at one level this is true, if by "nothing" we mean "nothing unusual." It is hardly earth-shattering news to discover that a married man in a position of power had a clandestine sexual relationship with a younger, subordinate woman. It happens all the time. Nor is engaging in sexual activities in the workplace (in this case the Oval Office) at all exceptional. After all, many a male academic has had sex with students in his office. Finally, the fact that a man confronted with the exposure of his tawdry secrets responds with evasive half-truths is not exactly shocking: it is what most straight men do when they find themselves in this situation.

The making of a political scandal out of such highly conventional sexual behaviour should give us pause for thought, and may explain feminists' reluctance to participate in public condemnation of Clinton. Most of us would not wish to identify ourselves with the political agenda of those seeking to whip up moral outrage around these events. If we were to side with those crying for impeachment, and had any sense of justice, we would logically need to call for the sacking of a good proportion of the professional middle-class male population. Having said this, I do not think feminists should let Clinton off the hook. Indeed, it is precisely because his behaviour *is* so conventional and so predictable that we should subject it

Reprinted by permission of Sage Publications Ltd, from Stevi Jackson, "A Conventional Affair" in *Sexualities*, Vol. 2(2), 1999, pp. 250–253. Copyright © 1999.

to scrutiny. The whole affair, including public and media reaction to it, says a great deal about contemporary heterosexual relations—and it is this which should be the focus of feminist critique.

To start from basic first principles, any sexual relationship between an older man in an institutionalized position of power and a younger, subordinate woman constitutes an abuse of power. It also exacerbates the gender hierarchy on which heterosexuality is founded. However, we still live in a world where heterosexuality relations usually couple older men with younger women, often with parallel inequalities in income, power, and status, and these relationships are often formed within organizational hierarchies. In this sense, the Clinton–Lewinsky relationship is simply an extreme version of everyday heterosexuality. Moreover, power "works" as an incitement to sexual desire for many women—who are attracted to prominent men because they are the centre of attention. Men in such positions benefit sexually from their power, as they benefit in other ways, whether or not they actually seek to do so. This is why heterosexual relationships within institutional hierarchies are so problematic, even where no harassment is involved.

As a woman caught up in such a power relationship, Monica Lewinsky in many ways exemplifies the contradictory character of 1990s female sexuality. She is not a classic victim: she seems to have made much of the running and her actions could be read as those of a sexually assertive young woman who has seen what she wanted and gone for it. But is a woman who discusses her knickers the first time she is alone with a man being sexually assertive or merely more sexually *explicit* in conveying her availability than was once common? She does not appear to have been empowered by this encounter. Quite apart from the fact that she ended up on her knees, she also bought into all the commonplace illusions of romantic love which rendered her emotionally vulnerable and ultimately powerless within the relationship. Her situation demonstrates the difficulties faced by women when they try to assert agency within heterosexual relations: they are still up against the institutionalized gender hierarchy of heterosexuality and their desires themselves, however actively pursued, remain constrained by the erotics of domination and subordination.

Clinton, it is said, cheated on his wife. I come from that generation of feminists who maintain a critical stance on monogamy and hence I do not see sexual "infidelity" as the worst crime a man can commit—although I do see being dishonest about it as an act of betrayal. It is difficult, however, to know what level of deception we are dealing with here. Hillary Clinton is an intelligent woman and I find it hard to believe that she was convinced by her husband's public denials; I'm sure she knows very well the sort of man she is married to. It is, however, painful to see this woman, who began by challenging much of the traditional "first lady" role, first reduced to playing that role to the hilt and now cast in the part of the wronged but loyal wife. Were I in her shoes I would find this far more humiliating than any hurt caused by her husband's extramarital sex.

And what about the sex? It is rather ironic that the issue of "what counts as sex" has made its way on to the public agenda in this context. Feminists have been trying to raise this question since the early 1970s when we first challenged the equation of sex with heterosexual penetration. When Clinton made his famous assertion that he did "not have sexual relations with that woman" he was, of course, simply deploying the conventional definition of what sex is. Interestingly, Monica Lewinsky seems to have concurred; tapes of her telephone conversations recorded her saying that she was not having sex, "just fooling around." Much more could be written about this, but I want to say something about the fact that most of the sexual contact in question consisted of Lewinsky performing oral sex on Clinton.

Here I find myself in agreement with Andrea Dworkin's assessment that this, as a *non-reciprocal* activity, is "the most fetishistic, heartless, cold sexual exchange that one could imagine" (1998: 50). I have no political or aesthetic objection to the practice of female-on-male oral sex; in the context of a sensual meeting of bodies, where this is one of many pleasures given and received, it is fine. But Lewinsky serviced Clinton while he had telephone conversations. He wasn't even fully engaged with the act; it is almost disembodied sex, as if his penis was being manipulated without him being implicated at all. Perhaps he was stating a truth when he said he did not have "sexual relations." This reveals a great deal about male (hetero)sexuality, about the ability of men to divorce body and mind, to localize their sexuality in their genitals. In what is still, for me, one of the best books on masculinity ever written, Emmanuel Reynaud characterizes male (hetero)sexuality as a form of frigidity, bound up with men's perception of penetrative sex as an act of appropriation, fueled by a desire for power rather than sensual pleasure. He could have been describing Bill Clinton when he wrote:

> He does not abandon himself to his pleasure; he confines it within the limits of his penis, and generally seeks it in his mind and on a woman's body . . . his desexualised body jerks between his penis and his head. (Reynaud 1981: 62–3)

Note

Many of these ideas were worked through in a late night kitchen-table discussion with Rosemary Hennessy. I have drawn on some of the points she made.

References

Dworkin, Andrea (1998) 'Slick Willy and the Silent Sisters', *Trouble & Strife* 37: 50–1. [reprinted, with additional commentary by Dworkin, from *The Guardian*, 29 January 1998]

Reynaud, Emmanual (1981) *Holy Virility*. London: Pluto Press.

Robert Staples

Stereotypes of Black Male Sexuality: The Facts Behind the Myths

It is difficult to think of a more controversial role in American society than that of the black male. He is a visible figure on the American scene, yet the least understood and studied of all sex–race groups in the United States. His cultural image is typically one of several types: the sexual super-stud, the athlete, and the rapacious criminal. That is how he is perceived in the public consciousness, interpreted in the media, and ultimately how he comes to see and internalize his own role. Rarely are we exposed to his more prosaic role as worker, husband, father, and American citizen.

The following essay focuses on the stereotypical roles of black male heterosexuality, not to reinforce them, but to penetrate the superficial images of black men as macho, hypersexual, violent, and exploitative. Obviously, there must be some explanation for the dominance of black men in the nations' negative statistics on rape, out-of-wedlock births, and premarital sexual activity. This is an effort to explore the reality behind the image.

Black Manhood

As a starting point, I see the black male as being in conflict with the normative definition of masculinity. This is a status which few, if any, black males have been able to achieve. Masculinity, as defined in this culture, has always implied a certain autonomy and mastery of one's environment. It can be said that not many white American

males have attained this ideal either. Yet, white males did achieve a dominance in the nuclear family. Even that semblance of control was largely to be denied black men. During slavery he could receive the respect and esteem of his wife, children, and kinsmen, but he had no formal legal authority over his wife or filial rights from his children. There are numerous and documented instances of the slave-owning class's attempts to undermine his respect and esteem in the eyes of his family.[1]

Beginning with the fact that slave men and women were equally subjugated to the capricious authority of the slaveholder, the African male saw his masculinity challenged by the rape of his woman, sale of his children, the rations issued in the name of the woman and children bearing her name. While those practices may have presaged the beginning of a healthier sexual egalitarianism than was possible for whites, they also provoked contradictions and dilemmas for black men in American society. It led to the black male's self-devaluation as a man and set the stage for internecine conflict within the black community.

A person's sex role identity is crucial to their values, life-style, and personality. The black man has always had to confront the contradiction between the normative expectations attached to being male in this society and the proscriptions on his behavior and achievement of goals. He is subjected to societal opprobrium for failing to live up to the standards of manhood on the one hand and for being super macho on the other. It is a classical case of "damned if you do and damned if you don't." In the past there was the assertion that black men were effeminate because they were raised in households with only a female parent or one with a weak father figure. Presently, they are being attacked in literature, in plays, and at conferences as having succumbed to the male chauvinist ideal.

Although the sexual stereotypes apply equally to black men and women, it is the black male who has suffered the worst because of white notions of his hypersexuality. Between 1884 and 1900 more than 2,500 black men were lynched, the majority of whom were accused of sexual interest in white women. Black men, it was said, had a larger penis, a greater sexual capacity, and an insatiable sexual appetite. These stereotypes depicted black men as primitive sexual beasts, without the white male's love for home and family.[2] These stereotypes persist in the American consciousness.

It is in the area of black sexual behavior, and black male sexuality in particular, that folk beliefs are abundant but empirical facts few. Yet public policy, sex education, and therapeutic programs to deal with the sex-related problems of black people cannot be developed to fit their peculiar needs until we know the nature and dynamics of black sexual behavior. Thus, it is incumbent upon researchers to throw some light on an area enmeshed in undocumented myths and stereotypes.

Sexuality of the Male Adolescent

The Kinsey data, cited by Bell,[3] reveal that black males acquire their knowledge about condoms at a later age than white males. The white male learns about sexual intercourse at a later age than black males. Because of poorer nutrition, the black male reaches puberty at a later age than his white male counterpart. A critical distinction between black and white males was the tendency of the more sexually repressed white male to substitute masturbation, fellatio, and fantasy for direct sexual intercourse. Masturbation, for instance, was more likely to be the occasion of the first ejaculation for the white male while intercourse was for the black male. A larger percentage of white males

reported being sexually aroused by being bitten during sexual activity, seeing a member of the opposite sex in a social situation, seeing themselves nude in the mirror or looking at another man's erect penis, hearing dirty jokes, reading sadomasochistic literature, and viewing sexy pictures. Conversely, black males tended to engage in premarital intercourse at earlier ages, to have intercourse, and to reach orgasm more frequently. As Bell notes in his analysis of these data, the black male's overabundance of sexuality is a myth. The sexuality of black and white men just tends to take different forms and neither group has any more self-control or moral heroism than the other.

Among young black American males, sexual activity begins at an earlier age, is more frequent, and involves more partners. Apparently white males are more likely to confine their associations in the adolescent years with other men. Larson and his associates found that black male adolescents were twice as likely to be romantically involved with women than white males.[4] The kind of rigid gender segregation found in white culture is largely absent from black society. For example, blacks are less likely to be associated with all male clubs, organizations, or colleges.

The sexual code of young black males is a permissive one. They do not, for example, divide black women into "good" (suitable for marriage) and "bad" (ineligible for marriage) categories. In the lower income groups, sexual activity is often a measure of masculinity. Thus, there is a greater orientation toward premarital sexual experimentation. In a study of premarital sexual standards among blacks and whites in the 1960s, Ira Reiss found that the sexual permissiveness of white males could be affected by a number of social forces (e.g., religion), but the black male was influenced by none of them.[5] Leanor Johnson and this author found that few black male adolescents were aware of the increased risk of teenage pregnancy, but there was an almost unanimous wish not to impregnate their sexual partner. Another survey of black male high school students reported their group believed that a male respects his partner when he uses a condom.[6]

Poverty and the Black Father

The period of adolescence, with its social, psychological and physical changes (particularly sex-role identity and sexuality), is the most problematic of the life cycle stages. The prolongation of adolescence in complex technological society and the earlier onset of puberty have served to compound the problem. While adolescents receive various messages to abandon childlike behavior, they are systematically excluded from adult activity such as family planning. This exclusion is justified not only by their incomplete social and emotional maturity, but by their lack of marketable skills which are necessary to command meaningful status-granting jobs. Unskilled adolescents are further disadvantaged if they are members of a minority racial group in a racially stratified society.

Parenthood at this stage of the life cycle is most undesirable. Yet, recent upsurges in teenage pregnancy and parenthood have occurred, specifically among females younger than 14. Approximately 52% of all children born to black women in 1982 were conceived out of wedlock. Among black women under age 20, about 75% of all births were out of wedlock compared with only 25% of births to young white women.[7] Although the rate of white out-of-wedlock pregnancy is increasing and that of non-whites decreasing, black unwed parenthood remains higher than that of whites.

Because life and family support systems of black males are severely handicapped by the effects of poverty and discrimination, the consequences of becoming a father in adolescence are more serious for the minority parent. Many family planning agencies offer counseling to the unwed mother, while the father is usually involved only superficially or punitively—as when efforts are made to establish legal paternity as a means for assessing financial responsibility. This omission, however, is not unique to black males. It is, perhaps, the single fact of inadequate economic provision which has resulted in the social agencies' premature conclusion that unwed fathers are unwilling to contribute to the future of their child and the support of the mother. Furthermore, sociological theory purports that slavery broke the black man's sense of family responsibility. Thus, it is assumed that black women do not expect or demand that black men support them in raising their children.

Family Planning

Recent evidence, however, suggests that the matrifocality of present theory and social services is myopic. Studies have demonstrated that most unwed fathers are willing to face their feelings and responsibilities.[8] The findings suggest that unmarried black males do not consider family planning a domain of the female, but rather a joint responsibility to be shared by both parents.[9]

Throughout the world one of the most important variables affecting birth rates is the male attitude toward family planning and the genesis of this attitude. Too often we are accustomed to thinking of reproduction as primarily a female responsibility. Since women are the main bearers and main rearers of children in our society, we tend to believe that they should be primarily concerned with planning the size of a family and developing those techniques of contraception consistent with the family's earning power, their own health and happiness, and the psychological well-being of their children.

However, in a male-dominated world it is women who are given the burden of having and raising children, while it is often men who determine what the magnitude of that burden should be. Unfortunately, the male's wishes in regard to the size of his family are not contingent on the effect of childbearing on the female partner, but are often shaped by his own psychological and status concerns.

Within many societies there is an inseparable link between men's self-image and their ability to have sexual relations with women and the subsequent birth of children from those sexual acts. For example, in Spanish-speaking cultures this masculine norm is embedded in the concept of "machismo." "Machismo," derived from the Latin word "masculus," literally means the ability to produce sperm and thus sire—abilities which define the status of a man in society. In male-dominated society other issues involved in reproduction are subordinated to the male's desire to affirm his virility, which in turn confirms his fulfillment of the masculine role. The research literature tells us that the male virility cult is strongest in countries and among groups where the need for family planning is greatest.

Thus, we find that in underdeveloped countries—and among low-income ethnic groups in industrialized societies, including much of the black population in the U.S.—men are resistant to anything but natural controls on the number of children they have. Studies show that males who strongly believe that their masculine status is associated with their virility do not communicate very well with their wives on the subject of family planning. As a result the wives are less effective in limiting their families to the number of children they desire.

Sexual Aggression

Sexual attacks against women are pervasive and sharply increasing in this country. The typical rapist is a black male and his victim is most often a black female. However, the most severe penalties for rape are reserved for black males accused of raping white women. Although 50% of those convicted for rape in the South were white males, over 90% of those executed for this crime in that region were black. Most of their alleged victims were white. No white male has ever been executed for raping a black woman.[10]

As is probably true of white females, the incidence of rape of black women is underreported. Lander reported that an eight-year-old girl has a good chance of being exposed to rape and violence if she is a member of the black underclass.[11] While widespread incidents of this kind are rooted in the sexist socialization of all men in society, it is pronounced among black men who have other symbols of traditional masculinity blocked to them. Various explanations have been put forth to explain why black men seem to adopt the atti-

tudes of the majority group toward black women. Poussaint believes that because white men have historically raped black women with impunity, many black males believe they can do the same.[12]

Sexual violence is also rooted in the dynamics of the black dating game. The majority of black rape victims know their attacker—a friend, relative, or neighbor. Many of the rapes occur after a date and are what Amir describes as misfired attempts at seduction.[13] A typical pattern is for the black male to seek sexual compliance from his date, encounter resistance which he thinks is feigned, and proceed to forcibly obtain his sexual gratification from her. Large numbers of black men believe sexual relations to be their "right" after a certain amount of dating.

Rape, however, is not regarded as the act of a sexually starved male but rather as an aggressive act toward females. Students of the subject suggest that it is a long-delayed reaction against authority and powerlessness. In the case of black men, it is asserted that they grow up feeling emasculated and powerless before reaching manhood. They often encounter women as authority figures and teachers or as the head of their household. These men consequently act out their feelings of powerlessness against black women in the form of sexual aggression. Hence, rape by black men should be viewed as both an aggressive and political act because it occurs in the context of racial discrimination which denies most black men a satisfying manhood.

Manhood in American society is closely tied to the acquisition of wealth. Men of wealth are rarely required to rape women because they can gain sexual access through other means. A female employee who submits to the sexual demands of a male employer in order to advance in her job is as much an unwilling partner in this situation as is the rape victim. The rewards for her sexual compliance are normatively sanctioned, whereas the rapist does not often have the resources to induce such sexual compliance. Moreover, the concept of women as sexual property is at the root of rape. This concept is peculiar to capitalistic, western societies rather than African nations (where the incidence of rape is much lower). For black men, rape is often an act of aggression against women because the kinds of status men can acquire through success in a job is not available to them.

Recommendations

To address the salient issues in black male sexuality, I offer the following recommendations:

1. An educational program for black men must be designed to sensitize them to the need for their responsibility for, and participation in, family planning. This program will best be conducted by other men who can convey the fact that virility is not in and of itself the measure of masculinity. Also, it should be emphasized that the use of contraception—or obtaining a vasectomy—does not diminish a male's virility.

2. An overall sex education program for both sexes should begin as early as kindergarten, before the male peer group can begin to reinforce attitudes of male dominance. Sex education courses should stress more than the physiological aspects in its course content. Males should be taught about the responsibility of men in sex relations and procreation. Forms of male contraception should be taught along with female measures of birth control.

3. The lack of alternative forms of role fulfillment available to many men, especially in industrialized societies, must be addressed. In cases of unemployment and underemployment, the male often resorts to the virility cult because it is the only outlet he has for a positive self-image and prestige within his peer group. Thus, we must provide those conditions whereby men can find meaningful employment.

4. Lines of communication must be opened between men and women. A supplement to the educational program for men should be seminars and workshops involving both men and women. Hopefully, this will lead to the kind of dialog between men and women that will sensitize each of them to the feelings of the other.

Notes

1. Robert Staples, *The Black Family: Essays and Studies.* (Belmont, CA: Wadsworth, 1978.)

2. Robert Staples, *Black Masculinity*, (San Francisco: The Black Scholar Press, 1982.)

3. Alan P. Bell, "Black Sexuality: Fact and Fancy" in R. Staples. ed., *The Black Family: Essays and Studies*, pp. 77–80.

4. David Larson, et al., "Social Factors in the Frequency of Romantic Involvement Among Adolescents." *Adolescence* 11: 7–12, 1976.

5. Ira Reiss, *The Social Context of Premarital Sexual Permissiveness.* (New York: Holt, Rinehart and Winston, 1968.)

6. Leanor Johnson and Robert Staples, "Minority Youth and Family Planning: A Pilot Project." *The Family Coordinator* 28: 534–543, 1978.

7. U.S. Bureau of the Census, *Fertility of American Women.* (Washington, D.C.: U.S. Government Printing Office, 1984.)

8. Lisa Connolly, "Boy Fathers." *Human Behavior* 45: 40–43, 1978.

9. B. D. Misra, "Correlates of Males' Attitudes Toward Family Planning" in D. Bogue, ed., *Sociological Contributions to Family Planning Research.* (Chicago: Univ. of Chicago Press, 1967), pp. 161–167.

10. William J. Bowers, *Executions in America.* (Lexington Books, 1974.)

11. Joyce Lander, *Tomorrow's Tomorrow: The Black Woman.* (Garden City, New York: Doubleday, 1971.)

12. Alvin Poussaint, *Why Blacks Kill Blacks.* (New York: Emerson-Hall, 1972.)

13. Menachim Amir, "Sociocultural Factors in Forcible Rape" in L. Gross, ed., *Sexual Behavior.* (New York: Spectrum Publications, 1974), pp. 1–12.

Tomás Almaguer

Chicano Men: A Cartography of Homosexual Identity and Behavior

The sexual behavior and sexual identity of Chicano male homosexuals is principally shaped by two distinct sexual systems, each of which attaches different significance and meaning to homosexuality. Both the European-American and Mexican/Latin-American systems have their own unique ensemble of sexual meanings, categories for sexual actors, and scripts that circumscribe sexual behavior. Each system also maps the human body in different ways by placing different values on homosexual erotic zones. The primary socialization of Chicanos into Mexican/Latin-American cultural norms, combined with their simultaneous socialization into the dominant European-American culture, largely structures how they negotiate sexual identity questions and confer meaning to homosexual behavior during adolescence and adulthood. Chicano men who embrace a "gay" identity (based on the European-American sexual system) must reconcile this sexual identity with their primary socialization into a Latino culture that does not recognize such a construction: there is no cultural equivalent to the modern "gay man" in the Mexican/Latin-American sexual system.

How does socialization into these different sexual systems shape the crystallization of their sexual identities and the meaning they give to their homosexuality? Why does only a segment of homosexually active Chicano men identify as "gay"? Do these men primarily consider themselves *Chicano* gay men (who retain primary emphasis on their ethnicity) or *gay* Chicanos (who place primary emphasis on their sexual preference)? How do Chicano homosexuals structure their sexual conduct, especially the sexual roles and relationships into which they enter? Are they structured along lines of power/dominance firmly rooted in a patriarchal Mexican culture that privileges men over women and the masculine over the feminine? Or do they reflect the ostensibly more egalitarian sexual norms and practices of the European-American sexual system? These are among the numerous questions that this paper problematizes and explores.

We know little about how Chicano men negotiate and contest a modern gay identity with aspects of Chicano culture drawing upon more Mexican/Latin-American configurations of sexual meaning. Unlike the rich literature on the Chicana/Latina lesbian experience, there is a paucity of writings on Chicano gay men.[1] There does not exist any scholarly literature on this topic other than one unpublished study addressing this issue as a secondary concern (Carrillo and Maiorana). The extant literature consists primarily of semi-autobiographical, literary texts by authors such as John Rechy, Arturo Islas, and Richard Rodriguez.[2] Unlike the writings on Chicana lesbianism, however, these works fail to discuss directly the cultural dissonance that Chicano homosexual men confront in reconciling their primary socialization into Chicano family life with the sexual norms of the dominant culture. They

An edited version of the original article appeared in *Differences: A Journal of Feminist Cultural Studies* 3:2(1991), pp. 75–100. Reprinted with permission. I gratefully acknowledge the valuable comments on an earlier version of this article by Jackie Goldsby, David Halperin, Teresa de Lauretis, Bob Blauner, Carla Trujillo, Patricia Zavella, Velia Garcia, and Ramón Gutiérrez.

415

offer little to our understanding of how these men negotiate the different ways these cultural systems stigmatize homosexuality and how they incorporate these messages into their adult sexual practices.

In the absence of such discussion or more direct ethnographic research to draw upon, we must turn elsewhere for insights into the lives of Chicano male homosexuals. One source of such knowledge is the perceptive anthropological research on homosexuality in Mexico and Latin America, which has direct relevance for our understanding of how Chicano men structure and culturally interpret their homosexual experiences. The other, ironically, is the writings of Chicana lesbians who have openly discussed intimate aspects of their sexual behavior and reflected upon sexual identity issues. How they have framed these complex sexual issues has major import for our understanding of Chicano male homosexuality. Thus, the first section of this paper examines certain features of the Mexican/Latin-American sexual system which offer clues to the ensemble of cultural meanings that Chicano homosexuals give to their sexual practices. The second section examines the autobiographical writings of Chicana lesbian writer Cherríe Moraga. I rely upon her candid discussion of her sexual development as ethnographic evidence for further problematizing the Chicano homosexual experience in the United States.

The Cartography of Desire in the Mexican/Latin-American Sexual System

American anthropologists have recently turned their attention to the complex meaning of homosexuality in Mexico and elsewhere in Latin America. Ethnographic research by Joseph M. Carrier, Roger N. Lancaster, Richard Parker, Barry D. Adam, and Clark L. Taylor has documented the inapplicability of Western European and North American categories of sexual meaning in the Latin American context. Since the Mexican/ Chicano population in the U.S. shares basic fea-

tures of these Latin cultural patterns, it is instructive to examine this sexual system closely and to explore its impact on the sexuality of homosexual Chicano men and women.

The rules that define and stigmatize homosexuality in Mexican culture operate under a logic and a discursive practice different from those of the bourgeois sexual system that shaped the emergence of contemporary gay/lesbian identity in the U.S. Each sexual system confers meaning to homosexuality by giving different weight to the two fundamental features of human sexuality that Freud delineated in the *Three Essays on the Theory of Sexuality*: sexual object choice and sexual aim. The structured meaning of homosexuality in the European-American context rests on the sexual object-choice one makes—i.e., the biological sex of the person toward whom sexual activity is directed. The Mexican/Latin-American sexual system, on the other hand, confers meaning to homosexual practices according to sexual aim— i.e., the act one wants to perform with another person (of either biological sex).

The contemporary bourgeois sexual system in the U.S. divides the sexual landscape according to discrete sexual categories and personages defined in terms of sexual preference or object choice: same sex (homosexual), opposite sex (heterosexual), or both (bisexual). Historically, this formulation has carried with it a blanket condemnation of all same-sex behavior. Because it is non-procreative and at odds with a rigid, compulsory heterosexual norm, homosexuality traditionally has been seen as either 1) a sinful transgression against the word of God, 2) a congenital disorder wracking the body, or 3) a psychological pathology gripping the mind. In underscoring object choice as the crucial factor in defining sexuality in the U.S., anthropologist Roger Lancaster argues that "homosexual desire itself, without any qualifications, stigmatizes one as a homosexual" (116). This stigmatization places the modern gay man at the bottom of the homosexual sexual hierarchy. According to Lancaster, "the object-choice of the homosexual emarginates him from male power, except insofar as he can serve as a negative example and . . . is positioned outside the operational rules of normative (hetero)sexuality" (123–24).

Unlike the European-American system, the Mexican/Latin-American sexual system is based on a configuration of gender/sex/power that is articulated along the active/passive axis and organized through the scripted sexual role one plays.[3] It highlights sexual aim—the act one wants to perform with the person toward whom sexual activity is directed—and gives only secondary importance to the person's gender or biological sex. According to Lancaster, "it renders certain organs and roles 'active,' other body passages and roles 'passive,' and assigns honor/shame and status/stigma accordingly" (123). It is the mapping of the body into differentiated erotic zones and the unequal, gender-coded statuses accorded sexual actors that structure homosexual meaning in Latin culture. In the Mexican/Latin-American context there is no cultural equivalent to the modern gay man. Instead of discrete sexual personages differentiated according to sexual preference, we have categories of people defined in terms of the role they play in the homosexual act. The Latin homosexual world is divided into *activos* and *pasivos* (as in Mexico and Brazil) and *machistas* and *cochóns* (in Nicaragua).

Although stigma accompanies homosexual practices in Latin culture, it does not equally adhere to both partners. It is primarily the anal–passive individual (the *cochón* or *pasivo*) who is stigmatized for playing the subservient, feminine role. His partner (the *activo* or *machista*) typically "is not stigmatized at all and, moreover, no clear category exists in the popular language to classify him. For all intents and purposes, he is just a normal . . . male" (Lancaster 113). In fact, Lancaster argues that the active party in a homosexual drama often gains status among his peers in precisely the same way that one derives status from seducing many women (113). This cultural construction confers an inordinate amount of meaning to the anal orifice and to anal penetration. This is in sharp contrast to the way homosexuality is viewed in the U.S., where the oral orifice struc-

tures the meaning of homosexuality in the popular imagination. In this regard, Lancaster suggests the lexicon of male insult in each context clearly reflects this basic difference in cultural meaning associated with oral/anal sites (111). The most common derisive term used to refer to homosexuals in the U.S. is "cocksucker." Conversely, most Latin American epithets for homosexuals convey the stigma associated with their being anally penetrated.

Consider for a moment the meaning associated with the passive homosexual in Nicaragua, the *cochón*. The term is derived from the word *colchón* or mattress, implying that one gets on top of another as one would a mattress, and thereby symbolically affirms the former's superior masculine power and male status over the other, who is feminized and indeed objectified (Lancaster 112). *Cochón* carries with it a distinct configuration of power, delineated along gender lines that are symbolically affirmed through the sexual role one plays in the homosexual act. Consequently, the meaning of homosexuality in Latin culture is fraught with elements of power/dominance that are not intrinsically accorded homosexual practices in the U.S. It is anal passivity alone that is stigmatized and that defines the subordinate status of homosexuals in Latin culture. The stigma conferred to the passive role is fundamentally inscribed in gender-coded terms.

> "To give" (*dar*) is to be masculine, "to receive" (*recibir, aceptar, tomar*) is to be feminine. This holds as the ideal in all spheres of transactions between and within genders. It is symbolized by the popular interpretation of the male sexual organ as active in intercourse and the female sexual organ (or male anus) as passive. (Lancaster 114)

This equation makes homosexuals such as the *pasivo* and *cochón* into feminized men; biological males, but not truly men. In Nicaragua, for example, homosexual behavior renders "one man a machista and the other a cochón. The machista's honor and the cochón's shame are opposite sides of the same coin" (Lancaster 114).

Male Homosexual Identity and Behavior in Mexico

Some of the most insightful ethnographic research on homosexuality in Mexico has been conducted by anthropologist J. M. Carrier. Like other Latin American specialists exploring this issue, Carrier argues that homosexuality is construed very differently in the U.S. and in Mexico. In the U.S., even one adult homosexual act or acknowledgment of homosexual desire may threaten a man's gender identity and throw open to question his sexual identity as well. In sharp contrast, a Mexican man's masculine gender and heterosexual identity are not threatened by a homosexual act as long as he plays the inserter's role. Only the male who plays the passive sexual role and exhibits feminine gender characteristics is considered to be truly homosexual and is, therefore, stigmatized. This "bisexual" option, an exemption from stigma for the "masculine" homosexual, can be seen as part of the ensemble of gender privileges and sexual prerogatives accorded Mexican men. Thus it is primarily the passive, effeminate homosexual man who becomes the object of derision and societal contempt in Mexico.

The terms used to refer to homosexual Mexican men are generally coded with gendered meaning drawn from the inferior position of women in patriarchal Mexican society. The most benign of these contemptuous terms is *maricón*, a label that highlights the non-conforming gender attributes of the (feminine) homosexual man. Its semantic equivalent in the U.S. is "sissy" or "fairy" (Carrier, "Cultural Factors" 123–24). Terms such as *joto* or *puto*, on the other hand, speak to the passive sexual role taken by these men rather than merely their gender attributes. They are infinitely more derogatory and vulgar in that they underscore the sexually non-conforming nature of their passive/receptive position in the homosexual act. The invective associated with all these appellations speaks to the way effeminate homosexual men are viewed as having betrayed the Mexican man's prescribed gender and sexual role. Moreover, it may be noted that the Spanish feminine word *puta* refers to a female prostitute while its male form *puto* refers to a passive homosexual, not a male prostitute. It is significant that the cultural equation made between the feminine, anal-receptive homosexual man and the most culturally-stigmatized female in Mexican society (the whore) share a common semantic base.[4]

Carrier's research suggests that homosexuality in Mexico is rigidly circumscribed by the prominent role the family plays in structuring homosexual activity. Whereas in the U.S., at least among most European-Americans, the role of the family as a regulator of the lives of gay men and lesbians has progressively declined, in Mexico the family remains a crucial institution that defines both gender and sexual relations between men and women. The Mexican family remains a bastion of patriarchal privilege for men and a major impediment to women's autonomy outside the private world of the home.

The constraints of family life often prevent homosexual Mexican men from securing unrestricted freedom to stay out late at night, to move out of their family's home before marriage, or to take an apartment with a male lover. Thus their opportunities to make homosexual contacts in other than anonymous locations, such as the balconies of movie theaters or certain parks, are severely constrained (Carrier, "Family Attitudes" 368). This situation creates an atmosphere of social interdiction which may explain why homosexuality in Mexico is typically shrouded in silence. The concealment, suppression, or prevention of any open acknowledgment of homosexual activity underscores the stringency of cultural dictates surrounding gender and sexual norms within Mexican family life. Unlike the generally more egalitarian, permissive family life of white middle-class gay men and lesbians in the U.S., the Mexican family appears to play a far more important and restrictive role in structuring homosexual behavior among Mexican men ("Family Attitudes" 373).

Given these constraints and the particular meanings attached to homosexuality in Mexican culture, same-sex behavior in Mexico typically unfolds in the context of an age-stratified hierarchy that grants privileges to older, more masculine men. It is very significant that in instances where two masculine, active men enter into a homosexual encounter, the rules that structure gender-coded homosexual relations continue to operate with full force. In these exchanges one of the men—typically he who is defined as being more masculine or powerful—assumes the active, inserter role while the other man is pressed into the passive, anal-receptive role. Moreover, men who may eventually adopt both active and passive features of homosexual behavior typically do not engage in such reciprocal relations with the same person. Instead, they generally only play the active role with one person (who is always viewed as being the more feminine) and are sexually passive with those they deem more masculine than themselves ("Cultural Factors" 120–21).

In sum, it appears that the major difference between bisexually-active men in Mexico and bisexual males in the U.S. is that the former are not stigmatized because they exclusively play the active, masculine, inserter role. Unlike in the North American context, "one drop of homosexuality" does not, ipso facto, make a Mexican male a *joto* or a *maricón*. As Carrier's research clearly documents, none of the active inserter participants in homosexual encounters ever considers himself a "homosexual" or to be "gay" ("Mexican Male" 83). What may be called the "bisexual escape hatch" functions to insure that the tenuous masculinity of Mexican men is not compromised through the homosexual act; they remain men, *hombres*, even though they participate in this sexual behavior. Moreover, the Mexican sexual system actually militates against the construction of discernable, discrete "bisexual" or "gay" sexual identities because these identities are shaped by and draw upon a different sexual system and foreign discursive practices. One does not, in other words, become "gay" or "lesbian" identified in Mexico because its sexual system precludes such an identity formation in the first place. These "bourgeois" sexual categories are simply not relevant or germane to the way gender and sexual meanings are conferred in Mexican society.

Implications for Chicano Gay Men in the U.S.

The emergence of the modern gay identity in the U.S. and its recent appearance in Mexico have implications for Chicano men that have not been fully explored. What is apparent, however, is that Chicanos, as well as other racial minorities, do not negotiate the acceptance of a gay identity in exactly the same way white American men do. The ambivalence of Chicanos vis-à-vis a gay sexual identity and their attendant uneasiness with white gay/lesbian culture do not necessarily reflect a denial of homosexuality. Rather, I would argue, the slow pace at which this identity formation has taken root among Chicanos is attributable to cultural and structural factors which differentiate the experiences of the white and non-white populations in the U.S.

Aside from the crucial differences discussed above in the way homosexuality is culturally constructed in the Mexican/Latin-American and European- or Anglo-American sexual systems, a number of other structural factors also militate against the emergence of a modern gay identity among Chicano men. In this regard, the progressive loosening of familial constraints among white, middle-class homosexual men and women at the end of the nineteenth century, and its acceleration in the post–World War II period, structurally positioned the white gay and lesbian population to redefine their primary self-identity in terms of their homosexuality. The shift from a family-based economy to a fully developed wage labor system at the end of the nineteenth century dramatically freed European-American men and women from the previously confining social and economic world of the family. It allowed both white men and the white "new woman" of the period to transgress the stifling gender roles that previously bound them to a compulsory heterosexual norm.[5] Extricating the nuclear family from its traditional role as a primary unit of production enabled homosexually inclined individuals to forge a new sexual identity and to develop a culture and community that were not previously possible. Moreover, the tremendous urban migration ignited (or precipitated) by World War II accelerated this process by drawing thousands of homosexuals into urban settings where the possibilities for same-sex intimacy were greater.

It is very apparent, however, that the gay identity and communities that emerged were overwhelmingly white, middle class, and male-centered. Leading figures of the first homophile organizations in the U.S., such as the Mattachine Society, and key individuals shaping the newly emergent gay culture were primarily drawn from this segment of the homosexual population. Moreover, the new communities founded in the postwar period were largely populated by white men who had the resources and talents needed to create "gilded" gay ghettos. This fact has given the contemporary gay community—despite its undeniable diversity—a largely white, middle class, and male form. In other words, the unique class and racial advantages of white gay men provided the foundation upon which they could boldly carve out the new gay identity. Their collective position in the social structure empowered them with the skills and talents needed to create new gay institutions, communities, and a unique sexual subculture.

Despite the intense hostility that, as gay men, they faced during that period, nevertheless, as white gay men, they were in the best position to risk the social ostracism that this process engendered. They were *relatively* better situated than other homosexuals to endure the hazards unleashed by their transgression of gender conventions and traditional heterosexual norms. The diminished importance of ethnic identity among these individuals, due principally to the homogenizing and integrating impact of the dominant racial categories which defined them foremost as white, undoubtedly also facilitated the emergence of gay identity among them. As members of the privileged racial group—and thus no longer viewing themselves primarily as Irish, Italian, Jewish,

Catholic, etc.—these middle-class men and women arguably no longer depended solely on their respective cultural groups and families as a line of defense against the dominant group. Although they may have continued to experience intense cultural dissonance leaving behind their ethnicity and their traditional family-based roles, they were now in a position to dare to make such a move.

Chicanos, on the other hand, have never occupied the social space where a gay or lesbian identity can readily become a primary basis of self-identity. This is due, in part, to their structural position at the subordinate ends of both the class and racial hierarchies, and in a context where ethnicity remains a primary basis of group identity and survival. Moreover, Chicano family life requires allegiance to patriarchal gender relations and to a system of sexual meanings that directly militate against the emergence of this alternative basis of self-identity. Furthermore, factors such as gender, geographical settlement, age, nativity, language usage, and degree of cultural assimilation further prevent, or at least complicate, the acceptance of a gay or lesbian identity by Chicanos or Chicanas respectively. They are not as free as individuals situated elsewhere in the social structure to redefine their sexual identity in ways that contravene the imperatives of minority family life and its traditional gender expectations. How they come to define their sexual identities as gay, straight, bisexual or, in Mexican/Latin-American terms, as an *activo, pasivo,* or *macho marica,* therefore, is not a straightforward or unmediated process. Unfortunately, there are no published studies to date exploring this identity formation process.

However, one unpublished study on homosexual Latino/Chicano men was conducted by Hector Carrillo and Horacio Maiorana in the spring of 1989. As part of their ongoing work on AIDS within the San Francisco Bay Area Latino community, these researchers develop a typology capturing the different points in a continuum differentiating the sexual identity of these men. Their preliminary typology is useful in that it delineates the way homosexual Chicanos/Latinos integrate elements of both the North American and Mexican sexual systems into their sexual behavior.

The first two categories of individuals, according to Carrillo and Maiorana, are: 1) Working-class Latino men who have adopted an effeminate gender persona and usually play the passive role in homosexual encounters (many of them are drag queens who frequent the Latino gay bars in the Mission District of San Francisco); and 2) Latino men who consider themselves heterosexual or bisexual, but who furtively have sex with other men. They are also primarily working class and often frequent Latino gay bars in search of discrete sexual encounters. They tend to retain a strong Latino or Chicano ethnic identity and structure their sexuality according to the Mexican sexual system. Although Carrillo and Maiorana do not discuss the issue, it seems likely that these men would primarily seek out other Latino men, rather than European-Americans, as potential partners in their culturally-circumscribed homosexual behavior.

I would also suggest from personal observation that these two categories of individuals occasionally enter into sexual relationships with middle-class Latinos and European-American men. In so doing, these working-class Latino men often become the object of the middle-class Latino's or the white man's colonial desires. In one expression of this class-coded lust, the effeminate *pasivo* becomes the boyish, feminized object of the middle-class man's colonial desire. In another, the masculine Mexican/Chicano *activo* becomes the embodiment of a potent ethnic masculinity that titillates the middle-class man who thus enters into a passive sexual role.

Unlike the first two categories of homosexually active Latino men, the other three have integrated several features of the North American sexual system into their sexual behavior. They are more likely to be assimilated into the dominant European-American culture of the U.S. and to come from middle-class backgrounds. They include 3) Latino men who openly consider themselves gay and participate in the emergent gay Latino subculture in the Mission district; 4) Latino men who consider themselves gay but do not participate in the Latino gay subculture, preferring to maintain a primary identity as Latino and only secondarily a gay one; and, finally, 5) Latino men who are fully assimilated into the white San Francisco gay male community in the Castro District and retain only a marginal Latino identity.

In contrast to the former two categories, Latino men in the latter three categories are more likely to seek European-American sexual partners and exhibit greater difficulty in reconciling their Latino cultural backgrounds with their gay lifestyle. In my impressionistic observations, these men do not exclusively engage in homosexual behavior that is hierarchically differentiated along the gender-coded lines of the Mexican sexual system. They are more likely to integrate both active and passive sexual roles into their sexuality and to enter into relationships in which the more egalitarian norms of the North American sexual system prevail. We know very little, however, about the actual sexual conduct of these individuals. Research has not yet been conducted on how these men express their sexual desires, how they negotiate their masculinity in light of their homosexuality, and, more generally, how they integrate aspects of the two sexual systems into their everyday sexual conduct.

In the absence of such knowledge, we may seek clues about the social world of Chicano gay men in the perceptive writings of Chicana lesbians. Being the first to shatter the silence on the homosexual experience of the Chicano population, they have candidly documented the perplexing issues Chicanos confront in negotiating the conflicting gender and sexual messages imparted by the coexisting Chicano and European-American cultures. The way in which Chicana lesbians have framed these problems, I believe, is bound to have major significance for the way Chicano men reconcile their homosexual behavior and gay sexual identity within a Chicano cultural context. More than any other lesbian writer's, the extraordinary work of Cherríe Moraga articulates a lucid and complex analysis of the predicament that the middle-class Chicana lesbian and Chicano gay man face in this society. A brief examination of her autobiographical writings offers important insights into the complexities and contradictions that may characterize the experience of homosexuality for all Chicanos and Chicanas in the U.S.

Cherríe Moraga and Chicana Lesbianism

An essential point of departure in assessing Cherríe Moraga's work is an appreciation of the way Chicano family life severely constrains the Chicana's ability to define her life outside of its stifling gender and sexual prescriptions. As a number of Chicana feminist scholars have clearly documented, Chicano family life remains rigidly structured along patriarchal lines that privilege men over women and children.[6] Any violation of these norms is undertaken at great personal risk because Chicanos draw upon the family to resist racism and the ravages of class inequality. Chicano men and women are drawn together in the face of these onslaughts and are closely bound into a family structure that exaggerates unequal gender roles and suppresses sexual non-conformity.[7] Therefore, any deviation from the sacred link binding husband, wife, and child not only threatens the very existence of la familia but also potentially undermines the mainstay of resistance to Anglo racism and class exploitation. "The family, then, becomes all the more ardently protected by oppressed people and the sanctity of this institution is infused like blood into the veins of the Chicano. At all costs, la familia must be preserved," writes Moraga. Thus, "we fight back . . . with our families—with our women pregnant, and our men as indispensable heads. We believe the more severely we protect the sex roles within the family, the stronger we will be as a unit in opposition to the anglo threat" (*Loving* 110).

These cultural prescriptions do not, however, curb the sexually non-conforming behavior of certain Chicanos. As in the case of Mexican homosexual men in Mexico, there exists a modicum of freedom for the Chicano homosexual who retains a masculine gender identity while secretly engaging in the active homosexual role. Moraga has perceptively noted that the Latin cultural norm inflects the sexual behavior of homosexual Chicanos: "Male homosexuality has always been a 'tolerated' aspect of Mexican/Chicano society, as long as it remains 'fringe' . . . But lesbianism, in any form, and male homosexuality which openly avows both the sexual and the emotional elements of the bond, challenge the very foundation of la familia" (111). The openly effeminate Chicano gay man's rejection of heterosexuality is typically seen as a fundamental betrayal of Chicano patriarchal cultural norms. He is viewed as having turned his back on the male role that privileges Chicano men and entitles them to sexual access to women, minors, and even other men. Those who reject these male prerogatives are viewed as non-men, as the cultural equivalents of women. Moraga astutely assesses the situation as one in which "the 'faggot' is the object of Chicano/Mexicano's contempt because he is consciously choosing a role his culture tells him to despise. That of a woman" (111).

The constraints that Chicano family life imposed on Moraga herself are candidly discussed in her provocative autobiographical essays "La Guera" and "A Long Line of Vendidas" in *Loving in the War Years*. In recounting her childhood in Southern California, Moraga describes how she was routinely required to make her brother's bed, iron his shirts, lend him money, and even serve him cold drinks when his friends came to visit their home. The privileged position of men in the Chicano family places women in a secondary, subordinate status. She resentfully acknowledges that "to this day in my mother's home, my brother and father are waited on, including by me" (90). Chicano men have always thought of themselves as superior to Chicanas, she asserts in unambiguous terms: "I have never met any kind of Latino who . . . did not subscribe to the basic belief that men are better" (101). The insidiousness of the patriarchal ideology permeating Chicano family life even shapes the way a mother defines her relationships with her children: "The daughter must constantly earn the mother's love, prove her fidelity to her. The son—he gets her love for free" (102).

Moraga realized early in life that she would find it virtually impossible to attain any meaningful autonomy in that cultural context. It was only in the Anglo world that freedom from oppressive gender and sexual strictures was remotely possible. In order to secure this latitude, she made a necessary choice: to embrace the white world and reject crucial aspects of her Chicana upbringing. In painfully honest terms, she states:

> I gradually became anglocized because I thought it was the only option available to me toward gaining autonomy as a person without being sexually stigmatized. . . . I instinctively made choices which I thought would allow me greater freedom of movement in the future. This meant resisting sex roles as much as I could safely manage and that was far easier in an anglo context than in a Chicano one. (99)

Born to a Chicana mother and an Anglo father, Moraga discovered that being fair-complexioned facilitated her integration into the Anglo social world and contributed immensely to her academic achievement. "My mother's desire to protect her children from poverty and illiteracy" led to their being "anglocized," she writes; "the more effectively we could pass in the white world, the better guaranteed our future" (51). Consequently her life in Southern California during the 1950s and 1960s is described as one in which she "identified with and aspired toward white values" (58). In the process, she "rode the wave of that Southern California privilege as far as conscience would let me" (58).

The price initially exacted by anglicization was estrangement from family and a partial loss of the nurturing and love she found therein. In reflecting on this experience, Moraga acknowledges that "I have had to confront that much of what I value about being Chicana, about my family, has been subverted by anglo culture and my cooperation with it. . . . I realized the major reason

for my total alienation from and fear of my classmates was rooted in class and culture" (54). She poignantly concedes that, in the process, "I had disavowed the language I knew best—ignored the words and rhythms that were closest to me. The sounds of my mother and aunts gossiping— half in English, half in Spanish—while drinking cerveza in the kitchen" (55). What she gained, on the other hand, was the greater autonomy that her middle-class white classmates had in defining their emergent sexuality and in circumventing burdensome gender prescriptions. Her movement into the white world, however, was viewed by Chicanos as a great betrayal. By gaining control of her life, Moraga became one of a "long line of vendidas," traitors or "sell-outs," as self-determined women are seen in the sexist cultural fantasy of patriarchal Chicano society. This is the accusation that "hangs above the heads and beats in the hearts of most Chicanas, seeking to develop our own autonomous sense of ourselves, particularly our sexuality" (103).

Patriarchal Chicano culture, with its deep roots in "the institution of heterosexuality," requires Chicanas to commit themselves to Chicano men and subordinate to them their own sexual desires. "[The Chicano] too, like any other man," Moraga writes, "wants to be able to determine how, when, and with whom his women—mother, wife, and daughter—are sexual" (110–11). But "the Chicana's sexual commitment to the Chicano male [is taken as] proof of her fidelity to her people" (105). "It is no wonder," she adds, that most "Chicanas often divorce ourselves from conscious recognition of our own sexuality" (119). In order to claim the identity of a Chicana lesbian, Moraga had to take "a radical stand in direct contradiction to, and in violation of, the women [sic] I was raised to be" (117); and yet she also drew upon themes and images of her Mexican Catholic background. Of its impact on her sexuality Moraga writes:

> I always knew that I felt the greatest emotional ties with women, but suddenly I was beginning to consciously identify those feelings as sexual. The more potent my dreams and fantasies

became and the more I sensed my own exploding sexual power, the more I *retreated* from my body's messages and into the region of religion. By giving definition and meaning to my desires, religion became the discipline to control my sexuality. Sexual fantasy and rebellion became "impure thoughts" and "sinful acts." (119)

These "contrary feelings," which initially surfaced around the age of twelve, unleashed feelings of guilt and moral transgression. She found it impossible to leave behind the Catholic Church's prohibitions regarding homosexuality, and religious themes found their way into how she initially came to define herself as a sexual subject—in a devil-like form. "I wrote poems describing myself as a centaur: half-animal/half-human, hairy-rumped and cloven-hoofed, como el diablo. The images emerged from a deeply Mexican and Catholic place" (124).

As her earliest sexual feelings were laden with religious images, so too were they shaped by images of herself in a male-like form. This is understandable in light of the fact that only men in Chicano culture are granted sexual subjectivity. Consequently, Moraga instinctively gravitated toward a butch persona and assumed a male-like stance toward other women.

> In the effort to avoid embodying la chingada, I became the chingón. In the effort not to feel fucked, I became the fucker, even with women. . . . The fact of the matter was that all those power struggles of "having" and "being had" were played out in my own bedroom. And in my psyche, they held a particular Mexican twist. (126)

In a candid and courageously outspoken conversation with lesbian activist Amber Hollibaugh, Moraga recounts that

> . . . what turned me on sexually, at a very early age, had to do with the fantasy of capture, taking a woman, and my identification was with the man. . . . The truth is, I do have some real gut-level misgivings about my sexual connection with capture. It might feel very sexy to imagine "taking" a woman, but it has some-

times occurred at the expense of my feeling, sexually, like I can surrender myself to a woman; that is, always needing to be the one in control, calling the shots. It's a very butch trip and I feel like this can keep me private and protected and can prevent me from fully being able to express myself. (Moraga and Hollibaugh 396)

Moraga's adult lesbian sexuality defined itself along the traditional butch/femme lines characteristic of lesbian relationships in the post-war period.[8] It is likely that such an identity formation was also largely an expression of the highly gender-coded sexuality imparted through Chicano family life. In order to define herself as an autonomous sexual subject, she embraced a butch, or more masculine, gender persona, and crystallized a sexual desire for feminine, or femme, lovers.

The Final Frontier: Unmasking the Chicano Gay Man

Moraga's experience is certainly only one expression of the diverse ways in which Chicana lesbians come to define their sense of gender and experience their homosexuality. But her odyssey reflects and articulates the tortuous and painful path traveled by working-class Chicanas (and Chicanos) who embrace the middle-class Anglo world and its sexual system in order to secure, ironically, the "right to passion expressed in our own cultural tongue and movements" (136). It is apparent from her powerful autobiographical writings, however, how much her adult sexuality was also inevitably shaped by the gender and sexual messages imparted through the Chicano family.

How this complex process of integrating, reconciling, and contesting various features of both Anglo and Chicano cultural life are experienced by Chicano gay men, has yet to be fully explored. Moraga's incisive and extraordinarily frank autobiographical account raises numerous questions about the parallels in the homosexual development of Chicana lesbians and Chicano gay men. How, for example, do Chicano male homosexuals internalize and reconcile the gender-specific prescriptions of Chicano culture? How does this primary socialization impact on the way they define their gender personas and sexual identities? How does socialization into a patriarchal gender system that privileges men over women and the masculine over the feminine structure intimate aspects of their sexual behavior? Do most Chicano gay men invariably organize aspects of their sexuality along the hierarchical lines of dominance/subordination that circumscribe gender roles and relationships in Chicano culture? My impression is that many Chicano gay men share the Chicano heterosexual man's underlying disdain for women and all that is feminine. Although it has not been documented empirically, it is likely that Chicano gay men incorporate and contest crucial features of the Mexican/Latin-American sexual system into their intimate sexual behavior. Despite having accepted a "modern" sexual identity, they are not immune to the hierarchical, gender-coded system of sexual meanings that is part and parcel of this discursive practice.

Until we can answer these questions through ethnographic research on the lives of Chicano gay men, we must continue to develop the type of feminist critique of Chicano male culture that is so powerfully articulated in the work of lesbian authors such as Cherríe Moraga. We are fortunate that courageous voices such as hers have irretrievably shattered the silence on the homosexual experience within the Mexican American community. Her work, and that of other Chicana lesbians, has laid a challenge before Chicano gay men to lift the lid on their homosexual experiences and to leave the closeted space they have been relegated to in Chicano culture. The task confronting us, therefore, is to begin interpreting and redefining what it means to be both Chicano and gay in a cultural setting that has traditionally viewed these categories as a contradiction in terms. This is an area of scholarly research that can no longer be left outside the purview of Chicano Studies, Gay and Lesbian Studies, or even more traditional lines of sociological inquiry.

Notes

1. See, for example, the writings by Chicana and Latina lesbians in Ramos; Alarcón, Castillo, and Moraga; Moraga and Anzaldúa; and Anzaldúa. See also the following studies on Latinas: Arguelles and Rich; Espin; and Hidalgo and Hidalgo-Christensen.

2. See Bruce-Novoa's interesting discussion of homosexuality as a theme in the Chicano novel.

3. There is a rich literature documenting the ways in which our sexuality is largely structured through sexual scripts that are culturally defined and individually internalized. See, for example, Gagnon and Simon; Simon and Gagnon; and Plummer. What is being referred to here as the Mexican/Latin-American sexual system is part of the circum-Mediterranean construction of gender and sexual meaning. In this regard, see the introduction and essays in Gilmore. For further discussion of this theme in the Mexican context, see Alonso and Koreck. Their essay, which uses many of the same sources as the present essay, explores male homosexual practices in Mexico in relation to AIDS.

4. In "Birth of the Queen," Trumback has perceptively documented that many of the contemporary terms used to refer to homosexual men in Western Europe and the United States (such as queen, punk, gay, faggot, and fairy) also were at one time the slang term for prostitutes (137). See also Alonso and Koreck, 111–113.

5. For a broad overview of the development of a gay and lesbian identity and community in the United States, see D'Emilio; D'Emilio and Freedman; and Katz. A number of articles in the important anthology edited by Duberman, Vicinus, and Chauncey document the white middle class–centered nature of gay/lesbian identity construction and community formation.

6. Some of the very best research in Chicano studies has been conducted by Chicana feminists who have explored the intersection of class, race, and gender in Chicanas' lives. Some recent examples of this impressive scholarship include Zavella; Segura; Pesquera; and Baca-Zinn.

7. This solidarity is captured in the early Chicano movement poster fittingly entitled "La Familia." It consists of three figures in a symbolic pose: a Mexican woman, with a child in her arms, is embraced by a Mexican man, who is centrally positioned in the portrait and a head taller. This poster symbolized the

patriarchal, male-centered privileging of the heterosexual, nuclear family in Chicano resistance against white racism. For a provocative discussion of these themes in the Chicano movement, see Gutiérrez.

8. For an interesting discussion of the butch/femme formulation among working-class white women at the time, see Davis and Kennedy; and Nestle.

References

Adam, Barry D. "Homosexuality without a Gay World: Pasivos y Activos en Nicaragua." *Out/Look* 1.4 (1989): 74–82.

Alarcón, Norma. "Chicana's Feminist Literature: A Re-vision Through Malintzin/or Malintzin: Putting Flesh Back on the Object." Moraga and Anzaldúa 182–90.

Alarcón, Norma, Ana Castillo, and Cherríe Moraga, eds. *Third Woman: The Sexuality of Latinas*. Berkeley: Third Woman, 1989.

Alonso, Ana Maria, and Maria Theresa Koreck. "Silences: 'Hispanics,' AIDS, and Sexual Practices." *differences: A Journal of Feminist Cultural Studies* 1.1 (1989): 101–24.

Anzaldúa, Gloria. *Borderlands/La Frontera: The New Mestiza*. San Francisco: Spinsters, 1987.

Arguelles, Lourdes, and B. Ruby Rich. "Homosexuality, Homophobia, and Revolution: Notes Toward an Understanding of the Cuban Lesbian and Gay Male Experience, Part 1." *Signs: Journal of Woman in Culture and Society* 9 (1984): 683–99.

———. "Homosexuality, Homophobia, and Revolution: Notes Toward an Understanding of the Cuban Lesbian and Gay Male Experience, Part 2." *Signs: Journal of Women in Culture and Society* 11 (1985): 120–36.

Baca-Zinn, Maxine. "Chicano Men and Masculinity." *The Journal of Ethnic Studies* 10.2 (1982): 29–44.

———. "Familism Among Chicanos: A Theoretical Review." *Humboldt Journal of Social Relations* 10.1 (1982–83): 224–38.

Blackwood, Evelyn, ed. *The Many Faces of Homosexuality: Anthropological Approaches to Homosexual Behavior*. New York: Harrington Park, 1989.

Bruce-Novoa, Juan. "Homosexuality and the Chicano Novel." *Confluencia: Revista Hispanica de Cultura y Literatura* 2.1 (1986): 69–77.

Carrier, Joseph M. "Cultural Factors Affecting Urban Mexican Male Homosexual Behavior." *The Archives of Sexual Behavior: An Interdisciplinary Research Journal* 5.2 (1976): 103–24.

———. "Family Attitudes and Mexican Male Homosexuality." *Urban Life: A Journal of Ethnographic Research* 5.3 (1976): 359–76.

———. "Gay Liberation and Coming Out in Mexico." Herdt 225–53.

———. "Mexican Male Bisexuality." *Bisexualities: Theory and Research*. Ed. F. Klein and T. Wolf. New York: Haworth, 1985. 75–85.

Carrillo, Hector, and Horacio Maiorana. "AIDS Prevention Among Gay Latinos in San Francisco: From Behavior Change to Social Change." Unpublished ms., 1989.

Davis, Madeline, and Elizabeth Lapovsky Kennedy. "Oral History and the Study of Sexuality in the Lesbian Community: Buffalo, New York, 1940–1960." Duberman 426–40.

D'Emilio, John. "Capitalism and Gay Identity." Snitow, Stansell, and Thompson 100–13.

———. *Sexual Politics, Sexual Communities: The Making of a Homosexual Minority in the United States, 1940–1970*. Chicago: U of Chicago P, 1983.

D'Emilio, John, and Estelle B. Freedman. *Intimate Matters: A History of Sexuality in America*. New York: Harper, 1988.

Duberman, Martin Bauml, Martha Vicinus, and George Chauncey Jr., eds. *Hidden from History: Reclaiming the Gay and Lesbian Past*. New York: NAL, 1989.

Espin, Oliva M. "Cultural and Historical Influences on Sexuality in Hispanic/Latin Women: Implications for Psychotherapy." *Pleasure and Danger: Exploring Female Sexuality*. Ed. Carol Vance. London: Routledge, 1984, 149–63.

———. "Issues of Identity in the Psychology of Latina Lesbians." *Lesbian Psychologies*. Ed. Boston Lesbian Psychologies Collective. Urbana: U of Illinois P, 1987. 35–55.

Freud, Sigmund. *Three Essays on the Theory of Sexuality*. 1905. *The Standard Edition of the Complete Psychological Works of Sigmund Freud*. Trans. and ed. James Strachey. Vol. 7. London: Hogarth, 1953. 123–243.

Gagnon, John H., and William Simon. *Sexual Conduct: The Social Sources of Human Sexuality*. Chicago: Aldine, 1973.

Gilmore, David D., ed. *Honor and Shame and the Unity of the Mediterranean*. No. 22, Washington: American Anthropological Association, 1987.

Goldwert, Marvin. "Mexican Machismo: The Flight from Femininity." *Psychoanalytic Review* 72.1 (1985): 161–69.

Gutiérrez, Ramón. "Community, Patriarchy, and Individualism: The Politics of Chicano History and the Dream of Equality." Forthcoming in *American Quarterly*.

Herdt, Gilbert, ed. *Gay and Lesbian Youth*. New York: Haworth, 1989.

Hidalgo, Hilda, and Elia Hidalgo-Christensen. "The Puerto Rican Lesbian and the Puerto Rican Community." *Journal of Homosexuality* 2 (1976–77): 109–21.

———. "The Puerto Rican Cultural Response to Female Homosexuality." *The Puerto Rican Woman*. Ed. Edna Acosta-Belen. New York: Praeger, 1979. 110–23.

Islas, Arturo. *Immigrant Souls*. New York: Morrow, 1990.

———. *The Rain God: A Desert Tale*. Palo Alto, CA: Alexandrian, 1984.

Katz, Jonathan Ned. *Gay/Lesbian Almanac: A New Documentary*. New York: Harper, 1983.

Lancaster, Roger N. "Subject Honor and Object Shame: The Construction of Male Homosexuality and Stigma in Nicaragua." *Ethnology* 27.2 (1987): 111–25.

Martin, Robert K. "Knights-Errant and Gothic Seducers: The Representation of Male Friendship in Mid-Nineteenth Century America." Duberman 169–82.

Moraga, Cherríe. *Loving in the War Years: Lo que nunca pasó por sus labios*. Boston: South End, 1983.

Moraga, Cherríe, and Gloria Anzaldúa, eds. *This Bridge Called My Back: Writings by Radical Women of Color*. Watertown, MA: Persephone, 1981.

Moraga, Cherríe, and Amber Hollibaugh. "What We're Rollin Around in Bed With: Sexual Silences in Feminism." Snitow, Stansell, and Thompson 394–405.

Nestle, Joan. "Butch–Fem Relationships: Sexual Courage in the 1950s." *Heresies* 12 (1981): 21–24.

Newton, Esther. "The Mythic Mannish Lesbian: Radcliffe Hall and the New Woman." Duberman 281–93.

Parker, Richard. "Youth Identity, and Homosexuality: The Changing Shape of Sexual Life in Contemporary Brazil." Herdt 269–89.

———. "Masculinity, Femininity, and Homosexuality: On the Anthropological Interpretation of Sexual Meanings in Brazil." Blackwood 155–64.

Paz, Octavio. *Labyrinth of Solitude: Life and Thought in Mexico*. New York: Grove, 1961.

Pesquera, Beatriz M. "Work and Family: A Comparative Analysis of Professional, Clerical and Blue-Collar Chicana Workers." PhD diss. U of California, Berkeley, 1985.

Plummer, Kenneth. "Symbolic Interaction and Sexual Conduct: An Emergent Perspective." *Human Sexual Relations*. Ed. Mike Brake. New York: Pantheon, 1982. 223–44.

Ramos, Juanita, ed. *Compañeras: Latina Lesbians*. New York: Latina Lesbian History Project, 1987.

Rechy. John. *City of Night*. New York: Grove, 1963.

———. *Numbers*. New York: Grove, 1967.

———. *Rushes*. New York: Grove, 1979.

———. *The Sexual Outlaw*. New York: Grove, 1977.

Rodriguez, Richard. *Hunger of Memory: The Education of Richard Rodriguez, An Autobiography*. Boston: Godine, 1982.

———. "Late Victorians: San Francisco, AIDS, and the Homosexual Stereotype." *Harper's Magazine* Oct. 1990: 57–66.

Rupp, Leila J. "Imagine My Surprise: Woman's Relationships in Mid-Twentieth Century America." Duberman 395–410.

Segura, Denise. "Chicana and Mexican Immigrant Women in the Labor Market: A Study of Occupational Mobility and Stratification." PhD diss. U of California, Berkeley, 1986.

———. "Chicana and Mexican Immigrant Women at Work: The Impact of Class, Race, and Gender on Occupational Mobility." *Gender and Society* 3.1 (1989): 37–52.

———. "The Interplay of Familism and Patriarchy on Employment Among Chicana and Mexican Women." *Renato Rosaldo Lecture Series* 5 (1989): 35–53.

Simon, William, and John H. Gagnon. "Sexual Scripts: Permanence and Change." *Archives of Sexual Behavior* 15.2 (1986): 97–120.

Smith-Rosenberg, Carroll. "Discourses of Sexuality and Subjectivity: The New Woman, 1870–1936." Duberman 264–80.

Snitow, Ann, Christine Stansell, and Sharon Thompson, eds. *Powers of Desire: The Politics of Sexuality*. New York: Monthly Review, 1983.

Taylor, Clark L. "Mexican Male Homosexual Interaction in Public Contexts." Blackwood 117–36.

Trumbach, Randolph. "The Birth of the Queen: Sodomy and the Emergence of Gender Equality in Modern Culture, 1660–1750." Duberman 129–40.

Zavella, Patricia. *Women's Work and Chicano Families: Cannery Workers of the Santa Clara Valley*. Ithaca: Cornell UP, 1987.

Susan D. Cochran
Vickie M. Mays

Sociocultural Facets of the Black Gay Male Experience

Prior to the appearance of AIDS in this country, studies on the sexual preferences and behaviors of gay men generally ignored the specific experiences of Black men (Bell, Weinberg, and Hammersmith 1981). With the press of the AIDS epidemic to develop baseline information on men's intimate behaviors, this tendency rarely to study Black gay men, or to do so in the same manner as White gay men, persists. While many researchers may recognize the importance of possible cultural differences, their approach has been to assume that Black gay men would be more like White gay men than Black heterosexuals. Questionnaires, sampling procedures, and topics of focus have been more consistent with White gay men's experiences (see Becker and Joseph 1988, for a comprehensive review of behavior change studies). This proclivity has resulted in an emergence of comparisons between Black and White men using White gay standards of behavior that may be obscuring our understanding of important psychosocial determinants of sexual behaviors in Black gay men. Given the differences that have been observed in family structure and sexual patterns between Black and White heterosexuals, there is no empirical basis upon which to assume

that Black gay men's experience of homosexuality would perfectly mimic that of Whites (Bell, Weinberg, and Hammersmith 1981). Indeed, very little is known empirically about the lives of Black gay men (Mays and Cochran 1987), though there are some indications, discussed below, that they are more likely to engage in activities that place them at greater risk for HIV infection.

In the absence of any data we need to proceed cautiously with assumptions that imply anything other than [that] same-sex *activities* of Black gay men resemble those of White gay men. This caution is particularly true for AIDS studies that purport to study psychosocial behavior. Studies of this type report not only on behavior but also attempt to describe motivations and circumstances that lead to the behavior. In the absence of a set of questions or framework incorporating important cultural, ethnic, and economic realities of Black gay men, interpretations emanating from a White gay male standard may be misleading.

Development of a Black Gay Identity

In recent years, researchers (Spanier and Glick 1980; Staples 1981; Guttentag and Secord 1983) have noted differences between Whites and Blacks in their intimate heterosexual relationships. Differential sociocultural factors presumably influence the development and specific structure of sexual behavior within Black heterosexual relationships. These factors include the unavailability of the same ethnic group partners, fewer social and financial resources, residential immobility, and lack of employment opportunities. Many of these same conditions may surround the formation, maintenance, and functioning of Black gay male relationships.

Popular writings in past years by Black gay men describe the difficulty in finding other Black gay men for potential partners, the lack of a visible Black gay community, an absence of role models, and the dearth of Black gay male social or professional organizations (Soares 1979; Beame 1983). While gay bars, gay baths, and public places existed where White gay men gathered, some of these were off limits to Black gay men either due to actual or perceived racism within the White gay community or the danger of passing through White neighborhoods in order to participate in gay community activities. Thus, expectations that the experiences of Black gay men are identical to those of White gay men seem unwarranted.

In examining differences between Blacks and Whites in the emergence of a homosexual orientation, Bell, Weinberg, and Hammersmith (1981) found that, for the White males, pre-adult sexual feelings appeared to be very important. In contrast, among Black males, childhood and adolescent sexual activities, rather than feelings, were stronger predictors of the development of adult homosexual sexual orientation. Thus, Blacks started to act at an earlier age on their sexual inclinations than Whites did (Bell, Weinberg, and Hammersmith 1981). This would be consistent with Black–White differences in the onset of heterosexual sexual activity if socioeconomic status is not statistically controlled for (Wyatt, personal communication).

The typical conceptualization of sexual orientation is that individuals are located in terms of their sexual feelings and behaviors on a bipolar dimension where one extreme is heterosexuality, the other is homosexuality, and lying somewhere in between is bisexuality (Bell and Weinberg 1978). This definition does not include ethnicity or culture as an interactive factor influencing the expression of sexual behavior or sexual orientation. For example, Smith (1986) makes a dis-

tinction between Black gays and gay Blacks complicating the demarcation between homosexuality and bisexuality:

> Gay Blacks are people who identify first as being gay and who usually live outside the closet in predominantly white gay communities. I would estimate that they amount to roughly ten percent of all Black homosexuals. Black gays, on the other hand, view our racial heritage as primary and frequently live "bisexual front lives" within Black neighborhoods. (p. 226)

These two groups are probably quite different in both social activities and sexual behaviors. The Black gay man, strongly identified with Afro-American culture, will often look and behave much like the Black heterosexual man except in his sexual behavior. The extent to which his same-sex partners are integrated into his family and social environment may be a function of his class status (Soares 1979). It has long been noted by Blacks that there are differences, both in values and behaviors, between middle-class and working-class Blacks. There is no reason to assume that within the Black gay community such diversity would not persist. While Smith (1986) has described the Black gay community in only two dimensions we would be remiss if we stopped here. There is a growing population of Black gays who have forged an identity acknowledging both statuses:

> At times I cried just remembering how it is to be both Black and gay during these truly difficult times. But here we are, still proud and living, with a culture all our own. (Sylvester, p. 11, 1986)

We know less about the behavior of Black men who identify as bisexual and least about those Black men who engage in same-sex sexual behavior but identify as exclusively heterosexual. When the factor of social class is added the distinction between homosexuality and heterosexuality may become even more blurred. Among lower socioeconomic Black men, those engaged in same-sex sexual activities, regardless of their sexual object choices, may appear on the surface no different from Black heterosexuals. If the support systems of Black gay men are like those of Black lesbians (Cochran and Mays 1986), fewer economic resources result in a greater reliance on a Black social network (both gay and heterosexual) for tangible and emotional support, a strong tendency to live in predominantly ethnic neighborhoods, and the maintenance of emotionally and economically close family ties.

This extensive integration into the Black heterosexual world may not only be a function of fewer economic resources, but also of ethnic identification. The culture of gay life, generally perceived to be White, may not be synonymous with the norms of Black culture. Choices of how to dress, what language to use, where to live, and whom to have as friends are all affected by culture. The White gay community, while diverse, has developed norms concerning language, social behavior, and other demarcations (Warren 1974) that may not mesh well with certain subgroups of Black gays. For example, in the past there has been a heavy emphasis in the gay White community (except among the middle-aged, middle-class closeted gay men) on socializing in public places—bars, beaches, and resorts (Warren, 1974). In contrast, the Black gay community places greater emphasis on home entertainment that is private and not public, perhaps as a holdover from the days when discrimination in many public places was common. This pattern of socializing would facilitate the development of a distinct Black gay culture (Soares 1979).

It is perhaps this difference in socializing that has frustrated health educators attempting to do AIDS education through the social network in gay bars. Generally, they have found that they do not reach a significant number of Black men using this technique. An understanding of the Black gay community makes salient that risk reduction strategies should focus on "risk behaviors" and *not* "risk groups." Emphasizing risk reduction strategies that rely on group membership requires

a social and personal identification by Black men that for many may not be relevant.

Sexual Behavior

Bell and Weinberg, in a 1978 study comparing sexual activities of White and Black gay men, found that Blacks were more likely to report having engaged in anal sex, both passively and actively, than White gay men. In terms of our current knowledge of AIDS, this appears to be one of the highest risk factors for contracting the HIV virus (Friedland and Klein 1987).

A second aspect of Black gay men's sexuality is that they may be more bisexual in their behaviors than White gay men. Evidence for this comes again from Bell and Weinberg (1978) who reported that Black gay men were significantly more likely to have engaged in heterosexual coitus (22 percent) in the previous twelve months than White gay men (14 percent). This seems to be borne out nationally by the AIDS statistics. Among male homosexual/bisexual AIDS patients, Black men are more likely than White men to be classified as bisexual (30 percent versus 13 percent) rather than homosexual (70 percent versus 87 percent). Due to the intense homophobia in the Black community and the factors we discussed above, men may be more likely to remain secretive regarding their homosexual activities (Mays and Cochran 1987). This may provide a mode of transmission of the AIDS virus outside of an already identified high risk group.

There are several other differences between Black and White gay men noted in the Kinsey Institute data that have implications for contracting the HIV virus. Looking at sexual behavior both pre- and post-Stonewall, Black gay men, in comparison to White gay men, were more likely to be sexually active across ethnic boundaries and less likely to report that their sexual partners were strangers (Gebhard and Johnson 1979; Bell and Weinberg 1978). Sexual practices post-Stonewall underwent profound change in the gay community. Black gay men were a part of that change

(Gebhard and Johnson 1979; Bell and Weinberg 1978). However, these differences in meeting partners or choice of partners remain. They are apparently less malleable to change than specific risk-related sexual behaviors.

While the 1978 Bell and Weinberg study was conducted on a small sample in the San Francisco area, it is suggestive of the need for further research to assess the prevalence of risk behaviors and strategies most effective for decreasing risk. Indeed, a recent report of ethnically based differences in syphilis incidence rates (Landrum, Beck-Sague, and Kraus 1988) suggests Black gay men are less likely than White gay men to be practicing "safer sex." Sexual behavior has multiple determinants and it is important that variables such as culture, ethnic identification, and class be incorporated into health education programs designed to promote sexual behavior change by Black men.

Intravenous Drug Use

IV drug use is more common in the Black community (Gary and Berry 1985), which may explain the higher than expected prevalence of Blacks in the co-categories of IV drug user and homosexual/bisexual male. HIV infection is endemic among IV drug users in the urbanized Northeast who themselves are most likely to be Black (Ginzburg, MacDonald, and Glass 1987). Ethnic differences exist between the percentage of homosexual/bisexual men with AIDS who are also IV drug users; for White gay and bisexual men with AIDS, 9 percent have histories of IV drug use, while for Blacks the figure is 16 percent. Black gays and bisexual men who do not use IV drugs may also be at increased risk because they are more likely than Whites to be sexual partners of Black men who are IV drugs users. In the Bell and Weinberg study (1978), 22 percent of White men had never had sex with a Black man, whereas for Black respondents, only 2 percent had never had sex with a White man.

Alcohol as a Cofactor

Recently, alcohol use has been implicated as a cofactor facilitating the occurrence of high risk sexual behavior among gay men (Stall et al. 1986). In predicting alcohol use among Black gay and bisexual men, one might expect that normative use patterns will be influenced by what is common behavior in both the Black community and gay community.

Norms for alcohol use in the Black community reflect a polarization of attitudes, shaped on the one hand by traditional religious fundamentalism and rural southern heritage and on the other by a focus on socializing in environments where drinking is common, such as bars, nightclubs, and home parties (Herd 1986). This latter norm is more prevalent in urban Black communities. Blacks and Whites vary in small ways in their drinking patterns, although Blacks are more likely to suffer negative consequences, including alcohol-related mortality and morbidity, from their drinking than are Whites. Current rates of mortality due to liver cirrhosis indicate that rates are 10 times higher in Black men aged 25–34 as compared to White males. While drinking is found across all socioeconomic groups of Blacks, health and social problems associated with drinking have been found more often in low income urban Blacks (Lex 1987). Similarly, for this group it was found that Black males 30–59 were most likely to use alcohol to face the stress of everyday life situations. This is the group most affected by HIV infection.

Within the gay male community, alcohol abuse is a serious problem (Icard and Traunstein 1987). This may result from both the sociocultural stress of discrimination and the tendency for gay-oriented establishments to be drinking establishments as well. Thus, gay men frequently socialize in environments where alcohol consumption is normative.

Black gay and bisexual men, depending upon their relative identification with the Black or gay community, would be expected to demonstrate behavior consistent with these norms. For some, this might mean a high level of abstinence apart from social drinking consistent with other Black Americans; for others, alcohol consumption might more closely resemble that of White gay men with concomitantly higher rates of alcohol dependency.

Crossing Traditional Risk Groups' Boundaries

Early AIDS epidemiologic tracking programs conceptualize the disease as a result of the gay lifestyle (Mays 1988). Indeed, now discarded names for different manifestations of the illness included Gay-related Immunodeficiency Disease and Gay cancer. This focus on discrete risk factors continues to the present, although the additional populations of IV drug abusers, hemophiliacs, persons born in Haiti and Central Africa, and recipients of blood transfusions after 1978 have been added to the list. For Whites, this approach is highly successful, describing the presumed HIV transmission vector in 94 percent of cases; for native-born Blacks, the percentage of cases accurately labeled by a single risk factor (including the combination of IV drug use and male homosexual sexual contact) drops to 88 percent (Cochran 1987). This underscores the reality that sociocultural factors varying across ethnic groups strongly influence individuals' behavior, and by this their risk of contracting HIV.

For Black gay and bisexual men, the reliance on highly specified risk groups (or factors) ignores the fundamental nature of their behavioral location in society. The multiplicity of their identities may indirectly increase their risk for HIV infection by exposing them to more diverse populations (Grob 1983).

First, as Blacks, they are behaviorally closer to two epicenters of the AIDS epidemic. IV drug use and foreign-born Blacks (primarily those from Haiti and Central Africa where HIV infection is more common). Social and behavioral segregation by ethnic status is still a reality of the American experience and Black gay and bisexual men suffer, like other Blacks, from pervasive racism.

As we noted above, if their social support systems are similar to what we know of Black lesbians (Cochran and Mays 1986), extensive integration into the Black heterosexual community is common. Behaviorally, this may include both IV drug use and heterosexual activity with HIV infected individuals. Thus Black gay and bisexual men are at increased risk for HIV infection simply by virtue of being Black.

Second, as men who have sex with other men, Black gay and bisexual men are often members of the broader gay community in which ethnicity probably reflects the general U.S. population (84 percent White). Black gay and bisexual men may have relatively open sexual access to White men, although racism in the community may preclude other forms of socializing (Icard 1985). Data from the Bell and Weinberg study (1978) suggest several interesting differences, as well as similarities, between White and Black gay men. Blacks reported equivalent numbers of sexual partners, both lifetime (median = 100–249 partners) and in the previous 12 months (median = 20–50), as Whites. Although they were significantly less likely than White gay men to engage in anonymous sexual contacts (51 percent versus 79 percent of partners), more than two-thirds reported that more than half their sexual partners were White men. In contrast, none of the White respondents reported that more than half their partners were Black. It should be kept in mind, however, that a greater percentage of the White sample (14 percent) was recruited at bath houses than the Black sample (2 percent). Nevertheless, at least sexually, Black gay men appear to be well integrated into the gay community. Therefore, Black gay and bisexual men are also at higher risk for HIV infection because they are behaviorally close to another epicenter of the AIDS epidemic: the gay male community.

Third, as a social grouping unto itself, the Black gay and bisexual male community may be more diverse than the White gay community (Icard 1985). Some men identify more closely with the Black community than the gay community (Black gay men); others find their primary emotional affinity with the gay community and not the Black community (gay Black men). To the extent that this diversity of identity is reflected in behavioral diversity as well, HIV transmission may be greatly facilitated (Denning 1987).

Thus Black gay and bisexual men are individuals often located behaviorally at the crossroads of HIV transmission. Their multiple social identities make it more likely that the practicing of high risk behavior, whether sexual or needle-sharing, will occur in the presence of HIV.

Perceptions of Risk

There may be a reluctance among Black gay and bisexual men to engage in risk reduction behaviors because of the perception by some members of the Black community that AIDS is a "gay White disease," or a disease of intravenous drug users (Mays and Cochran 1987). In addition, many risk reduction programs are located within outreach programs of primarily White gay organizations. These organizations often fail to attract extensive participation by Black gay men.

Research findings suggest that the personal perception of being at risk is most often influenced by accurate knowledge of one's actual risk and personal experiences with the AIDS epidemic (McKusick, Horstman, and Coates 1985). There may be a variety of reasons why Black gay and bisexual men do not see themselves as at risk. These include the notion of relative risk and a lack of ethnically credible sources for encouraging risk perceptions (Mays and Cochran 1988). Relative risk refers to the importance of AIDS in context with other social realities. For example, poverty, with its own attendant survival risks, may outweigh the fear of AIDS in a teenager's decision to engage in male prostitution. Economic privilege, more common in the White gay community, assists in permitting White gay men to focus their energies and concerns on the AIDS epidemic. For Black gay men of lesser economic privilege other pressing realities of life may, to some extent, diffuse such concerns. Credible

sources relate to the issues that we have presented here of ethnic identification. Black gay men who are emotionally and behaviorally distant from the White community may tend to discount media messages from White sources.

References

Bakeman, R., J. Lumb, R. E. Jackson, and P. N. Whitley. 1987. "The Incidence of AIDS among Blacks and Hispanics." *Journal of the National Medical Association* 79: 921–928.

Beame, T. 1983. "Racism from a Black Perspective." In *Black Men/White Men: A Gay Anthology*. M. J. Smith ed. San Francisco: Gay Sunshine Press.

Becker, M. H. and J. G. Joseph. 1988. "AIDS and Behavioral Change to Reduce Risk: A Review." *American Journal of Public Health* 78: 394–410.

Bell, A. P. and M. S. Weinberg. 1978. *Homosexualities: A Study of Diversity among Men and Women*. New York: Simon & Schuster.

Bell, A. P., M. S. Weinberg, and S. K. Hammersmith. 1981. *Sexual Preference: Its Development in Men and Women*. Bloomington: Indiana University Press.

Bureau of the Census. 1983. "General Population Characteristics, 1980." U.S. Department of Commerce: U.S. Government Printing Office.

Centers for Disease Control, Acquired Immunodeficiency Syndrome (AIDS) Weekly Surveillance Report, United States AIDS Activity, Center for Infectious Diseases, April 4, 1988.

Centers for Disease Control. 1987. "Human Immunodeficiency Virus Infection in the United States: A Review of Current Knowledge." *Morbidity and Mortality Weekly* 36 (Suppl. no. S-6): 1–48.

Cochran, S. D. 1987. "Numbers That Obscure the Truth: Bias in Data Presentation." Paper presented at the meetings of the American Psychological Association, New York, August.

Cochran, S. D. and V. M. Mays. 1986. "Sources of Support among Black Lesbians." Paper presented at the meetings of the American Psychological Association, Washington, D.C., August.

Cochran, S. D., V. M. Mays, and V. Roberts. 1988. "Ethnic Minorities and AIDS." In *Nursing Care of Patients with AIDS/ARC*, A. Lewis ed., pp. 17–24. Maryland: Aspen Publishers.

Denning, P. J. 1987. "Computer Models of AIDS Epidemiology." *American Scientist* 75: 347–351.

Friedland, G. H. and R. S. Klein. 1987. "Transmission of the Human Immunodeficiency Virus." *New England Journal of Medicine* 317: 1125–1135.

Friedman, S. R., J. L. Sotheran, A. Abdul-Quader, B. J. Primm, D. C. Des Jarlais, P. Kleinman, C. Mauge, D. S. Goldsmith, W. El-Sadr, and R. Maslansky. 1987. "The AIDS Epidemic among Blacks and Hispanics." *The Milbank Quarterly* 65, Suppl. 2.

Gary, L. E. and G. L. Berry. 1985. "Predicting Attitudes toward Substance Use in a Black Community: Implications for Prevention." *Community Mental Health Journal* 21: 112–118.

Gebhard, P. H. and A. B. Johnson. 1979. *The Kinsey Data: Marginal Tabulations of the 1938–1963 Interviews Conducted by the Institute for Sex Research.* Philadelphia: W. B. Saunders Co.

Ginzburg, H. M., M. G. MacDonald, and J. W. Glass. 1987. "AIDS, HTLV-III Diseases, Minorities and Intravenous Drug Abuse." *Advances in Alcohol and Substance Abuse* 6: 7–21.

Gottlieb, M. S., H. M. Schanker, P. Fan, A. Saxon, J. D. Weisman, and I. Posalki. 1981. "Pneumocystic Pneumonia—Los Angeles." *Morbidity and Mortality Weekly Report* 30: 250–252.

Grob, G. N. 1983. "Diseases and Environment in American History." In *Handbook of Health, Health Care, and the Health Professions,* D. Mechanic, ed., pp. 3–23. New York: Free Press.

Guttentag, M. and P. F. Secord. 1983. *Too Many Women: The Sex Ratio Question.* Beverly Hills, Calif.: Sage Publications.

Herd, D. 1986. "A Review of Drinking Patterns and Alcohol Problems among U.S. Blacks." In *Report of the Secretary's Task Force on Black and Minority Health*: Volume 7, M. Heckler ed. USDHHS.

Icard, L. 1985. "Black Gay Men and Conflicting Social Identities: Sexual Orientation versus Racial Identity." *Journal of Social Work and Human Sexuality* 4: 83–93.

Icard, L., and D. M. Traunstein. 1987. "Black, Gay, Alcoholic Men: Their Character and Treatment." *Social Casework* 68: 267–272.

Landrum, S., C. Beck-Sague, and S. Kraus. 1988. "Racial Trends in Syphilis among Men with Same-Sex Partners in Atlanta, Georgia." *American Journal of Public Health* 78: 66–67.

Lex, B. W. 1987. "Review of Alcohol Problems in Ethnic Minority Groups." *Journal of Consulting and Clinical Psychology* 55 (3): 293–300.

Macdonald, D. I. 1986. "Coolfont Report: A PHS Plan for the Prevention and Control of AIDS and the AIDS Virus." *Public Health Reports* 101: 341–348.

Mays, V. M. 1988. "The Epidemiology of AIDS in U.S. Blacks: Some Problems and Projections." Unpublished manuscript.

Mays, V. M. and S. D. Cochran. 1987. "Acquired Immunodeficiency Syndrome and Black Americans: Special Psychosocial Issues." *Public Health Reports* 102: 224–231.

———. "Issues in the Perception of AIDS Risk and Risk Reduction Activities by Black and Hispanic Women." *American Psychologist* 1988; 43: 11.

McKusick, L., W. Horstman, and T. J. Coates. 1985. "AIDS and Sexual Behavior Reported by Gay Men in San Francisco." *American Journal of Public Health* 75: 493–496.

Morgan, W. M. and J. W. Curran. 1986. "Acquired Immunodeficiency Syndrome: Current and Future Trends." *Public Health Reports* 101: 459–465.

Samuel, M. and W. Winkelstein. 1987. "Prevalence of Human Immunodeficiency Virus in Ethnic Minority Homosexual/Bisexual Men." *Journal of the American Medical Association* 257: 1901 (letter).

Smith, M. C. 1986. "By the Year 2000." In *In the Life: A Black Gay Anthology,* J. Beam ed. Boston: Alyson Publications.

Soares, J. V. 1979. "Black and Gay." In *Gay Men: The Sociology of Male Homosexuality,* M. P. Levine, ed. New York: Harper & Row Publishers.

Spanier, G. B. and P. C. Glick. 1980. "Mate Selection Differentials between Whites and Blacks in the United States." *Social Forces* 58: 707–725.

Stall, R. S., L. McKusick, J. Wiley, T. J. Coates, and D. G. Ostrow. 1986. "Alcohol and Drug Use during Sexual Activity and Compliance with Safe Sex Guidelines for AIDS: The AIDS Behavioral Research Project." *Health Education Quarterly* 13: 359–371.

Staples, R. 1981. *The Changing World of Black Singles.* Connecticut: Greenwood Press.

Sylvester. 1986. Foreword. In *In the Life: A Black Gay Anthology,* J. Beam ed. Boston: Alyson Publications.

Warren, C. A. B. 1974. *Identity and Community Formation in the Gay World.* New York: John Wiley & Sons.

PART EIGHT

Men in Families

Are men still taking seriously their responsibilities as family breadwinners? Are today's men sharing more of the family housework and childcare than those in previous generations? The answers to these questions are complex, and often depend on which men we are talking about and what we mean when we say "family."

Many male workers long ago won a "family wage," and with it made an unwritten pact to share that wage with a wife and children. But today, as Barbara Ehrenreich argues in her influential book *The Hearts of Men*, increasing numbers of men are revolting against this traditional responsibility to share their wages, thus contributing to the rapidly growing impoverishment of women and children. Ehrenreich may be correct, at least with respect to the specific category of men who were labeled "yuppies" in the 1980s. But if we are looking at the growing impoverishment of women and children among poor, working-class, and minority families, the causes have more to do with dramatic shifts in the structure of the economy—including skyrocketing unemployment among young black males—than they do with male irresponsibility. Increasing numbers of men have no wage to share with a family.

But how about the New Dual-Career Family? Can we look to this emerging family type as a model of egalitarianism? Arlie Hochschild's research indicates that the growth of the two-career family has not significantly altered the division of labor in the household. Women still, she argues, work a "second shift" when they return home from their paid-work job.

One of the most significant issues of the 1990s is fatherhood. Are men becoming more nurturing and caring fathers, developing skills, like the men in Hollywood films such as *Three Men and a Baby*, or simply loving their children more than life itself, as in *Ransom, Jingle All the Way*, and so many others? The articles in this section cause us to expand the debate about fatherhood, recognizing the variety of fatherhoods that are evidenced by different groups of men, such as gay fathers (Brian Miller), Chicano fathers (Scott Coltrane), and black fathers (Michael Hanchard).

Photo courtesy of Sue Sattel.

ARTICLE 43

Arlie Hochschild

The Second Shift: Employed Women Are Putting in Another Day of Work at Home

Every American household bears the footprints of economic and cultural trends that originate far outside its walls. A rise in inflation eroding the earning power of the male wage, an expanding service sector opening up jobs for women, and the inroads made by women into many professions—all these changes do not simply go on around the American family. They occur *within* a marriage or living-together arrangement and transform it. Problems between couples, problems that seem "unique" or "marital," are often the individual ripples of powerful economic and cultural shock waves. Quarrels between husbands and wives in households across the nation result mainly from a friction between faster-changing women and slower-changing men.

The exodus of women from the home to the workplace has not been accompanied by a new view of marriage and work that would make this transition smooth. Most workplaces have remained inflexible in the face of the changing needs of workers with families, and most men have yet to really adapt to the changes in women. I call the strain caused by the disparity between the change in women and the absence of change elsewhere the "stalled revolution."

If women begin to do less at home because they have less time, if men do little more, and if the work of raising children and tending a home requires roughly the same effort, then the questions of who does what at home and of what

From *The Second Shift* by Arlie Hochschild and Ann Machung. Copyright © 1989 by Arlie Hochschild. Used by permission of Viking Penguin, a division of Penguin Putnam Inc. This excerpt also appeared in a slightly different form in *New Age Journal* (Sept./Oct. 1989).

"needs doing" become a source of deep tension in a marriage.

Over the past 30 years in the United States, more and more women have begun to work outside the home, and more have divorced. While some commentators conclude that women's work *causes* divorce, my research into changes in the American family suggests something else. Since all the wives in the families I studied (over an eight-year period) worked outside the home, the fact that they worked did not account for why some marriages were happy and others were not. What *did* contribute to happiness was the husband's willingness to do the work at home. Whether they were traditional or more egalitarian in their relationship, couples were happier when the men did a sizable share of housework and child care.

In one study of 600 couples filing for divorce, researcher George Levinger found that the second most common reason women cited for wanting to divorce—after "mental cruelty"—was their husbands' "neglect of home or children." Women mentioned this reason more often than financial problems, physical abuse, drinking, or infidelity.

A happy marriage is supported by a couple's being economically secure, by their enjoying a supportive community, and by their having compatible needs and values. But these days it may also depend on a shared appreciation of the work it takes to nurture others. As the role of the homemaker is being abandoned by many women, the homemaker's work has been continually devalued and passed on to low-paid housekeepers, babysitters, or day-care workers. Long devalued by men, the contribution of cooking, cleaning, and care-giving is now being devalued as mere drudgery by many women, too.

In the era of the stalled revolution, one way to make housework and child care more valued is for men to share in that work. Many working mothers are already doing all they can at home. Now it's time for men to make the move.

If more mothers of young children are working at full-time jobs outside the home, and if most couples can't afford household help, who's doing the work at home? Adding together the time it takes to do a paid job and to do housework and child care and using estimates from major studies on time use done in the 1960s and 1970s, I found that women worked roughly 15 more hours each week than men. Over a year, they worked an extra month of 24-hour days. Over a dozen years, it was an extra year of 24-hour days. Most women without children spend much more time than men on housework. Women with children devote more time to both housework and child care. Just as there is a wage gap between men and women in the workplace, there is a "leisure gap" between them at home. Most women work one shift at the office or factory and a "second shift" at home.

In my research, I interviewed and observed 52 couples over an eight-year period as they cooked dinner, shopped, bathed their children, and in general struggled to find enough time to make their complex lives work. The women I interviewed seemed to be far more deeply torn between the demands of work and family than were their husbands. They talked more about the abiding conflict between work and family. They felt the second shift was *their* issue, and most of their husbands agreed. When I telephoned one husband to arrange an interview with him, explaining that I wanted to ask him how he managed work and family life, he replied genially, "Oh, this will *really* interest my *wife*."

Men who shared the load at home seemed just as pressed for time as their wives, and as torn between the demands of career and small children. But of the men I surveyed, the majority did not share the load at home. Some refused outright. Others refused more passively, often offering a loving shoulder to lean on, or an understanding ear, as their working wife faced the conflict they both saw as hers. At first it seemed to me that the problem of the second shift *was* hers. But I came to realize that those husbands who helped very little at home were often just as deeply affected as their wives—through the resentment their wives felt toward them and through their own need to steel themselves against that resentment.

A clear example of this phenomenon is Evan Holt, a warehouse furniture salesman who did very little housework and played with his four-year-old son, Joey, only at his convenience. His wife, Nancy, did the second shift, but she resented it keenly and half-consciously expressed her frustration and rage by losing interest in sex and becoming overly absorbed in Joey.

Even when husbands happily shared the work, their wives *felt* more responsible for home and children. More women than men kept track of doctor's appointments and arranged for kids' playmates to come over. More mothers than fathers worried about a child's Halloween costume or a birthday present for a school friend. They were more likely to think about their children while at work and to check in by phone with the babysitter.

Partly because of this, more women felt torn between two kinds of urgency, between the need to soothe a child's fear of being left at day-care and the need to show the boss she's "serious" at work. Twenty percent of the men in my study shared housework equally. Seventy percent did a substantial amount (less than half of it, but more than a third), and 10 percent did less than a third. But even when couples more equitably share the work at home, women do two thirds of the daily jobs at home, such as cooking and cleaning—jobs that fix them into a rigid routine. Most women cook dinner, for instance, while men change the oil in the family car. But, as one mother pointed out, dinner needs to be prepared every evening around six o'clock, whereas the car oil needs to be changed every six months, with no particular deadline. Women do more child care than men, and men repair more household appliances. A child needs to be tended to daily, whereas the repair of household appliances can often wait, said the men, "until I have time." Men thus have more control over when they make their contributions than women do. They may be very busy with family chores, but, like the executive who tells his secretary to "hold my calls," the man has more control over his time.

Another reason why women may feel under more strain than men is that women more often do two things at once—for example, write checks and return phone calls, vacuum and keep an eye on a three-year-old, fold laundry and think out the shopping list. Men more often will either cook dinner *or* watch the kids. Women more often do both at the same time.

Beyond doing more at home, women also devote proportionately more of their time at home to housework than men and proportionately less of it to child care. Of all the time men spend working at home, a growing amount of it goes to child care. Since most parents prefer to tend to their children than to clean house, men do more of what they'd rather do. More men than women take their children on "fun" outings to the park, the zoo, the movies. Women spend more time on maintenance, such as feeding and bathing children—enjoyable activities, to be sure, but often less leisurely or "special" than going to the zoo. Men also do fewer of the most undesirable household chores, such as scrubbing the toilet.

As a result, women tend to talk more intensely about being overtired, sick, and emotionally drained. Many women interviewed were fixated on the topic of sleep. They talked about how much they could "get by on": six and a half, seven, seven and a half, less, more. They talked about who they knew who needed more or less. Some apologized for how much sleep they needed—"I'm afraid I need eight hours of sleep"—as if eight was "too much." They talked about how to avoid fully waking up when a child called them at night, and how to get back to sleep. These women talked about sleep the way a hungry person talks about food.

If, all in all, the two-job family is suffering from a speedup of work and family life, working mothers are its primary victims. It is ironic, then, that often it falls to women to be the time-and-motion experts of family life. As I observed families inside their homes, I noticed it was often the mother who rushed children, saying, "Hurry up! It's time to go," "Finish your cereal now," "You can do that later," or "Let's go!" When a bath needed to be crammed into a slot between 7:45 and 8:00, it was often the mother who called out, "Let's see who can take their bath the quickest!" Often a younger child would rush out, scurrying to be first in bed, while the older and wiser one stalled, resistant, sometimes resentful: "Mother is always rushing us." Sadly, women are more often the lightning rods for family tensions aroused by this speedup of work and family life. They are the villains in a process in which they are also the primary victims. More than the longer hours and the lack of sleep, this is the saddest cost to women of their extra month of work each year.

Raising children in a nuclear family is still the overwhelming preference of most people. Yet in the face of new problems for this family model we have not created an adequate support system so that the nuclear family can do its job well in the era of the two-career couple. Corporations have done little to accommodate the needs of working parents, and the government has done little to prod them.

The Reagan and Bush administrations said they were "pro-family" but confused being pro-family with being against women's work outside the home. During a time when more than 70 percent of wives and mothers work outside the home (the rate is still climbing), the Reagan administration's Panel on the Family offered as its pro-family policy only a package of measures against crime, drugs, and welfare. In the name of protecting the family, the Republicans proposed to legitimize school prayer and eliminate family-planning services. They did nothing to help parents integrate work and family life. We have to ask, when marriages continue to end because of the strains of this life, is it pro-family or anti-family to make life in two-job families so very hard? As working parents become an interest group, a voting block, and a swing vote in elections, the issue of policies to ease life in two-job families is likely to become a serious political issue in years ahead.

We really need, as sociologist Frank Furstenberg has suggested, a Marshall Plan for the family. After World War II we saw that it was in our best interests to aid the war-torn nations of Europe. Now—it seems obvious in an era of growing concern over drugs, crime, and family instability—it is in our best interests to aid the overworked two-job families right here at home. We should look to other nations for a model of what could be done. In Sweden, for example, upon the birth of a child every working couple is entitled to 12 months of paid parental leave— nine months at 90 percent of the worker's salary, plus an additional three months at about three hundred dollars a month. The mother and father are free to divide this year off between them as they wish. Working parents of a child under eight have the opportunity to work no more than six hours a day, at six hours' pay. Parental insurance offers parents money for work time lost while visiting a child's school or caring for a sick child. That's a true pro-family policy.

A pro-family policy in the United States could give tax breaks to companies that encourage job sharing, part-time work, flex time, and family leave for new parents. By implementing comparable worth policies we could increase pay scales for "women's" jobs. Another key element of a pro-family policy would be instituting fewer-hour, more flexible options—called "family phases"—for all regular jobs filled by parents of young children.

Day-care centers could be made more warm and creative through generous public and private funding. If the best form of day-care comes from the attention of elderly neighbors, students, or grandparents, these people could be paid to care for children through social programs.

In these ways, the American government would create a safer environment for the two-job family. If the government encouraged corporations to consider the long-range interests of workers and their families, they would save on long-range costs caused by absenteeism, turnover, juvenile delinquency, mental illness, and welfare support for single mothers.

These are real pro-family reforms. If they seem utopian today, we should remember that in the past the eight-hour day, the abolition of child labor, and the vote for women seemed utopian, too. Among top-rated employers listed in *The 100 Best Companies to Work for in America* are many offering country-club memberships, first-class air travel, and million-dollar fitness centers. But only a handful offer job sharing, flex time, or part-time work. Not one provides on-site day-care, and only three offer child-care deductions: Control Data, Polaroid, and Honeywell. In his book *Megatrends*, John Naisbitt reports that 83 percent of corporate executives believed that more men feel the need to share the responsibilities of parenting; yet only 9 percent of corporations offer paternity leave.

Public strategies are linked to private ones. Economic and cultural trends bear on family relations in ways it would be useful for all of us to understand. The happiest two-job marriages I saw during my research were ones in which men and women shared the housework and parenting. What couples called good communication often meant that they were good at saying thanks to one another for small aspects of taking care of the family. Making it to the school play, helping a child read, cooking dinner in good spirits, remembering the grocery list, taking responsibility for cleaning up the bedrooms—these were the silver and gold of the marital exchange. Until now, couples committed to an equal sharing of housework and child care have been rare. But, if we as a culture come to see the urgent need of meeting the new problems posed by the second shift, and if society and government begin to shape new policies that allow working parents more flexibility, then we will be making some progress toward happier times at home and work. And as the young learn by example, many more women and men will be able to enjoy the pleasure that arises when family life is family life, and not a second shift.

Brian Miller

Life-Styles of Gay Husbands and Fathers

The words "gay husband" and "gay father" are often regarded as contradictions in terms. This notion is hinted at in Anita Bryant's widely quoted non sequitur, "Homosexuals recruit because they cannot reproduce." Researchers estimate, however, that in America there are six million gay husbands and fathers (Bozett 1987; Schulenberg 1985). Why do these men marry and have children? How do they organize their lives? What are their difficulties and joys as a consequence of their behavior?

To address these questions, 50 gay husbands and fathers were contacted in 1976 by means of multiple-source chain-referral samples. At first interview, 24 of the men were living with their wives; three years later at the second interview, only three had intact marriages. Approximately two-thirds of the respondents have been followed to the present and all of them are now separated (Humphreys and Miller 1980a). To show the modal developments in gay husbands' and fathers' life-styles, the data are organized along a four-point continuum: Covert Behavior, Marginal Involvement, Transformed Participation, and Open Endorsement.

Covert Behavior

Early in adult life, gay husbands and fathers tend to regard their homosexual feelings as nothing more than genital urges. They are reluctant to refer to either themselves or their behavior as gay:

Revised and updated from an article in *Gay Men: The Sociology of Male Homosexuality* by Martin P. Levine. New York: Harper & Row, 1979.

"I hate labels" is a common response to questions about sexual orientation. These men have unstable self-concepts—one day thinking they are homosexual and another day thinking they are not. Their reluctance to label their same-sex activity as homosexual is not because they hate labels per se; indeed they strive to present themselves to others under a heterosexual label. Rather, they dislike a label that calls attention to behaviors they would prefer to forget.

Premarital homosexual experiences are often explained away with "It's only a phase" or "God, was I drunk last night!" These men report such activities prior to marriage as arranging heterosexual double-date situations in which they would perform coitus in the back seat of the car, for example, while fantasizing about the male in the front seat. Others report collaborating with a buddy to share a female prostitute. These ostensibly heterosexual acts allowed the men to buttress their sense of heterosexuality while gratifying homosexual urges. During the premarital period, respondents discounted gay life-styles and romanticized heterosexual family living as the only way to achieve the stable home life, loyal companionship, and fatherhood they desired.

These men married in good faith, thinking they could overcome their gay desires; they did not believe they were deceiving their spouses. In fact, most men broached the issue of their homosexual feelings to their wives before marriage, but the information was usually conveyed in an oblique manner and downplayed as inconsequential. This kept their future wives from thinking that they might be marrying homosexuals. Wives' denials of their husbands' homosexuality were further facilitated by the fact that half the women, at

443

their nuptials, were pregnant by the men they were marrying.

In the early years of marriage, high libido provided husbands with easy erections for coitus. Respondents report, however, that this situation tended to deteriorate shortly after the birth of the first child. Increasingly, they found themselves fantasizing about gay erotica during coitus.

Marriage engulfs the men in a heterosexual role, making them marginal to the gay world. Their social isolation from others who share their sexual interests burdens them with "I'm-the-only-one-in-the-world" feelings. These men, realizing their behavior is inconsistent with their heterosexual reputation, try to reduce their anxiety and guilt by compartmentalizing gay and nongay worlds. One respondent said: "I never walk in the door without an airtight excuse of where I've been." Some men avoid the strain of remembering stories by intimidating the wife into silence: "She knows better than to question my whereabouts. I tell her, 'I get home when I get home; no questions asked.'" In these respects, respondents have parallels to their adulterous heterosexual counterparts (Libby and Whitehurst 1977).

Extramarital sex for respondents usually consists of clandestine, impersonal encounters in parks, tearooms, or highway rest stops, with hitchhikers or male hustlers. (Regarding this, single gays sometimes comment, "Married gays give the rest of us a bad name.") Occasionally, furtiveness itself becomes eroticized, making the men sexually dysfunctional in calmer contexts. Recreational, gay scenes such as dances, parties, and gay organizations are not used by respondents, primarily because they dread discovery and subsequent marital dissolution. Many are further limited by fears that their jobs would be threatened, by lack of geographical access to gay institutions, or by religious scruples. In fact, these men are largely unaware of gay social events in their communities and have little idea of how to participate in them. They tend to be ideologically ambivalent about the gay world, sometimes thinking of it as exotic, and other times condemning it as "superficial, unstable, full of blackmail and vio-

lence." Given their exposure to only the impersonal homosexual underground, and not to loving gay relationships, their negative perception is somewhat justified. As long as they remain marginal to the gay world, the likelihood of their participation in safe, fulfilling gay relationships remains minimal (Miller and Humphreys 1980).

Some men regard their homosexual desires not as an orientation, but as a compulsion: "I don't want to do these things, but I'm driven to do them." Other accounts that explain away their homosexual behavior, emphasize its nonseriousness, and minimize its consequences include (1) "I might be okay if my wife learned to give good blow jobs." (2) "I only go out for it when I'm drunk or depressed." (3) "I go to the truck-stop and meet someone. We're just a couple of horny married guys relieving ourselves. That's not sex. [It] doesn't threaten my marriage like adultery would." (4) "Sex with men is a minor aspect of my life that I refuse to let outweigh more important things."

The respondent who gave this last account also presented conflicting evidence. He spent time, effort, and anxiety in rearranging his schedule to accommodate sex, spending money on his car and fuel to search for willing men, constructing intricate stories to fool work associates and family, and buying his wife penance gifts. He also experienced near misses with police and gay bashers. Still, he viewed all this as only a "minor aspect" of his life.

Another rationalization is "I'm not really homosexual since I don't care if it's a man, woman or dog that's licking my cock. All I want is a hole." Further questioning, however, made clear that this respondent was not looking for just any available orifice. He stated that it was equally important that he persuade the most attractive man available to fellate him.

Another account is the "Eichmann dodge." Men may claim, like Eichmann, that they are the victims of other men's desire, inadvertently caught up and swept along by the events, thereby absolving themselves of responsibility. Men stating this rationalization, however, are often skilled at seducing others into making the first move. Some gay husbands and fathers claim that they limit themselves to one special "friendship" and that no one else of their sex could excite them. If they think of homosexuality at all, they conceive it as promiscuous behavior done by degenerates, not by people like themselves who are loyal and who look conventional.

These accounts help respondents deny homosexuality while practicing it. They find it difficult to simultaneously see themselves as worthwhile persons and as homosexuals, and to reconcile their masculine self-image with the popular image of gays as effeminate. The most they can acknowledge is that they get together with other men to ejaculate and that they fantasize about men during sex with their wives. In spite of their rationalizations, however, these men report considerable anxiety and guilt about maintaining their compartmentalized double lives.

Respondents are reluctant to rate their marriages as "happy," typically referring to them as "duties." The ambivalence is expressed by one who said: "My wife is a good person, but it's funny, I can't live with this marriage and I can't live without it." Respondents report conflict with wives who object to the disproportionate time these men spend away from home, neglecting parental responsibilities. The men view alternatives to marriage as limited, not seeing life in the gay world as a viable option. They find it difficult to talk about their children and express guilt that their work and sex schedules do not allow them to spend as much time with their children as they would like. Nevertheless, most of the men report that their children are the main reason for remaining married: "In this horrible marriage, [the children] are the consolation prize."

Marginal Involvement

Respondents at this point on the continuum engage in homosexual behavior and have a gay self-identity. However, these men are marginal to the gay community since they have heterosexual public identities, and are often living with their wives.

Still, they are much more comfortable with their homoerotic desires than are those in the Covert Behavior group and are more disclosing about their sexual orientation to other gays.

Compared with men in the previous group, Marginally Involved respondents have an expanded repertoire of sexual outlets. They sometimes compile telephone-number lists of sex partners and have limited involvement with small networks of gay friends. The men maintain secrecy by using post office boxes or separate office phones for gay-related business. Fake identities and names may be constructed to prevent identification by sexual partners. Employing male "masseurs" or maintaining a separate apartment for gay sex provide other relatively safe outlets. Consequently, these men are less likely to encounter police entrapment or gay bashers. Gay bars are somewhat inaccessible since they often start too late, and the men cannot regularly find excuses for extended absences from home. Some men resort to lunch-hour or presupper "quickies" at the baths.

In spite of these measures, respondents report many facade-shattering incidents with heterosexuals. Such difficulties include being caught on the street with a gay friend whose presence cannot be explained, blurting out praise about an event, then remembering it was attended with a gay friend, not one's wife, and transferring body lice or a venereal disease from a hustler to the wife, an especially dangerous occurrence in this time of AIDS (Pearson 1986). Many respondents, however, continue to deny wives' knowledge about their homosexuality: "I don't think my wife really knows. She's only mentioned it a couple of times, and only when she was too drunk to know what she was saying."

Men who travel as part of their business or who have loosely structured working hours enjoy relative freedom. For them, absences and sexual incidents may be more easily covered. A minority of men, specifically those in artistic and academic fields, are able to mix their heterosexual and homosexual worlds. Their circle is that of the relatively wealthy and tolerant in which the epithet "perversion" is replaced by the more neutral "eccentricity," and variant behavior is accepted as long as the man is discreet and does not "rub the wife's nose in it." Several respondents socialize openly with similarly situated men or with gay sex partners whom wives and others ostensibly know as merely work assistants or friends of the family.

Because Marginally Involved respondents are "out" to some audiences and not to others, they sometimes resemble, as one man said, "a crazy quilt of contradictions." This is emphasized by playing word games with questioners or with those who try to penetrate their defenses. Playing the role of the eccentric and giving mixed messages provide a smokescreen for their emotional whereabouts from both gays and nongays.

This adjustment, however, is tenuous and respondents are often ambivalent about maintaining their marriages. They fantasize about life as a gay single, and entertain ideas of divorce. The guilt these respondents experience is sometimes reflected in what might be called Santa Claus behavior. They shower their children—and sometimes their wives—with expensive gifts to counteract feelings that they have done a terrible thing to their family by being homosexual: "It's the least I can do for having ruined their chance to grow up in a normal home." Using credit cards to manage guilt has many of these men in serious debt and laboring as workaholics.

Like men in the first category, these men regret that performing their breadwinner, husband, and homosexual roles leaves little time for the father role. Nevertheless, they are reluctant to leave their marriages, fearing permanent separation from their children. They also fear community stigma, ambivalently regard the gay world, and are unwilling to endure the decreased standard of living necessitated by divorce.

Over time, it becomes increasingly difficult for these men to reconcile their discordant identities as husband and as homosexual. Although some are able to routinize compartmentalization, others find sustaining the necessary maneuvers for secrecy to be not worth it. Conspiracies of si-

lence and denial within the families become strained, if not transparent. Respondents tend to seek closure by communicating, directly and indirectly, their orientational needs to wives and by becoming more explicit in their methods of making gay contacts. Others are exposed by vice arrests or by being victimized by men they solicit. Most wives are surprised by the direct confrontation. Respondents are surprised that their wives are surprised since respondents may have thought their wives already knew, and tacitly accepted it. Initially wives often react with disbelief, revulsion, and anger: "I feel betrayed." This frequently gives way to a feeling of couple solidarity, that "we can conquer the problem together." When this is the adaptation, respondents do not come out of the closet so much as take their wives into the closet with them.

Couples try a variety of techniques to shore up the marriages. Respondents may seek therapy to "cure" their homosexuality. Some men generously offer wives the freedom to experience extramarital affairs, too, although it appears this is done mostly to relieve respondents' guilt since they know that wives are unlikely to take them up on the offer. When wives do not put the offer to the test, respondents further console their guilt by interpreting this as evidence that the wives are "frigid" or low in "sex drive," although data from the wives dispute this characterization (Hays and Samuels 1988).

Some couples try instituting new sexual arrangements: a *ménage à trois,* or the husband is allowed out one night a week with gay friends. In the former interaction, wives tend to report feeling "used" and, in the latter, men tend to report feeling they are on a "leash."

Sexual conflicts spill into other domestic areas. Tardiness or missed appointments lead to wives' suspicions and accusations and general marital discord. One man calls this compromise period "white-knuckle heterosexuality." By negotiating ground rules that reinstate partial denial and by intellectualizing the situation, some couples maintain for years the compromise period. This uneasy truce ends if ground rules are repeatedly violated and when the wife realizes (1) that her husband finds men sexier than herself, (2) that he is unalterably gay, (3) that her primary place as object of permanent affection is challenged, and (4) that she has alternatives and can cope without the marriage. Wives gradually come to resent romanceless marriages with men who would rather make love to another man, and the homosexual husbands come to resent, as one man said, being "stifled in a nuptial closet."

Couples who remain married after disclosure tend not to have rejected divorce, but rather to have an indefinite postponement of it: "After the children leave home." "After the finances are in order." Other considerations that keep the couples together include religious beliefs, family pressure, wives' dependence, and the perceived nonviability of the gay world.

In most cases, the immediate impetus for ending the marriage is the husband's establishment of a love relationship with another man. As such relationships intensify, men begin to reconstruct the gay world as favorable for effecting companionship and social stability. It is usually wives, however, who take action to terminate the marriages. Painful as this experience is, it somewhat eases the men's guilt for causing marital dissolution.

Transformed Participation

Respondents who reach this point on the continuum engage in homosexual behavior and have self-identities—and to a limited extent, public identities—that reflect acceptance of their behavior. These men generally have come out as gay and left their wives.

Acculturation into the gay world involves three areas of concern for respondents: (1) disadvantage of advanced age and late arrival on the scene, (2) the necessity of learning new gay social definitions and skills, and (3) the need to reconcile prior fantasies to the realities of the gay world. Once respondents no longer live with wives and children, they begin to increase their contacts with the gay world and their marginality to it decreases.

They may now subscribe to gay publications, join gay religious congregations, and go to gay social and political clubs and private gay parties. They experience a rapid expansion of gay consciousness and skills and take steps to form close friendships with others of their sexual orientation.

Moving out of the closet, these men report a stabilization of self-concept and a greater sense of psychological well-being. Their attitudes toward homoerotic behavior become more relaxed and better integrated into their everyday lives. Most experience a change in body image, exemplified by improved physical fitness and increased care with their appearance. Many report the elimination of nervous and psychosomatic disorders such as ulcers, excessive fatigue, and back aches, as well as substance abuse.

These respondents' sexual orientation tends to be known by significant others with two exceptions: their employers and children. Secrecy sometimes exists with employers since respondents believe the legal system does not protect their interests should they be dismissed for being gay (Levine 1981).

Relatively little openness about homosexuality also exists with these respondents' children. Typically, only older children (if any) are told, and it is not considered a topic for general discussion. There is fear that, if the man's gayness becomes known in the community, his employer might find out or his ex-wife might become irked and deny him child visits. Successful legal appeal for gay people in such matters is difficult, a situation these men perceive as legally sanctioned blackmail.

In line with this, most respondents, rather than living with their children, have visiting schedules with them. They do not have the financial resources either to persuade their ex-wives to relinquish the children or to hire care for them while devoting time to their own careers.

Men who are able to terminate marriages without their spouse's discovering their homosexuality avoid this problem. However, fear of subsequent exposure and loss of children through a new court order remains and prompts some men to stay partially closeted even after marital dissolution. In spite of these fears, the degree of passing and compartmentalization of gay and nongay worlds is much less for men at this point on the continuum than for those who are Covert and Marginal.

Open Endorsement

Respondents who reach this point on the continuum not only engage in homosexual behavior and have a self-identity reflective of the behavior but also openly champion the gay community. Although they come from the full range of economic backgrounds, they tend to have high social and occupational resources. Some have tolerant employers; some are full-time gay activists; others are self-employed, often in businesses with largely gay clienteles.

Proud of their newfound identity, these men organize their world, to a great extent, around gay cultures. Much of their leisure, if not occupation, is spent in gay-related pursuits. They have experienced unhappy marriages and divorce, the struggle of achieving a gay identity, and now feel they have arrived at a satisfactory adjustment. These men, consequently, distinguish themselves in ideology from respondents in other categories. For example, what the others refer to as "discretion," men in this category call "duplicity" and "sneaking around." Moreover, what closeted men see as "flaunting," openly gay respondents call "being forthright" and "upfront."

Respondents' efforts in constructing this new life are helped not only by having a gay love relationship, but by the Gay Liberation Movement (Humphreys and Miller 1980b). Parallel processes are at work whereby the building of a personal gay identity is facilitated by the larger cultural context of increasing gay pride and diversification of gay institutions and heritage (Adam 1987; Harry and DeVall 1978; Murray 1979). Still, coming out is not easy or automatic. This is partly due to the fact that there is no necessary conjunction among sexual behavior fantasy, self-identity, and object of affectional attachment. Although there is a strain toward consistency for most people among these components of sexuality, this is not invariably so. The ways these components change over time and the combinations in which they link with each other are multiple (Miller 1983; Simon and Gagnon 1969).

Men who reach the Open Endorsement point often have fears that their father and ex-husband statuses could distance them from single gays. Sometimes respondents fear that single gays, similar to nongays, regard them with confusion, curiosity, or pity. Integrating gay and father roles requires patience, since it is often difficult for respondents to find a lover who accepts him and his children as a "package deal," and the gay father may feel he has not enough time and energy to attend to both children and a lover. Selecting a lover who is also a gay father is a common solution to this situation.

Most respondents who have custody of their children did not experience court custody battles but gained custody because the mother did not want the children or because the children, being allowed to choose, chose to live with their fathers. Respondents who live with their children are more likely to have a close circle of gay friends as their main social outlet, rather than participating primarily in gay commercial establishments (McWhirter and Mattison 1984).

Men at this point on the continuum have told their children about their homosexuality. They report children's reaction to be more positive than expected and, when there is a negative reaction, it generally dissipates over time (Miller 1979). Children's negative reactions centered more on the parent's divorce and subsequent household changes than on the father's homosexuality per se. Daughters tend to be more accepting of their father's homosexuality than sons, although most children feel their father's honesty brings them closer together. Children report few instances of neighborhood homophobia directed against them, possibly because the children try to disclose only to people they know will react favorably. There is no indication that the children of gay fathers are disproportionately homosexual themselves although, of the children who turned out to be gay, there were more lesbian daughters than gay sons. Wives and relatives sometimes worry that gay men's children will be molested by him or his gay friends. Evidence from this study supports earlier research findings that indicate such fears are unwarranted (Bozett 1987).

Discussion

The general tendency is for the Covert Behavior respondents to move toward Open Endorsement. There are several caveats, however, about this movement. For example, the continuum should not be construed as reifying transient states into types. Additionally, movement out of marriage into an openly gay identity is not unilateral. There are many negotiations back and forth, in and out of the closet. There is not a finite number of stages; not everyone becomes publicly gay and not everyone passes through every step. Few respondents move easily or accidentally through the process. Rather, each level is achieved by a painful search, negotiating with both oneself and the larger world.

The event most responsible for initiating movement along the continuum and reconstructing gay fathers' perceptions of the gay community is the experience of falling in love with another man. By contrast, factors hindering movement along the continuum include inability to perceive the gay world as a viable alternative as well as perceived lack of support from other gays, economic difficulty, family pressure, poor health, wives' dependence, homophobia in respondents or community, and moral/religious scruples.

This study has several findings. Gayness and traditional marital relationships are perceived by the respondents as discordant compared to relationships established when they move into the gay world. Although respondents perceive gayness as incompatible with traditional marriage, they perceive gayness as compatible with fathering. Highly compartmentalized life-styles and deceit sometimes repress open marital conflict, but unresolved tension characterizes respondents' marriages. In contrast, men who leave their spouses

and enter the gay world report gay relationships to be more harmonious than marital relationships. They also report fathering to be more salient once having left their marriages. Men who come out perceive less discrimination from family, friends, and co-workers than those who are closeted anticipate. Wives tend to be upset by their husbands' revelations, but respondents are typically surprised by the positive reactions of their children and their parents.

Future prospects for gay fathers hinge largely on the success of the gay liberation movement. If these men can politicize their status, if they can see their difficulties stemming from social injustice and society's homophobic conditioning rather than personal inadequacy, and if they can redefine themselves, not as deviants, but as an oppressed minority, self-acceptance is improved. This helps lift their depression and externalize anger—anger about prejudice and about wasting their precious early years in the closet. Further, it minimizes their guilt and eases adjustment into the gay community (Miller 1987).

As the gay liberation movement makes alternatives for fathering available within the gay community, fewer gays are likely to become involved in heterosexual marriages and divorce. Adoption, surrogate parenting, and alternative fertilization are some of the new ways single gays can now experience fatherhood (Miller 1988). If current trends continue, there will be a proliferation of family life-styles so that parenthood becomes available to all regardless of sexual orientation.

References

Adam, B. (1987). *The rise of a gay and lesbian movement.* Boston: Hall.

Bozett, F. W. (1987). *Gay and lesbian parents.* New York: Praeger.

Harry, J. & DeVall, W. (1978). *The social organization of gay males.* New York: Praeger.

Hays, D. & Samuels, A. (1988). Heterosexual women's perceptions of their marriages to bisexual or homosexual men. In F. W. Bozett (Ed.), *Homosexuality in the family.* New York: Haworth.

Humphreys, L. & Miller, B. (1980A). Keeping in touch: Maintaining contact with stigmatized respondents. In W. Shaffir, R. Stebbins & A. Turowetz (Eds.), *Field work experience: Qualitative approaches in social research.* New York: St. Martin's.

Humphreys, L. & Miller, B. (1980B). Identities in the emerging gay culture. In J. Marmor (Ed.), *Homosexual behavior: A modern reappraisal.* New York: Basic.

Levine, M. (1981). Employment discrimination against gay men. In P. Stein (Ed.), *Single life.* New York: St. Martin's.

Libby, R. & Whitehurt, R. (1977). *Marriage and alternatives.* Glenview, IL: Scott, Foresman.

McWhirter, D. & Mattison, A. (1984). *The male couple.* Englewood Cliffs, NJ: Prentice-Hall.

Miller, B. (1979). Gay fathers and their children. *Family Coordinator* 28: 544–552.

Miller, B. (1983). Foreword. In M. W. Ross (Ed.), *The married homosexual man.* London: Routledge & Kegan Paul.

Miller, B. (1987). Counseling gay husbands and fathers. In F. W. Bozett (Ed.), *Gay and lesbian parents.* New York: Praeger.

Miller, B. (1988). Preface. In F. W. Bozett (Ed.), *Homosexuality in the family.* New York: Haworth.

Miller, B. & Humphreys, L. (1980). Lifestyles and violence: Homosexual victims of assault and murder. *Qualitative Sociology* 3: 169–185.

Murray, S. (1979). The institutional elaboration of a quasi-ethnic community. *International Review of Modern Sociology* 9: 165–177.

Pearson, C. (1986). *Good-by, I love you.* New York: Random House.

Schulenberg, J. (1985). *Gay parenting.* New York: Doubleday.

Simon, W. & Gagnon, J. (1969). On psychosexual development. In D. Goslin (Ed.), *Handbook of socialization theory and research.* New York: Rand McNally.

ARTICLE 45

Scott Coltrane

Stability and Change in Chicano Men's Family Lives

One of the most popular pejorative American slang terms to emerge in the 1980s was "macho," used to describe men prone to combative posturing, relentless sexual conquest, and other compulsive displays of masculinity. Macho men continually guard against imputations of being soft or feminine and thus tend to avoid domestic tasks and family activities that are considered "women's work." Macho comes from the Spanish *machismo*, and although the behaviors associated with it are clearly not limited to one ethnic group, Latino men are often stereotyped as especially prone toward macho displays.[1] This chapter uses in-depth interviews with twenty Chicano couples to explore how paid work and family work are divided. As in other contemporary American households, divisions of labor in these Chicano families were far from balanced or egalitarian, and husbands tended to enjoy special privileges simply because they were men. Never-

This article is based on a study of Dual-Earner Chicano Couples conducted in 1990–1992 by Scott Coltrane with research assistance from Elsa Valdez and Hilda Cortez. Partial funding was provided by the Academic Senate of the University of California, Riverside, and the UCR Minority Student Research Internship Program. Included here are analyses of unpublished interview excerpts along with selected passages from three published sources: (1) Coltrane, *Family Man: Fatherhood, Housework, and Gender Equity* (New York: Oxford University Press, 1994); (2) Coltrane and Valdez, "Reluctant Compliance: Work/Family Role Allocation in Dual-Earner Chicano Families," in Jane C. Hood (ed.), *Men, Work, and Family* (Newbury Park, CA: Sage, 1994); and (3) Valdez and Coltrane, "Work, Family, and the Chicana: Power, Perception and Equity," in Judith Frankel (ed.), *Employed Mothers and the Family Context* (New York: Springer, 1993).

theless, many couples were allocating household chores without reference to gender, and few of the Chicano men exhibited stereotypical macho behavior.

Chicanos, or Mexican-Americans, are often portrayed as living in poor farm-worker families composed of macho men, subservient women, and plentiful children. Yet these stereotypes have been changing, as diverse groups of people with Mexican and Latin-American heritage are responding to the same sorts of social and economic pressures faced by families of other ethnic backgrounds. For example, most Chicano families in the United States now live in urban centers or their suburbs rather than in traditional rural farming areas, and their patterns of marital interaction appear to be about as egalitarian as those of other American families. What's more, Chicanos will no longer be a numerical minority in the near future. Because of higher-than-average birth rates and continued in-migration, by the year 2015 Chicano children will outnumber Anglos in many southwest states, including California, Texas, Arizona, and New Mexico.[2]

When family researchers study white couples, they typically focus on middle-class suburban households, usually highlighting their strengths. Studies of ethnic minority families, in contrast, have tended to focus on the problems of poor or working-class households living in inner-city or rural settings. Because most research on Latino families in the United States has not controlled for social class, wife's employment status, or recency of immigration, a narrow and stereotyped view of these families as patriarchal and culturally backward has persisted. In addition, large-scale studies of "Hispanics" have failed to distinguish between divergent groups of people with Mexican, Central American, South American, Cuban, Puerto Rican, Spanish, or Portuguese ancestry. In contrast, contemporary scholars are beginning to look at some of the positive aspects of minority families and to focus on the economic and institutional factors that influence men's lives within these families.[3]

In 1990 and 1991, Elsa Valdez and I interviewed a group of twenty middle-class Chicano couples with young children living in Southern California. We were primarily interested in finding out if they were facing the same sorts of pressures experienced by other families, so we selected only families in which both the husband and the wife were employed outside the home—the most typical pattern among young parents in the United States today. We wanted to see who did what in these families and find out how they talked about the personal and financial pushes and pulls associated with raising a family. We interviewed wives and husbands separately in their homes, asking them a variety of questions about housework, child care, and their jobs. Elsewhere, we describe details of their time use and task performance, but here I analyze the couples' talk about work, family, and gender, exploring how feelings of entitlement and obligation are shaped by patterns of paid and unpaid labor.[4]

When we asked husbands and wives to sort sixty-four common household tasks according to who most often performed them, we found that wives in most families were responsible for housecleaning, clothes care, meal preparation, and clean-up, whereas husbands were primarily responsible for home maintenance and repair. Most routine child care was also performed by wives, though most husbands reported that they made substantial contributions to parenting. Wives saw the mundane daily housework as an ever-present burden that they had to shoulder themselves or delegate to someone else. While many wives did not expect the current division of labor to change, they did acknowledge that it was unbalanced. The men, although acknowledging that things weren't

exactly fair, tended to minimize the asymmetry by seeing many of the short repetitive tasks associated with housekeeping as shared activities. Although there was tremendous diversity among the couples we talked to, we observed a general pattern of disagreement over how much family work the other spouse performed.

The sociologist Jesse Bernard provides us with a useful way to understand why this might be. Bernard suggested that every marital union contains two marriages—"his" and "hers."[5] We discovered from our interviews and observations that most of the husbands and wives were, indeed, living in separate marriages or separate worlds. Her world centered around keeping track of the countless details of housework and child care even though she was employed. His world centered around his work and his leisure activities so that he avoided noticing or anticipating the details of running a home. Husbands "helped out" when wives gave them tasks to do, and because they almost always complied with requests for help, most tended to assume that they were sharing the household labor. Because much of the work the women did was unseen or taken for granted by the men, they tended to underestimate their wives contributions and escaped the full range of tensions and strains associated with family work.

Because wives remained in control of setting schedules, generating lists for domestic chores, and worrying about the children, they perceived their husbands as contributing relatively little. A frequent comment from wives was that their husbands "just didn't see" the domestic details, and that the men would not often take responsibility for anticipating and planning for what needed to be done. Although many of the men we interviewed maintained their favored position within the family by "not seeing" various aspects of domestic life and leaving the details and planning to their wives, other couples were in the process of ongoing negotiations and, as described below, were successful at redefining some household chores as shared endeavors.

Concerning their paid work, the families we interviewed reported that both husbands and wives had jobs because of financial necessity. The men made comments like, "we were pretty much forced into it," or "we didn't really have any choice." Although most of the husbands and wives were employed full-time, only a few accepted the wife as an equal provider or true breadwinner. Using the type of job, employment schedule, and earnings of each spouse, along with their attitudes toward providing, I categorized the couples into main-provider families and co-provider families.[6] Main-provider couples considered the husband's job to be primary and the wife's job to be secondary. Co-provider couples in contrast, tended to accept the wife's job as permanent, and some even treated the wife's job as equally important to her husband's. Accepting the wife as an equal provider, or considering the husband to have failed as a provider, significantly shaped the couples' divisions of household labor.

Main-Provider Families

In just under half of the families we interviewed, the men earned substantially more money than their wives and were assumed to be "natural" breadwinners, whereas the women were assumed to be innately better equipped to deal with home and children. Wives in all of these main-provider families were employed, but the wife's job was often considered temporary, and her income was treated as "extra" money and earmarked for special purposes.[7] One main-provider husband said, "I would prefer that my wife did not have to work, and could stay at home with my daughter, but finances just don't permit that." Another commented that his wife made just about enough to cover the costs of child care, suggesting that the children were still her primary responsibility, and that any wages she earned should first be allocated to cover "her" tasks.

The main-provider couples included many wives who were employed part-time, and some who worked in lower-status full-time jobs with wages much lower than their husband's. These women took pride in their homemaker role and readily accepted responsibility for managing the

household, although they occasionally asked for help. One part-time bookkeeper married to a recent law-school graduate described their division of labor by saying, "It's a given that I take care of children and housework, but when I am real tired, he steps in willingly." Main-provider husbands typically remained in a helper role: in this case, the law clerk told his wife, "Just tell me what to do and I'll do it." He said that if he came home and she was gone, he might clean house, but that if she was home, he would "let her do it." This reflects a typical division of labor in which the wife acts as household manager and the husband occasionally serves as her helper.[8]

This lawyer-to-be talked about early negotiations between he and his wife that seemed to set the tone for current smoldering arguments about housework:

> When we were first married, I would do something and she wouldn't like the way that I did it. So I would say, "OK, then, you do it, and I won't do it again." That was like in our first few years of marriage when we were first getting used to each other, but now she doesn't discourage me so much. She knows that if she does, she's going to wind up doing it herself.

His resistance and her reluctance to press for change reflect an unbalanced economy of gratitude.[9] When he occasionally contributed to housework or child care, she was indebted to him. She complimented him for being willing to step in when she asked for help, but privately lamented the fact that she had to negotiate for each small contribution. Firmly entrenched in the main-provider role and somewhat oblivious to the daily rituals of housework and child care, he felt justified in needing prodding and encouragement. When she did ask him for help, she was careful to thank him for dressing the children or for giving her a ten-minute break from them. While these patterns of domestic labor and inequities in the exchange of gratitude were long-standing, tension lurked just below the surface for this couple. He commented, "My wife gets uptight with me for agreeing to help out my mom, when she feels she can't even ask me to go to the store for her."

Another main-provider couple reflected a similar pattern of labor allocation, but claimed that the arrangement was fair to them both. The woman, a part-time teacher's aide, acknowledged that she loved being a wife and mother and "naturally" took charge of managing the household. She commented, "I have the say so on the running of the house, and I also decide on the children's activities." Although she had a college degree, she described her current part-time job as "ideal" for her. She was able to work twenty hours per week at a neighborhood school and was home by the time her own children returned home from their school. While she earned only $6,000 per year, she justified the low salary because the job fit so well with "the family's schedule." Her husband's administrative job allowed them to live comfortably since he earned almost $50,000 annually.

This secondary-provider wife said that they divided household tasks in a conventional manner: She did most all of the cleaning, cooking, clothes-care, and child-care tasks, while he did the yard work, home repairs, and finances. Her major complaints were that her husband didn't notice things, that she had to nag him, and that he created more housework for her. "The worst part about the housework and child care is the amount of nagging I have to do to get him to help. Also, for example, say I just cleaned the house; he will leave the newspaper scattered all over the place or he will leave wet towels on the bathroom floor."

When asked whether there had been any negotiation over who would do what chores, the husband responded, "I don't think a set decision was made, it was a necessity." His wife's response was similar, "It just evolved that way, we never really talked about it." His provider role was taken for granted, but occasionally she voiced some muted resentment. For example, she commented that it upset her when he told her that she should not be working because their youngest child was only five years old. As an afterthought, she mentioned that she was sometimes bothered by the fact that she had not advanced her career, or

worked overtime, since that would have interfered with "the family's" schedule.

In general, wives of main-providers not only performed virtually all housework and child care, but both spouses accepted this as "natural" or "normal." Main provider husbands assumed that financial support was their "job" or their "duty." When one man was asked about how it felt to make more money than his wife, he responded by saying: "It's my job, I wouldn't feel right if I didn't make more money. . . . Any way that I look at it, I have to keep up my salary, or I'm not doing my job. If it costs $40,000 to live nowadays and I'm not in a $40,000-a-year job, then I'm not gonna be happy."

This same husband, a head mechanic who worked between 50 and 60 hours per week, also showed how main-provider husbands sometimes felt threatened when women begin asserting themselves in previously all-male occupational enclaves:

> As long as women mind their own business, no problem with me. . . . There's nothing wrong with them being in the job, but they shouldn't try to do more than that. Like, if you get a secretary that's nosy and wants to run the company, hey, well, we tell her where to stick it. . . . When you can't do my job, don't tell me how to do it.

The mechanic's wife, also a part-time teacher's aide, subtly resisted by "spending as little time on housework as I can get away with." Nevertheless, she still considered it her sole duty to cook, and only when her husband was away at National Guard training sessions did she feel she could "slack off" by not placing "regular meals" on the family's table each night.

The Provider Role and Failed Aspirations

Wives performed most of the household labor in main-provider couples, but if main-provider husbands had failed career aspirations, more domestic work was shared. What appeared to tip the economy of gratitude away from automatic male privilege was the wife's sense that the husband had not fulfilled his occupational potential. For example, one main-provider husband graduated from a four-year college and completed two years of post-graduate study without finishing his Master's Thesis. At the time of the interview, he was making about $30,000 a year as a self-employed house painter, and his wife was making less than half that amount as a full-time secretary. His comments show how her evaluation of his failed or postponed career aspirations led to more bargaining over his participation in routine housework:

> She reminds me that I'm not doing what we both think I should be doing, and sometimes that's a discouragement. I might have worked a lot of hours, and I'll come home tired, for example, and she'll say, "You've gotta clean the house," and I'll say, "Damn I'm tired, I'd like to get a little rest in," but she says "you're only doing this because it's been your choice." She tends to not have sympathy for me in my work because it was more my choice than hers.

He acknowledged that he should be doing something more "worthwhile," and hoped that he would not be painting houses for more than another year. Still, as long as he stayed in his current job, considered beneath him by both of them, she would not allow him to use fatigue from employment as a way to get out of doing housework:

> I worked about 60 hours a week the last couple of weeks. I worked yesterday [Saturday], and today—if it had been my choice—I would have drank beer and watched TV. But since she had a baby shower to go to, I babysitted my nephews. And since we had you coming, she kind of laid out the program: "You've gotta clean the floors, and wash the dishes and do the carpets. So get to it buddy!" [Laughs.]

This main-provider husband capitulated to his wife's demands, but she still had to set tasks for him and remind him to perform them. In responding to her "program," he used the strategy of claimed incompetence that other main-provider husbands also used. While he admitted that he was proficient at the "janitorial stuff," he was careful to point out that he was incapable of dusting or doing the laundry:

> It's amazing what you can do when you have little time and you just get in and do it. And I'm good at that. I'm good at the big cleaning, I'm good at the janitorial stuff. I can do the carpet, do the floors, do all that stuff. But I'm no good on the details. She wants all the details just right, so she handles dusting, the laundry, and stuff like that. . . . You know, like I would have everything come out one color.

By re-categorizing some of the housework as "big cleaning," this husband rendered it accountable as men's work. He drew the line at laundry and dusting, but he had transformed some household tasks, like vacuuming and mopping, into work appropriate for men to do. He was complying, albeit reluctantly, to many of his wife's requests because they agreed that he had not fulfilled "his" job as sole provider. He still yearned to be the "real" breadwinner and shared his hope that getting a better paying job would mean that he could ignore the housework:

> Sharing the house stuff is usually just a necessity. If, as we would hope in the future, she didn't have to work outside the home, then I think I would be comfortable doing less of it. Then she would be the primary house-care person and I would be the primary financial-resource person. I think roles would change then, and I would be comfortable with her doing more of the dishes and more of the cleaning, and I think she would too. In that sense, I think traditional relationships—if traditional means the guy working and the woman staying home—is a good thing. I wouldn't mind getting a taste of it myself!

A similar failed aspirations pattern was found in another main-provider household, in spite of the fact that the husband had a college degree and a job as an elementary-school teacher. While his wife earned less than a sixth of what he did, she was working on an advanced degree and coordinated a nonprofit community program. In this family, unlike most of the others, the husband performed more housework than he did child care, though both he and his wife agreed that she did more of both. Nevertheless, he performed these household chores reluctantly and only in response to prodding from his wife: "Housework is mostly her responsibility. I like to come home and kick back. Sometimes she has to complain before I do anything around the house. You know when she hits the wall, then I start doing things."

This main-provider husband talked about how his real love was art, and how he had failed to pursue his dream of being a graphic artist. The blocked occupational achievement in his case was not that he didn't make good money in a respected professional job, but that he was not fulfilling his "true" potential. His failed career goals increased her willingness to make demands on him, influenced their division of household labor, and helped shape feelings of entitlement between them: "I have talents that she doesn't have. I guess that's one of my strongest strengths, that I'm an artist. But she's very disappointed in me that I have not done enough of it . . ."

Another main-provider husband held a job as a telephone lineman, and his wife ran a family day-care center out of their home, which earned her less than a third of what he made. She talked about her regrets that he didn't do something "more important" for a living, and he talked about her frequent reminders that he was "too smart for what I'm doing." Like the other failed-aspirations husbands, he made significant contributions to domestic chores, but his resentment showed when he talked about "the wife" holding a job far from home:

> What I didn't like about it was that I used to get home before the wife, because she had to commute, and I'd have to pop something to eat. Most of the time it was just whatever I happened to find in the fridge. Then I'd have to go pick up the kids immediately from the babysitter, and sometimes I had evening things to do, so what I didn't like was that I had to figure out a way to schedule baby watch or baby sitting.

Even when main-provider husbands began to assume responsibility for domestic work in response to "necessity" or "nagging," they seemed to cling to the idea that these were still "her" chores. Coincidentally, most of the secondary-provider wives reported that they received little help unless they "constantly" reminded their husbands. What generally kept secondary-provider wives from resenting their husband's resistance was their own acceptance of the homemaker role and their recognition of his superior financial contributions. When performance of the male-provider role was deemed to be lacking in some way—i.e., failed aspirations or low occupational prestige—wives' resentment appeared closer to the surface, and they were more persistent in demanding help from their husbands.

Ambivalent Co-providers

Over half of the couples we interviewed were classified as co-providers. The husbands and wives in these families had more equal earnings and placed a higher value on the wife's employment than those in main-provider families, but there was considerable variation in terms of their willingness to accept the woman as a full and equal provider. Five of the twelve husbands in the co-provider group were ambivalent about sharing the provider role and were also reluctant to share most household tasks. Compared to their wives, ambivalent co-provider husbands usually held jobs that were roughly equivalent in terms of occupational prestige and worked about the same number of hours per week, but because of gender bias in the labor market, the men earned significantly more than their wives. Compared to main-provider husbands, they considered their wives' jobs to be relatively permanent and important, but they continued to use their own job commitments as justification for doing little at home. Ambivalent co-provider husbands' family obligations rarely intruded into their work lives, whereas their wives' family obligations frequently interfered with their paid work. Such asymmetrically permeable work/

family boundaries are common in single-earner and main-provider families, but must be supported with subtle ideologies and elaborate justifications when husbands and wives hold similar occupational positions.[10]

Ambivalent co-provider husbands remained in a helper role at home, perceiving their wives to be more involved parents and assuming that housework was also primarily their wives' responsibility. The men used their jobs to justify their absence from home, but most also lamented not being able to spend more time with their families. For instance, one husband who worked full time as a city planner was married to a woman who worked an equal number of hours as an office manager. In talking about the time he put in at his job, he commented, "I wish I had more time to spend with my children, and to spend with my wife too, of course, but it's a fact of life that I have to work." His wife, in contrast, indicated that her paid job, which she had held for fourteen years, did not prohibit her from adequately caring for her three children, or taking care of "her" household chores. Ambivalent co-provider husbands did not perform significantly more housework and child care than main-provider husbands, and generally did fewer household chores than main-provider husbands with failed career aspirations.

Not surprisingly, ambivalent co-provider husbands tended to be satisfied with their current divisions of labor, even though they usually admitted that things were "not quite fair." One junior-high-school teacher married to a bilingual-education program coordinator described his reactions to their division of family labor:

> To be honest, I'm totally satisfied. When I had a first-period conference, I was a little more flexible; I'd help her more with changing 'em, you know, getting them ready for school, since I didn't have to be at school right away. Then I had to switch because they had some situation out at fifth-period conference, so that now she does it a little bit more than I do, and I don't help out with the kids as much in the morning because I have to be there an hour earlier.

This ambivalent co-provider clearly saw himself as "helping" his wife with the children, yet made light of her contributions by saying she does "a little bit more than I do." He went on to reveal how his wife did not enjoy similar special privileges due to her employment, since she had to pick up the children from day care every day, as well as taking them to school in the mornings:

> She gets out a little later than I do, because she's an administrator but I have other things outside. I also work out, I run, and that sort of gives me a time away, to do that before they all come here. I have community meetings in the evenings sometimes, too. So, I mean, it might not be totally fair—maybe 60/40—but I'm thoroughly happy with the way things are.

While he was "thoroughly happy" with the current arrangements, she thought that it was decidedly unfair. She said, "I don't like the fact that it's taken for granted that I'm available. When he goes out he just assumes I'm available, but when I go out I have to consult with him to make sure he is available." For her, child care was a given; for him, it was optional. He commented, "If I don't have something else to do, then I'll take the kids."

Ambivalent co-provider husbands also tended to talk about regretting that their family involvements limited their careers or personal activities. For instance the school teacher discussed above lamented that he could not do what he used to before he had children:

> Having children keeps me away from thinking a lot about my work. You know, it used to be, before we had kids, I could have my mind geared to work—you know how ideas just pop in, you really get into it. But with kids it doesn't get as—you know, you can't switch. It gets more difficult, it makes it hard to get into it. I don't have that freedom of mind, you know, and it takes away from aspects of my work, like doing a little bit more reading or research that I would like to do. Or my own activities, I mean, I still run, but not as much as I used to. I used to play basketball, I used to coach, this and that . . .

Other ambivalent co-provider husbands talked about the impact of children on their careers and personal lives with less bitterness and more appreciation for establishing a relationship with their children. Encouraged by their wives to alter their priorities, some reinterpreted the relative importance of career and family commitments:

I like the way things are going. Let's put it this way. I mean, it's just that once you become a parent, it's a never-ending thing. I coach my kid for example, this past week we had four games. . . . I just think that by having a family that your life becomes so involved after awhile with your own kids, that it's very difficult. I coached at the varsity level for one year, but I had to give it up. I would leave in the morning when they were asleep, and I would get out of coaches' meetings at ten or eleven at night. My wife said to me, "Think about your priorities, man; you leave when the kids are asleep, come back when they are asleep." So I decided to change that act. So I gave it up for one year, and I was home all the time. Now I am going to coach again, but it's at lower levels, and I'll be home every day. I have to make adjustments for my family. Your attitude changes, it's not me that counts anymore.

Whereas family labor was not shared equally in this ambivalent co-provider couple, the husband, at his wife's urging, was beginning to accept and appreciate that his children were more important than his job. He was evaluating his attachment to his children on his wife's terms, but he was agreeing with her, and he had begun to take more responsibility for them.

Many of these husbands talked about struggles over wanting to spend more time on their careers, and most did not relinquish the assumption that the home was the wife's domain. For example, some ambivalent co-provider couples attempted to alleviate stress on the wife by hiring outside help. In response to a question about whether their division of labor was fair, a self-employed male attorney said, "Do you mean fair like equal? It's probably not equal, so probably it wouldn't be fair, but that's why we have a housekeeper." His wife, a social worker earning only ten percent less than he, said that the household was still her responsibility, but that she now had fewer tasks to do: "When I did not have help, I tended to do everything, but with a housekeeper, I don't have to do so much." She went on to talk about how she wished he would do more with their five- and eight-year-old children, but speculated that he probably would as they grew older.

Another couple paid a live-in babysitter/housekeeper to watch their three children during the day while he worked full-time in construction and she worked full-time as a psychiatric social worker. While she labeled the outside help as "essential," she noted that her husband contributed more to the mess than he did to its clean-up. He saw himself as an involved father because he played with his children, and she acknowledged this, but she also complained that he competed with them in games as if he were a child himself. His participation in routine household labor was considered optional, as evidenced by his comment, "I like to cook once in a while."

Co-providers

In contrast, about a third of the couples we interviewed fully accepted the wife's long-term employment, considered her career to be just as important as his, and were in various stages of redefining household labor as men's work. Like the ambivalent couples discussed above, full co-provider spouses worked about the same number of hours as each other, but on the whole, these couples worked more total hours than their more ambivalent counterparts, though their annual incomes were a bit lower. According to both husbands and wives, the sharing of housework and child care was substantially greater for full co-providers than for ambivalent co-providers, and also much more balanced than for main-providers.

Like ambivalent co-providers, husbands in full co-provider families discussed conflicts between work and family and sometimes alluded to the ways that their occupational advancement was limited by their commitments to their children. One husband and wife spent the same number of hours on the job, earned approximately the same amount of money, and were employed as engineering technicians for the same employer. When we asked him how his family involvement had affected his job performance, he responded by saying, "It should, OK, because I really need to spend a lot more time learning my work, and I haven't really put in the time I need to advance in the profession. I would like to spend, I mean I *would* spend, more time if I didn't have kids. I'd like to be able to play with the computer or read books more often." Although he talked about conflicts between job and family, he also emphasized that lost work time was not really a sacrifice because he valued time with his children so highly. He did not use his job as an excuse to get out of doing child care or housework, and he seemed to value his wife's career at least as much as his own:

> I think her job is probably more important than mine because she's been at that kind of work a lot longer than I have. And at the level she is— it's awkward the way it is, because I get paid just a little bit more than she does, I have a higher position. But she definitely knows the work a lot more, she's been doing the same type of work for about nine years already, and I've only been doing this type of engineering work for about two-and-a-half years, so she knows a lot more. We both have to work, that's for sure.

Recognition of their roughly equivalent professional status and the need for two equal providers affected this couple's division of parenting and housework. The husband indicated that he did more child care and housework than his wife, and she gave him much credit for his efforts, but in her interview, she indicated that he still did less than half. She described her husband's relationship with their seven-year-old son as "very caring," and noted that he assists the boy with homework more than she does. She also said that her husband did most of the heavy cleaning and scrubbing, but also commented that he doesn't clean toilets and doesn't always notice when things get dirty. The husband described their allocation of housework by saying, "Maybe she does less than I do, but some of the things she does, I just will not do. I will not dust all the little things in the house. That's one of my least favorite things, but I'm more likely to do the mopping and vacuuming." This husband's comments also revealed some ongoing tension about whose housework standards should be maintained. He said, "She has high standards for cleanliness that you would have to be home to maintain. Mind tend to acknowledge that you don't always get to this stuff because you have other things to do. I think I have a better acceptance that one priority hurts something else in the background."

While this couple generally agreed about how to raise their son, standards for child care were also subject to debate. He saw himself as doing more with his son than his wife, as reflected in comments such as "I tend to think of myself as the more involved parent, and I think other people have noticed that, too." While she had only positive things to say about his parenting, he offered both praise and criticism of her parenting:

> She can be very playful. She makes up fun games. She doesn't always put enough into the educational part of it, though, like exploring or reading. . . . She cherishes tune-up time [job-related study or preparation], and sometimes I feel she should be using that time to spend with him. Like at the beach, I'll play with him, but she'll be more likely to be under the umbrella reading.

Like many of the other husbands, he went on to say that he thought their division of labor was unfair. Unlike the others, however, he indicated that he thought their current arrangements favored *her* needs, not his:

> I think I do more housework. It's probably not fair, because I do more of the dirtier tasks. . . . Also, at this point, our solution tends to favor her free time more than my free time. I think that has more to do with our personal backgrounds. She has more personal friends to do things with, so she has more outside things to do whereas I say I'm not doing anything.

In this family, comparable occupational status and earnings, coupled with a relatively egalitarian ideology, led to substantial sharing of both child care and housework. While the husband tended to take more credit for his involvement than his wife gave him, we can see a difference between their talk and that of some of the families discussed above. Other husbands sometimes complained about their wife's high standards, but they also treated housework, and even parenting, as primarily *her* duty. They usually resented being nagged to do more around the house and failed to move out of a helper role. Rarely did such men consider it *their* duty to anticipate, schedule, and take care of family and household needs. In this co-provider household, in contrast, the gendered allocation of responsibility for child care and housework was not assumed. Because of this, negotiations over housework and parenting were more frequent than in the other families. Since they both held expectations that each would fulfill both provider and caretaker roles, resentments came from both spouses—not just from the wife.

Our interviews suggest that it might be easier for couples to share both provider and homemaker roles when, like the family above, the wife's earnings and occupational prestige equal or exceed those of her husband. For instance, in one of the couples reporting the most sharing of child care and housework, the wife earned $36,000 annually as the executive director of a non-profit community organization and a consultant, and her husband earned $30,000 as a self-employed general contractor. This couple started off their marriage with fairly conventional gender-role expectations and an unbalanced division of labor. While the husband's ideology had changed somewhat, he still talked like most of the main-provider husbands:

> As far the household is concerned, I divide a house into two categories: one is the interior and the other is the exterior. For the interior, my wife pushes me to deal with that. The exterior, I'm left to it myself. So, what I'm basically saying is that generally speaking, a woman does not deal with the exterior. The woman's main concern is with the interior, although there is a lot of deviation.

In this family, an egalitarian belief system did not precede the sharing of household labor. The wife was still responsible for setting the "interior" household agenda and had to remind her husband to help with housework and child care. When asked whether he and his wife had arguments about housework, this husband laughed and said, "All the time, doesn't everybody?"

What differentiated this couple from most others, is that she made more money than he did and had no qualms about demanding help from him. While he had not yet accepted the idea that interior chores were equally his, he reluctantly performed them. She ranked his contributions to child care to be equal to hers, and rated his contributions to housework only slightly below her own. While not eagerly rushing to do the cooking, cleaning, or laundry, he complied with occasional reminders and according to his wife, was "a better cleaner" than she was.

His sharing stemmed, in part, from her higher earnings and their mutual willingness to reduce his "outside chores" by hiring outside help. Unlike the more ambivalent co-providers who hired housekeepers to do "her" chores, this couple hired a gardener to work on the yard so they could both spend more time focusing on the children and the house. Rather than complaining about their division of labor, he talked about how he has come to appreciate his situation:

> Ever since I've known my wife, she's made more money than I have. Initially—as a man—I resented it. I went through a lot of head trips about it. But as time developed, I appreciated it. Now I respect it. The way I figure it is, I'd rather have her sharing the money with me than sharing it with someone else. She has her full-time job and then she has her part-time job as a consultant. The gardener I'm paying $75 per week, and I'm paying someone else $25 per week to make my lunch, so I'm enjoying it! It's self-interest.

The power dynamic in this family, coupled with their willingness to pay for outside help to reduce his chores, and the flexibility of his self-employed work schedule, led to substantial sharing of cooking, cleaning, and child care. Because she was making more money and working more hours than he was, he could not emulate other husbands in claiming priority for his provider activities.

A similar dynamic was evident in other co-provider couples with comparable earnings and career commitments. One male IRS officer married to a school teacher now made more money than his wife, but talked about his feelings when she was the more successful provider:

> It doesn't bother me when she makes more money than me. I don't think it has anything to do with being a man. I don't have any hangups about it, I mean, I don't equate those things with manhood. It takes a pretty simple mind to think that way. First of all, she doesn't feel superior when she has made more money.

The woman in this couple commented that her husband was "better" at housework than she was, but that she still had to nag him to do it. Although only two wives in our sample of Chicano families earned more than their husbands, the reversal of symbolic provider status seemed to raise expectations for increased family work from husbands. The husbands who made less than their wives performed significantly more of the housework and child care than the other husbands.

Even when wives' earnings did not exceed the husbands', some co-providers shared the homemaker role. A male college-admissions recruiter and his executive-secretary wife shared substantial housework and child care according to mutual ratings. He made $29,000 per year working a 50 hour week, while she made $22,000 working a 40 hour week. She was willing to give him more credit than he was willing to claim for child care, reflecting her sincere appreciation for his parenting efforts, which were greater than those of other fathers she knew. He placed a high value on her mothering and seemed to downplay the possibility that they should be considered equal parents. Like most of the men in this study, the college-recruiter husband was reluctant to perform house-cleaning chores. Like many co-providers, however, he managed to redefine some routine household chores as a shared responsibility. For instance, when we asked him what he liked least about housework, he laughingly replied, "Probably those damn toilets, man, and the showers, the bathrooms, gotta scrub 'em, argghh! I wish I didn't have to do any of that, you know the vacuuming and all that. But it's just a fact of life."

Even though he did more than most husbands, he acknowledged that he did less than his wife, and admitted that he sometimes tried to use his job to get out of doing more around the house. But whereas other wives often allowed husbands to use their jobs as excuses for doing less family work, or assumed that their husbands were incapable of performing certain chores like cooking or laundry, the pattern in this family resembled that of the failed-aspirations couples. In other words, the wife did not assume that housework was "her" job, did not accept her husband's job demands as justification for his doing less housework, and sometimes challenged his interpretation of how much his job required of him. She also got her husband to assume more responsibility by refraining from performing certain tasks. He commented:

> Sometimes she just refuses to do something. . . . An example would be the ironing, you know, I never used to do the ironing, hated it. Now it's just something that happens. You need something ironed, you better iron it or you're not gonna have it in the morning. So, I think, you know, that kinda just evolved. I mean, she just gradually quit doing it so everybody just had to do their own. My son irons his own clothes, I iron my own clothes, my daughter irons her own clothes, the only one that doesn't iron is the baby, and next year she'll probably start.

The sociologist Jane Hood, whose path-breaking family research highlighted the importance of provider role definition to marital power, describes this strategy as "going on strike," and suggests that it is most effective when husbands feel the specific task *must* be done.[11] Since appearing neat and well-dressed was a priority for this husband, when his wife stopped ironing his clothes, he started doing it himself. Because he felt it was important for his children to be "presentable" in public, he also began to remind them to iron their own clothes before going visiting or attending church.

While many co-provider couples reported that sharing housework was contingent upon ongoing bargaining and negotiation, others focused on how it evolved "naturally." One co-provider husband, director of a housing agency, reported that he and his wife didn't negotiate; "we pretty much do what needs to be done." His wife, an executive secretary, confirmed his description, and echoed the ad-hoc arrangements of many of the role-sharing couples: "We have not had to negotiate. We both have our specialties. He is great with dishes, I like to clean bathrooms. He does most of the laundry. It has worked out that we each do what we like best."

Although sharing tasks sometimes increases conflict, when both spouses assume that household tasks are a shared responsibility, negotiation can also become less necessary or contentious. For example, a co-provider husband who worked as a mail carrier commented, "I get home early and start dinner, make sure the kids do their homework, feed the dogs, stuff like that." He and his wife, an executive secretary, agreed that they rarely talk about housework. She said, "When I went back to work we agreed that we both needed to share, and so we just do it." While she still reminded him to perform chores according to her standards or on her schedule, she summed up her appreciation by commenting, "at least he does it without complaining." Lack of complaint was a common feature of co-provider families. Whereas many main-provider husbands complained of having to do "her" chores, the co-providers rarely talked about harboring resentments. Main-provider husbands typically lamented not having

the services of a stay-at-home wife, but co-provider husbands almost never made such comparisons.

Summary and Discussion

For these dual-earner Chicano couples, we found conventional masculine privilege as well as considerable sharing in several domains. First, as in previous studies of ethnic minority families, wives were employed a substantial number of hours and made significant contributions to the household income. Second, like some who have studied Chicano families, we found that couples described their decision-making to be relatively fair and equal.[12] Third, fathers in these families were more involved in child rearing than their own fathers had been, and many were rated as sharing a majority of child care tasks. Finally, while no husband performed fully half of the housework, a few made substantial contributions in this area as well.

One of the power dynamics that appeared to undergird the household division of labor in these families was the relative earning power of each spouse, though this was modified by factors such as occupational prestige, provider role status, and personal preference. In just under half of the families, the wife earned less than a third of the family income, and in all of these families the husband performed little of the routine housework or child care. In two families, wives earned more than their husbands, and these two households reported sharing more domestic labor than others. Among the other couples who shared housework and child care, there was a preponderance of relatively balanced incomes. In the two families with large financial contributions from wives, but little household help from husbands, couples hired housekeepers to reduce the wives' household workload.

While relative income appeared to make a significant difference in marital power, we observed no simple or straightforward exchange of market resources for domestic services. Other factors like failed career aspirations or occupational status influenced marital dynamics and helped explain why some wives were willing to push a little harder for change in the division of household labor. In almost every case, husbands reluctantly responded to requests for help from wives. Only when wives explicitly took the initiative to shift some of the housework burden to husbands did the men begin to assume significant responsibility for the day-to-day operation of the household. Even when they began to share the housework and child care, men tended to do some of the less onerous tasks like playing with the children or washing the dinner dishes. When we compared these men to their own fathers, or their wives' fathers, however, we could see that they were sharing more domestic chores than the generation that preceded them.

Acceptance of wives as co-providers and wives' delegation of a portion of the homemaker role to husbands were especially important to creating more equal divisions of household labor in these families. If wives made lists for their husbands or offered them frequent reminders, they were more successful than if they waited for husbands to take the initiative. Remaining responsible for managing the home and children was cause for resentment on the part of many wives, however. Sometimes wives were effective in getting husbands to perform certain chores, like ironing, by stopping doing it altogether. For other wives, sharing evolved more "naturally," as both spouses agreed to share tasks or performed the chores that they preferred.

Economies of gratitude continually shifted as the ideology, career attachments, and feelings of entitlement of each spouse changed over time. For some main-provider families, this meant that wives were grateful for husbands' "permission" to hold a job, or that wives worked harder at home because they felt guilty for making their husbands do any of the housework. Main-provider husbands usually let their job commitments limit their family work, whereas their wives took time off from work to care for a sick child or to attend a parent–teacher conference.

Even in families where co-provider wives had advanced degrees and earned high incomes, some wives' work/family boundaries were more permeable than their husbands', like the program director married to a teacher who was a "perpetual" graduate student and attended "endless" community meetings. While she was employed more hours than he, and made about the same amount of money, she had to "schedule him" to watch the children if she wanted to leave the house alone. His stature as a "community leader" provided him with subterranean leverage in the unspoken struggle over taking responsibility for the house and children. His "gender ideology," if measured with conventional survey questions, would undoubtedly have been characterized as "egalitarian," because he spoke in broad platitudes about women's equality and was washing the dishes when we arrived for the interviews. He insisted on finishing the dishes as he answered my questions, but in the other room, his wife confided to Elsa in incredulous tones, "He *never* does that!"

In other ambivalent co-provider families, husbands gained unspoken advantage because they had more prestigious jobs than their wives, and earned more money. While these highly educated attorneys and administrators talked about how they respected their wives' careers, and expressed interest in spending more time with their children, their actions showed that they did not fully assume responsibility for sharing the homemaker or parenting role. To solve the dilemma of too little time and too many chores, two of these families hired housekeepers. Wives were grateful for this strategy, though it did not alter inequities in the distribution of housework and child care, nor in the allocation of worry.

In other families, the economy of gratitude departed dramatically from conventional notions of husband as economic provider and wife as nurturing homemaker. When wives' earnings approached or exceeded their husbands', economies of gratitude shifted toward more equal expectations, with husbands beginning to assume that they must do more around the house. Even in these families, husbands rarely began doing more chores without prodding from wives, but they usually did them "without complaining." Similarly, when wives with economic leverage began expecting more from their husbands, they were usually successful in getting them to do more.

Another type of leverage that was important, even in main-provider households, was the existence of failed aspirations. If wives expected husbands to "make more" of themselves, pursue "more important" careers, or follow "dream" occupational goals, then wives were able to get husbands to do more around the house. This perception of failed aspirations, if held by both spouses, served as a reminder that husbands had no excuse for not helping out at home. In these families, wives were not at all reluctant to demand assistance with domestic chores, and husbands were rarely able to use their jobs as excuses for getting out of housework.

The economies of gratitude in these families were not equally balanced, but many exhibited divisions of household labor that contradicted cultural stereotypes of macho men and male-dominated families. Particularly salient in these families was the lack of fit between their own class position and that of their parents. Most of the parents were Mexican immigrants with little education and low occupational mobility. The couples we interviewed, in contrast, were well-educated and relatively secure in middle-class occupations. The couples could have compared themselves to their parents, evaluating themselves to be egalitarian and financially successful. While some did just that, most compared themselves to their Anglo and Chicano friends and coworkers, many of whom shared as much or more than they did. Implicitly comparing their earnings, occupational commitments, and perceived aptitudes, husbands and wives negotiated new patterns of work/family boundaries and developed novel justifications for their emerging arrangements. These were not created anew, but emerged out of the popular culture in which they found themselves. Judith

Stacey labels such developments the making of the "postmodern family," because they signal "the contested, ambivalent, and undecided character of contemporary gender and kinship arrangements."[13] Our findings confirm that families are an important site of new struggles over the meaning of gender and the rights and obligations of men and women in each other and over each other's labor.

One of the most provocative findings from our study has to do with the class position of Chicano husbands and wives who shared household labor: white-collar, working-class families shared more than upper-middle-class professionals. Contrary to findings from nationwide surveys predicting that higher levels of education for either husbands or wives will be associated with more sharing, the most highly educated of our well-educated sample of Chicano couples shared only moderate amounts of child care and little housework.[14] Contrary to other predictions, neither was it the working-class women in this study who achieved the most balanced divisions of labor.[15] It was the middle occupational group of women, the executive secretaries, clerks, technicians, teachers, and mid-level administrators who extracted the most help from husbands. The men in these families were similarly in the middle in terms of occupational status for this sample—administrative assistants, a builder, a mail carrier, a technician—and in the middle in terms of income. What this means is that the highest status wives—the program coordinators, nurses, social workers, and office managers—were not able to, or chose not to, transform their salaries or occupational status into more participation from husbands. This was probably because their husbands had even higher incomes and more prestigious occupations than they did. The lawyers, program directors, ranking bureaucrats, and "community leaders" parlayed their status into extra leisure at home, either by paying for housekeepers or ignoring the housework. Finally, Chicana wives at the lowest end of the occupational structure fared least well. The teacher's aides, entry-level secretaries, day-care providers, and part-time employees did the bulk of the work at home whether they were married to mechanics or lawyers. When wives made less than a third of what their husbands did, they were only able to get husbands to do a little more if the men were working at jobs considered "below" them—a telephone lineman, a painter, an elementary-school teacher.

Only Chicano couples were included in this study, but results are similar to findings from previous interviews with Anglo couples.[16] My interpretation is that the major processes shaping divisions of labor in middle-class Chicano couples are approximately the same as those shaping divisions of labor in other middle-class couples. This is not to say that ethnicity did not make a difference to the Chicano couples we interviewed. They grew up in recently immigrating working-class families, watched their parents work long hours for minimal wages, and understood firsthand the toll that various forms of racial discrimination can take. Probably because of some of these experiences, and their own more recent ones, our informants looked at job security, fertility decisions, and the division of household labor somewhat differently than their Anglo counterparts. In some cases, this can give Chicano husbands in working-class or professional jobs license to ignore more of the housework, and might temper the anger of some working-class or professional Chicanas who are still called on to do most of the domestic chores. If these findings are generalizable, however, it is those in between the blue-collar working-class and the upper-middle-class professionals that might be more likely to share housework and childcare.

Assessing whether these findings apply to other dual-earner Chicano couples will require the use of larger, more representative samples. If the limited sharing observed here represents a trend— however slow or reluctant—it could have far-reaching consequences. More and more Chicana mothers are remaining full-time members of the paid labor force. With the "postindustrial" expansion of the service and information sectors of the economy, Chicanos and Chicanas will be increasingly likely to enter white-collar middle-class

occupations. As more Chicano families fit the occupational profile of those we studied, we may see more assumption of housework and child care by Chicano men. Regardless of the specific changes that the economy will undergo, we can expect Chicano men and women, like their Anglo counterparts, to continue to negotiate for change in their work and family roles.

Notes

1. For a discussion of how the term machismo can also reflect positive attributes of respect, loyalty, responsibility and generosity, see Alfredo Mirandé, "Chicano Fathers: Traditional Perceptions and Current Realities," pp. 93–106, in *Fatherhood Today*, P. Bronstein and C. Cowan, eds. (New York: Wiley, 1988).

2. For reviews of literature on Latin-American families and projections on their future proportionate representation in the population, see Randall Collins and Scott Coltrane, *Sociology of Marriage and the Family* (Chicago: Nelson Hall, 1994); William A. Vega, "Hispanic Families in the 1980s," *Journal of Marriage and the Family* 52(1990): 1015–1024; and Norma Williams, *The Mexican-American Family* (New York: General Hall, 1990).

3. Maxinne Baca Zinn, "Family, Feminism, and Race in America," *Gender & Society* 4(1990): 68–82; Mirandé, "Chicano Fathers"; Vega, "Hispanic Families"; and Williams, *The Mexican-American Family*.

4. See Coltrane, *Family Man: Fatherhood, Housework, and Gender Equity* (New York: Oxford University Press, 1994); Coltrane and Valdez, "Reluctant Compliance: Work/Family Role Allocation in Dual-Earner Chicano Families," in *Men, Work, and Family*, Jane C. Hood, ed. (Newbury Park, CA: Sage, 1994) and Valdez and Coltrane, "Work, Family, and the Chicana: Power, Perception and Equity," in *Employed Mothers and the Family Context*, Judith Frankel, ed. (New York: Springer, 1993). I thank Hilda Cortez, a summer research intern at the University of California, for help in transcribing some of the interviews and for providing insight into some of the issues faced by these families.

5. Jessie Bernard, *The Future of Marriage* (New York: World, 1972).

6. See Jane Hood, 1986. "The Provider Role: Its Meaning and Measurement." *Journal of Marriage and the Family* 48: 349–359.

7. Hood, "The Provider Role."

8. See Coltrane, "Household Labor and the Routine Production of Gender." *Social Problems* 36: 473–490.

9. I am indebted to Arlie Hochschild, who first used this term in *The Second Shift* (New York: Viking, 1987). See also Karen Pyke and Scott Coltrane, "Entitlement, Obligation, and Gratitude in Remarriage: Toward a Gendered Understanding of Household Labor Allocation."

10. I am indebted to Joseph Pleck for his conceptualization of "asymmetrically permeable" work/family boundaries ("The Work-Family Role System." *Social Problems* 24: 417–427).

11. Jane Hood, *Becoming a Two-Job Family*, p. 131.

12. See, for example, V. Cromwell and R. Cromwell, 1978. "Perceived Dominance in Decision Making and Conflict Resolution among Anglo, Black, and Chicano Couples." *Journal of Marriage and the Family* 40: 749–760; G. Hawkes and M. Taylor, 1975. "Power Structure in Mexican and Mexican-American Farm Labor Families." *Journal of Marriage and the Family* 37: 807–81; L. Ybarra, 1982. "When Wives Work: The Impact on the Chicano Family." *Journal of Marriage and the Family* 44: 169–178.

13. Judith Stacey, 1990. *Brave New Families*. New York: Basic Books, p. 17.

14. See, for instance, Donna H. Berardo, Constance Shehan, and Gerald R. Leslie, "A Residue of Tradition: Jobs, Careers, and Spouses' Time in Housework." *Journal of Marriage and the Family* 49(1987): 381–390; Catherine E. Ross, "The Division of Labor at Home." *Social Forces* 65(1987): 816–833.

15. Patricia Zavella. 1987. *Women's Work and Chicano Families*. Ithaca, NY: Cornell University Press; Stacey, *Brave New Families*.

16. See, for example, Hochschild, *Second Shift*; Hood, *Two-Job Family*; Coltrane, *Family Man*.

Michael C. Hanchard

On "Good" Black Fathers

After observing my then two-year-old daughter and I playing with each other at a summer event during graduate school, a black woman graduate student I knew walked up to us with a big smile and said, "It's so nice to see a black man who spends so much time with his child," adding a serious tone that reduced her voice to a conspiratorial whisper: "There's not too many black men who spend time with their children these days, you know," before she walked away. My daughter, oblivious to the exchange, continued with her demand that I flip her one more time (for the third time!). I was stunned.

How could this woman make such a statement, I thought to myself, when she herself was a product of a household with a responsible father (of whom she often spoke)? Had the dynamics of black communities—middle- and working-class—changed that much over the course of one generation to make the term *black father* an oxymoron, and cavorting with my daughter an exception? Like many other people in the United States, black or otherwise, I had heard and read the statistics and data on the number of black men who helped produce children but who were not "heading households," which has come to be understood as not living with the mother of his child. This has also come to be equated with, I believe, being an absent, irresponsible or non-parent.

These two assumptions are not, however, only part of the rhetoric about the crisis of black fatherhood. They are inextricably related to more

general assumptions about fatherhood, domesticity, and masculinity in these United States. Rarely, though, are discussions about black fatherhood linked to a broader conjuncture of societal forces that have shaped the present moment. Consequently, relations between black women, black men, and their children are rarely considered against the backdrop of rising divorce rates, family dysfunction, and cultural conservatism in the nation as a whole.

Embedded in my fellow graduate student's comments to me during that afternoon barbecue were parts of this discussion, the presumptions about the culpability of black men in impeding our ability to reproduce and nurture ourselves. That moment in which I was identified as a presence in my daughter's life became a barometer and lightning rod for black male parenting. In contrast to most mothers I know, who are automatically considered parents, young fathers like myself who are also parents are often treated like some sort of novelty. The fact of my blackness made my public act of parenting seem like an even greater novelty. While the widely voiced concern can be attributed to the circumstances under which black men, as fathers and individuals, find themselves at the present time, it is also a variation on a recurrent theme over the course of U.S. history, politics, and public policy about the very ability of African-Americans to care for themselves as a people, from slave quarters in Mississippi to the south side of Chicago, from Strivers Row in Harlem to Shaker Heights in Cleveland and points elsewhere. Whereas once African-Americans, like other people of African descent, were considered intellectually incapable of attending to their own self-governance, they are now interpreted by many who hold conservative as well as liberal positions as being culturally incapable—that is, without the moral and ethical imperatives—to raise and take care of families. The so-called "crisis of the black male," a topic of debate among members of black communities and their attendant institutions, policy makers, the religious right, rap musicians, and others, is often segregated from society at large by a language that assumes that black men and the communities that spawned them can be interpreted only through the lens of slavery and discrimination, as if these two features of U.S. society and culture affected only black people.

As those of any color who are involved in the lives of children know, parenting involves much more than an afternoon barbecue or any other public event in which people who supposedly love one another perform the usual niceties of hugging, kissing, and embracing in ways that suggest to the world outside that all is well within. Biographies of celebrities both living and dead, talk shows, television documentaries, and published research by specialists on families have provided ample grounds for suggesting that while the image of a loving, mutually supportive family with two ever present parents is not an absolute myth, there are few actual families that resemble the conventional, "traditional" model of the nuclear family. At the same time, those individuals and families whose lives do not resemble the mythic family are not, by definition, either bad people or bad parents.

Most people fall somewhere in between the models for families that more closely resemble a facade on a Hollywood movie lot than an actual case of domesticity or the entirely dysfunctional ensembles of disfigured humanity that family arrangements sometimes turn out to be. Most parents struggle with issues of divorce, fidelity, time and budgetary constraints, ornery relatives, and other thorny subjects within the context of their families and individual identities. Black people are no different.

What does distinguish black fathers, mothers, and their children from the present "crisis of the family" is that black people have struggled through various crisis and moments—as families and individuals—ever since their arrival into the New World as slaves four centuries ago. The very condition of slavery presupposed the absence or negation of family, since slavery operated on the premise that slaves belonged to no one other than slave owners themselves. From the dawn of slavery, people of African descent in the United States resisted their comprehensive but incomplete domination at the hands of slave masters by maintaining whatever possible links with family members on other plantations, or by forging familial ties where these were none, such as those between shipmates and their offspring.

I briefly recall this history simply to suggest that the present "crisis" of the black family in general and black males in particular has a prior history, and it is but a variation on a theme. With this in mind, I would like to make a basic point about the need to recognize the creative responses African-American communities have had to the responsibilities of fatherhood that have not fit within the parameters of the mythic constructions of fatherhood, the family, masculinity, and domesticity. Discussions of black fatherhood that attempt to force black males into a model of parenting that few people—male or female—white, black, or otherwise, adhere to in the contemporary United States should be viewed with suspicion against this historical and contemporary backdrop. Unfortunately, as my own personal example suggests, members of the African-American community, often in an effort to portray a sense of the cohesiveness and respectability so often denied by broader society, reproduce the same myths about parenting and family responsibility that imprison them within the very stereotypes they have been struggling for so long to break free of.

While I do not want to suggest that we ignore or dismiss nasty legacies of domestic and other forms of violence within black communities, teenage pregnancies, and a litany of other maladies that have been perpetrated and perpetuated by black men, I do want to suggest that we view discussions about the "crisis of the black male" with skepticism as long as the more general crises weighing over black people are ignored. Ultimately, the debates about the black male are less about black maleness and responsibility than about the variety of racially and economically discriminatory circumstances, both inside and outside black communities, that black males often find themselves in and react to, regardless of their parenting status.

An example of the ways in which the stereotypes of black dysfunction plague even the most successful black families regardless of their specific circumstances again comes from a personal experience, involving a girlfriend of my daughter. This child, whom I will call Rachel, was my daughter's best friend in the first grade. Donna (for the purposes of this essay), Rachel's mother, was a hardworking woman. She not only raised Rachel but worked at a demanding managerial job, held leadership positions in church and community organizations, and raised her stepson's infant daughter in her home. Neither Donna nor her husband were wealthy by any means, but they are able to provide not only for themselves but for their extended family as well, in both material and spiritual terms. They lived in a modest one-family home in the black section of a very segregated city. Donna would sometimes allow several days to pass before reading through the material in the school folder that Rachel brought home every day, which included past homework and exercises as well as information about upcoming school events. Like most working parents I know, regardless of socioeconomic status, it was a constant struggle to juggle domestic and professional responsibilities. With perhaps the exception of male single parents, I believe it is safe to say that women parents have greater home responsibilities than their male counterparts, and Donna was no exception.

Ms. Mason, her daughter's teacher, reprimanded Rachel one day for not having her folder materials checked by a parent, one of the rules of her classroom. After receiving a note from Rachel's teacher on the matter, Donna immediately called my wife and told her something like the following: "The next time I brought Rachel to school, I had a talk with the teacher, to let her know that just because I hadn't looked at her folder did not mean I didn't check her homework," adding "because I'm a good black parent."

A good black parent. What does that mean? There are several conditions that these four words could imply. A black person cannot simply be a parent; they are a black parent. But to be a black parent is simply not enough; one must be a good black parent. How does being a good black parent differ from being a good white parent, or simply a white or any other hued parent? What links Donna and me in this example is the manner in which both of us lurk between the categories already created for us and acted upon in a racist society. The identities of our lives are multiple: parent, spouse, counsel, friend, son and daughter, and so on. The stereotypes that we supposedly inhabit are singular: suspect parent. We are suspect parents because we are suspect human beings, suspected by the ideologies of racial discrimination to be something less than the norm, less than ideal.

Donna is a prime example of how black people both in and out of conventional families respond to these stereotypes of negativity. There is little doubt, I think, in her statement about her ability to be a good parent or the ability of others in her position to do the same. There is doubt, though, about the capability of certain members of white society to see her that way. This, unfortunately, is part of the legacy of black performance in public life in the United States. One of the cultural responses of blacks in virtually every profession since emancipation has been that black people must be nearly perfect in their undertakings, lest a little slip-up here or there (unchecked class assignments, for example) be taken as not only individual incompetence but a collective shortcoming. This is echoed in the personal narratives, biographies of people like Benjamin O. Davis of the U.S. Army, sports legends Jackie Robinson and Joe Louis, performers like Wilma Rudolph and Lena Horne. It is also echoed in everyday people's daily lives, as Donna's example illustrates.

The example of her life is instructive because of the way in which it combines the activities of both conventional nuclear and extended families (community, in a word) that extends beyond narrower definitions of family. First, given the realities of teenage pregnancy, the ravages of crack, undereducation, unemployment, and other plagues of working-class black communities, black mothers and fathers cannot afford—I repeat, cannot afford—to operate exclusively under the nuclear family rubric. In no way am I declaring myself "anti-family" in the way that political and cultural conservatives claim that leftists advocate. I realize that families of all colors have had to adjust and adapt to the changing realities of the 1990s in the United States, where even middle- and upper-middle-class parents no longer operate with the assurance that their children will be able to fare as well as or better than they have. Black communities must not allow the focus on "the crisis of the black family" to obscure the larger problems of this precarious time. Simply put, if the majority of U.S. communities, which includes African-Americans, are neither products of nor participants in a two-parent family, then why should African-Americans be expected to adhere to a more restrictive notion of family that serves as an ideal more than a reality and, ultimately, was designed with another group of people in mind?

All this relates to the politics of black fatherhood since, invariably, black men who sire and/or nurture children can be fathers only in relation to their children, husbands and/or lovers in relation to their wives and/or companions, sons in relation to their parents. When viewed in isolation, black fatherhood becomes a fetish of machismo and conventional masculinity rather than a practical component of family life within immediate and extended families and communities. When viewed in isolation, the black family becomes but another receptacle for dominant values and ideals that do not work for the dominant social group in the first place but are utilized to tell African-Americans, once again, that they don't measure up.

A recent example of the effects of distorted images upon African-American males comes from the state of New Jersey, where Republican governor Christine Whitman started a controversy in March 1995 during an interview when she stated that young black ghetto men in Newark proudly considered siring children out of wedlock a matter of adding "jewels to the crown." Ms. Whitman, who is certainly no ghetto dweller, obtained this information from a black mother in Newark who informed her that this was the reality of black male parental responsibility in that city.

The governor has had to respond to the outcry over this statement from a variety of sources in black communities in New Jersey, including young black fathers who have children out of wedlock and are responsible parents. Participants in the Young Fathers' Program in Newark,[1] a program that had been in existence eight years prior to Ms. Whitman's statement, as well as other collectives of young fathers, have informed the governor of the seriousness of their programs and their good-parenting practices regardless of their marital status. In a meeting with the governor in June of the same year, several members of the Young Fathers' Program and lifelong Newark residents told Ms. Whitman that they had never heard of the "jewels in the crown" phrase uttered by the young black mother.

At various times in the ensuing months, the governor reiterated that she had been merely repeating something said to her. It was a statement she neither confirmed nor endorsed. During her June meeting with Young Fathers' Program participants, she stated, "I didn't stigmatize anybody."

While she may have made what one would call an "honest mistake" (certainly impolitic), she still misses the point, but she does so in a way that is useful for this article. Those young men were already stigmatized by the fact that they did not operate within the conventional two-family model. Her statement, to my mind, can be viewed only as naive or disingenuous when seen in the context of two arenas of public debate that relate to this controversy, family values and the disintegration of the black family.

More subtle indignations, however, emerge when we consider the fact that a white, female governor who presides over some of the most blighted and underfunded cities in the entire country would accept the comments of one person of any race to characterize the behavior of an entire class of individuals. Would she have relayed these comments in such an offhand, unmediated manner if the individuals in question were young white men from Princeton or Upper Montclair, New Jersey, two of the state's most affluent neighborhoods? Would she have even believed the comments of a single person from the neighborhood? We may never know the answer to these two questions, but it is significant that in most cases involving white parenting such questions are rarely posed. My guess is that part of the reason she relied so easily upon one black mother's depiction of unwed fathers is because it corresponded so easily with common assumptions about young black men.

Tellingly, in her June 1995 meeting with the program participants she explained that her statement was a rendering of "a comment that someone said to me, by someone who said this was what happened, whether it was on her block or what, I don't know." Ironically, her explanation reveals the pressures of what I shall call "racial translation," which are often imposed upon blacks in their interaction with whites in the United States. Before making such a statement, wouldn't it have made sense for Ms. Whitman to determine whether her informant was talking about young black men in general or a few on the woman's block? This is a depressingly familiar scenario in which the comments of one black individual as "racial translator" become the opinion of depiction of black people as a whole, much in the same way that the negative actions of one or several black individuals are often perceived as being symptomatic of black communities or the entire black race.

The similarities between the responses of these young black fathers and Donna are striking. Both felt the need to respond to others' characterizations that did not correspond with the realities of their daily lives. Like my own identity as a father, their identities as parents reside somewhere in between stereotypes and the starkest cases of parental neglect and abuse. What distinguishes these young men from Donna and myself is that poverty, undereducation, and unemployment render them socially naked. They do not have the trappings of middle-class respectability that would shield them from the accusations and characterizations of irresponsibility in the way that middle-class whites or minorities do. One only has to think of the surprise and shock echoed in voices and journalistic reports when a case of middle-class abuse is uncovered (parents who lock their infant children in the house to go on a vacation, for example) to obtain a sense of what notions of middle-class respectability can obscure. This is not restricted to young black men, either; the poor in general are symbolically victimized by these characterizations, as they are deemed to be the underside of what good parenting is all about.

In an age where both parents work and only three percent of families in the United States rely solely on a male breadwinner, parents who live with their children don't always have ample time to spend with them. In many middle- and upper-middle-class households (black and white) it is not uncommon to find nannies performing the functions of parents, who spend less and less time at home. Years of neglect and inattention have taken their toll on many prep school-educated Ivy League-bound adolescents, just as it has upon the "latchkey" children in working-class homes who are alone, locked inside their homes while their parents are at work. I mention these things to suggest what should be an obvious point; *no class or race has a monopoly on good or bad parenting.* Seemingly "external" societal factors have as much impact upon family dynamics as internal ones.

When one adds relational discord, physical and psychoemotional violence, incest, alcoholism, poverty, depression, and a range of other personal travails that have domestic repercussions, some children are better off without their biological or adoptive parents. This further erodes the all-or-nothing distinctions made between parents who live with their children and those who do not. The behavioral imprint left upon children in dysfunctional households can affect not only immediate family members but successive generations as well. With males of any color, children who witnessed or experienced physical and non-physical violence are likely to reproduce such violence in their own families.

At a conference in Fort Lauderdale, Florida, in October 1994, six present and former professional football players—all black—participated in a forum on domestic violence against women. Having witnessed their fathers break the arms and blacken eyes of their mothers and traumatize everyone in their presence at the same time, several of these men in turn heaped similar forms of violence upon their girlfriends and spouses. This cycle, as these men came to recognize, has to be broken before there are any realistic prospects for improved family dynamics among people of African descent. The reason I mention these particular men is to suggest that such labels, for example, "wife beater," could apply to a broad array of males, from the aforementioned men to O. J. Simpson. Eradicating domestic and other forms of intracommunity violence often means coming to terms with memories of violence inflicted upon them by a previous generation—by mothers, fathers, relatives, or family friends.

To discuss "the black family" without consideration of the myriad forms of violence and its consequences for black men as well as black women is to engage in the sort of blissful denial of negative, abusive "family values" that have existed as long as families have. Such violence has often operated as a primary cause of drug abuse, predation by young males, teenage runaways, suicide, depression, among other phenomena that characterize what family specialists refer to as "at-risk youth." If we are concerned with the preservation of family values—"African," "Afro-

Centric," or otherwise—let us make sure about just what it is we are preserving.

Here is where more complex understandings of the relationship between family and community become crucial for deeper probings of the politics of black fatherhood. In much of black conservative discussions about responsibility for teenage pregnancy (public statements and writings by Stanley Crouch and Glenn Loury provide two examples), there is often a nostalgic evocation of a bygone era when young women were sanctioned within black communities for having children out of wedlock. Suspending for the moment whether this was actually true even in some (certainly not all) black communities, or whether this was or is viable coping strategy for young teenage mothers, there is virtually no mention in this rhetoric of popular community sanctions against woman beaters or men who too readily and too violently spank their children. Should this nostalgic rhetoric be preserved? Should the silence about these issues be preserved? As usual, women political and cultural activists remain at the forefront of this discussion within the black community. Billye Avery, founder of the National Black Women's Health Project, is one example of a black woman political activist who has worked on these issues, often to the deaf ears of her male counterparts in the struggle for racial equality. Queen Latifah and Karyn White, two popular contemporary artists, have both produced effective music and videos on the theme of domestic violence within black families.[2] Certainly there are others, created largely by black women, that address domestic-violence issues, but there needs to be an ongoing dialogue about these issues in black communities and institutions. Family coherence should not be confused with individual abuse, intimidation, and oppression. Nor should discussion of the failings of particular black men in this regard be automatically considered a threat to the black male.

All of these concerns, from notions of community and extended families to domestic violence, impact upon black fathers and the politics of their being. An example of this occurred while riding a bus one day with two young black men from a summer program, which I was mentoring. I became the mediator in an argument about "proper" parenting philosophies for black men, a discussion that was prompted, I believe, by the presence of my daughter Jenna.

One young man from Kentucky stated that if he were a parent, he would raise his boy and girl children differently since boys, men in the making, had to be taught not to cry, not wear their emotions on their sleeves and commit other acts that would make them be perceived as weak. In contrast, the other young man, who hailed from Boston, said that he would not raise his girl child any differently from his son, since men too need to cry and express their emotions. "Plus," he added with emphasis, "it's rough out here on the sisters these days. They've got to be tough, too. They need all the help they can get."

And so they do. The task for progressive black males, as fathers, lovers, friends, and "brothers" in both senses of the term, is to understand black masculinity as merely one facet of their humanity. Like me, these two young men exist somewhere in between negative stereotypes and ideal-types. Together, in dialogue, they were not only coming to terms with what it meant to be re-sponsible black men in the contemporary United States, but with what it meant to be fuller human beings.

Notes

1. The Young Fathers' Program was founded in 1987 after a successful pilot program initiated in 1986. The program, which is housed in the New Jersey Medical School in Newark, is designed to assist young black and latino men between fifteen and twenty-three in meeting the emotional, financial, and social demands of fatherhood. Its services include educational and employment training for young men and their families, family support and counseling to reduce the risk of neglect and abuse within these families. As of June 1995, approximately one thousand young fathers have utilized the program's services. For more information contact (201) 982-5277.

2. See Queen Latifah's 1993 hit "U.N.I.T.Y" and Karyn White's incisive 1995 production, aptly entitled "I'd Rather Be Alone." Both ably capture the problems inherent in static categorizations of the nuclear family which do not address the reasons why, in some instances, it is healthier for people not to be in their nuclear family relationships, ones that cause unnecessary emotional and physical disfigurement.

PART NINE

Masculinities in the Media

Men are daily bombarded with images of masculinity—in magazines, television, movies, music, even the Internet. We see what men are supposed to look like, act like, be like. And social scientists are only now beginning to understand the enormous influence that the media have in shaping our ideas about what it means to be a man.

For one thing, it's clear that the media can create artificial standards against which boys as well as girls measure themselves. Just as idealized human female models can only approximate the exaggeratedly large breasts and exaggeratedly small waistline of Barbie, virtually no men can approach the physiques of the cartoon version of Tarzan or

even G.I. Joe. The original G.I. Joe had the equivalent of 12.2-inch biceps when he was introduced in 1964. Ten years later, his biceps measured 15.2 inches. By 1994, he had 16.4-inch biceps, and today his biceps measure 26.8 inches—nearly 7 inches larger than Mark McGwire's 20-inch muscles. "Many modern figures display the physiques of advanced bodybuilders and some display levels of muscularity far exceeding the outer limits of actual human attainment," notes Dr. Harrison Pope, a Harvard psychiatrist.

Media masculinities create standards against which men measure themselves. No wonder we often feel like we fail the test of physical manhood. At the same time, the media encourage us to evaluate and judge the manhood of others by those same standards. As the articles in this section suggest, we are constantly "seeing" masculinity, whether on late night television (Jocelyn Hollander), in the movies (Peter Lehman), in commercials (Lance Strate), and even in pornography (Richard Fung). Any effort to understand—let alone transform—masculinity must take account of the ways in which we see ourselves reflected through the lenses that record our fantasy lives.

As G.I. Joe Bulks Up, Concern For the 98-Pound Weakling

Just as Barbie dolls have taunted little girls with an impossible ideal of the female body, G.I. Joes have morphed over the last three decades into muscle-bound hunks that can harm the self-esteem of boys, according to a new study.

Dr. Harrison Pope, a Harvard psychiatrist, studied the evolution of American action figures over the last 30 years to learn whether there was a connection between the toys and an increase in "body-image disturbances" among men. Pope and his researchers purchased G.I. Joes and other action figures manufactured since the 1960s, measured their waists, chests and biceps, then calculated the figures for a 6-foot man. The results were stark.

"Many modern figures display the physiques of advanced bodybuilders and some display levels of muscularity far exceeding the outer limits of actual human attainment," according to the study, published this month in the International Journal of Eating Disorders.

More research is needed to determine the effect on boys and, ultimately, adult men, the study warned, but added, "the impact of toys should not be underestimated." Male action toys accounted for $949 million in manufacturers' shipments in 1994, and action figures were $687 million of the total, the study said.

The study noted one exception to the bulking-up trend: Barbie's longtime boyfriend, Ken.

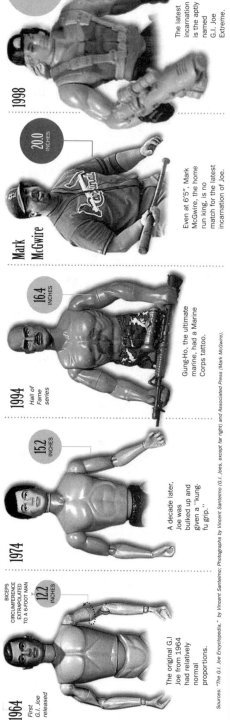

1964
First G.I. Joe released

BICEPS CIRCUMFERENCE EXTRAPOLATED TO A 6-FOOT MAN
12.2 INCHES

The original G.I Joe from 1964 had relatively normal proportions.

1974
15.2 INCHES

A decade later, Joe was bulked up and given a "kung-fu grip."

1994
Hall of Fame series
16.4 INCHES

Gung-Ho, the ultimate marine, had a Marine Corps tattoo.

Mark McGwire
20.0 INCHES

Even at 6'5", Mark McGwire, the home run king, is no match for the latest incarnation of Joe.

1998
26.8 INCHES

The latest incarnation is the aptly named G.I. Joe Extreme.

Sources: "The G.I. Joe Encyclopedia," by Vincent Santelmo; Photographs by Vincent Santelmo (G.I. Joes, except far right) and Associated Press (Mark McGwire).

N.Y. Times News Service

Reprinted with permission of *The New York Times*.

476

Jocelyn A. Hollander

Doing *Studs*: The Performance of Gender and Sexuality on Late-Night Television

"We always start out watching Nightline, but we just can't help taking a peek. Then we're hooked. Why? Is it putty-faced Mark DeCarlo's smarmy repartée? Is it the lewd double-entendres written for the contestants by the show's uncredited geniuses? Is it the slow-witted mooks who punch each other's shoulders when they answer correctly? Or is it the user-friendly babes? Yes! Yes, it's all that."

Rolling Stone (May 14, 1992)

"Gender, not religion, is the opiate of the masses."

Erving Goffman, "The Arrangement Between the Sexes" (1977)

Popular conceptions of gender center around the seemingly huge differences between women and men—in behavior, talk, and even feelings—and the "war of the sexes" that results. Books, magazines, and film share with most traditional scholarly work on gender the assumption that gender is a dichotomous attribute possessed by individuals. Whether they believe that gender is biologically innate or socioculturally determined, these authors imply that gender—the social expression of maleness or femaleness—is something that individuals *have*.

In contrast to these approaches, an increasing number of scholars have begun to theorize gender as something that is enacted rather than possessed, something that must be constantly achieved rather than simply expressed. For example, West and her colleagues (West and Zimmer-

man 1987; West and Fenstermaker 1993, 1995) define gender not as a characteristic of individuals, but as "the activity of managing situated conduct in light of normative conceptions of attitudes and activities appropriate for one's sex category" (West and Zimmerman 1987: 127). They contend that gender is "not simply an aspect of what one is, but, more fundamentally, it is something that one *does,* and does recurrently, in interaction with others" (140). When we interact with others, we manage our behavior in order to confirm our gender. According to Fox, "a woman (or man) must earn the label of "feminine" (or "masculine") through traditional sex-appropriate behavior, and one must act feminine (or masculine) continually in order to retain this label" (1977: 809–10; see also Goffman 1976, 1977; Kessler and McKenna 1978; Connell 1987, 1995; Bem 1993; Thorne 1994; Bornstein 1994; Lorber 1994).

The performative nature of gender is rarely salient; because we perform gender (and see others perform gender) continually from the time we are children, gender performances tend to be invisible unless they are inadequate or interrupted. Nonetheless, individuals are constantly performing gender, and these performances are not only a means of claiming membership in a gender category but a strategy for constructing identity and image. My goal in this paper is to demonstrate *how* gender is performed, and identity is constructed, through interaction. It is important to recognize, however, that these actions do not take place in a vacuum; they are constrained by, and simultaneously reinforce, social structures (Lorber 1994).

The performance of gender can be seen clearly on television, where actors tend to play stereotypical roles and where, even in nondramatic media, the pressures for successful self-presentation are high because of the public nature of the performance. In this analysis, I focus on a television performance that purports to be realistic and in which gender is central: the late-night dating game show *Studs.*[1]

Studs premiered on the Fox television network in mid-1991, and from the beginning, its popularity was enormous. Although the show finally ended production in 1994, it sparked a series of similar "kiss and tell" shows, both in the US and internationally. *Studs* is clearly a caricature of real-life dating. However, I suggest that it mirrors—and indeed, provides a stark view of—some of the gendered elements of everyday interaction. In addition, shows such as this help create the cultural context in which this interaction takes place.

The basic premise of *Studs* is the same as that of most dating shows: the contestants—in this case, two men—each go on blind dates with three women (for a total of six dates), and then return to the show to answer questions about their dates. The sequence of events in the half-hour program is as follows: host Mark DeCarlo introduces "the ladies" (whom I will call the "dates"), who are seated on a couch to stage right. He presents their names, ages, and professions, and then asks them, "So what are you looking for in a guy?" After each woman has answered, "DeCarlo introduces the two "studs," who literally bound onto the set and

sit on a couch to stage left. Once this introductory sequence is complete, the contest begins. The body of the show consists of three guessing sequences separated by advertisement breaks. In the first, De-Carlo asks the first "stud" contestant a preliminary question (for example, "What's the first thing you notice when you look at a woman?") and, after the contestant has answered, says, "Well, we asked them what they thought when they first saw you, and here's what they said." Then, three quotes attributed[2] to the "dates" are flashed onto the screen. The contestant selects a quote, and guesses which woman has said it. If he is correct, DeCarlo tosses him a decorated fabric heart, which the contestant affixes to his clothing. De-Carlo questions the "date" and/or the "stud" about the quote, and then the process is repeated for a second turn. If the contestant answers incorrectly, he receives no heart (and no second turn), but DeCarlo still questions the women about the quotes. This guessing process is repeated for the second contestant.

In the second sequence, this guessing process is repeated, but with different questions. Typically, the preliminary question is about dating behavior (e.g., "How do you make the first move on a date?") and the quotes similarly address romantic dating behavior (e.g., "We asked them about your romantic moves, and here's what they told us.").

The third sequence follows a different format. DeCarlo alternately asks the two men questions beginning with, "According to the ladies, who's most likely to . . .?" Common endings include "kiss a woman's hand," "wear makeup," "fall asleep during sex," "be a peeping tom," or "sell his sperm for rent money"; in all cases, the questions reflect on the contestant's gender, sexuality, or both. After the contestant guesses, the women say the correct name in unison. Correct answers earn the contestant a heart, and both correct and incorrect answers are followed by an explanation from one of the women.

Winning the game is a complicated process. First, a contestant must earn more hearts than his "co-stud" by answering questions correctly. Second, he must choose which woman he would like to date again, *and* that woman must also choose him. The men present their choices verbally at the end of the show, after explaining why they did not choose the other women; the women reveal their choices by uncovering a written name, but do not have the opportunity to describe the reasons behind their choices. If all of these conditions are met, the winning contestants go on an all-expenses-paid "fantasy date" to the destination of the stud's choice; in the case of a tie, both winning couples receive a fantasy date.

Two variations on this general sequence should be noted. First, there is another, more ambiguous way to be a successful "stud": a contestant who answers all questions correctly is crowned "King Stud" and decorated with a shiny gold necklace with "STUD" in large gold letters. However, being King Stud does not entitle a contestant to further dates or prize money. Second, occasional episodes are "reversal shows," in which two women play the "stud" roles (they are described as "studettes" and are eligible to become "Queen Stud") and three men play the "date" roles. Interestingly, these reversal shows are always "theme shows," featuring some unusual type of women (e.g., hot mud oil wrestlers or construction workers) and are often part of some larger theme week such as "Fantasy Week" or "Wild Women Week." Apparently some justification is necessary for women to play the typically masculine role.

To examine the performance of gender on *Studs,* I videotaped 18 episodes between October 29 and December 9, 1992. I transcribed these episodes, also noting the contestants' nonverbal behaviors and the audience members' responses. The basic unit of analysis is the communication turn; I define this unit to include not only conversational turns, but also gestures and other nonverbal actions.[3] I examine these communication turns within several contexts. First, I analyze a particular communication turn in relation to the speaker's other turns: how does the turn interact with what the contestant has said or done previously? In other words, is the contestant's performance internally consistent? Similarly, I analyze

turns in relation to the other contestants' turns. Often, both the stud and his date will describe a particular date: are their separate accounts mutually supportive or contradictory? When there is inconsistency in a speaker's own turns, or between the accounts of the stud and the date, I analyze the circumstances of the contradiction: do contradictions occur on some topics more than others? How are the contradictions resolved, and what are the consequences for the speakers?

The third type of context is that of role, or the particular part being performed. In fact, there are two types of roles performed by each person on *Studs.* First, each contestant plays a specific role on the show—i.e., that of "stud/studette" or "date." This role is symbolized by the couch on which a contestant is seated—studs sit to stage left, dates to stage right—and the contestants' performance of these roles presumably ends when their participation in the show ends. However, each contestant also performs a second, more permanent, role: that of being a woman or man in everyday life. These roles are signalled by the performers' appearance and behavior; as Kessler and McKenna (1978) note, although people generally believe they assign gender based on physical features such as genitals or genes, they rarely see these features and it is in fact social behavior that triggers gender assignment in everyday life. West and Zimmerman call these two types of roles "situated identities" and "master identities," respectively: the first type is "assumed and relinquished as the situation demands," while the second is constant across diverse situations (1987: 128). The reversal nights on *Studs,* during which women play the "studette" roles and men play the "date" roles, highlight the differences between these two types of roles or identities.

Finally, I examined the contestants' communication turns in the context of the *Studs*-like genre (or frame, in the Goffmanian sense) of performances—what Bauman (1986) has termed "burlesque performance." The game show is ultimately a source of entertainment for viewers, and the contestants' job is to provide an entertaining performance. In this genre, sexual innuendo, hyperbole, and outrageous double entendre are legitimized and expected; in fact, skillful performance requires that contestants imply as much risqué behavior as possible. In this context, a good story can be personally beneficial to the performer, even if the story does not present the self in a favorable light. The expectations of this genre enable the situated "stud" and "date" roles to be played; nonetheless, the normative expectations of the contestants' master (gender) identities still exist, and it is in the management of these often conflicting demands that the contestants show their most skillful gender performances.

Performing Gender: Studs, Studettes, and Their Dates

According to West and Zimmerman, "doing gender means creating differences between girls and boys and women and men, differences that are not natural, essential, or biological. Once the differences have been constructed, they are used to reinforce the 'essentialness' of gender" (1987: 137). Bem calls this process "gender polarization": the organization of social life around perceived differences between women and men. Gender polarization "defines mutually exclusive scripts for being male and female," and also "defines any person or behavior that deviates from those scripts as problematic" (1993: 81). On *Studs,* differences are created and maintained in myriad ways. The initial structure of the set and the show, the non-verbal gestures and positions of the contestants, the stories they tell about the dates, and the statements they make about men and women—all of these serve to construct and emphasize gendered differences between the "studs" and their "dates."

Setting the Scene

From the first moment of *Studs,* the male and female contestants are separated and treated as different. Men and women are always seated on opposite sides of the stage, and their numbers are always unequal. The fact that there are always more "dates" than "studs" means that at least one "date" is never chosen. Because the "dates" are nearly always women, at least one woman is always left out of the final pairings.

As the show begins, the "dates" sit demurely to stage right, while the "studs" run onstage soon after and often engage in some sort of clowning as they sit down to stage left. The host always rises and shakes hands with the "studs," but never with the dates; at the end of the show he congratulates only the winning "stud."[4] The physical separation of the sexes results from the show's focus on heterosexual dating—mixing the participants might suggest a less orthodox bisexual pairing of contestants. This separation, together with the contrasting entrances of the contestants onto the stage and their differential treatment by the host, serves to emphasize the differences, rather than the similarities, between the men and women.

The contestants' clothing is perhaps the most salient marker of difference and gender.[5] With very few exceptions, the female contestants wear some sort of revealing clothing: short, tight miniskirts, low-cut shirts or blouses, skin-tight bodysuits, or some variation on these. High heels are *de rigueur.* Even when the episode is a "theme show" that would demand some other sort of dress from the women (female construction workers, for example), the women's outfits conform to these guidelines as much as possible (for example, both construction workers wore tight jeans shorts and low-cut, midriff-baring tops along with their work boots). Occasionally, a female contestant does not conform to this implicit dress code (for example, wearing a calf-length rather than thigh-length skirt); in my sample of episodes, these women are less likely to be chosen as desired future dates.

The men's clothing, in contrast, serves to emphasize masculine strength rather than feminine curves. Their clothing is seldom revealing; the only exception to this rule is that highly muscular men occasionally wear shorts or sleeveless shirts that emphasize their muscled arms and legs. Form-fitting jeans and cowboy boots are the most common dress for men. This stereotypical attire is, of course, indicated by the stud and date roles the contestants are playing, as well as by the burlesque genre: the task of the contestants is to be as sexually suggestive as possible. In a heterosexual context, this task requires a polarization of the sexes, which is precisely the effect produced by the contestants' clothing. Interestingly, however, even when the stud/date roles are reversed—i.e., the women are seated to stage left—the contestants' clothing remains the same, suggesting that it is not only the situated roles that produce these differences, but the gendered "master identities" of the actors.

Bodies in Motion

Another indicator of gendered performance is the nonverbal communication acts performed by the contestants. This category includes the positioning of the contestants' bodies and the gestures they make in reaction to others' communication turns. Although sitting and moving need not be gender-specific activities, these behaviors are markedly different for the "studs" and their "dates."

The most subtle of the nonverbal expressions, and the most constant across the duration of the show, is body positioning. Without exception, the women in this sample of shows sit in a "feminine" way: legs together or tightly crossed, arms held close to their bodies. Some of this positioning might be accounted for by the mode of dress adopted by the women: miniskirts do not lend themselves to sitting with legs apart on national television. Nonetheless, even when the female contestants wear longer skirts, pants, or shorts, their body positioning is the same.

The mens' body positioning contrasts sharply with that of the women. From the moment they sit down on the couch, the men sit widely, legs apart or crossed knee-to-ankle, arms often extended from their bodies along the back or on the arm of the couch. The men's bodies seem to take up all the space allotted—they often appear to be crowded on their couch—whereas the women seem to be trying to take up as little space as possible. This difference between the men's and women's body positions persists even in reversal episodes.

The contestants' gestures mirror their body positions. In general, the men make big, expansive gestures. When they are introduced, they clap with their arms spread widely; they punch each other playfully, slap each other on the back, raise or pump their fists in the air, and so on. These gestures are most obvious when the men win a heart or are the subject of some particularly bawdy comment. When they receive a heart, they slap it forcefully onto their bodies; in both situations, they clap vehemently and are congratulated by their "co-stud" through mock punching, elbowing, high fives, and the like.

The women, in contrast, use small, contained gestures. When they are introduced, they nearly always give small, cute waves, smile at the camera, and then clap for themselves with their arms close to their sides. In contrast to the friendly camaraderie evident between the male contestants, the women never interact physically with each other, and rarely interact verbally. In the reversal shows, they press rather than slap the hearts they win onto their bodies. When they are the subject of some highly sexual comment, the women may laugh, clap quietly, or hide their faces in embarrassment; other than these gestures, running their fingers through their hair or adjusting their clothes are their only motions. Again, these nonverbal behaviors do not change when the stud/date roles are reversed; here too, master identity seems to override situated identity when the two are in conflict.

Overall, the men's body language is expansive and active: they run onstage, take up all the available space when seated and move freely and frequently. The women's body language is dramatically different: they fold themselves into a minimum amount of space, make small, infrequent gestures, and generally sit passively for the duration of the show. This active/passive distinction is further emphasized by the separation of the women and men onstage and by the host's behavior: he interacts frequently with the men but rarely with the women. Thus, men's gender performances entail activity and interaction; women's center around display. This differentiation heightens the perceived polarization of men and women.

Gender Prescriptions

The first time the "dates" speak on *Studs* is during the introductory sequence when host DeCarlo asks them each, "What are you looking for in a guy?" (or, in the case of a reversal show, "What are you looking for in a woman?"). A selection of these responses follows:

Q: What kind of guy are you looking for?

A: A big, strong *man.*

A guy I could get along with, a good personality, and dresses nice. Tall, lean, mean rock-and-rollers.

A guy who's sexy, casual, clean-cut, and conservative.

Q: What are you looking for in a woman?

A: Someone who's going to put up a big challenge—make me work for what I want.

A woman with a nice firm athletic body, a woman who looks conservative, but likes to get wild.

A woman who knows what she wants, and knows how to use what she's got.

I like a woman who has a nice body, long legs, nice breasts, and a little bit of, you know, an airhead. [Mark: You like an airheaded girl.] Yeah. [Mark: Why's that?] You don't have to worry about what they're going to say, you don't have to go into complications, you can just let things happen.

These responses constitute both gender performances on the part of the speaker and gender prescriptions for the "studs" or "studettes." Most obviously, these statements tell the other contestants (and, indirectly, the audience members) what is expected of them: what gendered characteristics or behaviors are necessary in order to be desirable. To be successfully masculine, one should be big, strong, and sexy; to be successfully feminine, one should have a nice body, be an airhead, like to get wild, and so on. These kinds of demands are predictable from the genre of the show; yet once gain they serve to highlight differences between women and men. Unfortunately, it is difficult to determine how the two types of roles—the situated stud/date roles and the master gender identities—affect these comments, because only those playing the "date" roles are asked what kind of person they are looking for.

In terms of performance, these prescriptive statements situate the speakers as masculine or feminine, emphasizing their sexuality—and, perhaps more important, their *hetero*sexuality—and defining the speaker as the type of man or woman who values the qualities desired in the other sex. For example, the man who said he liked "airheaded women" can now be categorized as the kind of man who values airheads; the man who asked for "someone who's going to put up a big challenge—make me work for what I want" can now be categorized as a very different type of man.

These prescriptive statements also serve as a reference point for the speaker's other communication turns. Having made this kind of prescription, the speaker later can be judged as behaving consistently or inconsistently ("Aha! She said she likes tall, lean, mean rock-n-rollers, and yet she chose a man who is a short, sweet, classical violinist!") and thus as putting on a credible or less-than-credible performance. In addition, the other performers can also be judged with respect to these prescriptions: the statements define "stud success" and thus, implicitly, "stud failure." Host DeCarlo often uses the prescriptions as an opportunity to joke about the kind of man who would *not* fit the requirements for "stud." For example, on one episode featuring "pirate Harley girls," DeCarlo made the following jokes:

MARK: What kind of guy do you like, Stephanya?

STEPHANYA: A big, strong *man.*

MARK: Someone who would ride maybe like a 150 moped, perhaps?

MARK: And Martine, I'm sure Alastair Cook is your type, right?

MARTINE: [laughs] Alastair Cook??? Well, I don't know about him. I like men that are strong, rough, and ready.

DeCarlo's jokes make it clear that "real studs" are not Alastair Cook kinds of men—quiet, intelligent, reserved—and that they ride big, powerful motorcycles, not small mopeds. These types of exchanges demonstrate that gender is negotiated through interaction—and imposed by some on others—rather than simply expressed or spontaneously performed. Through interaction with each other and with the host, the contestants on *Studs* enact gendered behaviors and collaboratively define what kind of qualities are necessary in order to be attractive to others.

Telling Stories

A final way in which gender is constructed and performed is through the use of stories. There has been growing attention in recent years to the phenomenon of storytelling as a means of describing and understanding social life (for example, see Bauman 1986; Read 1987; Plummer 1995). Narratives about the contestants' dates are the core of *Studs*. It is through the stories that the audience is told what "really" happened on the dates and that the quality of the contestants' performances—both as dating partners and as bawdy storytellers—can be assessed. These stories not only describe the events that occurred on the dates, but also make sense of them by giving the events order and meaning, and evaluate them by defining the events and the actors as good or bad, proper or improper. At the same time, they serve to construct a social, gendered identity for the storyteller and his or her date.

Stories on *Studs* are generally prompted by the quotes from the dates, which are flashed onto the screen and which are almost uniformly sexually suggestive.[6] A sampling of these quotes:

"He bucked around the room with the force of a lovesick bronco."

"A couple of warm splashes and his boxers were bubbling over."

"A few short grunts and I was ready to worship the king."

"I started to giggle when he kissed that rear end."

"You gotta love a woman who can handle a really big crankshaft."

"For a little girl, she can sure gulp a whole lot of foam."

The sexual implications of these comments are clear. After the contestant has guessed which of the dates is responsible for one of the quotes, De-Carlo asks the date to explain the quote, thereby prompting storytelling. One of the most interesting facets of these stories is that when the date is female, the story is often a repair sequence of sorts: although she has purportedly made the bawdy comment herself, her explanation of it is generally a denial or minimization of the sexual behavior it implies. Some examples:

QUOTE: "One mighty shove from behind and I was seeing stars."

EXPLANATION: Well, it was night, it was late and we were at the park and . . . and it was a starlit night and he was pushing me on the swing, from behind.

QUOTE: "A few quick slurps and he was spilling his seeds all over the table."

EXPLANATION: He had some melon, some watermelon, and he had some juice, and the seeds, it's from the seeds, from the watermelon, that fell on the plate.

QUOTE: "One mighty plunge and the log was soaking wet."

EXPLANATION: We went to Disneyland, so we went on Splash Mountain, and so all the way down he held my hands up so I could get wet in front of him, blocking him.

Thus, although the burlesque genre of the show and the roles the women play within that genre demand sexually suggestive comments, the women also seem to be expected to deny the very sexuality they profess. These contradictory demands do not appear to apply to men: in my sample of shows, no male contestant ever denied a sexual encounter. In fact, one man insinuated that a sexual encounter had occurred, but later apologized to the woman for making this suggestion, assuring the audience that nothing had happened.

When men's sexuality or sexual behavior is described, men react very differently than women: they applaud enthusiastically, and they generally engage in some congratulatory behavior with the other male contestant—back-slapping, high fives, or pumping raised fists. In contrast, when it is implied that the women have engaged in sexual behavior beyond simply kissing, they often appear embarrassed (for example, covering their faces with their hands) and attempt to deny or minimize the occurrence. Moreover, the other women never acknowledge that the sexual behavior has occurred, let alone congratulate the others on their conquest. The implications of this kind of sexuality for women and men are very different: men tend to be seen as studs, women as sluts (Kimmel 1993; Orenstein 1994).

From these differences, I suggest that the participants in *Studs* are performing and constructing identity along two linked dimensions: gender (masculinity/femininity) and sexuality. For men these dimensions are congruent: for both masculinity and sexuality, more is always better. Using the tools described above—positions, gestures, statements, and stories—men emphasize their masculinity and the differences between themselves and women. They also emphasize their sexuality, implying that sexual encounters took place and congratulating each other when sexually suggestive comments are made. Thus for men, sexuality reinforces masculinity, and vice versa. A man who is highly sexual is seen as more masculine; a man who is more masculine is assumed to be more sexual.

For women, however, the dimensions of femininity and sexuality are at least partially opposed. Like the "studs," the female contestants use verbal and nonverbal communication to emphasize their femininity and their differences from men. In terms of sexuality, however, the women's task is more complicated. On the one hand, the women must appear sexually provocative, both in their appearance and in their comments about the dates. On the other hand, however, there seems to be strong pressure to mask or minimize this sexuality. The racy quotes, although appropriate to the bur-

lesque frame of the show, constitute gender transgressions for the women. In order to repair these transgressions, and maintain a credible gender performance, the women must dispel the implication of sexual behavior created by the quotes. This dichotomy between gender and sexuality is reminiscent of the good girl/bad girl distinction of past decades (Fox 1977), when men would be attracted to "bad girls," whose sexuality was evident, but desire to marry "good girls," whose sexuality was hidden. The performance of gender on *Studs* suggest that in the 1990s, this distinction has shifted from one between women to one *within* women: to be considered attractive, women must be both sexually provocative *and* sexually restrained—both a "bad girl" *and* a "good girl." Performing both of these roles requires a subtle, skillful balancing act between conflicting demands.

But are these demands made by the situated "date" role that women usually play on the show, or by their master identity as women? These two identities can be teased apart by examining the role-reversal episodes in which women play the "stud" roles and men play the "date" roles. In these episodes, several interesting changes in gender performance occur. First, sexuality seems to become more acceptable for women. There is even greater use of sexual innuendo (by both women and men), and the women are not as quick to deny sexual events, as in this example:

QUOTE: "A rip here, a tear there, and lips and clothes were everywhere."

MARK: What does that mean, Milton?

MILTON: What that means is we were having a pretty good time when we left the bar, and we pretty much did the streets of San Diego.

MARK: So how'd your date with Miltie end up, Tracy? After you're driving around the city streets for a while . . .

TRACY: It ended up the next morning.

MARK: Fun evening?

TRACY: Yeah, kinda sticky. [Audience: "Wooo . . ."] He poured a can, he poured Dr Pepper on me.

In this narrative, there is an acknowledgement of female sexual behavior that is rarely found in the stories of women playing the "date" role. Interestingly, this type of acknowledgement was also more frequent during "theme" episodes that legitimated unconventional female behavior. For example, the following story was told on an episode featuring "pirate Harley girls" during "Wild Women Week":

QUOTE: "A couple of warm splashes and his boxers were bubbling over."

STEPHANYA: We went jacuzzi-hopping at a couple condos, different condos actually . . .

MARK: How do you jacuzzi-hop?

STEPHANYA: Well you get half-naked and you jump from jacuzzi to different jacuzzi.

MARK: So you weren't wearing a bathing suit.

STEPHANYA: Um, no, I was wearing his boxers actually.

ACE: I helped her get into them . . .

MARK: And?

ACE: I did. It was fun. It took a while before we got in the jacuzzi, but it was fun, it was a very fun date.

MARK: So you just crash these places when you go?

STEPHANYA: Yeah. That's the fun part, getting in, and then, well actually that's not the real fun part, but yeah. [laughs]

OTHER WOMEN: Oh yeah?? Oh yeah??

STEPHANYA: Stop it! [pointing to other women]

In both of these situations—when women play the "stud" role and when they are characterized as "Wild Women"—gender transgression is legitimated, and open acknowledgement of sexuality becomes more acceptable. On the other hand, both women still perform a modified repair sequence: Tracy attributes the stickiness of the evening to having had soda poured on her, while Stephanya cuts short the other women's sexual innuendo.

Thus even on the reversal and theme shows, sexuality that is too overt must be repaired. For example, both of these exchanges took place on reversal shows:

QUOTE: "Her savage growl made me feel like king of the jungle."

MARK: Why, what'd you talk about?

MILTON: We talked about wet things, oceans, and you know, fun things we don't want to talk about here.

MARK: What'd you talk about with Milt? Fill me in, Trace. [Tracy covers her face, looking embarrassed]

TRACY: Well, we just basically talked about getting together and going somewhere because everything was just so spur-of-the-moment, but we like that.

QUOTE: "One night of wild passion, and I was a mass of throbbing flesh."

MARK: Yeah? Want to explain that, Darryl?

DARRYL: I don't think my couch will ever be the same again.

MARK: What were you doing on the couch?

DARRYL: Um, major kissing, caressing, and then loving.

MARK: How long was she over there?

DARRYL: Come on! Uh, it was a while.

MARK: It was a while. How long was it, Sherry?

SHERRY: I left at like 1, 1:30, somewhere around that. He had to work, so . . .

MARK: What were you going on the couch?

SHERRY: Watching TV.

MARK: What were you watching?

SHERRY: *Home Improvements.*

MARK: *Home Improvements?* That's on at one in the morning now? Pretty romantic, Darryl?

DARRYL: I think it was working into that, but she had to leave.

MARK: Would you have wanted it to go on longer?

DARRYL: Of course.

MARK: Sure. How about you, Sherry?

SHERRY: [unenthusiastically] Yeah.

Because of the reversal show setup, the male "dates" give the first descriptions of the events. Host DeCarlo then asks the women about the dates, and, as is obvious in the stories above, the women often give very different accounts than the men, even when asked exactly the same questions as the men. In the first story, when asked about the phone conversation, Milton says they discussed "wet things, oceans, and you know, fun things we don't want to talk about here." De-Carlo immediately turns to the female "studette" and asks her precisely the same question, to which she answers, "Well, we just basically talked about getting together and going somewhere." The contestants are describing the same conversation in response to the same question, but his response implies sexuality while hers denies it.

The same difference occurs in the second story: DeCarlo asks Darryl what he and his date were doing on the couch, and he answers, "Major kissing, caressing, and then loving," implying extensive sexual behavior. However, when DeCarlo asks Sherry the same question, she responds, "Watching TV." No only does she deny that sexual behavior occurred, she also flatly contradicts her date. Female contestants, despite their role as "studettes," still both imply and deny sexuality, although there is a tendency to acknowledge more sexual behavior when the women are in the "studette" role than in the "date" role. Male contestants, on the other hand, seem to become even more overtly sexual in their quotes and stories when they are in the "date" role—perhaps needing to display masculinity and sexuality even more clearly in order to overcome the feminine implications of the role—although this apparent difference may also be due to the fact that those in the "date" role generally have more opportunities to tell stories.

Thus, women and men experience different demands for sexuality and gender on *Studs.* While men are expected to be both highly masculine and highly sexual, women must balance the conflicting demands of femininity and sexuality. Although this conflict appears to be exacerbated by the "date" role they usually play, it is not eliminated by switching roles. Some other set of expectations, constant across roles, appears to be responsible. There are two possible explanations: the burlesque genre of the show, or the master gender identities that the participants hold despite their varying roles. I hypothesize that it is identity, not genre, that produces these differences between men and women. Because the burlesque genre thrives on bawdy performances, if the genre were the more pressing source of expectations I would expect the women to be more, rather than less, sexually suggestive. The master identity of "woman," however, prescribes restrained sexuality. It is this force, then, that I suggest is ultimately responsible for the different performances of men and women on *Studs.* West and Zimmerman suggest that "to be successful, marking or displaying gender must be finely fitted to situations and modified or transformed as the occasion demands. Doing gender consists of managing such occasions so that, whatever the particulars, the outcome is seen and seeable in context as gender-appropriate" (1987: 135). The reversal episodes on *Studs* illustrate how gender can be negotiated even when performing gender-atypical roles.

Multiple Performances

Although I have focused here on the performance of gender on *Studs,* it is clear that gender is not the only identity being constructed in this context. A number of scholars (e.g., Spelman 1988; Hill Collins 1990; hooks 1984) have criticized studies that attempt to analyze gender separately from other statuses such as race and class, arguing that this approach tends to privilege white, middle-class experiences and ignore the experiences of poor people and people of color. In their recent paper, "Doing Difference" (1995), West and Fenstermaker take up this challenge, and argue that individuals "do race" and "do class" at the same time that they "do gender." All interactions, they write, "regardless of the participants or the outcome, are simultaneously 'gendered,' 'raced,' and 'classed'" (1995: 13). Although their attempts to provide a model for understanding these intersections was only partially successful (see critiques in Hill Collins et al. 1995, for example), their argument that race, class, and gender affect individuals and interaction simultaneously is important. I would add that sexual orientation and age are also implicated in most interactions. These performances are interwoven with the gender performances of the *Studs* contestants.

Most salient, perhaps, is the construction of sexuality. The burlesque nature of *Studs* induces both men and women to display sexuality—but, although never stated explicitly, this sexuality is always *hetero*sexuality. The link between gender and heterosexual orientation is absolute and unquestioned on *Studs*: to be a successful "stud" or "studette," one must be both attracted to and desired by the opposite sex. Alternative sexualities— homosexuality or bisexuality, for example, or even heterosexual women being assertively sexual—are never mentioned directly. Because traditional heterosexuality is assumed, other sexual possibilities need not even be mentioned; this silence both reflects and reinforces the hegemony of heterosexuality. Despite the invisibility of homosexuality or bisexuality, sexuality on *Studs* is constructed via implicit contrast with these other possibilities. In examples discussed earlier in this paper, judgments about the type of masculinity desirable in a "stud" (strength, roughness, and so on) were conveyed through contrast with less valued masculinities: Alastair Cook types and men who ride mopeds rather than powerful motorcycles. A similar type of contrastive process occurs during the third guessing sequence in each episode, in which the host asks the "studs" to guess which man is more likely to perform a number of behaviors, such as kissing a woman's hand or wearing makeup. In each case, differences within gender categories are constructed and evaluated. Connell describes this process as "the construction of hierarchies of authority and centrality within the major gender categories" (1987: 109). In the hierarchy of masculinities constructed on

Studs, heterosexuality is valued over homosexuality and other less stereotypically "masculine" or "feminine" sexualities.

The construction of race is more subtle, but equally powerful. There is almost complete racial segregation on *Studs.* There is never any mixing of African American and white contestants; there are only all-black and all- or mostly-white episodes. Occasionally, one Asian American or Latina woman is included in an otherwise all-white episode; in contrast, there were no Asian American or Latino men among the male "studs" in my sample. As with gender, "the accomplishment of race consists of creating differences among members of different race categories—differences that are neither natural nor biological" (West and Fenstermaker 1995: 25). On *Studs,* this creation of difference is accomplished in part by assigning participants of different racial and ethnic categories to separate episodes. This separation of racial groups both mirrors and reproduces existing segregation in the wider world. The message about race here is clear: interracial contact, especially sexual contact, is unthinkable. It is taken for granted that whites and blacks will not be interested in each other as dating partners. The only racial mixing possible involves white men and Asian or Latina women; men of color do not date white women in the world constructed by *Studs.*

Race is also accomplished *within* racially homogeneous episodes. As West and Fenstermaker note, "the accomplishment of race, class, and gender does not require categorical diversity among the participants" (1995: 31). On the all-white (or mostly white) episodes, race is never discussed. There is no questioning of the racial segregation of participants, and no references to race ever occurred in the verbal interactions among contestants. These silences are telling: one of the hallmarks of privileged status is that privilege is taken for granted and not even noted unless it disappears (Frankenberg 1993). To these white participants, race does not seem to be a salient feature of interaction.[7]

Race is mentioned much more frequently (although obliquely) on the all-black episodes.[8]

The most frequent comments refer to skin tone. For example, when asked what she was "looking for in a guy," one African American contestant said she wanted a "nice chocolate guy"; another stated that her ideal man would be a "tall, dark guy with smooth skin." Skin color is discussed later in this same episode, when a female "date" comments that "I thought he was going to be light skinned, but he was dark." Other race-related comments referred to hair texture and style and clothing choices. Through these comments, the participants evaluate others' appearance and behavior in terms of racialized categories, and make it clear which of these categories are more highly valued. These evaluations also serve as performances of race for the speakers, locating them as the type of people who prefer certain characteristics. It is also important to note that these statements simultaneously enact other statuses as well as race: by saying that she wants "a tall, dark guy with smooth skin," the speaker accomplishes gender, sexuality, and race.

The construction of age and class is more subtle, but also important, in these episodes. Virtually all the episodes of *Studs* focus on young adults in their twenties. Although the age of the typical contestant undoubtedly mirrors that of the target audience, it nonetheless suggests that only young adults are sexual and desirable. One episode in my sample did involve middle-aged adults, and demonstrated clearly that people in their late 30s, 40s, and 50s can be as sexually provocative as young adults. However, this was the only episode with contestants over age 35 in both the formal sample of 18 shows used for this analysis and the much larger informal sample of episodes I watched; on *Studs,* as in much of the media, the sexuality of middle-aged and older adults is invisible.

Another age-related pattern on *Studs* was that the men were generally older than the women they dated. For example, on one typical episode, the "studs" were age 23 and 27; their "dates" were 20, 21, and 23. The age gap was even more pronounced when the contestants were older; in the episode mentioned above, the "studs" were 49 and

52; their "dates" were 37, 41, and 43. Here again, the patterns illustrated on *Studs* both reflect and reinforce patterns of domination in the wider world. Women are encouraged to pair with older, more powerful men; romances between older women and younger men are invisible, or are met with derision and even disgust. These patterns, while not necessarily harmful in individual cases, reinforce men's power over women in the aggregate.

Messages about social class were similarly embedded in these episodes. In the opening sequence, contestants are introduced by their name, age, and occupation, thereby providing hints about their class position. It was not clear from this sample of episodes whether contestants were deliberately matched on class position as they were with respect to age and race, although there were some indications that this might be the case. For example, in one episode, women who were described as a nutritionist, a secretary, and a community college student—all white-collar occupations—were matched with an economics student and a hotel "guest services rep." The youth of many of the participants, however, made a more conclusive analysis difficult.

What was clear from these episodes, however, was that financial generosity, and the class status it implies, was important—but only for men. On several occasions in these episodes, men's willingness to spend money on a date was assessed. For example, one woman reported that her date had "stiff[ed] the waiter at Red Lobster." The host probed for more details:

MARK: Did you give the waiter at Red Lobster a tip?

MICHAEL: Oh yeah.

MARK: How much?

MICHAEL: Five. . .

MARK: Five dollars.

MARION: Because I made you give it to him.

MARK: Why weren't you going to give him a tip? Was it bad service? If the service is crappy, I don't tip people either.

MARION: No, the service was great, it's just that . . . I don't know what happened, he just really embarrassed me, actually.

Indeed, one of the few things male contestants are criticized for is appearing stingy, either by not spending enough money on the date or by failing to leave a generous tip in restaurants. These kinds of assessments were never made of women. Thus it is the interaction of gender and class that is important here; these statuses cannot be considered individually.

Conclusions

Recipes for Success

Becker (1991) suggests that one way to understand a social phenomenon is to devise a "recipe" for its creation. This analogy is particularly appropriate when discussing performance, because the recipes can be understood as a sort of script for actors. In this spirit, then, I offer the following recipes for studhood and studettehood. Although my comments below refer to the social context of *Studs,* I suggest that these recipes apply to everyday interaction as well:

Recipe for Studhood	Recipe for Studettehood
1 Be big.	1 Be small.
2 Be strong.	2 Be beautiful.
3 Be (hetero)sexual.	3 Be (hetero)sexually provocative . . .
4 Be young.	4 but not too sexual.
5 Be generous.	5 Be young.
6 Desire a studette of the same race and similar (or younger) age as yourself.	6 Desire a stud of the same race and similar (or older) age as yourself.

To be a successful stud, a man should be big and strong (qualities many of the women say they are looking for at the beginning of the show). He should dress in "manly" clothes—jeans and boots are ideal, unless of course the man is particularly muscular, in which case he may wear clothes that reveal and emphasize his strength. He should also be big in terms of body position and gestures: he should move in a masculine fashion, sitting so as to take up the maximum space, gesturing widely and engaging in playful, ritualistic aggression with other men when introduced or when sexual comments are made. On dates, the man should engage in sexual behavior if possible (although being overly boorish or overly hesitant may lead to criticism from his dates). He should be young and, as discussed above, he should be generous with his money. A stud should look for and ultimately select a woman who embodies the qualities of a studette; heterosexuality and masculinity are tightly linked. Finally, a stud should focus only on women of the same race and similar (or younger) age as himself as possible sexual partners.

Women who aspire to studettehood have very different requirements. As with men, they should be young. However, they should be small, not big, and beautiful, not strong: the most consistently admired women are thin (although buxom) and conventionally pretty. The way the women sit and move emphasizes their smallness: they sit in a way that minimizes the amount of space they take up, and their gestures are small and contained. Like men, women should also be sexually attractive and provocative: on *Studs,* their official quotes about the dates should be as racy and sexually suggestive as possible. In particular circumstances—if they are playing the "studette" role, or if they are "wild women," women may admit to some sexual activity. However, they should not be *too* sexual. After making suggestive comments, they should deny that sexual activity has occurred, although this denial may be less robust if they are playing the "studette" role. Thus their job is to be sexually provocative but still maintain the appearance of virtue. And finally, women should desire, and ultimately select, a man who is also a stud— but one of the same race and similar (or older) age as herself. Each of these requirements serves to maximize the differences between women and men, constructing gender as dichotomous.

Gender as Performance

The main argument of this paper is that gender is not something we have, but something we do in interaction with others. Although the performance of gender may be habitual and therefore taken for granted, we are constantly, skillfully, enacting what it means to be masculine or feminine in both our situational and cultural contexts. The behavior of the contestants on *Studs* provides a glimpse of precisely how gender is performed. Because gender is so salient in this context, its performance is obvious.

I want to emphasize three additional points. First, I contend in this paper that the enactments of gendered behavior exemplified by *Studs* are skillful performances rather than the expression of innate qualities. However, an important feature of these performances is that they are perceived to be natural expressions of underlying masculinity and femininity. Bem (1993) calls this "biological essentialism": the belief that gender polarization is "the natural and inevitable consequence of the intrinsic biological natures of women and men" (1993: 2). Although great skill is required to juggle the conflicting demands of gender and situational roles, there is never any acknowledgement of these talents, nor any hint that gender might be enacted differently. Thus this view of gender is consistent with Goffman's contention that gender "is not instinctive but is socially learned and socially patterned; it is a socially defined category which employs a particular expression, and a socially established schedule which determines when these expressions will occur. And this is so even though individuals come to employ expressions in what is sensed to be a spontaneous and unselfconscious way, that is, uncalculated, unfaked, natural" (1976: 7).

The second point is that although gender is a constructed performance, rather than an innate characteristic, it does not follow that gender performance is voluntary or consequence-free. Although the men and women on *Studs* clearly choose to participate in the show, the details of their roles, as well as their everyday behaviors as

men and women, are constrained and subject to evaluation and sanction. Properly performing gendered behavior elicits social approval (e.g., applause and whistles from the audience), "stud success," being chosen for future dates, and so on. Improper performance, on the other hand, is socially punished by disapproval (e.g., booing, groaning, or lack of applause from the audience), "stud failure," and being passed over for future dates.

Examples of gender transgression—and the consequences it entails—were visible, although infrequent, in these episodes of *Studs*.[9] For instance, one male participant admitted using self-tanning lotion—a practice associated with femininity. This participant, who worked as a bouncer at a bar, commented, "I work during the day, I don't get out into the sun. So when I get back to the bar, I put some tanning stuff on my face, everyone was ragging on me, 'Aw, you're putting on makeup.'" The derision with which such transgressive behavior is met is evidenced both in the comments he reports and in the response of the studio audience, who groaned, "Ohhhh . . . ," when he admitted using this product.

Women also suffer consequences for gender transgression. For example, one woman was particularly open in her admission of sexual behavior, as is evident in the following exchange:

LARRY: "He blazed a trail across my belly like 1,000 horny homesteaders" has got to be Cheryl.

CHERYL: Yep.

MARK: There you go! All right Cheryl, when last we left Larry's loveboat . . .

CHERYL: Well, we came back from dinner, and we're on the balcony, and he's still determined on that bikini.

MARK: How did he do?

CHERYL: Very well.

MARK: Uh huh. How did . . .

LARRY: I told her I like tall girls, and she said, well, it might be nice to have a tall girl with legs wrapped around you, but she said it's a lot more fun to have short girl tryin'.

Although it was clear from Cheryl's comments—and from her selection of Larry at the end of the show as her preferred future date—that she had enjoyed her date with him, Larry did not choose her for future dates. Why? As he put it, "because I've already seen everything she's got." Gender transgression, such as admitting sexuality in women, is punished.

Finally, I want to emphasize that individuals' enactments of gender and other statuses are not solo performances. Individuals do perform gendered behaviors, but they do so in interaction with other people and in specific contexts that provide opportunities to perform gender, set expectations for gendered behavior, and then evaluate this behavior. On *Studs,* there are several types of interaction that work together to construct gender. First, the performers evaluate each other's comments and behaviors, both on and off the set. For example, consider this set of conversations reported by a "date":

> QUOTE: "One quick shake and he was finally satisfied."
> MARK: What kind of shake are you talking about?
> NICOLE: I mean a handshake. Um, him and Patrick had talked, and said I don't kiss on the first date, which I don't. And he analyzed me for like two hours asking me why I don't kiss on the first date.
> MARK: Why don't you?
> NICOLE: I just don't, that's something that I, I'm not interested in doing, so I don't—
> MARK: Okay. So in your whole life, you've never kissed on the first date.
> NICOLE: No. I didn't say all that, I didn't say that, I just said—
> MARK: You did! You said, "I don't kiss on the first—"
> NICOLE: I, I said I don't! That's, that's, that's now. [Audience: laughter]

> MARK: Well, that's about as clear as you can get it.

In this example, Nicole reports that the two "studs" discussed her refusal to kiss on the first date (a behavior which implicates both gender and sexuality) both with her and with each other.[10] Clearly, her choice not to kiss was not evaluated positively. The host then probes for an explanation for this choice—a second type of interaction that elicits comments from the "date"—and then evaluates it (negatively, in this case).

Another type of interaction involves the studio audience's response to the contestants. In the example above, the audience laughs at Nicole when an apparent inconsistency is found in her performance (i.e., she asserted that she didn't kiss on first dates, but then acknowledged having done so). Laughter is only one kind of audience response; there are a number of other common audience reactions that evaluate the success or failure of the participants' performances. For example, the audience rewards adherence to expectations about gender and sexuality by applauding, whistling, and saying, "Wooooo!":

> QUOTE: "His skin's as soft as satin panties."
> AUDIENCE: "Wooooo!"

The audience also makes it clear when gender transgressions have occurred, by laughing, hissing, booing, or groaning ("Ohhhh!"), as in these examples:

> QUOTE: "I didn't kiss him, but I'm sure the girl he left with did."
> AUDIENCE: "Ohhhhh!"
> QUOTE: "He's a really big tipper—if you've got change for a quarter."
> AUDIENCE: "Ohhhhh!"

Through these interactions, expectations for behavior are set, individual performances are evaluated, and alternative masculinities and femininities are suppressed. The range of performances permissible on *Studs* is highly restricted;

individuals may choose to transgress, but they do so at the risk of evaluation and social sanction.

Is *Studs* just trivial entertainment, or does it have a deeper message? My suspicion is that the situated stud and date roles performed on *Studs* are simply stereotyped exaggerations of everyday gender performances. Nonetheless, my conclusions are limited by the fact that this analysis explores only one context, and, moreover, that this context is clearly unusual: as well as being part of a specialized genre, it is exceptionally public, at least partially scripted, and probably edited. On the other hand, this show was extremely popular; in my informal discussions and presentations of this paper, the overwhelming majority of my colleagues and students had seen the show at least once. Although many viewers criticize the show for its sexism, racism, and a host of other faults, I suspect that its gender prescriptions and performances may influence even critical viewers. Recent studies documenting the effects of viewing attractive models on subjects' perceptions of self and others (for example, see Kenrick and Gutierres 1989) also suggest these effects. I suggest that performance of gender on *Studs* and in other media serves to both model and reinforce the more subtle gender performances found in everyday behavior and thus to recreate existing differences and hierarchies based on gender, race, age, class, and sexuality. The stylized interactions on *Studs* illustrate how these statuses (and the institutional-level hierarchies they represent) are simultaneously constructed and maintained through everyday interaction. West and Zimmerman argue that "if we do gender appropriately, we simultaneously sustain, reproduce, and render legitimate the institutional arrangements that are based on sex category" (1987: 146). Examining the micro-level processes of interaction shows both how enmeshed these systems of hierarchy are—and how difficult they are to resist.

Notes

1. Of course, even "spontaneous" television entertainment, such as talk and game shows, is highly scripted. Nonetheless, these shows remain a good site for studies of gender performance. First, the scripts themselves illustrate popular conceptions of and prescriptions for gender. Second, the gendered behavior of performers that goes beyond these already-gendered roles shows the compulsory nature of gender performance. Participants are still responsible for their individual gender performances, even when playing scripted roles.

2. The credits following the show include this disclaimer: "Contestants' answers which appear on screen are the contestants' own, but may have been paraphrased or edited by the producer."

3. A conversational turn is defined as "a single contribution of a speaker to a conversation" (Crystal 1987: 432); communication turns similarly represent discrete contributions, either verbal or nonverbal, to an interaction.

4. The host's role is clearly intended to be neutral: he wears a suit to distinguish him from the younger, more casually-dressed participants, and although in fact unmarried, he wears a gold wedding band to signify that he is not sexually available. Although this role may be sexually neutral, however, it is not gender neutral. The host is clearly aligned with the male "studs" rather than the female "dates." He stands up to greet the male contestants when they arrive on stage, congratulates them after the show, asks them whether they consider the game's rules to be "fair enough," and engages the men in playful joking. He performs none of these behaviors with the female participants.

5. The amount of choice the contestants have regarding attire is unknown. However, the fact that there is some variation in dress suggests that they have at least some control over their clothing choices.

6. A second type of quote occurs regularly, although considerably less frequently: Derisive comments about the "studs" appearance or behavior. For example, the sample of episodes I use here included comments such as "He's the handsomest man on the planet . . . if you live on the planet of the apes" and "Food swirled through his mouth like clothes in a dryer."

7. Of course, this may be less true for the Asian American and Latina women who appear on the otherwise all-white episodes.

8. These episodes are infrequent, so I am generalizing here from a sample of only three episodes.

9. The relative lack of gender resistance is probably due in part to processes of self-selection. Those who choose to transgress the normative boundaries of gender and sexuality are unlikely to volunteer to participate in a television show focused around conventional notions of heterosexuality. If such individuals did volunteer to participate, moreover, they are not likely to be chosen as contestants. In this way, resistance becomes invisible: the contradictory goals of resistors and gatekeepers both result in the marginalization of those who choose to resist gender expectations.

10. Note women's presumed responsibility for determining and policing sexual boundaries.

References

Bauman, Richard. 1986. *Story, Performance, and Event: Contextual Studies of Oral Narrative.* Cambridge: Cambridge University Press.

Becker, Howard S. 1991. Personal communication.

Bem, Sandra Lipsitz. 1993. *The Lenses of Gender.* New Haven, CT: Yale University Press.

Bornstein, Kate. 1994. *Gender Outlaw: On Men, Women, and the Rest of Us.* New York, NY: Vintage.

Clark, Herbert H. 1985. "Language Use and Language Users," in *The Handbook of Social Psychology,* G. Lindzey and E. Aronson (eds), 3rd edn. New York, NY: Random House, pp. 179–231.

Connell, Robert W. 1987. *Gender and Power: Society, the Person, and Sexual Politics.* Stanford, CA: Stanford University Press.

———. 1995. *Masculinities.* Berkeley, CA: University of California Press.

Crystal, David. 1987. *The Cambridge Encyclopedia of Language.* Cambridge: Cambridge University Press.

Fox, Greer Litton. 1977. " 'Nice Girl': Social Control of Women Through A Value Construct." *Signs* 2(4): 805–17.

Frankenberg, Ruth. 1993. *White Women, Race Matters: The Social Construction of Whiteness.* Minneapolis, MN: University of Minnesota Press.

Garfinkel, Harold. 1967. *Studies in Ethnomethodology.* Englewood Cliffs, NJ: Prentice-Hall.

Goffman, Erving. 1976. *Gender Advertisements.* New York, NY: Harper and Row.

———. 1977. "The Arrangement Between the Sexes." *Theory and Society* 43: 301–31.

———. 1974. *Frame Analysis: An Essay on the Organization of Experience.* Cambridge, MA: Harvard University Press.

Henley, Nancy M. 1977. *Body Politics: Power, Sex, and Nonverbal Communication.* New York, NY: Simon and Schuster.

Hill Collins, Patricia. 1990. *Black Feminist Thought.* New York, NY: Routledge.

———, Lionel A. Maldonado, Dana Y. Takagi, Barrie Thorne, Lynn Weber, and Howard Winant. 1995. "On West and Fenstermaker's 'Doing Difference'." *Gender and Society* 9(4): 491–506.

hooks, bell. 1984. *From Margin to Center.* Boston, MA: South End.

Kenrick, Douglas T., Sara E. Gutierres, and Laurie L. Goldberg. 1989. "Influence of popular erotica on judgments of strangers and mates." *Journal of Experimental Social Psychology* 25(2): 159–67.

Kessler, Suzanne J. and Wendy McKenna. 1978. *Gender: An Ethnomethodological Approach.* New York, NY: John Wiley and Sons.

Kimmel, Michael. 1993. "Clarence, William, Iron Mike, Tailhook, Senator Packwood, Spur Posse, Magic . . . and Us," in *Transforming a Rape Culture,* E. Buchwald, P. R. Fletcher and M. Roth (eds). Minneapolis, MN: Milkweed, pp. 121–38.

Lorber, Judith. 1994. *Paradoxes of Gender.* New Haven, CT: Yale University Press.

Orenstein, Peggy. 1994. *SchoolGirls: Young Women, Self-Esteem, and the Confidence Gap.* New York, NY: Anchor.

Plummer, Ken. 1995. *Telling Sexual Stories: Power, Change and Social Worlds.* London: Routledge.

Read, Stephen J. 1987. "Constructing Causal Scenarios: A Knowledge Structure Approach to Causal Reasoning." *Journal of Personality and Social Psychology* 52(2): 288–302.

Spelman, Elizabeth. 1988. *Inessential Women: Problems of Exclusion in Feminist Thought.* Boston, MA: Beacon Press.

Thorne, Barrie. 1994. *Gender Play: Girls and Boys in School.* New Brunswick, NJ: Rutgers.

"We Always Start Watching . . ." *Rolling Stone,* 14 May 1992: 89.

West, Candace, and Don. H. Zimmerman. 1987. "Doing Gender." *Gender and Society* 1(2): 125–51.

———, and Sarah Fenstermaker. 1993. "Power, Inequality, and the Accomplishment of Gender: An Ethnomethodological View," in *Theory on Gender/Feminism on Theory,* ed. Paula England. New York, NY: Aldine de Gruyter, pp. 151–73.

———. 1995. "Doing Difference." *Gender and Society* 9(1): 8–37.

ARTICLE 48

Peter Lehman

In an Imperfect World, Men with Small Penises Are Unforgiven

The Presentation of the Penis/Phallus in American Films of the 1990s

Reservoir Dogs (1992) begins with a dark screen as we hear a man saying, "Let me tell you what 'Like a Virgin's' all about. It's all about a girl who digs a guy with a big dick. It's her song. It's a metaphor for big dicks." After he finishes, the blank screen yields to the image of a group of men sitting in a restaurant talking. One of them (played by Quentin Tarantino, the film's writer and director) has spoken the lines we just heard. Moments later, amid the wandering conversation, he says, "You guys are like making me lose my train of thought. I was saying something. What was it? . . . What the fuck was I talking about?" After one of his companions puts him back on track, he continues, "Let me tell you what 'Like a Virgin's' about. It's all about this . . . regular fuck machine. I'm talking morning, day, night—dick, dick, dick, dick, dick, dick." "How many dicks is that?" someone asks. "A lot," another answers.

Both the question and the answer are oddly appropriate for the talk about penises that characterizes several recent American films as well as the news media in the 1990s. In *Running Scared: Masculinity and the Representation of the Male Body* (Lehman 1993), I argued that work on the repre-

Author's Note: *I would like to thank Chris Holmlund, Robert Eberwein, Melanie Magisos, Russell Merritt, and William Luhr for their comments and revision suggestions. I am particularly indebted to an anonymous reviewer for* Men and Masculinities.

From *Men and Masculinities*, Vol. 1, No. 2, pp. 123–137, copyright © 1998 Sage Publications, Inc. Reprinted by permission of Sage Publications, Inc.

sentation of the penis is important since, until very recently, nearly all critical attention has been focused on the phallus. This nearly exclusive attention to the symbolic realm has had the unfortunate effect, among others, of perpetuating the very phallic mystique that such work seeks to deconstruct. The penis in our culture either is hidden from sight, or its representation is carefully regulated for specific ideological purposes. Centering the penis may seem the ultimate patriarchal tyranny, but it is no coincidence that the most traditional men have been comfortable with the silence surrounding the penis and its absence or careful regulation within representation. Silence about and invisibility of the penis contribute to a phallic mystique. The penis is and will remain centered until such time as we turn the critical spotlight on it; paradoxically, we have to center the penis so that eventually it may be decentered. Richard Dyer's 1982 article, "Don't Look Now: The Male Pin-Up," began important work on the penis/phallus relationship and the manner in which it structures certain notions of masculinity and representations of the male body. As Barbara de Genevieve (1991) puts it, "To unveil the penis is to unveil the phallus is to unveil the social construction of masculinity" (p. 4). It is within this perspective that it is important that we understand the chatter and joking about penises in films of the 1990s.

When the penis is shown in our culture, such representations are carefully regulated, as in the pornographic discourse that attempts to make an impressive spectacle of the penis or in contemporary medical discourse that attempts to represent the "normal" or statistically average penis. What these and other discourses do is suppress anything resembling the variety and range of actual penises, which thus remain mysterious and become the subject of curiosity, the object of scorn and humor, or the unseen object of phallic worship. It is precisely within this context that we can understand the seemingly unlimited public appetite for gossip and information surrounding the Bobbitt case and other news stories that center discussion of penises. Predictably, some people felt that Howard Stern reached an all-time television low during his 1993 New Year's eve show when he waved $15,000 in front of John Bobbitt as enticement to drop his pants and let the nation see what a reattached penis looked like (Ring out the old 1994, 33). Yet, such antics seem to me not far removed from recent newspaper articles in Oakland, Tucson, San Antonio, and Phoenix about new surgical techniques for penis enlargement (Kanigel 1995; Schmidt 1995; Hosteteler 1994) or a recent *Arizona Daily Star* story with a large headline, "Urologist Debunks Myths Surrounding the Area below Men's Belts" (Cobb 1994, C6). One of the myths is, predictably, "Myth 7: Penis size matters."

We have created an environment in which inquiring minds want to know, laugh, snicker, speculate, and worship the hidden penis. Lisa Kemler, one of Lorena Bobbitt's lawyers, remarked after the case, "This case was not about a penis. . . . Everyone was so consumed with that. But that's not what this case is really about. It was really about a life" (Bobbitt cleared 1994, 1A). She is, of course, correct on both counts. The reason, however, that everyone was too "consumed" with the penis is that the one real taboo that remains in our culture is that disallowing of anything resembling a mature and explicit representation of the actual organ that is the subject of all this media attention, be it in the news or the movies—for such representation would destroy the cherished patriarchal myth that the penis can sustain such never-ending fascination and be worthy of setting entire narratives in motion or dominating a trial involving life-

and-death issues and matters of the most profound social and cultural importance.

I have elsewhere documented in detail how American films of the 1970s and 1980s have been laced with chatter about the penis (Lehman 1990), frequently taking the form of fleeting penis-size jokes, and while the 1990s promises to continue this pattern (there are, for example, two such jokes in 1994's *Mrs. Doubtfire*), there exists a significant variation of which *Reservoir Dogs* is a prime example. Talk about the penis has been occurring nearer the beginning of some films and, in several extreme instances, even sets the narrative events in motion. This development is not entirely without precedent. *The Witches of Eastwick* (1987) begins with three women talking about their penis-size preferences, and, in a variation that involves no language, the plot of *Robocop* (1987) is set in motion when a female police officer is distracted by looking at a man's penis as he finishes urinating. Similarly, the entire narrative momentum in *Hard to Kill* (1990) begins when Steven Seagal awakens from a coma of many years immediately after a nurse lifts the sheets and sighs about the waste of his impressive sexual endowment. Clint Eastwood's *Unforgiven* (1992) and *A Perfect World* (1993) are currently the most significant films to conform to this pattern, but before turning attention to them, I want to return to *Reservoir Dogs*.

The gangster in *Reservoir Dogs* completes his interpretation (which, despite his occupation, is something of a scholarly analysis) of "Like a Virgin" as follows:

> Then one day she meets this John Holmes motherfucker and it's like "Whoa baby." I mean this cat is like Charles Bronson in *The Great Escape*—he's big in tunnels . . . pain, pain . . . it hurts. It shouldn't hurt . . . but when this cat fucks her it hurts—it hurts just like it did the first time. See, the pain is reminding the fuck machine what it was like to be a virgin—hence, "Like a Virgin."

Viewers of the film, like the Harvey Keitel character, may complain that they've "got Madonna's big dick coming out of [their] left ear" since this constant chatter about big dicks seems distracting in relation to the gangster story that is "coming out of [their] right" ear.

Although in many films this chatter about penises occurs only once, such is not the case in *Reservoir Dogs.* Once the gangster story proper begins, we are treated to another dick-talking session, this time as a group of the gangsters drive to a big meeting where they will be briefed by their leader. The driver announces his desire to tell a story. When the others continue talking, he yells, "Shut up! I'm trying to tell a story here." The story is about a woman who seeks vengeance on her lover.

> So anyway, one night she plays it real cool. She waits for this bag of shit to get real drunk. He falls asleep on the fucking couch. She sneaks up on him and she puts whacko glue on his dick and glues his dick to his belly.

"Jesus Christ!" the Keitel character exclaims amid general groans of disgust. "They had to call the paramedics to cut the prick loose," the driver concludes, and they all share a good laugh. The film cuts to the leader addressing the men, "You guys like to tell jokes and giggle and kid around, huh? Giggling like a bunch of young broads in a school yard."

Once again, the film viewer is likely to feel like there is someone's dick coming out of one ear while the gangster story is coming out of the other. What do these dicks have to do with the gangster story? *Reservoir Dogs* is a remarkable and coherent film and one that has been read by Robert Hilferty (1992) as possessing a homosexual subtext. In any case, whether homosexual or not, the film deals centrally with the intimacies of male bonding, and talk about the penis relates to that context. The dick talk in this film is linked to both age and generation; the young men feel a need to talk about penises, which relates to the notions of masculinity they struggle with. The older man either ignores them or scolds them for this type of behavior. For the younger man seated on Keitel's left, big dicks are an important part of masculinity, while for the older man seated on his right,

they seem to hold no interest; he leafs through his address book during the conversation, muttering to himself. This seating arrangement suggests that the masculine obsession with penility is replaced by senility with advancing age. When the penis is no longer central to masculinity, only its decline and ruin are left.

Despite this rich context for the dick talking in *Reservoir Dogs,* I would caution against an overly thematic reading, especially of the metaphoric kind the character played by the film's director offers of "Like a Virgin." Like many recent films, *Reservoir Dogs* seems to sense some connection between penises and its subject matter, but it does not know precisely what that connection is. What makes *Reservoir Dogs* unique in this regard is that it gives formal expression to this somewhat bizarre state of affairs. Indeed, in both cases the characters doing the dick talking voice their frustration with the manner in which they are interrupted ("What the fuck was I saying?" and "I'm trying to tell a story here."), and their stories themselves appear like digressions and interruptions in the film. And other characters make this clear in both cases. Keitel's character is literally distracted from his conversation with the boss in the restaurant, and the boss scolds the men for acting like giggling schoolgirls immediately following the second dick discussion. Indeed, Keitel's left and right ear dilemma neatly summarizes the cacophonic disruption that such digressive talk creates in most of these films. The filmmakers need to talk about penises (which they never show) for reasons that are not fully clear even to them, although such talk interrupts their films and the stories they are trying to tell. While such talk in *Reservoir Dogs* is far from being totally digressive, it interrupts the film's narration in a manner mirroring that in which the narrators of the penis stories are themselves interrupted.

In *True Lies* (1994), by contrast, the filmmakers seem to know exactly why they talk about penis size. In that film, a pathetic used-car salesman masquerades as a glamorous spy who is like the one played by Arnold Schwarzenegger. When caught and asked why he engaged in such behavior, he blurts out, "I'm not a spy. I'm nothing. . . . I have to lie to women to get laid and I don't score much. I got a little dick; it's pathetic." He then wets his pants. This "nothing" man, the pretender to the true masculinity that Schwarzenegger represents, is primarily marked by the "little dick" and secondarily by his inability, due to fear, to control his bladder. The character reappears briefly at the end of the film when he once again wets his pants.

In my earlier analysis of the virtual epidemic of penis-size jokes in Hollywood films of the 1970s, 1980s, and early 1990s, I hypothesized that their presence could be accounted for in a number of quite different ways including fear of the collapse of the alleged dramatic visual marker of sexual difference, veiled homoerotic desire given a heterosexual veneer by the women who frequently tell the jokes and make the judgments, and, in relation to the last point, male masochism that revels in being judged against a phallic standard and found lacking (Lehman 1993).

While I still believe that all those dynamics are present, it now seems to me that two additional things have to be considered. First, *True Lies* makes dramatically clear that to maintain our belief in the powerful phallic sexuality of an Arnold Schwarzenegger, we have to believe in the pathetic failed sexuality of men with small penises. How can we worship big penises in a world without small penises? (It might be interesting, incidentally, to consider the comic pairing of Schwarzenegger and Danny DeVito in *Twins,* 1988, and *Junior,* 1994, from this perspective—the presence of the small man even further dramatizes Schwarzenegger's large stature.) Second, my analysis of 1970s and 1980s penis-size jokes and chatter reveals an entrenched binary opposition between big and small penises, with small men being the pathetic objects of the jokes and large men being the, frequently implicit, desirable ideal. Something new, however, is emerging in some 1990s films that unexpectedly breaks this dichotomy and suggests that the ideal of the large penis may not be what it's cracked up to be and may, in fact, even be dangerous.

When the function of the penis is to serve as the privileged sign of visual sexual difference, the logical direction of crisis about penis size is that which emerges in Michel Foucault's (1980) edition of *Herculine Barbin: Being the Recently Discovered Memoirs of a Nineteenth-Century French Hermaphrodite.* Two medical documents referring to Adelaide Herculine Barbin are of particular interest here. Dr. Chesnet examined Barbin when as a teenager "she" was living in a convent. Much attention is given to what he calls a "penial body," which measures four to five centimeters. "This little member, which because of its dimensions is as far removed from the clitoris as it is from the penis in its normal state, can, according to Alexina, swell, harden, and lengthen" (p. 126). Later in the report, he refers to "a sort of imperforate penis, which might be a monstrously developed clitoris" (p. 127). In a published autopsy report in Foucault, E. Goujon makes similar observations. At one point, Barbin's sexual organ is described as a "large clitoris rather than a penis; in fact, among women we sometimes see the clitoris attain the size of the index finger" (p. 131). When the dimensions of the penis are given later, it is again noted that "in size [it] did not exceed the clitoris of some women," and it is finally simply referred to as "the erectile organ (penis or clitoris)" (pp. 131–35). The crisis surrounding the penis in the Barbin case is that the external organ is presumed to be the visual marker of sexual difference, and size is key to distinguishing between it and a clitoris.

Something much different is happening in *True Lies,* in which the small penis serves to set off not the clitoris but the large penis. In effect, these penis-size jokes no longer pretend to be about the collapse of sexual difference or about female pleasure. If in Foucault's analysis, Barbin is sacrificed to the nineteenth-century need to determine an individual's true sex, the pathetic used-car salesman with the "little dick" is sacrificed on the altar of late-twentieth-century worship of true masculinity—such is our need to believe in Schwarzenegger's masculinity. The small penis, in other words, far from being an embarrassment for masculinity, becomes its very ground. By making fun of some characters whose penises do not measure up to the phallic mystique, we ensure that mystique with the implicit assumption that some do measure up. Hence, rather than reveal the gap between the penis and the phallus, such films revel in its denial.

As in *Reservoir Dogs,* however, the penis talk in *True Lies* takes place within a complex context. The scenes of high-tech tracking and interrogation of Schwarzenegger's wife's sexual activities reveal how desperately insecure his masculinity is. He may seem like the phallic ideal in comparison to the used-car salesman, but the ideal is not what it seems to be. The true masculinity that Schwarzenegger embodies is itself a form of true lies. He requires the highest technology the government can offer and is assisted by a SWAT team when he captures his wife, who is about to engage in infidelity. He then breaks her down in an interrogation scene in which he stands behind a two-way mirror. Although critics frequently singled out this scene as particularly misogynistic, it in fact can be read quite the opposite. The extremes to which Schwarzenegger goes to catch his wife and wring a confession from her expose an astonishing level of insecurity. The dynamics of the scene enable the audience to laugh at Schwarzenegger and his male partner rather than simply identify with them and enjoy the powerful manner in which they brutally terrorize the woman. Nevertheless, by the end of the film, when he rises into view at a skyscraper to rescue his daughter who has been kidnapped, he appears to have a powerful jet between his legs. As outrageous as the phallic imagery of the plane is, Schwarzenegger commands it masterfully.

Clint Eastwood's *Unforgiven* and *A Perfect World* are particularly interesting films to analyze within this context of 1990s films that grapple with the penis/phallus conundrum for two reasons. They foreground and integrate these issues narratively and thematically, and since Eastwood himself has been one of the major stars to shape and embody masculinity in cinema since the mid-

1960s, these films in part reflect back on his star persona.

Unforgiven begins in midaction with a cowboy slashing the face of a whore. Another prostitute explains, "All she done when she seen he had a teensy little pecker is give a giggle. That's all." This event sets the entire narrative in motion since the prostitutes offer a bounty for the guilty man and his companion. If the cowboy at the beginning of the film is found to be literally lacking in the privileged cultural sign of masculinity, we quickly find that all the men are symbolically plagued by similar problems. William Munny (Clint Eastwood) has trouble mounting his horse due to his age, and the young cowboy who somewhat maniacally assembles the posse and leads them is, for all practical purposes, blind. In another image closely related to the film's opening emphasis on the penis, an Eastern writer becomes so scared during a tense confrontation that he wets his pants. Thus, like *True Lies,* the film contains references to and images of perhaps the two most humiliating possibilities surrounding the dual functions of the penis as a sexual and a urinary organ: sexual smallness and loss of bladder control due to fear. The image of masculinity that permeates *Unforgiven* is one of men with small penises who piss in their pants and have trouble mounting and staying on their horses and even seeing who they are shooting at and pursuing.

This integration of a reference to a small penis into complex and carefully developed imagery about the myth of masculinity within the Western genre recalls Robert Altman's similar integration of a penis-size joke in *McCabe and Mrs. Miller* (1971). Dennis Bingham (1994) notes that the script for *Unforgiven* was written by David Webb Peoples in 1975 and that it was "apparently inspired" by Altman's film (p. 232). Although the consequences in Altman's film are much different, once again a prostitute laughs at a cowboy with a small penis, this time when another whore whispers in her ear and indicates with her fingers the man's sexual smallness. As I have shown in a detailed analysis of that film (Lehman 1990,

119–23), Altman not only weaves this joke into a complex critique of the mystique of the Western hero but also into a comparison with the female body, since the dialogue makes clear that one of the whores is sexually small both in her vagina and her breasts.

Similarly, in *Unforgiven* Eastwood extends his careful development of male body imagery to a comparison with the female body. After Munny is beaten in a fight, he regains consciousness to see the scarred whore from the opening scene nursing him. "I must look kinda like you now, huh?" Munny remarks. "You don't look nothing like me, Mister," she quickly responds. Although Munny later calls himself ugly and tries to reassure her that she is "a beautiful woman," her initial response is unsentimentally accurate. In Hollywood films, when a beautiful woman's face is scarred, it nearly always indicates a loss of power stemming from the cultural assumption that women derive power from the passive possession of beauty. When a man's face is similarly disfigured, it nearly always means that he is a tough, active character, the scars proving that he has been tested and survived. He is, in other words, more powerful as a result of his scarred face. The scarred whore in *Unforgiven* hires others to avenge the irreparable loss she has suffered; the battered Munny does the job just fine himself, emerging as a powerful, demonic figure. The cosmetic damage he has suffered is, to say the least, not just like that of the woman.

But the body imagery in *Unforgiven* is even further complicated not by contrasting the male body with the female body but, rather, by unexpectedly contrasting the film's initial emphasis on the cowboy with the small penis with a gunslinger with a large one. During a jail conversation, the sheriff, Little Bill Daggett (Gene Hackman), whose name is of no small interest here, tells the Eastern writer about a gunfighter who died in a shoot-out with "English Bob," the man whose biography he is writing. The gunfighter was nicknamed "Two-Gun Corky," even though he only carried one gun. "Corky never carried two guns, although he should have," the sheriff observes before explaining how he got the nickname. "He had a dick that was so big, it was longer than the barrel on that Walker colt that he carried." Corky's mistake, we are told, was "to stick that thing of his into this French lady that English Bob here was kinda sweet on." Corky is killed in an ensuing fight when the gun he is using blows up in his hand. The sheriff draws the moral, "You see though, if Corky had had two guns instead of just a big dick; he would have been there right to the end to defend himself." I will return to this image of the large penis as posing a danger to its possessor after considering *A Perfect World*.

Although the comparisons with *Unforgiven* were inevitable, very few critics saw much of a connection between that film and *A Perfect World*, Eastwood's next directorial effort. The former appeared to be a film of epic range that looked back on much of the history of the genre and on Eastwood's persona as it was developed in the films of Sergio Leone and Don Diegel, while the latter appeared to be a minor action film with none of the ambitious sweep of its predecessor. Yet, penis size emerges overtly once again in *A Perfect World*, and it is once again woven into the fabric of the film. The convict who escapes from prison with Butch Haynes (Kevin Costner) is represented from the outset as revolting. This is in keeping with a tradition within the male action film, which I have analyzed elsewhere in relation to *The Man Who Shot Liberty Valance*, in which the hero and the villain are similar to each other (Luhr and Lehman 1977). In this variation, the escapees are the "bad" male system, but there is a dichotomy within that system with a good male (Haynes) and a bad male (his companion). They are further contrasted with a "good" male system, the law, which is also composed of the good lawman, Red Garnett (Clint Eastwood), and a sleazy officer who sexually harasses a young woman assigned to the case.

In a pivotal scene that is once again near the beginning of the film, Haynes leaves the boy they have kidnapped with his partner in the car and goes into a store. At Haynes's instructions, the boy, in the front seat, holds a cocked gun pointed at the head of the man sitting in the back seat. The boy has no pants on since he was kidnapped in his underpants. The man talks to the boy about shooting and surmises that he has never shot a gun before. Leaning forward, he tells the boy that they are going to have a "man-to-man" talk, asks him whether he is a man, and, saying, "Let's see what you got down there," reaches down to his underpants, pulls the hand out, looks down, and observes, "Kinda puny ain't it?" The boy, distracted by looking down, is disarmed. The man then begins to molest him. The boy escapes from the car and runs into a field followed by the man, who now appears absolutely diabolical and degenerate. Moments later Haynes kills him.

A truly remarkable scene, however, occurs later in the film when Haynes is alone with the boy in the car. When the boy is reluctant to undress and put on a pair of new pants in front of him, Haynes asks, "Are you embarrassed because I might see your pecker?" "It's puny," the boy replies. When Haynes guesses who told him that, he says, "Let me see," assuring the boy that he will tell him the truth. In a two-shot through the car door window, we see the profile of the boy's head as he pulls down his underpants and Haynes leans forward, looks directly down at his groin, and reports, "Hell no, Philip. Good size for boy your age." We then see a close-up of the boy beaming with pride. The spectacle of an actor of Costner's importance looking at a penis for the express purpose of determining its size in a scene that not only shows him looking but also announces in a dialogue why he is looking is undoubtedly the most narratively and visually centered example to date within a virtual epidemic of such penis preoccupied scenes within Hollywood films. Why is it there?

At one level, the scene uniquely dramatizes why penis-size anxiety so riddles our culture. It condenses a long, drawn out, psychoanalytic experience for boys into a few brief, dramatic moments. The "bad" convict plants the idea in the little boy's mind that he is sexually inadequate, linking the "puny" penis to symbolic issues of

masculinity, including guns and shooting. The "good" convict eliminates that anxiety from the boy's psyche (much like he literally eliminates the bad convict from the narrative), in effect making him feel good about himself. The manner in which the boy smiles indicates just how important this moment is. The scene is intensely emotional since it dramatizes how important it is for the boy's psychic development that he feel good about his penis and also how fundamentally good and humane Haynes is for reversing the damage done by the bad convict. Since the little boy's father has abandoned the family, Haynes becomes a kind of good-father figure here, giving the boy what he needs and what he himself never had when he was growing up. For all the talk and joking about penis size that riddles recent Hollywood films, *A Perfect World* provides a rare, serious, indeed profound context for that preoccupation. It is no exaggeration to say that the scene, in its extremely condensed and dramatic form, may help explain why the subject has been so pervasive, if less integrated, in so many other movies. Male subjectivity is, in this scene, formed around the penis. From this perspective, penis size does matter, and for a boy to feel good about his penis is important. Haynes fulfills both literal and symbolic functions of the absent father in this film and, for the fulfillment of the latter, the penis-size scene is crucial—for if *Unforgiven* unlooses an ugly and "bad" masculinity resulting from the cowboy with a small penis who cuts up a whore, *A Perfect World* suggests that Haynes (the good version of such a bad cowboy) has prevented the formation of precisely such a masculinity within the boy.

But the scene functions in yet another way that shows just how much the good and bad male systems are like each other in the male action film. There are many ways that Haynes could fulfill the function of the good father by relieving the boy's anxiety. Like his evil partner, however (they are two sides of the same coin), Haynes affirms the very importance of penis size in masculine identity. By telling the boy that he will evaluate him and tell him the truth, Haynes implies that the answer could be that he is indeed "puny" and that looking at the flaccid penis is important to determine whether this is the case. He makes the boy feel good, in other words, because his penis is of good size. Yet, he could tell the boy, for example, that penis size does not matter and that growing up to be a man has nothing to do with big or small penises. As Michael Renov (1980) has shown in a different context, when films present two male systems (one good and one bad), the bad within the good system goes unnoticed because we are so glad to see the evil male get his punishment. In *A Perfect World*, we are so likely to be overjoyed with the manner in which Haynes stops the damage to the boy's psyche begun by his partner that we do not notice that, in the process, he emphasizes and affirms the same principle.

Although we may miss the connection between Haynes and his evil partner in that particular scene because it is structured to make us identify with Haynes's good-guy version of the persona, part of what makes *A Perfect World* so complex is the disturbing manner in which other scenes virtually insist on us seeing the connection. This aspect of the film reaches its zenith in the scene with the black family. After seeing the father slap his son, Haynes literally goes into a sadistic, murderous rage that is only contained by Philip when he shoots him. Although reminiscent of, for example, the murderous rage that Ethan Edwards in *The Searchers* bears toward his niece (Lehman 1990), this is one of the most extreme and graphically disturbing instances in all of the action cinema of the normally hidden bad part emerging within a "good" character. This exact same complexity lies at the center of *Unforgiven,* in which Gene Hackman's character is simultaneously highly likable and frighteningly egomaniacal and sadistic. And, of course, William Munny himself swings between poles of kindness and generosity (e.g., his treatment of the scarred whore when she offers him sex) and the most vicious and brutally excessive masculinity when he turns his murderous rage loose at the film's climax.

Before returning to *Unforgiven,* however, I want to detour through *The Last Seduction* (1994), another film in which a major portion of the narrative is set in motion by penis size. A young man in a bar tries to pick up a woman, who turns him down without showing any interest. He leans over and whispers in her ear that he is "hung like a horse." He then turns to walk away and she calls him back, referring to him as "Mr. Ed." Staring at his groin she asks him to show her. She tells him to sit down, unzips his pants, then puts her hand in and feels around. When he asks her what she is doing, she says "looking for a certain horse-like quality." Apparently satisfied that he has it, she invites him to bed. It is all downhill from there for this well-hung, confident stud. By the time the film is over, he is framed by the woman for murders he did not commit and for which capital punishment awaits him. Similarly, after she is taken into custody by a black private detective, she manages to kill him and escape by convincing him to show her whether it is true that all black men are well hung. He takes off his seat belt to unzip his pants and, in an appropriation of phallic machinery worthy of Schwarzenegger in *True Lies,* she crashes the car so hard that his body is thrown through the windshield.

The fate of the central character in *The Last Seduction* and, to a lesser extent, that of the private detective bear comparison with that of the well-hung gunfighter described in *Unforgiven*. Nearly all the penis-size jokes and references I have traced through so many films of the 1970s, 1890s, and early 1990s either make fun of small ones or glorify big ones. *Unforgiven* and *The Last Seduction,* on the other hand, imply that being too small is not the only danger. Indeed, it is literally dangerous to be too big—it can kill a man. It is within this context that the scene in the car between Haynes and the boy in *A Perfect World* can be most fully understood. The film does not glorify the alleged phallic power of the large penis but, rather, implies the importance of the "normal" penis to the psychic development of the boy. As soon as the concept of normality is invoked, however, one can be either above or below the norm, have either too much or too little. Just like one can be too smart for one's own good, apparently in the 1990s one can also be too big for one's own good. Being normal is safest.

The continuing preoccupation with penis size in Hollywood films of the 1990s causes critical bewilderment and misjudgment in those rare instances in which reviewers acknowledge it. In his *New Yorker* review of *Nell,* Terrence Rafferty (1994) accuses the film of being hopelessly muddled and writes,

> In the nuttiest scene, Jerry and Paula try to cure Nell of her fear of men . . . by giving her a glimpse of the good Doctor's penis; he strips in the moonlight, Nell giggles girlishly, and her lifelong phobia vanishes into the night air. (p. 108)

Although countless other scenes could qualify for the dubious distinction of being the "nuttiest" in this film, the scene is indeed ludicrous for all the reasons Rafferty (1994) suggests: Nell is instantly cured and, as he goes on to note, she remains entirely pure and innocent. I, however, would emphasize an aspect of the scene that Rafferty overlooks: it is also shot and edited in a ludicrous manner. We see a frontal view of Jerry as he approaches Nell with a towel wrapped around his waist. We get the predictable penis-size joke when Paula urges Jerry on by telling him that "it's no big deal," and he responds self-deprecatingly by adding, "believe me, it's no big deal." He then takes his towel off for the benefit of Nell, who watches from the lake in which she is swimming. As soon as he takes the towel off, however, he sits down and we only see him in profile. One might very well wonder by what logic a man wishing to display his penis sits down to do so. Although Paula says seeing a penis is "no big deal," Hollywood thinks otherwise. Although it may be no big deal for Paula, it is for the audience of this film, who must be protected from its sight. Needless to say, the same is not true for the sight of Nell's nude body, over which the camera lingers long and lovingly—and, of course, innocently.

What is this "nutty" scene doing in the film? I think it can only be understood within Hollywood's current preoccupation with talking about the penis while keeping it covered up. It is pre-cisely this structure that guarantees that penises are a big deal. *Nell,* along with such films as *True Lies, Unforgiven, A Perfect World,* and *The Last Seduction,* conforms to a deep-seated need in current Hollywood films to narratively center the penis and circle around it in a manner so extreme that audiences may soon begin to wonder just how much longer this can go on without showing penises.

Robert Cauthorn's (1994) positive review of *The Last Seduction* is revealing in this regard. Like Rafferty's (1994) review of *Nell,* Cauthorn's review of *The Last Seduction* is generally very perceptive. He complains, however, of "several glaring flaws."

> Chief among these is a somewhat juvenile take on sex that conflicts with the movie's more sophisticated spirit. Bridget has this thing for asking men to whip out their penises at inappropriate moments, and the men slavishly respond. "The Last Seduction" actually uses one such scene to resolve a critical moment. (p. E14)

He might very well add that if one instance resolves a crucial scene, the other actually sets the narrative in motion. Just like it is not particularly helpful to call the penis scene in *Nell* the "nuttiest" scene in the film, it is not helpful to call the penis scenes in *The Last Seduction* "juvenile." Such critical responses brush over an important cultural preoccupation that must be understood.

If *Reservoir Dogs, Unforgiven,* and *A Perfect World* all indicate that the answer to the question, "How many dicks is that?" in recent Hollywood films is "a lot," they also indicate that the answer to the related question we might pose, "What is the meaning of all these dicks?" may be varied and complicated. In most films, like *Mrs. Doubtfire,* the dick talk merely supplies fleeting and usually forgettable moments that equate masculinity with big penises and small penises with its pitiable and/or comic collapse. Something much more complex is happening in *Reservoir Dogs, The Last Seduction, Unforgiven,* and *A Perfect World.* All of these films explore and question the place of the penis in the formation of male subjectivity or within the construction of mythic, phallic masculinity.

The dangers associated with the large penis in *The Last Seduction* and *Unforgiven* may reveal a growing awareness among filmmakers that we have long confused the penis with the phallus in our culture. Both the sexually predatory young man in *The Last Seduction* and Two-Gun Corky in *Unforgiven* act on an arrogant assumption of, respectively, their sexual and physical prowess based on their large penises. The young man presumes he will be able to conquer the woman he desires, and Corky presumes that he will be able to kill all his opponents with one gun. Both men have confused their literal endowment with symbolic power, and both are sadly mistaken. Indeed, the manner in which Corky's gun backfires in his hand bears comparison with the car crash that kills the private "dick" in *The Last Seduction*. The woman driving the car is keenly aware of this male confusion when she seizes phallic power and crashes the car, forcibly ejecting the man at precisely the moment that he has unbuckled his seat belt to show her his presumably large penis. As this scene shows, even the large penis and the phallus are two separate things, and the woman with no penis can seize the phallus just as well as any man and perhaps better than a man who feels secure in his endowment. Near the end of *The Last Seduction*, we learn that the overly confident, well-hung young man had years earlier fallen in love with and married a woman who he did not know was actually a man—his endowment and his powers are clearly quite separate!

It is, of course, too soon to predict whether the very recent notion that big penises pose a deadly threat to their possessors will become a trend in Hollywood films. Both *Unforgiven* and *A Perfect World*, however, reveal a 1990s continuing preoccupation with the importance of penis size and the undesirability of small ones, as well as a new caution against the usual reification of the "big dick" as the desired alternative. On the contrary, these films seem to desire a concept of normality in which either extreme is dangerous. As such, their insistence on the importance of the

"normal" penis is much like their insistence on "normal" forms of masculinity. Coming from Clint Eastwood, who somewhat gloriously personified powerful, phallic masculinity for a quarter century, this desire to abandon the excesses of such a form of masculinity has added significance. Dennis Bingham (1994) notes of stars like Eastwood and Schwarzenegger that "machismo cannot hold for long and eventually must call attention to its own considerable artifice" (p. 245). But Eastwood wants to do more than expose the artifice; he seems to have developed an almost nostalgic desire for a masculine norm that makes machismo appear grotesque. If only Haynes in *A Perfect World* had had a normal family life with a father, if only the little boy he kidnaps had such a normal life with such a father, if only Munny at the beginning of *Unforgiven* was normal and had not grown too soft, if only we lived in a perfect world where both literally and symbolically masculinity and male sexuality were all in the "normal" range, no one would be unforgiven.

References

Bingham, Dennis. 1994. *Acting male: Masculinities in the films of James Stewart, Jack Nicholson, and Clint Eastwood.* New Brunswick, NJ: Rutgers University Press.

Bobbitt cleared as temporarily insane in attack. 1994. *The Arizona Daily Star,* 22 January, 1A–5A.

Cauthorn, Robert. 1994. Review of *The Last Seduction. Arizona Daily Star,* 18 November, E14.

Cobb, Nathan. 1994. Urologist debunks myth surrounding the area below men's belts. *Arizona Daily Star,* 19 January, 6C.

Dyer, Richard. 1982. Don't look now: The male pin-up. *Screen* 23 (34): 61–73.

Foucault, Michel. 1980. *Herculine Barbin: Being the recently discovered memoirs of a nineteenth-century French hermaphrodite,* translated by Richard McDougall. New York: Pantheon.

Genevieve, Barbara de. 1991. Masculinity and its discontents. *Camerawork* 18 (3/4): 3–5.

Hilferty, Robert. 1992. Review of *Reservoir Dogs. Cineaste* 19 (4): 79–81.

Hosteteler, Darrin. 1994. A groin concern. *New Times,* 5–11 January, 5.

Kanigel, Rachele. 1995. Penile surgery risky process, study warns. *Oakland Tribune,* 26 April, A9–A10.

Lehman, Peter. 1990. Texas 1868/America 1956: The searchers. In *Close viewings: An anthology of new film criticism,* edited by Peter Lehman. Tallahassee: Florida State University Press.

———. 1993. *Running scared: Masculinity and the representation of the male body.* Philadelphia: Temple University Press.

Luhr, William, and Peter Lehman. 1977. *Authorship and narrative in the cinema: Issues in contemporary aesthetics and criticism.* New York: G. P. Putnam.

Rafferty, Terrence. 1994. Review of *Nell, The New Yorker,* 19 December, 108.

Renov, Michael. 1980. From identification of ideology: The male system of Hitchcock's *Notorious. Wide Angle* 4 (1): 30–37.

Ring out the old, gross out the new. 1994. *Newsweek,* 17 February, 33.

Schmidt, Becky Whitestone. 1995. Men unzipping wallets to change penis size. *Arizona Daily Star,* 15 May, B8. Originally published in *San Antonio Express-News.*

A R T I C L E   4 9

Lance Strate

Beer Commercials

A Manual on Masculinity

Jocks, rock stars, and pick-up artists; cowboys, construction workers, and comedians; these are some of the major "social types" (Klapp 1962) found in contemporary American beer commercials. The characters may vary in occupation, race, and age, but they all exemplify traditional conceptions of the masculine role. Clearly, the beer industry relies on stereotypes of the man's man to appeal to a mainstream, predominantly male target audience. That is why alternate social types, such as sensitive men, gay men, and househusbands, scholars, poets, and political activists, are noticeably absent from beer advertising. The manifest function of beer advertising is to promote a particular brand, but collectively the commercials provide a clear and consistent image of the masculine role; in a sense, they constitute a guide for becoming a man, a rulebook for appropriate male behavior, in short, a manual on masculinity. Of course, they are not the only source of knowledge on this subject, but nowhere is so much information presented in so concentrated a form as in television's 30-second spots, and no other industry's commercials focus so exclusively and so exhaustively on images of the man's man. Most analyses of alcohol advertising acknowledge the use of masculine characters and themes, but only focus on their persuasive function (see, for example, Atkin 1987; Finn & Strickland 1982, 1983; Hacker, Collins, & Jacobson 1987; Jacobson, Atkins, & Hacker 1983). In my own research on beer commercials (Postman, Nystrom, Strate, &

Weingartner 1987; Strate 1989, 1990), the ads are analyzed as a form of cultural communication and a carrier of social myths, in particular, the myth of masculinity. A similar approach is taken by Craig (1987) in his analysis of Super Bowl advertising, and by Wenner (1991) in his analysis of beer commercials and television sports. A major concern in my research has been the relationship between alcohol advertising and drinking and driving, a problem especially among young, unmarried men. Drawing on that research, I will discuss here the ways in which the myth of masculinity is expressed in beer commercials.

Myths, according to semioticians such as Roland Barthes (1972), are not falsehoods or fairy tales, but uncontested and generally unconscious assumptions that are so widely shared within a culture that they are considered natural, instead of recognized as products of unique historical circumstances. Biology determines whether we are male or female; culture determines what it *means* to be male or female, and what sorts of behaviors and personality attributes are appropriate for each gender role. In other words, masculinity is a social construction (Fejes 1989; Kimmel 1987a). The foundation may be biological, but the structure is manmade; it is also flexible, subject to change over time and differing significantly from culture to culture. Myth, as a form of cultural communication, is the material out of which such structures are built, and through myth, the role of human beings in inventing and reinventing masculinity is disguised and therefore naturalized (and "biologicized"). The myth of masculinity is manifested in myriad forms of mediated and nonmediated communication; beer commercials are only one such form, and to a large extent, the ads merely reflect preexisting cultural conceptions of the man's man. But in reflecting the myth, the commercials also reinforce it. Moreover, since each individual expression of a myth varies, beer ads also reshape the myth of masculinity, and in this sense, take part in its continuing construction.

Myths provide ready-made answers to universal human questions about ourselves, our relationships with others and with our environment. Thus, the myth of masculinity answers the question: What does it mean to be a man? This can be broken down into five separate questions: What kinds of things do men do? What kinds of settings do men prefer? How do boys become men? How do men relate to each other? How do men relate to women? Let us now consider the ways in which beer commercials answer these questions.

What kinds of things do men do? Although advertisers are prevented from actually showing an individual drinking beer in a television commercial, there is no question that drinking is presented as a central masculine activity, and beer as the beverage of choice. Drinking, however, is rarely presented as an isolated activity, but rather is associated with a variety of occupational and leisure pursuits, all of which, in one way or another, involve overcoming challenges. In the world of beer commercials, men work hard and they play hard.

Physical labor is often emphasized in these ads, both on and off the job. Busch beer features cowboys riding horses, driving cattle, and performing in rodeos. Budweiser presents a variety of blue-collar types, including construction workers, lumberjacks, and soldiers (as well as skilled laborers and a few white-collar workers). Miller Genuine Draft shows men working as farm hands and piano movers. But the key to work is the challenge it poses, whether to physical strength and endurance, to skill, patience, and craftsmanship, or to wit and competitive drive in the business world. The ads do associate hard work with the American dream of economic success (this theme is particularly strong in Budweiser's campaign), but it is also presented as its own end, reflecting the Puritan work ethic. Men do not labor primar-

ily out of economic necessity nor for financial gain, but rather for the pride of accomplishment provided by a difficult job well done; for the respect and camaraderie of other men (few women are visible in the beer commercial workplace); for the benefit of family, community, and nation; and for the opportunity to demonstrate masculinity by triumphing over the challenges work provides. In short, work is an integral part of a man's identity.

Beer is integrated with the work world in three ways. *First,* it is represented in some commercials as the product of patient, skillful craftsmanship, thus partaking of the virtues associated with the labor that produced it; this is particularly apparent in the Miller beer commercials in which former football player Ed Marinaro takes us on a tour of the Miller brewery. In effect, an identity relationship between beer and labor is established, although this is overshadowed by the identification between beer and nature discussed below. *Second,* beer serves as a reward for a job well done, and receiving a beer from one's peers acts as a symbol of other men's respect for the worker's accomplishment—"For all you do, this Bud's for you." Beer is seen as an appropriate reward not just because drinking is pleasurable, but because it is identified with labor, and therefore can act as a substitute for labor. Thus, drinking beer at the end of the day is a symbolic reenactment of the successful completion of a day's work. And *third,* beer acts as a marker of the end of the work day, the signal of quitting time ("Miller time"), the means for making the transition from work to leisure ("If you've got the time, we've got the beer"). In the commercials, the celebration of work completed takes on a ritualistic quality, much like saying grace and breaking bread signal the beginning of meal time; opening the can represents the opening of leisure time.

The men of beer commercials fill their leisure time in two ways: in active pursuits usually conducted in outdoor settings (e.g., car and boat racing, fishing, camping, and sports; often symbolized by the presence of sports stars, especially in Miller Lite ads) and in "hanging out," usually in bars. As it is in work, the key to men's active play is the challenge it provides to physical and emotional strength, endurance, and daring. Some element of danger is usually present in the challenge, for danger magnifies the risks of failure and the significance of success. Movement and speed are often a part of the challenge, not only for the increased risk they pose, but also because they require immediate and decisive action and fine control over one's own responses. Thus, Budweiser spots feature automobile racing; Michelob's music video-like ads show cars moving in fast-motion and include lyrics like "I'm overheating, I'm ready to burn, got dirt on my wheels, they're ready to turn"; Old Milwaukee and Budweiser commercials include images of powerboat, sailboat, and canoe racing; Busch beer features cowboys on galloping horses; and Coors uses the slogan, "The Silver Bullet won't slow you down." Activities that include movement and speed, along with displays of coordination, are particularly troubling when associated with beer, in light of social problems such as drinking and driving. Moreover, beer commercials portray men as unmindful of risks, laughing off danger. For example, in two Miller Genuine Draft commercials, a group of young men are drinking and reminiscing; in one they recall the time when they worked as farm hands, loading bales of hay onto a truck, and the large stack fell over. In the other, the memory is of moving a piano, raising it up by rope on the outside of a building to get it into a third-story apartment; the rope breaks and the piano crashes to the ground. The falling bales and falling piano both appear dangerous, but in the ads the men merely joke about the incidents; this attitude is reinforced visually as, in both cases, there is a cut from the past scene to the present one just before the crash actually occurs.

When they are not engaged in physical activity, the men of beer commercials frequently seek out symbolic challenges and dangers by playing games such as poker and pool, and by watching professional sports. The games pose particular challenges to self-control, while spectator sports allow for vicarious participation in the drama of

challenge, risk, and triumph. Even when they are merely hanging out together, men engage in verbal jousts that contain a strong element of challenge, either in the form of good-natured arguments (such as Miller Lite's ongoing "tastes great—less filling" conflict) or in ribbing one another, which tests self-control and the ability to "take it." A sense of proportion and humor is required to overcome such challenges, which is why jokers and comedians are a valued social type in the myth of masculinity. Women may also pose a challenge to the man's ability to attract the opposite sex and, more important, to his self-control.

The central theme of masculine leisure activity in beer commercials, then, is challenge, risk, and mastery—mastery over nature, over technology, over others in good-natured "combat," and over oneself. And beer is integrated into this theme in two ways: one obvious, the other far more subtle. At the overt level, beer functions in leisure activities as it does in work: as a reward for challenges successfully overcome (the race completed, the big fish landed, the ribbing returned). But it also serves another function, never explicitly alluded to in commercials. In several ways drinking, in itself, is a test of mastery. Because alcohol affects judgment and slows reaction time, it intensifies the risks inherent in movement and speed, and thereby increases the challenge they represent. And because it threatens self-control, drinking poses heightened opportunities for demonstrating self-mastery. Thus beer is not merely a reward for the successful meeting of a challenge in masculine work and leisure, but is itself an occasion for demonstrating mastery, and thus, masculinity. Beer is an appropriate award for overcoming challenge because it is a challenge itself, and thereby allows a man to symbolically reenact his feat. It would be all but suicidal for advertisers to present drinking as a challenge by which the masculine role can be acted out; instead, they associate beer with other forms of challenge related to the myth of masculinity.

What kinds of settings do men prefer? In beer commercials, the settings most closely associated with masculinity are the outdoors, generally the natural environment, and the self-contained world of the bar. The outdoors is featured prominently as both a workplace and a setting for leisure activity in ads for Busch beer, Old Milwaukee, Miller Genuine Draft, and Budweiser. As a workplace, the natural environment provides suitable challenge and danger for demonstrating masculinity, and the separation from civilization forces men to rely only on themselves. The height of masculinity can be attained when the natural environment and the work environment coincide, that is, when men have to overcome nature in order to survive. That is why the cowboy or frontiersman is the archetypical man's man in our culture. Other work environments, such as the farm, factory, and office, offer their own form of challenge, but physical danger is usually downplayed and the major risk is economic. Challenge and danger are also reduced, but still present, when nature is presented as a leisure environment; male bonding receives greater emphasis, and freedom from civilization becomes freedom for men to behave in a boyish manner.

In the ads, nature is closely associated with both masculinity and beer, as beer is presented as equivalent to nature. Often, beer is shown to be a product that is natural and pure, implying that its consumption is not harmful, and perhaps even healthy. Moreover, a number of beers, including Rolling Rock, Heinekan's Old Style, and Molson's Golden, are identified with natural sources of water. This identification is taken even further in one Busch beer commercial: We see a cowboy on horseback, herding cattle across a river. A small calf is overcome by the current, but the cowboy is able to withstand the force of the river and come to the rescue. The voice-over says, "Sometimes a simple river crossing isn't so simple. And when you've got him back, it's your turn. Head for the beer brewed natural as a mountain stream." We then see a six-pack pulled out of clear running water, as if by magic. The raging water represents the power and danger of nature, while the mountain stream stands for nature's gentler aspect. Through the voice-over and the image of the hand

pulling the six-pack from the water, beer is presented as identical with the stream, as bottled nature. Drinking beer, then, is a relatively safe way of facing the challenge of raging rivers, of symbolically reenacting the taming of the frontier.

Beer is identified with nature in a more general way in the ads for Old Milwaukee, which are usually set in wilderness environments that feature water, such as the Florida Everglades, and Snake River, Wyoming. In each ad, a group of men is engaged in recreational activities such as high-speed air-boating, flat-bottom boat racing, or fishing. Each commercial begins with a voice-over saying something like, "The Florida Everglades and Old Milwaukee both mean something great to these guys." Each ad includes a jingle, which says, "There's nothing like the flavor of a special place and Old Milwaukee beer." In other words, Old Milwaukee is equivalent to the special place. The place is special because it is untouched by civilization, allowing men to engage in forms of recreation not available elsewhere. It therefore must be fairly inaccessible, but since beer is presented as identical to the place, drinking may act as a substitute for actually going there.

Beer is also identified with nature through animals. For example, the symbol of Busch beer, found on its label and in its commercials, is a horse rearing on its hind legs, a phallic symbol that also evokes the idea of the untamed. And in another Busch ad, a young rodeo rider is quickly thrown from his mount; trying to cheer him up, an older cowboy hands him a beer and says, "Here. This one don't buck so hard." Thus, the identification of beer and nature is made via the horse. Drinking beer is like rodeo-riding, only less strenuous. It is a challenge that the rider can easily overcome, allowing him to save face and reaffirm masculinity. Budweiser beer also uses horses as a symbol: The Budweiser Clydesdales, a breed of "draft" horse. Whereas the Busch Stallion represents the frontier wilderness, the Clydesdales stand for the pastoral. Also, Colt 45 malt liquor, by its very name, invokes images of the Old West, horses, and of course guns, another phallic symbol. Another way in which beer is identified with nature and animals is through Budweiser's "Spuds McKenzie" and Stroh's "Alex," both dogs that behave like humans; both are in turn identified with masculinity as they are male characters, and canines are the animals most closely associated with masculinity.

As a setting for masculine activity, the bar runs a close second to nature, and many commercials seem to advertise bar patronage as much as they do a particular brand of beer. Of course, the drinking hall has a venerable history in Western culture as a center for male socializing and tests of skill, strength, and drinking ability. It is a setting featured prominently in the myths and legends of ancient Greece, and in Norse and Old English sagas. The pub is a popular setting in British literature, as is the saloon in the American Western genre. Like its predecessors, the bar of the beer commercial is presented as a male-dominated environment, although it sometimes serves as a setting for male-female interaction. And it is generally portrayed as a relaxed and comfortable context for male socializing, as well as a place where a man can find entertainment and excitement. The bars are immaculate and smokeless, and the waitresses and bartenders are always friendly; thus, along with nature, bars are the ideal male leisure environment. The only exception is the Bud Light bar, where men who are so uninformed as to ask for "a light" rather than a specific brand are subjected to pranks by the bartenders; still, even in this case the practical jokes are taken in stride, reaffirming the customer's masculinity.

It is worth noting that in the romanticized barroom of beer commercials, no one ever pays for his drinks, either literally or in terms of alcohol's effects. In other words, there are no consequences to the men's actions, which is consistent with the myth of masculinity's tendency to ignore or downplay risk and danger. The bar is shown as a self-contained environment, one that, like the outdoors, frees men from the constraints of civilization, allowing them to behave irresponsibly. Moreover, most settings featured as drinking-places in beer commercials are probably places

that people would drive to—and drive home from. Because the action is confined to these settings, however, the question of how people arrived and how they will get home never comes up.

How do boys become men? In the world of beer commercials, boys become men by earning acceptance from those who are already full-fledged members of the community of men. Adult men are identified by their age, their size, their celebrity, and their positions of authority in the work world and/or status in a bar. To earn acceptance, the younger man must demonstrate that he can do the things that men do: take risks, meet challenges, face danger courageously, and dominate his environment. In the workplace, he demonstrates this by seizing opportunities to work, taking pride in his labor, proving his ability, persisting in the face of uncertainty, and learning to accept failure with equanimity. Having proven that he can act out the masculine role, the initiate is rewarded with beer. As a reward, beer symbolizes the overcoming of a challenge, the fulfilling of the requirements for group membership. The gift of beer also allows the adult male to show his acceptance of the initiate without becoming emotional. Beer then functions as a symbol of initiation and group membership.

For example, one of Budweiser's most frequently aired commercials during the 1980s features a young Polish immigrant and an older foreman and dispatcher. In the first scene, the dispatcher is reading names from a clipboard, giving workers their assignments. Arriving late, which earns him a look or displeasure from the foreman, the nervous young man takes a seat in the back. When he is finally called, the dispatcher stumbles over the immigrant's foreign name. The young man walks up to the front of the room, corrects the dispatcher's mispronunciation—a risky move, given his neophyte status, but one that demonstrates his pride and self-confidence. He receives his assignment, and the scene then shifts to a montage of the day's work. At the beginning, he drops a toolbox, spilling its contents, a mishap noted by the foreman; by the end of the day, however, he has demonstrated his ability and has earned the respect of his co-workers. The final scene is in a crowded tavern; the young man walks through the door, making his way to the bar, looking around nervously. He hears his name called, turns around, and the foreman, sitting at the bar, hands him a beer. In both the first and final scene, the immigrant begins at the back of the room, highlighting his outsider status, and moves to the front as he is given a chance to prove himself. The commercial's parallelism is not just an aesthetic device, but a mythic one as well. Having mastered the challenge of work, the neophyte receives the reward of a beer, which is both a symbol of that mastery and an invitation to symbolically reenact his feat. By working hard and well, he gains acceptance in the work world; by drinking the beer, he can also gain acceptance into the social world of the bar. The foreman, by virtue of his age, his position of authority, and his position sitting at the bar in the center of the tavern, holds the power of confirmation in both worlds.

The theme of initiation is also present in a subtle way in the Bud Light ads in which someone orders "a light," is given a substitute such as lamp or torch, and then corrects himself, asking for a "Bud Light." As one of the commercials revealed, the bartenders play these pranks because they are fed up with uninformed customers. The bizarre substitutions are a form of hazing, an initiation into proper barroom etiquette. The mature male is familiar with brands of beer, knows what he wants, and shows decisiveness in ordering it. Clearly, the individuals who ask for "a light" are inexperienced drinkers, and it is important to keep in mind that, to the barroom novice (and especially to the underage drinker), bars and bartenders can seem very threatening. While the substitute "lights" come as a surprise to the patrons, and thus threaten their composure, they are a relatively mild threat. The customers are able to overcome this challenge to their self-control, correct their order, and thereby gain entry into barroom society.

The biological transition from childhood to adulthood is a gradual one, but in traditional cul-tures, it is symbolized by formal rituals of initiation, rites of passage which mark the boundary between childhood and adulthood, clearly separating these two social positions. In our own culture, there are no initiation rites, and therefore the adolescent's social position is an ambiguous one. A number of events and activities do serve as symbols of adulthood, however. The commercials emphasize entry into the work world as one such step; financial independence brings the freedom of adulthood, while work is an integral part of the adult male's identity. As a symbol of initiation into the work world, beer also functions as a symbol of adulthood. And although this is never dealt with in the commercials, drinking in and of itself is a symbol of adulthood in our culture, as is driving, particularly in the eyes of underage males. Bars are seen as exclusively adult environments, and so acceptance in bars is a further sign of manhood. In the commercials, bars and workplaces complement each other as environments in which initiation into adulthood can be consummated.

How do men relate to each other? In beer commercials, men are rarely found in solitary pursuits (and never drink alone), and only occasionally in one-to-one relationships, usually involving father-son or mentor-protégé transactions. The dominant social context for male interaction is the group, and teamwork and group loyalty rank high in the list of masculine values. Individualism and competition, by contrast, are downplayed, and are acceptable only as long as they foster the cohesiveness of the group as a whole. Although differences in status may exist between members of the group and outsiders, within the group equality is the rule, and elitism and intellectualism are disdained. This reflects the American value of egalitarianism and solidifies the importance of the group over individual members. The concept of group loyalty is extended to community and to country, so that patriotism is also presented as an important value for men.

The emotional tenor of relationships among men in beer commercials is characterized by self-restraint. Generally, strong emotions are eschewed, especially overt displays of affection. In the workplace, mutual respect is exhibited, but respect must be earned through ability and attitude. In leisure situations, humor is a major element in male interactions. Conversations among men emphasize joking, bragging, storytelling, and good-natured insults. The insults are a form of symbolic challenge; taking a ribbing in good spirit is a demonstration of emotional strength and self-mastery. By providing a controlled social context for the exchange of challenges and demonstrations of ego strength and self-control, the group provides continuous reinforcement of the members' masculinity. Moreover, gathering in groups provides men with the freedom to act irresponsibly; that is, it allows men to act like boys. This is particularly the case in the Miller Lite ads that feature retired sports stars, comedians, and other celebrities.

In beer commercials, drinking serves several important functions in promoting group solidarity. Beer is frequently the shared activity that brings the group together, and in the ads for Miller Genuine Draft, sharing beer acts as a reminder of the group's identity and history. Thus, beer becomes a symbol of group membership. It also serves as a means for demonstrating the group's egalitarian values. When one man gives a beer to another, it is a sign of acceptance, friendship, or gratitude. In this role, beer is also a substitute for overt display of affection. Although the commercials never deal with why beer takes on this role, the answer lies in the effects of alcohol. Certainly, its function as mood enhancer can have a positive influence on group interaction. And, as previously discussed, alcohol itself constitutes a challenge, so that drinking allows each member of the group to publicly demonstrate his masculinity. Alcohol also lowers inhibitions, making it easier for men to show their affection for one another. The well-known saying that you cannot trust a man who does not drink reflects the popular conception that under the influence of alcohol, men become more open and honest. Moreover, the effects of drinking on physical coordination make a man less of an immediate threat. All these properties contribute to beer's role as a medium of male bonding and a facilitator of group solidarity.

In general, men are not portrayed as loners in beer commercials, and in this respect the ads differ markedly from other expressions of the myth of masculinity. There are no isolated Marlboro men in the Busch frontier, for example. When he saves the calf from being swept away by the river, the Busch cowboy appears to be on his own, but by the time he is ready for his reward, another cowboy has appeared out of nowhere to share his beer. In another Busch ad, a jingle with the following lyrics is heard: "There's no place on earth that I'd rather be, than out in the open where it's all plain to see, if it's going to get done it's up to you and me." In this way, the ideal of individual self-reliance that is so central to the American myth of the frontier is transformed into group self-reliance. In the world of beer commercials, demonstrating one's masculinity requires an audience to judge one's performance and confirm one's status. Moreover, the emphasis the ads place on beer drinking as a group activity undermines the idea that it is in any way problematic. One of the most widespread stereotypes of problem drinkers is that they are solitary and secretive loners. The emphasis on the group in beer commercials plays on the common misconception that drinking, when it is done socially and publicly, cannot be harmful.

How do men relate to women? Although the world of beer commercials is often monopolized by men, some of the ads do feature male-female interaction in the form of courtship, as well as in more established relationships. When courtship is the focus, the image of the man's man gives way to that of the ladies' man, for whom seduction is the highest form of challenge. And while the obvious risk in courtship is rejection by the opposite sex, the more significant danger in beer ads is loss of emotional self-control. The ladies' man must remain cool, confident, and detached when faced with the object of his desires. This social type is exemplified by Billy Dee Williams, who plays on his romantic image in Colt 45 commercials. Strangely enough, Spuds McKenzie, Budweiser's "party animal," also fits into this category, insofar as he, like Alex, is treated like a human being. In his ads, Spuds is surrounded by the Spudettes, three beautiful young women who dance with him, serve him, even bathe him. The women are attractive enough to make most males salivate like Pavlov's dogs, but Spuds receives their attentions with casual indifference (and never betrays the insecurities that haunt his cousin Snoopy when the *Peanuts* dog assumes his "Joe Cool" persona). While the commercials do not go so far as to suggest bestiality, there is no question that Spuds is a stud.

Emotional control is also demonstrated by the male's ability to divide his attention. For example, in one Michelob commercial, a young woman is shown leaning over a jukebox and selecting a song; her expression is one of pure pleasure, and she seems lost in thought. Other scenes, presumably her memories, show her dancing in the arms of a handsome young man. His arms are around her neck, and he is holding in one hand, behind her back, a bottle of beer. This image emphasizes the difference between the myths of masculinity and femininity; her attention is focused entirely on him, while his interests extend to the beer as well as the woman. According to the myth of masculinity, the man who loses control of his emotions in a relationship is a man who loses his independence, and ultimately, his masculinity; dividing attention is one way to demonstrate self-control. Michelob also presents images of ladies' men in the form of popular musicians, such as the rock group Genesis, rock star Eric Clapton, and popular vocalist Frank Sinatra. Many male pop stars have reputations as sexual athletes surrounded by groupies; in the ads, however, they function as modern troubadours, providing a romantic backdrop for lovers and facilitating social interaction. Acting, like Spuds McKenzie, as mascots for the beer companies, they imply that the beer they are identified with serves the same functions.

By far the most sexist of beer commercials, almost to the point of farce, are the Colt 45 ads

featuring Billy Dee Williams. One of these, which is divided into three segments, begins with Williams saying: "There are two rules to remember if you want to have a good time: Rule number one, never run out of Colt 45. Rule number two, never forget rule number one." In the next segment, Williams continues: "You want to know why you should keep plenty of Colt 45 on hand? You never know when friends might show up." As he says this, he opens a can and a woman's hand reaches out and takes it. In the third segment, he concludes, "I don't claim you can have a better time with Colt 45 than without it, but why take chances?" As he says this, the camera pulls back to reveal Williams standing, and an attractive woman sitting next to him. The ad ends with a picture of a Colt 45 can and the slogan, "The power of Colt 45: It works every time." There are a number of ways to interpret this pitch. First, malt liquor has a higher alcohol content than beer or ale, and therefore is a more *powerful* beverage. Second, the ad alludes to alcohol's image as an aphrodisiac, despite the fact that it actually reduces male potency. As noted, the Colt 45 pistol is a phallic symbol, while the slogan can be read as a guarantee against impotency—"it works every time." Third, it can be seen as referring to alcohol's ability to make men feel more confident about themselves and more interested in the opposite sex. And fourth, it plays on the popular notion that getting a woman drunk increases her desire for and willingness to engage in sex. Williams keeps Colt 45 on hand not just for himself, but for "friends," meaning "women." His secret of seduction is getting women to drink. In the ad, the woman is eager to drink Colt 45, implying that she will be just as eager to make love. The idea that a woman who drinks is "looking for it" is even clearer in a second ad.

This commercial begins with the title "Billy Dee Williams on Body Language." Moving through an outdoor party, Williams says, "You know, body language tells you a lot about what a person is thinking. For instance, that means she has an interest in the finer things in life." As he says this, the camera pans to show an attractive woman sitting at a bar alone, holding her necklace. She shifts her position and strokes her hair, and Williams says, "That means she also wants a little fun in her life, but only with the right man." At this point, the woman fills her glass with Colt 45, as Williams says, "And now she's pouring Colt 45 and we all know what that means." He then goes over to her and asks if she would mind if he joined her, and she replies, "You must have read my mind." Williams responds, "Something like that," and the ad ends with the same slogan as the first. What is implied in this commercial is that any woman who would sit by herself and drink must be looking to get picked up; she is sending out signals and preparing herself to be seduced. And although she is making herself approachable, she must wait for Williams to make the first move. At the same time, the woman appears to be vain, fondling her jewelry and hair. And in both ads, the women are seated while Williams stands. This portrayal of the woman's woman, based on the myth of femininity, is the perfect counterpart to Williams' image as a ladies' man.

When the commercials depict more established relationships, the emphasis shifts from romance and seduction to male activities in which women are reduced largely to the role of admiring onlookers. Men appear to value their group of friends over their female partners, and the women accept this. Women tend to be passive, not participating but merely watching as men perform physical tasks. In other words, they become the audience for whom men perform. For the most part, women know their place and do not interfere with male bonding. They may, however, act as emotional catalysts for male interaction, bringing men together. Occasionally, a woman may be found together with a group of men, presumably as the girlfriend or wife of one of the group members. Here, the presence of women, and their noninterference, indicates their approval of masculine activity and male bonding, and their approval of the role of beer in these situations. Even when a group of men acts irresponsibly and/or boyishly,

the presence of a woman shows that this behavior is socially sanctioned.

Alternate images of femininity can be found in beer commercials, but they are generally relegated to the background; for the most part, the traditional roles of masculinity and femininity are upheld. One exception is a Michelob Light ad that features Madeline Kahn. Introduced by a male voice-over, "Madeline Kahn on having it all," she is lying on her side on a couch, wearing an expensive-looking gown and necklace, and holding a bottle of beer. Kahn does a short humorous monologue in which she acknowledges her wealth and glamour, and the scene shifts to a shot of the beer, as the male voice-over says, "Michelob Light. You *can* have it all." While this represents something of a concession to changing conceptions of femininity, the advertisers hedge their bets. The male voice-over frames, and in a sense controls, Kahn's monologue, while Kahn's position, lying on her side, is a passive and seductive one. To male viewers, the commercial can easily imply that "having it all" includes having a woman like her.

Conclusion

In the world of beer commercials, masculinity revolves around the theme of challenge, an association that is particularly alarming, given the social problems stemming from alcohol abuse. For the most part beer commercials present traditional, stereotypical images of men, and uphold the myths of masculinity and femininity. Thus, in promoting beer, advertisers also promote and perpetuate these images and myths. Although targeted at an adult audience, beer commercials are highly accessible to children; between the ages of 2 and 18, American children may see as many as 100,000 of these ads (Postman et al. 1987). They are also extremely attractive to children: humorous, exciting, and offering answers to questions about gender and adulthood. And they do have an impact, playing a role in social learning and attitude formation (Wallack, Cassady, & Grube

1990). As Postman (1979) argues, television constitutes a curriculum, one that children spend more time with than in schoolrooms. Beer commercials are a prominent subject in television's curriculum, a subject that is ultimately hazardous to the intellectual as well as the physical health of the young. The myth of masculinity *does* have a number of redeeming features (facing challenges and taking risks are valuable activities in many contexts), but the unrelenting one-dimensionality of masculinity as presented by beer commercials is clearly anachronistic, possibly laughable, but without a doubt sobering.

References

Atkin, C. K. (1987). Alcoholic-beverage advertising: Its content and impact. *Advances in Substances Abuse (Suppl.) 1,* 267–287.

Barthes, R. (1972). *Mythologies* (A. Lavers, Ed. and Trans.). New York: Hill & Wang. (Original work published 1957).

Craig, S. (1987, March). *Marketing American masculinity: Mythology and flow in the Super Bowl telecasts.* Paper presented at the annual meeting of the Popular Culture Association, Montreal.

Fejes, F. (1989). Images of men in media research. *Critical Studies in Mass Communication, 6*(2), 215–221.

Finn, T. A., & Strickland, D. (1983). The advertising and alcohol abuse issue: A cross media comparison of alcohol beverage advertising content. In M. Burgeon (Ed.), *Communication yearbook* (pp. 850–872). Beverly Hills, CA: Sage.

Hacker. G. A., Collins R., & Jacobson, M. (1987). *Marketing booze to blacks.* Washington, DC: Center for Science in the Public Interest.

Jacobson, M., Atkins, R., & Hacker, G. (1983). *The booze merchants: The inebriating of America.* Washington, DC: Center for Science in the Public Interest.

Kimmel, M. (Ed.). (1987a). *Changing men: New directions in research on men and masculinity.* Newbury Park, CA: Sage.

Strate, L. (1989). The mediation of nature and culture in beer commercials. *New Dimensions In Communications, Proceedings of the 47th Annual New York State Speech Communication Association Conference 3,* 92–95.

Strate, L. (1990, October). *The cultural meaning of beer commercials.* Paper presented at the Advances in Consumer Research Conference, New York.

Wenner, L. (1991). One part alcohol, one part sport, one part dirt, stir gently: Beer commercials and television sports. In L. R. Vande Berg & L. A. Wenner (Eds.), *Television criticism: Approaches and applications.* New York: Longman.

Richard Fung

Looking for My Penis: The Eroticized Asian in Gay Video Porn

Several scientists have begun to examine the relation between personality and human reproductive behavior from a gene-based evolutionary perspective. . . . In this vein we reported a study of racial difference in sexual restraint such that Orientals > whites > blacks. Restraint was indexed in numerous ways, having in common a lowered allocation of bodily energy to sexual functioning. We found the same racial pattern occurred on gamete production (dizygotic birthing frequency per 100: Mongoloids, 4; Caucasoids, 8; Negroids, 16), intercourse frequencies (premarital, marital, extramarital), developmental precocity (age at first intercourse, age at first pregnancy, number of pregnancies), primary sexual characteristics (size of penis, vagina, testis, ovaries), secondary sexual characteristics (salient voice, muscularity, buttocks, breasts), and biologic control of behavior (periodicity of sexual response predictability of life history from onset of puberty), as well as in androgen levels and sexual attitudes.[1]

This passage from the *Journal of Research in Personality* was written by University of Western Ontario psychologist Philippe Rushton, who enjoys considerable controversy in Canadian academic circles and in the popular media. His thesis, articulated throughout his work, appropriates biological studies of the continuum of reproductive strategies of oysters through chimpanzees and posits that degree of "sexuality"—interpreted as penis and vagina size, frequency of intercourse, buttock and lip size—correlates positively with criminality and sociopathic behavior and inversely with intelligence, health, and longevity. Rushton sees race as the determining factor and places East Asians (Rushton uses the word *Orientals*) on one end of the spectrum and blacks on the other. Since whites fall squarely in the middle, the position of perfect balance, there is no need for analysis, and they remain free of scrutiny.

Notwithstanding its profound scientific shortcomings, Rushton's work serves as an excellent articulation of a dominant discourse on race and sexuality in Western society—a system of ideas and reciprocal practices that originated in Europe simultaneously with (some argue as a conscious justification for[2]) colonial expansion and slavery. In the nineteenth century these ideas took on a scientific gloss with social Darwinism and eugenics. Now they reappear, somewhat altered, in psychology journals from the likes of Rushton. It is important to add that these ideas have also permeated the global popular consciousness. Anyone who has been exposed to Western television or advertising images, which is much of the world, will have absorbed this particular constellation of stereotyping and racial hierarchy. In Trinidad in the 1960s, on the outer reaches of the empire, everyone in my schoolyard was thoroughly versed in these "truths" about the races.

Historically, most organizing against racism has concentrated on fighting discrimination that stems from the intelligence-social behavior variable assumed by Rushton's scale. Discrimination based on perceived intellectual ability does, after all, have direct ramifications in terms of education and employment, and therefore for survival. Until recently, issues of gender and sexuality remained a low priority for those who claimed to speak for the communities.[3] But antiracist strategies that fail to subvert the race-gender status quo are of seriously limited value. Racism cannot be narrowly defined in terms of race hatred. Race is a factor in even our most intimate relationships.

The contemporary construction of race and sex as exemplified by Rushton has endowed black people, both men and women, with a threatening hypersexuality. Asians, on the other hand, are collectively seen as undersexed.[4] But here I want to make some crucial distinctions. First, in North America, stereotyping has focused almost exclusively on what recent colonial language designates as "Orientals"—that is East and southeast Asian peoples—as opposed to the "Orientalism" discussed by Edward Said, which concerns the Middle East. This current, popular usage is based more on a perception of similar physical features—black hair, "slanted" eyes, high cheek bones, and so on—than through a reference to common cultural traits. South Asians, people whose backgrounds are in the Indian subcontinent and Sri Lanka, hardly figure at all in North American popular representations, and those few images are ostensibly devoid of sexual connotation.[5]

Second, within the totalizing stereotype of the "Oriental," there are competing and sometimes contradictory sexual associations based on nationality. So, for example, a person could be seen as Japanese and somewhat kinky, or Filipino and "available." The very same person could also be seen as "Oriental" and therefore sexless. In addition, the racial hierarchy revamped by Rushton is itself in tension with an earlier and only partially eclipsed depiction of *all* Asians as having an undisciplined and dangerous libido. I am referring to the writings of the early European explorers and missionaries, but also to antimiscegenation laws and such specific legislation as the 1912 Saskatchewan law that barred white women from employment in Chinese-owned business.

Finally, East Asian women figure differently from men both in reality and in representation. In "Lotus Blossoms Don't Bleed," Renee Tajima points out that in Hollywood films:

> There are two basic types: the Lotus Blossom Baby (a.k.a. China Doll, Geisha Girl, shy Polynesian beauty, et al.) and the Dragon Lady (Fu Manchu's various female relations, prostitutes, devious madames). . . . Asian women in film are, for the most part, passive figures who exist to serve men—as love interests for white men (re: Lotus Blossoms) or as partners in crime for men of their own kind (re: Dragon Ladies).[6]

Further:

> Dutiful creatures that they are, Asian women are often assigned the task of expendability in a situation of illicit love. . . . Noticeably lacking is the portrayal of love relationships between Asian women and Asian men, particularly as lead characters.[7]

Because of their supposed passivity and sexual compliance, Asian women have been fetishized in dominant representation, and there is a large and growing body of literature by Asian women in the oppressiveness of these images. Asian men, however—at least since Sessue Hayakawa, who made a Hollywood career in the 1920s of representing the Asian man as sexual threat[8]—have been consigned to one of two categories: the egghead/wimp, or—in what may be analogous to the lotus blossom-dragon lady dichotomy—the kung fu master/ninja/samurai. He is sometimes dangerous, sometimes friendly, but almost always characterized by a desexualized Zen asceticism. So whereas, as Fanon tells us, "the Negro is eclipsed. He is turned into a penis. He *is* a penis,"[9] the Asian man is defined by a striking absence down there. And if Asian men have no sexuality, how can we have homosexuality?

Even as recently as the early 1980s, I remember having to prove my queer credentials before being admitted with other Asian men into a Toronto gay club. I do not believe it was a question of a color barrier. Rather, my friends and I felt that the doorman was genuinely unsure about our sexual orientation. We also felt that had we been white and dressed similarly, our entrance would have been automatic.[10]

Although a motto for the lesbian and gay movements has been "we are everywhere," Asians are largely absent from the images produced by both the political and the commercial sectors of the mainstream gay and lesbian communities. From the earliest articulation of the Asian gay and lesbian movements, a principal concern has therefore been visibility. In political organizing, the demand for a voice, or rather the demand to be heard, has largely been responded to by the problematic practice of "minority" representation on panels and boards.[11] But since racism is a question of power and not of numbers, this strategy has often led to a dead-end tokenistic integration, failing to address the real imbalances.

Creating a space for Asian gay and lesbian representation has meant, among other things, deepening an understanding of what is at stake for Asians in coming out publicly.[12] As is the case for many other people of color and especially immigrants, our families and our ethnic communities are a rare source of affirmation in a racist society. In coming out, we risk (or feel that we risk) losing this support, though the ever-growing organizations of lesbian and gay Asians have worked against this process of cultural exile. In my own experience, the existence of a gay Asian community broke down the cultural schizophrenia in which I related on the one hand to a heterosexual family that affirmed my ethnic culture and, on the other, to a gay community that was predominantly white. Knowing that there was support also helped me come out to my family and further bridge the gap.

If we look at commercial gay sexual representation, it appears that the antiracist movements have had little impact: the images of men and male beauty are still of *white* men and *white* male beauty. These are the standards against which we

compare both ourselves and often our brothers— Asian, black, native, and Latino.[13] Although other people's rejection (or fetishization) of us according to the established racial hierarchies may be experienced as oppressive, we are not necessarily moved to scrutinize our own desire and its relationship to the hegemonic image of the white man.[14]

In my lifelong vocation of looking for my penis, trying to fill in the visual void, I have come across only a handful of primary and secondary references to Asian male sexuality in North American representation. Even in my own video work, the stress has been on deconstructing sexual representation and only marginally on creating erotica. So I was very excited at the discovery of a Vietnamese American working in gay porn.

Having acted in six videotapes, Sum Yung Mahn is perhaps the only Asian to qualify as a gay porn "star." Variously known as Brad Troung or Sam or Sum Yung Mahn, he has worked for a number of different production studios. All of the tapes in which he appears are distributed through International Wavelength, a San Francisco–based mail order company whose catalog entries feature Asians in American, Thai, and Japanese productions. According to the owner of International Wavelength, about 90 percent of the Asian tapes are bought by white men, and the remaining 10 percent are purchased by Asians. But the number of Asian buyers is growing.

In examining Sum Yung Mahn's work, it is important to recognize the different strategies used for fitting an Asian actor into the traditionally white world of gay porn and how the terms of entry are determined by the perceived demands of an intended audience. Three tapes, each geared toward a specific erotic interest, illustrate these strategies.

Below the Belt (1985, directed by Philip St. John, California Dream Machine Productions), like most porn tapes, has an episodic structure. All the sequences involve the students and *sense* of an all-male karate *dojo*. The authenticity of the setting is proclaimed with the opening shots of a gym full of *gi*-clad, serious-faced young men going through their weapons exercises. Each of the main actors is introduced in turn; with the exception of the teacher, who has dark hair, all fit into the current porn conventions of Aryan, blond, shaved, good looks.[15] Moreover, since Sum Yung Mahn is not even listed in the opening credits, we can surmise that this tape is not targeted to an audience with any particular erotic interest in Asian men. Most gay video porn exclusively uses white actors; those tapes having the least bit of racial integration are pitched to the specialty market throughout outlets such as International Wavelength.[16] This visual apartheid stems, I assume, from an erroneous perception that the sexual appetites of gay men are exclusive and unchangeable.

A Karate dojo offers a rich opportunity to introduce Asian actors. One might imagine it as the gay Orientalist's dream project. But given the intended audience for this video, the erotic appeal of the dojo, except for the costumes and a few misplaced props (Taiwanese and Korean flags for a Japanese art form?) are completely appropriated into a white world.

The tape's action occurs in a gym, in the students' apartments, and in a garden. The one scene with Sum Yung Mahn is a dream sequence. Two students, Robbie and Stevie, are sitting in a locker room. Robbie confesses that he has been having strange dreams about Greg, their teacher. Cut to the dream sequence, which is coded by clouds of green smoke. Robbie is wearing a red headband with black markings suggesting script (if indeed they belong to an Asian language, they are not the Japanese or Chinese characters that one would expect). He is trapped in an elaborate snare. Enter a character in a black *ninja* mask, wielding a *nanchaku*. Robbie narrates: "I knew this evil samurai would kill me." The masked figure is menacingly running the nanchaku chain under Robbie's genitals when Greg, the teacher, appears and disposes of him. Robbie explains to Stevie in the locker room: "I knew that I owed him my life, and I knew I had to please him [long pause] in any way that he wanted." During that pause we cut back to the dream. Amid more puffs of smoke, Greg, carrying a man in his arms, approaches a low plat-

form. Although Greg's back is toward the camera, we can see that the man is wearing the red headband that identifies him as Robbie. As Greg lays him down, we see that Robbie has "turned Japanese"! It's Sum Yung Mahn.

Greg fucks Sum Yung Mahn, who is always face down. The scene constructs anal intercourse for the Asian Robbie as an act of submission, not of pleasure: unlike other scenes of anal intercourse in the tape, for example, there is no dubbed dialogue on the order of "Oh yeah . . . fuck me harder!" but merely ambiguous groans. Without coming, Greg leaves. A group of (white) men wearing Japanese outfits encircle the platform, and Asian Robbie, or "the Oriental boy," as he is listed in the final credits, turns to lie on his back. He sucks a cock, licks someone's balls. The other men come all over his body; he comes. The final shot of the sequence zooms in to a close-up of Sum Yung Mahn's headband, which dissolves to a similar close-up of Robbie wearing the same headband, emphasizing that the two actors represent one character.

We now cut back to the locker room. Robbie's story has made Stevie horny. He reaches into Robbie's pants, pulls out his penis, and sex follows. In his Asian manifestation, Robbie is fucked and sucks others off (Greek passive/French active/bottom). His passivity is pronounced, and he is never shown other than prone. As a white man, his role is completely reversed: he is at first sucked off by Stevie, and then he fucks him (Greek active/French passive/top). Neither of Robbie's manifestations veers from his prescribed role.

To a greater extent than most other gay porn tapes, *Below the Belt* is directly about power. The hierarchical dojo setting is mild for its evocation of dominance and submission. With the exception of one very romantic sequence midway through the tape, most of the actors stick to their defined roles of top or bottom. Sex, especially anal sex, as punishment is a recurrent image. In this genre of gay pornography, the role-playing in the dream sequence is perfectly apt. What is significant, however, is how race figures into the equation. In a tape that appropriates emblems of Asian power (karate), the only place for a real Asian actor is as a caricature of passivity. Sum Yung Mahn does not portray an Asian, but rather the liberalization of a metaphor, so that by being passive, Robbie actually becomes "Oriental." At a more practical level, the device of the dream also allows the producers to introduce an element of the mysterious, the exotic, without disrupting the racial status quo of the rest of the tape. Even in the dream sequence, Sum Yung Mahn is at the center of the frame as spectacle, having minimal physical involvement with the men around him. Although the sequence ends with his climax, he exists for the pleasure of others.

Richard Dyer, writing about gay porn, states that:

> although the pleasure of anal sex (that is, of being anally fucked) is represented, the narrative is never organized around the desire to be fucked, but around the desire to ejaculate (whether or not following from anal intercourse). Thus, although a level of public representation of gay men may be thought of as deviant and disruptive of masculine norms because we assert the pleasure of being fucked and the eroticism of the anus, in our pornography this takes a back seat.[17]

Although Tom Waugh's amendment to this argument—that anal pleasure is represented in individual sequences[18]—also holds true for *Below the Belt*, as a whole the power of the penis and the pleasure of ejaculation are clearly the narrative's organizing principles. As with the vast majority of North American tapes featuring Asians, the problem is not the representation of anal pleasure per se, but rather that the narratives privilege the penis while always assigning the Asian the role of bottom; Asian and anus are conflated. In the case of Sum Yung Mahn, being fucked may well be his personal sexual preference. But the fact remains that there are very few occasions in North American video porn in which an Asian fucks a white man, so few, in fact, that International Wavelength promotes the tape *Studio X* (1986) with the blurb "Sum Yung Mahn makes history as the first Asian who fucks a non-Asian."[19]

Although I agree with Waugh that in gay as opposed to straight porn "the spectator's positions in relation to the representations are open and in flux,"[20] this observation applies only when all the participants are white. Race introduces another dimension that may serve to close down some of this mobility. This is not to suggest that the experience of gay men of color with this kind of sexual representation is the same as that of heterosexual women with regard to the gendered gaze of straight porn. For one thing, Asian gay men are men. We can therefore physically experience the pleasures depicted on the screen, since we too have erections and ejaculations and can experience anal penetration. A shifting identification may occur despite the racially defined roles, and most gay Asian men in North America are used to obtaining pleasure from all-white pornography. This, of course, goes hand in hand with many problems of self-image and sexual identity. Still, I have been struck by the unanimity with which gay Asian men I have met, from all over this continent as well as from Asia, immediately identify and resist these representations. Whenever I mention the topic of Asian actors in American porn, the first question I am asked is whether the Asian is simply shown getting fucked.

Asian Knights (1985, directed by Ed Sung, William Richhe Productions), the second tape I want to consider, has an Asian producer–director and a predominantly Asian cast. In its first scenario, two Asian men, Brad and Rick, are seeing a white psychiatrist because they are unable to have sex with each other:

Rick: We never have sex with other Asians. We usually have sex with Caucasian guys.

Counselor: Have you had the opportunity to have sex together?

Rick: Yes, a coupla times, but we never get going.

Homophobia, like other forms of oppression, is seldom dealt with in gay video porn. With the exception of safe sex tapes that attempt a rare blend of the pedagogical with the pornographic, social or political issues are not generally associated with the erotic. It is therefore unusual to see one of the favored discussion topics for gay Asian consciousness-raising groups employed as a sex fantasy in *Asian Knights*. The desexualized image of Asian men that I have described has seriously affected our relationships with one another, and often gay Asian men find it difficult to see each other beyond the terms of platonic friendship or competition, to consider other Asian men as lovers.

True to the conventions of porn, minimal counseling from the psychiatrist convinces Rick and Brad to shed their clothes. Immediately sprouting erections, they proceed to have sex. But what appears to be an assertion of gay Asian desire is quickly derailed. As Brad and Rick make love on the couch, the camera cross-cuts to the psychiatrist looking on from an armchair. The rhetoric of the editing suggests that we are observing the two Asian men from his point of view. Soon the white man takes off his clothes and joins in. He immediately takes up a position at the center of the action—and at the center of the frame. What appeared to be a "conversion fantasy" for gay Asian desire was merely a ruse. Brad and Rick's temporary mutual absorption really occurs to establish the superior sexual draw of the white psychiatrist, a stand-in for the white male viewer, who is the real sexual subject of the tape. And the question of Asian–Asian desire, though presented as the main narrative force of the sequence, is deflected, or rather reframed from a white perspective. Sex between the two Asian men in this sequence can be related somewhat to heterosexual sex in some gay porn films, such as those produced by the Gage brothers. In *Heatstroke* (1982), for example, sex with a woman is used to establish the authenticity of the straight man who is about to be seduced into gay sex. It dramatizes the significance of the conversion from the sanctioned object of desire, underscoring the power of the gay man to incite desire in his socially defined superior. It is also tied up with the fantasies of (female) virginity and conquest in Judeo-Christian and other patriarchal societies. The therapy session sequence of *Asian Knights* also suggests parallels to representations of lesbians in straight porn, representations that are not meant to eroticize women loving women, but rather to titillate and empower the sexual ego of the heterosexual male viewer.

Asian Knights is organized to sell representations of Asians to white men. Unlike Sum Yung Mahn in *Below the Belt*, the actors are therefore more expressive and sexually assertive, as often the seducers as the seduced. But though the roles shift during the predominantly oral sex, the Asians remain passive in anal intercourse, except that they are now shown to want it! How much this assertion of agency represents a step forward remains a question.

Even in the one sequence of *Asian Knights* in which the Asian actor fucks the white man, the scenario privileges the pleasure of the white man over that of the Asian. The sequence begins with the Asian reading a magazine. When the white man (played by porn star Eric Stryker) returns home from a hard day at the office, the waiting Asian asks how his day went, undresses him (even taking off his socks), and proceeds to massage his back.[21] The Asian man acts the role of the mythologized geisha of "the good wife" as fantasized in the mail-order bride business. And, in fact, the "house boy" is one of the most persistent white fantasies about Asian men. The fantasy is also a reality in many Asian countries where economic imperialism gives foreigners, whatever their race, the pick of handsome men in financial need. The accompanying cultural imperialism grants status to those Asians with white lovers. White men who for various reasons, especially age, are deemed unattractive in their own countries, suddenly find themselves elevated and desired.

From the opening shot of painted lotus blossoms on a screen to the shot of a Japanese garden that separates the episodes, from the Chinese pop music to the chinoiserie in the apartment, there is a conscious attempt in *Asian Knights* to evoke a particular atmosphere.[22] Self-conscious "Oriental" signifiers are part and parcel of a colonial fantasy—and reality—the empowers one kind of gay man over another. Though I have known Asian men in dependent relations with older, wealthier white men, as an erotic fantasy the house boy scenario tends to work one way. I know of no scenarios of Asian men and white house boys. It is not the representation of the fantasy that offends, or even the fantasy itself, rather the uniformity with which these narratives reappear and the uncomfortable relationship they have to real social conditions.

International Skin (1985, directed by William Richhe, N'wayvo Richhe Productions), as its name suggests, features a Latino, a black man, Sum Yung Mahn, and a number of white actors. Unlike the other tapes I have discussed, there are no "Oriental" devices. And although Sum Yung Mahn and all the men of color are inevitably fucked (without reciprocating), there is mutual sexual engagement between the white and non-white characters.

In this tape Sum Yung Mahn is Brad, a film student making a movie for his class. Brad is the narrator, and the film begins with a self-reflexive "head and shoulders" shot of Sum Yung Mahn explaining the scenario. The film we are watching supposedly represents Brad's point of view. But here again the tape is not targeted to black, Asian, or Latino men; though Brad introduces all of these men as his friends, no two men of color ever meet on screen. Men of color are not invited to participate in the internationalism that is being sold, except through identification with white characters. This tape illustrates how an agenda of integration becomes problematic if it frames the issue solely in terms of black–white, Asian–white mixing; it perpetuates a system of white-centeredness.

The gay Asian viewer is not constructed as a sexual subject in any of this work—not on the screen, not as a viewer. I may find Sum Yung Mahn attractive, I may desire his body, but I am always aware that he is not meant for me. I may lust after Eric Stryker and imagine myself as the Asian who is having sex with him, but the role the Asian plays in the scene with him is demean-

ing. It is not that there is anything wrong with the image of servitude per se, but rather that it is one of the few fantasy scenarios in which we figure, and we are always in the role of servant.

Are there then no pleasures for an Asian viewer? The answer to this question is extremely complex. There is first of all no essential Asian viewer. The race of the person viewing says nothing about how race figures in his or her own desires. Uniracial white representations in porn may not in themselves present a problem in addressing many gay Asian men's desires. But the issue is not simply that porn may deny pleasures to some gay Asian men. We also need to examine what role the pleasure of porn plays in securing a consensus about race and desirability that ultimately works to our disadvantage.

Though the sequences I have focused on in the preceding examples are those in which the discourses about Asian sexuality are most clearly articulated, they do not define the totality of depiction in these tapes. Much of the time the actors merely reproduce or attempt to reproduce the conventions of pornography. The fact that, with the exception of Sum Yung Mahn, they rarely succeed—because of their body type, because Midwestern-cowboy-porn dialect with Vietnamese intonation is just a bit incongruous, because they groan or gyrate just a bit too much—more than anything brings home the relative rigidity of the genre's codes. There is little seamlessness here. There are times, however, when the actors appear neither as simulated whites nor as symbolic others. There are several moments in *International Skin*, for example, in which the focus shifts from the genitals to hands caressing a body; these moments feel to me more "genuine." I do not mean this in the sense of an essential Asian sexuality, but rather a moment is captured in which the actor stops pretending. He does not stop acting, but he stops pretending to be a white porn star. I find myself focusing on moments like these, in which the racist ideology of the text seems to be temporarily suspended or rather eclipsed by the erotic power of the moment.

In "Pornography and the Doubleness of Sex for Women," Joanna Russ writes:

> Sex is ecstatic, autonomous and lovely for women. Sex is violent, dangerous and unpleasant for women. I don't mean a dichotomy (i.e., two kinds of women or even two kinds of sex) but rather a continuum in which no one's experience is wholly positive or negative.[35]

Gay Asian men are men and therefore not normally victims of the rape, incest, or other sexual harassment to which Russ is referring. However, there is a kind of doubleness, of ambivalence, in the way that Asian men experience contemporary North American gay communities. The "ghetto," the mainstream gay movement, can be a place of freedom and sexual identity. But it is also a site of racial, cultural, *and* sexual alienation sometimes more pronounced than that in straight society. For me sex is a source of pleasure, but also a site of humiliation and pain. Released from the social constraints against expressing overt racism in public, the intimacy of sex can provide my (non-Asian) partner an opening for letting me know my place—sometimes literally, as when after we come, he turns over and asks where I come from.[24] Most gay Asian men I know have similar experiences.

This is just one reality that differentiates the experiences and therefore the political priorities of gay Asians and, I think, other gay men of color from those of white men. For one thing we cannot afford to take a libertarian approach. Porn can be an active agent in representing *and* reproducing a sex–race status quo. We cannot attain a healthy alliance without coming to terms with these differences.

The barriers that impede pornography from providing representations of Asian men that are erotic and politically palatable (as opposed to correct) are similar to those that inhibit the Asian documentary, the Asian feature, the Asian experimental film and videotape. We are seen as too peripheral, not commercially visible—not the general audience. *Looking for Langston* (1988),[25] which is the first film I have seen that affirms

rather than appropriates the sexuality of black gay men, was produced under exceptional economic circumstances that freed it from the constraints of the marketplace.[26] Should we call for an independent gay Asian pornography? Perhaps I do, in a utopian sort of way, though I feel that the problems in North America's porn conventions are manifold and go beyond the question of race. There is such a limited vision of what constitutes the erotic.

One major debate about race and representation has shifted from an emphasis on the image to a discussion of appropriation and control of production and distribution—who gets to produce the work. But as we have seen in the case of *Asian Knights*, the race of the producer is no automatic guarantee of "consciousness" about these issues or of a different product. Much depends on who is constructed as the audience for the work. In any case, it is not surprising that under capitalism, finding my penis may ultimately be a matter of dollars and cents.

Notes

I would like to thank Tim McCaskell and Helen Lee for their ongoing criticism and comments, as well as Jeff Nunokawa and Douglas Crimp for their invaluable suggestions in converting the original spoken presentation into a written text. Finally, I would like to extend my gratitude to Bad Object-Choices for inviting me to participate in "How Do I Look?"

1. Phillipe Rushton and Anthony F. Bogaert, University of Western Ontario, "Race versus Social Class Difference in Sexual Behavior: A Follow-up Test of the r/K Dimension," *Journal of Research in Personality* 22 (1988): 259.

2. Feminists of color have long pointed out that racism is phrased differently for men and women. Nevertheless, since it is usually heterosexual (and often middle-class) males whose voices are validated by the power structure, it is their interests that are taken up as "representing" the communities. See Barbara Smith, "Toward a Black Feminist Criticism," in *All the Women Are White, All the Blacks Are Men, But Some of Us Are Brave:*

Black Women's Studies (Old Westbury, N.Y.: The Feminist Press, 1982), 182.

3–4. The mainstream "leadership" within Asian communities often colludes with the myth of the model minority and the reassuring desexualization of Asian people.

5. In Britain, however, more race–sex stereotypes of South Asians exist. Led by artists such as Pratibha Parmar, Sunil Gupta, and Hanif Kureishi, there is also a growing and already significant body of work by South Asians themselves, which takes up questions of sexuality.

6. Renee Tajima, "Lotus Blossoms Don't Bleed: Images of Asian Women," *Anthologies of Asian American Film and Video* (New York: A distribution project of Third World Newsreel, 1984), 28.

7. Ibid, 29.

8. See Stephen Gong, "Zen Warrior of the Celluloid (Silent) Years: The Art of Sessue Hayakawa," *Bridge* 8, no. 2 (Winter 1982–83): 37–41.

9. Frantz Fanon, *Black Skin, White Masks* (London: Paladin, 1970), 120. For a reconsideration of this statement in the light of contemporary black gay issues, see Kobena Mercer, "Imaging the Black Man's Sex," in *Photography/Politics: Two*, ed. Pat Holland, Jo Spence, and Simon Watney (London: Comedia/Methuen 1987); reprinted in *Male Order: Unwrapping Masculinity*, ed. Rowena Chapman and Jonathan Rutherford (London: Lawrence and Wishart 1988), 141.

10. I do not think that this could happen in today's Toronto, which now has the second largest Chinese community on the continent. Perhaps it would not have happened in San Francisco. But I still believe that there is an onus on gay Asians and other gay people of color to prove our homosexuality.

11. The term *minority* is misleading. Racism is not a matter of numbers but of power. This is especially clear in situations where people of color constitute actual majorities, as in most former European colonies. At the same time, I feel that none of the current terms are really satisfactory and that too much time spent on the politics of "naming" can in the end be diversionary.

12. To organize effectively with lesbian and gay Asians, we must reject self-righteous condemnation of "closetedness" and see coming out more as a process or a goal, rather than as a prerequisite for participation in the movement.

13. Racism is available to be used by anyone. The conclusion that—because racism = power + prejudice— only white people can be racist is Eurocentric and simply wrong. Individuals have varying degrees and different sources of power, depending on the given moment in a shifting context. This does not contradict the fact that, in contemporary North American society, racism is generally organized around white supremacy.

14. From simple observation, I feel safe in saying that most gay Asian men in North America hold white men as their idealized sexual partners. However, I am not trying to construct an argument for determinism, and there are a number of outstanding problems that are not easily answered by current analyses of power. What of the experience of Asians who are attracted to men of color, including other Asians? What about white men who prefer Asians sexually? How and to what extent is desire articulated in terms of race as opposed to body type or other attributes? To what extent is sexual attraction exclusive and/or changeable, and can it be consciously programmed? These questions are all politically loaded, as they parallel and impact the debates between essentialists and social constructionists on the nature of homosexuality itself. They are also emotionally charged, in that sexual choice involving race has been a basis for moral judgment.

15. See Richard Dyer, *Heavenly Bodies: Film Stars and Society* (New York: St. Martin's Press 1986). In his chapter on Marilyn Monroe, Dyer writes extensively on the relationship between blondness, whiteness, and desirability.

16. Print porn is somewhat more racially integrated, as are the new safe sex tapes—by the Gay Men's Health Crisis, for example—produced in a political and pedagogical rather than a commercial context.

17. Richard Dyer, "Coming to Terms," *Jump Cut*, no. 30 (March 1985): 28.

18. Tom Waugh, "Men's Pornography, Gay vs. Straight," *Jump Cut*, no. 30 (March 1985): 31.

19. *International Wavelength News* 2, No. 1 (January 1991).

20. Tom Waugh, "Men's Pornography, Gay vs. Straight," 33.

21. It seems to me that the undressing here is organized around the pleasure of the white man in being

served. This is in contrast to the undressing scenes, in, say, James Bond films, in which the narrative is organized around undressing as an act of revealing the woman's body, an indicator of sexual conquest.

22. Interestingly, the gay video porn from Japan and Thailand that I have seen has none of this Oriental coding. Asianness is not taken up as a sign but is taken for granted as a setting for the narrative.

23. Joanna Russ, "Pornography and the Doubleness of Sex for Women," *Jump Cut*, no. 32 (April 1986): 39.

24. Though this is a common enough question in our postcolonial, urban environments, when asked of Asians it often reveals two agendas: first, the assumption that all Asians are newly arrived immigrants and, second, a fascination with difference and sameness. Although we (Asians) all supposedly look alike, there are specific characteristics and stereotypes associated with each particular ethnic group. The inability to tell us apart underlies the inscrutability attributed to Asians. This "inscrutability" took on sadly ridiculous proportions when during World War II the Chinese were issued badges so that white Canadians could distinguish them from "the enemy."

25. Isaac Julien (director), *Looking for Langston* (United Kingdom: Sankofa Film and Video 1988).

26. For more on the origins of the black film and video workshops in Britain, see Jim Pines, "The Cultural Context of Black British Cinema," in *Blackframes: Critical Perspectives on Black Independent Cinema*, ed. Mybe B. Cham and Clair Andrade-Watkins (Cambridge, Mass.: MIT Press 1988), 26.

PART TEN

Men, Movements and the Future

Q: Why did you decide to record again?

A: Because *this* housewife would like to have a career for a bit! On October 9, I'll be 40, and Sean will be 5 and I can afford to say, "Daddy does something else as well." He's not accustomed to it—in five years I hardly picked up a guitar. Last Christmas our neighbors showed him "Yellow Submarine" and he came running in, saying, "Daddy, you were singing . . . Were you a Beatle?" I said, "Well—yes, right."

—John Lennon, interview for *Newsweek*, 1980

Are men changing? If so, in what directions? Can men change even more? In what ways should men

be different? We posed many of these questions at the beginning of our exploration of men's lives, and we return to them here, in the book's last section, to examine the directions men have taken to enlarge their roles, to expand the meaning of masculinity, to change the rules.

The articles in this section address the possibility and the direction of change for men: how shall we, as a society, address the questions raised by men's increasing exploration of the meaning of our lives? The articles in this section explore the movements and organizations designed to engage with men in the process of transformation. bell hooks argues that feminists, and especially African American feminists, need to see men as potential allies, while Robert Allen describes the gender politics of the Million Man March. The "Statement of Principles" of the National Organization for Men Against Sexism (NOMAS) provides an alternative way to frame these issues of gender, sexual, and racial equality. And Michael Kimmel's essay explores a variety of recent events in the continuing redefinition of masculinity and suggests some of the ways we transform masculinity in the future.

bell hooks

Men: Comrades in Struggle

Feminism defined as a movement to end sexist oppression enables women and men, girls and boys, to participate equally in revolutionary struggle. So far, contemporary feminist movement has been primarily generated by the efforts of women—men have rarely participated. This lack of participation is not solely a consequence of anti-feminism. By making women's liberation synonymous with women gaining social equality with men, liberal feminists effectively created a situation in which they, not men, designated feminist movement "women's work." Even as they were attacking sex role divisions of labor, the institutionalized sexism which assigns unpaid, devalued, "dirty" work to women, they were assigning to women yet another sex role task: making feminist revolution. Women's liberationists called upon all women to join feminist movement but they did not continually stress that men should assume responsibility for actively struggling to end sexist oppression. Men, they argued, were all-powerful, misogynist oppressors—the enemy. Women were the oppressed—the victims. Such rhetoric reinforced sexist ideology by positing in an inverted form the notion of a basic conflict between the sexes, the implication being that the empowerment of women would necessarily be at the expense of men.

As with other issues, the insistence on a "woman only" feminist movement and a virulent anti-male stance reflected the race and class background of participants. Bourgeois white women,

especially radical feminists, were envious and angry at privileged white men for denying them an equal share in class privilege. In part, feminism provided them with a public forum for the expression of their anger as well as a political platform they could use to call attention to issues of social equality, demand change, and promote specific reforms. They were not eager to call attention to the fact that men do not share a common social status; that patriarchy does not negate the existence of class and race privilege or exploitation; that all men do not benefit equally from sexism. They did not want to acknowledge that bourgeois white women, though often victimized by sexism, have more power and privilege, are less likely to be exploited or oppressed, than poor, uneducated, nonwhite males. At the time, many white women's liberationists did not care about the fate of oppressed groups of men. In keeping with the exercise of race and/or class privilege, they deemed the life experiences of these men unworthy of their attention, dismissed them, and simultaneously deflected attention away from their support of continued exploitation and oppression. Assertions like "all men are the enemy," "all men hate women" lumped all groups of men in one category, thereby suggesting that they share equally in all forms of male privilege. One of the first written statements which endeavored to make an anti-male stance a central feminist position was "The Redstocking Manifesto." Clause III of the manifesto reads:

> We identify the agents of our oppression as men. Male supremacy is the oldest, most basic form of domination. All other forms of exploitation and oppression (racism, capitalism, imperialism, etc.) are extensions of male

supremacy: men dominate women, a few men dominate the rest. All power situations throughout history have been male-dominated and male-oriented. Men have controlled all political, economic, and cultural institutions and backed up this control with physical force. They have used their power to keep women in an inferior position. All men receive economic, sexual, and psychological benefits from male supremacy. All men have oppressed women. (1970, p. 109)

Anti-male sentiments alienated many poor and working class women, particularly non-white women, from feminist movement. Their life experiences had shown them that they have more in common with men of their race and/or class group than bourgeois white women. They know the sufferings and hardships women face in their communities; they also know the sufferings and hardships men face and they have compassion for them. They have had the experience of struggling with them for a better life. This has been especially true for black women. Throughout our history in the United States, black women have shared equal responsibility in all struggles to resist racist oppression. Despite sexism, black women have continually contributed equally to anti-racist struggle, and frequently, before contemporary black liberation effort, black men recognized this contribution. There is a special tie binding people together who struggle collectively for liberation. Black women and men have been united by such ties. They have known the experience of political solidarity. It is the experience of shared resistance struggle that led black women to reject the anti-male stance of some feminist activists. This does not mean that black women were not willing to acknowledge the reality of black male sexism. It does mean that many of us do not believe we will combat sexism or woman-hating by attacking black men or responding to them in kind.

Bourgeois white women cannot conceptualize the bonds that develop between women and men in liberation struggle and have not had as many positive experiences working with men politically. Patriarchal white male rule has usually devalued female political input. Despite the prevalence of sexism in black communities, the role black women play in social institutions, whether primary or secondary, is recognized by everyone as significant and valuable. In an interview with Claudia Tate (1983), black woman writer Maya Angelou explains her sense of the different role black and white women play in their communities:

> Black women and white women are in strange positions in our separate communities. In the social gatherings of black people, black women have always been predominant. That is to say, in the church it's always Sister Hudson, Sister Thomas, and Sister Wetheringay who keep the church alive. In lay gatherings it's always Lottie who cooks, and Mary who's going to Bonita's where there is a good party going on. Also, black women are the nurturers of children in our community. White women are in a different position in their social institutions. White men, who are in effect their fathers, husbands, brothers, their sons, nephews, and uncles say to white women or imply in any case: "I don't really need you to run my institutions. I need you in certain places and in those places you must be kept—in the bedroom, in the kitchen, in the nursery, and on the pedestal." Black women have never been told this. . . .

Without the material input of black women, as participants and leaders, many male-dominated institutions in black communities would cease to exist; this is not the case in all white communities.

Many black women refused participation in feminist movement because they felt an anti-male stance was not a sound basis for action. They were convinced that virulent expressions of these sentiments intensify sexism by adding to the antagonism which already exists between women and men. For years black women (and some black men) had been struggling to overcome the tensions and antagonisms between black females and males that is generated by internalized racism (i.e., when the white patriarchy suggests one group has caused the oppression of the other). Black women were saying to black men, "we are not one another's enemy," "we must resist the socialization that teaches us to hate ourselves and one another." This affirmation of bonding between black women and men was part of anti-racist struggle. It could have been a part of feminist struggle had white women's liberationists stressed the need for women and men to resist the sexist socialization that teaches us to hate and fear one another. They chose instead to emphasize hate, especially male woman-hating, suggesting that it could not be changed. Therefore no viable political solidarity could exist between women and men. Women of color, from various ethnic backgrounds, as well as women who were active in the gay movement, not only experienced the development of solidarity between women and men in resistance struggle, but recognized its value. They were not willing to devalue this bonding by allying themselves with anti-male bourgeois white women. Encouraging political bonding between women and men to radically resist sexist oppression would have called attention to the transformative potential of feminism. The anti-male stance was a reactionary perspective that made feminism appear to be a movement that would enable white women to usurp white male power, replacing white male supremacist rule with white female supremacist rule.

Within feminist organizations, the issue of female separatism was initially separated from the anti-male stance; it was only as the movement progressed that the two perspectives merged. Many all-female sex-segregated groups were formed because women recognized that separatist organizing could hasten female consciousness-raising, lay the groundwork for the development of solidarity between women, and generally advance the movement. It was believed that mixed groups would get bogged down by male power trips. Separatist groups were seen as a necessary strategy, not as a way to attack men. Ultimately, the purpose of such groups was integration with equality. The positive implications of separatist organizing were diminished when radical feminists, like Ti Grace Atkinson, proposed sexual separatism as an ultimate goal of feminist movement. Reac-

tionary separatism is rooted in the conviction that male supremacy is an absolute aspect of our culture, that women have only two alternatives: accepting it or withdrawing from it to create subcultures. This position eliminates any need for revolutionary struggle and it is in no way a threat to the status quo. In the essay "Separate to Integrate," Barbara Leon (1975) stresses that male supremacists would rather feminist movement remain "separate and unequal." She gives the example of orchestra conductor Antonia Brico's efforts to shift from an all-women orchestra to a mixed orchestra, only to find she could not get support for the latter:

> Antonia Brico's efforts were acceptable as long as she confined herself to proving that women were qualified musicians. She had no trouble finding 100 women who could play in an orchestra or getting financial backing for them to do so. But finding the backing for men and women to play together in a truly integrated orchestra proved to be impossible. Fighting for integration proved to be more a threat to male supremacy and, therefore, harder to achieve.
>
> The women's movement is at the same point now. We can take the easier way of accepting segregation, but that would mean losing the very goals for which the movement was formed. Reactionary separatism has been a way of halting the push of feminism. . . .

During the course of contemporary feminist movement, reactionary separatism has led many women to abandon feminist struggle, yet it remains an accepted pattern for feminist organizing, e.g. autonomous women's groups within the peace movement. As a policy, it has helped to marginalize feminist struggle, to make it seem more a personal solution to individual problems, especially problems with men, than a political movement which aims to transform society as a whole. To return to an emphasis on feminism as revolutionary struggle, women can no longer allow feminism to be another arena for the continued expression of antagonism between the sexes. The time has come for women active in feminist movement to develop new strategies for including men in the struggle against sexism.

All men support and perpetuate sexism and sexist oppression in one form or another. It is crucial that feminist activists not get bogged down in intensifying our awareness of this fact to the extent that we do not stress the more unemphasized point which is that men can lead life affirming, meaningful lives without exploiting and oppressing women. Like women, men have been socialized to passively accept sexist ideology. While they need not blame themselves for accepting sexism, they must assume responsibility for eliminating it. It angers women activists who push separatism as a goal of feminist movement to hear emphasis placed on men being victimized by sexism; they cling to the "all men are the enemy" version of reality. Men are not exploited or oppressed by sexism, but there are ways in which they suffer as a result of it. This suffering should not be ignored. While it in no way diminishes the seriousness of male abuse and oppression of women, or negates male responsibility for exploitative actions, the pain men experience can serve as a catalyst calling attention to the need for change. Recognition of the painful consequences of sexism in their lives led some men to establish consciousness-raising groups to examine this. Paul Hornacek (1977) explains the purpose of these gatherings in his essay "Anti-Sexist Consciousness-Raising Groups for Men":

> Men have reported a variety of different reasons for deciding to seek a C-R group, all of which have an underlying link to the feminist movement. Most are experiencing emotional pain as a result of their male sex role and are dissatisfied with it. Some have had confrontations with radical feminists in public or private encounters and have been repeatedly criticized for being sexist. Some come as a result of their commitment to social change and their recognition that sexism and patriarchy are elements of an intolerable social system that needs to be altered . . .

Men in the consciousness-raising groups Hornacek describes acknowledge that they benefit from patriarchy and yet are also hurt by it. Men's groups, like women's support groups, run the risk of overemphasizing personal change at the expense of political analysis and struggle.

Separatist ideology encourages women to ignore the negative impact of sexism on male personhood. It stresses polarization between the sexes. According to Joy Justice, separatists believe that there are "two basic perspectives" on the issue of naming the victims of sexism: "There is the perspective that men oppress women. And there is the perspective that people are people, and we are all hurt by rigid sex roles." Many separatists feel that the latter perspective is a sign of co-optation, representing women's refusal to confront the fact that men are the enemy—they insist on the primacy of the first perspective. Both perspectives accurately describe our predicament. Men *do* oppress women. People *are* hurt by rigid sex role patterns. These two realities co-exist. Male oppression of women cannot be excused by the recognition that there are ways men are hurt by rigid sex roles. Feminist activists should acknowledge that hurt—it exists. It does not erase or lessen male responsibility for supporting and perpetuating their power under patriarchy to exploit and oppress women in a manner far more grievous than the psychological stress or emotional pain caused by male conformity to rigid sex role patterns.

Women active in feminist movement have not wanted to focus in any way on male pain so as not to deflect attention away from the focus on male privilege. Separatist feminist rhetoric suggested that all men shared equally in male privilege, that all men reap positive benefits from sexism. Yet the poor or working class man has been socialized via sexist ideology to believe that there are privileges and powers he should possess solely because he is male often finds that few if any of these benefits are automatically bestowed him in life. More than any other male group in the United States, he is constantly concerned about the contradiction between the notion of masculinity he was taught and his inability to live up to that notion. He is usually "hurt," emotionally scarred because he does not have the privilege or power society has taught him "real men" should possess. Alienated, frustrated, pissed off, he may attack, abuse, and oppress an individual woman or women, but he is not reaping positive benefits from his support and perpetuation of sexist ideology. When he beats or rapes women, he is not exercising privilege or reaping positive rewards; he may feel satisfied in exercising the only form of domination allowed him. The ruling class male power structure that promotes his sexist abuse of women reaps the real material benefits and privileges from his actions. As long as he is attacking women and not sexism or capitalism, he helps to maintain a system that allows him few, if any, benefits or privileges. He is an oppressor. He is an enemy to women. He is also an enemy to himself. He is also oppressed. His abuse of women is not justifiable. Even though he has been socialized to act as he does, there are existing social movements that would enable him to struggle for self-recovery and liberation. By ignoring these movements, he chooses to remain both oppressor and oppressed. If feminist movement ignores his predicament, dismisses his hurt, or writes him off as just another male enemy, then we are passively condoning his actions.

The process by which men act as oppressors and are oppressed is particularly visible in black communities, where men are working class and poor. In her essay "Notes For Yet Another Paper on Black Feminism, or Will The Real Enemy Please Stand Up?" (1979) black feminist activist Barbara Smith suggests that black women are unwilling to confront the problem of sexist oppression in black communities:

> By naming sexist oppression as a problem it would appear that we would have to identify as threatening a group we have heretofore assumed to be our allies—Black men. This seems to be one of the major stumbling blocks to beginning to analyze the sexual relationships/sexual politics of our lives. The phrase "men are not the enemy" dismisses feminism and the reality of patriarchy in one breath and also overlooks some major realities. If we cannot

entertain the idea that some men are the enemy, especially white men and in a different sense Black men, too, then we will never be able to figure out all the reasons why, for example, we are beaten up every day, why we are sterilized against our wills, why we are being raped by our neighbors, why we are pregnant at age twelve, and why we are at home on welfare with more children than we can support or care for. Acknowledging the sexism of Black men does not mean that we become "manhaters" or necessarily eliminate them from our lives. What it does mean is that we must struggle for a different basis of interaction with them.

Women in black communities have been reluctant to publicly discuss sexist oppression, but they have always known it exists. We too have been socialized to accept sexist ideology and many black women feel that black male abuse of women is a reflection of frustrated masculinity—such thoughts lead them to see that abuse is understandable, even justified. The vast majority of black women think that just publicly stating that these men are the enemy or identifying them as oppressors would do little to change the situation; they fear it could simply lead to greater victimization. Naming oppressive realities, in and of itself, has not brought about the kinds of changes for oppressed groups that it can for more privileged groups, who command a different quality of attention. The public naming of sexism has generally not resulted in the institutionalized violence that characterized, for example, the response to black civil rights struggles. (Private naming, however, is often met with violent oppression.) Black women have not joined the feminist movement not because they cannot face the reality of sexist oppression; they face it daily. They do not join feminist movement because they do not see in feminist theory and practice, especially those writings made available to masses of people, potential solutions.

So far, feminist rhetoric identifying men as the enemy has had few positive implications. Had feminist activists called attention to the relationship between ruling class men and the vast majority of men, who are socialized to perpetuate and maintain sexism and sexist oppression even as they reap no life-affirming benefits, these men might have been motivated to examine the impact of sexism in their lives. Often feminist activists talk about male abuse of women as if it is an exercise of privilege rather than an expression of moral bankruptcy, insanity, and dehumanization. For example, in Barbara Smith's essay, she identifies white males as "the primary oppressor group in American society" and discusses the nature of their domination of others. At the end of the passage in which this statement is made she comments: "It is not just rich and powerful capitalists who inhibit and destroy life. Rapists, murderers, lynchers, and ordinary bigots do too and exercise very real and violent power because of this white male privilege." Implicit in this statement is the assumption that the act of committing violent crimes against women is either a gesture or an affirmation of privilege. Sexist ideology brainwashes men to believe that their violent abuse of women is beneficial when it is not. Yet feminist activists affirm this logic when we should be constantly naming these acts as expressions of perverted power relations, general lack of control over one's actions, emotional powerlessness, extreme irrationality, and in many cases, outright insanity. Passive male absorption of sexist ideology enables them to interpret this disturbed behavior positively. As long as men are brainwashed to equate violent abuse of women with privilege, they will have no understanding of the damage done to themselves, or the damage they do to others, and no motivation to change.

Individuals committed to feminist revolution must address ways that men can unlearn sexism. Women were never encouraged in contemporary feminist movement to point out to men their responsibility. Some feminist rhetoric "put down" women who related to men at all. Most women's liberationists were saying "women have nurtured, helped, and supported others for too long—now we must fend for ourselves." Having helped and supported men for centuries by acting in complicity with sexism, women were suddenly encouraged to withdraw their support when it came to the issue of "liberation." The insistence on a concentrated focus on individualism, on the primacy of self, deemed "liberatory" by women's liberationists, was not a visionary, radical concept of freedom. It did provide individual solutions for women, however. It was the same idea of independence perpetuated by the imperial patriarchal state which equates independence with narcissism and lack of concern with triumph over others. In this way, women active in feminist movement were simply inverting the dominant ideology of the culture—they were not attacking it. They were not presenting practical alternatives to the status quo. In fact, even the statement "men are the enemy" was basically an inversion of the male supremacist doctrine that "women are the enemy"—the old Adam and Eve version of reality.

In retrospect, it is evident that the emphasis on "man as enemy" deflected attention away from focus on improving relationships between women and men, ways for men and women to work together to unlearn sexism. Bourgeois women active in feminist movement exploited the notion of a natural polarization between the sexes to draw attention to equal rights effort. They had an enormous investment in depicting the male as enemy and the female as victim. They were the group of women who could dismiss their ties with men once they had an equal share in class privilege. They were ultimately more concerned with obtaining an equal share in class privilege than with the struggle to eliminate sexism and sexist oppression. Their insistence on separating from men heightened the sense that they, as women without men, needed equality of opportunity. Most women do not have the freedom to separate from men because of economic inter-dependence. The separatist notion that women could resist sexism by withdrawing from contact with men reflected a bourgeois class perspective. In Cathy McCandless' essay "Some Thoughts About Racism, Classism, and Separatism," she makes the point that separatism is in many ways a false issue because "in this capitalist economy, none of us are truly separate" (1979). However, she adds:

Socially, it's another matter entirely. The richer you are, the less you generally have to acknowledge those you depend upon. Money can buy you a great deal of distance. Given enough of it, it is even possible never to lay eyes upon a man. It's a wonderful luxury, having control over who you lay eyes on, but let's face it: most women's daily survival still involves face-to-face contact with men whether they like it or not. It seems to me that for this reason alone, criticizing women who associate with men not only tends to be counterproductive, it borders on blaming the victim. Particularly if the women taking it upon themselves to set the standards are white and upper or middle class (as has often been the case in my experience) and those to whom they apply these rules are not.

Devaluing the real necessities of life that compel many women to remain in contact with men, as well as not respecting the desire of women to keep contact with men, created an unnecessary conflict of interest for those women who might have been very interested in feminism but felt they could not live up to the politically correct standards.

Feminist writings did not say enough about ways women could directly engage in feminist struggle in subtle, day-to-day contacts with men, although they have addressed crises. Feminism is politically relevant to the masses of women who daily interact with men both publicly and privately, if it addresses ways that interaction, which usually has negative components because sexism is so all-pervasive, can be changed. Women who have daily contact with men need useful strategies that will enable them to integrate feminist movement into their daily life. By inadequately addressing or failing to address the difficult issues, contemporary feminist movement located itself on the periphery of society rather than at the center. Many women and men think feminism is happening, or happened, "out there." Television tells them the "liberated" woman is an exception, that she is primarily a careerist. Commercials like the one that shows a white career women shifting from work attire to flimsy clothing exposing flesh, singing all the while "I can bring home the bacon,

fry it up in the pan, and never let you forget you're a man" reaffirm that her careerism will not prevent her from assuming the stereotyped sex object role assigned women in male supremacist society.

Often men who claim to support women's liberation do so because they believe they will benefit by no longer having to assume specific, rigid sex roles they find negative or restrictive. The role they are most willing and eager to change is that of economic provider. Commercials like the one described above assure men that women can be breadwinners or even "the" breadwinner, but still allow men to dominate them. Carol Hanisch's essay "Men's Liberation" (1975) explores the attempt by these men to exploit women's issues to their own advantage, particularly those issues related to work:

> Another major issue is the attempt by men to drop out of the work force and put their women to work supporting them. Men don't like their jobs, don't like the rat race, and don't like having a boss. That's what all the whining about being a "success symbol" or "success object" is really all about. Well, women don't like those things either, especially since they get paid 40% less than men for working, generally have more boring jobs, and rarely are even allowed to be "successful." But for women working is usually the only way to achieve some equality and power in the family, in their relationship with men, some independence. A man can quit work and pretty much still remain the master of the household, gaining for himself a lot of free time since the work he does doesn't come close to what his wife or lover does. In most cases, she's still doing more than her share of the housework in addition to wife work and her job. Instead of fighting to make his job better, to end the rat race, and to get rid of bosses, he sends his woman to work—not much different from the old practice of buying a substitute for the draft, or even pimping. And all in the name of breaking down "role stereotypes" or some such nonsense.

Such a "men's liberation movement" could only be formed in reaction to women's liberation in an attempt to make feminist movement serve the opportunistic interests of individual men. These men identified themselves as victims of sexism, working to liberate men. They identified rigid sex roles as the primary source of their victimization and though they wanted to change the notion of masculinity, they were not particularly concerned with their sexist exploitation and oppression of women. Narcissism and general self-pity characterized men's liberation groups. Kanisch concludes her essay with the statement:

> Women don't want to pretend to be weak and passive. And we don't want phony, weak, passive acting men any more than we want phony supermen full of bravado and little else. What women want is for men to be honest. Women want men to be bold—boldly honest, aggressive in their human pursuits. Boldly passionate, sexual and sensual. And women want this for themselves. It's time men became boldly radical. Daring to go to the root of their own exploitation and seeing that it is not women or "sex roles" or "society" causing their unhappiness, but capitalists and capitalism. It's time men dare to name and fight these, their real exploiters.

Men who have dared to be honest about sexism and sexist oppression, who have chosen to assume responsibility for opposing and resisting it, often find themselves isolated. Their politics are disdained by antifeminist men and women, and are often ignored by women active in feminist movement. Writing about his efforts to publicly support feminism in a local newspaper in Santa Cruz, Morris Conerly explains:

> Talking with a group of men, the subject of Women's Liberation inevitably comes up. A few laughs, snickers, angry mutterings, and denunciations follow. There is a group consensus that men are in an embattled position and must close ranks against the assaults of misguided females. Without fail, someone will solicit me for my view, which is that I am 100% for Women's Liberation. That throws them for a loop and they start staring at me as if my eyebrows were crawling with lice.

They're thinking, "What kind of man is he?" I am a black man who understands that women are not my enemy. If I were a white man with a position of power; one could understand the reason for defending the status quo. Even then, the defense of a morally bankrupt doctrine that exploits and oppresses others would be inexcusable.

Conerly stresses that it was not easy for him to publicly support feminist movement, that it took time:

> . . . Why did it take me some time? Because I was scared of the negative reaction I knew would come my way by supporting Women's Liberation. In my mind I could hear it from the brothers and sisters. "What kind of man are you?" "Who's wearing the pants?" "Why are you in that white shit?" And on and on. Sure enough, the attacks came as I had foreseen but by that time my belief was firm enough to withstand public scorn.
>
> With growth there is pain . . . and that truism certainly applied in my case.

Men who actively struggle against sexism have a place in feminist movement. They are our comrades. Feminists have recognized and supported the work of men who take responsibility for sexist oppression—men's work with batterers, for example. Those women's liberationists who see no value in this participation must re-think and re-examine the process by which revolutionary struggle is advanced. Individual men tend to become involved in feminist movement because of the pain generated in relationships with women. Usually a woman friend or companion has called attention to their support of male supremacy. Jon Snodgrass introduces the book he edited, *For Men Against Sexism: A Book of Readings* (1977), by telling readers:

> While there were aspects of women's liberation which appealed to men, on the whole my reaction was typical of men. I was threatened by the movement and responded with anger and ridicule. I believed that men and women were oppressed by capital, but not that women were oppressed by men. I argued that "men are op-

pressed too" and that it's workers who need liberation! I was unable to recognize a hierarchy of inequality between men and women (in the working class) not to attribute it to male domination. My blindness to patriarchy, I now think, was a function of my male privilege. As a member of the male gender case, I either ignored or suppressed women's liberation.

My full introduction to the women's movement came through a personal relationship. . . . As our relationship developed, I began to receive repeated criticism for being sexist. At first I responded, as part of the male backlash, with anger and denial. In time, however, I began to recognize the validity of the accusation, and eventually even to acknowledge the sexism in my denial of the accusations.

Snodgrass participated in the men's consciousness-raising groups and edited the book of readings in 1977. Towards the end of the 1970s, interest in male anti-sexist groups declined. Even though more men than ever before support the idea of social equality for women, like women they do not see this support as synonymous with efforts to end sexist oppression, with feminist movement that would radically transform society. Men who advocate feminism as a movement to end sexist oppression must become more vocal and public in their opposition to sexism and sexist oppression. Until men share equal responsibility for struggling to end sexism, the feminist movement will reflect the very sexist contradictions we wish to eradicate.

Separatist ideology encourages us to believe that women alone can make feminist revolution—we cannot. Since men are the primary agents maintaining and supporting sexism and sexist oppression, they can only be successfully eradicated if men are compelled to assume responsibility for transforming their consciousness and the consciousness of society as a whole. After hundreds of years of anti-racist struggle, more than ever before non-white people are currently calling attention to the primary role white people must play in anti-racist struggle. The same is true of the struggle to eradicate sexism—men have a primary role to play. This does not mean that they are better equipped to lead feminist movement; it does mean that they should share equally in resistance struggle. In particular, men have a tremendous contribution to make to feminist struggle in the area of exposing, confronting, opposing, and transforming the sexism of their male peers. When men show a willingness to assume equal responsibility in feminist struggle, performing whatever tasks are necessary, women should affirm their revolutionary work by acknowledging them as comrades in struggle.

References

Angelou, Maya. 1983. "Interview." In *Black Women Writers at Work*, edited by Claudia Tate. New York: Continuum Publishing.

Hanisch, Carol. 1975. "Men's Liberation," Pp. 60–63 in *Feminist Revolution*. New Paltz, NY: Redstockings.

Hornacek, Paul. 1977. "Anti-Sexist Consciousness Raising Groups for Men." In *A Book of Readings for Men Against Sexism*, edited by Jon Snodgrass. Albion: Times Change Press.

Leon, Barbara. 1975. "Separate to Integrate." Pp. 139–44 in *Feminist Revolution*. New Paltz, NY: Redstockings.

McCandless, Cathy. 1979. "Some Thoughts About Racism, Classism, and Separatism." Pp. 105–15 in *Top Ranking*, edited by Joan Gibbs and Sara Bennett. New York: February Third Press.

"Redstockings Manifesto." 1970. Page 109 in *Voices from Women's Liberation*, edited by Leslie B. Tanner. New York: Signet, NAL.

Smith, Barbara. 1979. "Notes for Yet Another Paper on Black Feminism, Or Will the Real Enemy Please Stand Up." *Conditions: Five* 2 (2): 123–27.

Snodgrass, Jon (ed.). 1977. *A Book of Readings for Men Against Sexism*. Albion: Times Change Press.

Robert L. Allen

Racism, Sexism, and a Million Men

It was one of the few times in recent memory when black men were on the front pages of newspapers and featured on national television, and the news wasn't about murders, drugs, riots or sports. The news was about a huge, dignified and morally powerful gathering by African American men from all walks of life throughout the nation.

The men came at the behest of Minister Louis Farrakhan, but, as Jesse Jackson suggested, the organizers of the march were as much Newt Gingrich and the racist backlash that now grips the country.

The Million Man March tapped an urgent need in the black community for men to stand up for justice and the principles of self-determination, self-reliance and respect for self and others. In this sense it was not so much a protest demonstration as it was an affirmation. It affirmed the dignity and humanity of black men. For many of the men there, it was also the occasion for making a commitment to the struggle for justice in society and the rebuilding of communities and families.

The march provoked a wide-ranging discussion in the black community of a host of issues, including the role of black nationalism, whether black people should remain bound to the two-party system, and the relationship between the sexes within the family, to name a few.

Indeed, the march touched a deep longing in black communities for stable, safe and loving families. All too many of us have experienced the dissolution of family life under the horrific pressures of depression-level unemployment, wholesale incarceration of black men, and a draconian welfare system that forces men to leave their families if the women and children are to get assistance. We have experienced the intimate violence that often accompanies family breakdown.

Under these circumstances the desire for some semblance of wholesome family life is more than understandable.

Nevertheless, as more black men are coming to realize, this cannot be achieved by men reclaiming their "rightful" place as head of the family anymore than a safe and stable society can be achieved by whites taking their "rightful" place as the superior race, or a safe and stable world be achieved by multinational corporations taking their "rightful" place as dictators of a new international order.

I believe many supporters and organizers of the march understood that we cannot go back to a patriarchal system that never really worked in the black community. The call for male responsibility and respect for women at the march was not necessarily a demand for patriarchal privilege; it was as much an admission of the harm done by irresponsibility and lack of respect, and a call for men to join with women in rebuilding families that have been damaged by social oppression. This will require a new notion of masculinity—not the old idea of a manhood based on domination and submission, but one based on mutual respect and mutual responsibility. Without justice, mutual respect and mutual responsibility we will never achieve stability and safety (much less love) in our homes nor in the society at large.

Black men are not the enemies of women, but the ideology of male supremacy is the enemy of all of us, for it beguiles us into accepting white supremacist notions of domination, and the "nor-

Reprinted by permission from *The Black Scholar*, Volume 25 (4), 1995, pages 24–26.

malization" of violence as the means to maintain control over others.

Historically, black men and women in America have been victims of brutal and systematic violence. Our communities have been terrorized by the lynching (and castration) of thousands of black men by white men, and the rape (and murder) of thousands of black women by white men. Today white mob violence and police brutality continue unabated.

African American men know intimately the violent capabilities of other men. It is a tragedy that some of us have internalized the violence of this racist/sexist society and brought it into our communities and our homes. The injuries done by racism to black men's bodies and spirits are sometimes devastating, but this can never justify transforming that hurt into rage and violence against black women's bodies and spirits. We may not yet be able to stop the violence of the racist state, but self-inflicted violence in our communities and homes is something we can stop. Black men, who well know the lash of white male violence, have a special responsibility to stand with black women and children against all forms of violence. Black men must hold each other responsible for challenging sexism in our community as we all challenge the racism of white America.

In this regard, the pledge proposed by Minister Farrakhan—disavowing wife abuse, abuse of children, and the use of misogynist language—was an affirming and healing gesture.

We must also challenge the sexism and homophobia that would deny legitimacy to women-headed families and same-sex families. African Americans have a long and wonderful tradition of multiform family structures. How many of us have been raised by grandmothers, siblings, "aunts" and "uncles" (many of whom may not have been blood kin)? In our community it is well accepted that the parents are those who do the parenting, irrespective of blood ties, and families are composed of those who feel they are "family." When we refer to each other as "brothers" and "sisters" we are not necessarily speaking biologi-

cally but of a deeply felt kinship of common experience. That experience unites us all—men and women, straight and gay—into a vibrant, creative, soulful family.

The black women and gays who took part in the march were in fact treated with respect, and women were featured prominently among the speakers. Perhaps this reflected the marchers' understanding that we do not elevate ourselves by belittling, dominating or attacking other members of our family. We gain respect and self-esteem by joining with others in the collective struggle against our common oppression.

Patriarchy is one form of capitalist oppression, with the patriarchal household as a microcosm of class relations in the capitalist nation-state. Yet the mockery and scorning of black men by white scholars and the white establishment for not being successful patriarchs generates a terrible pressure to "act like men" and a humiliating social stigma if we fail to measure up, if we fail to demonstrate the semblance of masculine power if not its substance. Some black men have let their anger at this double-bind trap them in destructive and self-destructive behavior, but others, including without doubt many in the march, have sought to be responsible partners, husbands and fathers who also challenge the system of oppression.

Abuse and violence arise from a system of racial and sexual oppression. To stop the violence, rebuild our families and our communities we must challenge the power structures, institutions and socially constructed roles upon which sexism and racism are based. This is a big task, but one which each of us can undertake in many ways—in our homes, in our schools, in our communities. We can offer our children new models of non-violent, supportive male and female behavior. We can affirm each other in finding healing responses to the pain and hurt we have suffered. We can educate young people about empowering ways to counter racism and sexism. We can confront institutionalized oppression and violence. We can support movements and organizations that are working for progressive social change. In sum, black men and women working together in small groups and large, in families and communities, can build community responses to the system of inequality and the cycle of violence that blight our lives.

The real meaning of the Million Man March will be expressed in homes, community meetings and political gatherings where the men who supported the march use their experience to catalyze progressive change. Already gatherings have been held in various cities to strategize ways of dealing with black economic development and the issue of reparations, housing and the homeless, voter registration and independent politics, youth and education. Networking between communities and organizations is taking place. Efforts are being made to form local branches of a National African American Leadership Summit. Women as well as men are actively involved in these efforts. These are significant initiatives that have flowed from the march; they deserve serious consideration and support as ways for realizing the hopes that the march represented.

It is true that the African American community has been wounded by the evils of racism and sexism, but the struggle for justice is itself a salve for our wounds and an affirmation of our humanity—and our manhood and our womanhood are expressed above all in our common humanity.

The National Organization for Men Against Sexism

Statement of Principles

The National Organization for Men Against Sexism is an activist organization of men and women supporting positive changes for men. NOMAS advocates a perspective that is pro-feminist, gay-affirmative, and committed to justice on a broad range of social issues including race, class, age, religion, and physical abilities. We affirm that working to make this nation's ideals of equality substantive is the finest expression of what it means to be men.

We believe that the new opportunities becoming available to women and men will be beneficial to both. Men can live as happier and more fulfilled human beings by challenging the old-fashioned rules of masculinity that embody the assumption of male superiority.

Traditional masculinity includes many positive characteristics in which we take pride and find strength, but it also contains qualities that have limited and harmed us. We are deeply supportive of men who are struggling with the issues of traditional masculinity. As an organization for changing men, we care about men and are especially concerned with men's problems, as well as the difficult issues in most men's lives.

As an organization for changing men, we strongly support the continuing struggle of women for full equality. We applaud and support the insights and positive social changes that feminism has stimulated for both women and men. We oppose such injustices to women as economic and legal discrimination, rape, domestic violence, sexual harassment, and many others. Women and men can and do work together as allies to change the injustices that have so often made them see one another as enemies.

One of the strongest and deepest anxieties of most American men is their fear of homosexuality. This homophobia contributes directly to the many injustices experienced by gay, lesbian, and bisexual persons, and is a debilitating restriction for heterosexual men. We call for an end to all forms of discrimination based on sexual–affectional orientation, and for the creation of a gay-affirmative society.

We also acknowledge that many people are oppressed today because of their race, class, age, religion, and physical condition. We believe that such injustices are vitally connected to sexism, with its fundamental premise of unequal distribution of power.

Our goal is to change not just ourselves and other men, but also the institutions that create inequality. We welcome any person who agrees in substance with these principles to membership in the National Organization For Men Against Sexism.

Michael S. Kimmel

Clarence, William, Iron Mike, Tailhook, Senator Packwood, Spur Posse, Magic . . . and Us

The 1990s may be remembered as the decade in which America took a crash course on male sexuality. From the national teach-in on sexual harassment that emerged from Clarence Thomas's confirmation hearings, to accusations about sexual harassment against Senator Robert Packwood, to the U.S. Navy Tailhook scandal, to Magic Johnson's revelation that he is infected with the HIV virus, to William Kennedy Smith's and Mike Tyson's date rape trials, to the trials of lacrosse players at St. John's University and high school athletes at Glen Ridge, New Jersey, we've had a steady discussion about male sexuality, about a sexuality that is more about predatory conquest than pleasure and connection.

And there's no end in sight—which explains the title of this essay. In the immediate aftermath of the Clarence Thomas confirmation hearings, the media claimed, as if with one voice, that the hearings would have a "chilling effect" on American women—that women would be far less likely to come forward and report incidents of sexual harassment for fear that they would be treated in the same shameful way as Anita Hill was by the Senate Judiciary Committee. Have the media ever been more wrong?

Since then, we've had less of a "chilling effect, and more of a national thaw, as women have come forward in record numbers to report cases of sexual harassment, date rape, and acquaintance rape. "Every woman has her Clarence Thomas,"

commented one woman, sadly surveying the workplace over the past two decades. In an op-ed essay in the *New York Times*, novelist Mary Lee Settle commented that Anita Hill had, "by her heroic stance, given not only me but thousands of women who have been silenced by shame the courage and the need to speak out about what we have tried for so long to bury and forget."

Currently, corporations, state and local governments, universities, and law firms are scrambling to implement procedures to handle sexual harassment. Most seem motivated more out of fear of lawsuits than out of general concern for women's experiences; thus, they are more interested in adjudicating harassment *after the fact* than in developing mechanisms to prevent it. In the same way, colleges and universities are developing strategies to handle the remarkable rise in date and acquaintance rape, although only a few are developing programs on prevention.

With more women coming forward now than ever before, many men have reacted defensively; "Men on Trial" has been the common headline linking Smith and Thomas in the media. But it's not *men* on trial here, it's *masculinity*, or, rather, a definition of masculinity that leads to certain behaviors that we now see as problematic and often physically threatening. Under prevailing definitions, men have been and are the "politically incorrect" sex.

But why have these issues emerged now? And why are issues such as sexual harassment and date rape the particular issues we're facing. Since it is certain that we will continue to face these issues for the rest of the decade, how can we understand these changes? And, most important, what can we do about it? How can we change the meanings of masculinity so that sexual harassment and date rape will disappear from our workplaces and our relationships?

The Social Construction of Male Sexuality

To speak of transforming masculinity is to begin with the way men are sexual in our culture. As social scientists now understand, sexuality is less a product of biological urges and more about the meanings that we attach to those urges, meanings that vary dramatically across cultures, over time, and among a variety of social groups within any particular culture. Sexual beings are made, not born. John Gagnon, a well-known theoretician of this approach, argues in his book *Human Sexualities* that

> People learn when they are quite young a few of the things that they are expected to be, and continue slowly to accumulate a belief in who they are and ought to be through the rest of childhood, adolescence, and adulthood. Sexual conduct is learned in the same ways and through the same processes; it is acquired and assembled in human interaction, judged and performed in specific cultural and historical worlds.

And the major item in that assemblage, the chief building block in the social construction of sexuality, is gender. We experience our sexual selves through a gendered prism. The meanings of sex to women and to men are very, very different. There really are a "his" and "hers" when it comes to sex. Just one example: think about the difference in the way we view a man or a woman who has a lot of different partners—the difference, say, between a stud and a slut.

The rules of masculinity and femininity are strictly enforced. And difference equals power. The difference between male and female sexuality reproduces men's power over women, and, si-

multaneously, the power of some men over other men, especially of the dominant, hegemonic form of manhood—white, straight, middle-class—over marginalized masculinities. Those who dare to cross over—women who are sexually adventurous and men who are sexually passive—risk being seen as *gender*, not sexual, nonconformists. And we all know how homophobia links gender nonconformity to homosexuality. The stakes are high if you don't play along.

Sexual behavior confirms manhood. It makes men feel manly. Robert Brannon has identified the four traditional rules of American manhood: (1) No Sissy Stuff: Men can never do anything that even remotely suggests femininity. Manhood is a relentless repudiation and devaluation of the feminine. (2) Be a Big Wheel: Manhood is measured by power, wealth, and success. Whoever has the most toys when he dies, wins. (3) Be a Sturdy Oak: Manhood depends on emotional reserve. Dependability in a crisis requires that men not reveal their feelings. (4) Give 'em Hell: Exude an aura of manly daring and aggression. Go for it. Take risks.

These four rules lead to a sexuality built around accumulating partners (scoring), emotional distance, and risk taking. In locker rooms and on playgrounds across the country, men are taught that the goal of every encounter with women is to score. Men are supposed to be ever ready for sex, constantly seeking sex, and constantly seeking to escalate every encounter so that intercourse will result, since, as one of my students once noted, "It doesn't count unless you put it in."

The emotional distancing of the sturdy oak is considered necessary for adequate male sexual functioning, but it leads to some strange behaviors. For example, to keep from ejaculating "too soon," men may devise a fascinating array of distractions, such as counting, doing multiplication tables in their heads, or thinking about sports.

Risk taking is a centerpiece of male sexuality. Sex is about adventure, excitement, danger. Taking chances. Responsibility is a word that seldom turns up in sexual discourse. And this of course has serious medical side effects; the possibilities include STDs, impregnation, and AIDS—currently the most gendered disease in American history.

To rein in this constructed male "appetite," women have been assigned the role of asexual gatekeeper; women decide, metaphorically and literally, who enters the desired garden of earthly delights, and who doesn't. Women's sexual agency, women's sense of entitlement to desire, is drowned out by the incessant humming of male desire, propelling him ever forward. A man's job is to wear down her resistance. One fraternity at a college I was lecturing at last year offered seminars to pledges on dating etiquette that appropriated the book of business advice called *Getting to Yes.*

Sometimes that hum can be so loud that it drowns out the actual voice of the real live woman that he's with. Men suffer from socialized deafness, a hearing impairment that strikes only when women say "no."

Who Are the Real Sexual Revolutionaries?

Of course, a lot has changed along the frontiers of the sexual landscape in the past two decades. We've had a sexual revolution, after all. But as the dust is settling from the sexual revolution, what emerges in unmistakably fine detail is that it's been women, not men, who are our era's real sexual pioneers. Of course, we men like to think that the sexual revolution, with its promises of more access to more partners with less emotional commitment, was tailor-made for male sexuality's fullest flowering. But in fact it's been women's sexuality that's changed in the past two decades, not men's. Women now feel capable, even *entitled*, to sexual pleasure. They have learned to say "yes" to their own desires, claiming their own sexual agency.

And men? We're still dancing the same tired dance of the sexual conquistadors. Look, for a minute, at that new late-night game show *Studs.*

Here are the results of the sexual revolution in media miniature. The men and women all date one another, and from implicit innuendo to explicit guffaws, one assumes that every couple has gone to bed. What's not news is that the men are joking about it; what *is* news is that the women are equally capable of it.

Now some might argue that this simply confirms that women can have "male sex," that male sexuality was victorious because we've convinced women to be more like us. But then why are so many men wilting in the face of desiring women? Why are the offices of sex therapists crammed with men who complain not of premature ejaculation (the most common sexual problem twenty years ago—a sexual problem that involves being a bit overeager) but of what therapists euphemistically call "inhibited desire." That is, these men don't want to have sex now that all these women are able to claim their sexual rights.

Date Rape and Sexual Predation, Aggression, and Entitlement

As women have claimed the right to say "yes," they've also begun to assert their rights to say "no." Women are now demanding that men be more sexually responsible and are holding men accountable for their sexual behaviors. It is women who have changed the rules of sexual conduct. What used to be (and in many places still is) called male sexual etiquette—forcing a woman to have sex when she says no, conniving, coercing, pushing, ignoring efforts to get you to stop, getting her so drunk that she loses the ability (or consciousness) that one needs to give consent—is now defined as date rape.

In one recent study, by psychologist Mary Koss at the University of Arizona, forty-five percent of all college women said that they had had some form of sexual contact against their will. A full twenty-five percent had been pressed or forced to have sexual intercourse against their will. And Patricia Bowman, who went home with William

Kennedy Smith from Au Bar in Palm Beach, Florida, knows all about those statistics. She testified that when she told Smith that she'd called her friends, and she was going to call the police, he responded, "You shouldn't have done that. Nobody's going to believe you." And, indeed, the jury didn't. I did.

I also believed that the testimony of three other women who claimed they were sexually assaulted by Smith should have been allowed in the trial. Such testimony would have established a pattern not of criminal assault, but of Smith's obvious belief in sexual *entitlement*, that he was entitled to press his sexual needs on women despite their resistance, because he didn't particularly care what they felt about it.

And Desiree Washington knows all about men who don't listen when a woman says no. Mike Tyson's aggressive masculinity in the boxing ring was sadly translated into a vicious misogyny with his ex-wife Robin Givens and a predatory sexuality, as evidenced by his behavior with Desiree Washington. Tyson's "grandiose sense of entitlement, fueled by the insecurities and emotions of adolescence," as writer Joyce Carol Oates put it, led to a behavior with women that was as out of control as homosocial behavior inside the ring.

Tyson's case underscores our particular fascination with athletes, and the causal equation we make between athletes and sexual aggression. From the St. John's University lacrosse team, to Glen Ridge, New Jersey, high school athletes, to dozens of athletic teams and individual players at campuses across the nation, we're getting the message that our young male athletes, trained for fearless aggression on the field, are translating that into a predatory sexual aggression in relationships with women. Columnist Robert Lipsyte calls it the "varsity syndrome—winner take all, winning at any cost, violence as a tool, aggression as a mark of masculinity." The very qualities we seek in our athletes are exactly the qualities we do not want in young men today. Rather, we want to encourage respect for others, compassion, the ability to listen, and attention to process rather than the end goal. Our task is to make it clear that what we want from our athletes when they are on the playing field is *not* the same as what we want from them when they are playing the field.

I think, though, that athletes only illustrate a deeper problem: the problem of men in groups. Most athletes play on teams, so much of their social life and much of a player's public persona is constructed through association with his teammates. Another homosocial preserve, fraternities, are the site of most gang rapes that occur on college campuses, according to psychologist Chris O'Sullivan, who has been studying gang rape for several years. At scores of campus and corporate workshops over the past five years, women have shared the complaint that, while individual men may appear sympathetic when they are alone with women, they suddenly turn out to be macho louts capable the vilest misogynistic statements when they are in groups of men. The members of the U.S. Navy Tailhook Association are quite possibly decent, law-abiding family men when they are alone with their families. But put them together at a convention, and they become a marauding gang of hypermasculine thugs who should be prosecuted for felonious assault, not merely slapped on their collective wrists.

I suppose it's true that the members of Spur Posse, a group of relatively affluent Southern California adolescent boys, are also "regular guys." Which makes their sexual predation and homosocial competition as chilling as it is revealing of something at the heart of American masculinity. Before a large group of young women and girls—one as young as ten!—came forward to claim that members of Spur Posse had sexually assaulted and raped them, these guys would have been seen as typical high school fellas. Members of the group competed with one another to have sex with the most girls and kept elaborately coded scores of their exploits by referring to various athletes' names as a way of signifying the number of conquests. Thus a reference to "Reggie Jackson" would refer to 44, the number on his jersey, while

"David Robinson" would signify 50 different conquests. In this way, the boys could publicly compete with one another without the young women understanding that they were simply the grounds for homosocial competition.

When some of these young women accused the boys of assault and rape, many residents of their affluent suburb were shocked. The boys' mothers, particularly, winced when they heard that their fifteen-year-old sons had had sex with 44 or 50 girls. A few expressed outrage. But the boys' fathers glowed with pride. "That's my boy," they declared in chorus. They accused the girls of being sluts. And we wonder where the kids get it from?

Spur Posse is only the most recent example of the way masculine sexual entitlement is offered to boys as part of their birthright. Transforming a rape culture is going to mean transforming a view of women as the vessels through which men can compete with one another, trying to better their positions on the homosocial ladders of success and status.

What is it about groups that seems to bring out the worst in men? I think it is because the animating condition for most American men is a deeply rooted fear of other men—a fear that other men will view us as less than manly. The fear of humiliation, of losing in a competitive ranking among men, of being dominated by other men— these are the fears that keep men in tow and that reinforce traditional definitions of masculinity as a false definition of safety. Homophobia (which I understand as more than the fear of homosexual men; it's also the fear of other men) keeps men acting like men, keeps men exaggerating their adherence to traditional norms, so that no other men will get the idea that we might really be that most dreaded person: the sissy.

Men's fear of being judged a failure as a man in the eyes of other men leads to a certain homosocial element within the heterosexual encounter: men often will use their sexual conquest as a form of currency to gain status among other men. Such homosocial competition contributes to the strange hearing impairment that men experience in any sexual encounter, a socialized deafness that leads us to hear "no" as "yes," to escalate the encounter, to always go for it, to score. And this is occurring just at the moment when women are, themselves, learning to say "yes" to their own sexuality, to say "yes" to their own desire for sexual pleasure. Instead of our socialized deafness, we need to become what Langston Hughes called "articulate listeners": we need to trust women when they tell us what they want, and when they want it, and what they don't want as well. If we listen when woman say "no," then they will feel more trusting and open to saying "yes" when they feel that. And we need to listen to our own inner voices, our own desires and needs. Not the voices that are about compulsively proving something that cannot be proved, but the voices that are about connection with another and the desires and passions that may happen between two equals.

Escalating a sexual encounter beyond what a woman may want is date rape, not sex; it is one of the most important issues we will face in the 1990s. It is transforming the sexual landscape as earlier sexual behaviors are being reevaluated in light of new ideas about sexual politics. We have to explore the meaning of the word *consent*, explore our own understandings, and make sure that these definitions are in accord with women's definitions.

From the Bedroom to the Boardroom

Just as women have been claiming the right to say "yes" and demanding the right to say "no" and have it listened to and respected in the sexual arena, they've also transformed the public arena, the workplace. As with sexuality, the real revolution in the past thirty years has been women's dramatic entry into the labor force in unprecedented numbers. Almost half of the labor force is female. I often demonstrate this point to my classes by asking the women who intend to have careers to raise their hands. All do. Then I ask them to keep their hands raised if their mothers have had a career outside the home for more than ten years.

Half put their hands down. Then I ask them to keep their hands raised if their grandmothers had a career for ten years. Virtually no hands remain raised. In three generations, they can visibly see the difference in women's working lives. Women are in the work force to stay, and men had better get used to having them around.

That means that the cozy boy's club—another homosocial arena—has been penetrated by women. And this, just when that arena is more suffused with doubt and anxieties than ever before. We are, after all, a downwardly mobile culture. Most Americans are less successful now than their parents were at the same age. It now takes two incomes to provide the same standard of living that one income provided about a generation ago. And most of us in the middle class cannot afford to buy the houses in which we were brought up. Since men derive their identity in the public sphere, and the primary public arena where masculinity is demonstrated is the workplace, this is an important issue. There are fewer and fewer big wheels and more and more men who will feel as though they haven't made the grade, who will feel damaged, injured, powerless—men who will need to demonstrate their masculinity all over again. Suddenly, men's fear of humiliation and domination are out in the open, and there's a convenient target at which to vent those anxieties.

And now, here come women into the workplace in unprecedented numbers. It now seems virtually impossible that a man will go through his entire working life without having a woman colleague, co-worker, or boss. Just when men's economic breadwinner status is threatened, women appear on the scene as easy targets for men's anger. Thus sexual harassment in the workplace is a distorted effort to put women back in their place, to remind women that they are not equal to men in the workplace, that they are still just women, even if they are in the workplace.

It seems to me that this is the context in which to explore the meaning of sexual harassment in our society. The Clarence Thomas confirmation hearings afford men a rare opportunity to do some serious soul searching. What is sexual

harassment about? And why should men help put an end to it?

One thing that sexual harassment is usually *not* about, although you couldn't convince the Senate Judiciary Committee of this, is a matter of one person telling the truth and the other person lying. Sexual harassment cases are difficult and confusing precisely because there are often a multiplicity of truths. "His" truth might be what appears to him as an innocent indication of sexual interest by harmless joking with the "boys in the office" (even if those "boys" happen to include women workers). "Her" truth is that those seemingly innocent remarks cause stress and anxiety about promotion, firing, and sexual pressure.

Judge Thomas asserted during the course of his testimony that "at no time did I become aware, either directly or indirectly, that she felt I had said or done anything to change the cordial nature of our relationship." And there is no reason to assume that he would have been aware of it. But that doesn't mean his words or actions did not have the effect that Professor Hill states, only that she was successful in concealing the resulting trauma from him—a concealment that women have carefully developed over the years in the workplace.

Why should this surprise us? Women and men often experience the same event differently. Men experience their behavior from the perspective of those who have power, women from the perspective of those upon whom that power is exercised.

If an employer asks an employee for a date, and she declines, perhaps he has forgotten about it by the time he gets to the parking lot. No big deal, he says to himself. You ask someone out, and she says "no." You forget about it. In fact, repairing a wounded male ego often *requires* that you forget about it. But the female employee? She's now frozen, partly with fear. What if I said yes? Would I have gotten promoted? Would he have expected more than a date? Will I now get fired? Will someone else get promoted over me? What should I do? And so, she will do what millions of women do in that situation: she calls her friends, who counsel her to let the matter rest and get on with her work. And she remembers for a long, long time. Who, therefore, is likely to have a better memory: those in power or those against whom that power is deployed?

This is precisely the divergence in experience that characterizes the controversies spinning around Senator Bob Packwood. Long a public supporter of women's causes, Senator Packwood also apparently chased numerous women around office desks, clumsily trying to have affairs with them. He claims, now, that alcoholism caused this behavior and that he doesn't remember. It's a good thing that the women remember. They often do.

Sexual harassment is particularly volatile because it often fuses two levels of power: the power of employers over employees and the power of men over women. Thus what may be said or intended as a man to a woman is also experienced in the context of superior and subordinate, or vice versa. Sexual harassment in the workplace results from men using their public position to demand or exact social relationships. It is the confusion of public and private, bringing together two arenas of men's power over women. Not only are men in positions of power in the workplace, but we are socialized to be the sexual initiators and to see sexual prowess as a confirmation of masculinity.

Sexual harassment is also a way to remind women that they are not yet equals in the workplace, that they really don't belong there. Harassment is most frequent in those occupations and workplaces where women are new and in the minority, like surgeons, firefighters, and investment bankers. "Men see women as invading a masculine environment," says Louise Fitzgerald, a University of Illinois psychologist. "These are guys whose sexual harassment has nothing whatever to do with sex. They're trying to scare women off a male preserve."

When the power of men is augmented by the power of employer over employee, it is easy to understand how humiliating and debilitating sexual harassment can be, and how individual women would be frightened about seeking redress. The workplace is not a level playing field. Subor-

dinates rarely have the resources to complain against managers, whatever the problem.

Some men were confused by Professor Hill's charges, others furious about sexual harassment because it feels as though women are changing the rules. What used to be routine behavior for men in the workplace is now being called sexual harassment. "Clarence Thomas didn't do anything wrong that any American male hasn't done," commented Dale Whitcomb, a thirty-two-year-old machinist. How right he was. The fact that two-thirds of men surveyed said they would be complimented if they were propositioned by a woman at work gives some idea of the vast gulf between women's and men's perceptions of workplace sexual conduct.

Although men surely do benefit from sexual harassment, I believe that we also have a stake in ending it. First, our ability to form positive and productive relationships with women colleagues in the workplace is undermined by it. So long as sexual harassment is a daily occurrence and women are afraid of their superiors in the workplace, innocent men's behaviors may be misinterpreted. Second, men's ability to develop social and sexual relationships that are both ethical and exciting is also compromised. If a male boss dates a subordinate, can he really trust that the reason she is with him is because she *wants* to be? Or will there always be a lingering doubt that she is there because she is afraid not to be or because she seeks to please him because of his position?

Currently, law firms and corporations all over the country are scrambling to implement sexual harassment policies, to make sure that sexual harassment will be recognized and punished. But our challenge is greater than admonition and post hoc counseling. Our challenge will be to prevent sexual harassment *before* it happens. And that means working with men. Men must come to see that these are not women who happen to be in the workplace (where, by this logic, they actually don't belong), but workers who happen to be women. And we'll need to change the meaning of success so that men don't look back at their careers when they retire and wonder what it was all for, whether any of it was worth it. Again, we'll need to change the definition of masculinity, dislodging it from these misshapen public enactments, including the capacity to embrace others as equals within it, because of an inner security and confidence that can last a lifetime. It is more important than ever to begin to listen to women, to listen with a compassion that understands that women's and men's experiences are different, and an understanding that men, too, can benefit from the elimination of sexual harassment.

AIDS as a Men's Disease

Surely, men will benefit from the eradication of AIDS. Although we are used to discussing AIDS as a disease of gay men and IV drug users, I think we need to see AIDS as a men's disease. Over ninety percent of all AIDS patients are men; AIDS is now the leading cause of death for men aged thirty-three to forty-five nationwide. AIDS is American men's number one health problem, and yet we rarely treat it as a men's issue. But AIDS is also the most gender-linked disease in American history. No other disease has attacked one gender so disproportionately, except those to which only one sex is susceptible, such as hemophilia or uterine or prostate cancer. AIDS *could* affect both men and women equally (and in Africa that seems to be closer to the case). But in the United States, AIDS patients are overwhelmingly men.

(Let me be clear that in no way am I saying that one should not be compassionate for women AIDS patients. Of course one must recognize that women are as likely to get AIDS from engaging in the same high-risk behaviors as men. But that's precisely my point. Women don't engage in those behaviors at rates anything like men.)

One is put at risk for AIDS by engaging in specific high-risk behaviors, activities that ignore potential health risks for more immediate pleasures. For example, sharing needles is both a de-

fiant flaunting of health risks and an expression of community among IV drug users. And the capacity of high-risk sexual behaviors—unprotected anal intercourse with a large number of partners, the ability to take it, despite any potential pain— are also confirmations of masculinity.

And so is accumulation—of money, property, or sexual conquests. It's curious that one of America's most lionized heroes, Magic Johnson, doesn't seem to have been particularly compassionate about the possibility of infection of the twenty-five hundred women he reported he slept with. Johnson told *Sports Illustrated* that as a single man, he tried to "accommodate as many women as I could, most of them through unprotected sex." Accommodate? When he protested that his words were misunderstood, he told the *New York Times*, "I was a bachelor, and I lived a bachelor's life. And I'm paying the price for it. But you know I respect women to the utmost." (I suppose that Wilt Chamberlain, who boasted in his autobiography that he slept with over twenty thousand women, respected them almost ten times as much.)

As sociologists have long understood, stigmatized gender identity often leads to exaggerated forms of gender-specific behavior. Thus, those whose masculinity is least secure are precisely those most likely to enact behavioral codes and hold fast to traditional definitions of masculinity. In social science research, hypermasculinity as compensation for insecure gender identity has been used to explain the propensity for homophobia, authoritarianism, racism, anti-Semitism, juvenile delinquency, and urban gangs.

Gay men and IV drug users—the two largest risk groups—can be seen in this light, although for different reasons. The traditional view of gay men is that they are not "real men." Most of the stereotypes revolve around effeminacy, weakness, passivity. But following the Stonewall riots of 1969, in which gay men fought back against a police raid on a gay bar in Greenwich Village, New York, and the subsequent birth of the Gay Liberation Movement, a new gay masculinity emerged in major cities (see Kleinberg 1990; Levine 1991). The "clone," as the new gay man was called, dressed in hypermasculine garb (flannel shirts, blue jeans, leather); had short hair (not at all androgynous) and a mustache; and was athletic, highly muscular. In short, the clone looked more like a "real man" than most straight men.

And the clones—who comprised roughly one-third of all gay men living in the major urban enclaves of the 1970s (see Bell and Weinberg 1980)—enacted a hypermasculine sexuality in steamy back rooms, bars, and bathhouses, where sex was plentiful, anonymous, and very hot. No unnecessary foreplay, romance, or post-coital awkwardness. Sex without attachment. One might even say that, given the norms of masculinity (that men are always seeking sex, ready for sex, wanting sex), gay men were the only men in America who were getting as much sex as they wanted. Predictably, high levels of sexual activity led to high levels of sexually transmitted diseases, such as gonorrhea, among the clones. But no one could have predicted AIDS.

Among IV drug users, we see a different pattern, but with some similar outcomes when seen from a gender perspective. The majority of IV drug users are African-American and Latino, two groups for whom the traditional avenues of successful manhood are blocked by poverty and racism. More than half of the black men between eighteen and twenty-five in our cities are unemployed, and one in four are in some way involved with the penal system (in jail, on probation, under arrest). We thus have an entire generation structurally prevented from demonstrating its manhood in that most traditional of ways—as breadwinners.

The drug culture offers an alternative. Dealing drugs can provide an income to support a family as well as the opportunity for manly risks and adventure. The community of drug users can confirm gender identity; the sharing of needles is a demonstration of that solidarity. And the ever-present risk of death by overdoes takes hyper-masculine bravado to its limits.

Who Asked for It?

The victims of men's adherence to these crazy norms of masculinity—AIDS patients, rape victims, victims of sexual harassment—did not become victims intentionally. They did not "ask for it," and they certainly do not deserve blame. That some women today are also sexual predators, going to swank bars or waiting outside athletes' locker rooms or trying to score with male subordinates at work, doesn't make William Kennedy Smith, Mike Tyson, Magic Johnson, or Clarence Thomas any less predatory. When predatory animals threaten civil populations, we warn the population to stay indoors, until the wild animals can be caught and recaged. When it's men on the prowl, women engage in a voluntary curfew, unless they want to risk being attacked.

And the men—the date rapists, the sexual harassers, the AIDS patients—are not "perverts" or "deviants" who have strayed from the norms of masculinity. They are, if anything, overconformists to destructive norms of male sexual behavior. Until we change the meaning of manhood, sexual risk-taking and conquest will remain part of the rhetoric of masculinity. And we will scatter the victims, both women and men, along the wayside as we rush headlong towards a testosterone-infected oblivion.

The Sexual Politics of Safety

What links the struggle against sexual harassment, date and acquaintance rape, and AIDS is that preventing all of them requires that *safety* become the central term, an organizing principle of men's relationships with women, as well as with other men. The politics of safety may be the missing link in the transformation of men's lives, in their capacity for change. Safety is more than the absence of danger, although that wouldn't be such a bad thing itself. Safety is pro-active, the creation of a space in which all people, women and men, gay and straight, and of all colors, can experience and express the fullness of their beings.

Think for a moment about how the politics of safety affects the three areas I have discussed in this essay. What is the best way to prevent AIDS? To use sterile needles for intravenous drug injections and to practice "safer sex." Sterile needles and safer sex share one basic characteristic: they both require that men act responsibly. This is not one of the cardinal rules of manhood. Safer sex programs encourage men to have fewer partners, to avoid certain particularly dangerous practices, and to use condoms when having any sex that involves the exchange of bodily fluids. In short, safer sex programs encourage men to stop having sex like men. To men, you see, "safer sex" is an oxymoron, one of those juxtapositions of terms that produce a nonsensical outcome. That which is sexy is not safe, that which is safe is not sexy. Sex is about danger, risk, excitement; safety is about comfort, softness, and security.

Seen this way, it is not surprising to find, as some researchers have found, that one-fourth of urban gay men report that they have not changed their unsafe sexual behaviors. What is, in fact, astonishing is that slightly more than three-fourths *have* changed and are now practicing safer sex.

What heterosexual men could learn from the gay community's response to AIDS is how to eroticize that responsibility—something that women have been trying to teach men for decades. Making safer sex into sexy sex has been one of the great transformations of male sexuality accomplished by the gay community. And straight men could also learn a thing or two about caring for one another through illness, supporting one another in grief, and maintaining a resilience in the face of a devastating disease and the callous indifference of the larger society.

Safety is also the animating condition for women's expression of sexuality. While safety may be a turnoff for men (comfort, softness, and security are the terms of postorgasmic detumescence, not sexual arousal), safety is a precondition for sexual agency for women. Only when women feel safe can they give their sexuality full expression. For men, hot sex leaves a warm afterglow; for women, warmth builds to heat, but warmth is not created by heat.

This perspective helps explain that curious finding in the sex research literature about the divergence of women's and men's sexualities as they age. We believe that men reach their sexual peak at around eighteen, and then go into steady, and later more precipitous, decline for the rest of their lives; while women hit their sexual stride closer to thirty, with the years between twenty-seven and thirty-eight as their peak years. Typically, we understand these changes as having to do with differences in biology—that hormonal changes find men feeling soft and cuddly just as women are getting all steamed up. But aging does not produce such changes in every culture; that is, biology doesn't seem to work the same way everywhere.

What biological explanations leave out is the way that men's and women's sexualities are related to each other, and the way that both are shaped by the institution of marriage. Marriage makes one's sexuality more predictable—the partner, the timing, the experience—and it places sex *always* in the context of the marital relationship. Marriage makes sex safer. No wonder women find their sexuality heightening—they finally feel safe enough to allow their sexual desires to be expressed. And no wonder men's sexuality deflates—there's no danger, risk, or excitement left.

Safety is a precondition for women's sexual expression. Only when a woman is certain, beyond the shadow of a doubt, that her "no" means "no," can she ever say "yes" to her own sexual desires. So if we men are going to have the sexual relationships with exciting, desiring women that we say we want, then we have to make the environment safe enough for women to express their desires. We have to make it absolutely certain to a woman that her "no" means "no"—no matter how urgently we feel the burning of our own desires.

To do this we will need to transform the definition of what it means to be a real man. But we have to work fast. AIDS is spreading rapidly, and date rape and sexual harassment are epidemic in the nation's colleges and workplaces. As AIDS spreads, and as women speak up about these issues, there are more and more people who need our compassion and support. Yet compassion is in relatively short supply among American men, since it involves the capacity of taking the role of the other, of seeing ourselves in someone else's shoes, a quality that contradicts the manly independence we have so carefully cultivated.

Sexual democracy, just like political democracy, relies on a balance between rights and responsibilities, between the claims of the individual and the claims of the community. When one discusses one's sexual rights—that each person, every woman and man, has an equal right to pleasure—men understand immediately what you mean. Women often look delighted and a little bit surprised. Add to the Bill of Sexual Rights a notion of responsibility, in which each of us treats sexual partners as if they had an integrity equal to our own, and it's the men who look puzzled. "Responsibility? What's that got to do with sex? I thought sex was about having fun."

Sure it is, but it's also political in the most intimate sense. Sexual democracy doesn't have to mean no sex. It means treating your partner as someone whose lust is equal to yours and also as someone whose life is equally valuable. It's about enacting in daily life one's principles, claiming our rights to pleasure, and making sure that our partners also feel safe enough to be able to fully claim theirs. This is what we demand for those who have come to America seeking refuge—safety—from political tyranny. Could we ask any less for those who are now asking for protection and refuge from millennia of sexual tyranny?

Coda: 1999

For the past few days, the nation has stared at the pictures of Eric Harris and Dylan Klebold, trying to understand the unfathomable—how these two young boys could arm themselves to the teeth

and open fire on their classmates and teachers. We'll stare at those pictures as the explanations begin to pour in from the experts and the pundits alike.

We'll hear from psychologists who'll draw elaborate profiles of misfits and loners, of adolescent depression and acting out. Cultural critics on the right will throw some blame on Goth music, Marilyn Manson, violent video games, the Internet. More liberal critics will tell us it's guns. President Clinton chimed in about violence in the media. Perhaps we'll soon hear about fatherlessness or the disappearance of modesty. The Denver school board has already banned the wearing of black trench coats.

All the while we will continue to miss the point—even though it is staring right back at us: The killers were middle-class white boys who live in gun states.

Skeptical? Try a little thought experiment: imagine that the killers in Littleton—and in Pearl, Mississippi; Paducah, Kentucky; Springfield, Oregon; and Jonesboro, Arkansas—were all black girls from poor families who lived in New Haven, Connecticut; Newark, New Jersey; or Providence, Rhode Island.

I believe we'd now be having a national debate about inner-city poor black girls. The entire focus would be on race, class, and gender. The media would invent a new term for their behavior, as they did with "wilding" a decade ago after the attack on the Central Park jogger. We'd hear about the culture of poverty; about how living in the city breeds crime and violence; about some putative natural tendency among blacks towards violence. Someone would even blame feminism for causing girls to become violent in vain imitation of boys.

Yet the obvious fact that these school killers were all middle-class white boys seems to have escaped everyone's notice.

In these cases, actually, it's unclear that class or race played any part in the shootings, although the killers in Colorado did target some black students. But that's the point: Imagine the national reaction if black boys had targeted whites in school shootings. We would assume that race alone explained the tragedy. (Some would, of course, blame rap music and violent movies.) Or if poor boys had targeted those with the fancy cars, we'd assume that class-based resentment caused the boy's rage. (That Dylan Klebold drove a BMW has not prompted the Denver school board to consider banning those cars, has it?)

That all these murders were committed by young boys with guns raises not a ripple. We continue to call them "teens," "youth," or "children" rather than what they really are: boys.

Yet gender is the single most obvious and intractable difference when it comes to violence in America. Men and boys are responsible for 95 percent of all violent crimes in this country. Every day, 12 boys and young men commit suicide—7 times the number of girls. Every day 18 boys and young men die from homicide—10 times the number of girls.

From an early age, boys learn that violence is not only an acceptable form of conflict resolution, but one that is admired. Four times more teenage boys than teenage girls think fighting is appropriate when someone cuts into the front of a line. Half of all teenage boys get into a physical fight each year.

The belief that violence is manly is not a trait carried on any chromosome, not soldered into the wiring of the right or left hemisphere, not juiced by testosterone. (It is still the case that half the boys don't fight, most don't carry weapons, and almost all don't kill: are they not boys?) Boys learn it.

They learn it from their fathers, nearly half of whom own a gun. They learn it from a media that glorifies it, from sports heroes who commit felonies and get big contracts, from a culture saturated in images of heroic and redemptive violence. They learn it from each other.

And this parallel education is made more lethal in states where gun control laws are most lax, where gun lobbyists are most powerful, because all available evidence suggests that all the

increases in the deadliness of school violence is attributable to guns. Boys have resorted to violence for a long time, but sticks and fists and even the occasional switchblade do not create the bloodbaths of the past few years. Nearly 90 percent of all homicides among boys aged 15 to 19 are firearm related, and 80 percent of the victims are boys. If the rumble in *West Side Story* were to take place today, the death toll would not be just Riff and Bernardo, but all the Sharks and all the Jets—and probably several dozen bystanders.

Some will throw up their hands and sigh that "boys will be boys." In the face of these tragic killings, such resignation is unacceptable. And it doesn't answer the policy question; it begs the question. If boys have a natural propensity toward violence and aggression, do we organize society to maximize that tendency, or to minimize it?

Perhaps the most sensible reform that could come from these tragedies is stricter gun control laws, at least on assault weapons and handguns. Far more sweeping—and necessary—is a national meditation on how our ideals of manhood became so entangled with violence.

Make no mistake: Eric Harris and Dylan Klebold were real boys. In a sense, they weren't deviants, but over-conformists to norms of masculinity that prescribe violence as a solution. Like real men, they didn't just get mad, they got even. Until we transform that definition of manhood, this terrible equation of masculinity and violence will add up to an increasing death toll at our nation's schools.

Note

My thinking on these issues has benefitted enormously from collaborative work with Michael Kaufman and the late Martin Levine. The material in the sections on sexual harassment and AIDS draws from that collaborative work, and I am grateful to them for their insights and support.

CONTRIBUTORS

ROBERT ALLEN is Senior Editor of *The Black Scholar* and a member of the Board of Directors of The Oakland Men's Project, a community education organization dealing with sexism, racism, and male violence. He is also co-editor, with Herb Boyd, of *Brotherman: The Odyssey of Black Men in America* (1995).

TOMÁS ALMAGUER is Associate Professor of American Studies at the University of California, Santa Cruz, and Associate Professor of Sociology and American Culture at the University of Michigan, Ann Arbor. His book, *Racial Fault Lines: The Historical Origins of White Supremacy*, will be published by University of California Press this fall.

MAXINE BACA ZINN teaches in the Department of Sociology at Michigan State University. She has written widely in the area of family relations, Chicano studies, and gender studies, including (most recently) *Women of Color in U.S. Society* (with Bonnie Thorton Dill), *Diversity in Families* (with Stanley Eitzen 1990), and *The Reshaping of America* (1989).

JEFFREY R. BENEDICT is with the New England Law School in Boston. He has published in the area of male college athletes' sexual violence against women.

TIM BENEKE is a freelance writer and editor living in the San Francisco Bay Area. He is the author of *Men on Rape* and *Proving Manhood*.

SUSAN BORDO is the Otis A. Singletary Chair in the Humanities at the University of Kentucky. Her books include *Unbearable Weight: Feminism, Western Culture and the Body*, *Twilight Zones: The Hidden Life of Cultural Images from Plato to O. J.*, and *The Male Body*, from which this essay is adapted.

A. AYRES BOSWELL is a supervisor at a foster care agency in New York City. She works with abused and neglected children, trying to achieve permanency in the children's lives either by reunification with their birth parents or by locating adoptive resources.

PHILIPPE BOURGOIS is Research Fellow, San Franciso Urban Institute and Associate Professor of Anthropology at San Francisco State University.

GEOFFREY CANADA is President of Rheedlen Centers for Children and Families in New York City. He was awarded a Heinz Award in 1995 for his leadership in nurturing and protecting children.

CRAIG CENTRIE is Executive Director of El Museo Francisco Oller y Diego Rivera, a Latino art gallery in Buffalo, New York. He is an adjunct faculty member of American Studies at SUNY Buffalo and is completing his Ph.D. in Social Foundations at SUNY Buffalo.

SUSAN D. COCHRAN currently teaches at California State University, Northridge.

SCOTT COLTRANE is Associate Professor of Sociology at the University of California, Riverside. His research on families, gender, and the changing role of fathers has appeared in various scholarly journals. He is co-author (with Randall Collins) of *Sociology of Marriage and the Family* (1992), and the author of *Family Man: Fatherhood, Housework, and Gender Equity* (1996).

R. W. CONNELL is Professor of Education, University of Sydney. His most recent works include *Gender and Power* (1987), *Staking a Claim: Feminism, Bureaucracy and the State* (with Suzanne Franzway and Dianne Court) and *Masculinities* (1996).

ANGELA COWAN is a postgraduate student in the Department of Sociology at the University of Newcastle. Her thesis topic is an investigation of the discursive world of young children. She is a trained primary school schoolteacher and has worked as an observer on a number of psychiatric research projects.

TODD W. CROSSET is Assistant Professor of Sport Studies at the University of Massachusetts, Amherst. He is author of *Outsiders in the Clubhouse: The World of Women's Professional Golf* (1995).

TIMOTHY CURRY is in the Department of Sociology at the Ohio State University.

RAFAEL DIAZ is a social worker and developmental psychologist who is on the faculty of AIDS Prevention Studies at University of California, San Francisco. His current research project is a "sociocultural model of HIV risk in Latino gay men."

MARTIN ESPADA is author of five books of poetry, most recent *City of Coughing and Dead Radiators* and *Imagine the Angels of Bread*. A former tenant lawyer, he teaches literature at University of Massachusetts, Amherst.

YEN LE ESPIRITU is professor of Ethnic Studies at the University of California, San Diego. She is the author of *Asian American Panethnicity: Bridging Institutions and Identities, Filipino American Lives,* and *Asian American Women and Men: Labor, Laws, and Love.* She is also serving as the President of the Association of Asian American Studies.

ANN FAUSTO-STERLING is Professor of Medical Science in the Division of Biology and Medicine at Brown University. She is the author of *Myths of Gender: Biological Theories about Women and Men,* and has also written broadly about the role of race and gender in the construction of scientific theory and the role of such theories in the construction of race and gender.

JULES FEIFFER is a syndicated cartoonist and was a regular contributor to *The Village Voice.*

CLYDE W. FRANKLIN II was Professor of Sociology at the Ohio State University. His research focused largely on black masculinity. His numerous publications included *The Changing Definition of Masculinity* and *Men and Society.*

RICHARD FUNG is a writer and independent video producer in Toronto, Canada. He has produced

tapes including "Fighting Chance: Gay Asian Men and HIV" (1980) and "My Mother's Place" (1990), while contributing articles to *Fuse* magazine and *Moving the Image: Independent Asian Pacific American Media Arts* (1991).

THOMAS J. GERSCHICK is Assistant Professor of Sociology at Illinois State University. His research focuses on identity, and marginalized and alternative masculinities.

PATTI A. GIUFFRE is a Ph.D. candidate in sociology at the University of Texas at Austin. Her dissertation focuses on the management of sexuality in organizations and sexual harassment in different workplace contexts.

MICHAEL HANCHARD is a Professor of Political Science at Northwestern University. He is the author of *Orpheus and Power: Afro-Brazilian Social Movements in Rio de Janeiro and Sao Paolo, 1945–1988.* He is currently working on a project on race, modernity, and the politics of the African dispora.

ARLIE HOCHSCHILD is Professor of Sociology at University of California, Berkeley. Her books include *The Managed Heart: Commercialization and Human Feeling* and *The Second Shift: Working Parents and the Revolution at Home.*

JOCELYN HOLLANDER is Assistant Professor of Sociology at the University of Oregon. Her research focuses on how gender, race, class, and sexuality are constructed through everyday interaction and on the consequences of these constructions for both individuals and social structures. Her current project explores the gendered construction of vulnerability and dangerousness in conversation. She is co-author, with Judith A. Howard, of *Gendered Situations, Gendered Selves* (1997).

BELL HOOKS is a writer and lecturer who speaks on issues of race, class, and gender. She teaches at CUNY Graduate Center. Her books include *Ain't I a Woman, Feminist Theory,* and *Talking Back.* Her column, "Sisters of the Yam," appears monthly in *Z* magazine.

STEVI JACKSON is Professor of Women's Studies and Director of the Centre of Women's Studies at the University of York. She is the author of *Christine Delphy* and co-editor of *Feminism and Sexuality* and *Contemporary Feminist Theories*.

ELLEN JORDAN is Senior Lecturer in the Department of Sociology at the University of Newcastle. She was for many years a teacher in primary schools. Her major research interests are women's work in nineteenth-century Britain and gender construction in early childhood.

MICHAEL KAUFMAN is the author or editor of several books on men and masculinity including *Cracking the Armor: Power, Pain, and the Lives of Men* (1993), *Theorizing Masculinities* (1994), and *Beyond Patriarchy* (1987). He lives in Toronto, Canada, and is active in efforts to end violence against women and in anti-sexist education for young men.

ROBIN D. G. KELLEY is a Professor of History and Africana at New York University and the author of *Hammer and Hoe: Alabama Communists During the Great Depression* (1990) and *Race Rebels* (1994).

MICHAEL S. KIMMEL is Professor of Sociology at SUNY at Stony Brook. His books include *Changing Men* (1987), *Men Confront Pornography* (1990), *Men in the United States* (1992), *Manhood in America* (1996), *The Politics of Manhood* (1996) and *The Gendered Society* (2000). He is the editor of *masculinities*, a scholarly journal, and National Spokesperson for the National Organization for Men Against Sexism (NOMAS).

BARBARA KRUGER is a graphic artist in New York City.

PETER LEHMAN is a Professor in the Interdisciplinary Humanities Program and the Hispanic Research Center at Arizona State University. He is author of *Running Scared: Masculinity and the Representation of the Male Body* and the editor of *Defining Cinema*.

PETER LYMAN is University Dean of Libraries at the University of California, Berkeley.

PAT MAHONY is Professor of Education at Roehampton Institute, London. She has worked for many years in the areas of equal opportunities and teacher education. Her books include *Schools for the Boys?, Promoting Quality and Equality in Schools*, and *Changing Schools*.

MANNING MARABLE is Professor and Director of the Center for African American Studies at Columbia University.

VICKIE M. MAYS currently teaches at University of California, Los Angeles.

MARK A. MCDONALD is a lecturer in Sport Studies at the University of Massachusetts, Amherst.

C. SHAWN MCGUFFEY is a doctoral student in the Department of Sociology at the University of Massachusetts, Amherst. McGuffey's research interests include the sociology of childhood, family, and interracial marriage patterns through the lens of critical race feminism. He is currently researching how children understand and experience race, class, gender, and sexuality at the New England summer camp.

MICHAEL A. MESSNER is Associate Professor of Sociology and Gender Studies at the University of Southern California. He is co-editor of *Through the Prism of Difference: Readings on Sex and Gender* (1997). His books include *Power at Play: Sports and the Problem of Masculinity* (1992), and *Politics of Masculinities: Men in Movements* (1997).

ADAM STEPHEN MILLER was a master's degree student in journalism at University of Michigan and an organizer of an Internet disability support group. He died in 1997.

BRIAN MILLER is a psychotherapist in West Hollywood, California. He writes a popular advice column for the gay community called "Out for Good." Besides gay husbands and fathers, he has researched victims of anti-gay violence.

PETER M. NARDI is Professor of Sociology at Pitzer College. He has published articles on AIDS, anti-gay crimes and violence, magic and magicians, and alcoholism and families. His books include

Men's Friendships (1993) and *Growing Up Before Stonewall* (1994), with David Sanders and Judd Marmor. He has served as co-president of the Los Angeles chapter of the Gay and Lesbian Alliance Against Defamation.

TIMOTHY NONN received his Ph.D. at the Graduate Theological Union in Berkeley and wrote a dissertation on faith and masculinity among poor men. He has a background in community organizing among rural and urban poor and refugees. He has published several articles on religion, gender, and poverty.

GARETH PALMER is Senior Lecturer in Media Production at the University of Salford. His two areas of research are masculinity and documentary.

JENNIFER L. PIERCE is Associate Professor of Sociology at the University of Minnesota. She is author of *Gender Trials: Emotional Lives in Contemporary Law Firms* (California 1995).

AMIRA PROWELLER is Assistant Professor of Foundations of Education at DePaul University. She is the author of *Constructing Female Identities: Meaning Making in an Upper Middle Class Youth Culture.*

B. LINSAY RICH is an Assistant Professor of Sociology at Transylvania University, specializes in gender, work, and inequality; and currently has a wide-lens focus on multiculturalism. This focus is now trained on the interethnic issues emerging with the rapidly growing Hispanic/Latino presence in the Bluegrass region of Central Kentucky.

EBET ROBERTS is a photographer in New York City.

M. ROCHLIN is the creator of "The Heterosexual Questionnaire."

LILLIAN B. RUBIN is a Research Associate at the Institute for the Study of Social Change at University of California, Berkeley, and a psychotherapist in private practice. Her books include *Intimate Strangers, Just Friends, Erotic Wars, Worlds of Pain,* and, most recently, *Families on the Fault Line* and *The Transcendant Child.*

DON SABO is a Professor of Social Sciences at D'Youville College in Buffalo, New York. He has co-authored *Humanism in Sociology, Jock: Sports & Male Identity,* and *Sport, Men and the Gender Order: Critical Feminist Perspectives.* His most recent books include, *Sex, Violence and Power in Sports: Rethinking Masculinity,* and *Men's Health & Illness: Gender, Power & the Body.* He has conducted many national surveys on gender issues in sport, is a trustee of the Women's Sports Foundation, and co-authored the 1997 Presidents' Council on Physical Fitness and Sports report "Physical Activity & Sport in the Lives of Girls."

RITCH C. SAVIN-WILLIAMS is at Cornell University. He is co-editor, with Kenneth M. Cohen, of *The Lives of Lesbians, Gays, and Bisexuals* (Harcourt Brace College Publishers 1996).

JASON SCHULTZ is a diversity management consultant and freelance writer. He has helped start dozens of profeminist men's groups on college campuses around the U.S. and serves on the executive board of SPEAKOUT: The National Student Coalition Against Campus Sexual Violence. His work has been featured in *The New York Times, Rolling Stone,* and *Ms.* Magazine. He is an honors graduate of Duke University in women's studies and public policy and currently attends law school at U.C. Berkeley.

JOAN B. SPADE is Associate Professor of Sociology at Lehigh University. Her previous publications have focused on the interstices of work and family, including the effects of men's and women's parental values. She is currently examining the effects of grouping students in middle schools.

ROBERT STAPLES is in the Department of Sociology at the University of California, San Francisco. He has written widely on black families and gender issues, including his book, *Black Masculinity.*

GLORIA STEINEM is a founding editor of *Ms.*, and the author of *Outrageous Acts and Everyday Rebellions* and *Revolution from Within.*

JOHN STOLTENBERG, a frequent speaker and workshop leader at colleges and conferences, is the radical feminist author of *Refusing to Be a Man: Essays on Sex and Justice* (revised edition 2000), *The End of Manhood: Parables on Sex and Selfhood* (revised edition 2000) and *What Makes Pornography "Sexy"?* (1994). He is represented by Program Corporation of America (www.speakerspca.com).

LANCE STRATE is Assistant Professor of Communications at Fordham University. He is co-author, with Neil Postman, Christine Nystrom, and Charles Weingartner of *Myths, Men and Beer: An Analysis of Beer Commercials on Broadcast Television* and is working on a book on the relationship between media environments and concepts of the hero.

KAREN WALKER is completing her doctorate in the Department of Sociology at the University of Pennsylvania.

LOIS WEIS is Professor of Sociology of Education at SUNY Buffalo. Author of numerous books and articles about race, class and gender, her most recent works include *Working Class Without Work* (1990) and *Beyond Silenced Voices* (with Michele Fine 1993).

CHRISTINE L. WILLIAMS is Professor of Sociology at the University of Texas at Austin. She is author of *Gender Differences at Work* (1989), *Still a Man's World* (1997), and editor of *Doing "Women's Work": Men in Nontraditional Occupations* (1993).